I0874746

Fundamentals of EU VAT Law

Fundamentals of EU VAT Law

Third Edition

Ad van Doesum
Herman van Kesteren
Simon Cornielje
Frank Nellen

Wolters Kluwer

Published by:
Kluwer Law International B.V.
PO Box 316
2400 AH Alphen aan den Rijn
The Netherlands
E-mail: lrs-sales@wolterskluwer.com
Website: www.wolterskluwer.com/en/solutions/kluwerlawinternational

Sold and distributed by:
Wolters Kluwer Legal & Regulatory U.S.
920 Links Avenue
Landisville, PA 17538
United States of America
E-mail: customer.service@wolterskluwer.com

ISBN 978-94-035-0879-5

e-Book: ISBN 978-94-035-0889-4
web-PDF: ISBN 978-94-035-0899-3

© 2025 Ad van Doesum, Herman van Kesteren, Simon Cornielje & Frank Nellen

All rights are reserved, including those for text and data mining, AI training, and similar technologies. No part of this publication may be reproduced, stored in a retrieval system, or transmitted in any form or by any means, electronic, mechanical, photocopying, recording, or otherwise, without written permission from the publisher. Permission to use this content must be obtained from the copyright owner.

About the Authors

Prof Dr Ad van Doesum (1975) is Professor of European Value Added Tax (VAT) Law at Maastricht University, the Netherlands. He is also the Head of PwC's Knowledge Centre in the Netherlands and is an honorary judge in the 's-Gravenhage (The Hague) Court.

Professor Van Doesum has broad experience in national and international VAT Law and particular expertise in the complex VAT issues attached to collaboration between organizations. He received his Law Degree (Tax Law) at Leiden University, the Netherlands, in 1998. In 2009, he obtained his doctorate with his thesis 'Contractual Cooperative Arrangements and VAT'.

Ad van Doesum has authored and co-authored numerous publications on national and European VAT law and is regularly invited to speak on indirect taxation at conferences and seminars around the world. He is on the editorial boards of the Dutch Encyclopaedia on VAT ('Vakstudie omzetbelasting') and the International VAT Monitor. Also, he is a member of the permanent committee of contributors to leading tax publications and is a correspondent for various other journals.

Prof Dr Herman van Kesteren (1961) is Professor of Tax Law at Tilburg University, the Netherlands. Until his retirement on 1 July 2024, he was also an Indirect Taxes Partner at PwC in Amsterdam. He is an honorary judge in the 's-Hertogenbosch Court of Appeals and in the 's-Gravenhage (The Hague) Court of First Instance.

Herman received his Law Degree (Major in tax) at Leiden University, the Netherlands, and lectured European VAT at this university before transferring to Tilburg University, the Netherlands, in 2000, where he was appointed professor in the field of VAT in 2003.

Herman has often been a (guest) lecturer, both in the Netherlands and abroad, for academic scholars as well as for tax practitioners. He serves as a lecturer in several international programmes and is chair of the board of the section of VAT specialists of the Dutch Association of Tax Advisors.

Herman is also a regular speaker at seminars and conferences regarding the European Union (EU) VAT Law. He actively contributes to thought leadership in the area of VAT and has written several books on VAT and numerous articles for legal periodicals and contributed to several papers.

Prof Dr Simon Cornielje (1983) is Professor of Indirect Tax Law at VU University in Amsterdam, the Netherlands. He is also a partner at PwC in Amsterdam, the Netherlands, with over 17 years of experience. Simon mainly advises multinational businesses on their indirect tax position, among others in the consumer market industry and the financial services sector. He is also responsible for knowledge management and litigation in the field of indirect tax.

Simon obtained his Law Degree at Maastricht University, the Netherlands, in 2007. In 2016, he obtained his doctorate with his thesis 'Mergers and acquisitions in European VAT' at Tilburg University, the Netherlands.

Simon is a regular speaker at seminars and conferences on European VAT and is an author and co-author of numerous publications on EU VAT law. He is on the editorial board of the *Tijdschrift voor Fiscaal ondernemingsrecht*, an author and editor for the *Cursus Belastingrecht Omzetbelasting* and a contributor to several legal periodicals. In 2019, Simon was awarded the *Stevens* Award ('*Stevensprijs*') for excellence in academic writing on tax law.

Dr Frank Nellen (1982) is Associate Professor (VAT and Customs Law) at Maastricht University, the Netherlands. He is also a director with Baker Tilly in Utrecht, the Netherlands, specializing in knowledge management and tax advisory in international settings. From 2008 until 2016, he worked as an indirect tax advisor with KPMG Meijburg & Co, Eindhoven, the Netherlands. He is a member of the Dutch Association of Tax Advisors.

Frank has an academic background in business (MSc International Business, Maastricht University), economics (MSc Tax Economics, Tilburg University, the Netherlands) and law (LLM Tax Law, Maastricht University). In 2017, he obtained his Doctorate in Tax Law from Maastricht University in connection with his thesis 'Information Asymmetries in EU VAT'. He is a regular speaker at seminars and conferences on tax law and contributes to a variety of legal periodicals. In 2024, Frank received the *Jaap van den Berge* award for his academic publications on tax law.

Besides his work in the area of VAT and customs, Frank is a novelist with Overamstel/Holland Diep, a major literary publishing house based in Amsterdam. His second novel, *De onzichtbaren* (UK: 'The invisibles'), received the Dutch Bookstore Award in 2024 and was shortlisted for the Libris Literature Prize and the E. du Perron prize.

Table of Contents

Preface

The purpose of the book is to provide the reader with an understanding of the fundamentals of EU VAT law. It aims to give the reader a deep insight into the systematics, the functioning and the principles of the European VAT system. To that end, not only does the book contain a description of the EU VAT system but it also explains the rationale of the system and more specifically of various provisions in EU VAT legislation. It puts the elements of the VAT system in perspective and shows how the various elements are linked to each other.

The book provides a clear overview of the EU VAT system. It separates essentials from side-issues without losing an eye for details. As such, the book is intended to serve as a book of reference for tax law practitioners and researchers. Moreover, because of its emphasis on the rationale and systematics of the EU VAT system, the book is very suitable as a stepping stone to further research in the field of VAT. It also makes the book an ideal textbook for advanced students who want to study EU VAT law.

The focus lies on the fundamentals of VAT law from a *European* perspective. The book describes the relevant VAT provisions fluidly, regardless of their place in the EU VAT legislation, rather than simply discussing each and every provision in the VAT Directive and VAT Regulation in the order in which they have been included therein. For that same reason, the book contains a number of chapters in which VAT topics, such as immovable property, importation and exportation and intra-Community transactions (ICTs) are discussed thematically. Also, the authors chose to minimize including summaries of case law because including such summaries would go against the objective of creating a textbook which puts the elements of the VAT system in perspective. Instead, the focus lies on the rules of law which can be deduced from the Court of Justice of the European Union (CJEU) case law in the context of the provisions to which the cases relate.

Authors have to make choices as to subject coverage and have to decide what to put in and to leave out. Particularly in the field of VAT, it is virtually impossible to include each and every detail, provision and case. Although we, as authors of this book, strived to include all key elements of the VAT system, only you as a reader will be able to assess whether we succeeded in our efforts of creating a complete, clear, up-to-date, yet not overdetailed book. Therefore, we welcome any suggestions on how to further improve the book in the future.

This third edition of the book reflects the latest state of affairs in EU VAT law. Among other things, it contains all key CJEU cases up to 15 August 2024, the rules introduced in the VAT package (including the new distance sales rules, the rules on platforms and the one-stop shop (OSS) mechanism) and the new VAT rates structure.

We truly hope that this book satisfies a widely felt need and that it will be an inspiration for many to continue studying this particular type of tax law. Studying VAT should no longer be a tax to your brain.

The copy was closed on 15 August 2024. Developments after that date have only been sporadically incorporated.

Prof Dr Ad van Doesum
Prof Dr Herman van Kesteren
Prof Dr Simon Cornielje
Dr Frank Nellen

List of Abbreviations and Glossary

B2B	Business to Business (Transactions Carried Out Between Taxable Persons)
B2C	Business to Consumers (Transactions Carried Out Between a Taxable Person and a Non-taxable Person)
B2H(ybrid)	Cross-Border Supply of Goods Within the EU by a Taxable Person to a Non-taxable Legal Person
B2Me	Transfer of Own Goods by a Taxable Person from One Member State to Another Member State
C2C	Consumer to Consumer (Transactions Between Non-taxable Persons)
CCC	Customs Community Code – Council Regulation 2913/92 of 12 October 1992 Establishing the Community Customs Code, [1992] OJ L302/1
CJEU	Court of Justice of the European Union The CJEU is the collective term for the European Union's judicial arm. The institution consists of three separate courts, each enjoying its own specific jurisdiction. One of them, the Court of Justice (CJ) which was formerly known as the European Court of Justice (ECJ), is the Court which deals with (among other cases) VAT cases. In order to prevent the mixed use of 'CJ' and 'ECJ' throughout this book, all CJ/ECJ case law is referred to as 'CJEU' case law
CMR	Convention Relative Au Contrat De Transport International De Marchandises Par Route. A 'CMR' document is a standardized document for cross-border transport of cargo by road
CPP	Card Protection Plan
CTP	Certified Taxable Person

DA	Delegated Act Commission Delegated Regulation (EU) 2015/2446 of 28 July 2015 Supplementing Regulation (EU) No 952/2013 of the European Parliament and of the Council as Regards Detailed Rules Concerning Certain Provisions of the Union Customs Code, [2015] OJ L 343
DB	Defined Benefit
DC	Defined Contribution
EEIG	European Economic Interest Grouping
EU	European Union
First VAT Directive	First Council Directive 67/227/EEC of 11 April 1967 on the Harmonization of Legislation of Member States Concerning Turnover Taxes [1967] OJ 071/1301–03
GST	Goods and Services Tax
IA	Implementing Act Commission Implementing Regulation (EU) 2015/2447 of 24 November 2015 Laying Down Detailed Rules for Implementing Certain Provisions of Regulation (EU) No 952/2013 of the European Parliament and of the Council Laying Down the Union Customs Code, [2015] OJ L 343
ICA	Intra-Community Acquisition of Goods
ICDS	Intra-Community Distance Sales of Goods
ICS	Intra-Community Supply of Goods
ICT	Intra-Community Transaction
ID	Identification
IOSS	Import One-Stop Shop
(M)OSS	(Mini) One-Stop Shop
MTIC	Missing Trader Intra-Community
NATO	North Atlantic Treaty Organization
OECD	Organisation for Economic Co-operation and Development
OSS	One-Stop Shop
QRM	Quick Reaction Mechanism
SE	Societas Europaea
Second VAT Directive	Second Council Directive 67/228/EEC of 11 April 1967 on the Harmonization of Legislation of Member States Concerning Turnover Taxes – Structure and Procedures for Application of the Common System of Value Added Tax [1967] OJ 071/1303–12
Sixth VAT Directive	Council Directive 77/388/EEC of 17 May 1977 on the Harmonization of the Laws of the Member States Relating to Turnover Taxes – Common System of Value Added Tax: Uniform Basis of Assessment [1977] OJ L145/1 TFEU Treaty on the Functioning of the European Union
SME	Small- and Medium-Sized Enterprise
SPV	Single-Purpose Voucher
STS	Simplified Triangulation Scheme

TBE	Telecommunications, Broadcasting or Electronic
TEDB	Taxes of Europe Database
TEU	Treaty on European Union, OJ C 202, 7.6.2016, p. 13–46.
TFEU	Treaty on the Functioning of the European Union, OJ C 202, 7.6.2016, p. 47–390.
Thirteenth VAT Directive	Thirteenth Council Directive 86/560/EEC of 17 November 1986 on the Harmonization of the Laws of the Member States Relating to Turnover Taxes – Arrangements for the Refund of Value Added Tax to Taxable Persons Not Established in Community Territory [1986] OJ L326/40
TOGC	Transfer of Going Concern
TOMS	Tour Operators' Margin Scheme
UCC	Union Customs Code Regulation (EU) No 952/2013 of 10 October 2013 of the Parliament and of the Council of 9 October 2013 Laying Down the Union Customs Code, [2013] OJ L269
VAT	Value Added Tax
VAT Directive	Council Directive 2006/112/EC of 28 November 2006 on the Common System of Value Added Tax [2006] OJ L347/1
VAT Implementing Regulation	Council Implementing Regulation (EU) No 282/2011 of 15 March 2011 Laying Down Implementing Measures for Directive 2006/112/EC on the Common System of Value Added Tax (Recast) [2011] OJ L 77/1 as Amended by Council Implementing Regulation (EU) No 1042/2013 of 7 October 2013 Amending Implementing Regulation (EU) No 282/2011 as Regards the Place of Supply of Services [2013] OJ L284/1
ViDA	VAT Rules in the Digital Age
VIES	VAT Information Exchange System

CHAPTER 1
Introduction

1.1 INTRODUCTION[1]

The roots of the value added tax (VAT), which is currently levied in all European Union (EU) Member States, lie in the ancient past.[2] Some argue that special taxes that were levied on the slave trade in the Roman Empire can be regarded as a form of turnover tax.[3] Turnover taxes were certainly known in medieval times; in Spain, for example, the Crown levied a general sales tax, called the *Alcabala* as early as the fourteenth century.[4] The basis for the 'modern' turnover tax system can be found in the period immediately after the First World War, when Germany imposed the *Umsatzsteuer*, in 1918. Turnover taxes were also implemented in other European countries to cover the costs of crisis or war.[5] For example, France (1920) and Belgium (1921) also introduced general turnover taxes to cover the expenses of the First World War. For similar reasons, in 1940, the UK introduced a number of excise duties that – taken together – might be regarded as a general turnover tax. The Netherlands (1934) introduced a turnover tax to cover the expenses of the Great Depression. Although turnover taxes often have been introduced as 'temporary' measures, in most European countries, they became permanent.

Turnover taxes were among the first taxes that were harmonized in what is now the EU. In 1967, the Member States of what was then the European Economic Community – Belgium, France, West Germany, the Netherlands, Italy and Luxembourg – committed themselves to harmonize their turnover taxes. They chose to implement a common system of turnover tax in the form of a VAT.

Nowadays, VAT is an important revenue-generating tax in all EU Member States and is also used as a basis to calculate the EU's own resources. In the EU as a whole, VAT is responsible for generating approximately EUR 1,075 billion per year in tax revenues.[6] In 2021, VAT-based resources amounted to EUR 17.97 billion and 11% of

1. *See also* A.J. van Doesum & F. Nellen, *VAT in a Day* (Fonds Indirect Tax 2021). Available at: https://ssrn.com/abstract=3867201 (accessed 16 August 2024).
2. For example: A. Schenk & O. Oldman, *Value Added Tax: A Comparative Approach* (Cambridge 2007), pp. 2-5; R.F. Brederode, *Systems of General Sales Taxation: Theory, Policy and Practice* (Kluwer Law International 2009), p. 5 and J.C.L. Huiskamp, *De omzetbelasting in internationaal verband* (Kluwer 1966), pp. 9-12.
3. *See* J.C.L. Huiskamp, *De omzetbelasting in internationaal verband* (Kluwer 1966), p. 11.
4. *See* K. Brown, 'Alcabala', in J. Michael Francis (ed.), *Iberia and the Americas: Culture, Politics, and History: A Multidisciplinary Encyclopedia*, Vol. 1 (ABC-CLIO Transatlantic relations series 2006), pp. 57-58 and R.F. Brederode, *Systems of General Sales Taxation: Theory, Policy and Practice* (Kluwer Law International 2009), p. 5. The introduction of the *Alcabala* in what is now the Netherlands was a trigger for the Dutch Revolt (1566 or 1568-1648). *See* F.H.M. Grapperhaus, *Alva en de Tiende Penning* (Walburg Pers 1982).
5. *See also* R. Grabower, *Die Geschichte der Umsatzsteuer unde ihre Gestaltung im Inland und im Ausland* (C. Heymann 1925) and J.C.L. Huiskamp, *De omzetbelasting in internationaal verband* (Kluwer 1966).
6. European Commission, CASE, G. Poniatowski, M. Bonch-Osmolovskiy, A. Śmietanka, A. Sojka, *VAT Gap in the EU: Report 2023* (Publications Office of the European Union, Luxembourg, 2023), https://data.europa.eu/doi/10.2778/911698 (accessed 13 November 2024). According to this study, an estimated EUR 60.6 billion in VAT revenues was lost due to non-compliance or non-collection in 2021. This equates to 5.3% of the total expected VAT revenue of 27 Member States in 2021.

the EU's total own resources.[7] These revenues play a huge role in the budgetary policy-making of the EU and of the individual Member States, in particular. It is likely that in many Member States, the importance of VAT will continue to grow in the years to come.

1.2 TERMINOLOGY: 'CONSUMPTION TAX', 'INDIRECT TAX', 'TURNOVER TAX' AND 'VAT'[8]

Consumption taxes may be defined as taxes that aim at taxing the private consumption of goods and/or services of private individuals. In this respect, the term 'consumption' can be interpreted in various ways.[9] Is a consumption tax simply a tax on everything a private consumer consumes,[10] is it a tax that effectively taxes income (at the time it is consumed),[11] or is it rather a tax on the expenditure of private consumers?[12] In our view, there is some truth in each of these interpretations. We believe that a consumption tax, such as the European VAT that is currently in place, is a tax on everything a private consumer consumes, albeit that it effectively takes the expenditure of private individuals as the criterion to establish the monetary value of that consumption. This can be understood if one realizes that: (1) it is difficult to define 'consumption' (is a bottle of whisky 'consumed' if the consumer drops it on the floor just after he purchased the bottle?); (2) there may be an interval between the purchase (expenditure) and the actual consumption of a good or service; (3) a good may be 'consumed' over a long period of time (e.g., the 'consumption of a building'); and (4) the monetary value of a consumed good or service must be established in order to levy a consumption tax. All these factors make it necessary to abstract out of the actual goal of taxing consumption and rather look at what the expenditures of a private individual are.

Theoretically, it would be conceivable to levy a consumption tax in a direct way, that means directly on the final consumer (measured by referencing their expenditure).[13] In a direct consumption tax, each consumer would report their consumption on a periodical basis and pay the consumption tax accordingly. Obviously, this means that there would be many taxpayers, and the administrative burden for them would be

7. *Ibid.*
8. *See also* J. Reugebrink, *Omzetbelasting* (9th ed., Kluwer 1997) and R.F. Brederode, *Systems of General Sales Taxation: Theory, Policy and Practice* (Kluwer Law International 2009).
9. A.J. van Doesum & G.J. van Norden, *Omzetbelasting* (17th ed., Kluwer 2023), pp. 5-6.
10. C.P. Tuk, *Wet op de omzetbelasting 1968* (Kluwer 1979), p. 33.
11. H.J. Tehler, *Die Umsatzsteuer als angewandte Verkehr- und/oder Verbrauchsteuer* (Köln 1986) and G. Schmölders, in *Handbuch der Finanzwissenschaft II* (Tübingen 1956), pp. 636 et seq.
12. J. Reugebrink, *Omzetbelasting* (Deventer, Kluwer 1990), p. 6 and C.K. Sullivan, 'Indirect Taxation and Goals of the European Community', in Shoup (ed.), *Fiscal Harmonization in Common Markets*, Vol. II (Columbia University Press 1967), p. 13.
13. The terms 'direct tax' and 'indirect tax' are also used to indicate that some taxes (direct taxes) are 'assessed upon property, business or income of the individual who is to pay the tax', whereas other taxes (indirect taxes) are 'levied upon commodities before they reach the consumer who ultimately pay(s) the taxes as part of the market price of the commodity'. *See* A. Schenk & O. Oldman, *Value Added Tax: A Comparative Approach* (Cambridge 2015), p. 5.

rather heavy.[14] Moreover, such a system of taxation would seem to be quite difficult for the tax authorities to control. It is probably for those reasons that consumption taxes are levied indirectly rather than directly. Rather than that the consumption/expenditures being taxed directly with the private individuals, it is the supply of goods and services by suppliers (entrepreneurs) that is taxed. The general idea is that consumption and the supply of goods and services are two sides of the same coin. By taxing the supply, eventually, private consumption is taxed. The implicit assumption is that the entrepreneur who supplies the goods and services will include the amount of the consumption tax in its prices. It is important to realize that taxing consumption in an indirect manner effectively implies that a further abstraction from the idea of taxing private consumption is accepted. The fact that a consumption tax is levied in an indirect manner implies that it takes the *form* of a transaction tax. As we will see, the form of the tax as a transaction tax creates norms in itself.[15]

The term 'turnover tax' refers to a collection of different forms of consumption tax, of which the 'VAT' is one manifestation.[16] In other words, VAT is a specific form of a turnover tax and thus also of a 'consumption tax'.[17] As the definition of the term 'consumption tax' already suggests, there are various types of consumption tax. Basically, there are two classes of a consumption tax: specific consumption taxes and general consumption taxes. Under a specific consumption tax, only certain goods and/or services are taxed. Typically, excise duties fall within this category of consumption tax. In an ideal form of a general consumption tax,[18] a tax is levied on (ultimately) the consumption of *all* goods and services that are (eventually) consumed. According to Article 1(2) VAT Directive, EU VAT is a general tax on consumption.

General taxes on consumption can take different forms. They may be single-stage taxes, as is the case with certain sales taxes, or they may be multiple-stage taxes. In a multiple-stage tax, the tax is imposed on supplies made in more than one leg of the production and distribution chain. EU VAT is a multiple-stage tax; in fact, it is an all-stage tax, since – up to and including the retail trade stage – the tax is levied on all supplies of goods and services made (*see*: Article 1(2) VAT Directive).

Before the harmonization of turnover taxes in the EU, all Member States that formed the European Communities at that time, except for France, had introduced

14. *See*, on whether personal expenditure tax is practicable: N. Kaldor, *An Expenditure Tax* (Allen & Unwin 1955). *See also* S. Cnossen, *De belasting van de toekomst? (Inaugural Speech)* (Kluwer 1978) and A. Schenk & O. Oldman, *Value Added Tax: A Comparative Approach* (Cambridge 2015), pp. 5-8.
15. A.H.R.M. Denie, *De overheid in de omzetbelasting (Dissertation)* (Kluwer 1987), p. 50.
16. For example: CJEU 20 May 1976, Case 111/75 *Impresa Costruzioni comm. Quirino Mazzalai v Ferrovia del Renon*, ECLI:EU:C:1976:68. *See also* A. Tait, *Value Added Tax: International Practice and Problems* (International Monetary Fund 1988), pp. 3-39.
17. Article 401 VAT Directive is the only provision in the VAT Directive in which the term 'turnover tax' is used. We note that the CJEU interprets this provision such that Member States are in principle not allowed to introduce any VAT in addition to the EU VAT. We refer to section 1.11.
18. With many general consumption taxes, certain goods and services are either exempted or are taxed at reduced rates. Such exemptions and reduced rates are deviations from the general character of the tax. However, since they are merely exceptions, they do not alter the character of a tax from that of a specific consumption tax.

all-stage *cascading* turnover taxes. This cascading effect occurred because taxable persons making taxed supplies could not recover the VAT which was charged to them (i.e., they could not recover the turnover tax on their purchases). Consequently, the turnover tax would become a cost component of their prices, on which again turnover tax would be chargeable. The turnover tax would thereby 'cascade'. For reasons that we will explain in section 1.6, the founding Member States replaced their turnover tax systems with a non-cascading turnover tax system. Non-cascading turnover tax systems are commonly referred to as 'VAT' or goods and services tax ('GST') systems. In fact, the goods and services taxes that are levied in Australia and New Zealand are turnover taxes in the form of VATs.

A non-cascading turnover tax requires that the taxable person carrying out a taxable transaction is in some way not burdened with the tax that is charged in a previous leg of the supply chain. The tax payable to the tax authorities under a non-cascading subtractive VAT can be calculated by using either an additive method or a subtractive method. An additive method entails that a taxable person must periodically establish the value of its economic factors for production and apply a tax rate to the aggregate value.[19] A subtractive method can either be devised by applying a tax rate to the difference between the sales and the purchases of a company (accounts-based method) or by applying a tax rate separately to the sales and separately to the purchases and then balancing these amounts off against each other (invoice-based method). The EU VAT is a turnover tax of the latter type. Figure 1.1 serves to illustrate the distinction between the various types of turnover tax.

Figure 1.1 Various Types of Turnover Tax[20]

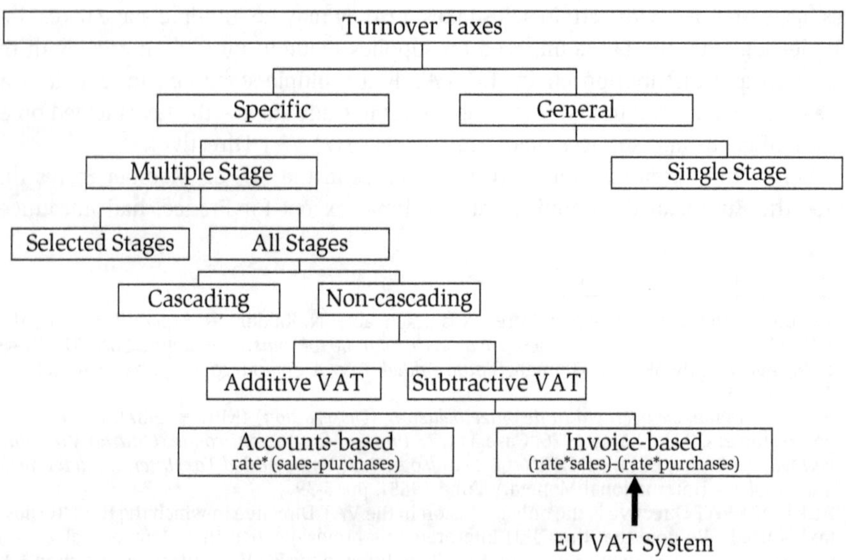

19. *See*, on the addition method of VAT: A. Schenk & O. Oldman, *Value Added Tax: A Comparative Approach* (Cambridge 2015), pp. 33-36.
20. Based on: J. Reugebrink, *Omzetbelasting* (9th edn, Kluwer 1997), p. 47.

1.3 EU VAT: A CONSUMPTION TAX, A TAX ON EXPENDITURE OR A TRANSACTION TAX?

Article 1(2) VAT Directive indicates that EU VAT is a 'general tax on consumption'. Therefore, it can be characterized as a consumption tax. Yet, it is clear from Article 2 VAT Directive that effectively 'transactions' are taxed. Therefore, EU VAT could be characterized as a transaction tax. However, EU VAT could also be characterized as an 'expenditure tax' because it (indirectly) only taxes the expenditure of consumers and not their actual consumption.

The question of how EU VAT may best be characterized is, in fact, a question of what the 'purpose' of EU VAT is. Usually, the 'purpose' of a tax concerns who and what must be taxed. In our view, it is clear that the purpose of EU VAT law is to generally tax the consumption of private consumers. This general consumption tax takes the form of a transaction tax. As a consequence, ultimately only consumption for which private consumers have paid is taxed.

With regard to the question of who must be taxed under EU VAT, we note the following. According to the Court of Justice of the European Union (CJEU) in *Hong Kong Trade Development Council*, the burden of VAT must eventually be borne by the final consumer.[21] That is the final person in the chain of transactions, who cannot pass on the amount of the tax. Most final consumers are natural persons, but sometimes that person is a legal person or just operates as an entity not having legal personality under the national civil law of a Member State (e.g., partnerships in most jurisdictions). Where a person's activity consists exclusively in providing services free of charge, there is no basis of assessment, and such services are, therefore, not subject to VAT. In such circumstances, the person providing those services must be treated the same as a final consumer because he is at the final stage of the production and distribution chain. If public bodies which carry out supplies for a consideration operate within a special legal regime especially made for them, and provided that they do not compete with private entrepreneurs, they also will be treated as final consumers. We refer to Chapter 2, on taxable persons.

As regards the question of what must be taxed, it is clear that the purpose of the VAT Directive is to tax the private consumption of goods and services. The transactions carried out by taxable persons serve as a proxy for the expenditures that were required to purchase goods and services. The expenditures, in turn, serve as a proxy for the consumption of those goods and services.

1.4 BASIC MECHANISM OF THE EU VAT SYSTEM[22]

With a view to taxing private consumption in an indirect manner, one could argue that it is unnecessary to tax supplies of goods and services between taxable persons, and

21. CJEU 1 April 1982, Case 89/81 *Staatssecretaris van Financiën v Hong Kong Trade Development Council*, ECLI:EU:C:1982:121.
22. A.J. van Doesum & F. Nellen, *VAT in a Day* (Fonds Indirect Tax 2021). Available at: https://ssrn.com/abstract=3867201 (accessed 16 August 2024), pp. 8-11.

that it would be sufficient to only tax supplies of goods and services to private persons: only the latter supplies lead to final consumption. The taxable person (the person who enables a private consumer to consume, by supplying a good or service to him) could simply include the VAT due in the total price that the consumer pays for the supply. Under the assumption that this 'recharging' of VAT is perfect, the burden of VAT is thus borne by the consumer – even though the taxable person is held liable to transfer the VAT to the tax authorities. Nonetheless, EU VAT subjects *all* transactions (in every stage of the production and distribution process) to taxation. The EU VAT thus is an all-stage turnover tax. It is levied and collected through a system of 'fractional payments'. In each stage of the supply chain, the tax authorities collect a small amount of the total VAT due on the final product. An advantage of this system of fractional payments is that the risk of incorrect filing of VAT, or even tax fraud, is spread over the entire supply chain, divided into smaller amounts than the total amount of VAT on the eventual consumption.

To ensure that taxable persons do not carry the burden of VAT and that ultimately only *private* consumption is taxed, taxable persons are allowed to deduct VAT that has been charged to them by other taxable persons, insofar as they use the input transactions for their own taxed output transactions. In that way, the right of deduction safeguards the 'neutrality' of VAT.[23] The result is that every taxable person pays VAT over the value he or she adds to the good or service. Cascading of VAT generally does not occur because VAT is not levied on VAT. The next example illustrates the basic functioning of the VAT system (Figure 1.2).

Figure 1.2 The Basic Functioning of the VAT System

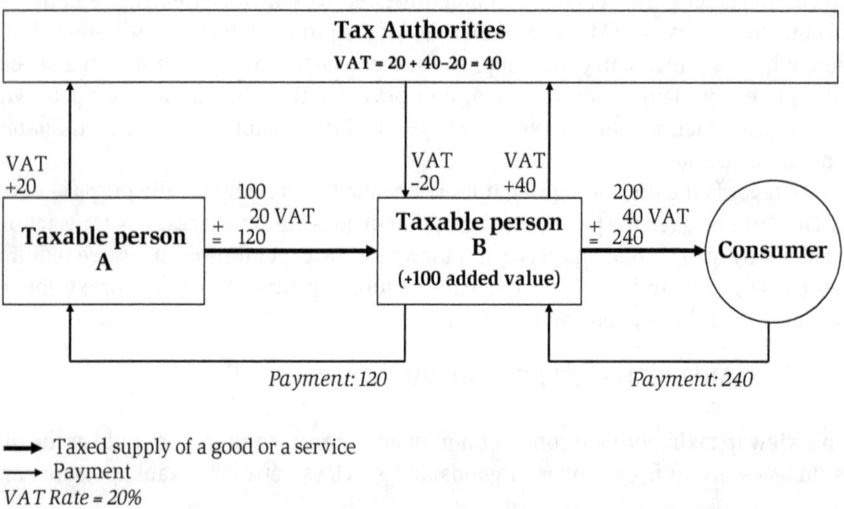

23. Cf. OECD International VAT/GST Guidelines, https://www.oecd.org/en/publications/international-vat-gst-guidelines_9789264271401-en.html (accessed 27 August 2024).

In the example above, taxable person A supplies goods or services with a value of EUR 100 to taxable person B. A charges 20% VAT on the supply to B. B pays an amount of EUR 100 + EUR 20 VAT = EUR 120 to A. A declares EUR 20 of VAT in his VAT return and pays the EUR 20 in VAT to the tax authorities. Next, B supplies this good or service he purchased to the end-consumer for a total amount of EUR 200 (excluding VAT). B charges 20% VAT over the amount of this supply to the end-consumer. The consumer pays a total of EUR 200 + EUR 40 VAT = EUR 240 to B. Subsequently, B declares the EUR 40 of VAT in his VAT return. However, B can also deduct on his VAT return the VAT charged to him by A, which was EUR 20. The result is that B effectively pays an amount of EUR 40–EUR 20 = EUR 20 to the tax authorities. Thus, the tax authorities receive the total VAT payment of EUR 40 VAT in two different payments at two different moments in the production and distribution chain (EUR 20 of VAT via A and EUR 20 of VAT via B). However, the consumer bears the entire burden of the VAT, paying EUR 40 of VAT on the purchase, and cannot deduct this VAT.

1.5 ADVANTAGES AND DISADVANTAGES OF TURNOVER TAXES[24]

The main advantage of turnover taxes, from a government perspective, lies in the stable revenue that general taxes on consumption generate at relatively low rates and relatively low costs of collection. General turnover taxes are levied equally on almost all members of society,[25] and due to the fact that they are usually included in the prices of goods or services, the perceived tax burden is also low.[26]

Indeed, over the years, EU VAT has proven to be a stable tax which, from the government's perspective, is levied in a relatively straightforward way. Because it has been harmonized, it is less prone to be used by the Member States for tax competition (striving to create a more attractive investment climate than other Member States) than direct taxes, such as corporate income tax. Nor is VAT subject to some of the (other) disadvantages inherent to personal income and corporate taxation. For example, assessing and collecting tax on income and corporate revenues is an administratively burdensome and costly process. Moreover, levying taxes on income and labour has a negative impact on economic market conditions. Direct taxes on labour and corporate

24. *See also* A. Tait, *Value Added Tax: International Practice and Problems* (International Monetary Fund 1988), pp. 3-39.
25. It should be noted that this does not necessarily imply that general turnover taxes adhere to the principle of (proportional) equality. It has been argued that general turnover taxes, and in particular VAT systems, have a regressive effect, i.e., in relation to in relation their income, it imposes a greater burden on the poor than on the rich.
26. *De La Feria and Walpole* who point out that consumption taxes are less visible to taxpayers than income taxes and that taxpayers often underestimate the burden associated with them. In other words, their tax salience, namely the extent to which taxpayers account for their cost when making decisions, is low. This phenomenon is also referred to as the fiscal illusion or Mill's hypothesis. *See* R. de la Feria & M. Walpole, *The Impact of Public Perceptions on General Consumption Taxes* (2020) 67/5 British Tax Review, pp. 637-669.

revenues share an almost direct relationship with the market economy. When economic circumstances decline, direct tax revenues also immediately decline. Additionally, taxes on labour are sensitive to an ageing population; as people live longer, the retirement period during which they do not pay taxes on labour increases accordingly, but they remain spending their income (based on their former employment and accumulated capital). VAT does not – or at least to a lesser extent – have these downsides, which explains the ongoing worldwide shift from direct taxation (income tax and corporation tax) to indirect taxation (VAT).

This shift to indirect taxation also raises some concerns. Indirect taxes – compared to direct taxes – are focused on transactions (taxable object) rather than on the person from which the tax is levied (taxable subject). As a consequence, indirect taxes generally do not take into account the personal circumstances of the taxable person. They are even considered to be regressive taxes.[27] The shift to indirect taxation also causes concerns because it would seem that it is difficult for VAT systems to adapt to the digitalization and globalization of the world's economy. More and more products can be supplied in a digital form these days. For example, books, films and newspapers no longer need to be supplied on a carrier medium but can be supplied online (downloaded or streamed). Such changes entail that supplies that used to be supplies of goods can now take the form of supplies of services. It is difficult for tax authorities to enforce the (tax) law on service providers that have no physical presence in or link with an EU country. Even though the EU has invested much effort in simplifying the VAT obligations for non-EU service suppliers (e.g., One-Stop-Shop regimes), it remains to be seen whether this will be sufficient to get the majority of those suppliers to comply with EU VAT law. These concerns may dissuade the Member States from relying too heavily on just one form of taxation. In our view, Member States will better off in the long run if they can find an optimal balance between direct and indirect taxation (the optimal 'tax mix').

1.6 THE HARMONIZATION OF TURNOVER TAXES[28]

In this section, we will discuss the rationale behind and the process of harmonizing of turnover taxes in the EU. We will explain why the Member States chose to implement a turnover tax in the form of a VAT. We will explain that notwithstanding the adoption of a common system of VAT, the harmonization process was not completed at all and that, in fact, this is an ongoing process.[29]

27. This is particularly true for VAT. *See*: Rita de la Feria & Artur Swistak, *Designing a Progressive VAT*, 2024, Working Paper WP/24/78, International Monetary Fund, Washington, D.C. Available from: https://doi.org/10.5089/9798400271830.001 (accessed 13 November 2024).
28. *See also* R. de La Feria, *The EU VAT System and the Internal Market* (*Dissertation*) (IBFD 2006).
29. *See also* N. Campbell, 'The European Court of Justice: Friend or Foe', in M. Lang, et al. (eds), *ECJ: Recent Developments in Value Added Tax, the Evolution of European VAT Jurisprudence and Its Role in the EU Common VAT System* (Linde 2014), p. 362 and S. Cornielje, *The Costly Stalemate of EU VAT Harmonization* (2022) EC Tax Review, pp. 85-96 https://doi.org/10.54648/ecta2022007.

1.6.1 Main Reasons for Harmonizing Turnover Taxes Throughout the EU

Before the creation of the European Community (now: EU) and before the adoption of the first and second VAT Directives, each European country had its own turnover tax. At that time, Belgium, West Germany, the Netherlands, Italy and Luxembourg all had implemented multiple-stage, cascading turnover taxes.[30] These cumulative, multiple-stage turnover taxes had important disadvantages:[31]

(1) Where goods are to be exported, they must be relieved of the burden of tax, to prevent the tax from being a distortive factor in international trade. However, with a cumulative tax, the actual burden of the tax on a product depends on the number of stages in the supply chain. This makes it virtually impossible to calculate the exact amount of the tax burden on a product. Lump sums or estimations may be used to overcome such difficulties to a certain extent, but they are complex and difficult to control.
(2) Since in a cumulative system of turnover tax the actual burden of the tax depends on the number of stages in the supply chain, cumulative turnover taxes are considered as encouraging vertical concentration (integration) of enterprises.[32]

VAT does not have these disadvantages.[33] Therefore, the initial Member States chose to adopt a VAT system as a common system of turnover taxes in their effort to harmonize the turnover taxes (*see* section 1.2).

In 1957, Belgium, France, West Germany, the Netherlands, Italy and Luxembourg adopted the treaty establishing the European Economic Community ('Treaty of Rome').[34] The preamble to the Treaty of Rome recognized that the removal of existing obstacles called for concerted action in order to guarantee a steady expansion, a balanced trade and fair competition. More specifically, Article 99 Treaty of Rome (now Article 113 TFEU) of that treaty provided:

> The Commission shall consider in what way the law of the various Member States concerning turnover taxes, excise duties and other forms of indirect taxation, including compensatory measures applying to exchanges between Member States, can be harmonized in the interest of the Common Market.

To fulfil its obligation under this provision, the European Commission sought advice on how the indirect taxes could be harmonized. Three sub-groups were

30. In France, the cumulative turnover tax was replaced by a non-cumulative VAT in 1953.
31. Reports of the Sub-Groups A, B and C, January 1962, in: *The EEC Reports on Tax Harmonisation* (IBFD 1969), p. 13.
32. *See also* J. Owens, *The Move to VAT* (1996) 2 Intertax, pp. 45-52 https://doi.org/10.54648/taxi1996010.
33. At the time, West Germany found that its cumulative turnover tax hindered its trade with France, which already adopted a VAT system. Conversely, France discovered that its VAT system was beneficial for its had international trade. *See* J. Reugebrink, *Omzetbelasting* (6th edn, Kluwer 1990), pp. 41-42.
34. Treaty Establishing the European Economic Community, 25 March 1957, 298 U.N.T.S. 11.

appointed to carry out a study and to advise on the harmonization of turnover taxes. In the course of 1962, the Commission of the European Economic Community released the General Report of Sub-Groups A, B and C appointed for the study of the various possibilities for the harmonization of turnover taxes. On 1 February 1963, the Report of the Fiscal and Financial Committee (the so-called Neumark Report) was released. Even though both reports had a very different approach, style and structure, their conclusion was the same: the existing cumulative turnover taxes had to be replaced by a common system of VAT. It was identified that cumulative turnover taxes intrinsically hindered international trade and caused other distortions to trade, such as vertical integration of enterprises. Moreover, it was considered that:

(1) the maintenance of tax frontiers caused barriers to the free circulation of goods; and
(2) the multiplicity of tax systems caused complications in relation to international trade.[35]

On the basis of these studies, the Member States decided to implement a system of harmonized VAT.

1.6.2 The Harmonization Process

The introduction of a harmonized VAT in the Member States was brought about by means of Council Directives. The Council Directives in the field of VAT serve as a blueprint for the national VAT legislation of the Member States. Each state is required to transpose the VAT Directives into national law. However, Member States are free to choose the way that best serves their economies and national legal orders. It is the result that counts. The result is that ideally, all Member State levy VAT in the same manner, even though the legal systems of the Member States are not identical.[36] Nonetheless, VAT Directives do not provide for the unification of VAT law. The VAT Directives contain options and derogations for the Member States and – since Directives must be transposed into, rather than simply copied to national law – the interpretation of the provisions implementing the Directives is not necessarily identical in all Member States. As a consequence, even nowadays, EU VAT is not completely harmonized. The harmonization of VAT in the EU has been shown to be a difficult process. In fact, the current state of the EU VAT system is the result of a gradual harmonization of national laws[37] and is still only partial.[38] This slow pace of

35. Reports of the Sub-Groups A, B and C, January 1962, in: *The EEC Reports on Tax Harmonisation* (IBFD 1969), p. 13.
36. A.J. van Doesum & F. Nellen, *VAT in a Day* (Fonds Indirect Tax 2021). Available at: https://ssrn.com/abstract=3867201 (accessed 16 August 2024), p. 12.
37. A. van Dongen, *De harmonisatie van de btw (Dissertation)* (Sdu Fiscale en Financiële Uitgevers 2007), p. 405.
38. CJEU 5 December 1989, Case C-165/88 *ORO Amsterdam Beheer BV and Concerto BV v Inspecteur der Omzetbelasting Amsterdam*, ECLI:EU:C:1989:608, para. 21.

harmonization can be understood, if one realizes that the harmonization process is subject to two counteracting forces:[39]

(1) On one side there is the conservatism of Member States. After all, VAT is an important budgetary instrument for the Member States. For that reason alone, they do not want to give up sovereignty in the field of VAT, which slows down the harmonization. In this sense, the many options and derogations in the VAT Directives should primarily be understood to result from a lack of (political) agreement between the Member States on specific subjects.
(2) On the other side, there are the functions of VAT as a Community tax. The first function was worded in the preamble of the First Directive: a harmonized VAT prevents distortion of trade and competition in a common market. A well-functioning common market is unthinkable without a harmonized VAT. The second function is connected with the introduction of the Sixth Directive. Member States contribute a percentage of the uniform basis of assessment for VAT to the Community. This implies that the provisions, except perhaps for those about rates and administrative obligations, should be interpreted uniformly across the EU, in order to ensure that all Member States carry a proportional burden. This force strengthens the necessity of harmonization.

It is important to understand that the harmonization process is not solely in the hands of the European legislator but is also subject to rulings of the CJEU. By ruling that the EC Treaty has created an autonomous legal order which is an integral part of the legal orders of Member States and for which the Member States have relinquished a part of their sovereignty, the CJEU opened the gates to (among other things) the harmonization of VAT. The idea of 'Community concepts' (now: Union concepts) of law has been a major step towards a truly harmonized VAT.[40] Yet, full harmonization of VAT is still miles away.[41]

1.7 HISTORY OF EU VAT LEGISLATION

In this section, we provide a concise overview of the history of EU VAT legislation.

1.7.1 The First and Second VAT Directives

The First and Second VAT Directives[42] mark the inception of the EU VAT system. The First VAT Directive merely stipulated that the Member States had to replace their

39. A. van Dongen, *De harmonisatie van de btw* (*Dissertation*) (Sdu Fiscale en Financiële Uitgevers 2007), p. 407.
40. *Ibid.*
41. *See also* S. Cornielje, *The Costly Stalemate of EU VAT Harmonization* (2022) 2 EC Tax Review, pp. 85-96 https://doi.org/10.54648/ecta2022007.
42. First Council Directive 67/227/EEC of 11 April 1967 on the harmonisation of legislation of Member States concerning turnover taxes [1967] OJ 071/1301–03 and Second Council Directive

turnover taxes with a VAT system with a right of deduction of input VAT. The Second VAT Directive contained the outline of this European VAT system. It laid down the structure of the tax and the way it should be applied. The Member States retained their autonomy as regards the application of exemptions and rates.

1.7.2 The Sixth VAT Directive

On 21 April 1970, the European Council adopted a decision on the replacement of financial contributions from the Member States to the European Communities by a system of own resources of the European Communities.[43] The Member States' contribution was to be calculated on the basis of (among other things) a certain percentage of the taxable base of the VAT in each Member State. This called for a uniform manner of determining a basis of assessment and thus for further harmonization of VAT. Moreover, it was acknowledged that further progress should be made in the effective removal of restrictions on the movement of persons, goods, services and capital and the integration of national economies. The objective of the creation of a common market resembling a real internal market was also an important reason for a further step in the harmonization process.

This next step was taken on 17 May 1977, when the Member States adopted the Sixth VAT Directive.[44] This had to be implemented in all Member States on 1 January 1979. The Directive detailed the coverage of VAT and the rate structure. It provided for more specific rules regarding the taxable person, taxable event, taxable amount and exemptions. Even though its objective was to further harmonize the VAT system, the Sixth VAT Directive still contained numerous options and derogations for the Member States. In most cases, the cause of this failure to come to a far-reaching harmonization lay in the absence of political will or courage to create uniform rules. When the Sixth VAT Directive entered into force, the Second VAT Directive was withdrawn. The First VAT Directive was not repealed. Until the first of January 2007, the Sixth VAT Directive was the legal basis upon which the national VAT regimes rested.

1.7.3 Proposals to Further Harmonize the VAT System

The EC Treaty required the abolition of internal fiscal frontiers by 1 January 1993. This called for further changes to the VAT legislation. From a technical point of view, the best way to achieve the complete abolition of fiscal frontiers in the EU would be to treat the entire European Community (now: EU) as one country, which is, for example, already the case under customs law. Such an approach would require VAT to be levied

67/228/EEC of 11 April 1967 on the harmonisation of legislation of Member States concerning turnover taxes – Structure and procedures for application of the common system of value added tax [1967] OJ 071/1303–12.

43. Council Decision of 21 April 1970 on the Replacement of Financial Contributions from Member States by the Communities' own Resources (70/243 ECSC, EEC, Euratom), p. 19.
44. Council Directive 77/388/EEC of 17 May 1977 on the harmonization of the laws of the Member States relating to turnover taxes – Common system of value added tax: uniform basis of assessment [1977] OJ L145/1.

by an 'EU Tax Administration' on the basis of one set of rules identically applicable in all Member States. Differences in VAT rates could no longer exist. However, a fully harmonized VAT system would also require a mechanism for the distribution of the centrally collected VAT revenues over the Member States. Effectively, this would mean that the EU would collect the VAT directly, take its own resources out of this revenue, and then distribute the remaining revenues across the Member States. Obviously, such a drastic change to the way in which VAT is levied would require the Member States to give up an important part of their sovereignty in tax matters. From a more practical perspective, a serious objection against such a centralized VAT is that the collection of VAT and the redistribution of VAT revenue over the Member States involves vast flows of money between the EU and the Member States.

In 1987, the Commission submitted proposals to fundamentally amend the VAT system, without going as far as creating a 'true' internal market. The general idea was that VAT on supplies within (what is now) the EU should be levied in the Member State of origin, i.e., in the Member State where the supplier is established. This idea was in line with one of the conclusions of the Neumark Report,[45] which was drafted in the 1960s. Taxation, according to the origin principle, would mean supplies to customers in another Member State being treated identically to supplies to the customers within the same Member State. Thus, the supplier would charge the VAT of his Member State on the supply. Furthermore, it was proposed that a taxable person could deduct 'foreign' VAT through its own (local) VAT return, thereby also aligning purchases in other Member State to purchases in the same Member State. Effectively, such a system would entail that a Member State had to refund (or allow for deduction) VAT which was remitted by the supplier to the tax authorities of another Member State. Without any further measures, it was believed that such a system would cause budgetary imbalances, i.e., a shift of tax revenue from importing countries to exporting countries.[46] Discrepancies in the VAT rates between the Member States would also lead to imbalances. To overcome those problems, the Commission proposed that a compensation mechanism (i.e., a 'VAT clearing system') be put in place. The Member State that refunded the (foreign) VAT to the customer (Member State of destination) was to be compensated by the Member State that taxed the supply (Member State of origin). It was proposed that effectively, only net balances (aggregated VAT collected on supplies minus aggregated refunds of VAT on purchases within a Member State) would have to be settled between the Member States. However, soon after these plans were adopted by the Commission, it became clear that the Member States did not want to implement such a clearing system. Yet, it was also clear that it was neither desirable nor possible to further postpone the abolition of fiscal frontiers.

45. Neumark Report (1962): Report of the Fiscal and Financial Committee on Tax Harmonization in the Common Market, in *The EEC Reports on Tax Harmonisation* (IBFD 1969), p. 13.

46. Only four Member States would increase their VAT revenue, whereas all other Member States would lose VAT revenue. *See* F. Vanistendael, *A Proposal for a Definitive VAT System. Taxation in the Country of Origin at the Rate of the Country of Destination Without Clearing* (1995) 1 EC Tax Review, pp. 45-53 https://doi.org/10.54648/ecta1995005.

1.7.4 The Abolition of Fiscal Frontiers and the Introduction of the Transitional System (1993)

Not long after it became clear that the Member States were unwilling to introduce a clearinghouse mechanism, certainly not before 1 January 1993, the Commission came up with an alternative: the transitional system for ICTs.

These measures were included in the Sixth VAT Directive and entered into force as from 1 January 1993. Although it was only intended as a temporary system, to cover the interval between 1 January 1993 and 1 January 1997 (the date on which the Member States were supposed to come with a definitive system), the transitional system obtained a permanent character after all. It is still in place, even though it is still referred to as the 'transitional system'.

Under the transitional system, as the main rule, taxation was to take place in the Member State of destination. With respect to supplies of goods, this was achieved through creating a system of (exempt) intra-Community supplies ('ICSs') in the Member State of origin and (taxed) intra-Community acquisitions ('ICAs') in the Member State of destination. It was intended that this transitional system would only apply until 1997 and that the Member States would use the intervening years to adopt a definitive system. History shows that the Member States have been unable to agree upon a definitive system. Therefore, the transitional system has been extended and is still in place. It is now an integral part of the current VAT Directive. However, in 2017 the European Commission has issued a series of proposals that eventually should replace the transitional system with a definitive VAT system.[47] It was proposed that as of 2022 the system of (exempt) ICSs in the Member State of origin and (taxed) ICAs in the Member State of destination is replaced with a system in which only a single taxable event (the Intra-union supply) would take place in case of a cross-border sale of goods. The proposals currently remain on the table but have not been adopted by the Member States, and we believe it is doubtful whether they ever will.

1.8 THE CURRENT STATE OF EU VAT LEGISLATION

In this section, we describe the most important EU legislative products relating to VAT that are currently in place.

1.8.1 The VAT Directive

When the First and the Sixth VAT Directives were adopted, the world was very different from how it looks now. For example, there were still fiscal frontiers between the Member States, there was no internet, and electronically supplied services were unthinkable. Since then, a lot has changed. In order to keep pace with reality, the Sixth

47. *See* most notably Proposal for a Council Directive amending Directive 2006/112/EC as regards the introduction of the detailed technical measures for the operation of the definitive VAT system for the taxation of trade between Member States, COM (2018)329.

VAT Directive was amended numerous times. Some of these changes were very substantial (for instance, the introduction of the transitional measures regarding ICSs). The effect of the many changes to the Sixth VAT Directive became more and more incomprehensible for insiders and had even become mysterious for outsiders. Moreover, the order of the provisions in the Sixth VAT Directive was not always logical.

In 2006, for reasons of clarity and rationalization, the Council completely overhauled the Sixth VAT Directive, 'recasting' it. This resulted in Directive 2006/112/EC.[48] We refer to this as the 'VAT Directive'. On 1 January 2007, the Directive entered into force. Since that date, it has been the main piece of legislation in EU VAT. The First and Second VAT Directives have been repealed.

The (recast) VAT Directive brought together and logically arranged the various provisions spread out over various Directives into one piece of legislation. Even though the existing provisions were changed substantially and put in a different order, the (recast) VAT Directive contained few material changes. Article 411(2) VAT Directive stipulates that references to repealed (VAT) Directives shall be construed as references to the VAT Directive and must be read in accordance with the correlation table contained in Annex XII to that VAT Directive. This provision removes the need to change all other legislative products that referred to the Sixth Directive. Likewise, it implies that all CJEU decisions which refer to the articles of the Sixth VAT Directive, in principle, keep their relevance for the explanation and interpretation of the corresponding articles in the VAT Directive.[49] In this book, we refer to the articles of the VAT Directive unless it is necessary to refer to the corresponding old articles.

On 12 February 2008, the VAT Directive underwent its most significant material change since the abolition of the internal frontiers in 1993 (*see* section 1.7.4). On that date, new rules on the place of supply of services were adopted.[50] The reason for these changes was that it had become clear that the realization of the internal market, globalization, deregulation and technology change – all combined – created enormous changes in the volume and pattern of trade in services. Nowadays, it is increasingly possible for a number of services to be supplied at a distance. Modernization and simplification called for fundamental changes to the manner in which services were to be taxed. In essence, the new rules stipulated that as a main rule, cross-border services supplied to (another) taxable person were to be taxed according to the destination principles. Services supplied to a non-taxable person were, in principle, to be taxed according to the origin principle. Because it was expected that some of the changes made to the place of supply of services could have a considerable impact on the budget of the Member States, it was decided that a smooth transition required that these changes should be introduced over time. Consequently, the first changes were scheduled for 2010, with further changes in 2011, 2013 and – lastly – in 2015. In Chapter 4, we will further explain the place of supply rules. In 2017 and 2019, yet

48. Council Directive 2006/112/EC of 28 November 2006 on the common system of value added tax [2006] OJ L347/1.
49. CJEU 12 November 2020, Case C-42/19 *Sonaecom SGPS SA v Autoridade Tributária e Aduaneira*, ECLI:EU:C:2020:913, para. 29.
50. Council Directive 2008/8/EC of 12 February 2008 amending Directive 2006/112/EC as regards the place of supply of services [2008] OJ L44/1.

another important changes were adopted, focussing on the VAT treatment of e-commerce transactions (*see* Chapters 4, 13 and 14).[51] In December 2022, the European Commission published its VAT in a Digital Age ('ViDA') proposal.[52] The proposal consists of three separate pillars that in combination seek to modernize the VAT system to make it better fitting to today's digital world. The first pillar is a proposal for a new real-time digital reporting system based on e-invoicing that is aimed at introducing an EU-wide system for electronic invoicing and electronic reporting of VAT obligations. The second pillar is aimed at establishing a Single EU VAT registration for businesses selling to consumers across the EU and contains several measures to make VAT registrations in other Member States than the Member State of establishment of the taxable person obsolete. The third pillar contains updated rules for the platform economy. Most notably, it aims to create a fiction to make platforms that act as an intermediary for the short-term rental of accommodation and passenger transport liable for all VAT due with respect to transactions concluded on their platforms. Until now, the third pillar has proved to be the proposals' Achilles heel. Adoption of the proposal was stopped by Estonia as they did not agree to the third-pillar measures. On 5 November 2024, however, the Economic and Financial Affairs Council (ECOFIN) of the EU finally adopted the ViDA package following the adoption of compromises to the original proposals made to satisfy all 27 Member States. Due to substantial changes made by the Council in the directive, the European Parliament will be consulted (again), and subsequently the text of the directive will need to be formally adopted by the Council before it can enter into force.

1.8.2 The Refund Directives

In addition to the VAT Directive, there are two other Directives in the field of VAT that should not go unmentioned in the context of this book.[53] The first one is Directive 2008/9/EC,[54] which deals with refunds of VAT to taxable persons that are established in another Member State than the Member State of refund. It builds further on Article 171(1) VAT Directive. The second is Directive 86/560/EEC[55] (referred to as the

51. Council Directive (EU) 2017/2455 of 5 December 2017 amending Directive 2006/112/EC and Directive 2009/132/EC as regards certain value added tax obligations for supplies of services and distance sales of goods [2017] OJ L 348/7 and Council Directive (EU) 2019/1995 of 21 November 2019 amending Directive 2006/112/EC as regards provisions relating to distance sales of goods and certain domestic supplies of goods [2019] OJ L310/1.
52. European Commission, Proposal for a Council Directive amending Directive 2006/112/EC as regards VAT rules for the digital age, COM(2022) 701 final.
53. For completeness' sake, we note other Directives that are relevant in the field of VAT: Directive 2009/132/EC (VAT-free importation), Directive 2006/79/EC (private consignments) and Directive 2007/74/EC (travellers' allowances).
54. Council Directive 2008/9/EC of 12 February 2008 laying down detailed rules for the refund of value added tax, provided for in Directive 2006/112/EC (the VAT Directive) to taxable persons not established in the Member State of refund but established in another Member State [2008] OJ L44/23.
55. Thirteenth Council Directive 86/560/EEC of 17 November 1986 on the harmonization of the laws of the Member States relating to turnover taxes – Arrangements for the refund of value added tax to taxable persons not established in Community territory [1986] OJ L326/40.

'Thirteenth VAT Directive'), which further details Article 171(2) VAT Directive. It deals with refunds of VAT to taxable persons established outside the EU. We will further elaborate on these Directives in Chapter 10.

1.8.3 The VAT Implementing Regulation

Traditionally, the harmonization of VAT, excise duties and direct taxation were realized by means of Directives. This changed in 2005 when the European Council adopted VAT Implementing Regulation 1777/2005/EC,[56] which entered into force on 1 July 2006. It was amended a couple of times within a few years. With a view to the changes to the place of supply rules for services in 2010 (and following years), which required a number of substantial changes, for reasons of clarity and rationalization, on 15 March 2011, a recast VAT Implementing Regulation was adopted.[57]

The main purpose of the VAT Implementing Regulation is to ensure that the application of the VAT system complies more fully with the objective of the internal market in cases where divergences in the application have arisen or may arise, which are incompatible with the proper functioning of such internal market.[58] In other words: it serves to further detail certain provisions in the VAT Directive. However, since a Directive needs to be transposed into national law in order to have effect, while a regulation has direct effect (i.e., it does *not* need to be transposed into national legislation to have an effect), the relation between these two legal instruments is the cause of some friction.[59]

The legal basis for the VAT Implementing Regulation can be found in Article 397 of the VAT Directive. The latter is derived from Article 291(2) of the TFEU. This article states that:

> where uniform conditions for implementing legally binding Union acts are needed, those acts shall confer implementing powers on the Commission, or, in duly justified specific cases and in the cases provided for in Articles 24 and 26 of the Treaty on European Union, on the Council.

With respect to implementing acts adopted by the *Commission*, the CJEU ruled that such acts must not conflict with the act they are implementing.[60] The VAT Implementing Regulation, however, is an implementing act adopted by the *Council*.

---

56. Council Regulation (EC) No 1777/2005 of 17 October 2005 laying down implementing measures for Directive 77/388/EEC on the common system of value added tax [2005] OJ L288/1.
57. Council Implementing Regulation (EU) No 282/2011 of 15 March 2011 laying down implementing measures for Directive 2006/112/EC on the common system of value added tax (recast) [2011] OJ L 77/1 as amended by Council Implementing Regulation (EU) No 1042/2013 of 7 October 2013 amending Implementing Regulation (EU) No 282/2011 as regards the place of supply of services [2013] OJ L284/1.
58. Preambule to the VAT Implementing Regulation, point 2.
59. *See* I. Lejeune & B. Mesdom, *Taxable Amount in the Case of Credit Card Payments in the Light of the New EU Regulation* (2006) 1 International VAT Monitor, pp. 23-29. *See also* CJEU 28 February 2023, Case C-695/22 *Fenix International Ltd v Commissioners for Her Majesty's Revenue and Customs*, ECLI:EU:C:2023:127.
60. CJEU 15 October 2014, Case C-65/13, *European Parliament v European Commission*, ECLI: EU:C:2014:2289.

Nonetheless, the CJEU ruled in *Fenix* that, in this regard, no distinction should be made depending on whether the implementing act is adopted by the Commission or the Council.[61] Consequently, the condition that the implementing act must not conflict with the act it is implementing applies to the VAT Implementing Regulation. According to the CJEU, an implementing measure:

> merely specifies the provisions of the legislative act concerned where it is intended solely, in general or in certain specific cases, to clarify the scope of those provisions or to determine the detailed rules for their application, provided, however, that in so doing, that measure avoids any contradiction with the objectives of those provisions and does not in any way alter the normative content of that act or its scope of application.[62]

In 2017 and 2019, important changes to the VAT Implementing Regulation were made with respect to the application of VAT to e-commerce transactions (*see* Chapters 4, 13 and 14).[63] The ViDA package again contains amendments to the VAT Implementing Regulation (*see* section 1.8.1).

1.9 OTHER KEY SOURCES OF EU VAT LAW

In this section, we highlight other key sources of EU VAT law. We note that there are certainly more sources of EU VAT law than those described in this section. However, for the purposes of this book, we feel that the sources described in this and in the previous section are sufficient for a thorough understanding of the fundamentals of EU VAT law.

1.9.1 CJEU Case Law

An important source of EU VAT law is the case law of the CJEU. Simply put, as regards VAT, the task of the CJEU is to explain and interpret the provisions in the VAT Directive. The CJEU has already ruled in over a thousand cases in the field of VAT. In fact, VAT is one the CJEU's largest case law generating domains. CJEU case law has *ex tunc* effect: the CJEU's interpretation of the rule of law must be regarded as having been applicable from the outset.

61. CJEU 28 February 2023, Case C-695/20 *Fenix International Limited v Commissioners for Her Majesty's Revenue and Customs*, ECLI:EU:C:2023:127.
62. *Ibid.*, para. 50. With respect to Article 9a of the VAT Implementing Regulation the CJEU ruled that the provision is valid because it does not supplement or amend Article 28 of the VAT Directive.
63. Council Implementing Regulation (EU) 2017/2459 of 5 December 2017 amending Implementing Regulation (EU) No 282/2011 laying down implementing measures for Directive 2006/112/EC on the common system of value added tax [2017] OJ L 348/32 and Council Implementing Regulation (EU) 2019/2026 of 21 November 2019 amending Implementing Regulation (EU) No 282/2011 as regards supplies of goods or services facilitated by electronic interfaces and the special schemes for taxable persons supplying services to non-taxable persons, making distance sales of goods and certain domestic supplies of goods [2019] OJ L 313/14.

It is settled CJEU case law that the CJEU cannot apply EU law to a given case, nor give judgment on the validity of a measure of national law with regard to it. The CJEU's task is to interpret EU law.[64] National courts may refer to the CJEU if the interpretation of Union law is unclear to them. In some cases, national courts are even required to refer to the CJEU on the interpretation of Union law.[65] The CJEU may also be asked to give its interpretation on a rule of Union law in case of a so-called infringement procedure. Thus, the CJEU provides national courts with guidelines on how rules of Union law should be interpreted. It speaks for itself that this also applies in the field of VAT.

Following a proposal by the CJEU in December 2022, a change has been made to the TFEU and the Statute of the Court of Justice, making it possible for the CJEU to refer preliminary questions on VAT and several other topics to the General Court as a way to deal with the extensive workload of the CJEU.[66] As of October 2024, the General Court holds the authority to issue preliminary ruling in the field of among others VAT. Preliminary questions by the courts of the Member States will still be referred to the CJEU but will in principle be forwarded to the General Court. Exceptions are possible if a case goes beyond the specific area of VAT and, for example, also includes questions on the Charter of the European Union. In specific situations, the CJEU may reassess the decisions by the General Court.

1.9.2 Explanatory Notes

Sometimes the European Commission publishes so-called explanatory notes.[67] These aim at providing a better understanding of the EU legislation. However, they are not legally binding and only provide practical and informal guidance about how EU law should be understood and applied on the basis of the views of the Commission's Directorate General for Taxation and Customs Union. Moreover, these notes are a work in progress, not a final product, and reflect the state of play at a certain point in time in accordance with the knowledge and experience available. Over time, it is expected that additional elements may be needed. As they are not legally binding, are a work in progress and are extensive (some explanatory notes consist of 90 pages or more), we feel that even though they may entertain a trained VAT expert, there is a risk that they

64. Cf. CJEU 20 May 1976, Case 111/75 *Impresa Costruzioni comm. Quirino Mazzalai v Ferrovia del Renon*, ECLI:EU:C:1976:68.
65. There is no need for a national court to refer to the CJEU, if the interpretation of rules of Union law is clear (*acte claire*) or has already been clarified by the CJEU (*acte eclairé*).
66. Regulation (EU, Euratom) 2024/2019 of the European Parliament and of the European Council of 11 April 2024 amending Protocol No 3 on the Statute of the Court of Justice of the European Union, OJ L, 12.8.2024.
67. With respect to the so-called place of supply provisions in the '2015 package', or 'Mini one-stop shop' (*see* Chapters 4 and 16) the European Commission published so-called explanatory notes. Also with regard to the place of supply rules on services connected with immovable property explanatory notes have been published. *See*: https://taxation-customs.ec.europa.eu/taxation/vat/commission-guidelines-vat_en (accessed 15 November 2024).

will confuse rather than enlighten businesses, especially those that cannot afford to hire professional VAT experts.[68]

1.9.3 Derogations for Member States

On the basis of Article 395 VAT Directive, Member States may be authorized to introduce special measures derogating from the provisions of the VAT Directive, in order to simplify the procedure for collecting VAT or for preventing certain forms of tax evasion or avoidance. However, the introduction of such special rules requires that the Member State sends an application to the Commission and provides all the necessary information. The Commission will then notify the other Member States and present to the Council either an appropriate proposal or, should it object to the derogation requested, a communication setting out its objections (Article 395(2) VAT Directive). Over the years, numerous derogations have been approved.[69] Since the derogations that had been granted appeared to be useful for other Member States (that did not ask for a derogation) as well, Directive 2006/69/EC was adopted on 24 July 2006.[70] This Directive, amending (what is now) the VAT Directive gives Member States the option of applying special rules to simplify the application of VAT or to counter tax avoidance and evasion without having to seek individual authorization. Furthermore, Directive 2010/23/EU of 16 March 2010 introduced Article 199a VAT Directive, which allowed the Member States until 30 June 2015 and for a minimum period of two years, to provide that with respect to certain supplies, the person liable for payment of VAT is another taxable person than the supplier. The Member States do not have to await the approval of the European Commission to implement such measures, but they do need to inform the Commission on the implementation thereof. This mechanism of derogation is commonly referred to as the 'Quick Reaction Mechanism' (QRM). Article 80 VAT Directive contains a general mechanism, not requiring prior approval, for derogative measures with respect to the taxable amount.[71]

68. In that regard, we welcome the fact that the Commission also took the initiative to publish a (non-legally binding, work in progress) 'Guide to the Mini One Stop Shop', which at least clarifies this part of the changes in the 2015 package and 'only' take up 31 pages, https://taxation-customs.ec.europa.eu/document/download/ca213281-027c-4ade-9a07-0c60e8929242_en?filename=one-stop-shop-guidelines_en.pdf (accessed 27 August 2024).
69. *See* for a list of the derogations that have been approved, https://taxation-customs.ec.europa.eu/document/download/b71ba13e-4e65-440a-a4ee-e1787e833998_en?filename=2024.04.19_vat_index_derogations.pdf (accessed 27 August 2024).
70. Council Directive 2006/69/EC of 24 July 2006 amending Directive 77/388/EEC as regards certain measures to simplify the procedure for charging value added tax and to assist in countering tax evasion or avoidance, and repealing certain Decisions granting derogations [2006] OJ L 221/9.
71. *See* for a list of derogations based on Articles 80 and 199a VAT Directive, https://taxation-customs.ec.europa.eu/system/files/2016-09/vat_derogations_options_directive_112-06_en.pdf (accessed 7 November 2023).

1.9.4 VAT Committee Guidelines and European Commission Communications

Furthermore, Article 398 VAT Directive is a source of EU VAT law in itself. This provision deals with the so-called VAT Committee. The function of the VAT Committee is to promote the uniform application of the provisions of the VAT Directive. However, it is only an advisory committee and has no legislative powers. Consequently, the VAT Committee cannot take legally binding decisions. The guidelines which the VAT Committee adopts after examining questions raised by the Commission or a Member State do not bind the European Commission or the Member States, which are free not to follow them. However, the VAT Committee guidelines can be regarded as 'soft law'. The same is true with respect to – for example – the non-legally binding 'communications' by the European Commission.[72]

1.10 THE RELATION BETWEEN PRIMARY EU LAW, SECONDARY EU LAW AND NATIONAL LAW

In this section, we discuss the relation between the various legal instruments that are relevant to the application of EU VAT. First, we will explain that there are different layers of law: primary EU law, secondary EU law and national law. Then we will discuss how VAT should be applied if national law is not identical to or even not in conformity with secondary EU law.

Please note that the purpose of this section is to provide a concise introduction to EU law, focusing on the domain of VAT. For a more in-depth analysis of EU law and the relation between primary EU law, secondary EU law and national law, we refer to the widely available literature on EU law.

1.10.1 Introduction: Layers of VAT Law

In *Van Gend en Loos*, the CJEU ruled that the European Economic Community (now: the EU) constitutes a new legal order of international law for the benefit of which the states have limited their sovereign rights, albeit within limited fields, and the subjects of which comprise not only the Member States but also their nationals.[73] EU law is an integral part of the legal system of the Member States, thus forming part of their own law. In *Costa v ENEL*, the CJEU confirmed that subject to conditions, Union law takes

72. For example: Communication from the Commission to the Council and the European Parliament on the VAT group option provided for in Article 11 of Council Directive 2006/112/EC on the common system of value added tax, COM (2009) 325 final, http://eur-lex.europa.eu/LexUriServ/LexUriServ.do?uri=COM:2009:0325:FIN:EN:PDF (accessed 13 November 2024).
73. CJEU 5 February 1963, Case 26/62 *NV Algemene Transport- en Expeditie Onderneming van Gend & Loos v Netherlands Inland Revenue Administration*, ECLI:EU:C:1963:1.

precedence over the national law of Member States (doctrine of the primacy of EU law).[74]

It is not uncommon to make a distinction between primary and secondary EU law.

Primary EU Law

The main sources of primary law are the Treaty on European Union (TEU) and the Treaty on the Functioning of the European Union (TFEU). With respect to VAT, the most relevant component of primary EU law is the TFEU. This treaty can be seen as a contract concluded by countries (Member States) through which they created supranational bodies which are entitled to make and interpret supranational legislation (Directives, regulations, decisions, recommendations and opinions). The most relevant bodies (from a VAT perspective) are the European Council, the European Commission, the European Parliament and the Court of Justice of the EU and (as an ancillary body) the European Economic and Social Committee.

Secondary EU Law

The legislative products of the aforementioned supranational bodies together form secondary Community law. Sources of secondary EU law are legal instruments based on the treaties and include unilateral secondary law[75] and conventions and agreements.[76] In the field of VAT, the main items of secondary EU law are the VAT Directive (as well as the Refund Directives and some Directives indirectly relating to VAT) and the VAT Implementing Regulation (*see* section 1.8).

Sometimes a third source of EU law is determined, referred to as supplementary sources of EU law. This category consists of elements of law not provided for by the treaties and includes, for example (but is not limited to), CJEU case law (*see* section 1.9.1) and general principles of law (both of a secondary and of a primary EU law level). Hereinafter, we only refer to and distinguish between primary EU law (including case law and general principles associated with primary EU law) and secondary EU law (including case law and general principles associated with secondary EU law).

Primary and secondary EU law can be considered as two 'layers' of EU law. National law transposing a Directive can be considered as forming a third layer of law. More specific to the field of VAT, the main source of primary EU law is the TFEU; the main sources of secondary EU law are the VAT Directive and the VAT Implementing Regulation; while the main source of national law is each Member State's national act implementing the VAT Directive. Figure 1.3 serves to illustrate this.

74. CJEU 15 July 1964, Case 6-64 *Flaminio Costa v ENEL*, ECLI:EU:C:1964:66. *See also* Treaty of Lisbon, Declaration No 17.
75. For example: communications and recommendations, white and green papers.
76. For example: regulations, Directives, decisions, opinions and recommendations.

Figure 1.3 Layers of Law

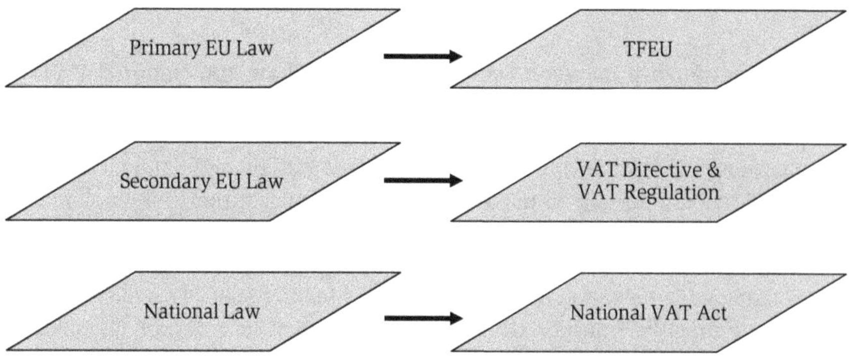

Union law consists not only of written but also unwritten (customary) law. Some general principles of law have been laid down in the TEU (e.g., the subsidiarity principle,[77] the principle of Union loyalty[78] and the prohibition of discrimination based on nationality)[79] but others are not (e.g., the principles of equivalence, effectiveness, legal certainty, protection of legitimate expectations and of interpretation prohibiting the abuse of Union law).

The CJEU plays a central role in identifying and interpreting the unwritten general principles of EU law. The legal basis for this role of the CJEU may be found in Article 19 TEU. This provision indicates that the CJEU shall ensure that in the interpretation and application of the treaties, the law is observed. The CJEU interprets the term 'the law' in such a manner that it covers both written and unwritten law. Consequently, both written and unwritten law are fundamentals of the Union legal order. More specifically, the CJEU identified various general (unwritten) principles of EU law, such as (but not limited to): the principles of equivalence, effectiveness and legal certainty, the principle of the protection of legitimate expectations, and the principle of interpretation prohibiting the abuse of Union law. The importance of these principles in practice should not be underestimated: many new problems cannot simply be solved by just applying a provision in the written law. Often, courts invoke principles of law in order to come to a decision.[80] It is difficult to determine whether the unwritten principles (being supplementary EU law) should be attributed to the first layer of EU law (primary EU law), to the second layer of EU law (secondary EU law) or to both layers.

We are inclined to attribute them to the first layer of primary EU law. After all, that is also where the written principles of EU law are to be found. However, the unwritten principles of EU law are, in a way, the 'DNA' of each and every provision of

77. Article 5 TEU.
78. Article 4(3) TEU.
79. Article 18 TEU.
80. T. Koopmans, *Judicial Activism and Procedural Law* (1993) 1/2 European Review of Private Law, p. 78 https://doi.org/10.54648/erpl1993006.

primary and secondary EU law. Therefore, one may take the view they are inherent to both primary and secondary EU law and that they do not even form a *separate* source of EU law.

1.10.2 Relationship Between Secondary EU VAT Law and National VAT Law

When analysing the relationship between secondary EU law and national law in the field of VAT, it is important to make a distinction between the VAT Implementing Regulation and the VAT Directive as sources of secondary EU law.

The reason for that is that a Directive must be implemented in, i.e., *transposed* into national law by the national legislator of each Member State. This means that the VAT Directive must be transposed into national law first in order for the rules laid down in it to be applicable.[81] Implementation of a Directive does not require that a Member State must literally copy the text of the Directive into its national legislation. Rather, Member States are free to choose the form and methods (and wording) in order to ensure that national legislation achieves the same results as the provisions in the Directive.[82] A Directive does not have direct effect in its entirety. Only if certain conditions are met specific provisions in a Directive will have direct effect. This also applies to the VAT Directive.

Conversely, if the European legislator uses the instrument of a Regulation instead of a Directive, no implementation of (secondary) EU law in national law is necessary because Regulations are *directly applicable*. When rules of national law conflict with a Regulation, such as the VAT Implementing Regulation, the rules of the (VAT) Regulation take precedence because a Regulation has in its entirety direct effect.[83] However, the European legislator can only use the form of a Regulation if all Member States unanimously decide to harmonize a specific area of EU law. Directives are the ideal instruments if there is not enough political will or courage to fully harmonize an area of EU law. It is because of this that Directives are used widely in the field of taxation.

Considering these differences between the VAT Directive and the VAT Implementing Regulation, we focus on the relation between the VAT Implementing Regulation and national VAT law in section 1.10.2.1. Next, in section 1.10.2.2, we focus on the relation between the VAT Directive(s) and the national VAT law.

81. *See*, however, section 1.10.2.2.2 with respect to the so-called direct effect.
82. CJEU 19 January 1982, Case 8/81 *Ursula Becker v Finanzamt Münster-Innenstadt*, ECLI:EU:C:1982:7, para. 17.
83. The provisions of an implementing act (the VAT Implementing Regulation) must, first, comply with the essential general aims pursued by the legislative act which those provisions are expected to clarify (the VAT Directive), and second, be necessary or appropriate for the uniform implementation of that act without supplementing or amending it, even as to its non-essential elements. CJEU 28 February 2023, Case C-695/20 *Fenix International Limited v Commissioners for Her Majesty's Revenue and Customs*, ECLI:EU:C:2023:127, paras 44 and 45.

1.10.2.1 Relationship Between the VAT Implementing Regulation and National VAT Law

A Regulation is generally applicable, is binding in its entirety, and is directly applicable in all Member States (*see* Article 288 TEU). That implies that a Regulation can be considered as a 'European law'. Consequently, a Regulation does not need to be transposed into the national law of a Member State: it is directly binding upon EU institutions, Member States and individuals. Even though a normative hierarchy exists between basic Regulations and implementing Regulations, both types of Regulation have direct effect. This means that the VAT Implementing Regulation, which lays down implementing measures for the VAT Directive, has direct effect. Both taxpayers and tax authorities can directly rely on the provisions of the VAT Implementing Regulation.

One of the consequences of the direct effect of the VAT Implementing Regulation is that if a situation occurs in which the rules of national law are disadvantageous in comparison with the rules laid down in the VAT Implementing Regulation, a taxable person can directly invoke the VAT Implementing Regulation to obtain the advantageous effect of the VAT Implementing Regulation. Conversely, the tax authorities of a Member State can use the VAT Implementing Regulation against a taxable person to prevent that taxable person from obtaining advantages laid down in national VAT law which are contrary to EU law.

1.10.2.2 Relationship Between the VAT Directive and National VAT Law

As opposed to a Regulation, a Directive does not automatically have a general direct effect. A Directive is binding as to the result to be achieved upon each Member State to which it is addressed. However, it leaves to the national authorities of each Member State the choice of form and methods.[84] Thus, a Directive must be transposed into national law in order for the rules to have effect, yet implementing does not mean that the text of the Directive must be copied exactly to national law. Consequently, national laws implementing Directives often use different wordings than the text of the VAT Directive they implement. Moreover, the fact that the text of a Directive does not need to be copied exactly into national law is one of the reasons why it may occur that the national law implementing a Directive is contrary to the Directive itself.

If the national VAT legislation is not consistent with the VAT Directive, it must first be established whether the rule(s) of national VAT law nevertheless can be interpreted in a manner that is in accordance with the VAT Directive ('reconciliatory interpretation' of the national (VAT) act, *see* section 1.10.2.2.1). If this proves to be impossible, then, subject to conditions, a provision in the VAT Directive may have direct effect (i.e., overrule the rule of national law, *see* section 1.10.2.2.2).

84. *Ibid.*

1.10.2.2.1 Reconciliatory (Compatible) Interpretation of the VAT Directive

If a rule of national VAT law is not identical to the corresponding rule in the VAT Directive, it should first be checked whether it is possible to interpret the rule of national law such that it is in conformity with the VAT Directive.[85] The national courts (and, in our view, also other institutions of Member States, such as the tax authorities) are required to interpret domestic law, and in particular, legislative provisions specifically adopted for the purpose of implementing the requirements of a Directive, so far as possible, in light of the wording and the purpose of the Directive concerned, in order to achieve the result sought by the Directive and consequently comply with the third paragraph of Article 288 TFEU.[86] This is called 'reconciliatory interpretation' or 'compatible interpretation'.

The obligation to interpret domestic law in accordance with a Directive applies irrespective of whether it adversely affects private individuals.[87] The question is how far a national court (or any other institution applying a provision specifically adopted for the purpose of implementing the requirements of a Directive) must and can go in interpreting the national provisions in light of the VAT Directive. In this regard, it is important to acknowledge that Union law does not demand interpretation of national law in conformity with Directives *contra legem*.[88] However, if indeed the application of interpretive methods recognized by national law enables a consistent interpretation of that national law, the national court (or other Member State institution) is bound to use those methods in order to achieve the result sought by the Directive.

1.10.2.2.2 Direct (Vertical) Effect of a Directive

The fact that Regulations are directly applicable, and consequently by their nature capable of producing direct effects, does not mean that other types of EU legislation cannot produce similar effects. As the CJEU confirmed in *Ratti,*[89] it would be incompatible with the binding effect which Article 288 TFEU gives to Directives to exclude on principle the possibility that persons can rely on the obligations imposed by these Directives. This would be particularly the case where EU authorities have, by means of Directive, placed the Member States under a duty to adopt a certain course of action.

85. For example: CJEU 13 November 1990, Case C-106/89 *Marleasing SA v La Comercial Internacional de Alimentacion SA*, ECLI:EU:C:1990:395, para. 8: 'the national court called upon to interpret it [the national law, authors] is required to do so, as far as possible, in the light of the wording and the purpose of the Directive in order to achieve the result pursued by the latter and thereby comply with the third paragraph of Article 189 of the Treaty'.
86. Cf. Opinion of Advocate General Kokott of 7 September 2006, Case C-369/04 *Hutchison 3G UK Ltd and Others v Commissioners of Customs and Excise,* ECLI:EU:C:2006:523, para. 143.
87. *Ibid.*, para. 147.
88. CJEU 16 June 2005, Case C-105/03 *Criminal proceedings against Maria Pupino,* ECLI:EU:C:2005:386, para. 4 and Opinion of Advocate General Kokott of 7 September 2006, Case C-369/04 *Hutchison 3G UK Ltd and Others v Commissioners of Customs and Excise,* ECLI:EU:C:2006:523, para. 150 and CJEU 8 May 2019, Case C-566/17 *Związek Gmin Zagłębia Miedziowego w Polkowicach v Szef Krajowej Administracji Skarbowej,* ECLI:EU:C:2019:390.
89. CJEU 5 April 1979, Case 148/78 *Criminal proceedings against Tullio Ratti,* ECLI:EU:C:1979:110.

The effectiveness of such an act would be weakened if persons were prevented from relying on it in legal proceedings. Consequently, the CJEU ruled that a Member State which has not adopted the implementing measures may not rely, as against individuals, on its own failure to perform the obligations which the Directive entails.[90]

In the landmark case of *Van Gend en Loos*, the CJEU introduced the principle of 'direct effect' of provisions in a Directive. From *Van Duyn*[91] and *Verbond Nederlandse Ondernemers*[92] ('*VNO*') it follows that a Directive has a direct effect when its provisions are unconditional and sufficiently clear and precise:

> It would be incompatible with the binding effect attributed to a Directive by article 189 to exclude, in principle, the possibility that the obligation which it imposes may be invoked by those concerned. In particular, where the Community authorities have, by Directive, imposed on member states the obligation to pursue a particular course of conduct, the useful effect of such an act would be weakened if individuals were prevented from relying on it before their national court and if the latter were prevented from taking it into consideration as an element of Community law. This is especially so when the individual invokes a provision of a Directive before a national court in order that the latter shall rule whether the competent national authorities, in exercising the choice which is left to them as to the form and the methods for implementing the Directive, have kept within the limits as to their discretion set out in the Directive.[93]

However, a Directive can only produce a direct effect if it has not been implemented within the prescribed period[94] or if the provision defines rights which individuals are able to assert against the state.[95]

Thus, wherever the provisions of a Directive appear to be unconditional and sufficiently precise, those provisions may, in the absence of implementing measures adopted within the prescribed period, be relied upon against any national provision which is incompatible with the Directive, or in so far as the provisions define rights which individuals are able to assert against the state. They then have a direct effect.[96] However, no direct effect can be invoked by the state – that has failed to take the

90. *Ibid.*
91. CJEU 4 December 1974, Case 41-74 *Yvonne van Duyn v Home Office,* ECLI:EU:C:1974:133.
92. CJEU 1 February 1977, Case 51/76 *Verbond van Nederlandse Ondernemingen v Inspecteur der Invoerrechten en Accijnzen,* ECLI:EU:C:1977:12.
93. *Ibid.*
94. So long as the period prescribed for the Member States to incorporate the provisions of a Directive into their national legislation has not expired, the Directive cannot have direct effect; such effect only arises at the end of the period prescribed and in the event of default by the Member State concerned. CJEU 5 April 1979, Case 148/78 *Criminal proceedings against Tullio Ratti,* ECLI:EU:C:1979:110.
95. CJEU 5 April 1979, Case 148/78 *Criminal proceedings against Tullio Ratti,* ECLI:EU:C:1979:110. *See also* B. Terra & P. Wattel, *European Tax Law* (Kluwer 2012), p. 116.
96. From *British Film Institute,* it can be inferred that a partial direct effect is conceivable. The CJEU considered that: 'In so far as that provision [*authors: Article 13A(1)(n) of the Sixth Directive*] allows the Member States a discretion in determining the exempted cultural services, it does not satisfy the conditions (...) for being capable of being relied on directly before the national courts.' CJEU 15 February 2017, Case C-592/15 *Commissioners for Her Majesty's Revenue and Customs v British Film Institute,* ECLI:EU:C:2017:117, para. 24.

appropriate implementing measures – against individuals where the Directive is disadvantageous for such individual in comparison to the national provisions.[97]

1.10.2.2.3 Symmetrical and Asymmetrical Reliance on the VAT Directive

In the previous paragraph we discussed the rule that where the treatment of certain activities is more favourable under the VAT Directive than under the national VAT Act, and the provision in the Directive at issue is not implemented in a timely or correct fashion, the taxable person may rely upon the European provision directly, as long as the provision is sufficiently precise, clear and unconditional ('direct effect').

A particular feature of VAT is that the VAT treatment of output transactions is relevant not only to the question of whether and to what amount VAT is chargeable on supply but also to the question of whether input VAT can be deducted. A right of deduction exists only insofar as a taxable person has used the goods and services he purchased for his taxed transactions. Consequently, if a taxable person invokes the direct effect of an (e.g., wrongfully implemented) exemption in the VAT Directive, systematically, no corresponding right of deduction should exist. However, the taxable person invoking the direct effect as regards the application of the exemption, on the one hand, might argue that on the other hand, he can rely on national law with respect to the right of deduction. He may take the position that since under national law (due to the incorrect implementation of the exemption), the output transaction is considered a taxed transaction, a corresponding right of deduction exists under national law. Then a result is achieved, which is not in line with system neutrality (*see* section 1.12.1). Similarly, if a transaction is wrongfully exempted by the national VAT legislation, the related input VAT will not be recoverable under that national regime. Then, a taxable person may argue that he can rely on the national rule only to the extent that the output transaction is exempted, and that he can invoke the direct effect of the VAT Directive just for the recovery of input VAT. In both situations, the taxable person achieves 'the best of both worlds': no VAT chargeable on his output transaction, and a full right of deduction on his purchases. This mechanism is referred to as 'asymmetrical reliance on the VAT Directive'.[98]

The CJEU does not accept asymmetrical reliance on the VAT Directive. In *VDP Dental,* it considered:

> Therefore, an undertaking like VDP, which objects to national legislation such as that at issue in the main proceedings on the ground that it is inconsistent with the Sixth Directive, can rely directly on the provisions of that Directive for the purpose of securing a decision that the supplies of dental prostheses concerned are liable to VAT and, consequently, deduct input VAT relating to such supplies.[99]

97. CJEU 8 October 1987, Case 80/86 *Kolpinghuis Nijmegen,* ECLI:EU:C:1987:431.
98. Opinion of Advocate General Kokott of 7 September 2006, Case C-401/05 *VDP Dental Laboratory NV v Staatssecretaris van Financiën,* ECLI:EU:C:2006:537, para. 95.
99. CJEU 14 December 2006, Case C-401/05 *VDP Dental Laboratory NV v Staatssecretaris van Financiën,* ECLI:EU:C:2006:792, para. 41.

In *VDP Dental II/X bv/Nobel Biocare Nederland BV*, the CJEU confirmed that where an exemption from VAT provided for by national law is incompatible with the VAT Directive, a taxable person cannot benefit from both that exemption and the right to deduct.[100]

In our opinion, this means that only a symmetrical reliance on the VAT Directive is acceptable.[101] If the VAT treatment by the Directive (both in terms of the deduction of input VAT and the chargeability of VAT on the output transactions) is more favourable than the VAT treatment under the national VAT Act of both the inputs and outputs, a taxable person can invoke the direct effect of a rule in the VAT Directive, but then he has to accept the VAT consequences of that rule for both his inputs and his outputs.

Sometimes, it can only be established in hindsight that a taxable person has enjoyed the benefits of an asymmetrical reliance on the VAT Directive. For example, if a taxable person deducted the input VAT in good faith (relying on domestic rules or national case law) and at a later stage – based on later CJEU case law – it turns out that the output transaction had to be exempted (instead of being taxed, as national VAT law stipulated), it needs to be examined whether the deduction made by the taxable person must be left undisturbed based on the principles of the protection of legitimate expectations and legal certainty.

1.10.2.2.4 Direct (Horizontal) Effect of the Directive

An interesting question is whether a person can rely on a (not correctly transposed) Directive against another person. From *Faccini Dori,*[102] the answer to this question seems to be negative because Directives are addressed to the Member States and should, therefore, not be capable of creating of themselves obligations for individuals or corporations who would be unaware of such obligations on the basis of national law.[103] In *Faccini Dori*, Ms Faccine Dori had wanted to cancel a contract that she had concluded with an Italian company at Milan's central railway station for an English language correspondence course. She wanted to execute her right to rely on a European Directive that provided for the possibility to cancel contracts negotiated away from a company's business premises. That Directive, however, had not been transposed into Italy's national legislation. The Court ruled that in the absence of measures transposing the Directive within the prescribed time limit, consumers could not derive from the Directive itself a right of cancellation as against traders with whom they had concluded

100. CJEU 26 February 2015, Joined Cases C-144/13, C-154/13 and C-160/13 *VDP Dental Laboratory NV v Staatssecretaris van Financiën (C-144/13) Staatssecretaris van Financiën v X BV (C-154/13) and Nobel Biocare Nederland BV (C-160/13)*, ECLI:EU:C:2015:116, para. 40.
101. However, it is possible to rely on the VAT Directive with regard to a single transaction, and to rely on domestic legislation with regard to another transaction. *See* CJEU 3 September 2014, C-589/12 *Commissioners for Her Majesty's Revenue and Customs and GMAC UK plc*, ECLI: EU:C:2014:2131.
102. CJEU 14 July 1994, Case C-91/92 *Paola Faccini Dori v Recreb Srl*, ECLI:EU:C:1994:292.
103. B. Terra & J. Kajus, *A Guide to the European VAT Directives, Introduction to European VAT*, Vol. 1 (IBFD 2014), pp. 166-167.

a contract, or enforce such a right in a national court. In essence, this means that Directives cannot produce horizontal effect, even if the relevant provisions are unconditional and sufficiently precise.

However, from *Feuerbestattungsverein Halle*, it follows that something like a horizontal effect *does* seem to exist in the case of Directives that have already been implemented.[104] A private company running a crematorium in the town of Halle believed it experienced a different VAT treatment from a crematorium operated by a body governed by public law in the adjacent city of Lutherstadt-Eisleben. The company asserted that the non-taxation or under-taxation by the German tax authorities of the public body in Lutherstadt-Eisleben was unlawful. The Court ruled:

> Therefore, individuals are entitled to rely before national courts, against the Member State concerned, on the provisions of a Directive which appear, so far as their subject-matter is concerned, to be unconditional and sufficiently precise whenever the full application of the Directive is not in fact secured, that is to say, not only where the Directive has not been implemented or has been implemented incorrectly, but also where the national measures correctly implementing the Directive are not being applied in such a way as to achieve the result sought by it (Case C-62/00 Marks & Spencer [2002] ECR I-6325, paragraph 27).
>
> ...
>
> ... a private person who is in competition with a body governed by public law and alleges that that body is, in respect of the activities in which it engages as a public authority, treated as a non-taxable person for VAT purposes or under-taxed is entitled to rely, before the national court, on the second subparagraph of Article 4(5) of the Sixth Directive.[105]

Although this case deals with the interpretation of a very specific VAT rule, written for public bodies (*see* Chapter 2, section 2.7), and even though one of the parties involved was indeed (a public body of) a Member State, one may conclude that it is conceivable that one taxpayer whose position is directly affected by the VAT treatment of another person, is – by relying on a provision of a European Directive – eventually able to influence the tax position of that other individual (in this case, the public legal entity). This could be considered a kind of horizontal effect. However, we are not inclined to take this as far as saying that the CJEU accepted (full) horizontal effect of the VAT Directive.

1.10.3 Relationship Between Primary EU Law and National Law

In section 1.10.2, we discussed the relationship between secondary EU law and national law. However, in some cases, primary EU law plays a direct role in the application of the VAT rules. In this section, we will discuss the basics of the relationship between primary EU law and national law.

---

104. CJEU 8 June 2006, Case C-430/04 *Finanzamt Eisleben v Feuerbestattungsverein Halle eV*, ECLI:EU:C:2006:374.
105. *Ibid.*, paras 29 and 31.

1.10.3.1 *Direct (Vertical) Effect of Unwritten Primary EC Law*

If national implementing provisions do not conflict with secondary EU law (simply) because nothing is arranged at that level, taxable persons have to look beyond the secondary EU law level (the Directive) to safeguard their EU rights. Effectively, this implies the need to test the application of national provisions against one or more unwritten EU principles. This is what happened in - for example - *Marks & Spencer.*[106]

The national provision at issue was a rule by which the UK reduced from six to three years the period within which repayment may be sought of wrongly paid VAT. The UK provided that the new time limit was to apply immediately to all claims made after the date of enactment of that legislation, and to claims made between that date and an earlier date, being that of the entry into force of the legislation, as well as to claims for repayment made before the date of entry into force which were still pending on that date. No rule in the VAT Directive explicitly prevented the UK government from reducing the above period, but Marks & Spencer appealed against this national measure by arguing that the rule was a breach of Community law, in particular, a breach of three unwritten principles of primary EU law: the principle of legal certainty, effectiveness and of the protection of legitimate expectations.

The CJEU agreed with Marks & Spencer. According to the CJEU, limitation periods must be fixed in advance in order to safeguard the legal certainty principle,[107] but the principle of effectiveness must also be safeguarded. The aim of that principle is that it should not become virtually impossible or excessively difficult for individuals to exercise rights conferred by Community law. Accordingly, legislation such as that at issue, the retroactive effect of which deprives individuals of any possibility of exercising a right which they previously enjoyed with regard to the repayment of VAT, must be held to be incompatible with the principle of effectiveness. The United Kingdom government maintained that the principle of the protection of legitimate expectations was not relevant in this dispute. It submitted that determination of the procedural rules governing claims for the recovery of overpayments of VAT was entirely a matter of domestic law, subject only to the observance of the Community law principles of equivalence and effectiveness. If the principle of the protection of legitimate expectations was applicable in the dispute in the main proceedings, the only expectation would be that individuals are entitled to have their claims dealt with in accordance with the procedural rules of national law, which happened in the present case. But the CJEU ruled that it had consistently held that the principle of the protection of legitimate expectations forms part of the EU legal order, and must be observed by the Member States when they exercise the powers conferred on them by the EU.[108] The Court has

106. CJEU 11 July 2002, Case C-62/00 *Marks & Spencer plc v Commissioners of Customs & Excise,* ECLI:EU:C:2002:435.
107. CJEU 15 July 1970, Case 41-69 *ACF Chemiefarma NV v Commission of the European Communities,* ECLI:EU:C:1970:71, para. 19.
108. CJEU 26 April 1988, Case 316/86 *Hauptzollamt Hamburg-Jonas v Firma P. Krücken,* ECLI:EU:C:1988:201, para. 22; CJEU 1 April 1993, Joined Cases C-31/91-C-44/91 *SpA Alois Lageder and others v Amministrazione delle Finanze dello Stato,* ECLI:EU:C:1993:132, para. 33; CJEU 3 December 1998, Case C-381/97 *Belgocodex SA v Belgian State,* ECLI:EU:C:1998:589, para. 26

held, in particular, that a legislative amendment retroactively depriving a taxable person of a right to deduction he has derived from the Sixth Directive (now: VAT Directive) is incompatible with the principle of the protection of legitimate expectations.[109] Thus, unwritten primary EU law prevailed over (written) national law.

1.10.3.2 Direct (Vertical) Effect of Written Primary EU Law

Sometimes, a national provision seems to be compatible with secondary EU law, but uncertainty remains regarding the question of whether that measure is also in line with the primary EU rules, like the written rules in the TFEU regarding freedoms. It is apparent from *FCE Bank*[110] that the sequence in which a national provision is to be tested against secondary or primary EU rules is that the first step is to test the national rule against secondary EU law. Only if the rule does not conflict with secondary EU law, the same rule (being both the national and secondary EU rule at the same time) to be tested against primary EU law. The Court ruled in *FCE Bank*:

> As Advocate General Léger pointed out in point 74 of his Opinion, a finding that a national law or practice is incompatible with the Sixth Directive dispenses with the need to consider whether the fundamental freedoms laid down by the Treaty, such as the freedom of establishment, have been infringed.
>
> …
>
> It follows from the foregoing that the Italian administrative practice is incompatible with the Sixth Directive, and it is not necessary to rule on the breach of Article 43 EU.[111]

Taxable persons can rely directly on provisions of EU law and therefore, also on the Treaty provisions, if they are sufficiently precise and clear, and are unconditional. From *Van Gend & Loos*[112] it follows that EU law takes precedence over domestic law (*see* section 1.10.2.2.2). Based on these principles, individuals or businesses may, in proceedings against a Member State, rely on a sufficient, precise, clear and unconditional Treaty provision to override incompatible domestic provisions of that Member State which has failed to implement the Treaty concerned correctly and in time. A test against the Treaty should not be made where complete harmonization at the level of secondary EU law has been achieved.[113] The test of a national implementing provision

---

and CJEU 8 June 2000, Case C-396/98 *Grundstückgemeinschaft Schloßstraße GbR v Finanzamt Paderborn,* ECLI:EU:C:2000:303, para. 44.

109. CJEU 8 June 2000, Case C-396/98 *Grundstückgemeinschaft Schloßstraße GbR v Finanzamt Paderborn,* ECLI:EU:C:2000:303, para. 47.
110. CJEU 23 March 2006, Case C-210/04 *Ministero dell'Economia e delle Finanze and Agenzia delle Entrate v FCE Bank plc,* ECLI:EU:C:2006:196.
111. *Ibid.*, paras 50-52.
112. CJEU 5 February 1963, Case 26/62 *NV Algemene Transport- en Expeditie Onderneming van Gend & Loos v Netherlands Inland Revenue Administration,* ECLI:EU:C:1963:1.
113. CJEU 14 December 2004, Case C-309/02 *Radlberger,* ECLI:EU:C:2004:799, paras 53 and 56-57. *See also* CJEU 5 May 1982, Case 15/81 *Gaston Schul I,* ECLI:EU:C:1982:135 and P.J.G. Kapteyn & P. Verloren van Themaat, *Het recht van de Europese Unie en van de Europese Gemeenschappen* (Kluwer 2003), pp. 385-87.

in the field of VAT - which has proved to be in line with the Directive, or at least not to be conflicting with it - is basically little more than a comparison of a Directive provision with primary EU law.

An example of a successful claim concerning a Treaty provision (Article 56 TFEU, free movement of services)[114] in the field of VAT is to be found in *Lease Plan Luxembourg SA*.[115] The Court ruled in this case that it was contrary to Article 59 of the Treaty (the predecessor of Article 56 TFEU) for national rules to provide that taxable persons not established in Belgium, who apply for a refund of VAT in accordance with the Eighth Directive, are entitled to interest only at a lower rate than that applied to the interest paid to taxable persons established in Belgium (and also within a shorter timeframe). Nothing was stipulated at a Directive level to prohibit or allow this. It was, therefore, necessary to look beyond the horizon of the VAT Directive to achieve the result that persons not established in Belgium would get the same interest rate as local entrepreneurs.

A test against the Treaty or other sources of primary EU law will not always lead to a result in favour of the taxable person. Where a taxable person wants to rely upon a special national regime which is advantageous to him but not in line with a source of secondary EU law (for instance, the VAT Directive), the tax authorities might - under certain conditions - take up the chance to prove that that regime is a form of state aid. That is what happened in *Heiser*.[116] When Austria became a member of the EU, it had to change its VAT legislation. One of the changes was that services provided by medical professionals were no longer taxed but exempted. The VAT Directive (Sixth VAT Directive at that time) prescribes that the original deduction of input VAT must be adjusted if capital goods are no longer used for taxed purposes. Based on a special Austrian transitional rule, these medical specialists, however, were not required to adjust the input VAT they had incurred on capital goods in the past. According to the CJEU in the *Heiser* case, Article 92 of the Treaty (now: Article 107 TFEU) was to be interpreted as meaning that a national rule providing that the changeover for medical practitioners from taxable to exempt status for the purposes of VAT should not, in relation to goods that continued to be used in the business, entail that the reduction of input tax already deducted, as prescribed by Article 20 of the Sixth Directive, must be classified as state aid. The advantage received must be repaid to the state that provided it. From this case law, it can be deduced that the belief that the taxable person can *always* rely on a national provision which is more favourable to him than a measure of secondary EU law which is not correctly implemented in his domestic legislation, while perhaps true, is nevertheless sometimes meaningless. If it turns out that the national VAT measure is a form of state aid, the (initial) advantage will be lost before it can effectively be enjoyed, or if it has been enjoyed, it must be repaid.

---

114. The free movement of services is established in Article 56 TFEU, with further guidance in Articles 57-62 TFEU.
115. CJEU 7 May 1998, Case C-390/96 *Lease Plan Luxembourg SA v Belgian State*, ECLI: EU:C:1998:206.
116. CJEU 3 March 2005, Case C-172/03 *Wolfgang Heiser v Finanzamt Innsbruck*, ECLI: EU:C:2005:130.

Until now, most claims on the Treaty have come from individual taxpayers. For example, in *Schmelz*, a natural person invoked are consistent with Article 12 EC (non-discrimination, now Article 18 TFEU), Article 43 EC (freedom of establishment, now Article 49 TFEU), Article 49 EC (freedom to provide services, now Article 56 TFEU) and with the general principle of equal treatment.[117] Ingrid Schmelz was a taxable person (a small enterprise) established in Germany who wanted to apply the special regime for small enterprises in Austria. However, the application of this special regime was restricted to Austrian-based businesses and was, therefore, denied by the Austrian tax authorities, on the basis that the regime was restricted to entrepreneurs who were established in Austria. As the territorial restriction of the Austrian provision regarding small enterprises was in line with the Directive, testing it against the Directive would have no effect. The only remedy that could be expected came from testing the Directive and national provisions against the EU Treaty, however, without much success.

The question referred was, in essence, the following:

> Does the wording 'as well as supplies of goods and services effected by a taxable person who is not established in the territory of the country' as mentioned in the Directive [in Article 24(3) and in Article 28i of the Sixth Council Directive] and a scheme transposing this provision into national law infringe the Treaty, in particular the principle of non-discrimination (Article 12 EC),[118] the freedom of establishment (Article 43 EC et seq.),[119] the freedom to provide services (Article 49 EC et seq.),[120] or fundamental rights under Community law (the Community-law principle of equal treatment) because the provision has the effect that Union citizens who are not established in the territory of the relevant country are excluded from the exemption under Article 24(2) of the Sixth Directive (Special scheme for small undertakings), whilst Union citizens who are established in the territory of the relevant country are able to claim this exemption where the relevant Member State grants an exemption for small undertakings in accordance with the Directive?[121]

The Court ruled that in this particular case, it followed from the fact that small undertakings established outside Austria excluded from the benefit of the VAT exemption rendered the provision of services in Austria less attractive for those small undertakings. Consequently, it entailed a restriction on the freedom to provide services. In those circumstances, it is necessary to examine the possible justification for the territorial restriction. The Court found such a justification:

> ... it appears that, at this stage in the evolution of the VAT system, the objective which consists in guaranteeing the effectiveness of fiscal supervision in order to combat fraud, tax evasion and possible abuse and the objective of the scheme for small undertakings, which is to support the competitiveness of such undertakings,

117. CJEU 26 October 2010, Case C-97/09 *Ingrid Schmelz v Finanzamt Waldviertel*, ECLI: EU:C:2010:632.
118. Currently Article 18 TFEU.
119. Articles 49-55 TFEU.
120. Article 56 TFEU.
121. CJEU 26 October 2010, Case C-97/09 *Ingrid Schmelz v Finanzamt Waldviertel*, ECLI: EU:C:2010:632, para. 26.

> justify, first, limiting the applicability of the VAT exemption to the activities of small undertakings established in the territory of the Member State in which the VAT is due and, second, the annual turnover generated to be taken into account being that generated in the Member State in which the undertaking is established.[122]

As a result, the territorial restriction of the Austrian provision regarding small enterprises appeared (test 1) to be in line with both secondary EU law (the VAT Directive) and (test 2) in line with primary EU law.[123]

1.11 BASIC FEATURES OF EU VAT LAW

Article 1(2) VAT Directive describes the basic features of EU VAT. These features can be summarized as followed:

(1) It is a general tax on consumption.
(2) The tax is exactly proportional to the price of the goods and services.
(3) It is levied in all stages of the production and distribution process up to and including the retail trade stage.
(4) Taxable persons have a right of deduction.

On the basis of Article 401 VAT Directive, Member States may maintain or introduce taxes on insurance contracts, taxes on betting and gambling, excise duties, stamp duties or, more generally, any taxes, duties or charges *which cannot be characterized as turnover taxes*, provided that the collection of those taxes, duties or charges does not give rise, in trade between the Member States, to formalities connected with the crossing of frontiers. According to the CJEU, taxes, duties and charges must, in any event, be regarded as being prohibited under Article 401 VAT Directive, if they exhibit the '*essential characteristics of VAT*', even if they are not identical to VAT in all points.[124] It is settled CJEU case law that the essential characteristics of VAT are as follows:[125]

122. *Ibid.*, para. 71.
123. The special scheme for small enterprises has been changed (changes will enter into force on 1 January 2025). One of the changes is that the territorial restriction has been removed. *See* Council Directive (EU) 2020/285 of 18 February 2020 amending Directive 2006/112/EC on the common system of value added tax as regards the special scheme for small enterprises and Regulation (EU) No 904/2010 as regards the administrative cooperation and exchange of information for the purpose of monitoring the correct application of the special scheme for small enterprises, [2020] OJ L 62/13.
124. CJEU 29 April 2004, Case C-308/01 *GIL Insurance Ltd and Others v Commissioners of Customs & Excise*, ECLI:EU:C:2004:252, para. 32.
125. For example: CJEU 3 March 1988, Case 252/86 *Gabriel Bergandi v Directeur général des impôts*, ECLI:EU:C:1988:112, para. 15; CJEU 7 May 1992, Case C-347/90 *Aldo Bozzi v Cassa Nazionale di Previdenza ed Assistenza a favore degli Avvocati e dei Procuratori legali*, ECLI:EU:C:1992:200, para. 12; CJEU 17 September 1997, Case C-130/96 *Fazenda Pública v Solisnor-Estaleiros Navais SA, also represented: Ministério Pùblico*, ECLI:EU:C:1997:416, para. 14; CJEU 17 September 1997, Case C-28/96 *Fazenda Pública v Fricarnes SA*, ECLI:EU:C:1997:41, para. 38; CJEU 29 April 2004, Case C-308/01 *GIL Insurance Ltd and Others v Commissioners of Customs & Excise*,

(1) VAT applies generally to transactions relating to goods or services;
(2) it is proportional to the price of those goods or services, whatever the number of transactions carried out;
(3) it is charged at each stage of the production and distribution process; and, finally
(4) it is imposed on the added value of goods and services since the tax payable on a transaction is calculated after deducting the tax paid on the previous transaction.

It would seem that the essential characteristics as identified by the CJEU in the context of Article 401 VAT Directive are very similar, if not identical to those which can be derived from Article 1(2) VAT Directive. Therefore, we believe it is safe to say that those are the basic features of EU VAT Law. In this section, we will further elaborate on each of those basic features.

1.11.1 A General Tax on Consumption

As we indicated in section 1.3, it follows from Article 1(2) VAT Directive, that EU VAT is a 'general tax on consumption'. In fact, the CJEU considers it as a basic principle of VAT that it is a consumption tax designed to be borne only by the final consumer.[126] Unlike *special* consumption taxes such as excise duties, which only aim to tax specific goods or specific categories of goods, a general consumption tax aims at taxing all consumption of goods and services. In principle, EU VAT indeed applies to all goods and services. This general character of the tax requires that exceptions to the general application of the tax, such as exemptions and reduced rates, are to be interpreted strictly.[127]

In section 1.3, we also explained that EU VAT takes the form of a transaction tax. The transactions carried out by taxable persons serve as a proxy to the expenditures that were required to purchase goods and services. The expenditures, in turn, serve as a proxy for the consumption of those goods and services.

It should be noted that EU VAT only aims at taxing consumption taking place within the EU. Moreover, consumption should be taxed in one Member State only. For this reason, EU VAT law contains special arrangements for cross-border transactions.

ECLI:EU:C:2004:252, para. 33; CJEU 11 October 2007, Joined Cases C-283/06 and C-312/06 *KÖGÁZ rt and Others v Zala Megyei Közigazgatási Hivatal Vezetője (C-283/06) and OTP Garancia Biztosító rt v Vas Megyei Közigazgatási Hivatal (C-312/06)*, ECLI:EU:C:2007:598, para. 37; CJEU 15 January 2009, Case C-502/07 *K-1 sp. z o.o. v Dyrektor Izby Skarbowej w Bydgoszczy*, ECLI:EU:C:2009:11, para. 17 and CJEU 29 July 2010, Case C-188/09 *Dyrektor Izby Skarbowej w Białymstoku v Profaktor Kulesza, Frankowski, Jóźwiak, Orłowski sp. J*, ECLI: EU:C:2010:454, para. 47.

126. CJEU 6 October 2005, Case C-291/03 *MyTravel plc v Commissioners of Customs & Excise, ECLI:EU:C:2005:591*, para. 30.

127. *See*, for example: CJEU 2 July 2020, Case C-231/19 *Blackrock Investment Management (UK) Limited v Commissioners for Her Majesty's Revenue and Customs*, ECLI:EU:C:2020:513, para. 22 and CJEU 6 May 2010, Case C-94/09 *European Commission v French Republic*, ECLI: EU:C:2010:253, para. 29.

Goods and services that are 'imported' into a Member State must be taxed in the same way as local goods and service, and 'exported' goods and services to other countries must be relieved from the burden of VAT as much as possible. Turnover taxes levied under a common system of VAT need taxation at the point of 'imports' of goods, and refund of taxes for 'exported' goods, as well as special rules for services which are, or are not, consumed within the territory of the country. We put imported and exported here in quotation marks because trade between Member States of the EU is normally indicated as intra-Community trade (or intra-Union), and formally only trade (of goods) with third countries may be called 'import' and 'export'. We refer to Chapters 4, 13 and 14 dealing with the place of supply, ICTs and importation and exportation.

1.11.2 Exactly Proportional to the Price of Goods or Services

The essential characteristic that EU VAT is exactly proportional to the price of goods and services is closely connected to the fact that EU VAT is intended (1) as an all-stage tax (*see* section 1.11.3) and (2) as a neutral tax (*see* section 1.1.12).

If a consumption tax is levied at all stages of the supply chain, the same good or the same service will be taxed multiple times, depending on the length of the supply chain. This will cause double taxation and/or cascading of tax if no specific measures are taken. As we indicated in section 1.2, the turnover taxes which were in place in most Member States before the introduction of the EU VAT system, were indeed turnover taxes which were not exactly proportional to the prices of the goods and services. The adverse consequences of that (*see* section 1.6), formed an important reason for choosing a VAT system to be applied throughout the EU. Proportionality of the VAT system is mainly achieved by allowing taxable persons to deduct the VAT that was charged to them from the VAT that is chargeable by them and by applying a tax rate to each supply. Under this system, the tax, calculated as a percentage of the value of the supply, is no longer deductible when the chain of transactions has come to an end. The tax is ultimately charged to the final consumer, who cannot pass on the amount of the tax, making the tax neutral for businesses and taxing the private consumption only once.

1.11.3 Charged at Each Stage of the Production and Distribution Process

In section 1.2, we explained that a consumption tax can be designed as a single-stage tax. However, single-stage taxes have various disadvantages. For example, single-stage taxes levied at the start of the supply chain require complex legislation in order to ensure that no cascading of tax will occur. If a single-stage tax is levied at the wholesale level, specific measures must be taken in order to ensure that supplies made directly to private consumers are taxed against the proper (estimated) retail prices. An important drawback of a single-stage tax which is levied at the retail level is that its correct application heavily depends on the quality of the taxable persons at that stage in the supply chain. In fact, one of the reasons for choosing an all-stage tax in the EU is the advantage of 'fractional payments' of VAT (*see* section 1.4), spreading the risks of non-compliance over all stages in the production and distribution chain.

1.11.4 The Right of Deduction

The right of deduction has been referred to as the cornerstone of the EU VAT system. As we will explain in section 1.12.1, the right of deduction is necessary to achieve the goal of a neutral consumption tax. The right of deduction also functions as a self-cleaning mechanism in the VAT system. This is because taxable persons cannot deduct VAT that has been incorrectly charged, or if they do not possess a correct invoice for the purchase. Therefore, the right of deduction forms an incentive to a taxable person purchasing goods or services from another taxable person to check the correct application and invoicing of VAT by the latter. In Chapter 10, we will discuss the right of deduction in more detail.

1.12 FUNDAMENTAL PRINCIPLES UNDERLYING THE VAT SYSTEM

When applying EU VAT law, not only do the rules laid down in the VAT Directives, the VAT Implementing Regulation and other sources of law (*see* sections 1.8 and 1.9) play a role but also more general principles of EU law are of importance. For example, in VAT cases the CJEU has often referred to general fundamental law principles such as (but not limited to) the principle of legal certainty, the principle of protection of legitimate expectations,[128] the principle of equal treatment, the principle of proportionality,[129] the principle of respect for the rights of the defence,[130] the principle of prohibiting abusive practices[131] and the principle of prohibiting tax fraud.[132] Moreover, specific principles connected to the very nature of VAT are applied. Examples of such 'system principles' are the principles that VAT is a consumption tax designed to be borne only by the final consumer[133] and the destination and origin principle. On

128. CJEU 14 September 2006, Joined Cases C-181/04-C-183/04 *Elmeka NE v Ypourgos Oikonomikon*, ECLI:EU:C:2006:563, para. 31.
129. CJEU 10 July 2008, Case C-484/06 *Fiscale eenheid Koninklijke Ahold NV v Staatssecretaris van Financiën*, ECLI:EU:C:2008:394, para. 32.
130. CJEU 3 July 2014, Joined Cases C-129/13 and C-130/13 *Kamino International Logistics BV (C-129/13) and Datema Hellmann Worldwide Logistics BV (C-130/13) v Staatssecretaris van Financiën*, ECLI:EU:C:2014:2041 and CJEU 18 December 2008, Case C-349/07 *Sopropé – Organizações de Calçado Lda v Fazenda Pública*, ECLI:EU:C:2008:746.
131. CJEU 21 February 2006, Case C-255/02 *Halifax plc, Leeds Permanent Development Services Ltd and County Wide Property Investments Ltd v Commissioners of Customs & Excise*, ECLI:EU:C:2006:121.
132. For example: CJEU 18 December 2014, Joined Cases C-131/13, C-163/13 and C-164/13 *Staatssecretaris van Financiën v Schoenimport 'Italmoda' Mariano Previti vof (C-131/13) and Turbu.com BV (C-163/13) and Turbu.com Mobile Phones BV (C-164/13) v Staatssecretaris van Financiën*, ECLI:EU:C:2014:2455.
133. CJEU 6 October 2005, Case C-291/03 *MyTravel plc v Commissioners of Customs & Excise, ECLI:EU:C:2005:591*, para. 30. *Also see*: R. de la Feria, 'EU VAT Principles as Interpretative Aids to EU VAT Rules: The Inherent Paradox', in M. Lang, et al. (eds), *CJEU: Recent Developments in Value Added Tax 2015* (Linde 2016), p. 5.

occasion, the CJEU has even considered the right of deduction (*see* Article 168 VAT Directive) as a fundamental (system) principle, as an integral part of the VAT scheme.[134]

The principle of neutrality combines elements of general law principles and system principles of EU VAT. As we will explain in section 1.12.1, the CJEU has distinguished multiple dimensions of the 'principle of neutrality': it is both a reflection in the field of VAT of the general principle of equal treatment and a system principle of EU VAT, essentially entailing that VAT should be strictly proportional to the prices of the goods and services.

Although general principles of EU law play an important role in the field of VAT, it would go beyond the purpose of this book to elaborate on all these principles. We refer to the general literature on (principles of) EU law. The system principles, such as the destination principle, will be discussed in Chapter 4, dealing with the allocation of taxation rights between Member States (the so-called place of supply rules). Because of its importance to the application of the EU VAT system, we will focus on the principle of neutrality. Nonetheless, we feel that this book would be incomplete if we were not to address the principle of prohibiting abusive practices and the principle of prohibiting tax fraud. For that reason, we will elaborate on these principles in sections 1.12.2 and 1.12.3.

1.12.1 The Principle of Neutrality[135]

From the preamble of the VAT Directive, it follows that it is intended that the VAT system should attain the highest degree of neutrality.[136] The VAT Directive does not explain what 'neutrality' is. In the same preamble, also the term 'neutrality in competition' is used.[137] Again, the VAT Directive does not explain the meaning of this term. According to the CJEU, the principle of neutrality is a fundamental principle that underlies the common system of VAT, and which follows from Article 2 of the First and Sixth Directives (now Article 1(2) VAT Directive).[138] Basically, the principle of neutrality has two aspects.

First of all, there is an 'economic' aspect. In this context, the neutrality principle entails that VAT should be exactly proportional to the price of the goods and services. This aspect is closely related to the purpose and the design of the EU VAT system and

134. CJEU 22 December 2010, Case C-277/09 *The Commissioners for Her Majesty's Revenue & Customs v RBS Deutschland Holdings GmbH*, ECLI:EU:C:2010:810, para. 39.
135. *See* A.J. van Doesum, *Contractuele samenwerkingsverbanden in de btw (Dissertation)* (Kluwer 2009), pp. 31-34.
136. Preamble, point 5 VAT Directive.
137. Preamble, point 7 VAT Directive.
138. For example: CJEU 6 July 2006, Joined Cases C-439/04 and C-440/04 *Axel Kittel v Belgian State (C-439/04) and Belgian State v Recolta Recycling SPRL (C-440/04)* ECLI:EU:C:2006:446, para. 49; CJEU 8 June 2000, Case C-98/98 *Commissioners of Customs and Excise v Midland Bank plc* ECLI:EU:C:2000:300, para. 29 and CJEU 27 November 2003, Case C-497/01 *Zita Modes Sàrl v Administration de l'enregistrement et des domains* ECLI:EU:C:2003:644, para. 37.

is, therefore, also referred to as the principle of 'system neutrality'.[139] Second, there is a 'legal' aspect to the principle of neutrality in VAT, which is, in fact, the reflection in the field of VAT of the (general) principle of equal treatment.[140]

The principle of neutrality in its meaning of 'system neutrality' has its origins in the idea that the levy of VAT should ideally not distort the optimal allocation of overall wealth. However, it is generally accepted that taxation, in whatever form, will always have an effect on economic activities. Even though this may be true, system neutrality does create specific norms to which EU VAT law should adhere. On numerous occasions, the CJEU has used the principle of system neutrality to purposefully interpret EU VAT law.[141] The first norm following from the principle of system neutrality is that EU VAT law should not lead to the concentration of businesses in the production and distribution chain. As Article 1(2) VAT Directive explicitly states, VAT is a general tax on consumption, which should be exactly proportional to the price of the goods and services, however many transactions take place in the production and distribution process before the stage at which the tax is charged. Thus, the length of the production and distribution chain should not affect the amount of VAT that ultimately burdens a good or a service and thus should not affect businesses' decisions to concentrate or combine their businesses. System neutrality also means that VAT should not cascade (no VAT on VAT) throughout the supply chain and that double taxation or non-taxation must not occur. After all, if VAT cascades in the supply chain, or if double- or non-taxation occurs, VAT will no longer be exactly proportional to the prices and likely have an effect on business decisions. In this respect, the right of deduction is the ultimate expression of the principle of system neutrality. It ensures that businesses (taxable persons) are not burdened with VAT. As we will show in Chapter 8, under current EU VAT law, full system neutrality is an unattainable utopia as long as exemptions without a right of deduction continue to exist.

As indicated earlier, the principle of neutrality also has a legal aspect. According to the CJEU, it can be considered as the reflection in the field of VAT of the general principle of equal treatment.[142] Thus, it forms a special manifestation of an overall EU law principle. It is applicable in respect of similar services and goods which are (thus)

139. Cf. A.H. Bomer, *De doorwerking van algemene rechtsbeginselen in de BTW* (dissertation) (Kluwer 2012).

140. Cf. CJEU 8 June 2006, Case C-106/05 *L.u.P. GmbH v Finanzamt Bochum-Mitte* ECLI:EU:C:2006:380, para. 48 (and the case law cited); CJEU 10 April 2008, Case C-309/06 *Marks & Spencer plc v Commissioners of Customs & Excise* ECLI:EU:C:2008:211, para. 49; CJEU 10 July 2008, Case C-484/06 *Fiscale eenheid Koninklijke Ahold NV v Staatssecretaris van Financiën* ECLI:EU:C:2008:394, para. 36 and CJEU 18 December 2008, Case C-488/07 *Royal Bank of Scotland plc v The Commissioners of Her Majesty's Revenue & Customs* ECLI:EU:C:2008:750, para. 27.

141. For example: CJEU 19 September 2000, Case C-454/98 *Schmeink & Cofreth AG & Co. KG v Finanzamt Borken and Manfred Strobel v Finanzamt Esslingen* ECLI:EU:C:2000:469; CJEU 29 April 2004, Case C-137/02 *Finanzamt Offenbach am Main-Land v Faxworld Vorgründungsgesellschaft Peter Hünninghausen und Wolfgang Klein GbR* ECLI:EU:C:2004:267 and CJEU 29 October 2009, Case C-29/08 *Skatteverket v AB SKF* ECLI:EU:C:2009:665.

142. CJEU 10 July 2008, Case C-484/06 *Fiscale eenheid Koninklijke Ahold NV v Staatssecretaris van Financiën* ECLI:EU:C:2008:394, para. 36.

in competition with each other.[143] According to the CJEU, its scope is limited, in the sense that an infringement of the principle of fiscal neutrality may be envisaged only as between competing traders.[144] Therefore, the general principle of equal treatment merely serves as a *lex generalis* in the field of VAT. In the context of EU VAT law, this general principle of equal treatment can be applied only:

> ... in matters relating to tax, by other kinds of discrimination which affect traders who are not necessarily in competition with each other but who are nevertheless in a similar situation in other respects.[145]

Not only does the principle of (legal) neutrality serve as the reflection in the field of VAT of the principle of equal treatment, it also serves as a principle safeguarding the objective of neutrality of competition (which, after all, implies equal treatment of similar situations). The preamble to the VAT Directive connects the objective of equal treatment to that of neutrality in competition:

> The common system of VAT should, even if rates and exemptions are not fully harmonized, result in neutrality in competition, such that within the territory of each Member State similar goods and services bear the same tax burden, whatever the length of the production and distribution chain.[146] For this reason, one could argue that the legal aspect of the neutrality principle has an economic dimension too.

The purpose of the application of the principle of (legal) neutrality/neutrality of competition is to ensure that similar goods and services - or, in a broader sense, similar economic transactions - are treated equally for VAT purposes.[147] For instance, this means that the same VAT rate should be applied to similar goods.[148] The principle of (legal) neutrality or neutrality of competition also extends to the taxable person, ensuring that individuals or entities in similar situations are treated equally. Neutrality in legal form is a natural extension of this principle.[149] Another important aspect of the principle of (legal) neutrality/neutrality of competition is its connection to the simplicity of the system, which is closely related to the principle of effectiveness of the system. This relationship is based on the idea that a complex VAT system imposes greater challenges on small businesses compared to larger, better-organized businesses.[150]

In an international context, the two aspects of the principle of neutrality together form the norm that goods and services which are supplied to a customer in another

143. *Ibid.*; CJEU 27 April 2006, Joined Cases C-443/04 and C-444/04 *H.A. Solleveld (C-443/04) and J.E. van den Hout-van Eijnsbergen (C-444/04) v Staatssecretaris van Financiën* ECLI:EU:C:2006:257, para. 35 and case law there cited. Also *See* CJEU 10 April 2008, Case C-309/06 *Marks & Spencer plc v Commissioners of Customs & Excise* ECLI:EU:C:2008:211, para. 47.
144. CJEU 10 April 2008, Case C-309/06 *Marks & Spencer plc v Commissioners of Customs & Excise* ECLI:EU:C:2008:211, para. 49.
145. *Ibid.*
146. Point 7 of the preamble to the VAT Directive.
147. CJEU 22 May 2008, Case C-162/07 *Ampliscientifica Srl and Amplifin SpA v Ministero dell'Economia e delle Finanze and Agenzia delle Entrate,* ECLI:EU:C:2008:301, para. 25.
148. For example: CJEU 10 April 2008, Case C-309/06 *Marks & Spencer plc v Commissioners of Customs & Excise,* ECLI:EU:C:2008:211, para. 47.
149. CJEU 29 March 2012, Case C-436/10 *Belgian State v BLM SA,* ECLI:EU:C:2012:185, para. 26.
150. ABC Report, January 1962, in *The EEC Reports on Tax Harmonisation* (IBFD 1969), p. 25.

country should be relieved from the burden of the VAT in the supplier's country. This norm is referred to as the 'external neutrality' of VAT. External neutrality relates to system neutrality because it serves to ensure that VAT does not become a tax on businesses, thereby influencing their business decisions. It relates to legal neutrality because it contributes to achieving the goal that the consumption of similar goods and services is taxed equally. Furthermore, it relates to the neutrality of competition because it ensures that goods and services which are supplied/purchased cross-border and those which are supplied/purchased locally eventually carry the same burden of VAT. Indeed, the CJEU confirmed that distortion of competition between (supplies by) local and foreign businesses must be prevented within the EU, in the interests of the goal of an internal market:

> In order to attain the objective of ensuring equal conditions of taxation for the same transaction, no matter in which Member State it is carried out, the common system of VAT was intended, according to the preamble to the Second Directive, to replace the turnover taxes in force in the various Member States.[151]

The exemption with a right of deduction for supplies of goods that are exported to customers outside the EU is a clear expression of the external neutrality (Article 148 VAT Directive). It entirely relieves the goods from the burden of EU VAT. Conversely, the taxation of goods that are imported from outside the EU into the EU is also a good example of the functioning of the principle of external neutrality (Article 30 VAT Directive).

Even though the CJEU considers the principle of neutrality as a 'fundamental principle of the common system of VAT established by the relevant Community legislation',[152] it is not a rule of primary law.[153] It is merely a principle of interpretation to be applied concurrently with other principles of interpretation, such as the principle of strict interpretation of exemptions.

1.12.2 Principle of Prohibition of Abuse Community Law ('*Fraus Legis*')

In EU VAT, the objective character of the transaction in question is decisive for its VAT treatment. For that reason, it was contended that in VAT, the principle of (the prohibition of) abuse of Community law (also referred to as 'abuse of rights', or *fraus legis*) could not be applied, since a precondition to the application of this principle is that transactions are carried out with the principal aim at the accrual of a tax advantage.[154] Moreover, it was believed that in the field of VAT, economic and

151. CJEU 3 October 2006, Case C-475/03 *Banca popolare di Cremona Soc. coop. arl v Agenzia Entrate Ufficio Cremona*, ECLI:EU:C:2006:629, paras 20 and 23 and CJEU 10 July 2008, Case C-484/06 *Fiscale eenheid Koninklijke Ahold NV v Staatssecretaris van Financiën*, ECLI: EU:C:2008:394, para. 28.
152. CJEU, 19 September 2000, Case C-454/98 *Schmeink & Cofreth AG & Co. KG v Finanzamt Borken and Manfred Strobel v Finanzamt Esslingen*, ECLI:EU:C:2000:469, para. 59.
153. CJEU 19 July 2012, Case C-44/11 *Finanzamt Frankfurt am Main V-Höchst v Deutsche Bank AG*, ECLI:EU:C:2012:484, para. 45.
154. CJEU 21 February 2008, Case C-425/06 *Ministero dell'Economia e delle Finanze v Part Service Srl*, ECLI:EU:C:2008:108.

commercial realities, as fundamental criteria for the application of the common system of VAT,[155] made the application of the principle of abuse of law redundant.

However, since the CJEU's ruling in *Halifax*, it is clear that the principle of prohibiting abusive practices also applies to the sphere of VAT.[156] The CJEU has held on various occasions that preventing possible tax evasion, avoidance and abuse is an objective recognized and encouraged by the Sixth Directive (now: VAT Directive).[157] As such, the CJEU has progressively contributed to a better understanding of the functioning of this principle in the field of VAT.[158] Moreover, the CJEU ruled that the principle of the prohibition of abuse of rights is applicable, regardless of any national measure giving effect to it in the domestic legal order, even with respect to transactions undertaken prior to its judgment in *Halifax*.[159]

The purpose and effect of the principle that the abuse of rights is prohibited are to bar wholly artificial arrangements which do not reflect economic reality and are set up with the essential aim of obtaining a tax advantage.[160] In our view, there is an important difference between an abuse of law and a case of fraud. Although a fraud could be considered an abuse, an abuse does not necessarily mean that fraud is committed. In case of an abuse of tax law, it is considered that no rules have been broken, but that they 'merely' have been applied to a situation that was principally artificially created to obtain a tax advantage. In the case of a tax fraud, rules have been deliberately broken in order to unlawfully obtain a tax advantage. We note that the CJEU does not always make a clear distinction between abusive practices and

155. Cf. CJEU 20 June 2013, Case C-653/11 *Her Majesty's Commissioners of Revenue and Customs v Paul Newey*, ECLI:EU:C:2013:409, para. 42 and the case law cited.
156. CJEU 21 February 2006, Case C-255/02 *Halifax plc, Leeds Permanent Development Services Ltd and County Wide Property Investments Ltd v Commissioners of Customs & Excise*, ECLI: EU:C:2006:121. *See also* (from the same date) CJEU 21 February 2006, Case C-419/02 *BUPA Hospitals Ltd and Goldsborough Developments Ltd v Commissioners of Customs & Excise*, ECLI:EU:C:2006:122 and CJEU 21 February 2006, Case C-223/03 *University of Huddersfield Higher Education Corporation v Commissioners of Customs & Excise*, ECLI:EU:C:2006:124. *See* with respect to the EU law origin of this principle: R. de la Feria, *Prohibition of Abuse (Community) Law: The Creation of a New General Principle of EC Law Through Tax* (2008) 45/2 Common Market Law Review, pp. 395-441 https://doi.org/10.54648/cola2008027.
157. CJEU 20 June 2013, Case C-653/11 *Her Majesty's Commissioners of Revenue and Customs v Paul Newey*, ECLI:EU:C:2013:409, para. 46.
158. *See* CJEU 21 February 2008, Case C-425/06 *Ministero dell'Economia e delle Finanze v Part Service Srl*, ECLI:EU:C:2008:108; CJEU 22 December 2010, Case C-103/09 *The Commissioners for Her Majesty's Revenue and Customs v Weald Leasing Ltd*, ECLI:EU:C:2010:804; CJEU 20 June 2013, Case C-653/11 *Her Majesty's Commissioners of Revenue and Customs v Paul Newey*, ECLI:EU:C:2013:409 and CJEU 22 November 2017, Case C-256/17 *Edward Cussens and Others v T. G. Brosman*, ECLI:EU:C:2017:881.
159. CJEU 22 November 2017, Case C-256/17 *Edward Cussens and Others v T. G. Brosman*, ECLI:EU:C:2017:881.
160. CJEU 22 May 2008, Case C-162/07 *Ampliscientifica Srl and Amplifin SpA v Ministero dell'Economia e delle Finanze and Agenzia delle Entrate*, ECLI:EU:C:2008:301, para. 28; CJEU 27 October 2011, Case C-504/10 *Tanoarch s.r.o. v Daňové riaditeľstvo Slovenskej republiky*, ECLI:EU:C:2011:707, para. 51 and CJEU 12 July 2012, Case C-326/11 *J.J. Komen en Zonen Beheer Heerhugowaard BV v Staatssecretaris van Financiën*, ECLI:EU:C:2012:461, para. 35. *See also* E. Traversa, 'Prevention of Evasion, Avoidance and Abuse in the EU VAT Law', in M. Lang, et al. (eds), *ECJ: Recent Developments in Value Added Tax, the Evolution of European VAT Jurisprudence and Its Role in the EU Common VAT System* (Linde 2014), pp. 40-42.

fraudulent practices. For example, on numerous occasions, the CJEU has simply considered that preventing tax evasion, avoidance and abuse is an objective recognized and encouraged by the VAT Directive[161] and (thus) that EU law cannot be relied on for abusive *or fraudulent* ends.[162] Nevertheless, we believe that this does not imply that the CJEU does not acknowledge that there is a difference between abusive practices which do not involve any tax fraud and abusive practices that do. This is underlined by the fact that the consequences of considering a scheme as a tax abuse are different (redefine the transactions, *see* below) than those of a scheme that involves a tax fraud (denial of a VAT exemption or a right of deduction, *see* section 1.12.3).

The application of the principle of abuse of law is subject to strict criteria because it entails a breach of the principle of legal certainty. Therefore, it can only be applied if:[163]

(1) the transactions concerned, notwithstanding the formal application of the conditions laid down by the relevant provisions of the VAT Directive and the national legislation transposing it, result in the accrual of a tax advantage;
(2) the grant of that tax advantage would be contrary to the purpose of those provisions; and
(3) it is apparent from a number of objective factors that the essential (principal)[164] aim of the transactions concerned is to obtain a tax advantage.

From these conditions, the following points can be inferred:

(1) There must be a tax advantage as a result of the transactions concerned. In this regard, we believe that obtaining a cash flow advantage can also be considered a 'tax advantage'.
(2) The tax advantage must be contrary to the purpose of the provisions of the VAT Directive. In this respect, it should be noted that if a taxable person in the context of its normal commercial activities is not (fully) entitled to deduct input VAT, it is contrary to the principle of tax neutrality and, therefore, contrary to the purpose of the rules of the VAT Directive if such a taxable

161. CJEU 29 April 2004, Joined Cases C-487/01 and C-7/02 *Gemeente Leusden (C-487/01) and Holin Groep BV cs (C-7/02) v Staatssecretaris van Financiën*, ECLI:EU:C:2004:263, para. 76 and CJEU 22 November 2017, Case C-256/17 *Edward Cussens and Others v T. G. Brosman*, ECLI:EU:C:2017:881, para. 27.
162. CJEU 12 May 1998, Case C-367/96 *Alexandros Kefalas and Others v Elliniko Dimosio (Greek State) and Organismos Oikonomikis Anasygkrotisis Epicheiriseon AE (OAE)*, ECLI:EU:C:1998:222, para. 20; CJEU 23 March 2000, Case C-373/97 *Dionysios Diamantis v Elliniko Dimosio (Greek State) and Organismos Ikonomikis Anasygkrotisis Epicheiriseon AE (OAE)*, ECLI:EU:C:2000:150, para. 33 and CJEU 3 March 2005, Case C-32/03 *I/S Fini H v Skatteministeriet*, ECLI:EU:C:2005:128, para. 32.
163. CJEU 21 February 2006, Case C-255/02 *Halifax plc, Leeds Permanent Development Services Ltd and County Wide Property Investments Ltd v Commissioners of Customs & Excise*, ECLI:EU:C:2006:121, paras 74 and 75.
164. CJEU 21 February 2008, Case C-425/06 *Ministero dell'Economia e delle Finanze v Part Service Srl*, ECLI:EU:C:2008:108.

person, creates a situation in which he - on the basis of the formal rules - is allowed to (fully) deduct input VAT.[165]

(3) The principal aim of the transactions must be to obtain the tax advantage. This means that the prohibition of abuse is not applicable where the transactions leading to the tax advantage can be sufficiently explained from a business or commercial perspective other than the mere attainment of such tax advantage.[166]

(4) It is up to a national court to determine whether the transactions concerned are principally aimed at obtaining a tax advantage. In that regard, the national courts must ascertain whether the contractual terms of the transactions do not genuinely reflect economic reality.[167] Thus, a national court should take into account the substance of the transactions concerned and may take into consideration whether they are artificial. Legal, economic and/or personal links between the parties involved in the scheme, may be indications of the artificial nature of the transactions.[168] A finding that there was an abusive practice is inferred, not from the nature of the commercial operations usually engaged in by the party which made the transactions in question, but from the object and effects of those transactions, as well as their purpose.[169]

Where an abusive practice has been found to exist, the transactions involved must be redefined so as to re-establish the situation that would have prevailed in the absence of the transactions constituting that abusive practice.[170] Or, in other words, if the transactions concerned do not genuinely reflect economic reality, the contractual terms (or elements thereof)[171] would have to be redefined so as to re-establish the situation that would have prevailed in the absence of the transactions constituting that abusive practice.[172] However, the redefinition by the national court must go no further than is necessary for the correct charging of the VAT and the prevention of tax evasion.[173]

165. *See also* J. Swinkels, *VAT-Saving Solutions and Abuse of Law* (2007) 18/5 International VAT Monitor, pp. 331 et seq.
166. CJEU 21 February 2006, Case C-255/02 *Halifax plc, Leeds Permanent Development Services Ltd and County Wide Property Investments Ltd v Commissioners of Customs & Excise,* ECLI:EU:C:2006:121, para. 75.
167. CJEU 20 June 2013, Case C-653/11 *Her Majesty's Commissioners of Revenue and Customs v Paul Newey,* ECLI:EU:C:2013:409, paras 48-50.
168. Cf. J. Swinkels, *VAT-Saving Solutions and Abuse of Law* (2007) 18/5 International VAT Monitor, pp. 331-342.
169. CJEU 22 December 2010, Case C-103/09 *The Commissioners for Her Majesty's Revenue and Customs v Weald Leasing Ltd,* ECLI:EU:C:2010:804, para. 44.
170. CJEU 21 February 2006, Case C-255/02 *Halifax plc, Leeds Permanent Development Services Ltd and County Wide Property Investments Ltd v Commissioners of Customs & Excise,* ECLI:EU:C:2006:121, para. 98.
171. CJEU 22 December 2010, Case C-103/09 *The Commissioners for Her Majesty's Revenue and Customs v Weald Leasing Ltd,* ECLI:EU:C:2010:804, para. 53.
172. CJEU 20 June 2013, Case C-653/11 *Her Majesty's Commissioners of Revenue and Customs v Paul Newey,* ECLI:EU:C:2013:409, para. 50.
173. CJEU 22 December 2010, Case C-103/09 *The Commissioners for Her Majesty's Revenue and Customs v Weald Leasing Ltd,* ECLI:EU:C:2010:804, para. 52.

Even though the CJEU has already resolved quite a few issues regarding the abuse of law doctrine, many questions still remain unanswered. For example: how should the redefinition of abusive transactions take place: should they be ignored or should their conditions be redefined? It is beyond doubt that in the years to come, the CJEU will be asked to shed more light on the functioning of this legal principle.

1.12.3 Principle of Prohibition of Tax Fraud

It is settled CJEU case law that the principle of fiscal neutrality prevents any general distinction between lawful and unlawful transactions (also *see*: Chapter 2, section 2.4.10).[174] However, as we indicated in section 1.12.2, it is also settled CJEU case law that prevention of tax evasion, avoidance and abuse is an objective recognized and encouraged by the VAT Directive.[175] EU law cannot be relied on for abusive or fraudulent ends.[176] Consequently, if a taxable person commits a tax fraud, he cannot rely on the VAT Directive to obtain the advantages of an exemption or a right of deduction.[177] A right of deduction or exemption is to be refused by the national authorities and courts, even in the absence of provisions of national law providing for

174. CJEU, 6 July 2006, Joined Cases C-439/04 and C-440/04 *Axel Kittel v Belgian State (C-439/04) and Belgian State v Recolta Recycling SPRL (C-440/04)*, ECLI:EU:C:2006:446, para. 50.
175. CJEU 29 April 2004, Joined Cases C-487/01 and C-7/02 *Gemeente Leusden (C-487/01) and Holin Groep BV cs (C-7/02) v Staatssecretaris van Financiën*, ECLI:EU:C:2004:263, para. 76; CJEU 21 February 2006, Case C-255/02 *Halifax plc, Leeds Permanent Development Services Ltd and County Wide Property Investments Ltd v Commissioners of Customs & Excise*, ECLI:EU:C:2006:121, para. 71; CJEU, 6 July 2006, Joined Cases C-439/04 and C-440/04 *Axel Kittel v Belgian State (C-439/04) and Belgian State v Recolta Recycling SPRL (C-440/04)*, ECLI:EU:C:2006:446, para. 54 and CJEU 21 June 2012, Joined Cases C-80/11, C-142/11 *Mahagében Kft v Nemzeti Adó- és Vámhivatal Dél-dunántúli Regionális Adó Főigazgatósága (C-80/11) and Péter Dávid v Nemzeti Adó- és Vámhivatal Észak-alföldi Regionális Adó Főigazgatósága (C-142/11)*, ECLI:EU:C:2012:373, para. 41, CJEU 18 December 2014, Joined Cases C-131/13, C-163/13 and C-164/13 *Staatssecretaris van Financiën v Schoenimport 'Italmoda' Mariano Previti vof (C-131/13) and Turbu.com BV (C-163/13) and Turbu.com Mobile Phone's BV (C-164/13) v Staatssecretaris van Financiën*, ECLI:EU:C:2014:2455, para. 42, CJEU 22 November 2017, Case C-251/16 *Edward Cussens and Others v T. G. Brosman*, ECLI:EU:C:2017:881 and CJEU 1 December 2022, Case C-512/21 *Aquila Part Prod Com*, ECLI:EU:C:2022:950.
176. CJEU 12 May 1998, Case C-367/96 *Alexandros Kefalas and Others v Elliniko Dimosio (Greek State) and Organismos Oikonomikis Anasygkrotisis Epicheiriseon AE (OAE)*, ECLI:EU:C:1998:222, para. 20; CJEU 23 March 2000, Case C-373/97 *Dionysios Diamantis v Elliniko Dimosio (Greek State) and Organismos Ikonomikis Anasygkrotisis Epicheiriseon AE (OAE)*, ECLI:EU:C:2000:150, para. 33 and CJEU 3 March 2005, Case C-32/03 *I/S Fini H v Skatteministeriet*, ECLI:EU:C:2005:128, para. 32. *See also* P. Pistone, 'Anti-avoidance Rules', in M. Lang & I. Lejeune (eds), *Improving VAT/GST: Designing a Simple and Fraud-Proof Tax System* (IBFD 2014), pp. 591-602.
177. For example: CJEU 7 December 2010, Case C-285/09 *Criminal proceedings against R*, ECLI:EU:C:2010:742 and CJEU 18 December 2014, Joined Cases C-131/13, C-163/13 and C-164/13 *Staatssecretaris van Financiën v Schoenimport 'Italmoda' Mariano Previti vof (C-131/13) and Turbu.com BV (C-163/13) and Turbu.com Mobile Phone's BV (C-164/13) v Staatssecretaris van Financiën*, ECLI:EU:C:2014:2455.

such refusal and even with respect to situations predating *Halifax*.[178] Although the CJEU has never referred to it as a 'principle', given its position in EU VAT law and its relation to the principle of prohibition of abuse of law (*see* section 1.12.2), we feel safe in referring to this as the 'principle of prohibition of tax fraud'.

The application of this principle is not restricted to (taxable) persons carrying out fraudulent transactions themselves. It can also apply if the (taxable) person that does not carry out the fraudulent transaction himself, but knew, or should have known, that, by the transaction relied on as a basis for the right concerned, it was participating in evasion of VAT committed in the context of a chain of supplies, he may be refused the benefit of the rights to deduction of, exemption from or refund of VAT.[179] This is irrespective of whether or not he profited from the resale of the goods. According to the CJEU, in such a situation, the taxable person aids the perpetrators of the fraud and becomes their accomplice. Effectively, he is then treated identically to a real fraudster. Conversely, the supplier can rely on the application of the exemption or deduction if he acted in good faith and took every step which could reasonably be asked of the supplier to satisfy itself that the transaction which it had carried out had not resulted in its participation in tax fraud.[180] We refer to section 13.11 on carrousel fraud.

The approach of denying a right of deduction of, or an exemption from VAT in case of (participation in) a tax fraud, has its advantages. For example, it would seem that it makes it more difficult to carry out fraudulent transactions, and due to its deterrent effect is apt to prevent them.[181] Furthermore, it prevents the occurrence and/or spreading of fraud because it creates incentives in the supply chain for traders to take every precaution, which could reasonably be required of them to ensure that their transactions are not connected with fraud, be it the fraudulent evasion of VAT or other fraud. However, it also has its disadvantages. For example, it breaches external neutrality and is difficult to reconcile with the objective character of VAT. Furthermore, one may argue that denying a right of deduction or an exemption amounts to a punishment of the taxable person who is believed to have committed fraud or who is believed to be an accomplice to that fraud. One may question whether criminal law contains more safety nets than VAT law for determining whether a taxable person committed fraud or was an accomplice to that fraud. In our view, tax authorities and courts should exercise restraint when applying this principle of prohibition of tax fraud.

178. CJEU 18 December 2014, Joined Cases C-131/13, C-163/13 and C-164/13 *Staatssecretaris van Financiën v Schoenimport 'Italmoda' Mariano Previti vof (C-131/13) and Turbu.com BV (C-163/13) and Turbu.com Mobile Phone's BV (C-164/13) v Staatssecretaris van Financiën*, ECLI:EU:C:2014:2455.
179. *Ibid.*
180. For example: CJEU 6 September 2012, Case C-273/11 *Mecsek-Gabona Kft v Nemzeti Adó- és Vámhivatal Dél-dunántúli Regionális Adó Főigazgatósága*, ECLI:EU:C:2012:547, para. 53.
181. CJEU, 6 July 2006, Joined Cases C-439/04 and C-440/04 *Axel Kittel v Belgian State (C-439/04) and Belgian State v Recolta Recycling SPRL (C-440/04)*, ECLI:EU:C:2006:446, para. 58.

1.13 HOW TO APPLY THE VAT DIRECTIVE (THE VAT DETERMINATION SCHEME)

The structure of the VAT Directive provides for a method that enables solving complex VAT cases. The structure of the Directive is set out in Table 1.1.

Table 1.1 Structure of the VAT Directive

Preambles		
Title I	Subject matter and Scope	*(Articles 1-4)*
Title II	Territorial scope	*(Articles 5-8)*
Title III	Taxable persons	*(Articles 9-13)*
Title IV	Taxable transactions	*(Articles 14-30b)*
Title V	Place of taxable transactions	*(Articles 31-61)*
Title VI	Chargeable event and chargeability of VAT	*(Articles 62-71)*
Title VII	Taxable amount	*(Articles 72-92)*
Title VIII	Rates	*(Articles 93-129a)*
Title IX	Exemptions	*(Articles 131-166)*
Title X	Deductions	*(Articles 167-192)*
Title XI	Obligations of taxable persons and certain non-taxable persons	*(Articles 192a-280)*
Title XII	Special schemes	*(Articles 281-369zc)*
Title XIII	Derogations	*(Articles 370-396)*
Title XIV	Miscellaneous	*(Articles 397-401)*
Title XV	Final Provisions	*(Articles 402-414)*

The structure of the VAT Directive is, in our view, presented in a rational manner, consistent with the principle of better regulation. After the preamble, in which the main objectives of the harmonized VAT system are set out, and the reasons for the amendments of the last version of the Directive are clarified, there are some introductory provisions (of which some admittedly are highly technical, such as Article 4 about 'acquisitions of second-hand goods not subject to VAT'). Perhaps the introductory Title I of all the titles is the least accessible, and not really welcoming to those who wish to familiarize themselves with this Directive for the first time. But after Title II about the territorial scope of the Directive, there is an order which even people with only basic knowledge of VAT will soon recognize: taxable person, taxable transaction, place of transactions, etc.

From this structure, we derive the so-called VAT Determination scheme, which can be used to virtually solve each VAT case in a clear and systematic manner. The steps in this determination scheme reflect the structure of the VAT Directive from which it has been derived. Below, the VAT determination scheme is rendered (the relevant provisions in the VAT Directive relating to each step are included in this overview):[182]

1. Who (Taxable person)
   Article 9–13 VAT Directive
2. What (Taxable transactions)
   Article 14–30b VAT Directive
3. Where (Place of supply)
   Article 31–61 VAT Directive
4. When and how (Chargeable event and the chargeability of VAT)
   Article 62–71 VAT Directive
5. How much (Taxable amount/VAT rates)
   Article 72–92 VAT Directive
   Article 93–129a VAT Directive
6. Exemptions
   Article 131–166 VAT Directive
7. Deductions
   Article 167–192 VAT Directive
8. Liability (Person liable for payment of VAT)
   Article 192a–212 VAT Directive
9. Administrative obligations
   Article 213–280 VAT Directive
10. Special schemes and derogations
    Article 281–369zc VAT Directive
    Article 370–396 VAT Directive.

In the following sections, we discuss the above stages in the determination scheme in more detail. This book largely follows the structure of the VAT Directive/VAT determination scheme, albeit that it also contains some topical chapters (such as 'Immovable property', 'Intra-Community transactions' and 'Importation and exportation of goods').

1.13.1 Applying the VAT Determination Scheme

In this section, we provide an overview of the application of the VAT rules contained in the VAT Directive, using the VAT determination scheme as a guideline. Setting aside the topical chapters in this book, we will devote a separate chapter to each of the steps.

1.13.1.1 Taxable Person

For VAT purposes, the taxable person is anyone who independently carries out economic activities, whatever the purpose or result (Article 9). He has to account for VAT with regard to supplies of tangible assets (goods) and services to the extent that they are made within the territory of a specific Member State. There are special rules –

182. *See also* A.J. van Doesum & F. Nellen, *VAT in a Day* (Fonds Indirect Tax 2021). Available at: https://ssrn.com/abstract=3867201 (accessed 16 August 2024).

among others – for VAT grouping (Article 11), occasional activities (Article 12) and bodies governed by public law (Article 13).

1.13.1.2 Taxable Transactions

The Directive provides a limitative list of those supplies that can be considered to be a supply of goods (Articles 14-19). The concept of 'services', on the other hand, is described as 'all supplies that do not constitute a supply of a good' (Articles 24-29). Besides goods and services, the Directive contains two more taxable events that relate to cross-border trade. First, the importation of goods from third countries (in short: any state or territory to which the treaty (or treaties) is (are) not applicable)[183] is subject to VAT, regardless of the status of the person who imports them (Article 30). Next to this, the ICA by taxable persons – purchases of goods by businesses in other Member States – has also been a taxable event since 1993 (Articles 20-23). That is the acquisition of the right to dispose of goods 'as if one were the owner'. The goods must also be transported to another Member State, usually the Member State in which the acquirer is established. This acquisition is the mirror image of the straightforward ICS. The ICS is also a taxable supply, but it is not separately mentioned in the Directive because it is seen as a regular supply of a good (*see* Article 14 VAT Directive).

1.13.1.3 The Place of Supply

Only transactions which are deemed to be made within a single Member State are subject to the VAT legislation of, and may, therefore, be levied by, that particular Member State (supply of goods: Articles 31-39; acquisitions: Articles 40-42; services: Articles 43-59b; importation of goods: Articles 60-61). All sums of VAT (after subtraction of the deductible amounts of input VAT) will eventually turn up in the treasury of that Member State. For all cross-border transactions – transactions of goods that are transported in accordance with the supply to another country, or services that are made by a taxable person in one territory to a person in another territory – it needs to be determined where such transactions take place for VAT purposes. All the criteria necessary to establish this can be found in the VAT Directive. For the supply of goods, the basic rule is that the supply is deemed to take place where the goods are at the moment of the supply if they are not being transported (Article 31). If they are transported in accordance with the supply, the place of supply will be the country where the transport starts (Article 32). In most of those cases, VAT will not actually be levied as the supply of the goods leaving the country is subject to an exemption (zero-rate supply). In the country of arrival of the goods, VAT will be levied from the importer of record upon importation of the goods (Article 60) or – if it concerns another EU Member State – VAT becomes due for the acquirer on the acquisition of the goods

183. *See* further Article 5(3) and (4) VAT Directive. Third territories are a separate category of excluded territories. They are different from third countries and belong to the Customs territory of the EU, but the VAT Directive is not applicable in those territories. The territories concerned are listed in Article 6 of the VAT Directive.

(Article 40). Services to taxable persons – thus between businesses – are taxable in the country where the recipient of the service is established (Article 44). Services to non-taxable persons (made by taxable persons to final consumers and those (legal) persons who are non-taxable persons) are deemed to take place in the country where the service provider is established (Article 45). There are some exceptions to these two main rules. For instance, the supplies connected to immovable property are taxable in the country where the immovable property is situated; and specific scientific, sporting, cultural services are taxable in the country where they are physically carried out.

Intra-Community Transactions

Since 1 January 1993, a special regime has been applicable to intra-Community trade. Initially, this regime was called a transitional measure, as it was meant to be replaced by a final system after a few years (in principle, by 1997). There was, however, not enough political will among the Member States to set up such a final system. It is, therefore, the case that the current – at first temporary – the measure is now accepted to be a definitive system, and it is no longer referred to as being 'transitional'. It may be good to remember that the VAT system itself was also introduced in most countries as a temporary measure. This is perhaps one of the reasons why most tax people are sceptical whenever the legislator introduces a new temporary measure.

Nevertheless, the current system is working rather well. Most entrepreneurs comply with the rules. Most of them make straightforward ICSs of goods, which means that there is a physical flow of goods from one Member State to another between two taxable persons using their VAT ID numbers. This results in an exempt (or zero-rated) supply in the country of departure and an acquisition in the country of arrival. In reality, there are nonetheless a variety of cross-border transactions within the EU, e.g., ICSs with just one party involved (bringing stock from one Member State to another), or transactions with more than two parties. Until 1 January 2010, the services directly related to ICSs had their own special regimes regarding the place of supply. Since that date, most of these services fall within the scope of the main rule for the determination of the place of supply of services which means that the service is deemed to take place at the country of destination (in the country where the taxable person who orders the service is based).

As already indicated in section 1.7.4., in 2017, the European Commission has issued a series of proposals that eventually should replace the transitional system with a definitive VAT system.[184] It was proposed that as of 2022 the system of (exempt) ICSs in the Member State of origin and (taxed) ICAs in the Member State of destination is replaced with a system in which only a single taxable event (the Intra-union supply) would take place in case of a cross-border sale of goods. It is as of yet unclear whether this newly proposed system will gather enough political support to replace the temporary system currently in place.

184. *See* most notably Proposal for a Council Directive amending Directive 2006/112/EC as regards the introduction of the detailed technical measures for the operation of the definitive VAT system for the taxation of trade between Member States, COM (2018)329.

Importation and Exportation

For all trade with third countries – as far as transactions with goods are concerned – where goods really cross the border of the EU, the expressions 'importation' (for incoming goods) and 'exportation' (for outgoing goods) can be used. Some European traders will still use the term 'export' if they sell and transport goods to entrepreneurs in other Member States, but that is not correct from a legal point of view: it is an ICS. Third countries are all countries outside the territory of the EU, as specified in Articles 5-8 of the VAT Directive. All export supplies are subject to an exemption (zero rate). Goods will, therefore, leave the country free of any VAT. It is up to the (third) country of destination whether they want to tax the importation with local VAT. In opposite situations – if goods are imported into one of the countries of the EU and brought into free circulation – VAT will be levied in the country of importation (importation takes place regardless whether the importer reports the importation or not, so also smuggling and removal of goods from bonded warehouses will result in an importation). Importation can take place regardless of the capacity of the importer, which means that even a private individual who brings goods from a third territory into his or her own country makes an importation from a VAT point of view. In order to avoid too great an administrative burden, there is a threshold. If private persons remain below this threshold, they do not need to report the importation, nor need they pay any VAT upon importation.

The taxable base for the calculation of the VAT on importation is the customs value. This encompasses all taxes (excluding VAT), all additional expenses such as transport costs, handling, packaging and insurance relating to the transport to the place of destination. The VAT rates on importation are, of course, the same as those on domestic supplies. Sometimes the VAT on importation can be suspended by applying special customs regimes. As VAT on importation is mostly deductible for the importer of record, for most entrepreneurs, it is a zero-rate operation in the end.

1.13.1.4 Chargeable Event and the Chargeability of VAT

Basically, VAT becomes chargeable at the time that the supply is made. Member States may, however, determine another tax point, like the moment that the invoice is issued or paid, or where an invoice is not issued or is issued late, within a specified period from the date of the taxable event.

1.13.1.5 Taxable Amount and VAT Rates

The taxable amount includes everything which constitutes the consideration obtained or to be obtained by the supplier, in return for the supply, from the customer or a third party. Member States must apply a standard rate of VAT, which is fixed by each Member State as a percentage of the taxable amount and which is the same for the supply of goods and for the supply of services. The rate applicable to the ICA must be the same as the rate applied to the supply of like goods within the territory of the

Member State. The standard rate can not be less than 15%. Member States may apply two reduced rates of a minimum of 5% and an exemption with deductibility of the VAT paid at the preceding stage. In addition, Member States are allowed to apply another super reduced rate between 5% and 0%. Member States may apply the reduced rates (of a minimum of 5%) to supplies of goods or services covered in a maximum of 24 points in Annex III. The super reduced rate lower than the minimum of 5% and the exemption with deductibility of the VAT paid at the preceding stage may only be applied to supplies of goods or services covered in specific points of Annex III (e.g., foodstuffs, books). Some Member States also apply a zero rate for ICSs and for supplies of goods to third countries (exportation). One has to keep in mind that this is just a technical rate. The Directive uses the expression 'exemption' with the right to deduction of input VAT (to be distinguished from exempt supplies without the right to deduction), and treat the ICSs and export supplies, therefore, as exempt supplies. The only reason why these Member States use the term 'zero rate' instead of 'exemption' is that they were used to this terminology before the coming into force of the Directive and because it is more practical to reserve the set phrase 'exemption' for 'true' exemptions (without the right to deduct the input VAT).

1.13.1.6 Exemptions

As noted above, the Directive encompasses two forms of exemption: exemptions with the right to deduct the related input VAT, and exemptions without that right. The first type is generally applicable to cross-border transactions (ICSs and export supplies), the latter is applied on supplies which are listed in Articles 132 and 135 of the VAT Directive. These supplies are largely exempt because they are (supposed to be) in the public interest (like medical care, education, sporting, etc.) or relate to immovable property (leasing and selling of immovable property) or have a financial character. Under some circumstances, the last category of the exemption – that does not give rise to a deduction of the related input VAT – can lead to an accumulation of input VAT. This depends on whether the exemption occurs at the end or in the middle of the supply chain. If it occurs at the end of the chain, the exemption will not lead to an accumulation of non-deductible input VAT. This is different, however, if the exemption takes place in the middle or at the beginning of the chain. The effect materializes as the party making the exempt supply incorporates the non-deductible input VAT in his selling price. The next party whose activity is not exempt has no right to deduct this hidden VAT and has to charge VAT on the value of his supplies, including this hidden input VAT. For this reason, and because exemptions are exceptions to the main rule that principally all supplies are taxed with VAT, the CJEU has consistently ruled that exemptions have to be interpreted strictly.

1.13.1.7 Deductions

From the VAT that the taxable person is liable to pay can be deducted the VAT that is charged to him by other taxpayers. In addition, VAT on incoming transactions, e.g., on

ICAs, on importation or that is shifted to him on the basis of the reverse charge mechanism, can be deducted from the VAT that he is liable to pay on his output transactions. If the input VAT exceeds the amount of output VAT, the taxpayer is entitled to reclaim this surplus from the tax authorities (the Member States may, however, carry forward the excess to the following period). Even if he makes supplies in another Member State, he is still entitled to recover the local VAT (of his own Member State) that is charged to him via his regular VAT return. He may only reclaim input VAT by means of an invoice drawn up in accordance with the Directive and national law. Not all supplies give rise to a deduction of input VAT (for instance, if supplies are exempt on the basis of Articles 132 and 135). If the taxpayer uses goods and services both for taxed and non-taxed supplies, he must calculate his deductible proportion (pro rata).

1.13.1.8 Liability

The question with regard to the liability for payment of VAT is twofold. First, one needs to know which person – the supplier or the purchaser – must pay the VAT to the tax authorities. Second, the liability issue refers to the question of at what time the supply is deemed to take place for VAT purposes.

Generally speaking, it is the person who makes the supply who is liable to pay the VAT to the tax authorities. However, under conditions, it can be the person to whom the supply is made that must pay the VAT. If the latter is the case, the expression used to refer to this switch of liability is 'reverse charge mechanism'.

1.13.1.9 Administrative Obligations

VAT that becomes due and the deductible input VAT arising in the same period must be reported in the VAT return relating to that period. The net amount must be paid to the tax authorities. In some cases, taxable persons must submit not only a VAT return but also recapitulative statements of the supplies they made in a tax period.

The invoice is certainly an important document. VAT can only be recovered if the recipient holds an invoice that has been drawn up correctly. In that respect, one might say that an invoice is a legal tender. The Directive and national VAT Acts contain detailed descriptions of invoice requirements. Only in exceptional cases can VAT be reclaimed without holding an invoice drawn up in accordance with the Directive or national law.

1.13.1.10 Special Schemes and Derogations

The VAT Directive contains six special schemes for levying VAT. These special schemes are laid down in Title XII of the VAT Directive and concern: (i) small- and medium-sized enterprises (SMEs), (ii) farmers, (iii) travel agents, (iv) second-hand goods, works of art, collector's items and antiques, (v) investment gold and (vi) non-established taxable persons supplying electronic services to non-taxable persons (hereinafter also referred to as: 'one-stop shop' (OSS)). The first three schemes are designed to cope with foreseen difficulties in levying VAT with respect to certain categories of taxable persons according to the normal regime. The fourth and fifth schemes were introduced to remove foreseen difficulties when applying the normal VAT regime to specific supplies. The last scheme was introduced to provide for administrative simplification in order to achieve an increase in VAT compliant behaviour. In Chapter 15, we will elaborate further on these special schemes and derogations.

CHAPTER 2
Taxable Persons

2.1 THE 'TAXABLE PERSON' IN A VAT SYSTEM

The ultimate goal of the EU's VAT system is to tax private consumption.[1] However, consumption is only taxed indirectly. In principle, only businesses, rather than private consumers, are considered as taxable persons for VAT. EU VAT is collected from businesses (and by businesses from consumers), instead of directly from consumers. Clearly, it is easier to collect tax from a relatively small group of businesses than from all EU citizens individually (which would be the case with a direct consumption tax).[2] Under this system of *indirect taxation*, businesses operate as intermediaries for the tax authorities in collecting the tax on consumption.

Wherever businesses enable consumers (or other businesses) to consume or spend, consumption tax (VAT) can be levied. However, where consumers spend their money on goods and services supplied by non-taxable suppliers, no consumption tax will be levied under a VAT system, regardless of the fact that such goods and services will be consumed. Imperfect taxation of consumption is often the result of a VAT system that does not rely on the direct taxation of consumption.

While the collection costs of VAT are relatively low for tax authorities, it should be observed that businesses incur costs when collecting the VAT from their customers and remitting that VAT to the tax authorities. This administrative burden should not be underestimated.[3] It encompasses both time (labour costs) and usually also other costs (e.g., IT costs). Yet these businesses are not paid for their assistance in collecting the tax. Although it is the intention of the EU to keep the administrative burden as low as possible, collecting VAT and all the associated administration is nevertheless a formidable administrative burden.

Notwithstanding the administrative burden, having the taxable person status has an important benefit. Taxable persons can recover VAT on goods and services charged to them. In principle, this right of recovery takes the form of a right of deduction, whereby businesses deduct the VAT on their purchases from the VAT on their sales.[4]

Through this system of recovery of input VAT, businesses are relieved of the direct fiscal burden of the tax. Their 'productive consumption' remains untaxed, allowing VAT to function as a tax on private consumption rather than on businesses themselves.

1. Article 1(2) VAT Directive.
2. A direct consumption tax as an alternative for an income tax was advocated by N. Kaldor, *An Expenditure Tax* (London 1955).
3. It is estimated that compliance costs for businesses range from 2% to as much as 8% of VAT collection. *See* Communication from the Commission to the European Parliament, the Council and the European and Social Committee on the future of VAT Towards a simpler, more robust and efficient VAT system tailored to the single market, COM (2011) 851 final, p. 6. It has been held that VAT is the most burdensome for business of all taxes (*see*: S. Eichfelder & F. Vaillancourt, *Tax Compliance Costs: A Review of Cost Burdens and Cost Structures*, Arqus discussion paper 178 (November 2014), available online at: http://www.arqus.info/mobile/paper/arqus_178.pdf (accessed 16 August 2024)). Also *see*: R. Highfield, M. Walpole & C. Evans, *A Proposal for the Development and Testing of a Diagnostic Tool for Assessing VAT Compliance Costs*, International VAT Monitor May/June 2017, pp. 228-239 https://doi.org/10.59403/2epk5e0.
4. Article 168 VAT Directive and further.

The notion of 'taxable person' should be defined as broadly as possible in order that VAT is given a sufficiently wide scope to comprise all stages of production, distribution and the provision of services.[5] This broad definition is crucial for VAT to achieve its ultimate goal of taxing all private consumption.

2.1.1 Taxable Person Status and Capacity

The EU VAT system applies exclusively to transactions carried out by 'a taxable person acting as such'. Therefore, it is essential to determine both whether a person meets the objective criteria for taxable person status and whether a person with taxable person status 'acts as such' (i.e., performs activities in its capacity as a taxable person). For example, if a one-man business (sole proprietor) supplies a used car, it must be established whether the supply is made privately or in the capacity of a taxable person. The operational capacity of a person with taxable status also impacts his right to deduct VAT. Only VAT incurred by a taxable person acting as such is eligible for recovery (*see* Chapter 10).

The capacity in which a person operates essentially comes down to the questions whether an activity carried out by a person must be considered as (a part of) an economic activity and/or whether that activity is carried out independently. For example, if a one-man business supplies a used car, is that an economic activity in the course of his business? Or is that an activity carried out as a private person, i.e., not in the course of his business? What is the correct VAT treatment if a director-shareholder provides management services to his limited liability company? Does he provide such services independently, i.e., as a taxable person, or does he provide the services as an employee to the limited liability company?

As questions related to the taxable person capacity arise only once the taxable person status has been established, we will first address the taxable person status, followed by the taxable person capacity in the subsequent sections.

2.1.2 Procedural and Substantive Effects of Taxable Person Status and Capacity

Being recognized as a taxable person and acting accordingly carries both substantive and procedural consequences. If individuals meet all the criteria outlined in Article 9 of the VAT Directive, they will be acknowledged as a taxable person and receive a VAT registration number in the Member State where their business is established. If they operate in multiple Member States or countries, they may be required to register in each of those jurisdictions. It is important to note, however, that a business with taxable person status may not necessarily conduct all its activities in that capacity (*see* section 2.1.1).

5. Cf. CJEU 29 April 2004, Case C-137/02 *Finanzamt Offenbach am Main-Land v Faxworld Vorgründungsgesellschaft Peter Hünninghausen und Wolfgang Klein GbR*, ECLI:EU:C:2004:267.

The most significant consequence of having the taxable person status is the obligation to remit VAT to the tax authorities, for amounts invoiced and charged to customers. Another aspect of being a taxable person and acting as such is that only taxable persons have the right to apply for exemptions or zero rates on intra-Community supplies of goods (ICSs). Additionally, only taxable persons acting as such are entitled to recover VAT incurred on supplies provided to them, paid upon importation, and intra-Community acquisitions (ICAs). The determination of whether a customer is a taxable person or not is relevant when applying the rules regarding the place of supply of services.

In addition to these substantive consequences related to the taxable person status and capacity of the supplier or customer, there are also procedural and administrative effects. In Chapter 15, we will delve into the administrative requirements concerning the identification for VAT purposes of the suppliers of goods and services. The most significant formal consequences are the following. All invoices issued by a taxable person must comply with all requirements outlined in the VAT Directive (Articles 217-240) and in the local VAT legislation if his customer is also a taxable person. Furthermore, the taxable person must file VAT returns that report all transactions, including deemed or fictitious supplies, imports, stock transfers, purchases, and ICAs (Articles 250-261). Those engaged in ICSs and services must submit sales listings containing the names of customers who purchased intra-Community goods and services (Articles 262-271). Additionally, they are required to complete Intrastat forms, which provide statistical information about their intra-Community (intra-EU) flows of goods, through the monthly Intrastat declaration. Finally, ledgers that meet the requirements set forth by the Directive and local legislation must be maintained (Article 243).

2.1.3 Basic Criteria for Taxable Person Status

According to Article 9(1) VAT Directive, a taxable person is any person who independently carries out in any place any economic activity, whatever the purpose or result of that activity. The following elements of this definition can be identified. They play a key role in determining whether a person can be regarded as a *taxable* person or not:

(1) any person;
(2) in any place;
(3) economic activity;
(4) independently.

These key elements will be analysed in the following subsections.

2.2 ANY PERSON

In an indirect tax, such as the EU VAT, it is important to have a broad definition of the taxable person concept to ensure that the ultimate goal of taxing private consumption is achieved (*see* section 2.1). Moreover, it is essential that the taxable person concept is applied in a uniform manner in all Member States. Consequently, the taxable person concept, and thereby its constituting elements ('any person', 'independently', 'economic activity') are uniform concepts of Union Law.[6] Regarding the concept of any person, this implies that neutrality of legal form is an inherent feature of the taxable person concept in EU VAT (*see* section 2.2.1). Even so, it is apparent that it is generally easier to identify a 'person' if it is a natural or legal person than when if it concerns 'something' without legal personality. For example, how does one determine if a contractual form of cooperation between natural or legal persons amounts to the creation of a new person which exists separately from the participants?

In this regard, the Court of Justice sometimes gives the impression of treating the term 'any person' merely as a grammatical construct. Moreover, the CJEU has ruled that the term 'any person' used in Article 9(1) VAT intends to give the notion of 'taxable person' a broad definition focused on independence in the pursuit of an economic activity.[7] However, it appears that the Court is more concerned with determining the extent to which a legal subject (entity, person) demonstrates independence in conducting economic activities rather than identifying the relevant legal subject itself.[8] Consequently, in its case law, the CJEU puts much emphasis on the existence of an economic activity and whether that activity is carried out independently. When independence in the exercise of an economic activity can be established, implicitly it has been established that a 'person' (entity) relevant for VAT exists. According to the CJEU, the criterion of independence concerns allocation of the transaction concerned to a particular person or entity.[9] By allocating a transaction to a person, that person is (implicitly) identified. If a combination of persons does not reveal its identity *vis-à-vis* third parties,[10] it cannot be a person (a legal subject bearing rights and obligations) and will not be possible to allocate any transactions to that combination. This may explain why in CJEU case law the concepts of 'any person' and 'independently' somewhat overlap. Moreover, if a combination of persons is not capable of acting for its own account, it is also not possible to allocate a transaction to that combination. Arguably, a combination can only act for its own account if it possesses a set of delineated assets

6. *See*, for example: CJEU 4 December 1990, Case C-186/89 *W. M. van Tiem v Staatssecretaris van Financiën*, ECLI:EU:C:1990:429, para. 25 and CJEU 29 April 2004, Case C-137/02 *Finanzamt Offenbach am Main-Land v Faxworld Vorgründungsgesellschaft Peter Hünninghausen und Wolfgang Klein GbR*, ECLI:EU:C:2004:267, para. 29.
7. CJEU 12 October 2016, Case C-340/15 *Christine Nigl and Others v Finanzamt Waldviertel*, ECLI:EU:C:2016:764, para. 27.
8. CJEU 16 September 2020, Case C-312/19 *XT v Valstybine mokesčių inspekcija prie Lietuvos Respublikos finansų ministerijos and Vilniaus apskrities valstybine mokesčių inspekcija prie Lietuvos Respublikos finansų ministerijos*, ECLI:EU:C:2020:711, para. 40. Also *see*: A.J. van Doesum & G.J. van Doesum, *Een onafhankelijk persoon (An Independent Person)*, WFR2023/225.
9. CJEU 16 September 2020, Case C-312/19 *XT v Valstybine mokesčių inspekcija prie Lietuvos Respublikos finansų ministerijos and Vilniaus apskrities valstybine mokesčių inspekcija prie Lietuvos Respublikos finansų ministerijos*, ECLI:EU:C:2020:711, para. 40.
10. *See*, for example: CJEU 16 September 2020, Case C-312/19 *XT v Valstybine mokesčių inspekcija prie Lietuvos Respublikos finansų ministerijos and Vilniaus apskrities valstybine mokesčių inspekcija prie Lietuvos Respublikos finansų ministerijos*, ECLI:EU:C:2020:711, paras 46 and 47.

over which it can exert its will to engage in transactions with third parties.[11] Using criteria, such as acting in the own account and on own responsibility and bearing risks, which are typically the criteria to determine if a person (once identified) acts independently, are also relevant in identifying whether a 'person' exists in the first place. We refer to section 2.5 on 'Independently'.

2.2.1 Neutrality of Legal Form

The legal form of a business is a matter of choice. The various legal forms available to a business depend largely on national civil law. The purpose of the VAT Directive is, *inter alia,* to have a common system of VAT based on a uniform definition of taxable persons. This objective might be jeopardized if the preconditions for being a taxable person were to differ from one Member State to another, as well as the conditions governing the legal form of a business under civil law. Therefore, from a VAT perspective, the legal form of a business should be irrelevant.

Indeed, the taxable person status does not depend on a specific legal form of a business. Even if the form of a business is not recognized as a 'legal person' under civil law, that business (or combination of persons) can in itself be considered as 'any person' from a VAT perspective and potentially as a taxable person.[12] All persons – natural or legal, both public and private, even entities devoid of legal personality – which, in an objective manner, satisfy the criteria set out in Article 9 VAT Directive must be regarded as being taxable persons for the purposes of VAT.[13] Consequently, self-employed persons (one-person businesses), private and public legal entities[14] (such as private or public limited companies, European Economic Interest Groupings (EEIGs) and the Societas Europaea (SE)), and also joint ventures and partnerships that – according to their national legislation – may lack legal personality can be considered as taxable persons under Article 9(1) VAT Directive. In the *Heerma* case,[15] the CJEU considered that partnerships governed by Dutch civil law are not legal persons in their own right. However, they do have the de facto independence of companies, which are legal persons and may carry on economic activities independently. According to the

11. B. Willemsen, *Op eigen benen in de btw, NLF-W 2023/34*, para. 2.3.
12. CJEU 12 October 2016, Case C-340/15 *Christine Nigl and Others v Finanzamt Waldviertel*, ECLI:EU:C:2016:764, para. 27.
13. CJEU 29 September 2015, Case C-276/14 *Gmina Wrocław v Minister Finansów ('Gmina Wrocław II')* ECLI:EU:C:2015:635, para. 28 and CJEU 12 October 2016, Case C-340/15 *Christine Nigl and Others v Finanzamt Waldviertel*, ECLI:EU:C:2016:764, para. 27.
14. *See also* CJEU 29 September 2015, Case C-276/14 *Gmina Wroclaw v Minister Finansów ('Gmina Wrocław II')*, ECLI:EU:C:2015:635, para. 33. The question was whether municipal budgetary entities could independently carry out economic activities. In *Gmina Wroclaw II* the CJEU did not check whether such an entity can be considered as a 'person', as mentioned in Article 9 VAT Directive. Instead, it simply referred to such a budgetary entity as 'a person' (*see* para. 34: 'to check whether the person concerned performs his activities in his own name'). The CJEU decided that the municipality, such as the Municipality of Wrocław, and its budgetary entities, must be regarded as one and the same taxable person within the meaning of Article 9(1) VAT Directive.
15. CJEU 27 January 2000, Case C-23/98 *Heerma and Maatschap J. Heerma en K. Heerma-Graanstra*, ECLI:EU:C:2000:46.

CJEU, the consequence of this de facto independence is that it is the partnership and not the partner or partners running the business, which is to be considered as the taxable person. The partner in a partnership can act in his capacity as a representative of the partnership, in which situation it is irrelevant whether the partner himself is a taxable person or not. All the supplies or purchases he makes as a representative are made in the name and on behalf of the partnership.

However, it is conceivable that a partner does not act in his capacity as a representative of the partnership, but rather in his own name and on his own behalf. In that situation, he can be considered as a taxable person in his own right. Then, the partner and the partnership of which he is part are considered as separate taxable persons. A partner may even derive his own taxable person status solely on account of supplies he makes to the partnership in which he is a partner. In *Heerma*, the CJEU decided that where a person's sole economic activity consisted of the letting of an item of tangible property to a company or a partnership, such as a partnership governed by Dutch civil law, of which he is a member, that letting under such conditions must be regarded as an independent activity.

2.2.2 European Legal Entities

By means of Council Regulation (EEC) 2137/85 on the EEIG, a new European law entity was launched. The purpose of the grouping is to facilitate or develop the economic activities of its members by a pooling of resources, activities or skills. It was the idea that this should produce better results than the members acting alone. Therefore, an EEIG's activities must be related to the economic activities of its members, although they may not replace them. For the same reason, it was considered that the EEIG should not make profits for itself. Consequently, it was provided that any profits would be apportioned among the members and for direct tax purposes be taxed accordingly.

This European law entity never became very popular, due to the fact that the Member States had to make too many compromises in order to realize the Regulation. There were simply too many complex conditions that the EEIG had to meet in relation to the advantages that they could obtain.

On 20 December 2000, the Council created a new European law entity and adopted the EC Statute on the 'SE', which consisted – among other legislative items – of an SE Regulation.[16] Terra and Kajus indicate that even though the SE is not – as originally envisaged – an actual Community legal form independent of national laws, the SE is more of a success than the EEIG.[17] In addition, on 22 July 2003, a Statute for a European Cooperative Society was adopted, also consisting of a Regulation.[18]

16. Regulation (EC) 2157/2001 [2001] OJ L294/1–21 amended by Regulation (EC) 885/2004 [2004] OJ L168/1–13.
17. B. Terra & J. Kajus, *A Guide to the European VAT Directives, Introduction to European VAT*, Vol. 1 (IBFD 2021), p. 447.
18. Proposals to introduce a Societas Privata Europaea (SPE), a European private limited company comparable to a BV, Ltd, GmbH, etc. have been tabled. However, since no political consensus could be reached, these proposals have been withdrawn. Subsequently, the Commission

It is beyond doubt that businesses taking any of these legal forms are to be seen as 'any person', as referred to in Article 9 VAT Directive. With respect to the EEIG, Article 5 VAT Implementing Regulation clarifies that an EEIG which supplies goods or services for consideration to its members or to third parties shall be a taxable person within the meaning of Article 9(1) VAT Directive.

2.2.3 A Marital Community

According to the CJEU, a marital community cannot, in principle, be considered as 'any person' in terms of Article 9 VAT Directive. In *HE*, the CJEU considered that the marital community formed by the spouses HE (Hundt-Eswein) as a result of their marriage did not itself carry out an economic activity either as a civil law partnership with its own legal personality or in a form which, although without legal personality, was, in fact, able to act independently.[19] The spouses, in that case, merely acted jointly in purchasing land and building a property. Therefore, the marital community could not be considered as 'any person', let alone as a 'taxable person'. Similarly, in *WG*, the CJEU considered that spouses carrying out an agricultural activity in the same holding, using property forming part of the marital community of property, should be considered as separate taxable persons where each of those spouses carries out an economic activity independently.[20]

2.3 IN ANY PLACE

The taxable person concept in EU VAT has a worldwide scope. Again, this broad scope is necessary to attain the ultimate goal of taxing private consumption. The worldwide scope of the taxable person concept bears a strong relation to the place of supply rules. The mere fact that a person is a taxable person does not mean that he must register and remit VAT in the EU.

2.3.1 Nationality

Any person meeting the criteria of Article 9 will be treated as a taxable person according to that provision, regardless of where that person is (within or outside the EU), and regardless of what their 'nationality' might be. Even an Egyptian car manufacturer established in Tokyo falls within the scope of Article 9 VAT Directive and is a taxable person for EU VAT purposes. This does not automatically mean that the Egyptian car manufacturer must register for VAT in the EU and remit EU VAT. That will

proposed legislative measures to introduce a European Single-member Private Limited Liability Companies ('Societas Unius Personae'), which were withdrawn in July 2018.

19. CJEU 21 April 2005, Case C-25/03 *Finanzamt Bergisch Gladbach v HE (Hundt-Eswein)*, ECLI:EU:C:2005:241.
20. CJEU 24 March 2022, Case C-697/20 *W.G. v Dyrektor Izby Skarbowej w L.*, ECLI:EU:C:2022:210.

only be the case if the manufacturer carries out taxable transactions in the EU for which he is liable to pay VAT in the EU (*see* Chapter 4 on the place of supply).

2.3.2 Place of Establishment

In section 2.3, we explained that the taxable person status does not depend on the place of establishment of a business. In a tax system focusing primarily on supplies made by taxable persons (the object of taxation) instead of concentrating on taxable persons making those supplies (the subject of taxation), the question of where *a supply* is taxed is logically more relevant than where *the taxable person* must be taxed.[21]

Nevertheless, it would be incorrect to conclude that for the purposes of VAT, the place where a supplier or recipient is based is completely irrelevant. For example, the VAT grouping option in Article 11 VAT Directive is limited to persons that are established in the territory of the same Member State (*see* section 2.6.6). Furthermore, the place of establishment is relevant with respect to the determination of the place of supply (i.e., which country is entitled to levy VAT on the supply). As regards cross-border services between businesses ('B2B services'), it is crucial to know where the *recipient* of the service is established (*see* Chapter 4).[22] For supplies made by businesses to private consumers ('B2C services'), the place of business of the *supplier* must be known in order to establish where (in which country) the taxable supply is taxed.[23]

Most businesses are based in just one country. However, in a global economy, it is very common for businesses to operate across borders and to be based in multiple jurisdictions. Some multinationals choose to set up separate companies in the various jurisdictions in which they are active, whereas others choose to merely set up branches (or 'filials'). The primary place of establishment of a company that sets up branches in other jurisdictions is also referred to as its 'place of business', 'place of establishment', 'seat' or – in practice – 'head office'. This will usually be the place where the management of the legal entity is based (we refer to section 4.5.2 on the place of establishment). Of less relevance is the 'nationality' of the law under which the legal entity was incorporated. For example, if a certain legal entity is incorporated under French business law, and the management of that legal entity is based in Brussels, it will be considered to be a Belgian-based business for VAT purposes (also *see* Article 10 VAT Implementing Regulation).

Branches that are set up by the head office shall be regarded as a 'fixed establishment' for VAT purposes if they meet certain criteria. A fixed establishment is regarded as a secondary place of establishment for VAT purposes. In *Berkholz,* the Court ruled that a fixed establishment requires a certain minimum size and the permanent presence of both the human and technical resources necessary for the provision of the service. Article 11 VAT Implementing Regulation echoes this definition. Typically, (foreign) subsidiaries are not considered as fixed establishments of

21. Conversely, earnings-based taxes, such as income tax focus on the taxable person.
22. *See* Article 44 VAT Directive.
23. *See* Article 45 VAT Directive.

their parent company. However, it follows from *Dong Yang* that it cannot be ruled out that a subsidiary can be a fixed establishment.[24] According to the CJEU, that depends on the substantive conditions for a fixed establishment, which must be assessed in the light of economic and commercial realities. From a conceptual and practical perspective, we do not agree with this ruling. We rather subscribe to Advocate General Kokott's view that for reasons of simplicity and legal certainty, a subsidiary company cannot constitute a fixed establishment, except in cases of abuse.[25] Cases such as *Berlin Chemie*[26] and *Cabot Plastics*[27] confirm that a legal entity should not be considered as a fixed establishment too easily. The existence of a fixed establishment cannot depend solely on the legal status of the entity concerned. Moreover, the CJEU confirmed that the fact that a service supplier and the recipient of the services are linked and belong to the same group, while being legally independent of each other, and that a company has a subsidiary in another Member State does not, in itself, mean that it also has its fixed establishment there. In section 4.5.2.3, we further outline the 'fixed establishment' concept.[28]

As previously mentioned, the place of establishment of a business establishment is not relevant in determining the existence of an economic activity or taxable person status. It is important to highlight that a secondary place of business, known as a fixed establishment, is in principle not treated as a separate taxable person but rather as a physical presence of a taxable person operating in another territory. The fact that a fixed establishment is viewed as an extension of the foreign taxable person's entity is emphasized by the principle that supplies made between the two places of business are not considered supplies made for third parties and therefore fall outside the scope of the VAT system.[29] For instance, if the head office hires out personnel to one of its fixed establishments, VAT should not be charged (unless the head office or the branch is part of a local VAT group).[30] Conversely, if the same head office provides the same service to a third party within its own country, local VAT must be charged. It is worth noting that the existence of a fixed establishment can impact the recovery of input VAT.[31] For further details, please refer to Chapter 10, section 10.2.4.2.2.

24. CJEU 7 May 2020, Case C-547/18 *Dong Yang Electronics Sp. z o.o. v Dyrektor Izby Administracji Skarbowej we Wrocławiu*, ECLI:EU:C:2020:350.
25. Opinion of Advocate General Kokott of 14 November 2019, Case C-547/18 *Dong Yang Electronics Sp. z o.o. v Dyrektor Izby Administracji Skarbowej we Wrocławiu*, ECLI:EU:C:2019:976.
26. CJEU 7 April 2022, Case C-333/20 *Berlin Chemie A. Menarini SRL v Administraţia Fiscală pentru Contribuabili Mijlocii Bucureşti – Direcţia Generală Regională a Finanţelor Publice Bucureşti*, ECLI:EU:C:2022:291.
27. CJEU 29 June 2023, Case C-232/22 *Cabot Plastics Belgium SA v État Belge*, ECLI:EU:C:2023:530.
28. CJEU 4 July 1985, Case 168/84 *Gunter Berkholz v Finanzamt Hamburg-Mitte-Altstadt*, ECLI:EU:C:1985:299, para. 18. Also *see*: Article 11 VAT Implementing Regulation.
29. CJEU 23 March 2006, Case C-210/04 *FCE Bank – Ministro dell'Economia e delle Finanze. Agenzia delle Entrate*, ECLI:EU:C:2006:196. *See* however sections 2.6.6.2. and 3.6.2.
30. CJEU 17 September 2014, C-7/13 *Skandia America Corp. v Skatteverket*, ECLI:EU:C:2014:2225 and CJEU 11 March 2021, Case C-812/19 *Danske Bank A/S, Danmark, Sverige Filial v Skatteverket*, ECLI:EU:C:2021:196.
31. *See*, for example: CJEU 2 September 2013, Case C-388/11 *Le Crédit Lyonnais v Ministre du Budget, des Comptes publics et de la Réforme de l'État*, ECLI:EU:C:2013:541, Order of the Court of 21 June 2016, Case C-393/15 *Dyrektor Izby Skarbowej w Krakowie v ESET spol. s r.o. sp. z o.o.*

2.4 ECONOMIC ACTIVITY

The interpretation of the concept of a 'taxable person' relies on specific criteria, as mentioned previously. These criteria include the presence of a person (any person, in any place) engaged in economic activity and acting independently. The previous paragraphs have discussed the terms 'any person' and 'in any place'. In this subsection, our focus shifts to understanding the meaning of the concept of 'economic activity'.

2.4.1 Broad Interpretation

Article 9(1) VAT Directive states that:

> Any activity of producers, traders or persons supplying services, including mining and agricultural activities and activities of the professions, shall be regarded as 'economic activity'. The exploitation of tangible or intangible property for the purposes of obtaining income therefrom on a continuing basis shall in particular be regarded as an economic activity.

The wording of this provision indicates the term 'economic activity' is a rather broad concept. Indeed, it is important to interpret the term 'economic activity' in a broad manner. Should the concept be interpreted too restrictively, the possibility exists that certain transactions, ultimately leading to consumption, would escape taxation. Such an effect is not in line with the aim of VAT (as a general tax) to tax all supplies of goods and services.[32] For the same reasons, the term economic activity has an objective character.

2.4.2 Objective Character: Whatever the Purpose or Result

The CJEU has consistently affirmed that the term 'economic activity' has an objective character in the sense that the activity is considered per se and without regard to its purpose or results.[33] This means that the activity itself is evaluated independently and that it is irrelevant whether the activities of a person are conferred to him upon by law, are regulated by law, are carried out in the public interest and/or without any business or commercial objective. The objective character of an economic activity is clearly

---

Oddział w Polsce, ECLI:EU:C:2016:481 and CJEU 24 January 2019, Case C-165/17 *Morgan Stanley & Co International plc v Ministre de l'Économie et des Finances*, ECLI:EU:C:2019:58.

32. A.J. van Doesum & F. Nellen, *VAT in a Day* (Fonds Indirect Tax, 2021). Available at: https://ssrn.com/abstract=3867201 (accessed 16 August 2024), pp. 19 and 20.

33. *See*, for example: CJEU 26 March 1987, Case 235/85 *Commission of the European Communities v Kingdom of the Netherlands*, ECLI:EU:C:1987:161, para. 10; CJEU 12 September 2000, Case C-260/98 *Commission of the European Communities v Hellenic Republic*, ECLI:EU:C:2000:4292, para. 28, CJEU 29 October 2009, Case C-246/08 *Commission of the European Communities v Republic of Finland*, ECLI:EU:C:2009:671, para. 40, CJEU 26 June 2007, Case C-284/04 *T-Mobile Austria GmbH and Others v Republik Österreich*, ECLI:EU:C:2007:381, para. 35 and CJEU 30 March 2023, Case C-612/21 *Gmina O. v Dyrektor Krajowej Informacji Skarbowej*, ECLI: EU:C:2023:279, para. 33.

emphasized in the wording of Article 9 of the VAT Directive itself. According to this article, an activity can be deemed economic 'whatever the purpose or results of that activity'. In fact, whether an activity is profitable or not is in principle irrelevant. An activity is, as a general rule, categorized as 'economic' where it is permanent and is carried out in return for remuneration, which is received by the person carrying out the activity.[34] Thus, a key criterion for categorizing an activity as 'economic' is that it is permanent and carried out in exchange for remuneration received by the person conducting the activity. Consequently, activities that are consistently provided free of charge are not subject to VAT since they cannot constitute a basis of assessment as observed in *Hong Kong Development Council*.[35] A person who exclusively provides supplies for free can therefore not be considered a taxable person for VAT purposes. Instead, he will be assimilated to a final consumer because he is at the final stage of the production and distribution chain.[36] Therefore, for an activity to qualify as an economic activity, it must result in supplies *for consideration*.[37] It does not necessarily mean that a person must generate income with every supply he makes. The crucial factor is whether, in an overall assessment, the person aims to generate income on a continuous basis. In this regard, it is understandable that the CJEU ruled that if a person solely bears the risks of loss without any prospect of profit, this becomes a relevant factor when determining the economic nature of an activity.[38]

2.4.3 Terminology: Economic Activities Versus Supplies of Goods and Services

The term 'economic activity' does not consistently carry the same meaning. In Article 9 of the VAT Directive, the EU legislator employs this term to define the VAT status of the person engaged in such activities. In this context, it clearly refers to the *whole business activity* (or an autonomous part of it) of a person. The economic activity comprises various activities, such as – but not limited to – purchasing goods and services ('input transactions'), producing goods and services ('internal activities'), as well as supplying goods and services ('output transactions').

By contrast, the CJEU occasionally employs the term as a synonym for *individual transactions* or as a descriptor for a group of individual supplies sharing a similar

34. CJEU 13 June 2018, Case C-421/17 *Szef Krajowej Administracji Skarbowej v Polfarmex Spółka Akcyjna w Kutnie*, ECLI:EU:C:2018:432, para. 38, CJEU 15 April 2021, Case C-846/19 *EQ v Administration de l'Enregistrement, des Domaines et de la TVA*, ECLI:EU:C:2021:277, para. 47 and CJEU 30 March 2023, Case C-612/21 *Gmina O. v Dyrektor Krajowej Informacji Skarbowej*, ECLI:EU:C:2023:279, para. 33.
35. CJEU 1 April 1982, Case 89/81 *Hong-Kong Trade Development Council v Staatssecretaris van Financiën*, ECLI:EU:C:1982:121, para. 11.
36. *Ibid.*, para. 10.
37. CJEU 14 February 1985, Case 268/83 *D.A. Rompelman and E.A. Rompelman-Van Deelen v Minister van Financiën*, ECLI:EU:C:1985:74.
38. CJEU 30 March 2023, Case C-612/21 *Gmina O. v Dyrektor Krajowej Informacji Skarbowej*, ECLI:EU:C:2023:279, para. 38 and CJEU 30 March 2023, Case C-616/21 *Dyrektor Krajowej Informacji Skarbowej v Gmina L.*, ECLI:EU:C:2023:280, para. 47.

nature.[39] This discrepancy can be attributed to the two-step process involved in determining the existence of an economic activity as we will outline below. The initial step involves establishing whether a person engages in transactions for consideration. Subsequently, it is necessary to determine whether the person's activities, in a broader sense, are conducted with the intention of generating income on a continuous basis. It is important to note that although these steps can be derived from CJEU case law, the CJEU itself does not consistently adhere to strict application of these steps.[40] Consequently, interpreting case law on this matter often presents challenges.

2.4.4 Step 1: Economic Activity and Supplies for Consideration

In order for a supply of goods or services to fall within the scope of VAT, the supply must, first, constitute a supply of goods or services for consideration, within the meaning of Article 2(1)(a) and (c) VAT Directive, and, second, have been carried out in the course of an economic activity, within the meaning of Article 9(1) VAT Directive, with the result that the person concerned has also acted as a taxable person.[41] Thus, the first step in establishing the economic nature of an activity is to assess whether it corresponds to one of the chargeable events defined in Article 2 VAT Directive.[42]

This means that for an economic activity to exist, it is necessary (but not sufficient) that the person in question carries out supplies of services or goods for consideration. Already in the landmark case *Hong Kong Development Council*, the CJEU clarified a person who solely carries out supplies free of charge is not a taxable person (*see* section 2.4.2).[43] But even if there is a payment, a supply may not be 'for consideration'.

This is because a supply of services or goods for consideration requires the existence of a direct link between the supply and the remuneration. A direct link exists if there is a legal relationship between the supplier and the recipient of the supply pursuant to which there is reciprocal performance, the remuneration received by the provider of the service constituting the value actually given in return for the service

39. If the CJEU refers to the full business operation of the taxable person, it commonly uses wordings, such as 'the economic activity as a whole'. *See*, for example: CJEU 8 February 2007, Case C-435/05 *Investrand BV v Staatssecretaris van Financiën*, ECLI:EU:C:2007:87, para. 29. If the CJEU refers to a group or bundle of activities with a similar nature within the furtherance of this 'economic activity as a whole', it uses expressions like: 'all his economic activities' (CJEU 8 February 2007, Case C-435/05 *Investrand BV v Staatssecretaris van Financiën*, ECLI:EU:C:2007:87, para. 22).
40. CJEU 2 June 2016, Case C-263/15 *Lajvér Meliorációs Nonprofit Kft. and Lajvér Csapadékvízrendezési Nonprofit Kft. v Nemzeti Adó- és Vámhivatal Dél-dunántúli Regionális Adó Főigazgatósága (NAV)*, ECLI:EU:C:2016:392.
41. CJEU 30 March 2023, Case C-612/21 *Gmina O. v Dyrektor Krajowej Informacji Skarbowej*, ECLI:EU:C:2023:279, para. 24 and CJEU 30 March 2023, Case C-616/21 *Dyrektor Krajowej Informacji Skarbowej v Gmina L.*, ECLI:EU:C:2023:280, para. 24.
42. CJEU 12 May 2016, Case C-520/14 *Gemeente Borsele v Staatssecretaris van Financiën and Staatssecretaris van Financiën v Gemeente Borsele*, ECLI:EU:C:2016:334, para. 21.
43. CJEU 1 April 1982, Case 89/81 *Hong-Kong Trade Development Council v Staatssecretaris van Financiën*, ECLI:EU:C:1982:121.

supplied to the recipient.[44] In order to be regarded as the value actually given in return for the service supplied, the remuneration must remain reasonable in relation to the service supplied in that it must not remunerate only part of the services supplied or to be supplied to the point of breaking the direct link between the services supplied and the consideration.[45] For a direct link to exist, it is however not necessary for the remuneration to exceed the costs of the supply.[46] It is also irrelevant whether the price of the supply is lower or higher than the open market value.[47] Furthermore, the fact that compensation is determined not on the basis of individualized services but on a flat-rate and annual basis to cover the operating costs of a company is not in itself, such as to affect the direct link between the supply of services made and the consideration received.[48] In Chapter 3, section 3.4, we will address the 'for consideration' criterion more elaborately.

In *Commission v Finland*, the CJEU ruled that the legal advice services provided by public legal aid offices did not constitute an economic activity, even though the legal aid offices received payments.[49] According to the CJEU, the receipt of a payment does not, per se, mean that a given activity is economic in nature.[50] The consideration must be received *in return for* the supply. The payments received by the public legal aid offices only covered part of the fees set by the national legislation. The remainder part of the fees was financed out of public funds. The part payment by the recipients in that particular case had to be regarded more as a fee than as consideration in the strict sense. Furthermore, as the CJEU observed, the fees largely depended upon the recipient's income and assets. Therefore, the CJEU ruled that the link between the legal aid services provided by public offices and the payment to be made by the recipients was not sufficiently direct for that payment to be regarded as consideration for those services. Consequently, the services could not be regarded as economic activities.

44. CJEU 3 March 1994, Case C-16/93 *R.J. Tolsma v Inspecteur der Omzetbelasting Leeuwarden*, ECLI:EU:C:1994:80, para. 14.
45. CJEU 21 December 2023, Case C-288/22 *TP v Administration de l'enregistrement, des domaines et de la TVA*, ECLI:EU:C:2023:1024, para. 34.
46. CJEU 30 March 2023, Case C-612/21 *Gmina O. v Dyrektor Krajowej Informacji Skarbowej*, ECLI:EU:C:2023:279, para. 27 and CJEU 30 March 2023, Case C-616/21 *Dyrektor Krajowej Informacji Skarbowej v Gmina L.*, ECLI:EU:C:2023:280, para. 36.
47. CJEU 20 January 2005, Case C-412/03 *Hotel Scandic Gåsabäck AB v Riksskatteverket*, ECLI:EU:C:2005:47, para. 22 and CJEU 2 June 2016, Case C-263/15 *Lajvér Meliorációs Nonprofit Kft. and Lajvér Csapadékvízrendezési Nonprofit Kft. v Nemzeti Adó- és Vámhivatal Dél-dunántúli Regionális Adó Főigazgatósága (NAV)*, ECLI:EU:C:2016:392, para. 45. *See*, however, Article 80 VAT Directive. We refer to Chapter 6, section 6.12.
48. CJEU 27 March 2014, Case C-151/13 *Le Rayon d'Or SARL v Ministre de l'Économie et des Finances*, ECLI:EU:C:2014:185, paras 36 and 37 and CJEU 29 October 2015, Case C-174/14 *Saudaçor – Sociedade Gestora de Recursos e Equipamentos da Saúde dos Açores SA v Fazenda Pública*, ECLI:EU:C:2015:733, para. 36.
49. CJEU 29 October 2009, Case C-246/08 *Commission of the European Communities v Republic of Finland*, ECLI:EU:C:2009:671.
50. Also *see*: CJEU 26 June 2007, Case C-369/04 *Hutchison 3G UK Ltd and Others v Commissioners of Customs and Excise*, ECLI:EU:C:2007:382, para. 39. We note that the reference the CJEU makes to Case C-343/95 *Diego Calì & Figli* does not make much sense.

The two-step approach to establishing the economic nature of an activity also becomes clear from *Gemeente Borsele*.[51] The Dutch municipality of Borsele offered a transport service for children to schools in their area. For these transport services, Borsele used the services of other transport companies, and these transport companies charged Borsele inclusive of Dutch VAT for the transport services. About one-third of the parents of the schoolchildren using the school transport paid a contribution on the basis of their financial capacity to Borsele, which was around 3 % of the total costs of the school transport paid by Borsele to the transport companies. The remaining part of the transport costs (97 %) was financed by Borsele from public funds. Hence, Borsele recovered, through the contributions that it received, only a small part of the costs incurred. Even though one-third of the parents paid a contribution that was not linked to the number of kilometres travelled per day, the cost price per journey for each pupil transported, or the frequency of the journeys, those payments were to be considered as a consideration directly linked to the services. However, that did not automatically mean that the services constitute an economic activity. The existence of supplies *for consideration* is a necessary but not a sufficient condition to economic activities. The analysis of whether an economic activity exists also requires taking a broader perspective on the activities performed, in which all the circumstances in which the services are supplied have to be examined. This is the second step in the two-step approach. In this step, a comparison can be made between the circumstances in which the services are supplied and the circumstances in which such services are usually supplied. Other factors, such as the number of customers and the amount of earnings, may also be taken into account. The CJEU indicates that in an overall assessment, the payments received by Borsele bear more similarities with a fee than with consideration for a service.[52] It considered that the circumstances in which the transport services were supplied compared to the circumstances in which such services are usually provided were critically different from 'normal' passenger transport services. As the CJEU puts it, Borsele did not offer the services on the general passenger transport market but rather appeared to be a beneficiary and final consumer of transport services which it acquired from transport undertakings with which it dealt and which it made available to parents of pupils as part of its public service activities. Even though it may be so that one-third of the parents paid for the transport services, the CJEU considered that there was no genuine link between the amount paid and the services supplied.[53] Consequently, the CJEU found no economic activity to be present.

2.4.5 Step 2: Economic Activity and the Objective to Obtain Income

Although supplies for consideration (*see* section 2.4.4) are a *necessary* precondition to the existence of an economic activity, they are not a *sufficient* precondition.[54] In order

51. CJEU 12 May 2016, Case C-520/14 *Gemeente Borsele v Staatssecretaris van Financiën and Staatssecretaris van Financiën v Gemeente Borsele*, ECLI:EU:C:2016:334.
52. *Ibid.*, para. 33.
53. *Ibid.*, para. 34.
54. *Ibid.*, para. 28.

to establish whether an activity is an economic activity, a broader evaluation of the activity is required to see if there is indeed an objective to obtain income on a continuous basis: does the person as a whole have this objective? According to the second paragraph of Article 9(1) VAT Directive, any activity of producers, traders or persons supplying services, including mining and agricultural activities and activities of the professions, must be regarded as 'economic activity'. The third paragraph of the same provision determines that the exploitation of tangible or intangible property for the purposes of obtaining income therefrom on a continuing basis must, in particular, also be regarded as an economic activity. This idea of obtaining income on a continuous basis reflects the general idea of what distinguishes an activity from an 'economic activity'. It follows that an activity can only be an economic activity if its purpose is to generate income thereby. The CJEU acknowledges that it is difficult to establish a precise definition of economic activity. Yet, it confirmed that an activity is generally classified as economic where it is permanent and is carried out in return for remuneration which is received by the person carrying out the activity,[55] which implies that the remuneration itself must be regarded as having a continuing basis.[56] It has ruled that to establish the economic nature of an activity, all the circumstances in which the activity concerned is carried out have to be examined, by making a case-by-case assessment, referring to the typical conduct of an active entrepreneur in the field concerned.[57]

From CJEU case law, relevant factors can be distilled on the basis of which the economic character of an activity can be established and a comparison with 'the typical conduct of an active entrepreneur in the field' can be made. In our view, the following non-exhaustive[58] factors may be relevant to ascertain whether the activity concerned is an economic activity:

- The nature of the goods[59] and services.[60]
- The actual length of the period during which the supplies are made.[61]

55. CJEU 15 April 2021, Case C-846/19 *EQ v Administration de l'Enregistrement, des Domaines et de la TVA*, ECLI:EU:C:2021:277, para. 47 and CJEU 21 December 2023, Case C-288/22 *TP v Administration de l'enregistrement, des domaines et de la TVA*, ECLI:EU:C:2023:1024, para. 42.
56. CJEU 13 December 2007, Case C-408/06 *Landesanstalt für Landwirtschaft v Franz Götz*, ECLI:EU:C:2007:789, para. 18, CJEU 13 June 2019, Case C-420/18 *IO v Inspecteur van de rijksbelastingdienst*, ECLI:EU:C:2019:490, para. 27 CJEU 15 April 2021, Case C-846/19 *EQ v Administration de l'Enregistrement, des Domaines et de la TVA*, ECLI:EU:C:2021:277, para. 55 and CJEU 21 December 2023, Case C-288/22 *TP v Administration de l'enregistrement, des domaines et de la TVA*, ECLI:EU:C:2023:1024, para. 42.
57. CJEU 12 May 2016, Case C-520/14 *Gemeente Borsele v Staatssecretaris van Financiën and Staatssecretaris van Financiën v Gemeente Borsele*, ECLI:EU:C:2016:334, para. 29, CJEU 30 March 2023, Case C-612/21 *Gmina O. v Dyrektor Krajowej Informacji Skarbowej*, ECLI: EU:C:2023:279, para. 35 and CJEU 30 March 2023, Case C-616/21 *Dyrektor Krajowej Informacji Skarbowej v Gmina L.*, ECLI:EU:C:2023:280, para. 43.
58. *See*: CJEU 26 September 1996, Case C-230/94 *Renate Enkler v Finanzamt Homburg*, ECLI: EU:C:1996:352, paras 28 and 29.
59. *Ibid.*, paras 26 and 27.
60. In our view, what applies to supplies of goods also applies to supplies of services in this regard.
61. CJEU 26 September 1996, Case C-230/94 *Renate Enkler v Finanzamt Homburg*, ECLI: EU:C:1996:352, para. 29.

- The number of customers.[62]
- The amount of earnings.[63]
- The receipt of income on a continuous basis (the continuity of the remuneration).[64]
- The taking of active steps to market property by mobilizing resources similar to those deployed by a producer, a trader or a person supplying services within the meaning of the second subparagraph of Article 9(1) VAT Directive.[65]
- Employment of staff equipped for the activity concerned.[66]
- The recurrent nature of the activity.[67]
- The part of the costs which is recovered by amounts received in return for supplies of services in comparison with the part of the costs which is being financed by public funds.[68]
- An inherently loss-generating cash flow, coupled with an extraordinary level of uncertainty regarding the potential recovery of the incurred costs.[69]

It is important to acknowledge that while these factors may hold relevance, they should not be regarded as an exhaustive list of conditions for the existence of an economic activity. It is crucial to emphasize that these conditions must be evaluated on a case-by-case basis, considering the customary practices of other taxable persons in the same sector. Therefore, depending on the specific circumstances (such as the involvement of a public body),[70] certain factors may be pertinent, while others may not be applicable.

62. *Ibid.* We note that having only one customer does not necessarily mean that there is no economic activity. *See*, for example: CJEU 27 January 2000, Case C-23/98 *Heerma and Maatschap J. Heerma en K. Heerma-Graanstra*, ECLI:EU:C:2000:46 and CJEU 13 June 2019, Case C-420/18 *IO v Inspecteur van de rijksbelastingdienst*, ECLI:EU:C:2019:490, para. 30.
63. CJEU 26 September 1996, Case C-230/94 *Renate Enkler v Finanzamt Homburg*, ECLI:EU:C:1996:352, para. 29.
64. CJEU 2 June 2016, Case C-263/15 *Lajvér Meliorációs Nonprofit Kft. and Lajvér Csapadékvízrendezési Nonprofit Kft. v Nemzeti Adó- és Vámhivatal Dél-dunántúli Regionális Adó Főigazgatósága (NAV)*, ECLI:EU:C:2016:392, para. 33 and CJEU 13 June 2019, Case C-420/18 *IO v Inspecteur van de rijksbelastingdienst*, ECLI:EU:C:2019:490, para. 27.
65. CJEU 15 September 2011, Joined Cases C-180/10 and C-181/10 *Jarosław Słaby v Minister Finansów (C-180/10) and Emilian Kuć and Halina Jeziorska-Kuć v Dyrektor Izby Skarbowej w Warszawie (C-181/10)*, ECLI:EU:C:2011:589, para. 39 and CJEU 19 July 2012, Case C-263/11 *Ainārs Rēdlihs v Valsts ieņēmumu dienests*, ECLI:EU:C:2012:497, para. 36.
66. CJEU 30 March 2023, Case C-616/21 *Dyrektor Krajowej Informacji Skarbowej v Gmina L.*, ECLI:EU:C:2023:280, para. 44.
67. *Ibid.*
68. CJEU 12 May 2016, Case C-520/14 *Gemeente Borsele v Staatssecretaris van Financiën and Staatssecretaris van Financiën v Gemeente Borsele*, ECLI:EU:C:2016:334, paras 33, and 34, CJEU 30 March 2023, Case C-612/21 *Gmina O. v Dyrektor Krajowej Informacji Skarbowej*, ECLI:EU:C:2023:279, para. 38 and CJEU 30 March 2023, Case C-616/21 *Dyrektor Krajowej Informacji Skarbowej v Gmina L.*, ECLI:EU:C:2023:280, para. 46.
69. CJEU 30 March 2023, Case C-612/21 *Gmina O. v Dyrektor Krajowej Informacji Skarbowej*, ECLI:EU:C:2023:279, para. 39.
70. For example, the factor that part of the costs which is recovered by amounts received in return for supplies of services in comparison with the part of the costs which is being financed by public funds seems to be particularly relevant for public bodies and of less relevance to holding companies.

For example, in *IO*, the CJEU explicitly indicated that the criterion of 'taking active steps to market property' deals specifically with the VAT treatment of the sale of land labelled as private assets and that such steps on the market are – in that particular context – a precondition for the existence of an economic activity.[71]

In *SPÖ Landesorganisation Kärnten*, the concept of 'supplies for consideration' is almost equated with the notion of 'economic activities'.[72] SPÖ Landesorganisation Kärnten carried out advertising services to other groups of the SPÖ. If we understand the case correctly, part of the costs for these services was invoiced to the other groups of SPÖ. Nonetheless, the CJEU considered that this activity did not allow the generation of revenue on a continuing basis. The CJEU considered that the only income obtained on a continuing basis by SPÖ comes from public funding and the party members' contributions, that income having been raised, in particular, to cover losses made by the activity at issue in the main proceedings.[73] According to the CJEU, the SPÖ's activity is the development of informed political opinion with a view to participation in the exercise of political power. In carrying out that activity, the SPÖ does not, however, participate in any market. Consequently, the advertising activities did not constitute an economic activity.

Similarly, in *Gemeente Borsele* (*see* section 2.4.4), the objective of obtaining income on a continuous basis was not met.[74] However, unlike in *SPÖ Landesorganisation Kärnten*, the CJEU explicitly refers to the aforementioned relevant factors to determine whether the activities are economic activities. It then adds that the Gemeente Borsele does not offer services on the general passenger transport market.[75] This resembles the criterion of participation on a market which the CJEU used in *SPÖ Landesorganisation Kärnten*.

This criterion of market participation originates from the *T-Mobile Austria* case.[76] One of the questions asked to the CJEU was whether the allocation by way of an auction by a Member State of frequency use rights for mobile telecommunication constitutes an 'economic activity'. The CJEU pointed out that the issuing of authorizations to use ether frequencies falls exclusively within the competence of the Member State concerned. Therefore, the issue of the frequency rights constitutes a necessary precondition for the access of economic operators to the mobile telecommunications market. Consequently, it cannot constitute *participation in that market* by the competent national authority. Only the operators, who are the holders of the rights granted, operate on the relevant market by exploiting the property in question for the purpose of obtaining income therefrom on a continuing basis.[77]

---

71. CJEU 13 June 2019, Case C-420/18 *IO v Inspecteur van de rijksbelastingdienst*, ECLI:EU:C:2019:490.
72. CJEU 6 October 2009, Case C-267/08 *SPÖ Landesorganisation Kärnten v Finanzamt Klagenfurt*, ECLI:EU:C:2009:619.
73. *Ibid.*, para. 23.
74. CJEU 12 May 2016, Case C-520/14 *Gemeente Borsele v Staatssecretaris van Financiën and Staatssecretaris van Financiën v Gemeente Borsele*, ECLI:EU:C:2016:334, para. 26.
75. *Ibid.*, para. 35.
76. CJEU 26 June 2007, Case C-284/04 *T-Mobile Austria GmbH and Others v Republik Österreich*, ECLI:EU:C:2007:381.
77. *Ibid.*, paras 41 and 42.

It is unclear whether the market participation criterion is a criterion that only applies in the case of activities in the public interest (such as in *T-Mobile Austria, SPÖ Landesorganisation Kärnten, Gemeente Borsele*). In our view, it would make sense to apply this criterion in all situations because it perfectly reflects the core of what makes an activity 'economic'. The CJEU's rulings in *Słaby and Kuć and in Rēdlihs* suggest broader applicability of the participation on a market criterion: if a person takes active steps to market property by mobilizing resources similar to those deployed by a producer, a trader or a person supplying services,[78] he, in fact, 'participates in a market'. From that viewpoint, it is difficult to understand the CJEU's ruling in the *Fuchs* case on photovoltaic installations.[79] The CJEU ruled that the operation of a photovoltaic installation on or adjacent to a house which is used as a dwelling, which is designed such that the electricity produced is: (i) always less than the electricity privately consumed by its operator, and (ii) supplied to the network in exchange for income on a continuing basis, is an economic activity. It must be noted that the photovoltaic installation at issue in the main proceedings produced electricity, which is supplied to the network in exchange for income on a continuing basis. In essence, this is what made the activity 'economic' in the eyes of the CJEU. In our view, the CJEU could easily have taken a different direction, though. If one observes the criteria listed at the beginning of this paragraph, clearly, there are factors that undermine the economic character of this activity. Moreover, it is difficult to see that someone with solar panels on his or her house 'participates in a market' and/or takes active steps to market its products (electricity). We note that any 'overproduction' by a house-owner cannot – at the current state of technology – efficiently be stored. It is automatically guided into the electricity network, and the house-owner will only draw electricity from that network in case his consumption exceeds the production of the solar panels. The CJEU seems to have overlooked the fiscal-administrative impact of the judgment: in various Member States, house-owners with solar panels on their roofs became taxable persons, granting them a right of deduction but also imposing administrative burdens upon them. From the viewpoint of the tax authorities, it was (and is!) not an easy task to monitor all these 'new' taxable persons.

2.4.6 The Mere Exercise of the Right of Ownership

The mere exercise of ownership does not constitute an economic activity. This can be conferred from *Polysar*, where the CJEU ruled that the mere acquisition of financial holdings in other undertakings does not amount to the exploitation of property for the purpose of obtaining income therefrom on a continuing basis because any dividend

78. *See*: CJEU 15 September 2011, Joined Cases C-180/10 and C-181/10 *Jarosław Słaby v Minister Finansów (C-180/10) and Emilian Kuć and Halina Jeziorska-Kuć v Dyrektor Izby Skarbowej w Warszawie (C-181/10)*, ECLI:EU:C:2011:589, para. 39 and CJEU 19 July 2012, Case C-263/11 *Ainārs Rēdlihs v Valsts ieņēmumu dienests*, ECLI:EU:C:2012:497, para. 36.
79. CJEU 20 June 2013, Case C-219/12 *Finanzamt Freistadt Rohrbach Urfahr v Unabhängiger Finanzsenat Außenstelle Linz*, ECLI:EU:C:2013:413.

yielded by that holding is merely the result of ownership of the property.[80] We refer to Chapter 11 on shares and other securities. Similarly, the CJEU considered in *Słaby and Kuć* that a person who divides a plot of land into 64 pieces and sells each piece separately, in principle, merely exercises his right of ownership. However, as the CJEU adds, that is not the case where that person takes active steps to market property by mobilizing resources similar to those deployed by a producer, a trader or a person supplying services within the meaning of the second subparagraph of Article 9(1) VAT Directive (*see* section 2.4.5).[81]

When private individuals deposit money in a savings account at a bank, it is typical for them to receive interest payments, which essentially provide them with a continuous income stream. However, despite the objective nature of the term 'economic activity', placing money in a savings account is not considered an economic activity. This is primarily because depositing money in a savings account is viewed as the 'mere exercise of the right of ownership'. The CJEU's ruling in *Harnas & Helm* seems to confirm this.[82] The CJEU ruled that the mere acquisition of ownership in and the mere holding of bonds is not an economic activity. According to the CJEU, the activity of a bondholder may be defined as a form of investment that does not extend further than straightforward asset management. The income from the bonds derives from the mere fact of holding them, which entitles the holder to payments of interest. Such interest cannot, therefore, be regarded as a return on an economic activity or transaction carried out by the bondholder since it derives from the mere ownership of the bonds.[83] In our view, this may be different if - for example - a holding company issues bonds to its subsidiaries and actively determines the conditions and the interest rates of the bonds, thereby exceeding the mere exercise of the rights of ownership.[84]

2.4.7 Exploitation of Property

According to the third paragraph of Article 9(1) VAT Directive, the exploitation of tangible or intangible property for the purposes of obtaining income therefrom on a continuing basis must, in particular, be regarded as an economic activity.

Exploitation is a special form of economic activity. Examples of this kind of economic activity are the granting of loans, the leasing of immovable or movable property, and the licensing of patents. Generally speaking, economic activities require a regular supply of goods or services, or at least the intention to supply these on a regular basis. The required frequency relates to the supplies, and not so much to the

80. CJEU 20 June 1991, Case C-60/90 *Polysar Investement Netherlands BV v Inspecteur der Invoerrechten en Accijnzen*, ECLI:EU:C:1991:268, para. 13. Also *see*: CJEU 20 June 1996, Case C-155/94 *Wellcome Trust Ltd v Commissioners of Customs and Excise*, ECLI:EU:C:1996:243, para. 32.
81. CJEU 15 September 2011, Joined Cases C-180/10 and C-181/10 *Jarosław Słaby v Minister Finansów (C-180/10) and Emilian Kuć and Halina Jeziorska-Kuć v Dyrektor Izby Skarbowej w Warszawie (C-181/10)*, ECLI:EU:C:2011:589, para. 39.
82. CJEU 6 February 1997, Case C-80/95 *Harnas & Helm CV v Staatssecretaris van Financiën*, ECLI:EU:C:1997:56.
83. *Ibid.*, para. 18.
84. *See*, for example: Dutch Supreme Court, 23 September 2011, Case 10-00383, V-N 2011/47.14.

flow of income that is generated by the supplies: the flow of income is a logical result of frequently carrying out activities for consideration. Where the economic activity is a kind of exploitation, a single activity (e.g., the signing of a lease contract) is sufficient to obtain a continuous flow of income. The legislator only seems to refer to this class of activity to avoid any doubt that even *one* lease agreement or *one* loan agreement can constitute an economic activity, as long as the consideration, the flow of income, is *on a continuing basis*.

In *Enkler*, the CJEU provided for important guidelines on how to determine whether property is exploited to obtain income therefrom.[85] Mrs Enkler was employed in her husband's tax consultancy firm. On 15 September 1984, she notified the tax authorities that she was carrying on the business of hiring out motor caravans. Subsequently, she bought a motor caravan which she leased to her husband and – over a period of three years – twice to third parties. Mrs Enkler deducted the VAT on the purchase of the motor caravan (and paid VAT on the lease of the motor caravan to her husband and to third parties). The CJEU was asked (among other things) whether the hiring out of the caravan could be considered as being done for the purpose of obtaining income therefrom on a continuing basis, in terms of what is now Article 9(1) second paragraph VAT Directive. The CJEU indicated that although criteria based on the results of the activity in question cannot in themselves make it possible to determine whether the activity is carried on for the purpose of obtaining income on a continuing basis, the actual length of the period for which the property is hired, the number of customers and the amount of earnings are also factors which, forming part of the circumstances of the case as a whole, may be taken into account with others when that question is under consideration (*see* section 2.4.5).

In *Van Tiem*, the CJEU confirmed that the income from the exploitation must be obtained on a continuous basis. Mr Van Tiem (only) granted a building right over a plot of land to his own BV (a Dutch limited risk company) for a period of 18 years, in return for an annual consideration. Under Dutch VAT law, this was considered a (one-time) supply of a good. However, the CJEU ruled that in accordance with the principle of neutrality, the term 'exploitation' refers to all transactions, whatever their legal form, by which it is sought to obtain income from the goods in question on a continuing basis.[86] Therefore, the grant by an owner of immovable property to a third party of a building right over that property must be deemed to be an exploitation of the property if that right is granted in return for a consideration for a specified period. That condition must be deemed to be satisfied when, as was the case in the main proceedings, the building rights are granted for a period of 18 years in return for an annual consideration.

Although the CJEU in *Van Tiem* seemed to suggest that exploitation can involve even a single transaction (the grant of a building right, which was treated as one supply of goods), in other cases, the Court has appeared to decide that exploitation requires

85. CJEU 26 September 1996, Case C-230/94 *Renate Enkler v Finanzamt Homburg*, ECLI:EU:C:1996:352.
86. CJEU 4 December 1990, Case C-186/89 *W. M. van Tiem v Staatssecretaris van Financiën*, ECLI:EU:C:1990:429.

more than one transaction. For example, in *Floridienne*, the CJEU ruled (emphasis added):

> Where a holding company makes capital available to its subsidiaries, that activity may of itself be considered an economic activity, consisting in exploiting that capital with a view to obtaining income by way of interest therefrom on a continuing basis, *provided that it is not carried out merely on an occasional basis* … .[87]

Article 9(1), second paragraph VAT Directive states that the exploitation of property must be carried out with the 'purpose of obtaining income therefrom on a continuing basis'. This suggests that the purpose of obtaining income on a continuing basis is only relevant in relation to property exploitation. However, CJEU case law clarifies that the same purpose is necessary for activities other than the exploitation of property (i.e., 'normal activities', such as supplies of groceries or providing advisory services). There are even instances where the CJEU considered 'normal' supplies of services as the 'exploitation of property'. For instance, in the case of *SPÖ Landesorganisation Kärnten*, the CJEU referred to advertising services as exploitation.[88] From our perspective, advertising services should not be considered as a form of exploitation of tangible or intangible property in terms of Article 9(1), second paragraph VAT Directive. Instead, they should be viewed as a straightforward economic activity falling under the first paragraph of that provision. In *Rēdlihs* too, the CJEU equated 'normal' supplies of goods with the exploitation of property:

> [it must] be observed in this respect that such supplies may fall within the scope of continuous exploitation of tangible property. The fruits of tangible property, such as timber from a forest, may, by their very nature and depending on their characteristics and, in particular, their age, not be suitable for immediate economic exploitation, as a certain period of time may be objectively necessary before those fruits can become amenable to economic exploitation. Nevertheless, that does not mean that the supplies of timber which have taken place in the meantime, as a result of alleged force majeure, do not come within the scope of exploitation of tangible property for the purposes of obtaining income therefrom on a continuing basis within the meaning of the second subparagraph of Article 9(1) VAT Directive.[89]

By referring to exploitation, it appears that the CJEU wants to make a point that a (normal) economic activity requires a flow of transactions, which will create a flow of income on a continuous basis. In other words: it seems that CJEU is indicating that a continuing activity generating proceeds is a prerequisite to all economic activities.

---

87. CJEU 14 November 2000, Case C-142/99 *Floridienne SA and Berginvest SA v Belgian State*, ECLI:EU:C:2000:623, para. 28.
88. CJEU 6 October 2009, Case C-267/08 *SPÖ Landesorganisation Kärnten v Finanzamt Klagenfurt*, ECLI:EU:C:2009:619.
89. CJEU 19 July 2012, Case C-263/11 *Ainārs Rēdlihs v Valsts ieņēmumu dienests*, ECLI: EU:C:2012:497, para. 37.

2.4.8 Regular and Incidental Activities

In the previous section, we explained that both 'normal' activities and the 'exploitation of property' require that they generate an income on a continuous basis. This already implies for 'normal' activities that they are carried out on a regular basis. Indeed, it is generally accepted that incidental supplies, in principle, are excluded from the notion of 'economic activities'. A decisive component of the notion 'economic activity' is that ('normal') supplies must be made on a regular basis. However, the necessity for supplies to occur regularly is not explicitly stated within the VAT Directive. Instead, it is a conclusion drawn through indirect inference.

Article 12(1) of the VAT Directive grants Member States the flexibility to consider specific occasional suppliers as taxable persons.[90] This provision would be unnecessary if occasional supplies were automatically classified as economic activities.

However, not all scholars share this view. For example, Terra and Kajus have a different view, believing Article 12 to be rather confusing:[91]

> Incorrectly, in our view, many commentators derive from this provision that activities must have a certain frequency in order to be qualified as relevant economic activities. Admittedly, Article 9(1), second subparagraph requires obtaining income from exploitation on a continuing basis, but as we have seen in *Van Tiem* the purchase and immediate granting of building rights are economic activities. Also the sale of shares in one lot in a single day can be an economic activity (see the Opinion of AG Lenz in *Wellcome Trust* ...) or the auctioning of a UMTS licence (see the opinion of AG Kokott ...). What is meant in Article 12 RVD, is that a person who is not a taxable person (either since he is an employee, or since it is not his intention to act as entrepreneur performing an occasional activity or, objectively, his activity lacks the characteristics of a business) can be treated as a taxable person, e.g. with regard to the supply of a building.

We agree that it is uncertain whether it is necessary for an activity to involve frequently performed supplies (or at least to maintain the intention of performing multiple supplies) in order to be recognized as an economic activity for VAT purposes. Nonetheless, we believe that the general concept of economic activity requires a certain (envisaged) frequency (repetition). We assume that that requirement is less important for forms of exploitation (such as the purchase and immediate granting of building rights, in *Van Tiem*) because, for these types of economic activity, the regularity aspect is guaranteed by the fact that the consideration is on a continuing basis. We recall that with respect to exploitation, the CJEU applied a stricter approach in *Floridienne* than it

90. Article 12(1) VAT Directive provides Member States with the option of regarding as a taxable person anyone who carries out, on an occasional basis, a transaction relating to the activities referred to in the second subparagraph of Article 9, and in particular, either of the following transactions: (a) the supply, before first occupation, of a building or parts of a building and of the land on which the building stands; or (b) the supply of building land. *See* section 9.5.1.
91. *See* B. Terra & J. Kajus, *A Guide to the European VAT Directives, Introduction to European VAT*, Vol. 1 (IBFD 2021), p. 381.

did in *Van Tiem*. There can only be 'exploitation' 'if it is not carried out merely on an occasional basis'.[92]

2.4.9 The Start and the End of an Economic Activity

In this section, we will discuss the start and the end of an economic activity.

2.4.9.1 The Start of an Economic Activity: Preparatory Acts

On the basis that one needs to throw out a sprat to catch a mackerel, it is not surprising that starting entrepreneurs incur VAT on their initial investments before those investments generate any income. The principle of neutrality requires that in spite of the fact that no output transactions are being carried out (yet), this input VAT is fully and immediately deductible. If this were to be different, an arbitrary distinction was to exist between investment expenditure incurred before the actual start of a business and expenditure incurred after the start of that business.[93] Moreover, it would create an unequal level playing field between start-ups and existing businesses. Therefore, the CJEU ruled in *Rompelman* that preparatory acts must themselves also be treated as constituting economic activity if the person carrying out these acts has the intention of engaging in activities for which a consideration will be obtained. This intention must be supported by objective evidence.[94] That is an important requirement because it prevents the acquisition of a dwelling automatically being considered as a preparatory act, from which the acquirer can derive taxable person status.

Besides the nature of the acquired assets, other circumstances, such as certificates to set up a special business activity, can be indicative of a business intention. Also, the time elapsing between the initial investment and the actual use of that investment can be decisive, according to the CJEU in *Lennartz*.[95] In *INZO*, the CJEU decided that even the commissioning of a feasibility study to investigate whether the envisaged activity will ever be technically possible and profitable may be regarded as an economic activity.[96] It follows from *Breitsohl* that the right to deduct the VAT paid on investments with a view to the realization of a planned economic activity still exists even where the tax authority is aware, from the time of the first tax assessment, that the economic activity envisaged will not be taken up.[97] From this case law, it follows that the first investment expenditure incurred for the purposes of and with the view to

92. CJEU 14 November 2000, Case C-142/99 *Floridienne SA and Berginvest SA v Belgian State*, ECLI:EU:C:2000:623, para. 28.
93. CJEU 14 February 1985, Case 268/83 *D.A. Rompelman and E.A. Rompelman-Van Deelen v Minister van Financiën*, ECLI:EU:C:1985:74, para. 23.
94. CJEU 14 February 1985, Case 268/83 *D.A. Rompelman and E.A. Rompelman-Van Deelen v Minister van Financiën*, ECLI:EU:C:1985:74.
95. CJEU 11 July 1991, Case C-97/90 *Hansgeorg Lennartz v Finanzamt München III, ECLI: EU:C:1991:315*.
96. CJEU 29 February 1996, Case C-110/94 *Intercommunale voor zeewaterontzilting (INZO) v Belgian State* [1996] ECR I-00857.
97. CJEU 8 June 2000, Case C-400/98 *Finanzamt Goslar v Brigitte Breitsohl*, ECLI:EU:C:2000:304.

commencing a business must be regarded as an economic activity and that the burden is on the taxable person to prove this.

In cases such as *ITH Comercial,*[98] *Skellefteå*[99] and *Vittamed,*[100] the CJEU reaffirmed the principles previously established in cases like *Rompelman*, *INZO*, and *Breitsohl*. However, the CJEU rulings in *ITH Comercial*, *Skellefteå*, and *Vittamed* also clarify that when such a taxable person no longer intends to employ the purchased goods and services to conduct taxable output transactions, or if they are used for exempt transactions, the mechanism for adjustment outlined in Articles 184 to 187 of the VAT Directive should be applied. The adjustment mechanism essentially ensures that where a taxable person, on the basis of his intended use for taxed transactions, initially deducts the VAT charged to him in relation to the purchase of capital goods, but at a later stage it turns out that the actual use of the goods and/or services he purchased is different, the amount of the VAT which was initially deducted is calibrated. Detailed information can be found in Chapter 10, section 10.6. Interestingly, the CJEU's rulings in cases like *Rompelman*, *INZO*, and *Breitsohl* could be interpreted as having created expectations for businesses, which were later altered by the rulings in *ITH Comercial*, *Skellefteå*, and *Vittamed*.[101] These later rulings make it evident that, as long as the adjustment period for capital goods has not expired, a portion of the initially deducted VAT may have to be adjusted (repaid).

In *Ryanair*, the CJEU confirmed that the first investment expenditure incurred for the purposes of and with the view to commencing a business must be regarded as an economic activity also applies to holding companies. A company holds shares in a subsidiary, which holding is accompanied by direct or indirect involvement in the management of the companies in which the holding has been acquired, if that entails carrying out transactions that are subject to VAT, is considered as a taxable person (*see* Chapter 11). A (future) holding company must be considered a taxable person if it carries out preparatory acts which are part of a proposed acquisition of shares in another company with the intention of pursuing an economic activity consisting of involvement in the management of that other company by providing management services subject to VAT.[102]

2.4.9.2 The Start of an Economic Activity: Companies 'In Formation'

When a one-person business or a partnership converted to a private (or public) limited company, it is generally assumed that this new private or public company is considered

98. CJEU 12 November 2020, Case C-734/19 *ITH Comercial Timişoara SRL*, ECLI:EU:C:2020:919.
99. CJEU 18 May 2021, Case C-248/20 (order), *Skatteverket v Skellefteå Industrihus AB*, ECLI:EU:C:2021:394.
100. CJEU 6 October 2022, Case C-293/21 *UAB 'Vittamed technologijos' v Valstybine mokesčių inspekcija*, ECLI:EU:C:2022:763.
101. *See*: M. Lamensch, *Order in Skellefteå Industrihus AB: A Reversal of the INZO, Ghent Coal Terminal and Breitsohl Jurisprudence?* (2022) 3 EC Tax Review.
102. CJEU 17 October 2018, Case C-249/17 *Ryanair Ltd v The Revenue Commissioners*, ECLI:EU:C:2018:834, para. 19.

as a new taxable person, separate from the preceding one-person business or partnership.[103] Consequently, when activities take place *before* the registration of the new company, these are performed by a different person, namely the limited company (or plc) 'in formation' ('i.f.'). Terra and Kajus mention in this respect:

> The consequence (at least theoretically, we are aware that not all Member States are sound in the doctrine) is that the plc or ltd, once registered, cannot claim deduction of the input VAT incurred by the ltd or plc i.f. during the pre-registration period. This is different when a private limited company is transformed into a public limited company, or vice versa, since the person is not changing, but mainly the applicable corporate law.[104]

According to the CJEU, there may be a right of deduction with the preceding business, which can be based on the taxed activities of the private or public limited company. In *Faxworld*, the CJEU ruled that a German 'Vorgründungsgeschellschaft', which had no intention to set up an economic activity for itself but only existed to acquire goods and services that would finally be used by the Faxworld AG, could be regarded as a taxable person.[105]

2.4.9.3 The End of an Economic Activity

As we indicated in section 2.4.9.1, a person having the intention to carry out economic activities is considered to be a taxable person, even though no output transaction has been carried out. In *Rompelman*, the CJEU indicated that the rationale is that if initial investments do not give the investor taxable person status, the VAT on the investments cannot be deducted. Ultimately, such non-deductible VAT will be included ('hidden') in the price of the taxable transactions once the business is commenced, and subsequently, the hidden VAT will be a part of the prices of other taxable persons further down the supply chain as well. In the end, the result is that private consumption is taxed more than once. This – from a systematic perspective – undesirable effect is usually referred to as the 'cascading of VAT'.[106]

A comparable adverse outcome would ensue if a business undergoing liquidation were unable to deduct VAT on its inputs, in the event that the costs arising from its economic activities were incurred after the cessation of those economic activities. *Fini H*, owing to a non-termination clause in the lease, had to continue paying business rent and charges on a property which it had leased for the purpose of carrying on a restaurant business until the normal expiry of the lease.[107] The CJEU ruled that the

103. *See* for a critical analysis of this presumption A.J. van Doesum, *Contractuele samenwerkingsverbanden in de btw* (*Dissertation*) (Kluwer 2009), pp. 510 et seq.
104. B. Terra & J. Kajus, *A Guide to the European VAT Directives, Introduction to European VAT*, Vol. 1 (IBFD 2021), pp. 452.
105. *See* CJEU 29 April 2004, Case C-137/02 *Finanzamt Offenbach am Main-Land v Faxworld Vorgründungsgesellschaft Peter Hünninghausen und Wolfgang Klein GbR*, ECLI:EU:C:2004:267.
106. *See* A.J. van Doesum & F. Nellen, *VAT in a Day* (Fonds Indirect Tax, 2021). Available at: https://ssrn.com/abstract=3867201 (accessed 16 August 2024), p. 20.
107. CJEU 3 March 2005, Case C-32/03 *I/S Fini H v Skatteministeriet*, ECLI:EU:C:2005:128.

same considerations as it had applied in – among others – *Rompelman*, dictated that transactions, such as the payments, which *Fini H* continued to have to make during the period over which its restaurant business was wound up must be regarded as forming part of the economic activity. According to the CJEU, the duration of the obligation to pay the rent and the charges on those premises has no bearing on the existence of an economic activity, provided that that period of time is strictly necessary to complete the winding-up of the business. Therefore, the costs, in principle, were to be regarded as being directly and immediately linked to the restaurant business and *Fini H* was allowed to deduct the VAT on those costs. In later cases, the CJEU has ruled that when there is no longer an intention to carry out taxable supplies, the VAT which was initially deducted in respect of capital goods may have to be adjusted. In this regard, it is important that the use to which the goods or services are put, or intended to be put, merely determines the extent of the *initial* deduction and the extent of any adjustments in the course of the following periods; it does not affect whether the right of deduction *arises.*[108] Thus, if an economic activity is terminated, the right of deduction is not retroactively removed, but rather its extent is adjusted through the adjustment mechanism as laid down in Article 184 and further of the VAT Directive (*see* Chapter 10, section 10.6). This explains why in *Vittamed* the CJEU ruled that if a taxable person no longer has – and will never have – any intention of using the capital goods for the purposes of taxed transactions an adjustment of the deducted VAT is to be made.[109]

Furthermore, we note that the termination of an economic activity does not imply that goods can reach a consumer free from taxation, even if no supplies have ever been made (the business does not take off). If a business is liquidated even before the envisaged economic activity materializes, goods are either supplied to third parties during liquidation, which constitutes a taxable transaction, or they are transferred for personal use. On the basis of Article 18(c) VAT Directive, a deemed supply occurs if a taxable person terminates its economic activity and retains the goods in private (*see* Chapter 3, section 3.2.5.4). A similar mechanism for services is laid down in Article 26 VAT Directive (*see* Chapter 3, section 3.3.2.2).

2.4.10 Illegal Transactions

The principle of fiscal neutrality precludes differentiation between lawful and unlawful transactions.[110] Therefore, in principle, illegal transactions are taxed in the same way as legal transactions. However, goods whose release into the economic and commercial channels of the EU is absolutely precluded and whose illegal importation or supply can give rise only to penalties under the criminal law, are not taxable. From the CJEU case law, it follows that an illegal transaction takes place outside the scope of VAT if:

108. CJEU 12 November 2020, Case C-734/19 *ITH Comercial Timişoara SRL*, ECLI:EU:C:2020:919, para. 33.
109. CJEU 6 October 2022, Case C-293/21 *UAB 'Vittamed technologijos' v Valstybine mokesčių inspekcija*, ECLI:EU:C:2022:763.
110. CJEU 5 July 1988, Case 289/86 *Vereniging Happy Family Rustenburgerstraat v Inspecteur der Omzetbelasting*, ECLI:EU:C:1988:360, para. 20.

(1) the importation and supply of the goods are subject to a total prohibition on marketing in all the Member States, with the exception of strictly controlled economic channels for use for medical and scientific purposes;
(2) the products such have special characteristics: their harmfulness is generally recognized; and
(3) all competition between a lawful economic sector and an unlawful sector is precluded; the principle of fiscal neutrality is not affected if the supply is not taxed.

The importation of counterfeit money[111] and the supply of narcotic drugs[112] are not subject to VAT. However, VAT is payable on the supply of counterfeit perfumes.[113] The organization of unlawful games of chance is subject to VAT but can be exempt.[114] The illegal export of computer systems for strategic purposes was exempt, with a right to deduction of input VAT.[115] The renting out of space for the sale of narcotic drugs is in itself not an illegal activity, and hence subject to VAT.[116]

2.4.11 Fraudulent and Abusive Activities

It is settled CJEU case law that the objective criteria which form the basis of the concepts of 'supply of goods effected by a taxable person acting as such' and 'economic activity' are not met where tax is evaded by the taxable person himself.[117] In our view, the ultimate consequence of this is that a person who exclusively carries out fraudulent or abusive activities cannot be considered as a taxable person. This implies that his output supplies are not subject to VAT and that he does not have a right of deduction. Where a person also carries out legal activities for which he is considered as a taxable person, the question arises whether he acts in his *capacity* of a taxable person when he carries out fraudulent transactions.

2.4.12 Economic Activities and the Capacity of Taxable Person

Being recognized as a taxable person does not necessarily entail that all goods and services supplied by such a person are subject to VAT. This also applies to the person's

111. CJEU 6 December 1990, Case C-343/89 *Max Witzemann v Hauptzollamt München-Mitte*, ECLI:EU:C:1990:445.
112. CJEU 28 February 1984, Case 294/82 *Senta Einberger v Hauptzollamt Freiburg ('Einberger II')*, ECLI:EU:C:1984:81 and CJEU 5 July 1988, Case 269/86 *W. J. R. Mol v Inspecteur der Invoerrechten en Accijnzen*, ECLI:EU:C:1988:359.
113. CJEU 28 May 1998, Case C-3/97 *Criminal Proceedings against John Charles Goodwin and Edward Thomas Unstead*, ECLI:EU:C:1998:263.
114. CJEU 11 June 1998, Case C-283/95 *Karlheinz Fischer v Finanzamt Donaueschingen*, ECLI:EU:C:1998:276.
115. CJEU 2 August 1993, Case C-111/92 *Wilfried Lange v Finanzamt Fürstenfeldbruck*, ECLI:EU:C:1993:345.
116. CJEU 29 June 1999, Case C-158/98 *Staatssecretaris van Financiën v Coffeeshop 'Siberië' vof*, ECLI:EU:C:1999:334.
117. CJEU 6 July 2006, Joined Cases C-439/04 and C-440/04 *Axel Kittel v Belgian State (C-439/04) and Belgian State v Recolta Recycling SPRL (C-440/04)*, ECLI:EU:C:2006:446, para. 53.

purchases. Not all purchases of goods and services by a taxable person are, by definition, made in the capacity of a taxable person. Some activities by such a taxable person are treated as outside the scope of VAT because the connection with the economic activity concerned is sometimes simply not strong enough to consider them part of that economic activity. Hereinafter, we will discuss the question of whether transactions that are somehow distinct from the regular activity because their nature is different from the other business activities (we will refer to them as ancillary activities, *see* section 2.4.12.1), and activities which form the extension of an economic activity (*see* section 2.4.12.2) must be regarded as being integrated into that economic activity or not. Transactions in which it is clear that the goods or services are supplied by a taxable person acting as such, but which are nonetheless not considered as subject to VAT, are referred to in this chapter as non- taxable supplies (section 2.4.12.3).

2.4.12.1 Ancillary Activities

If a taxable person starts a new (economic) activity next to his existing economic activities, he will be regarded as having taxable status and capacity for both activities. A butcher who starts selling groceries in addition to meat products will have taxable status and capacity for both activities.

If a natural person who has a taxable person status carries out hobby activities, those hobby activities are, in principle, not a part of his economic activities. He does not carry them out in his capacity as a taxable person. If, for example, a butcher sells items from his private record collection on eBay, such a sale is not a taxable supply for VAT. There may be a point, however, on which the selling of records through eBay is not to be considered as a hobby activity anymore but meets the criteria of an economic activity itself. The butcher then has two parallel economic activities for which he has both taxable person status and taxable person capacity.

In *Kostov,* the CJEU seemingly took a different approach. The CJEU addressed the question of whether a natural person who had already been registered as a taxable person (i.e., who had taxable person status) for the activities of being and operating as a bailiff and who entered into a new, one-off transaction concerning immovable property, which was distinct from his regular activities as a bailiff, acted in his capacity as a taxable person.[118] According to the CJEU, a natural person who is already a taxable person in respect of his activities as a self-employed bailiff must be regarded as a 'taxable person' in respect of *any other economic activity* carried out occasionally, provided that that activity constitutes an activity within the meaning of Article 9(1) VAT Directive. Although this latter addition: 'provided that that activity constitutes an activity within the meaning of Article 9(1) VAT Directive' leaves room for a reconciliatory interpretation with the basic principles set out above, the ruling in *Kostov* created some doubt on the CJEU's view to ancillary activities.

118. CJEU 13 June 2013, Case C-62/12 *Galin Kostov v Direktor na Direktsia 'Obzhalvane i upravlenie na izpalnenieto' – Varna pri Tsentralno upravlenie na Natsionalnata agentsia za prihodite,* ECLI:EU:C:2013:391, paras 28-30.

Although we can see that in a way, the ruling in *Kostov* observes fiscal neutrality,[119] the CJEU could have taken a different approach. For example, it could have decided that any person who makes a supply on an occasional basis, whether he is already a taxable person or not, must prove his intention to make such a supply on a regular basis before being treated as a taxable person with respect to those supplies. The factors that we listed in section 2.4.5 should be decisive for determining whether the ancillary activity forms part of the economic activity. It would, in our view, be particularly fitting to check whether the person took active steps to market its property by mobilizing resources similar to those deployed by a producer, a trader or a person supplying services.[120] This approach would certainly help in determining whether activities on online platforms (e.g., eBay) and in the sharing economy (e.g., Airbnb, BlaBlacar) are to be considered as economic activities in a neutral manner.[121]

2.4.12.2 Direct, Permanent and Necessary Extension

In section 2.4.12.1, we discussed ancillary activities that are somewhat detached from a taxable person's economic activity and which may, in their own regard, be regarded as economic activities. A different situation is the one in which a taxable person performs activities that are closely connected to a taxable person's economic activities, but which are of a non-economic nature in their own regard. Such non-economic activities may be 'drawn' into the economic activity of a taxable person if it is the 'direct, permanent and necessary extension' of that economic activity.

The concept of direct, permanent and necessary extension was first introduced by the CJEU in the case of *Régie Dauphinoise*[122] where a property management company which held monies received on behalf of clients in its own bank account until they were due to be paid over and was allowed to retain the interest earned. The CJEU ruled that the supplies were not incidental because the receipt of the interest was a 'direct, permanent and necessary extension of the taxable activity of property management'. Accordingly, the amount of interest received had to be included in the denominator of the fraction used to calculate the deductible proportion.

The extension doctrine has become part of the standard set of case law with respect to dealings in shares. For example, in *Harnas & Helm*, the CJEU indicated that the holding of shares and bonds may fall within the scope of VAT, where they

119. The CJEU's ruling safeguards that whether the supply is made by a taxable person who makes such supplies regularly, or by a taxable person who is only incidentally engaged in such an activity, the treatment will be the same: both (competing) transactions are treated in the same way for VAT purposes.
120. CJEU 15 September 2011, Joined Cases C-180/10 and C-181/10 *Jarosław Słaby v Minister Finansów (C-180/10) and Emilian Kuć and Halina Jeziorska-Kuć v Dyrektor Izby Skarbowej w Warszawie (C-181/10)*, ECLI:EU:C:2011:589.
121. *See*: I. Grlica, *How the Sharing Economy Is Challenging the EU VAT System* (2017) 28/2 International VAT Monitor, pp. 124-131.
122. CJEU 11 July 1996, Case C-306/94 *Régie Dauphinoise – Cabinet A. Forest SARL v Ministre du Budget*, ECLI:EU:C:1996:290. para. 18.

constitute the direct, permanent and necessary extension of the taxable activity.[123] We refer to Chapter 11, section 11.4.3. In *Floridienne-Berginvest*,[124] the CJEU had to decide on the nature of the granting of loans by a holding company to its subsidiaries to which it supplied administrative, accounting, information technology and general management services. The CJEU noted that the holding company merely reinvested the dividends paid by their subsidiaries in loans to those subsidiaries without there being any link with the management services provided to the subsidiaries. Therefore, the interest on the loans constituted income resulting from ownership of the debts owed by the subsidiaries, or even income from credit transactions incidental to the main activity, namely the holding of shares, and thus fell outside the scope of VAT. The loans could also not be subjected to VAT on the ground that they were the direct, permanent and necessary extension of the supply of the taxable services to the subsidiaries. The loans were neither necessarily nor directly linked to services supplied.[125] In our view, a clear example of a direct, permanent and necessary extension of an economic activity was identified by Advocate General Kokott in her opinion in *Ryanair*.[126] She considered that the strategic takeover of (the shares in) an undertaking by which the acquiring company pursues the aim of extending or modifying its operating business is to be regarded as such a direct, permanent and necessary extension of a taxable activity. Although it is not in itself an economic activity, it constitutes a measure aimed at (extended) taxable turnover.[127] Unfortunately, the CJEU did not confirm this view of the Advocate General.

We note that if an activity is the direct, permanent and necessary extension of an economic activity, it cannot be classified as 'incidental' for the purposes of Article 174(2) VAT Directive (*see* Chapter 10, section 10.4.1.1).[128]

2.4.12.3 Non-taxable Supplies and Non-economic Activities

It follows directly from Article 9 VAT Directive that 'economic activities' are an essential element of the notion of 'taxable person'. Persons who do not carry out any economic activity do not have taxable person status. That means that – for example – persons who do not seek any consideration for any of their activities, or persons whose income is obtained by an activity which is seen as a result of a passive 'activity' (mere ownership), rather than of a more active one, persons who supply securities within the

123. CJEU 6 February 1997, Case C-80/95 *Harnas & Helm CV v Staatssecretaris van Financiën*, ECLI:EU:C:1997:56.
124. CJEU 14 November 2000, Case C-142/99 *Floridienne SA and Berginvest SA v Belgian State*, ECLI:EU:C:2000:623, paras 29 and 32.
125. *Ibid.*, para. 29.
126. Opinion of Advocate General Kokott of 3 May 2018, Case C-249/17 *Ryanair Ltd v The Revenue Commissioners*, ECLI:EU:C:2018:301.
127. *Ibid.*, para. 38.
128. CJEU 29 October 2009, Case C-174/08 *NCC Construction Danmark A/S v Skatteministeriet*, ECLI:EU:C:2009:669.

framework of investment activities with shares and other securities[129] or persons who are - less likely - to carry out strictly forbidden activities, do not perform economic activities and are, therefore, not considered as having taxable person status. Such activities must be seen as being completely dissociated from economic activity. These transactions or events are commonly referred to (as in this book), as 'non-economic activities'.

It may occur that a person carries out activities that are *partly* economic and *partly* non-economic. For example, if a natural person has a one-man business, he will be considered as carrying out economic activities when he acts in his capacity of that one-man business. However, when he acts in his private capacity, those activities in his private capacity are typically not considered to be economic activities.

Businesses run by private legal persons can also be engaged in both economic and non-economic activities (e.g., if they carry out charitable activities free of charge or passive holding activities next to their economic activities).[130] Similarly, public legal entities operating in their capacity as public authorities are also often engaged in economic activities and non-economic activities.

Non-economic activities are necessarily activities which fall outside the scope of VAT. Thus, a supply of goods or services, which is not an economic activity, is also a 'non-taxable transaction'.[131] However, a non-taxable transaction is not necessarily a non-economic activity. For example, the transfer of a going concern under Articles 19 and 29 is clearly an economic activity, yet it constitutes a non-taxable transaction by legal fiction (in those Member States which have implemented the provisions).

It is important to realize that not all non-taxable supplies (those which are made for free, a transfer of a going concern, the issuing of new shares, etc.) or non-taxable events (such as purchases of shares or other items) are of the same nature. In this respect, we note that not all non-taxable supplies and events are in the same way related to the economic activity concerned. In *Sveda*, Advocate General Kokott seems to support the idea that certain non-taxable supplies may be seen as supplied or taking place within the framework of the economic activity.

We agree that some non-taxable supplies seem to be more related to economic activities than others. We suppose that the making available of a recreational path to the public for free, as in *Sveda*,[132] or the provision of parking space for customers for free, or the transfer of a going concern, as in *Abbey National*, are all strongly related to

129. In which, for instance, Securenta was involved: CJEU 13 March 2008, Case C-437/06 *Securenta Göttinger Immobilienanlagen und Vermögensmanagement AG v Finanzamt Göttingen* [2008] ECR 01597.

130. *See*, for example: *Vereniging Noordelijke Land- en Tuinbouw Organisatie* (which was a cooperative) and *Securenta* (which was an incorporated company). CJEU 12 February 2009, Case C-515/07 *Vereniging Noordelijke Land- en Tuinbouw Organisatie v Staatssecretaris van Financiën*, ECLI:EU:C:2009:88 and CJEU 13 March 2008, Case C-437/06 *Securenta Göttinger Immobilienanlagen und Vermögensmanagement AG v Finanzamt Göttingen*, ECLI: EU:C:2008:166.

131. For example: CJEU 1 April 1982, Case 89/81 *Hong-Kong Trade Development Council v Staatssecretaris van Financiën*, ECLI:EU:C:1982:121.

132. For example: CJEU 22 October 2015, Case C-126/14 *'Sveda' UAB v Valstybine mokesčių inspekcija prie Lietuvos Respublikos finansų ministerijos*, ECLI:EU:C:2015:712.

the economic activity of the taxable person in question. It is in this regard not helpful that the CJEU is inconsistent in using the term 'non-economic activities' (*see* section 2.4.3). It sometimes uses the term to refer to activities without any 'economic nature' and sometimes to refer to activities that do have an economic nature but are non-taxable transactions. Therefore, the term 'non-economic activity' bears the danger of causing confusion. Accordingly, we use the more neutral terms 'non-taxable supplies' or 'non-taxable events' when referring to 'outside the scope transactions' which are not entirely dissociated from the (other) economic activities of a taxable person.

The question of in what capacity a taxable person carries out the activities (i.e., whether the activity in question is an economic or a non-economic activity) is relevant not only with respect to the calculation of the output VAT (the VAT on his supplies) but also with respect to the calculation of the amount of recoverable input VAT (the VAT on his purchases, intra-Community acquisitions and importations). We refer to Chapter 10, section 10.3.2.

2.4.12.4 Holding Companies, Dealings in Shares and Other Securities

Dealing in shares and other securities raises questions about the capacity in which a taxable person operates. This is because the acquisition, holding and sale of shares are not considered economic activities in themselves. Consequently, a mere holding company cannot be regarded as a taxpayer. However, the acquisition, holding and sale of shares may, in certain circumstances, be an economic activity after all. Notably, this is the case if the holding of shares is accompanied by direct or indirect involvement in the management of the company in which the holding has been acquired, insofar as the involvement of that kind entails carrying out transactions which are subject to VAT (holding of shares by a 'controlling, active parent company').[133] Since this has become a rather complex subject matter, we discuss the EU VAT treatment of holding companies, dealings in shares and other securities separately in Chapter 11.

2.4.12.5 Asset Labelling (Lennartz Principle)

If a natural person independently carries out an economic activity, he will obtain taxable person status. That does not necessarily mean that with everything he does, he acts in that capacity. He may very well act in his capacity as a non-taxable person/end-consumer. This is of particular relevance when he incurs VAT on purchases goods or services. Depending on the capacity in which he acts, he may have a right of deduction.

133. The CJEU's ruling in W-GmbH appears to undermine the carefully constructed framework established in previous case law and its interpretation. The ruling could be interpreted to suggest that holding shares in a subsidiary does not constitute an economic activity, even if a holding company provides management services for a fee to that subsidiary. However, for now, we assume that it was not the CJEU's intention to depart from its previous case law. CJEU 8 September 2022, Case C-98/21 *Finanzamt R v W-GmbH*, ECLI:EU:C:2022:645.

However, in the case of the purchase of assets, it also depends on how the assets are labelled. In this subsection, we will, therefore, discuss the concept of asset labelling.

2.4.12.5.1 Time: Assignment as Business Asset

The answer to the question regarding in what capacity a (taxable) person acts is of particular relevance if the taxable person can either act in his capacity as a taxable person, or in the capacity as a private consumer. If the (taxable) person purchases goods in his capacity as a taxable person, he should, in principle, be relieved immediately and completely from the burden of VAT because VAT should be neutral to taxable persons. However, if the taxable person purchases goods or services in his capacity as a private consumer, there should be no right of deduction because VAT aims at taxing private consumption. Unfortunately, it is not always clear in what capacity a taxable person purchases goods and/or services.

In *Lennartz*, the CJEU ruled:[134]

> A taxable person who uses goods for the purposes of an economic activity has the right on the acquisition of those goods to deduct input tax in accordance with the rules laid down in Article 17 of the Sixth Directive, however small the proportion of business use.

After this ruling, it became settled CJEU case law that a taxable person may choose whether or not to integrate into his business, part of an asset that is given over to his private use.[135] If the taxable person chooses to treat capital goods used both for business and private purposes as business goods, the VAT due as input tax on the acquisition of those goods is, in principle, wholly and immediately deductible.[136] This 'principle' is commonly referred to as the 'asset labelling theory' or the '*Lennartz* principle'.

However, in order for this case law to be applicable, it is a requirement that the capital goods must have been purchased by a taxable person, acting in the capacity of a taxable person. Indeed, as the CJEU considered in *Bakcsi*:

> In such a case, it is necessary to determine whether the goods have been acquired by the taxable person acting, at least in part, as such, that is to say, for the purposes of his economic activities within the meaning of Art. 4 Sixth VAT Directive, [currently Art. 9 VAT Directive]. This is a question of fact to be determined in the light of all the circumstances of the case, including the nature of the goods concerned and the period between the acquisition of the goods and their use for the purposes of the taxable person's economic activities (*see*, to this effect, *Lennartz*, paragraph 21 and 35).[137]

134. CJEU 11 July 1991, Case C-97/90 *Hansgeorg Lennartz v Finanzamt München III*, ECLI: EU:C:1991:315, para. 35, operative part.
135. For example: CJEU 8 May 2003, Case C-269/00 *Wolfgang Seeling v Finanzamt Starnberg*, ECLI:EU:C:2003:254, para. 40.
136. *Ibid.*, para. 41.
137. CJEU 8 March 2001, Case C-415/98 *Laszlo Bakcsi v Finanzamt Fürstenfeldbruck*, ECLI: EU:C:2001:136.

Unfortunately, this does not provide much guidance. It seems that the intention of the purchaser is decisive with respect to the answer to the question of in what capacity a capital good is purchased. If a natural person who has acquired goods exclusively for his private use, subsequently puts those goods to economic use, no recovery of input VAT is possible.[138] However, if the acquirer has the intention to use the capital good used for *both* business and private purposes, he has the discretion to allocate that capital good that is fully, or partly, or not at all to the business. This leads us to the conclusion that goods that have been acquired to be used exclusively for business purposes may not be partially allocated ('labelled') as a private asset. They are necessarily to be treated as business assets, i.e., it is assumed that they have been bought exclusively in the capacity as a taxable person. Conversely, capital goods that are used exclusively for private purposes cannot be labelled as business assets at all. This raises various questions. How relevant is the nature of the good with respect to the possibility of labelling the good as a business asset? How long, after the acquisition of the item, does the taxable person keep the right to allocate a mixed-used capital good to either the business assets or private assets? What are the consequences of an incorrect allocation (labelling), and does it give rise to an obligation to adjust the original allocation when the circumstances change in such a way that the goods are not used any longer for one of both purposes? Some of these questions were partially answered by the CJEU in *Petar Kezic.*[139] Mr Kezic had acquired plots of land, some of which had been assigned to his private assets and others to his business. He had built, in his capacity as a taxable person, upon all of those plots of land, a shopping centre. This centre was sold, together with the plots of land on which the building was erected. The CJEU ruled that the sale of the plots of land, which were assigned to his private assets, must be subject to VAT since that person, at the time of that transaction, acted as such. This ruling shows that under specific circumstances – like those in this case – the label 'private asset' can be removed from the asset and changed into the label 'business asset' where the person concerned has taken active steps to market property by mobilizing resources among which private property and the carrying out on that land of preparatory work to make development possible.[140] He also made use of widespread marketing techniques.

---

138. Advocate General Kokott has proposed a review of the CJEU case law confirming this principle. *See*: Opinion of Advocate General Kokott of 19 April 2018, Case C-140/17 *Szef Krajowej Administracji Skarbowej v Gmina Ryjewo*, ECLI:EU:C:2018:273.
139. CJEU 9 July 2015, Case C-331/14 *Petar Kezic s.p. Trgovina Prizma v Republika Slovenija*, ECLI:EU:C:2015:456, paras 24-28.
140. A comparable mechanism, although in a different area than asset labelling, can be observed in the sphere of dealings in shares. If an actively involved holding company sells the shares in its subsidiary, one would expect that the sale of such shares – like the holding of those shares – is an economic activity. However, under specific circumstances, for example, if the holding company uses the proceeds of the sale of the shares for the sole benefit of its shareholders, the shares are 'relabelled' from 'economic' to 'non-economic'. The sale of those shares suddenly becomes a non-economic activity, even though their acquisition and holding was an economic activity. *See* Chapter 11.

2.4.12.5.2 Scope: Business Versus Private Assets

In *Charles & Charles*, the CJEU provided clear guidelines on applying the asset labelling rules (the *Lennartz* principle).[141] When an item is used for both business and private purposes, the taxable person may choose to allocate this item in full, or in part, to either his business and/or his private assets. The Court considered:

> Should the taxable person choose to treat capital goods used for both business and private purposes as business goods, the input VAT due on the acquisition of those goods is, in principle, immediately deductible in full.[142]

The CJEU also observed the following:

> It follows from Art. 6(2)(a) Sixth VAT Directive, [currently Art. 26(1)a VAT Directive] that when the input VAT paid on goods forming part of the assets of a business is wholly or partly deductible, their use for the private purposes of the taxable person or of his staff or for purposes other than those of his business is treated as a supply of services for consideration.[143]

From the CJEU case law on asset labelling, it was not immediately clear whether the asset labelling theory only applied to capital goods that were used for both business and private purposes, or also to capital goods that were used for both business and non-economic activities (other than private use). However, in *Vereniging Noordelijke Land- en Tuinbouw Organisatie* ('VNLTO'), the CJEU indicated that legal entities do not have the right to fully allocate goods or services acquired and actually used for both economic and non-economic activities to the business assets.[144] VNLTO was an association that carried out not only taxable activities but also non-taxable activities, namely, promotion of the general interests of its members. The CJEU ruled that such a body is not entitled to label capital goods and services as business assets when it uses the assets for both economic and non-economic activities. Entities like VNLTO are supposed to acquire those goods and services in full or in part outside the framework of the business, i.e., not in the capacity as a taxable person. Following this ruling, the

141. CJEU 14 July 2005, Case C-434/03 *P. Charles en T. S. Charles-Tijmens v Staatssecretaris van Financiën* [2005] ECR I-07037.
142. *Ibid.*, para. 24. *See also* CJEU 11 July 1991, Case C-97/90 *Hansgeorg Lennartz v Finanzamt München III*, ECLI:EU:C:1991:315, para. 26; CJEU 8 March 2001, Case C-415/98 *Laszlo Bakcsi v Finanzamt Fürstenfeldbruck*, ECLI:EU:C:2001:136, para. 25 and CJEU 8 May 2003, Case C-269/00 *Wolfgang Seeling v Finanzamt Starnberg*, ECLI:EU:C:2003:254, para. 41.
143. CJEU 14 July 2005, Case C-434/03 *P. Charles en T. S. Charles-Tijmens v Staatssecretaris van Financiën*, ECLI:EU:C:2005:463, para. 25.
144. CJEU 12 February 2009, Case C-515/07 *Vereniging Noordelijke Land- en Tuinbouw Organisatie v Staatssecretaris van Financiën*, ECLI:EU:C:2009:88. The Dutch Supreme Court asked in an earlier case – CJEU 2 June 2005, Case C-378/02 *Waterschap Zeeuws Vlaanderen v Staatssecretaris van Financiën*, ECLI:EU:C:2005:335 – does a body governed by public law have, as regards a capital item acquired by it which it supplies for consideration to a third party, in respect of which supply it must be regarded as a taxable person, a right to adjust the turnover tax paid in respect of that acquisition pursuant to Article 20 (in particular, paras 2 and 3) of the Sixth Directive in so far as it has used that item for activities in which it engages as a public authority under Article 4(5) of that directive? There was no need for the Court to answer this question, as it decided that Waterschap Zeeuw Vlaanderen was not engaged in economic activities at the moment of the acquisition of the capital good.

right to label mixed-used goods to their business assets in full seems to be restricted to self-employed persons and partnerships.[145]

2.4.12.5.3 Rules on Asset Labelling since 1 January 2011

Since 1 January 2011, the VAT Directive has contained specific rules on asset labelling. Article 168a(1) VAT Directive stipulates that expenditures related to immovable property forming part of the business assets of a taxable person and used both for purposes of the taxable person's business and for his private use or that of his staff, or, more generally, for purposes other than those of his business, will be deductible only up to the proportion of the property's use for purposes of the taxable person's business. Member States are allowed to apply the same rules for movable capital items forming part of the business assets as they specify (Article 168a(2) VAT Directive). Under these new rules, self-employed persons are still entitled to allocate mixed-used capital items to the business assets in full or in part but are allowed only to deduct the input VAT on the expenditures related to these items only in so far as these items are used for business purposes. *See* section 10.7.1.2.1.

2.5 INDEPENDENTLY

In this section, we discuss the condition of the taxable person status and capacity that a person must carry out an economic activity 'independently'. From CJEU case law, it can be learned that independence must first[146] be assessed under Article 10 VAT Directive. This entails that it must be established whether there is no 'employer-employee relationship' as regards working conditions, remuneration and the employer's liability.[147] If the conclusion of such assessment is that there is independence in terms of Article 10 VAT Directive, then the next step is to further examine whether there is – more generally – also independence in terms of Article 9 VAT Directive. In that regard, it must be established whether there is an 'independence in the exercise of the economic activity'. This can be assessed by testing whether the person concerned performs his activities in his own name, on his own behalf and under his own responsibility and whether he bears the economic risk associated with carrying out those activities. The implication of this two-step approach is that even if an employer-employee relationship may not exist (Article 10), the person concerned may still not act

145. CJEU 19 July 2012, Case C-334/10 *X v Staatssecretaris van Financiën*, ECLI:EU:C:2012:473.
146. In *TP*, the CJEU seems to have reversed the order in which 'independence' should be examined. Where in *IO*, it first examined independence in terms of Article 10 VAT Directive and second independence in terms of Article 9 VAT Directive, it considered in *TP* that a test against Article 10 is only relevant if the test against Article 9(1) was successfully carried out. CJEU 21 December 2023, Case C-288/22 *TP v Administration de l'enregistrement, des domaines et de la TVA*, ECLI:EU:C:2023:1024, para. 50.
147. CJEU 13 June 2019, Case C-420/18 *IO v Inspecteur van de rijksbelastingdienst*, ECLI:EU:C:2019:490, para. 39.

'independently' in terms of Article 9 VAT Directive, if - for example - he does not act in his own name and own account and/or does not bear any economic risk.[148]

We note that the independence referred to in Article 9 VAT Directive is assessed by reference to the carrying out of economic activities. Whether or not an entity is independent *vis-à-vis* another entity, is in this regard, irrelevant.[149] Furthermore, the CJEU has confirmed that the same criteria for assessing the condition of independence in the pursuit of economic activities may apply to public and private persons.[150]

2.5.1 Exclusion of Employed Persons

The expression 'independently' in - what is now Article 10 VAT Directive - is intended in particular to exclude from taxation wage-earners who are bound to their employer by a contract of service.[151] The element 'independently' in Article 9 VAT Directive is defined in negative terms in Article 10 VAT Directive:[152]

> The condition in Article 9(1) that the economic activity be conducted 'independently' shall exclude employed and other persons from VAT in so far as they are bound to an employer by a contract of employment or by any other legal ties creating the relationship of employer and employee as regards working conditions, remuneration and the employer's liability.

The overarching criterion in Article 10 VAT Directive is whether an employer-employee type relationship exists. The provision sets out three criteria for determining whether such a relationship exists, pertaining to working conditions, remuneration and liability.[153]

The 'independently' element has been subject to debate in various CJEU cases. The first two cases before the CJEU considered both professions that were governed by public law, notaries and bailiffs in *Commission v Netherlands,*[154] and tax collectors in *Ayuntamiento de Sevilla.*[155] In *Commission v Netherlands,* the CJEU decided that the notaries and bailiffs act independently because they carry out their activities *on their own account and on their own responsibility*. They are free, subject to certain limits imposed by statue, to arrange how they perform their work, and they themselves receive the emoluments which make up their income.

In *Van der Steen,* the CJEU ruled that a director-majority shareholder who had a 100% ownership of the shares in a Dutch BV could not be seen as a taxable person

148. CJEU 13 June 2019, Case C-420/18 *IO v Inspecteur van de rijksbelastingdienst,* ECLI:EU:C:2019:490.
149. Opinion of advocate general Jääskinen of 30 June 2015, Case C-276/14 *Gmina Wrocław v Minister Finansów ('Gmina Wrocław II'),* ECLI:EU:C:2015:431, paras 50-58.
150. CJEU 29 September 2015, Case C-276/14 *Gmina Wroclaw v Minister Finansów ('Gmina Wrocław II'),* ECLI:EU:C:2015:635, para. 35.
151. Annex A (point 2) to the Second VAT Directive.
152. Opinion of advocate general Jääskinen of 30 June 2015, Case C-276/14 *Gmina Wrocław v Minister Finansów ('Gmina Wrocław II'),* ECLI:EU:C:2015:431, para. 39.
153. *Ibid.*
154. CJEU 26 March 1987, Case 235/85 *Commission v Netherlands,* ECLI:EU:C:1987:161.
155. CJEU 25 July 1991, Case C-202/90 *Ayuntamiento de Sevilla v Recaudadores de Tributos de las Zonas primera y segunda,* ECLI:EU:C:1991:332.

because of the existence of a contract of employment.[156] It follows from this case that a natural person carrying out all work in the name and on behalf of a company that is a taxable person pursuant to a contract of employment binding him to that company, of which he is also the sole shareholder, the sole manager and the sole member of staff, is not himself a taxable person.

A member of a supervisory board of a foundation under Dutch civil law did not act independently, even though he operated under a contract of assignment rather than under a contract of employment.[157] The CJEU considered that no relationship of subordination existed with regard to the employment conditions vis-à-vis the foundation or the supervisory board. The reason for this was that the board member was not bound by any instructions, in particular, when determining their working methods. This was underlined by the fact that the supervisory task of a board member is simply not compatible with a relationship of subordination. Thus, on the basis of Article 10 VAT Directive, it appeared that the board member acted independently. However, based on a more general assessment of the criterion of independence in light of Article 9 VAT Directive, it was apparent that the board member did not act in his own name, for his own account or under his own responsibility. He received a fixed fee for his activities and, therefore, did not bear any economic risks. Consequently, he was found not to have sufficient independence in the pursuit of his economic activities and, therefore, not to have taxable person status. Similarly, the CJEU effectively ruled that a member of the board of directors of several public limited companies incorporated under Luxembourg law does not act independently in terms of Article 9(1) VAT Directive, despite the fact that that member is free to arrange how he or she performs his or her work, receives the emoluments making up his or her income, acts in his or her own name and is not subject to an employer-employee relationship. A board member in such a capacity does not act on their own behalf or under their own responsibility and does not assume the economic risk associated with their activity.[158]

2.5.2 Bearing Risks

Excluding persons from being able to operate independently, as mentioned in Article 10 VAT Directive (employed persons), is one thing; determining that someone indeed acts independently is another thing. In order to establish whether someone acts independently, the CJEU (also) takes into account the fact that the person in question bears the 'economic risk' entailed in their activities.[159] In *Ayuntamiento de Sevilla*, the

156. CJEU 18 October 2007, Case C-355/06 *J.A. van der Steen v Inspecteur van de Belastingdienst Utrecht-Gooi/kantoor Utrecht*, ECLI:EU:C:2007:615.
157. CJEU 13 June 2019, Case C-420/18 *IO v Inspecteur van de rijksbelastingdienst*, ECLI:EU:C:2019:490.
158. CJEU 21 December 2023, Case C-288/22 *TP v Administration de l'enregistrement, des domaines et de la TVA*, ECLI:EU:C:2023:1024. We note that TP deals with a situation of a board member which is rather specific to Luxembourg. Consequently, the decision can in our view not be automatically applied to board members in other Member States.
159. Cf. CJEU 25 July 1991, Case C-202/90 *Ayuntamiento de Sevilla v Recaudadores de Tributos de las Zonas primera y segunda*, ECLI:EU:C:1991:332.

tax collectors' profit did not depend only on the amount of taxes collected but also on the expenses incurred on staff and equipment in connection with their activity.[160] The fact that the tax collectors were subject to disciplinary control by the government in the first case, and that the Spanish state could be held liable for the conduct of the tax collectors in the second, did not in itself form sufficient grounds for regarding them as persons bound by legal ties to an employer. In *Wroclaw,* the CJEU decided with regard to municipal budgetary entities (of the Polish city of Wroclaw) that those entities did not bear the required economic risk associated with carrying out economic activities since they did not own their own property, did not generate their own earnings and did not bear the costs of those activities.[161] Moreover, any earnings generated were assigned to the budget of the Municipality of Wrocław and the expenses were directly attributed to the budget of that municipality.

2.5.2.1 Bearing Risks and Branches

In section 2.3.2, we briefly touched upon the concept of a 'fixed establishment'. In *Berkholz,* the CJEU defined a fixed establishment as having 'a certain minimum size and both the human and technical resources necessary for the provision of the service which are permanently present'.[162] In *FCE Bank,* the CJEU considered that the 'bearing of economic risk' is also a factor to take into account when determining whether an establishment is a 'fixed establishment' or a separate taxable person.[163]

FCE Bank was a bank established in the UK with an establishment in Italy. The Italian branch received various services from FCE Bank UK. According to the Italian tax authorities, these supplies of services were subject to VAT in Italy. However, the CJEU decided that the Italian branch of FCE Bank could not be considered as a taxable person (separate from its head office) because it did not act independently, because it did not bear the economic risk arising from its business. The bank, as a legal person, bore all risks associated to the business (such as those as customers defaulting on the repayment of loans) and was, therefore, the subject of supervision of its financial strength and solvency in the Member State of origin (the UK). The CJEU also attached importance to the fact that the Italian branch had no endowment capital. This too indicated that the risk associated with the economic activity lay wholly with FCE Bank in the UK. The *FCE Bank* case demonstrates how the condition that a person must act 'independently' is also used to determine whether a branch has sufficient autonomy to be treated as a separate taxable person distinct from the head office.

Although the central question in *FCE Bank* was whether a branch can perform taxable supplies to its head office, the CJEU based its ruling by interpreting the concept of acting 'independently'. It seems that the CJEU is not so much concerned with

160. *Ibid.*
161. CJEU 29 September 2015, Case C-276/14 *Gmina Wroclaw v Minister Finansów ('Gmina Wrocław II'),* ECLI:EU:C:2015:635, paras 34-39.
162. CJEU 4 July 1985, Case 168/84 *Gunter Berkholz v Finanzamt Hamburg-Mitte-Altstadt,* ECLI:EU:C:1985:299, para. 18. *Also see*: Article 11 VAT Implementing Regulation.
163. CJEU 23 March 2006, Case C-210/04 *Ministero dell'Economia e delle Finanze and Agenzia delle Entrate v FCE Bank plc,* ECLI:EU:C:2006:196.

identifying the legal subject(s) for VAT ('any person') as with determining the extent to which a legal subject demonstrates independence in the exercise of an economic activity. The CJEU focuses on attributing an activity to 'something'. However, in doing so, the implicit judgment is made that this 'something' is a VAT legal entity (any person). In our view, it is systematically more correct to first establish whether a fixed establishment can be considered as a VAT legal entity ('any person') in its own right. Should the conclusion be that the fixed establishment is a separate VAT entity (person) from its head office, it should second be assessed whether it carries out an economic activity 'independently'. The CJEU, however, seems to take a different approach by focusing on interpreting the concept of 'independence'. It departs from the idea that only an independent operating person engaged in making economic activities can make taxable supplies to other persons. For this reason, the CJEU examined whether the branch of FCE Bank could be treated as a separate, independently operating taxable person.

We observe that in *FCE Bank*, the CJEU made no reference to Article 10 VAT Directive, which clarifies the condition of acting 'independently' in the context of a relationship of employer and employee. In our view, that is correct because the independence in the context of a branch has no relation whatsoever with a contract of employment or any other legal ties creating the relationship of employer and employee. Yet, in FCE Bank, the CJEU interprets the concept of 'independent'. This, however, is a different type of 'independence' than the independence referred to in Article 10 VAT Directive (*see* section 2.5). As can be observed from *Gmina Wrocław II*, Article 9 VAT Directive requires 'independence in the pursuit of an economic activity'.[164] According to the CJEU, it must be established whether the person concerned performs his activities in his own name, on his own behalf and under his own responsibility and whether he bears the economic risk associated with carrying out those activities. Indeed, this is what the CJEU examines in *FCE Bank*.

Another landmark judgment that needs reference here is *Skandia America Corporation.*[165] The central question, in this case, was whether the supplies of externally purchased services from the company's main establishment in a third country to its branch in a Member State constituted taxable transactions if the branch belonged to a VAT group in the Member State. On the one hand, the branch forms part of the head office's legal entity, and on the other hand, the branch forms part of the VAT group to which its head office does not belong. The CJEU decided that the FCE Bank principle did not apply in a situation like this and that transactions between head office and the VAT group (of which the fixed establishment is a member) are subject to VAT. In *Danske Bank*, the CJEU delivered a ruling on how to deal with a 'reverse' Skandia situation.[166] The CJEU was asked whether taxable services were being provided by a Danish head office, which was part of a Danish VAT Group, to its fixed

164. CJEU 29 September 2015, Case C-276/14 *Gmina Wrocław v Minister Finansów ('Gmina Wrocław II')*, ECLI:EU:C:2015:635, para. 28.
165. CJEU 17 September 2014, Case C-7/13 *Skandia America Corp. (USA), filial Sverige v Skatteverket*, ECLI:EU:C:2014:2225, paras 25-32.
166. CJEU 11 March 2021, Case C-812/19 *Danske Bank A/S, Danmark, Sverige Filial v Skatteverket*, ECLI:EU:C:2021:196.

establishment located in Sweden. The CJEU essentially ruled that this was the case. According to the CJEU, only persons established in one Member State can be part of a VAT Group. Foreign establishments cannot be part of a VAT Group and must therefore be seen as separate taxable persons in relation to that VAT Group. In our view, the ruling in *Danske Bank* raises a conceptual difficulty because it suggests that if a head office is part of a VAT Group, the fixed establishment must be considered as 'any person' separate from its head office. This is difficult, if not impossible, to reconciliate with the *FCE Bank* principle. We refer to section 2.6.6.

2.5.2.2 Bearing Risks and a Contract of Employment

In *Van der Steen*, the bearing of economic risk was the determining factor when testing whether a sole director-shareholder was independent.[167] The director and sole shareholder, Van der Steen, had a contract of employment with his own company.

Under Article 10 VAT Directive, this was an indication that Van der Steen did not act independently. Also, on the basis of the employment contract, he would receive a salary from his company, regardless of what happened with the company. Van der Steen did not bear any economic business risk in acting as manager and performing the work in the course of the company's dealings with third parties. This implied that under Article 9 VAT Directive, Van der Steen did not act independently in the exercise of the economic activity. Consequently, Van der Steen was not considered to be acting independently when he acted in the course of his employment contract. Following the CJEU's decision, a director with a majority shareholding is not a separate taxable person for VAT when he carries out activities or taxable transactions within the scope of his employment contract and on behalf of the company.

In *IO*, a board member did *not* work under a contract of employment. Under Article 10 VAT Directive, this was an indication that the board member acted independently. However, in terms of Article 9 VAT Directive, there was no independence in the exercise of an economic activity. The CJEU considered that the board member concerned did not bear any economic risk because he received a fixed fee, which did not depend on his participation in meetings or on the hours actually worked. Unlike an entrepreneur, he, therefore, did not have a significant influence on his income and expenditure. Moreover, where a member of such a supervisory board is negligent in the performance of his duties, that member's remuneration cannot be directly affected since, according to the articles of association of the foundation in question, such a failure to perform his duties can lead to the resignation of that member only after a specific procedure has been followed.[168]

167. CJEU 18 October 2007, Case C-355/06 *J.A. van der Steen v Inspecteur van de Belastingdienst Utrecht-Gooi/kantoor Utrecht*, ECLI:EU:C:2007:615.
168. CJEU 13 June 2019, Case C-420/18 *IO v Inspecteur van de rijksbelastingdienst*, ECLI: EU:C:2019:490, para. 42. *See also*: CJEU 21 December 2023, Case C-288/22 *TP v Administration de l'enregistrement, des domaines et de la TVA*, ECLI:EU:C:2023:1024.

2.5.3 Independently and the Capacity of Taxable Person

Just like the criterion of economic activity (*see* section 2.4.12), the criterion of independence is decisive for both taxable person status and capacity. For example, a part-time drawing teacher at a school who is also a successful painter and regularly sells paintings to art-lovers does not carry out his teaching activities in the capacity of taxable person since those activities are not performed independently, but he does carry out his painting activities in the taxable person capacity since those activities are performed independently.

2.6 VAT GROUPING[169]

In this section, we discuss the 'VAT Grouping' concept laid down in Article 11 VAT Directive.

2.6.1 Basic Principles of VAT Grouping

Article 11 VAT Directive provides Member States with the option of introducing VAT grouping schemes into their national legislation. Two or more persons established within a Member State, who, while being legally independent, are closely bound to one another by financial, economic and organizational links, may be treated as a single taxable person for VAT purposes.[170] If a Member State exercises this option, the result is that where the material conditions are met, a group of companies becomes a single taxable person. If a VAT group is formed, for VAT purposes it takes the place of the individual members.[171] This means, for example, that the VAT number of the VAT group has to be used on invoices, and the VAT group will file a single VAT return. Transactions between members of the group are outside the scope of VAT and, therefore, will not be taxed. The right to deduct input VAT is based on the activities of the VAT group taken together.

169. The initial text of this section is largely based on: A.J van Doesum, H. van Kesteren & G.J. van Norden, *The Internal Market and VAT: Intra-Group Transactions of Branches, Subsidiaries and VAT Groups* (2007) 1 EC Tax Review https://doi.org/10.54648/ecta2007005 and A.J. van Doesum & G.J. van Norden, *T(w)o Become One: The Communication from the Commission on VAT Grouping* (2009) 6 British Tax Review, pp. 657-667.

170. European Commission, Communication on the VAT Group option provided for in Article 11 of Council Directive 2006/112/EC on the common system of value added tax COM (2009) 325 final, p. 2.

171. CJEU 22 May 2008, Case C-162/07 *Ampliscientifica Srl and Amplifin SpA v Ministero dell'Economia e delle Finanze and Agenzia delle Entrate*, ECLI:EU:C:2008:301, CJEU 17 September 2014, Case C-7/13, *Skandia America Corp. (USA), filial Sverige v Skatteverket*, ECLI:EU:C:2014:2225 and CJEU 18 November 2020, Case C-77/19, *Kaplan International colleges UK Ltd v The Commissioners for Her Majesty's Revenue and Customs*, ECLI: EU:C:2020:934.

In *Norddeutsche Gesellschaft für Diakonie mbH ('NDG')* and *Finanzamt T v S.*, the CJEU gave the impression of deviating from the core of these basic principles.[172] The CJEU seemed to suggest that it is conceivable that a legal relationship exists between an entity forming part of a VAT group and the other members of that group, so that the supplies made by that entity may be liable to VAT. In our view, such an interpretation of Article 11 VAT Directive would go against the idea that the VAT Grouping concept ultimately recognizes, at the level of the taxable person, the existence of a group of companies as an economic unit, in line with fiscal neutrality and economic reality (*see* section 2.6.2). In *Finanzamt T (II)*, the CJEU restored law and order by indicating that its rulings in *NDG* and *Finanzamt T* (I) should not be interpreted as meaning that supplies within a VAT group are subject to VAT. The CJEU ruled that even where the VAT due or paid by the recipient of those services cannot be subject to an input deduction, supplies within a VAT group are not subject to VAT.[173]

2.6.2 The *Ratio Legis* of VAT Grouping

Although the European Commission was of the opinion that the VAT grouping facility could lead to distortions within the EU, the Explanatory Memorandum to the proposal for a Sixth VAT Directive makes it clear that the VAT grouping facility was wanted for reasons of administrative simplification, and because of the scope it offered to combat abuse (e.g., the splitting up of a single undertaking into several taxable persons, so that each might benefit from a special scheme).[174] However, the application of the VAT grouping facility was restricted to the territory of a single Member State. This restriction was mainly intended to avoid distortions, which it was presumed would result from applying the facility more broadly (also including foreign companies). However, many of the supposed distortions would by no means be a result of the facility as such, but rather would be caused by the fact of some Member States applying the facility while others do not. The facility is, after all, based on an optional provision. But even if all the Member States apply the VAT grouping regime, the risk of distortions – at a European level – would arise as the criteria under which a VAT group can exist, 'the financial, organizational and economic links' (*see* section 2.6.4), are not defined by the VAT Directive, which could easily result in different interpretations by the Member States.

From the Explanatory Memorandum to the proposal for a Sixth Directive, it follows that the rationale behind the VAT grouping facility is administrative simplification and combat of abuse.[175] However, in *Van Paassen*, the European Commission explicitly acknowledged that the VAT grouping concept is based on the German

172. CJEU 1 December 2022, Case C-141/20 *Finanzamt Kiel v Norddeutsche Gesellschaft für Diakonie mbH.*, ECLI:EU:C:2022:943 and CJEU 1 December 2022, Case C-269/20 *Finanzamt T v S.*, ECLI:EU:C:2022:944.
173. CJEU 11 July 2024, Case C-184/23 *Finanzamt T v S*, ECLI:EU:C:2024:599; CJEU 11 July 2024, Case C-184/23 *Finanzamt T v S*, ECLI:EU:C:2024:599, 'Finanzamt T (II)'.
174. Explanatory Memorandum to the proposal for a Sixth Directive of 20 June 1973, COM (73)950.
175. *Ibid. See also* S. Pfeiffer, 'Written Comment to the Keynote Paper Taxable Persons', in M. Lang, et al. (eds), *ECJ: Recent Developments in Value Added Tax, the Evolution of European VAT Jurisprudence and Its Role in the EU Common VAT System* (Linde 2014), pp. 98-99.

Organschaft concept.[176] Indeed, from the documents for discussion at a sitting of the European Parliament with respect to the proposal for a Second Directive, it would appear that the Commission has long held this view.[177] Nevertheless, it is not something the Commission recalled in its 2009 VAT Grouping Communication.

Based on the *Organschaft* concept, structurally linked persons must be considered a single legal entity for both company law and tax purposes. This is, in fact, the reflection in German law of the (general) group idea in which the group forms a single company.[178] We, therefore, believe that the (underlying) *ratio legis* of Article 11 VAT Directive is to offer the Member States the possibility of recognizing, at the level of the taxable person, the existence of the economic unit.

From CJEU case law since the introduction of the Sixth VAT Directive, it is clear that the principle of neutrality of legal form and the principle of economic reality are fundamental criteria for applying the common system of VAT.[179] Because both are fundamental to the VAT system as a whole, the principles are also crucial to the VAT grouping regime. Indeed, VAT grouping does justice to both neutrality of legal form and economic reality. On the one hand, the neutrality of legal form calls for a VAT grouping regime as it should make no difference whether an economic unit is incorporated as a single legal person or, for business or civil law reasons, as several legal persons. On the other hand, the principle of economic reality also calls for a VAT grouping regime since it allows for corresponding treatment as a single entity from a VAT perspective of that which is regarded as such from an economic perspective.

In our view, the VAT grouping option should no longer be an *option* for the Member States. The *ratio legis* of VAT grouping calls for the application of one and the same VAT grouping regime in all Member States. However, it seems unlikely that the Member States will ever be able to agree to such an amendment of Article 11 VAT Directive.

2.6.3 Advantages and Disadvantages of VAT Grouping

Usually, VAT grouping merely results in a reduction of the administrative burden for its members. However, in some cases, it may lead to substantial financial advantages (VAT savings). This happens, for instance, if one of the members of the VAT group carries out supplies to one or more of the other members, which supplies would have

176. *See* written comments of the Commission in: CJEU 12 June 1979, Cases 181-229/78 *Ketelhandel P. van Paassen BV and Denkavit Dienstbetoon BV*, ECLI:EU:C:1979:151.
177. Cf. B.G. van Zadelhoff, *Belastingplichtige in de BTW* (Kluwer 2008), p. 35.
178. *See* L. Timmerman, *Over multinationale ondernemingen en medezeggenschap van werknemers* (*Dissertation*) (Kluwer 1988), p. 59, who indicates that the group can be regarded as a business in its own right.
179. CJEU 29 April 2004, Case C-137/02 *Finanzamt Offenbach am Main-Land v Faxworld Vorgründungsgesellschaft Peter Hünninghausen und Wolfgang Klein GbR*, ECLI:EU:C:2004:267, para. 28; CJEU 20 February 1997, Case C-260/95 *DFDS A/S v Commissioners of Customs and Excise*, ECLI:EU:C:1997:77, para. 23 and CJEU 28 June 2007, Case C-73/06 *Planzer Luxembourg v Sàrl-Bundeszentralamt für Steuern*, ECLI:EU:C:2007:397, para. 43. *See* on the neutrality of legal form in more detail: A.J. van Doesum, *Contractuele samenwerkingsverbanden in de btw* (*Dissertation*) (Kluwer 2009), pp. 136, 162-163 and 519.

been exempted if they were made to third parties. Had the supplier not been part of the VAT group (making taxed supplies to third parties), it would not be entitled to a deduction, and its prices would be increased by the non-deductible input tax. Where the supply is made internally – within the VAT group – it is treated as a non-taxable event, and the input tax will, in principle, not be blocked since that input tax is supposed to be related to the supplies made by the VAT group to third parties. Moreover, VAT grouping may have cash flow advantages in cases where the group no longer has to pre-finance VAT.

Member States may deem these advantages to be unjustified, although, in our opinion, it remains to be seen whether and in what situations such tax advantages are unjustified. But even if they are unjustified, Member States are well equipped to take away any of those advantages. Article 11 VAT Directive offers Member States the tools to ensure that VAT grouping does not become a vehicle for tax fraud (tax evasion) or avoidance. In our view, obtaining a tax advantage through VAT grouping certainly does not constitute tax fraud. Also, it does not necessarily entail tax evasion or avoidance. Nevertheless, it follows from *Stichting Goed Wonen I* that Member States are free to exercise choice offered by the VAT Directive, while at the same time permitted to set conditions in so far as these do not materially alter the nature of choice offered.[180] Member States are, therefore, free to adopt measures to counter VAT advantages caused by VAT grouping that they deem unjustified or undesirable.

2.6.4 Material Conditions to VAT Grouping

In this section, we will elaborate on the material conditions to VAT grouping. It goes without saying that in Member States that have not availed themselves of the VAT grouping option, these conditions are of no relevance. It should also be noted that Article 11 VAT Directive does not have direct effect.[181]

2.6.4.1 'Any Persons'

On the basis of the English text of Article 11 VAT Directive, 'any person' may be included in a VAT group. In its 2009 report on VAT grouping, the European Commission took the position that only 'taxable persons' can be part of a VAT group.[182]

However, this ignores the fact that Article 11 VAT Directive specifically refers to 'persons', not to 'taxable persons'. Moreover, in our view, the VAT grouping concept is a supplement to the concept of taxable persons. It allows for treating as one from a VAT perspective that is regarded as one from an economic perspective, thereby safeguarding the principle of neutrality. Furthermore, groups of companies may

180. CJEU 4 October 2001, Case C-326/99 *Stichting Goed Wonen I*, ECLI:EU:C:2001:506.
181. CJEU 16 July 2015, Case C-108/14 *Beteiligungsgesellschaft Larentia + Minverva mbH & Co. KG v Finanzamt Nordenham*, ECLI:EU:C:2015:496, para. 50.
182. European Commission, Communication on the VAT Group option provided for in Article 11 of Council Directive 2006/112/EC on the common system of value added tax COM (2009) 325 final, p. 2.

include entities that are not taxable persons *stricto senso*,[183] simply because from an economic perspective, they should be regarded as one together with the group companies that are taxable persons. As indicated before, the VAT grouping facility recognizes the single economic unit for VAT purposes. If non-taxable persons are an integral part of this single economic unit, they should also fall within the scope of the VAT grouping regime. Indeed, in *Commission v Ireland* and in *Commission v The Kingdom of the Netherlands*,[184] the CJEU ruled that taxable person status is not a requirement for inclusion in a VAT group, albeit that the CJEU based its decision on a rather literal interpretation of Article 11 VAT Directive.

Based on the above, we can draw the conclusion that only 'persons' can be included in a VAT group. Clearly, a relevant question is whether only the local branch of a foreign company can be a member of the local VAT group, or whether the foreign head office must also be included in the local VAT group. We will discuss this issue in section 2.6.6.2.

Another question that deals with the scope of the wording 'person' as referred to in Article 11 VAT Directive is the following. In Germany, the question arose whether it was in conformity with Union law that in Germany, the right to form a VAT group was solely reserved to entities with legal personality and linked to the controlling company of that group in a relationship of subordination. Based on that local German rule, limited partnerships (not having legal personality) could not be included in a German VAT group.[185] It was not correct, according to the CJEU, to limit the scope of the notion person in such a way that only those entities with legal personality and linked to the controlling company of that group in a relationship of subordination could form a VAT group with the controlling company. This is only allowed where those two requirements constitute measures that are appropriate and necessary in order to achieve the objectives of seeking to prevent abusive practices or behaviour or to combat tax evasion or tax avoidance (it was for the referring court to determine whether that was the case in Germany). In *M GmbH*, the CJEU added that Member States must not apply criteria to demonstrate the existence of financial links (*see* section 2.6.5) that exclusively pertain to certain types of legal entities.[186]

---

183. Entities that come to mind include active holding companies that receive no remuneration for their activities. In CJEU 20 June 1991, Case C-60/90 *Polysar Investement Netherlands BV v Inspecteur der Invoerrechten en Accijnzen*, ECLI:EU:C:1991:268, the Court found that holding companies that merely acquire and hold shares in other companies are not to be regarded as taxable persons on a stand-alone basis.
184. CJEU 9 April 2013, Case C-85/11 *European Commission v Ireland*, ECLI:EU:C:2013:217 and CJEU 25 April 2013, Case C-65/11 *European Commission v Kingdom of the Netherlands*, ECLI:EU:C:2013:265.
185. CJEU 16 July 2015, Case C-108/14 *Beteiligungsgesellschaft Larentia + Minverva mbH & Co. KG v Finanzamt Nordenham*, ECLI:EU:C:2015:496, paras 34-46.
186. CJEU 15 April 2021, Case C-868/19 *M-GmbH v Finanzamt für Körperschaften*, ECLI:EU:C:2021:285.

2.6.4.2 Excluded Sectors

Some Member States exclude specific sectors or only apply the VAT grouping concept to certain sectors. According to the CJEU, Sweden and Finland were allowed to restrict the scope of the VAT grouping regime to specific parts of the economy - financial institutions.[187] In order to prevent tax evasion and avoidance, and in accordance with the second paragraph of Article 11 VAT Directive, Sweden and Finland had decided to restrict the possibility of forming a VAT group to those undertakings which were placed, directly or indirectly, under the supervision of the Finance Inspectorate and which were, therefore, covered by a public monitoring system. According to the CJEU, the European Commission had failed to show convincingly that, in light of the need to combat tax evasion and avoidance, that measure was not well founded.

It would seem from this case law that it is only possible for Member States to exclude specific sectors if the exclusion is based on the 'anti-abuse' second paragraph of Article 11 VAT Directive.

2.6.5 The Condition of 'Financial, Economic and Organizational Links'

In order to form a VAT group, there has to be a financial, economic and organizational link between the members of the VAT group.

In our view, the conditions are independent concepts of Union law.[188] In *Norddeutsche Gesellschaft für Diakonie* and in *Finanzamt T v S.*, the CJEU considered that it is important, for the uniform application of VAT Directive that the concept of 'close financial links' is given an autonomous and uniform interpretation.[189] In our view, the same holds true for the economic and organizational link. Therefore, these conditions should be uniformly interpreted in all Member States. This would also be in line with the purpose of the VAT Directive, which attempts to found a common system of VAT upon a uniform definition of 'taxable persons'.[190] Yet, Member States still seem to apply their own interpretation of the conditions.[191] With a view to (silently) harmonizing the interpretation of the conditions, in its 2009 Communication on VAT Grouping, the European Commission gave its views on how these links have to be established:[192]

187. CJEU 25 April 2013, Case C-74/11 *European Commission v the Republic of Finland*, ECLI: EU:C:2013:266, para. 39.
188. Also *see*: Value Added Tax Committee, Working Paper No 918, taxud.c.1(2017)982178 - EN, available at: https://bit.ly/32KLz8N (accessed 30 August 2023, 14:40).
189. CJEU 1 December 2022, Case C-141/20 *Finanzamt Kiel v Norddeutsche Gesellschaft für Diakonie mbH.*, ECLI:EU:C:2022:943, para. 65 and CJEU 1 December 2022, Case C-269/20 *Finanzamt T v S.*, ECLI:EU:C:2022:944, para. 37.
190. CJEU 4 December 1990, Case C-186/89 *W.M. van Tiem v Staatssecretaris van Financiën*, ECLI:EU:C:1990:429, para. 25 and CJEU 29 April 2004, Case C-137/02 *Finanzamt Offenbach am Main-Land v Faxworld Vorgründungsgesellschaft Peter Hünninghausen und Wolfgang Klein GbR*, ECLI:EU:C:2004:267, para. 29.
191. *See*: S. Pfeiffer, *VAT Grouping from a European Perspective* (IBFD 2015), pp. 123-156.
192. In its 2017 working paper, the VAT Committee further analysed the meaning of these three, available at: https://bit.ly/32KLz8N (accessed 30 August 2023, 14:40).

- The financial link: over 50% in capital or in voting rights or bases on a franchise contract. The financial link has to guarantee that one company has actual control of another.
- The economic link: the principal activity of the group of members is of the same nature or the activities of the group members are complementary or interdependent, or one member of the group carries out activities which are wholly or substantially to the benefit of other members.
- The organizational link: shared or at least partially shared management structure.

At first glance, the definitions suggested by the Commission seem rather broad compared to those currently applied by some Member States. This is particularly apparent with respect to the financial link condition, which is defined by reference to a percentage of participation in the capital or in voting rights (over 50%), or by reference to a franchise contract.[193] According to the Commission, this guarantees that one company has actual control over another. However, according to the CJEU, the EU legislature has not intended to reserve the benefit of the VAT group scheme only to entities in a relationship of subordination with the controlling company of the group's undertakings considered. Although the existence of such a relationship of subordination allows it to be presumed that relations between the persons concerned are close, it cannot, however, in principle, be regarded as a condition which is necessary for the constitution of a VAT group.[194] We believe that participation, both direct and indirect (through subsidiaries), leads to a financial link. Moreover, in our view, companies can be linked via a company in a different country. If – for example, a holding company which is established in Germany holds all shares (including the voting rights) in two subsidiaries which are established in the Netherlands, the two Dutch subsidiaries are financially linked through their German parent company. With respect to the financial link, the CJEU has confirmed that it should not be interpreted restrictively.[195] The economic link is defined by reference to the existence of at least one of the following three situations of economic cooperation: (a) the principal activity of the group members is of the same nature, or (b) the activities of the group members are complementary or interdependent, or (c) one member of the group carries out activities which are wholly or substantially to the benefit of the other members. Lastly, the organizational link is defined by reference to the existence of a shared or partially shared management structure.

Although the definition provided by the Commission for the economic link can be considered quite liberal compared to those currently applied by some Member States, we nevertheless feel that even so, it unnecessarily restricts the scope for establishing

193. Denmark, for example, requires a 100% participation in the capital, whereas Austria requires a 75% participation in the capital. *See* G. Michie, 'Value Added Tax on Financial Services in the European Union', in Han Kogels (ed.), *Consumption Taxation on Financial Services, Cahiers de Droit Fiscal International*, Vol. 88b (Kluwer Law International 2003), p. 226.

194. CJEU 1 December 2022, Case C-141/20 *Finanzamt Kiel v Norddeutsche Gesellschaft für Diakonie mbH.*, ECLI:EU:C:2022:943, para. 68.

195. CJEU 15 April 2021, Case C-868/19 *M-GmbH v Finanzamt für Körperschaften*, ECLI:EU:C:2021:285, para. 45.

VAT groups. Neither administrative simplification nor combat of abuse prescribes a strict interpretation of the economic link test.[196] Moreover, such an interpretation would also conflict with the principle of neutrality. Multinationals, especially but also domestic or regional groups of companies, will often have group companies that do not meet the economic link condition as formulated by the Commission. For example, if one group company is active in the chemicals sector and another is active in the fast-moving consumer goods sector, and the two do not conduct intercompany activities or deliver supplies, no economic link would be present. This example immediately demonstrates that by applying separate and restrictive criteria for this type of link, certain economic units would fall outside the scope of the VAT grouping facility, whereas on the basis of the *ratio legis* for VAT grouping, they should not.

These problems do not occur if the *ratio legis* for VAT grouping is taken as a starting point. As demonstrated, the basic idea behind VAT grouping is to treat as one from a VAT viewpoint that may be regarded as one from an economic viewpoint. In our view, determining whether one entity 'controls' other entities is the crucial test to establish whether a single economic unit is present.[197] Given the basic idea behind VAT grouping, this should also be the determining test for VAT purposes. In Germany, where the *Organschaft* concept originates, this is, in fact, the determining test.[198] Ultimately, this is also the criterion currently used in the United Kingdom. We, therefore, advocate applying a 'control test' to determine whether a VAT group exists. From that perspective, it makes more sense to test the links jointly, as a whole, rather than separately.

Although it would seem that the Commission's technique of testing the links separately is different from the proposed 'control technique' of testing the links jointly, these methods are, in fact, not that different. If the financial and organizational links, as defined by the Commission, are considered together, the Commission, in essence, already applies a control test. Basically, the decisive factor is whether an entity controls another entity by means of participation in capital or in voting rights, whereby this control should be formalized in at least a partially shared management structure. If the Commission were to propose applying the economic link condition more liberally than it suggests in the Communication, or indeed the abolition of that condition, this would, in effect, achieve the same result as the control technique proposed here.

2.6.6 Territorial Restriction of VAT Grouping

Article 11 VAT Directive stipulates that only persons 'established in the territory of that Member State' can be part of a VAT group. This is commonly referred to as the 'territorial restriction of VAT grouping'. In this section, we discuss the territorial restriction of VAT grouping.

196. Explanatory Memorandum to the proposal for a Sixth Directive of 20 June 1973, COM (73)950.
197. G.J. van Norden, *Het concern in de btw (Dissertation)* (Kluwer 2007), pp. 224-226.
198. D. Rau & G. Flick, *Kommentar zum Umsatzsteuergesetz* (2015) 8, § 2 and O.-G. Lippross, *Umsatzsteuer*, Grüne Reihe, Vol. 11 (Erich Fleischer Verlag, Achim 2005), p. 289.

2.6.6.1 Foreign Subsidiaries and VAT Grouping

Article 11 VAT Directive limits the formation of VAT groups to the territory of a single Member State. Persons who are closely bound to one another by financial, economic and organizational links, while established in the EU but not in a single Member State, are treated differently than such persons established within a single Member State. The question has been posed to what extent this difference in treatment is compatible with the freedom of establishment as laid down in Article 43 EC Treaty (currently Article 49 TFEU).[199] So far, the CJEU has not been able to provide a ruling on this matter.

2.6.6.2 Branches, Fixed Establishments and VAT Grouping

In *FCE Bank*,[200] the CJEU confirmed that a head office and its fixed establishment are both parts of one and the same taxable person. A taxable person can – if all conditions are fulfilled – become a part of a VAT group. However, Article 11 VAT Directive stipulates that only persons 'established in the territory of that Member State' can be part of a VAT group. A head office and a fixed establishment can both be considered as 'establishments' of the same taxable person. Hence, it can be argued that such a 'person' is established (either through its head office or its fixed establishment) in the territory of the Member State (of the VAT group).[201] However, it is clear from CJEU case law that the CJEU does not accept that a head office is part of a foreign VAT group which includes its fixed establishment (*Skandia America Corporation*)[202] nor that a

199. A.J. van Doesum, H.W.M. van Kesteren & G.J. van Norden, *The Internal Market and VAT: Intra-Group Transactions of Branches, Subsidiaries and VAT Groups* (2007) 1 EC Tax Review, pp. 35-43 https://doi.org/10.54648/ecta2007005. Also *see*: opinion of Advocate General Kokkott of 23 April 2020, Case C-77/19 *Kaplan International Colleges UK Ltd v The Commissioners for Her Majesty's Revenue and Customs*, ECLI:EU:C:2020:302, para. 62.

200. CJEU 23 March 2006, Case C-210/04 *FCE Bank – Ministro dell'Economia e delle Finanze. Agenzia delle Entrate*, ECLI:EU:C:2006:196.

201. If a foreign head office or if a foreign fixed establishment were in principle eligible to be included in a (national) VAT Group (this was the case in the Netherlands, until 1 January 2024) the question arises of how to test whether the financial, organizational and economic link conditions are fulfilled. If a foreign head office or if a foreign fixed establishment were to be part of a VAT group, how does one test, for example, the economic link, considering the fact that the foreign element typically serves a different customer base or even engages in a different type of activity? The case law of the CJEU has the effect that it is no longer possible to include foreign group entities in a fiscal unity, but due to the smaller group of entities (i.e., only those which are primarily or secondarily established in the VAT group's Member State) that can potentially belong to a fiscal unity, it may be more likely that the financial, economic and organizational link criteria can be fulfilled.

202. CJEU 17 September 2014, Case C-7/13 *Skandia America Corp. v Skatteverket*, ECLI: EU:C:2014:2225. *Also see*, for instance, Working Paper No 485, 17 February 2015, Value Added Tax Committee of the European Commission, CJEU Case C-7/13 *Skandia America*: VAT group, taxud.c.1(2015)747072 – EN, Brussels, and VAT Expert Group, VEG No 047, Brussels, 31 August 2015, taxud.c.1(2015)3986774 – EN, VAT grouping and judgment in Case C-7/13 (*Skandia America Corp.* (USA)).

fixed establishment is part of a foreign VAT group that includes the head office (*Danske Bank*).[203]

In *Skandia America Corporation*, the CJEU accepted as a given fact that in Sweden (only) branches of foreign companies can participate in a VAT group and that this Member State explicitly excludes the opportunity for the main establishment in the foreign country to participate in a Swedish VAT group. This approach is, in fact, in line with the view of the European Commission as communicated consistently by the Commission since 2009.[204] The CJEU ruled that if a branch belongs to a local VAT group and the foreign head office is excluded from that local VAT group, the supplies made between the head office and the branch as part of the VAT group are, in principle, taxable. Effectively, this means that the branch is dissociated from its head office. Conceptually, this raises the question if a branch which is dissociated from its head office can still be considered as a 'person'[205] in terms of Article 11 VAT Directive and therefore can still be recognized as a person eligible for inclusion in a VAT group.[206] In this sense, *Skandia America Corporation* results in a circular reasoning.

In *Danske Bank*, the CJEU ruled on a situation that can be seen as the opposite of the situation in *Skandia America Corporation*.[207] A Danish head office formed part of a Danish VAT group which made supplies to a Swedish branch. The CJEU ruled that the Swedish branch could not be considered as a part of the Danish VAT group. The VAT group of which the head office is a member and the branch must be regarded as separate taxable persons where head office provides that branch with services and imputes the costs thereof to the branch. Here too, from a conceptual perspective, it is difficult to accept that a branch which is dissociated from its head office because the latter forms part of a VAT group automatically becomes a 'person'. Such a 'headless' figure in our view cannot be characterized as a self-contained, autonomous person (able to enter into agreements on its own behalf and for its own expenses).

Given the conceptual issues the CJEU has created with its approach in *Skandia America Corporation* and *Danske Bank*, we wonder if alternative approaches could have been viable too. In this regard, it is important to acknowledge that including primary or secondary establishments abroad in VAT groups may lead to VAT advantages. This is, for example, the case where a fixed establishment abroad 'supplies' services to a group company, other than its head office, that is part of the same VAT

203. CJEU 11 March 2021, Case C-812/19 *Danske Bank A/S, Danmark, Sverige Filial v Skatteverket*, ECLI:EU:C:2021:196.
204. Communication of the Commission to the Council and the European Parliament on the VAT group option provided for in Article 11 of Council Directive 2006/112/EC on the common system of value added tax (COM 2009), *see*, in particular, sections 3.2 and 3.3.2.2.
205. Its intellectual nexus (the general management) generally resides in another territory (the main place of business). Such a 'headless' figure cannot easily be characterized as a self-contained, autonomous person (able to enter into agreements on its own behalf and for its own expenses).
206. The Commission in Working Paper No 485 states on page 24 that it does not seem to find this a problem: 'This seems to be in line with the position that a branch could be considered a taxable person (the VAT group, distinct from its head office).' Working Paper No 485, 17 February 2015, Value Added Tax Committee of the European Commission, CJEU Case C-7/13 *Skandia America*: VAT group, taxud.c.1(2015)747072 – EN, Brussels.
207. CJEU 11 March 2021, Case C-812/19 *Danske Bank A/S, Danmark, Sverige Filial v Skatteverket*, ECLI:EU:C:2021:196.

group to which the head office belongs. Should this group company not be fully entitled to a deduction of input VAT if it was not part of the VAT group, supplies by the fixed establishment would be taxable. The VAT on those supplies would be a cost for that company. Conversely, if the company is part of a VAT group and the foreign fixed establishment as well, the supplies by the foreign fixed establishment and the company are not subject to VAT. In that situation, there is a VAT advantage, which could possibly be considered unjustifiable. In its 2009 Communication on VAT grouping, the European Commission took the position that this may even be regarded as tax evasion. According to the Commission, the phrase 'established in the territory of that Member State' includes businesses with their seat of economic activity in the territory of the Member State implementing the VAT grouping scheme but does not include those fixed establishments that are situated abroad. This entails that if (just) a head office becomes part of a VAT group, all transactions between the fixed establishment and the VAT group are subject to VAT.

In our view, applying a general territoriality restriction in this situation is not a proportionate measure to counter this VAT advantage. In particular, the territoriality restriction should not apply if the entities included in the VAT group are fully entitled to deduct input VAT, as no VAT advantage, VAT avoidance or distortion of competition occurs in such situations. Administrative difficulties that the tax authorities may incur, in our view, cannot justify the exclusion of foreign fixed establishments. Moreover, Member States have other, more proportionate means of preventing such advantages. First of all, Article 27 VAT Directive ('internal supplies of services') can be used to prevent unjustified VAT advantages. It would even appear that this provision is specifically intended for this purpose.[208] Second, it follows from *Stichting Goed Wonen I*[209] that Member States can adopt measures to counter unjustified VAT advantages if a VAT grouping scheme is applied. Third, should the unjustified VAT advantages at hand be regarded as 'tax fraud, tax evasion or tax avoidance', Article 11 VAT Directive itself offers Member States the means to prevent a VAT group from engaging in tax evasion or avoidance. The advantage of the 'options' presented here over the solutions adopted by the CJEU in *Skandia America Corporation* and *Danske Bank* is that they do not create the conceptual difficulties indicated above, while preventing that VAT advantages arise which are not in line with the overall concept and design of the EU VAT system.

2.6.7 Extraterritorial Effects of VAT Grouping

Article 11 VAT Directive does not allow for cross-border VAT grouping. It is also true that *all activities* of the group members fall within the scope of the VAT grouping

---

208. European Commission, Communication on the VAT group option provided for in Article 11 of Council Directive 2006/112/EC on the common system on value added tax COM (2009) 325 final *see*, in particular, sections 3.2 and 3.3.2.2.
209. CJEU 4 October 2001, Case C-326/99 *Stichting 'Goed Wonen' v Staatssecretaris van Financiën*, ECLI:EU:C:2001:506.

regime.[210] The ultimate consequence of this latter rule is that transactions of which the place of supply lies outside the Member State of the VAT group, also take place within the VAT grouping regime (and thus fall outside the scope of VAT). If, for example, a member of a Dutch VAT group were to make a local supply of goods in Portugal (whereby the goods are and remain physically located in Portugal) to a different member of the same Dutch VAT group, from a Portuguese perspective, the place of the supply is Portugal. Since Portugal currently does not allow VAT grouping, the supply is taxed in Portugal. However, from a Dutch perspective, since both parties are within the same VAT group, the supply is not subject to VAT at all. Following the Commission's view, the Portuguese tax authorities are, in effect, forced to accept a foreign VAT grouping regime.

If cross-border VAT grouping is not allowed from a fiscal sovereignty point of view (*see* section 2.6.6), the question arises whether a Member State without a VAT grouping regime should be forced to accept the consequences of a foreign VAT grouping regime. In *Danske Bank*, the CJEU considered that the existence of a VAT group in a Member State must, where appropriate, be taken into account for the purposes of taxation in other Member States, in particular when the latter assess the tax obligations of a branch established in their territory.[211] This strongly suggests that, referring to the example outlined above, Portugal must take into account the VAT group accepted by the Netherlands and deem the local supply in Portugal not subject to VAT. Apparently, national implementations of Article 11 VAT Directive must be respected by other Member States.[212]

2.7 PUBLIC BODIES

Public bodies, such as states, regional and local government authorities (provinces, municipalities, etc.), often charge VAT on the supplies they make to their 'customers'. The question may arise to what extent activities of a public authority are subject to VAT. As the underlying objective of the harmonized VAT system is to levy a tax on private consumption, it would be in line with that purpose if VAT were only to be levied where public bodies enable persons to consume goods and services. The question is whether there is still 'consumption' if a citizen pays involuntarily for 'goods' or 'services', i.e., if he is forced by law to make the payments. For example, if a citizen must pay for his driving licence or his marriage certificate, it can be argued that no consumption takes place. However, if the citizen pays for goods and services supplied by a public body, while he can purchase the same goods or services from

210. CJEU 22 May 2008, Case C-162/07 *Ampliscientifica Srl, Amplifin SpA v Ministero dell'Economia e delle Finanze, Agenzia delle Entrate*, ECLI:EU:C:2008:301.
211. CJEU 11 March 2021, Case C-812/19 *Danske Bank A/S, Danmark, Sverige Filial v Skatteverket*, ECLI:EU:C:2021:196, para. 33. Also *see*: S.B. Cornielje, *De grensoverschrijdende fiscale eenheid in de btw* (WFR 2022/49).
212. In our view, this contradicts with the fact that VAT grouping is an option available to Member States. We believe that a national VAT Group should only have the implication that national VAT is not levied on the internal transactions but should not have as a consequence that another Member State should have to wave its right to tax.

private entrepreneurs, it can hardly be denied that there is 'consumption'. Moreover, not taxing such supplies by public bodies would cause distortion of competition. Articles 9 and particularly 13 VAT Directive deal with these complications.

2.7.1 Basic Principles

Public bodies are not considered to be taxable persons in respect of activities in which they are engaged as public authorities. Although the wording of Article 13 VAT Directive suggests that public bodies do not have the *status* of a taxable person when they carry out activities in which they are engaged as public authorities, it is our view that Article 13 VAT Directive in effect provides that public bodies which independently carry out economic activities do not carry out such activities in the *capacity* of a taxable person.

2.7.1.1 Conditions to Article 13 VAT Directive

The case law on public bodies[213] can be summarized as follows.[214] Four conditions must be fulfilled in order to conclude that a public body does not act in the capacity of a taxable person:

(1) The activity in itself must be an economic activity.
(2) The activity must be carried out by a public body.
(3) The activity must be carried out under a special legal regime applicable to the public body.
(4) There must be no significant distortion of competition.

We discuss these four conditions in the next subsections.

2.7.1.2 Strict Interpretation of Article 13 VAT Directive

In our view, the national courts should interpret the 'exemption' of Article 13 VAT Directive strictly, as it entails a deviation from the general harmonized VAT system.[215] As a guideline, we believe that the national courts should take the underlying objective of the VAT system into consideration when assessing whether an activity of a public body is covered by Article 13 VAT Directive. That underlying objective is to tax private consumption.

213. *See, inter alia*: CJEU 17 October 1989, Joined Cases 231/87 and 129/88 *Ufficio distrettuale delle imposte dirette di Fiorenzuola d'Arda and others v Comune di Carpaneto Piacentino and others*, ECLI:EU:C:1989:381; CJEU 25 July 1991, Case C-202/90 *Ayuntamiento de Sevilla v Recaudadores de Tributos de las Zonas primera y segunda*, ECLI:EU:C:1991:332 and CJEU 26 June 2007, Case C-284/04 *T-Mobile Austria GmbH and Others v Republik Österreich*, ECLI:EU:C:2007:381.
214. Cf. A.J. van Doesum & F. Nellen, *VAT in a Day* (Fonds Indirect Tax, 2021). Available at: https://ssrn.com/abstract=3867201 (accessed 16 August 2024), pp. 23-25.
215. *See* CJEU 13 July 1989, Case 173/88 *Skatteministeriet v Morten Henriksen*, ECLI:EU:C:1989:329.

2.7.1.3 *Consequences of the Application of Article 13 VAT Directive*

If an activity carried out by the public body is covered by Article 13 VAT Directive, the consequences are on the one hand that no VAT is due in respect of the output transactions, and on the other hand that the related input tax is not recoverable. The public body is, in fact, treated in the same way as private individuals are treated by the VAT system.

As is the case for private consumers, the non-recoverable VAT on goods and services bought by a public body is de facto a tax burden on consumption. Nonetheless, public bodies are not really consuming goods and services; at least they are most probably not the final consumers the European legislator had in mind when designing the VAT system. Accordingly, there is little difference with the exemptions listed in Articles 132 and 135 VAT Directive. In principle, the supplier cannot deduct the input VAT attributable to such exempt supplies. However, since the supplier is considered to incorporate the non-deductible VAT in his prices to its customers, it is assumed that ultimately the private consumer's consumption is taxed. In this regard, the position of a public body can be different. It is not uncommon for public bodies to not request a specific remuneration in return for their activities. In such instances, they are unable to pass on the tax burden to the 'real' final consumers. Consequently, private consumption is untaxed. This unwelcome result can be avoided if public bodies are - where possible and appropriate - treated in the same way as regular taxed operating private enterprises. That enables them to recover (at least more of) their input tax, and insofar as they charge the public for their activities, they can transfer the burden to their customers. It is indeed in line with the objective of the VAT system to restrict the interpretation of the exemption that is permitted for public bodies.

2.7.2 The Activity in Itself Must Be an Economic Activity

From *T-Mobile Austria*, it follows that the conditions listed in sections 2.7.3, 2.7.4, and 2.7.5 do not need to be checked if the activity in itself does not constitute an economic activity in the sense of Article 9 VAT Directive.[216] In other words: it is of no use determining in what capacity a public body operates (Article 13 VAT Directive) if it does not have taxable person status in the first place.

In *T-Mobile Austria*, the Court ruled that a public body that sold Universal Mobile Telecommunications System frequencies via a public auction and that asked really significant amounts for these 'rights' was not engaged in economic activities as defined in Article 9(1) VAT Directive.[217] According to this ruling, a public authority executing conditions laid down in European legislation (in respect of the effective use of the frequency spectrum) which creates a *new* market in which players can participate and deal in those frequency rights, is not engaged in economic activities as defined in Article 9(1) VAT Directive. The assignment (new release) of those frequencies in itself

216. CJEU 26 June 2007, Case C-284/04 *T-Mobile Austria GmbH and Others v Republik Österreich*, ECLI:EU:C:2007:381.
217. *Ibid.*

does not entail active participation in this market by the authority assigning these rights. Therefore, there is no economic activity, and thus the conditions of Article 13 VAT Directive need not apply. In *Fluvius Antwerpen*, a network operator sued a consumer who had stolen electricity.[218] The CJEU was asked whether electricity theft by a consumer amounted to an economic activity by the network operator and if so if Article 13 VAT Directive was to be applied. The CJEU established that even though the consumer stole the electricity, the network operator carried out a taxable supply. The CJEU ruled that the involuntary supply of electricity which was the result of unlawful conduct on the part of a third party constitutes an economic activity of the network operator inasmuch as it gives rise to a risk inherent in its activity as an electricity distribution network operator. Since the supply of electricity is included in Annex I VAT Directive, it follows from Article 13, third paragraph VAT Directive that the network operator must be considered as a taxable person.

In *SPÖ*, the CJEU ruled that external advertising activities carried out by a section of a Member State's political party (the SPÖ) were not to be regarded as an economic activity.[219] According to the CJEU, the SPÖ carried out a communication exercise in keeping with the attainment of its political objectives and which sought to spread its ideas as a political organization.[220] In carrying out that activity, the Court ruled explicitly that the SPÖ did not, however, participate *in any market*.[221] A similar conclusion can be drawn from *Gemeente Borsele*: the municipality concerned did not offer services on the general passenger transport market and did, therefore, not carry out an economic activity (*see* sections 2.4.4 and 2.4.5).[222]

In our view, this case law makes the analysis complicated as to whether a certain activity by a public body is a taxable or non-taxable activity. Establishing whether a transaction takes place *in a market* or *outside the scope of any market* does not appear to be an easy task. In our view, it would have been more straightforward to consider the assignment of the frequency user rights by the public body as an economic activity according to Article 9(1) VAT Directive and, subsequently, to examine whether the same transaction eventually might be or have been a non-taxable event on the grounds mentioned in Article 13 VAT Directive.

In fact, as may be seen in *Gmina O.*[223] and *Gmina L.*,[224] the emphasis on the fulfilment of the precondition that there must be an economic activity before Article 13

218. CJEU 27 April 2023, Case C-677/21 *Fluvius Antwerpen v MX*, ECLI:EU:C:2023:348.
219. CJEU 6 October 2009, Case C-267/08 *SPÖ Landesorganisation Kärnten v Finanzamt Klagenfurt*, ECLI:EU:C:2009:619.
220. More specifically, the SPÖ's activity is the development of informed political opinion with a view to participation in the exercise of political power.
221. *Ibid.*, para. 24: 'By such activities, the SPÖ is therefore carrying out a communication exercise in keeping with attainment of its political objectives and which seeks to spread its ideas as a political organisation. More specifically, the SPÖ's activity, particularly through the intermediary of the Landesorganisation, is the development of informed political opinion with a view to participation in the exercise of political power. In carrying out that activity, the SPÖ does not however participate in any market.'
222. CJEU 12 May 2016, Case C-520/14 *Gemeente Borsele v Staatssecretaris van Financiën and Staatssecretaris van Financiën v Gemeente Borsele*, ECLI:EU:C:2016:334, para. 35.
223. CJEU 30 March 2023, Case C-612/21 *Gmina O. v Dyrektor Krajowej Informacji Skarbowej*, ECLI:EU:C:2023:279.

VAT Directive is to be tested largely strips the latter provision from its relevance. In *Gmina O.* and *Gmina L.*, the CJEU considers that to establish the existence of an economic activity, a case-by-case assessment, referring to the typical conduct of an active entrepreneur in the field concerned, must be made. Since public bodies hardly ever show the typical conduct of an active entrepreneur in any field, particularly when they act under a specific legal regime applicable to them (*see* section 2.7.4), it is by no means inconceivable that a review under Article 13 VAT Directive may only be possible in very exceptional cases.

2.7.3 The Activity Must Be Carried Out by a Public Body

In an infringement procedure against the Netherlands, the CJEU had to determine whether private individuals like notaries and bailiffs who perform official services because they exercise the powers of public authority by virtue of their appointment to public office, should be covered by the 'exemption' of Article 4(5) Sixth VAT Directive (currently Article 13 VAT Directive).[225] In the Netherlands, their activities were treated as 'exempted' (in fact, as 'non-taxable' activities) because they were performed within the scope of a special legal regime. According to the CJEU, however, notaries and bailiffs may not enjoy the exemption provided for in Article 4(5) Sixth VAT Directive. The reason for this is that they pursue those activities, not in the form of a *body* governed by public law, since they are not part of the public administration, but in the form of an independent economic activity carried out in the exercise of a liberal profession.

As a consequence of this case law, a private individual or a private legal person can, in principle, not be considered as a body governed by public law within the meaning of Article 13 VAT Directive.[226] Municipalities, provinces, the state and the like are part of the public administration, and therefore, public bodies, as mentioned in the provision concerned. However, the CJEU has also indicated that the concept of 'other bodies governed by public law' in Article 13 VAT Directive, must be given an autonomous and uniform interpretation throughout the EU.[227] This concept constitutes a residual category of bodies falling within the public authority other than those specifically mentioned in that provision.[228] That does not mean that if a private law body has powers conferred by public law, it is automatically an 'other body governed by public law'. Yet, having such powers is an essential characteristic specific to any

224. CJEU 30 March 2023, Case C-616/21 *Dyrektor Krajowej Informacji Skarbowej v Gmina L.*, ECLI:EU:C:2023:280.
225. CJEU 26 March 1987, Case 235/85 *Commission of the European Communities v Kingdom of the Netherlands*, ECLI:EU:C:1987:161.
226. A person which, not being part of the public administration, independently performs acts falling within the powers of the public authority cannot be classified as a body governed by public law within the meaning of that provision. CJEU 21 May 2008, Case C-456/07 *Karol Mihal v Daňový úrad Košice V.*, ECLI:EU:C:2008:293, para. 18 and CJEU 29 October 2015, Case C-174/14 *Saudaçor v Fazenda Publica*, ECLI:EU:C:2015:733, para. 57.
227. CJEU 29 October 2015, Case C-174/14 *Saudaçor v Fazenda Publica*, ECLI:EU:C:2015:733, para. 45.
228. *Ibid.*, para. 55.

public authority, and therefore, is a relevant factor in determining that the body must be classified as a 'body governed by public law'.[229] In *Saudaçor*, the CJEU accepted that a limited company following a process of transformation by decentralizing the functions of an existing state body could be classified as a body governed by public law within the meaning of Article 13(1) VAT Directive.[230] The private legal body in *Nagyszénás Településszolgáltatási* did not seem to enjoy the benefit of the doubt and – subject to verification by the referring court – was not considered an 'other body governed by public law'.[231]

2.7.4 The Activity Must Be Carried Out under a Special Legal Regime

Article 13 VAT Directive excludes activities engaged in by public authorities governed by public law where these activities can also be carried out by persons subject to private law. The legal regime applicable to the public body is, therefore, an important criterion. If a public body acts under a special legal regime applicable to it, its activities are not subject to VAT unless it acts under the same legal conditions as those that apply to private traders.

The requirement that the public body acts 'as a public authority' means, first, that bodies governed by public law are not automatically exempted in respect of all the activities in which they engage but only in respect of those which form part of their *specific duties as public authorities*,[232] and second, that an activity carried on by a private individual is not covered by Article 13 VAT Directive merely because it consists of acts falling within the *prerogatives* of a public authority. On the basis of these guidelines, the national courts have to classify the activities in question in light of this criterion.

In *Câmara Municipal do Porto*, the CJEU ruled that in determining 'if an activity is engaged in as public authority', the subject matter or purpose of the activity is irrelevant.[233] This has implications with respect to, for example, questions regarding parking services which are carried out by a public body. In this respect, it is not in itself determinative whether the land on which vehicles are parked is public or private property of the public authority.[234] The fact that the pursuit of an activity involves the use of public powers, such as authorizing or restricting parking on a public highway, or penalizing by fine infringements of parking regulations, shows that this activity is

229. *Ibid.*, para. 58 and CJEU 22 February 2018, Case C-182/17 *Nagyszénás Településszolgáltatási Nonprofit Kft. v Nemzeti Adó- és Vámhivatal Fellebbviteli Igazgatósága*, ECLI:EU:C:2018:91, para. 45.
230. CJEU 29 October 2015, Case C-174/14 *Saudaçor v Fazenda Publica*, ECLI:EU:C:2015:733, paras 61 and 62.
231. CJEU 22 February 2018, Case C-182/17 *Nagyszénás Településszolgáltatási Nonprofit Kft. v Nemzeti Adó- és Vámhivatal Fellebbviteli Igazgatósága*, ECLI:EU:C:2018:91.
232. *See* CJEU 11 July 1985, Case 107/84 *Commission v Federal Republic of Germany*, ECLI:EU:C:1985:332.
233. CJEU 14 December 2002, Case C-446/98 *Agenzia delle Entrate – Ufficio di Genova 1 v Porto Antico di Genova SpA*, ECLI:EU:C:2000:691.
234. *Ibid.*, para. 20.

subject to a public law regime.[235] In the Netherlands, for example, parking on public roads can only be authorized by a tax levied on parking by local government bodies. Parking in parking garages, or lands that can be closed by a barrier, can be engaged in by public as well as private bodies. Therefore, parking on public roads is not a taxable activity for the local governments, but parking in garages or lands that can be closed by a barrier is (also *see* section 2.7.5, on potential distortions of competition).

Admittedly, the condition that activities by public bodies are pursued 'under the special regime applicable to them' is not always very helpful to national courts. It is clear that it does not include activities pursued by them under the same legal conditions as those that apply to private traders. It leaves room for different interpretations by the various Member States, which in itself does not move the harmonization process in the right direction.

2.7.5 There Must Be No Significant Distortion of Competition

If the treatment of public bodies as non-taxable entities leads to significant distortion of competition, they will be regarded as acting in their capacity as a taxable person after all. For some activities, public bodies shall, in any case, be regarded as taxable persons unless the activities are carried out on such a small scale as to be negligible (*see* Annex I VAT Directive).

2.7.5.1 Distortion of Competition: Relevant Area

In the *Isle of Wight,* the CJEU addressed the question of whether the expression 'distortions of competition' should be determined by reference to the area or areas where the particular body in question provides off-street parking or by reference to the totality of the national territory of the Member State.[236]

In the *Isle of Wight,* it was questioned whether off-street parking services supplied by a public body fell within the scope of Article 13 VAT Directive. The local authorities concerned submitted that the expression 'distortions of competition' is properly to be ascertained with regard to a public body by public body basis, and not by reference to a hypothetical market which encompasses the totality of the national territory of any particular Member State. A contrary approach, they argued, would be inconsistent with the very concept of 'competition'. The VAT exemption conferred on each of those authorities, they argued, did not lead in any way to distortions of competition in relation to private providers or local authorities in, for example, Glasgow, let alone to 'significant' distortions. Similarly, a person who wished to shop on the Isle of Wight would not park his vehicle in Manchester.

The CJEU did not follow this line of reasoning. It ruled that the argument that distortions of competition must be evaluated having regard to each of the local markets

235. *Ibid.*
236. CJEU 16 September 2008, Case C-288/07 *Commissioners of Her Majesty's Revenue & Customs v Isle of Wight Council and Others,* ECLI:EU:C:2008:505.

on which the local authorities offer off-street parking assumes a systematic re-evaluation, on the basis of often complex economic analyses, of the conditions of competition on a multitude of local markets. It must, therefore, be evaluated by reference to the activity in question, as such, without such evaluation relating to any local market, in particular. The CJEU added that the expression 'would lead to' (in the same provision) is to be interpreted as encompassing not only actual competition but also potential competition, provided that the possibility of a private operator entering the relevant market is real, and not purely hypothetical.

Thus, the evaluation of whether there is a significant distortion of competition cannot be made relating to any local market in particular. The evaluation also cannot be confined to cases of distortion of actual competition. Potential competition is also relevant, provided that it is not purely hypothetical.[237] This means, for example, that the mere presence of private operators on the market, without account being taken of matters of fact, objective evidence or an analysis of the market, cannot demonstrate the existence either of actual or potential competition or of a significant distortion of competition.[238]

In *Salix*, the CJEU confirmed that public bodies are to be considered as taxable persons in respect of activities or transactions in which they engage as public authorities not only where their treatment as non-taxable persons would lead to significant distortions of competition to the detriment of their private competitors but also *where it would lead to such distortions to their own detriment.*[239] Salix leased a building to a public body. It wanted to waive the exemption for the lease of that building. However, that required – among other things – that the lessee could be considered a taxable person. Salix observed that the wording of the second subparagraph of Article 4(5) of the Sixth Directive (now Article 13 VAT Directive) refers without distinction to all 'significant distortions of competition', no matter who is the victim of them. However, the treatment of those bodies as non-taxable persons, which excludes them from the right to deduct input VAT, could also lead to distortions of competition to the detriment of the non-taxable person. Since competition is distorted, whether that be to the advantage of the bodies governed by public law or to that of their private competitors, it should be held that the principle of fiscal neutrality, the expression in the area of VAT of the principle of equal treatment, is infringed. Such an interpretation would be compatible with the protection of competition per se, without regard to the particular characteristics of the relevant individual operator. The CJEU followed this line of reasoning.

In National Roads Authority, the CJEU was asked whether a body governed by public law which carries on an activity consisting in providing access to a road on payment of a toll must be regarded as competing with private operators who collect tolls on other toll roads pursuant to an agreement with the public law body concerned

237. *Ibid.*

238. CJEU 19 January 2017, Case C-344/15 *National Roads Authority v The Revenue Commissioners*, ECLI:EU:C:2017:28, para. 44.

239. CJEU 4 June 2009, Case C-102/08 *Finanzamt Düsseldorf-Süd v Salix Grundstücks-Vermietungsgesellschaft mbH & Co. Objekt Offenbach KG*, ECLI:EU:C:2009:345.

under national statutory provisions. It was of particular importance in this case that there was no real possibility of a private operator entering the market in question by constructing a road that could compete with already existing national roads. Consequently, the CJEU held that there was no real competition with activities carried on by private operators, consisting of collecting tolls on other toll roads. Furthermore, the CJEU considered there was no potential competition either, in so far as the possibility of private operators carrying on the activity in question on the same conditions as the public body is purely theoretical. Accordingly, there was no real competition, actual or potential, between the public law body in question and private operators.[240]

2.7.5.2 Annex I VAT Directive

In any event, public bodies shall be regarded as taxable persons in respect of the activities listed in Annex I to the VAT Directive, provided that those activities are not carried out on such a small scale as to be negligible. Annex I, for instance, mentions telecommunications services; supply of water, gas, electricity and thermal energy; transport of goods; and activities of commercial publicity bodies.

Member States may consider activities of these bodies which are exempt under Articles 132, 135, 136, 371, 374 to 377, 378(2), 379(2) and 380-390 VAT Directive as activities which they *do* engage in as public authorities. The Member States must lay down an express provision in order to be able to rely on this option.

As regards the question of whether the Member States can rely on the option provided only if they have previously adopted an express legal provision to that effect, it should be pointed out that, according to the settled CJEU case law, the transposition of a Directive into domestic law does not necessarily require that its provisions be incorporated formally in express, specific legislation; a general legal context may be adequate for the purpose provided that it does indeed guarantee the full application of the directive in a sufficiently clear and precise manner.[241] However, according to the CJEU's ruling in *Salix*,[242] Member States must lay down an express provision in order to be able to rely on the option in question, according to which specific activities of bodies governed by public law that are exempt under that directive are considered as activities of public authorities.

240. CJEU 19 January 2017, Case C-344/15 *National Roads Authority v The Revenue Commissioners*, ECLI:EU:C:2017:28.
241. *See:* CJEU 28 February 1991, Case C-131/88 *Commission v Germany*, ECLI:EU:C:1991:87, para. 6; CJEU 15 November 2001, Case C-49/00 *Commission v Italy*, ECLI:EU:C:2001:611, para. 21 and CJEU 28 April 2005, Case C-410/03 *Commission v Italy*, ECLI:EU:C:2005:258, para. 60.
242. CJEU 4 June 2009, Case C-102/08 *Finanzamt Düsseldorf-Süd v Salix Grundstücks-Vermietungsgesellschaft mbH & Co. Objekt Offenbach KG*, ECLI:EU:C:2009:345, para. 58.

2.7.6 Horizontal Effect of Article 13 VAT Directive

The question may arise whether an individual can rely on a Directive that has not yet been (correctly) transposed into national legislation against another individual.[243] It is settled CJEU case law that this is not possible. For example, the CJEU has explicitly rejected this idea of 'horizontal effect' in a case about cancellation rights on the ground that Directives are addressed to the Member States and should, therefore, not be capable of creating of themselves obligations for individuals or corporations who would be unaware of such obligations on the basis of national law.[244]

Nevertheless, from *Feuerbestattungsverein Halle*, it appears that in the field of VAT, there may be something like a horizontal effect (in case of an already implemented, yet incorrectly executed Directive).[245]

The question was whether a private taxable person (a crematorium in the town of Halle) would be able to rely on the second subparagraph of Article 4(5) of the Sixth VAT Directive (currently Article 13 VAT Directive) in the circumstance where that taxable person was in competition with a body governed by public law (the city of Lutherstadt-Eisleben, which also operated a crematorium) and asserting that the non-taxation or under-taxation by the German tax authorities of that body was unlawful.

The CJEU ruled:

> 29. Therefore, individuals are entitled to rely before national courts, against the Member State concerned, on the provisions of a directive which appears, so far as their subject-matter is concerned, to be unconditional and sufficiently precise whenever the full application of the directive is not, in fact, secured, that is to say, not only where the directive has not been implemented or has been implemented incorrectly, but also where the national measures correctly implementing the directive are not being applied in such a way as to achieve the result sought by it (Case C62/00 *Marks & Spencer*, [2002] ECR I6325, paragraph 27).
>
> ...
>
> 32. ... A private person who is in competition with a body governed by public law and alleges that that body is, in respect of the activities in which it engages as a public authority, treated as a non-taxable person for VAT purposes or undertaxed is entitled to rely, before the national court, on the second subparagraph of Article 4(5) of Sixth Council Directive in proceedings, such as the main proceedings, between a private person and the national tax authorities.[246]

Although this concerns the interpretation of a very specific VAT rule which applies specifically to public bodies, this ruling may have a broader scope. Arguably, a taxpayer whose position is directly influenced by the way in which another taxable person is treated by the tax authorities is able eventually to affect the tax position of

243. B. Terra & J. Kajus, *A Guide to the European VAT Directives, Introduction to European VAT*, Vol. 1 (IBFD 2013), p. 160.
244. CJEU 14 July 1994, Case C-91/92 *Paola Faccini Dori v Recreb Srl*, ECLI:EU:C:1994:292.
245. CJEU 8 June 2006, Case C-430/04 *Finanzamt Eisleben v Feuerbestattungsverein Halle*, ECLI:EU:C:2006:374.
246. *Ibid.*, paras 29 and 32.

that other individual (in this case, the public body) by relying on a provision of a European Directive.

2.8 NEW MEANS OF TRANSPORT

Article 9(2) VAT Directive appoints as a taxable person any person who occasionally performs an intra-Community supply of a new means of transport. We refer to section 13.2.7 for a more detailed description of and the function of designating this form of activity as an economic activity.

CHAPTER 3
Taxable Transactions

3.1 INTRODUCTION

The principle of the common VAT system entails the application of VAT to goods and services (Article 1(2) VAT Directive). On the basis of Article 2(1) VAT Directive, there are four taxable events for VAT:

(1) the supply of goods for consideration;
(2) the supply of services for consideration;
(3) the ICA; and
(4) the importation of goods.

Although Article 2(1) VAT Directive denotes all four taxable events as 'transactions', strictly speaking, only supplies of goods and supplies of services can be regarded as such. Of the aforementioned four taxable events, the supplies of goods and the supplies of services are the most important taxable VAT events. Nonetheless, we will discuss all four taxable events in this chapter. However, since we will deal with intra-Community acquisitions (ICAs) of goods separately in Chapter 12, we will only discuss the ICAs of goods briefly in this chapter. Because we will focus on importations of goods separately in Chapter 13, we will also only briefly discuss the importations of goods in this chapter. Consequently, we concentrate on supplies of goods and supplies of services as taxable events for VAT in this chapter.

3.1.1 The Importance of Distinguishing Between Goods and Services

Bearing in mind that European VAT is a general tax on all goods and services, it seems illogical to make a distinction between supplies of goods and supplies of services. After all, they are all subject to VAT, the taxable amount is usually the same for both supplies of goods and supplies of services, and the VAT rate that applies to both is normally the standard rate. If, however, a distinction were not to be made between supplies of goods and supplies of services, more difficult EU VAT legislation would be required. By making a distinction, for example, the place of supply rules for supplies of goods can be kept relatively simple, whereas the place of supply rules for services (in particular Business to Consumers (B2C) services, *see* Chapter 4) are more complicated. The distinction between supplies of goods and services is also of relevance for determining whether exemptions apply (e.g., the exemption for supplies of immovable property) and the VAT rate that applies (e.g., the rebinding of a book is subject to the standard VAT rate, whereas the supply of a book can be subject to the reduced VAT rate).

3.1.2 Supplying Goods and Services or Supplying a Right to Goods and Services?[1]

On occasion, the CJEU has seemingly shifted the question of whether a good or service is supplied to the question of whether a right to the supply of such good or service is supplied. For example, in *MEO* and in *Vodafone*, the CJEU considers that the telephone subscription service supplied by these companies is 'formed by the right derived by the customer to benefit from the fulfilment of the obligations arising from that contract.[2] As a consequence, it was deemed irrelevant whether the customer actually made use of his or her rights under the subscription; in any case there was a supply of a service, even if the customer decided to cancel the contract. This echoes the CJEU's ruling in *Air France-KLM*, in which the Court considered that by selling an airline ticket, the customer obtains a right to the passenger transport service.[3] The CJEU indicated:

> Therefore, the consideration for the price paid when the ticket was purchased consists of the passenger's right to benefit from the performance of obligations arising from the transport contract, regardless of whether the passenger exercises that right, since the airline company fulfils the service by enabling the passenger to benefit from those services.[4]

If we understand the CJEU correctly, this means that the service commences when the ticket is purchased and is only completed when either the passenger arrives at his or her destination or does not board the plane before departure.[5] The taxable event (*see* Chapter 5) takes place over a longer period of time. This implies that the chargeable event (i.e., the moment when the supply is completed, *see* Article 63 VAT Directive) also takes place at either of these two moments. The chargeability of VAT (i.e., the moment when the Tax Authorities become entitled to formally claim the VAT), however, arises when the customer pays (typically a prepayment) or – if the Member State concerned implemented Article 66 of the VAT Directive – when the invoice is or should have been issued. Similarly, in *Asparuhovo*, the CJEU considered

1. This section is partly based on: A.J. van Doesum & F.N. Nellen, 'Taxable Amount and VAT Rates', in M. Lang, et al. (eds), *CJEU: Recent Developments in Value Added Tax 2020* (Vienna: Linde, 2022), p. 149.
2. CJEU 22 November 2018, Case C-295/17 *MEO – Serviços de Comunicações e Multimédia SA v Autoridade Tributária e Aduaneira*, ECLI:EU:C:2018:942 and CJEU 11 June 2020, Case C-43/19 *Vodafone Portugal – Comunicações Pessoais, SA v Autoridade Tributária e Aduaneira*, ECLI: EU:C:2020:465. para. 32.
3. According to the CJEU, a passenger transport service via air comprises the checking in and the boarding of passengers, the onboard reception of those passengers at the place of take-off agreed in the transport contract, the departure of the aircraft at the scheduled time, the transport of the passengers and their luggage from the place of departure to the place of arrival, the care of passengers during the flight, and, finally, their disembarkation in conditions of safety at the place of landing and at the time scheduled in that contract. *See*: CJEU 23 December 2015, Case C-250/14 *Air France-KLM and Hop!-Brit Air SAS v Ministère des Finances et des Comptes publics, ECLI:EU:C:2015:841*, para. 26.
4. CJEU 23 December 2015, Case C-250/14 *Air France-KLM and Hop!-Brit Air SAS v Ministère des Finances et des Comptes publics*, ECLI:EU:C:2015:841, para. 28.
5. CJEU 11 June 2020, Case C-43/19 *Vodafone Portugal – Comunicações Pessoais, SA v Autoridade Tributária e Aduaneira*, ECLI:EU:C:2020:465. para. 32.

that the entering into subscription contracts for consulting services constituted a supply which commences at the moment the subscription starts and is supplied, regardless of whether the customer actually makes use of the rights entailed in the subscription.[6]

It may be difficult to understand that even when no advice is actually provided, no passenger is actually transported and no telecommunication service is actually provided, for VAT purposes:

(1) the essence of these services is still the supply of advisory, transportation or telecommunication services; and
(2) the supply of these services is completed as soon as it becomes clear that the customer will not consume or use the service (e.g., upon cancellation, no-show).

In our view, the CJEU is not converting the (actual) supply of the advisory, passenger transport or telecommunication services to the supply of a 'right' to such services. The CJEU considers these 'non-consumed' services still as supplies of advice, passenger transportation and telecommunication services, starting at the moment at which a right to these services comes into existence.[7] One may question whether this is in line with 'economic reality' because even though the contract is a primary determinant of the essence of a transaction, other factors such as the actual conduct of the contracting parties may be taken into account.[8] The customer obtained a right to the services, and indeed insofar enjoyed a benefit, but never fully consumed the actual services (i.e., never enjoyed the actual advice, passenger transport or telecommunication services). Yet the services still derive their nature from the intended consumption. Also, the classification of a service does not depend on how parties classify the nature of the supply for their own purposes.[9] Furthermore, considering the essence of the supply as the supply to a 'right' does not contribute to a purposeful application of EU VAT either. Therefore, we believe that indeed the essence of a supply that takes a while to be completed is not to be based on the *right* to that supply but on the *essential features* of the performance/supply to which a right has been obtained. This should in our view be the case, even if a customer decides not to consume the supply before the

6. CJEU 3 September 2015, Case C-463/14 *Asparuhovo Lake Investment Company OOD v Direktor na Direktsia 'Obzhalvane i danachno-osiguritelna praktika' Varna pri Tsentralno upravlenie na Natsionalnata agentsia za prihodite*, ECLI:EU:C:2015:542.
7. The CJEU's case law on cancellations of contracts and no-shows is however difficult to reconcile with CJEU 18 July 2007, Case C-277/05 *Société thermale d'Eugénie-les-Bains v Ministère de l'Économie, des Finances et de l'Industrie*, ECLI:EU:C:2007:440. Yet, there are noticeable differences between the underlying facts of these cases. *See*: A.J. van Doesum & F.J.G. Nellen, 'Taxable Amount and VAT Rates', in M. Lang, et al. (eds), *CJEU: Recent Developments in Value Added Tax 2020* (Vienna: Linde, 2022), pp. 169-171.
8. CJEU 14 July 2011, Case C-464/10 *Henfling and Others*, ECLI:EU:C:2011:489. Also *see*: Ad van Doesum & Frank Nellen, *Economic Reality in EU VAT* (2020) 5 EC Tax Review, p. 219 https://doi.org/10.54648/ecta2020048.
9. Ad van Doesum & Frank Nellen, *Economic Reality in EU VAT* (2020) 5 EC Tax Review, p. 220 https://doi.org/10.54648/ecta2020048.

moment at which it should have been completed had it not been cancelled (which includes a no-show of the customer).

3.1.3 Vouchers

The VAT treatment of transactions involving the use of vouchers depends on the type of voucher. A distinction is made between a 'Single-Purpose Vouchers' (SPV) and Multi-Purpose Vouchers MPV (*see* Article 30a VAT Directive). This distinction is of relevance because in case of SPV it is considered that at the time of issuance and each transfer of the voucher, a supply of the goods and/or services represented by the voucher takes place and VAT will be come due (Article 30b(1) VAT Directive). In case of an MPV the supply of goods and/or services for which the voucher is redeemed only takes place at the time of redemption (Article 30b(2) VAT Directive). This distinction between SPV and MPV is particularly relevant in cases where the customer does not redeem the voucher. We will discuss the VAT consequences of vouchers in Chapter 6 in more detail.

3.2 SUPPLY OF GOODS

3.2.1 Elements of a Taxable Supply of Goods

Since VAT should be levied in as general a manner as possible, the concept of the 'supply of goods' is very broad. Following Article 2(1)(a) VAT Directive, the supply of goods for consideration within the territory of a Member State by a taxable person acting as such is subject to VAT. This provision thus requires that:

(1) the object of the transaction can be qualified as a 'good';
(2) the transaction itself can be regarded as a 'supply';
(3) which 'supply' is made 'for consideration';
(4) and which 'supply' is made 'within the territory of a Member State';
(5) 'by a taxable person acting as such'.

In Chapter 2, we discussed the last element of the taxable supply of goods, i.e., when does a taxable person act in his taxable person capacity ('as such'). In Chapter 4, we will discuss the place of supply rules on the basis of which it can be determined whether a supply is made 'within the territory of a Member State'. As regards supplies of goods as a taxable event for VAT, in this chapter we will focus on the first three elements: the concept of 'goods' (section 3.2.2), the definition of a 'supply' (sections 3.2.3-3.2.6) and the notion of 'for consideration' (section 3.4).

3.2.2 The Concept of 'Goods'

It is clear from Article 14(1) VAT Directive that only tangible, physical objects fall within the scope of the concept of 'goods'.[10] The concept is an independent concept of community law. It is, therefore, irrelevant if there is a (different) definition of 'goods' in the national (civil law) legislation of the Member States.

Even though the definition of goods seems plain and simple, it is not always easy to establish whether a supply is of goods or of services. As regards the supply of animals, one could doubt whether that is a supply of 'goods'. However, the CJEU ruled that animals are 'goods'.[11] Difficulties can also arise with respect to supplies of software. If, for example, a company supplies customized software on a carrier medium (e.g., a DVD), surely the carrier medium is a tangible, physical object. However, the value of the software exceeds the value of the carrier medium by far. In *Levob*, the CJEU ruled that where it is apparent that the customization of the software is neither minor nor ancillary but, on the contrary, predominates, the supply of the software on a carrier is to be regarded as a supply of services.[12] The supply of standard software on a data carrier constitutes a supply of goods.[13]

Article 15 VAT Directive, which is discussed below, expands the scope of the concept of goods. Certain supplies, even though they entail no supplies of tangible physical objects, are brought under the definition of supplies of goods, by treating expanding the scope of the concept of 'goods'.

3.2.2.1 Electricity, Gas, Heat, Refrigeration and the Like

Even though electricity, gas, heat, refrigeration and the like cannot be regarded as tangible, physical objects themselves, they are treated as tangible property for VAT purposes (Article 15(1) VAT Directive). The supply of electricity through an electricity network is, therefore, treated as a supply of goods.[14] Since Article 15(1) VAT Directive is not an optional provision, this is the case in all Member States.[15]

10. CJEU 17 May 2001, Cases C-322/99 and C-323/99 *Finanzamt Burgdorf v Hans-Georg Fischer and Finanzamt Düsseldorf-Mettmann v Klaus Brandenstein*, ECLI:EU:C:2001:280, paras 59 and 60.
11. CJEU 21 June 1988, Case 10/87 *The Queen v Commissioners of Customs and Excise ex parte Tattersalls Ltd*, ECLI:EU:C:1988:326 and CJEU 1 April 2004, Case C-320/02 *Förvaltnings AB Stenholmen v Riksskatteverket*, ECLI:EU:C:2004:213.
12. CJEU 27 October 2005, Case C-41/04 *Levob Verzekeringen BV and OV Bank NV v Staatssecretaris van Financiën*, ECLI:EU:C:2005:649.
13. Opinion of Advocate General Kokott, 12 May 2005, Case C-41/04 *Levob Verzekeringen BV and OV Bank NV v Staatssecretaris van Financiën*, ECLI:EU:C:2005:292, para. 55.
14. *See also* Council Directive 2003/92/EC of 7 October 2003 amending Directive 77/388/EEC as regards the rules on the place of supply of gas and electricity [2003] OJ L260/8-9.
15. We note that the supply of gas, electricity and thermal energy are also listed in Annex I of the VAT Directive. If a public authority undertakes an activity listed in Annex I, the authority must be treated as a taxable person in this respect unless the activity is carried out on such a small scale as to be negligible. Surprisingly, heat and refrigeration are not listed in this Annex. It is unclear why these elements are omitted.

3.2.2.2 *Rights Relating to Immovable Property*

Article 15(2) VAT Directive contains optional provisions for the Member States. The purpose of this provision is to safeguard a neutral application of the VAT, by treating transactions regarding immovable property that are economically equivalent to the supply of immovable property, the same as the immovable property or part thereof themselves.[16] In Chapter 9 we discuss the VAT aspects of transactions relating to immovable property.

Member States can regard as tangible property:

(1) certain interests in immovable property (Article 15(1)(a));
(2) rights in rem giving a right of use over immovable property (Article 15(1)(b));
(3) shares or interests equivalent to shares giving the holder thereof de jure or de facto rights of ownership or possession over immovable property or part thereof (Article 15(1)(c)).

In *Van Tiem*, the CJEU held that if a Member State exercised the option of Article 5(3) Sixth VAT Directive (Article 15(2) VAT Directive) to consider certain rights in rem to be tangible property, also the creation of such rights (for the benefit of another person) is considered as a transfer of immovable property, i.e., a supply of goods.[17] Therefore, not only the *transfer* but also the *creation* of such a right can be regarded as (supplies of) tangible property by Member States that implemented Article 15(2) VAT Directive. In fact, also the *transformation* of a right of perpetual usufruct into full immovable property ownership rights constitutes a supply of goods within the meaning of that provision.[18] In our view, the foregoing is also true for certain interests in immovable property mentioned in Article 15(1)(a), and for shares or interests equivalent to shares as referred to in Article 15(1)(c).

The scope of Article 15(2) VAT Directive does however not cover a sale and lease back transaction consisting of a combined and simultaneous grant, first, of an emphyteutic right by a taxable person to another taxable person, second, of a lease of real property by the latter taxable person to the first. In case of such a sale and lease back transaction, the grant of the emphyteutic right and of the leasing of real property must be considered together. They form a single supply, which is not to be classified as a supply of goods.[19]

It should be noted that Article 15(2) VAT Directive contains an option for the Member States. Consequently, Member States are at liberty to exercise choice offered

16. European Commission, Common System of Value Added Tax: Uniform Basis of Assessment. Proposal for a Sixth Council Directive on the harmonization of Member States concerning turnover taxes. Submitted to the Council by the Commission COM (73) 950 final, 20 June 1973. Bulletin of the European Communities, Supplement 11/73, pp. 9-10.
17. CJEU 4 December 1990, Case C-186/89 *W.M. van Tiem v Staatssecretaris van Financiën*, ECLI:EU:C:1990:429.
18. CJEU 25 February 2021, Case C-604/19 *Gmina Wrocław IV (Perpetual usufruct)*, ECLI: EU:C:2021:132.
19. CJEU 27 March 2019, Case C-201/18 *Mydibel SA v État belge*, ECLI:EU:C:2019:254.

to them. In *Stichting Goed Wonen*, the CJEU confirmed that the optional character of Article 15(2) VAT Directive entails that Member States may lay down certain conditions when implementing the provision since no provision of the Sixth VAT Directive (now: VAT Directive) in any way restricts the Member States' discretion in this regard.[20] The limitation is that the conditions laid down by the Member State in question must not alter the nature of choice afforded.

According to the CJEU's decision in *Centralan*, it is possible that two different persons, having different rights over a property, may both have the right to dispose it of as owner.[21] According to the CJEU, the various manifestations of the concept of co-ownership in the Member States' legal systems are such as to indicate that it is possible that more than one person may have the right to dispose of property as owner. In our view, *Centralan* does not make Article 15(2) VAT Directive redundant; this still has a function where the granting of interests, rights or shares in itself does not already lead to a transfer of the right to dispose of tangible property as owner.

3.2.3 Transfer of the Right to Dispose of Tangible Property as Owner

Article 14(1) VAT Directive provides that a 'supply of goods' shall mean the transfer of the right to dispose of tangible property as owner. That leaves the questions of what 'the transfer of the right to dispose of tangible property as owner' entails. From *Shipping and Forwarding Enterprise Safe,* it follows that the concept 'supply of goods' does not refer to the transfer of ownership in accordance with the procedures prescribed by the applicable national law. Rather, it covers any transfer of tangible property by one party, which empowers the other party actually to dispose it of as if he were the owner of the property.[22] It is an independent concept of community law.

In order to establish whether there is a supply of goods, it, therefore, need only be determined whether one party actually empowers the other party to dispose it of as if he were the owner of the property. In our view, this entails a twofold test. It must be established whether de jure (on the basis of the contract) one party actually empowers the other party to dispose of it as if he were the owner of the property, and it must also be established whether this takes place de facto. As regards the de jure right to dispose of the goods as owner, it is relevant whether the purchaser at any time obtains the right to decide in what way the goods must be used or to what end.[23] Decisive is whether the party to whom the right is transferred has the right to take decisions which are capable

20. CJEU 4 October 2001, Case C-326/99 *Stichting 'Goed Wonen' v Staatssecretaris van Financiën*, ECLI:EU:C:2001:506.
21. CJEU 15 December 2005, Case C-63/04 *Centralan Property Ltd v Commissioners of Customs & Excise*, ECLI:EU:C:2005:773.
22. CJEU 8 February 1990, Case C-320/88 *Staatssecretaris van Financiën v Shipping and Forwarding Enterprise Safe BV*, ECLI:EU:C:1990:61 and CJEU 6 February 2003, Case C-185/01 *Auto Lease Holland BV v Bundesamt für Finanzen*, ECLI:EU:C:2003:73.
23. CJEU 6 February 2003, Case C-185/01 *Auto Lease Holland BV v Bundesamt für Finanzen*, ECLI:EU:C:2003:73, para. 34.

of affecting the legal situation of the good or goods concerned, including, *inter alia*, the decision to sell it/them.[24]

Only if the other party obtains enough rights to use the goods as it sees fit *and* is actually in the position to use the goods as it sees fit, does a supply of goods take place. Using this twofold test, the supply of a good can be distinguished from the rental of a good. Were only the de facto test to be applied, this would not be possible.

3.2.3.1 Leasing

When a company leases goods to a customer, the lessee evidently obtains the de facto use of the goods, but it is open to question whether he also obtains the de jure right to dispose of the goods as owner. Basically, there are two forms of leasing: (1) financial lease, and (2) operational lease.[25] A financial lease usually involves periodic payments by the lessee to the lessor until the lessee has paid for the full cost of the asset together with a return on the finance provided. The lessee accepts substantially all the risks and rewards associated with ownership. Often, the lessor offers the lessee to purchase the asset at the end of the leasing period for an inviting price. An operational lease normally entails the lessee paying rental for the hire of the asset for a period of time, which is substantially less than the asset's useful life. The lessor retains most of the risks and rewards of ownership. A financial lease generally has more characteristics of a supply of goods, whereas an operational lease generally can be regarded as a supply of services.

A financial lease is in many ways comparable to a hire purchase agreement, albeit that in the case of a hire purchase agreement, the purchaser automatically becomes the owner of the asset that is the object of the agreement (*see* section 3.2.4.2). It is also not always easy to distinguish a finance lease from a sale with payment by instalments. For this reason, the European Commission proposed including a provision in the Sixth VAT Directive on the basis of which a financial lease was regarded as a supply of goods.[26] This particular provision, however, was not adopted in the final Sixth VAT Directive, and therefore, also did not make it into the current VAT Directive. In our view, it should not be the results of agreements comparable to financial lease agreements (such as hire purchase agreements) that influence the distinction between the supply of a good or supply of a service, but rather the purpose and aim of a financial lease agreement which should be decisive. Therefore, a financial lease agreement should not automatically be regarded as a supply of goods. Even though under such a lease agreement, it is likely

24. CJEU 23 April 2020, Case C-401/18 *Herst s.r.o. v Odvolací finanční ředitelství*, ECLI: EU:C:2020:295.
25. *See*, for the concept of so-called sale and lease back transactions and their VAT implications, CJEU 27 March 2019, Case C-201/18 *Mydibel SA v État belge*, ECLI:EU:C:2019:254. Also *see*: section 3.2.2.2.
26. This viewpoint was taken by the European Commission in the proposal for a Sixth VAT Directive. European Commission, Common System of Value Added Tax: Uniform Basis of Assessment. Proposal for a Sixth Council Directive on the harmonization of Member States concerning turnover taxes. Submitted to the Council by the Commission. COM (73) 950 final, 20 June 1973. Bulletin of the European Communities, Supplement 11/73, p. 10.

that the lessee will eventually purchase the asset, the fact that the ownership does not automatically shift from the lessor to the lessee at the end of the agreement cannot, in our view, be simply ignored. Moreover, the fact that the European Commission deemed it necessary to propose a specific provision on financial leases illustrates the fact that a financial lease cannot automatically be regarded as a supply of goods by itself. It is, therefore, conceivable that some Member States may consider a financial lease transaction as a supply of services, while others may consider such a transaction as a supply of goods.[27]

In *Eon Aset Menidjmunt OOD*, the CJEU considered that the leasing (of a car) was, in principle, to be regarded as a supply of services.[28] However, according to the CJEU, the lease of a motor vehicle under a financial leasing contract may present features that are comparable to those of the acquisition of capital goods.[29] We note that the CJEU considers the characterization of the leasing from the viewpoint of the lessee, rather than from the viewpoint of the lessor, by stating that a finance lease may present features of the 'acquisition' of capital goods. The reason for this seems to be that the underlying question is whether the lessee can deduct the VAT on the lease. Nonetheless, we believe that the CJEU's line of reasoning also applies to the classification of a (financial) leasing contract from the lessor's (the supplier's) perspective. In order to determine whether a (financial) leasing contract entails supply of goods or a supply of services, the CJEU has provided some guidelines. Where a financial leasing contract relating to a good (in this case, a motor vehicle) provides:

(1) that:
    (a) the ownership of that good is to be transferred to the lessee on the expiry of that contract, or
    (b) the lessee is to possess all the essential powers attached to the ownership of that good.
(2) in particular, all the rewards and risks incidental to legal ownership of that good are transferred to the lessee substantially, and
(3) the present value of the amount of the lease payments is practically identical to the market value of the property; the transaction must be treated as the supply of a good.[30]

In *NLB Leasing*, the CJEU confirmed that an operating lease must be distinguished from a finance lease, the nature of the latter being that substantially all the risks and rewards of legal ownership are transferred to the lessee.[31] Referring back to *Eon Aset Menidjmunt OOD*, the CJEU again indicated that the fact that a transfer of ownership is provided for on the expiry of the contract, or the fact that the present value of the lease payments is practically identical to the market value of the property,

27. For example, CJEU 22 December 2010, Case C-277/09 *The Commissioners for Her Majesty's Revenue & Customs v RBS Deutschland Holdings GmbH*, ECLI:EU:C:2010:810.
28. CJEU 16 February 2012, Case C-118/11 *Eon Aset Menidjmunt OOD v Direktor na Direktsia 'Obzhalvane I upravlenie na izpalnenieto' – Varna pri Tsentralno upravlenie na Natsionalnata agentsia za prihodite*, ECLI:EU:C:2012:97, para. 33.
29. *Ibid.*, para. 34.
30. Cf. *ibid.*, para. 40.
31. CJEU 2 July 2015, Case C-209/14 *NLB Leasing d.o.o. v Republika Slovenija*, ECLI:EU:C:2015:440, para. 28.

constitute, separately or together, criteria which permit a determination of whether a contract can be categorized as a finance lease. The CJEU also reiterated the criteria it formulated in *Eon Aset Menidjmunt OOD* on the basis of which an operating lease must be distinguished from a finance lease.[32]

In another case,[33] the CJEU noted that the label attached to a specific agreement for the hiring of a motor vehicle with an option to purchase (e.g., 'finance lease' or 'hire purchase') is not determinative of whether the supply is one of goods or services. The court went on to set the following test to determine whether a supply falls to be treated as goods under Article 14(2)(b) of the VAT Directive:

(a) the contract must include a clause expressly relating to the transfer of ownership of the goods; and
(b) objectively assessed, ownership of the goods should pass automatically through the normal performance, over the full term, of the contract.

The CJEU further clarified that if only first of the above test is met and the second is not met, i.e., where the transfer of ownership of the goods is not automatic and is one of a number of options available to the customer, the contract will not fall within Article 14(2)(b). However, in this case, the CJEU did not refrain from creating an exception to the second test and noted that the contract can fall within Article 14(2)(b), where the contractual instalments correspond to the market value of the goods, including financing and when the customer is not required to pay a substantial additional fee in order to exercise the option to purchase.

It is clear that a lease contract contains a financing element, i.e., there is an element in there of granting credit. The granting of credit in itself falls within the scope of the exemption of Article 135(1)(b) VAT Directive. In *Muys en De Winter*, the CJEU ruled that a supplier of goods or services who authorizes his customer to defer payment of the price, in return for payment of interest, is, in principle, making an exempt grant of credit within the meaning of that provision. However, where a supplier of goods or services grants his customer deferral of payment of the price, in return for payment of interest, only until delivery, that interest does not constitute consideration for the grant of credit but part of the consideration obtained for the supply of goods or services.[34] In *Volkswagen Financial Services*, the CJEU addressed the question of whether a finance lease contract should be split into a taxed element (rental service or supply of goods) and an exempt element (granting of credit).[35] Although, in many cases, the exempt element of a finance lease contract will be absorbed by the taxed element and thus form one single (taxed) supply for VAT purposes, it is conceivable that the elements should be split into two separate VAT transactions. This will, in our view, particularly be the

32. *Ibid.*, para. 30.
33. CJEU 4 October 2017, Case C-164/16 *Commissioners for Her Majesty's Revenue & Customs v Mercedes-Benz Financial Services UK Ltd*, ECLI:EU:C:2017:734, paras 29-34.
34. CJEU 27 October 1993, Case C-281/91 *Muys' en De Winter's Bouw- en Aannemingsbedrijf BV v Staatssecretaris van Financiën*, ECLI:EU:C:1993:855.
35. CJEU 18 October 2018, Case C-153/17 *Commissioners for Her Majesty's Revenue and Customs v Volkswagen Financial Services (UK) Ltd*, ECLI:EU:C:2018:845.

case if the interest rate is determined and calculated over a given period and is charged separately from the lease instalments.

3.2.3.2 Chain Transactions

A 'chain transaction' (*Reihengeschäft* in German) occurs if, for example, company A sells goods to company B, which sells the goods onwards to company C and company C in its turn sells the goods further to company D, while the goods are transported directly from company A to company D. This may be depicted as in Figure 3.1.[36]

Figure 3.1 Example of a Chain Transaction

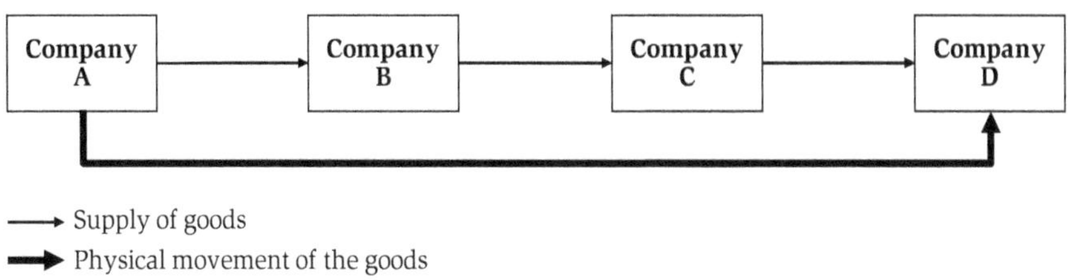

The amended proposal for a Sixth VAT Directive contained a provision on the basis of which the Member States could treat forward transactions as if there were a single supply from the first seller to the last buyer. This provision was, however, not included in the final version of the Sixth VAT Directive.[37] Strictly following the system of the VAT Directive, for each sale, it must be determined whether a 'transfer of the right to dispose of tangible property as owner' takes place. If each of the companies involved obtains the right to dispose of tangible property as owner at some point in time, three supplies of goods take place in the example above. The simplified triangulation scheme (STS) of Article 42 VAT Directive (*see* Chapter 12) confirms this viewpoint. This scheme is based on the presumption that chain transactions between three companies that are established in three different Member States represent two separate supplies of goods for VAT. From *EMAG,* it also follows that under current EU VAT legislation, successive supplies must be regarded as having followed each other in time, even if they only give rise to a single movement of goods. The intermediary companies (e.g., B) acquiring the goods can transfer the right to dispose of the goods as owner to the next company acquiring the goods (e.g., C) only if it has previously been transferred to the company (company B) by the previous company (company A), and therefore, the subsequent supply can take place only after the previous supply (the

36. In this example, all companies are taxable persons. Please note that a 'chain transaction' can also occur if there are only three companies involved or if more than four companies are involved.
37. European Commission, Common System of Value Added Tax: Uniform Basis of Assessment. Amendments to the Proposal for a Sixth Council Directive on the harmonization of legislation of Member States concerning turnover taxes. COM (74) 795 final, 26 July 1974.

supply between A and B) has been effected.[38] In our view, it is safe to conclude that chain transactions give rise to multiple, successive supplies of goods if, in each leg of the supply chain, the right to dispose of tangible property as owner is actually transferred.

Transactions are often carried out via intermediaries acting in their own name (and on their own account or on behalf of the principal). An intermediary acting in its own name takes part in the commercial supply chain. This means that on the basis of the main rules for the supply of goods (Article 14(1) VAT Directive) and for services (Article 24 VAT Directive), or on the basis of a specific rule written for commissionaires (also referred to as 'commission agents'), the relevant supply is normally made to and by an intermediary acting in its own name (*see* section 3.2.4.3).

In *Fast Bunkering Klaipėda*[39] ('*FBK*') and in *Vega International*,[40] the CJEU seems to accept that in a chain transaction, an intermediary who acts in its own name is, under specific circumstances, not buying and selling the goods. We will elaborate on this using an example of a three-party supply chain: principal (A), middleman (B) and customer (C). It follows from *FBK* and *Vega International* that the middleman (B) acting in his own name is – under specific circumstances – 'skipped' and the supply is considered as having been made directly by the first supplier (A) to the last party in the chain of transactions, being the customer (C). Although the main question which needed to be answered in *FBK* was whether the (local) zero rate (in the VAT Directive defined as an exemption with a right to recover the related input VAT) could be applied on the delivery of fuel to operators of vessels for navigation on the high seas, this case touches upon a more fundamental issue.

FBK (A) was a supplier of oil for seagoing vessels. If a seagoing vessel needed oil, it contacted a middleman (B), who acted in its own name. This middleman ordered the oil from FBK (A), who would then supply the oil directly to the customer (the seagoing vessel, C). Subsequently, FBK (A) would invoice B for the oil, and B would then invoice C for the supply of the oil. The CJEU ruled that goods which were delivered via an intermediary acting in his own name (B) were supplied directly to the operator (C) because the intermediary (B) was *neither in law nor in fact empowered to dispose of the fuel as if he were the owner*.

This raises the question of the conditions under which a middleman acting in its own name must be skipped for VAT purposes. In other words, under what circumstances does a supply still need to be seen as having been made to and by that intermediary person (which is still the common approach for most chain transactions), and under what circumstances, and on the basis of what criteria, must a supply be treated as one made directly by the first person in the chain to the last person?

38. CJEU 6 April 2006, Case C-245/04 *EMAG Handel Eder OHG v Finanzlandesdirektion für Kärnten*, ECLI:EU:C:2006:232.
39. CJEU 3 September 2015, Case C-526/13 *Fast Bunkering Klaipeda UAB v Valstybine mokesčių inspekcija prie Lietuvos Respublikos finansų ministerijos*, ECLI:EU:C:2015:536.
40. CJEU 15 May 2019, Case C-235/18 *Vega International Car Transport and Logistic – Trading GmbH v Dyrektor Izby Skarbowej w Warszawie*, ECLI:EU:C:2019:412.

FBK was not the first CJEU case in which a middleman was skipped. It had also occurred in *Auto Lease Holland ('ALH')*[41] (*see* section 3.2.3). At the time of that ruling, *ALH* was believed to be a specific solution in an extraordinary case. Now, after *FBK*, it seems to be less peculiar to skip the middleman, although we certainly do not believe it is the default VAT treatment of chain transactions. What makes the situations in *ALH* and in *FBK* so special is that in both cases, the intermediary had no other option than to transfer the legal ownership to the person who had already been brought by the original supplier in the position to dispose of the goods as if he were the owner.

For the CJEU, the main reason for skipping the intermediary was the fact that the right to dispose of the tangible property as owner was already with the customer at the time that the intermediary could transfer his (legal) rights. But the CJEU also referred in this respect to the considerations of Advocate General Sharpston,[42] which must, for cases like this, be taken into account as relevant criteria. The Advocate General came up with more circumstances under which, in her view, a supply must be seen as directly made by the original supplier (A) to the customer (C):

> Once fuel has been delivered into the tanks of a vessel used for navigation on the high seas, it is extremely difficult to conceive of its being 'disposed of' other than by consumption by the vessel concerned (and thus by its operator) in order to meet its energy requirements. Any alternative actual disposal by a legal owner of the fuel, other than the operator of the vessel, would seem to require physical intervention of an impractical kind. There is in practice no likelihood that the fuel will not be consumed for the vessel's needs, and it seems implausible that the intermediary, for the time that he may be legal owner, will wish to assume responsibilities of ownership (in the form of, for example, storage and insurance costs) in order to be able to dispose of it otherwise.[43]

The main practical impact of this decision is that the (original) suppliers of tangible goods involved in chain transactions have to determine whether they make their supply to their contract party (the intermediary) or directly to the final consumer, with whom they have no legal arrangements.[44] Making taxable supplies (of goods) to the contracting party rather than to parties with whom the supplier did not enter into a contract remains the default situation, but caution is advised. In cases where the supplier brings the customer of his intermediary irrevocably in the position to dispose of the goods as if he is the owner *before* the supplier sells and invoices the goods to the

41. CJEU 6 February 2003, Case C-185/01 *Auto Lease Holland BV v Bundesamt für Finanzen*, ECLI:EU:C:2003:73.
42. Opinion of Advocate General Sharpston of 5 March 2015, Case C526/13 *Fast Bunkering Klaipeda UAB v Valstybine mokesčių inspekcija prie Lietuvos Respublikos finansų ministerijos*, ECLI: EU:C:2015:156, para. 34.
43. *Ibid.*, para. 42.
44. Also *see*: VAT Committee, Working Paper No 907, Issues arising from recent judgments of the Court of Justice of the European Union, taxud.c.1(2016)3438314 – EN, available at: https://bit.ly/2uE0uj6 (accessed 16 August 2024).

intermediary, it completely changes the supply chain and the position of the intermediary.[45]

3.2.4 Mandatory Supplies of Goods

In section 3.2.2, we discussed the concept of 'goods'. By expanding the scope of the definition of the concept of 'tangible property' to include electricity, gas, heat, refrigeration and the like, and to certain rights relating to immovable property, the scope of the concept of the 'supply of goods' is broadened. The scope of the concept of 'supply of goods' can be expanded even further by treating certain activities relating to goods (as defined in Articles 14(1) and 15 VAT Directive) as a 'supply' of those goods.

Article 14(2) VAT Directive prescribes that the Member States shall treat as a supply of goods the transfer of property by order, the hire purchase of goods and the transfer of goods under a commissionaire contract (*see* sections 3.2.4.1-3.2.4.3). The CJEU has ruled that Article 14(2) of the VAT Directive constitutes a *lex specialis* against the general definition of a supply of goods under Article 14(1) VAT Directive.[46] The first provision is autonomous with regard to the latter. The provisions are to be interpreted independently from each other. The implication is that the conditions to Article 14(1) are irrelevant to the application of Article 14(2) VAT Directive to which separate conditions apply. In addition to Article 14(2), Article 16 VAT Directive requires that the Member States treat the application of goods for private use under certain conditions as a supply of goods (*see* section 3.2.4.4).[47]

3.2.4.1 The Transfer by Order

On the basis of Article 14(2)(a) VAT Directive, the transfer by an order made by or in the name of a public authority or in pursuance of the law, of the ownership of property against payment of compensation is a supply of goods. The legislative history offers no explanation with regard to this provision.

Arguably, a transfer by order against payment could already be covered by the general definition of a supply of goods of Article 14(1) VAT Directive. The reason why this article, which is a *lex specialis* in relation to Article 14(1),[48] was included in the Sixth VAT Directive (and later in the VAT Directive) is most likely that a payment of a

45. From a legal point of view, the intermediary will remain a buy-sell company, or a limited risk distributor or a commissionaire (so part of a commercial supply chain), but for VAT purposes will not be considered to be part of a supply chain.
46. CJEU 25 February 2021, Case C-604/19 *Gmina Wrocław IV (Perpetual usufruct)*, ECLI:EU:C:2021:132, para. 55 and CJEU 13 June 2018, Case C-665/16 *Gmina Wrocław III (Compensation for construction national road)*, ECLI:EU:C:2018:431, para. 36.
47. *See:* CJEU 14 July 2005, Case C-434/03 *P. Charles and T.S. Charles-Tijmens v Staatssecretaris van Financiën*, ECLI:EU:C:2005:463.
48. CJEU 13 June 2018, Case C-665/16 *Gmina Wrocław III (Compensation for construction national road)*, ECLI:EU:C:2018:431.

'compensation' is not always regarded as a payment of a 'consideration' (*see* section 3.4.4).[49] A supply of goods can only be subject to VAT if it is made for a consideration (*see* section 3.4). Therefore, without Article 14(2)(a) VAT Directive, the transfer of goods by order for compensation would not be subject to VAT. A public authority would then have a choice when it wants to acquire certain goods. It can either purchase the goods for payment consideration (the supply is then subject VAT) or acquire the goods by order against payment of compensation (the transfer would then not be subject to VAT). It seems that Article 14(2)(a) VAT Directive prevents public authorities having such a choice, and guarantees that the transfer of goods by order to a public authority is treated equally to the supply of goods to a public authority.[50] It safeguards the neutrality of the VAT system.[51]

Article 14(2) VAT Directive constitutes a *lex specialis* against the general definition of a supply of goods under Article 14(1) VAT Directive.[52] Therefore, the conditions for the application of Article 14(2)(a) VAT Directive are independent of those in Article 14(1) VAT Directive. In order for Article 14(2)(a) VAT Directive to apply, the following three cumulative requirements must be met:

(1) there has to be a transfer of ownership of property;
(2) the transfer of ownership has to occur 'by order made by or in the name of a public authority or in pursuance of the law'; and
(3) there has to be payment of compensation.[53]

Because the conditions for the application of Article 14(2)(a) VAT Directive are independent of those that are necessary for Article 14(1) VAT Directive to apply, the 'normal' criteria for a supply of goods do not apply (*see* section 3.2.3). Article 14(2)(a) VAT Directive refers not to the transfer of the power to dispose of property as owner, which is the case in paragraph 1 of that article, but, more explicitly, to the transfer of

49. Most language versions of the VAT Directive use a term similar to that of 'payment of compensation' (e.g., 'paiment d'une indemnité' in French and 'Zahlung einer Entschädigung' in German). However, the Dutch language version uses the term 'betaling van een vergoeding', which translates to 'payment of a consideration'.
50. Also *see*: Opinion of Advocate General Bobek of 22 February 2018, Case C-665/16 *Gmina Wrocław III (Compensation for construction national road)*, ECLI:EU:C:2018:112, paras 38 and 39.
51. In *Fluvius Antwerpen*, the CJEU does not seem to reject the idea that Article 14(2)(a) VAT Directive can also apply if a public body transfers ownership *to* another party. CJEU 27 April 2023, Case C-677/21 *Fluvius Antwerpen v MX*, ECLI:EU:C:2023:348.
52. Normally, a specific rule (*lex specialis*) overrides the general rule (*lex generalis*): '*lex specialis erogate legi generali*'. Even though the CJEU considers Article 14(2) VAT Directive a *lex specialis* in relation to Article 14(1) VAT Directive, it does not necessarily accept that 14(2)(a) overrides Article 14(1) VAT Directive. *See*, for example: CJEU 27 April 2023, Case C-677/21 *Fluvius Antwerpen v MX*, ECLI:EU:C:2023:348, para. 38. *See*, for a critical analysis: H.W.M. Van Kesteren, *Lex specialis. Voorrang en volgorde bij toetsen* (WFR 2023/222).
53. CJEU 3 June 2018, Case C-665/16 *Gmina Wrocław III (Compensation for construction national road)*, ECLI:EU:C:2018:431, para. 37 and CJEU 25 February 2021, Case C-604/19 *Gmina Wrocław IV (Perpetual usufruct)*, ECLI:EU:C:2021:132, para. 56.

ownership of that property.[54] Therefore, the requirement of a transfer of the right to dispose of a good as an owner, which is required for the application of Article 14(1) VAT Directive, is not a requirement for the application of Article 14(2)(a) VAT Directive. A transfer in the economic sense is not necessary.[55] Rather, it is the transfer of the ownership of property in the sense of the formal legal title that suffices for such a transaction to be regarded as a taxable 'supply of goods' under Article 14(2)(a) VAT Directive, on condition that the other requirements of that provision are fulfilled.[56]

The fact that Article 14(2) VAT Directive is a *lex specialis* to Article 14(1) also seems to imply that it is irrelevant whether all the constitutive elements of the concept of 'consideration' (*see* section 3.4) are met. It appears that it suffices that a 'compensation' paid is directly linked to the transfer of the ownership. As long as the payment of that compensation has become effective, this can even be an internal accounting transfer within a single budget.[57]

3.2.4.2 Hire Purchase and Sale on Deferred Terms

Where goods are first hired out for a period of time, and only at the end of that period are sold to the buyer under a single contract of 'hire/purchase', in fact, two supplies can be distinguished: (1) the supply of a service, being the rental of a good, and (2) the supply of a good at the end of the rental period. The same applies when goods are sold on deferred terms stipulating that ownership is to pass at the latest upon payment of the final instalment. However, in order to apply the same VAT regime to sales with payment by instalments and hire/purchase agreements or sales on deferred terms, the VAT Directive does not take the two supplies approach.[58]

On the basis of Article 14(2)(b) VAT Directive, both the actual handing over of goods pursuant to a contract for the hire of goods for a certain period and the sale of goods on deferred terms, which provides that in the normal course of events[59] ownership is to pass at the latest upon payment of the final instalment, are treated as a supply of goods. Even if according to the national law of a Member State legal title to the goods only passes at the end of the duration of the contract, for VAT purposes, a

54. CJEU 3 June 2018, Case C-665/16 *Gmina Wrocław III (Compensation for construction national road)*, ECLI:EU:C:2018:431, para. 40. Also *see*: CJEU 4 October 2017, Case C-164/16 *Commissioners for Her Majesty's Revenue & Customs v Mercedes-Benz Financial Services UK Ltd*, ECLI:EU:C:2017:734, para. 31.
55. CJEU 3 June 2018, Case C-665/16 *Gmina Wrocław III (Compensation for construction national road)*, ECLI:EU:C:2018:431, para. 38.
56. *Ibid.*, para. 41.
57. *Ibid.*, para. 45.
58. European Commission, Common System of Value Added Tax: Uniform Basis of Assessment. Proposal for a Sixth Council Directive on the harmonization of Member States concerning turnover taxes. Submitted to the Council by the Commission. COM (73) 950 final, 20 June 1973. Bulletin of the European Communities, Supplement 11/73, p. 10.
59. The phrase 'in the normal course of events' must be regarded as referring simply to the foreseeable performance of an agreement over its full term by the parties thereto, acting in good faith, in accordance with the principle that agreements must be kept. *See*: CJEU 4 October 2017, Case C-164/16 *Commissioners for Her Majesty's Revenue & Customs v Mercedes-Benz Financial Services UK Ltd*, ECLI:EU:C:2017:734, para. 36.

supply of goods is regarded as taking place at the beginning, when the goods are actually handed over to the buyer. The (potential) transfer of legal ownership at the end of the duration of the contract on the basis of national law is disregarded for VAT. The element of the (rental) service is also disregarded for VAT if the material conditions of Article 14(2)(b) VAT Directive are met. Some Member States treat certain leasing contracts as hire purchase contracts under Article 14(2)(b) VAT Directive (*see* section 3.2.3.1).

According to the CJEU, paragraph 2 of Article 14 VAT Directive constitutes a *lex specialis*, the conditions for the application of which are independent of those in paragraph 1.[60]

3.2.4.3 Commissionaire

A commissionaire acts in its own name but on behalf of another person (commonly called the 'principal'). Even though the so-called commissionaire fiction does not require a commissionaire to conceal the identity of its principal, the usefulness of the fiction can best be understood by considering a situation in which a principal does not want to reveal its identity to the customer and therefore engages a commissionaire (sometimes also referred to as a 'commission agent') who acts in its own name but on behalf of the principal. Where a commissionaire sells goods on behalf of his principal to a customer, it is, in fact, the principal who makes a supply of goods to the customer. Without any further arrangements, the customer receives an invoice for the supply from the commissionaire (who, after all, acts in his own name). However, the supply is, in fact, made by the principal. Under these circumstances, the customer would not receive a (correct) invoice from the supplier, making it impossible for the customer to deduct any VAT in relation to the supply. Only if the commissionaire discloses its principal, can it issue a correct invoice on behalf of the principal to the customer. This, however, may not be feasible from a commercial perspective. We underline that it is not *necessary* that the identity of the principal remains concealed from the customer(s). In this regard, the term 'undisclosed agent', which is commonly used in practice to refer to a commissionaire, is not entirely accurate. If the conditions of Article 14(2)(c) or Article 28 VAT Directive are met, the commissionaire fiction[61] applies.[62] There can be two types of commissionaire model: the sales commissionaire model and the purchase commissionaire model.[63]

60. CJEU 3 June 2018, Case C-665/16 *Gmina Wrocław III (Compensation for construction national road)*, ECLI:EU:C:2018:431, para. 36.
61. The CJEU has indicated that the commissionaire provisions are legal fictions by virtue of which the legal relationship between the principal and the commissionaire is reversed for the purposes of VAT. *See*: CJEU 14 July 2011, Case C-464/10 *Belgian State v Pierre Henfling and Others*, ECLI:EU:C:2011:489, para. 35.
62. Also *see*: A.J. van Doesum, *Revisiting the Commissionaire Fiction in EU VAT Law: Cause, Effect and the Role of Identical Supplies* (2024) 35/6 Intl. VAT Monitor, Journal Articles & Opinion Pieces IBFD (accessed 16 August 2024).
63. Opinion of Advocate General Kokott of 7 March 2024, Case C-87/23 *Biedrība 'Latvijas Informācijas un komunikācijas tehnoloģijas asociācija' v Valsts ieņēmumu dienests*, ECLI: EU:C:2024:222, para. 56.

Therefore, on the basis of Article 14(2)(c) VAT Directive, the transfer of goods pursuant to a contract under which commission is payable on purchase or sale is regarded supply of goods. Article 28 VAT Directive provides for services what Article 14(2)(c) VAT Directive provides for goods (*see* 3.3.2.1).

The CJEU interprets these two provisions in conjunction with each other.[64] These provisions create a legal fiction of two identical supplies of goods or services provided consecutively. That means that – in a sales commissionaire model – the principal is regarded to make a supply of goods (or services, *see* section 3.3.2.1) to the commissionaire, and the commissionaire is regarded to make a subsequent supply or services of goods to the customer. In a purchase commissionaire model, the commissionaire is regarded to purchase goods (or services, *see* section 3.3.2.1) from the supplier and to make a subsequent supply of those goods or services to the principal. Both (deemed) supplies have VAT consequences which are identical.[65] For VAT purposes, a commissionaire is not considered to render (intermediary) services to its principal. The sales commissionaire is deemed to buy and sell the goods (or services, *see* section 3.3.2.1), even though the commissionaire does not do so from a legal point of view. Therefore, the sales commissionaire's commission fee is the difference between the purchase price and the sales price of the commissionaire.

From *Gmina Wrocław III (Compensation for construction national road)*, it is clear that Article 14(2) of the VAT Directive constitutes a *lex specialis* against the general definition of a supply of goods under Article 14(1) VAT Directive.[66] Since Article 14(2)(c) and Article 28 VAT Directive are inextricably linked to each other, Article 28 should, in our view, be considered as a *lex specialis* to Article 24 VAT Directive. Consequently, Article 14(2)(c) is autonomous from Article 14(1), and Article 28 is autonomous from Article 24 VAT Directive. The implication is that the conditions to Articles 14(1)/24 are irrelevant to the application of Articles 14(2)/28 VAT Directive. One consequence of that is that it is *not* required for the application of the commissionaire fiction(s) that the (deemed) supply by the commissionaire (B) to the customer (C) is for consideration.[67] The legal fiction itself is sufficient for the deemed supply to be a taxable supply.

64. CJEU 14 July 2011, Case C-464/10 *Belgian State v Pierre Henfling and Others*, ECLI:EU:C:2011:489, para. 35; CJEU 4 May 2017, Case C-274/15 *European Commission v Grand Duchy of Luxembourg*, ECLI:EU:C:2017:333, para. 87, CJEU 9 December 2019, Case C-707/18 *Amărăşti Land Investment SRL v DirecŢia Generală Regională a FinanŢelor*, ECLI:EU:C:2019:1136, para. 37, CJEU 3 September 2015, Case C-526/13 *UAB 'Fast Bunkering Klaipeda' v Valstybine mokesčių inspekcija prie Lietuvos Respublikos finansų ministerijos*, ECLI:EU:C:2015:536, paras 32-34 and CJEU 12 November 2020, Case C-734/19 *ITH Comercial Timişoara SRL v Agenţia Naţională de Administrare Fiscală – Direcţia Generală Regională a Finanţelor Publice Bucureşti and Agenţia Naţională de Administrare Fiscală – Direcţia Generală Regională a Finanţelor Publice Bucureşti – Administraţia Sector 1 a Finanţelor Publice*, ECLI:EU:C:2020:919, para. 50.
65. *Ibid.*, para. 35.
66. CJEU 3 June 2018, Case C-665/16 *Gmina Wrocław III (Compensation for construction national road)*, ECLI:EU:C:2018:431, para. 36.
67. CJEU 9 December 2019, Case C-707/18 *Amărăşti Land Investment SRL v DirecŢia Generală Regională a FinanŢelor*, ECLI:EU:C:2019:1136, para. 42.

If indeed Article 14(2)(c) should be interpreted independent from Article 14(1) VAT Directive, a (deemed) supply under the commissionaire fiction should also not require that there is a transfer 'of the right to dispose of tangible property as owner' as referred to in the latter provision. However, in *Fast Bunkering*[68] the CJEU did seem to consider the criteria to the application of Article 14(1) as basic requirements to the application of Article 14(2)(c) VAT Directive.[69] In our view, *Fast Bunkering* and *Gmina Wrocław III (Compensation for construction national road)* are insofar incompatible.[70]

Article 14(2)(c) VAT Directive requires that there is a transfer of goods pursuant to a contract under which commission is payable on purchase or sale. The CJEU has interpreted the requirement of a 'contract under which commission is payable' as that the principal must give 'agency'. This means that there must be an agreement between the commission agent and the principal for the purpose of granting the agency concerned.[71] The VAT Directive does not provide in what form, written or oral, the agency must be given. Moreover, it appears that such agency agreement can originate from (civil) law.[72]

For completeness sake, we emphasize that, for the application of the scheme, it is not necessary for the intermediary to identify themselves as a 'commissionaire'. Anyone who, on his own name but on behalf of another person, supplies goods falls under the scheme. Intermediary persons who do not act in their own name but merely connect supplier and customer, however, are not covered by the commissionaire fiction. Such persons provide intermediary services. Examples include brokers, commercial agents, insurance intermediaries, etc.

3.2.4.4 The Application of Goods for Private Use

Article 16 VAT Directive provides that the application by a taxable person of goods forming part of his business assets for his private use or for that of his staff, or their

68. CJEU 3 September 2015, Case C-526/13 *Fast Bunkering Klaipeda UAB v Valstybine mokesčių inspekcija prie Lietuvos Respublikos finansų ministerijos*, ECLI:EU:C:2015:536.
69. *See*: H. van Kesteren & H. van Erp, 'Taxable Transactions', in M. Lang, et al. (eds), *CJEU: Recent Developments in Value Added Tax 2018* (Linde 2019), pp. 154-163.
70. What makes it difficult to understand these decisions is that, although there seems to be, in principle, a situation falling within the scope of Article 14(2) VAT Directive (*lex specialis*), the CJEU still assesses it against the criteria outlined in Article 14(1) VAT Directive (*lex generalis*). In *Gmina Wrocław III (Compensation for construction national road)* the CJEU ruled that Article 14(2) VAT Directive constitutes a *lex specialis* of the general concept of supply of goods in Article 14(1) VAT Directive. It indicated that the conditions of Article 14(1) were irrelevant for the application of Article 14(2) VAT Directive, for which separate criteria apply. This makes it more challenging to comprehend that in *Fast Bunkering* (and also in *Auto Lease Holland* and *Vega International*), the CJEU does attribute weight to the moment when ownership is transferred to the last party in the chain, as that is a criterion derived from the *lex generalis* of Article 14(1) VAT Directive.
71. CJEU 12 November 2020, Case C-734/19 *ITH Comercial Timişoara SRL v Agenţia Naţională de Administrare Fiscală – Direcţia Generală Regională a Finanţelor Publice Bucureşti and Agenţia Naţională de Administrare Fiscală – Direcţia Generală Regională a Finanţelor Publice Bucureşti – Administraţia Sector 1 a Finanţelor Publice*, ECLI:EU:C:2020:919, para. 52.
72. CJEU 21 January 2021, Case C-501/19 *UCMR – ADA Asociaţia pentru Drepturi de Autor a Compozitorilor v Asociatia culturala 'Suflet de Român'*, ECLI:EU:C:2021:50.

disposal free of charge or, more generally, their application for purposes other than those of his business, is considered as a supply of goods for consideration. The provision only applies if the VAT on the goods or the component parts thereof was wholly or partly deductible.[73]

The purpose of Article 16 is similar[74] to that of Article 26 VAT Directive (*see* section 3.3.2.2) and is closely related to the right of deduction (*see* Chapter 10). Both provisions aim at ensuring the equal treatment of taxable persons and consumers, preventing that final consumption remains untaxed.[75] Their goal is to prevent the non-taxation of goods included in the assets of a business that are applied or used for private purposes as well as services provided free of charge for private purposes.[76] A final customer does not have the right to deduction of input VAT and thus bears the costs of the VAT when he purchases goods. The same result is achieved by Articles 16 and 26 VAT Directive in cases where a taxable person purchases goods or services, deducts the VAT on those purchases, subsequently applies to goods or services for consumptive purposes but is then deemed to make a supply of goods or services for consideration.[77] The provisions can be regarded as a correction mechanism to the right of deduction for goods or services on which input VAT has been deducted but are applied for consumptive purposes.

The two provisions cannot be understood as entailing a general rule under which transactions that fall outside the scope of VAT are assumed to fall within these provisions.[78] Rather, they should be understood as covering situations in which goods

73. CJEU 23 April 2009, Case C-460/07 *Sandra Puffer v Unabhängiger Finanzsenat, Außenstelle Linz*, ECLI:EU:C:2009:254, para. 49.
74. CJEU 11 December 2008, Case C-371/07 *Danfoss A/S and AstraZeneca A/S v Skatteministeriet*, ECLI:EU:C:2008:711, para. 48.
75. CJEU 26 September 1996, Case C-230/94 *Renate Enkler v Finanzamt Homburg*, ECLI: EU:C:1996:352, para. 35; CJEU 16 October 1997, Case C-258/95 *Julius Fillibeck Söhne GmbH & Co. KG v Finanzamt Neustadt*, ECLI:EU:C:1997:491, para. 25; CJEU 17 May 2001, Cases C-322/99 and C-323/99 *Finanzamt Burgdorf v Hans-Georg Fischer and Finanzamt Düsseldorf-Mettmann v Klaus Brandenstein*, ECLI:EU:C:2001:280, para. 56; CJEU 20 January 2005, Case C-412/03 *Hotel Scandic Gåsabäck AB v Riksskatteverket*, ECLI:EU:C:2005:47, para. 23 and CJEU 11 December 2008, Case C-371/07 *Danfoss A/S and AstraZeneca A/S v Skatteministeriet*, ECLI:EU:C:2008:711, para. 46. *See also* European Commission, Common System of Value Added Tax: Uniform Basis of Assessment. Proposal for a Sixth Council Directive on the harmonization of Member States concerning turnover taxes. Submitted to the Council by the Commission. COM (73) 950 final, 20 June 1973. Bulletin of the European Communities, Supplement 11/73. Even though the case law mentioned above relates to services mentioned in Article 26 VAT Directive, we believe it is safe to argue that Article 26 VAT Directive and Article 16 VAT Directive have the same purpose.
76. *See* CJEU 16 October 1997, Case C-258/95 *Julius Fillibeck Söhne GmbH & Co. KG v Finanzamt Neustadt*, ECLI:EU:C:1997:491, para. 25, CJEU 30 September 2010, Case C-581/08 *EMI Group Ltd v The Commissioners for Her Majesty's Revenue and Customs*, ECLI:EU:C:2010:559, para. 17 and para. 30 and CJEU 16 September 2020, Case C-528/19 *Mitteldeutsche Hartstein-Industrie AG v Finanzamt Y*, ECLI:EU:C:2020:712, para. 59.
77. Following Article 168a VAT Directive, a different mechanism applies in case of mixed use of immovable property. In case of mixed use, it is not possible to deduct immediately all input VAT. *See also* Chapter 10.
78. *See* Opinion of Advocate General Mengozzi of 22 December 2008, Case C-515/07 *Vereniging Noordelijke Land- en Tuinbouw Organisatie v Staatssecretaris van Financiën*, ECLI: EU:C:2008:769, para. 38. *Also see* B.J.M. Terra & P.J. Wattel, *European Tax Law* (Kluwer 2012), p. 320.

or services are applied or used for purposes that are wholly extraneous to those of the taxable business.[79] However, they can apply only where the goods (or services) concerned are put to consumptive use, not where the goods are put to another use in a non-taxable activity (i.e., used for a non-economic activity).[80] In fact, if goods or services are used for purposes that do not hold any link with the economic activity, no right of deduction exists from the outset.[81] In our view, this also implies that Articles 16 and 26 VAT Directive cannot be applied if a taxable person purchases goods or services of which it is clear from the outset that the goods or services will *exclusively* be used for consumptive purposes (and thus not for the purposes of the taxable person's economic activity at all). After all, in such a situation, there is no objective link between the goods and/or services and the taxable person's taxable activity. It follows from CJEU case law that then no right of deduction originates.[82]

Articles 16 and 26 VAT Directive relate only to transactions effected free of charge. In this respect, it is irrelevant whether the consideration paid is higher or lower than the cost price.[83] We note that if a consideration is only symbolic, that in itself does not mean that the supply must be considered to have been carried out free of charge. It follows from *Scandic* that if a Member State wants to rule out the risk that businesses will use symbolic considerations to prevent Article 26 VAT Directive, it should take a specific action with respect to the rules with respect to the taxable amount (*see* Articles 395 and 80 VAT Directive). Nonetheless, a company making only supplies free of charge and/or for a symbolic consideration will not be considered as a taxable person (*see* Chapter 2). Furthermore, it should be noted that in an employer-employee relationship, a supply for consideration will be found to exist if the employee is required to give up a part of his or her salary as consideration for a good or service provided by the employer.[84] Then, Article 16 or 26 will not apply.

Article 16 VAT Directive effectively distinguishes between three categories of use for consumptive purposes:

(1) The application of goods forming for the taxable person's private use or for that of his staff.
(2) The disposal of goods free of charge.
(3) The application of goods for purposes other than those of his business.

---

79. *See* Opinion of Advocate General Sharpston of 23 October 2008, Case C-371/07 *Danfoss A/S and AstraZeneca A/S v Skatteministeriet*, ECLI:EU:C:2008:590, para. 38.
80. CJEU, 30 March 2006, Case C-184/04 *Uudenkaupungin kaupunki*, ECLI:EU:C:2006:214, para. 33, and CJEU 10 September 2014, Case C-92/13 *Gemeente 's-Hertogenbosch v Staatssecretaris van Financiën*, ECLI:EU:C:2014:2188, paras 25 and 26.
81. CJEU, 30 March 2006, Case C-184/04 *Uudenkaupungin kaupunki*, ECLI:EU:C:2006:214.
82. CJEU 14 September 2017, Case C-132/16 *Direktor na Direktsia 'Obzhalvane i danachno-osiguritelna praktika' – Sofia v 'Iberdrola Inmobiliaria Real Estate Investments' EOOD*, ECLI:EU:C:2017:683, CJEU 16 September 2020, Case C-528/19 *Mitteldeutsche Hartstein-Industrie AG v Finanzamt Y*, ECLI:EU:C:2020:712 and CJEU 1 October 2020, Case C-405/19 *Vos Aannemingen BVBA v Belgische Staat*, ECLI:EU:C:2020:785.
83. CJEU 20 January 2005, Case C-412/03 *Hotel Scandic Gåsabäck AB v Riksskatteverket*, ECLI:EU:C:2005:47, para. 24.
84. CJEU 20 January 2021, Case C-288/19 *QM v Finanzamt Saarbrücken*, ECLI:EU:C:2021:32.

The Taxable Person's Private Use or the Private Use of His Staff

It is settled case law that where capital goods are used both for business and for private purposes, the taxpayer has the choice of: (i) allocating those goods wholly to the assets of his business, (ii) retaining them wholly within his private assets, thereby excluding them entirely from the system of VAT, or (iii) integrating them into his business only to the extent to which they are actually used for business purposes (*see* Chapter 10, section 10.7, 'Asset Labelling').[85] If the taxable person chooses to treat movable capital goods used for both business and private purposes as business goods, he can, in principle, deduct all input VAT charged on the supply of those goods to him.[86] Subsequently, if the taxable person who wholly or partly deducted the input VAT paid on goods forming part of the assets of business applies those goods or uses those goods for the private purposes of the taxable person or of his staff, a correction to the deduction of the input VAT must be made.

The Disposal of Goods Free of Charge

Article 16 VAT Directive indicates that the disposal of goods free of charge[87] shall be treated as a supply of goods for consideration. It is in this respect in principle immaterial whether the disposal of the goods was for business purposes.[88] This implies that even if a taxable person makes a supply free of charge for business purposes (e.g., the handing out of a giveaway item to attract new customers),[89] in principle, a supply under Article 16 is regarded to take place. The Court of Justice derives this from an *a contrario* reasoning, including the second paragraph of Article 16(2) VAT Directive, which indicates that the application of goods for business use as samples or as gifts of small value shall not be treated as a supply of goods for consideration.[90] If supplies free of charge were not covered by the provisions of Article 16 VAT Directive, excluding samples and gifts of small value would be unnecessary. Apparently, the assumption is

85. CJEU 14 July 2005, Case C-434/03 *P. Charles and T.S. Charles-Tijmens v Staatssecretaris van Financiën*, ECLI:EU:C:2005:463, para. 23. *See also* CJEU 4 October 1995, Case C-291/92 *Finanzamt Uelzen v Dieter Armbrecht*, ECLI:EU:C:1995:304, para. 20; CJEU 8 March 2001, Case C-415/98 *Laszlo Bakcsi v Finanzamt Fürstenfeldbruck*, ECLI:EU:C:2001:136, paras 25 and 26; CJEU 8 May 2003, Case C-269/00 *Wolfgang Seeling v Finanzamt Starnberg*, ECLI:EU:C:2003:254, para. 40 and CJEU 21 April 2005, Case C-25/03 *Finanzamt Bergisch Gladbach v HE*, ECLI: EU:C:2005:241, para. 46.
86. CJEU 11 July 1991, Case C-97/90 *Hansgeorg Lennartz v Finanzamt München III*, ECLI: EU:C:1991:315, para. 26; CJEU 8 March 2001, Case C-415/98 *Laszlo Bakcsi v Finanzamt Fürstenfeldbruck*, ECLI:EU:C:2001:136, para. 25 and CJEU 8 May 2003, Case C-269/00 *Wolfgang Seeling v Finanzamt Starnberg*, ECLI:EU:C:2003:254, para. 41.
87. In our view, the term 'free of charge' in Articles 16 and 26(1)(b) VAT Directive should be interpreted as 'not for consideration'. The implication is that if a supply is not made for consideration in terms of Article 2 VAT Directive, it is a disposal or supply 'free of charge' under Article 16 or 26(1)(b) VAT Directive.
88. CJEU 27 April 1999, Case C-48/97 *Kuwait Petroleum (GB) Ltd v Commissioners of Customs & Excise*, ECLI:EU:C:1999:203, para. 22.
89. Provided that the supply of the giveaway item cannot be considered as being absorbed by another supply that is made for consideration. *See:* CJEU 5 October 2023, Case C-505/22 *Deco Proteste – Editores Lda v Autoridade Tributária e Aduaneira*, ECLI:EU:C:2023:731.
90. CJEU 27 April 1999, Case C-48/97 *Kuwait Petroleum (GB) Ltd v Commissioners of Customs & Excise*, ECLI:EU:C:1999:203, para. 22.

that supplies of goods free of charge also include business transactions free of charge, with the subsequent exclusion of samples or gifts of small value from the deemed supply for consideration. However, some nuance is warranted in this regard. In *Mitteldeutsche Hartstein-Industrie*,[91] the CJEU did not consider a deemed supply applicable, as in that instance, not subjecting the supply free of charge to VAT could not lead to a situation of untaxed final consumption or a violation of the principle of equal treatment.[92] In our view, this means that a disposal free of charge is only to result in a deemed supply if it otherwise gives rise to a situation of untaxed final consumption or a violation of the principle of equal treatment.

Application of Goods for Other Than Business Purposes

We believe that the category of 'application of goods for other than business purposes' is to be considered as a safety net covering situations where there is a withdrawal for private, consumptive purposes but not by the taxable person or his staff. This could include the application of goods for the benefit of the partners of a partnership or the director of an association. Support for this interpretation can be found in *Danfoss and AstraZeneca* and *VNLTO* in which the CJEU confirmed that with the phrase 'purposes other than business', there is, in fact, an implicit reference to the private purposes of the taxable person, his staff, or third parties.[93] This interpretation is also in line with the idea that Articles 16 and 26 VAT Directive cannot be understood as entailing general rules under which transactions that fall outside the scope of VAT are assumed to fall within these provisions (*see* above).

In case the business purposes of an application of goods clearly prevail over the private, consumptive purposes of such application, then the goods are being regarded as provided for purposes that are not other than those of the business. Hence, Article 16 VAT Directive will not apply.[94]

The *use of goods* forming (and remaining) part of the assets of a business for private use is regarded as a supply of services under Article 26(a) VAT Directive (*see* section 3.3.2.2).

91. CJEU 16 September 2020, Case C-528/19 *Mitteldeutsche Hartstein-Industrie AG v Finanzamt Y*, ECLI:EU:C:2020:712.
92. We assert that this also applies to services free of charge under Article 26(1)(b) VAT Directive. Cf. CJEU 16 September 2020, Case C-528/19 *Mitteldeutsche Hartstein-Industrie AG v Finanzamt Y*, ECLI:EU:C:2020:712, para. 58.
93. CJEU 11 December 2008, Case C-371/07 *Danfoss A/S and AstraZeneca A/S v Skatteministeriet*, ECLI:EU:C:2008:711 and CJEU 12 February 2009, Case C-515/07, *Vereniging Noordelijke Land- en Tuinbouw Organisatie v Staatssecretaris van Financiën ('VNLTO')*, ECLI:EU:C:2009:88. Also *see*: S.T.M. Beelen, *Aftrek van btw als belaste omzet ontbreekt (diss.)* (Deventer, Kluwer 2010), pp. 170-176.
94. *See*: CJEU 16 October 1997, Case C-258/95 *Julius Fillibeck Söhne GmbH & Co. KG v Finanzamt Neustadt*, ECLI:EU:C:1997:491 and CJEU 11 December 2008, Case C-371/07 *Danfoss A/S and AstraZeneca A/S v Skatteministeriet*, ECLI:EU:C:2008:711.

3.2.5 Optional Supplies of Goods

In addition to the (mandatory) deemed supplies of goods listed in Article 14(2) VAT Directive, Articles 14(3) and 18 VAT Directive allow for an even further expansion of the concept of 'supply of goods'. It is not quite clear why these provisions have been given the form of optional provisions. Under the Second VAT Directive and the proposal for a Sixth VAT Directive, they were mandatory provisions.[95]

3.2.5.1 Certain Works of Construction

Article 14(3) VAT Directive allows the Member States to regard the handing over of certain works of construction as a supply of goods.

Under the Second VAT Directive, Member States were required to consider the following transactions as supplies of goods:

(1) the delivery of movable property produced under a contract for work; and
(2) the delivery up of works of construction, including those in which movable property is incorporated in immovable property.

The first item, delivery of movable property produced under a contract for work, was further defined as 'the handing over by a contractor to his customer of movable property which he has made from materials and objects entrusted to him by the customer for this purpose, whether or not the contractor has provided a part of the products used'. As regards the second item, the delivery up of works of construction, Annex A (point 5) to the Second VAT Directive permitted the Member States to classify certain operations as supplies of services where, for specifically national reasons, they could not be considered as supplies of goods. Without giving a definition of 'works of construction', the Annex contained a list of examples of 'works of construction':

(1) the construction of buildings, bridges, roads, ports, etc., in performance of a building contract;
(2) earth-moving and planting of gardens;
(3) installation work (of central heating, for example);
(4) repairs to buildings, other than current maintenance.

Other work, such as simple repairs, cleaning, etc., could not be regarded as a supply of goods but was regarded as a supply of a service.[96]

---

95. European Commission, Common System of Value Added Tax: Uniform Basis of Assessment. Proposal for a Sixth Council Directive on the harmonization of Member States concerning turnover taxes. Submitted to the Council by the Commission. COM (73) 950 final, 20 June 1973. Bulletin of the European Communities, Supplement 11/73, p. 37.
96. Proposal for a Second Council Directive for the harmonization among Member States of turnover tax legislation, concerning the form and the methods of application of the common system of taxation on value added (submitted by the Commission to the Council on 14 April 1965), Explanatory Memorandum, Article 3, para. 2.f.

It seems that the Second VAT Directive sought a balance between discrepancies as regards the taxable amount, the time at which the charge to tax arises, the rate of tax and the rules for collection caused by differences in classification of the operations, on the one hand, and difficulties caused by the different concepts employed in the national laws, on the other hand.

In order to eliminate all sources of discrepancy, the European Commission proposed drawing up a list of operations to be treated as works of construction, in respect of which the detailed rules for the application of the tax are those laid down for supplies of goods. Consequently, under the proposal for the Sixth VAT Directive, Member States were required to treat the supply under a contract to make up work from customers' materials[97] and the handing over of a work of construction as defined in Article 6 of the proposed text as a supply of goods. On the basis of Article 6 of the proposal, 'works of construction' were:

(a) all works relating to buildings, bridges, roads, ports and other structures fixed to the ground, such as:
  - demolition;
  - construction, including foundations, supply of principal materials, fitting-out;
  - incorporation of moveable property in immoveable property, including all installation works;
  - extension, modification and renovation;
  - repairs and maintenance, other than day-to-day maintenance.

(b) work on preparing and improving land, such as foundation for work on industrial and residential developments, division into plots, levelling, installation of water supply and sewers, electricity supply installations, supporting walls, planting of gardens.

The final text of the Sixth VAT Directive was different from that of the proposal. The legislative history does not provide an insight into the reasons for these differences. The final text contained an *option* for the Member States to treat supplies under a contract to make up work from customers' materials[98] and the handing over of certain works of construction as supplies of goods (Article 5(5)(a) and (b) Sixth VAT Directive). The final text did not contain a definition of the concept of 'works of construction' (the proposed Article 6 was not adopted). Since the final text allows the Member States to treat certain works of construction as supplies of goods, it seems to us that - in principle - Member States are free to define the concept of works of construction. However, we believe that the list of proposed Article 6 may still be useful when interpreting the concept of 'works of construction'. From other text versions of

97. Defined as: 'the delivery by a contractor to his customer of movable property made or assembled by the contractor from materials or objects entrusted to him by the customer for this purpose, whether or not the contractor has provided a part of the products used'.
98. Defined as: 'the delivery by a contractor to his customer of movable property made or assembled by the contractor from materials or objects entrusted to him by the customer for this purpose, whether or not the contractor has provided any part of the materials used'.

the Sixth VAT Directive, it becomes even more clear that the concept relates to immovable property only.

In *Van Dijks' Boekhuis*, the CJEU explained the concept of 'production of goods from customers' materials'.[99] The CJEU confirmed that it is an independent concept of Community law and means the manufacture or assembly of movable property from materials furnished by the customer for that purpose. The CJEU ruled that the production of goods from customers' materials only takes place where a contractor produces a new article from the materials entrusted to him by his customer. The making of a new article implies the creation of an article that did not previously exist. According to the CJEU, a new article is produced when the work of the contractor results in an article whose function, according to generally accepted views, is different from that of the materials provided. A mere repair of a good, however radical it may be, which simply restores the function of the article handed over, does not amount in the creation of a new article.

Even though *Van Dijks' Boekhuis* relates to the manufacture or assembly of *movable* property rather than to works of construction relating to immovable property, we believe that it is relevant for both types of operations. Therefore, this case has remained of relevance even after the deletion, on 1 January 1996, of Article 5(5)(a) Sixth VAT Directive, on the supplies under a contract to make up work from customers' materials.[100] It was thought that the qualification of certain works on movable property as work carried out under a contract to make up work was a source of difficulty and should, therefore, be eliminated.[101] Indeed, some Member States regarded works on movable property as supplies of goods, while others treated it as supplies of services. This could give rise to double (non-)taxation in cross-border transactions.

Consequently, contract work relating to movable tangible property is regarded as a supply of services under the amended Sixth VAT Directive (and since 1 January 2007 under the VAT Directive).[102] Now, only construction works relating to *immovable* property fall within the scope of this provision. Thus, a Member State that desires to do so can regard the handing over of certain works of construction as a supply of goods if the construction leads to the creation of an immovable property that did not previously exist.

3.2.5.2 Internal Supplies

Article 18(a) VAT Directive optionally provides for a levy of VAT, even though no supply of goods for consideration takes place. The function of this provision is to

---

99. CJEU 14 May 1985, Case 139/84 *Van Dijks' Boekhuis BV v Staatssecretaris van Financiën*, ECLI:EU:C:1985:195.
100. Council Directive 95/7/EC of 10 April 1995 amending Directive 77/388/EEC and introducing new simplification measures with regard to value added tax – scope of certain exemptions and practical arrangements for implementing them [1995] OJ L102/18–24.
101. Preamble to Directive 95/7/EC.
102. *See* Chapter 4 on the place of supplies of such services. Article 17(2)(f) VAT Directive (Article 28a(5)(b), fourth indent, Sixth VAT Directive) provides that the transfer of the materials to be used in the contract work is not treated as an intra-Community supply (ICS).

prevent distortion of competition. In our view, it aims at situations where a taxable person not entitled to (full) deduction of input VAT, self-constructs (movable or immovable) goods in order to reduce the burden of VAT. After all, by self-constructing goods, the wage and profit components remain untaxed. The levy of VAT may affect the way businesses operate by interfering with regular trading patterns, which is not in conformity with the fundamental principle of neutrality of VAT. This is, in our view, the *ratio legis* of Article 18(a) VAT Directive.[103]

It appears that the CJEU attaches a different *ratio legis* to the provision. According to the CJEU, the purpose of Article 18(a) VAT Directive is to prevent that businesses that cannot deduct input VAT because of the fact that they make exempt output supplies are placed at a disadvantage as compared with competitors engaged in the same activity who use goods which they have obtained without paying VAT, by producing the goods themselves or, more generally, by obtaining them 'in the course of, [their] business'.[104]

The difference between both viewpoints is that different comparisons are made. In our view, Article 18(a) VAT Directive removes the difference between comparing businesses that can deduct input VAT and businesses that cannot deduct input VAT. The CJEU compares businesses that cannot deduct input VAT but purchase goods and services from third parties (and thus incur input VAT) with businesses that can also not deduct input VAT but obtained goods without paying VAT (and thus not incurring input VAT).

Whatever the case may be, Article 18(a) VAT Directive allows the Member States to treat as supplies of goods, the application by a taxable person for the purposes of his business of goods produced, constructed, extracted, processed, purchased or imported in the course of such business, where the VAT on such goods, had they been acquired from another taxable person, would not be wholly deductible. In our view, the term 'produced, constructed, extracted, processed etc.' means 'the making of a new good'. The criteria set out by the CJEU in *Van Dijk's Boekhuis* should be used in order to determine whether a good is created that did not previously exist (*see* section 3.2.5.1).

Example

Each month, a hospital purchases ready-made sterile culture medium for use in petri dishes intended for medical research. The third-party supplier of the culture medium issues an invoice for EUR 47,000. The total price contains costs for materials (EUR 15,000), labour costs (EUR 30,000) and a profit margin (EUR 2,000). On its invoice for the culture medium, the third-party supplier is required to charge 19% (standard rate in this particular Member State) VAT (EUR 8,930). The hospital cannot deduct the VAT as it makes exempt supplies of services itself (Article 132(1)(b) VAT Directive). The hospital's total cost price of the culture medium is, therefore, EUR 55,930. If the hospital decides to produce the culture medium itself, the cost price will consist of EUR

103. *See also* Opinion of Advocate General Mengozzi of 15 October 2015, Case C-128/14 *Het Oudeland Beheer*, ECLI:EU:C:2015:698, para. 36.

104. CJEU 8 November 2012, Case C-299/11 *Staatssecretaris van Financiën v Gemeente Vlaardingen*, ECLI:EU:C:2012:698.

17,850 materials (VAT inclusive) and EUR 30,000 labour costs. In that case, the total cost price is EUR 47,850. Therefore, if no internal supply takes place, the self-produced culture medium is EUR 8,080 cheaper than the culture medium purchased from a third-party supplier. The difference in this example is caused by the VAT component on the labour (EUR 5,700), the profit margin (EUR 2,000) and the VAT on the profit margin (EUR 380).

In the Netherlands, until January 2014, the internal supply of Article 18(a) VAT Directive was designed in such a way that during the production of goods, all input VAT was deductible. The idea was that all input VAT could be attributed to the taxed(!) internal supply, which was foreseeable. This internal supply was to take place at the moment the goods are first applied for their intended purpose.

Example

The hospital from the previous example produces the culture medium itself. From a third-party supplier, it purchases EUR 15,000 materials. The third-party supplier charges EUR 2,850 VAT on this supply. The hospital can deduct the EUR 2,850 VAT since it will effect an internal supply. In order to produce the culture medium, the hospital incurs EUR 30,000 labour costs. When the culture medium is first used in petri dishes for medical research, the hospital effects an internal supply. The taxable amount consists of the EUR 15,000 materials and the EUR 30,000 labour costs, thus EUR 45,000. Therefore, the hospital must pay 19% over EUR 45,000 = EUR 8,550 to the tax authorities. As a result, the total cost price of the culture medium is EUR 53,550. Even though this is not exactly the same cost price as the cost price when purchasing ready-made culture medium from a third-party supplier, the internal supply largely takes away the VAT incentive for the hospital to produce the culture medium itself. The difference (EUR 2,380) with the cost price ready-made culture medium (EUR 55,930) is caused by the profit margin element (EUR 2,000) and the VAT on the profit margin (EUR 380).

The preliminary questions in *Gemeente Vlaardingen* raised questions about whether this approach is correct in the CJEU's view. In *Gemeente Vlaardingen*, the CJEU ruled that the taxable amount of the internal supply does not include those costs components on which VAT has already been paid. Possibly, the CJEU does not want to see any deduction of cost components on which VAT has already been paid and an internal supply only including cost components for which no VAT has been paid. The Dutch Supreme Court, in the case of *Het Oudeland Beheer BV (Oudeland),*[105] asked further clarification from the CJEU in this regard. In this case, a taxable person established in the Netherlands for VAT purposes was granted a 20-year right in rem on land on which an unfinished building was located. An annual payment (ground rent) was due in return for granting this right. This was subject to VAT, with the taxable amount being equal to the capitalized value of the right. Oudeland deducted input VAT on this amount. Subsequently, it completed the construction of the building and

105. CJEU 18 April 2016, Case C-128/14 *Het Oudeland Beheer*, ECLI:EU:C:2015:698, para. 46. *See also* Opinion of Advocate General Mengozzi of 15 October 2015, Case C-128/14 *Het Oudeland Beheer*, ECLI:EU:C:2015:698.

deducted input VAT on the associated costs. It rented out 87.5% of the building exempt from VAT and exercised the option to subject the remaining 12.5% to VAT. Before the construction had been completed, the first ground rent payment was due. Oudeland stated that the renting out of the property should be considered a self-supply, that VAT was paid on the part of the building which was to be used for VAT-exempt purposes (i.e., the 87.5%), and that, therefore, no right to deduct the input VAT for that part of the building existed. It stated that the taxable amount should, therefore, be set at the cost of completing the construction of the building plus the annual ground rent payment. The CJEU concluded that the value of a right in rem granting its holder a right of use over immovable property and the cost of completing the office building built on the land in question might be included in the taxable amount of a supply, where the taxable person has already paid VAT on that value and that cost but also deducted the VAT immediately and in full. This decision of the CJEU was later confirmed by the Supreme Court of the Netherlands.

3.2.5.3 Application for the Purposes of Non-taxable Activities

In section 3.2.4.4, we discussed the deemed (or self-)supplies that take place if a taxable person applies goods for 'private use' (Article 16 VAT Directive). A similar provision applies to services that are used privately (Article 26 VAT Directive). This mechanism of deemed supplies ensures equal treatment as between a taxable person who applies goods or services for his own private use or for that of his staff and a final consumer who acquires goods or services of the same type. It aims at making corrections as regards the application for *private* use.

Article 18(b) VAT Directive also entails a deemed supply (which is mostly referred to as an internal supply). Its nature is, however, different from that of Articles 16 and 26 VAT Directive. It provides that a Member State may regard as a supply of goods for consideration the application of goods by a taxable person for the purposes of a non-taxable area of activity, where the VAT on such goods became wholly or partly deductible. We emphasize that the private use of goods or services cannot be regarded as the use of those goods or services for a non-taxable area of activity of a taxable person.[106] Therefore, Articles 16 and 26 VAT Directive have a different scope from Article 18(b) VAT Directive. Moreover, unlike Articles 16 and 26 VAT Directive, Article 18(b) VAT Directive is an optional provision for the Member States.

The purpose of Article 18(b) VAT Directive is to avoid the enjoyment of unjustified advantages by taxable persons who initially deduct input VAT, but who change the intended use of goods so that – in retrospect – no right of deduction should have existed.[107] It thus addresses situations in which a taxable person uses goods for other purposes than was initially intended. This may occur, for example, if the goods are applied for activities which are outside the scope of VAT ('non-taxable activities'),

106. CJEU 12 February 2009, Case C-515/07 *Vereniging Noordelijke Land- en Tuinbouw Organisatie v Staatssecretaris van Financiën*, ECLI:EU:C:2009:88, para. 38.
107. *See* A.J. van Doesum, 'Taxable Amount and VAT Rates', in M. Lang, et al. (eds), *CJEU: Recent Developments in Value Added Tax 2016* (Linde 2017), pp. 245-250.

or if goods are used for exempt rather than taxed supplies.[108] The Explanatory Memorandum to the proposal for the Sixth VAT Directive mentions that the same aim (of what is now Article 18(b) VAT Directive) could have been attained by means of adjustments to deductions already made. However, according to the Explanatory Memorandum, the technique of treating these transactions as taxable supplies was chosen for reasons of impartiality and simplicity. However, the provision is optional, and the Member States simply have the option to adjust the initial deduction of input VAT on the basis of the adjustment rules (Article 184 VAT Directive).[109]

Article 18(b) VAT Directive is, for example, applicable, when an association, on the one hand, promotes the general interests of the agricultural sector for which it does not receive any specific remuneration (non-taxable area of activity),[110] and on the other hand, provides a number of individual services to its members (taxable area of activity) for which it charges a fee. If that association purchases a computer to be exclusively used for the services to its members (for its taxable area of activity), it can deduct the input VAT on that computer. If at a later stage, the association decides to apply the computer for the non-taxable area of its activity (promotion of the agricultural sector), it is deemed to make the supply of goods for consideration if the Member State in question has implemented Article 18(b) VAT Directive.

3.2.5.4 Retention of Goods When Economic Activity Ends

When a taxable person ends its business, it is possible that goods that previously belonged to the business are no longer used for economic activities but are rather applied for private use. If the business deducted the VAT on those goods, the (former) taxable person or his successors would obtain goods on which the VAT became wholly or partly deductible, even though they are (now) applied for private use. As with Articles 16 and 26 VAT Directive, Article 18(c) VAT Directive prevents the acquisition

108. Article 18(b) VAT Directive should only apply if there is an 'application of goods by a taxable person for the purposes of a non-taxable area of activity'. An exempt area of activity is, in our view, a taxable area of activity, even though there is no VAT due on the supplies. Strictly speaking, a non-taxable area of activity is an area from which only activities are carried out which are outside the scope of VAT. Therefore, the wording of Article 18(b) VAT Directive does not seem to entirely cover its purpose.
109. In *BCR Leasing* the CJEU considered that: 'it should be made clear that the adjustment provided for in Articles 184 to 186 of the VAT Directive is an integral part of the VAT deduction scheme established by that directive (CJEU 18 October 2012, Case C-234/11 *TETS Haskovo AD v Direktor na Direktsia 'Obzhalvane I upravlenie na izpalnenieto – Varna pri Tsentralno upravlenie na Natsionalnata agentsia za prihodite'*, ECLI:EU:C:2012:644, para. 30). The foregoing considerations thus do not affect any right of the tax authorities to require adjustment on the part of a taxable person under the conditions prescribed in that regard in the VAT Directive.' CJEU 17 July 2014, Case C-438/13 *BCR Leasing IFN SA v AgenŢia NaŢională de Administrare Fiscală – DirecŢia generală de administrare a marilor contribuabili and AgenŢia*, ECLI:EU:C:2014:2093, para. 32. It would seem to us that the tax authorities cannot simultaneously require an adjustment of the input VAT under Articles 184-186 of the VAT Directive and an internal supply under Article 18(b) VAT Directive. In our view, the adjustment rules take precedence over the mechanism of Article 18(b) VAT Directive.
110. CJEU 12 February 2009, Case C-515/07 *Vereniging Noordelijke Land- en Tuinbouw Organisatie v Staatssecretaris van Financiën*, ECLI:EU:C:2009:88, para. 34.

of goods that are ultimately applied for private use, without payment of VAT. The retention of goods by a taxable person, or by his successors, when he ceases to carry out a taxable economic activity, where the VAT on such goods became wholly or partly deductible upon their acquisition or upon an internal supply (*see* section 3.2.5.2) is regarded as a supply of goods for consideration.

It should be noted that Article 18(c) VAT Directive applies only with the exception of the cases referred to in Article 19 VAT Directive. The latter provision entails the so-called no-supply rule (*see* section 3.6.3). This rule entails that the transfer of totality of assets or part thereof is not regarded as a taxable supply. According to the CJEU, the no-supply rule only applies if the transferee does not immediately liquidate the activity transferred and sell the stock.[111] If a transferee continues an economic activity with the totality of assets, Article 18(c) VAT Directive should indeed not apply since there is no application of goods for private use. It seems to us that Article 18(c) VAT Directive mentions unnecessarily that it applies 'with the exception of the cases referred to in Article 19 VAT Directive'.

3.2.6 Transfer of Goods to Another Member State

Where a taxable person merely transfers its own goods to another Member State, he is regarded as making a supply of goods for a consideration, even when he does not sell the goods to a third party. Since the goods are transferred from one Member State to another Member State in the course of this deemed supply, the supply is, in fact, a (deemed) ICS. Normally, such a deemed supply is exempted with credit (zero rated). In Chapter 13, we will deal with these deemed intra-Community supplies (ICSs) *in extenso*.

3.3 SUPPLY OF SERVICES

3.3.1 Everything Which Does Not Constitute a Supply of Goods

Since VAT is meant to be a general tax on consumption, the VAT Directive gives VAT a very wide scope. In section 3.2, we discussed the supplies of goods. However, a vast part of overall consumption consists of services. The general principle is that VAT is to be levied on all services supplied for consideration by a taxable person.[112] A supply of a service is any transaction which does not constitute a supply of goods (Article 24 VAT Directive). Strictly speaking, this is not quite accurate since the VAT Directive considers intra-Community acquisitions (ICAs) of goods and the importation of goods as taxable events in themselves and not as supplies of services. Moreover, the supply of a service requires that the supplier provides an identifiable recipient with an

111. CJEU 27 November 2003, Case C-497/01 *Zita Modes Sàrl v Administration de l'enregistrement et des domaines*, ECLI:EU:C:2003:644.

112. CJEU 20 June 2002, Case C-287/00 *Commission v Germany*, ECLI:EU:C:2002:388, para. 43 and CJEU 20 November 2003, Case C-8/01 *Taksatorringen*, ECLI:EU:C:2003:621, para. 36.

identifiable benefit.[113] Nonetheless, the overall idea is clear: everything (for consideration) that is not a supply, an ICA or an importation of goods, but does provide an identifiable customer with an identifiable benefit must be taxed as a supply of services.

Article 25 VAT Directive gives a few examples of what the concept of 'supply of services' encompasses. In Article 25 VAT Directive, it is explained that the assignment of intangible property, whether or not the subject of a document establishing a title, is a supply of services. Also, the obligation to refrain from an act, or to tolerate an act or situation, is regarded as a service. The same is true for the performance of services in pursuance of an order made by or in the name of a public authority or in pursuance of the law. The list in Article 25 VAT Directive is not meant to be exhaustive. Work on movable goods (repairs), the granting of a right, intermediation, medical treatments and education are also services. The scope of 'supplies of services' is almost endless, as is that of discussions on what the scope and nature of a particular service are.

Two examples based on recent case law may serve to demonstrate that the tax authorities and the supplier of a service can have different views on the exact nature of a certain service.

Example 1

In *Asparuhovo Lake Investment Company* the question was whether the term 'supply of services' included subscription contracts for the supply of consulting services, in particular, those of a legal, commercial or financial nature, under which a supplier had agreed to be available to the customer during the period of the contract, and had undertaken to refrain from entering into contracts with a similar subject matter with the customer's competitors. To put it differently, the question was whether the supply had the nature of several individual advisory services or a more continuous nature consisting of the supplier remaining available to customers to provide advisory services if they needed them, within the contract period.[114] The decision of the CJEU was that Article 24(1) of the VAT Directive must be interpreted as meaning that the term 'supply of services' includes subscription contracts for the supply of consulting services to an undertaking, in particular, those of a legal, commercial or financial nature, under which a supplier has agreed to be available to the customer during the term of the contract. The nature of the service was, therefore, a service with a more continuous character.[115]

113. CJEU 29 February 1996, Case C-215/94 *Jürgen Mohr v Finanzamt Bad Segeberg*, ECLI:EU:C:1996:72.

114. CJEU 3 September 2015, Case C-463/14 *Asparuhovo Lake Investment Company OOD v Direktor na Direktsia 'Obzhalvane i danachno-osiguritelna praktika' Varna pri Tsentralno upravlenie na Natsionalnata agentsia za prihodite*, ECLI:EU:C:2015:542.

115. *See also* CJEU 29 October 2015, C-174/14 *Saudaçor – Sociedade Gestora de Recursos e Equipamentos da Saúde dos Açores SA*, ECLI:EU:C:2015:733, para. 37. The Court ruled that: 'In the light of the permanent and continuous nature of the planning and management services provided by Saudaçor, the fact that that compensation is determined not on the basis of individualized services but on a flat-rate and annual basis to cover the operating costs of that company is not in itself such as to affect the direct link between the supply of services made and the consideration received, the amount of which is determined in advance on the basis of well-established criteria (*see*, CJEU 27 March 2014, Case C-151/13 *Le Rayon d'Or SARL v Ministre de l'Économie et des Finances*, ECLI:EU:C:2014:185, paras 36 and 37)'.

Example 2

In *Air France – KLM,*[116] parties wished to ascertain whether the issue by an airline company of tickets is (1) subject to VAT where those tickets have not been used by passengers and the latter are unable to receive a refund, or (2) has the character of a non-taxable contractual indemnity, in other words, a compensation for possible damages. According to the CJEU, if option (1) is applicable: the issue by an airline company of tickets is subject to VAT even where the tickets issued have not been used by passengers, and the latter are unable to obtain a refund for those tickets.

Apart from the above-mentioned examples of supplies of services, some activities that do not fall under the definition of services are considered as services by fiction. Some of these fictions are mandatory for the Member States (section 3.3.2), while others are optional for the Member States (section 3.3.3).

3.3.2 Mandatory Supplies of Services

In this section, we will discuss activities that the Member States must consider as supplies of services.

3.3.2.1 (Service) Commissionaire

As we discussed in section 3.2.4.3, it follows from Article 14(2)(c) VAT Directive that the transfer of goods pursuant to a contract under which commission is payable on purchase or sale is regarded as a supply of goods. On the basis of this provision, a principal in a commissionaire set-up is regarded to make a supply of goods to the commissionaire, and the commissionaire is regarded to make a subsequent supply of goods to the customer.

Article 28 VAT Directive is the equivalent of Article 14(2)(c) VAT Directive for services. However, from its wording, it is much clearer that the commissionaire is regarded as both purchasing and supplying services: the commissionaire 'shall be deemed to have received and supplied those services himself'. As we indicated in section 3.2.4.3, the CJEU interprets these two provisions in conjunction with each other.

Unlike Article 14(2)(c) VAT Directive, Article 28 VAT Directive (Article 6(4) Sixth VAT Directive) does not have a predecessor in the Second VAT Directive. Even the proposal for a Sixth VAT Directive did not contain a provision for services like Article 28 VAT Directive. It is unclear why this provision was eventually included in the Sixth VAT Directive (and later in the VAT Directive).[117] Since the CJEU interprets Article 28

116. CJEU 23 December 2015, Joined Cases C-250/14 and C-289/14 *Air France – KLM (C-250/14) and Hop! – Brit Air SAS, Ministère des Finances et des Comptes publics (C-289/14)*, ECLI: EU:C:2015:841.

117. Arguably, the *ratio legis* of Article 28 VAT Directive is a different one. Article 28 VAT Directive may be explained by the fact that Member States may have treated or are treating the figure of a commissionaire differently in their national (civil) law. Some Member States do not consider the commissionaire as a party to the underlying transaction (similar to an agent), while others

and 14(2)(c) VAT Directive conjunctively, we suffice here with a reference to section 3.2.4.3. We note that Article 9a VAT Implementing Regulation contains a clarification or rebuttable presumption on the applicability of Article 28 VAT Directive.[118] We refer to section 3.3.4.1.

3.3.2.2 Private Use of Goods and of Services

In section 3.2.4.4, we explained that a taxable person who applies goods from his business for his private use or for that of his staff, disposes of the goods free of charge or applies goods for purposes other than those of his business is regarded as making a supply of goods for consideration. The purpose is to prevent situations of untaxed final consumption and violations of the principle of equal treatment that may occur if the VAT on the purchase of a good is deducted, after which that good is used for consumptive purposes.

A similar mechanism applicable to services is laid down in Article 26 VAT Directive. We refer to section 3.2.4.4. However, in contrast to Article 16 VAT Directive (on the application of goods for private use), Member States may derogate from Article 26(1) VAT Directive regarding services, provided that such derogation does not lead to distortion of competition (Article 26(2) VAT Directive). Article 26(1) VAT Directive distinguishes two situations:

(1) The situation in which a taxable person *uses* goods forming part of the assets of a business for the private use of a taxable person or of his staff or for purposes other than those of his business.
(2) The situation in which a taxable person *supplies services free of charge* for his private use or for that of his staff or for purposes other than those of his business.

Use of (Movable)[119] *Goods*

Where Article 16 VAT Directive covers the *application of goods* for private use (the goods no longer form part of the assets of the business), under Article 26(1)(a) VAT Directive, the *use* of movable goods forming (and remaining) part of the assets of a business (taxable person) for the private use of a taxable person or of his staff or, more

do recognize the commissionaire as a party to it. The application of the commissionaire fictions serves to eliminate any differences between Member States in this regard. *See* A.J. van Doesum & H.W.M. van Kesteren, *De commissionair in de btw* (WFR 2021/109).

118. Since Article 9a VAT Implementing Regulation is to be regarded as a mere clarification or rebuttable presumption on the applicability of Article 28 VAT Directive *and* Articles 28 and 14(2)(c) VAT Directive must be interpreted conjunctively, the question arises whether the clarifications laid down in Article 9a VAT Implementing Regulation are also relevant to the application of Article 14(2)(c) VAT Directive. *See*: CJEU 28 February 2023, Case C-695/20 *Fenix International Limited v Commissioners for Her Majesty's Revenue and Customs*, ECLI: EU:C:2023:127.

119. Under Article 168a VAT Directive, a different mechanism applies for mixed use of immovable property. *See* Chapter 10.

generally, for purposes other than those of his business (together referred to as 'private use'), is regarded as a supply of services for consideration. The taxable amount of deemed supplies under Article 26(1)(a) is the 'full cost' of the service (*see* Chapter 6).

To a large extent, Article 26(1)(a) mirrors the categories of use for consumptive purposes of Article 16 VAT Directive. The provision only applies if the VAT on the goods was wholly or partly deductible. As is the case with Article 16 VAT Directive, this shows that Article 26(1)(a) VAT Directive is, in fact, a correction to the mechanism of full and immediate deduction of input VAT. However, unlike Article 16, it does not contain a category mirroring or echoing the category of 'disposal free of charge'. We therefore maintain that services provided 'free of charge' for business reasons fall outside the scope of Article 26(1)(a) VAT Directive. They do not lead to a deemed supply of services for consideration under that provision.[120]

Carrying Out of Services Free of Charge

Under Article 26(1)(b) VAT Directive, the supply of *services carried out free of charge* by a taxable person for his private use or for that of his staff or, more generally, for purposes other than those of his business (together referred to as 'private use'), is regarded as a supply of services for consideration. Unlike Articles 16 and 26(1)(a) VAT Directive, the condition that the provision only applies if the VAT on the services was wholly or partly deductible is not present. It is not entirely clear why this condition is omitted in Article 26(1)(b) VAT Directive.[121]

From CJEU case law it follows that Articles 16 and 26(1)(b) VAT Directive are not intended to establish a rule that transactions outside the scope of the system of VAT may be considered to be carried out for 'purposes other than those of the business' within the meaning of those provisions.[122] Thus, any application or use for so-called non-economic activities is not covered by these deemed supplies. However, where Article 16 VAT Directive applies to supplies free of charge, regardless of whether these supplies are made in the course of an economic activity, i.e., 'for business purposes',[123] Article 26(1)(b) appears to apply to situations where services are supplied for 'other

120. CJEU 17 November 2022, Case C-607/20 *GE Aircraft Engine Services Ltd v The Commissioners for Her Majesty's Revenue & Customs*, ECLI:EU:C:2022:884, paras 33 and 34 seem to confirm this.
121. A potential explanation is that Article 26(1)(b) VAT Directive also applies to services that are generated by the business itself. It ascertains, for example, that if an owner of a painting business orders his personnel to paint his (private) house, he is regarded as making a supply of services for consideration under Article 26(1)(b) and that if he provides his personnel with – for example – a (mobile) phone subscription for their private use, he is also regarded as making a supply of services for consideration. However, we note that if it is clear from the outset that externally purchased services will be exclusively used for the private purposes of employees, no right of deduction originates in the first place (*see* section 3.2.4.4). Applying a deemed service under Article 26(1)(b) VAT Directive in that situation will effectively amount to double taxation, which is not in line with the purpose of Article 26 nor the principle of neutrality.
122. *See*, for example: CJEU 12 February 2009, Case C-515/07, *Vereniging Noordelijke Land- en Tuinbouw Organisatie v Staatssecretaris van Financiën (VNLTO)*, ECLI:EU:C:2009:88, para. 38.
123. CJEU 27 April 1999, Case C-48/97 *Kuwait Petroleum (GB) Ltd v Commissioners of Customs & Excise*, ECLI:EU:C:1999:203.

than business purposes'. Arguably, 'services supplied for other than business purposes' in Article 26(1)(b) refers to services which are supplied for the *private* purposes of someone other than the taxable person (including his family) or his employees. This could, for example, be the private use by a partner in a partnership or the private use by the director of an association (*cf.* section 3.2.4.4). Any use free of charge for *business reasons* (such as the supply of an advice free of charge to attract a new customer) would in our view not trigger a deemed supply under Article 26(1)(b) VAT Directive. Due to the different configurations of Articles 16 and 26(1)(b), the CJEU's ruling in *Kuwait Petroleum* can in our view not be extended to Article 26(b) VAT Directive.[124]

Private Consumption Merely Incidental to the Requirements of the Business

In certain circumstances, the requirements of the business may make it necessary for the taxable person to provide goods or services to its employees or to business contacts. Sometimes, only the taxable person is able to provide the goods or services. He may even be obliged to do so. The personal benefit derived by employees from such supplies may then be of only secondary importance compared to the needs of the business. In those cases, the CJEU has accepted that Articles 16 and 26 VAT Directive do not apply. For example, a building firm that organized suitable transport free of charge for employees between their homes and the (various) workplaces pursuant to a collective agreement did not provide transport services for purposes other than those of the business.[125] The personal benefit derived by employees from such transport was regarded to be of only secondary importance compared to the needs of the business.[126] Similarly, in *Danfoss and AstraZeneca*, the CJEU ruled that although providing canteen meals to employees may constitute a use 'for other than business purposes', this may be different if the needs of the company require the employer to provide the meals.[127] The CJEU held that Article 26 VAT Directive does not cover the provision, free of charge, of meals in company canteens to business contacts in the course of meetings held on the company premises where there is objective evidence that those meals are provided for strictly business-related purposes. Likewise, Article 26 VAT Directive does not apply to the provision, free of charge, of meals by a company to its staff on its premises, if the needs of the company, such as the to ensure that work meetings are run smoothly and without interruption, require the employer to ensure that meals are provided. Even the offering of retail vouchers that were provided to employees in the context of an employee recognition and reward programme did not fall in the scope of

124. *See* however, CJEU 17 November 2022, Case C-607/20 *GE Aircraft Engine Services Ltd v The Commissioners for Her Majesty's Revenue & Customs*, ECLI:EU:C:2022:884, paras 33 and 34.
125. CJEU 16 October 1997, Case C-258/95 *Julius Fillibeck Söhne GmbH & Co. KG v Finanzamt Neustadt*, ECLI:EU:C:1997:491.
126. Also *see*: CJEU 18 July 2013, Case C-124/12 *AES-3C Maritza East 1 EOOD v Direktor na Direktsia 'Obzhalvane i upravlenie na izpalnenieto' pri Tsentralno upravlenie na Natsionalnata agentsia za prihodite, Plovdiv*, ECLI:EU:C:2013:488.
127. CJEU 11 December 2008, Case C-371/07 *Danfoss A/S and AstraZeneca A/S v Skatteministeriet*, ECLI:EU:C:2008:711.

Article 26(1)(b) VAT Directive.[128] The personal advantage which employees derived from the supply appeared to be merely incidental to the requirements of the business.

3.3.3 Optional Supplies of Services

As regards supplies of services, the VAT Directive only contains one option for the Member States. On the basis of Article 27 VAT Directive, they can regard as a supply of services for consideration 'the supply by a taxable person of a service for the purposes of his business, where the VAT on such a service, were it supplied by another taxable person, would not be wholly deductible'. This is often referred to as an 'internal supply' of services. The provision corresponds to Article 18(a) VAT Directive that allows for an internal supply of goods. The *ratio legis* of both provisions corresponds. They aim at preventing distortions of competition that are due to business without a right to full deduction of input VAT 'in sourcing' certain activities (e.g., a hospital that does its own laundry instead of sending it to a third-party laundry). In addition, Article 27 VAT Directive can be used by the Member States to prevent distortions of competition.[129] The taxable amount is the 'open market value' of the service supplied (*see* Article 77 VAT Directive).

It is unclear why, in order for the Member States to be allowed to apply the option of Article 27 VAT Directive, they must consult the VAT Committee prior to implementing said article. The legislative history of the Sixth VAT Directive/VAT Directive also provides no clues as to the condition that the goal of applying Article 27 VAT Directive must be the prevention of distortion of competition. Perhaps the reason is that without the latter condition, even the activity of personnel of a bank (who are not entitled to full deduction of input VAT) consisting of keeping its own books or of surveillance of the bank's vault would immediately lead to an internal supply. Moreover, it has been suggested that the condition prevents the Member States from taxing companies that are not entitled to the full deduction of input VAT in a disproportionate manner.[130]

3.3.4 Platform Provisions

The VAT Implementing Regulation and the VAT Directive both contain special rules that apply to so-called (online) platforms through which certain supplies of services (*see* section 3.3.4.1) and goods (*see* section 3.3.4.2) are made. These platform provisions are connected to and/or work similar as the commissionaire provisions of Articles 28 and 14(2)(c) VAT Directive (*see* sections 3.2.4.3 and 3.3.2.1).

128. CJEU 17 November 2022, Case C-607/20 *GE Aircraft Engine Services Ltd v The Commissioners for Her Majesty's Revenue & Customs*, ECLI:EU:C:2022:884.
129. A.J. van Doesum, H.W.M. van Kesteren & G.J. van Norden, *The Internal Market and VAT: Intra-Group Transactions of Branches, Subsidiaries and VAT Groups* (2007) 1 EC Tax Review, p. 40 https://doi.org/10.54648/ecta2007005 and A.J. van Doesum & G.J. van Norden, *T(w)o Become One, Current Note on the Communication from the Commission on VAT Grouping* (2009) 6 British Tax Review, pp. 657-667.
130. G.J. van Norden, *Het concern in de btw* (*Dissertation*) (Kluwer 2007), p. 299.

3.3.4.1 *Platforms: Electronic Services and Telecommunications Services via the Internet*

Article 9a VAT Implementing Regulation contains the so-called platform fiction for electronic services and telecommunications services via the internet. If such services are provided through a telecommunications network, an interface, or a portal such as an application marketplace (also referred to as a 'platform'), then, for the purposes of Article 28 VAT Directive, the platform through which the service is provided is generally considered to act in its own name but on behalf of the provider of these services.[131]

The purpose of this mechanism is to shift the responsibility for the payment of EU VAT concerning these services from individual 'underlying' providers to the platform through which these services are provided. For example, if a customer purchases an app via the app-store on his smartphone, then the (owner of the) app-store is considered as having purchased the app from the 'underlying supplier' and having supplied it to the customer. This way, the app-store, instead of the numerous underlying suppliers, is made responsible for the correct application of VAT to the customer's purchase. This is particularly relevant in case the customer is located in a different country than the underlying supplier because normally the destination principle will apply to B2C supplies of electronic services and telecommunications services via the internet.

The CJEU has ruled that the provision merely introduces the rebuttable presumption that a taxable person through whose intervention electronic services or internet-based telephone services are provided acts in its own name but on behalf of the person providing these services. It must not be seen as an *extension* of Article 28 VAT Directive.[132]

From *Fast Bunkering Klaipėda*[133] and *ITH Comercial,*[134] it can be established that Article 28 VAT Directive must be read in conjunction with Article 14(2)(c) VAT Directive (i.e., the commissionaire fiction for the supply of goods). Since the CJEU does not consider Article 9a VAT Implementing Regulation as an extension to the basic commissionaire provision of Article 28 VAT Directive, the conclusion imposes itself that Article 9a VAT Implementing Regulation should also be relevant to the interpretation of Article 14(2)(c) VAT Directive. This could, for example, imply that the commissionaire fiction does not apply if the underlying supplier ('principal') is

131. In the explanatory notes of 3 April 2014, from the European Commission on the EU VAT changes to the place of supply of TBE services that enter into force in 2015, there is further elaboration on the way the platform fiction works.

132. CJEU 28 February 2023, Case C-695/20 *Fenix International Limited v Commissioners for Her Majesty's Revenue and Customs*, ECLI:EU:C:2023:127.

133. CJEU 3 September 2015, Case C-526/13 *UAB 'Fast Bunkering Klaipeda' v Valstybine mokesčių inspekcija prie Lietuvos Respublikos finansų ministerijos*, ECLI:EU:C:2015:536.

134. CJEU 12 November 2020, Case C-734/19 *ITH Comercial Timişoara SRL v Agenţia Naţională de Administrare Fiscală – Direcţia Generală Regională a Finanţelor Publice Bucureşti and Agenţia Naţională de Administrare Fiscală – Direcţia Generală Regională a Finanţelor Publice Bucureşti – Administraţia Sector 1 a Finanţelor Publice*, ECLI:EU:C:2020:919.

expressly designated by the middleman as the one making the supply, and this is clearly indicated in the contractual arrangements between the parties.

3.3.4.2 *Platforms: Supplies of Goods*

Not only services but also a significant portion of online trade in goods takes place through 'platforms', such as Bol.com, Amazon, eBay, and Alibaba. Under the present rules for B2C supplies of goods, such (cross-border) supplies are generally taxed in accordance with the destination principle. If no further rules were to exist, the situation would arise where each taxable person making cross-border B2C supplies of goods through a platform would have to deal with the (not overly simple) rules for distance sales (*see* Chapters 13 and 14). For this reason, Article 14a VAT Directive introduces two platform fictions for B2C cross-border supplies of goods through platforms. With these fictions, the legislator ensures that tax authorities no longer have to deal with all individual underlying taxable persons offering their goods through the platform. Conveniently, the 'underlying suppliers' have little to no obligations. Only the platform is subject to VAT obligations.

A platform (Article 14a refers to a 'marketplace, platform, portal or similar means') that facilitates a cross-border B2C supply is deemed to have received and delivered the goods itself in the following situations:

(1) non-EU distance sales with a value of no more than EUR 150 via the platform; or
(2) supplies of goods within the EU by a non-EU established supplier to a non-taxable person via the platform.

It should be noted that the platform fictions for supplies of goods as outlined above are fictions in their own right in the sense that they do not depend on nor refer to the commissionaire fiction of Article 14(2)(c) VAT Directive (*see* section 3.2.4.3). There is also a noticeable difference with the platform fiction for electronic services and telecommunication services via the internet because the VAT Implementing Regulation does not contain any rules further detailing the platform fictions for supplies of goods. We outline the VAT rules on cross-border B2C supplies of goods in more detail in Chapters 13 and 14, sections 13.4.2.2 and 14.15, respectively.

3.4 FOR CONSIDERATION

3.4.1 The Concept of 'For Consideration'

Articles 14(1) and 24(1) VAT Directive must be read in conjunction with Article 2(1)(a) VAT Directive. Article 14(1) VAT Directive defines the concept of a 'supply of goods', and Article 24(1) VAT Directive defines the concept of a 'supply of services'. Article 2(1)(a) VAT Directive and Article 2(1)(c) VAT Directive hold that the supply of goods and services, respectively, *for consideration* within the territory of a Member State by a taxable person acting as such is subject to VAT.[135] Consequently, the transfer of the right to dispose of tangible property as owner or the supply of a service granting an identifiable benefit to an identifiable customer is only taxable if it occurs 'for consideration'. This is underlined by Articles 17 and 27 VAT Directive, which provide that certain supplies of goods and services that are *not* for consideration must (nonetheless) be treated as if they were effected for consideration. It follows from the above that VAT is chargeable only on the supply of goods and services effected for consideration.[136] VAT is based on the quid pro quo principle.[137] It follows from CJEU case law that a supply of goods is made 'for consideration', if:

(1) there is a legal relationship between the provider of the goods or services and the recipient pursuant to which there is reciprocal performance;
(2) the remuneration received by the provider of the goods or services constitutes the value actually given in return for the goods or services supplied to the recipient; and
(3) there is a direct link between the goods or the services provided and the consideration received.

Furthermore, it is clear from CJEU case law that the notion of 'consideration' is the subjective value, that is to say, the value actually received, and not a value estimated according to objective criteria. It is irrelevant *how* the consideration is paid: the payment of a price carried out through an accounting operation may be sufficient for a supply to be made 'for consideration', as long as the there is indeed a reciprocal performance and the accounting operation leads to some accrual of the own resources of the supplier.[138]

In *Coöperatieve Aardappelenbewaarplaats*, the CJEU established that the term 'consideration' is an independent concept of Community law.[139] Moreover, the CJEU ruled that in order for a service to be subject to VAT, there must be a direct link between the service provided and the consideration received. In our view, the direct link

135. The requirement that a supply of goods or services must be effected for consideration is closely connected to the taxable amount. The taxable amount is everything which constitutes consideration obtained or to be obtained by the supplier in return for the supply (*see* Article 73 VAT Directive). In Chapter 6, we will deal with the taxable amount in more detail.

136. *See inter alia*: CJEU 14 July 1998, Case C-172/96 *Commissioners of Customs & Excise v First National Bank of Chicago*, ECLI:EU:C:1998:354, para. 26; CJEU 27 April 1999, Case C-48/97 *Kuwait Petroleum (GB) Ltd v Commissioners of Customs & Excise*, ECLI:EU:C:1999:203, para. 26; CJEU 21 March 2002, Case C-174/00 *Kennemer Golf & Country Club v Staatssecretaris van Financiën*, ECLI:EU:C:2002:200, para. 39; CJEU 17 September 2002, Case C-498/99 *Town & County Factors Ltd v Commissioners of Customs & Excise*, ECLI:EU:C:2002:494, para. 18; CJEU 26 June 2003, Case C-305/01 *Finanzamt Groß-Gerau v MKG-Kraftfahrzeuge-Factoring GmbH*, ECLI:EU:C:2003:377, para. 47 and CJEU 29 April 2004, Case C-77/01 *Empresa de Desenvolvimento Mineiro SGPS SA (EDM) v Fazenda Pública*, ECLI:EU:C:2004:243, para. 86.

137. *See* on this principle in more detail: A.J. van Doesum, *Contractuele samenwerkingsverbanden in de btw (Dissertation)* (Kluwer 2009), p. 207.

138. Opinion of Advocate General Bobek of 22 February 2018, Case C-665/16 *Gmina Wrocław III (Compensation for construction national road)*, ECLI:EU:C:2018:112, paras 86-88.

139. CJEU 5 February 1981, Case 154/80 *Staatssecretaris van Financiën v Association coopérative 'Coöperatieve Aardappelenbewaarplaats GA'*, ECLI:EU:C:1981:38, para. 9.

criterion is indeed a fundamental element of the VAT system. After all, the ultimate goal of VAT is to tax consumption. For efficiency reasons, the legislator chooses not to directly tax the consumption, but rather the supplies by taxable persons for which the payments by the customers are the taxable amount. Only if there is a direct link between the supplies by the taxable persons and the payments by the customers, the spending of the customers is a measure of their consumption. A link between a supply and the consideration must be regarded as direct when the supply will not be made if no consideration is paid and when no consideration will be paid if the supply is not made.[140]

According to the CJEU, the provision of services for which no definite subjective consideration is received does not constitute a provision of services 'against payment' (i.e., for consideration).[141] Consequently, the CJEU ruled that an unascertained reduction in the value of the shares possessed by the members of the cooperative in question could not be regarded as a payment received by the cooperative providing services. It is apparent that the CJEU requires that the consideration is a subjective value, that is to say, the value actually received, and not a value estimated according to objective criteria. Moreover, that consideration must be capable of being expressed in money.[142] Even where the remuneration is, in fact, a supply of a good or a service, there can be a supply for consideration. The goods or services supplied must then be expressed in money.

In *Apple and Pear,* the CJEU confirmed that the concept of the supply of services effected for consideration presupposes the existence of a direct link between the service provided and the consideration received.[143] The Apple and Pear Development Council undertook activities funded by the mandatory charges imposed upon commercial growers of apples and pears in England and Wales. The activities related to the common interests of the growers. The benefits deriving from those activities accrued to the whole industry. It was established that no relationship existed between the level of

140. *See*: CJEU 2 June 1994, Case C-33/93 *Empire Stores Ltd v Commissioners of Customs and Excise,* ECLI:EU:C:1994:225, para. 16.
141. CJEU 5 February 1981, Case 154/80 *Staatssecretaris van Financiën v Association coopérative 'Coöperatieve Aardappelenbewaarplaats GA'*, ECLI:EU:C:1981:38.
142. CJEU 23 November 1988, Case 230/87 *Naturally Yours Cosmetics Limited v Commissioners of Customs and Excise,* ECLI:EU:C:1988:508, para. 16. Compare: CJEU 5 February 1981, Case 154/80 *Staatssecretaris van Financiën v Association coopérative 'Coöperatieve Aardappelenbewaarplaats GA'*, ECLI:EU:C:1981:38, para. 13; CJEU 27 March 1990, Case C-126/88 *Boots Company plc v Commissioners of Customs and Excise,* ECLI:EU:C:1990:136, para. 19; CJEU 2 June 1994, Case C-33/93 *Empire Stores Ltd v Commissioners of Customs and Excise,* ECLI-:EU:C:1994:225, para. 18; CJEU 24 October 1996, Case C-317/94 *Elida Gibbs Ltd v Commissioners of Customs and Excise,* ECLI:EU:C:1996:400, para. 27; CJEU 16 October 1997, Case C-258/95 *Julius Fillibeck Söhne GmbH & Co. KG v Finanzamt Neustadt,* ECLI:EU:C:1997:491, para. 13; CJEU 22 October 1998, Joined Cases C-308/96 and C-94/97 *Commissioners of Customs and Excise v T.P. Madgett, R.M. Baldwin and The Howden Court Hotel,* ECLI:EU:C:1998:496, para. 40; CJEU 29 March 2001, Case C-404/99 *Commission of the European Communities v French Republic,* ECLI:EU:C:2001:192, para. 38 (regarding service charges) and CJEU 20 January 2005, Case C-412/03 *Hotel Scandic Gåsabäck AB v Riksskatteverket,* ECLI: EU:C:2005:47, para. 21.
143. CJEU 8 March 1988, Case 102/86 *Apple and Pear Development Council v Commissioners of Customs and Excise,* ECLI:EU:C:1988:120.

the benefits which individual growers obtained from the services provided by the development council and the amount of the mandatory charges which they are obliged to pay. The question was whether the Apple and Pear Development Council supplied services 'for consideration'. The CJEU ruled that since there was no direct link present, the services were not conducted 'for consideration'. Hence, the Apple and Pear Development Council did not supply taxable services. From this case, it is clear that activities in the general interest rather than in the interest of an identifiable (group of) recipient(s) are not subject to VAT.

In *Tolsma*, the CJEU further refined the concept of 'for consideration'. Tolsma was an organ-grinder who played a barrel organ on the public highway in the Netherlands. During his musical performance, he offered passers-by a collecting tin for their donations. The passers-by voluntarily made donations, whose amount they determined as they wished. They did not request Tolsma to play the music for them. The donations did not depend on the musical service. Some persons placed money, sometimes a considerable sum, in the musician's collecting tin without lingering, whereas others listened to the music for some time without making any donation at all. The question was whether Tolsma supplied services 'for consideration'. According to the CJEU, a supply is 'for consideration' if there is a legal relationship between the provider of the service and the recipient pursuant to which there is reciprocal performance, the remuneration received by the provider of the service constituting the value actually given in return for the service supplied to the recipient.[144] The CJEU ruled that the 'supply of services effected for consideration' does not include an activity consisting of playing music on the public highway, for which no remuneration is stipulated, even if the musician solicits money and receives sums whose amount, however, is neither quantified nor quantifiable. Tolsma did not make taxable supplies of services.

It does not follow from *Apple and Pear* and *Tolsma* that contributions to associations cannot be the consideration for service. The CJEU decided in *Kennemer Golf- en Countryclub* that the annual subscription fees of members of a sports association can constitute consideration for the services provided by the association, even though members who do not use, or do not regularly use the association's facilities must still pay their annual subscription fees.

The CJEU confirmed its interpretation given in *Kennemer Golf- en Countryclub* in its rulings in *Le Rayon d'Or* and *Asparuhovo*.[145] In *Le Rayon d'Or*, a healthcare supplier charged a 'healthcare lump sum' for the permanent availability of the service provider to supply, at the appropriate time, the healthcare services required by the customers.

144. CJEU 3 March 1994, Case C-16/93 *R.J. Tolsma v Inspecteur der Omzetbelasting Leeuwarden*, ECLI:EU:C:1994:80, para. 14.

145. CJEU 27 March 2014, Case C-151/13 *Le Rayon d'Or SARL v Ministre de l'Économie et des Finances*, ECLI:EU:C:2014:185 and CJEU 3 September 2015, Case C-463/14 *Asparuhovo Lake Investment Company OOD v Direktor na Direktsia 'Obzhalvane i danachno-osiguritelna praktika' Varna pri Tsentralno upravlenie na Natsionalnata agentsia za prihodite*, ECLI:EU:C:2015:542.

In *Asparuhovo,* a consultancy firm entered into subscription contracts with its customers for the supply of consulting services, under which the supplier agreed - for a fixed weekly fee - to be exclusively available to the customer during the term of the contract.

The CJEU indicated that, in essence, where the supply of services is characterized, *inter alia*, by the permanent availability of the service provider in order to supply, at the appropriate time, the services required by the customer, it is not necessary, in order to find that there is a direct link between that service and the consideration received, to establish that a payment relates to a personalized supply of services at a specific time carried out at the request of a customer. In *Kennemer Golf- en Countryclub, Le Rayon d'Or* and in *Asparuhovo* there was a supply of taxable services, to which the fixed sum related, irrespective of the number of services provided and received in each case, namely the number of rounds of golf played or the amount of care provided. The fact that the services provided are neither defined in advance nor personalized and that the payment is made in the form of a lump sum, is also not such as to affect the direct link between the supply of services made and the consideration received, the amount of which is determined in advance on the basis of well-established criteria.[146] In a case about an organization for public broadcasting activities which was funded by a compulsory statutory charge paid by owners or possessors of a radio receiver and carried out by a radio broadcasting company created by law, the CJEU ruled that there is no legal relationship between the organization and the persons liable to pay the radio fee, in the course of which there is an exchange of reciprocal performance, or direct link between that public broadcasting service and that fee.[147] Similarly, the CJEU ruled that a public national television provider and viewers of their programmes are not linked by any contractual relationship or transaction in which a price was stipulated, or even by a voluntary legal commitment made by one party towards the other. Additionally, the access of those viewers to the audiovisual media services provided by that provider was free, and the activity concerned generally benefitted all potential viewers. Hence, the CJEU concluded that no supply 'for consideration' exists.[148]

Often, the existence of a legal relationship, entailing a reciprocal performance and a direct link between a supply and the remuneration go hand in hand. However, it is important to realize that each of these three elements must be present and that if one

146. CJEU 3 September 2015, Case C-463/14 *Asparuhovo Lake Investment Company OOD v Direktor na Direktsia 'Obzhalvane i danachno-osiguritelna praktika' Varna pri Tsentralno upravlenie na Natsionalnata agentsia za prihodite*, ECLI:EU:C:2015:542, paras 38 and 39.
147. CJEU 22 June 2016, Case C-11/15, *Odvolací finanční ředitelství v Český rozhlas*, ECLI: EU:C:2016:470.
148. CJEU 16 September 2021, Case C-21/20, *Balgarska natsionalna televizia v Direktor na Direktsia 'Obzhalvane i danachno-osiguritelna praktika' – Sofia pri Tsentralno upravlenie na NAP*, ECLI:EU:C:2021:743. The CJEU indicated that this case differs from *Le Rayon d'Or* because in the latter case, a direct link existed between the supply of services provided by a residential care home for the elderly to its residents and the 'healthcare lump sum', so that such a lump sum payment constituted consideration for the supply of care services. The CJEU attached importance to the facts that the media services did not benefit persons who are likely to be clearly identified, but all potential viewers. In addition, the amount of the subsidy was determined by reference to a flat-rate per programme hour, and without taking into account the identity or the number of users of the service provided. *Also see*: CJEU 27 March 2014, Case C-151/13 *Le Rayon d'Or SARL v Ministre de l'Économie et des Finances*, ECLI:EU:C:2014:185.

of them does not exist, the supply is not made 'for consideration'. For example, in *Posnania*, a taxable person transferred ownership of immovable property to the State Treasury in payment of tax arrears. The CJEU indicated that there was clearly a supply, clearly a payment and clearly a direct link between the supply and the payment. However, it ruled that there was no legal relationship entailing reciprocal performance because the obligation for a person to pay tax is unilateral in nature. It can only result in the statutory discharge of its tax debt, even if this is done by means of the provision of immovable property. Moreover, it is a compulsory charge. According to the CJEU, such a charge, whether it relates to a sum of money or to tangible property, does not result in any performance on the part of the public authority or, therefore, in any corresponding performance on the part of the taxable person. Therefore, the supply of immovable property in payment of tax is not made 'for consideration' and does not constitute a taxable supply, because there is no reciprocal performance.[149]

While the existence of a legal relationship is a *conditio sine qua non* for a supply for consideration to exist, on occasion, the CJEU seems to interpret the concept of a 'legal relationship' extensively.[150] For example, in *EQ*, a legal relationship was found to be present between a lawyer and the adults he was appointed to represent. Even though the lawyer was appointed by a judicial authority, and even though the adults lacked legal capacity in civil matters, the CJEU deemed a legal relationship between the lawyer and the adults to be present.[151] Also, in *Apcoa Parking Danmark*, the CJEU considered that accepting general terms and conditions creates a legal relationship. Consequently, control fees payable for parking in breach of the regulations constituted consideration for the provision of a parking space.[152] Another example of an extensive interpretation of the concept of 'legal relationship' can be found in *Fluvius Antwerpen*.[153] The case deals with a consumer who was caught unlawfully using electricity. On the basis of a Decree containing rules for determining the compensation representing the advantage unlawfully obtained by that consumer, an invoice was issued to the consumer. The CJEU considered that even if the supply of electricity has occurred without the conclusion of a contract, the relationship between the clandestine consumer and the electricity distribution network operator is governed by a Decree, a legal relationship exists on the basis of which there is a supply of goods (electricity) for consideration.

In our view, it is not only the existence of a legal relationship that is important but also the scope of that relationship. In that regard, we do not agree with the CJEU's ruling in *A Oy*.[154] In this case, a demolition company which under a demolition contract took on itself to carry out demolition works was allowed if the demolition waste

149. CJEU 11 May 2017, Case C-36/16 *Minister Finansów v Posnania Investment SA*, ECLI: EU:C:2017:361.
150. CJEU 27 April 2023, Case C-677/21 *Fluvius Antwerpen v MX*, ECLI:EU:C:2023:348, para. 31.
151. CJEU 15 April 2021, Case C-846/19 *EQ v Administration de l'Enregistrement, des Domaines et de la TVA*, ECLI:EU:C:2021:277.
152. CJEU 20 January 2022, Case C-90/20, *Apcoa Parking Danmark A/S v Skatteministeriet*, ECLI:EU:C:2022:37, para. 29.
153. CJEU 27 April 2023, Case C-677/21 *Fluvius Antwerpen v MX*, ECLI:EU:C:2023:348.
154. CJEU 10 January 2019, Case C-410/17 *Proceedings brought by A Oy*, ECLI:EU:C:2019:12.

contained scrap metal, to resell that scrap metal. In substance, the CJEU was asked whether the supply of demolition services was also made in exchange for the scrap metal contained in the waste. Even though the quantity and value of the scrap metal contained in demolition waste had not been agreed in the demolition contract, the CJEU found that the supply of scrap metal was a taxable transaction, suggesting that a legal relationship, a reciprocal performance and a direct link existed. In our view, this a rather extensive interpretation of what is the essence of the transactions which risks going beyond the bounds of legal certainty.

As a last note, we point out that the notion of 'compensation' under Article 14(2)(a) VAT Directive is different from the notion 'consideration' under Article 2(1)(a) VAT Directive.[155] We refer to section 3.2.4.1. Advocate General Bobek was of the view that 'compensation' can be seen as a standardized type of consideration provided for in the specific circumstances of expropriation.

3.4.2 Payments Which Are Low in Relative and Absolute Terms

As we indicated in section 3.4.1, a 'consideration' in terms of Article 2(1)(a) VAT Directive is a subjective value. This means that the consideration is the value which the supplier actually receives, and not a value estimated according to objective criteria. This subjective nature of the remuneration serves the 'real-time' application of VAT on invoices: it allows businesses to easily apply the VAT on their invoices when they are issued. However, the reason for taking the subjective value as the consideration is mainly explained by the purpose of VAT as a tax on private consumption. This legal character of VAT requires that the taxable amount approximates as closely as possible to the value of the consumption. If the consideration were to be an objective value, the consideration, and therefore, the taxable amount would not truly reflect the underlying consumption. Only in the case of tax evasion or avoidance, Member States may use an objective value, i.e., the 'open market value' (Article 80 VAT Directive). We refer to Chapter 6, sections 6.3 and 6.12. From the subjective nature of the consideration, it follows that it is, in principle, irrelevant whether remuneration is a price above or below the cost price of the goods and/or services supplied, in order for it to constitute a consideration for a supply.[156]

However, a distinction should be made between the level of the taxable transaction ('transaction level') and the level of the economic activity ('economic activity level'). This is related to the CJEU's case law with respect to the existence of an economic activity.

155. CJEU 13 June 2018, Case C-665/16 *Gmina Wrocław III (Compensation for construction national road)*, ECLI:EU:C:2018:431. Also *see*: Opinion of Advocate General Bobek of 22 February 2018, Case C665/16 *Gmina Wrocław III (Compensation for construction national road)*, ECLI: EU:C:2018:112, para. 62.

156. CJEU 20 January 2005, Case C-412/03 *Hotel Scandic Gåsabäck AB v Riksskatteverket* [2005] ECR I-00743, para. 22 and CJEU 12 May 2016, Case 520/14 *Gemeente Borsele v Staatssecretaris van Financiën and Staatssecretaris van Financiën v Gemeente Borsele*, ECLI:EU:C:2016:334, para. 26.

In Chapter 2, section 2.4, we explained that for a supply to come into the scope of VAT, two basic tests need to be passed. The first entails determining if a person carries out transactions 'for consideration' ('transaction level'). If that is the case, the second one is determining whether that person's activities, in a broader sense, are carried out with a view to obtaining income on a continuous basis ('economic activity level').

The CJEU has confirmed that at the transaction level, it is irrelevant for the purpose of establishing whether it was a transaction for consideration whether the price paid for a supply of a service is higher or lower than the cost price and, therefore, higher or lower than the open market value.[157] At an economic activity level, when establishing the taxable person status of a person or entity, it must be determined whether the activity is permanent and is carried out in return for remuneration which is received by the person carrying out the activity. This requires a case-by-case assessment, referring to the typical conduct of an active entrepreneur in the field concerned. In this regard, it may be relevant whether the person concerned set his prices to absorb his costs and to make a profit, whether a person only bears risks of loss without any prospect of profit and/or whether a structurally loss-making situation exists.[158] We refer to Chapter 2.

A closely related issue to the consideration that is low in relative or absolute terms is whether the consideration is paid *in return for* the supply. For example, if it can be substantiated that a fee is wholly paid on other grounds (e.g., charity) than as a remuneration for the supply, arguably, the supply is not made 'for consideration'. In our view, the CJEU's ruling in *Lajvér* leaves room for such an interpretation, where it considered that in the assessment of the existence of a direct link, it might be taken into account whether the *amount* has been determined on the basis of factors that do not sufficiently reflect the quid pro quo principle.[159] We expect that sooner or later, the CJEU will be asked to further clarify its case law on how to deal with situations in which payments which are low in relative and absolute terms are made.

157. CJEU 30 March 2023, Case C-616/21 *Dyrektor Krajowej Informacji Skarbowej v Gmina L.*, ECLI:EU:C:2023:280 and CJEU 30 March 2023, Case C-612/21 *Gmina O. v Dyrektor Krajowej Informacji Skarbowej*, ECLI:EU:C:2023:279.
158. CJEU 12 May 2016, Case 520/14 *Gemeente Borsele v Staatssecretaris van Financiën and Staatssecretaris van Financiën v Gemeente Borsele*, ECLI:EU:C:2016:334, CJEU 2 June 2016, Case C-263/15 *Lajvér Meliorációs Nonprofit Kft. and Lajvér Csapadékvízrendezési Nonprofit Kft. v Nemzeti Adó- és Vámhivatal Dél-dunántúli Regionális Adó Főigazgatósága (NAV)*, ECLI: EU:C:2016:392, CJEU 30 March 2023, Case C-616/21 *Dyrektor Krajowej Informacji Skarbowej v Gmina L.*, ECLI:EU:C:2023:280 and CJEU 30 March 2023, Case C-612/21 *Gmina O. v Dyrektor Krajowej Informacji Skarbowej*, ECLI:EU:C:2023:279.
159. CJEU 2 June 2016, Case C-263/15 *Lajvér Meliorációs Nonprofit Kft. and Lajvér Csapadékvízrendezési Nonprofit Kft. v Nemzeti Adó- és Vámhivatal Dél-dunántúli Regionális Adó Főigazgatósága (NAV)*, ECLI:EU:C:2016:392, para. 49. The CJEU instructed the referring court to 'to ascertain that the fee which the applicants in the main proceedings are planning to charge does not only partly remunerate the services supplied or to be supplied and that its amount has not been determined as a result of other possible factors that could, depending on the circumstances, call into question the direct link between the services supplied and the consideration.'

3.4.3 Barter Transactions

As discussed in the previous section, a supply may still be for consideration, if the remuneration is a supply of goods or services in itself ('barter transactions'). The consideration must then be expressed in an amount of money. According to the CJEU, however, the consideration is a subjective value, not a value estimated according to objective criteria. This poses particular difficulties in respect of barter transactions.

If a taxable person supplies a good in return for a different good (without paying an additional amount of money), the subjective consideration is the value which the recipient of the supply constituting the consideration for the supply of goods attributes to the goods which he is seeking to obtain. In practical terms, it is impossible for the supplier to know that value. Therefore, the CJEU decided in *Empire Stores* that the subjective value can only be the price that the supplier has paid for the article which he is supplying.[160] If he produced the goods himself, we believe that the value should be the cost price of the goods.

Where an exchange of services between taxable persons takes place, often there is no purchase price. Neither the VAT Directive nor CJEU case law provides for a solution in such circumstances. In our view, Article 75 VAT Directive should be applied analogously in order to reach a reasonable result, i.e., the consideration must be the full cost to the taxable person providing the service. Where the service consists of the granting of the use of a good, the full cost should be the depreciation proportionate to the time increased with the costs of maintenance and improvement. In other cases, the full cost should, in our view, be the amount of money that the supplier *does not receive* now that he claimed a remuneration in kind. The criterion defined by the CJEU in *Cooperative Aardappelenbewaarplaats* that the consideration is a subjective value, capable of being expressed in money, must be applied with more flexibility in case of barter transactions.[161] In Chapter 6, section 6.6.1.2, we will further elaborate on barter transactions.

3.4.4 Subsidies

Where a taxable person receives a 'subsidy', a relevant question is whether the amount received as a subsidy is, in fact, a consideration for a supply of goods or services. In particular, it must be determined whether a direct link exists between the supplies of goods or services and the subsidy. In practice, the answer to this question is decisive for the funding of the activities. This is because often, a public body that is not a taxable person grants the subsidy. In principle, such a public body cannot deduct any input VAT. If the subsidy is to be seen as a consideration for a supply, the taxable person receiving the subsidy is, in fact, regarded as making taxable supplies to the public body. The taxable person must charge VAT on his supplies. Under those circumstances, the

160. CJEU 2 June 1994, Case C-33/93 *Empire Stores Ltd v Commissioners of Customs and Excise*, ECLI:EU:C:1994:225, para. 19.
161. A.J. van Doesum, *Contractuele samenwerkingsverbanden in de btw* (*Dissertation*) (Kluwer 2009), p. 211.

public body will require the taxable person to pay the VAT out of the subsidy amount, leaving less of the subsidy for the actual subsidized activities.

In *Mohr*, a farmer received a compensation payment from the European Community for the definitive discontinuation of milk production.[162] Given the fact that VAT is designed as a general tax with an objective character, it is not all that strange that the German government took the view that Mr Mohr provided a service (discontinuation of milk production) for consideration (the compensation). A direct link seems to be present between the service and the consideration. After all, the compensation was a necessary condition for Mr Mohr to discontinue the milk production, the discontinuation of production being a necessary requirement for the European Community to pay the compensation. Nonetheless, the CJEU ruled that there was no consumption as envisaged in the VAT system. According to the CJEU, the European Community did not, by compensating Mr Mohr to cease the milk production, acquire goods or services for its own use. The European Community acted rather in the common interest of promoting the proper functioning of the Community milk market. The CJEU held that Mr Mohr had not made a supply of services for consideration.

In a similar case, *Landboden-Agrardienste*, the CJEU repeated that a transaction consisting of an undertaking given by a farmer to reduce production is not a taxable service because it does not give rise to any consumption.[163] The farmer does not provide services to an identifiable consumer or any benefit capable of being regarded as a cost component of the activity of another person in the commercial chain.

One might think that since it is inherent in a subsidy that it is granted in the common interest, and that, therefore – on the basis of *Mohr* and *Landboden-Agrardienste* – all subsidies (where only *two parties* are involved: (1) the supplier and (2) the subsidizing customer, mostly a public body) fall outside the scope of VAT. We believe that that view cannot be accepted.

It seems to us that, when determining the direct link between a service and a subsidy/compensation, one of the aspects that needs to be tested is whether there is identifiable consumption by an identifiable consumer. Only if there is identifiable consumption by an identifiable consumer, can there be a supply for consideration which is subject to VAT. If, for example, a ministry asks a consultancy firm for advice on how it can work more efficiently, we assume that the service supplied by the consultancy firm is identifiable and that the ministry is the identifiable consumer, and not the general public, which is only indirectly profiting from the service (in *Mohr* and *Landboden-Agrardienste* the general public was the unidentifiable customer, as no public body could primarily be identified as the customer).

One must keep in mind that some subsidies are granted in cases where *three parties* are involved:

(1) the supplier of a good or a service;

162. CJEU 29 February 1996, Case C-215/94 *Jürgen Mohr v Finanzamt Bad Segeberg*, ECLI:EU:C:1996:72.

163. CJEU 18 December 1997, Case C-384/95 *Landboden-Agrardienste GmbH & Co. KG v Finanzamt Calau*, ECLI:EU:C:1997:627.

(2) the customer who pays mostly a relatively low amount compared to the costs made by the supplier (and sometimes pays nothing); and
(3) a public authority that grants a price subsidy in order to make it possible for the supplier to make those supplies without incurring losses.

It is useful to distinguish the situation in which the customer pays nothing from that where he pays a low amount (lower than the normal price of the goods or services).

If the customer receives the supply for free, but the subsidizing public entity pays the full consideration for each supply which is made by the supplier to the customer(s), the supply will be considered as being a taxable supply made to the customer (who receives the identifiable benefit) but which is paid for by a third party. In such a case, the price subsidy is the full consideration of the supply. The situation in which a subsidy is granted and no more than two parties are involved differs, in that in the first case the paying (subsidizing) party is also the identifiable customer, whereas in the latter case the customer and the party who pays the consideration are different persons (parties).

In cases where the customer pays a relatively low amount, the price subsidies are part of the taxable amount of the supply that the supplier makes to the customer (assuming that all the requirements connected to a price subsidy are met). The supply to the customer is already a taxable transaction because the customer is the identifiable consumer who receives an identifiable benefit (good or service) and pays a (small) consideration that can be seen as being directly linked to the supply concerned. Whether the price subsidy is part of the taxable amount is, therefore, not as much an issue that needs to be discussed in this chapter about taxable events, but more an item that will be outlined in Chapter 6 on the taxable amount. Nonetheless, an example may serve to illustrate the concept of price subsidies in such a situation (as being part of the taxable amount).

Example

A museum receives a subsidy of EUR 5 from the government for each visitor it welcomes in a year. The visitor pays an entrance fee of EUR 10. It is assumed that the cost price of an entrance fee will be around EUR 15. Both the consumption (entrance to a museum) and the consumer (the visitor) are identifiable.

The payment by the visitor of EUR 10 in the example above makes the supply 'already' a *taxable supply* effected for consideration (according to Article 2 VAT Directive). Everything that is paid for a supply – even if it is received from a third party, like the government in this case – can be seen as part of the consideration. Consequently, the price subsidy is part of the taxable amount of the supply made by the museum to the visitor. Effectively, it is a third-party payment[164] or a subsidy directly

164. *See*, for example: CJEU 30 March 2023, Case C-616/21 *Dyrektor Krajowej Informacji Skarbowej v Gmina L.*, ECLI:EU:C:2023:280.

linked to the price of the supply ('price subsidy') which,[165] on the basis of Article 73 VAT Directive, is in any case part of the taxable amount.

In *Office des produits wallons*, the CJEU confirmed that for a subsidy to be directly linked to the price of supplies by a subsidized body, it is necessary that the subsidy is paid specifically to the subsidized body to enable it to provide particular goods or services to a third party.[166] According to the CJEU, that makes it necessary to verify at an early stage that the purchasers of the goods or services benefit from the subsidy granted to the subsidized body. The price payable by the purchaser must be fixed in such a way that it diminishes in proportion to the subsidy granted to the seller or supplier of the goods or services, which, therefore, constitutes an element in determining the price demanded by the latter. The ultimate test is whether the fact that a subsidy is paid to the supplier allows the supplier to sell the goods or supply the services at a price lower than he would have to demand in the absence of the subsidy. To that end, the price at which the goods are sold or the services are supplied may be compared in relation to their normal cost price, or it may be examined whether the amount of the subsidy has been reduced once those goods are no longer produced. If the factors examined are significant, it must be concluded that the part of the subsidy allocated to the production and supply of the goods or supply of the services constitutes a subsidy directly linked to the price.[167]

3.4.5 Compensation for Damages

It is generally accepted that compensation for damages does not constitute a consideration for supplies of goods or services. Arguably, the reason for this is that a compensation for damages does amount to (additional) consumption. From a more technical perspective, it can be observed that a compensation for damages is not paid *in return for* a supply and, therefore, does not constitute a 'consideration' as referred to in Article 2(1)(a) VAT Directive (*see* below).

In practice, it is not always easy to determine whether a payment is compensation for damages or rather the remuneration for a supply. This is complicated by the fact that according to Article 25 VAT Directive, the obligation to refrain from an act or to tolerate a situation is a service. It is, for example, questionable whether a payment received as compensation for damages under the condition that the matter will not be

165. Theoretically, in situations like these, a distinction can be made between a third-party payment and a 'price subsidy'. A third-party payment occurs if the supplier does not lower his price and simply receives (part of) the remuneration from someone else than the recipient of the supply. In case of a price subsidy, the supplier lowers his prices with the amount of the subsidy which he receives from someone else than the recipient of the supply. Economically, these two scenarios are very similar. Regardless of what scenario applies, Article 73 VAT Directive includes the amount received from the third party/subsidizing party.

166. CJEU 22 November 2001, Case C-184/00 *Office des produits wallons ASBL v Belgian State*, ECLI:EU:C:2001:629.

167. *Ibid.*, paras 15-17.

taken to court is not a consideration for service. In *Société thermale d'Eugenié-les-Bains*, the CJEU ruled on so-called no-show payments.[168] A hotel owner collected, by way of deposits, sums paid in advance by clients when reserving rooms. Those sums were either deducted from the amount to be paid for the accommodation later, or retained by the company in cases where clients cancelled their reservations. The CJEU decided that a sum paid as a deposit is to be regarded, where the client exercises the cancellation option available to him, and that sum is retained by the hotelier as a fixed cancellation charge paid as compensation for the loss suffered as a result of client default. According to the CJEU, there is no direct link with the supply of any service. The no-show payment was a compensation for damages rather than a consideration for service.[169] Similarly, in *SAWP*, the CJEU held that the obligation on producers and importers of blank media and of recording and reproduction devices to pay fees to holders of reproduction rights could not be regarded as resulting from the supply of a service for which it constitutes the direct consideration.[170] Those fees are intended to finance fair compensation for holders of reproduction rights. This fair compensation does not constitute the direct consideration for any supply of services because it is linked to the harm resulting for those right holders from the reproduction of their protected works without their authorization. In *Air France – KLM*,[171] the CJEU decided that the payment by the customer for a flight (as a passenger) which he did not make use of and for which payment could not be reclaimed from the airline, could not be treated as a non-taxable compensation for damages (no-show payment) but was the consideration for a taxable supply.[172] The right that the customer was supposed to have received consisted of the passenger's right to benefit from the performance of obligations arising from the transport contract, regardless of whether the passenger exercises that right since the airline company fulfils the service merely *by enabling the passenger to benefit from those services* (as already discussed in section 3.3.1).

3.4.6 Recharges of Costs

It is not uncommon for businesses to pass on costs to other parties if it is believed that the costs 'belong' to those other parties. If costs are recharged to another party, essentially two questions arise.

The first question is whether the payment following the recharge is to be regarded as a consideration for a (taxable) supply made by the taxable person that has recharged the costs. In our assessment, there are situations where no taxable transaction can be

168. CJEU 18 July 2007, Case C-277/05 *Société thermale d'Eugénie-les-Bains v Ministère de l'Économie, des Finances et de l'Industrie*, ECLI:EU:C:2007:440.
169. *Ibid.*
170. CJEU 18 January 2017, Case C-37/16 *Minister Finansów v Stowarzyszenie Artystów Wykonawców Utworów Muzycznych i Słowno-Muzycznych SAWP (SAWP)*, ECLI:EU:C:2017:22, paras 19-34.
171. CJEU 23 December 2015, Joined Cases C-250/14 and C-289/14 *Air France – KLM (C-250/14) and Hop! – Brit Air SAS, Ministère des Finances et des Comptes publics (C-289/14)*, ECLI:EU:C:2015:841.
172. *Ibid.*

found to exist.[173] It is important to acknowledge that the recharge itself is – from a VAT perspective – nothing more than a notification or request for payment. It is the payment itself that follows from such notification or request that may be relevant for VAT.

The second question relates to the extent to which the taxable person recharging the costs can deduct the VAT on goods or services it has purchased and for which it has passed on the costs. We refer to Chapter 10 on the Right of Deduction.[174]

As regards the first question on the existence of a taxable transaction, it is essential to ascertain whether the taxable person recharging the costs has conferred an identifiable benefit upon the other party, which can be directly linked with the payment stemming from the recharge.[175] In this context, it is irrelevant whether the full costs are recharged, a margin is added, or an amount less than the full costs is recharged.[176] In instances where the parties are interconnected, such as in the case of group companies, the determination of their capacity (whether as a third party or a shareholder) may influence the determination of whether a taxable transaction has occurred. This is because in such situations the recharge may be affected by the capital relationship. For example, a parent company may in fact decide that certain costs are allocated to a group company. In situations like that, it may be found that no identifiable benefit is provided to the other company and/or that no direct link can be established between a supply of goods or services and the payment following the recharge. In our view, the payment following such a recharge is not a directly linked remuneration for any supply of goods or services.

It should be noted that if the recharges do correspond with taxable transactions, it will be necessary to determine a taxable amount (unless the supplies are exempt). Normally, the taxable amount will simply be the amount of the recharge, unless the Member State concerned implemented the open market value rules as provided for in Article 80 of the VAT Directive.

173. Another important issue relates to the extent to which the taxable person recharging the costs can deduct the VAT on goods or services it has purchased and for which it has passed on the costs.

174. As for the right of deduction, the key question is usually whether the costs have been made in connection the taxable person's economic activity, whether they do not exceed what is necessary to allow that taxable person to carry out its economic activity and to what extent they are included in the price of the output transactions carried out by that taxable person. *See*, for example: CJEU 16 September 2020, Case C-528/19 *Mitteldeutsche Hartstein-Industrie AG v Finanzamt Y*, ECLI:EU:C:2020:712. However, the CJEU has confirmed that the right of deduction is not subject to a criterion relating to an increase in the taxable person's turnover or, more generally, to a criterion of economic profitability of the input transaction. CJEU 25 November 2021, Case C-334/20 *Amper Metal Kft v Nemzeti Adó- és Vámhivatal Fellebbviteli Igazgatósága*, ECLI:EU:C:2021:961, para. 30. We refer to Chapter 10.

175. Following Article 79(c) VAT Directive, a repayment of expenditure incurred in the name and on behalf of the customer and entered in the taxable person's books in a suspense account is excluded from the taxable amount (of any coinciding taxable transactions).

176. CJEU 11 March 2020, Case C-94/19 *San Domenico Vetraria SpA v Agenzia delle Entrate*, ECLI:EU:C:2020:193, para. 29 and CJEU 24 February 2022, Case C-605/20 *Suzlon Wind Energy Portugal – Energia Eólica Unipessoal, Lda v Autoridade Tributária e Aduaneira*, ECLI:EU:C:2022:116, para. 65.

3.4.7 Cost-Sharing and Other Pooling Agreements

It is quite common for businesses to cooperate on a contractual basis. Cooperation on a contractual basis can give businesses certain advantages that they cannot obtain on their own, without surrendering themselves completely to other businesses. Various levels of contractual cooperation can exist.[177] Parties working together can limit themselves to pooling certain assets, money ('cash pooling', 'cost-sharing'), or personnel. They can share risks or even form a new business ('joint venture', 'partnership', 'EEIG')[178] together. From a VAT perspective, cooperative contractual arrangements may lead to the creation of a new taxable person, separate from the participants.[179] Where the contractual cooperation is less overt, the general and objective character of the VAT system leads to the expectation that they provide taxable transactions for one another. They 'swap' activities, mostly services. However, for each activity in the course of a contract entailing cooperation between two separate taxable persons (not forming a VAT group), it must be determined whether, in fact, supplies of goods or services *for consideration* are effected. In some cases, in particular, when looking at certain cost-sharing agreements and certain (other) pooling agreements, a direct link which is required for a supply to be 'for consideration' cannot, or may only with great difficulty, be established. Moreover, the levy of VAT on activities within the framework of a contractual cooperation arrangement may lead to additional costs if the participants are not entitled to deduction of input VAT. In some cases, this may lead to accumulation of VAT in the production and distribution chain.

In some countries, activities within the framework of certain cost-sharing agreements remain outside the scope of VAT. This is, for instance, the case in the Netherlands. Costs shared (costs incurred and on-charged to other participants) under an agreement to share joint expenses are not to be seen as the consideration for services supplied, on condition that the actual expenses are divided among the participants on the basis of a distribution formula fixed and agreed on beforehand and on the condition that all participants, including the principal itself, bear the risk in respect of the costs in the same proportion.[180] In the UK, in some cases, paymaster services for associated companies remain outside the scope of VAT, being seen as disbursements.[181]

A legal basis in European VAT law to leave certain pooled costs, personnel or assets outside the scope of VAT is scarcely found. If there were to be a legal basis at all, it would be the CJEU's ruling in *EDM*.[182] However, in our view, *EDM* does not provide

177. For an overview and a model of various forms of contractual cooperation: A.J. van Doesum, *Contractuele samenwerkingsverbanden in de btw* (*Dissertation*) (Kluwer 2009).
178. Or EEIG, which is a legal entity based on European law to facilitate and encourage cross-border cooperation.
179. Cf. CJEU 27 January 2000, Case C-23/98 *Staatssecretaris van Financiën v J. Heerma*, ECLI:EU:C:2000:46.
180. *See* on agreements to share joint expenses further: A.J. van Doesum, *Contractuele samenwerkingsverbanden in de btw* (*Dissertation*) (Kluwer 2009).
181. VAT Notice 700/34, Staff, section 3.3, http://customs.hmrc.gov.uk/channelsPortalWebApp/downloadFile?contentID=HMCE_CL_000871 (accessed 22 December 2009).
182. CJEU 29 April 2004, Case C-77/01 *Empresa de Desenvolvimento Mineiro SGPS SA (EDM) v Fazenda Pública*, ECLI:EU:C:2004:243.

a solid basis for leaving activities in the framework of cost-sharing agreements outside the scope of VAT since the facts and circumstances in that case materially differ from those that apply in case of an agreement to share joint expenses. Moreover, in *EDM*, it was set out by the referring court and accepted by the CJEU that operations carried out by the members of three consortia were not paid for. Consequently, the CJEU held that the activities were not effected 'for consideration'.[183] Therefore, they could not be subject to VAT. There is a strong possibility that *EDM* does not contain any new insights into the scope of the VAT system. However, in her opinion in *TGE Gas*, Advocate General Kokott indicated that if the company, which is a member of an EEIG, contributes to the costs of that EEIG, no supplies for consideration take place if the sums relate to the general costs of the EIG's business activity.[184] Under such circumstances, the sums are not paid in return for any supply by the EEIG to the partner (TGE) and do not constitute consideration. The Advocate General draws an interesting parallel to the payments of dividends. It follows from *Cibo* that the payment of dividend does not constitute consideration because it solely depends on any profits having been realized (*see* Chapter 11). It can, therefore, not constitute consideration for a supply. If a member of an EEIG, such as TGE, is required to cover expenditure incurred only by virtue of his status as a Member, the payments made are simply the result of status as a member and do not, therefore, constitute consideration for a supply of services. The sums only represent an apportionment of the general costs of the EEIG among its members stemming from their duty to share in profits and to bear losses, but do not represent consideration for a specific activity.

As regards pooling arrangements under which the use of money ('cash pooling'), goods or immaterial assets are pooled, we believe that there may be situations in which the VAT system is inadequate to apply. If, for example, a vast number of participants to a pooling arrangement mutually supply services to all other participants, without any monetary considerations being paid, a direct link between the mutual services being supplied can, at some stage, no longer be effectively identified. Under four conditions, it can be argued that activities within the framework of such a pooling agreement remain outside the scope of VAT:

(1) There must be a vast number of participants involved in the arrangement.
(2) There must be objective evidence that the parties involved do not so much have the intention to mutually supply services aimed at obtaining a direct benefit from those services, but that they rather have the intention to indirectly obtain benefits from cooperating with other businesses and cannot or can only less efficiently obtain those benefits otherwise.
(3) All participants must contribute, and all participants must benefit.
(4) No cash payments for any activities within the framework of the contractual cooperation arrangement must be made (parties must settle on mutual terms).

183. *Ibid.*, paras 87 and 88.
184. Opinion of Advocate General Kokott of 3 May 2018, Case 16/17 *TGE Gas Engineering GmbH – Sucursal em Portugal v Autoridade Tributária e Aduaneira*, ECLI:EU:C:2018:302.

3.4.8 Capital Contributions to Companies and Partnerships[185]

From *KapHag*, it is clear that the entry of a new partner into a partnership in consideration for a contribution in cash, as well as the admission of a new partner into a partnership, is not a taxable transaction.[186] Capital contributions in cash are no taxable transactions or considerations for taxable transactions. This principle also applies to companies with share capital. In *Kretztechnik*, the CJEU confirmed in this regard that:

> 26. (...) a company that issues new shares is increasing its assets by acquiring additional capital, whilst granting the new shareholders a right of ownership of part of the capital thus increased. From the issuing company's point of view, the aim is to raise capital and not to provide services. As far as the shareholder is concerned, payment of the sums necessary for the increase of capital is not a payment of consideration but an investment or an employment of capital.
>
> 27. It follows that a share issue does not constitute a supply of goods or of services for consideration within the meaning of Article 2(1) of the Sixth Directive.[187]

In *W-GmbH,*[188] at first sight the CJEU seemed to confirm its previous case law in *KapHag* and *Kretztechnik*. It considered with respect to a contribution in kind that it 'comes under holding of shares', which does not amount to an economic activity, even though the contributing party is concerned also separately from the contribution supplied services for consideration to the subsidiary.[189] In Chapter 12 we will discuss the suggestion implied herein that the holding of shares and supplying services for consideration should be considered separately and that the holding of shares should never be considered an economic activity, even if it is accompanied by services for consideration. In this section we focus on two aspects:

(1) The CJEU's consideration in *W-GmbH* that a contribution in kind does not constitute an economic activity.
(2) The CJEU's ruling in *P. sp. z o.o.* (C-241/23) from which it appears that a contribution in kind does constitute a supply for consideration.

1. Contribution Not an Economic Activity?

As we indicated above, in *W-GmbH*, the CJEU considered that a contribution in kind does not constitute an economic activity. Although we agree that – in line with *KapHag* and *Kretztechnik* – a contribution in kind does not constitute a *taxable transaction*

185. This section reflects a part of the outcome of the research conducted by Ad van Doesum on contractual cooperative arrangements and VAT. *See* A.J. van Doesum, *Contractuele samenwerkingsverbanden in de btw (Dissertation)* (Kluwer 2009), pp. 540-580.
186. CJEU 26 June 2003, Case C-442/01 *KapHag Renditefonds 35 Spreecenter Berlin-Hellersdorf 3. Tranche GbR v Finanzamt Charlottenburg*, ECLI:EU:C:2003:381.
187. CJEU 26 May 2005, Case C-465/03 *Kretztechnik AG v Finanzamt Linz*, ECLI:EU:C:2005:320, paras 26 and 27.
188. CJEU 8 September 2022, Case C-98/21 *Finanzamt R v W-GmbH*, ECLI:EU:C:2022:645, para. 53.
189. *Ibid.*

because the payment of the sums[190] necessary for the increase of capital is not a payment of consideration but an investment or an employment of capital,[191] we still believe, nonetheless, that the CJEU has oversimplified the matter by stating that the contribution in kind is not an *economic activity*. In particular, we do not unconditionally subscribe to the CJEU's view that *because* contributions in kind are not economic activities, they therefore do not give rise to a right to deduct. In our view, there are three 'types' of contributions, which can arguably be considered as (directly linked to) economic activities, i.e., in which the exclusive reason does not lie outside the contributor's economic activity:[192]

(1) Strategic contribution.
This is, for example, a contribution in the framework of a strategic takeover. A strategic takeover occurs, for example, if a contributor takes (a majority of the) shares in a competitor from which the obligation arises to make a contribution.

(2) Accessory contribution.
This is, for example, the case if a contributor invests in a company from which it purchases goods and services that are required for the manufacture or supply of his own products or services (e.g., semi-finished products). Then, the investment is in fact an extension of the contributor's own economic activity (an accessory contribution).

(3) Controlling contribution.
If the contribution serves as a means to increase the contributor's controlling power over the company, allowing it to increase the supply of (management) services, the contribution may be considered as a 'controlling contribution'.

In these scenarios, we believe the contribution should be regarded as an economic activity and there should in principle be a right of deduction.

In *Polfarmex*, the CJEU ruled that if a limited company buys back shares in return for transferring immovable property, which was used in its economic activity, it carries out a taxable supply of immovable property, even though the transfer of the shares does not constitute an economic activity. In Chapter 11, we will explain that this ruling is difficult to reconcile with the notion of a capital relation between a shareholder and

190. In our view, this should not be restricted to payments in cash, but extended to payments in kind. After all, in EU VAT, there is no fundamental difference between payments in cash and in kind. *See*: CJEU 3 July 1997, Case C-330/95 *Goldsmiths (Jewellers) Ltd v Commissioners of Customs & Excise, ECLI:EU:C:1997:339*. *See* with respect to the valuation of barter transactions: R.M. Millar, *Illusory Supplies and Unacknowledged Discounts: VAT and Valuation in Consumer Transactions* (2003) 2 British Tax Review, pp. 153-184. *See* Chapter 3, section 3.4.

191. *See*: A.J. van Doesum, *Contractuele samenwerkingsverbanden in de btw* (*Dissertation*) (Kluwer 2009), pp. 540-580 and A.J. van Doesum, *Contributions to Partnerships from a European VAT Law Perspective*, (2010) 6 EC Tax Review https://doi.org/10.54648/ecta2010033.

192. *See*: A.J. van Doesum, 'Capital Contributions: VAT Neutrality, Economic Reality and Legal Certainty', in *EU Value Added Tax and Beyond, Essays in Honour of Ben Terra* (IBFD 2023), pp. 3-34.

a company and with the line of reasoning set out in cases such as *Kretztechnik* and *KapHag*.

2. Contribution in Kind Is a Taxable Transaction?

In *P. sp. z o.o.* (C-241/23), an investor obtained new shares in return for a contribution in kind. The CJEU ruled that the contribution constituted a supply for consideration.[193] The CJEU ruled that the contribution constituted a barter transaction, in which the shareholder provided real estate and in return acquired shares in P. sp. z o.o. According to the CJEU, there is a direct link between the transfer of the property and the acquisition of the shares. It is – as is evident from the fact that a taxable amount must be determined – a taxable supply.

This ruling creates tensions with the CJEU's previous case law in *Kretztechnik*, *KapHag* and in particular with *W-GmbH* in which the CJEU ruled that a contribution in kind did *not* constitute an economic activity (*see* above). There are however striking differences between *W-GmbH* and *P. sp. z o.o.* that perhaps can explain the difference between the two rulings. In *W-GmbH*, the contributor contributed services it purchased from third parties, without the partnership issuing new 'shares'. The contributions took place in proportion to each contributor's existing participation: thus, the ratios of interests in the partnerships did not change. In *P. sp. z o.o.*, the contributor who contributed an immovable property obtained new shares. Perhaps the CJEU considers the contribution by W-GmbH as a supply 'free of charge' (because no new shares are obtained), while the contribution to P. sp. z o.o. is a supply for consideration (because new shares are obtained). The idea behind *W-GmbH* could be that in case of a contribution in kind, for this contribution to be an economic one, one must not look for a link with any services that the investor (in addition to and separately from the contribution) supplies to the subsidiary, but to the contribution itself. It may be so that the CJEU believes that a contribution in kind is an economic activity (for which a right of deduction may exist) if that contribution itself can be regarded as a supply for consideration under Article 2(1)(a) of the VAT Directive.[194] A contribution 'free of charge' may then arguably 'come under holding of shares',[195] which does not amount to an economic activity; the mere holding of shares does not constitute an economic activity. Admittedly, however, it remains unclear whether the CJEU indeed holds this thought as its guiding principle. Moreover, this interpretation still creates ambiguities in its own right. This is because the ruling in *P. sp. z o.o.* (C-241/23) that the contribution constituted a supply for consideration is difficult to reconcile with the ruling in *Kretztechnik*, in which the CJEU on rather principal grounds ruled that the issue of new shares does not constitute a supply of services for consideration. It

193. CJEU 8 May 2024, Case C-241/23 *P. sp. z o.o. v Dyrektor Izby Administracji Skarbowej w Warszawie*, ECLI:EU:C:2024:392, para. 25.
194. *See*, however: A.J. van Doesum, *Contractuele samenwerkingsverbanden in de btw* (*Dissertation*) (Kluwer 2009), pp. 540-580 and A.J. van Doesum, *Contributions to Partnerships from a European VAT Law Perspective*, (2010) 6 EC Tax Review https://doi.org/10.54648/ecta2010033.
195. Cf. CJEU 8 September 2022, Case C-98/21 *Finanzamt R v W-GmbH*, ECLI:EU:C:2022:645, para. 53.

indicated that 'from the issuing company's point of view, the aim is to raise capital and not to provide services'. From the shareholder's perspective, the cash contribution following the taking of the shares is 'not a payment of consideration but an investment or an employment of capital'. The question is therefore why a shareholder obtaining new shares should be treated differently depending on the nature of his contribution: in cash or in kind? After all, it is settled CJEU case law that payments in cash are not to be treated differently from payments in kind.[196] Another perplexing issue lies in the application of the fiscal neutrality principle. Specifically, it seems contradictory that a contribution in kind in exchange for obtaining new shares is regarded as a supply within the scope of VAT (*P. sp. z o.o.*), whilst a contribution in kind leading to an increase in value of existing shares (without new ones being issued) does not constitute a supply for consideration *(W-GmbH)*.

In conclusion, there is still a fair amount of uncertainty as to whether a contribution in kind (goods, use of goods, intangibles, labour) may constitute a taxable supply or even an economic activity. The consequences of this lack of clarity are legal uncertainty and unequal treatment of similar transactions. It is inevitable that the CJEU will be impelled to elucidate these issues with greater precision in due course.

3.5 COMPOSITE SUPPLIES: ONE SINGLE SUPPLY OR VARIOUS SEPARATE SUPPLIES?[197]

Usually, it is not important whether a single supply is regarded as a supply of a good rather than as a supply of a service. However, there are situations in which the classification as a supply of a good or as a supply of services is relevant because the classification may, for example, affect the place of the supply (*see* Chapter 4), the application of an exemption (*see* Chapter 8) or the rate that applies (*see* Chapter 7). Determining the exact nature of a supply can be difficult where the transaction comprises a bundle of features and acts.

If, for example, a painter paints a house, he makes a supply of a good (the supply of paint) and a supply of a service (the application of the paint). A doctor who administers a drug to a patient by giving an intravenous injection makes a supply of a good (the medicine) and a supply of a service (the medical service of giving the injection). Basically, there are four options[198] conceivable when addressing the question of whether a transaction which comprises several elements is to be regarded as a single supply or as two or more distinct supplies:

196. CJEU 3 July 1997, Case C-330/95 *Goldsmiths (Jewellers) Ltd v Commissioners of Customs & Excise*, ECLI:EU:C:1997:339. *See* with respect to the valuation of barter transactions: R.M. Millar, *Illusory Supplies and Unacknowledged Discounts: VAT and Valuation in Consumer Transactions* (2003) 2 British Tax Review, pp. 153-184. *See* Chapter 3, section 3.4.

197. This section is partly based on: A.J. van Doesum & F. Nellen, 'Taxable Amount and VAT Rates', in M. Lang, et al. (eds), *CJEU: Recent Developments in Value Added Tax 2018* (Linde 2019), pp. 215-222.

198. CJEU 25 February 1999, Case C-349/96 *Card Protection Plan Limited v Commissioners of Customs and Excise*, ECLI:EU:C:1999:93.

(1) Each of the elements of the transaction is regarded as distinct and independent. The activities are split into separate supplies of goods or services. In the example above, this means that the painter and the doctor are regarded to make both a supply of a good (paint, medicine) and a supply of a service (painting of a house, medical service).
(2) None of the elements is considered the constituting principal element of the supply. Instead, both components of the supply are so closely linked to each other that they must be regarded as constituting a single supply[199] of its own nature ('sui generis'), with its own VAT consequences. It is difficult to apply this solution to the examples of the painter and the doctor above. The consequence would be that neither an exemption nor a reduced rate can be applied.
(3) The 'service' element is considered the constituting principal element of the supply, while one or more elements are to be regarded, by contrast, as ancillary services or supplies of goods which share the tax treatment of the principal service (exception 1, absorption). In the example above, this implies that the painter and the doctor are regarded to make a single supply of a service. The doctor's service is exempt under Article 132(1)(c) VAT Directive.
(4) The 'supply of a good' element is considered the constituting principal element of the supply, while one or more elements are to be regarded, by contrast, as ancillary services or supplies of goods which share the tax treatment of the principal supply of a good. In the example above, both the painter and the doctor make a single taxable supply of a good. No exemption applies. This does not seem to be a very likely outcome of the examples used.

From CJEU, case law rules can be derived on the basis of which composite supplies can be assessed. In this section, we discuss the issue of so-called composite supplies.

3.5.1 The CPP Doctrine

Card Protection Plan ('CPP') can be regarded as a milestone in the development of a doctrine on composite supplies.[200] CPP Ltd offered holders of credit cards a plan intended to protect them against financial loss and inconvenience resulting from the loss or theft of their cards, or of certain other items such as car keys, passports and insurance documents. The credit CPP included some services that – if judged on their individual merits – were categorized as insurance transactions (exempt) and other services that – if judged on their individual merits – were to be regarded as card registration services (taxed). The CJEU was asked whether the various services involved in the supply of the credit CPP might benefit wholly or in part from the insurance exemption.

199. *Ibid.*
200. CJEU 25 February 1999, Case C-349/96 *Card Protection Plan Limited v Commissioners of Customs and Excise*, ECLI:EU:C:1999:93.

In *CPP*, the CJEU provided a framework on the basis of which the VAT treatment of composite supplies should be determined. The CJEU has reiterated this framework many times since, and it now forms part of settled CJEU case law. The framework lays down the following rules for composite supplies:

(1) Splitting.
As a main rule, every supply (i.e., every element of the composite supply) must normally be regarded as distinct and independent. If that is the case, each element is treated as a separate service. In our view, this applies in a like manner to supplies of goods. If the main rule applies, each element of the composite supply has its own VAT consequences.

(2) Single supply from an economic point of view (exception 1).
As a first exception to the foregoing main rule, the supplies (i.e., all elements) are considered as constituting one single supply of its own nature (thus with its own VAT consequences), provided the supplies (elements) from an economic point of view comprise a single supply and should not be artificially split, so as not to distort the functioning of the VAT system. If this exception applies, the single supply should be evaluated on its own merits to determine its VAT consequences. This exception applies where the elements of the composite supply are all indispensable for carrying out the composite supply as a whole.[201] The characteristic elements of the transaction must be determined[202] from the perspective of the average consumer.[203] The body of evidence relied on for this purpose comprises various elements, the first of which, being of an intellectual nature and of decisive importance, seeks to establish whether or not the elements of the operation in question are indivisible[204] and its economic purpose, whether or not this is unique.[205] The second set of elements are of a substantive nature and not of decisive importance to the outcome of the analysis.[206] They support the analysis of the

201. CJEU 19 July 2012, Case C-44/11 *Finanzamt Frankfurt am Main V-Höchst v Deutsche Bank AG*, ECLI:EU:C:2012:484, para. 27.

202. CJEU 29 March 2007, Case C-111/05 *Aktiebolaget NN v Skatteverket*, ECLI:EU:C:2007:195, para. 22, CJEU 18 January 2018, Case C-463/16 *Stadion Amsterdam CV v Staatssecretaris van Financiën*, ECLI:EU:C:2018:22, para. 30 and CJEU 4 March 2021, Case C-581/19 *Frenetikexito – Unipessoal Lda v Autoridade Tributária e Aduaneira*, ECLI:EU:C:2021:167, para. 39.

203. CJEU 19 July 2012, Case C-44/11 *Finanzamt Frankfurt am Main V-Höchst v Deutsche Bank AG*, ECLI:EU:C:2012:484, para. 21 and CJEU 4 March 2021, Case C-581/19 *Frenetikexito – Unipessoal Lda v Autoridade Tributária e Aduaneira*, ECLI:EU:C:2021:167, para. 39.

204. CJEU 28 February 2019, Case C-278/18 *Manuel Jorge Sequeira Mesquita v Fazenda Pública*, ECLI:EU:C:2019:160, para. 30 and CJEU 4 March 2021, Case C-581/19 *Frenetikexito – Unipessoal Lda v Autoridade Tributária e Aduaneira*, ECLI:EU:C:2021:167, para. 39.

205. CJEU 2 July 2020, Case C-231/19 *Blackrock Investment Management (UK) Limited v Commissioners for Her Majesty's Revenue and Customs*, ECLI:EU:C:2020:513, para. 34 and CJEU 4 March 2021, Case C-581/19 *Frenetikexito – Unipessoal Lda v Autoridade Tributária e Aduaneira*, ECLI:EU:C:2021:167, para. 39.

206. CJEU 25 February 1999, Case C-349/96 *Card Protection Plan Limited v Commissioners of Customs and Excise*, ECLI:EU:C:1999:93, para. 31 and CJEU 4 March 2021, Case C-581/19 *Frenetikexito – Unipessoal Lda v Autoridade Tributária e Aduaneira*, ECLI:EU:C:2021:167, para. 39.

first elements, such as separate[207] or joint[208] access to the services concerned and the existence of a single invoice[209] or a separate invoice.[210]

(3) Single supply through 'absorption' (exception 2).
If the main rule does not apply and the elements of the composite supply are not to be considered as a single supply from an economic point of view, the elements may still be considered as being part of a single supply. This is the case if one or more elements are to be regarded as constituting the principal service, while one or more elements are to be regarded, by contrast, as ancillary services that share the tax treatment of the principal service. A service must be regarded as ancillary to a principal service if it from the average consumer's perspective does not constitute an aim in itself, but a means of better enjoying the principal service supplied. The fact that a single price is charged is not decisive. Even though the CJEU seemed to deem it relevant that a third party could, in principle, supply certain service-elements,[211] in *Field Fisher Waterhouse*, the CJEU confirmed that the existence of such a possibility is not decisive in itself.[212] If this exception to the main rule applies, the ancillary elements of the composite supply follow the VAT regime of the principal element of the composite supply.

3.5.2 VAT Treatment of Composite Supplies

It follows from CJEU case law that the consequences attached to the applicability of the first exception (single economic supply) are different from those attached to the second one (absorption). The line of CJEU case law on composite supplies can schematically be depicted as in Figure 3.2.

207. CJEU 17 January 2013, Case C-224/11 *BGZ Leasing sp. z o.o. v Dyrektor Izby Skarbowej w Warszawie*, ECLI:EU:C:2013:15, para. 43 and CJEU 4 March 2021, Case C-581/19 *Frenetikexito – Unipessoal Lda v Autoridade Tributária e Aduaneira*, ECLI:EU:C:2021:167, para. 39.
208. CJEU 8 December 2016, Case C-208/15 *Stock '94 Szolgáltató Zrt. v Nemzeti Adó- és Vámhivatal Dél-dunántúli Regionális Adó Főigazgatósága*, ECLI:EU:C:2016:936, para. 33 and CJEU 4 March 2021, Case C-581/19 *Frenetikexito – Unipessoal Lda v Autoridade Tributária e Aduaneira*, ECLI:EU:C:2021:167, para. 39.
209. CJEU 19 January 2012, Case C-117/11 *Purple Parking Ltd and Airparks Services Ltd v The Commissioners for Her Majesty's Revenue & Customs*, ECLI:EU:C:2012:29, para. 34 and CJEU 4 March 2021, Case C-581/19 *Frenetikexito – Unipessoal Lda v Autoridade Tributária e Aduaneira*, ECLI:EU:C:2021:167, para. 39.
210. CJEU 18 January 2018, Case C-463/16 *Stadion Amsterdam CV v Staatssecretaris van Financiën*, ECLI:EU:C:2018:22, para. 27 and CJEU 4 March 2021, Case C-581/19 *Frenetikexito – Unipessoal Lda v Autoridade Tributária e Aduaneira*, ECLI:EU:C:2021:167, para. 39.
211. CJEU 11 June 2009, Case C-572/07 *RLRE Tellmer Property sro v Finanční ředitelství v Ústí nad Labem*, ECLI:EU:C:2009:365.
212. CJEU 27 September 2012, Case C-392/11 *Field Fisher Waterhouse LLP v Commissioners for Her Majesty's Revenue and Customs*, ECLI:EU:C:2012:597.

Figure 3.2 Composite Supplies[213]

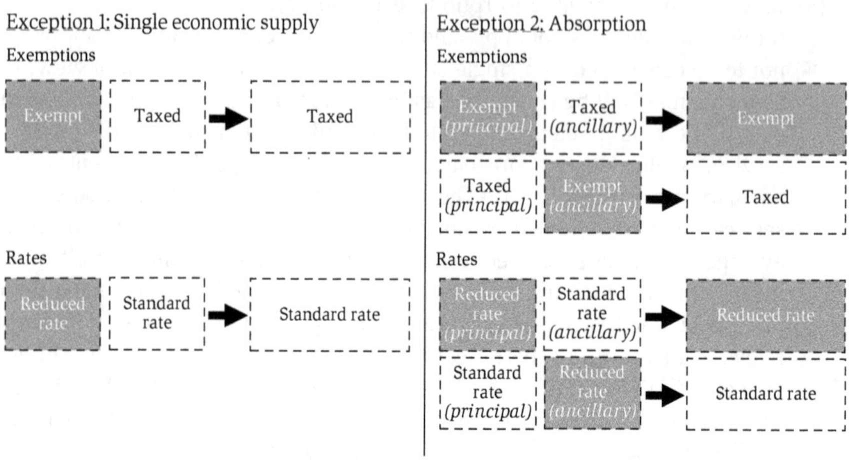

We will explain this line of CJEU case law below.

3.5.2.1 *Exception 1: Single Economic Supply*

In *Deutsche Bank*, the CJEU ruled that if a service, consisting of taxed and exempt elements, must be considered as a single economic supply for VAT purposes (i.e., the first exemption applies), that single supply cannot be exempted.[214] Exempting such supplies would go against the idea of a strict interpretation of the exemptions without a right of deduction in the VAT Directive. Similarly, in *Baštová*, the CJEU ruled that a single economic supply for VAT purposes, consisting of standard rated and reduced rated elements, can only be (wholly) taxed at the standard VAT rate.[215] An exception to this principle may arise if the exemption itself essentially relates to a combination of services, as is the case with management of special investment funds as defined by Member States cf. Article 135(1)(g) VAT Directive.[216] In such a scenario, it is conceivable that the entirety of the elements precisely falls within the description of the exemption, so that the application of that exemption to the combination of services does not entail an extensive interpretation of the relevant exemption.[217]

213. A.J. van Doesum & F. Nellen, 'Taxable Amount and VAT Rates', in M. Lang, et al. (eds), *CJEU: Recent Developments in Value Added Tax 2018* (Linde 2019), p. 218.
214. CJEU 19 July 2012, Case C-44/11 *Finanzamt Frankfurt am Main V-Höchst v Deutsche Bank AG*, ECLI:EU:C:2012:484, para. 43.
215. CJEU 10 November 2016, Case C-432/15 *Odvolací finanční ředitelství v Pavlína Baštová.*, ECLI:EU:C:2016:855.
216. CJEU 2 July 2020, Case C-231/19 *Blackrock Investment Management (UK) Limited v Commissioners for Her Majesty's Revenue and Customs*, ECLI:EU:C:2020:513.
217. The management of special investment funds is exempt, whereas the management of individual management funds is taxed. In *Blackrock*, the management services related to both special and individual management funds. The services constituted a single supply for VAT,

3.5.2.2 *Exception 2: Absorption*

Conversely, when a composite supply is considered as a single supply for VAT purposes on the basis of the absorption theory (exception 2), the ancillary elements of the supply follow the VAT treatment of the principal element. *CPP* is an example of such a situation, in which the ancillary element of a (in itself taxed) card registration service followed the VAT regime of the principal exempt insurance services. In *Stadion Amsterdam*, a case regarding the question of whether football stadium tours in combination with a visit to a museum is one single supply, the CJEU once more confirmed that it follows from the characterization of an operation comprising several elements as a single supply that that operation will be subject to one and the same rate of VAT.[218]

3.5.2.3 *Concrete and Specific Elements of a Single Supply, Elements Treated Differently?*

There is some CJEU case law which suggests that even if a composite supply is to be treated as a single supply for VAT purposes, constituent elements of the supply, which are concrete and specific, may be taxed differently from the other constituent elements of that single supply.[219] In the *Stadion Amsterdam* case, the CJEU attempted to mitigate the confusion its case law caused on 'concrete and specific elements'. To that end, in *Stadion Amsterdam*, the CJEU 'clarifies'[220] a number of its earlier rulings. According to the CJEU, there is a difference between the scope of the discretion left to the Member States by the VAT Directive (Annex III) as regards the (selective) application of a reduced rate (i.e., the application of reduced rates only to concrete and specific elements mentioned in Annex III) and the application of a reduced rate to a single

---

which must be the subject of a single tax treatment. The CJEU considered that the exemption of Article 135(1)(g) VAT Directive is defined exclusively in relation to the nature of the supply, i.e., operations for the management of special investment funds. The wording of that provision does not therefore permit the tax treatment of a single supply to be dissociated according to its uses. Moreover, the services supplied to Blackrock were designed for the purpose of managing investments of various kinds and could be used in the same way for the management of special investment funds as for the management of other funds. Therefore, the services could not be regarded as specifically for the management of special investment funds. Additionally, the CJEU considered that applying the exemption for special investment funds to the composite supply would result in the management of individual management funds - as part of the composite supply - to be exempt too. That goes against the principle of strict interpretation of the exemptions. On these grounds, among others, the CJEU found that the services should be the subject of a single tax treatment (the standard VAT rate). CJEU 2 July 2020, Case C-231/19 *Blackrock Investment Management (UK) Limited v Commissioners for Her Majesty's Revenue and Customs*, ECLI:EU:C:2020:513.

218. CJEU 8 January 2018, Case C-463/16 *Stadion Amsterdam CV v Staatssecretaris van Financiën*, ECLI:EU:C:2018:22, para. 26.
219. CJEU 8 May 2003, Case C-384/01 *European Commission v French Republic*, ECLI:EUEU:C:2003:264; CJEU 6 July 2006, Case C-251/05 *Talacre Beach Caravan Sales*, ECLI:EUEU:C:2006:451 and CJEU 6 May 2010, Case C-94/09 *European Commission v French Republic*, ECLI:EUEU:C:2010:253.
220. Arguably, the CJEU does not so much clarify its previous rulings as attempt to forcefully fit them into the mould of its other - more consistent - case law on composite supplies.

supply. Our conclusion is that only one VAT rate can be applied to a single supply.[221] We note that this single VAT treatment of such single supply may depend on the destination of the supplies of services concerned and may thus vary depending on the customer's status, for example, if the application of an exemption depends on how the services are used (*see* Article 132(1)(f) VAT Directive).[222]

3.5.2.4 Proportional Application of VAT Rates?

In *DSR*, the CJEU seems to have deviated from the idea that a single supply can only be taxed at one single VAT rate[223] In 2007, the VAT Directive contained provisions that allowed Member States, under certain conditions, to apply reduced rates for certain labour-intensive services, including 'renovation and repairing of private dwellings, excluding materials which account for a significant part of the value of the service supplied'. On the basis of a national provision implementing this reduced rate, DSR applied the reduced rate to the supply of its lift repair and maintenance services to shared facilities in a building that was used for both residential and non-residential purposes. The CJEU ruled that 'since renovation and repair services carried out in buildings used for non-residential purposes must remain subject to the application of the standard rate of VAT, a pro rata allocation should be made in the case of renovation and repair services relating to shared facilities in mixed-use buildings, which include units intended for private residential use and units intended for other purposes, such as commercial purposes'.[224] In our view, this ruling is not in line with the CJEU's earlier case law on the application of reduced VAT rates and exemptions in case of composite supplies if indeed the underlying assumption is that there was only one single supply (*see* sections 3.5.2.1 and 3.5.2.2).[225] In her opinion in *HPA – Construções SA*, Advocate General Kokott also draws the conclusion that the ruling in *DSR* can meaningfully only have been based on the assumption that there were two separable services.[226]

---

221. CJEU 2 July 2020, Case C-231/19 *Blackrock Investment Management (UK) Limited v Commissioners for Her Majesty's Revenue and Customs*, ECLI:EU:C:2020:513, paras 35 and 40. *Also See*: Opinion of Advocate-General Kokott, 7 September 2023, Case C-433/22 *Autoridade Tributária e Aduaneira tegen HPA – Construções SA*, ECLI:EU:C:2023:655, para. 2, footnote 2. For a critical analysis of the CJEU's ruling in Stadion Amsterdam, we refer to: A.J. van Doesum & F. Nellen, 'Taxable Amount and VAT Rates', in M. Lang, et al. (eds), *CJEU: Recent Developments in Value Added Tax 2018* (Linde 2019), pp. 215-222.
222. CJEU 2 July 2020, Case C-231/19 *Blackrock Investment Management (UK) Limited v Commissioners for Her Majesty's Revenue and Customs*, ECLI:EU:C:2020:513, para. 38. Also *see*: CJEU 4 May 2017, Case C-274/15 *European Commission v Grand Duchy of Luxembourg*, ECLI: EU:C:2017:333 and CJEU 20 November 2019, Case C-400/18 *Infohos v Belgische Staat*, ECLI:EU:C:2019:992.
223. CJEU 5 May 2022, Case C-218/21 *Autoridade Tributária e Aduaneira v DSR – Montagem e Manutenção de Ascensores e Escadas Rolantes SA*, ECLI:EU:C:2022:355.
224. *Ibid.*, para. 42.
225. *See*: A.J. van Doesum & F.J.G., 'Taxable Amount and VAT Rates', in M. Lang, et al. (eds), *CJEU: Recent Developments in Value Added Tax 2022* (Vienna, Linde 2024).
226. Opinion of Advocate-General Kokott, 7 September 2023, Case C-433/22 *Autoridade Tributária e Aduaneira tegen HPA – Construções SA*, ECLI:EU:C:2023:655, para. 2, footnote 2.

3.5.2.5 *Examples of Composite Supplies in CJEU Case Law*

Various examples of composite supplies can be found in CJEU case law. For instance, in *Morten Henriksen*, the CJEU ruled that letting of garages (taxable if considered as a single supply in its own right) closely linked to the letting of immovable (residential) property (exempt if considered as a single supply in its own right) encompassed a single composite economic transaction (exempt).[227] An example is also to be found in *Faaborg-Gelting Linien*.[228] The CJEU decided that restaurant transactions carried out on board ferries constitute supplies of services rather than supplies of goods. According to the CJEU, restaurant transactions are characterized by a cluster of features and acts; the provision of food is only one component of the composite supply in which services largely predominate. However, the CJEU made it also clear that where the transaction relates to takeaway food and is not coupled with services designed to enhance consumption on-the-spot in an appropriate setting, the transaction is not a single supply of a service. In our view, the supply of takeaway food should be considered a (single) supply of goods. In *Bertelsmann*, group companies of the Bertelsmann group gave bonuses in kind, such as books, records and bicycles, to customers who introduced new customers to Bertelsmann.[229] Bertelsmann also arranged for the delivery of the bonuses in kind. The CJEU was (among other things) asked whether the delivery of the bonuses in kind should be regarded as a single service or rather as a service incidental to the principal supply, which is the supply of the bonuses. The CJEU ruled that the supply and the delivery of the bonuses in kind together form a single transaction (a supply of goods). Referring to *CPP*, the CJEU considered the delivery incidental to the principal supply of the bonuses in kind, as the delivery service does not constitute for the customer an end in itself but a means of better enjoying the principal supply (of the bonuses).

In *Levob*, a US supplier provided Levob, an insurance company established in the Netherlands, with a standard computer program.[230] Levob was granted a non-transferable licence of unlimited duration. The actual software itself was supplied on a carrier medium. Levob acted as an importer of the product into the Netherlands. The contract under which the licence was granted and the software was supplied further stipulated that the software was to be customized by the US supplier. For each of the elements (licence, the supply of the software, the customization), a separate price was charged and paid. The CJEU was asked (among other things) if the provision of standard software developed, put on the market and recorded on a carrier by the supplier, and the subsequent customization thereof by the supplier to the purchaser's requirements, in consideration of the payment of separate prices, were to be regarded as two distinct supplies or as one single supply. The CJEU held that it would be artificial

227. CJEU 13 July 1989, Case 173/88 *Skatteministeriet v Morten Henriksen*, ECLI:EU:C:1989:329.
228. CJEU 2 May 1996, Case C-231/94 *Faaborg-Gelting Linien A/S v Finanzamt Flensburg*, ECLI: EU:C:1996:184.
229. CJEU 3 July 2001, Case C-380/99 *Bertelsmann AG v Finanzamt Wiedenbrück*, ECLI: EU:C:2001:372.
230. CJEU 27 October 2005, Case C-41/04 *Levob Verzekeringen BV and OV Bank NV v Staatssecretaris van Financiën*, ECLI:EU:C:2005:649.

to split the supply and subsequent customization of software. Therefore, even though separate prices were charged, the transactions were to be regarded as forming a single supply. Since the predominant element of that supply was the customization,[231] which is a service, the composite supply was regarded as a supply of services. We note that the CJEU did not take into consideration the fact that – since 19 March 2002 – its ruling implies that it accepts double taxation. Since that date, the physical importation of software on a carrier medium has been taxed whereby the (full) value of the software constitutes the taxable amount. If a (single) supply as in *Levob* takes place after 19 March 2002, both the importation and the service are taxable in the same country. The CJEU's ruling in *Levob* does not entail that the importation is also 'absorbed' by the supply of the principal service. Both the taxable amount of the importation and the supply of the service contain the (full) value of the software. If the customer, such as Levob, does not have a (full) right to deduction of input VAT, the same software is taxed twice.

More recently, the CJEU ruled that a nutrition monitoring service provided by a certified and authorized professional in sports facilities, potentially in the context of programmes that also include physical well-being and fitness services, constitutes a separate and independent supply of services ('splitting').[232] The provision of a subscription gift in return for taking out a subscription to periodicals constitutes a supply that is ancillary to the principal service of supplying periodicals ('absorption').[233]

3.5.3 Credit and Debit Cards

The case law mentioned above shows that, in practice, it is not always easy to determine whether a complex of transactions must be treated as separate supplies or as single, composite supplies.[234] Undoubtedly, there is even more case law at the national level of the Member States. In this respect, *Debenhams* cannot remain unmentioned.[235] Debenhams, a department store, operated a scheme aimed at avoiding accounting for output tax on the full ticket price of goods where the customer paid by credit or debit card. Normally, Debenhams had to pay a fee to the relevant card issuer for the exempt card-handling services supplied to Debenhams. Since the card issuers did not charge VAT on their services, there was no input VAT for Debenhams to recover. The card-handling services were, however, a component of the price Debenhams charged its customers. Consequently, Debenhams had to account for output VAT on the full

231. The importance of the customization of the basic software to make it useful for the professional activities of Levob and the extent, duration and cost of that customization were considered relevant elements in that regard.
232. CJEU 4 March 2021, Case C-581/19 *Frenetikexito – Unipessoal Lda v Autoridade Tributária e Aduaneira*, ECLI:EU:C:2021:167.
233. CJEU 5 October 2023, Case C-505/22 *Deco Proteste – Editores Lda v Autoridade Tributária e Aduaneira*, ECLI:EU:C:2023:731.
234. *See* for a more recent case, CJEU 16 April 2015, Case C-42/14 *Minister Finansów v Wojskowa Agencja Mieszkaniowa w Warszawie*, ECLI:EU:C:2015:229.
235. *Debenhams Retail Plc v Commissioners of Customs and Excise* (2004) EWHC 1540 (Ch). *See also*: D. Ladds & M. Chowdry, *Debenhams Retail Plc v Commissioners of Customs & Excise* (2004) 1 British Tax Review, pp. 26-36.

price of the goods. In order to remove the element of the credit card-handling services from the taxable amount of the supplies of goods to customers, Debenhams introduced a scheme. It was intended that credit or debit card customers would enter into two contracts: one with Debenhams for the sale of goods, and another with a wholly owned subsidiary of Debenhams, DCHS, by which the customer contracted with DCHS for exempt card-handling services. The UK Court nevertheless decided that there was only a single supply of goods by Debenhams to the customers. This ruling seems to be confirmed in Article 42 VAT Implementing Regulation. There, it is made clear that where a supplier of goods or services, as a condition of accepting payment by credit or debit card, requires the customer to pay an amount to himself for another undertaking, and where the total price payable by that customer is unaffected irrespective of how payment is accepted, that amount shall constitute an integral part of the taxable amount for the supply of the goods or services. In our view, that can only be true if the supply of the card-handling service and the supply of goods are together considered as one single supply of goods.

3.5.4 Two Suppliers, One Single Supply?

In all the above cases, the group of individual supplies, or the single (indivisible) supply, was made by a single supplier. In both *Part Service*[236] and in *Mapfre*,[237] the question was whether two suppliers who each made a supply to the same customer, the supplies being additional in nature, could be considered as making a single supply (with its own nature) to the customer (in which case both suppliers must charge and account for any VAT with respect to their own part in making the supply).[238] Whereas in *Part Service*, it seemed only possible to treat the additional supplies by different suppliers as one single supply by applying the principle of abuse of law, in *Mapfre*, the CJEU did not categorically rule out the possibility of treating both additional supplies by different suppliers as a single supply without referring to its case law on the abuse of right principle (there was no reference to *Part Service*, for instance). It must be stressed that in *Mapfre* the CJEU decided that in that particular case, the services by the different suppliers were not linked closely enough to be treated as one single supply, but the CJEU appeared to leave such a possibility open where it ruled:

> In those circumstances, and subject to determination by the referring court, a warranty such as that at issue in the main proceedings does not appear to be so

236. CJEU 21 February 2008, Case C-425/06 *Ministero dell'Economia e delle Finanze, formerly Ministero delle Finanze v Part Service Srl, company in liquidation, formerly Italservice Srl*, ECLI:EU:C:2008:108, para. 55: 'In that context, it may find it necessary to extend its analysis by seeking evidence of indications of the existence of an abusive practice, which is the concept with which the question referred is concerned'.
237. CJEU 16 July 2015, Case C-584/13 *Directeur général des finances publiques v Mapfre asistencia compania internacional de seguros y reaseguros SA*, and *Mapfre warranty SpA v Directeur général des finances publiques*, ECLI:EU:C:2015:488.
238. *Bookit* also seems to suggest that two suppliers can make a single supply for VAT. CJEU 26 May 2016, Case C-607/14 *Bookit Ltd v Commissioners for Her Majesty's Revenue and Customs*, ECLI:EU:C:2016:355.

> closely linked to the sale of the second-hand vehicle that those two transactions, provided, moreover, by two different suppliers, constitute an indivisible economic supply which it would be artificial to split. Consequently, they must, in principle, be considered to be distinct and independent transactions for VAT purposes.
>
> ... It is for the referring court to determine whether, having regard to the specific circumstances of the cases in the main proceedings, the sale of a second-hand vehicle and the warranty provided by an independent economic operator to the dealer selling that second-hand vehicle covering mechanical breakdowns which may affect certain parts of that vehicle are so interconnected that they must be regarded as constituting a single transaction or whether, on the contrary, they are independent transactions.[239]

With *Mapfre*, the CJEU added a whole new dimension to the discussion on the VAT treatment of composite supplies. Nonetheless, doubt remains, as in *KPC Herning,*[240] which is of a later date, the CJEU suggests, referring to *Kerrutt,*[241] which predates *Mapfre*, that the fact that legally distinct transactions carried out by different contractors cannot be classified as a single transaction for VAT.

3.6 NO SUPPLY OF GOODS OR SERVICES FOR CONSIDERATION

Despite the fact that the VAT Directive generally subjects all supplies of goods and services for consideration to taxation, there may be instances where there are supplies for consideration, but VAT cannot be applied. This occurs, for example, when the supplies of goods or services take place within the same legal entity (section 3.6.1) or within a VAT Group (section 3.6.2). Furthermore, the Union legislator has itself made an exception to the aforementioned principle in Articles 19 and 29 of the VAT Directive: the transfer of a totality of assets for consideration is nevertheless not subject to taxation by way of legal fiction (section 3.6.3). Additionally, within the framework of certain special schemes, the Union legislator has made an exception to the principle that all supplies of goods and services for consideration are subject to VAT (section 3.6.4).

3.6.1 Within the Same Legal Entity

Activities (supplies of goods or services) within the same taxable person are, in principle, not subject to tax. If, for example, the bookkeeping department of a business makes an overview of all costs incurred in relation to a specific product for the sales department, and the costs of this service by the bookkeeping department are allocated to the sales department, there is still no service for consideration for VAT purposes. It is an internal activity within the framework of the taxable person. Or, to put it differently, because the bookkeeping and the sales department cannot be regarded as

239. *Ibid.*, paras 57 and 58.
240. CJEU 4 September 2019, Case C-71/18 *Skatteministeriet v KPC Herning*, ECLI:EU:C:2019:660, paras 44-47.
241. CJEU 8 July 1986, Case 73/85 *Hans-Dieter and Ute Kerrutt v Finanzamt Mönchengladbach – Mitte*, ECLI:EU:C:1986:295.

'persons' from a VAT perspective (*see* Chapter 2), they cannot engage in a legal relationship. In *Tolsma*, the CJEU held that in order for a supply to be 'for consideration', there must be a 'legal relationship' between them. If there is no legal relationship, there cannot be a supply for consideration; hence, there cannot be a taxable event for VAT. In *FCE Bank*, the CJEU ruled that the branch of the head office was not an independent taxable person as it did not bear the economic risk arising from its business.[242] This reasoning was laid on the fact that the branch had no endowment capital, which meant that if a customer defaulted on a loan, the risk was borne entirely by the head office and not the branch. Consequently, the branch was dependent upon the head office and, with it, constituted a single taxable person. As such, no supply could exist for VAT purposes between the head office and the branch. This conclusion drawn in *FCE Bank* was further refined in *Skandia America Corporation*[243] and *Danske Bank*,[244] which have been discussed earlier in Chapter 2, section 2.6.6.2. The conclusion from these rulings is that where a branch (or a head office) belongs to a local VAT group and the head office (or the branch) is located abroad, the supplies between the head office and the branch are considered as supplies between two separate taxable persons, one of them being the VAT group (including the head office or the branch). We refer to Chapter 2, section 2.5.2.1.

3.6.2 Within a VAT Group

In Chapter 2, we showed that Article 11 VAT Directive allows the Member States to apply a so-called VAT grouping scheme. Under a VAT grouping scheme, persons established in the territory of a Member State who are legally independent, but financially, economically, and organizationally linked closely to one another, are treated as a single taxpayer. Consequently, the members of a VAT group are no longer identified separately for VAT, they can no longer file VAT declarations separately, and their intra-group supplies (supplies between the members of the VAT group) are non-existent for VAT.[245] Thus, supplies of goods or services for consideration between the members of a VAT group are not subject to VAT.[246] Supplies to persons who are

242. CJEU 23 March 2006, Case C-210/04 *Ministero dell'Economia e delle Finanze and Agenzia delle Entrate v FCE Bank plc.*, ECLI:EU:C:2006:196, para. 41.
243. CJEU 17 September 2014, Case C-7/13 *Skandia America Corp. v Skatteverket*, ECLI:EU:C:2014:2225.
244. CJEU 11 March 2021, Case C-812/19 *Danske Bank A/S, Danmark, Sverige Filial v Skatteverket*, ECLI:EU:C:2021:196.
245. CJEU 22 May 2008, Case C-162/07 *Ampliscientifica Srl, Amplifin SpA v Ministero dell'Economia e delle Finanze, Agenzia delle Entrate*, ECLI:EU:C:2008:301. *See* A.J. van Doesum & G.J. van Norden, *T(w)o Become One, Current Note on the Communication from the Commission on VAT Grouping* (2009) 6 British Tax Review, pp. 657-667.
246. In Chapter 2, section 2.6.1 we indicated that we cannot accept the CJEU's suggestion in *Norddeutsche Gesellschaft für Diakonie mbH ('NDG')* and *Finanzamt T v S.* that supplies within a VAT group are subject to VAT. As long as the CJEU has not answered the follow-up questions in the pending case *Finanzamt T v S.* II (C-184/23) to the contrary we hold that internal transactions are not subject to VAT. Obviously, it is possible that a deemed taxable supply occurs (*see* Articles 16, 18, 26 and in particular 27 VAT Directive). *See also* A.J. van Doesum,

partly excluded from the VAT group, as in *Skandia America Corporation* (*see* the previous section), are taxable.

3.6.3 Transfer of a Going Concern (Totality of Assets): The 'No-Supply Rule'

3.6.3.1 The Scope of the No-Supply Rule

On the basis of Article 19 VAT Directive, Member States may consider the transfer of a totality of assets or part thereof not to be a supply of goods, whether the transfer takes place for consideration or not, or as a contribution to a company. This rule is commonly called the 'no-supply rule' or referred to as TOGC (transfer of going concern). Article 29 VAT Directive provides that Article 19 VAT Directive applies in the same manner to services.

3.6.3.2 The Purpose of the No-Supply Rule

These provisions enable the Member States to facilitate transfers of undertakings or parts of undertakings by simplifying them and preventing cash flow disadvantages for the transferee.[247] When a Member State has made use of that option, the transfer of a totality of assets or part thereof is not regarded as a supply of goods or services for the purposes of the VAT Directive. Instead, if a transfer of a totality of assets (or part thereof) occurs, the person to whom the goods are transferred is to be treated as the successor to the transferor. Most Member States made use of this option in the VAT Directive, albeit that they apply different conditions to treat a transfer of a totality of assets or part thereof as a supply outside the scope of VAT.

3.6.3.3 The Concept of 'A Totality of Assets or Part Thereof'

The VAT Directive does not contain a definition of the concept of 'a transfer, whether for consideration or not or as a contribution to a company, of a totality of assets or part thereof'. It is, however, an independent concept of Union law. In *Zita Modes*, the CJEU ruled that it covers the transfer of a business or an independent part of an undertaking including tangible elements and, as the case may be, intangible elements which, together, constitute an undertaking or a part of an undertaking capable of carrying on an independent economic activity.[248] Conversely, it does not cover the simple transfer of assets, such as the sale of a stock of products.

H.W.M. van Kesteren & G.J. van Norden, *The Internal Market and VAT: Intra-Group Transactions of Branches, Subsidiaries and VAT Groups* (2007) 1 EC Tax Review, pp. 34-43 https://doi.org/10.54648/ecta2007005.

247. Also *see*: S.B. Cornielje, *Fusies en overnames in de Europese btw* (*Dissertation*) (Kluwer 2016).
248. CJEU 27 November 2003, Case C-497/01 *Zita Modes Sàrl v Administration de l'enregistrement et des domaines*, ECLI:EU:C:2003:644. Also *see*: CJEU 16 January 2023, Case C-729/21 *W. Sp. z o. o. v Dyrektor Izby Administracji Skarbowej w Łodzi*, ECLI:EU:C:2023:74.

It is not necessary that *all* assets are transferred. Even if some of the assets are not transferred but are hired out instead, the combination of the assets that *are* transferred may be regarded as a totality of assets. In this respect, it is required that the assets transferred are sufficient for the transferee to be able to carry on an independent economic activity on a lasting basis.[249]

In the first place, this implies that the transferee must acquire the possession of all goods (and services) that are necessary to carry out[250] the economic activity. However, there is no reason in principle why possession of those goods or services may not be transferred by means of a lease contract.[251] It should be noted that the lease itself does not fall inside the scope of the no-supply rule. If all the items necessary to pursue the economic activity are merely let, and no related property rights are transferred, no transfer of a going concern takes place.[252]

Second, this implies that the transferee must obtain more or less permanent possession of the goods (or services). Matters, such as the duration of the lease granted and the procedure agreed for terminating it, must be taken into account in an overall assessment of the transaction transferring the assets. After all, they may have a bearing on the assessment if they might make it impossible to carry on the economic activity on a lasting basis.[253]

3.6.3.4 No Immediate Liquidation Condition

It should be noted that in order for Article 19 VAT Directive to apply, the transferee must have had the intention to operate the business or the part of the undertaking transferred and not simply to immediately liquidate the activity concerned and sell the stock if any.[254] According to the CJEU in the aforementioned *Zita Modes*, there must be an intention to operate the business or the part of the undertaking transferred. However, it is not necessary that the transferee pursues the same type of economic activity as the transferor did prior to the transfer.

In principle, the transferee does not need to be a (fully) taxable person. However, if this is necessary to prevent distortion of competition, Member States may limit the application of the no-supply rule to transferees that are wholly liable to tax. Given the condition that the transferee must have the intention to operate the business or the part

249. CJEU 10 November 2011, Case C-444/10 *Finanzamt Lüdenscheid v Christel Schriever*, ECLI: EU:C:2011:724.
250. We note that the CJEU uses the wording the 'continuation of the economic activity'. However, from *Zita Modes* it follows that it is not necessary to continue the same economic activity. *See* section 3.6.3.4.
251. CJEU 10 November 2011, Case C-444/10 *Finanzamt Lüdenscheid v Christel Schriever*, ECLI: EU:C:2011:724, para. 36.
252. CJEU 19 December 2018, Case C-17/18 *Criminal proceedings against Virgil Mailat and Others*, ECLI:EU:C:2018:1038 and CJEU 28 February 2019, Case C-278/18 *Manuel Jorge Sequeira Mesquita v Fazenda Pública*, ECLI:EU:C:2019:160.
253. CJEU 10 November 2011, Case C-444/10 *Finanzamt Lüdenscheid v Christel Schriever*, ECLI: EU:C:2011:724, para. 42.
254. CJEU 19 December 2018, Case C-17/18 *Criminal proceedings against Virgil Mailat and Others*, ECLI:EU:C:2018:1038, para. 25.

of the undertaking transferred and not immediately liquidate the activity transferred and sell the stock, the transferee will ultimately become a taxable person the moment the transfer takes place. Member States can apply further conditions to prevent tax evasion or avoidance through the use of the no-supply rule. In our view, Member States must observe the principle of fiscal neutrality when applying further conditions. Moreover, any further conditions must be proportionate to prevent tax evasion or avoidance through the use of the no-supply rule.

3.6.3.5 Transfers of Shares under the No-Supply Rule?

Until the CJEU's ruling in *SKF*, it was generally conceived that the no-supply rule did not apply to transfers of shares in a company.[255] In *SKF*, the CJEU ruled that if an active holding company, which is to be regarded as a taxable person, disposes of all the shares in a wholly owned subsidiary (and of its remaining shareholding in a controlled company), the transfer of shares is an economic activity. More precisely, the transfer is to be regarded as a supply of services for consideration, which is exempt pursuant to Article 135(1)(f) VAT Directive. In *SKF*, the CJEU did not categorically reject the idea that the no-supply rule may apply to that transfer of shares.[256] It left it to the referring court to determine whether that is the case. From the CJEU's ruling, it seemed to follow that it is decisive whether the effect of the sale of shares in the subsidiary and in the controlled company was the total or partial disposal of the assets of the undertakings concerned. Apparently, the CJEU considered it to be necessary to 'look through' the shares in order to establish whether the no-supply rule applies to the disposal of those shares. We have difficulties fitting that in with the normal framework of the VAT system.[257] Moreover, it does not match with the CJEU's ruling in *DTZ Zadelhoff*, from which it follows that only in the event that a Member State used the option provided for in Article 15(2) VAT Directive (*see* section 3.2.2.2) to consider certain rights relating to immovable property as 'goods', is it possible to 'look through' the shares in a company.[258] In Case C-651/11 ('*X*'), the CJEU indeed clarified that shareholders are not owners of the assets of the undertaking in which they hold their shares. They are owners of the shares and, as such, are entitled to a dividend and to the communication of information and are involved in the adoption of important decisions for the management of the undertaking. According to the CJEU, the transfer of shares in a company cannot, irrespective of the size of the shareholding, be regarded as equivalent

255. CJEU 29 October 2009, Case C-29/08 *Skatteverket v AB SKF*, ECLI:EU:C:2009:665. *See also* J. Englisch, 'The Share Deal as a Non-taxable Transaction', in T. Ecker, M. Lang and I. Lejeune (eds), *The Future of Indirect Taxation* (Wolters Kluwer 2012), pp. 549-586.
256. CJEU 30 May 2013, Case C-651/11 *Staatssecretaris van Financiën v X BV*, ECLI:EU:C:2013:346, para. 33.
257. *See* in more detail on the disposal of shares and VAT: A.J. van Doesum, H.W.M. van Kesteren & G.J. van Norden, *Share Disposals and the Right of Deduction of Input VAT* (2010) 2 EC Tax Review, pp. 62-73 https://doi.org/10.54648/ecta2010008.
258. CJEU 5 July 2012, Case C-259/11 *DTZ Zadelhoff vof v Staatssecretaris van Financiën*, ECLI:EU:C:2012:423. *See also* A.J. van Doesum, *What Looks Like a Duck Is a Duck: Economic Purpose and Legal Reality in EU VAT Law* (2012) 2 World Journal of VAT, pp. 202-204 https://doi.org/10.5235/wjovl.1.2.202.

to the transfer of a totality of assets or part thereof unless the holding is part of an independent unit[259] which allows an independent economic activity to be carried out, and that activity is carried on by the transferee.[260]

3.6.4 Special Schemes

The VAT Directive contains a number of special schemes on the basis of which activities of a business in certain branches are effectively wholly or partially placed outside the scope of VAT. These special schemes are:

(1) special scheme for small enterprises;[261]
(2) common flat-rate scheme for farmers;[262]
(3) special scheme for travel agents;[263]
(4) special arrangements for second-hand goods, works of art, collectors' items and antiques;[264]
(5) special scheme for investment gold;[265]
(6) (Mini) One-Stop Shop ((M)OSS).[266]

The existence of these special schemes has to do with the apparent special position of certain participants on the market. They all cover only a part of the economic activities in the Internal Market. In Chapter 16, we will further analyse these special schemes.

3.7 INTRA-COMMUNITY ACQUISITIONS OF GOODS (ICAs)

In section 3.1, we indicated that on the basis of Article 2(1) VAT Directive, there are four taxable events for VAT. The first two are the supply of goods for consideration and the supply of services for consideration, which we discussed in the previous sections. Article 2(1) VAT Directive provides that the intra-Community acquisition (ICA) is also a taxable event.

An ICA occurs if a taxable person supplies goods to another taxable person, and the goods are physically moved from a Member State to another Member State in the course of that supply. An intra-Community supply (ICS) also takes place if a taxable person physically moves goods belonging to his business from a Member State to

259. It appears that the CJEU by this refers to the 'VAT Grouping' concept of Article 11 VAT Directive.
260. CJEU 30 May 2013, Case C-651/11 *Staatssecretaris van Financiën v X BV*, ECLI:EU:C:2013:346, para. 38.
261. Articles 281-294 VAT Directive.
262. Articles 295-305 VAT Directive.
263. Articles 306-310 VAT Directive.
264. Articles 311-343 VAT Directive.
265. Articles 344-356 VAT Directive.
266. Articles 358-369 VAT Directive.

another Member State. In some cases, an ICA takes place even though the purchaser is not a taxable person. In Chapter 12, we will discuss ICAs in more detail.

3.8 IMPORTATION OF GOODS

Where goods from outside the EU are brought into the EU, an importation of those goods takes place. The importation of goods is a taxable event for VAT. Even if the importer is not a taxable person for VAT purposes, VAT is due upon the importation of the goods (provided that no exemptions of special regimes apply). In Chapter 13, we will further discuss the importation of goods.

CHAPTER 4

Place of Supply

4.1 INTRODUCTION

To an increasing extent, national economies are dependent on international (global) trade. In this context, a central aspect of consumption taxation is the allocation of taxing competences between countries. Each country wants to have its fair share of tax revenues, without confronting businesses with unreasonable fiscal burdens (i.e., double taxation). Ideally, the legal framework of each tax system should ensure that neither double taxation nor non-taxation takes place. For direct taxation, bilateral tax treaties are the common instrument for allocating taxing rights.[1]

For VAT purposes, currently, no tax treaties exist.[2] Late in 2012, the first Organisation for Economic Co-operation and Development (OECD) Global Forum on VAT was held. The OECD countries concluded that it would be necessary to agree on a global framework for the application of VATs and GSTs to international trade, particularly in services and intangibles. The OECD developed international VAT/GST guidelines to address issues of double taxation and unintended double non-taxation. This work provides a unique basis for the creation of the future international standard for applying VAT to cross-border trade.[3]

The VAT Directive contains a detailed set of rules to allocate taxing competences both between the Member States and between the EU and non-EU countries. On the basis of these rules, which are often referred to as the 'place of supply rules', taxing competences in respect of each possible supply of goods and services are allocated to a certain country. The place of supply of goods is governed by Articles 31-39 VAT Directive, whereas the place of supply of services is laid down in Articles 43-59c VAT Directive. This chapter focuses on the place of supply rules in respect of supplies of goods and services. The allocation of taxing rights in the case of the so-called intra-Community acquisitions of goods ('ICAs') or importation of goods from non-EU countries is only briefly addressed. For a more detailed analysis in that respect, we refer to Chapters 13 and 14.

4.2 PRINCIPLES GOVERNING THE PLACE OF SUPPLY RULES

Generally, two main principles may govern the allocation of taxing rights in a consumption tax: the origin principle and the destination principle.[4] According to the origin principle, goods and services should be taxed in the country where they are produced. Also, if goods and services are supplied to another country, taxation ideally takes place in the country in which they are produced and supplied from. Upon acquisition of these goods and services in that other country, no tax is levied. For businesses, the advantage of a tax system based on the origin principle is that all their supplies of goods and services are subject to taxation in the country of establishment. An important disadvantage, however, is that local supplies and supplies from abroad

1. E.C.C.M. Kemmeren, *Principle of Origin in Tax Conventions: A Rethinking of Models* (*Dissertation*) (Pijnenburg 2001), p. 15 observes that the rationale for double tax conventions is often said to be the prevention of double taxation.
2. *See* T. Ecker, *A VAT/GST Model Convention* (*Dissertation*) (Amsterdam, IBFD 2013).
3. *See* OECD (2017), International VAT/GST Guidelines, OECD Publishing, Paris, https://doi.org/10.1787/9789264271401-en (accessed 17 August 2024).
4. *See* R.F. van Brederode, *Systems of General Sales Taxation* (Kluwer Law International 2009), pp. 201-264 on cross-border transactions in consumption tax systems. *See also* B. Terra, *The Place of Supply in European VAT* (Kluwer Law International 1998), pp. 4-5 and OECD (2017), International VAT/GST Guidelines, OECD Publishing, Paris, https://doi.org/10.1787/9789264271401-en (accessed 17 August 2024).

may be treated unequally, notably when the country from which the supplies are made applies a different tax rate than the country to which the supplies are made. An origin principle-based tax system holds an incentive to purchase goods and services from countries with a lower tax rate, or even without taxation. Moreover, such a system imposes an additional administrative burden on businesses, as they should recover input tax on goods and services purchased from abroad from foreign tax administrations.

According to the destination principle, goods and services are to be taxed in the country to which the goods and services are supplied (i.e., the country of destination).[5] Thus, when supplied from the country of origin to the country of destination, taxation ideally takes place in the latter. In a destination principle-based system, any input VAT on supplies of goods and services levied by the country of origin should be refunded. In that way, the goods and services leave that country tax-free. In turn, the country of destination is entitled to impose taxation upon acquisition of these goods and services. The country of destination applies the same VAT rate to identical goods or services, whatever place they originated from. Thus, an important advantage of destination principle-based taxation is that goods and services purchased locally are treated on equal terms with purchases from abroad. For businesses and tax administrations, a disadvantage may be that different tax treatments apply to domestic and cross-border supplies, which leads to additional administration and control measures.

Since VAT, as a general tax on consumption,[6] in theory, aims to burden consumption, it should also tax that consumption at the location where this consumption takes place.[7] As the concept of consumption does not provide for a sufficiently clear and practical norm, it is necessary to employ approximations (proxies) of the location where consumption takes place. Generally, it is believed that the destination principle provides for a proxy that is most in line with the general aim of taxing consumption. The VAT Directive takes the destination principle as a starting point. Consequently, many place of supply rules are worded in such a fashion that taxation takes place in the country of destination of the goods or services, thereby approximating the location where the commodities are (likely) to be consumed. For example, if a Polish consumer buys a television online from a web shop based in Germany, and the television is transported from Germany to Poland, the place of supply rule for that type of supply (intra-Community distance sale of goods)[8] establishes that taxing competences are allocated to the country where the goods are located at the time when

5. The destination and origin principles have a background in economics. In the context of EU VAT, they were employed by the authors of Tinbergen report (which enjoyed a strong focus on economics). *See* Report on the problems raised by the different turnover tax systems applied within the Common Market (Tinbergen Report), Committee of Experts, High Authority ECSC, 5 March 1953. Currently, the principles suffer from a certain extent of conceptual ambiguity. For further reading, refer to F.J.G. Nellen, *Information Asymmetries in EU VAT (diss)* (Datawyse 2017), p. 588.
6. Article 1(2) VAT Directive.
7. In her conclusion in the CJEU case of Heger (Opinion of A-G Sharpston of 7 March 2006 in Case C-166/05 *Heger*, ECLI:EU:C:2006:156, para. 47), A-G Sharpston notes that taxation of services at the place of consumption [...] 'is generally considered to be desirable'.
8. Article 14(4)(1) VAT Directive.

dispatch or transport of the goods to the customer ends, i.e., Poland.[9] Therefore, Polish VAT applies to the transaction.

Finally, we note that the place of supply rules constitute material VAT law that cannot, on a national level, be ignored or misapplied, not even when VAT fraud has taken place. In other words: Member States must respect their meaning and application and cannot (unilaterally) appropriate taxing competences in lieu of the provisions of VAT Directive.[10]

4.3 PLACE OF SUPPLY, VAT LIABILITY AND COMPLIANCE

The function of the place of supply rules is to allocate taxing competences to jurisdictions. The fact that the place of supply is located in a particular country does not determine who is liable to remit the payable VAT to the tax authorities in that country. On the basis of Article 193 VAT Directive, the main rule is that the VAT is payable by the taxable person that carries out a taxable supply of goods or services, whether or not that person is established within the country. In cross-border situations, this main rule would lead to disproportional administrative and compliance burdens for businesses. For example, if a US company provides services to a Spanish business customer, the place of that supply is located in Spain.[11] If the main rule were to be applied without restriction, the US company would be required to register for VAT purposes in Spain, charge Spanish VAT to the business customer, file a VAT return in Spain, and pay the VAT due to the Spanish tax authorities. Assuming the Spanish business customer is entitled to full deduction of input VAT, he can immediately deduct the Spanish VAT that the US company is charging him. On balance, there is no effect on the Spanish government budget.

To avoid unnecessary administrative and compliance burdens for (non-established) businesses, as illustrated by the example, the main rule on the liability of VAT knows some exceptions. In some cases, the recipient of a supply, instead of the supplier, is designated as the person liable for payment of VAT to the tax authorities. This is commonly known as the 'reverse charge mechanism'. In the above example, the reverse charge mechanism applies.[12] Consequently, the VAT liability is shifted from the US company to his Spanish business customer. Instead of the US company, the Spanish business customer is held liable to pay the Spanish tax authorities. He should report this VAT in his own Spanish VAT return as VAT due but can immediately deduct this amount on the same VAT return, resulting in a zero-balance. The reverse charge

9. Article 33(a) VAT Directive.
10. In CJEU 27 October 2022, Case C-641/21 *Climate Corporation Emissions Trading GmbH v Finanzamt Österreich*, ECLI:EU:C:2022:842), the CJEU has ruled that the place of supply of services cannot be altered in disregard of the wordings of the VAT Directive on the ground that the transaction at issue is vitiated by VAT evasion. A similar line of reasoning can be found in CJEU case law on the material norms for the taxable amount (CJEU 1 July 2021, Case C-521/19, *CB v Tribunal Económico-Administrativo Regional de Galicia*, ECLI:EU:C:2021:527).
11. Article 44 VAT Directive.
12. Article 196 VAT Directive.

mechanism, therefore, obviates the need for VAT registration in Spain and additional VAT compliance.

When dealing with cross-border situations, it is essential to keep a close eye on both the place of supply rules and the rules on VAT liability. They are closely connected but are different concepts that require separate interpretation and application. For further details on the liability of VAT, we refer to Chapter 12.

4.4 PLACE OF SUPPLY OF GOODS

4.4.1 Introduction

For the place of supply of goods, the main distinctive criterion is whether the goods are transported or not. Different rules apply to supplies of goods without transport and to supplies of goods with transport. The place where the customer is established or residing is not decisive.

4.4.2 Supply of Goods Without Transport

According to Article 31 VAT Directive, the place of supply of goods that are not dispatched or transported is the place where the goods are located at the time when the supply takes place. This is in accordance with the destination principle. It is assumed that the goods will be consumed in the country where the goods are located at the moment the goods are supplied.

4.4.3 Supply of Goods with Transport

4.4.3.1 Where Transport Begins

Article 32 VAT Directive contains the 'main' place of supply rule in case of dispatch or transport of goods. If goods are dispatched or transported by the supplier, or by the customer, or by a third person, the place of supply is the place where the goods are located at the time when dispatch or transport of the goods to the customer begins. This rule applies to supplies within the territory of a country but also to intra-Community supplies ('ICSs') from one Member State to another, as well as to export supplies to non-EU countries. Specific rules may apply, however, to so-called distance sales (*see* sections 4.4.3.2 and 4.4.3.3).

In principle, taxation at the place where the goods are located at the time of dispatch or transport of the goods does not fit with the destination principle. At first glance, it might appear that this place of supply rule leads to the taxation of cross-border supplies of goods according to the origin principle. This, however, is not true, as both ICSs from one Member State to another and exports of goods to non-EU countries are exempt while the supplier enjoys the right to deduct related input VAT.[13] The application of these exemptions ensures that the goods do not carry a tax burden from the country of origin – and thus leave that country free of VAT. This approach (i.e., a place of supply in the country of origin, coupled with an exemption with a right to deduct input VAT) is a choice of design made by the EU legislator. Other (non-EU) countries may achieve the same result by way of defining the place of supply in case of dispatch or transport of goods as the country where the transport of the goods ends. Both approaches are in line with the destination principle, even though they employ a different legal framework (different rules) to achieve that conformity.

From a systemic point of view, the place of supply rule of Article 32 VAT Directive only seems to apply to the supply that actually triggers the transport. When goods are supplied during the transport, e.g., on board a ship travelling from Hamburg to the Middle East, these supplies take place on board the ship and not at the place of departure. The territorial application of VAT is not extended to ships flying the flag of a Member State.[14] However, if dispatch or transport of the goods begins in a non-EU country, both the place of supply of any supply by the importer who is liable for import VAT and the place of any subsequent supply are within the Member State of importation of the goods (*see* section 4.4.3.4).

4.4.3.2 Distance Sales until 1 July 2021

The place of supply rule of Article 32 VAT Directive does not apply in all situations involving transport. One of the reasons for this is that in some situations, the application of Article 32 VAT Directive would lead to neutrality distortions. This is, for example, the case in connection with supplies of goods (distance sales) to non-taxable persons in an intra-Community context. If a private individual purchases goods locally in Denmark, those goods are taxed against the applicable Danish VAT rate of 25%. However, if he would instead place an order with a Luxembourg mail-order company, and Article 32 VAT Directive applies, these very same goods would only be taxed at the Luxembourg VAT rate of 16% VAT rate (i.e., the VAT rate applicable in the country where transport starts). Non-taxable persons would thus experience an incentive to buy goods from Member States with low VAT rates.

To mitigate this unequal treatment and neutrality distortion, the EU legislator has adopted a special provision for the supply of goods to non-taxable persons in other Member States and to taxable persons or non-taxable legal persons in other Member States whose ICAs are not subject to VAT pursuant to Article 3(1) VAT Directive. Commonly, such supplies are referred to as 'Intra-Community distance sales of

13. Articles 138 and 146 VAT Directive.
14. B. Terra, *The Place of Supply in European VAT* (Kluwer Law International 1998), p. 21. *See* for a different view Opinion of A-G Mancini of 6 June 1985 in Case 168/84 *Gunter Berkholz v Finanzamt Hamburg-Mitte-Altstadt*, ECLI:EU:C:1985:299.

goods'.[15] Until 1 July 2021, the so-called distance sales scheme was laid down in Articles 33-35 VAT Directive. The essence of the scheme was primarily conveyed by the (former) Article 33 VAT Directive, which stipulated that the place of supply of goods for Intra-Community distance sales is the place where the dispatch or transport of the goods to the customer ends. The *ratio* of the distance sales scheme was to prevent distortion of competition between suppliers established in different Member States, caused by the difference in applicable (general) VAT rates across the EU.

4.4.3.3 Distance Sales from 1 July 2021

Over the years, the distance sales scheme has become increasingly important, especially because of the exponential growth of the e-commerce economy.[16] In order to modernize the scheme, on 5 December 2017, the Council adopted Council Directive 2017/2455, the primary legislative instrument of the so-called VAT e-commerce package.[17] Accompanied by other instruments, the Directive aims to adapt the EU VAT legislation to the growth of, and to the (technological) developments within, the e-commerce sector.[18] By derogation from Article 32 VAT Directive (the 'main' place of supply rule in case of dispatch or transport of goods), the package contained a revised provision (the revised Article 33 VAT Directive) concerning the place of supply of goods in the context of distance sales, which has applied as from 1 July 2021:

(1) *Intra-Community distance sales of goods ('ICDS'):* The place of supply of intra-Community distance sales of goods shall be deemed to be the place where the goods are located at the time when dispatch or transport of the goods to the customer ends. The VAT implications of this category of transactions are further discussed in Chapter 13.[19]

---

15. Without such a provision, the internal market for B2C supplies of goods would have been disturbed dramatically, as all direct mail companies would have relocated to the Member State with the lowest VAT rate and would have started to supply their goods from that location.
16. *See* Council Directive (EU) 2017/2455 of 5 December 2017 amending Directive 2006/112/EC and Directive 2009/132/EC as regards certain value added tax obligations for supplies of services and distance sales of goods [2017] OJ L 348/7. In the recitals of which the EU legislator underlines the 'explosive growth of electronic commerce and, hence, of distance sales of goods.'
17. Council Directive (EU) 2017/2455 of 5 December 2017 [2017] OJ L 348/7.
18. *See* Council Implementing Regulation (EU) 2019/2026 of 21 November 2019 amending Implementing Regulation (EU) No 282/2011 as regards supplies of goods or services facilitated by electronic interfaces and the special schemes for taxable persons supplying services to non-taxable persons, making distance sales of goods and certain domestic supplies of goods [2019] OJ L 313/14; Council Directive (EU) 2019/1995 of 21 November 2019 amending Directive 2006/112/EC as regards provisions relating to distance sales of goods and certain domestic supplies of goods [2019] OJ L 310/1; Commission Implementing Regulation (EU) 2020/194 of 12 February 2020 laying down detailed rules for the application of Council Regulation (EU) No 904/2010 as regards the special schemes for taxable persons supplying services to non-taxable persons, making distance sales of goods and certain domestic supplies of goods [2020] OJ L 40/114.
19. *See* Article 33(a) VAT Directive. In short, Article 14(4)(1) VAT Directive defines an intra-Community distance sale of goods as a supply of goods dispatched or transported by or on behalf of the supplier, including where the supplier intervenes indirectly in the transport or dispatch of

(2) *Non-EU distance sales of goods in a three-country scenario*: The place of supply of distance sales of goods imported from third territories or third countries into a Member State other than that in which dispatch or transport of the goods to the customer ends, shall be deemed to be the place where the goods are located at the time when dispatch or transport of the goods to the customer ends. The VAT implications of this category of transactions are further discussed in Chapter 14.[20]

(3) *Non-EU distance sales of goods in a two-country scenario when the* Import One-Stop Shop *(IOSS) is used*: the place of supply of distance sales of goods imported from third territories or third countries into the Member State in which dispatch or transport of the goods to the customer ends shall be deemed to be in that Member State, on the condition that the special scheme IOSS is used for the reporting and payment of the VAT due.[21] The VAT implications of this category of transactions, as well as the details of the IOSS, are further discussed in Chapters 14 and 16.

The above place of supply rules for the place of supply of distance sales of goods are quite specific and, moreover, are strongly related to other legal concepts, such as the taxable event 'importation' and the 'IOSS'. For reasons of expedience and clarity, we discuss the place of supply rules in conjunction with these other concepts in separate sections in Chapters 13, 14 and 16.

4.4.3.4 Supplies by the Importer and Subsequent Supplies

In international trade, goods often move from the production phase to the consumption phase by means of extensive supply chains. For example, goods transported by ship from South Africa to Germany may very well be sold and supplied several times during transport. Clearly, the first supply of goods from an EU VAT perspective takes place in South Africa. Following Article 32, first sentence VAT Directive, the place of supply is the place where the goods are located at the time when transport of the goods to the customer begins – being South Africa.[22] Moreover, it is obvious that these goods are imported in Germany, and hence VAT will be levied there upon importation (Article 60 VAT Directive). The question, however, arises as to how taxing rights are to be allocated to the supplies of goods following the first supply (for which taxing rights were allocated to South Africa). Should the taxing rights for these supplies be allocated to South Africa, to Germany, or perhaps to no country at all since the goods are transported over international waters?

---

the goods, from a Member State other than that in which dispatch or transport of the goods to the customer ends. Various conditions apply.

20. *See* Article 33(b) VAT Directive. In short, Article 14(4)(2) VAT Directive defines non-EU distance sale of goods as a supply of goods dispatched or transported by or on behalf of the supplier, including where the supplier intervenes indirectly in the transport or dispatch of the goods, from a third territory or third country, to a customer in a Member State. Various conditions apply.
21. *See* Article 33(c) VAT Directive.
22. Also *see* sections 10.2.2.5, 12.2.3, 13.3.2.2.3 and 14.13.

If goods are imported from a third country by the supplier, Article 32, second paragraph holds a special provision on the determination of the place of the supply. Under this provision, both the place of supply by the supplier and any subsequent supply are considered to take place within the Member State of importation of the goods if:

(1) the dispatch or transport of the goods begins in a third territory or third country;
(2) the goods are imported by the supplier; and
(3) the importer/supplier is designated or recognized under Article 201 as liable for payment of VAT on importation.

The purpose of Article 32, second paragraph VAT Directive is to prevent the loss of VAT revenues. The idea is that – were it not for Article 32, second paragraph – persons without a right of deduction could purchase goods from outside the EU without those goods effectively being taxed in the end. If goods are supplied from outside the EU, the place of supply would be outside the EU (place of departure, *see* Article 32, first sentence VAT Directive). If subsequently, the supplier were to import the goods in a Member State, the importation would be taxed. However, on the basis of Article 168(e) VAT Directive, VAT due or paid in respect of the importation of goods into a Member State is recoverable, in so far as the goods and services are used for the purposes of the taxed transactions of a taxable person. Arguably, the supplier, in this example, can recover the VAT on importation because he uses the goods for the purposes of making a supply for which a right of deduction exists. The end result is then that the goods effectively remain completely untaxed (VAT-free). To prevent this from occurring, Article 32, second paragraph VAT Directive considers that the place of supply of the goods is not within a third country, but rather in the Member State of importation if the goods are imported[23] by a supplier who is designated or recognized as the person liable to pay the VAT on importation.[24]

4.4.4 Supply of Goods with Installation and Assembly

A special place of supply rule applies to goods that are installed or assembled by or on behalf of the supplier (so-called installation supplies). Article 36 VAT Directive stipulates that, where goods dispatched or transported by the supplier, by the customer or by a third person, are installed or assembled, with or without a trial run, by or on

23. The condition that the goods must be imported by the supplier means, in our view, that the supplier must be the person who is the debtor for customs duties under Article 4(12) CCC/Article 5(19) UCC.
24. Article 32, second paragraph VAT Directive does not need to be applied if the customer is liable to pay the VAT on importation, because in such a situation, there is no risk of VAT leakage (non-taxation). After all, either the customer cannot deduct the VAT on importation, or if he can deduct the VAT on importation, his subsequent supplies will be subject to VAT. This may explain why Article 32, second paragraph VAT Directive only applies if the supplier is the same person as 'the importer designated or recognised under Article 201 as liable for payment of VAT'.

behalf of the supplier, the place of supply is the place where the goods are installed or assembled. The VAT status of the customer (taxable person or non-taxable person) is not relevant. In most EU countries, the reverse charge mechanism applies to the installation supply, in case the supplier is not established in the country where the goods are supplied but the customer is. For a more extensive description of the reverse charge mechanism, we refer to Chapter 12.

Neither the VAT Directive nor the VAT Implementing Regulation contains a definition of the concepts of 'installation' or 'assembly' as used by this particular place of supply rule. Member States seem to interpret these concepts differently, which gives rise to discrepancies. Some Member States require a good to become immovable in order to qualify as an installed or assembled good, where other Member States regard the ratio between the value of the goods and the value of the installation/assembly service as decisive for the qualification as a so-called installation supply. This latter aspect relates to the subject of composite supplies, i.e., transactions that consist of multiple discernible elements. The question may rise whether an installation supply is one indivisible supply of a good or, alternatively, a combination of a supply of goods (i.e., the transfer of the right to dispose of the installed/assembled good) and a separate supply of services (i.e., the installation/assembly service). In *Aktiebolaget NN v Skatteverket*, the CJEU has ruled that the supply and installation of a fibre-optic cable linking two Member States and sited in part outside Community territory must be considered a supply of goods. Notably, the Court refers to the relevant circumstances that: (a) the cable was transferred to the client who will dispose of it as owner, (b) the price of the cable itself clearly represented the greater part of the total cost of that transaction, and (c) the supplier's services were limited to the laying of the cable without altering its nature and without adapting it to the specific requirements of the client.[25] In situations involving different types of installation supplies, the outcome may very well be different.[26]

The second paragraph of Article 36 VAT Directive prescribes that where the installation or assembly is carried out in a Member State other than that of the supplier, the Member State within the territory of which the installation or assembly is carried out shall take the measures necessary to ensure that there is no double taxation in that Member State. Although it is not fully clear what exactly could cause the double taxation, this paragraph may be meant to prevent that an installation supply carried out by a supplier established in another Member State is qualified as a regular ICS by the customer and, concurrently, as an installation supply by the supplier.

In principle, according to Article 17 VAT Directive, the transfer by a taxable person of goods forming part of his business assets from one Member State to another Member State shall be treated as a (deemed) supply of goods for consideration. However, following Article 17(2)(b) VAT Directive, the dispatch or transport of goods, for the purposes of a so-called installation supply by the supplier within the territory of the Member State of arrival of the goods, shall not be regarded as a transfer to another

25. CJEU 29 March 2007, Case C-111/05 *Aktiebolaget NN v Skatteverket*, ECLI:EU:C:2007:195.
26. *See* section 3.5 for further reading on the VAT treatment of composite supplies.

Member State. For a more extensive description of the provisions with respect to the transfer of own goods, we refer to Chapter 13.

4.4.5 Supply of Goods on Board Ships, Aircraft or Trains

For goods that are supplied on board ships, aircraft or trains during the section of a passenger transport operation effected within the EU, the place of supply shall be deemed to be at the point of departure of the passenger transport operation. This special place of supply rule is laid down in Article 37(1) VAT Directive. According to Article 37(2) VAT Directive, a 'section of a passenger transport operation effected within the Community' shall in this respect mean the section of the operation effected, without a stopover outside the Community, between the point of departure and the point of arrival of the passenger transport operation. According to Article 15 VAT Implementing Regulation, the section of a passenger transport operation shall be determined by the journey of the means of transport and not by the journey completed by each of the passengers. 'Point of departure' and 'point of arrival' are also defined in Article 37(2) VAT Directive and shall mean respectively the first and last scheduled points of passenger (dis)embarkation within the Community, where applicable respectively after and before a stopover outside the Community. In the case of a return trip, the return leg shall be regarded as a separate transport operation. As a result, goods bought on the outward leg of a return trip between Sicily and Majorca are subject to Italian VAT, whereas goods bought on the return leg are subject to Spanish VAT.

This special place of supply rule applies to all goods supplied on board of ships, aircraft or trains. In Article 37(3) VAT Directive, Member States are allowed to exempt, with deductibility of input VAT, the supply of goods for consumption on board. In many Member States, goods supplied on board for consumption on board, are, therefore, exempt from VAT. As a result, no VAT is paid on goods for consumption supplied on board ships, aircraft or trains. As the means of transport to which this special place of supply rule and VAT exemption apply, are defined quite precisely; we believe that these special rules are not applicable to the supply of goods on board other means of transport, such as coaches. The reason for a different VAT treatment does not follow from the preamble of the VAT Directive or the explanatory notes to the proposals for the Sixth VAT Directive.

4.4.6 Supply of Goods Through Distribution Systems (Gas, Electricity)

Pursuant to Article 15 VAT Directive, electricity, gas, heat, cooling energy and the like shall be treated as tangible property for VAT purposes. As a result, the place of supply is, in principle, defined by applying the rules for the place of supply of goods. The place of supply is either where the goods are located at the time of the supply (Article 31 VAT Directive) or if the goods are transported, the place of departure of the goods (Article 32 VAT Directive). However, it proved that electricity and gas were difficult to track physically. Consequently, it was difficult to determine the place of supply of such transactions. Directive 2003/92/EC, amending the Sixth VAT Directive, changed the place of supply of gas through a natural gas system situated within the territory of the EU or any network connected to such a system, the supply of electricity, and the supply of heat or cooling energy through heating or cooling networks to a taxable dealer. The supply is considered to take place where the taxable dealer (customer) is established, has a fixed establishment for which the goods are supplied or, where he has his permanent address or where he usually resides (Article 38 VAT Directive). Since European VAT aims at taxing private consumption, the place of supply of gas through a natural gas system situated within the territory of the EU or any network connected to such a system, the supply of electricity or the supply of heat or cooling energy through heating or cooling networks, is in all other situations the place where the customer has effective use and consumption of the goods (Article 39 VAT Directive). Where all or part of the gas, electricity or heat or cooling energy is not effectively consumed by the customer, those non-consumed goods are deemed to have been used and consumed at the place where the customer has established his business or has a fixed establishment for which the goods are supplied.

4.4.7 Intra-Community Supplies and Acquisitions of Goods

Before 1993, fiscal borders existed between the EU Member States. If goods were physically transported or dispatched in the course of a supply of goods from one Member State to another, the place of supply of goods was the Member State where the goods were located at the time when dispatch or transport of the goods to the customer began. In view of the destination principle, this export supply of goods was exempt, while the supplier enjoyed a right to deduct related input VAT. Upon importation in the other Member State, import VAT was levied. This system of export and import still exists for supplies of goods to non-EU countries from the EU Member States, and vice versa (*see* Chapter 14).

In 1993, the fiscal borders between the Member States were removed. As physical controls by customs officials were (in principle) no longer in place, VAT could not be levied upon importation in another Member State. Because of this change, the concepts of 'intra-Community supply' ('ICS') and 'intra-Community acquisition' ('ICA') were introduced for supplies of goods between taxable persons. If goods are physically transported or dispatched in the course of a supply from one Member State to another, an ICS takes place. The place of this supply is still the Member State where the goods are located at the time when dispatch or transport of the goods to the customer begins (Article 32 VAT Directive; *see* section 4.4.3.1). Following Article 138 VAT Directive an exemption with a right to deduction exists for the ICS, ensuring that taxation takes place in accordance with the destination principle. In the Member State where the transport of the goods ends, an ICA takes place (Article 40 VAT Directive), which is a separate taxable transaction from the (intra-Community) supply of goods (Articles 2(1)(b) and 20 VAT Directive). By means of this ICA, taxation on 'importation' takes place, albeit that no VAT is levied at the physical border. For a more in-depth analysis of ICSs and ICAs, we refer to Chapter 13.

4.4.8 Importation and Exportation of Goods

Where goods are dispatched or transported by the supplier, or by the customer, or by a third person, the place of supply is in principle the place where the goods are located at the time when dispatch or transport of the goods to the customer begins (Article 32, first paragraph VAT Directive). This means that the place of supply of a supply of goods from a Member State to a non-EU country (i.e., exportation of goods) is in that Member State. In view of the destination principle, no tax burden should rest on these goods, and therefore, an exemption with a right to deduct applies to the supply of goods (Article 146 VAT Directive). Assuming that the non-EU country to which the goods are dispatched or transported has a consumption tax comparable to EU VAT, taxation upon importation will take place.

In case of a supply of goods from a non-EU country to an EU Member State, two taxable transactions take place: (1) the supply of goods from the non-EU county (Article 2(1)(a) VAT Directive), and (2) the importation of goods in the EU Member State (Article 2(1)(d) VAT Directive). The place of supply of the supply of goods from the non-EU country to the EU Member State is in the non-EU country, as the dispatch or transport of the goods to the customer begins there (Article 32, first paragraph VAT Directive). Although the destination principle calls for the absence of a tax burden upon the exportation of the goods, it depends on the tax legislation of the particular non-EU country whether actual taxation takes place. The importation of goods in the EU Member State is subject to taxation there, as that is where the goods are located when they enter the Community (Article 60 VAT Directive). For a more in-depth analysis of importation and exportation of goods, we refer to Chapter 14.

4.5 PLACE OF SUPPLY OF SERVICES

4.5.1 Introduction

On 1 January 2010, the place of supply rules changed. Until then, the place of supply rules had not changed dramatically since the introduction of the Sixth VAT Directive, which applied from 1 January 1978, replacing the place of supply rules laid down in the Second VAT Directive, which was adopted on 11 April 1967. In the Sixth VAT Directive, the place of supply rules were predominantly based on the origin principle. Globalization, technology changes and the realization of the internal market created enormous changes in the volume and pattern of international trade in services. The cross-border supply of services became both easier and more common. After years of discussion between the EU Member States, the place of supply rules changed as of 1 January 2010.[27] The primary aim of the legislative changes was – where possible – to

27. Council Directive 2008/8/EC of 20 February 2008 amending Directive 2006/112/EC as regards the place of supply of services [2008] OJ L44/11.

levy VAT where actual consumption takes place.[28] As a result of the changes, the new place of supply rules for services adhered to a greater extent to the destination principle.[29] Furthermore, the changes mitigated the effect of the different VAT rates in the Member States. According to the EU legislator, this contributed to the realization of the internal market and the prevention of distortion of competition between service suppliers established in different Member States.

The scope of the place of supply rules is not limited to EU service suppliers and recipients. Therefore, it does not only apply to services rendered between (legal) persons established or residing in the EU but also to services rendered by/to (legal) persons established or residing outside the EU. Following the place of supply rules, most services rendered by non-EU suppliers to EU recipients are located in the EU. Additionally, most services rendered by EU suppliers to non-EU recipients are located outside the EU. These aspects contribute to the reduction of distortion of competition between EU suppliers and non-EU suppliers.

Since 1 January 2010, the place of supply rules for services are structured around two main rules. The first main rule applies to services rendered to taxable persons or customers who are regarded as such (Business to Business (B2B) supplies). The second main rule applies to services rendered to non-taxable persons (B2C supplies). Each of these main rules has its own set of exceptions. The main rules and exceptions for B2B and B2C supplies will be discussed in sections 4.5.3 and 4.5.4.

With respect to the rules determining the place of supply of services before 1 January 2010, the CJEU maintained that the main rule should not prevail over the exceptions.[30] We are of the opinion that this approach by the CJEU is still valid. The main rules, therefore, have no precedence over the exceptions. This means that in order to determine the place of supply of a service, it must first be assessed whether the service is covered by one of the exceptions. If not, either the main rule for B2B supplies or the main rule for B2C supplies applies. Most of the exceptions are described quite specifically. In order to determine whether an exception applies to a certain service, according to the CJEU, the criterion for determining the place in which services are deemed to be supplied is the nature of the services in question. Moreover, it is necessary in each case to take account of all the circumstances surrounding the service

28. *Ibid.*, para. 3. *See, inter alia*, original proposal for changing place of supply dated 23 December 2003, COM (2003)822 final, p. 2, and the amended proposal for changing the place of supply dated 20 July 2005, COM (2005)334 final, p. 2.
29. In the Second VAT Directive, the place of supply rules were also based on the destination principle, but another proxy was used to establish where consumption takes place. In the Second VAT Directive, the place of a service was, as a general rule, the place where the services provided, the right transferred or granted, or the object hired, is used or enjoyed. Since 2010, the (main) proxy used to establish the place where consumption takes place has been the place where the customer is established.
30. CJEU 26 September 1996, Case C-327/94 *Jürgen Dudda v Finanzgericht Bergisch Gladbach*, ECLI:EU:C:1996:355, para. 21; CJEU 6 March 1997, Case C-167/95 *Maatschap M.J.M. Linthorst, K.G.P. Pouwels en J. Scheren c.s. tegen Inspecteur der Belastingdienst/Ondernemingen Roermond*, ECLI:EU:C:1997:105, para. 11; CJEU 12 May 2005, Case C-452/03 *RAL (Channel Islands) Ltd and Others v Commissioners of Customs & Excise*, ECLI:EU:C:2005:289, para. 24 and CJEU 9 March 2006, Case C-114/05 *Ministre de l'Économie, des Finances et de l'Industrie v Gillan Beach Ltd*, ECLI:EU:C:2006:169, para. 15.

in question.[31] As the nature of the service in question is the decisive criterion, a service may be characterized as a supply of, e.g., an advertising service, even where it is not carried out by a supplier engaged in business as an advertising agency.[32] For the same reason, the rules for determining the place of supply must be applied to each transaction, also in case the services are supplied indirectly to the final customer and invoiced to an intermediate customer who in turn invoices them to the final customer: the services are to be classified based on their nature without taking into account the transactions carried out after the supply of the service.[33]

Although it might sound straightforward that the nature of a service is the decisive criterion for determining the place of supply of a service, in practice, it can be quite difficult to determine the exact nature of a supply – in particular, where the transaction comprises a bundle of features and acts. We refer to section 3.5 for a description of the circumstances to be taken into account when classifying a supply as one single supply or various separate supplies. Furthermore, the specific description of the exceptions easily results in different interpretations of the legal rule at hand or the nature of the respective service.

An explanation of some definitions used in the place of supply provisions is given in the VAT Implementing Regulation. A large number of implementing provisions aim at ensuring the uniform application of the place of supply rules so that the application of the VAT system complies more fully with the objective and proper functioning of the internal market. These implementing provisions contain specific rules in response to selective questions of application and are designed to achieve uniform treatment throughout the EU under those specific circumstances.

4.5.2 Place of Establishment

4.5.2.1 The Importance of the Place of Establishment for the Determination of the Place of Supply of Services

In the two main rules as well as in part of the specific provisions, the place of business of the service supplier and/or the customer plays an important role in determining the place of supply. To ensure the uniform application of the place of supply rules, concepts, such as the 'place where a taxable person has established his business, fixed establishment, permanent address' and the 'place where a person usually resides' must be interpreted in the same way in all EU Member States. Since 1 July 2011, these concepts have been defined in Articles 10-13 VAT Implementing Regulation. Article 10

31. CJEU 15 March 2001, Case C-108/00 *SPI*, ECLI:EU:C:2001:173, para. 19.
32. CJEU 17 November 1993, Case C-68/92 *Commission of the European Communities v French Republic*, ECLI:EU:C:1993:888, para. 17; CJEU 17 November 1993, Case C-69/92 *Commission of the European Communities v Grand Duchy of Luxembourg*, ECLI:EU:C:1993:889, para. 18 and CJEU 17 November 1993, Case C-73/92 *Commission of the European Communities v Kingdom of Spain*, ECLI:EU:C:1993:891, para. 15.
33. CJEU 5 June 2003, Case C-438-01 *Design Concept SA v Flanders Expo SA*, ECLI:EU:C:2003:325, paras 24-26.

(place of business) and Article 11 (fixed establishment) will be described in the next sections.[34]

4.5.2.2 Place of Business (Head Office)

Although the 'place of business' (in full: 'place where the business of a taxable person is established') has played an important role for the application of the place of supply of services since the Sixth VAT Directive, neither the Sixth VAT Directive nor the VAT Directive contained a definition of the concept. Apparently, in practice, there was not much discussion about the 'place of business', given the fact that no cases were brought before the CJEU concerning this concept. Article 10 VAT Implementing Regulation stipulates that, for the application of the main rules for the place of supply of services, laid down in Articles 44 and 45 VAT Directive, the place where the business of a taxable person is established shall be the place where the functions of the business' central administration are carried out. In order to determine this place, account shall be taken of the place where essential decisions concerning the general management of the business are taken, the place where the registered office of the business is located, and the place where management meets. We consider it a missed opportunity that the scope of Article 10 VAT Implementing Regulation is limited to Articles 44 and 45 VAT Directive, in which the main rules for the place of supply are laid down. In our view, the place of supply rules would have been applied in an even more uniform manner, in case the definition given in Article 10 VAT Implementing Regulation had been applied to other places of supply rules as well, e.g., Articles 38 and 58 VAT Directive. Earlier, in *Planzer*,[35] the European Court of Justice decided that similar factors should be taken into consideration when interpreting the term 'business' used in Article 1(1) Thirteenth Directive.[36]

Although Article 10 VAT Implementing Regulation contains a clear list of factors that should be taken into consideration when determining the place of establishment of a business, it might still be difficult to define this place, e.g., where essential decisions concerning the general management are taken in various offices, or where the registered office is located in another place than the place where essential management decisions are taken. For such cases in which the place of establishment of a business cannot be determined with certainty, the place where essential decisions concerning the general management of the business are taken shall take precedence.[37] However, when the 'place of business' of a customer needs to be determined on the basis of this

34. 'Permanent address of a natural person' and 'the place where a natural person usually resides' are defined in Articles 12 and 13 VAT Regulation.
35. CJEU 28 June 2007, Case C-73/06 *Planzer Luxembourg Sàrl v Bundeszentralamt für Steuern*, ECLI:EU:C:2007:397, para. 61.
36. Thirteenth Council Directive 86/560/EEC of 17 November 1986 on the harmonization of the laws of the Member States relating to turnover taxes – Arrangements for the refund of value added tax to taxable persons not established in Community territory [1986] OJ L326/40. The Thirteenth Directive contains the arrangements for the refund of VAT to taxable persons not established in the EU, *see* section 10.2.4.3.
37. The mere existence of a postal address may not be taken to be the place of establishment of a business of a taxable person.

criterion (e.g., when a supplier renders a B2B service, which is taxable where the customer has his 'place of business'),[38] the supplier may experience difficulty in obtaining sufficient information on, and proof of, the place where essential decisions are taken.[39]

4.5.2.3 Fixed Establishment

A taxable person can carry on his business through more than one establishment. If a taxable person acts from more than one country, the place of business in the other country than the country where the head office is established is under certain conditions qualified as a fixed establishment for VAT purposes. A taxable person with a fixed establishment in a (different) Member State, is essentially considered to be (secondarily) established in that Member State. The taxable person's head office is considered the primary place of establishment.

Fixed establishments play an important role in the determination of the place of supply of a service. The main rule for B2B services of Article 44 VAT Directive, for example, defines that the place of supply of a service rendered to a taxable person shall be the place where that person has established his business. However, if those services are provided to a fixed establishment of the taxable person located in a place other than the place where he has established his business, the place of supply shall be the place where that fixed establishment is located. Not only fixed establishments of the recipient of a service but also fixed establishments of the service supplier must be taken into consideration when determining the place of supply of a service. If a taxable person supplies services *from his place of business (head office)*, the head office is the supplier of the service, whereas the fixed establishment will, rather than the head office, be considered as the service supplier if the services are supplied *from the fixed establishment.* Also, for the application of the reverse charge mechanism,[40] it is essential to establish whether the service supplier and/or recipient of the service has a fixed establishment and if so, whether the services are supplied from and/or to this fixed establishment.

The VAT Directive does not define the concept of fixed establishment. However, the European Court of Justice has been asked several times to explain the concept; from its case law, one can conclude that a fixed establishment is an establishment that possesses a sufficient degree of permanence and a structure adequate, in terms of human and technical resources, to supply the services in question on an independent basis.[41] In its judgments on the definition of a fixed establishment (in the VAT

38. Article 44 VAT Directive.
39. *See* F. Nellen, *Information Asymmetries in EU VAT (diss.)* (Datawyse 2017), p. 368.
40. *See* section 12.3.5.
41. CJEU 4 July 1985, Case 168/84 *Berkholz v Finanzamt Hamburg-Mitte-Altstadt*, ECLI:EU:C:1985:299, para. 18; CJEU 2 May 1996, Case C-231/94 *Faaborg-Gelting Linien A/S v Finanzamt Flensburg*, ECLI:EU:C:1996:184, para. 17; CJEU 20 February 1997, Case C-260/95 *Commissioners of Customs and Excise v DFDS A/S*, ECLI:EU:C:1997:77, para. 20; CJEU 17 July 1997, Case C-190/95 *ARO Lease BV v Inspecteur van de Belastingdienst Grote Ondernemingen te Amsterdam*, ECLI:EU:C:1997:374, para. 16 and CJEU 7 May 1998, Case 390/96 *Lease Plan*

Directive), the European Court of Justice has emphasized that the place where the supplier has established his business is a primary point of reference inasmuch as there is no purpose in referring to another establishment from which the services are supplied unless reference to the place of business does not lead to a rational result for tax purposes or create a conflict with another Member State.[42]

In 2011, the EU legislator provided legal definitions of the concept of fixed establishment. The VAT Implementing Regulation currently contains no less than three definitions of the term 'fixed establishment'. The definition differs depending on the place of supply rule in which the term is used.

a) B2B Fixed Establishment

Article 11(1) VAT Implementing Regulation stipulates that, for the application of Article 44 of Directive 2006/112/EC, a 'fixed establishment' shall be any establishment, other than the place of establishment of a business, characterized by a sufficient degree of permanence and a suitable structure in terms of human and technical resources *to enable it to receive and use the services supplied to it for its own needs.*

b) B2C Fixed Establishment

According to Article 11(2) VAT Implementing Regulation, for the application of Articles 45, 56(2), 58 (until 31 December 2014) and 192a VAT Directive, a 'fixed establishment' shall be any establishment, other than the place of establishment of a business, characterized by a sufficient degree of permanence and a suitable structure in terms of human and technical resources *to enable it to provide the services which it supplies.*

Article 11(3) VAT Implementing Regulation clarifies that the fact of having a VAT ID number shall not in itself be sufficient to consider that a taxable person has a fixed establishment.

In our view, the question is to what extent the legal definitions have, in fact, improved legal certainty as regards the manner in which one is to understand the

Luxembourg SA v Belgian State, ECLI:EU:C:1998:206, para. 24. In the Eight VAT Directive, replaced on 1 January 2010 by Council Directive 2008/9, the term 'fixed establishment' is also used, but in combination with the words 'from which business transactions were effected'. It follows from CJEU case law that the expression 'fixed establishment from which business transactions are effected' in the Eighth Directive/Directive 2008/9, must be interpreted as regarding a non-resident taxable person as a person who does not have a fixed establishment carrying out taxable transactions in general. The existence of *active transactions* in the Member State concerned, therefore, constitutes the determining factor for exclusion of recourse to the Eighth Directive/Directive 2008/9. Similarly, the Court has held that the term 'transactions' used in the phrase 'from which business transactions are effected' can refer only to output transactions. *See* CJEU 16 July 2009, Case C-244/08 *Commission v Italy*, ECLI:EU:C:2009:478 and CJEU 25 October 2012, Joined Cases C-318/11 and C-319/11 *Daimler AG/Widex AS v Skatteverket*, ECLI:EU:C:2012:666.

42. CJEU 4 July 1985, Case 168/84 *Berkholz v Finanzamt Hamburg-Mitte-Altstadt*, ECLI: EU:C:1985:299, para. 17; CJEU 2 May 1996, Case C-231/94 *Faaborg-Gelting Linien A/S v Finanzamt Flensburg*, ECLI:EU:C:1996:184, para. 16; CJEU 20 February 1997, Case C-260/95 *Commissioners of Customs and Excise v DFDS A/S*, ECLI:EU:C:1997:77, para. 19; CJEU 17 July 1997, Case C-190/95 *ARO Lease BV v Inspecteur van de Belastingdienst Grote Ondernemingen te Amsterdam*, ECLI:EU:C:1997:374, para. 15 and CJEU 7 May 1998, Case 390/96 *Lease Plan Luxembourg SA v Belgian State*, ECLI:EU:C:1998:206, para. 24.

concept of the fixed establishment.[43] First, the legal definitions have a limited scope – as they are relevant only in the context of the application of specifically mentioned place of supply rules. Further, as also becomes apparent from CJEU case law – e.g., the *Welmory* case[44] – there still is considerable uncertainty as to the interpretation of the rather abstract concepts of 'sufficient degree of permanence', 'suitable structure' and 'human and technical resources' – especially when situations involve a high extent of digitalization and intangibility (e.g., in the electronic services sector).[45] For example, one may question whether the concept of the fixed establishment also covers situations involving the presence of a digitalized infrastructure (e.g., websites operated by means of servers *in situ*), or involving human and technical resources that are strictly external to the company that makes use of them (e.g., when staff is temporarily hired from an employment agency and equipment is temporarily rented from a rental company). The latter situation is addressed in *Titanium Ltd v Finanzamt Österreich*, concerning a company based in Jersey that lets immovable property in Austria without having its own staff present.[46] The CJEU rules that the property does not constitute a fixed establishment for VAT purposes. In the course of its judgment, the Court considers that the persons responsible for the property management in Austria were merely contractually appointed by the company, did not concern own staff, and enjoyed no important decision power. Thus, the property in Austria did not have any human resource enabling it to act independently. In our view, the judgment implies that *hired* staff (external staff that is not directly on the payroll of the company concerned) can constitute the required human resource of a fixed establishment only if the relationship between the hiring entity and the hired staff reflects the material characteristics of the classic employment relationship. Such material characteristics may include employer authority and decision power, and a quid pro quo in terms of labour (input) and salary (remuneration).[47]

Concerning the concept of fixed establishment, there is one more development worth mentioning. In 1997, the CJEU ruled in the *DFDS* case that a subsidiary that has

43. According to De la Feria, the concept is far from clear. *See* R. de la Feria, *On the Evolving VAT Concept of Fixed Establishment* (2021) 5&6 EC Tax Review https://doi.org/10.54648/ecta2021021. Similarly, *see* N. Şvidchi, *The Evolution and Uncertainties of the Fixed Establishment Concept* (2022) 26 Journal of Public Administration, Finance and Law https://doi.org/10.47743/jopafl-2022-26-27.
44. CJEU 16 October 2014, Case C-605/12 *Welmory*, ECLI:EU:C:2014:2298. Among others, this case concerned the question of whether a certain physical yet digitalized presence of a Cypriot company in Poland (i.e., operation of websites via servers) constituted a fixed establishment of VAT purposes in the latter Member State. Unfortunately, the CJEU does not directly address this question.
45. It is interesting to see that the Base Erosion and Profit Shifting Action Plans of the OECD also address the concept of permanent (fixed) establishment in consumption taxes, clearly in an attempt to explore a proper mode of application in the context of the new economy. *See* M. Merkx, *Fixed Establishments in European Value Added Tax: Base Erosion and Profit Shifting's Side Effects?* (2017) 1 EC Tax Review, pp. 36-44 https://doi.org/10.54648/ecta2017004.
46. CJEU 3 June 2021, Case C-931/19 *Titanium Ltd v Finanzamt Österreich*, ECLI:EU:C:2021:446.
47. *See* F. Nellen, *De ontwikkeling van het begrip vaste inrichting (BTW) in de internationale handel* (2021), Tijdschrift Fiscaal Ondernemingsrecht, pp. 19-26. For further reading on the importance of staff for fixed establishments, *see* N. Mediratta, *A Human-Free Structure: A 'Fixed Establishment' under EU VAT?* (2022) 10 European Taxation https://doi.org/10.59403/3v96vk2.

its own legal personality can, in certain instances, qualify as a fixed establishment of the parent company.[48] In its considerations, the Court referred to the need to take into account 'the actual economic situation' and the ambition to achieve a 'rational result for tax purposes' that does not allow for tax avoidance.[49] At that time, some regarded the judgment as enigmatic since the human and technical resources that constitute such a fixed establishment effectively belong to and are managed by an entity that is independent and has its own legal personality. In 2019, Advocate General Kokott opined that the CJEU had 'already distanced itself from the *DFDS* decision', the case facts of which were 'characterized by the particular circumstances of the risk of abuse of services'.[50] But then, in May 2020, the CJEU passed judgment in the *Dong Yang* case, reiterating that it is not impossible for VAT purposes that a subsidiary qualifies as a fixed establishment.[51] Whether or not such a fixed establishment is present depends on the material conditions as laid down in the VAT Implementing Regulation (Article 11), which need to be assessed in the light of the economic and commercial reality of the case at hand. The legal status of the subsidiary – i.e., the fact that it has its own legal personality – is not decisive in this regard. This judgment reinforced the *DFDS* approach and seemed to disregard the legal and economic disunion that characterizes entities which are legally independent. More recent case law, however, has in our view diluted the significance of the *Dong Yang* judgment. In *Berlin Chemie A. Menarini SRL*, the Court provided that a company which has its registered office in one Member State (Germany) does not have a fixed establishment in another Member State (Romania) on the ground that that company owns a subsidiary there that makes available to it human and technical resources under contracts by means of which that subsidiary provides, exclusively to it, marketing, regulatory, advertising and representation services that are capable of having a direct influence on the volume of its sales.[52] So, even though the German company enjoyed, by means of its capital ownership *and* the closed contract, extensive formal and actual control over the Romanian subsidiary, the human and technical assets of the latter still did not constitute a fixed establishment of the former.[53] Furthermore, the case *Cabot Plastics Belgium SA* concerned a toll manufacturer based in Belgium that, on the basis of tolling service contracts, processed goods

48. CJEU 20 February 1997, Case C-260/95 *Commissioners of Customs and Excise v DFDS A/S*, ECLI:EU:C:1997:77. In the case, the CJEU refers to the circumstances that the subsidiary is wholly owned by the parent company, and merely acts as an auxiliary organ of the latter.
49. *Ibid.*, paras 22 and 23.
50. Opinion of Advocate General Kokott of 14 November 2019, Case C-547/18 *Dong Yang Electronics Sp. z o.o. v Dyrektor Izby Administracji Skarbowej we Wrocławiu*, ECLI:EU:C:2019:976, paras 64 and 65.
51. CJEU 7 May 2020, Case C-547/18 *Dong Yang Electronics Sp. z o.o. v Dyrektor Izby Administracji Skarbowej we Wrocławiu*, ECLI:EU:C:2020:350.
52. CJEU 7 April 2022, Case C-333.20 *Berlin Chemie A. Menarini SRL*, ECLI:EU:C:2022:291.
53. The Romanian tax authorities in this case argued that the assets of the subsidiary constituted a fixed establishment of the company and that the services provided by the subsidiary were received, in Romania, by the fixed establishment (which consisted of the assets of the subsidiary). In our view, this position is incomprehensible if one considers the logic and systemics of EU VAT. The CJEU very directly rejects it by stating that the same means cannot be used to both provide and receive the same services (para. 54).

owned by an affiliated Swiss principal.[54] Also here, the CJEU unambiguously rules that the Swiss principal has no fixed establishment in Belgium, where the service provider is established. Following these judgments, we are of the opinion that considering the human and technical resources of a separate legal entity as the fixed establishment of another legal entity should be regarded as a highly exceptional and, for a variety of reasons, a fundamentally flawed approach, save certain instances that involve practices that are clearly abusive.[55]

c) Intervening Fixed Establishment

In case it has been established that the service supplier indeed has a fixed establishment as defined in Article 11 VAT Implementing Regulation, one must assess whether the service is rendered from the service supplier's place of business (head office) or from (one of) his fixed establishment(s). Further, in case the service recipient has a fixed establishment, one must assess whether the service is rendered to the recipient's place of business (head office) or to (one of) his fixed establishment(s). Articles 20-22 VAT Implementing Regulation describe the factors that should be taken into account in this respect.[56] Where a service supplier renders a service from its head office and the service is located in another country, in which the service supplier has a fixed establishment, the person liable to pay VAT depends on the role of the fixed establishment.

Article 196 VAT Directive stipulates that, in general, the person liable to pay VAT for cross-border B2B main rule services of Article 44 VAT Directive, is the person receiving the services if the taxable person rendering the services is not established in the customer's country.[57] According to Article 192a VAT Directive, for the purposes of the provisions on 'person liable to pay VAT', a taxable person who has a fixed establishment within the territory of the Member State where the tax is due shall be regarded as a taxable person who is *not* established within that Member State, provided that this fixed establishment does not intervene in that supply. The concept of 'intervene' is elaborated on in the VAT Implementing Regulation. From Article 53(1), we learn that, for the application of Article 192a VAT Directive, a fixed establishment as defined in Article 11(2) VAT Implementing Regulation shall be taken into consideration only when it is characterized by a sufficient degree of permanence and a suitable structure in terms of human and technical resources to enable it to make the supply of goods or services *in which it intervenes.* Pursuant to Article 53(2) VAT

54. CJEU 29 June 2023, Case C-232/33 *Cabot Plastics Belgium SA*, ECLI:EU:C:2023:530. For an analysis of this case, *see* K. Tourmous & A. Soldai, *VAT and the Concept of Fixed Establishment: The Cabot Plastics Belgium Case* (2023) 6 International VAT Monitor https://doi.org/10.59403/1bzw22c.
55. *See* F. Nellen, *De ontwikkeling van het begrip vaste inrichting (BTW) in de internationale handel* (2021), Tijdschrift Fiscaal Ondernemingsrecht, pp. 19-26. For further reading, *see* G.E. Zubeldia, *Turning a Subsidiary into a VAT Fixed Establishment: It Just Ain't So?* (2022) 4 International VAT Monitor https://doi.org/10.59403/qt6wjv.
56. Articles 20-22 VAT Regulation are discussed in section 12.3.5.1.
57. *See* to Chapter 12 for a further explanation of the person liable and reverse charge mechanism.

Implementing Regulation, the fixed establishment shall be considered as not intervening in the supply of goods[58] or services unless the technical and human resources of that fixed establishment are used by him for transactions *inherent in the fulfilment of the taxable supply* of those goods or services made within that Member State, before or during this fulfilment. It is left to the Member States and taxable person concerned to establish what intervention is considered to be inherent and what not. The only guidelines given in this respect are that, where the resources of the fixed establishment are only used for administrative support tasks, such as accounting, invoicing and collection of debt-claims, they shall not be regarded as being used for the fulfilment of the supply of goods or services. As there is a large grey area between mere administrative support and inherent transactions, we strongly doubt whether Article 53(2) provides a real clarification. We fear and have experienced in practice that this provision is explained differently by different Member States. Double (non-)taxation could be the undesirable result. Given *RBS Deutschland GmbH,*[59] it will be difficult for Member States to impose VAT assessments for underpaid VAT in case of double non-taxation, arguing abuse of law.

To avoid uncertainty and possible conflicts with the tax authorities, a taxable person can decide to issue the invoice under the VAT ID number attributed by the Member State of the fixed establishment. According to Article 53(2) VAT Implementing Regulation, the fixed establishment shall then be regarded as having intervened in the supply of goods or services made in that Member State unless there is proof to the contrary.

4.5.3 Business to Business Services (B2B Services)

In this section, we will discuss the place of supply rules for services supplied by a taxable person to another taxable person (B2B services). Since the rules on the place of supply of services are rather detailed, we deem it useful to provide the reader with the overview of the place of B2B services (Figure 4.1).[60]

58. Article 192a VAT Directive and Article 53 VAT Regulation also apply to the supply of goods, *see* section 12.3.5.1.
59. CJEU 22 December 2010, Case C-277/09 *The Commissioners for Her Majesty's Revenue & Customs v RBS Deutschland Holdings GmbH,* ECLI:EU:C:2010:810.
60. This overview is based on: A.J. van Doesum, H.W.M. van Kesteren, G.J. van Norden, & I.H.T. Reiniers, *The New Rules on the Place of Supply of Services in European VAT* (2008) 2 EC Tax Review, pp. 78-89 https://doi.org/10.54648/ecta2008056.

Figure 4.1 Overview Place of Supply Rules B2B Services

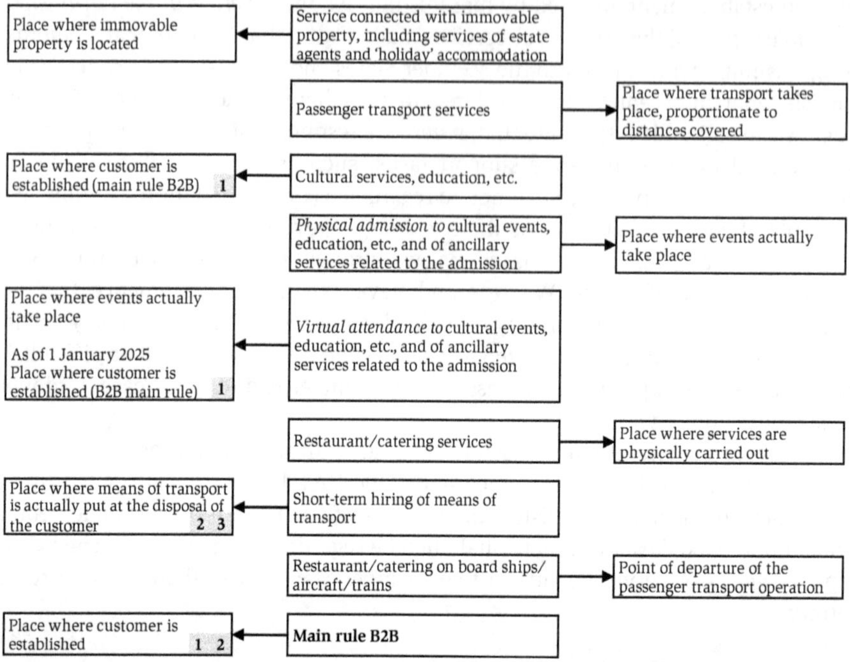

Key to Figure 4.1:

1 Where this overview refers for brevity to the place where the customer is established, the place of supply is where the customer has established his business, a fixed establishment to which the services are provided or where the customer has his permanent address or usually resides.

2 If a Member State implements the effective use and enjoyment rules (Article 59a VAT Directive), the place of supply is where the effective use and enjoyment of the service takes place.

3 Member States may implement the effective use and enjoyment rules (Article 59a VAT Directive) with regard to all services referred to in Article 56 VAT Directive. Therefore, also the place of hiring, other than short-term hiring, can be the place where the effective use and enjoyment ofthe service takes place.

4.5.3.1 *The Taxable Person Concept in the Context of the Place of Supply Rules*

Some place of supply rules – including the B2C and B2B main rules for the place of supply of services – depend on the VAT taxable status of the customer of a service. It is, therefore, important to determine whether or not a customer is a taxable person. For the purposes of applying the place of supply rules, Article 43(1) VAT Directive stipulates that a taxable person who also carries out activities or transactions that are not considered to be taxable supplies of goods or services in accordance with Article

2(1) VAT Directive shall be regarded as a taxable person in respect of all services rendered to him. This means that the place of supply of services rendered to taxable persons with both a taxable and a non-taxable sphere should always be considered to be located where these taxable persons are established (unless an exception applies). This rule contributes to the administrative simplification and greater legal certainty.

One can imagine the situation in which an entity carries out both economic and non-economic activities. In connection with such instances, the CJEU ruled in *TRR* that Article 9(2)(e) Sixth VAT Directive (currently Article 59(c) VAT Directive) must be interpreted as meaning that where the customer for consultancy services supplied by a taxable person established in another Member State carries out both an economic activity and an activity which falls outside the scope of those directives, that customer is to be regarded as a taxable person even where the supply is used solely for the purposes of the latter activity.[61] In other words, a taxable person who also carries out activities that are outside the scope of VAT is to be regarded as a taxable person for the place of supply rules, even though the services were received solely in respect of its activities outside the scope of VAT (non-taxable sphere). This judgment has been codified by the EU legislator in Article 43(1) VAT Directive.

Similarly, Article 43(2) VAT Directive states that a non-taxable legal person who is identified for VAT purposes shall be regarded as a taxable person for the purposes of applying the place of supply rules. Even though these legal persons are non-taxable persons, not the B2C main rule for the place of supply of services applies, but rather the B2B main rule. We believe that this provision was introduced for reasons of legal certainty and simplicity. Service suppliers who receive a VAT ID number from their foreign customer may, apart from the exceptions, assume that their services are taxable in the Member State that has issued this VAT ID number. In our view, it is quite remarkable that the new provision refers solely to legal persons. For a Community tax, such as VAT, national civil law qualifications, such as legal form and personality, should be of no relevance. On the basis of Article 43(2) VAT Directive, a non-taxable entity with a VAT ID number and legal personality is treated differently from a non-taxable entity without legal personality. In view of the neutrality of legal form that the EU VAT aspires to, we deem this dissimilar approach undesirable. Furthermore, the provision of Article 43(2) VAT Directive could give rise to VAT planning. A non-taxable legal person that purchases services from a foreign service supplier that is established in a Member State with a higher VAT rate than the Member State where the non-taxable legal person is established could decide to file a request to be identified for VAT purposes with the local tax authorities so as to 'shift' the place of supply of the services to the latter Member State. The non-taxable legal person can do this by opting to have its ICAs subject to taxation in the Member State where it is established.[62] For a more

61. CJEU 6 November 2008, Case C-291/07 *Kollektivavtalsstiftelsen TRR Trygghetsrådet v Skatteverket*, ECLI:EU:C:2008:609.
62. Articles 3(3) and 214(1)(b) VAT Directive. Article 17(2) VAT Regulation confirms that a non-taxable legal person who has exercised the option of making his intra-Community acquisitions of goods subject to VAT shall be regarded as a taxable person within the meaning of Article 43 VAT Directive. If the value of its yearly intra-Community acquisitions of goods

extensive description of the circumstances under which a non-taxable legal person is identified for VAT purposes, we refer to Chapter 13.[63]

4.5.3.2 *Criteria to Determine the Status and Capacity of the Customer*

The correct application of the rules governing the place of supply of services relies mainly on the status of the customer as a taxable or non-taxable person, and on the capacity in which he is acting. The VAT Implementing Regulation contains some rather detailed guidelines that the service supplier can use to determine the status and capacity of its customer.

In order to determine the customer's status as a taxable person, Articles 17 and 18 VAT Implementing Regulation establish what the supplier is required to obtain as evidence from his customer. Where Article 17 VAT Implementing Regulation stipulates as a general rule that the status of the customer shall be determined on the basis of Articles 9-13 and Article 43 VAT Directive, Article 18 VAT Implementing Regulation contains guidelines that the supplier can follow when establishing the status of its customer. According to Article 18(1) VAT Implementing Regulation, the supplier may, unless he has information to the contrary, regard a customer established within the Community as a taxable person:

(a) where the customer has communicated his individual VAT ID number to him, and the supplier obtains confirmation of the validity of that identification number and of the associated name and address in accordance with a Council Regulation on administrative cooperation and combating fraud in the field of VAT;[64]
(b) where the customer has not yet received an individual VAT ID number but informs the supplier that he has applied for it, and the supplier obtains any other proof which demonstrates that the customer is a taxable person or a non-taxable legal person required to be identified for VAT purposes and carries out a reasonable level of verification of the accuracy of the information provided by the customer, by normal commercial security measures, such as those relating to identity or payment checks.

Having access to an individual VAT ID number thus plays an important role, as also appears from Article 18(2) VAT Implementing Regulation, which stipulates that the supplier may, unless he has information to the contrary, regard a customer established within the Community as a non-taxable person when he can demonstrate that the customer has *not* communicated his individual VAT ID number to him.

---

exceeds a threshold of EUR 10,000, the non-taxable legal person has no choice but to register for VAT purposes in the Member State where the intra-Community acquisitions take place (Article 3(2) VAT Directive).

63. Articles 3(3) and 214(1) sub b VAT Directive.
64. Article 31 of Council Regulation (EU) No 904/2010 of 7 October 2010 on administrative cooperation and combating fraud in the field of value added tax (recast) [2010] OJ L268/1.

Although the guidelines in Article 18 VAT Implementing Regulation are intended to minimize administrative burdens and to maximize the legal certainty of the service supplier, we consider it not always easy for the service supplier to demonstrate that he has no contrary information and that a customer has not communicated his individual VAT ID number to him. Article 55 VAT Implementing Regulation can be helpful in this respect: it requires taxable persons to whom a VAT ID number has been attributed and non-taxable legal persons who are identified for VAT purposes when acting as such, to communicate their VAT ID number to their suppliers.

For customers established outside the EU, other items of proof will have to be collected to substantiate the VAT taxable status of the recipient. Article 18(3) VAT Implementing Regulation stipulates that the supplier may unless he has information to the contrary, regard a customer established outside the Community as a taxable person:

(a) if he obtains from the customer a certificate issued by the customer's competent tax authorities as confirmation that the customer is engaged in economic activities in order to enable him to obtain a refund of VAT under the Thirteenth Directive;[65]
(b) where the customer does not possess such a certificate if the supplier has the VAT number, or a similar number attributed to the customer by the country of establishment and used to identify businesses or any other proof which demonstrates that the customer is a taxable person and if the supplier carries out a reasonable level of verification of the accuracy of the information provided by the customer, by normal commercial security measures, such as those relating to identity or payment checks.

We note that Article 44 VAT Directive states that it applies when B2B main rule services are provided to a 'taxable person acting as such'. In the preamble of Council Directive 2008/8/EC,[66] it is considered that Article 43 VAT Directive should not extend to supplies of services received by a taxable person for his own personal use or that of his staff. In view of Article 43 VAT Directive, one may argue that the addition 'as such' only refers to the categories of supplies mentioned in the preamble, i.e., services for the taxable person's personal use or for his staff's use. This view is supported by Article 19 VAT Implementing Regulation, according to which a taxable person, or a non-taxable legal person deemed to be a taxable person, who receives services exclusively for private use, including use by his staff, shall, for the purpose of applying the B2B and B2C main rules for the place of supply of services (Articles 44 and 45 VAT Directive), be regarded as a non-taxable person. Unless he has information to the contrary, such as information on the nature of the services provided, the supplier may consider that

65. Thirteenth Council Directive 86/560/EEC of 17 November 1986 on the harmonization of the laws of the Member States relating to turnover taxes – Arrangements for the refund of value added tax to taxable persons not established in Community territory [1986] OJ L326/40.
66. Council Directive 2008/8/EC of 20 February 2008 amending Directive 2006/112/EC as regards the place of supply of services [2008] OJ L44/11, paras 4 and 19.

the services are for the customer's business use if, for that transaction, the customer has communicated his individual VAT ID number. Where one and the same service is intended for both private use, including use by the customer's staff, and business use, the supply of that service shall be covered exclusively by the main rule for B2B services, laid down in Article 44 VAT Directive, provided there is no abusive practice.

4.5.3.3 Main Rule B2B Services

The main rule for the place of supply of services rendered to taxable persons is laid down in Article 44 VAT Directive and states that the place of supply of services to a taxable person acting as such shall be the place where that person has established his business. However, if those services are provided *to a fixed establishment* of the taxable person located in a place other than the place where he has established his business, the place of supply of those services shall be the place where that fixed establishment is located. In the absence of such a place of establishment or fixed establishment, the place of supply of services shall be the place where the taxable person who receives such services has his permanent address or usually resides.

In practice, most B2B services are subject to this main rule for B2B services. The reason is that there are only a few exceptions to the B2B main rule, relating to very specific categories of the service industry – which are addressed in section 4.5.3.4. The broad scope of the new main rule is in agreement with the EU legislator's ambition to realize taxation at the place of consumption.[67] The following services are, among other services, subject to the main rule for B2B services (the list is not exhaustive):

(1) valuations of and work on movable tangible property;
(2) ancillary transport services, such as loading, unloading, handling and similar services;
(3) transport of goods;
(4) services by intermediaries;
(5) 'intellectual services', e.g., advertising, services of consultants, engineers, lawyers, accountants, banking and insurance transactions, etc.

If a service recipient (taxable person) carries on its business through more than one establishment in more than one country, the place of supply of the received B2B main rule services is in principle located in the head office's country unless the services are received by a fixed establishment that is using the service for its own needs. The principle that the head office takes precedence over the fixed establishments is confirmed in Article 21 VAT Implementing Regulation. For a service supplier, it will not always be easy to assess to which establishment of the recipient he provides his service, particularly not because the establishments are part of the same legal person. Furthermore, in practice, a head office often engages a service supplier for the

67. We note, however, that the place where the service recipient is established is not necessarily the place where actual consumption takes place. It is merely an approximation of the place of actual consumption.

provision of services directly to its fixed establishments. Article 22(1) VAT Implementing Regulation stipulates that, in order to identify the customer's fixed establishment to which the service is provided, the supplier shall examine the nature and use of the service provided. If the service supplier is unable to identify the fixed establishment to which the service is provided by means of the nature and use of the service provided, the supplier shall pay particular attention to whether the contract, the order form and the VAT ID number attributed by the Member State of the customer and communicated to him by the customer identify the fixed establishment as the customer of the service and whether the fixed establishment is the entity paying for the service. We expect that, in practice, the contract and VAT ID number communicated to the service supplier will be used to identify the establishment to which the service is provided. Where neither the nature and use of a service, nor the contract, order form and VAT ID number can be used to determine the receiving establishment, and where the services are supplied under a contract covering one or more services used in an unidentifiable and non-quantifiable manner, the supplier may legitimately consider that the services have been supplied to the customer's head office. Article 25 VAT Implementing Regulation provides that only the circumstances existing at the time of the chargeable event shall be taken into account. Any subsequent changes to the use of the service received shall not affect the determination of the place of supply, provided there is no abusive practice.

4.5.3.4 *Exceptions B2B Services*

4.5.3.4.1 Services Connected with Immovable Property

According to Article 47 VAT Directive, the place of supply of services connected with immovable property shall be the place where the immovable property is located. This exception applies, irrespective of the VAT taxable status of the customer and aims to tax services on the place of consumption of the service. For a definition of immovable property, we refer to section 9.4.

The most important service that falls under this provision is probably the lease of immovable property.[68] Article 47 VAT Directive mentions a variety of services that also fall within the scope of this exception: services of experts and estate agents, the provision of accommodation in the hotel sector or in sectors with a similar function, such as holiday camps or sites developed for use as camping sites, the granting of rights to use immovable property and services for the preparation and coordination of construction work, such as the services of architects and of firms providing on-site supervision. In our view, this list is illustrative rather than exhaustive.[69] Other services, not explicitly mentioned, can also qualify as services connected with immovable property. The CJEU ruled that there must be a 'sufficiently direct' connection with the

68. The definition of the concept of leasing or letting of immovable property is explained in section 9.6.1.
69. *See* Opinion of Advocate General Sharpston of 7 March 2006, Case C-166/05 *Rudi Heger GmbH v Finanzamt Graz-Stadt*, ECLI:EU:C:2006:156, para. 36.

immovable property. According to the CJEU, it would be contrary to the general scheme of this special place of supply rule to place within its scope every supply of services provided that has a connection, even a very tenuous one, with immovable property since a large number of services are connected in one way or another with immovable property. Thus, only supplies of services that have a sufficiently direct connection with immovable property come under this exception.[70] In *Heger*, the CJEU ruled that an immovable property must constitute a 'central and essential element' of a supply, in order to establish a sufficiently direct connection of a service with the immovable property.[71]

From the CJEU's considerations, we take that it is not sufficient that a service is connected with immovable property merely in a general sense.[72] Rather, the service must relate to expressly specific immovable property.[73] In addition, it is necessary that the supply of services relates to the immovable property itself. Under those circumstances, expressly specific immovable property should be considered a constituent element of a supply of services, in that it constitutes a central and essential element thereof.[74] As a result, for example, a storage service, which cannot be regarded as relating to the development, management or evaluation of immovable property, only falls within the scope of the special place of supply rule for immovable property if the recipient of that service is given a right to use all or part of expressly specific immovable property.[75]

Still, it is not always clear whether a service is 'sufficiently directly' connected to an immovable property. Because of Council Regulation 1042/2013 amending the VAT Implementing Regulation,[76] a new provision has been added to the VAT Implementing Regulation, which is intended to provide more guidance as to the scope of services that are sufficiently directly connected to immovable property. This new Article 31a(1) states that:

> services shall be regarded as having a sufficiently direct connection with immovable property in the following cases:

70. CJEU 7 September 2006, Case C-166/05 *Heger Rudi GmbH v Finanzamt Graz-Stadt,* ECLI:EU:C:2006:533, paras 23 and 24; CJEU 3 September 2009, Case C37/08 *RCI Europe v Commissioners for Her Majesty's Revenue and Customs,* ECLI:EU:C:2009:507, para. 36; CJEU 27 October 2011, Case C-530/09 *Inter-Mark Group sp. z o.o. sp. Komandytowa v Minister Finansów,* ECLI:EU:C:2011:697, para. 30 and CJEU 27 June 2013, Case C-155/12 *Minister Finansów v RR Donnelley Global Turnkey Solutions Poland Sp. z o.o.,* ECLI:EU:C:2013:434, para. 32.
71. CJEU 7 September 2006, Case C-166/05 *Heger Rudi GmbH v Finanzamt Graz-Stadt,* ECLI:EU:C:2006:533, para. 25.
72. *See* M.W. Horsthuis & F.J.G. Nellen, *Storage of Goods under EU VAT* (2013) 6 International VAT Monitor, para. 2.2.3.
73. CJEU 27 June 2013, Case C-155/12 *Minister Finansów v RR Donnelley Global Turnkey Solutions Poland Sp. z o.o.,* ECLI:EU:C:2013:434, para. 34.
74. CJEU 7 September 2006, Case C-166/05 *Heger Rudi GmbH v Finanzamt Graz-Stadt,* ECLI:EU:C:2006:533, para. 25 and CJEU 27 June 2013, Case C-155/12 *Minister Finansów v RR Donnelley Global Turnkey Solutions Poland Sp. z o.o.,* ECLI:EU:C:2013:434, para. 35.
75. CJEU 27 June 2013, Case C-155/12 *Minister Finansów v RR Donnelley Global Turnkey Solutions Poland Sp. z o.o.,* ECLI:EU:C:2013:434, para. 37.
76. Council Implementing Regulation (EU) No 1042/2013 of 7 October 2013 amending Implementing Regulation (EU) No 282/2011 as regards the place of supply of services [2013] OJ L284/1.

(a) where they are derived from an immovable property, and that property makes up a constituent element of the service and is central to, and essential for, the services supplied;
(b) where they are provided to, or directed towards, an immovable property having as their object the legal or physical alteration of that property.

Article 31a(2) and (3) contain a list of services that shall, in particular, respectively, be covered or not be qualified as 'sufficiently directly' connected to an immovable property. For example, the drawing up of plans for a building designated for a particular plot of land regardless of whether or not the building is erected and legal services relating to the conveyance or the transfer of a title to immovable property are mentioned as sufficiently directly connected services, whereas portfolio management of investments in real estate is not to be regarded as such. Article 31a applies as of 1 January 2017.

4.5.3.4.2 Passenger Transport Services

Article 48 VAT Directive provides that the place of supply of passenger transport services is the place where the transport takes place, proportionate to the distances covered. As a result, when passenger transport is being carried out on the territory of several countries, the service is partially located in every country where the transport actually takes place. This provision leads to the levying of VAT where the consumption takes place, yet at the same time implies a considerable administrative burden. The service supplier will have to register for VAT and charge VAT in every country where the transport takes place unless the reverse charge mechanism is applicable under the local VAT Act.

In *Trans Tirreno Express,*[77] the CJEU ruled that this specific rule does not prohibit a Member State from applying its VAT legislation to a transport operation effected between two points within its national territory, even where a part of that journey is completed outside its national territory (e.g., international waters), provided that it does not encroach on the tax jurisdiction of other states. As a result, in these circumstances, for national transport services, not only the distance covered in the respective country is subject to national VAT but also the distance covered outside the respective country may be subject to national VAT. In *Commission/France,* the CJEU decided that Member States may not be required to apply VAT to transport operations carried out within their territory in respect of that part of the journey occurring in or above international waters.[78]

We note that passenger transport services should be distinguished from the hiring of means of transport, for which a separate exception applies, depending on VAT taxable status of the customer and on the duration of the hiring. We refer to sections 4.5.3.4.6 and 4.5.4.2.9.

77. CJEU 23 January 1986, Case 283/84 *Trans Tirreno Express SpA v Ufficio provinciale IVA*, ECLI:EU:C:1986:31.
78. CJEU 13 March 1990, Case C-30/89 *Commission of the European Communities v French Republic*, ECLI:EU:C:1990:114.

4.5.3.4.3 Admission to Cultural, Educational and Suchlike Events

Article 53 VAT Directive provides that the place of supply of services in respect of *admission to* cultural, artistic, sporting, scientific, educational, entertainment or similar events, such as fairs and exhibitions, and of ancillary services related to the admission, supplied to a taxable person, shall be the place where those events actually take place. This specific rule aims to tax these services in the place of final consumption. Currently, access to such events falls under the provision, regardless of whether the access is physical or virtual. As per 1 January 2025, Article 53 VAT Directive mentions that the provision does not apply to admission to events where the attendance is virtual. Thus, from that date only physical access to such events falls under this place of service rule. Virtual attendance will then be covered by the B2B main rule (Article 44 VAT Directive).[79]

The categories of services mentioned in the provision (i.e., services in respect of admission to cultural etc. events) are generally complex by nature and often provided for a number of different recipients. Furthermore, the various categories of services also have the common feature that they are usually provided for specific events, and the place where those complex services are physically carried out is easy to identify since such events take place at specific locations.[80] As regards the criteria according to which a specified service is to be regarded as a cultural, educational or suchlike service, no particular artistic level is required, and it is not only services relating *inter alia* to artistic and entertainment activities but also services relating to merely similar activities that fall within the scope of this provision.[81] An activity (event) in respect of which the principal objective pursued by the supplier of services is the entertainment of its customers constitutes an entertainment or similar event.[82]

From Article 32 VAT Implementing Regulation, it follows that this special provision includes the supply of services of which the *essential* characteristics are the granting of the right of admission to an event in exchange for a ticket or payment, including payment in the form of a subscription, a season ticket or a periodic fee.[83] In particular, the right of admission to shows, theatrical performances, circus performances, fairs, amusement parks, concerts, exhibitions, and other similar cultural

79. This specific rule was adopted following the CJEU ruling in *Geelen* (CJEU 8 May 2019, Case C-568/17 *Staatssecretaris van Financiën v L.W. Geelen*, ECLI:EU:C:2019:388). *See* Council Directive (EU) 2022/542 of 5 April 2022 amending Directives 2006/112/EC and (EU) 2020/285 as regards rates of value added tax, OJ L107.
80. CJEU 9 March 2006, Case C-114/05 *Ministre de l'Économie, des Finances et de l'Industrie v Gillan Beach Ltd*, ECLI:EU:C:2006:169, paras 23 and 24; CJEU 7 October 2010, Case C-222/09 *Kronospan Mielec sp. z o.o. v Dyrektor Izby Skarbowej w Rzeszowie*, ECLI:EU:C:2010:593.
81. CJEU 26 September 1996, Case C-327/94 *Jürgen Dudda v Finanzgericht Bergisch Gladbach*, ECLI:EU:C:1996:355; CJEU 12 May 2005, Case C-452/03 *RAL (Channel Islands) Ltd and Others v Commissioners of Customs & Excise*, ECLI:EU:C:2005:289; CJEU 9 March 2006, Case C-114/05 *Ministre de l'Économie, des Finances et de l'Industrie v Gillan Beach Ltd*, ECLI:EU:C:2006:169 and CJEU 7 October 2010, Case C-222/09 *Kronospan Mielec sp. z o.o. v Dyrektor Izby Skarbowej w Rzeszowie*, ECLI:EU:C:2010:593.
82. CJEU 12 May 2005, Case C-452/03 *RAL (Channel Islands) Ltd and Others v Commissioners of Customs & Excise*, ECLI:EU:C:2005:289.
83. CJEU 13 March 2019, Case C-647/17 *Srf konsulterna AB*, ECLI:EU:C:2019:195.

events, sporting events, such as matches or competitions and educational and scientific events, such as conferences and seminars, fall within the scope of this provision. Following the new Article 33a VAT Implementing Regulation[84] the supply of tickets by an intermediary acting in his own name but on behalf of the organizer or by a taxable person, other than the organizer, acting on his own behalf, is covered by Article 53 (and Article 54(1)) VAT Directive. By means of this provision, taxation takes place where the event does, regardless of whether the tickets are distributed by the event organizer himself or by an intermediary ticket office.

In our view, one may wonder whether Article 53 VAT Directive also applies in cases in which participants do not have to buy a ticket. On the basis of Article 32 VAT Implementing Regulation, access to the event on the basis of a ticket as such seems not to be a hard condition, as long as there is a payment.[85] In our view, the question to ask is whether the essential characteristics of the respective event consist of granting admission to that event, irrespective of the organizational manner in which participants ultimately obtain admission. This also becomes apparent from the judgment in *Srf konsulterna AB*,[86] where the CJEU adds that admission to an event in the sense of Article 53 VAT Directive necessarily involves the possibility of attending and participating in that event. It is, therefore, not the right to enter a place which is paramount, but rather the right to participate in the specified event.[87] Similarly, in *SC Westside Unicat SRL*, the Court has provided that the provision does not apply to digital content creation services rendered by a video recording studio to the operator of an internet streaming platform.[88]

4.5.3.4.4 Restaurant and Catering Services

In Chapter 1, we set out that the main purpose of levying VAT is to tax consumption. Ideally, VAT is levied at the place where consumption takes place. For restaurant and catering services, this place can be identified quite easily. Thus, Article 55 VAT Directive stipulates that the place of supply of restaurant and catering services other than those physically carried out on board ships, aircraft or trains during the section of a passenger transport operation effected within the Community, shall be the place where the services are physically carried out. We interpret the words 'physically carried out' to mean that the country in which the food/drinks are served is regarded

84. Council Implementing Regulation (EU) No 1042/2013 of 7 October 2013 amending Implementing Regulation (EU) No 282/2011 as regards the place of supply of services [2013] OJ L284/1.
85. Article 32 VAT Regulation provides that services as meant by Article 53 VAT Directive shall include the supply of services of which the essential characteristics are the granting of the right of admission to an event in exchange for a *ticket or payment* (...).
86. CJEU 13 March 2019, Case C-647/17 *Srf konsulterna AB*, ECLI:EU:C:2019:195.
87. Finally, Article 33 VAT Regulation stipulates that such ancillary services shall include, in particular, the use of cloakrooms or sanitary facilities but shall not include mere intermediary services relating to the sale of tickets. In our opinion, many ancillary services which are directly related to the admission can also be regarded as being part of the service consisting of the admission to the event and can, therefore, not always be regarded as a separate service. *See* section 3.5 with respect to a single supply versus various separate supplies.
88. CJEU 23 November 2023, Case C-532/22 *SC Westside Unicat SRL*, ECLI:EU:C:2023:919.

as the place of supply, even if the food is prepared in another country. This provision applies not only to restaurant and catering services rendered to taxable persons but also to non-taxable persons.

Restaurant and catering services are defined in Article 6 VAT Implementing Regulation as services that consist of the supply of prepared or unprepared food or beverages or both, for human consumption, accompanied by sufficient support services allowing for the immediate consumption thereof. According to the CJEU, restaurant and catering services consist of 'a cluster of features and acts, of which the provision of food is only one component and in which services largely predominate.'[89] If the food and/or beverages are supplied without any other support services or with insignificant support services, the supply shall be considered a supply of goods rather than restaurant or catering services.[90]

4.5.3.4.5 *Restaurant and Catering Services on Board Ships/Trains/Aircraft*

In Article 57 VAT Directive, a special rule is laid down for establishing the place of supply of restaurant and catering services which are physically carried out on board ships, aircraft or trains during the section of a passenger transport operation effected within the Community. The place of supply of such a restaurant or catering service shall be at the point of departure of the passenger transport operation. In the case of a return trip, the return leg shall be regarded as a separate transport operation. As a result, passengers will be charged a different rate on the way back than on the way over. For *supplies of goods* on board ships, aircraft or trains during the section of a passenger transport operation effected within the Community, the place of supply is also the point of departure of the passenger transport operation.[91]

Article 57 VAT Directive and Articles 35-37 VAT Implementing Regulation contain rules to determine 'the section of a passenger transport operation effected within the Community' and 'the point of departure'. From these rules, we derive that restaurant and catering services carried out during a section subsequent to a departure from a place outside the Community, do not fall under this special provision, but fall within the scope of the place of supply rule for catering and restaurant services of Article 55 VAT Directive.

4.5.3.4.6 *Short-Term Hiring of Means of Transport*

The place of supply of the hiring of means of transport depends on the duration of the possession or use, on the means of transport hired and on the VAT status of the

89. *See also* CJEU 2 May 1996, Case C-231/94 *Faaborg-Gelting Linien A/S v Finanzamt Flensburg*, ECLI:EU:C:1996:184, para. 14.
90. This is in accordance with the CJEU judgment of 10 March 2011 in Joined Cases C-497/09 *Finanzamt Burgdorf v Manfred Bog*, C-499/09 *CinemaxX Entertainment GmbH & Co. KG v Finanzamt Hamburg-Barmbek-Uhlenhorst*, C-501/09 *Lothar Lohmeyer v Finanzamt Minden* and C-502/09 *Fleischerei Nier GmbH & Co. KG v Finanzamt Detmold*, ECLI:EU:C:2011:135.
91. *See* Article 37 EU VAT Directive.

customer. In this section, we discuss the rules for the hiring of means of transport to VAT taxable persons. The (additional) particular rules for the hiring of means of transport to non-taxable persons are described in section 4.5.4.2.9.

A definition of means of transport and a non-exhaustive list of vehicles that should be considered means of transport can be found in Article 38 VAT Implementing Regulation. From this definition and list, we learn that 'means of transport' is explained quite broadly. According to Article 56(1) VAT Directive and Article 40 VAT Implementing Regulation, the place of supply of short-term hiring of a means of transport shall be the place where the means of transport is actually put at the disposal of the customer, being the place where the customer or a third party acting on his behalf takes physical possession of it. The exception for short-term hiring of means of transport applies, irrespective of the VAT status of the customer. Article 56(3) VAT Directive stipulates that 'short-term' shall mean the continuous possession or use of the means of transport throughout a period of not more than 30 days and, in the case of vessels, not more than 90 days. If the leasing period is longer than 30 days (all means of transport except vessels) or longer than 90 days (vessels), the main B2B rule is applicable.[92] Given that the place of supply depends on the duration of the possession or use, the treatment of such a supply where one successive contract follows another needs some further clarification. Article 39(1) VAT Implementing Regulation stipulates that the contract shall serve as a presumption that may be rebutted by any means, in fact, or law in order to establish the actual duration of the continuous possession or use. Where hiring of one and the same means of transport is covered by consecutive contracts between the same parties or when an existing contract is extended, the duration shall be that of the continuous possession or use of the means of transport provided for under the contracts as a whole, according to Article 39(2) VAT Implementing Regulation. However, the duration of the short-term hire contract, or contracts preceding a contract which is regarded as long-term, shall not be called into question provided there is no abusive practice. This seems to suggest that where a short-term hire contract is extended to more than 30 days (or more than 90 days in the case of vessels), the lease during the initial hiring period is still regarded as a short-term lease (assuming no abuse takes place), whereas the lease during the extended period is regarded as a long-term lease. As a result, the place of supply of the first lease period will differ from the place of supply of the extension of the lease period.

If the effective use and enjoyment of short-term hiring of a means of transport are located outside the EU, whereas the means of transport is actually put at the disposal of the customer within the EU or vice versa, the place of supply will be where the effective use and enjoyment of the service takes place, provided that the Member State has implemented the effective use and enjoyment rules of Article 59a VAT Directive.[93]

92. Long-term hiring of means of transport to non-taxable persons does not fall within the scope of the B2C main rule, but is subject to a special place of supply for the long-term hiring of means of transport (*see* section 4.5.4.2.9).

93. *See* section 4.5.5 for a description of the effective use and enjoyment rules.

4.5.4 Business to Consumer Services (B2C Services)

In this section, we will discuss the place of supply rules for services supplied by a taxable person to a non-taxable person (B2C services). There are more exceptions to the main rule for B2C services than for B2B services, as illustrated by Figure 4.2.[94]

94. This overview is based on: A.J. van Doesum, H.W.M. van Kesteren, G.J. van Norden & I.T.H. Reiniers, *The New Rules on the Place of Supply of Services in European VAT* (2008) 2 EC Tax Review, pp. 78-89 https://doi.org/10.54648/ecta2008056.

Figure 4.2 Overview Place of Supply Rules B2C Services

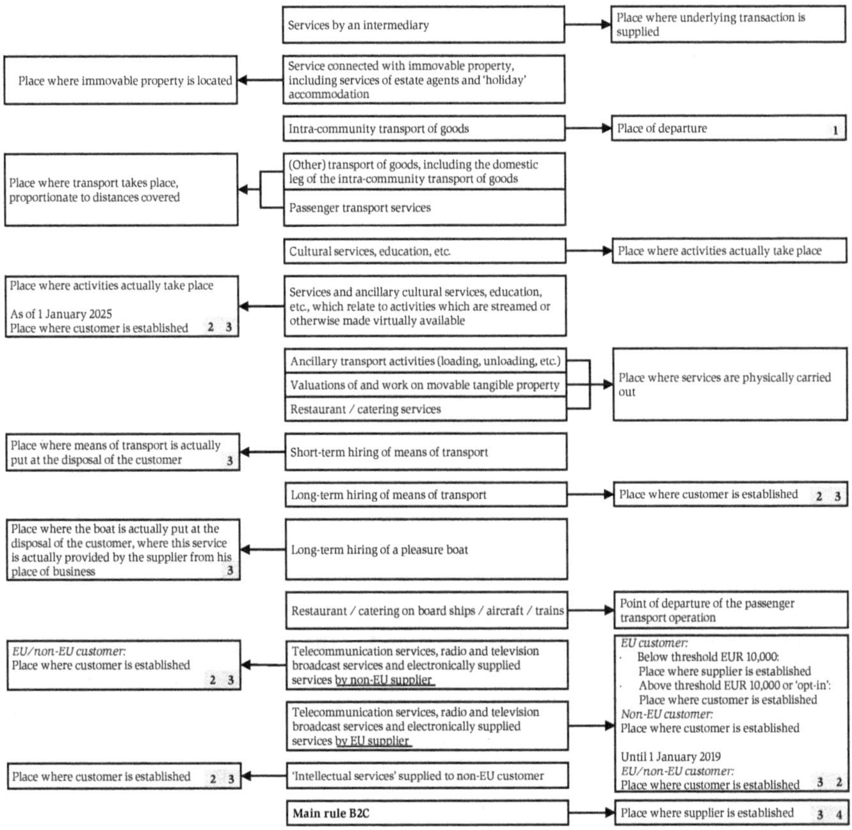

Key to Figure 4.2:

1 Member States need not apply the tax to that part of the intra-Community transport of goods to non-taxable persons corresponding to journeys made over water, which do not form part of the territory of the Community (Union).
2 Where this overview refers for brevity to the place where the customer is established, the place of supply is where the customer/non-taxable person is established, has his permanent address or usually resides.
3 If a Member State implements the effective use and enjoyment rules, the place of supply is where the effective use and enjoyment of the service take place.
4 Where this overview refers for brevity to the place where the supplier is established, the place of supply is where the supplier/taxable person has established his business, a fixed establishment from which the services are provided or where the supplier has his permanent address or usually resides.

4.5.4.1 *Main Rule B2C Services*

The general rule for B2C services, as laid down in Article 45 VAT Directive, states that the services take place where the supplier has established his business. If those services are provided from a fixed establishment of the supplier located somewhere other than the place where he has established his business, the place of supply of those services shall be the place where that fixed establishment is located. In the absence of such a place of establishment or fixed establishment, the place of supply of services shall be the place where the supplier has his permanent address or usually resides. According to Article 11(2) VAT Implementing Regulation, for the application of (among others) Article 45 VAT Directive, a 'fixed establishment' shall be any establishment, other than the place of establishment of a business, characterized by a sufficient degree of permanence and a suitable structure in terms of human and technical resources *to enable it to provide the services which it supplies.*[95]

It should be kept in mind that the B2C main rule only applies if the B2B main rule of Article 44 VAT Directive does not apply.[96] Article 43(1) VAT Directive stipulates that a taxable person who also carries out activities or transactions that are not considered to be taxable supplies of goods or services in accordance with Article 2(1) VAT Directive is regarded as a taxable person in respect of all services rendered to him. Similarly, Article 43(2) VAT Directive states that a non-taxable legal person who is identified for VAT purposes is regarded as a taxable person for the purposes of applying the place of supply rules. Although the recipient of the services in the first instance is not acting in the capacity of a taxable person and in the second situation not even has the status of a taxable person, he should be regarded as a taxable person for the application of the place of supply rules for services. Hence, in these instances, the B2B main rule applies instead of the B2C main rule.

A large number of exceptions apply to this main rule. In most cases, the exceptions reflect the principle that VAT should be levied at the place where final consumption takes place. However, concessions have been made in order to prevent a disproportionate administrative burden for businesses. First of all, 'consumption' and the 'place of consumption' are abstract terms that lack clear definitions; in practice, it is often difficult to pinpoint the act and place of consumption. Second, in case a supplier is not established in the Member State where consumption takes place, he would have to register for VAT purposes in order to report and pay the VAT due in that state.[97] These aspects underline that the B2C main rule is a concession to the practicality and effectiveness of taxation.

95. *See* section 4.5.2.3.
96. Also, none of the B2C exceptions should apply.
97. Note that in B2C situations, the liability of VAT cannot be shifted to the customer (since that customer is a non-taxable person/final consumer without a VAT registration).

4.5.4.2 *Exceptions B2C Services*

4.5.4.2.1 *Intermediary Services*

Article 46 deals with intermediary services - but not all. Only services by intermediaries who act *in the name and on behalf of* their principal fall within the scope of this provision. Intermediaries who act in their *own* name but on behalf of their principal are deemed to be part of the chain (in other words, he is deemed to receive a supply, as well as make one himself) (*see* Article 14(2)(c) VAT Directive where he takes part in a supply of goods and Article 28 VAT Directive where he takes part in a supply of services). If, for instance, such an intermediary is involved in the supply of a good, the supply of that good is deemed to be received and made by him, and the place of supply of the transactions is subject to the place of supply rules for goods.

The first type of intermediary - those who act in the name and on behalf of the principal - are mostly referred to as 'agents' ('true agents', or in British terminology, 'disclosed agents') and are subject to Article 46 VAT Directive. The second type of intermediaries is mostly referred to as 'commission agents' (commissionaires, or under British law, 'undisclosed agents'). These intermediaries do not fall within the scope of Article 46 but are subject to other places of supply rules.[98]

In this book, we will use the term 'agent' to refer to those intermediaries who act in the name and on behalf of the principal and 'commission agent' for those intermediaries who act in their own name but on behalf of their principal.

As noted above, Article 46 VAT Directive deals exclusively with 'agents'. According to Article 46 VAT Directive, the place of supply of services rendered to a non-taxable person by an intermediary (agent) shall be the place where the underlying transaction is supplied in accordance with the place of supply rules. Article 30 VAT Implementing Regulation provides that 'intermediary' services shall cover the services of intermediaries acting *in the name* and *on behalf of* the recipient of the service procured and the services performed by the intermediaries acting *in the name* and *on behalf* of the provider of the services procured.[99] This type of intermediary or agent shall thus be distinguished from a commission agent. We refer to Chapter 3 for further reading.

The underlying transaction thus defines the place of supply of the intermediary service. Would the underlying transaction be made by a non-taxable person and thus fall outside the scope of VAT, it follows from *Lipjes* that in order to determine the place of supply of the intermediary service, it does not matter that the principal transaction

98. In general commission agents purchase and sell items on behalf of a principal, usually a company. They conduct business under their own names, which affords a measure of anonymity to their principals.
99. Article 31 VAT Regulation stipulates that services supplied by intermediaries acting in the name of and on behalf of another person consisting of the intermediation in the provision of accommodation in the hotel sector or in sectors having a similar function shall fall within the scope of the special place of supply provision for intermediary services.

falls outside the scope of VAT. The place of supply of the underlying service should still be defined.[100]

4.5.4.2.2 *Services Connected with Immovable Property*

As this exception applies irrespective of the VAT status of the customer, we refer to section 4.5.3.4.1.

4.5.4.2.3 *Passenger Transport Services*

As this special provision is applicable both on services rendered to taxable persons and to non-taxable persons, we refer to section 4.5.3.4.2.

4.5.4.2.4 *(Intra-Community) Transport of Goods and Ancillary Transport Services*

For transport services rendered to non-taxable persons, a distinction is made between intra-Community transport of goods, other (non-intra-Community) transport of goods and ancillary transport services. Furthermore, there is a special provision for passenger transport services, which is discussed in section 4.5.3.4.2.

According to Article 51 VAT Directive, 'intra-Community transport of goods' shall mean any transport of goods in respect of which the place of departure and the place of arrival are situated within the territories of two different Member States. In this respect, 'place of departure' shall mean the place where transport of the goods *actually* begins, irrespective of distances covered in order to reach the place where the goods are located and 'place of arrival' shall mean the place where transport of the goods *actually* ends. As only the place of departure and arrival are of importance, the intra-Community transport of goods can take place partly outside the Community. Even an intermediate stopover (e.g., for cross-docking or other logistic purposes) outside the Community, in our view, does not prevent the transport from being an intra-Community transport of goods. According to Article 52 VAT Directive, however, Member States need not apply VAT to that part of the intra-Community transport of goods to non-taxable persons taking place over waters which do not form part of the territory of the Community. In *Commission/France*, the same was decided for passenger transport services.[101]

Article 50 VAT Directive provides that the place of supply of the intra-Community transport of goods to non-taxable persons shall be the place of departure. All other transport of goods services for non-taxable persons, being local transport services and transport services to or from a non-EU Member State, fall under Article 49 VAT

100. CJEU 27 May 2004, Case C-68/03 *Staatssecretaris van Financiën v D. Lipjes*, ECLI: EU:C:2004:325.
101. CJEU 13 March 1990, Case C-30/89 *Commission of the European Communities v French Republic*, ECLI:EU:C:1990:114.

Directive. These services are located where the transport takes place, proportionate to the distances covered. As a result, such an international transport of goods service will be located partially within the EU and partially outside the EU.

Article 54(a) VAT Directive provides that ancillary transport activities, such as loading, unloading, handling and similar activities, which are rendered to non-taxable persons, are located on the place where the services are physically carried out.

4.5.4.2.5 Cultural, Educational and Suchlike Services

Pursuant to Article 54(1) VAT Directive, the place of supply of services and ancillary services, relating to cultural, artistic, sporting, scientific, educational, entertainment or similar activities, such as fairs and exhibitions, including the supply of services of the organizers of such activities, supplied to a non-taxable person shall be the place where those activities actually take place. This rule aims to tax these services where final consumption effectively takes place. As from 1 January 2025, however, where the services and ancillary services relate to activities which are streamed or otherwise made virtually available, the place of supply shall be the place where the non-taxable person is established, has his permanent address or usually resides.[102]

4.5.4.2.6 Valuations of and Work on Movable Tangible Property

According to Article 54(2)(b) VAT Directive, the place of supply of valuations of and work on movable tangible property shall be the place where the services are physically carried out. Repair services will, in most cases, fall within the scope of this provision.

In *Linthorst*, the CJEU considered the term 'valuations' signifies examination of the physical condition or investigation of the authenticity of a good with a view to estimating its value or quantifying work to be carried out or the extent of damage sustained.[103] The CJEU held that the services principally and habitually performed by a veterinary surgeon do not fall within the concept of 'valuations'. With respect to the phrase 'work on movable tangible property', the CJEU considered that that phrase refers to purely physical action on movable tangible property that is, by nature, in principle neither scientific nor intellectual.[104] As the principal duties of a veterinary surgeon consist in the provision of therapeutic treatment administered to animals in

102. In *Geelen* (CJEU 8 May 2019, Case C-568/17 *Staatssecretaris van Financiën v L.W. Geelen*, ECLI:EU:C:2019:388), the CJEU ruled that a composite supply, such as the offering of erotic webcam sessions, constitutes an entertainment activity that actually takes place (and thus is taxable) where the service provider has established his business. Article 54(1) VAT Directive was subsequently adopted to tax such virtual services (from 1 January 2025 onwards) at the place where the customer is residing (as a proxy location for the place of consumption of the services). *See* Council Directive (EU) 2022/542 of 5 April 2022 amending Directives 2006/112/EC and (EU) 2020/285 as regards rates of value added tax, OJ L107.
103. CJEU 6 March 1997, Case C-167/95 *Maatschap M.J.M. Linthorst, K.G.P. Pouwels en J. Scheren c.s. tegen Inspecteur der Belastingdienst/Ondernemingen Roermond*, ECLI:EU:C:1997:105, para. 13.
104. *Ibid.*, para. 16.

accordance with scientific rules, the CJEU ruled that the services rendered by veterinary surgeons do neither qualify as work on movable tangible property.

The assembly of goods is a service that typically qualifies as a work on movable tangible property, according to Article 34 VAT Implementing Regulation, provided that the service consists only of the assembly by a taxable person of the various parts of a machine, all of which were provided to him by his customer. As an exception thereto, where the goods being assembled become part of immovable property, the service is not to be qualified as a work on movable property. Instead, this service probably qualifies as a service connected with immovable property, for which Article 47 VAT Directive stipulates that the place of supply is located where the immovable property is located, irrespective of the status of the recipient of the service.

4.5.4.2.7 *Restaurant and Catering Services*

As Article 55 VAT Directive is applicable both to services rendered to taxable persons and to non-taxable persons, we refer to section 4.5.3.4.4.

4.5.4.2.8 *Restaurant and Catering Services on Board Ships/Trains/Aircraft*

As Article 57 is applicable both to services rendered to taxable persons and to non-taxable persons, we refer to section 4.5.3.4.5.

4.5.4.2.9 *Hiring of Means of Transport*

The place of supply of the hiring of means of transport depends on the duration of the possession or use, on the means of transport and on the VAT taxable status of the customer. In section 4.5.3.4.6, we discussed the rules for the hiring of means of transport to VAT taxable persons. The (additional) particular rules for the hiring of means of transport to non-taxable persons are described in this section. For a definition of 'means of transport' and for a description of the distinction between 'short-term' and 'long-term' hiring, we refer to section 4.5.3.4.6.

According to Article 56(1) VAT Directive and Article 40 VAT Implementing Regulation, the place of supply of short-term hiring of a means of transport shall be the place where the means of transport is actually put at the disposal of the customer, being the place where the customer or a third party acting on his behalf takes physical possession of it. On the basis of Article 56(2) VAT Directive, the place of supply of *long-term* hiring of a means of transport, other than a pleasure boat, to a non-taxable person shall be the place where the customer is established, has his permanent address or usually resides.[105] Consequently, the place of supply of the long-term hiring of a

105. Article 24c VAT Regulation provides guidance for establishing the place of supply in case of B2C long-term hiring of means of transport. Following that provision it shall be presumed that the customer is established, has his permanent address or usually resides at the place identified as such by the supplier on the basis of two items of non-contradictory evidence as listed in

means of transport, other than a pleasure boat, will be located in the customer's home country, irrespective of the customer's status as a taxable person or not.[106] As a result, VAT on long-term hiring of a means of transport, other than a pleasure boat, is levied at the place where consumption likely takes place, and distortion of competition between service suppliers established in different Member States is prevented.

The long-term hiring (longer than 90 days) of a pleasure boat to a non-taxable person shall be the place where the pleasure boat is actually put at the disposal of the customer, where this service is actually provided by the supplier from his place of business or a fixed establishment situated in that place. The wording of this provision is not fully clear. In our opinion, the word 'where' at the beginning of the second part of the sentence can have different meanings. We do believe that the second part of the sentence is meant to provide that the exception for the long-term hiring of pleasure boats is only applicable if the boat is actually put at the customer's disposal from the supplier's place of business or from a fixed establishment.[107] If a pleasure boat, for example, is put at the customer's disposal in France, while the lessor is established in Spain, the exception is not applicable. The place of supply will, in this case, be located in the customer's country. This exception was probably introduced to combat VAT fraud, as pleasure boats are movable property with a possibly very high value.

For the hiring of movable tangible properties, other than means of transport, to a non-taxable person established outside the EU, the place of supply is defined on the basis of Article 59(g) VAT Directive.

If the effective use and enjoyment of a short-term hiring of a means of transport are located outside the EU, whereas the means of transport is actually put at the disposal of the customer within the EU or vice versa, the place of supply will be where the effective use and enjoyment of the service takes place, provided that the Member State has implemented the effective use and enjoyment rules of Article 59a VAT Directive.[108]

Article 24e VAT Regulation. These items are: (a) the billing address of the customer, (b) bank details, such as the location of the bank account used for payment or the billing address of the customer held by that bank, (c) registration details of the means of transport hired by the customer if registration of that means of transport is required at the place where it is used, or other similar information, and (d) other commercially relevant information. Both provisions apply from 1 January 2015. *See* Council Implementing Regulation (EU) No 1042/2013 of 7 October 2013 amending Implementing Regulation (EU) No 282/2011 as regards the place of supply of services [2013] OJ L284/1.

106. Either Article 56(2) VAT Directive applies (in B2C situations), or Article 44 VAT Directive (in B2B situations).

107. This interpretation of this exception is also based on the German, French and Dutch language versions of Article 56(2) VAT Directive. The German-language version uses the words 'sofern der Dienstleistungserbringer diese Dienstleistung tatsächlich vom Sitz seiner wirtschaftlichen Tätigkeit oder von einer festen Niederlassung an diesem Ort aus erbringt.' The French version states 'lorsque le service est effectivement fourni par le prestataire à partir du siège de son activité économique ou d'un établissement stable qui y est situé.' The Dutch version uses the words 'indien deze dienst daadwerkelijk door de dienstverrichter wordt verricht vanuit de zetel van zijn bedrijfsuitoefening of een vaste inrichting aldaar'.

108. *See* section 4.5.5.

4.5.4.2.10 *Electronically Supplied Services,*[109] *Telecommunication, Radio and Television Broadcasting Services*

Before 1 January 2015, the place of supply of such services to non-taxable persons[110] was:

(1) the country where the supplier was established if he was established in the EU;
(2) the country where the customer was established if the supplier was established outside the EU.

The rules before 1 January 2015 thus resulted in unequal treatment between B2C electronically supplied services, telecommunication and radio and television broadcasting services by EU services providers and such services supplied by non-EU service providers. Many businesses in the electronic services, telecommunication and television broadcasting sector were induced to establish their companies in Luxembourg, where they were liable to charge the (lower) Luxembourg VAT rate instead of the (higher) (standard) VAT rates of the Member State where the recipient was located. As this arrangement raised significant VAT revenues, the Luxembourg government was long opposed to any changes in the place of supply rules of electronic services, telecommunication and television broadcasting services. Other Member States would only accept the new place of supply rules, on the basis that the place of supply rules for the mentioned services would also change. Finally, a political agreement was reached, which implied that the place of supply rules for these services would only have effect from 1 January 2015. By postponing these measures from 1 January 2010 to 1 January 2015, and by (de facto) allowing Luxembourg financial compensation for the period from 1 January 2015 until 31 December 2018, the new place of supply rules were finally unanimously accepted. Paragraph 10 of the preamble to Directive 2008/08/EC is expressed as follows: 'Some of the changes made to the place of supply of services could have a considerable impact on the budget of member states. To ensure a smooth transition these changes should be introduced over time.' On 1 January 2015, new rules became effective. They were further amended with effect from 1 January 2019.

As a starting point, the current rules provide that the place of supply of electronically supplied services, telecommunication and radio and television broadcasting services is located in the customer's country if the customer is not a taxable person (Article 58(1) VAT Directive). The consequence is that the supplier of such services needs to comply with the rules of the customer's Member State. It was

109. *See* for an overview of the VAT treatment of electronic services in the EU as well as several other large jurisdictions, including Australia, Brazil, Canada, South Africa and Switzerland, F. Annacondia, 'VAT Aspects of Importation of Electronic Services', in H. van Arendonk, S. Jansen & R. van der Paardt (eds), *VAT in an EU and International Perspective, Essays in Honour of Han Kogels* (IBFD 2011), pp. 281-294.

110. As regards B2B supplies of such services, the place of supply was the place where the customer was established, and the reverse charge mechanism would apply.

considered that the burden for microbusinesses occasionally supplying such cross-border B2C services of having to comply with VAT obligations in customer's Member States was too high and should be reduced.[111] Therefore, a special regime applies to cross-border B2C supplies of such services by suppliers established in the EU that do not exceed EUR 10,000 (Article 59c(1) VAT Directive). If in the current and previous calendar year, this threshold is/was not exceeded (and the supplier did not 'opt-in' for taxation in the customer's Member State),[112] the place of supply of such B2C services supplied by EU suppliers is to be based on the main rule: where the supplier is located (Article 45 VAT Directive). Figure 4.3 serves to summarize the place of supply rules with respect to electronically supplied services, telecommunication and radio and television broadcasting services.[113]

111. Point 3 of the preamble to Council Directive 2017/2455 of 5 December 2017 amending Directive 2006/112/EC and Directive 2009/132/EC as regards certain value added tax obligations for supplies of services and distance sales of goods, OJ L 348, 29 December 2017.
112. Article 59c(3) VAT Directive.
113. Note that as from 1 January 2021, the threshold regime (Article 59c VAT Directive) also relates to intra-Community distance sales of goods. For further reading, *see* sections 4.4.3.3. and 13.4.2.2.

Figure 4.3 Place of Supply Rules with Respect to Cross-Border B2C Supplies of Electronically Supplied Services, Telecommunication and Radio and Television Broadcasting Services

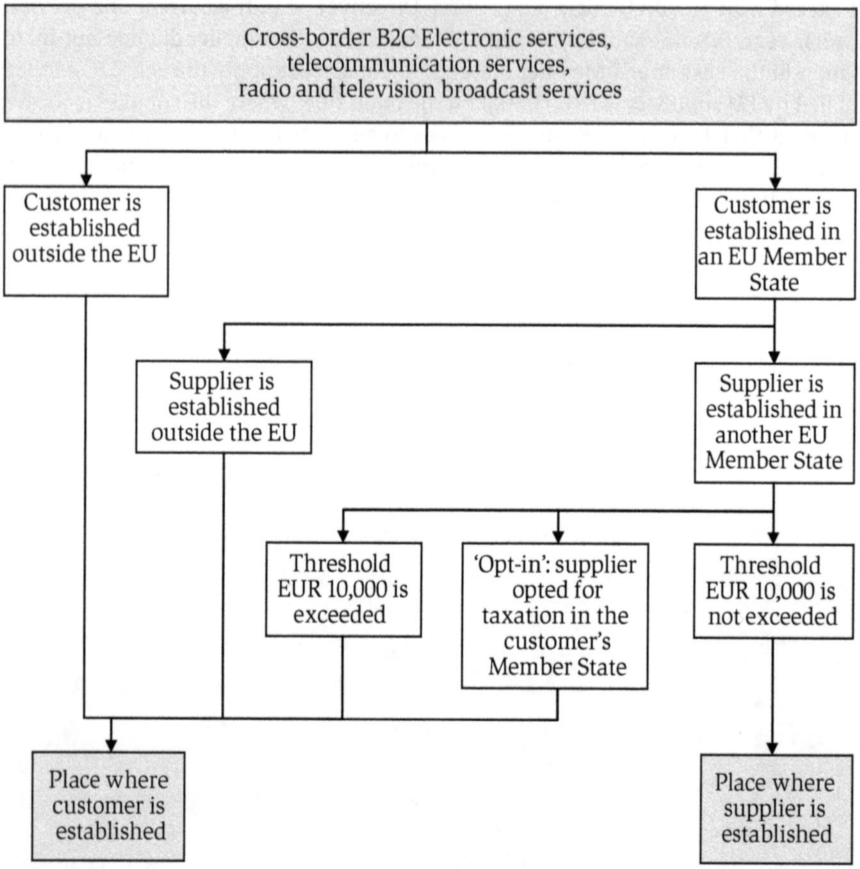

In a situation in which the threshold is exceeded, and consequently, the place of supply is where the customer is located, the supplier needs to comply with the rules of the customer's Member State. In order to simplify the levying of VAT, EU and non-EU suppliers of such services to non-taxable persons resident in the EU can apply the so-called OSS scheme. Articles 358-369 VAT Directive contain the rules on the OSS scheme with respect to telecommunications, broadcasting or electronic services supplied by taxable persons *not established within the Community*. Article 369a-369k VAT Directive contain the rules with respect to the OSS scheme for, *inter alia*, services supplied by taxable persons established within the Community but not in the Member State of consumption. This scheme allows taxable persons supplying telecommunication services, television and radio broadcasting services and electronically supplied services to non-taxable persons in the Member States in which they do not have an establishment to account for the VAT due on those supplies via a web portal in the Member State in which they are identified. We refer to Chapter 16.

Telecommunication services and radio and television broadcasting services have been further defined in Article 6a and 6b VAT Implementing Regulation. As regards electronically supplied services, the second paragraph of Article 58(1) VAT Directive indicates that when the supplier of a service and the customer communicate via e-mail, that shall not of itself mean that the service supplied is electronically supplied. Annex II to the VAT Directive contains a list of electronically supplied services:

(1) website supply, web-hosting, distance maintenance of programmes and equipment;
(2) supply of software and updating thereof;
(3) supply of images, text and information and making available of databases;
(4) supply of music, films and games, including games of chance and gambling games, and of political, cultural, artistic, sporting, scientific and entertainment broadcasts and events;
(5) supply of distance teaching.

This list is non-exhaustive, implying that other electronically supplied services not mentioned on the list also fall under this special provision. Service providers will have to assess whether their services qualify as electronically supplied services. In that regard, they can refer to Article 7 VAT Implementing Regulation, which defines 'electronically supplied services' as services which are delivered over the internet or an electronic network and the nature of which renders their supply essentially automated and involving minimal human intervention, and impossible to ensure in the absence of information technology. Moreover, this provision includes a more detailed list of services that are, and are not, to be regarded as electronically supplied services. Article 7(2)(f) VAT Implementing Regulation, in particular, refers to Annex I of the VAT Implementing Regulation, which contains further examples of electronically supplies services. Article 9a VAT Implementing Regulation sets out specific rules with respect to the supply of electronic services through a telecommunications network, an interface or a portal, such as a marketplace for applications.

Since it is so important to the determination of the place of supply of electronically supplied services, telecommunication and radio and television broadcasting services whether the customer is a taxable person, whether he acts in his capacity as a taxable person and where he is established, the VAT Implementing Regulation contains a number of presumptions and evidence rules on the basis of which the assessment of these factors can be made.

4.5.4.2.11 Intellectual Services Supplied to a Non-EU Customer

In this section, we discuss a special place of supply rule for several so-called intellectual services rendered to non-taxable persons.[114] The place of supply of these services depends on the place where the customer is established or has his permanent address or usually resides. According to Article 59 VAT Directive, the place of supply of intellectual services rendered to a non-taxable person who is established or has his permanent address or usually resides outside the EU is the place where that person is established, has his permanent address or usually resides.[115] In case the non-taxable customer of an intellectual service is established in the EU, the place of supply is located in the supplier's country on the basis of Article 45 VAT Directive (the B2C main rule).

Thus, in conjunction with Articles 44 and 45 VAT Directive, Article 59 VAT Directive leads to the following VAT treatment of intellectual services. If a non-EU recipient purchases an intellectual service, the place of supply will be located in the customer's country, either pursuant to Article 44 VAT Directive ('B2B'), or pursuant to Article 59 VAT Directive ('B2C').[116] A service supplier who renders intellectual services to an EU customer must, however, assess whether his customer is a taxable person according to Articles 9 and 43 VAT Directive. Article 43 VAT Directive simplifies this assessment. In case the recipient of the service provides the service supplier with a VAT ID number, the service is located in the recipient's country pursuant to Article 44 VAT Directive, while the service is located in the supplier's country pursuant to Article 45 VAT Directive in case the recipient does communicate a VAT ID number.

Article 59 VAT Directive has been introduced to prevent distortion of competition between EU and non-EU service suppliers. Would the place of supply of an intangible service rendered by an EU service provider to a non-EU customer be located in the EU, the EU service provider would find himself at a competitive disadvantage vis-à-vis his non-EU competitor(s).

The following services qualify as intellectual services for the purpose of Article 59 VAT Directive.

---

114. The term 'intangible services' is also used to refer to the services as listed in Article 59 VAT Directive. With 'B2B', we mean situations in which the service is rendered to a taxable person. With 'B2C', we mean situation in which the service is rendered to a non-taxable person.
115. For the determination of the place of supply on the basis of Article 59 VAT Directive, the nature of those services is decisive. When various services are provided, which for VAT purposes should be regarded as a single supply, the nature of this single supply should be established. In case such a single supply consists of various intellectual services, but as a whole constitutes a general, unspecified service of its own, the B2C main place of supply rule of Article 45 VAT Directive may apply instead of Article 59 VAT Directive. Under the former place of supply rules (those in effect up to 1 January 2010), certain Member States, for example, did not consider management services as intellectual services, but rather as main rule services.
116. Except in case the effective use and enjoyment rules lead to another place of supply; *see* section 4.5.5.

(a) Transfers and Assignments of Copyrights, Patents, Licences, Trademarks and Similar Rights

The transfer and assignment of copyrights, patents, licences, trademarks and similar rights fall within the scope of Article 59 VAT Directive. Although the VAT Directive does not contain a definition of these rights, it appears that at least all rights that are generally remunerated by means of royalty payments are included.

(b) Advertising Services

The CJEU has passed several judgments on the explanation of advertising services. In three cases brought before the CJEU by the Commission, the CJEU ruled that the concept of 'advertising services' is a Union law concept which must be interpreted uniformly in order to avoid instances of double taxation or non-taxation which may result from conflicting interpretations.[117] According to the CJEU, the concept of advertising necessarily entails the dissemination of a message intended to inform consumers of the existence and the qualities of a product or service, with a view to increase sales. Although that message is usually spread by means of spoken or printed words and/or pictures, by the press, radio and/or television, this can also be done by the partial or exclusive use of other means.[118] In these three cases, the European Commission took the view that some specific transactions could be regarded as advertising services, whereas the three involved Member States had explicitly excluded these transactions from the definition of 'advertising services'.[119]

From the CJEU judgment in *SPI*, it follows that the central criterion for determining the place where services are deemed to be supplied is the nature of the services in question. The special place of supply rule for advertising services, therefore, not only applies to advertising services supplied directly and invoiced by the supplier to a taxable advertiser but also to services supplied indirectly to the advertiser and invoiced to a third party who in turn invoices them to the advertiser.[120] The CJEU confirmed this judgment in *Design Concept*.[121]

117. CJEU 17 November 1993, Case C-68/92 *Commission of the European Communities v French Republic*, ECLI:EU:C:1993:888, para. 14; CJEU 17 November 1993, Case C-69/92 *Commission of the European Communities v Grand Duchy of Luxembourg*, ECLI:EU:C:1993:889, para. 15 and CJEU 17 November 1993, Case C-73/92 *Commission of the European Communities v Kingdom of Spain*, ECLI:EU:C:1993:891, para. 12.
118. CJEU 17 November 1993, Case C-68/92 *Commission of the European Communities v French Republic*, ECLI:EU:C:1993:888, para. 16; CJEU 17 November 1993, Case C-69/92 *Commission of the European Communities v Grand Duchy of Luxembourg*, ECLI:EU:C:1993:889, para. 17 and CJEU 17 November 1993, Case C-73/92 *Commission of the European Communities v Kingdom of Spain*, ECLI:EU:C:1993:891, para. 14.
119. The CJEU declared that these Member States had failed to fulfil their obligations under the VAT Directive by excluding, for example, the sale by an advertising agency to its customer of articles intended to be handed out to consumers, the production of advertising aids, the sale of movable tangible property in the context of an advertising campaign, and services provided in connection with a variety of public-relations events, such as press conferences, seminars, cocktail parties and recreational functions.
120. CJEU 15 March 2001, Case C-108/00 *Syndicat des producteurs indépendants (SPI) v Ministère de l'Economie, des Finances et de l'Industrie*, ECLI:EU:C:2001:173.
121. CJEU 5 June 2003, Case C-438/01 *Design Concept SA v Flanders Expo SA*, ECLI:EU:C:2003:325.

(c) The Services of Consultants, Engineers, Consultancy Firms, Lawyers, Accountants and Other Similar Services, as Well as Data Processing and the Provision of Information

In *Von Hoffman*, the CJEU held that the category of services of consultants, etc. does not refer to professions, such as those of lawyers, consultants, accountants or engineers, but to services. The Union legislature has used the professions mentioned in that provision as a means of defining the categories of services to which it refers.[122] The scope of this provision is limited to the services principally and habitually carried out as part of the professions listed in this provision. The CJEU held that the Union law definition of a lawyer does not cover the services of an arbitrator, as the purpose of services provided by a lawyer differs from the purpose of services provided by an arbitrator. For similar reasons, the services of an arbitrator cannot correspond to those of a consultant, engineer, consultancy bureau or accountant. None of the services principally and habitually provided as part of any of those professions concerns the settling of a dispute between two or more parties. Nor do the services of an arbitrator qualify as other similar services mentioned in this article, as this qualification also requires that the service serves the same purposes as the disparate activities mentioned, viewed separately.[123]

Given the fact that the scope of this provision is limited to the services principally and habitually carried out as part of the professions listed in this provision, a discussion often arises about management services. In some EU Member States, management services are regarded as services that are principally and habitually carried out as part of the professions listed in this provision, whereas in other EU Member States, e.g., the Netherlands, management services do not fall within the scope of this provision.[124] We believe that there is a decisive difference between services principally and habitually carried out by consultants, lawyers, accountants, etc., and management services because the former category mainly has a consultative character, while management services are not of a consultative nature.

Following the earlier formulated guidelines for the explanation of this provision, the CJEU ruled in *Commission/Germany* that the services of an executor do not fall within the scope of this provision. As for services principally and habitually carried out as part of a lawyer's profession, the CJEU has stated that these services aim to represent or defend the interests of a person.[125] Although lawyers are often chosen to be executors, the executor does not represent the testator but merely carries out his last wishes. According to the CJEU, the service of executing a will is of a specific nature that distinguishes it from the services principally and habitually carried out by a lawyer.[126]

122. CJEU 16 September 1997, Case C-145/96 *Bernd von Hoffmann v Finanzamt Trier*, ECLI: EU:C:1997:406, para. 15.
123. *Ibid.*, paras 16-24.
124. Dutch Supreme Court, 26 August 1998, No 33 595, BNB 1999/302.
125. CJEU 6 December 2007, Case C-401/06 *Commission of the European Communities v Bundesrepublik Deutschland*, ECLI:EU:C:2007:759, para. 36 and CJEU 16 September 1997, Case C-145/96 *Bernd von Hoffmann v Finanzamt Trier*, ECLI:EU:C:1997:406, para. 17.
126. CJEU 6 December 2007, Case C-401/06 *Commission of the European Communities v Bundesrepublik Deutschland*, ECLI:EU:C:2007:759, para. 37.

Executors' services can, therefore, not be considered to be lawyers' services, nor services similar to lawyers' services.

The supply consisting of the supply of standard software and subsequent customization to the specific requirements of a consumer is, in principle, to be regarded as forming a single supply for VAT purposes. This single supply qualifies as a supply of a service, which, according to the CJEU in *Levob*,[127] is likely to be carried out either by engineers or by other persons trained to carry out tasks that are similar to the activity of an engineer.

The CJEU decided in *Linthorst*[128] that the services of veterinary surgeons do not fall within the scope of intellectual services. Although veterinary surgeons' duties sometimes involve advisory or consultancy aspects, that fact is not enough to bring the principal and habitual activities of the profession of veterinary surgeon within the concepts of 'consultants' or 'consultancy firms', or to cause them to be regarded as 'similar services'.

Article 41 VAT Implementing Regulation stipulates that the service of translating texts shall be subject to this special provision.

(d) Obligations to Refrain from Pursuing or Exercising, in Whole or in Part, a Business Activity or a Right Referred to in This Provision

According to Article 25 VAT Directive, the obligation to refrain from an act, or to tolerate an act or situation, is a service. In section 3.4.5, we elaborated on the VAT treatment of compensation for damages. We have set out that it is questionable whether a payment received as compensation for damages under the condition that the matter will not be taken to court is not a consideration for a service. Furthermore, from case law of the CJEU,[129] it follows that not every payment received for ceasing activities is regarded as the consideration for a service. Only if there is identifiable consumption by an identifiable consumer, can there be a supply of a service for consideration which is subject to VAT.

(e) Banking, Financial and Insurance Transactions, Including Reinsurance, with the Exception of the Hire of Safes

It is generally assumed that this special provision has a wider scope than the exemptions for financial and insurance services laid down in Article 135(1)(a)-(g) VAT Directive.[130] There is little doubt that the place of supply of financial services that are

127. CJEU 27 October 2005, Case C-41/04 *Levob Verzekeringen BV and OV Bank NV v Staatssecretaris van Financiën*, ECLI:EU:C:2005:649.
128. CJEU 6 March 1997, Case C-167/95 *Maatschap M.J.M. Linthorst, K.G.P. Pouwels en J. Scheren c.s. tegen Inspecteur der Belastingdienst/Ondernemingen Roermond*, ECLI:EU:C:1997:105, para. 22.
129. CJEU 29 February 1996, Case C-215/94 *Jürgen Mohr v Finanzamt Bad Segeberg*, ECLI:EU:C:1996:72; CJEU 22 November 2001, Case C-184/00 *Office des produits wallons ASbl v Belgian State*, ECLI:EU:C:2001:629 and CJEU 18 December 1997, Case C-384/95 *Landboden-Agrardienste GmbH & Co. KG v Finanzamt Calau*, ECLI:EU:C:1997:627.
130. For example, B. Terra, *The Place of Supply in European VAT* (Kluwer Law International 1998), pp. 212-213 and O. Henkow, *Financial Activities in European VAT (Dissertation)* (Kluwer Law International 2008), pp. 232-233.

explicitly excluded from these exemptions (e.g., management and safekeeping of securities) and are provided to non-taxable persons residing outside the EU should also be located where the service recipient is residing. Moreover, Article 59(e) VAT Directive does not refer to the aforementioned exemptions at all. In *Swiss Re*, the CJEU held, however, that the concept of 'insurance transactions including reinsurance' in this special place of supply provision is defined the same as the interpretation of the term 'insurance and reinsurance transactions' which is employed in the exemption rule.[131] In *Deutsche Bank*, it was confirmed that the place of supply rule at issue has a broader scope than the exemptions for financial services, but has the same scope as the exemption for insurance services of Article 135(1)(a) VAT Directive.[132] In respect of insurance transactions, essentially identical terms are used in the place of supply and exemption provisions, whereas this is clearly not true for financial transactions.

(f) The Supply of Staff

This provision should not be confused with the supply of, e.g., a consulting service. In our view, the supply of staff requires that the recipient of the services will get the authority to instruct the 'employee' and that the 'employee' will work under the responsibility of the recipient of the service.

(g) The Hiring Out of Movable Tangible Property, with the Exception of All Means of Transport

This special provision applies to the hiring out of all movable tangible property, except for the hiring out of all means of transport. Other places of supply rules dealing with the hiring out of a means of transport are addressed in sections 4.5.3.4.6 and 4.5.4.2.9.

(h) Access to and Transport Through Natural Gas and Electricity Distribution Systems

The provision of access to, and transport or transmission through, natural gas and electricity distribution systems is regarded as a separate supply of services. It is thus (mostly) not part of the supply of gas or electricity. In 2003, the European Council adopted Directive 2003/92/EC on the place of supply of this service, coming into effect as of 1 January 2005. In 2009, the European Council adopted Directive 2009/162/EU,[133] which further clarifies the scope of this provision. The amended text that came into effect as from 1 January 2011 ensures that all services, including supplies relating to a transmission system or an upstream pipeline network, fall within the scope of this special provision. Furthermore, the special provision also applies to the supply of access to heating and cooling networks.

131. CJEU 22 October 2009, Case C-242/08 *Swiss Re Germany Holding GmbH v Finanzamt München für Körperschaften*, ECLI:EU:C:2009:647.
132. CJEU 19 July 2012, Case C-44/11 *Finanzamt Frankfurt am Main V-Höchst v Deutsche Bank AG*, ECLI:EU:C:2012:484.
133. Council Directive 2009/162/EU of 22 December 2009 amending various provisions of Directive 2006/112/EC on the common system of value added tax, OJ L10, 15 January 2010.

4.5.5 Effective Use and Enjoyment Rule

As set out in section 4.2, the place of supply rules not only govern the distribution of taxing competences between Member States but also apply in situations involving third countries. If a non-EU country levies a consumption tax (e.g., VAT, GST or sales tax), the EU place of supply rules may not match those of the non-EU country in question. Consequently, double taxation or double non-taxation may take place. Moreover, the different rules may trigger distortions of competition.

The VAT Directive contains an optional mechanism to prevent double (non-)taxation or distortion of competition caused by the differences between the EU place of supply rules and those of non-EU countries. In our opinion, this provision should have been implemented on an obligatory basis. Although the purpose of this provision is to prevent double taxation or non-taxation and the distortion of competition, its facultative nature implies that these undesirable effects can still manifest themselves in the context of cross-border transactions. Where appropriate, the application of the optional mechanism will result in taxation at the place of consumption of a service (where the effective use and enjoyment take place). The effective use and enjoyment mechanism overrule the (other) place of supply rules. It should be noted that the effective use and enjoyment rules can only be applied to services the place of supply of which is governed by Articles 44, 45, 54(1), second subparagraph, 56, 58 and 59 VAT Directive.

Two scenarios need to be distinguished here. The first one relates to Article 59a(a) VAT Directive, concerning situations in which, on the basis of the EU place of supply rules, a service is regarded to take place *within the EU*, whereas the effective use and enjoyment of that service are *outside the EU*. A Member State that has implemented Article 59(a) VAT Directive essentially gives up its right to levy VAT in favour of the non-EU country, where the effective use and enjoyment takes place.

The second scenario relates to Article 59a(b) VAT Directive. Most Member States have only implemented this second scenario – and some even partially. Article 59a(b) VAT Directive governs the situation in which, on the basis of the EU place of supply rules, a service is regarded as taking place outside the EU, whereas the effective use and enjoyment of that service take place within a Member State. As a last resort, the effective use and enjoyment rules may shift the place of supply to the Member State where the effective use and enjoyment takes place if and insofar as the Member State in question has implemented Article 59a(b) VAT Directive. This option has also been exercised by Italy. In *Athesia Druck* the CJEU decided that where an Italian supplier provides advertising services to a customer in a non-Member State, such a service takes place – according to the general rule – in the country where the recipient is established (in this particular case, in the non-Member State), but that the service is deemed to be supplied in Italy, provided that the effective use and enjoyment of the service take place in Italy. That is – according to the CJEU – the case with regard to advertising services, where the advertising material being supplied, was distributed from Italy. The CJEU argued that irrespective of the fact that the recipients of those services might be located throughout the world, the Italian media undoubtedly operates primarily in Italy.[134]

The exact meaning of the term 'effective use and enjoyment' is not defined in statutory EU VAT law. We believe, however, that it is a concept of Union law.[135] Member States nevertheless appear to have different interpretations of 'effective use and enjoyment'. From the viewpoint of legal certainty, we would, therefore, welcome any legal definition of the concept of 'effective use and enjoyment' in either the VAT Directive or the VAT Implementing Regulation.

134. CJEU 19 February 2009, Case C-1/08 *Athesia Druck Srl v Ministrero dell'Economia e delle Finanze, Agenzia delle Entrate*, ECLI:EU:C:2009:108, paras 28-30.

135. *See also* B. Terra, *The Place of Supply in European VAT* (Kluwer Law International 1998), p. 222.

CHAPTER 5

Chargeable Event, Chargeability and Payment of VAT

5.1 INTRODUCTION

When it has been established that a taxable event (supply of goods or services, intra-Community acquisition or import) has taken place and VAT is due at either the reduced or at the standard rate, it must be established *when* (at what moment) the VAT must be paid to the tax authorities. Point 24 of the preamble to the VAT Directive states that 'The concepts of chargeable event and of the chargeability of VAT should be harmonised if the introduction of the common system of VAT and of any subsequent amendments thereto are to take effect at the same time in all Member States.' The EU legislature thereby intended maximum harmonization of the date on which liability to pay VAT arises in all the Member States in order to ensure the uniform collection of that tax.[1] The VAT Directive, unfortunately, uses a terminology that over-complicates the determination of the moment at which the VAT must be paid to the tax authorities. In our view, that does not contribute to the objective of achieving maximum harmonization.

5.1.1 Taxable Events

It is critical to first determine which 'transactions' are subject to VAT. According to Article 2, under the heading of Title IV of the VAT Directive ('Taxable transactions') the following 'actions' or 'events' constitute (taxable) transactions: (1) the supply of goods, (2) the supply of services, (3) the ICA and (4) the importation of goods are 'taxable transactions'. As 'ICAs' and 'the importation of goods' are, strictly speaking, 'actions' rather than *transactions*, but nevertheless seen as matters which are subject to VAT (according to Article 2 VAT Directive), we mostly refer to these four categories of 'actions or events' as 'taxable events' rather than 'taxable transactions'.

Some supplies do not need much time to be completed, other supplies take more time to be finalized, while other supplies have a continuous nature. If a supply can be made instantly (e.g., the supply of a good by a shop), it is possible to pinpoint one particular moment in time as the moment at which the taxable event takes place. When a supply needs some time to be carried out (e.g., a tax adviser needs three days to write tax advice), the taxable event takes place over a period of three days. Some taxable events even have a continuous character (e.g., a subscription for a telephone line): then the supply may even take place over a longer period of time. Figure 5.1 serves to illustrate this.

1. CJEU 16 May 2013, Case C-169/12 *TNT Express Worldwide (Poland) sp. z o.o. v Minister Finansów*, ECLI:EU:C:2013:314, para. 31 and CJEU 2 May 2019, Case C-224/18 *Budimex S.A. v Minister Finansów*, ECLI:EU:C:2019:347, para. 22.

Figure 5.1 Moment or Period of the Taxable Event

I. Taxable event: supply of a good in a shop

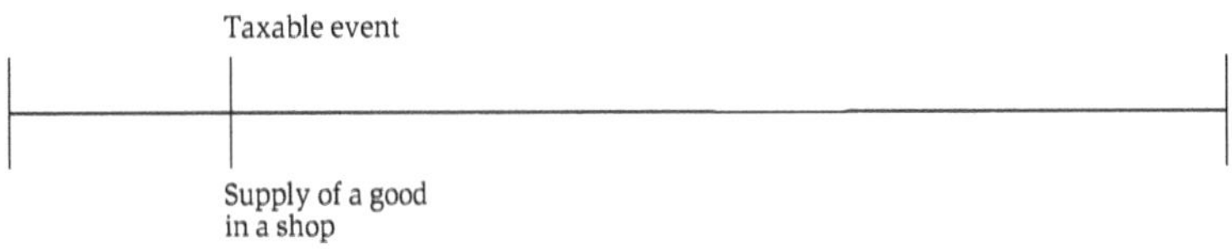

II. Taxable event: supply of tax advice

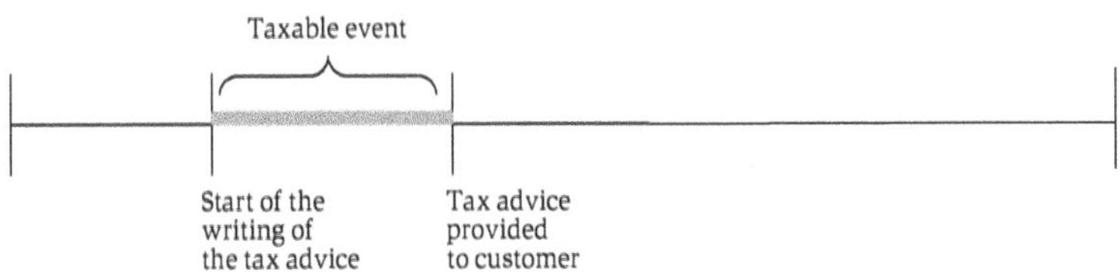

III. Taxable event: supply of a subscription for a telephone line

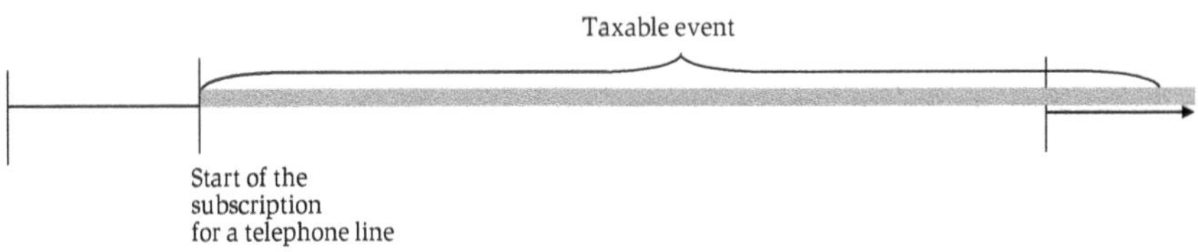

5.1.2 Chargeable Events

As a consequence of the occurrence of the 'taxable event', the VAT on that supply or event becomes due. There is a need, however, to distinguish between 'taxable events' and 'chargeable events', particularly when the taxable event itself cannot be pin-pointed to one moment in time but rather takes place over a period of time. In order to pinpoint a taxable event on a timeline (to appoint a single date) with the ultimate aim of ascertaining when a taxable event must be reported in the VAT return and when the VAT on that event must be paid, the legislator introduced the notion of the 'chargeable event'. The chargeable event seems to be the moment at which the taxable event has been completed (de facto, or by fiction).

Article 62(1) VAT Directive describes the *chargeable event* as the 'occurrence by virtue of which the legal conditions necessary for VAT to become chargeable are fulfilled'. The fact that a supply is carried out (the taxable event takes place) means that only if such a taxable event has been *completed,* all legal conditions necessary for VAT to become chargeable are fulfilled; hence the chargeable event takes place. At that moment, VAT becomes due in a material sense. The VAT Directive does not provide any options to the Member States as to the determination of the chargeable event.

As regards the example of the sale of a good in a shop, it is fairly easy to determine when the supply (taxable event) has been completed. This will be the moment at which the customer becomes the owner of the good. That will then also be the moment of the chargeable event. With respect to the tax advice in the previous example, things are also not too complicated. The completion of the taxable event will be when the tax advice is provided to the client. It will be more complicated to determine the moment at which a continuous supply is completed. Therefore, Article 64(2) VAT Directive contains the legal fiction that a continuous supply is regarded as being completed on expiry of each calendar year until such time as the supply of services comes to an end. This may be depicted as in Figure 5.2.

Figure 5.2 Moment of the Chargeable Event

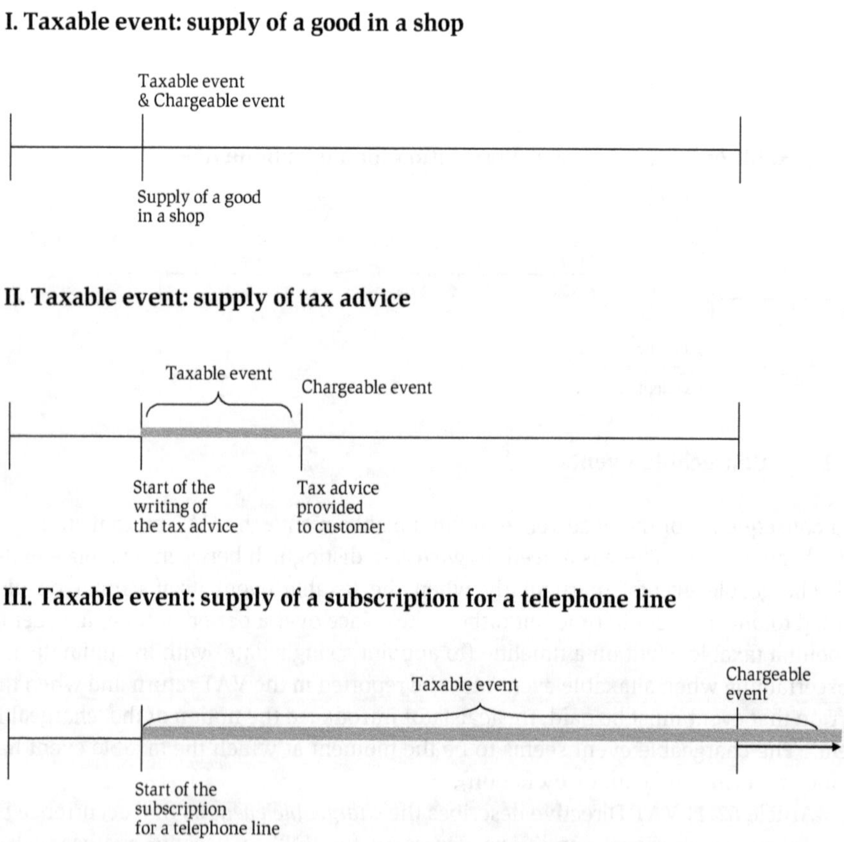

The chargeable event is not only the moment when the VAT materially becomes due[2] but - on the basis of Article 167 VAT Directive - also the moment when the recipient's right of deduction arises (provided that the material conditions for a right of deduction are fulfilled).[3] We refer to Chapter 10, section 10.2.3.

5.1.3 Chargeability (Moment at Which the VAT Becomes Formally Chargeable)

According to Article 63 VAT Directive, VAT becomes - as a general rule - chargeable at the occurrence of the chargeable event (i.e., when the taxable event has been completed). This means that VAT becomes 'formally' due at the moment of the chargeable event. 'Formally due' in this respect means that the tax authorities are entitled to claim the VAT from the person who is liable to remit and pay the VAT.

There are exceptions to the general rule that the VAT becomes chargeable at the same moment the chargeable event occurs. The chargeable event will not always coincide with the moment at which the VAT becomes chargeable in a formal sense (also referred to as the moment of 'chargeability'). The mere fact that the chargeable event occurs does not necessarily mean that the tax inspectorate in that particular Member State is also *entitled to claim* the VAT from the taxable person concerned. Thus, despite what may be expected from a terminology point of view, the moment of the completion of the taxable event, i.e., the moment of the chargeable event, is not always the moment at which VAT becomes chargeable (the 'chargeability of VAT' occurs), meaning the moment at which the tax authorities become entitled under the law to claim the tax from the person liable to pay (even though the time of payment may be deferred, *see* Article 62(2) VAT Directive). The moment at which the chargeability of VAT occurs (i.e., the tax authorities can actually claim the tax from the taxable person) very much depends on what option the Member State in question has chosen under Article 66 to determine *when* VAT becomes chargeable in the expressed formal sense.

It appears that Article 62(1) VAT Directive merely formalizes the material VAT due that arises when a transaction has been carried out and has been completed. Therefore, the distinction between the chargeable event and the time at which the VAT becomes chargeable seems to be only a distinction between the occurrence of a *material* VAT *due* (at the chargeable event) and a *formal* VAT *due* (in the sense that it may be claimed by the tax authorities).

In the examples used in the previous sections, the moment at which the VAT becomes chargeable (i.e., the 'chargeability' arises) is, as the main rule, the same moment as the moment at which the chargeable event takes place (Article 63 VAT

2. The term 'due' refers to an enforceable tax claim and therefore requires that the taxable person has an obligation to pay the amount of VAT which he seeks deduction of as input VAT. CJEU 29 March 2012, Case C-414/10, *VELECLAIR SA v Ministre du Budget, des Comptes publics et de la Réforme de l'État*, ECLI:EU:C:2012:183, para. 20.
3. CJEU 10 February 2022, Case C-9/20 *Grundstücksgemeinschaft Kollaustraße 136 v Finanzamt Hamburg-Oberalster*, ECLI:EU:C:2022:88.

Directive). However, if, for example, a Member State implemented Article 66(a) VAT Directive, the moment at which the VAT becomes chargeable (the chargeability of VAT arises) in that Member State can be the moment at which the invoice is issued. If the supplies in the previous examples were made in such a Member State, the diagrams would look as provided in Figure 5.3.

Figure 5.3 Moment of the Chargeability of VAT

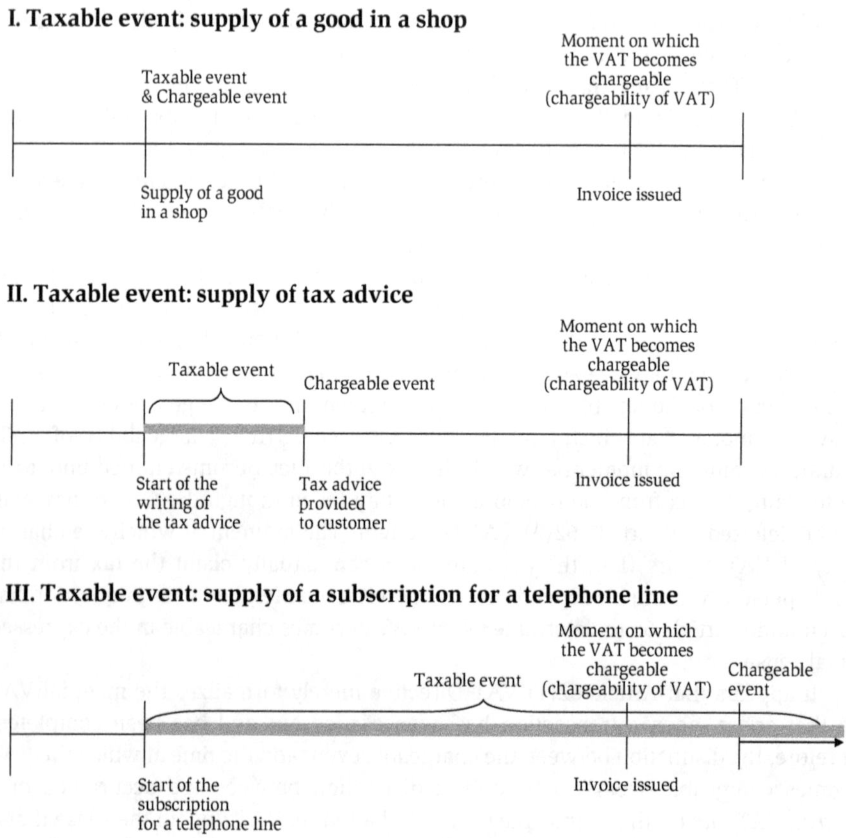

For clarity's sake, we note that often, in case of continuous supplies, the invoice is issued *after* the chargeable event takes place. Thus, in practice, in case of a subscription for a telephone line, the diagram would likely look as provided in Figure 5.4.[4]

4. Assuming that no prepayment takes place.

Figure 5.4 Taxable Event, Chargeable Event and Chargeability of VAT in Case of Continuous Supplies

III. Taxable event: supply of a subscription for a telephone line

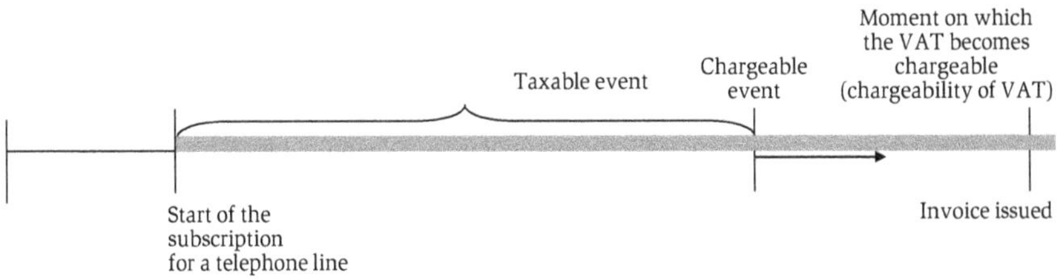

5.1.4 VAT Becomes Payable

A distinction has to be drawn between the concepts of taxable event, chargeable event, chargeability of tax, and that of the payment of the tax. VAT cannot become payable before it has become chargeable. Only after the point at which VAT has become chargeable (chargeability of VAT), is it relevant to determine whether there is effectively an amount of VAT payable to the tax authorities (*see* section 5.7).

The relevance of making a distinction between these different concepts can be illustrated on the basis of the following example. For instance, in a Member State that has chosen that VAT becomes chargeable no later than the time the invoice is issued (on the basis of the option given in Article 66(a) VAT Directive):

(1) the *taxable event* of hiring out a motor vehicle for the period of one month – let us say the month of March – will take place from 1 March until (and including) 31 March;
(2) the *chargeable event* takes place on 31 March since the service (the rental period) has been completed on that date (materially, the VAT becomes due);
(3) in this particular Member State, the VAT becomes chargeable (chargeability of VAT: the tax authorities are entitled to claim the VAT from the taxable person) at the moment that the VAT invoice is issued (let us assume on 23 April). The material VAT due has been formalized now and may, therefore, be claimed by the tax authorities;
(4) if the taxable person files VAT returns on a monthly basis, he will report this rental activity in his VAT return for the month of April (presumably) at the end of May, and will most probably be obliged to pay the VAT to the tax authorities at the same date (as the VAT has become payable).

Under normal circumstances, the trigger for the tax authorities to become legally entitled to claim the VAT is the point at which VAT becomes chargeable (under the general rule of Article 63 this coincides with the chargeable event), which causes the taxable person to become a debtor to the tax authorities in respect of the VAT on the supply. The commentary relating to the proposed Article 11 Sixth VAT Directive in the explanatory memorandum to the proposal for a Sixth VAT Directive is illustrative of this point:

> The determination of the event by virtue of which the tax becomes due (chargeable event) and the determination of the moment at which the tax authority becomes entitled to claim the tax (when the tax becomes chargeable) and the moment when the tax must be paid (liability payment of the tax) have given rise to numerous controversies. Under the laws of most of the Member States, the moment when the 'chargeable event' takes place is indistinguishable from that when the tax becomes chargeable. On the contrary however, for practical reasons, the tax usually does not become payable until a later date.

5.2 TAXABLE EVENT VERSUS CHARGEABLE EVENT

From the above, it almost seems that no distinction is made between the taxable event (the moment at or period in which the supply takes place) and the chargeable event (the completion – potentially by legal fiction – of the event by virtue of which the tax becomes materially due). However, as we indicated earlier, we believe that in a variety of situations, it is clearly possible to make a distinction between the taxable event and the chargeable event.

For example, with respect to situations which give rise to successive statements of accounts or successive payments, the supply of goods or of services is by fiction regarded as being completed on the expiry of the periods to which such statements of accounts or payments relate (Article 64(1) VAT Directive). Specific continuous supplies of goods and services over a period of time are to be regarded as being completed at intervals of no longer than one year (Article 64(2) VAT Directive). These rules are to be interpreted in such a way that although the taxable event needs a period of time to be completed or even has a continuing nature, the chargeable event is allocated to the moment in time at which they are actually completed (de facto) or at least at the moment that they are deemed to be completed for VAT purposes (de jure).[5]

Also with respect to the importation of goods, Article 71 VAT Directive provides that in the event of goods being placed under a customs arrangement upon their importation, i.e., their entry into the EU (Article 30 VAT Directive), the chargeable event and the chargeability of VAT shall only occur when the goods cease to be covered by a customs arrangement.[6] If that occurs, there is a difference between the taxable event (the importation, being the physical entry of goods in the EU) and the chargeable event (the occurrence by virtue of which the legal conditions necessary for VAT to

5. This is confirmed by the CJEU's ruling in CJEU 28 October 2021, Case C-324/20 *Finanzamt B v X-Beteiligungsgesellschaft mbH*, ECLI:EU:C:2021:880. The CJEU ruled that that the wording 'supplies which give rise to successive payments' in Article 64(1) VAT Directive should be interpreted as concerning only supplies the nature of which justify payment in instalments, namely those which are not performed on a single occasion, but repeated or continuous over a certain period.
6. According to the CJEU, the reference in the first paragraph of Article 61 and in the first subparagraph of Article 71(1) of the VAT Directive to 'one of the arrangements or situations

become chargeable (chargeability of VAT) are fulfilled, being the termination of the particular customs arrangement).

5.3 CHARGEABLE EVENT VERSUS CHARGEABILITY (THE MOMENT AT WHICH VAT BECOMES CHARGEABLE)

From the foregoing, it may be observed that in most Member States, it is not possible to make a clear distinction between the chargeable event and the moment at which the tax becomes chargeable (chargeability of VAT). However, in a Member State that made use of any of the options provided for in Article 66 VAT Directive, the occurrence of the chargeable event will be different from the moment at which the tax becomes chargeable (chargeability of VAT). For example, if the Member State provided that the VAT becomes chargeable no later than the time the payment is received (compare Article 66(b) VAT Directive), the moment of the chargeable event is different from the moment that the tax becomes chargeable (chargeability of VAT). Therefore, we believe it is correct to make a distinction between the chargeable event and the moment at which the VAT becomes chargeable (chargeability of VAT), i.e., the moment at which the VAT becomes materially due versus the moment at which the tax authorities may formally claim the VAT on the transaction from the taxable person.

In cases of payments on account (prepayments), Article 65 states that where a payment is to be made on account before the goods or services are supplied, VAT shall become chargeable on receipt of the payment and on the amount received.

We understand this provision as follows. The *taxable event* takes place at the time that the supplier is making the supply (as we indicated in section 5.1.1, some supplies do not need much time to be supplied, other supplies take more time to be finalized, while other supplies have a continuous nature). At the time that the supply is completed (de facto or by legal fiction), the *chargeable event* occurs. The *formal* moment at which VAT becomes chargeable, however, takes place at the time of the prepayment. Illustrative of this distinction is the CJEU's ruling in *Air France-KLM* (also *see*: Chapter 3, section 3.3.1).[7]

In *Air France-KLM*, the CJEU had to decide on the question at what moment VAT becomes due in respect of the supply of (flight) tickets, which are eventually not used by the customer (so-called no-show). Although the CJEU's ruling is not very clear, we believe that the CJEU considers that the taxable event of supplying a ticket (i.e., supplying the service) takes place over a period between the issuing of the ticket and the moment at which the customer is brought to his destination, or – in case of a no-show – the moment at which the plane departs without the customer. The taxable event thus takes a while to be completed. The chargeable event pinpoints the taxable event on a single moment at the timeline. In *Air France-KLM*, the chargeable event

referred to in Article 156' must be interpreted as meaning that that reference includes free zones. CJEU 1 June 2017, Case C-571/15 *Wallenborn Transports SA v Hauptzollamt Gießen*, ECLI: EU:C:2017:417, para. 44.

7. CJEU 23 December 2015, Joined Cases C-250/14 and C-289/14 *Air France-KLM (C-250/14) and Hop!-Brit Air SAS, Ministère des Finances et des Comptes publics*, ECLI:EU:C:2015:841.

seems to be the moment at which the taxable event is completed (completion of the travel or – in case of a no-show – departure of the plane). Since the customers already paid for their tickets in advance, the chargeability of VAT arises at the moment of the prepayment.

The question of whether the normal rate, lower rate or an exemption is to be applied depends on the assumed nature of the supply, as it will have at the time that all legal conditions are fulfilled to become chargeable in a more material sense, being the moment of the chargeable event. If, however, the VAT rate in a particular Member State changes (it becomes higher or lower than expected at the moment of the prepayment), the definitive applicable rate depends on the moment at which the tax became chargeable (the moment of the prepayment). In other words: in case of a VAT rate change, it is not the taxable event nor the chargeable event which determines whether the old or the new VAT applies. The moment at which the VAT becomes chargeable (chargeability of VAT) decides which VAT rates are applicable. The moment at which the VAT becomes chargeable (chargeability of VAT) is also particularly relevant with respect to the right of deduction of input VAT. Article 167 VAT Directive provides that a right of deduction arises at the time the deductible tax becomes chargeable.

5.4 CHARGEABILITY OF VAT VERSUS THE TIME AT WHICH VAT BECOMES PAYABLE

The mere fact that VAT has become chargeable under Article 62(2) VAT Directive does not necessarily mean that the (net) VAT must immediately be paid to the tax authorities. The time of *payment* of VAT that is chargeable may be deferred. Under normal circumstances, the (net) VAT needs only to be paid at the moment the VAT return must be filed, or even after that moment. According to Article 250 VAT Directive, taxable persons that make taxable transactions are required to file a periodical VAT return, setting out all the information needed to calculate the tax that has become chargeable. The point at which the taxable person must file a VAT return over a tax period (of normally one, two or three months – *see* Article 252 VAT Directive) in principle determines the moment at which that (net) VAT must actually be paid (assuming that there is VAT payable). As a rule, this moment occurs at the same moment at which the VAT return must be submitted (Article 206 VAT Directive). However, Member States may choose to require payment *after* the filing of the VAT return (Article 206 VAT Directive), since Member States may set a different date for payment of the net amount of VAT. Also, Member States may require payment of the net amount of VAT at an earlier moment than that of the filing of the VAT return. For example, Member States may require interim payment as soon as the tax has become chargeable. Consequently, the moment at which the tax must be paid to the tax authorities differs per Member State.[8]

8. CJEU 20 October 1993, Case C-10/92 *Maurizio Balocchi v Ministero delle Finanze dello Stato*, ECLI:EU:C:1993:846.

5.5 CONCLUSION WITH REGARD TO THE RELEVANT MOMENTS OF LEVYING VAT

It follows from the above that – strictly speaking – four concepts should be distinguished. These four concepts are to be defined as follows.

1. Taxable Event

This is the moment at or the period in which a 'transaction' (*see* Article 2(1) VAT Directive) takes place.

2. Chargeable Event

The moment at which the event occurs on which the legal conditions are fulfilled for the tax to become due (the moment that the taxable event is completed or deemed to be completed).

3. Moment at Which the Tax Becomes Chargeable (Chargeability of VAT)

The moment at which the tax authorities legally become entitled to claim the tax.

4. Moment at Which the Tax Becomes Payable

The moment at which the tax must be paid to the tax authorities.

5.6 TAXABLE EVENTS AND THEIR OWN SPECIFIC RULES

Following the overall system of the VAT Directive, each type of taxable transaction (event) has its own set of rules determining when the chargeable event takes place. Articles 63-67 VAT Directive contain the main rules as regards supplies of goods and services, Articles 68-69 VAT Directive those as regards the ICAs of goods, and Articles 70-71 VAT Directive those regarding the importation of goods.

Below, we will first discuss the chargeable event with respect to the supplies of goods and services. Subsequently, we will discuss the moment at which the VAT becomes chargeable. Then, we will discuss the moment at which the tax becomes payable. Lastly, in sections 5.6.2, 5.6.3 and 5.6.4, we will address the chargeable event and the chargeability of VAT in the case of ICAs and importations of goods.

5.6.1 Supplies of Goods and Services

In this section, we will discuss the chargeable event and the chargeability of VAT with respect to supplies of goods and services.

5.6.1.1 Main Rule

As a main rule, Article 63 VAT Directive provides that the 'chargeable event shall occur and the VAT shall become chargeable when the goods or the services are supplied'. As regards supplies of goods and services, in principle, the chargeable event and the moment at which the tax becomes chargeable coincide. However, there are various exceptions to this main rule. In any event, these exceptions may not lead to a chargeable event that occurs at a *later* moment than the moment at which the goods or the services are supplied. From the *Mazzalai* case, it follows that the moment at which the chargeable event occurs cannot be deferred beyond the moment when the service or services are provided in full (i.e., only possible for the time at which the VAT becomes chargeable). It seems to us that this also applies to supplies of goods.[9] The moment when the supply of goods or service is made (is completed or fulfilled: chargeable event) cannot be identified with that when the invoice is issued, or a payment on account is made if the issuance of the invoice or the payment on account[10] takes place after the supply has been carried out.

As set out above, the moment at which tax becomes chargeable must at least be advanced to the moment before the supply is completed on the receipt of a payment and on the amount received (Article 65 VAT Directive: regarding prepayments). It may even be advanced if the Member State applies the option to derogate from Article 65 (prepayments) by applying the rule that VAT becomes chargeable no later than the time the invoice is issued (for the prepayment). The VAT Directive contains both imperative and optional provisions that require Member States to move up the moment at which the VAT becomes chargeable.

It is important to realize that the rules for supplies which give rise to successive statements of account or successive payments (Article 64(1) VAT Directive), the rules for cross-border continuous supplies (Article 62(2) VAT Directive) and the rules concerning payments on account (Article 65 VAT Directive) overrule the main rule (Article 63 VAT Directive). In this regard, the CJEU has ruled that Article 65 VAT Directive, relating to prepayments ('payments are made on account before the goods or services are supplied') constitutes a derogation from the rule laid down in Article 63 and, as such, must be interpreted strictly.[11] In our view, the same applies to Articles 62(2) and 64(1) VAT Directive.

We will discuss these derogations from the main rule of Article 63 VAT Directive in the next sections.

9. Consequently, the CJEU held that national provisions which make the moment when the service is provided coincide with that when the consideration is paid are not compatible with the Second VAT Directive. In our view, this ruling is still relevant under the VAT Directive. CJEU 20 May 1976, Case 111-75 *Impresa Costruzioni comm. Quirino Mazzalai tegen Ferrovia del Renon*, ECLI:EU:C:1976:68.

10. In the English text of *Mazzalai* case, the CJEU refers to the issuance of invoices and the making of payments on account as 'transactions'. In our view, such activities cannot be considered as 'transactions', but should rather be referred to as 'deeds', 'acts' or 'activities', as is the case in other language versions of the ruling. We prefer to reserve the term 'transactions' for the taxable transactions in Article 2 VAT Directive, in particular for supplies of goods or services. CJEU 20 May 1976, Case 111-75 *Impresa Costruzioni comm. Quirino Mazzalai tegen Ferrovia del Renon*, ECLI:EU:C:1976:68, para. 17.

11. CJEU 21 February 2006, Case C-419/02 *BUPA Hospitals Ltd and Goldsborough Developments Ltd v Commissioners of Customs & Excise*, ECLI:EU:C:2006:122, para. 45; CJEU 13 March 2014, Case C-107/13 *FIRIN OOD v Direktor na Direktsia 'Obzhalvane i danachno-osiguritelna praktika' – Veliko Tarnovo pri Tsentralno upravlenie na Natsionalnata agentsia za prihodite*, ECLI: EU:C:2014:151, para. 35 and CJEU 19 December 2018, Case C-422/17 *Szef Krajowej Administracji Skarbowej v Skarpa Travel sp. z o.o. w Krakowie*, ECLI:EU:C:2018:1029, para. 33.

5.6.1.2 *Options Available to Member States*

Article 66 VAT Directive contains optional derogations to the rules on the designation of the moment at which the VAT becomes chargeable for certain transactions or certain categories of taxable persons. The limitation of the options for the Member States to 'certain transactions or certain categories of taxable persons'[12] suggests that Member States that avail themselves of either one of the options available are required to specify the transactions or categories of taxable persons for which a different moment of chargeability of VAT is set.[13]

Member States may provide that VAT is to become chargeable:

(1) no later than the time the invoice is issued (Article 66(a) VAT Directive);
(2) no later than the time the payment is received (Article 66(b) VAT Directive); or
(3) where an invoice is not issued or is issued late, within a specified period from the date of the chargeable event (Article 66(c) VAT Directive).

As from 1 January 2013, the Member States' option to designate a specified period from the date of the chargeable event (the third option) has become more detailed. From that date, in principle, Member States are allowed to designate as the moment at which the VAT becomes chargeable a time no later than the expiry of the time limit for the issue of invoices imposed by the Member States (*see* Article 222, second paragraph VAT Directive). However, if a Member State has not imposed a time limit for issue of invoices, that Member State may fall back on the option that was already available before 1 January 2010. The Member State may set as the moment at which the VAT becomes chargeable a moment, which lies within a specified period from the date of the chargeable event.

However, Member States are not allowed to designate a different moment at which the VAT becomes chargeable in respect of supplies of services for which the customer is required to self-assess for VAT under the reverse charge mechanism (Article 196 VAT Directive). To those supplies of services, the main rule applies (Article 63 VAT Directive), which means that the VAT becomes chargeable when the services are supplied.[14]

Also, with respect to intra-Community transfers of own goods (*see* sections 13.2.5 and 13.6), Member States cannot set their own rules with respect to the chargeable event and the chargeability of VAT. With respect to those intra-Community transfers of goods, Article 67 contains specific rules.

12. The exact English text is: 'certain categories of taxable person', which seems to be incorrect.
13. However, the CJEU has ruled that the Member State which avails itself of the derogation is not required to lay down detailed rules for documentation and recording of the completed service and the payment for it whenever the invoice or document serving as invoice has not been issued or the price has not been received. Therefore, 'certain transactions' may include 'all' services (CJEU 26 October 1995, Case C-144/94 *Ufficio IVA di Trapani v Italittica SpA*, ECLI: EU:C:1995:355). In our view, the same applies to supplies of goods.
14. *See also* B. Terra & P. Wattel, *European Tax Law* (Kluwer 2012), p. 345.

The ultimate consequence of Article 66 VAT Directive (regarding optional derogations with respect to the moment at which the VAT becomes chargeable: 'chargeability') is that in the Member States which made use of one or more of the options provided, the VAT may become chargeable *before or after* the chargeable event took place since Article 66 VAT Directive only alters the moment at which the VAT is to become chargeable (chargeability) and not the moment of the chargeable event itself.

5.6.1.3 Successive Statements on Account and Successive Payments

In cases where a supply of goods or services takes a period to be completed, the supply may give rise to successive statements of account or successive payments. If, for example, a constructor builds an extension to a house, the supply will take a period to be completed. Nonetheless, the constructor will require successive payments to be made as the alterations advance. In that situation, the supply will be regarded as (already) completed on expiry of the periods to which such statements of account or payments relate (Article 64(1) VAT Directive). The consequence is that, on the basis of the aforementioned main rule of Article 63 VAT Directive, in principle, a chargeable event occurs, and the VAT becomes chargeable on the expiry of each period.[15] Each time the constructor receives a payment, he will be required to account for the VAT relating to that payment.

As we explained in Chapter 3, section 3.2.4.2 Article 14(2)(b) VAT Directive stipulates that both the actual handing over of goods pursuant to a contract for the hire of goods for a certain period and the sale of goods on deferred terms, which provides that in the normal course of events ownership is to pass at the latest upon payment of the final instalment, is treated as a supply of goods for VAT purposes. That supply of goods is regarded as taking place at the beginning when the goods are actually handed over to the buyer. Therefore, VAT must be charged at the moment the goods are handed over.[16] For that reason, Article 64(1) VAT Directive provides that a periodical chargeability does not occur in case the supply of goods which gives rise to successive statements of account or successive payments consists in the hire of goods for a certain period or the sale of goods on deferred terms, as referred to in Article 14(2)(b) VAT Directive.

Under Article 64(1) VAT Directive, the supply of services which give rise to successive statements of account or successive payments, shall be regarded as being completed on expiry of the periods to which such statements of account or payments

15. *See also* CJEU 3 September 2015, Case C-463/14 *Asparuhovo Lake Investment Company OOD v Direktor na Direktsia 'Obzhalvane i danachno-osiguritelna praktika' Varna pri Tsentralno upravlenie na Natsionalnata agentsia za prihodite*, ECLI:EU:C:2015:542.
16. In *Muys en De Winter*, the CJEU confirmed that the interest element is to be excluded from the taxable base of the (future) instalments, since a supplier of goods or services who authorizes his customer to defer payment of the price, in return for payment of interest, is in principle making an exempt grant of credit within the meaning of that provision. CJEU 27 October 1993, Case C-281/91 *Muys' en De Winter's Bouw- en Aannemingsbedrijf BV v Staatssecretaris van Financiën*, ECLI:EU:C:1993:855.

relate. In our view, this rule also applies if the services are (locally) supplied on a continuous basis. If a business supplies a continuous telephone subscription service locally, each time a period to which a payment relates expires, the supply of the service shall be regarded as being completed. That means that the chargeable event and the chargeability of VAT occur on the expiry of that period.[17]

In *Asparuhovo Lake Investment Company OOD*, one of the questions raised was whether, in case of subscription contracts for consulting services, the chargeable event and the chargeability of the tax occur upon the expiry of the period in respect of which the payment has been agreed, irrespective of whether and how often the customer makes use of the supplier's services.[18] Under the relevant contract, the service supplier had essentially agreed to be permanently available to the customer in order to provide it with consulting services. The supplier was remunerated by means of fixed sums paid periodically. The CJEU ruled that the supply must be regarded as having been completed at the end of each period to which the payments relate.[19] In other words, the chargeable event took place, and the chargeability of VAT occurred at the end of each payment period. Interestingly, the CJEU adds that it is irrelevant in this regard whether or not the service provider has actually provided advice to its customer during that period. Apparently, the CJEU considers that the nature of the service is not so much the provision of concrete consultancy services but the being available for the customer. This suggests that such a service has a continuous nature. Whether a service is supplied on a continuous basis, is, however, only relevant for the application of Article 64(2) VAT Directive, which relates to continuous cross-border supplies of goods (*see* section 5.6.1.5) and cross-border supplies of services (*see* below).

5.6.1.4 Continuous Cross-Border Supplies of Services

As a main rule, the supplier is the person liable to pay the VAT to the tax authorities. However, in a number of situations, particularly in cross-border situations, the VAT on a supply is due by the customer, rather than by the supplier. This is called the 'reverse charge mechanism', *see* Chapter 12, section 12.3.[20] If, for example, a business supplies an advisory service to a company established in another Member State, the place of supply will be where the customer is established (Article 44 VAT Directive, *see* Chapter 4, section 4.5.3). Article 196 VAT Directive stipulates that the customer is payable by

17. This is the case in which a Member State did not make use of any of the options provided for in Article 66 VAT Directive. In Figure 5.3, we depicted an example in which a Member State implemented the option of Article 66(a) VAT Directive, so that the VAT becomes chargeable no later than the time the invoice is issued. That explains why in the example in Figure 5.3, the chargeable event and the chargeability do not coincide. Also *see* Figure 5.4.
18. CJEU 3 September 2015, Case C-463/14 *Asparuhovo Lake Investment Company OOD v Direktor na Direktsia 'Obzhalvane i danachno-osiguritelna praktika' Varna pri Tsentralno upravlenie na Natsionalnata agentsia za prihodite*, ECLI:EU:C:2015:542.
19. Also *see*: CJEU 29 November 2018, Case C-548/17 *Finanzamt Goslar v baumgarten sports & more GmbH*, ECLI:EU:C:2018:970, para. 28.
20. The 'reverse charge mechanism' is also referred to as 'the transfer mechanism of the tax obligation'. *See*: ECJ 15 March 2007, Case C-35/05 *Reemtsma Cigarettenfabriken GmbH v Ministero delle Finanze*, ECLI:EU:C:2007:167, para. 32.

the customer (reversed charged). However, if an intra-Community supply of services continues over a lengthy period, for example, in the case of B2B telecommunications services, there is a risk that the supplier, who is required to file a recapitulative statement (*see*: Article 262(c), *see* Chapter 15, section 15.6) and the customer, who is required to record the services in his VAT return, do so at different moments. Article 64(2) VAT Directive enables transactions to be declared by the vendor and the purchaser during the same period so that the information submitted can be cross-checked efficiently. Moreover, it ensures uniform rules for charging VAT so that service providers do not have to comply with charging rules that vary according to their customer's place of establishment in order to be able to declare these transactions.[21] Article 64(2) VAT Directive (regarding supplies with a continuous nature) provides that a supply that continues for more than a year, and for which the VAT is payable by the customer under Article 196 VAT Directive, is considered as being completed on expiry of each calendar year until the services come to an end.

However, if the continuous supplies give rise to statements of account or interim payments during the period in which the supplies are made, in principle, Article 64(1) applies. Consequently, the supply will be regarded as completed insofar as and at the moment at which payment is made. Then, the chargeable event occurs, and the VAT becomes chargeable at the moment of the payment. Since usually, the aforementioned B2B telecommunications services give rise to interim payments, the intra-Community cross-border B2B supplies of telecommunications services will normally be considered as completed each time the customer makes a payment. The customer must account for the VAT on those supplies under the reverse charge mechanism.

In 2010, Article 64(2) VAT Directive (regarding supplies with a continuous nature) was amended. It was found appropriate that the continuous supply of goods from one Member State to another over a period of more than one calendar month should be regarded as being completed at the end of each calendar month.[22] Thus, continuous ICSs deemed to be completed on the expiry of each calendar month.

The above rules on the chargeable event in the case of continuous supplies, other than those that cover a period which exceeds one year and does not give rise to statements of account or payments during that period, can be set aside by the Member States. Article 64(2), last sentence VAT Directive gives the Member States the option to provide that continuous supplies of goods or services over a period of time are to be regarded as being completed at least at intervals of one year. Moreover, different rules apply if payments on account are made (*see* Article 65 VAT Directive, discussed section 5.3) or if a Member State designates a different moment as the moment in which VAT is to become chargeable (*see* Article 66 VAT Directive, discussed section 5.6.1.2). Different rules also apply to ICSs (*see* Article 67 VAT Directive, discussed in section 5.6.2).

21. *See* Proposal for a Council Directive amending Directive 2006/112/EC on the common system of value added tax to combat tax evasion connected with ICTs, COM (2008) 147 final, pp. 5 and 7.
22. *See* the third recital of the Preamble to the Council Directive 2010/45/EU of 13 July 2010 amending Directive 2006/112/EC on the common system of value added tax as regards the rules on invoicing [2010] OJ L189/1.

5.6.1.5 Continuous Cross-Border Supplies of Goods

Although it may be difficult to imagine that a good is supplied continuously, it must be borne in mind that under Article 15(1) VAT Directive, electricity, gas, heat, refrigeration and the like are considered to be goods, from a VAT point of view (*see* Chapter 3, section 3.2.2.1). Such goods can be supplied continuously.

Prior to 1 January 2013, the VAT Directive contained no specific obligatory provision on the chargeable event in case of continuous supplies of goods. However, Member States have the option to deem a continuous supply of goods duration of which exceeds a year as being completed at least once a year (Article 64, last sentence VAT Directive).

Since 1 January 2013, a specific rule is applicable for continuous ICSs or transfers of goods. If the duration of such exempt supplies (*see* Article 138 VAT Directive) exceeds a year, they shall be regarded as being completed on expiry of each calendar month, until the supplies or transfers come to an end. As a departure from that rule, Member States will still have the option of deeming a continuous supply of goods as being completed at least once a year.

5.6.1.6 Payments on Account

Sometimes, a supplier of goods or services requires the customer to make a (partial) payment before he supplies the goods or services ('a payment on account' or 'prepayment'). Normally, a payment on account will particularly be required if the goods or services are expensive. One can imagine that when a customer orders an expensive sofa, the supplier, who must place an order with (and make a payment to) the sofa-factory, will require a prepayment for the sofa. That way, he can reduce the financing costs of his order with the factory and, at the same time, create an incentive for the customer to comply with the sales agreement. If a prepayment is made, VAT becomes chargeable on receipt of the payment on the amount received (Article 65 VAT Directive), unless a Member State made use of one of the possibilities for derogation provided for in Article 66 VAT Directive, because Article 66 overrules Article 65 VAT Directive (*see* section 5.6.1.2).

In order for the tax to become chargeable when the customer has made a payment on account, all the relevant information concerning the chargeable event, namely the future delivery or future performance, must already be known and therefore, in particular, when the payment on account is made, the goods or services must be precisely identified. Payments on account of supplies of goods or services that have not yet been clearly identified cannot be subject to VAT. For that reason, a lump sum prepayment for drugs and prostheses referred to in general terms in a list which could be altered at any time and from which the buyer may possibly select articles was not considered a payment on account.[23]

23. CJEU 21 February 2006, Case C-419/02 *BUPA Hospitals Ltd and Goldsborough Developments Ltd v Commissioners of Customs & Excise*, ECLI:EU:C:2006:122.

5.6.2 ICSs

Article 67(1) VAT Directive provides that in the case of an exempt (with the right to deduct input VAT, *see* Chapter 10, section 10.2.4.2.3) ICS or intra-Community transfer of goods, the VAT is chargeable on the 15th day following the month in which the chargeable event occurs.

5.6.3 ICAs

The chargeable event with respect to ICAs is set at the moment at which the taxable event (the intra-Community acquisition) takes place. Thus, with respect to ICAs, the VAT Directive (Article 68) explicitly determines that the taxable event and the chargeable event coincide.[24] Therefore, it is relevant to establish at what moment the ICA takes place.

The second paragraph of Article 68 VAT Directive sets this moment as the point at which 'the supply of similar goods is regarded as being effected within the territory of the relevant member state'. The idea is that the ICA in the Member State of arrival of the goods is to take place at the same moment as the corresponding ICS in the Member State of departure of the goods. This parallelism is important for the functioning of the system of ICTs, for the ICSs must be reported on the VAT return and on the recapitulative statement. This information is matched against the ICAs reported in the Member State of the recipient of the goods. That is only possible if both the ICS and the ICA are reported in the same tax period. In our view, Article 68 VAT Directive does not fully guarantee this parallelism. This is because it does not set the chargeable event at the moment at which the ICS (in the Member State of departure of the goods) takes place, but rather sets it at the moment at which a similar supply of goods is regarded as being effected in the Member State of arrival of the goods. Although under the main rules the chargeable event for supplies of goods will be identical in all Member States (i.e., when the goods are supplied, *see* section 5.1.2), it is possible that – due to optional provisions regarding the chargeable event for continuous supplies of goods in Article 64(2) VAT Directive – the chargeable event of the supply in the Member State of departure is different from the chargeable event of a similar supply in the Member State of arrival. However, the text of this provision changed on 1 January 2013, after which date, full parallelism exists, even if it concerns continuous ICSs.[25]

24. Article 69 VAT Directive echoes this idea: as a main rule, the VAT on an ICA becomes chargeable on the issue of the invoice (for the intra-Community supply) or on the fifteenth day of the month following that in which the chargeable event occurs, where no invoice has been issued before that date. *See*: CJEU 9 September 2021, Case C-855/19 *G. Sp. z o.o. v Dyrektor Izby Administracji Skarbowej w Bydgoszczy*, ECLI:EU:C:2021:714.

25. Council Directive 2010/45/EU of 13 July 2010 amending Directive 2006/112/EC on the common system of value added tax as regards the rules on invoicing.

5.6.4 Importation of Goods

As regards goods that are imported, the chargeable event is the moment at which the goods are imported (Article 70 VAT Directive). If the goods are immediately placed under a customs arrangement or situation referred to in Article 156 VAT Directive (or under a temporary importation arrangement with a total exemption for import duty/an external transit arrangement), the chargeable event and the chargeability of VAT are postponed. We refer to Chapter 14 on importation and exportation.

5.7 PAYMENT ARRANGEMENTS

A distinction has to be drawn between, on the one hand, the concepts of chargeable event and chargeability of tax, and, on the other hand, that of the payment of the tax. VAT cannot become payable before it has become chargeable. Only after the point at which VAT has become chargeable, is it relevant to determine whether there is effectively an amount of VAT payable to the tax authorities.[26]

Input VAT can, in principle, be deducted from the VAT that is payable. Therefore, there will only be an amount of VAT payable, if the balance of output VAT and input VAT is positive. Any surplus VAT must be paid to the tax authorities.

As regards the moment at which the net amount of VAT must be paid, the main rule is that the person that is held liable to pay the VAT (*see* Chapter 12), must pay the VAT to the tax authorities, when submitting the VAT return (Article 206 VAT Directive). However, Member States may set a different date for payment or may require interim payments to be made. Consequently, the moment at which the net amount of VAT must be paid to the tax authorities differs per Member State. Nonetheless, all Member States are under an obligation to take all legislative and administrative measures appropriate for ensuring the collection of all the VAT due on its territory. In that regard, Member States are required to check taxable persons' returns, accounts and other relevant documents, and to calculate and collect the tax due.[27] Although the text of Article 206 VAT Directive suggests that a Member State may either set a different date for payment *or* require interim payments to be made, we believe that Member States should be able to do both.

In case the reverse charge applies, or if a person is jointly liable for the payment of VAT, Member States are required to ensure that the net amount of VAT will be paid to the tax authorities and (in the Member States that require interim payments) that interim payments are made.

There are specific rules on the payment arrangements regarding investment gold ICAs by certain acquirers, as well as for the importation of goods (*see* Articles 208, 209, 210 and 211 VAT Directive). Because of their specific nature, we will not further elaborate on those rules. There are also specific rules concerning the payment

26. CJEU 20 October 1993, Case C-10/92 *Maurizio Balocchi v Ministero delle Finanze dello Stato*, ECLI:EU:C:1993:846.
27. CJEU 17 July 2008, Case C-132/06 *Commission of the European Communities v Italian Republic*, ECLI:EU:C:2008:412.

arrangements in case the special scheme for electronically supplied services applies to such supplies of a non-established taxable person. The non-established taxable person must pay the VAT when submitting the VAT return (Article 367 VAT Directive).

In the event that the amount of VAT payable is insignificant, Member States may release taxable persons from the payment of the VAT due. The VAT Directive does not contain a definition of the term 'insignificant' in this respect.

CHAPTER 6

Taxable Amount

6.1 INTRODUCTION

If a taxable person carries out a taxed supply of goods or services, for which he is liable to pay the VAT, he must determine how much VAT he must charge to his customer and report in his VAT return. For that, he needs to establish the amount to which he can apply the VAT rate. The amount to which VAT is applied is commonly referred to as the 'taxable amount'.

Chapter VII of the VAT Directive deals with the determination of the taxable amount (Articles 72-92 VAT Directive). Normally, the taxable amount is the price that the supplier charges for its goods or services whereby there should be a direct link between the supply and the consideration. In addition, the VAT Directive contains specific provisions determining which elements must be included and which must be excluded from the taxable amount. Furthermore, specific rules exist with respect to – for example, but not limited to – price adjustments, cancellations, returns and discounts. The VAT Directive even contains (optional) rules on the application of an 'open market value' under specific circumstances. Also, Chapter VII of the VAT Directive contains provisions on the determination of the taxable amount in cases where there is – for example – a deemed supply, an ICA or importation of goods.

All in all, it is clear that there is more to the taxable amount in EU VAT law than one might expect at first sight. Therefore, we will elaborate on the taxable amount in this chapter.

6.2 THE PROPORTIONALITY OF VAT AND THE TAXABLE AMOUNT

Article 1(2) VAT Directive states that:

> VAT entails the application to goods and services of a general tax on consumption exactly proportional to the price of the goods and services.

The fact that it is proportional to the price of the goods or services concerned is one of the essential characteristics of EU VAT.[1] According to the CJEU, the principle that VAT must be proportionate can relate only to the taxable amount.[2] Article 73 VAT Directive stipulates that the taxable amount for supplies of goods and services is everything that constitutes the consideration *obtained or to be obtained by the supplier*, in return for the supply, including subsidies directly linked to the price of the supply. Thus, even though the objective of EU VAT is to tax consumption and to measure that consumption by the expenditures of final consumers, in the end, the taxable amount is determined by what the taxable person actually receives or should receive as consideration for his supplies.[3] Indeed, the CJEU, on occasion, has ruled that the taxable amount for a supply of services is represented by the 'consideration actually received' for that supply.[4] The underlying reason for using the receipts of suppliers rather than the payments by customers as a taxable amount clearly lies within the indirect character of the tax (*see* Chapter 1, section 1.2).

1. CJEU 31 March 1992, Case C-200/90 *Dansk Denkavit ApS and P. Poulsen Trading ApS, supported by Monsanto-Searle A/S v Skatteministeriet*, ECLI:EU:C:1992:152, para. 11; CJEU 8 June 1999, Joined Cases C-338/97, C-344/97 and C-390/97 *Erna Pelzl and Others v Steiermärkische Landesregierung (C-338/97), Wiener Städtische Allgemeine Versicherungs AG and Others v Tiroler Landesregierung (C-344/97) and STUAG Bau-Aktiengesellschaft v Kärntner Landesregierung (C-390/97)*, ECLI:EU:C:1999:285, para. 25 and CJEU 11 October 2007, Joined Cases C-283/06 and C-312/06 *KÖGÁZ rt and Others v Zala Megyei Közigazgatási Hivatal Vezetője (C-283/06) and OTP Garancia Biztosító rt v Vas Megyei Közigazgatási Hivatal (C-312/06)*, ECLI:EU:C:2007:598, para. 40.
2. CJEU 24 October 2013, Case C-440/12 *Metropol Spielstätten Unternehmergesellschaft (haftungsbeschränkt) v Finanzamt Hamburg-Bergedorf*, ECLI:EU:C:2013:687, para. 38.
3. CJEU 19 June 2003, Case C-149/01 *First Choice Holidays*, ECLI:EU:C:2003:358, paras 28-31 and the case law cited and CJEU 24 October 2013, Case C-440/12 *Metropol Spielstätten Unternehmergesellschaft (haftungsbeschränkt) v Finanzamt Hamburg-Bergedorf*, ECLI:EU:C:2013:687, para. 38.
4. *See, inter alia* CJEU 27 March 1990, Case C-126/88 *Boots Company plc v Commissioners of Customs and Excise*, ECLI:EU:C:1990:136, para. 19; CJEU 17 September 2002, Case C-498/99 *Town & County Factors Ltd v Commissioners of Customs & Excise*, ECLI:EU:C:2002:494, para. 27 and CJEU 19 July 2012, Case C-377/11 *International Bingo Technology SA v Tribunal Económico-Administrativo Regional de Cataluña (TEARC)*, ECLI:EU:C:2012:503, para. 25. *See* A.J. van Doesum, 'Taxable Amount', in M. Lang, et al. (eds), *ECJ: Recent Developments in Value Added Tax, the Evolution of European VAT Jurisprudence and Its Role in the EU Common VAT System* (Linde 2014), pp. 177-233. In our view, as for a supply of goods, the taxable amount is represented by the 'consideration actually received' for that supply.

6.3 THE TAXABLE AMOUNT IS A SUBJECTIVE VALUE

With a consumption tax, such as EU VAT, the taxable amount is a key element because, in the end, it is decisive – together with the applicable VAT rate – in determining the tax burden on private consumption. If a taxable amount estimated according to objective criteria were to be used, the amount of VAT levied would not be related to consumption at all. That does not match the legal character and the indirect form of EU VAT. Therefore, the taxable amount for VAT purposes must be a subjective value.[5] This means that the consideration is the value actually received in each specific case, and not a value estimated according to objective criteria.[6] Even if a price is – from an objective economic perspective, compared to prices on the market – too low or too high, the taxable amount should still be the actual sales price, in order to reflect the actual consumption taking place. Article 80 VAT Directive contains, subject to conditions, an exception to this main principle which is laid down in Article 73 VAT Directive.

The legal character of VAT requires that the taxable amount approximates the value of the consumption as closely as possible. Arguably, the value of consumption is best approximated by the spending power that the consumer sacrifices in order to obtain the good or service to be consumed. After all, the prices paid by customers reflect their consumption. However, taxing customers' expenditures in a direct manner is considered as not being feasible (also *see* Chapter 1, section 1.2) because taxing the customers' expenditures directly would impose a heavy burden on taxpayers and tax authorities. Therefore, EU VAT taxes transactions, carried out by taxable persons, being the 'opposite side' of an expenditure. It should be noted that as a consequence, not all private consumption is taxed (e.g., private consumption following a supply by a non-taxable person is, in principle, not taxed). Therefore, it is safe to say that taxable transactions can be considered as mere proxies to consumption.[7]

The subjective character of the taxable amount also implies that the taxable amount may not – in principle[8] – *exceed* the sum finally received by the supplier.[9] Indeed, it is a fundamental principle of the VAT Directive, that the basis of assessment is the consideration actually received, the corollary of which is that the tax authorities

5. In this respect, the term 'subjective' is used to describe the value placed by the parties on key elements in a transaction. *See* the Opinion of Advocate General Fennelly of 27 June 1996, Case C-288/94 *Argos Distributors Ltd v Commissioners of Customs & Excise*, ECLI:EU:C:1996:398, para. 21.
6. CJEU 1 April 1982, Case 89/81 *Staatssecretaris van Financiën v Hong-Kong Trade Development Council*, ECLI:EU:C:1982:121, para. 13; CJEU 23 November 1988, Case 230/87 *Naturally Yours Cosmetics Limited v Commissioners of Customs and Excise*, ECLI:EU:C:1988:508, para. 16; Case C-126/88; CJEU 27 March 1990, Case C-126/88 *Boots Company plc v Commissioners of Customs and Excise*, ECLI:EU:C:1990:136 and CJEU 24 October 1996, Case C-317/94 *Elida Gibbs Ltd v Commissioners of Customs and Excise*, ECLI:EU:C:1996:400, para. 27.
7. A.J. van Doesum, 'Taxable Amount', in M. Lang, et al. (eds), *ECJ: Recent Developments in Value Added Tax, the Evolution of European VAT Jurisprudence and Its Role in the EU Common VAT System* (Linde 2014), pp. 177-233.
8. For example, Article 80 VAT Directive.
9. CJEU 24 October 1996, Case C-317/94 *Elida Gibbs Ltd v Commissioners of Customs and Excise*, ECLI:EU:C:1996:400, para. 28.

may not in any circumstances require an amount of VAT exceeding the tax received by the taxable person.[10]

6.4 THE TAXABLE AMOUNT MUST BE EXPRESSED IN MONEY

Not only should the taxable amount be a subjective value but should also be capable of being expressed in money.[11] After all, a tax needs to be expressed in monetary terms.

Normally, the sales price of the goods or services constitutes the taxable amount. If no specific price is agreed, but a consideration is, in fact, paid in return for a supply, the amount actually received by the supplier constitutes the taxable amount. Therefore, we believe that it is not necessary that the exact amount of a consideration is known upfront for it to constitute a taxable amount. As a result, success- or contingency fees should, in principle, be considered to form the taxable amount.[12]

The sales price may be agreed upon as a sum of money, as a payment in kind or as a combination of both (*see* sections 6.6.1.1 and 6.6.1.2). If the payment is wholly or partially in kind, the consideration must still be capable of being expressed in money.[13] The subjective value of a (partial) consideration in kind for the supplier must, to that end, be 'transformed' to a sum of money, which is to be subjected to VAT. Therefore, a consumption tax system should provide for means to determine the relevant taxable amount in such situations.

The VAT Directive contains several provisions for determining the taxable amount in specific circumstances.[14] The most important ones will be addressed in this chapter.

---

10. CJEU 26 January 2012, Case C-588/10 *Minister Finansów v Kraft Foods Polska SA*, ECLI:EU:C:2012:40, para. 27.
11. For example: CJEU 5 February 1981, Case 154/80 *Staatssecretaris van Financiën v Coöperatieve Aardappelenbewaarplaats*, ECLI:EU:C:1981:38, para. 13.
12. CJEU 10 November 2016, Case C-432/15 *Odvolací finanční ředitelství v Pavlína Baštová* suggests that some fees that rely on a certain result can remain outside the scope of EU VAT. Because of the specific nature and facts of that case (supply of a horse by a taxable person to the organizer of horse races whereby only the owners of winning horses received a remuneration), we do not believe that it leads to any general conclusions on the EU VAT treatment of success or contingency fees. On the contrary, we believe it would be counter to the purpose of the directive if its scope would be limited to considerations the amount and payment of which are certain upfront.
13. CJEU 5 February 1981, Case 154/80 *Staatssecretaris van Financiën v Coöperatieve Aardappelenbewaarplaats* [1981] ECR 00445; CJEU 23 November 1988, Case 230/87 *Naturally Yours Cosmetics Ltd v Commissioners of Customs and Excise*, ECLI:EU:C:1988:508; CJEU 27 March 1990, Case C-126/88 *The Boots Company plc v The Commissioners of Customs and Excise*, ECLI:EU:C:1990:136 and CJEU 24 October 1996, Case C-288/94 *Argos Distributors Ltd v Commissioners of Customs and Excise*, ECLI:EU:C:1996:398.
14. Deemed supplies (self-supplies and internal supplies: Articles 74-77 VAT Directive), in case the supplier also charges taxes, duties, levies or incidental expenses to his customer (Article 78), for price discounts (Article 79), for the prevention of tax evasion or avoidance (Article 80), special regimes for second-hand goods and the like and investment gold (Articles 81-82), intra-Community acquisitions of goods (Articles 83-84), importation of goods (Articles 85-89), cancellation, refusal, total or partial non-payment, price reduction after the supply (Article 90), exchange rates (Article 91) and returnable packing material (Article 92).

6.5 A HARMONIZED TAX BASE

Title VII contains the rules with respect to the determination of the taxable amount. The purpose of the provisions in this Title is to harmonize the taxable amount to the greatest extent possible.[15] A harmonized tax base in EU VAT is important to prevent distortions of competition and to safeguard the EU's own resources, of which the tax base in VAT forms a constituent element. Consequently, the EU VAT regime for determining the taxable amount does not leave much discretion or room for interpretation to the Member States. This regime is intended, *inter alia,* to ensure that VAT is applied at each marketing stage on the price or value of the goods at that stage. It, therefore, precludes the application of taxation arrangements in which VAT is determined, once only, on the price at the first marketing stage.[16]

6.6 CONSIDERATION

In this section, we will further elaborate on the concept of the 'consideration'. To facilitate this, it is useful to have a closer look at the text of Article 73 VAT Directive, containing the main rule with respect to the determination of the taxable amount. Article 73 VAT Directive reads as follows:

> In respect of the supply of goods or services, other than as referred to in Articles 74 to 77, the taxable amount shall include everything which constitutes consideration obtained or to be obtained by the supplier, in return for the supply, from the customer or a third party, including subsidies directly linked to the price of the supply.

When analysing this provision, it is apparent that the following elements are key to the concept of the 'taxable amount':

(1) The taxable amount shall include everything which constitutes consideration.
(2) The consideration must be obtained or to be obtained by the supplier.
(3) The consideration must be 'in return' for the supply (usually referred to as the 'direct link criterion').
(4) The consideration must be obtained from the customer or a third party.
(5) The consideration includes subsidies directly linked to the price of the supply.

In the following subsections, we will discuss each of these elements of the taxable amount concept.

15. *See* Preamble to the VAT Directive, para. 25: 'The taxable amount should be harmonized so that the application of VAT to taxable transactions leads to comparable results in all the Member States.' and CJEU 25 May 1993, Case C-18/92 *Chaussures Bally SA v Belgian State,* ECLI: EU:C:1993:212, para. 12: 'The purpose of that provision is therefore, as may be seen from the ninth recital in the preamble to the Sixth Directive, to harmonize the taxable amount'.
16. CJEU 6 July 1995, Case C-62/93 *BP Soupergaz Anonimos Etairia Geniki Emporiki-Viomichaniki kai Antiprossopeion v Greek State,* ECLI:EU:C:1995:223.

6.6.1 Everything Which Constitutes Consideration

The word 'consideration' suggests that the taxable amount requires a legal relationship based on the 'quid pro quo' principle, meaning that a supply of goods or services by one party is contingent upon a payment of money or in kind by the other party. As we will show in section 6.6.3, this is underlined by the fact that a consideration must be given 'in return for the supply'. Thus, Article 73 VAT Directive strongly indicates the requirement of a direct link between a supply and the consideration.

Furthermore, it is apparent from the words 'everything which constitutes consideration' that the consideration need not be an amount of money. A consideration can also be paid 'in kind'. We will further elaborate on considerations in kind in section 6.6.1.2. The word 'everything' also indicates that the amount or value of the compensation for the goods or services is irrelevant for it to be considered as a 'consideration'. We will discuss 'low' and/or 'symbolic' considerations in section 6.6.1.3 and the single considerations which are paid in return for supplies consisting of multiple elements in section 6.6.1.4.

6.6.1.1 Monetary Consideration (Foreign Currencies)

In most cases, the consideration is an amount expressed in money. The determination of the taxable amount is then rather straightforward. However, complications may arise if the consideration is expressed in a foreign currency.

According to normal business practice, monetary amounts can be paid in the currency of the Member State involved or paid in a foreign currency. This will generally depend on the commercial and contractual arrangements in place between parties.

Article 91(2), first paragraph VAT Directive contains the main rule on the determination of the taxable amount in case foreign currency is used to determine the taxable amount of a transaction (other than the importation of goods).[17] It stipulates that the exchange rate applicable shall be the latest selling rate recorded, at the time VAT becomes chargeable, on the most representative exchange market or markets of the Member State concerned, or a rate determined by reference to that or those markets, in accordance with the rules laid down by that Member State.

Article 91(2), second paragraph VAT Directive contains an exception. It requires the Member States to accept the use of the latest exchange rate published by the European Central Bank at the time the tax becomes chargeable instead. Conversion between currencies other than the euro shall be made by using the euro exchange rate of each currency. Member States may require that they be notified of the exercise of this option by the taxable person.

17. Article 92(1) VAT Directive states that where the factors used to determine the taxable amount on importation are expressed in a currency other than that of the Member State in which assessment takes place, the exchange rate shall be determined in accordance with the Community provisions governing the calculation of the value for customs purposes.

However, for some transactions, or for certain categories of taxable persons, Member States may use the exchange rate determined in accordance with the Community provisions in force governing the calculation of the value for customs purposes.

6.6.1.2 *Consideration in Kind (Barter Transactions)*[18]

Conceptually, supplies of goods or services for which a consideration in kind is paid (barter transactions) must be taxed in the same way as supplies for which a monetary consideration is paid. Both from the perspective of the legal character of VAT (to tax all consumption), and also from a neutrality perspective, it is necessary to tax barter transactions and to determine a taxable amount, expressed in money. Indeed, in *Goldsmiths*, the CJEU ruled that transactions for which the consideration is in money and transactions for which the consideration is in kind are similar transactions from a VAT perspective, and should, therefore, be treated identically for VAT purposes.[19]

A payment in kind is considered as a (return) supply. If the person making the payment in kind is not a taxable person, the payment in kind (the return supply) is not a taxable supply.

Conversely, if the person making the payment in kind is a taxable person (acting as such), the payment in kind (the return supply) is a taxable supply. Then, there are two taxable supplies: the (initial) supply of a good or service by the supplier (a taxable person) and the return supply by the purchaser (here, also a taxable person). If such a payment in kind is made between two taxable persons who have a full right of deduction, the calculation of the taxable amount is more or less an academic exercise. After all, both parties can fully deduct the VAT on the supply and the return supply, respectively. However, if one of the taxable persons involved in the barter is not fully entitled to a deduction of input tax, the determination of the taxable amount of the return supply (a consideration in kind) suddenly becomes more relevant. For example, if a local retailer provides shirts with his firm's logo to a local soccer club (making exempt supplies under Article 132(1)(m) VAT Directive, thus not entitled to full deduction of input VAT) in return for an advertising service by the soccer club, two questions arise:

(1) What is the taxable amount on which the local retailer should calculate the VAT to the local soccer club (which VAT the soccer club will not be able to deduct)?

18. *See* Chapter 3, section 3.4.3. Also *see* A.J. van Doesum, 'Taxable Amount', in M. Lang, et al. (eds), *ECJ: Recent Developments in Value Added Tax, the Evolution of European VAT Jurisprudence and Its Role in the EU Common VAT System* (Linde 2014), pp. 177-233.

19. CJEU 3 July 1997, Case C-330/95 *Goldsmiths (Jewellers) Ltd v Commissioners of Customs & Excise*, ECLI:EU:C:1997:339. *See* with respect to the valuation of barter transactions: R.M. Millar, *Illusory Supplies and Unacknowledged Discounts: VAT and Valuation in Consumer Transactions* (2003) 2 British Tax Review, pp. 153-184.

(2) What is the taxable amount of the return supply by the local soccer club that also affects its right to deduction (the pro rata; *see* Chapter 10 on Deduction of Input VAT)?[20]

Since the taxable amount is the central topic in this chapter, we will focus on the first question here. We will discuss the following scenarios:

(1) Goods bartered for goods.
(2) Goods bartered for services.
(3) Goods partially bartered for services.
(4) Services bartered for services.

6.6.1.2.1 Goods Bartered for Goods

In the case of a barter of goods, the consideration for a supply of a good (e.g., a pencil) is the value of the other good (e.g., a sharpener) that is received in return and the other way around. The consideration taken as the taxable amount in respect of such a supply of a good (the pencil) is a subjective value since the taxable amount is the consideration actually received, and not a value estimated according to objective criteria.[21] In order for the value to be used as the taxable amount to be a subjective value, the taxable amount of the supply of the pencil by the supplier A must be the value which he attaches to the sharpener that he receives in return from B and must correspond to the amount which supplier of the pencil A is prepared to spend for that purpose.[22] Because there is no monetary value agreed, that value can only be the price which A as the *supplier* of the pencil has paid for the pencil (i.e., the purchase price of the pencil). The taxable amount of the supply of the sharpener by B is determined in exactly the same manner, which means that the taxable amount consists of the purchase price of the

20. It does not follow directly from the VAT Directive that the taxable amount of Article 73 VAT Directive is the decisive factor for the calculation of the deductible proportion under Article 174 VAT Directive. Articles 73 and 174 VAT Directive use different wordings in this respect. In Article 73, the term 'everything which constitutes consideration obtained or to be obtained' is used. Article 174 uses the term 'total amount of turnover'. However, in *International Bingo*, the CJEU coupled Article 11(1)(a) Sixth VAT Directive (now: Article 73 VAT Directive) to Article 19(1) Sixth VAT Directive (now: Article 174 VAT Directive). Since there is no principal difference between a consideration in money and in kind, we believe that the payment of a consideration in kind is also relevant for calculating the pro rata. *See* CJEU 19 July 2012, Case C-377/11 *International Bingo Technology SA v Tribunal Económico-Administrativo Regional de Cataluña (TEARC)*, ECLI:EU:C:2012:503. *See also* A.J. van Doesum, 'Taxable Amount', in M. Lang, et al. (eds), *ECJ: Recent Developments in Value Added Tax, the Evolution of European VAT Jurisprudence and Its Role in the EU Common VAT System* (Linde 2014), pp. 177-233.
21. CJEU 1 April 1982, Case 89/81 *Staatssecretaris van Financiën v Hong-Kong Trade Development Council*, ECLI:EU:C:1982:121, para. 13; CJEU 23 November 1988, Case 230/87 *Naturally Yours Cosmetics Ltd v Commissioners of Customs and Excise*, ECLI:EU:C:1988:508, para. 16; CJEU 27 March 1990, Case C-126/88 *Boots Company plc v Commissioners of Customs and Excise*, ECLI:EU:C:1990:136, para. 19 and CJEU 24 October 1996, Case C-317/94 *Elida Gibbs Ltd v Commissioners of Customs and Excise*, ECLI:EU:C:1996:400, para. 27.
22. CJEU 2 June 1994, Case C-33/93 *Empire Stores Ltd v Commissioners of Customs and Excise*, ECLI:EU:C:1994:225, para. 19.

sharpener. Perhaps counterintuitively, this means that different amounts of VAT may be due for each of the supplies that constitute the barter.

6.6.1.2.2 Goods Bartered for Services

Instead of consisting of a good, the consideration for a supply of goods may[23] consist in a provision of services, and so constitute the taxable amount for a supply of goods.[24] This is the case in the example used above of the local soccer club, which is sponsored (in kind) by a local retailer. It is also the example of *Empire Stores*.[25]

In *Empire Stores*, the CJEU clarified that in order for the consideration of a supply of goods made for a consideration in kind consisting of service, the taxable amount of the supply of the goods must, in principle, be based on the value which the supplier[26] of the goods attributes to it.[27] The CJEU's ruling is a bit confusing in this regard:

> Where that value [eds.: the value of the goods] is not a sum of money agreed between the parties, it must, in order to be subjective, be the value which the recipient of the services [eds.: in this case the recipient of the services is actually the same person as the person making the supply of the goods] constituting the consideration for the supply of goods attributes to the services which he [eds.: the supplier of the goods] is seeking to obtain and must correspond to the amount which he [eds.: the supplier of the goods] is prepared to spend for that purpose. Where, as here, the supply of goods is involved, that value can only be the price which the supplier [eds.: of the goods] has paid for the article which he is supplying without extra charge in consideration of the services in question.[28]

It follows from the citation above that since it is virtually impossible to determine what value the supplier of the goods attributes to the service that he receives, the value which the customer attributes to the supply can be *objectified*. The CJEU ruled that the value must correspond to the amount which the supplier of the goods is prepared to spend for that purpose. Effectively, this means that the cost price of the goods supplied constitutes the taxable amount.

Empire Stores was a mail-order company selling goods by catalogue. Under one of its schemes, referred to as the 'self-introduction scheme', *Empire Stores* offered potential customers the possibility of choosing one article from a list. That article could be supplied without extra charge once they had filled in a form requesting personal details. That form was designed to establish their creditworthiness. Another condition was that *Empire Stores* had approved the completed form and that the potential customer had placed an order for goods from its sales catalogue or had made at least a

23. There must be a direct link between the supply of goods and the provision of services and the value of those services must be capable of being expressed in monetary terms.
24. CJEU 23 November 1988, Case 230/87 *Naturally Yours Cosmetics Ltd v Commissioners of Customs and Excise*, ECLI:EU:C:1988:508, paras 11, 12 and 16.
25. CJEU 2 June 1994, Case C-33/93 *Empire Stores Ltd v Commissioners of Customs and Excise*, ECLI:EU:C:1994:225.
26. What the supplier would like to receive is what the recipient would like to give up.
27. CJEU 2 June 1994, Case C-33/93 *Empire Stores Ltd v Commissioners of Customs and Excise*, ECLI:EU:C:1994:225.
28. *Ibid.*, para. 19.

first payment in respect of such an order. The Court ruled that Article 11A(1)(a) Sixth VAT Directive (now Article 73 VAT Directive) must be interpreted 'as meaning that the taxable amount in respect of an article supplied without extra charge to a person who introduces herself or another person as a potential new customer is distinct from the taxable amount in respect of the goods bought from the supplier by the new customer and corresponds to the price paid by the supplier for that article.' So indeed, the taxable amount of the supply made by *Empire Stores* should have been calculated on how Empire Stores valued the services it received from its (potential) customers. This value could be estimated on the offer made by *Empire Stores* to provide the customer with the goods concerned; in other words, the purchase price of that product.

6.6.1.2.3 Services Bartered for Services

The rules given in *Empire Stores* certainly provide some guidance as to the calculation of the taxable amount of supplies of goods in return for services. However, if a barter transaction consists of the exchange of two services, the application of the principles set out in *Empire Stores* may not be easy. The reason for that is that, in practice, it would not always be easy to calculate the cost price of a service, particularly not if that service was generated internally. In our view, such a situation calls for further objectification.

In *Orfey*,[29] there was an exchange of a service (the granting of a building right) for another service (the construction services). In those circumstances, it is not possible to use the purchase price of goods as the taxable amount. It would seem logical to use the purchase price of the services as the taxable amount. However, as is often the case with services, a purchase price may not exist because the services were generated by the service supplier itself. If even in case of an exchange of services, the taxable amount must be a subjective value, it would, in our view, be incorrect to use the purchase price of similar services as the taxable amount. After all, such a value is an objective value that comes very close to or is even similar to the open market value of Article 72 VAT Directive. Therefore, it would seem to be more in line with the idea of a subjective value to use the cost price/full cost of (generating) the service as the taxable amount (*see* Article 75 VAT Directive).

Even though, from a theoretical perspective it would be correct to apply the cost price/full cost method, in practice, applying this method could be problematic with respect to services, as it may well be that with respect to the supplying of services, relatively few costs are attributable to the supply, even if overhead costs are proportionally included in the calculation of the full costs of the services. Moreover, even if both parties in a barter transaction have a full right of deduction, using the cost price/full cost method may be inconvenient. This is because if the parties involved must issue an invoice for their taxable transactions, and if they must use the cost price as the taxable amount, they are effectively forced to reveal their cost price (and thus

29. CJEU 19 December 2012, Case C-549/11 *Direktor na Direktsia v Orfey Balgaria EOOD*, ECLI:EU:C:2012:832.

their 'margin') to each other. From a commercial perspective, this hardly seems acceptable.

In view of the aforementioned complications, it may be more feasible to use the purchase price of similar services as the taxable amount after all and accept that in barter transactions, it is not always feasible to use a true subjective value as the taxable amount. These are complications that may easily exceed a local soccer club's VAT knowledge.

6.6.1.2.4 *Summary of Barters Without Extra Charges*

In summary, if goods are bartered against goods or services, the consideration taken as the taxable amount in respect of such a supply of goods is a subjective value.[30] Consequently, the taxable amount must be the value which the supplier of the goods attributes to the goods or services which he is seeking to obtain and must correspond to the amount which he is prepared to spend for that purpose.[31] Therefore, if a good is exchanged for another good or a service, the value of the service received can only be the price that the *supplier* has paid for the goods which he is supplying without extra charge to his customer.[32] In that respect, the CJEU held in *Bertelsmann* that all the expenses borne by the supplier of goods to obtain the supply of services, including the costs of incidental services (e.g., transport costs) which are connected to the supply of the goods, make up the purchase price (and thus the taxable amount) of his supply of goods.[33] In cases of an exchange of a service for another service it may be more practical to use the purchase price of similar services (instead of the purchase price of the service actually supplied) as the taxable amount after all, and accept that in barter transactions, it is not always feasible to use a true subjective value as the taxable amount.

6.6.1.2.5 *Goods Bartered for Services and an Extra Charge*

Sometimes, the consideration *partially* consists of an amount paid in money and *partially* of a payment in kind. In such cases, both components of the consideration have to be regarded as constituting the taxable amount. In *Naturally Yours*, the CJEU explained how the taxable amount should be established in cases like that.[34] The Court

30. CJEU 1 April 1982, Case 89/81 *Staatssecretaris van Financiën v Hong-Kong Trade Development Council*, ECLI:EU:C:1982:121, para. 13; CJEU 23 November 1988, Case 230/87 *Naturally Yours Cosmetics Ltd v Commissioners of Customs and Excise*, ECLI:EU:C:1988:508, para. 16; CJEU 27 March 1990, Case C-126/88 *Boots Company plc v Commissioners of Customs and Excise*, ECLI:EU:C:1990:136, para. 19 and CJEU 24 October 1996, Case C-317/94 *Elida Gibbs Ltd v Commissioners of Customs and Excise*, ECLI:EU:C:1996:400, para. 27.
31. CJEU 2 June 1994, Case C-33/93 *Empire Stores Ltd v Commissioners of Customs and Excise*, ECLI:EU:C:1994:225, para. 19.
32. *Ibid.*
33. CJEU 3 July 2001, Case C-380/99 *Bertelsmann AG v Finanzamt Wiedenbrück*, ECLI:EU:C:2001:372.
34. CJEU 23 November 1988, Case 230/87 *Naturally Yours Cosmetics Ltd v Commissioners of Customs and Excise*, ECLI:EU:C:1988:508.

repeated that the taxable basis for a supply of goods within the meaning of Article 11A(1)(a) Sixth VAT Directive (now Article 73 VAT Directive) is made up of everything which is received directly in connection with the supply and represents the consideration for it, the latter being a *subjective value* which must be capable of being expressed in monetary terms. Naturally Yours (the wholesaler) supplied goods (the inducement) to another taxable person (beauty consultant) for a monetary consideration which was less than that at which identical goods were supplied to the retailer for resale to the public. The purpose of this was to enable the beauty consultants to stimulate (by reselling or giving away the inducement) natural persons to arrange a gathering at which further goods of the wholesaler could be sold by the beauty consultant. It was also clear to both parties that if eventually no such gathering was held, the inducement was to be returned to Naturally Yours or paid for at its wholesale price. According to the CJEU, the taxable amount for the inducement was the sum of the monetary consideration *and* of the value of a service provided by the beauty consultant to Naturally Yours.

This service consists of applying the inducement to procure the services of another person or in rewarding that person for those services; the value of the service provided by the beauty consultant must be regarded as being equal to the difference between the price actually paid for that product and its normal wholesale price.

Given the subjective nature of the consideration in EU VAT, one might expect that the value of the services supplied by the beauty consultant should have been established at the value Naturally Yours assigned to those services (being the difference between the price actually paid in cash for that product and the *purchase* price of the product). By establishing that the value of the consideration must be regarded as being equal to the difference between the price actually paid in cash for that product and its 'normal wholesale' price, a certain (further) objectification seems to have been applied instead.[35] However, it should be noted that Naturally Yours had no other clients than the beauty consultants and that the normal price, as mentioned by the Court, was the price which was always charged to those 'own' beauty consultants. Also, the fact that the inducement was given by Naturally Yours to the beauty consultant only if the gathering was indeed organized, indicated that Naturally Yours assigned a subjective value to those services established at the value of the price reduction: exactly this amount had to be paid by the beauty consultant as no such gathering was held. The Court seems to be consistent in deciding that the value of a consideration in kind must be established at the value that the supplier assigns to what he receives in return for his own supply. It would seem that the most suitable method to calculate this subjective value depends on the facts and circumstances of each individual case.

This may not always be easy. For example, in *A Oy* it was ruled that where a demolition company agrees to demolish a building of another taxable person, but it adjusts the price it charges for that service based on the fact that it can resell any scrap metal it finds in the demolition waste, the supply of scrap metal to the demolition

35. *See* for a critical analysis of this case: R.M. Millar, *Illusory Supplies and Unacknowledged Discounts: VAT and Valuation in Consumer Transactions* (2003) 2 British Tax Review, pp. 153-184.

company is to be regarded as a supply of goods.[36] The consideration for that supply of goods is the value that the demolition company takes into account in the calculation of the price quoted for carrying out the demolition works. This is even the case if the quantity and value of the scrap metal contained in demolition waste has not been agreed in the demolition contract. This could make it quite difficult to attribute a value to the part of the consideration paid in kind (the supply of scrap metal) as it may be completely subjective what value the demolition company attributes to the scrap metal in setting its price for the demolition service.

6.6.1.3 Low or Symbolic Remunerations

In Chapter 3, section 3.4.2, we discussed the issue of payments, which are low in relative and absolute terms. The issue we discussed was whether such relatively and absolutely low payments constitute a consideration in terms of Article 2(1) VAT Directive at a transaction level and whether an economic activity could exist in such a case at a taxable person level. Once it has been established that the supply is indeed a supply for consideration by a taxable person in the course of his economic activity, the taxable amount of such supply is to be determined. The ultimate goal of VAT is to tax all private consumption, whereby the customer's expenditures are used as a proxy for consumption. Therefore, it is necessary that the taxable amount in EU VAT, in principle, matches with the expenditures made by customers. Consequently, regardless of whether a consideration paid by a customer is – from an objective economic perspective, and in comparison to normal market prices – too high or too low, the price paid (the expenditure) is, in principle, decisive for the determination of the taxable amount. The taxable amount is, indeed, a subjective value.

This means that even if a supply for consideration in the course of an economic activity is made for a remuneration below the cost price of the supply, that (low) remuneration is considered as the taxable amount for the supply. The CJEU confirmed this in *Scandic Gåsabäck* by stating:

> the fact that the price paid for an economic transaction is higher or lower than the cost price is irrelevant to the question whether a transaction is to be regarded as a 'transaction effected for consideration'. The latter concept requires only that there be a direct link between the supply of goods or the provision of services and the consideration actually received by the taxable person.[37]

The question arises whether the taxable amount must still be the subjective value if a remuneration is only of a symbolic nature. Arguably, if a taxable person carries out a supply for a very low or symbolic amount, the supply is not a taxable supply. We refer to Chapter 3, section 3.4.2.

Clearly, a distinction has to be made between the consideration that needs to be obtained within the context of Article 9 VAT Directive (can an activity carried out for

36. CJEU 10 January 2019, Case C-410/17 *A Oy*, ECLI:EU:C:2019:12.
37. CJEU 20 January 2005, Case C-412/03 *Hotel Scandic Gåsabäck AB v Riksskatteverket*, ECLI: EU:C:2005:47, para. 22.

a symbolic remuneration constitute an economic activity?), and the requirement of Article 2 VAT Directive (can an activity carried out for a symbolic remuneration constitute a 'supply for consideration'?) that supplies must be effected for a consideration in order to be taxable.[38] The latter consideration is also the taxable amount of the supply pursuant to Article 73 VAT Directive.

With regard to the finding that a transaction is carried out for a consideration and can be seen as a taxable supply as mentioned in Article 2(1) VAT Directive, the CJEU made clear in *Hotel Scandic* that where an activity is carried out by a taxable person for the purpose of receiving a remuneration, it constitutes a taxable supply even if the consideration is (far) below the cost price of such a supply.[39] There is no reason to exclude such supplies delivered by taxable persons from the scope of the VAT legislation.[40] Such low considerations can very well be based on rational, pragmatic and commercially motivated decisions of the supplier.

However, in order to establish whether there is an economic activity pursuant to Article 9 VAT Directive, *other criteria* must be met. In *Borsele*,[41] even where (some) supplies are effected for a consideration as mentioned in Article 2(1) VAT Directive, there will be no economic activity on the basis of Article 9 VAT Directive (*Hong Kong* case)[42] because there is no genuine link between the income and the services provided that is required for an economic activity as meant in Article 9(1) second paragraph. As a result, the receipt of a payment for a transaction will not itself be sufficient to constitute an economic activity. Although they receive remuneration for their activities, some suppliers, like some public bodies, do not operate as a regular economic operator on the market (as in *T-Mobile Austria and Others*) and are supposed not to be engaged in economic activities.[43] Other suppliers (operators with a private legal form) may ask merely a symbolic remuneration for their activities and will for that reason not be seen as real economic operators and subsequently not be seen as being engaged in economic activities as mentioned in Article 9 VAT Directive either (*Commission v France*).[44]

We agree that persons who exclusively carry out transactions for a remuneration of a symbolic nature do not carry out an economic activity and are, therefore, not to be

38. Opinion of Advocate General Kokott of 23 December 2015, Case C-520/14 *Gemeente Borsele v Staatssecretaris van Financiën*, ECLI:EU:C:2015:855, para. 44.
39. *Ibid.*
40. Only if symbolic remunerations are used to avoid self-supplies (Articles 395 and 80 VAT Directive) or to prevent tax evasion or avoidance.
41. CJEU 12 May 2016, Case C-520/14 *Gemeente Borsele v Staatssecretaris van Financiën*, ECLI:EU:C:2016:334. *See also* CJEU 13 December 2007, Case C-408/06 *Landesanstalt für Landwirtschaft v Franz Götz* EU:C:2007:789, para. 21 and CJEU 29 October 2009, Case C-246/08 *Commission of the European Communities v Republic of Finland*, ECLI:EU:C:2009:671, para. 38.
42. If a person only carries out transactions free of charge, that person will not obtain taxable person status (*see* Chapter 2, section 2.4.2). CJEU 1 April 1982, Case 89/81 *Hong-Kong Trade Development Council v Staatssecretaris van Financiën*, ECLI:EU:C:1982:121.
43. CJEU 26 June 2007, Case C-284/04 *T-Mobile Austria GmbH and Others v Republik Österreich*, ECLI:EU:C:2007:381.
44. Following *Commission v French Republic*, supplies made out of generosity, are outside the scope of VAT because they cannot be regarded as an 'economic activity': 'Where, because of the amount of the rent, the lease must necessarily be regarded as involving a concession and not as constituting an economic activity within the meaning of the directive, the deduction initially

considered as taxable persons. However, persons that already have the taxable person status (because they regularly carry out taxable transactions for consideration) which also carry out transactions for a symbolic remuneration will be required to pay VAT on those latter supplies (unless a Member State took specific measures to apply an 'open market value') if there is a genuine link between the amounts paid and the supplies made.[45] The mere fact that a person with the taxable person status makes a supply for a symbolic remuneration does not automatically mean that he does so in a capacity different from his taxable person capacity.[46]

6.6.1.4 *Composite Supplies and the Taxable Amount*

The determination of the taxable amount is preceded by the determination of the nature of the supply. This order of things is particularly relevant if the supply consists of multiple elements ('composite supplies', *see* Chapter 3, section 3.5). If a composite supply is made, it is imperative to establish whether the elements constituting the composite supply must be considered as separate supplies of goods and/or services, or whether the elements form a single supply from a VAT perspective.

If the total fee for a composite supply is EUR 1,000 and the supply is to be seen as a single supply, the taxable amount for that single supply is EUR 1,000. If the elements of the composite supplies must be regarded as separate supplies of goods and/or services, the fee must partially be attributed to each of the supplies. The allocation of the fee to the supplies is of particular importance if the supplies are taxed differently (e.g., different place of supply rules applicable, reduced rates, exemptions). For example, in *BGZ Leasing*, the CJEU ruled that the supply of insurance services for a leased item and the supply of the leasing services themselves must, in principle, be

---

made is adjusted and the time-limit for that adjustment may be extended up to 10 years.' CJEU, 21 September 1988, Case 50/87 *Commission of the European Communities v French Republic* ECLI:EU:C:1988:429, para. 21.

45. CJEU 12 May 2016, Case C-520/14 *Gemeente Borsele v Staatssecretaris van Financiën*, ECLI:EU:C:2016:334.
46. There might be a difference in the treatment of public legal entities and private legal entities. With regard to private legal entities the CJEU seems to check only once whether such a person has the status of taxable person and whether that person is engaged in economic activities or not. Almost automatically every new or additional transaction, even if the nature of the transaction is different from the other transactions, – and irrespective of amount charged – seems to be made within the scope of that economic activity and will be subsequently treated as taxable transactions according to Article 2 VAT Directive. With regard to public legal entities, the CJEU seems to check every time that a public legal entities starts up a new activity, whether such a new (distinct) activity is an economic activity in itself pursuant to Article 9 VAT Directive. CJEU 13 June 2013, Case C-62/12 *Galin Kostov v Direktor na Direktsia 'Obzhalvane I upravlenie na izpalnenieto' – Varna pri Tsentralno upravlenie na Natsionalnata agentsia za prihodite*, ECLI:EU:C:2013:391 and CJEU 12 May 2016, Case C-520/14 *Gemeente Borsele v Staatssecretaris van Financiën*, ECLI:EU:C:2016:334. The case law of the CJEU does not seem to be very consistent in this regard. Compare, for instance, the mentioned *Kostov* case and the *Wellcome Trust* case: CJEU 20 June 1996, Case C-155/94 *Wellcome Trust Ltd v Commissionairs of Customs and Excise*, ECLI:EU:C:1996:243.

regarded as distinct and independent supplies of services for VAT purposes.[47] However, the CJEU left it up to the national court to determine whether the transactions at issue were so closely linked that they should be regarded as constituting a single supply after all. If the supply were to be a single (taxed) supply, for which only a fee of EUR 1,000 is charged, that full amount would constitute the taxable amount. Then VAT needs to be calculated on the consideration, being EUR 1,000. Conversely, if the elements of such a supply are to be considered as separate services, the part of the remuneration of EUR 1,000 attributable to the leasing services is taxed, whereas the remainder is exempt.

This leaves the question of how a total price should be attributed to the various services for which this price is the consideration. The VAT Directive contains no rules in this respect.[48] It would seem that there are basically two methods: one based on actual costs and the other on market value. In *MyTravel,* the CJEU ruled – albeit in the context of the special scheme for travel agents – that the market value method should be applied unless the method based on the criterion of actual costs accurately reflects the actual structure of the package (of services).[49]

6.6.2 Consideration Obtained or to Be Obtained

Article 73 VAT Directive mentions that the taxable amount shall include everything which constitutes consideration *obtained or to be obtained* by the supplier. This has two important implications.

First of all, it means that if a supplier obtains more than he charged for the supply, the surplus is also part of the consideration. For example, if a customer pays an amount of EUR 150 for a product, instead of the advertised sales price of EUR 100, the surplus of EUR 50 is also part of the taxable amount. It should be noted that the condition in Article 73 VAT Directive that the consideration must be paid 'in return for the supply' (*see* section 6.6.3, below) also applies to the surplus. For example, if a customer pays the advertised price of EUR 100 for dinner at a restaurant, but leaves an amount of EUR 150 on the table, the surplus of EUR 50 (the 'tip') is only a part of the taxable amount if it is indeed paid for the restaurant service. However, it may well be that the surplus is not paid to the restaurant supplying the restaurant service, but to the waiter for this exceptional good care. Then, it can be argued that the surplus is not a part of the consideration.

A second implication of the text of Article 73 VAT Directive is that not only the amount which the supplier received forms the taxable amount but that also amounts which he should receive (amounts which are 'to be obtained') are part of the taxable amount. This part of the article seems particularly aimed at including amounts that are invoiced to a customer but not (yet) paid in the taxable amount. In *Connoisseur*

47. CJEU 17 January 2013, Case C-224/11 *BGI Leasing sp. z o.o. v Dyrektor Izby Skarbowej w Warszawie,* ECLI:EU:C:2013:15.
48. *See* with respect to credit card payment services, Article 42 VAT Regulation.
49. CJEU 6 October 2005, Case C-291/03 *MyTravel plc v Commissioners of Customs & Excise,* ECLI:EU:C:2005:591.

Belgium BVBA, the CJEU ruled that amounts that could have been invoiced on the basis of the contractual arrangements between a supplier and its customer, but in fact, were not invoiced, after all, are excluded from the taxable amount.[50]

6.6.2.1 Payment by Credit or Debit Card

Usually, when a customer pays for a good or service using a credit card, the credit card company will charge a fee to the retailer. In practice, if the price of a supply of goods is met by the purchaser by means of a credit card payment, effectively the credit card company will pay the purchase price to the supplier, after deduction of a percentage as commission in payment for the service rendered by the credit card company to the supplier of the goods. From the supplier's perspective, this means he receives less for his supplies when a customer pays with a credit card. The question has been asked whether the amount paid by retailers to credit card companies may be deducted from the taxable amount which the retailers charge to their customers. It follows from *Bally* that the answer to that question is 'no'.[51] The CJEU ruled that the sum which the credit card company deducted from the sales price as a commission for its credit card services must be included in the taxable amount on which the supplier, as the taxable person, must pay tax to the tax authorities.

In an attempt to reduce the taxable amount in the case of credit card payments, suppliers (retailers) may seek to create a situation in which the credit card company's commission is paid separately by the customer, either to the retailer or to the credit card company directly. However, this will not have the intended effect. According to Article 42 VAT Implementing Regulation, if a supplier of goods or services, as a condition of accepting payment by credit or debit card, requires the customer to pay an amount to himself or another undertaking, and where the total price payable by that customer is unaffected irrespective of how payment is accepted, that amount constitutes an integral part of the taxable amount for the supply of the goods or services. We consider this to be in line with the concept of VAT as a general tax on consumption. After all, the total amount to be paid for the supply of goods or services is fixed, regardless of how payment is accepted (credit card, debit card or cash). The fact that the supplier pays part of the payment he receives to someone else (e.g., the credit or debit card organization) does not - from the customer's perspective - affect the amount consumed.

6.6.2.2 Prepayments

In most cases, the supplier will have made his supply before he is paid by his customer. However, sometimes the customer pays *before* the supply is actually made to him. Under those circumstances, the prepayment is considered to fall within the scope of the phrase 'consideration obtained' as mentioned in Article 73 VAT Directive. Moreover, if

50. CJEU 9 December 2011, Case C-69/11 *Connoisseur Belgium BVBA*, ECLI:EU:C:2011:825.
51. CJEU 25 May 1993, Case C-18/92 *Chaussures Bally SA v Belgian State*, ECLI:EU:C:1993:212.

prepayments were not to be considered as (a part of) the consideration, this would lead to non-taxation, which goes against the legal character and the neutrality of VAT.

The VAT becomes due at the moment the prepayment is received. According to Article 65 VAT Directive, where a payment is to be made on account before the goods or services are supplied, VAT is chargeable on receipt of the payment and on the amount received. We will further elaborate on this in Chapter 5.

6.6.2.3 Gaming Machines[52]

In *RAL*, the CJEU confirmed that the activity consisting of making available to the public, for consideration, slot gaming machines installed in entertainment arcades, is a supply of services.[53] The principal objective of such activity is the entertainment of slot machine users and not financial gain on their part. The same applies to other forms of gaming activities, such as 'spot the ball'[54] and 'bingo'[55] games.

However, in respect of games that allow users to win amounts of money, the determination of the taxable amount is generally perceived to be complex. It is commonly accepted that the stakes inserted by players are an essential part of the taxable amount. The central question is whether the prices which must be paid as winnings to players should be excluded from the taxable amount. In *Glawe*, the CJEU took the opportunity to answer that question.[56] In that case, where a taxable person exploited gaming machines, the proportion of the stakes which was paid out as winnings was mandatorily fixed by law in advance at 60%. Moreover, the operator of the gaming machines could not physically touch the money that was reserved for paying out the winnings. Consequently, that money could not be regarded as forming part of the consideration for the provision of the machine to the players, nor as the price for any other service provided to the players, such as giving them the opportunity of winning, or the payment of winnings itself. Therefore, the CJEU ruled that in the case of gaming machines offering the possibility of winning, the taxable amount does not include the statutorily prescribed proportion of the total stakes inserted, which corresponds to the winnings paid out to the players.[57] The net cash receipts - the takings minus the VAT owed - constitute the taxable amount.

52. A.J. van Doesum, 'Taxable Amount', in M. Lang, et al. (eds), *ECJ: Recent Developments in Value Added Tax, the Evolution of European VAT Jurisprudence and Its Role in the EU Common VAT System* (Linde 2014), pp. 177-233.
53. CJEU 12 May 2005, Case C-452/03 *RAL (Channel Islands) Ltd and Others v Commissioners of Customs & Excise*, ECLI:EU:C:2005:289.
54. *See* CJEU 17 September 2002, Case C-498/99 *Town & County Factors Ltd v Commissioners of Customs & Excise*, ECLI:EU:C:2002:494.
55. *See* CJEU 19 July 2012, Case C-377/11 *International Bingo Technology SA v Tribunal Económico-Administrativo Regional de Cataluña (TEARC)*, ECLI:EU:C:2012:503.
56. CJEU 5 May 1994, Case C-38/93 *H.J. Glawe Spiel- und Unterhaltungsgeräte Aufstellungsgesellschaft mbH & Co. KG v Finanzamt Hamburg-Barmbek-Uhlenhorst*, ECLI:EU:C:1994:188.
57. However, Advocate General Jacobs did not believe that the particular workings of the slot machines in question in *Glawe*, or the fact that the minimum winnings paid out were fixed by law, were critical to the Court's ruling. *See* Opinion of Advocate General Jacobs of 20 March 1997, Case C-283/95 *Karlheinz Fischer v Finanzamt Donaueschingen*, ECLI:EU:C:1997:167, para. 58.

In *Glawe*, the operator of the gaming machines could not physically touch the money that was to be paid out as winnings. This, however, is apparently not a necessary requirement for these amounts not to be included in the taxable amount.[58] To that extent, *International Bingo* contributes to the understanding of the concept of the 'consideration actually received'. The fact that national legislation fixes in advance the portion of the bingo card price which must be returned to players as winnings is sufficient to conclude that such portion of the bingo card price cannot be regarded as forming part of the 'consideration actually received' by the organizer of the game for the supply of the service provided to players. Conversely, if the organizer of a game has the full amount of the entry fees freely at his disposal, those (full) amounts should be included in the taxable amount.[59]

In *Metropol Spielstätten*, the CJEU was asked whether a Member State was allowed to use the cash receipts after a set interval in a slot machine, which consists of stakes inserted by various players minus the winnings paid to various players in that time interval, as the taxable amount, or whether a direct link with *specific* stakes inserted by *individual* players was required. The referring court observed that if the cash receipts from gaming machines after a set interval were to be used, there would no longer be a direct link with what a specific user paid (inserted as a stake and received as a winning) for one particular service (playing the game on the machine). In other words: at the level of the individual player, the VAT would no longer be strictly proportional to the prices, according to the referring court. The CJEU pointed out that with regard to Article 73 VAT Directive, what the customer pays is not so relevant as what the supplier receives, or should receive, and that the referring court ought to have known from *Glawe* that the taxable amount consists of the cash receipts after a set interval.[60] After all, the net cash receipts form the proportion of the stakes which the operator can actually take for himself.

6.6.3 Direct Link: 'In Return for the Supply'

On the basis of Article 2(1) VAT Directive, only supplies of goods and services 'for consideration' are subject to VAT. The term 'consideration' is a uniform concept of Union law.[61] In order for a supply to be 'for consideration', there must be a direct link between the service provided and the consideration received. We refer to Chapter 3, section 3.4. Article 73 VAT Directive reiterates this direct link condition where it contains the phrase 'in return for the supply'. Indeed, the CJEU confirmed in *Bertelsmann* that the term 'consideration' requires a direct link between the supply and the remuneration.

58. Cf. CJEU 14 July 1998, Case C-172/96 *Commissioners of Customs & Excise v First National Bank of Chicago*, ECLI:EU:C:1998:354.
59. CJEU 17 September 2002, Case C-498/99 *Town & County Factors Ltd v Commissioners of Customs & Excise*, ECLI:EU:C:2002:494.
60. CJEU 24 October 2013, Case C-440/12 *Metropol Spielstätten Unternehmergesellschaft (haftungsbeschränkt) v Finanzamt Hamburg-Bergedorf*, ECLI:EU:C:2013:687, paras 38-40.
61. CJEU 5 February 1981, Case 154/80 *Staatssecretaris van Financiën v Association coopérative 'Coöperatieve Aardappelenbewaarplaats GA'*, ECLI:EU:C:1981:38, para. 9.

Since the direct link criterion is an element of both the 'for consideration' criterion of Article 2(1) VAT Directive and of the 'in return for the supply' criterion of Articles 73 et seq. of the VAT Directive, sometimes both elements overlap. For example, in *Société thermale d'Eugénie-les-Bains*, the question was addressed whether deposits, paid in the context of contracts relating to supplies of hotel services, which are retained by the hotel in the event of cancellation, should be considered as:

(a) a remuneration for the reservation service and, as such, subject to VAT; or
(b) cancellation payments made to compensate for the loss suffered as a result of the default of the customer, which have no direct connection with any service supplied for consideration and, as such, are not subject to VAT.[62]

The CJEU ruled that deposits, as described above, do 'not constitute the fee for a service and [form] no part of the taxable amount for VAT purposes'. This underlines the connection between the 'for consideration' criterion and the 'in return for the supply' criterion. According to the CJEU deposits are to be regarded, where the client exercises the cancellation option available to him and that sum is retained by the hotelier, as a fixed cancellation charge paid as compensation for the loss suffered as a result of client default, and as having no direct connection with the supply of any service for consideration; as such, they are not subject to VAT. This does not mean, however, that all cancellation fees will remain outside the scope of VAT. From *Air France/KLM* and *MEO*, it may be derived that generally, the taxable amount is not reduced in situations where the payment due by the customer that does not show up or cancels, is equal to the amount that would be payable for the (cancelled) service anyway.[63] The reasoning of the CJEU in this instance seems to be that the amount due upon the early termination of the contract seeks to guarantee the operator a minimum contractual remuneration for the service provided. As such, the payment due upon termination is regarded as part of the total remuneration obtained by the service provider, although in effect, no service is provided anymore. Based upon this same reasoning, from *Vodafone Portugal*, it follows that a cancellation payment by a customer can be part of the taxable amount even if that cancellation payment is separately determined in the contract and as such lower than what would normally be payable for the (cancelled) service.[64]

62. CJEU 18 July 2007, Case C-277/05 *Société thermale d'Eugénie-les-Bains v Ministère de l'Économie, des Finances et de l'Industrie*, ECLI:EU:C:2007:440.
63. CJEU 23 December 2015, Joined Cases C-250/14 and C-289/14 *Air France-KLM/ Hop!-Brit Air SAS v Ministère des Finances et des Comptes publics*, ECLI:EU:C:2015:841 and CJEU 22 November 2018, Case C-295/17 *MEO – Serviços de Comunicações e Multimédia SA v Autoridade Tributária e Aduaneira*, ECLI:EU:C:2018:942.
64. CJEU 11 June 2020, Case C-43/19 *Vodafone Portugal – Comunicações Pessoais, SA v Autoridade Tributária e Aduaneira*, ECLI:EU:C:2020:465.

6.6.4 From the Customer or a Third Party ('Third-Party Payments')

Typically, a supplier will receive the consideration in return for his supplies from his customer. However, it may occur that someone other than the recipient of the supply pays the consideration to the supplier, in full or partially. If no special rules were drawn up, VAT could be avoided by having others pay for supplies. For this reason, Article 73 VAT Directive stipulates that not only considerations obtained from the customer constitute (a part of) the taxable amount but also considerations obtained from third parties. As long as a direct link can be established between the supply and the consideration, it is irrelevant who actually makes the payment. Even if a third party only makes a partial payment, VAT cannot be avoided. The total amount which the supplier obtains or should obtain for the supply remains the taxable amount. This also makes sense from a conceptual point of view. After all, it is consumption that should be taxed, and it is, therefore, irrelevant who actually pays for that consumption.

6.6.5 Subsidies Directly Linked to the Price of the Supply

In Chapter 3, section 3.4.3, we discussed under what circumstances a subsidy must be regarded as the consideration for a supply. Basically, a subsidy is considered to be a consideration for a supply if the entity granting the subsidy obtains a specific benefit from the taxable person obtaining the subsidy. In this respect, much depends on the exact conditions relating to the subsidy. Simply put, the mere fact that a remuneration for a supply is called a 'subsidy' does not prevent that remuneration from forming the consideration, i.e., the taxable amount for a supply. Usually, subsidies that are directly linked to the price of supplies are referred to as 'price subsidies'.

It may occur that a public authority pays a price subsidy to another person than the person making the supply for which the subsidy is the consideration. Such a price subsidy is effectively a specific form of third-party payment. Such subsidies are also included in the taxable amount. This was confirmed in *Office des produits wallons ASBL*, in which the CJEU ruled that for the purposes of Article 73 VAT Directive, 'subsidies directly linked to the price' must be interpreted as covering only subsidies which constitute the whole or part of the consideration for a supply of goods or services and which are paid by a third party to the seller or supplier.[65]

Also, in *Office des produits wallons ASBL*, the CJEU indicated that the mere fact that a subsidy may affect the price of the goods or services supplied by the recipient of the subsidy is not enough to make that subsidy taxable.[66] For the subsidy to be directly

65. CJEU 22 November 2001, Case C-184/00 *Office des produits wallons ASBL v Belgian State*, ECLI:EU:C:2001:629. *See also* CJEU 13 June 2002, Case C-353/00 *Keeping Newcastle Warm Ltd v Commissioners of Customs and Excise*, ECLI:EU:C:2002:369.

66. The CJEU indicated that operating subsidies covering a part of running costs nearly always affect the cost price of the goods and services supplied by the subsidized body. In so far as it offers specific goods or services, that body can normally do so at prices which it would be unable to offer if were obliged at the same time both to pass on its costs and make a profit. CJEU 22 November 2001, Case C-184/00 *Office des produits wallons ASBL v Belgian State*, ECLI: EU:C:2001:629, para. 11.

linked to the price of such supplies, it is also necessary that it be paid specifically to the recipient of the subsidy to enable it to provide particular goods or services. Only in that event can the subsidy be regarded as consideration for the supply of goods or services, and therefore, be taxable.[67] The CJEU provided the following guidelines as to how to establish whether a subsidy constitutes a consideration:[68]

(1) The price of the goods or services must, in principle, be determined not later than the time of the triggering event.
(2) The undertaking to pay the subsidy made by the person who grants it has as its corollary the right of the beneficiary to receive it since a taxable supply has been made by the latter.
(3) That link between the subsidy and the price must appear unequivocally following a case-by-case analysis of the circumstances underlying the payment of that consideration.
(4) It is not necessary for the price of the goods or services – or a part of the price – to be ascertained. It is sufficient for it to be ascertainable.

6.7 INCLUDED AND EXCLUDED ELEMENTS

The initial price paid is the starting point for determining the taxable amount. If the price of the good or service supplied is later adjusted (through discounts, a promotion, etc.), the taxable amount can also be adjusted under certain conditions. The VAT Directive contains special provisions that deal with price adjustments, prices in different currencies and other specific circumstances. Article 78 VAT Directive stipulates that certain elements must be included in the taxable amount. Conversely, Article 79 VAT Directive excludes certain elements from the taxable amount. In section 6.7.1, we will discuss the inclusions, and we will discuss the exclusions in section 6.7.2. Section 6.7.3 deals with a specific rule on amounts relating to returnable packing, which may either be included or excluded.

6.7.1 Inclusions

On the basis of Article 78 VAT Directive, the following elements must be included in the taxable amount:

(1) Taxes, duties, levies and charges.
(2) Incidental expenses.

These inclusions will be discussed in sections 6.7.1.1 and 6.7.1.2, respectively.

67. CJEU 22 November 2001, Case C-184/00 *Office des produits wallons ASBL v Belgian State*, ECLI:EU:C:2001:629, para. 12.
68. *Ibid.*, para. 13. *See also* CJEU 15 July 2004, Case C-381/01 *Commission of the European Communities v Italian Republic*, ECLI:EU:C:2004:441.

6.7.1.1 *Taxes, Duties, Levies and Charges*

According to Article 73 VAT Directive, the taxable amount includes everything which constitutes consideration for a supply of goods or services. Arguably, taxes, duties, levies and charges which are 'as such' recharged by a supplier to his customer cannot be considered as being charged 'in return for the supply'. They do not generally represent any added value and do not constitute the financial consideration for the supply of goods or services.[69]

However, sometimes taxes, duties levies and charges – even though they are not a part of the consideration for the supply – bear a strong link with that supply. If that is the case, Article 78(a) VAT Directive may apply. On the basis of that provision, taxes, duties, levies and charges, excluding the VAT itself, are to be included in the taxable amount.

In our view, Article 78(a) VAT Directive is a *lex specialis* to Article 73 VAT Directive.[70] Consequently, when answering the question of whether a tax, duty, levy or charge forms a part of the taxable amount, Article 78(a) VAT Directive should be checked first.

It is settled CJEU case law that the (answer to the) question of whether the chargeable event for the tax coincides with that for VAT is a decisive factor for the purposes of establishing the existence of a direct link between the taxes, duties, levies or charges and the supply.[71] In other words: if the tax, duty, levy or charge is triggered by a *supply*, it must be included in the taxable amount for VAT of that supply. For that reason, the CJEU in *De Danske Bilimportører* ruled that a car registration duty was not to be included in the taxable amount.[72] The taxable event for the car registration duty did not coincide with that for VAT: cars could be supplied without having been registered, and could be registered without being supplied. The CJEU ruled in a similar way with respect to an Austrian car registration duty.[73] The land use taxes in *Lisboagás* could also not be included in the taxable amount on the basis of Article 78(a) VAT Directive because the taxable events for the land use taxes and VAT did not coincide (the land use taxes were included in the taxable amount for other reasons, though – *see*

69. *See also* A.J. van Doesum & H.W.M. van Kesteren, *Taxes, Duties, Levies and Charges as Part of the Taxable Amount for Value Added Tax* (2017) 1 EC Tax Review, p. 45 https://doi.org/10.54648/ecta2017005.

70. CJEU 27 March 1990, Case C-126/88 *Boots Company plc v Commissioners of Customs and Excise*, ECLI:EU:C:1990:136, paras 15 and 16 and CJEU 3 July 2001, Case C-380/99 *Bertelsmann AG v Finanzamt Wiedenbrück*, ECLI:EU:C:2001:372, para. 15.

71. CJEU 1 June 2006, Case C-98/05 *De Danske Bilimportører v Skatteministeriet*, ECLI:EU:C:2006:363, para. 17; CJEU 20 May 2010, Case C-228/09 *European Commission v Republic of Poland*, ECLI:EU:C:2010:295, para. 30; CJEU, 22 December 2010, Case C-433/09 *European Commission v Republic of Austria*, ECLI:EU:C:2010:817, para. 34; CJEU 5 December 2013, Joined Cases C-618/11, C-637/11 and C-659/11 *TVI – Televisão Independente SA v Fazenda Pública*, ECLI:EU:C:2013:789, paras 37 and 39 and CJEU 11 June 2015, Case C-256/14 *Lisboagás GDL – Sociedade Distribuidora de Gás Natural de Lisboa SA v Autoridade Tributária e Aduaneira*, ECLI:EU:C:2015:387, para. 29.

72. CJEU 1 June 2006, Case C-98/05 *De Danske Bilimportører v Skatteministeriet*, ECLI:EU:C:2006:363.

73. CJEU 22 December 2010, Case C-433/09 *European Commission v Republic of Austria*, ECLI:EU:C:2010:817.

below). In *TVI*, a screening tax did fall in the scope of Article 78(a) VAT Directive because the chargeable event for the screening tax coincides with that for the VAT payable on commercial advertising screening services.[74]

In order to determine whether the taxable events of the tax, duty, levy or charge, on the one hand, and VAT, on the other hand, coincide, the CJEU seems to also take into consideration whether the tax, duty, levy or charge is payable in the name and/or for the account of the supplier or in the name and/or account of the recipient of the supply.[75] The more responsibilities with respect to the tax, duty, levy or charge lie with the supplier, the sooner it will be assumed that the tax, duty, levy or charge coincides with VAT and thus must be included in the taxable amount. If the responsibilities with respect to tax, duty, levy or charge completely lie with the recipient of the supply, Article 78(a) VAT Directive will normally not apply. Instead, if the tax, duty, levy or charge is paid in the name and for the account of the recipient of the supply, it may even be regarded as a suspense account under Article 79(c) VAT Directive (*see* section 6.7.2.3).

Sometimes, taxes, duties, levies and charges are not recharged 'as such'. This is the case if the supplier does not really pass on the tax, duty, levy or charge as such but merely incorporates the costs of such tax, duty, levy or charge in the price of its supply. The tax, duty, levy or charge is then a cost component of the supply, just like any other cost component. Under such circumstances, the tax, duty, levy or charge still does not represent any added value and is still not directly linked to the supply but is simply a cost that is born by the supplier 'for the needs of making the supply'.[76] According to the CJEU, it is in this respect principally irrelevant whether the tax, duty, levy or charge are passed on as separate items on the invoice, or as part of the total price for the goods or service.[77] However, in our view, if the tax, duty, levy or charge is not listed as separate line items on an invoice, it will be difficult to establish whether it is merely passed on, or whether it is, in fact, a part of the costs of making the supply of goods or services. So far, the CJEU has not given any directions as to how to determine if taxes, duties, levies and charges are part of the cost price if they are listed as separate line items on an invoice. It seems to us that the criteria to be applied in order to determine whether a tax, duty, levy or charge is not charged 'as such' are still rather unclear. We foresee more CJEU case law on this matter.

The final point is that - for obvious reasons - Article 78(a) VAT Directive excludes VAT itself from the taxable amount. However, if non-EU VAT, GST or sales tax is paid in respect of a supply which is also subject to EU VAT, that non-EU VAT, GST or sales tax is to be regarded as part of the taxable amount. For example, in case of a B2B supply of services for which a non-EU service provider raises an invoice including non-EU VAT, GST or sales tax, the EU business recipient should include the non-EU VAT, GST or sales tax in the taxable amount when calculating the EU VAT due

74. CJEU 5 December 2013, Case C-659/11 *TVI - Televisão Independente SA v Fazenda Pública*, ECLI:EU:C:2013:789, para. 41.
75. CJEU 28 July 2011, Case C-106/10 *Lidl & Companhia v Fazenda Pública*, ECLI:EU:C:2011:526.
76. Cf. CJEU 11 June 2015, Case C-256/14 *Lisboagás GDL - Sociedade Distribuidora de Gás Natural de Lisboa SA v Autoridade Tributária e Aduaneira*, ECLI:EU:C:2015:387, paras 31 and 35.
77. *Ibid.*, para. 34.

under the reverse charge mechanism.[78] Strictly speaking, also incorrectly charged foreign EU VAT in respect of a B2B service should be included in the taxable amount, when an EU business recipient is determining the taxable amount of VAT which is lawfully due under the reverse charge mechanism.

6.7.1.2 *Incidental Expenses*

On the basis of Article 78(b) VAT Directive, the taxable amount includes incidental expenses, such as commission, packing, transport and insurance costs, charged by the supplier to the customer. Member States may even regard expenses covered by a separate agreement as incidental expenses. This is a rather peculiar option for the Member States, as it does not seem consistent with established case law on the question of single supply versus multiple supplies (*see* section 6.6.1.4).

Typically, incidental expenses are expenses made by the supplier, which he recharges as separate items on his invoice to his customer on the basis of their contractual arrangements. The supplier should have made the expenses in his own name in order to be regarded as incidental expenses. Examples of this type of expense are costs of insurance, packing, transport, travel, postage and other out-of-pocket expenses.

Interest may be regarded as an incidental expense, depending on the situation. According to *Muys and De Winter's Bouw- en Aannemingsbedrijf BV*, where the supplier of goods agrees that the purchaser, in return for payment of interest, should defer payment of the price until delivery, the taxable amount includes that interest, even if the agreement treats it as distinct from the purchase price of the goods.[79] If an extension of payment is granted for a period after the time of supply, interest may be regarded as a consideration for separate VAT-exempt granting of credit.

6.7.2 Exclusions

According to Article 79 VAT Directive, the taxable amount shall not include the following factors:

(a) price reductions by way of discount for early payment;
(b) price discounts and rebates granted to the customer and obtained by him at the time of the supply;
(c) amounts received by a taxable person from the customer, as repayment of expenditure incurred in the name and on behalf of the customer, and entered in his books in a suspense account.

In the following subsections, we will discuss each of these factors separately.

78. *See* Chapter 4, section 4.5.3 on the B2B place of supply rules and Chapter 12, section 12.3 on the application of the reverse charge mechanism.
79. CJEU 27 October 1993, Case C-281/91 *Muijs' en De Winter's Bouw- en Aannemingsbedrijf BV v Staatssecretaris van Financiën*, ECLI:EU:C:1993:855.

6.7.2.1 *Price Reductions (Early Payment)*

Pursuant to Article 79(a) VAT Directive, price reductions by way of discount for early payment are excluded from the taxable basis. In our view, such price reductions are not to be included in the taxable basis anyway, regardless of this specific provision. Perhaps, the legislator, when drafting this provision, had situations in mind where the discount has already reduced the supplier's original price. In such a situation, there is nothing to adjust or reduce if the customer pays in good time. If this is indeed the idea behind this provision, the provision merely ensures that the initial price (including the discount for early payment) forms the taxable base and that the amount of the discount does not need to be added to the taxable amount.

However, if the customer pays after the discount period has expired, he has no right, for obvious reasons, to receive a discount for early payment. If the supplier had already taken the price reduction into account (assuming that the customer would pay in time), the supplier will have to charge the additional amount of VAT due on the – in hindsight – incorrectly granted discount. He needs to report this additional VAT in his VAT return.

6.7.2.2 *Price Discounts (At the Time of the Supply)*

Price reductions which are granted immediately are taken into account directly, on the basis of Article 79(b) VAT Directive. These reductions are different from early payment discounts, as they are not granted under the condition that the payment must be made before a certain day. Immediate price reductions are excluded anyway, without the need for adjustment afterwards. In our view, Article 79(b) VAT Directive is redundant because price reductions which are granted at the time of the supply are not included in the taxable amount on the basis of Article 73 VAT Directive in the first place. They represent amounts that are typically *not* paid 'in return for the supply'. For example, if a retailer advertises a price of EUR 100 for a certain product but offers it to a specific customer for EUR 90, it is clear that the taxable amount is EUR 90 already on the basis of Article 73.

6.7.2.3 *Suspense Accounts*

Article 79(c) VAT Directive provides that amounts received by a taxable person from the customer as repayment of expenditure incurred in the name and on behalf of the customer, and entered in his books in a suspense account, are to be excluded from the taxable amount, under the further condition that proof of the actual amount of the expenditure must be furnished, and that he does not deduct any VAT which may have been charged.

From the wording of this provision, it immediately becomes clear that it can only apply if a taxable person receives amounts which he is not legally entitled to. He merely receives such amounts in the name and on behalf of the customer and only enters these amounts in his books as a suspense account. Therefore, a suspense account, as mentioned in Article 79(c) VAT Directive, requires that the recipient of the service has a *direct* relationship of private or public law character with the person charging the costs in the first place.

A common example of a suspense account, as mentioned in Article 79(c) VAT Directive, is the situation in which a building firm arranges a building permit for a customer. If the customer of the building firm requests and obtains a permit from – for example – the municipality directly, no VAT will be charged on such licence, as it is granted by the municipality in its capacity as a public body (Article 13 VAT Directive). However, if the building constructor requests and obtains the permit in the name and on behalf of his customer, and recharges the costs of the permit to the customer, the question arises as to whether that amount is a part of the total remuneration for the construction services. Article 79(c) VAT Directive makes clear that such amounts can be seen as a suspense account. The building firm must furnish proof of the actual amount of the expenditure referred to in Article 79(c) VAT Directive and may not deduct any VAT which may have been charged.[80]

It is somewhat unclear how Articles 73 and 79(c) VAT Directive interrelate. In our view, Article 79(c) VAT Directive merely confirms what Article 73 VAT Directive already states: only amounts 'in return for the supply' are part of the taxable amount. Amounts received in the name and for the account of another party are not received 'in return for the supply' and thus do not belong to the taxable amount. Accordingly, Article 79(c) VAT Directive seems merely a clarification of and not an exception to Article 73 VAT Directive.

6.7.2.4 *Cancellation, Refusal, Total or Partial Non-payment, Price Reduction after the Supply*[81]

Article 73 VAT Directive stipulates that the taxable amount comprises all sums which make up the consideration which has been or is to be obtained by the supplier from the purchaser. Article 90(1) VAT Directive provides that the taxable amount shall be reduced accordingly in the case of:[82]

(1) cancellation; or
(2) refusal; or
(3) total or partial non-payment; or
(4) where the price is reduced after the supply takes place.

80. In this example, one may assume that no VAT will be charged on the permit, assuming that the municipality acts in its capacity as a non-taxable person when granting the licence.
81. A.J. van Doesum, 'Taxable Amount', in M. Lang, et al. (eds), *ECJ: Recent Developments in Value Added Tax, the Evolution of European VAT Jurisprudence and Its Role in the EU Common VAT System* (Linde 2014), pp. 177-233 and A.J. van Doesum & Frank Nellen, 'Taxable Amount & VAT Rates', in M. Lang, et al. (eds), *CJEU: Recent Developments in Value Added Tax 2018* (2019), pp. 191-222.
82. CJEU 26 January 2012, Case C-588/10 *Minister Finansów v Kraft Foods Polska SA*, ECLI: EU:C:2012:40, para. 21.

Article 90 VAT Directive reads as follows:

1. In the case of cancellation, refusal or total or partial non-payment, or where the price is reduced after the supply takes place, the taxable amount shall be reduced accordingly under conditions which shall be determined by the member states.
2. In the case of total or partial non-payment, member states may derogate from paragraph 1.

In some language versions of the VAT Directive, Article 90(1) provides for a fifth situation in which the taxable amount shall be reduced: termination of a contract for non-performance because it has become impossible to perform or because the terms are excessively onerous.[83] With respect to the third (in some language versions, the fourth) situation, Member States are allowed to derogate from Article 90(1) VAT Directive (*see* Article 90(2) VAT Directive). This is based on the idea that in certain circumstances and because of the legal situation prevailing in the Member State concerned, non-payment of consideration may be difficult to establish or may only be temporary.[84] From *Di Maura*, it follows that the derogation of Article 90(2) VAT Directive does not give the Member States the option to exclude the reduction of the taxable amount in cases of partial or total non-payment altogether.[85] In fact, if it is reasonably likely that a non-payment is definitive, Member States must allow for a reduction of the taxable amount.[86]

It would not be in conformity with the VAT Directive if the taxable amount were to exceed the sum finally received by the supplier.[87] After all, it is a fundamental principle of the VAT Directive, that the basis of assessment is the consideration actually received, the corollary of which is that the tax authorities may not in any circumstances charge an amount of VAT exceeding the tax paid by the taxable person.[88] This can explain the *ratio legis* of Article 90(1) VAT Directive. Indeed, from the commentary of the Economic and Social Committee to the proposal for the Sixth VAT Directive, it can be understood that Article 90 VAT Directive is to safeguard the neutrality of VAT. CJEU case law confirms this. For example, in *Elida Gibbs*, the CJEU ruled that:

83. For example, the Dutch and the Italian language versions of Article 90(1) VAT Directive. *See* the Opinion of Advocate General La Pergola of 27 February 1997, Case C-330/95 *Goldsmiths (Jewellers) Ltd v Commissioners of Customs & Excise*, ECLI:EU:C:1997:339.
84. CJEU 3 July 1997, Case C-330/95 *Goldsmiths (Jewellers) Ltd v Commissioners of Customs & Excise*, ECLI:EU:C:1997:339, para. 18.
85. CJEU 23 November 2017, Case C-246/16 *Enzo Di Maura v Agenzia delle Entrate – Direzione Provinciale di Siracusa*, ECLI:EU:C:2017:887.
86. CJEU July 2019, Case C-242/18 *'UniCredit Leasing' EAD v Direktor na Direktsia 'Obzhalvane i danachno-osiguritelna praktika' – Sofia pri Tsentralno upravlenie na Natsionalnata agentsia za prihodite (NAP)*, ECLI:EU:C:2019:558.
87. CJEU 24 October 1996, Case C-317/94 *Elida Gibbs Ltd v Commissioners of Customs and Excise*, ECLI:EU:C:1996:400, para. 28; CJEU 3 July 1997, Case C-330/95 *Goldsmiths (Jewellers) Ltd v Commissioners of Customs & Excise*, ECLI:EU:C:1997:339, para. 15 and CJEU 23 November 2017, Case C-246/16 *Enzo Di Maura v Agenzia delle Entrate – Direzione Provinciale di Siracusa*, ECLI:EU:C:2017:887.
88. CJEU 26 January 2012, Case C-588/10 *Minister Finansów v Kraft Foods Polska SA*, ECLI: EU:C:2012:40, para. 27.

> That interpretation is borne out by Article 11(C)(1) of the Sixth Directive [now Article 90(1) VAT Directive, *eds.*] which, in order to ensure the neutrality of the taxable person's position, provides that, in the case of cancellation, refusal or total or partial non-payment, or where the price is reduced after the supply takes place, the taxable amount is to be reduced accordingly under conditions to be determined by the member states.[89]

In *Goldsmiths*, the CJEU confirmed that in accordance with the principle of neutrality, Article 90 defines the cases in which the Member States are required to ensure that the taxable amount is reduced accordingly. That provision, therefore, requires the Member States to reduce the taxable amount and, consequently, the amount of VAT payable by the taxable person whenever, after a transaction has been concluded, part or all of the consideration has not been received by the taxable person.[90] Reduction of the taxable amount is not required in cases where the service supplier has, in fact, received all the payments in consideration for the service which he supplied or where, without the agreement having been refused or cancelled, the recipient of that service is no longer liable to the taxable person for the agreed price.[91] Consequently, we hold that the purpose of Article 90 VAT Directive is to ensure that the VAT is strictly proportional to the price actually received for supplies that are actually made. That way, the neutrality of VAT is safeguarded. As such, in *Almos*, the CJEU considered that Article 90(1) fulfils the conditions for it to have direct effect[92] and that taxable persons may rely on Article 90(1) before national courts against the Member State to obtain a reduction of their taxable amount for VAT, even if that Member State did not (correctly) implement Article 90(1).[93]

From *Elida Gibbs*, it follows that Article 90(1) can also lead to a reduction of the taxable amount in cases where a price reduction is allowed to the final consumer by way of a money-back coupon, even if the money is paid back by the manufacturer whose initial supply is made to the wholesaler (and not the final consumer).[94] However, the scope of Article 90(1) does not extend to the situation where a travel agent, acting as an intermediary, grants to the final consumer, on the travel agent's own initiative and at his own expense, a price reduction on the principal service provided by the tour operator.[95] On the basis of *Euler Hermes*, Article 90(1) can also not be applied in a situation where an insurance company which, under a contract for the

89. CJEU 24 October 1996, Case C-317/94 *Elida Gibbs Ltd v Commissioners of Customs and Excise*, ECLI:EU:C:1996:400, para. 30.
90. CJEU 3 July 1997, Case C-330/95 *Goldsmiths (Jewellers) Ltd v Commissioners of Customs & Excise*, ECLI:EU:C:1997:339, para. 16. *See also* CJEU 26 January 2012, Case C-588/10 *Minister Finansów v Kraft Foods Polska SA*, ECLI:EU:C:2012:40, para. 27.
91. CJEU 2 July 2015, Case C-209/14 *NLB Leasing d.o.o. v Republika Slovenija*, ECLI:EU:C:2015:440.
92. CJEU 5 May 2014, Case C-337/13, *Almos Agrárkülkereskedelmi Kft v Nemzeti Adó- és Vámhivatal Közép-magyarországi Regionális Adó Főigazgatósága*, ECLI:EU:C:2014:328, para. 34.
93. *Ibid.*, para. 40. *See also* A.J. van Doesum, 'Non-payments is EU VAT', in M. Lang, et al. (eds), *CJEU: Recent Developments in Value Added Tax 2021* (Linde 2022).
94. CJEU 24 October 1996, Case C-317/94 *Elida Gibbs Ltd v Commissioners of Customs and Excise*, ECLI:EU:C:1996:400. *See also* CJEU 20 December 2017, Case C-462/16 *Finanzamt Bingen-Alzey v Boehringer Ingelheim Pharma GmbH & Co. KG*, ECLI:EU:C:2017:1006.
95. CJEU 16 January 2014, Case C-300/12 *Finanzamt Düsseldorf-Mitte v Ibero Tours GmbH*, ECLI:EU:C:2014:8.

insurance of trade debts, pays the insured person, by way of compensation following non-payment of a debt to that insured person, part of the taxable amount of the taxable transaction at issue (the transaction between the insured person and its customer) including VAT, even though, pursuant to that contract, that part of the debt together with all associated rights have been assigned to that insurer.[96] The reasoning of the CJEU in this respect is that the compensation by the insurance company to the insured person constitutes a (third party) payment to the insured person, for its supply to its customer. As a result, no situation of non-payment exists at the level of the insured party. Moreover, the insurer may also not reduce its taxable amount on the basis of Article 90(1), as the insurer did not provide a taxable supply to the customer (of the insured person) for which the outstanding amount can be a taxable amount, even though the debt together with all associated rights have been assigned to that insurer.

Article 90(1) VAT Directive allows the Member States to set the conditions to a reduction of the taxable amount. According to the CJEU, Article 90(1) VAT Directive gives the Member States a margin of discretion, *inter alia, as to the formalities to be complied with* by taxable persons vis-à-vis the tax authorities of those states in order to ensure that, where the price is reduced after the supply has taken place, the taxable amount is reduced accordingly.[97] Such measures must have as little effect as possible on the objectives and principles of the VAT Directive and may not, therefore, be used in such a way that they would have the effect of undermining VAT neutrality. As such in *ELVOSPOL* it was ruled that Member States may not set as a condition that a reduction of the taxable amount under Article 90 can only be effectuated if the debts have arisen outside a time period of six months preceding the declaration of bankruptcy of a taxable person.[98] Member States can only set conditions in so far as those conditions do not make it impossible or excessively difficult to reduce the taxable amount.

6.7.3 Inclusions or Exclusions

Article 92 VAT Directive contains an option for the Member States to either include or exclude amounts relating to returnable packing material in/from the taxable amount.

6.7.3.1 Returnable Packaging Material

As regards the costs of returnable packaging materials, Member States may take one of the following measures:

96. CJEU 9 February 2023, Case C-482/21 *Euler Hermes SA Magyarországi Fióktelepe v Nemzeti Adó- és Vámhivatal Fellebbviteli Igazgatósága*, ECLI:EU:C:2023:83.
97. CJEU 3 July 1997, Case C-330/95 *Goldsmiths (Jewellers) Ltd v Commissioners of Customs & Excise*, ECLI:EU:C:1997:339, para. 23.
98. CJEU 11 November 2021, Case C-398/20 *ELVOSPOL s.r.o. v Odvolací finanční ředitelství*, ECLI:EU:C:2021:911.

(a) exclude them from the taxable amount and take the measures necessary to ensure that this amount is adjusted if the packaging materials are not returned;
(b) include them in the taxable amount and take the measures necessary to ensure that this amount is adjusted if the packaging materials are, in fact, returned.

According to the Explanatory Memorandum to the Proposal for the Sixth VAT Directive, the purpose of excluding the cost of returnable packaging is to avoid having to adjust the taxable amount each time, as is normally the case, the packaging is returned by the customer.[99]

6.8 DEEMED SUPPLIES

In sections 3.3.2.2 and 3.2.5.2, we explained that the VAT Directive contains two 'types' of provisions on the basis of which a taxable person is deemed to make a supply of goods or services, even though he did not actually carry out a taxable supply.

The first type is the 'self-supply' of goods and services (Articles 16 and 26 VAT Directive). This type of 'deemed supplies' provides for a correction mechanism for goods and services on which input VAT has been deducted but are applied for private purposes.[100] The purpose is to ensure equal treatment as between a taxable person who applies goods for his own private use, for that of his staff or of others, and a final consumer who acquires goods or services of the same type.[101]

The second type of 'deemed supplies' consists of the so-called internal supplies. In Chapter 3, section 3.2.5.2, we elaborated on the (confusion with respect to the) purpose of the provisions containing the internal supplies (Articles 18(a) and 27 VAT Directive). They aim at preventing distortions of competition that are due to businesses without a full right of deduction 'in sourcing' certain activities.

In this section, we will discuss the determination of the taxable amount of both types of deemed supplies.

---

99. Explanatory Memorandum to the proposal for a Sixth Directive of 20 June 1973, COM (73)950.
100. Article 26(b) VAT Directive does not contain the condition that input VAT must have been deducted. *See* Chapter 3, section 3.3.2.2.
101. CJEU 26 September 1996, Case C-230/94 *Renate Enkler v Finanzamt Homburg* [1996] ECR I-04517, para. 35; CJEU 16 October 1997, Case C-258/95 *Julius Fillibeck Söhne GmbH & Co. KG v Finanzamt Neustadt* [1997] ECR I-05577, para. 25; CJEU 17 May 2001, Cases C-322/99 and C-323/99 *Finanzamt Burgdorf v Hans-Georg Fischer and Finanzamt Düsseldorf-Mettmann v Klaus Brandenstein* [2001] ECR I-04049, para. 56; CJEU 20 January 2005, Case C-412/03 *Hotel Scandic Gåsabäck AB v Riksskatteverket*, ECLI:EU:C:2005:47, para. 23 and CJEU 11 December 2008, Case C-371/07 *Danfoss A/S and AstraZeneca A/S v Skatteministeriet*, ECLI-:EU:C:2008:711, para. 46. *See also* European Commission, Common System of Value Added Tax: Uniform Basis of Assessment. Proposal for a Sixth Council Directive on the harmonization of Member States concerning turnover taxes. Submitted to the Council by the Commission. COM (73) 950 final, 20 June 1973. Bulletin of the European Communities, Supplement 11/73. Even though the case law mentioned above relates to services mentioned in Article 26 VAT Directive, we believe it is safe to argue that Article 26 VAT Directive and Article 16 VAT Directive have the same purpose.

6.8.1 Self-Supply and Internal Supply of Goods

In the case of a self-supply (Article 16 VAT Directive) or an internal supply (Article 18 VAT Directive) of goods, no consideration is available to form the taxable amount for these supplies. However, in order to levy VAT, a taxable amount must be determined. To this end, Article 74 VAT Directive is introduced.

Pursuant to this provision, the taxable amount is the purchase price of the goods or of similar goods or, in the absence of a purchase price, the cost price, determined at the time when the application, disposal or retention takes place. In *Y KG*, it was ruled that Article 74 must be interpreted as meaning that the 'cost price' in the sense of that provision includes not only direct manufacturing or production costs but also indirectly attributable costs, such as financing costs, whether or not those costs have been subject to input VAT.[102] In our view, this is surprising as there is no systematic necessity to include costs which have not been subject to VAT in the taxable amount for a deemed supply, as in those cases there is no risk of untaxed final consumption. In this respect, *Y KG* also does not seem to fit the principles set out in cases like *Kühne*[103] and *Mohsche.*[104]

With regard to the taxable amount of internal supplies of goods (Article 18(a) VAT Directive), it follows from *Gemeente Vlaardingen*[105] and *Het Oudeland Beheer BV*[106] that the taxable amount must include the costs of acquiring land on which a building is constructed to the extent that the taxable person has paid VAT and deducted that VAT (in full or partially) when he acquired the land. With respect to the application of Article 18(c) VAT Directive, on the basis of *Marinov*, in the event of the cessation of the taxable economic activity, the taxable amount of the transaction is the value of the goods in question determined at the time of that cessation, which, therefore, takes into account the change in the value of those assets between their acquisition and the cessation.[107]

6.8.2 Self-Supply and Internal Supply of Services

Articles 26 and 27 VAT Directive contain the provisions for self-supplies of services and internal supplies of services, respectively.

Article 75 VAT Directive states that in respect of the supply of services, as referred to in Article 26 VAT Directive, where goods forming part of the assets of a business are used for private purposes or services are carried out free of charge; the taxable amount

102. CJEU 25 April 2024, Case C-207/23 *Y KG v Finanzamt X*, ECLI:EU:C:2024:352.
103. CJEU 27 June 1989, Case 50/88 *Kühne v Finanzamt München III*, ECLI:EU:C:1989:262.
104. CJEU 25 May 1993, Case C-193/91 *Finanzamt München III v Mohsche*, ECLI:EU:C:1993:203.
105. CJEU 8 November 2012, Case C-299/11 *Staatssecretaris van Financiën v Gemeente Vlaardingen*, ECLI:EU:C:2012:698.
106. CJEU 28 April 2016, Case C-128/14 *Staatssecretaris van Financiën v Het Oudeland Beheer BV*, ECLI:EU:C:2016:306.
107. CJEU 8 May 2013, Case C-142/12 *Hristomir Marinov v Direktor na Direktsia 'Obzhalvane i upravlenie na izpalnenieto' – grad Varna pri Tsentralno upravlenie na Natsionalna agentsia za prihodite*, ECLI:EU:C:2013:292, para. 33.

shall be the *full cost* to the taxable person of providing the services. This basis must have been chosen because it reflects the costs that the taxable person has offered to make this self-supply. In *Wollny*,[108] the CJEU had to decide on the legal sustainability of a special calculation method as used by Germany, and more specifically, on the interpretation of the wording 'full costs'. The *Finanzgericht München* asked the CJEU how the term 'full cost' in Article 11(A)(1)(c) of the Sixth VAT Directive (currently Article 75 VAT Directive) was to be interpreted. It asked whether the 'full costs' for a privately used dwelling in a building that formed part of the assets of a business include, in addition to recurring expenses, the annual depreciation for the wear and tear of buildings and/or the annual proportion of the acquisition and production cost that has given rise to a right to deduct VAT. The CJEU decided that in these circumstances, the notion of 'full costs' does not preclude the taxable amount for VAT from being fixed at a portion of the acquisition or construction costs of the building, established in accordance with the length of the period for adjustment of deductions concerning VAT provided for in Article 184 VAT Directive.

Also, in *Van Laarhoven*, it was ruled that although the Member States have a certain margin of discretion as regards the principles governing the determination of those costs, and such a margin permits, to a certain extent, flat-rate methods of calculation, it must be ensured that any flat-rate method of calculating the VAT payable by the taxable person satisfies, in particular, the principle of proportionality, in that such a flat-rate determination must necessarily be proportional to the extent of private use of the goods at issue.[109]

Article 77 VAT Directive rules that in respect of an internal supply of a service, as referred to in Article 27 VAT Directive, the taxable amount shall be the open market value of the service supplied. This taxable basis is different from the taxable basis for self-supplies. The reason to take another approach for internal supplies is that the underlying objective of an internal supply is to prevent distortions of competition between those taxable persons who make these supplies for themselves on those who make them for the market. The open market value is, therefore, the most suitable basis. The open market value is defined in Article 72 VAT Directive (*see* section 6.12).

6.8.3 Intra-Community Transfer of Own Goods ('Intra-Community B2Me Transactions')

If a company moves its own stock from one (warehouse in one) Member State to another (warehouse in another) Member State, clearly there is no supply of goods between two parties. However, in such situations, Article 17(1) VAT Directive by legal fiction deems that an intra-Community supply (ICS) takes place in the Member State of departure or dispatch, and an intra-Community acquisition (ICA) is effected in the

108. CJEU 14 September 2006, Case C-72/05 *Hausgemeinschaft Jörg und Stefanie Wollny v Finanzamt Landshut*, ECLI:EU:C:2006:573.
109. CJEU 16 February 2012, Case C-594/10 *T.G. van Laarhoven tegen Staatssecretaris van Financiën*, ECLI:EU:C:2012:92.

Member State of arrival of the goods. In Chapter 13, section 13.6, we will further elaborate on these deemed supplies, which we refer to as 'B2Me transactions'.

Normally, the determination of a taxable amount for such taxable events seems rather unnecessary because such transactions are often carried out by parties that can apply for an exemption (with a right of deduction, Article 138 VAT Directive) to the supply and have a full right of deduction as regards the VAT on the ICA. However, this is not always the case. Moreover, a taxable amount must be determined in order to be able to file a correct recapitulative statement (*see* Chapter 13, Intra-Community transactions (ICTs)).

Article 76 VAT Directive deals with the determination of the taxable amount of such B2Me supplies. The taxable amount is the purchase price of the goods or of similar goods or, in the absence of a purchase price, the cost price, determined at the time the transfer takes place. Since the corollary of an ICS (even if it is a deemed supply) is an ICA, a B2Me intra-Community supply leads to an ICA in the Member State of arrival of the goods. Consequently, a taxable amount for that acquisition must be determined. Article 83, last paragraph, VAT Directive provides for just that. The taxable amount of the ICA following a B2Me intra-Community supply is the purchase price of the goods or of similar goods or, in the absence of a purchase price, the cost price, determined at the time of the supply. We refer to Chapter 13, section 13.3.2.2.5.

6.9 INTRA-COMMUNITY ACQUISITION OF GOODS (ICAs)

In section 6.8.3, we discussed the determination of the taxable amount for intra-Community acquisitions (ICAs) following 'B2Me intra-Community supplies of goods'. Article 83, first sentence states the taxable amount applicable to straightforward ICAs of goods. In respect of the ICA, Article 83 VAT Directive determines that the taxable amount must be established on the basis of the same factors as are used to determine the taxable amount for the supply of the same goods within the territory of the Member State concerned. It is logical that the calculation of the supply and the acquisition is calculated by the same method. Otherwise, it would create mismatches between the Member States. For the determination of the taxable amount in more specific acquisitions – like those of the acquisitions of excise goods – we refer to Article 84 VAT Directive. In Chapter 13, section 13.3.3.2.5, we will further discuss the taxable amount for ICAs.

6.10 IMPORTATION OF GOODS

In respect of the importation of goods, the taxable amount must be the value for customs purposes, determined in accordance with the Union provisions in force. Articles 85-89 VAT Directive deal with the calculation of the taxable amount of imported goods.

The taxable amount of imported goods must include the following factors, insofar as they are not already included: (a) taxes, duties and other charges due outside the Member State of importation, and those due by reason of importation, excluding the VAT to be levied; and (b) incidental expenses, such as commission, packing, transport, and insurance costs, incurred up to the first place of destination (the place mentioned on the consignment note or on any other document under which the goods are imported into the Member State of importation),[110] within the territory of the Member State of importation as well as those resulting from transport to another place of destination within the Union if that other place if known when the chargeable event occurs.

The taxable amount does not include: (a) price reductions by way of discount for early payment (*see also* section 6.7.2.1); or (b) price discounts and rebates granted to the customer and obtained by him at the time of importation.

Where goods, temporarily exported from the Union, are reimported after having undergone repair, processing, adaptation, making up or reworking outside the Union, Member States shall take steps to ensure that the tax treatment of the goods for VAT purposes is the same as that which would have been applied had the repair, processing, adaptation, making up or reworking been carried out within their territory.

There are special rules for the calculation of the taxable amount of importation of works of art. We refer to Article 89 VAT Directive. Also, *see* Chapter 14, section 14.8.

6.11 SPECIAL REGIMES

For an in-depth description of the special regimes such as the special scheme for travel agents, the special arrangements for second-hand goods, works of art, collectors' items and antiques and the special scheme for investment gold and the implications of those regimes for the taxable amount in specific circumstances, we refer to Chapter 16.

6.12 OPEN MARKET VALUE[111]

As mentioned in section 6.2, the main rule for the determination of the taxable amount for VAT purposes is that the taxable amount comprises all sums which make up the consideration which has been or is to be obtained by the supplier from the purchaser. The taxable amount is a subjective value. Normally, this is the sales price of the goods or services, or as Article 73 VAT Directive puts it more precisely: 'all sums which make up the consideration which has been or is to be obtained by the supplier from the purchaser'.

110. If no such mention is made, the first place of destination shall be deemed to be the place of the first transfer of cargo in the Member State of importation (Article 86(2), last sentence VAT Directive).

111. A.J. van Doesum, 'Taxable Amount', in M. Lang, et al. (eds), *ECJ: Recent Developments in Value Added Tax, the Evolution of European VAT Jurisprudence and Its Role in the EU Common VAT System* (Linde 2014), pp. 177-233.

If parties agree on a consideration (price), which is lower than usual (i.e., lower than objective market value), this consideration is still the taxable amount for VAT. However, Article 80 VAT Directive contains an exception to the main principle laid down in Article 73 VAT Directive. Article 80 VAT Directive allows the Member States to apply the so-called open market value as the taxable amount for a supply. It is an optional provision, which some Member States, such as Bulgaria, have implemented. The *ratio legis* of this provision is to prevent tax evasion or avoidance in cases where the Member States would suffer a loss of tax revenues through the use by taxable persons of connected parties to derive tax benefits.[112] It should be noted that 'connected' is a very broad concept here: it covers 'family or other close personal ties, management, ownership, membership, financial or legal ties as defined by the member state'.

According to the CJEU, if a supply is made between two (connected) taxable persons who have a full right of deduction, using an artificially low or high price for their mutual supplies, that in itself cannot lead to tax evasion or avoidance or to any tax benefits.[113] However, one could imagine that an artificially low or high price might have an impact on later adjustments of the VAT that was initially deducted by the recipient of the supply (*see* Articles 184, 186, 187 and in particular Article 188 VAT Directive) and therefore, may lead to a tax benefit in years after that in which the goods (or services, depending on the implementation of Article 190 VAT Directive) have been acquired. Nonetheless, where both parties to a supply have a full right of deduction, in principle, the tax is entirely neutral for both parties and will remain so whatever the price charged.[114] If one of the (connected) parties involved does *not* have a full right of deduction, using an artificially low or high price may lead to tax evasion or avoidance. If the *supplier* does not have a full right of deduction, he can optimize his proportional deduction of input VAT on general costs (pro rata, *see* Chapter 10, section 10.4) by applying an artificially high price to his taxed supplies or an artificially low price to his exempt supplies. If the *recipient* of the supply does not have a full right of deduction, non-deductible VAT with the recipient can be prevented by using an artificially low price. Article 80 VAT Directive may serve to prevent such 'tax benefits', 'loss of tax

112. *See* Article 80(1) VAT Directive and recital 26 in the preamble to the VAT Directive, which states that: 'To prevent loss of tax revenues through the use of connected parties to derive tax benefits, it should, in specific limited circumstances, be possible for Member States to intervene as regards the taxable amount of supplies of goods or services and intra-Community acquisitions of goods.' *See also* recital 3 in the preamble to Directive 2006/69 which adds: 'to ensure that there is no loss of tax through the use of connected parties to derive tax benefits'.
113. CJEU 26 April 2012, Joined Cases C-621/10 and C-129/11 *Balkan and Sea Properties ADSITS (C-621/10) and Provadinvest OOD (C-129/11) v Direktor na Direktsia 'Obzhalvane i upravlenie na izpalnenieto' – Varna pri Tsentralno upravlenie na Natsionalnata agentsia za prihodite*, ECLI:EU:C:2012:248, para. 47.
114. *See* the Opinion of Advocate General Sharpston of 26 January 2012, Joined Cases C-621/10 and C-129/11 *Balkan and Sea Properties ADSITS (C-621/10) and Provadinvest OOD (C-129/11) v Direktor na Direktsia 'Obzhalvane i upravlenie na izpalnenieto' – Varna pri Tsentralno upravlenie na Natsionalnata agentsia za prihodite*, ECLI:EU:C:2012:41, para. 30.

revenue', 'tax evasion' or 'tax avoidance' from occurring. Member States can use open market value instead of the 'subjective value' of Article 73 VAT Directive.

Article 72 VAT Directive contains a definition of the term 'open market value'. It is the full amount that, in order to obtain the goods or services in question at that time, a customer at the same marketing stage at which the supply of goods or services takes place, would have to pay, under conditions of fair competition, to a supplier at arm's length within the territory of the Member State in which the supply is subject to tax. In the case of a supply of goods, the open market value is an amount that is not less than the purchase price of goods or of similar goods or, in the absence of a purchase price, the cost price, determined at the time of supply if no comparable supply of goods can be ascertained. In respect of services, an amount that is not less than the full cost to the taxable person of providing the service is the open market value if no comparable supply of goods or services can be ascertained.

Most Member States – not surprisingly – are proving reluctant to apply this more objective taxable base. The subjective taxable amount is indeed something deserving to be protected. Entrepreneurs may have an expectation that the invoiced amount is also the taxable amount. Such an expectation should not be disturbed lightly. Only if certain tax planning schemes are applied too freely, and the tax authorities are proving reluctant to apply the principle of prohibition of abuse because the obligation to prove that the main objective of the structure is tax avoidance is too labour intensive, Member States could consider introducing the open market value as a means to combat those structures. In practice, various elements need to be addressed, such as how the measure should be applied, how the invoice should look like, how the right to deduction should be calculated in case of customers with a partial right to deduction and how this measure should be applied in cross-border situations.[115] It follows, however, from *Balkan and Sea Properties* and *Provadinvest* that the conditions of application laid down in Article 80 VAT Directive are exhaustive and, consequently, national legislation cannot, on the basis of that provision, provide that the taxable amount is to be the open market value of the transaction in cases other than those listed in that provision.[116]

6.13 VOUCHERS

6.13.1 Vouchers and EU VAT

Using a voucher in a taxable transaction can have consequences for the taxable amount, the time of a transaction, and even in certain circumstances, the place of

115. *See* for a more in-depth analyses D. Ramsdahl Jensen, 'Transfer Pricing Principles VAT/GST v. Direct Taxation', in M. Lang, et al. (eds), *Value Added Tax and Direct Taxation, Similarities and Differences* (IBFD 2009), pp. 877-900.
116. CJEU 26 April 2012, Joined Cases C-621/10 and C-129/11 *Balkan and Sea Properties en Provadinvest*, ECLI:EU:C:2012:248.

taxation. Uncertainty about the correct tax treatment can, however, be problematic for cross-border transactions and for chain transactions in the commercial distribution of vouchers. Despite the fact that the European market for vouchers is huge,[117] for a long time, no specific rules for the VAT treatment or the taxable amount of vouchers were to be found in the VAT Directive. Because of the lack of harmonization with respect to the VAT treatment of vouchers, vouchers – in all their manifestations – were treated differently by the various Member States. This caused mismatches in taxation, leading to double- or non-taxation. The latter effect, in turn, contributes to tax avoidance, and created barriers to business innovation.[118]

In 2016, after a long legislative process, a proposal for harmonized rules on the treatment of vouchers was accepted.[119] The VAT Directive was amended as per 2019.

6.13.2 Single-Purpose and Multi-Purpose Vouchers

Under the 2019 rules, Article 30bis VAT Directive defines a voucher as an instrument where there is an obligation to accept it as consideration or part consideration for a supply of goods or services and where the goods or services to be supplied, or the identities of their potential suppliers are either indicated on the instrument itself or in related documentation, including the terms and conditions of use of such instrument. The article goes on to define two types of vouchers: the single-purpose voucher and the multi-purpose voucher. Single-purpose vouchers (Article 30bis (2) VAT Directive) are vouchers for which it is clear from the outset what the VAT treatment of the supply of goods or services that can be obtained with the vouchers will be, including the place of supply and the amount of VAT due. Multi-purpose vouchers (Article 30bis (3) VAT Directive) are all other vouchers, meaning that this concept entails any voucher within the definition of Article 30bis (1) VAT Directive, for which not all elements of the VAT treatment of the supply of goods or services that the voucher can be exchanged for are known upfront. From *M Gbr*, it follows that the qualification of a voucher as a single-purpose voucher depends solely on the conditions laid down in that provision, which include the requirement that the place of supply of services to end consumers, to which that voucher relates, must be known at the time of the issue of that voucher, irrespective of the fact that the voucher is the subject of transfers between taxable persons acting in their own name and established in the territory of Member States

117. J.B.O. Bijl, *VAT, Vouchers, Rights and Payments: The VAT Treatment of Vouchers* (2013) 3 EC Tax Review, p. 115 https://doi.org/10.54648/ecta2013014.
118. The Proposal for a Council Directive amending Directive 2006/112/EC on the common system of value added tax, as regards the treatment of vouchers, COM (2012)206 ('the Proposal'), https://eur-lex.europa.eu/legal-content/EN/TXT/?uri=CELEX:52012PC0206 (accessed 17 August 2024).
119. Council Directive (EU) 2016/1065 of 27 June 2016 amending Directive 2006/112/EC as regards the treatment of vouchers, OJ L 177/9.

other than that in which those end consumers are located.[120] From *DSAB Destination Stockholm*, it follows that the supply of a city card, that gave the cardholder access to multiple attractions in Stockholm, use of passenger transport services as well as sightseeing tours with other organizers, should be treated as a voucher on the basis of Article 30bis VAT Directive and more specifically as a multi-purpose voucher, since the VAT due on the specific services (some could benefit from a reduced rate or an exemption) would not be known at the time of issuance of that instrument.[121] The fact that as a result of the limited validity period of the card, the average consumer would not be expected to be able to benefit from all the services offered was deemed irrelevant in this respect.

The transfer of a single-purpose voucher is treated as the supply of goods or services that the voucher represents. As a result, VAT becomes due at the moment of issue or transfer of a single-purpose voucher, as if it were the supply of goods or services that, in reality, will first occur when the voucher is used. For the determination of the taxable amount of single-purpose voucher, the basic rule of Article 73 VAT Directive applies, meaning that the taxable amount will be formed by the subjective value attributed to the voucher by the issuer or seller of the voucher and the buyer. As a consequence of treating the issue or transfer of the single-purpose voucher as the moment to tax the eventual return of the voucher for goods or services, the actual handing over of the goods or the actual provision of the services in return for a single-purpose voucher will not be regarded as an independent chargeable event.

Where it is a multi-purpose voucher, the issue, supply or transfer of such a voucher does not in itself create a taxable supply. The main reason for this is that not all the relevant information concerning the chargeable event – namely, the future delivery or future performance – are known at the moment a multi-purpose voucher is purchased. For example, in the case of a multi-purpose voucher, the nature and the quantity of goods or services are unknown at the moment of the purchase of the voucher. Indeed, a multi-purpose voucher can be used as a means of payment for a range of products and/or services. Therefore, on the basis of Article 30ter (2) VAT Directive, the relevant supply only occurs at the moment that the supplier makes his concrete supply in return for the redemption of the multi-purpose voucher.

Article 73a VAT Directive provides for a specific rule on the determination of the taxable amount for the supply of goods or services provided in respect of a multi-purpose voucher. It provides that the taxable amount is equal to the consideration paid for the voucher or, in the absence of information on that consideration, the monetary value indicated on the multi-purpose voucher itself or in the related documentation, less the amount of VAT relating to the goods or services supplied.

120. CJEU 18 April 2024, Case C-68/23 *M Gbr v Finanzamt O (Bons à usage unique)*, ECLI: EU:C:2024:342.
121. CJEU 28 April 2022, Case C-637/20 *Skatteverket v DSAB Destination Stockholm AB*, ECLI: EU:C:2022:304.

It must be noted that applying this provision could raise some practical questions. For example, if a multi-purpose voucher with a monetary value of 10 indicated on it, is issued for no consideration (as a promotional activity), then the question would be what the appropriate taxable amount should be upon return of the voucher for goods or services. It would be reasonable to assume that the taxable amount should be the monetary value indicated on the voucher, but the text of Article 73a suggests that such amount will only be relevant in the absence of information on the consideration paid for the voucher. If it is known to the business accepting the multi-purpose voucher in question, that the consideration paid for the voucher is naught, it could be argued that the taxable amount of its supply of goods or services is naught as well. Also, it is pointed out that in situations where the issuer or seller of the multi-purpose voucher and the business accepting the voucher as consideration are two distinct (taxable) persons, taking either the consideration paid for the voucher or the monetary value of the voucher as the taxable amount, may well lead to taxing an amount that deviates from the amount of remuneration that the acceptant actually receives from the issuer.[122] That result could be seen to be undesirable. *DSAB Destination Stockholm* provided an opportunity for the Court to clarify the rules around the determination of the taxable amount of multi-purpose vouchers.[123] A-G *Capeta* offered an interesting take that rather surprisingly included levying VAT over the unused parts of the city card against the standard rate, which seems to go directly against the grain of the concept and treatment of a multi-purpose voucher.[124] However, as the questions referred by the Swedish referring court did not necessitate this, the CJEU refrained from confirming or denying this view.[125] We expect further case law with respect to this issue.

6.13.3 Other Vouchers and Case Law

It should be noted that the scope of the voucher-rules in Article 30bis-30ter VAT Directive is quite limited. It does not cover all instruments that – in common parlance – would be covered by the concept of a 'voucher'. For example, discount vouchers or coupons will, in principle, not be covered by the definition of Article 30bis (1). As a result, most CJEU case law on the treatment of vouchers – in the broader, common parlance sense, has not lost its relevance after the introduction of the new rules.

---

122. It could be argued that this is not in line with CJEU 24 October 1996, Case C-288/94 *Argos Distributors Ltd v Commissioners of Customs and Excise*, ECLI:EU:C:1996:398. *See also* J.B.O. Bijl, *The EU VAT Treatment of Vouchers in the Context of Promotional Activities* (dissertation) (Kluwer 2019), pp. 298-299.
123. CJEU 28 April 2022, Case C-637/20 *Skatteverket v DSAB Destination Stockholm AB*, ECLI: EU:C:2022:304.
124. Opinion of Advocate General Capeta of 24 February 2022, Case C-637/20 *Skatteverket v DSAB Destination Stockholm AB*, ECLI:EU:C:2022:131.
125. CJEU 28 April 2022, Case C-637/20 *Skatteverket v DSAB Destination Stockholm AB*, ECLI: EU:C:2022:304.

A remarkably large number of CJEU cases on vouchers (in the broad sense) originate from the UK. Possibly, this has something to do with the popularity of vouchers as a marketing instrument in the UK.[126] To explain the VAT treatment of vouchers in EU law, it is first important to recall that under current EU VAT law, the taxable amount of a supply is reduced if a discount or price reduction is granted after the supply takes place (*see* Article 90 VAT Directive, described in section 6.7.2.4). Second, in practice, it is not always the supplier granting a discount or a price reduction to the end-consumer directly, this occurring via other parties in the supply chain (e.g., resellers). The CJEU's rulings in *Argos* and *Elida Gibbs* are illustrative in this respect.

Argos sold vouchers to a buyer ('the employer') at a discount and promised subsequently to accept these vouchers at their face value in full or part payment of the price of goods purchased by customers who were not the buyers of the voucher ('the employees').[127] Let us assume that the employer bought 100 vouchers with a face value of GBP 50 (and a total face value GBP 5,000) for GBP 4,000. The employees did not know the actual price at which the vouchers were sold by Argos to their employer (GBP 4,000: GBP 40 for each voucher). According to the Court, the consideration represented by the vouchers for the supplies of goods eventually made by Argos to the employees was the sum actually received by Argos upon the sale of the vouchers (GBP 4,000). It is, therefore, that sum, and not the face value of the vouchers (GBP 5,000 in total), which, in accordance with the provision concerned in the VAT Directive (currently Article 73), must be adopted as the taxable amount for application of VAT to the sale in respect of which the voucher was accepted in payment.

In *Elida Gibbs,* a manufacturer (Elida Gibbs) distributed – via magazines – money-off coupons to stimulate the general public to purchase its products (soap and the like). Readers could redeem these coupons with retailers.[128] The manufacturer compensated the retailers on its turn. Next to this, other coupons were distributed, namely cash-back coupons. Those coupons were attached to the products. The customers could reclaim the face value from Elida Gibbs. Elida Gibbs was wondering whether it was obliged to charge and remit VAT on the original supplier's price (the price it had charged to the retailer) without taking into account the discount supplied to them, or was entitled to charge and remit VAT on the original supplier's price minus the discounts. The Court ruled that Elida Gibbs had the right to deduct the provided discounts from the original prices. Also, in cases where money-off coupons are distributed, the taxable amount must be established on the original supplier's price minus the discount indicated on the coupon and refunded. In cases of cash-back coupons, that taxable amount is also the original supplier's price minus the amount of

126. The gift voucher, gift card and stored value solutions market is big business in the UK. *See* http://www.gcva.co.uk/ (accessed 17 August 2024).
127. CJEU 24 October 1996, Case C-288/94 *Argos Distributors Ltd v Commissioners of Customs and Excise*, ECLI:EU:C:1996:398.
128. CJEU 24 October 1996, Case C-317/94 *Elida Gibbs Ltd v Commissioners of Customs and Excise,* ECLI:EU:C:1996:400.

discount indicated on the coupon and the amounts actually refunded by the wholesaler. According to the Court, this interpretation necessarily followed from the principle that the taxable amount serving as a basis for the VAT to be collected by the tax authorities cannot exceed the consideration actually paid by the final consumer which is the basis for calculating the VAT ultimately borne by him and from the principle of neutrality of the tax whereby within each country similar goods should bear the same tax burden whatever the length of the production and distribution chain. Furthermore, the Court considered that the VAT system is not disturbed as a result of that interpretation since there is no need to readjust the taxable amount for the intermediate transactions. That amount remains unchanged since, for those transactions, observance of the principle of neutrality is ensured by application of the conditions for deduction set out in the Directive, which enable the intermediate links in the distribution chain, such as wholesalers and retailers, to pay to the tax authorities only the part of the VAT representing the difference between the price paid by each to his supplier and the price at which he supplied the goods to his purchaser.

6.14 TRANSFER PRICING AND VAT[129]

A recurrent topic of debate concerns the effects of transfer pricing adjustments for direct tax purposes on the taxable amount for VAT. In 2017, the VAT Committee published a working paper on the possible VAT effects of transfer pricing adjustments.[130] Also, in literature, the topic has gained quite some attention.[131] Key questions are whether transfer pricing adjustments lead to (retroactive) adjustments to the taxable amounts for VAT of supplies made throughout the year? If any retroactive adjustments need to be made to the taxable amounts for VAT, what are the implications for the VAT returns, EC Sales lists and interests? What if a year-end adjustment does not lead to an adjustment of the taxable amount for VAT? Can intercompany payments (which follow from year-end adjustments) then be regarded as the remuneration for any service rendered? Or are year-end adjustments merely to be regarded as financial transactions outside the scope of EU VAT after all?

In our view, transfer pricing adjustments at the initiative of the tax authorities that take place after the tax returns have been filed (ex post), often referred to as

129. R. van den Brekel, A.J. van Doesum & H.W.M. van Kesteren, *VAT Effects of Year-End Transfer Pricing Adjustments* (2017) 4 EC Tax Review, pp. 182-192 https://doi.org/10.54648/ecta2017020.

130. Value Added Tax Committee, 28 February 2017, Working Paper 923, Possible VAT Implications of Transfer Pricing, taxud.c.1 (2016) 1280928 – EN.

131. *See, e.g.*: I. Rouberol, *Interactions Between Transfer Pricing and VAT Adjustments in the European Union* (2016) 9(10) International VAT Monitor, pp. 316-319 https://doi.org/10.59403/nyqq8p and M. Schippers, *BEPS and Transfer Pricing but What About VAT and Customs?* (2016) 3 EC Tax Review, pp. 174-179 https://doi.org/10.54648/ecta2016018 and R. van den Brekel, A.J. van Doesum & H.W.M. van Kesteren, *VAT Effects of Year-End Transfer Pricing Adjustments* (2017) 4 EC Tax Review, pp. 182-192 https://doi.org/10.54648/ecta2017020.

'primary transfer pricing adjustments' generally do not have VAT implications. The same applies to so-called Corresponding Transfer Pricing Adjustments.[132] Also, Secondary Transactions and Secondary Adjustments generally do not attract VAT.[133]

Compensating adjustments[134] often in the form of so-called year-end adjustments[135] may, but do not necessarily have VAT effects. Year-end adjustments can be carried out in various manners. They can be made through book-entry adjustments but may also be made by paying/receiving service fees (e.g., a 'marketing fee') or by actually adjusting the prices of previous supplies. Often, year-end adjustments are made by issuing debit or credit notes.[136]

Year-end adjustments may have VAT effects if the transfer pricing adjustments are not exclusively made in the tax accounts but are also reflected in the commercial books. However, identifying a legal relationship between the related parties and determining a direct link between the price adjustments and either previous supplies or (marketing) services is key to establish any VAT effects. Furthermore, in order for a year-end adjustment to trigger VAT, it must be established that one party provided an identifiable benefit to the other (related) party. It may be a complex affair to establish any direct link between adjustment payments and the (potentially diverse) goods and services which were supplied in previous phases. If indeed a year-end adjustment passes above tests and indeed has VAT effects, it can have considerable (administrative) implications for the parties involved. For example, changing the taxable amount for VAT retroactively requires the parties involved to adjust their VAT and statistical filings (VAT returns, EC Sales Lists, Intrastat reports), and raises complex questions as regards the adjustment of deductions and unduly charged VAT (cf. Article 203 VAT

132. Corresponding Transfer Pricing Adjustments are adjustments to the tax liability of the related party enterprise in a second tax jurisdiction made by the tax administration of that second jurisdiction, corresponding to a primary adjustment made by the tax administration in the first tax jurisdiction (applying the primary adjustment), so that the allocation of profits by the two jurisdictions is consistent. *See*: R. van den Brekel, A.J. van Doesum & H.W.M. van Kesteren, *VAT Effects of Year-End Transfer Pricing Adjustments* (2017) 4 EC Tax Review, pp. 182-192 https://doi.org/10.54648/ecta2017020.
133. A secondary adjustment is an adjustment that arises from imposing tax on a secondary transaction, such as levying dividend withholding tax on a deemed dividend. Asserting the existence of a constructive dividend, equity contribution or loan is referred to as a 'secondary transaction'. *See*: R. van den Brekel, A.J. van Doesum & H.W.M. van Kesteren, *VAT Effects of Year-End Transfer Pricing Adjustments* (2017) 4 EC Tax Review, pp. 182-192 https://doi.org/10.54648/ecta2017020.
134. A compensating adjustment is an adjustment to the transfer prices at the initiative of the taxable person. *See*: OECD Transfer Pricing Guidelines for Multinational Enterprises and Tax Administrations 25 (July 2010), Glossary.
135. Year-end adjustments are compensating adjustments made at the end of a year. *See* OECD Transfer Pricing Guidelines (July 2010), para. 3.71.
136. A. Bakker & B. Obuoforibo, *Transfer Pricing and Customs Valuation: Two Worlds to Tax as One* (Amsterdam: IBFD 2009). and Alain Charlet & David Holmes, *Determining the Place of Taxation of Transactions under VAT/GST: Can Transfer Pricing Principles Help?* (2010) 21(6) International VAT Monitor, p. 432.

Directive). Moreover, as regards upward adjustments from the perspective of the supplier, or downward adjustments from the perspective of the customer, we do not exclude the possibility that in some Member States, year-end adjustments ultimately hold the risk of VAT assessments, fines, and interest liability.

CHAPTER 7

Rates

7.1 INTRODUCTION

As with any tax, rates are an important feature of European VAT. Based on the taxable amount and the applicable VAT rate, the VAT amount chargeable and due can be calculated. The rules governing VAT rates are covered in Title VIII of the VAT Directive (Articles 93-129). Up until 1 January 1993, the Member States had the freedom to define the applicable VAT rates themselves. As a result of the abolition of the fiscal frontiers as of that date, the need for harmonization of VAT rates increased, as differences in rates between Member States can incentivize shopping in low-rate Member States. This is especially true for an origin-based VAT system. However, although the Sixth Directive and subsequently the VAT Directive have put some boundaries as to the minimum standard rate (15%) and the application of reduced rates, as of yet Member States have not been able to harmonize VAT rates in any substantial way (*see* section 7.2). However, as a result of the increasing shift to application of the destination principle in B2C transactions (among other things:

distance selling rules in Article 33 VAT Directive, *see* Chapter 4, sections 4.4.3.2 and 4.4.3.3 and the place of supply rules for electronically supplied services, telecommunication, radio and television broadcasting services, *see* Chapter 4, section 4.5.4.2.10), the need for rate harmonization has diminished. This has even led to an adjustment of the VAT Directive that entered into force in 2022 that provides some more flexibility for Member States to determine and change the VAT rates they apply to different products.[1] The rules enable the Member States, in addition to the two reduced rates of a minimum of 5% and an exemption with deductibility of the VAT paid at the preceding stage currently allowed, to apply another super reduced rate between 5% and 0%. Member States may apply the reduced rates (of a minimum of 5%) to supplies of goods or services covered in a maximum of 24 points in Annex III. The super reduced rate lower than the minimum of 5% and the exemption with deductibility of the VAT paid at the preceding stage may only be applied to supplies of goods or services covered in specific points of Annex III (e.g., foodstuffs, books). Also, Article 98, second paragraph, sub b stipulates that Member States that applied on 1 January 2021 reduced rates lower than the minimum of 5% or were granting exemptions with a right to deduct the VAT paid at the preceding stage to supplies of goods or services covered in *more* than seven points in Annex III will have to limit the application of those reduced rates or the granting of those exemptions by 1 January 2032 or by the adoption of the definitive arrangements referred to in Article 402 (i.e., the introduction of an origin-based VAT system, which requires some form of rate harmonization), whichever is the earlier.

7.2 HARMONIZATION OF VAT RATES

7.2.1 The Need for Harmonization

An origin-based VAT system that suits the purposes of the internal market requires VAT rate harmonization in order to not distort competition. Consequently, it can be seen as surprising that the changes to the VAT rate structure in 2022 – although they did not go so far as originally proposed[2] – give Member States more possibilities to deviate from one another in the application of reduced rates. Indeed, some have argued that giving more discretion in rate policy to the Member States is in effect de-harmonizing and as such in breach of Article 113 TFEU.[3] Although the change was justified by arguing that in a VAT system that is increasingly based on the destination principle, the need for rate harmonization is vastly diminished, we are of the view that the change is unfortunate both from the (historical) context of EU VAT harmonization (*see* section 7.2.2) and from the perspective of a broadly accepted view of experts on

1. Council Directive (EU) 2022/542 of 5 April 2022 amending Directives 2006/112/EC and (EU) 2020/285 as regards rates of value added tax, OJ L 107, 6.4.2022, pp. 1-12.
2. *See* Proposal for a COUNCIL DIRECTIVE amending Directive 2006/112/EC as regards rates of value added tax, COM(2018)20.
3. R. de la Feria & M. Schofield, *Towards an [Unlawful] Modernized EU VAT Rate Policy* (2017) EC Tax Review 2, pp. 89-95 https://doi.org/10.54648/ecta2017010.

the ineffectiveness and compliance burden attributed to the application of (multiple) reduced rates (*see* section 7.2.3).

7.2.2 History of Rate Harmonization

In 1963, before the introduction of the Sixth VAT Directive, the European Commission released a report on the various possibilities for the harmonization of turnover taxes. The report discussed the difference in tax rates between the Member States. The Commission pointed out that a difference in tax rates would affect the principle of equal conditions of competition between the Member States. To avoid such distortions, the Commission emphasized that the turnover tax should be levied at equal rates.[4]

In 1986, various Member States signed the Single European Act, established to provide a further economic integration and to encourage political cooperation.[5] This Single European Act made reference to the creation of the European internal market as of the end of 1992. Following the preamble of the VAT rate Directive, abolition of fiscal controls at the frontiers was required as a first step to complete the internal market. To avoid distortion, the abolition of these fiscal controls also implies that the number of rates and rate levels are sufficiently close.

The VAT rate Directive, therefore, amended the Sixth VAT Directive on certain points in 1992. Among others, a minimal standard rate of 15% was introduced, and the number of reduced rates was limited to a maximum of two. Also, Annex H was attached to the Sixth VAT Directive (currently Annex III to the VAT Directive), including a limited list of goods and services on which the reduced rate could be applied.

On 1 December 2010, the European Commission released its Green Paper on the future of VAT.[6] This Green Paper invited all interested parties to provide their response to some questions raised in respect of the future of VAT. According to the general conclusions in this Green Paper, the difference in VAT rates leads to additional compliance costs. The use of reduced rates is an obstacle to the proper functioning of the internal market. It is furthermore open to the question of whether the use of reduced rates is the most suitable instrument to pursue policy objectives, such as the redistribution of income.

Reduced rates make the EU VAT system more complex, thereby increasing administrative and compliance costs. On the other hand, the application of reduced rates distorts households' spending patterns and can give rise to economically inefficient outcomes, when the choice of consumers is driven by tax rather than commercial considerations. This evaluation also indicated that reducing the dissimilarity of the

---

4. The EEC reports on Tax Harmonization, The Report of The Fiscal and Financial Committee and the Reports of The Sub-Groups A, B and C (Amsterdam, International Bureau of Fiscal Documentation, 1963).
5. Single European Act [1987] OJ L169/1.
6. Green Paper On the future of VAT. 'Towards a simpler, more robust and efficient VAT system'. COM (2010) 695 final, 1 December 2010.

VAT rates structure between the Member States by 50 % could increase the trade within the EU by 9.8 %, leading to an increased Gross Domestic Product of 0.7 %.

Following the aforementioned Green Paper, in December 2011, the European Commission released a Communication on the future of VAT, with the aim of increasing the efficiency of the VAT system. The Communication discussed the fundamental features of the VAT system and defined the priority areas for further action in the coming years.[7] One of the priority actions was a review of the current VAT rates structure. The Commission put forward the following guiding principles for this review:

(1) Abolition of those reduced rates, which constitute an obstacle to the proper functioning of the internal market. Reduced rates justified in the past can have distorting effects today because the economic, business and legal environments have changed in the meantime.
(2) Abolition of reduced rates on goods and services whose consumption is discouraged by other EU policies. Examples of such goods and services are those which are harmful to the environment, health and welfare.
(3) Similar goods and services should be subject to the same VAT rate, and progress in technology should be taken into account in this respect so that the challenge of convergence between the online and the physical environment is addressed.

On 8 October 2012, the Commission opened a public consultation, seeking the opinions of stakeholders. On 29 April 2013, the summary report of this consultation was published.[8] Most inputs were provided by national or European associations, a large majority of them representing sectors currently benefiting from reduced VAT rates and opposed to their abolition or advocating their extension. These responses do not necessarily fit with the above-mentioned three guiding principles of the Commission but do underline the sensitivity of a review, and potentially modernization, of the current VAT rate structure. According to the Commission, the input provided by the stakeholders will be an important part of the assessment process of the VAT rates structure.

7.2.3 Expert Views on VAT Rate Policy

Various Member States have also commissioned tax experts to perform a study on the position of VAT within their tax system. In the UK, the Institute for Fiscal Studies has

7. Communication from the Commission to the Parliament, Council and the European Economic and Social Committee on the future of VAT. 'Towards a simpler, more robust and efficient VAT system tailored to the single market.' COM (2011) 851 final, 6 December 2011.
8. European Commission, Summary report of the outcome of the public consultation on the review of existing legislation on VAT reduced rates (8 October 2012-4 January 2013).

presented the Mirrlees Review,[9] containing an analysis of the UK tax system. The Review was published in September 2011 and also addresses the impact of VAT. Pursuant to this Review, there are better instruments to redistribute income than the use of reduced rates (on, for example, food and children's clothing). The Review also emphasizes the administration and compliance burden when using different rates. When reforming the current tax system, the Review suggests removing the zero rate and reduced rates and applying the standard rate to a wider range of goods. Poor households could be compensated for their losses by the government, while the revenue of the government would still increase. A similar study has been published in the Netherlands.[10] In the area of VAT, the Dutch committee also suggests the introduction of a uniform VAT rate and increasing the share of VAT in the total amount of tax revenue.

However, as *De La Feria* and *Walpole* point out, regardless of the fact that (1) applying more than one rate of VAT gives rise to significant legal difficulties, creates economic distortions, and it (2) is at best unclear whether it actually has the social and distributional effects that it aims to achieve, from a political and policy point of view, the allure of introducing and applying reduced rates proves hard to resist.[11] The 2022 changes to the VAT rate structure in the VAT Directive seem a perfect case in point.[12] Although there are many political and practical issues attached to the introduction of a uniform VAT rate, we feel the benefits have been sufficiently demonstrated. On balance, we, therefore, advocate the introduction of a uniform and ideally harmonized VAT rate. As indicated in section 7.1, the 2022 adjustment of the VAT rate structure in the VAT Directive is – unfortunately – a move in the opposite direction.

7.3 STANDARD RATE

Following Article 96 VAT Directive, Member States shall apply a standard rate of VAT, which shall be fixed by each Member State as a percentage of the taxable amount. The standard rate shall be the same for the supply of goods and for the supply of services. This reflects the fact that European VAT is a general tax on consumption, which should cover all stages of production and distribution of goods as well as services in the most general manner as possible. In order to achieve fiscal neutrality between goods that are supplied locally and goods that are acquired from the other EU Member States or

9. Sir J. Mirrlees, et al., *Dimensions of Tax Design, The Mirrlees Review* (Oxford University Press 2010).
10. Studiecommissie Belastingstelsel, led by S. van Weeghel, 'Continuïteit en vernieuwing: Een visie op het belastingstelsel' (2010) https://www.tweedekamer.nl/kamerstukken/detail/detail?id=2010D17436&did=2010D17436 (accessed 27 November 2024).
11. R. de la Feria & M. Walpole, *The Impact of Public Perceptions on General Consumption Taxes* (2020) 67/5 British Tax Review, pp. 637-669.
12. Also *see:* M. Merkx et al., *The EU Council's New Agreement on VAT Rates Is a Poisonous Gift to Member States, Citizens, and Businesses* (2021) 104 Tax Notes International, p. 1337. https://www.taxnotes.com/tax-notes-international/value-added-tax/eu-councils-new-agreement-vat-rates-poisonous-gift-member-states-citizens-and-businesses/2021/12/20/7cpjq (accessed 17 August 2024).

imported from non-EU countries, the standard rate also applies to ICAs[13] and imports of goods.[14] In this way, for example, it makes no difference for a German hospital, which cannot or can only partly deduct input VAT,[15] whether it purchases medical equipment in Germany or from elsewhere in the EU. In any case, the German standard VAT rate applies.

According to Article 97 VAT Directive, the standard rate may not be less than 15.

The VAT Directive does not specify a maximum value for the standard rate, although in view of the harmonization of VAT rates, to do so would appear logical. Apparently, Member States could not formally agree on a maximum rate. A gentlemen's agreement, however, exists on the basis of which Member States should not introduce a standard VAT rate higher than 25%. Except for Hungary, which introduced a rate of 27% as of 1 January 2012, up until now, all Member States have respected the agreement. The Taxes of Europe Database (TEDB) can be used to find a VAT rate applied by the Member States on specific products.[16] The information in the database is provided and kept up to date by the Member States.

As a general trend VAT rates tend to increase. Increasing the standard VAT rate has proved to be an effective way of generating additional government income especially in times of budgetary constraints, such as the 2008 economic and financial crisis and the COVID pandemic. The way VAT is administered and collected makes it a quick and economical means of generating cash, compared to other taxes. Also, the option to swiftly adapt and change the rate makes VAT a very flexible fiscal tool. However, a decrease of the VAT rate in times of economic prosperity proves to be much less popular with governments.

7.4 REDUCED RATES

7.4.1 Rationale Behind Reduced Rates

Under the Second VAT Directive, it was left up to the Member States to decide upon the supplies of goods and services to which they would apply a reduced rate. From the preamble of the Second VAT Directive, it can be derived that the application of reduced rates was allowed for social and economic reasons. The Sixth VAT Directive initially also left it up to the Member States to determine the supplies of goods and services to which a reduced rate could be applied. On 19 October 1992, the Member States decided to amend the Sixth VAT Directive and to include a limited list of goods and services to which the reduced rate could be applied. In the VAT Directive, this list is included in Annex III. Typical goods and services that may be subjected to a reduced rate include food and beverages, pharmaceutical products, books, admission to cultural amenities, hotel accommodation, restaurant and catering services and use of sporting facilities.

---

13. Article 94(1) VAT Directive.
14. Article 94(2) VAT Directive.
15. *See* Article 132(1)(b) VAT Directive and Chapter 8.
16. https://ec.europa.eu/taxation_customs/tedb/#/home (accessed 27 August 2024).

Although European VAT lacks an extensive legislative history, generally speaking, the reasons for the introduction of reduced rates are similar to those for applying for VAT exemptions without a right to recover VAT. Basically, the introduction of a reduced rate will be based on one of the following grounds:

- easing the VAT burden on people with a low income;
- supporting social and cultural causes;
- human suffering;
- fiscal, technical reasons;
- economic reasons; or
- environmental reasons.

Easing the VAT burden on people with a low income is sometimes regarded as an indication that European VAT is a tax that is based on the ability to pay principle. The concept of that principle implies that all people should support the state's finances on the basis of their financial position: people with a higher income should pay more taxes than people with a lower income. Even a VAT with reduced rates, however, has a regressive effect. People with a low income will still encounter an absolute tax burden due to VAT paid in relation to their consumption. Moreover, VAT will be regressive for the remainder of the people, who, in percentage terms, will consume less of their income as their income increases. In our view, the existence of reduced rates is no indication that European VAT is based on the ability to pay principle, especially as no reference to this end can be found in preparatory documents of the European Commission or in final legislative documents. Nevertheless, the reduced rates decreases the regressive effect of the tax. However, in order to really strengthen the progression in European VAT for people with a low income, a tax credit via the personal income tax or an increase in transfer payments would be preferable to reduced rates.[17] As the Commission indicated, from an economic point of view, reduced VAT rates do have an income distribution effect, but alternative instruments, such as direct subsidies or incentives, are considered to be more targeted and, therefore, more efficient.[18]

The TEDB can be used to find a VAT rate applied by the Member States on specific products.[19] The information in the database is provided and kept up to date by the Member States.

17. In this respect, *see also* B. Terra & J. Kajus, *Commentary: A Guide to the Recast VAT Directive* (IBFD 2019), section 8.4.4. Available online at: https://research.ibfd.org/#/doc?url=/collections/evdcom/html/evdcom_recast_chap08.html (accessed 27 August 2024 – please note that this is a password-restricted website).
18. European Commission, Summary report of the outcome of the public consultation on the review of existing legislation on VAT reduced rates (8 October 2012-4 January 2013), p. 5.
19. https://ec.europa.eu/taxation_customs/tedb/#/home (accessed 27 August 2024).

7.4.2 Supplies to Which a Reduced Rate Can Be Applied

Since 2022, Member States may apply two reduced rates (of a minimum of 5%) to supplies of goods or services covered in a maximum of 24 points in Annex III. They may also apply a super reduced rate lower than the minimum of 5% and an exemption with deductibility of the VAT paid at the preceding stage, although those may only be applied to supplies of goods or services covered in specific points of Annex III (e.g., foodstuffs, books). By means of a transitional rule, Article 98, second paragraph, sub b stipulates that Member States that applied on 1 January 2021 reduced rates lower than the minimum of 5% or were granting exemptions with a right to deduct the VAT paid at the preceding stage to supplies of goods or services covered in *more* than seven points in Annex III will have to limit the application of those reduced rates or the granting of those exemptions by 1 January 2032 or by the adoption of the definitive arrangements referred to in Article 402 (i.e., the introduction of an origin-based VAT system, which requires some form of rate harmonization), whichever is the earlier. In the *European Commission v French Republic*, the European Commission questioned whether the application of both a reduced rate and a standard rate on the supply of services by undertakers infringed Article 98(1) VAT Directive. According to the European Commission, the artificial separation of the service of transporting the body by vehicle (subject to the reduced French rate) from the whole supply of services by undertakers (further subject to the standard rate) led to an effective rate of taxation corresponding to an average rate that was lower than the standard French rate. The CJEU mentioned that exceptions, such as the application of a reduced rate, should be interpreted strictly. The CJEU presents a twofold condition. First, for the purposes of the application of the reduced rate, the supply at issue should constitute a concrete and specific aspect of that category of supply, as set out in Annex III to the VAT Directive. Second, the application of the reduced rate should comply with the principles of fiscal neutrality. Since both conditions were met, the French government could apply a reduced rate to the service of transporting the body by a vehicle while applying a standard rate to the remaining part of the supply of undertakers.[20]

As of 1 January 2010, electronically supplied services (as mentioned in Article 56(1)(k) VAT Directive) are explicitly excluded from the application of a reduced rate.

Annex III covers a wide range of supplies of goods and services that may benefit from a reduced rate. This Annex, among others, provides the application of a reduced rate on foodstuffs, medical equipment, admission to shows and theatres and admission to sporting events. Most cases of the CJEU referring to the application of the reduced rates concern challenges by the European Commission, especially the interpretation of the goods and services listed in Annex III are subject of discussion. For example, in *European Commission v Kingdom of the Netherlands*, it was questioned whether the Netherlands was allowed to apply a reduced rate on the supply of horses if these horses were not intended for preparation of foodstuffs for human and animal consumption (as indicated in point 1 of Annex III). The CJEU decided that, within the EU, horses are not

20. CJEU 6 May 2010, Case C-94/09 *European Commission v French Republic*, ECLI:EU:C:2010:253.

normally intended for consumption. Only if a horse is supplied for slaughter, in order to be used in the preparation of foodstuffs, may it be subject to the reduced rate.[21]

On the basis of Article 100 VAT Directive, the Council may, in accordance with Article 93 of the EC Treaty, decide to alter the list of goods and services set out in Annex III. The last time the Annex was amended was by means of Directive 2009/47/EC.[22] Pursuant to the preamble of this Directive, it may be justified to exclude the supply of alcoholic and/or non-alcoholic beverages when applying the reduced rate to the supply of restaurant and catering services. This exclusion was included in point 12a of Annex III. The application of reduced rates for certain social and health reasons was also included, as well as a clarification and update to technical progress of the reference to books.

Although most provisions in the VAT Directive concern concepts of Union law, there sometimes may be scope for different interpretations by the Member States. To that end, the VAT Regulation[23] contains common provisions for implementing and interpretation of the VAT Directive. According to the preamble of the Regulation, it should be ensured that the application of the VAT system complies more fully with the objective of the internal market. The VAT Regulation primarily not only focuses on the place of supply rules but also clarifies the application of the reduced rate in one specific case. According to Article 43 VAT Regulation, the 'provision of holiday accommodation', as referred to in Annex III to the VAT Directive, also includes the hiring out of tents, caravans or mobile homes installed on camping sites and used as accommodation. From paragraph 31 of the preamble to the VAT Regulation, we take that it apparently was felt necessary to clarify this point.

In 2018, the VAT Directive was amended in order to allow for the application of the reduced rate to e-books and other electronically supplied publications, in order to align VAT rates for electronically supplied publications with lower VAT rates for publications that are supplied on physical means of support.[24]

An important issue when dealing with VAT rates is the question of whether the activities at hand for VAT purposes constitute a single (composite) supply or separate supplies. Especially in the case of customers that are private individuals or VAT-exempt taxable persons, the question arises whether activities on a stand-alone basis that would be subject to the standard VAT rate could also benefit from a reduced rate that is applicable to the other activities that are carried out. Such questions should be addressed on the basis of the general principles that the CJEU has laid down in cases,

21. CJEU 3 March 2011, Case C-41/09 *European Commission v Kingdom of the Netherlands*, ECLI:EU:C:2011:108.
22. Council Directive 2009/47/EC of 5 May 2009 amending Directive 2006/112/EC as regards reduced rates of value added tax [2009] OJ L116/18.
23. Council Implementing Regulation (EU) No 282/2011 of 15 March 2011 laying down implementing measures for Directive 2006/112/EC on the common system of value added tax [2011] OJ L77/1.
24. Council Directive (EU) 2018/1713 of 6 November 2018 amending Directive 2006/112/EC as regards rates of value added tax applied to books, newspapers and periodicals.

such as *Madgett & Baldwin*, *Card Protection Plan* and *Aktiebolaget NN*.[25] We refer to section 3.5, where this case law is discussed extensively. Here, however, we would like to point out that on the basis of *Stadion Amsterdam*, in cases of a single supply that consists of two elements that supplied in itself would have a different VAT rate, only one of the VAT rates should be applied.[26] *Talacre Beach Caravan Sales Ltd* can be seen as an exception that confirms this general rule.[27] The case relates to the applicable VAT rate on a supply consisting of a caravan, including its contents. Although the specific goods were considered to be part of a single supply, VAT was levied at two different rates. The CJEU indicated that the zero rate, applicable to the supply of the caravan, was based on the 'old' VAT Act of the United Kingdom, from before 1 January 1991. Since the application of the zero rate derogates from the general principles of VAT, it should be interpreted strictly. Therefore, the UK was allowed to levy VAT at a standard rate on the supply of the contents of the caravan, even though the caravan and its contents were considered as a single supply.

7.4.3 Special Provisions on Reduced Rates

Besides the reduced rates for supplies of goods and services, as set out in its Annex III, the VAT Directive provides for some special provisions to apply a reduced rate. When the Council adopted the VAT rate Directive in 1992, it was considered that, during the transitional period, certain derogations concerning the number and level of rates should be possible. Based on these derogations, some exceptions to Articles 98-101 VAT Directive were agreed upon. The initial intention was that the transitional period would ultimately end on 31 December 1996. Currently, the transitional regime is still in place, and it will not be replaced by a final regime in the foreseeable future. Therefore, the Member States may still apply special reduced rates to certain supplies of goods and services.

Article 103 VAT Directive provides for a reduced rate on the importation of certain works of art, collectors' items and antiques, while Articles 104 and 105 allow Austria, Greece and Portugal to use, in certain regions, rates which are different from the 'normal' standard and reduced rate.

Article 105a and b provide for transitional rules for Member States that applied reduced rates on 1 January 2021, in line with EU law but not in line with the 2022 adjustment to the VAT rate structure.

---

25. CJEU 25 February 1999, Case C-349/96 *Card Protection Plan Ltd v Commissioners of Customs & Excise*, ECLI:EU:C:1999:93 and CJEU 29 March 2007, Case C-111/05 *Aktiebolaget NN v Skatteverket*, ECLI:EU:C:2007:195.
26. CJEU 18 January 2018, Case C-463/16 *Stadion Amsterdam CV v Staatssecretaris van Financiën*, ECLI:EU:C:2018:22.
27. *Talacre Beach* (CJEU 6 July 2006), Case C-251/05 *Talacre Beach Caravan Sales Ltd v Commissioners of Customs & Excise*, ECLI:EU:C:2006:451. Also *see*: CJEU 3 April 2008, Case C-442/05 *Finanzamt Oschatz v Zweckverband zur Trinkwasserversorgung und Abwasserbeseitigung Torgau-Westelbien*, ECLI:EU:C:2008:184 and CJEU 6 May 2010, Case C-94/09 *European Commission v French Republic*, ECLI:EU:C:2010:253.

Article 129a is a temporary provision, allowing Member States to apply a reduced rate or grant an exemption with a right to deduct input VAT in respect of the supply of COVID-19 in vitro diagnostic medical devices and services closely linked to those devices.

7.4.4 Labour-Intensive Services

Member States are allowed to apply a reduced rate to particular labour-intensive services.[28] This reduced rate can be applied to hairdressing and cleaning of private households, among other activities. The reduced rate was introduced in 1999, with the intention to lower unemployment and to reduce the incentive for businesses to join or remain in the informal economy. To avoid a possible negative impact on the internal market and tax neutrality, the reduced rate on labour-intensive services was strictly limited to a list of services, and to a certain period of time.[29]

The Communication on VAT rates other than standard VAT rates which the Commission presented to the European Parliament and the Council in 2007 concluded that the application of reduced VAT rates to locally supplied services is of no concern for the functioning of the internal market and may, under certain conditions, have positive effects in terms of job creation and of combating the informal economy.[30] In view thereof, the possibility to apply a reduced rate to particular labour-intensive services has been relieved of its temporary character. Following Directive 2009/47/EC,[31] the labour-intensive services have been added to Annex III to the VAT Directive, now consisting of all supplies for which the Member States can introduce a (normal) reduced rate. As studies have failed to unequivocally demonstrate the effectiveness of the reduced rate for labour-intensive services with respect to either job creation or combating the informal economy, we feel that there is insufficient ground to maintain this specific reduced rate. From a political point of view, however, there currently seems to be no incentive to abolish it.

7.5 ZERO RATE OR EXEMPTION WITH CREDIT

Besides a standard rate and reduced rates, Member States may also apply for exemptions with deduction of input VAT to certain supplies of goods and services. These exemptions are also referred to as exemptions with credit. In practice, these exemptions function as a zero rate: 0% VAT is charged on the supplies, whereas input VAT in respect of these supplies can be deducted. Although technically incorrect, the

28. *See* points 10a, 10b, 19, 20 and 21 of Annex III to the VAT Directive.
29. Council Directive 1999/85/EC of 22 October 1999 amending Directive 77/388/EEC as regards the possibility of applying on an experiment basis a reduced VAT rate on labour-intensive services [1999] OJ, L277/34.
30. Communication from the Commission to the Council and the European Parliament on VAT rates other than standard VAT rates, COM (2007) 380 final, 5 July 2007, https://eur-lex.europa.eu/legal-content/EN/TXT/?uri=CELEX:52007DC0380 (accessed 28 January 2025).
31. Council Directive 2009/47/EC of 5 May 2009 amending Directive 2006/112/EC as regards reduced rates of value added tax [2009] OJ L116/18.

exemptions with deduction of input VAT in some Member States are also addressed as zero rates. Typical examples of exemptions with credit are those applied to ICSs of goods to the other Member States and to supplies of goods to non-EU countries.[32]

The exemptions with credit (Articles 138-166 VAT Directive) differ importantly from the exemptions without credit (Articles 132-137 VAT Directive). For example, if a taxable person makes an ICS, in which context the goods are transported to a taxable person in another Member State, he is not only allowed to apply an exemption ('zero rate'), but he can also deduct the input VAT on costs relating to this supply. When the same taxable person is providing a service as mentioned in Article 132 VAT Directive, he is, however, allowed to apply an exemption to his supply, but he cannot recover the input VAT on costs relating to the supply. Although the outputs are also exempt in the latter case, the inputs, in fact, lead to a tax burden for the taxable person. Clearly, an exemption without credit cannot be compared with a zero rate. We refer to Chapter 8 in which the exemptions are discussed in more detail.

32. *See* Chapters 12 and 13.

CHAPTER 8

Exemptions

8.1 INTRODUCTION

The effect of VAT exemptions is that suppliers do not have to charge VAT on supplies to their customers. The VAT Directive identifies several categories of VAT exemptions. The main distinction, however, is between exemptions without the right to deduct input VAT, and those with this right. The first category of exemptions exists for various reasons. The relevant supplies are exempt because they are (supposed to be) in the public interest (like medical care, education, sports), or are by nature difficult to tax (financial services), or relate to immovable property, the 'consumption' of which is stretched over longer periods of time (sale of immovable property). The second category of exemptions (with a right to deduct) generally relates to cross-border transactions (intra-Community supplies (ICSs) and export supplies).

The exemptions in the first category, those without the right to deduct input VAT, are laid down in Articles 132-137 VAT Directive. Following Article 168 VAT Directive, no input VAT can be deducted for supplies subject to those exemptions. The basic concept behind the exemptions without the right to deduct input VAT is to ensure that the prices of exempt supplies for consumers should be kept as low as possible, and should not be increased by VAT. Where an exemption applies in the final stage of a supply chain (supplier–final consumer), this aim is achieved. Under those circumstances, no VAT is due on this supply and therefore, the total price of the supply is lower for the final consumer. However, under some circumstances, the application of an exemption earlier in the supply chain than in the final stage may lead to tax cascading. This effect materializes as the party making the exempt supply incorporates his non-deductible input VAT in his selling price of supplies to a party that can deduct input VAT. This next party, whose activity is not exempt, has no right to deduct the hidden VAT incurred, and charges VAT on the value of his supplies, thus including the hidden input VAT that he has incurred as part of his purchases. For this reason, and because exemptions are exceptions to the main rule that principally all supplies are taxed with VAT, the CJEU has ruled consistently that exemptions must be interpreted strictly.[1]

Exemptions in the second category, those with the right to deduct input VAT, are laid down in Articles 138-166 VAT Directive. In practice, these exemptions are often referred to as zero rates, although technically, they are exemptions and not rates. The most important exemptions in this category relate to intra-Community supplies of goods (supplies of goods from one Member State to another, i.e., ICSs) and exports of goods (supplies of goods from a Member State to a third country). Suppliers making exempt supplies of this kind are entitled to deduct all input VAT on their purchases on the basis of Article 169(b) VAT Directive. Tax cascading does not occur with the second category of exemptions.

8.2 APPLICATION AND INTERPRETATION OF EXEMPTIONS

Within a consumption tax, exemptions may be designed either with an objective character (exempting transactions) or with a subjective character (exempting persons). In order to achieve neutrality as regards the way consumption is taxed, objective exemptions are to be preferred to subjective ones. After all, similar consumption should be treated equally, regardless of the identity of the party making the supply, which leads to that consumption. The exemptions in the VAT Directive generally have an objective nature, although occasionally, the qualifications of the supplier are relevant for the application of the exemption. Mostly, the objective pursued by the exemption dictates such a legislative approach. That is the case, for example, for the exemption for medical care. As the objective is to ensure that the exemption applies solely to services provided by persons with the appropriate professional medical qualification, the status of the supplier is made relevant.[2] The exemptions with a right to deduct input VAT are generally more objective than those without a right of deduction. That is because their background is more objective and can primarily be found in the destination principle and the intention not to tax international trade.

As with all legal provisions, the VAT exemptions laid down in Articles 132-137 VAT Directive require interpretation. On the basis of settled case law, the exemptions without a right to deduction have their own independent meaning in Union law, and

1. For example: CJEU 15 June 1989, Case 348/87 *Stichting Uitvoering Financiële Acties v Staatssecretaris van Financiën*, ECLI:EU:C:1989:246 and more recently, CJEU 26 May 2016, Case C-607/14 *Bookit, Ltd v Commissioners for Her Majesty's Revenue and Customs*, ECLI:EU:C:2016:355.
2. *See* CJEU 27 April 2006, Cases C-443/04 and C-444/04 *H.A. Solleveld and J.E. van den Hout-van Eijnsbergen v Staatssecretaris van Financiën*, ECLI:EU:C:2006:257.

they must, therefore, be given a Union definition.[3] Although Article 131 VAT Directive states that the Member States are to lay down the conditions for exemptions in order to ensure the correct and straightforward application of the exemptions and to prevent any possible evasion, avoidance or abuse, those conditions cannot affect the definition of the subject matter of the exemptions envisaged.[4] Given the pan-European nature of the VAT Directive, the answer to the question of whether a specific transaction is subject to or exempt from VAT cannot depend on its classification in national law.[5] Moreover, the need for uniform interpretation of Union law makes it impossible for the text of a provision, in case of doubt, to be considered in isolation. On the contrary, it requires that it be interpreted and applied in the light of the versions existing in the other official languages.[6]

According to established case law, the terms used to specify the exemptions without a right to deduct are to be interpreted strictly since they constitute exceptions to the general principle that VAT is to be levied on all goods and services supplied by a taxable person.[7] As a general consumption tax, European VAT should be levied as widely as possible. Therefore, exemptions should be interpreted strictly, and exceptions to these exemptions broadly.[8] However, the interpretation of the terms used in exemption provisions must be consistent with the objectives pursued by those exemptions and must comply with the requirements of the principle of fiscal neutrality inherent in a common system of VAT.[9] Thus, the requirement of strict interpretation does not mean that the terms used to specify the exemptions should be construed in

3. For example: CJEU 12 September 2000, Case C-358/97 *Commission of the European Communities v Ireland*, ECLI:EU:C:2000:425; CJEU 12 June 2003, Case C-275/01 *Sinclair Collis Ltd v Commissioners of Customs and Excise*, ECLI:EU:C:2003:341 and CJEU 18 November 2004, Case C-284/03 *Belgian State v Temco Europe SA*, ECLI:EU:C:2004:730.
4. CJEU 2002, Case C287/00 *Commission v Germany*, ECLI:EU:C:2002:388 and CJEU 26 May 2005, Case C-498/03 *Kingscrest Associates Ltd, Montecello Ltd v Commissioners of Customs and Excise*, ECLI:EU:C:2005:322.
5. CJEU 11 January 2001, Case C-76/99 *Commission of the European Communities v French Republic*, ECLI:EU:C:2001:12 and CJEU 16 January 2003, Case C-315/00 *Rudolf Maierhofer v Finanzamt Augsburg-Land*, ECLI:EU:C:2003:23.
6. CJEU 2 April 1998, Case C-296/95 *The Queen and Commissioners of Customs and Excise v EMU Tabac SARL, The Man in Black Ltd and John Cunningham*, ECLI:EU:C:1998:152; CJEU 17 June 1998, Case C-321/96 *Wilhelm Mecklenburg v Kreis Pinneberg – Der Landrat*, ECLI:EU:C:1998:300 and CJEU 26 May 2005, Case C-498/03 *Kingscrest Associates Ltd, Montecello Ltd v Commissioners of Customs and Excise*, ECLI:EU:C:2005:322.
7. *See*, for example, CJEU 15 June 1989, Case 348/87 *Stichting Uitvoering Financiële Acties v Staatssecretaris van Financiën*, ECLI:EU:C:1989:246 and more recently CJEU 26 May 2016, Case C-607/14 *Bookit, Ltd v Commissioners for Her Majesty's Revenue and Customs*, ECLI: EU:C:2016:355.
8. CJEU 26 June 2003, Case C-305/01 *Finanzamt Groß-Gerau v MKG-Kraftfahrzeuge-Factoring GmbH*, ECLI:EU:C:2003:377 and CJEU 28 October 2010, Case C-175/09 *Commissioners for Her Majesty's Revenue and Customs v AXA UK PLC*, ECLI:EU:C:2003:377.
9. CJEU 6 November 2003, Case C-45/01 *Christoph-Dornier-Stiftung für Klinische Psychologie v Finanzamt Gießen*, ECLI:EU:C:2003:595.

such a way as to deprive the exemptions of their intended effect.[10] From *Deutsche Bank*, it follows that the principle of fiscal neutrality cannot extend the scope of an exemption in the absence of clear wording to that effect. That principle is not a rule of primary law which can condition the validity of an exemption but is a principle of interpretation to be applied concurrently with the principle of strict interpretation of exemptions.[11] The CJEU has used the principle of fiscal neutrality in several cases to interpret exemptions. In *Fischer*, for example, the CJEU held that since unlawful transactions in the operation of a game of chance are in competition with lawful activities, the principle of fiscal neutrality precludes their being treated differently for VAT purposes.[12] Also, in *Gregg & Gregg*, the CJEU grounded its judgment that private persons can be regarded as 'organizations', as mentioned in Article 135(1)(g) VAT Directive on the principle of fiscal neutrality.[13]

The exemptions with a right to deduction are laid down in Articles 138-166 VAT Directive. Similar to the exemptions without a right to deduct input VAT, the exemptions with a right to deduct input VAT are exceptions to the general principle that VAT is to be levied on all goods and services supplied by a taxable person. From *Velker Oil*, *Cimber Air* and *A Oy*, for example, it follows that exemptions with a right to deduction also should be interpreted strictly.[14] However, the requirement of strict interpretation does not mean that the terms used to specify the exemptions should be construed in such a way as to deprive those exemptions of their intended effect.[15]

8.3 EXEMPTIONS FOR ACTIVITIES IN THE PUBLIC INTEREST

In this section, we will discuss the exemptions for activities 'in the public interest'.

10. For example: CJEU 14 June 2007, Case C-445/05 *Werner Haderer v Finanzamt Wilmersdorf*, ECLI:EU:C:2007:344; CJEU 11 December 2008, Case C-407/07 *Stichting Centraal Begeleidingsorgaan voor de Intercollegiale Toetsing v Staatssecretaris van Financiën*, ECLI:EU:C:2008:713 and CJEU 19 November 2009, Case C-461/08 *Don Bosco Onroerend Goed BV v Staatssecretaris van Financiën*, ECLI:EU:C:2009:722.
11. CJEU 19 July 2012, Case C-44/11 *Finanzamt Frankfurt am Main V-Höchst v Deutsche Bank AG*, ECLI:EU:C:2012:484.
12. CJEU 11 June 1998, Case C-283/95 *Karlheinz Fischer v Finanzamt Donaueschingen*, ECLI-:EU:C:1998:276. *See also* section 8.4.5.
13. CJEU 7 September 1999, Case C-216/97 *Jennifer Gregg and Mervyn Gregg v Commissioners of Customs and Excise*, ECLI:EU:C:1999:390. *See also* section 8.3.8.
14. CJEU 26 June 1990, Case C-185/89 *Staatssecretaris van Financiën v Velker Oil International Oil Company Ltd NV*, ECLI:EU:C:1990:262; CJEU 16 September 2004, Case C-382/02 *Cimber Air A/S v Skatteministeriet*, ECLI:EU:C:2004:534 and CJEU 19 July 2012, Case C-33/11 *A Oy*, ECLI: EU:C:2012:482. *See also* CJEU 3 September 2015, Case C-526/13 *Fast Bunkering Klaipėda UAB v Valstybinė mokesčių inspekcija prie Lietuvos Respublikos finansų ministerijos*, ECLI: EU:C:2015:536.
15. For example: CJEU 18 October 2007, Case C-97/06 *Navicon SA v Administración del Estado*, ECLI:EU:C:2007:609 and CJEU 19 July 2012, Case C-33/11 *A Oy*, ECLI:EU:C:2012:482.

8.3.1 General

Chapter 2 of Title IX of the VAT Directive deals with the exemptions for certain activities in the public interest. These are exemptions without the right to deduct input VAT. Certain activities in the public interest were considered so valuable to consumers that an exemption seemed in order. The exemptions are set out in Articles 132-134 VAT Directive and relate to various activities in the public interest, such as public postal services, medical care, education and sports. According to *Matthias Hoffmann*, the heading of Chapter 2 'Exemptions for certain activities in the public interest' does not entail a restriction to the possibilities of exemption, even not if the activities are provided primarily for commercial purposes.[16] Not every activity performed in the public interest is exempt, but only those which are listed and described in great detail.[17] The exemptions are thus defined by their wording in Articles 132-134 VAT Directive.

Pursuant to Article 131 VAT Directive, the exemptions shall apply without prejudice to other Union provisions and in accordance with conditions which the Member States shall lay down for the purposes of ensuring the correct and straightforward application of those exemptions, and of preventing any possible evasion, avoidance or abuse. Member States are thus not only given the opportunity to introduce conditions for a correct and straightforward application of the exemptions but are also specifically given the possibility to lay down conditions in order to prevent evasion, avoidance or abuse. Although the latter possibility generally is to be supported, a generic provision allowing the Member States so much legislative freedom is not in line with the Union law character of the exemptions. It is a step away from harmonization, which, especially in the field of the exemptions, should not be allowed, as the exemptions are exceptions to the general rule that all supplies of goods and services are taxed. According to *Commission v Germany* and *Kingscrest*, however, the freedom of Member States is more limited than might appear from the wording of Article 131 VAT Directive. The CJEU explicitly decided that the conditions the Member States may introduce must not affect the definition of the subject matter of the exemptions envisaged.[18] The risk of non-uniform application of the exemptions across the Member States is, therefore, somewhat mitigated.

8.3.2 Public Postal Services

The first category of activities exempted from VAT, in view of their public interest, is public postal services. Pursuant to Article 132(1)(a) VAT Directive, Member States

16. CJEU 3 April 2003, Case C-144/00 *Matthias Hoffmann*, ECLI:EU:C:2003:192.
17. For example: CJEU 14 June 2007, Case C-434/05 *Stichting Regionaal Opleidingen Centrum Noord-Kennemerland/West-Friesland (Horizon College) v Staatssecretaris van Financiën*, ECLI: EU:C:2007:343 and CJEU 16 October 2008, Case C-253/07 *Canterbury Hockey Club, Canterbury Ladies Hockey Club v The Commissioners for Her Majesty's Revenue and Customs*, ECLI: EU:C:2008:571.
18. CJEU 20 June 2002, Case C287/00 *Commission of the European Communities v Federal Republic of Germany*, ECLI:EU:C:2002:388 and CJEU 26 May 2005, Case C-498/03 *Kingscrest Associates Ltd, Montecello Ltd v Commissioners of Customs and Excise*, ECLI:EU:C:2005:322.

shall exempt the supply by the public postal services of services other than passenger transport and telecommunications services, and the supply of goods incidental thereto. In the initial proposal for a Sixth VAT Directive, the European Commission proposed to also exempt telecommunication services. In view of the considerable investments made with respect to telecommunications, however, the introduction of an exemption denying the right of input VAT deduction was not regarded as sensible. Accordingly, the exemption was limited to public postal services.

It follows from *Commission v Germany* that the term 'public postal services' refers to the actual organizations which engage in the supply of the services to be exempted.[19] In order to be covered by the postal exemption, services must be performed by one or more bodies, which (together) may be described as 'the public postal service' in the organic sense of that expression. Contrary to German practice, the postal exemption thus did not apply to the mere long-distance transportation between two post offices carried out by a transport undertaking. Postal services provided by (private) companies other than the postal services are, in principle, not exempt. In a liberalized European postal market, this gives rise to distortion of competition, and the issue was raised in *TNT Post UK Ltd.*[20] Member States grant a licence to one, traditionally the national, mail company for providing the so-called universal postal service, which includes at least one delivery to every address and one collection from every access point every working day at affordable and uniform prices.[21] According to the CJEU, the concept of 'public postal services' must be interpreted to cover operators, whether they are public or private, who undertake all or part of the universal postal service.[22] Moreover, the postal exemption applies to the supply by the public postal services acting as such - that is, in their capacity as an operator who undertakes to provide all or part of the universal postal service in a Member State - of services other than passenger transport and telecommunications services, and the supply of goods incidental thereto. Competitors that do not undertake all or part of the universal postal services, therefore, cannot apply the exemption, although their postal services offerings to clients may be very similar. Bodies that provide only a part of the universal postal service can apply the exemption, meaning that universal postal service can be divided over several providers.[23] The exemption, however, does not apply to supplies of postal services or of goods incidental thereto for which the terms have been

19. CJEU 11 July 1985, Case 107/84 *Commission of the European Communities v Federal Republic of Germany*, ECLI:EU:C:1985:332.
20. CJEU 23 April 2009, Case C-357/07 *The Queen, on the application of TNT Post UK Ltd v The Commissioners for Her Majesty's Revenue and Customs*, ECLI:EU:C:2009:248.
21. *See* Directive 97/67/EC of the European Parliament and of the Council of 15 December 1997 with regard to the full accomplishment of the internal market of Community postal services as last amended by Directive 2008/6/EC of the European Parliament and of the Council of 20 February 2008 (Postal Directive).
22. From CJEU 30 April 2020, Case C-661/18 *CTT – Correios de Portugal v Autoridade Tributária e Aduaneira*, ECLI:EU:C:2020:335, it follows that in Portugal postal bill-payment services were VAT-exempt until 2013.
23. CJEU 16 October 2019, Joined Cases C-4/18 and C-5/18 *Michael Winterhoff v Finanzamt Ulm and Jochen Eisenbeisvv Bundeszentralamt für Steuern (C-4/18) and Jochen Eisenbeis, acting as liquidator in the insolvency of JUREX GmbH v Bundeszentralamt für Steuern (C-5/18)*, ECLI:EU:C:2019:860.

individually negotiated. Those activities do not fall within the scope of the universal postal service and, therefore, are outside the scope of the exemption. For these activities, a more or less level playing field exists.

As far back as 2000, the European Commission had suggested in its communication to the European Council and the European Parliament on the new VAT strategy abolition of the postal exemption.[24] The public postal services are increasingly operating in a competitive postal market. Distortion of competition is inevitable if only the public postal services is exempted, while the postal services of their competitors are taxed. In order to comply with the principle of neutrality in VAT and to prevent distortion of competition, all postal services should be liable to VAT, regardless of the status of the postal service supplier. In 2003 the European Commission presented its proposal for a Directive regarding VAT on services provided in the postal sector.[25] The key aim of the proposal was the removal of the postal exemption. In 2004, the Commission delivered a (slightly) amended proposal, which, however, still included the abolition of the exemption.[26] This dossier proved to be a difficult one from a political point of view. Member States were unable to agree on the terms and conditions to modernize VAT legislation as regards postal services. Finally, on 16 April 2013, the proposal was withdrawn.

8.3.3 Hospital and Medical Care

Article 132(1)(b) VAT Directive provides for an exemption of hospital and medical care and closely related activities undertaken by bodies governed by public law or, under social conditions comparable with those applicable to bodies governed by public law, by hospitals, centres for medical treatment or diagnosis and other duly recognized establishments of a similar nature. Article 132(1)(c) VAT Directive contains an exemption for medical care in the exercise of the medical and paramedical professions. It follows from consistent CJEU case law that the first exemption covers all services supplied in a hospital environment, while the latter exemption covers medical services provided outside such a framework, both at the private address of the person providing the care and at the patient's home or at any other place.[27] The two exemptions, which have separate fields of application, are intended to regulate all exemptions of medical services in the strict sense.

The concept of 'medical care', as mentioned in Article 132(1)(b) VAT Directive, is intended to cover services which have, as their purpose the diagnosis, treatment and,

24. Communication from the Commission to the Council and the European Parliament, 'A strategy to improve the operation of the VAT system within the context of the internal market', 7 June 2000, COM (2000) 348 final.
25. Proposal for a Council Directive amending Directive 77/388/EEC as regards value added tax on services provided in the postal sector, 5 May 2003, COM (2003) 234 final.
26. Amended proposal for a Council Directive amending Directive 77/388/EEC as regards value added tax on services provided in the postal sector, 8 July 2004, COM (2004) 468 final.
27. For example, CJEU 10 September 2002, Case C-141/00 *Ambulanter Pflegedienst Kügler GmbH v Finanzamt für Körperschaften I in Berlin*, ECLI:EU:C:2002:473 and CJEU 10 June 2010, Case C-262/08 *CopyGene A/S v Skatteministeriet*, ECLI:EU:C:2010:328.

in so far as possible, cure of diseases or health disorders.[28] While 'medical care' must have a therapeutic aim, it does not necessarily follow that the therapeutic purpose of a service must be confined within a particularly narrow compass. Medical services effected for prophylactic purposes may benefit from exemption under Article 132(1)(b) VAT Directive. Even in cases where the persons who are the subject of examination or other medical intervention of a prophylactic nature are not suffering from any disease or health disorder, the inclusion of those services within the meaning of 'medical care' is consistent with the objective of reducing the cost of healthcare which objective justifies the exemption. Accordingly, medical services supplied for the purpose of protecting, including maintaining or restoring human health, may benefit from the exemption.

Not only hospital and medical care are included in the scope of the exemption but also activities closely related thereto. Although no definition is provided of the concept of 'closely related activities', it can be assumed that the VAT Directive legislator intended to exempt supplies ancillary to hospital and medical care. According to the CJEU, the aforementioned concept does not call for an especially narrow interpretation since the exemption of activities closely related to hospital and medical care is designed to ensure that the benefits flowing from such care are not hindered by the increased costs of providing it that would follow if it, or closely related activities, were subject to VAT. As a result, the taking of a sample and the transmission of that sample to a specialized laboratory constitute a service that is closely related to the analysis so that they must be treated the same as the VAT-exempt analysis and, therefore, must also be VAT-exempt.[29] The same is true for an activity consisting in compiling an individual file, including the user's clinical record, which entitles the user to purchase 'traditional thermal cure' medical care within a spa establishment, where those files set out data relating to the user's state of health, planned and prescribed medical care as well as the manner in which that care is to be administered which must be consulted for the provision of care and to achieve the therapeutic objectives pursued.[30] However, the transportation, for clinics and laboratories, of human organs and samples of human origin for the purposes of medical analysis or medical or therapeutic care, by a third party who is self-employed, cannot be regarded as activities closely related to hospital and medical care.[31] Also, the supply of telephone services and the hiring out of televisions to inpatients are not exempt.[32] Likewise, the dispatch of a kit for collecting blood from the umbilical cord of newborn babies and the testing and processing of that blood and, where appropriate, the storage of stem cells contained in it for possible

28. For example: CJEU 6 November 2003, Case C-45/01 *Christoph-Dornier-Stiftung für Klinische Psychologie v Finanzamt Gießen*, ECLI:EU:C:2003:595; CJEU 8 June 2006, Case C-106/05 *L.u.P. GmbH v Finanzamt Bochum-Mitte*, ECLI:EU:C:2006:380 and CJEU 10 June 2010, Case C-262/08 *CopyGene A/S v Skatteministeriet*, ECLI:EU:C:2010:328.
29. CJEU 11 January 2001, Case C-76/99 *Commission of the European Communities v French Republic*, ECLI:EU:C:2001:12.
30. CJEU 13 January 2022, Case C-513/20 *Autoridade Tributária e Aduaneira v Termas Sulfurosas de Alcafache SA*, ECLI:EU:C:2022:18.
31. CJEU 2 July 2015, Case C-334/14 *État belge v Nathalie De Fruytier*, ECLI:EU:C:2015:437.
32. CJEU 1 December 2005, Cases C-394/04 and C-395/04 *Diagnostiko & Therapeftiko Kentro Athinon-Ygeia AE v Ipourgos Ikonomikon*, ECLI:EU:C:2005:734.

future therapeutic use, cannot be considered as an activity closely related to hospital and medical care. These activities are merely potentially related to therapeutic use, which has not been performed, commenced or yet envisaged.[33] However, in specific situations, a transaction in itself may not be regarded as an activity closely related to hospital and medical care but, under strict conditions, the exemption can nevertheless be applied. In *Klinikum Dortmund*, the CJEU ruled that the supply of cytostatic drugs prescribed in the course of outpatient cancer treatment by doctors working in an independent capacity in a hospital is not exempt from VAT under Article 13A(1)(c) Sixth VAT Directive (now Article 132(1)(b) VAT Directive) unless that supply is physically and economically indissociable from the principal supply of medical care.[34]

A delicate issue is whether plastic surgery and other cosmetic treatments are to be regarded as exempt hospital and medical care. The exemption is intended to cover only services that have as their purpose the diagnosis, treatment and, in so far as possible, the cure of diseases or health disorders. In *PFC Clinic*, the CJEU decided that plastic surgery and other cosmetic treatments fall within the concepts of 'medical care' where those services are intended to diagnose, treat or cure diseases or health disorders or to protect, maintain or restore human health.[35] The subjective understanding of the patient undergoing plastic surgery or cosmetic treatment is not decisive in determining whether that intervention has a therapeutic purpose. The fact that such services are supplied or undertaken by a licensed member of the medical profession, or that the purpose of such services is determined by such a professional may, however, influence the assessment of whether such interventions fall within the concept of 'medical care'. The view of the medical professional as to the aim of the services is, therefore, key to the applicability of the exemption, which fits with the purpose of the exemption.

Similar to other exemptions, the exemption for hospital and medical care is not only defined by means of the supplies made but also by the status of the suppliers. The exemption only applies to supplies by bodies governed by public law or under social conditions comparable with those applicable to bodies governed by public law, hospitals, centres for medical treatment or diagnosis and other duly recognized establishments of a similar nature. The nature of the exemption, in combination with the importance of healthcare, seems to provide for sufficient justification for limitation of the exemption to certain suppliers. However, from *I GmbH* it follows that application of the exemption under national legislation cannot be denied for private hospitals which supply similar services under social conditions comparable with those applicable to bodies governed by public law.[36]

Following Article 133 VAT Directive, Member States may, in each individual case, set certain conditions for the application of this exemption to supplies made by

33. CJEU 10 June 2010, Case C-86/09 *Future Health Technologies Ltd v The Commissioners for Her Majesty's Revenue and Customs*, ECLI:EU:C:2010:334. *See also* CJEU 10 June 2010, Case C-262/08 *CopyGene A/S v Skatteministeriet*, ECLI:EU:C:2010:328 in this respect.
34. CJEU 13 March 2014, Case C-366/12 *Finanzamt Dortmund-West v Klinikum Dortmund GmbH*, ECLI:EU:C:2014:143.
35. CJEU 21 March 2013, Case C-91/12 *Skatteverket v PFC Clinic AB*, ECLI:EU:C:2013:198. Following this judgment the same applies to Article 132(1)(c) VAT Directive.
36. CJEU 7 April 2022, Case C-228/20 *I GmbH v Finanzamt H*, ECLI:EU:C:2022:275.

bodies other than those governed by public law (*see* section 8.3.19). From *Dornier*, it follows that Article 133 does not affect the discretion Member States enjoy under Article 132(1)(b) to allow the exemption for 'other duly recognized establishments of a similar nature'.[37] In any case, the exemption for hospital and medical care does not apply to supplies of goods and services if the conditions of Article 134 VAT Directive are met. No exemption applies (a) where the supply is not essential to the transactions exempted, or (b) where the basic purpose of the supply is to obtain additional income for the body in question through transactions which are in direct competition with those of commercial enterprises subject to VAT (*see* section 8.3.19).

8.3.4 Medical Care

Pursuant to Article 132(1)(c) VAT Directive, Member States shall exempt the provision of medical care in the exercise of the medical and paramedical professions as defined by the Member State concerned. This exemption covers medical services provided outside a hospital environment, whether at the private address of the person providing the care or at the patient's home or at any other place.[38] The exemption of Article 132(1)(b) VAT Directive covers all medical services supplied in a hospital environment. The exemption of Article 132(1)(c) VAT Directive only relates to medical care provided to persons and does not extend to services provided by veterinary surgeons.[39] Since the exemption is not dependent on the legal form of the taxable person providing the medical or paramedical services, medical services provided by a foundation governed by private law and carried out by employed psychotherapists are exempt.[40] This is in line with the principle of fiscal neutrality, which is indifferent to the legal form in which medical services are performed.[41]

It follows from consistent CJEU case law that the exemption has the objective of preventing medical care from becoming inaccessible on account of the increased costs that would follow if that care were VAT taxed.[42] The provision does not exempt all services which may be affected in the exercise of the medical and paramedical professions but only 'provision of medical care', which constitutes an independent concept of Union law. Services effected in the exercise of those professions remain

37. CJEU 6 November 2003, Case C-45/01 *Christoph-Dornier-Stiftung für Klinische Psychologie v Finanzamt Gießen*, ECLI:EU:C:2003:595.
38. For example: CJEU 10 September 2002, Case C-141/00 *Ambulanter Pflegedienst Kügler GmbH v Finanzamt für Körperschaften I in Berlin*, ECLI:EU:C:2002:473 and CJEU 10 June 2010, Case C-262/08 *CopyGene A/S v Skatteministeriet*, ECLI:EU:C:2010:328.
39. CJEU 24 May 1988, Case 122/87 *Commission of the European Communities v Italian Republic*, ECLI:EU:C:1988:256.
40. CJEU 6 November 2003, Case C-45/01 *Christoph-Dornier-Stiftung für Klinische Psychologie v Finanzamt Gießen*, ECLI:EU:C:2003:595.
41. *See also* CJEU 10 September 2002, Case C-141/00 *Ambulanter Pflegedienst Kügler GmbH v Finanzamt für Körperschaften I in Berlin*, ECLI:EU:C:2002:473.
42. For example: CJEU 11 January 2001, Case C-76/99 *Commission of the European Communities v French Republic*, ECLI:EU:C:2001:12 and CJEU 10 September 2002, Case C-141/00 *Ambulanter Pflegedienst Kügler GmbH v Finanzamt für Körperschaften I in Berlin*, ECLI:EU:C:2002:473. *See also* M. Gabriël, *The Hindering Effect of EU VAT on the Access to Health Care* (*Dissertation*) (Datawyse - Universitaire Pers Maastricht 2018), p. 107.

taxed if they do not correspond to the concept of 'the provision of medical care'. Even if other services provided by doctors may share the characteristics of activities in the public interest, it follows from *D. v W.* that Article 132(1)(c) VAT Directive does not exempt from VAT every activity performed in the public interest, but only those which are listed and described in great detail.[43] In that case, it was established that the exemption does not apply to services consisting in establishing the genetic affinity of individuals through biological tests. The services did not provide care to persons by diagnosing and treating a disease or any other health disorder. Following established case law, the 'provision of medical care' must have a therapeutic aim, which includes medical services effected for prophylactic purposes.[44] This does not mean that the medical care in question should be supplied within the framework of a confidential relationship between the patient and the person providing the care in order to fall within the scope of the exemption.[45] Medical services effected for a purpose other than that of protecting human health, including maintaining or restoring it, may not benefit from the exemption. Such services, although performed in the exercise of a medical profession, include, for example, giving certificates as to a person's medical condition for purposes, such as entitlement to a war pension, and medical examinations conducted with a view to the preparation of an expert medical report regarding issues of liability and the quantification of damages for individuals contemplating personal injury litigation.[46] Similarly, services consisting in verifying the accuracy of an insured person's diagnosis of serious illness, in order to determine the best possible health care with a view to the insured person's recovery and to ensure where that risk is covered by the insurance contract and where the insured person so requests that the medical treatment is provided abroad are not covered by the exemption.[47] Following *Klinikum Dortmund* (*see* section 8.3.3. on hospital care), not every supply by a medical professional, such as a doctor, is VAT-exempt. From *Solleveld*, it is clear that Member States have the discretion to define the paramedical professions and the medical care coming within the scope of the professions mentioned in Article 132(1)(c) VAT Directive.[48] However, in the exercise of that discretion, Member States must comply with the objective pursued by the said provision, which is to ensure that the exemption applies solely to services provided by persons with the required professional qualifications, and the principle of fiscal neutrality.[49] As regards fiscal neutrality, it needs to be established whether services of certain paramedical professionals are of equivalent

43. CJEU 14 September 2000, Case C-384/98 *D. v W.*, ECLI:EU:C:2000:444.
44. For example: CJEU 20 November 2003, Case C-212/01 *Margarete Unterpertinger v Pensionsversicherungsanstalt der Arbeiter*, ECLI:EU:C:2003:625 and CJEU 20 November 2003, Case C-307/01 *Peter d'Ambrumenil, Dispute Resolution Services Ltd v Commissioners of Customs and Excise*, ECLI:EU:C:2003:627.
45. CJEU 18 September 219, Case C-700/17 *Finanzamt Kyritz v Wolf-Henning Peters*, ECLI:EU:C:2019:753.
46. CJEU 20 November 2003, Case C-307/01 *Peter d'Ambrumenil, Dispute Resolution Services Ltd v Commissioners of Customs and Excise*, ECLI:EU:C:2003:627.
47. CJEU 24 November 2022, Case C-458/21 *CIG Pannónia Életbiztosító*, ECLI:EU:C:2022:924.
48. CJEU 27 April 2006, Cases C-443/04 and C-444/04 *H.A. Solleveld and J.E. van den Hout-van Eijnsbergen v Staatssecretaris van Financiën*, ECLI:EU:C:2006:257.
49. *See also* CJEU 27 June 2019, Case C-597/17 *Belgisch Syndicaat van Chiropraxie and Others v Ministerraad*, ECLI:EU:C:2019:544, para. 25.

quality to the services of (para)medical professionals that the Member States have recognized as persons that may apply the exemption, having regard to the professional qualifications of the latter.

8.3.5 Supply of Human Organs, Blood and Milk

On the basis of Article 132(1)(d) VAT Directive, Member States are held to exempt the supply of human organs, blood and milk. While most exemptions relate to supplies of services, this exemption deals with supplies of goods. On the basis of *TMD*, the exemption is only applicable to supplies of human organs, blood and milk, where such supply contributes directly to healthcare or for therapeutic purposes.[50] From *De Fruytier (I)*, it follows that the exemption does not apply to the activity of transporting human organs and samples for hospitals and laboratories. Such a transport activity merely involves physically moving the goods concerned from one place to another and does not equate to a supply of goods.[51]

8.3.6 Dental Services and Supply of Dental Prostheses

Article 132(1)(e) VAT Directive provides for an exemption of the supply of services by dental technicians in their professional capacity and the supply of dental prostheses by dentists and dental technicians. As most Member States will have included dentists in their definition of medical and paramedical professions, services provided by dentists will fall under the scope of the exemption for medical care of Article 132(1)(c) VAT Directive (*see* section 8.3.4). The exemption of Article 132(1)(e) VAT Directive, therefore, seems supplementary to the exemption for medical care. The exemption has the objective of preventing dental care from becoming inaccessible on account of the increased costs that would follow if that care were VAT taxed.[52] As is confirmed in *VDP Dental Laboratory*, the exemption for the supply of dental prostheses is not only defined according to the nature of the goods supplied but also according to the status of the supplier.[53] Therefore, not all supplies of dental prostheses are VAT-exempt, but only those which are made by the members of two particular professions, namely dentists and dental technicians. According to Article 370 jo. Annex X, Part A(1) VAT Directive, Member States may continue to subject the dental supplies mentioned in Article 132(1)(e) VAT Directive. Also, the Member States which have already exempted these supplies and also allowed the right to opt for taxation may maintain the option to tax on the basis of Article 371 VAT Directive. The different VAT treatment of

50. CJEU 5 October 2016, Case C-412/15 *TMD Gesellschaft für transfusionsmedizinische Dienste GmbH v Finanzamt Kassel II – Hofgeismar*, ECLI:EU:C:2016:738.
51. CJEU 3 June 2010, Case C-237/09 *Belgian State v Nathalie De Fruytier*, ECLI:EU:C:2015:437.
52. CJEU 14 December 2006, Case C-401/05 *VDP Dental Laboratory NV v Staatssecretaris van Financiën*, ECLI:EU:C:2006:792.
53. *Ibid.*

dental supplies across the Member States causes distortion of competition.[54] This is illustrated perfectly by *Eurodental.*[55] In this case, the CJEU decided that a supply exempt under Article 132(1)(e) VAT Directive did not give the right to deduct input VAT, even when it concerned an intra-Community supply (ICS) to another Member State, and regardless of the VAT system applicable in that other Member State where the intra-Community acquisition (ICA) took place. Suppliers established in that Member State, however, are entitled to deduct input VAT, which clearly shows the distortion of competition. We, therefore, favour complete harmonization and abolition of all derogations, including the one discussed here. In addition to the exemptions for dental activities, Member States may apply a reduced VAT rate to the provision of dental care in so far as those services are not already exempt. Paragraph 17 of Annex III to the VAT Directive provides for this possibility (*see* Chapter 7).

8.3.7 Cost-Sharing Exemption

Article 132(1)(f) VAT Directive contains the so-called cost-sharing exemption. The provision exempts the supply of services by independent groups of persons, who are carrying on an activity which is exempt from VAT, or in relation to which they are not taxable persons, for the purpose of rendering to their members the services directly necessary for the exercise of that activity. Those groups must merely claim from their members an exact reimbursement of their share of the joint expenses, and the application of the exemption should not likely cause distortion of competition. Although the exemption was limited to services supplied by independent groups of persons to members carrying on medical or paramedical activities in the proposal to the Sixth VAT Directive,[56] there is, in our view, nothing to suggest that the material scope is still limited to supplies to members that are active in the medical sector. Following *Taksatorringen,*[57] in many Member States, it was common ground that the cost-sharing exemption was not even limited to activities in the public interest but could also include an 'independent group' providing services to members carrying out activities that are exempt under Article 135 VAT Directive. From *DNB Banka*, it follows that such reading of *Taksatorringen* is misguided. The cost-sharing exemption is limited to independent groups that perform services for members whose activities are exempt on the basis of Article 132 VAT Directive.[58]

---

54. For an illustration of that effect, *see* a court case regarding the same company, but of a more recent date: CJEU 26 February 2015, Joined Cases C-144/13, C-154/13 and C-160/13 *VDP Dental Laboratory NV v Staatssecretaris van Financiën (C-144/13) and Staatssecretaris van Financiën v X BV (C-154/13) and Nobel Biocare Nederland BV (C-160/13)*, ECLI:EU:C:2015:116.
55. CJEU 7 December 2006, Case C-240/05 *Administration de l'enregistrement et des domaines v Eurodental Sarl*, ECLI:EU:C:2006:763.
56. Explanatory Memorandum to the proposal for a Sixth Directive of 20 June 1973, COM (73) 950. *See also* Opinion of Advocate General Mischo of 3 October 2002, Case C-8/01 *Assurandør-Societetet et v Skatteministeriet*, ECLI:EU:C:2002:562, para. 108.
57. CJEU 20 November 2003, Case C-8/01 *Assurandør-Societetet, acting on behalf of Taksatorringen v Skatteministeriet*, ECLI:EU:C:2003:621.
58. CJEU 21 September 2017, Case C-326/15 *'DNB Banka' AS v Valsts ieņēmumu dienests*, ECLI:EU:C:2017:719. *See also* CJEU 21 September 2017, C-616/15 *Commission v Germany*,

The cost-sharing exemption removes some of the negative effects of the VAT exemptions without a right of deduction. In fact, its rationale is 'to create an exemption from VAT in order to avoid an entity offering certain services from being required to pay that tax when it has found it necessary to cooperate with other entities by means of a common structure set up to undertake activities essential to the provision of those services'.[59] Hence, its goal is to prevent VAT from becoming a distortive factor when a group of persons finds it necessary to cooperate. Moreover, it ensures that the objectives of certain other exemptions are met (e.g., reducing the cost of medical care).[60]

As the wording of the exemption is not very clear, Member States not only apply the exemption differently but also in contradictory ways.[61] Basically, the conditions to the exemption are:

(1) There is an 'independent group of persons'.
In *SUFA*, the CJEU ruled that the exemption can only apply if the group has at least two members.[62] Fiscal neutrality requires that the legal form of a group does not determine whether or not the exemption can apply. Therefore, the legal form of the group is, in our view, irrelevant to the application of the exemption.[63] In our view, not only legal persons (such as associations, foundations or capital companies) but also entities without legal personality under the national civil law of a Member State (such as partnerships), in principle – subject to the other conditions of Article 132(1)(f) VAT Directive – are eligible as independent groups of persons.
(2) The group supplies services to its members.
The exemption only applies to services to the members. Hence, any services from the members to the independent group fall outside the scope of Article 132(1)(f) VAT Directive. Where an independent group outsources tasks to a third party, that third party cannot apply the exemption to its services to the independent group.[64] The exemption applies even if the services are supplied to only one or several of the members.[65] Moreover, the application of the exemption to services to members is not waived if the independent group also supplies (taxed) services to other parties than the members of the group.

ECLI:EU:C:2017:721 and CJEU 21 September 2017, Case C-605/15 *Minister Finansów v Aviva Towarzystwo Ubezpieczeń na Iycie S.A. w Warszawie*, ECLI:EU:C:2017:718.

59. CJEU 11 December 2008, Case C-407/07 *Stichting Centraal Begeleidingsorgaan voor de Intercollegiale Toetsing v Staatssecretaris van Financiën*, ECLI:EU:C:2008:713, para. 37.
60. *See* A.J. van Doesum, *Contractuele samenwerkingsverbanden in de btw (Dissertation)* (Kluwer 2009).
61. Value Added Tax Committee, Working Paper No 654, taxud.d.1(2010)123337.
62. CJEU 15 June 1989, Case 348/87 *Stichting Uitvoering Financiële Acties v Staatssecretaris van Financiën*, ECLI:EU:C:1989:246.
63. *See* A.J. van Doesum, *Contractuele samenwerkingsverbanden in de btw (Dissertation)* (Kluwer 2009).
64. CJEU 15 June 1989, Case 348/87 *Stichting Uitvoering Financiële Acties v Staatssecretaris van Financiën*, ECLI:EU:C:1989:246.
65. CJEU 11 December 2008, Case C-407/07 *Stichting Centraal Begeleidingsorgaan voor de Intercollegiale Toetsing (CBIT) v Staatssecretaris van Financiën*, ECLI:EU:C:2008:713.

(3) The services are 'directly necessary' for the exercise of the member's 'exempt' or 'non-taxable' activities.
Since exemptions are an exception to the main rule, they must be interpreted strictly. Nonetheless, we believe that the interpretation of the exemption, and that of the term 'directly necessary', should not be so strict that it makes the practical application of the exemption virtually impossible. In our view, the relevant test is whether the members would have purchased the services from the group if they were not carrying out their exempt or non-taxable activities *and* whether the group would have been supplying the services to the members if they were not to carry out the exempt or non-taxable activities. The mere fact that a certain member carries out taxed activities besides his exempt or non-taxable activities does not preclude the application of the exemption, although the exemption will only apply in so far as those services are directly necessary for the members' exempt or non-taxable activities[66] As indicated, the cost-sharing exemption is limited to independent groups that perform services for members whose activities are exempt on the basis of Article 132 VAT Directive, excluding persons whose activities are exempt on the basis of Article 135 VAT Directive.

(4) The independent group merely claims an 'exact reimbursement of costs' of each member's share of the 'joint expenses'.
It is, in principle, not allowed for the group to include a profit margin in the fees that are charged to its members. In our view, surpluses arising with the independent group at the end of an accounting year should not preclude the application of the exemption.[67] We subscribe to the European Commission's view that direct tax consequences which may flow from (transfer) pricing policy imposed by the VAT Directive should have no impact on the VAT treatment of the services provided by the group.[68] However, if the transfer pricing adjustments entail a de facto extra retroactive charge to the members, there may no longer be an exact reimbursement of costs. The term 'expenses' indicates that costs, not being expenses (such as depreciation of assets) cannot be shared under the cost-sharing exemption. However, it seems fair that such costs are to be shared under the exemption because that better reflects economic reality. The VAT that the independent group cannot deduct (because it supplies exempt services) is a cost that in itself can be shared and reimbursed by the members.[69]

66. CJEU 4 May 2017, Case C-274/15 *Commission v Luxembourg*, ECLI:EU:C:2017:333. *See also* Value Added Tax Committee, Working Paper No 654, taxud.d.1(2010)123337.
67. *See* by analogy: CJEU 14 June 2007, Case C-434/05 *Stichting Regionaal Opleidingen Centrum Noord-Kennemerland/West-Friesland (Horizon College) v Staatssecretaris van Financiën*, ECLI-:EU:C:2007:343, para. 33.
68. Value Added Tax Committee, Working Paper No 654, taxud.d.1(2010)123337.
69. The EC considers this to be a requirement. Value Added Tax Committee, Working Paper No 450, TAXUD/1650/04–EN.

(5) The exemption is 'not likely to cause distortion of competition'.
In *Taksatorringen*, the CJEU clarified that the condition that the exemption is not likely to cause distortion of competition entails a test as to whether it is the VAT exemption in itself which is not liable 'to give rise to distortions of competition on a market in which competition will in any event be affected by the presence of an operator which provides services for its members and which is prohibited from seeking profits'. In this respect, the only relevant test is if, irrespective of any taxation or exemption, the groups are assured of keeping their members as customers. If so, 'there is no reason to take the view that it is the exemption granted them that closes the market to independent operators'. Thus, it must be checked whether the independent group would be able to retain its members if its services were not exempt.[70] In our view, this will be difficult to prove in practice.

In several Member States, such as Belgium, France and Portugal, the cost-sharing exemption can only be applied if the members of the cost-sharing association have a relatively small percentage of VAT taxed supplies. Generally, a threshold of 10% is applied. This type of condition is believed to be an interpretation of the condition that the cost-sharing exemption is not likely to cause distortion of competition. In the Netherlands, for example, this condition is interpreted in such a way that certain supplies of services are deemed to cause distortion of competition and thus are excluded from exemption (e.g., IT related services).

8.3.8 Welfare and Social Security Work

According to Article 132(1)(g) VAT Directive, Member States shall exempt the supply of services and of goods closely linked to welfare and social security work, including those supplied by old people's homes, by bodies governed by public law or by other bodies recognized by the Member State concerned as being devoted to social well-being.[71] From *Kingscrest,* it can be derived that the exemption is intended to reduce the cost of supplies in the field of welfare and social security work and to make them more accessible to the individuals who may benefit from them.[72] In view of the principle of neutrality, the term 'bodies' does not exclude from the exemption natural persons

70. CJEU 20 November 2003, Case C-8/01 *Assurandør-Societetet, acting on behalf of Taksatorringen v Skatteministeriet,* ECLI:EU:C:2003:621.
71. Under Article 13A(1)(g) Sixth VAT Directive. The last part of this sentence reads: 'or by other organizations recognized as charitable by the Member State concerned'. Following para. 3 of the preamble of the VAT Directive, the wording of this Directive will not, in principle, bring about material changes in the existing VAT legislation. Therefore, we feel that the current wording of Article 132(1)(g) VAT Directive has no different meaning than the aforementioned wording in the Sixth VAT Directive.
72. CJEU 26 May 2005, Case C-498/03 *Kingscrest Associates Ltd, Montecello Ltd v Commissioners of Customs and Excise,* ECLI:EU:C:2005:322.

running a business,[73] nor does it exclude private profit-making entities.[74] In *Ambulanter Pflegedienst Kügler*, it was decided that the provision of general care and domestic help by an outpatient care service to persons in a state of physical or economic dependence is to be regarded as the supply of services closely linked to welfare and social security work.[75] This case shows the complementary function of the exemption for welfare and social security work to the exemption for hospital and medical care of Article 132(1)(b) VAT Directive. From *'go fair' Zeitarbeit*, it follows, however, that the exemption does not include the provision of temporary care workers to inpatient and outpatient care establishments.[76]

Intermediary services provided with respect to welfare and social security work can benefit from the exemption if (i) the welfare and social security work itself is VAT-exempt, (ii) the intermediary service is of such a nature or quality that the principle of the intermediary could not be assured of obtaining a service of the same value without the assistance of the intermediary, and (iii) the basic purpose of the intermediary services is not to obtain additional income for the service provider by carrying out transactions which are in direct competition with those of commercial enterprises liable to VAT.[77] In our view, this last condition directly follows from Article 134(b) VAT Directive but is not as such a condition contained in Article 132(1)(g) VAT Directive.

In *Momtrade Ruse*, it was ruled that the exemption may be applied for services provided to natural persons residing in a Member State other than that in which the service provider has established the seat of his economic activity.[78] In such a case, it is the Member State of establishment of the service provider that may assess whether the nature of those services and the characteristics of that company for the purposes of determining whether the services fall within the concept of 'provision of services [...] closely linked to social assistance and social security [...] carried out by [...] [a body recognized] as having a social character by the Member State concerned', within the meaning of Article 132(1)(g).

Following Article 133 VAT Directive, Member States may, in each individual case, set certain conditions for the application of this exemption to supplies made by bodies other than those governed by public law (*see* section 8.3.19). In any case, the exemption for welfare and social work does not apply to supplies of goods and services if the conditions of Article 134 VAT Directive are met. No exemption applies (a) where

73. CJEU 7 September 1999, Case C-216/97 *Jennifer Gregg and Mervyn Gregg v Commissioners of Customs and Excise*, ECLI:EU:C:1999:390. This case reverses CJEU 11 August 1995, Case C-453/93 *W. Bulthuis-Griffioen v Inspecteur der Omzetbelasting*, ECLI:EU:C:1995:265, in which the CJEU had ruled otherwise.
74. CJEU 26 May 2005, Case C-498/03 *Kingscrest Associates Ltd, Montecello Ltd v Commissioners of Customs and Excise*, ECLI:EU:C:2005:322.
75. CJEU 10 September 2002, Case C-141/00 *Ambulanter Pflegedienst Kügler GmbH v Finanzamt für Körperschaften I in Berlin*, ECLI:EU:C:2002:473.
76. CJEU 12 March 2015, Case C-594/13 *'go fair' Zeitarbeit OHG v Finanzamt Hamburg-Altona*, ECLI:EU:C:2015:164.
77. CJEU 9 February 2006, Case C-415/04 *Staatssecretaris van Financiën v Stichting Kinderopvang Enschede*, ECLI:EU:C:2006:95.
78. CJEU 11 May 2023, Case C-620/21 *MOMTRADE RUSE OOD*, ECLI:EU:C:2023:395.

the supply is not essential to the transactions exempted, or (b) where the basic purpose of the supply is to obtain additional income for the body in question through transactions which are in direct competition with those of commercial enterprises subject to VAT (*see* section 8.3.19).

In addition to the exemption, Member States may apply a reduced VAT rate to the supply of services and goods by bodies recognized as being devoted to social well-being by the Member State and engaged in welfare and social security work, where these supplies are not VAT-exempt. Paragraph 15 of Annex III to the VAT Directive provides for this possibility (*see* Chapter 7).

8.3.9 Supplies Closely Linked to the Protection of Children and Young Persons

Under Article 132(1)(h) VAT Directive, an exemption applies to the supply of services and of goods closely linked to the protection of children and young persons by bodies governed by public law or by other organizations recognized by the Member State concerned as being devoted to social well-being. There are no commentaries on this exemption. Under Article 13A(1)(h) Sixth VAT Directive, the last part of Article 135(1)(h) VAT Directive reads: 'or by other organizations recognized as charitable by the Member State concerned'. It follows from *Kingscrest* that 'organizations recognized as charitable by the Member State concerned' does not exclude private profit-making entities. On the basis of paragraph 3 of the preamble of the VAT Directive, the wording of this Directive will not, in principle, bring about material changes in the existing VAT legislation, i.e., the Sixth VAT Directive. Therefore, we feel that private profit-making entities fall within the scope of Article 132(1)(h) VAT Directive, provided that all other conditions are met. Reference is made to section 8.3.8 as regards intermediary services since the principles set out with respect to the exemption of Article 132(1)(g) VAT Directive apply similarly to the exemption of Article 132(1)(h) VAT Directive.

Following Article 133 VAT Directive, Member States may, in each individual case, set certain conditions for the application of this exemption to supplies made by bodies other than those governed by public law (*see* section 8.3.19). In any case, the exemption for supplies closely linked to the protection of children and young persons does not apply to supplies of goods and services if the conditions of Article 134 VAT Directive are met. No exemption applies (a) where the supply is not essential to the transactions exempted, or (b) where the basic purpose of the supply is to obtain additional income for the body in question through transactions which are in direct competition with those of commercial enterprises subject to VAT (*see* section 8.3.19).

8.3.10 Education

Article 132(1)(i) VAT Directive exempts the provision of children's or young people's education, school or university education, vocational training or retraining, including the supply of services and of goods closely related thereto, by bodies governed by public law having such as their aim or by other organizations recognized by the

Member State concerned as having similar objects. The exemption is intended to ensure that the levy of VAT does not increase the costs of education so that the VAT does not hinder access to the benefits of education.[79] Article 132(1)(i) VAT Directive contains no definition of the various forms of education covered by that provision. These forms are nevertheless to be considered as independent concepts of Union law. From *Horizon College*, it can be taken that the transfer of knowledge and skills between a teacher and students is a particularly important element of educational activity. The educational activity referred to in Article 132(1)(i) VAT Directive consists of a combination of elements which include, along with those relating to the teacher/student relationship, also those which make up the organizational framework of the establishment concerned. The making available of a teacher to another school cannot be regarded as an activity capable of being covered by the term 'education'.[80] Pursuant to Article 44 VAT Implementing Regulation, exempt vocational training or retraining services include instruction relating directly to a trade or profession, as well as any instruction aimed at acquiring or updating knowledge for vocational purposes. The duration of a vocational training or retraining course is irrelevant in this respect.

On the basis of established case law, a supply can only be regarded as a supply closely related to an exempt service if it is in itself essential for that exempt service.[81] Supplies that can be considered as supplies closely related to education include, for example, the sale and lease of schoolbooks. From *Commission v Germany*, it follows that research projects undertaken by state universities against consideration cannot benefit from the exemption. Taxation of such research projects does not amount to hindering access to the benefits of education.[82] Those research activities are subject to the general rule and thus are taxed. According to *Horizon College*, the making available, for consideration, of a teacher to another school in which that teacher temporarily carries out teaching duties under the responsibility of that school, may constitute a supply of services 'closely related' to education if such a teacher placement is a means of better enjoying the education deemed to be the principal service.[83] From *Brockenhurst College*, it follows that even restaurant and entertainment services provided to third parties by students of a college specializing in catering, hospitality and performing arts, may be regarded as supplies 'closely related' to the principal supply of education, provided that those services are essential to the students' education and that their basic purpose is not to obtain additional income for that establishment by carrying

79. CJEU 20 June 2002, Case C-287/00 *Commission of the European Communities v Federal Republic of Germany*, ECLI:EU:C:2002:388.
80. CJEU 14 June 2007, Case C-434/05 *Stichting Regionaal Opleidingen Centrum Noord-Kennemerland/West-Friesland (Horizon College) v Staatssecretaris van Financiën*, ECLI:EU:C:2007:3433.
81. CJEU 1 December 2005, Cases C-394/04 and C-395/04 *Diagnostiko & Therapeftiko Kentro Athinon-Ygeia AE v Ipourgos Ikonomikon*, ECLI:EU:C:2005:734 and CJEU 9 February 2006, Case C-415/04 *Staatssecretaris van Financiën v Stichting Kinderopvang Enschede*, ECLI:EU:C:2006:95.
82. CJEU 20 June 2002, Case C-287/00 *Commission of the European Communities v Federal Republic of Germany*, ECLI:EU:C:2002:388.
83. CJEU 14 June 2007, Case C-434/05 *Stichting Regionaal Opleidingen Centrum Noord-Kennemerland/West-Friesland (Horizon College) v Staatssecretaris van Financiën*, ECLI:EU:C:2007:3433.

out transactions which are in direct competition with those of commercial businesses.[84] It is noteworthy that, apparently, the principle of neutrality, in this case, is regarded from the perspective of the service provider rather than that of the guests or other restaurateurs. For the exemption, it is decisive whether or not the school is looking to obtain an additional income, whereas one could argue that from a competition perspective, that circumstance is irrelevant for both the guests at the restaurant (that will be of the view that they consume a meal at Brockenhurst college rather than a service closely related to an exempt education service) or other restaurateurs that may well experience a competitive disadvantage regardless of that circumstance.

Following *MDDP*, Article 132(1)(i) VAT Directive must be interpreted as meaning that this provision does not preclude educational services provided for commercial purposes by bodies not governed by public law from being exempt from VAT.[85] However, it does preclude a general exemption of all supplies of educational services, without consideration of the objects pursued by non-public organizations providing those services. In other words, for private organizations to be able to make use of the exemption, they must fulfil the condition of pursuing objects similar to those of bodies governed by public law.[86]

Following Article 133 VAT Directive, Member States may, in individual cases, set certain conditions for the application of this exemption to supplies made by bodies other than those governed by public law (*see* section 8.3.19). In any case, the exemption for education does not apply to supplies of goods and services if the conditions of Article 134 VAT Directive are met. No exemption applies (a) where the supply is not essential to the transactions exempted, or (b) where the basic purpose of the supply is to obtain additional income for the body in question through transactions which are in direct competition with those of commercial enterprises subject to VAT (*see* section 8.3.19).

8.3.11 Private Education

Pursuant to Article 132(1)(j) VAT Directive, Member States shall exempt tuition given privately by teachers and covering school or university education. This exemption is supplementary to the educational exemption of Article 132(1)(i) VAT Directive. Basically, these measures aim to exempt both public and private education. This is also apparent from *Eulitz*, which makes clear that for both exemptions, 'education' encompasses the transfer of knowledge and skills between a teacher and students as a particularly important element, but consists of a combination of elements, including those relating to the teacher-student relationship, and also those which make up the

84. CJEU 4 May 2017, Case C-699/15 *Commissioners for Her Majesty's Revenue & Customs v Brockenhurst College*, ECLI:EU:C:2017:344.
85. CJEU 28 November 2013, Case C-319/12 *Minister Finansów v MDDP sp. z o.o. Akademia Biznesu, sp. Komandytowa*, ECLI:EU:C:2013:778.
86. *See also* CJEU 28 April 2022, Case C-612/20 *Happy Education SRL*, ECLI:EU:C:2022:314.

organizational framework of the establishment concerned.[87] As the CJEU observed in *Werner Haderer*, the VAT Directive itself does not provide for a definition of 'school or university education'. On the basis of *A&G Fahrschule*, the concept of 'school or university education' generally refers to 'an integrated system for the transfer of knowledge and skills covering a wide and diversified set of subjects, and to the furthering and development of that knowledge and those skills by the pupils and students in the course of their progress and their specialisation in the various constituent stages of that system.'[88] In this respect, the CJEU ruled that the concept is not limited to education which leads to examinations for the purpose of obtaining qualifications, or which provides training for the purposes of carrying out a professional or trade activity, but includes other activities which are taught in schools and universities in order to develop pupils' or students' knowledge and skills, provided that those activities are not purely recreational.[89] From *Werner Haderer*, it also follows that tuition given privately by teachers requires that teachers provide their services on their own account and at their own risk in order for the exemption to apply. A direct contractual link between the recipients of the tuition and the teacher who provides it, however, is not necessary. Such a contractual link often exists with persons other than the recipient, such as the parents of pupils or students.

8.3.12 Supply of Staff by Religious or Philosophical Institutions

Pursuant to Article 132(1)(k) VAT Directive, Member States shall exempt the supply of staff by religious or philosophical institutions for the purpose of the activities referred to in Article 132(1)(b), (g), (h) and (i) VAT Directive and with a view to spiritual welfare. Unfortunately, the proposal for a Sixth VAT Directive does not contain the background for the exemption, nor does it provide for guidance as regards the interpretation of the exemption. It follows from the provision that a condition for the exemption to apply is that the supply of staff is for the purpose of hospital and medical care (b), welfare and social security work (g), protection of children (h) or children's or young people's education (i). At first sight, it seems unclear whether the provision exempts both the supply of staff for the purpose of the aforementioned activities and the supply of staff with a view to spiritual welfare, or only the supply of staff for these purposes if this supply is with a view to spiritual welfare. If the supply of staff for the purpose of the aforementioned activities would indeed be VAT-exempt, this could very well give rise to distortion of competition, as only religious or philosophical institutions would be able to benefit from the exemption. In that case, it would seem logical to include a condition in the VAT Directive, which would aim at preventing distortion of competition. This, for example, has been done with respect to the cost-sharing

87. CJEU 28 January 2010, Case C-473/08 *Ingenieursbüro Eulitz GbR Thomas und Marion Eulitz v Finanzamt Dresden I*, ECLI:EU:C:2010:47.
88. CJEU 14 March 2019, Case C-449/17 *A & G Fahrschul-Akademie GmbH v Finanzamt Wolfenbüttel*, ECLI:EU:C:2019:202.
89. CJEU 14 June 2007, Case C-445/05 *Werner Haderer v Finanzamt Wilmersdorf*, ECLI:EU:C:2007:344.

exemption of Article 132(1)(f) VAT Directive and the exemption for non-profit-making organizations of Article 132(1)(l) VAT Directive (*see* sections 8.3.7 and 8.3.13). As such a condition is not included in Article 132(1)(k) VAT Directive, we feel that the supply of staff for the purpose of hospital and medical care, etc., is only VAT-exempt if this supply of staff is with a view to spiritual welfare.[90]

8.3.13 Non-profit-Making Organizations

Article 132(1)(l) of the VAT Directive concerns non-profit-making organizations with aims of a political, trade-union, religious, patriotic, philosophical, philanthropic or civic nature. The article provides for an exemption for the supply of services, and the supply of goods closely linked thereto, to the members of such organizations in their common interest in return for a subscription fixed in accordance with the organizations' rules. This exemption, however, must not be likely to cause distortion of competition. Obviously, the exemption only becomes relevant when the relevant organizations are to be regarded as taxable persons on the basis of Article 9 VAT Directive. In view of *Apple & Pear Development Council* and *Kennemer Golf & Country Club,*[91] it should also be determined whether the supplies in return for a fixed subscription can be considered as taxable supplies against consideration, as mentioned in Article 2 VAT Directive (*see* section 3.4.1). Only then can the exemption provided by Article 132(1)(l) VAT Directive apply. It follows from *The Institute of the Motor Industry* that the expression 'trade-union' in Article 132(1)(l) means specifically an organization whose main objective is to defend the collective interests of its members – whether they are workers, employers, independent professionals or traders carrying on a particular economic activity – and to represent them vis-à-vis the appropriate third parties, including the public authorities.[92] A non-profit-making organization whose main objective is to defend and represent the collective interests of its members satisfies the criterion of exercising an activity in the public interest, which is the basis of the exemptions set out in the aforementioned provision, in so far as it provides its members with a representative voice and strength in negotiations with third parties.

Following Article 133 VAT Directive, Member States may, in each individual case, set certain conditions for the application of this exemption to supplies made by bodies other than those governed by public law (*see* section 8.3.19). In any case, the exemption for supplies of non-profit-making organizations does not apply to supplies of goods and services if the conditions of Article 134 VAT Directive are met. No exemption applies (a) where the supply is not essential to the transactions exempted, or (b) where the basic purpose of the supply is to obtain additional income for the body

90. *See also* D.B. Bijl, M.E. van Hilten & D.G. van Vliet, *Europese BTW en Nederlandse omzetbelasting* (Kluwer 2001), p. 232.
91. CJEU 8 March 1988, Case 102/86 *Apple and Pear Development Council v Commissioners of Customs and Excise*, ECLI:EU:C:1988:120 and CJEU 21 March 2002, Case C-174/00 *Kennemer Golf & Country Club v Staatssecretaris van Financiën*, ECLI:EU:C:2002:200.
92. CJEU 12 November 1998, Case C-149/97 *The Institute of the Motor Industry v Commissioners of Customs and Excise*, ECLI:EU:C:1998:536.

in question through transactions which are in direct competition with those of commercial enterprises subject to VAT (*see* section 8.3.19).

8.3.14 Sport and Physical Education

The supply of certain services closely linked to sport or physical education by non-profit-making organizations to persons taking part in sport or physical education is exempt under Article 132(1)(m) VAT Directive. The exemption is intended to encourage sport and physical education but is not a general exemption of all supplies of services linked to the practice of sports and physical education.[93] Moreover, the rationale of this exemption is to be seen against the background of Article 165(1) second subparagraph, TFEU, according to which the Union is to contribute to the promotion of European sporting issues while taking account of the specific nature of the sport, its structures based on voluntary activity and its social and educational function.[94] The activities of non-profit-making sports clubs are exempt provided that they are closely linked to the practice of sport or physical education and are made to persons practising sports or physical education.[95] Article 132(1)(m) VAT Directive covers taking part in sports and physical education in general and does not require, in order to be applicable, that the sporting activity in question be practised at a particular level, for example, at a professional level, nor that the activity be practised in a particular way, namely in a regular or organized manner or in order to participate in sports competitions. The provision has the objective of encouraging certain activities in the public interest, namely services closely linked to sport or physical education, which are provided by non-profit-making organizations to persons taking part in sport or physical education. Accordingly, the provision seeks to promote such participation by large sections of the population.[96]

Following *Kennemer Golf & Country Club*, the categorization of an organization as non-profit-making must be based on all the organization's activities. Moreover, the term 'non-profit-making' is to be interpreted as meaning that an organization may be categorized as not systematically aiming to make a profit, even if it systematically seeks to achieve surpluses, which it then uses for the purposes of the provision of its services.[97] From *Canterbury Hockey Club*, it follows that not only sports clubs supplying services to persons taking part in sports can benefit from the exemption, but in

93. CJEU 12 January 2006, Case C-246/04 *Turn- und Sportunion Waldburg*, ECLI:EU:C:2006:22 and CJEU 16 October 2008, Case C-253/07 *Canterbury Hockey Club, Canterbury Ladies Hockey Club v The Commissioners for Her Majesty's Revenue and Customs*, ECLI:EU:C:2008:571.
94. Opinion A-G Szpunar, 15 June 217, Case C-90/16 *The English Bridge Union Limited*, ECLI: EU:C:2017:464.
95. For example: CJEU 21 March 2002, Case C-174/00 *Kennemer Golf & Countryclub v Staatssecretaris van Financiën*, ECLI:EU:C:2002:200 and CJEU 12 January 2006, Case C-246/04 *Turn- und Sportunion Waldburg*, ECLI:EU:C:2006:22.
96. *See* CJEU 21 February 2013, Case C-18/12 *Město Žamberk v Finanční ředitelství v Hradci Králové*, ECLI:EU:C:2013:95 and CJEU 19 December 2013, Case C-495/12 *Commissioners for Her Majesty's Revenue and Customs v Bridport and West Dorset Golf Club Ltd*, ECLI:EU:C:2013:95.
97. CJEU 21 March 2002, Case C-174/00 *Kennemer Golf & Countryclub v Staatssecretaris van Financiën*, ECLI:EU:C:2002:200.

principle, also associations of sports clubs, such as in this case the English Hockey Association.[98] In view of the principle of fiscal neutrality, the organizational structure particular to the sporting activity should not affect the application of the exemption. Although this might appear to be a wide application of the principle of fiscal neutrality, we feel it is in line with the overall purpose of the exemption. Next to this exemption, Member States may introduce a reduced VAT rate for admission to sporting events and the use of sporting facilities (*see* paragraphs 13 and 14 of Annex III to the VAT Directive, and Chapter 7).

Following Article 133 VAT Directive, Member States may, in each individual case, set certain conditions for the application of this exemption to supplies made by bodies other than those governed by public law (*see* section 8.3.19).[99] In any case, the exemption for sport and physical education does not apply to supplies of goods and services if the conditions of Article 134 VAT Directive are met. No exemption applies (a) where the supply is not essential to the transactions exempted, or (b) where the basic purpose of the supply is to obtain additional income for the body in question through transactions which are in direct competition with those of commercial enterprises subject to VAT (*see* section 8.3.19).

8.3.15 Cultural Services

On the basis of Article 132(1)(n) VAT Directive, Member States shall exempt the supply of certain cultural services and the supply of goods closely linked thereto by bodies governed by public law or by other cultural bodies recognized by the Member State concerned. The term 'certain' is not very precise and seems to leave it to the discretion of the individual Member States to determine which cultural services fall within the scope of the exemption. The rather vague exemption is most likely caused by the fact that the Member States could not agree on the exact cultural activities that should be VAT-exempt. In the proposal for a Sixth VAT Directive, specific services were addressed, such as the supply of services by theatres, cinema clubs, concert halls, museums, libraries, public parks, botanical or zoological gardens and educational exhibitions. The current VAT Directive, as well as its predecessor, the Sixth VAT Directive, however, provides for a general exemption for certain cultural services and no longer contains specific VAT-exempt cultural activities. In our view, Article 132(1)(n) VAT Directive offers the Member States a discretionary power to exempt certain cultural services. As such, it follows from the *British Film Institute* that this exemption does not have direct effect, as the Member States can decide to exempt 'certain' cultural services while subjecting others to tax.[100] This also becomes apparent from Annex III to the VAT Directive, which allows Member States to introduce a

98. CJEU 16 October 2008, Case C-253/07 *Canterbury Hockey Club, Canterbury Ladies Hockey Club v The Commissioners for Her Majesty's Revenue and Customs*, ECLI:EU:C:2008:571.
99. *See* CJEU 13 July 2017, Case C-633/15 *London Borough of Ealing v Commissioners for Her Majesty's Revenue and Customs*, ECLI:EU:C:2017:544.
100. CJEU 15 February 2017, Case C-592/15 *Commissioners for Her Majesty's Revenue and Customs v British Film Institute*, ECLI:EU:C:2017:117.

reduced VAT rate for admission to shows, theatres, circuses, fairs, amusement parks, concerts and similar cultural events and facilities (*see* Chapter 7). In general, the cultural sector will prefer a reduced VAT rate with the right to deduct input VAT to an exemption without such a right of deduction.

The exemption only applies to cultural services provided by bodies governed by public law or by other cultural bodies recognized by the Member State concerned. In *Matthias Hoffmann*, the CJEU decided that national legislature may exclude individual artists from the benefit of the exemption since the exemption from VAT of bodies other than public law bodies is expressly subjected to the recognition of the relevant Member State.[101] The principle of fiscal neutrality does not preclude this, as there is no distortion of competition unless cultural services of the same type are subjected without justification to a different regime. According to the CJEU, the services of soloists and of bodies are different. However, if the Member States want to treat cultural services of cultural bodies and individual artists similarly, Article 132(1)(n) VAT Directive does not prevent them from doing so.

Following Article 133 VAT Directive, Member States may, in each individual case, set certain conditions for the application of this exemption to supplies made by bodies other than those governed by public law (*see* section 8.3.19). In any case, the exemption for cultural services does not apply to supplies of goods and services if the conditions of Article 134 VAT Directive are met. No exemption applies (a) where the supply is not essential to the transactions exempted, or (b) where the basic purpose of the supply is to obtain additional income for the body in question through transactions which are in direct competition with those of commercial enterprises subject to VAT (*see* section 8.3.19).

8.3.16 Fund-Raising Events

Pursuant to Article 132(1)(o) VAT Directive, Member States shall exempt the supply of services and goods, by organizations whose activities are exempt pursuant to points (b), (g), (h), (i), (l), (m) and (n), in connection with fund-raising events organized exclusively for their own benefit, provided that the exemption is not likely to cause distortion of competition. Supplies of goods and services to raise funds by organizations active in the field of hospital and medical care (b), welfare and social security work (g), protection of children (h), children's or young people's education (i), non-profit-making activities (l), sport or physical education (m) and cultural services (n), therefore, are VAT-exempt. The exemption was not mentioned prior to the adoption of the Sixth VAT Directive. It basically extends the scope of the other exemptions mentioned in the provision, while also offering administrative simplification as well as a financial advantage (i.e., no VAT on supplies in the context of a fund-raising event). Following Article 132(2) VAT Directive, Member States may introduce any restrictions necessary to the exemption, in particular, as regards the number of events or the amount of receipts that give entitlement to the exemption.

101. CJEU 3 April 2003, Case C-144/00 *Matthias Hoffmann*, ECLI:EU:C:2003:192.

Moreover, Member States may introduce measures to prevent distortion of competition.

8.3.17 Transport Services for Sick or Injured Persons

The supply of transport services for sick or injured persons in vehicles specially designed for the purpose, by duly authorized bodies, is VAT-exempt on the basis of Article 132(1)(p) VAT Directive. This exemption was not mentioned prior to the adoption of the Sixth VAT Directive. The exemption is likely to be introduced to extend the scope of the exemptions for hospital and medical care (Article 132(1)(b) VAT Directive) and for other medical care (Article 132(1)(c) VAT Directive). Although the term 'vehicles' seems to relate to land vehicles only, we feel that transport services by other means of transport specially designed for the purpose of transporting sick or injured persons should also be covered by the exemption. In our view, the principle of neutrality dictates that, for example, transport services by helicopter ambulance should also be VAT-exempt.

8.3.18 Public Radio and Television

Article 132(1)(q) VAT Directive provides for an exemption of the activities, other than those of a commercial nature, carried out by public radio and television bodies. As indicated in section 8.3.15, the proposal for a Sixth VAT Directive contained a detailed list of VAT-exempt cultural activities. In its comments on the proposal, the European Economic and Social Committee wondered why state radio and television was not exempt, whereas similar cultural services were exempt. Most likely, on that basis, the exemption for public radio and television was introduced in EU VAT legislation. The main element in identifying a public radio and television body as such, in our view, is public funding. Other elements to be taken into consideration could be special obligations, such as coverage of a certain territory or linguistic area.[102] In our opinion, the legal status of public radio and television bodies (either a public body or a private body) should not be decisive for the application of the exemption. We should stress that it follows from *Český rozhlas* that the exemption only applies if public radio and television bodies actually perform their non-commercial activities for payment.[103] If not, they do not make taxable supplies against consideration, as mentioned in Article 2 VAT Directive, and no exemption can apply. Commercial activities of public radio and television bodies, such as broadcasting commercials and selling TV guides, are not VAT-exempt. Input VAT on costs related to these activities can be deducted. Following

102. Guideline of the VAT Committee, 53rd meeting. Available from: https://taxation-customs.ec.europa.eu/document/download/474e7e57-7e01-4de0-ac94-e55537e505ae_en?filename=guidelines-vat-committee-meetings_en.pdf (accessed 17 August 2024). *See also* B. Terra & J. Kajus, *A Guide to the European VAT Directives, Introduction to European VAT*, Vol. 1 (IBFD 2013), para. 9.2.17.
103. CJEU 22 June 2016, Case C-11/15 *Odvolací finanční ředitelství v Český rozhlas*, ECLI:EU:C:2016:470.

BNT, any input VAT related to both commercial activities and non-commercial activities for no consideration can only be deducted in part on the basis of a so-called pre-pro rata (*see also* Chapter 10, section 10.5).[104]

8.3.19 Additional Conditions

Articles 133 and 134 VAT Directive contain additional conditions for the application of the exemptions for certain activities in the public interest. While the first provision offers the Member States the possibility to introduce certain additional conditions, the latter provision contains mandatory conditions.

Following Article 133 VAT Directive, Member States may, in each individual case, set certain conditions for the application of specifically addressed exemptions to supplies made by bodies other than those governed by public law. It should be noted that these conditions cannot be applied in the case of bodies governed by public law.[105] This does not seem to be in line with the principle of fiscal neutrality but may be explained by the nature of the exemption at hand, which are exemptions in the public interest. The exemptions are the following and are mentioned in Article 132(1) VAT Directive: (b) hospital and medical care, (g) welfare and social security work, (h) supplies closely connected to the protection of children and young persons, (i) education, (l) private education, (m) sport and physical education, and (n) cultural services. Member States may apply one or more of the following conditions:

(a) the bodies in question must not systematically aim to make a profit, and any surpluses nevertheless arising must not be distributed, but must be assigned to the continuance or improvement of the services supplied;
(b) those bodies must be managed and administered on an essentially voluntary basis by persons who have no direct or indirect interest, either themselves or through intermediaries, in the results of the activities concerned;
(c) those bodies must charge prices which are approved by the public authorities or which do not exceed such approved prices or, in respect of those services not subject to approval, the prices charged must be lower than those charged for similar services by commercial enterprises subject to VAT;
(d) the exemptions must not be likely to cause distortion of competition to the disadvantage of commercial enterprises subject to VAT.

---

104. CJEU 16 September 2021, Case C-21/20 *Balgarska natsionalna televizia v Direktor na Direktsia 'Obzhalvane i danachno-osiguritelna praktika' – Sofia pri Tsentralnoupravlenie na NAP*, ECLI:EU:C:2021:743.
105. The only exception is the condition of Article 133(d) VAT Directive (i.e., 'the exemptions must not be likely to cause distortion of competition to the disadvantage of commercial enterprises subject to VAT'). On the basis of the second subparagraph of Article 133 VAT Directive, Member States which on 1 January 1989 applied VAT to the transactions referred to in Article 132(1)(m) and (n) VAT Directive are allowed to apply this condition also when the said supply of goods or services by bodies governed by public law is granted exemption. *See* in this respect CJEU 13 July 2017, Case C-633/15 *London Borough of Ealing v Commissioners for Her Majesty's Revenue and Customs*, ECLI:EU:C:2017:544.

Following *Kennemer Golf & Country Club,* the additional condition that the Member States may apply, mentioned in Article 133(a) VAT Directive, is to be interpreted as meaning that an organization may be categorized as not systematically aiming to make a profit, even if it systematically seeks to achieve surpluses which it then uses for the purposes of the provision of its services.[106] From *Zoological Society of London,* it can be taken that the additional condition mentioned in Article 133(b) VAT Directive refers only to members of that body who are designated in accordance with its constitution to direct it at the highest level, as well as other persons who, without being designated by the constitution, do, in fact, direct it in that they make the decisions of last resort concerning the policy of that body, especially in the financial area, and carry out the higher supervisory tasks. Moreover, the words 'on an essentially voluntary basis' refer to the members who compose the organs entrusted with the management and administration of a body of the kind referred to in that provision and those persons who, without being designated by the constitution, do in fact direct it and also refer to the reward which the latter may receive, habitually or exceptionally, from that body.[107] As a result, the Zoological Society, which operated two zoological gardens, was able to benefit from the exemption, although some of the society's paid employees were involved in its management and administration. This decision seems in line with the objective of the exemption for cultural services and the function of the additional conditions.

Pursuant to Article 134 VAT Directive, the exemptions for certain activities in the public interest do not apply to supplies of goods and services if additional conditions are not met. The exemptions in question are the same as those mentioned in Article 133 VAT Directive. The additional conditions, therefore, apply to the following exemptions mentioned in Article 132(1) VAT Directive: (b) hospital and medical care, (g) welfare and social security work, (h) supplies closely connected to the protection of children and young persons, (i) education, (l) private education, (m) sport and physical education and (n) cultural services. No exemption applies:

(a) where the supply is not essential to the transactions exempted;
(b) where the basic purpose of the supply is to obtain additional income for the body in question through transactions that are in direct competition with those of commercial enterprises subject to VAT.

8.4 EXEMPTIONS FOR OTHER ACTIVITIES

In this section, we will discuss the exemptions for activities other than those mentioned in Article 132 VAT Directive.

106. CJEU 21 March 2002, Case C-174/00 *Kennemer Golf & Countryclub v Staatssecretaris van Financiën*, ECLI:EU:C:2002:200.
107. CJEU 21 March 2002, Case C-267/00 *Commissioners of Customs and Excise v Zoological Society of London*, ECLI:EU:C:2002:202.

8.4.1 General

Chapter 3 of Title IX of the VAT Directive deals with exemptions for other activities. Similar to the exemptions included in Chapter 2, these are exemptions without the right to deduct input VAT. The exemptions are justified for reasons of general policy common to all the Member States and are set out in Articles 135-137 VAT Directive. The exemptions relate to specific transactions, such as insurance and financial services, betting, lotteries and gambling, supplies of immovable property and leasing and letting of immovable property.

Article 131 VAT Directive also applies to the exemptions for other activities. On the basis of that provision, Member States are held to lay down conditions for the purposes of ensuring the correct and straightforward application of these exemptions and of preventing any possible evasion, avoidance or abuse. As this is a general provision that applies to almost all exemptions, we refer to section 8.3.1 in this respect.

8.4.2 Insurance and Reinsurance Transactions[108]

Article 135(1)(a) VAT Directive exempts insurance and reinsurance transactions, including related services performed by insurance brokers and insurance agents from VAT. Therefore, no VAT is chargeable on the insurance premiums that the insured pays to insurance companies. Likewise, reinsurance premiums paid by insurance companies to reinsurers are not taxed with VAT. The payment of damages is outside the scope of VAT as such payment does not constitute consideration for a supply of goods or services.

The VAT Directive does not provide clear guidance on the interpretation of the exemption. Following consistent CJEU case law, the expression 'insurance transactions' means that the insurer undertakes, in return for prior payment of a premium, to provide the insured, in the event of materialization of the risk covered, with the service agreed when the contract was concluded.[109] The service can either be the payment of an amount of money or a service in kind (e.g., a repair service).[110] Following *Skandia*, an insurance transaction necessarily implies the existence of a contractual relationship between the provider of the insurance service and the person whose risks are covered by the insurance (the insured party).[111] From *CPP*, it follows that the exemption is not

108. This section is derived from A.J. van Doesum & G.J. van Norden 'Financial Services', in M. Lang & I. Lejeune (eds), *Improving VAT/GST: Designing a Simple and Fraud-Proof Tax System* (IBFD 2014), pp. 591-602.
109. For example: CJEU 25 February 1999, Case C-349/96 *Card Protection Plan Ltd (CPP) v Commissioners of Customs & Excise*, ECLI:EU:C:1999:93; CJEU 8 March 2001, Case C-240/99 *Försäkringsaktiebolaget Skandia (publ)*, ECLI:EU:C:2001:140; CJEU 20 November 2003, Case C-8/01 *Assurandør-Societetet, acting on behalf of Taksatorringen v Skatteministeriet*, ECLI: EU:C:2003:621 and CJEU 2 October 2009, Case C-242/08 *Swiss Re Germany Holding GmbH v Finanzamt München für Körperschaften*, ECLI:EU:C:2009:647.
110. CJEU 7 December 2006, Case C-13/06 *Commission of the European Communities v Hellenic Republic*, ECLI:EU:C:2006:765.
111. CJEU 8 March 2001, Case C-240/99 *Försäkringsaktiebolaget Skandia (publ)*, ECLI: EU:C:2001:140.

limited to services provided by insurance companies and that only the nature of the services provided is relevant.[112] In our view, this is in line with the concept of fiscal neutrality. However, not all transactions carried out by insurers are VAT-exempt. For example, it follows from *Global Companhia de Seguros* that activities that consist of the purchase and sale of parts from written-off vehicles by a car insurer are outside the scope of the exemption.[113] *Swiss Re* shows that a transfer for consideration of a portfolio of life reinsurance contracts by a reinsurance company is not an exempt insurance transaction, as it does not meet the aforementioned criteria for an insurance transaction.[114] Depending on the circumstances at issue and the legislation of the Member State concerned, no VAT may be due because the transfer can be regarded as a so-called TOGC, as mentioned in Article 29 VAT Directive.

From *Swiss Re*, it can also be derived that the VAT exemption for reinsurance transactions applies if an insurance company pays a reinsurance premium to a reinsurance company, whereby the insurance company remains the party that issues insurance policies to its own policyholders.

Services related to insurance and reinsurance transactions performed by insurance brokers and insurance agents are also VAT-exempt. In *Arthur Andersen*, finding prospects and introducing them to an insurer was regarded as an essential aspect of the work of an insurance agent. The supply of 'back office' services to an insurer, however, was not regarded as an exempt insurance intermediation service.[115] Also, the outsourcing of claims settlement services to a third party that acts on behalf of the insurance company is not exempt.[116] From *Taksatorringen*, it follows that the expression 'services related to insurance and reinsurance transactions performed by insurance brokers and insurance agents' refers only to services provided by professionals who have a relationship with both the insurer and the insured party, it being stressed that the broker is no more than an intermediary.[117] Following *J.C.M. Beheer BV*, the fact that an insurance broker or agent does not have a direct relationship with the parties to the insurance contract (either the insurer or the insured) in which conclusion he has been instrumental, but merely an indirect relationship with them through another intermediary who has a direct relationship with either of the parties to the insurance contract, does not prevent the exemption from applying.[118] Not only regular intermediation but also so-called sub-intermediation is VAT-exempt. In the current marketplace, the latter

---

112. CJEU 25 February 1999, Case C-349/96 *Card Protection Plan Ltd (CPP) v Commissioners of Customs & Excise*, ECLI:EU:C:1999:93.
113. CJEU 9 March 2023, Case C-42/22 *Generali Seguros SA, formerly Global – Companhia de Seguros, SA v Autoridade Tributária e Aduaneira*, ECLI:EU:C:2023:183.
114. CJEU 2 October 2009, Case C-242/08 *Swiss Re Germany Holding GmbH v Finanzamt München für Körperschaften*, ECLI:EU:C:2009:647. *See* on the concept of intermediation of insurance and financial services: C. Bohn Jespersen, *Intermediation of Insurance and Financial Services in European VAT (Dissertation)* (Wolters Kluwer 2011).
115. CJEU 3 March 2005, Case C-472/03 *Staatssecretaris van Financiën v Arthur Andersen & Co. Accountants c.s.*, ECLI:EU:C:2005:135.
116. CJEU 17 March 2016, Case C-40/15 *Minister Finansów v Aspiro SA*, ECLI:EU:C:2016:172.
117. CJEU 20 November 2003, Case C-8/01 *Assurandør-Societetet, acting on behalf of Taksatorringen v Skatteministeriet*, ECLI:EU:C:2003:621.
118. CJEU 3 April 2008, Case C-124/07 *J.C.M. Beheer BV v Staatssecretaris van Financiën*, ECLI:EU:C:2008:196.

type of intermediation occurs more and more. A wider interpretation of the exemption that the CJEU applied in *J.C.M. Beheer BV* seems in line with these market developments.

8.4.3 Financial Services[119]

In this section, we will discuss the exemptions with respect to financial services.

8.4.3.1 Granting and Negotiation of Credit

Pursuant to Article 135(1)(b) VAT Directive, an exemption applies to the granting and negotiation of credit and the management of credit by the person granting it. From *Velvet & Steel* and *Swiss Re*, it can be derived that the purpose of the exemption is to avoid an increase in the cost of consumer credit.[120] The exemption applies to credit granted by banks and financial institutions but is not limited to that type of credit. Credit granted by other taxable persons also falls within the scope of the exemption. The principle of neutrality requires this equal treatment. For example, from *Vega International*, it follows that a company that provides fuel cards to its subsidiaries in order to facilitate purchases of fuel, and as such, pre-finances the fuel purchases against payment of a 2% surcharge, provides credit in the sense of the VAT exemption.[121] Not only is the regular granting of interest-bearing loans exempt, but the granting of deferral payment for a supply of goods or services in return for payment of interest may also be exempt. For, in *Muys' en De Winter's*, it was confirmed that a supplier who authorizes his customer to defer payment of the price, in return for payment of interest, is, in principle, making an exempt grant of credit.[122] However, where a supplier grants his customer deferral of payment of the price, in return for payment of interest only until delivery, that interest does not constitute consideration for the grant of credit, but part of the consideration obtained for the supply.

The exemption is restricted to the management of credit by the person granting it. Situations in which a third party manages the credit are excluded from the exemption. This restriction raises questions in the field of securitizations. Here, the management of the credit is usually carried out by the financial institution that has transferred its loan portfolio to a special purpose vehicle (SPV). As of the date of the transfer, the SPV is granting the credit, thereby, in principle, excluding the management of the credit by the financial institution from the exemption. There is no clear reason why the exemption

119. This section is derived from A.J. van Doesum & G.J. van Norden 'Financial Services', in M. Lang & I. Lejeune (eds), *Improving VAT/GST: Designing a Simple and Fraud-Proof Tax System* (IBFD 2014), pp. 531-590.
120. CJEU 19 April 2007, Case C-455/05 *Velvet & Steel Immobilien und Handels GmbH v Finanzamt Hamburg-Eimsbüttel*, ECLI:EU:C:2007:232 and CJEU 2 October 2009, Case C-242/08 *Swiss Re Germany Holding GmbH v Finanzamt München für Körperschaften*, ECLI:EU:C:2009:647.
121. CJEU 15 May 2019, Case C-235/18 *Vega International Car Transport and Logistic – Trading GmbH v Dyrektor Izby Skarbowej w Warszawie*, ECLI:EU:C:2019:412.
122. CJEU 27 October 1993, Case C-281/91 *Muys' en De Winter's Bouw- en Aannemingsbedrijf BV v Staatssecretaris van Financiën*, ECLI:EU:C:1993:855.

should be restricted in this manner. However, the negotiation of credit can benefit from the exemption. Possibly, the *ratio legis* of this exemption is that without it, the two archetypes of intermediaries would be treated differently for VAT purposes. For, without an exemption for the negotiation of credit, intermediaries, acting in the name and on account of a client, cannot apply the exemption, whereas intermediaries acting in their own name but on account of a client (so-called commissionaires) can apply the VAT exemption on the basis of the fiction embedded in Article 28 VAT Directive.[123] The exemption for negotiation of credit removes this inequality and provides for equal VAT treatment. In recent years there has been increasing use of intermediaries in the financial services sector. In some situations, more than one intermediary is involved in concluding an agreement for the granting of credit by one party to another (so-called sub-agency). Following *Volker Ludwig*, the fact that an intermediary has no contractual link with any of the parties to a credit agreement, to the conclusion of which agreement he has contributed, nor does he establish direct contact with any of those parties, does not preclude the service of the intermediary being exempt negotiation of credit.[124]

8.4.3.2 Credit Guarantees

Article 135(1)(c) VAT Directive exempts the negotiation of, or any dealings in, credit guarantees or any other security for money and the management of credit guarantees by the person who is granting the credit. A notable example of a transaction under this exemption is a bank guarantee. The term 'guarantee' is not defined in the VAT Directive, nor has it previously been considered in CJEU case law either. According to AG Jääskinen in his opinion in *Skandinaviska Enskilda Banken*, a guarantee is essentially an assurance that, in the case of default by another, the person acting as a guarantor will undertake the necessary performance, usually payment, that the defaulting party has failed to make.[125] It follows from *Velvet & Steel* that transactions exempt on the basis of Article 135(1)(c) VAT Directive should relate to the sphere of financial transactions.[126] Therefore, the provision excludes from the exemption obligations, which are non-pecuniary, such as the obligation to renovate a property.

8.4.3.3 Current Accounts, Payments and Transfers

On the basis of Article 135(1)(d) VAT Directive, transactions, including negotiation, concerning deposit and current accounts, payments, transfers, debts, cheques and other negotiable instruments, but excluding debt collection, are exempt. *SDC* can be

123. On the basis of this provision, where a taxable person acting in his own name but on behalf of another person takes part in a supply of services, he shall be deemed to have received and supplied those services himself.
124. CJEU 21 June 2007, Case C-453/05 *Volker Ludwig v Finanzamt Luckenwalde*, ECLI:EU:C:2007:369.
125. Opinion of AG Jääskinen of 16 December 2010, Case C540/09 *Skandinaviska Enskilda Banken AB Momsgrupp v Skatteverket*, ECLI:EU:C:2011:137.
126. CJEU 19 April 2007, Case C-455/05 *Velvet & Steel Immobilien und Handels GmbH v Finanzamt Hamburg-Eimsbüttel*, ECLI:EU:C:2007:232.

considered as the directional case with respect to this exemption.[127] The CJEU set out the conditions for a transaction to be exempt under Article 135(1)(d) VAT Directive. As for all exemptions, this exemption should be interpreted strictly because it is an exception to the general rule that all taxable transactions are taxed with VAT. In order for the exemption to apply, the services should, viewed broadly, form a distinct whole, in effect fulfilling the specific, essential functions of an exempt service. In order for a transaction to be recognized as 'a transaction concerning transfers', the services provided must have the effect of transferring funds and entail changes in the legal and financial situation. An exempt service must be distinguished from a mere physical or technical supply, such as making a data-handling system available to a bank. In *SDC*, the CJEU left it to the national court to examine the extent of the responsibility of the service provider vis-à-vis its customers, in particular, the question of whether its responsibility is restricted to technical aspects, or whether it extends to the specific, essential aspects of the transactions.

Although the criteria for applying this exemption may seem fairly straightforward, in practice, they give rise to several discussions between taxpayers and tax administrations. The interpretation of the SDC-criteria has been the subject of a number of CJEU cases on the scope of the exemption for payments and transfers. From cases like *Nordea*, *Bookit*, *DPAS* and *Cardpoint*, it may be derived that there seems to be very little scope to apply the exemption on services performed by entities that are not able to actually debit one account and credit the other in order to effectuate a payment or a transfer of funds.[128] Consequently, the exemption seems to have a somewhat subjective nature, as it is difficult to envisage what provider can meet the SDC-criteria, outside of banking institutions. Differences between the language versions of *SDC* certainly do not contribute to a uniform interpretation of the exemption at issue. In the English language version of *SDC*, for example, the term 'responsibility' is used, which is similar to the terms *responsabilité* and *Verantwortung* that are used in the French- and German-language versions. In the Dutch language version, however, the term *aansprakelijkheid* is used, which translates as 'liability' and refers to a totally different legal concept to 'responsibility'.[129] Besides legal uncertainty within the territory of Member States, *SDC* has led to legal uncertainty in cross-border situations. The interpretation of *SDC* in the various Member States tends to differ, leading to an uneven playing field.

Debt collection is explicitly excluded from the exemption. However, there is no definition of the term 'debt collection' in the VAT Directive. As debt collection is an exception to the exemption, it is to be interpreted broadly. Debt collection refers to

127. CJEU 5 June 1997, Case C-2/95 *Sparekassernes Datacenter (SDC) v Skatteministeriet*, ECLI:EU:C:1997:278.

128. CJEU 28 July 2011, Case C-350/10 *Nordea Pankki Suomi Oyj*, ECLI:EU:C:2011:532; CJEU 26 May 2016, Case C-607/14 *Bookit, Ltd v Commissioners for Her Majesty's Revenue and Customs*, ECLI:EU:C:2016:355; CJEU 25 July 2018, Case C-5/17 *Commissioners for Her Majesty's Revenue and Customs v DPAS Limited*, ECLI:EU:C:2018:592 and CJEU 3 October 2019, Case C-42/18 *Finanzamt Trier v Cardpoint GmbH, legal successor to Moneybox Deutschland GmbH*, ECLI:EU:C:2019:822.

129. In CJEU 28 July 2011, Case C-350/10 *Nordea Pankki Suomi Oyj*, ECLI:EU:C:2011:532, the same difference in terminology can be found.

financial transactions designed to obtain payment of a pecuniary debt.[130] As a result of technological progress, the amount and variety of payment solutions have increased rapidly. Payments can be made by means of the internet, (smart)phone and other equipment. Businesses receive offers from service providers to improve their outgoing and incoming payment flows. All these developments lead to new service provisions that should have a clear VAT treatment. However, there is only a thin line between exempt payment-handling services and VAT taxed debt collection. *Axa UK* dealt with the handling of payments on behalf of dentists in respect of payment plans under which patients agreed to pay their respective dentists a fixed monthly sum in return for a specified level of dental care. The CJEU ruled that the exemption does not apply to those services. It even concluded in *DPAS* that the same was true if this service was contractually provided to the patients, instead of the dentists, thus suggesting that a (taxable) debt collection service can be provided to the person whose debt is being collected.[131]

Following *MKG*, it is clear that factoring is also to be treated as an activity that is excluded from the exemption. Factoring must be regarded as constituting merely a variant of the more general concept of debt collection.[132] According to the CJEU, a factoring company that purchases debts, assuming the risk of the debtor's default, supplies a service to its clients consisting essentially in relieving them of the debt recovery operations and of the risk of the debts not being paid. In return, the clients owe payment to the factoring company corresponding to the difference between the face value of the debts which they have assigned to the factoring company and the amount the factoring company pays them for these debts. The CJEU's ruling perhaps raised more questions than it answered. If the factoring company indeed provided services, should the transfer of the debts still be considered as an exempt transfer, or should it be disregarded for VAT purposes? How should securitization transactions and the sale of non-performing loans be treated? In *GFKL*, the CJEU decided that a business that, at its own risk, purchases defaulted debts at a price below their face value, does not carry out a supply of services within the meaning of Article 2 VAT Directive. The difference between the face value of the assigned debts and the purchase price of those debts does not constitute the consideration for a service, but a reflection of the actual economic value of the debts at the time of their assignment, which results from the fact that they are doubtful, and from the increased risk of default of the debtors.[133] Transfers of non-performing loans should not be treated as 'regular' factoring. In our view, a different VAT treatment is in line with the character of both types of

130. CJEU 26 June 2003, Case C-305/01 *Finanzamt Groß-Gerau v MKG-Kraftfahrzeuge-Factoring GmbH*, ECLI:EU:C:2003:377 and CJEU 28 October 2010, Case C-175/09 *Commissioners for Her Majesty's Revenue and Customs v AXA UK PLC*, ECLI:EU:C:2010:646.

131. CJEU 25 July 2018, Case C-5/17 *Commissioners for Her Majesty's Revenue and Customs v DPAS Limited*, ECLI:EU:C:2018:592. *See* on the DPAS-case P. Gamito, *Is an Instruction to Make a Payment an Exempt Supply for VAT Purposes?* (2018) 4 EC Tax Review, pp. 218-224 https://doi.org/10.54648/ecta2018023.

132. CJEU 26 June 2003, Case C-305/01 *Finanzamt Groß-Gerau v MKG-Kraftfahrzeuge-Factoring GmbH*, ECLI:EU:C:2003:377.

133. CJEU 27 October 2011, Case C-93/10 *Finanzamt Essen-NordOst v GFKL Financial Services AG*, ECLI:EU:C:2011:700.

transactions. A factoring company, in essence, provides a service to its clients, offering to collect their debts in combination with a financing arrangement. This is not the essence of a non-performing loans transaction. The purchaser of such loans is not providing any services to the seller of those loans but is merely acting as a purchaser.

8.4.3.4 Currency, Bank Notes and Coins

On the basis of Article 135(1)(e) VAT Directive, Member States shall exempt transactions, including negotiation, concerning currency, banknotes and coins used as legal tender, with the exception of collectors' items, that is to say, gold, silver or other metal coins or banknotes which are not normally used as legal tender or coins of numismatic interest.[134] In a general tax on consumption, such as EU VAT, consumption should be taxed. EU VAT taxes this consumption by levying tax with respect to private expenditure. However, the means of the exchange necessary to make these expenditures, i.e., money, should not be taxed. This seems the reason why transactions concerning currency, banknotes and coins are VAT-exempt. In order for the exemption to apply the currency, banknotes and coins should be used as legal tender. The exemption is not applicable in the case of collectors' items, namely gold, silver or other metal coins or banknotes, which are not normally used as legal tender, or coins of numismatic interest. In principle, transactions with respect to these banknotes and coins are VAT taxed. However, the margin scheme or the special scheme for investment gold may apply.[135]

Transactions, including *negotiation* regarding currencies, are exempt under Article 135(1)(e) VAT Directive. In modern life, virtual currencies (like bitcoins) are also used as a means to pay for goods and services, and some undertakings specialize in the exchange of virtual currencies for traditional currencies and vice versa. In *David Hedqvist,* the CJEU ruled that transactions which consist of the exchange of traditional currency for units of the bitcoin virtual currency and vice versa, in return for payment of a sum equal to the difference between, on the one hand, the price paid by the operator to purchase the currency and, on the other hand, the price at which he sells that currency to his clients, constitute the supply of services for consideration within the meaning of Article 135(1)(e) and are exempt from VAT.[136]

8.4.3.5 Shares and Other Securities

Article 135(1)(f) VAT Directive exempts transactions, including negotiation, but not management or safekeeping, in shares, interests in companies or associations, debentures and other securities, but excluding documents establishing title to goods, and the rights or securities referred to in Article 15(2) VAT Directive. From *CSC Financial Services,* it follows that transactions in securities refer to transactions liable to create,

---

134. Pursuant to Article 45 VAT Implementing Regulation, the exemption does not apply to so-called platinum nobles.
135. *See* Articles 311 et seq. and Articles 344 et seq. VAT Directive.
136. CJEU 22 October 2015, Case C-264/14 *Skatteverket v David Hedqvist,* ECLI:EU:C:2015:718.

alter or extinguish parties' rights and obligations in respect of securities.[137] Moreover, the CJEU held that nothing, in principle, precludes an exempt transaction in securities from being broken down into a number of separate services. In the case of outsourcing in the field of securities, the exemption may still apply, although only a part of the transactions in securities is outsourced.

From a business perspective, the question arises as to whether the sale of (shares in) a subsidiary falls within the scope of the exemption (we refer to Chapter 11, section 11.6). If so, this sale is VAT-exempt, which precludes the deduction of input VAT on costs directly attributable to the sale.[138] From a theoretical point of view, we believe that a consumption tax, such as VAT, should not create a tax burden for businesses that dispose of (shares in) their subsidiaries. These businesses should have a right to reclaim all VAT on costs related to such disposal because they incur these costs in the course of their business activities. In the context of share disposals, there is no private consumption to be taxed. However, given the technical structure of the current EU VAT system, input VAT deduction should nevertheless be disallowed.

Management and safekeeping of shares and other securities are excluded from the exemption. The terms 'management' and 'safekeeping' are not defined in the VAT Directive. The reason for excluding management and safekeeping from the exemption seems to be their administrative nature. Administrative activities do not involve alteration of legal and financial positions of the parties concerned, which, according to *SDC* and *CSC*, is necessary to benefit from the exemption.[139] The question, however, is whether services like asset management and global custody should be regarded as 'management' and 'safekeeping' of shares, as mentioned in Article 135(1)(f) VAT Directive.

Asset management services are generally understood to be services whereby the asset manager will not only identify an investment opportunity but will also have the authority to act upon the occurrence of such opportunity by acquiring or disposing of assets on behalf of its clients within the mandate granted to it.[140] According to *Deutsche Bank AG*, portfolio management services cannot benefit from the exemption of Article 135(1)(f) VAT Directive in situations where the asset manager not only determines the purchase and sale of securities but also implements that determination by buying and selling the securities in so far as it relates to transactions in securities or the negotiation of such transactions.[141] The CJEU established that the portfolio management effectively

137. CJEU 13 December 2001, Case C-235/00 *Commissioners of Customs & Excise v CSC Financial Services Ltd*, ECLI:EU:C:2001:696.
138. This also follows from CJEU 6 April 1995, Case C-4/94 *BLP Group plc v Commissioners of Customs & Excise*, ECLI:EU:C:1995:107. If the shares were to be sold to a party established outside the EU, however, full deduction of directly attributable input VAT would be possible on the basis of Article 169(c) VAT Directive.
139. CJEU 5 June 1997, Case C-2/95 *Sparekassernes Datacenter (SDC) v Skatteministeriet*, ECLI:EU:C:1997:278 and CJEU 13 December 2001, Case C-235/00 *Commissioners of Customs & Excise v CSC Financial Services Ltd.*, ECLI:EU:C:2001:696.
140. E. van Kasteren, *How Recent CJEU Referrals May Place Increased Pressure on the VAT Position of Asset Managers* (2011) 6 Derivatives & Financial Instruments, p. 335 https://doi.org/10.59403/kdm61n.
141. CJEU 19 July 2012, Case C-44/11 *Finanzamt Frankfurt am Main V-Höchst v Deutsche Bank AG*, ECLI:EU:C:2012:484.

consisted of two elements: analysing and monitoring the investor's assets, and the purchase and sale of securities, which for VAT purposes constituted a single supply. This single supply cannot be regarded as a transaction in securities.

Transactions in documents establishing title to goods, and the rights or securities referred to in Article 15(2) VAT Directive are also excluded from the exemption. Considering that documents establishing title to goods, in fact, give their holders the right to dispose of these goods as owners explain the exclusion from the exemption. The supply of such a document implies the supply of the right to dispose of the very good it establishes title to. The supply of these documents should not be covered by an exemption; only the underlying supply of goods should be relevant for VAT.

Article 135(1)(f) reads as follows: 'transactions, including *negotiation* ... in shares.' The notion 'negotiation' is a common expression and used in several provisions regarding exemptions (as already discussed above, and as further discussed in the sections below). The main issue in *DTZ Zadelhoff* was the question of when a taxable person is considered to be *negotiating with regard to shares and other securities*.[142] In that case, the question arose whether the notion 'negotiation in shares' covers intermediary services, such as those carried out by DTZ Zadelhoff. DTZ Zadelhoff negotiated between the owners of immovable property and the potential customers of that immovable property. At the start of the negotiation, it was uncertain whether the negotiation would eventually relate to the supply of immovable property itself (direct supply of immovable property), or would relate to the disposal of shares in a legal entity that would hold the immovable property (indirect supply of immovable property). The first option would certainly lead to a taxed intermediary service; the second option would lead - at least that was the issue - to an exempt intermediary service, being negotiation relating to a share dealing. It was clear from the start that the customer was primarily interested in the immovable property, and that the shares were only meant as 'carriers' (or, in other words, 'a means of transport') of the immovable property concerned. Nevertheless, the CJEU ruled that if the underlying transaction of the negotiation takes the form of a share dealing finally, the negotiation will have the nature of an exempted intermediary service, being the negotiation of a share dealing as meant in Article 135(1)(f).[143]

142. *See also* A.J. van Doesum, *Commentary* to *DTZ Zadelhoff, What Looks Like a Duck Is a Duck: Economic Purpose and Legal Reality in EU VAT Law* (2012) 2 World Journal of VAT https://doi.org/10.5235/wjovl.1.2.202.

143. CJEU 5 July 2012, Case 257/11 *DTZ Zadelhoff vof v Staatssecretaris van Financiën*, ECLI: EU:C:2012:423, para. 42. We note that the exception to the exemption provided for in the second indent of that provision ('but excluding documents establishing title to goods, and the rights or securities referred to in Article 15(2) VAT Directive') is not applicable if the Member State has not availed itself of the possibility provided by Article 5(3)(c) of the Sixth Directive of considering shares or interests equivalent to shares giving the holder thereof de jure or de facto rights of ownership or possession over immovable property to be tangible property.

8.4.3.6 Management of Special Investment Funds

Article 135(1)(g) VAT Directive provides for an exemption of the management of special investment funds as defined by the Member States.[144] From *Abbey National* and *JP Morgan Fleming Claverhouse*, it is clear that a particular purpose of the exemption is to facilitate investment in securities for (small) investors by means of investment undertakings. The provision is intended to ensure that VAT is fiscally neutral as regards the choice between direct investment in securities and investment through undertakings for collective investment.[145] The wording of the provision seems to leave quite some room for the Member States to define the scope of the exemption. This is somewhat difficult to reconcile with the general idea that exemptions should have an independent meaning in Community law, and with the intention of having a harmonized VAT throughout the EU. Nonetheless, CJEU case law has contributed to further harmonization in this respect. For example, through reference to particular language versions of the exemption, it was decided in *Abbey National* that the concept of 'management' of special investment funds has its own independent meaning in Community law, whose content the Member States may not alter.[146]

From *JP Morgan Fleming Claverhouse*, it follows that the Member States do not have full discretion to define the concept of 'special investment funds'.[147] In the exercise of their power to define the concept, Member States must respect the objective of the exemption, which is to facilitate investment in securities for investors through investment undertakings, while guaranteeing the principle of fiscal neutrality. The Member States, therefore, are not allowed to exclude investment funds from the exemption if they are in competition with investment funds that can benefit from the exemption. From *Fiscale Eenheid X*, it follows that this criterion of competition is met if a fund is subject to specific state supervision.[148]

In *Wheels Common Investment Fund Trustees Ltd*, the question was raised whether certain UK pension schemes should be regarded as special investment funds, as mentioned in Article 135(1)(g) VAT Directive.[149] Given the legal differences in pension schemes, Member States currently treat pension schemes differently for VAT purposes. In *Wheels Common Investment Fund Trustees Ltd*, the CJEU held that the

144. For more background to this so-called fund exemption *see* G.J. van Norden, 'Collective Investment Vehicles and VAT in a Changing Environment', in Hein Vermeulen (ed.) *The Tax Treatment of CIVs and REITs* (IBFD 2013), pp. 201-228.
145. CJEU 4 May 2006, Case C-169/04 *Abbey National plc, Inscape Investment Fund v Commissioners of Customs & Excise*, ECLI:EU:C:2006:28 and CJEU 28 June 2007, Case C-363/05 *JP Morgan Fleming Claverhouse Investment Trust plc, The Association of Investment Trust Companies v The Commissioners of HM Revenue and Customs*, ECLI:EU:C:2007:391.
146. CJEU 4 May 2006, Case C-169/04 *Abbey National plc, Inscape Investment Fund v Commissioners of Customs & Excise*, ECLI:EU:C:2006:28.
147. CJEU 28 June 2007, Case C-363/05 *JP Morgan Fleming Claverhouse Investment Trust plc, The Association of Investment Trust Companies v The Commissioners of HM Revenue and Customs*, ECLI:EU:C:2007:391.
148. CJEU 9 December 2015, Case C-595/13 *Staatssecretaris van Financiën v Fiscale Eenheid X NV cs*, ECLI:EU:C:2015:801.
149. CJEU 4 March 2013, Case C-424/11 *Wheels Common Investment Fund Trustees Ltd*, ECLI: EU:C:2013:144.

defined benefit (DB) pension schemes at issue were not qualifying funds under EU VAT law, and therefore, supplies of investment management services to such schemes should not be exempt from VAT. According to the CJEU, DB pension schemes do not display the characteristics of special investment funds, as they are not open to investment by the public, employees do not bear the investment risk, and employers' contributions are made as a consequence of legal obligation to the employee, rather than in the course of an investment activity.[150]

In *ATP Pension Services*, so-called defined contribution (DC) pension schemes were addressed.[151] In a DB pension scheme, such as at issue in *Wheels Common Investment Fund Trustees Ltd*, a specified monthly benefit is promised on retirement that is predetermined by a formula based on the employee's earnings history, tenure of service and age, rather than depending directly on individual investment returns. Under a DC pension scheme, the contributions of the employer and employee are defined and known in advance, but the future benefit to be paid out is not. Therefore, DC pension schemes appear to have more characteristics in common with 'regular' investment funds. From *ATP Pension Services*, one can take that, under the circumstances, DC pension schemes indeed can be regarded as special investment funds, as mentioned in Article 135(1)(g) VAT Directive. To this end, it is relevant whether the DC pension schemes are funded by the persons to whom the retirement benefit is to be paid, whether they invest using a risk-spreading principle, and whether the pension customers bear the investment risk. In that regard, it is of little consequence that the contributions are paid by the employer, that the amount paid in is based on collective agreements between labour-market organizations, that there are different ways of paying out the funds invested, that contributions are deductible under income tax law, or that it is possible to add an insurance element which is ancillary to the other services provided.

In the investment fund sector, quite often, third-party financial service providers are used. This gives rise to the question of whether the exemption applies to their services. Following *Abbey National*, the exemption covers the services performed by a third-party manager in respect of the administrative management of the fund if, viewed broadly, they form a distinct whole and are specific to, and essential for, the management of the fund.[152] In its decision, the CJEU, in fact, applied the same criteria for the interpretation of the exemption as were used in *SDC* with respect to the exemption mentioned in Article 135(1)(d) VAT Directive (*see* section 8.4.3.3).[153] For example, fund accounting services can benefit from the exemption on the basis of *Abbey National*. On the basis of *GfBk Gesellschaft für Börsenkommunikation mbH* investment advice provided to a fund manager whose fund management services are

150. *See also* CJEU 18 July 2013, Case C-26/12 *Fiscale eenheid PPG Holdings BV cs te Hoogezand v Inspecteur van de Belastingdienst/Noord/kantoor Groningen*, ECLI:EU:C:2013:526.
151. CJEU 13 March 2014, Case C-464/12 *ATP Pension Service A/S v Skatteministeriet*, ECLI:EU:C:2014:139.
152. CJEU 4 May 2006, Case C-169/04 *Abbey National plc, Inscape Investment Fund v Commissioners of Customs & Excise*, ECLI:EU:C:2006:28.
153. CJEU 5 June 1997, Case C-2/95 *Sparekassernes Datacenter (SDC) v Skatteministeriet*, ECLI:EU:C:1997:278.

VAT-exempt can fall within the scope of the exemption.[154] According to the CJEU, investment advice services are VAT-exempt if intrinsically connected to the activity characteristic of a special investment fund, thereby constituting the specific and essential functions of the management of such a fund. Recommendations as to the purchase and sale of assets are, in the view of the CJEU, intrinsically connected to the activities of a fund, and should be able to benefit from the exemption. In *K & DBKAG*, it was ruled that tax-related services consisting in ensuring that the income received from a special investment fund by the unit-holders is taxed in accordance with national law and the grant of a right to use software which is used exclusively to carry out calculations which are essential for risk management and performance measurement fall within the scope of the exemption.[155] From *BlackRock*, it follows that if a fund manager purchases a single service of management for its funds and uses it for both taxable activities (non-special investment funds) and the VAT-exempt management of a special investment fund, the exemption cannot be applied on such purchase.[156]

Special investment funds may also be regarded as investment companies, in which capital (immovable property) is pooled by several investors. These investors usually bear the risk connected with the management of the assets assembled in those companies with a view to purchasing, owning, managing and selling immovable property in order to derive a profit therefrom. That profit is normally distributed to all unit-holders in the form of a dividend. Those unit-holders stand to benefit also from any increase in the value of their holding. Under those conditions and provided that the Member State concerned has made those companies subject to specific state supervision, the management of such a special investment fund is exempt. However, the exempt management will not cover the actual management of the immovable property of a special investment fund.[157]

8.4.4 Postage Stamps

On the basis of Article 135(1)(h) VAT Directive, a VAT exemption applies to the supply at face value of postage stamps valid for use within their respective territory, fiscal stamps and other similar stamps. This exemption exists alongside the exemption of Article 132(1)(a) VAT Directive for public postal services. It is not particularly clear what the reason is behind the additional exemption for postage stamps. From the Second Report, it can be derived that the European Commission felt an exemption was necessary for the importation of postage stamps. According to the Commission, imposing VAT on the importation of postage stamps was likely to create discrimination in relation to supplies of stamps having the same function within the importing

154. CJEU 7 March 2013, Case C-275/11 *GfBk Gesellschaft für Börsenkommunikation mbH v Finanzamt Bayreuth*, ECLI:EU:C:2013:141.
155. CJEU 17 June 2021, Cases C-58/20 and C-59/20 *K and DBKAG v Finanzamt Österreich, anciennement Finanzamt Linz*, ECLI:EU:C:2021:491.
156. CJEU 2 July 2020, Case C-231/19 *Blackrock Investment Management (UK) Limited v Commissioners for Her Majesty's Revenue and Customs* ECLI:EU:C:2020:513.
157. CJEU 9 December 2015, Case C-595/13 *Staatssecretaris van Financiën v Fiscale Eenheid X NV cs*, ECLI:EU:C:2015:801.

country, i.e., (exempt) stamps issued by the postal authorities of that country and supplied directly by them.[158] Although the VAT Directive contains two separate exemptions, some Member States (e.g., the Netherlands) have chosen only to implement the general exemption for postal services under Article 135(1)(h) VAT Directive. A separate exemption, however, is required where the Member States make use of fiscal stamps or other similar stamps. If a Member State does not use such stamps, a specific provision obviously is not necessary.

As indicated in section 8.3.2, in 2003, the European Commission presented a proposal for a Directive regarding VAT on services provided in the postal sector.[159] This proposal also included the removal of the exemption for postage stamps. In 2004, the Commission delivered a (slightly) amended proposal, which, however, maintained the abolition of the exemption.[160] The Member States appeared to be unable to agree on the terms and conditions necessary to revise VAT legislation as regards postal services. On 16 April 2013, the proposal was withdrawn.

8.4.5 Betting, Lotteries and Gambling

Article 135(1)(i) VAT Directive provides for an exemption for betting, lotteries and other forms of gambling, subject to the conditions and limitations laid down by each Member State. The *ratio legis* for this exemption is probably the fact that several Member States already levied national taxes with respect to gambling. Also, it was most likely considered to be difficult to determine the taxable amount for gambling.[161]

Following consistent CJEU case law, the exemptions are Union law concepts and thus should be interpreted similarly in all Member States.[162] This should equally apply to the exemption for betting, lotteries and other forms of gambling. On the other hand, Article 135(1)(i) VAT Directive seems to offer the Member States the possibility of determining the scope of the exemption themselves. After all, the provision requires the Member States to exempt betting, lotteries and other forms of gambling, but this is subject to the conditions and limitations laid down by each Member State. This delicate balance can also be found with other exemption, such as the exemption for management of special investment funds laid down in Article 135(1)(g) VAT Directive (*see* section 8.4.3.6).

It follows from *Fischer* that the principle of fiscal neutrality also applies when the Member States exercise their power to lay down the conditions and limitations of the exemption for betting and gambling. Following the principle of neutrality, the unlawful

158. Second report from the Commission on the application of the common system of value added tax, submitted in accordance with Article 34 of the Sixth Directive, COM (88) 799 final, pp. 36 et seq.
159. Proposal for a Council Directive amending Directive 77/388/EEC as regards value added tax on services provided in the postal sector, 5 May 2003, COM (2003) 234 final.
160. Amended proposal for a Council Directive amending Directive 77/388/EEC as regards value added tax on services provided in the postal sector, 8 July 2004, COM (2004) 468 final.
161. Explanatory Memorandum to the proposal for a Sixth Directive of 20 June 1973, COM (73)950.
162. For example: CJEU 11 January 2001, Case C-76/99 *Commission of the European Communities v French Republic*, ECLI:EU:C:2001:12 and CJEU 16 January 2003, Case C-315/00 *Rudolf Maierhofer v Finanzamt Augsburg-Land*, ECLI:EU:C:2003:23.

operation of a game of chance falls within the scope of the exemption when the corresponding lawful activity carried out by a licensed casino is exempt.[163] Similarly, it was decided in *Linneweber* that national legislation, which exempts the operation of all games of chance and gaming machines where it is carried out in licensed public casinos but does not exempt the operation of the same activity by entrepreneurs other than those running casinos, is not in line with Article 135(1)(g) VAT Directive.[164] Moreover, *Linneweber* makes clear that this provision has direct effect, in the sense that an operator of games of chance or gaming machines can rely upon that provision before national courts to prevent national legislation, which is inconsistent with the provision. In order to benefit from the exemption, services should actually be betting, lottery or gambling services. It is necessary that an offer of a chance of winning is made to customers placing bets in consideration for accepting the risk of having to pay for winnings.[165] According to *United Utilities*, for example, call centre services to a telephone bookmaking organizer, which entails the staff of the call centre accepting bets on behalf of the organizer, cannot be regarded as a betting service.[166]

8.4.6 Supply of a Building

Article 135(1)(j) VAT Directive exempts the supply of a building or parts thereof, and of the land on which it stands, other than the supply of building land referred to in Article 12(1)(a) VAT Directive. Immovable property has a special position in the framework of consumption taxes. Given the fact that immovable property, in principle, lasts for years if not decades, and generally cannot be completely consumed, it seems odd to levy a consumption tax each time a specific immovable property is supplied. Moreover, immovable property is often also supplied by private persons. For these reasons, the supply of immovable property is exempt from consumption taxes. This also applies with regard to European VAT. As a general rule, supplies of a building or parts thereof, and of the land on which it stands, are exempt.

On the basis of Article 137(1)(b) VAT Directive, however, Member States may allow taxable persons a right of option for taxation (*see* section 8.4.10). If such an option is introduced and used with respect to a supply of a building from one taxable person to another taxable person, which is entitled to a deduction of input VAT, tax cascading is avoided. The design of the option, however, differs per Member State. This is likely to be partially caused by the fact that some Member States levy a real estate transfer tax next to VAT on supplies of immovable property.

The supply, before first occupation, of a building or parts of a building and of the land on which the building stands, referred to in Article 12(1)(a) VAT Directive, is, in

163. CJEU 11 June 1998, Case C-283/95 *Karlheinz Fischer v Finanzamt Donaueschingen*, ECLI:EU:C:1998:276.
164. CJEU 17 February 2005, Cases C-453/02 and C-462/02 *Finanzamt Gladbeck v Edith Linneweber and Finanzamt Herne-West v Savvas Akritidis*, ECLI:EU:C:2005:92.
165. CJEU 13 July 2006, Case C-89/05 *United Utilities Plc v Commissioners of Customs & Excise*, ECLI:EU:C:2006:469, para. 26.
166. CJEU 13 July 2006, Case C-89/05 *United Utilities Plc v Commissioners of Customs & Excise*, ECLI:EU:C:2006:469.

any case, excluded from the exemption. This exclusion is introduced because it was felt that new immovable property should be taxed in a consumption tax. Pursuant to Article 12(2) VAT Directive, Member States may determine the conditions of application of the criterion concerning first occupation to transformations of buildings and the land on which they stand. Member States are granted this freedom in order to counter abusive practices. We refer to Chapter 9, which deals specifically with immovable property, for a more in-depth analysis of this exemption.

8.4.7 Supply of Land

Pursuant to Article 135(1)(k) VAT Directive, an exemption applies to the supply of land which has not been built on, other than the supply of building land as referred to in Article 12(1)(b) VAT Directive. The reasons for exempting the supply of land are effectively the same as for the supply of buildings (*see* section 8.4.6). On the basis of Article 137(1)(c) VAT Directive, Member States may allow taxable persons a right of option for taxation of a supply of land which has not been built on. We refer to section 8.4.10 in this respect. The supply of building land referred to in Article 12(1)(b) VAT Directive is, in any case, excluded from the exemption. We refer to Chapter 9, which deals specifically with immovable property, for a more in-depth analysis of this exemption.

8.4.8 Leasing of Immovable Property

Article 135(1)(l) VAT Directive provides for an exemption of the leasing or letting of immovable property. From the Explanatory Memorandum to the proposal for a Sixth VAT Directive, it follows that the Member States generally exempted the letting of immovable property on technical, economic and social grounds.[167]

Article 135(2) VAT Directive excludes four categories of supplies of services from the exemption for leasing of immovable property. First, an exclusion applies to the provision of accommodation, as defined in the laws of the Member States, in the hotel sector or in sectors with a similar function, including the provision of accommodation in holiday camps or on sites developed for use as camping sites. Second, the letting of premises and sites for the parking of vehicles is excluded from the exemption. Third, the letting of permanently installed equipment and machinery is subject to VAT. Finally, the hire of safes is also not exempt.

On the basis of Article 137(1)(d), Member States may allow taxable persons a right of option for taxation in respect of the leasing or letting of immovable property. If they choose to do so, Member States have to lay down the detailed rules governing the exercise of that option. Member States may, however, restrict the scope of that right of option. We refer to Chapter 9, which deals specifically with immovable property, for a more in-depth analysis of the VAT exemption for leasing of immovable property.

167. Explanatory Memorandum to the proposal for a Sixth Directive of 20 June 1973, COM (73) 950.

8.4.9 Technical Exemption

Article 136 VAT Directive contains a very specific exemption with a technical character. In short, paragraph (a) of this provision exempts supplies of goods which are solely used for specifically listed exempt activities,[168] if those goods have not given rise to deductibility. For example, if a school supplies used school desks that have been used solely for exempt educational activities, the supply is exempt. The *ratio legis* for this exemption is that no double taxation should occur. Without this provision, no deduction would be allowed at the moment of purchase of goods, which after being used for exempt purposes, are taxed upon disposal. Following paragraph (b) of the provision, an exemption applies to the supply of goods on the acquisition or application of which VAT was not deductible pursuant to Article 176 VAT Directive. This is a standstill provision, on which basis Member States may continue certain input VAT limitations they had in the past. Moreover, on the basis of Article 176 VAT Directive, VAT is in no circumstances deductible in respect of expenditure, which is not strictly for business purposes, such as expenditure on luxuries, amusements or entertainment. If for whatever reason, goods are supplied to which input VAT deduction is denied on the basis of Article 176 VAT Directive, an exemption applies to that supply. This exemption is also introduced in order to avoid double taxation.

8.4.10 Option to Tax

According to Article 137(1) VAT Directive, Member States may allow taxable persons a right of option for taxation in respect of certain specifically mentioned transactions. On the basis of Article 137(2) VAT Directive, Member States are to lay down detailed rules governing the exercise of the option to tax. Moreover, Member States may restrict the scope of the option to tax. It is for the Member States to assess whether they should or should not introduce the right of option, depending on what they consider to be expedient in the situation existing in their country at a given time.[169] When the Member States use their ability to restrict the scope of the right of option and to determine the arrangements for its exercise, they are to observe the general objectives and principles of the VAT Directive, in particular, the principle of fiscal neutrality and the requirement for correct, straightforward and uniform application of the exemptions.[170]

168. The activities exempted under Articles 132 (exemptions for certain activities in the public interest), 135 (exemptions for other activities), 371 (original transitional exemptions), 375 (transitional exemptions for Greece), 376 (transitional exemptions for Spain), 377 (transitional exemptions for Portugal), 378(2) (transitional exemptions for Austria), 379(2) (transitional exemptions for Finland) and 380-390 (transitional exemptions for Member States which more recently entered the EU) VAT Directive.
169. *See* CJEU 3 December 1998, Case C-381/97 *Belgocodex SA v Belgian State*, ECLI:EU:C:1998:589 and CJEU 12 January 2006, Case C-246/04 *Turn- und Sportunion Waldburg v Finanzlandesdirektion für Oberöstereich*, ECLI:EU:C:2006:22.
170. *See* CJEU 4 October 2001, Case C-326/99 *Stichting Goed Wonen v Staatssecretaris van Financiën*, ECLI:EU:C:2001:506 and CJEU 12 January 2006, Case C-246/04 *Turn- und Sportunion Waldburg v Finanzlandesdirektion für Oberöstereich*, ECLI:EU:C:2006:22.

The specifically mentioned transactions for which an exemption may be introduced are the following:

(a) the financial transactions referred to in Article 135(1)(b)-(g);
(b) the supply of a building or of parts thereof, and of the land on which the building stands, other than the supply referred to in point (a) of Article 12(1);
(c) the supply of land which has not been built on other than the supply of building land referred to in point (b) of Article 12(1);
(d) the leasing or letting of immovable property.[171]

The option to tax removes one of the systematic disadvantages of the VAT exemptions. For example, if a taxable person opts to tax its financial services supplied to businesses, which then have a right to recover the VAT on those services (B2B supplies), the problem of tax cascading in the production and distribution chain is removed. However, as regards B2C supplies, the option to tax does not contribute to a better functioning of the VAT system. In general, Member States have only made use of the possibility to introduce an option to tax in a B2B context. Only seven Member States have introduced an option to tax financial services: Austria, Belgium, Bulgaria, Estonia, France, Germany and Lithuania. It should be noted that the option to tax can only be exercised for financial services, as mentioned in Article 135(1)(b)-(g) VAT Directive. The Member States, therefore, are not allowed to grant an option to tax in respect of insurance services, as mentioned in Article 135(1)(a) VAT Directive. Far more Member States, including Denmark, Germany, the Netherlands and Poland, have introduced an option for taxation in respect of the supply and leasing of immovable property. Given the importance of leasing of immovable property in daily practice, especially the negative effect of the exemption in that context should be removed. For lessees able to deduct input VAT in full, an exemption for the lease of immovable property leads to tax cascading. The landlord will include non-deductible input VAT in the lease instalments he charges to the lessee. The lessee, in turn, will incorporate this 'hidden' VAT in the prices of his supplies and charge (actual) VAT with respect to the 'hidden' VAT. The option for taxation prevents this tax cascading. This is in line with the nature of VAT as a general consumption tax and meets the requirements from practice.

Because the introduction of the option to tax as well as the conditions for the application of this option are left to the discretion of the Member States, distortion of competition between taxable persons established in the various Member States is bound to occur.[172] Clearly, the optional character is not in line with the fundamental principle of fiscal neutrality, which serves to attain the objective to eliminate, as far as possible, factors which may distort conditions of competition, whether at national or

171. *See* respectively, sections 8.4.3, 8.4.6, 8.4.7 and 8.4.8.
172. *See* in respect of financial services S. Poddar, 'Consumption Taxes: The Role of the Value-Added Tax', in P. Hohohan (ed.), *Taxation of Financial Intermediation: Theory and Practise for Emerging Economies* (World Bank and Oxford University Press 2003), p. 368.

Union level.[173] As a result of the option to tax in the VAT Directive, in the financial sector, in particular, the playing field is far from level. If the option to tax is to be used at all in the EU VAT system, we advocate shifting the power to apply the option to tax from the Member States to the taxable persons, and to introduce harmonized standards throughout the EU for applying the option to tax.

8.5 EXEMPTIONS FOR ICTs

The main difference between the exemptions dealt with in section 8.4, and the exemptions for intra-Community transactions (ICTs) lies in the right to deduct input VAT. In contrast with the first category of exemptions, the second category of exemptions allows the deduction of input VAT. The reason for exempting certain ICTs does not relate to the public interest or technical reasons, but rather relates to the destination principle. Goods supplied from one Member State to another Member State should, in principle, be taxed in the latter Member State, the country of destination.

The system for ICTs was introduced in the context of the abolition of fiscal frontiers within the EU as of 1 January 1993. The system of exportation and importation of goods (which still exists today for supplies to and from third countries) was then replaced by the ICT system. Although both systems differ in a technical sense, their basic features do not. A taxable person supplying goods from Member State A to another taxable person in Member State B, supplies goods from Member State A, which are exempt under Article 138 VAT Directive. This is referred to as an intra-Community supply (ICS). The other taxable person in Member State B receives the goods there and should report VAT due in respect of a so-called ICA. This is a separate taxable transaction (Article 20 VAT Directive). This is similar to a regime in which an exempt exportation of goods takes place in the country of dispatch of goods, and a taxed importation of goods takes place in the country of arrival of the goods. Under the ICT regime, the tax authorities, however, have far less control due to the abolition of the fiscal frontiers and thus of the related border checks.

Section 1 of Chapter 4 of Title IX of the VAT Directive (Articles 138-139) deals with exemptions related to intra-Community supplies of goods (ICSs). Section 2 of that Chapter holds the exemptions for intra-Community acquisitions (ICAs) of goods (Articles 140-141). Section 3, consisting of one provision, exempts the supply of intra-Community transport of goods to and from the islands making up the autonomous regions of the Azores and Madeira, as well as the supply of transport of goods between those islands. As Chapter 13 deals specifically with intra-Community transactions (ICTs), we refer to that chapter.

8.6 EXEMPTIONS ON IMPORTATION

Similar to the exemptions for ICTs, the exemptions on importation also endow the right to deduct input VAT. The exemptions on importation are dealt with in Chapter 5 of

173. Point 4 of the preamble to the VAT Directive.

Title IX of the VAT Directive (Articles 143-145). If the importation of goods from non-EU countries were not to be taxed, not all consumption of goods in the EU would be taxed with EU VAT. In order to ensure neutrality between goods purchased domestically and goods purchased from non-EU countries, the taxable event of importation of goods is introduced in Article 2(d) VAT Directive. Taxation upon the importation of goods is also in line with the destination principle. As Chapter 14 deals specifically with importation and exportation, we refer to that chapter.

8.7 EXEMPTIONS ON EXPORTATION

The exemptions on exportation also allow the right to deduct input VAT. These exemptions are introduced on the basis of the destination principle. Goods that leave the EU should be released from the burden of VAT. By exempting supplies of goods to non-EU countries and allowing deduction of input VAT, this aim is achieved. The exemptions on exportation are dealt with in Chapter 6 of Title IX of the VAT Directive (Articles 146-147). As Chapter 14 deals specifically with importation and exportation, we refer to that chapter.

8.8 EXEMPTIONS RELATED TO INTERNATIONAL TRANSPORT

The exemptions related to international transport are dealt with in Chapter 7 of Title IX of the VAT Directive (Articles 148-150).[174] The supply of certain vessels and aircraft is exempt from VAT with a right of deduction of input VAT. The objective pursued is to facilitate the international transport of goods or persons.[175] The exemptions will probably be based on the fact that these means of transport generally are used outside the EU. Generally, the owners of the aforementioned vessels and aircraft will have a full right of deduction. Nonetheless, the exemption in practice is very valuable to businesses purchasing these means of transport, in view of the cash flow advantage resulting from the application of the exemption.

Pursuant to Article 148(c) VAT Directive an exemption applies to the supply of vessels used for navigation on the high seas and carrying passengers for reward, or used for the purpose of commercial, industrial or fishing activities, or for rescue or assistance at sea, or for inshore fishing. Likewise, Article 148(f) VAT Directive provides for an exemption for the supply of aircraft used by airlines operating for reward chiefly on international routes. According to *Cimber Air*, the provision also applies to aircraft which operate on domestic routes but are used by airlines chiefly operating for reward on international routes.[176] Although perhaps not in line with the supposed *ratio legis* of the provision, the legal wording is clear and includes such aircraft. From *Cimber Air*, it also follows that airlines operating chiefly on international routes are those whose operations on non-international routes are found to be considerably less extensive than

174. We will not address Article 149 VAT Directive as it contains a specific exemption for Portugal.
175. CJEU 4 May 2017, Case C-33/16 *A Oy*, ECLI:EU:C:2017:339.
176. CJEU 16 September 2004, Case C-382/02 *Cimber Air A/S v Skatteministeriet*, ECLI:EU:C:2004:534.

their international activities. All information which indicates the relative importance of the type of operations concerned may be taken into account, in particular, turnover. According to *A Oy*, the airlines that can benefit from the exemption include airlines that operate international charter flights to meet demand from undertakings and private persons. Furthermore, the exemption also applies to the supply of an aircraft to an operator, which is not in itself an airline operating chiefly on international routes, but which acquires that aircraft for the purposes of exclusive use thereof by such an undertaking.[177]

In addition, to the supply of the above-mentioned vessels, certain other supplies relating to those vessels are exempt. Article 148(a) VAT Directive exempts the supply of goods for the fuelling and provisioning of such vessels, with the exception, in the case of vessels used for inshore fishing, of ships' provisions. It follows from *Velker Oil* that the exemption only applies to the supply of goods to a vessel operator who will use those goods for fuelling and provisioning and cannot be extended to the supply of those goods effected at a previous stage in the commercial chain.[178] There is, however, no requirement that the goods should be actually loaded on board the vessel at the time of their supply to the vessel operator. In *A Oy*, the CJEU seemed to depart somewhat from *Velker Oil*. As the CJEU indicated in *A Oy*, an extension of the exemption in *Velker Oil* to stages prior to the final supply of goods made directly to the vessel operator was ruled out, in particular, because such an exemption would require the Member States to set up means of supervision and monitoring in order to be sure of the ultimate use of the goods in question. Surprisingly, in the more recent *Fast Bunkering Klaipeda* case the CJEU ruled that a supplier of fuel for seagoing vessels that supplied its products to the vessels via intermediaries could apply the exemption on its supplies if the transfer to those intermediaries of the ownership in the products took place at the earliest at the same time when the operators of vessels used for navigation on the high seas were actually entitled to dispose of those goods as if they were the owners.[179] In other words, in situations where the intermediary is only informed of the quantity and price of the oil supplied to the vessel after the bunkering has taken place, the supply has to be regarded as a direct supply of goods (a transfer of the power to dispose of as owner) from the principal supplier to the (operator of) the vessel, thus disregarding the intermediary in the supply chain. In this way, it is possible that the exemption is, in fact, applicable in earlier stages of the supply chain, albeit that in those cases, it seems that the earlier stage is seen as the final supply, regardless of legal relations and obligations stating otherwise. The approach of the CJEU, in this case, garnered some scrutiny but is generally understood as applicable only in very specific situations.[180]

177. CJEU 19 July 2012, Case C-33/11 *A Oy*, ECLI:EU:C:2012:482.
178. CJEU 26 June 1990, Case C-185/89 *Staatssecretaris van Financiën v Velker Oil International Oil Company Ltd NV*, ECLI:EU:C:1990:262.
179. CJEU 3 September 2015, Case C-526/13 UAB *'Fast Bunkering Klaipeda' v Valstybine mokesčių inspekcija prie Lietuvos Respublikos finansų ministerijos*, ECLI:EU:C:2015:536.
180. *See* Value Added Tax Committee, Working Paper No 907, taxud.c.1(2016)3438314, Value Added Tax Committee, Working Paper No 934, taxud.c.1(2017)6158402 and the Guidelines resulting from the 109th meeting of 1 December 2017 Document E – taxud.c.1(2018)5913820 – 954 (1/1), No 6.

Although the Court's interpretation of the scope of the exemption worked out favourably for the litigant (Fast Bunkering Klaipeda), the judgment has led to considerable ambiguity as regards the manner in which the concept of a supply of goods and the treatment of chain transactions and the scope of Article 14(2)(c) VAT Directive (*see* Chapter 3, sections 3.2.3-3.2.4.3) are to be understood.

The modification, repair, maintenance, chartering and hiring of these vessels, and the supply, hiring, repair and maintenance of equipment, including fishing equipment, incorporated or used therein is also exempt on the basis of Article 148(c) VAT Directive. In *Navicon,* it was explicitly decided that this exemption covers both full and partial chartering of vessels.[181] The supply of other services to meet the direct needs of these vessels or of their cargoes is exempt as well, under Article 148(d) VAT Directive. From *A Oy,* it follows that Article 148(d) can also apply on services provided prior to the final stage of the commercial chain, for example, services provided by a subcontractor to an economic operator, which then re-invoices them to a freight forwarder or transporter.[182] Article 148(b) VAT Directive exempts the supply of goods for the fuelling and provisioning of fighting ships, falling within the combined nomenclature (CN) code 8906 10 00, leaving their territory and bound for ports or anchorages outside the Member State concerned.

Similar exemptions exist for certain supplies relating to aircraft used by airlines operating for reward chiefly on international routes. Following Article 148(e) VAT Directive, the supply of goods for the fuelling and provisioning of these aircraft is exempt. Moreover, on the basis of Article 148(f) VAT Directive, the supply, modification, repair, maintenance, chartering and hiring of these aircraft, and the supply, hiring, repair and maintenance of equipment incorporated or used therein are exempt. Furthermore, Article 148(g) VAT Directive exempts the supply of other services that meet the direct needs of these aircraft or of their cargoes.

The rationale behind Article 150 VAT Directive is not quite clear. Apparently, Member States could not fully agree on the final wording of the provision and granted a possibility to the European Commission to propose an amended scope of the above-mentioned exemptions. According to the provision, the Commission shall, where appropriate, as soon as possible, present to the European Council proposals designed to delimit the scope of these exemptions and to lay down the detailed rules for their implementation. Up until now, the Commission has not made use of this possibility. Pending the entry into force of the provisions, Member States may limit the scope of the exemptions referred to in Article 148(a) and (b) VAT Directive.

8.9 EXEMPTIONS RELATING TO CERTAIN TRANSACTIONS TREATED AS EXPORTS

The exemptions relating to certain transactions treated as exports are dealt with in Chapter 8 of Title IX of the VAT Directive (Articles 151-152). Article 151(1) VAT

181. CJEU 18 October 2007, Case C-97/06 *Navicon SA v Administración del Estado,* ECLI: EU:C:2007:609.
182. CJEU 4 May 2017, Case C-33/16 *A Oy,* ECLI:EU:C:2017:339.

Directive contains several specific exemptions for supplies of goods and services to international organizations. In short, the following supplies of goods and services are exempt:

a) supplies under diplomatic and consular arrangements;
   aa) supplies to the European Community, the European Atomic Energy Community, the European Central Bank or the European Investment Bank, or to the bodies set up by the Communities to which the Protocol of 8 April 1965 on the privileges and immunities of the European Communities applies, within the limits and under the conditions of that Protocol and the agreements for its implementation or the headquarters agreements, in so far as it does not lead to distortion of competition;
b) supplies to international bodies, other than those referred to under aa), recognized as such by the public authorities of the host member states, and to members of such bodies, within the limits and under the conditions laid down by the international conventions establishing the bodies or by headquarters agreements;
c) supplies within a member state which is a party to the North Atlantic Treaty, intended either for the armed forces of other states party to that treaty for the use of those forces, or of the civilian staff accompanying them, or for supplying their messes or canteens when such forces take part in the common defence effort;
d) supplies to another member state, intended for the armed forces of any state which is a party to the North Atlantic Treaty, other than the member state of destination itself, for the use of those forces, or of the civilian staff accompanying them, or for supplying their messes or canteens when such forces take part in the common defence effort;
e) supplies to the armed forces of the United Kingdom stationed on the island of Cyprus, which are for the use of those forces, or of the civilian staff accompanying them, or for supplying their messes or canteens.

Following Article 49 VAT Implementing Regulation, the exemption also applies to electronic services that are supplied by non-EU service providers under the OSS mechanism of Articles 357-369 VAT Directive (*see* Chapter 16 on Special regimes). Pending the adoption of common tax rules, the above-mentioned exemptions are subject to the limitations laid down by the host Member State. This is once again an example of a lack of harmonization. It will require political will to establish common tax rules. Taking into account that this particular subject is not a priority for the European Commission, different rules will apply among the Member States. It is specific to this exemption that it may also be shaped as a VAT refund rather than as an exemption. Following Article 151(2) VAT Directive, in cases where goods are not dispatched or transported out of the Member State in which the supply takes place, and in case of services, the exemption may be granted by means of a VAT refund. Although the technique is different, the final result is the same: international organizations are freed from the burden of VAT.

According to Article 152 VAT Directive, Member States shall exempt the supply of gold to central banks. Not only are domestic supplies of gold exempt but also the intra-Community acquisition (ICA, Article 140(b) VAT Directive) and the importation

(Article 143(1)(k) VAT Directive) of gold by central banks is VAT-exempt. Central banks can, therefore, acquire gold without the additional cost of non-deductible input VAT.

8.10 EXEMPTION FOR THE SUPPLY OF SERVICES BY INTERMEDIARIES

Chapter 9 of Title IX of the VAT Directive contains only one provision. According to Article 153, Member States shall exempt the supply of services by intermediaries, acting in the name and on behalf of another person, where they take part in the transactions referred to in Chapters 6, 7 and 8 VAT Directive,[183] or of transactions carried out outside the EU. In order for the exemption to apply, the place of supply of the intermediary services should be located in one of the Member States. The place of supply rules effective prior to 1 January 2010 contained a rather complicated set of rules in this respect. Under the new place of supply rules, B2B intermediary services are taxable in the jurisdiction where the recipient of the services is established (Article 44 VAT Directive). B2C intermediary services are taxable in the jurisdiction where the underlying transaction is supplied (Article 46 VAT Directive; *see* Chapter 4).[184] On the basis of this exemption, a French intermediary acting in the name and on behalf of a French business in respect of the latter's supplies of goods to the United States can, for example, exempt his intermediary services. This is because the supplies of goods from his client are exempt as export supplies under Article 146 VAT Directive. Following the destination principle, the intermediary services carried out in respect of goods that leave the EU should indeed be free of VAT. This is also the mirror image of the VAT treatment of intermediary services upon importation. According to Article 86(1)(b) VAT Directive, commissions incurred up to the first place of destination within the territory of the Member State of importation should be included in the taxable amount of the import at hand.

The exemption of Article 153 VAT Directive does not apply to travel agents who, in the name and on behalf of travellers, supply services which are carried out in the other Member States. For travel agents, a separate regime applies, the so-called Tour Operators' Margin Scheme ('TOMS'; *see* Chapter 16 on Special Regimes).

8.11 EXEMPTIONS FOR TRANSACTIONS RELATING TO INTERNATIONAL TRADE

The exemptions for transactions relating to international trade are dealt with in Chapter 10 of Title IX of the VAT Directive (Articles 154-166). Articles 154-163 VAT Directive contain provisions regarding customs warehouses, warehouses other than customs warehouses and similar arrangements, whereas Articles 164 and 165 VAT Directive

183. In short, export supplies, supplies related to international transport and supplies to international organizations; *see* respectively sections 8.7, 8.8 and 8.9.

184. Both for B2B and for B2C intermediary services an exception exists for intermediation related to real estate. *See* Article 47 VAT Directive and Chapter 4, sections 4.5.3.4.1 and 4.5.4.2.2.

deal with transactions exempted with a view to export and in the framework of trade between the Member States. These arrangements are rather specific. Therefore, we will focus on their main characteristics and not go into too much detail. The background of these exemptions seems to be that international trade should not unnecessarily be obstructed by levying VAT. In international trade, foreign suppliers are often part of the supply chain. If these traders established abroad supply goods, application of an exemption avoids registration with and payment of VAT to the tax authorities, which their customers can typically deduct. Where these foreign traders purchase goods, exempting the supplies of goods to them avoids a difficult VAT refund procedure. On many occasions, these supply chains (in the end) lead to the exportation of the goods anyway, so an exemption does not appear inappropriate.

The taxable 'importation of goods' event occurs when the goods are imported, i.e., when they physically enter the EU. At the same moment, VAT becomes chargeable. However, as long as the goods are placed under a customs arrangement or situation as mentioned in Article 157 VAT Directive, the chargeable event will not occur (yet), and no VAT will become chargeable (yet).[185] According to this provision, Member States may exempt the following transactions:

(a) the supply of goods which are intended to be presented to customs and, where applicable, placed in temporary storage;
(b) the supply of goods which are intended to be placed in a free zone or in a free warehouse;
(c) the supply of goods which are intended to be placed under customs warehousing arrangements or inward processing arrangements;
(d) the supply of goods which are intended to be admitted into territorial waters in order to be incorporated into drilling or production platforms, for purposes of the construction, repair, maintenance, alteration or fitting-out of such platforms, or to link such drilling or production platforms to the mainland;
(e) the supply of goods which are intended to be admitted into territorial waters for the fuelling and provisioning of drilling or production platforms.

All these arrangements are those defined as such by the Community customs provisions in force. Although goods that are brought under a customs procedure appear not to be located in the EU, they formally are. Therefore, the place of supply of such goods is within the EU. In order to avoid taxation, the above-mentioned exemptions are designed. Remarkably, the exemptions are optional rather than mandatory for the Member States, which for a harmonized tax, such as EU VAT, would have seemed the more obvious arrangement.

Pursuant to Article 157 VAT Directive, Member States may also exempt:

185. *See* Chapter 14.

(a) the importation of goods which are intended to be placed under warehousing arrangements other than customs warehousing;
(b) the supply of goods which are intended to be placed, within their territory, under warehousing arrangements other than customs warehousing.

Goods that are not subject to excise duty and are intended to be supplied at the retail stage may only be brought under a customs warehousing arrangement. Other warehousing arrangements are not allowed. In addition, Article 159 VAT Directive exempts the supply of services relating to the supply of goods, as mentioned under (b). On the basis of that provision, the supply of services relating to the supply of goods referred to in Article 156 VAT Directive is also exempt.

Pursuant to Article 164(1) VAT Directive, Member States may, after consulting the VAT Committee, exempt the following transactions carried out by, or intended for, a taxable person up to an amount equal to the value of the exports carried out by that person during the preceding 12 months:

(a) intra-Community acquisitions of goods made by the taxable person, and imports for and supplies of goods to the taxable person, with a view to their exportation from the Community as they are or after processing;
(b) supplies of services linked with the export business of the taxable person.[186]

Under the system of the Sixth VAT Directive *with* fiscal frontiers, Article 16(2) (currently Article 164 VAT Directive) formed an extension of Article 15(2) (currently Article 146(b) VAT Directive). According to Terra and Kajus, the latter provision provided for an exemption of the supply of goods dispatched or transported to a destination outside the territory of a Member State by or on behalf of the purchaser not established within the territory, while the former provision provided for an exemption of the supply of goods to a taxable person established within the territory, intending to export them as they are, or after processing.[187] Although Article 15(2) clearly required that the purchaser must be established outside the territory, some Member States permitted, in general, an exempt supply to purchasers immediately exporting the goods, provided the purchaser (or even subsequent purchasers) could provide the vendor with a notification of exportation. Since the abolition of the fiscal frontiers within the EU, this is no longer possible for supplies of goods between the Member States. Article 164 VAT Directive, however, can still apply to supplies of goods to non-EU countries.

186. According to Article 164(2) VAT Directive, where Member States exercise the option of exemption Article 164(1), they shall, after consulting the VAT Committee, apply that exemption also to transactions relating to supplies carried out by the taxable person, in accordance with the conditions specified in Article 138, up to an amount equal to the value of the supplies carried out by that person, in accordance with the same conditions, during the preceding 12 months. Following Article 165 VAT Directive, Member States may set a common maximum amount for the aforementioned exempt transactions.
187. B. Terra & J. Kajus, *A Guide to the European VAT Directives, Introduction to European VAT*, Vol. 1 (IBFD 2014), para. 15.6, p. 1068.

According to Article 166 VAT Directive, the European Commission shall, where appropriate, as soon as possible, present to the European Council proposals concerning common arrangements for applying VAT to the exempt transactions discussed in this section. So far, the European Commission has taken no action in this respect, nor is any action expected in the near future.

CHAPTER 9

Immovable Property

9.1 INTRODUCTION

There are several reasons why immovable property deserves its own dedicated chapter. First, the VAT treatment of supplies involving immovable property is governed by an extensive set of rules, which contain numerous exceptions. Additionally, many of these rules are discretionary for Member States, resulting in variations in the VAT treatment of immovable property across different Member States.

Moreover, at a national level, VAT in many cases is not the sole transaction tax imposed on supplies and acquisitions of immovable property. Often, the VAT rules intertwine with real estate transfer taxes. Consequently, the VAT treatment of immovable transactions is often perceived as complex.

Compounding the complexity, for many businesses, transactions involving immovable property are not their primary focus but rather occasional endeavours. Nevertheless, such transactions typically involve substantial amounts of money and entail costs, including cash flow costs. These last two factors render transactions involving immovable property an especially high-risk area.

Given these circumstances, we believe it is appropriate to allocate a separate chapter specifically addressing the VAT treatment of immovable property.

9.2 TAXING IMMOVABLE PROPERTY UNDER THE EU VAT SYSTEM

The purpose of VAT is to tax private consumption of goods and services (*see* Chapter 1, 'Introduction'). It is a general tax on consumption, aiming at taxing all consumption of goods and services. The broad base of the tax implies that the consumption of immovable property, and any services derived from such property, should also be taxed. However, immovable property has certain characteristics that complicate this ambition.[1] First of all, immovable property typically has a long lifecycle. It is not consumed immediately upon purchase, but gradually over time. Second, immovable property generally appreciates over time. Third, during its lifespan, immovable property may switch back and forth from the production to the consumption sphere. As a last and fourth point, the CJEU has considered that the sale of an old building generates relatively little value added as compared to a sale of a new building.[2]

The combination of these characteristics means that supplies involving immovable property are prone to cause a cascading of VAT. To prevent such an occurrence that would go against the principle of neutrality (*see* Chapter 1, 'Introduction'), EU VAT law contains specific rules on the taxation of supplies involving immovable property.

Due to the options for the Member States contained in the VAT Directive with respect to the taxation of supplies with respect to immovable property, the rules with respect to the taxation of supplies involving immovable property vary between the

1. Cf. R.F. van Brederode (ed.), *Immovable Property under VAT: A Comparative Analysis* (Kluwer Law International 2011), pp. 1-3.
2. CJEU 4 September 2019, Case C-71/18 *Skatteministeriet v KPC Herning*, ECLI:EU:C:2019:660, para. 57.

Member States.[3] While it would seem that this contradicts the objective of the VAT Directive to harmonize the turnover tax systems of EU Member States, the differences between the Member States as regards the taxation of immovable property can be understood if one considers the following.

As the term 'immovable property' suggests, a most particular characteristic of such property is that it is – by nature – immovable. This implies that it is relatively easy to determine the place of its consumption. Moreover, since immovable property is bound to a certain location, the chances of distortions of competition occurring as a result of Member States applying different rules on the taxation of immovable property seem to be remote.[4] Also, it is important to realize that civil law, and in particular land law, vary considerably between the Member States, making a full harmonization of the VAT rules relating to immovable property less straightforward. In addition, fully harmonizing the VAT rules with respect to immovable property would be more or less pointless if other taxes on real estate transactions are not harmonized at all.

Since the purpose of this book is to provide an insight into the fundamentals of EU VAT law rather than into the details of the application of EU VAT law in all Member States, we will describe in this chapter the rules on taxing immovable property under EU VAT from a more general perspective, taking the provisions relating to this subject in the VAT Directive and VAT Implementing Regulation as our guiding light.

9.3 TRANSACTIONS INVOLVING IMMOVABLE PROPERTY

Roughly, three categories of rules can be derived from the VAT Directive and the VAT Implementing Regulation on the VAT treatment of supplies of goods or services involving immovable property ('transactions involving immovable property'):

(1) *Rules regarding the supply of immovable property.*
The VAT Directive contains a number of special provisions with respect to taxable person status, the notion of 'supply' of immovable property, the place of supply and – most noteworthy – the exemption (and the exceptions thereto) from the VAT of supplies of immovable property. Furthermore, there are some specific rules on the taxable amount, VAT rate and the liability to pay the VAT relating to supplies of immovable property. We will discuss these rules in section 9.5.

(2) *Rules regarding the leasing or letting of immovable property.*
Similar types of provisions to those relating to the supply of immovable property exists with respect to the leasing or letting of immovable property. We will discuss these rules in section 9.6.

---

3. *See* R.F. van Brederode (ed.), *Immovable Property under VAT: A Comparative Analysis* (Kluwer Law International 2011), pp. 1-3 and C. Amand, G. Schellmann & R. Vermeulen, *Immovable Property and VAT: Lessons from Past Experience* (2005) 16/5 International VAT Monitor, pp. 325-334.
4. *See*, however, C. Amand, G. Schellmann & R. Vermeulen, *Immovable Property and VAT: Lessons from Past Experience* (2005) 16/5 International VAT Monitor, pp. 325-334.

(3) *Rules regarding services connected with immovable property.*
This category of rules primarily focuses on determining the place of supply of services connected to immovable property. These rules have already been dealt with extensively in Chapter 4 ('Place of Supply'), so we will only highlight them in section 9.7.

9.4 THE CONCEPT OF 'IMMOVABLE PROPERTY'

In this section, we will discuss the concept of 'immovable property'. The VAT Directive itself does not contain a definition of the term 'immovable property'. Moreover, it does not define the terms 'supply of immovable property' or 'leasing of immovable property'. Article 13b VAT Implementing Regulation does contain a definition of the term 'immovable property', but the exact scope of this definition is not entirely clear (*see* section 9.4.1).

Since both the supply and the leasing of immovable property are exempt supplies, these terms have their own independent meaning in Union law and must, therefore, be given a Union definition. The interpretation of the concept of (a supply or a leasing of) immovable property cannot depend on that given by the civil law of a Member State.[5] In our view, there are no valid reasons for interpreting the term 'immovable property' differently depending on whether the transaction involving an immovable property is a supply of a service (leasing/letting) or a supply of goods. Therefore, we feel safe when deriving a definition of 'immovable property' from CJEU case law, which applies to both the 'supply of immovable property' and to the 'leasing or letting of immovable property'.

In practice, immovable property is often also referred to as 'real estate'. It would seem that the terms 'immovable property' and 'real estate' are synonyms. Whatever the case may be, in this chapter, we make no principal distinction between 'immovable property' and 'real estate'. For consistency's sake, we will use the term 'immovable property' throughout this chapter unless the context requires differently.

9.4.1 Definition of the Term 'Immovable Property'

Article 13b VAT Implementing Regulation contains a definition of the concept of 'immovable property'. According to points 11 and 18 of the preamble to Regulation (EU) No 1042/2013, by which Article 13b was inserted, the reason for including such a definition in the Regulation was to ensure the uniform tax treatment of supplies of 'services connected with immovable property' as referred to in Article 47 VAT Directive (*see* section 9.7).[6] This suggests that the definition is only relevant for the application

5. CJEU 16 January 2003, Case C-315/00 *Rudof Maierhofer v Fianzamt Augsburg-Land*, ECLI: EU:C:2003:23, paras 25-26 and CJEU, 15 November 2012, Case C-532/11 *Susanne Leichenich v Ansbert Peffekoven and Ingo Horeis*, ECLI:EU:C:2012:720, para. 17.
6. For some reason, the preamble uses the words 'introduction of that concept', but it would seem to us that Regulation (EU) No 1042/2013 does not introduce the concept of immovable property, but rather explains it.

of Article 47 VAT Directive.[7] Also, its placing in Chapter V 'Place of Taxable Transactions' indicates that the definition is only applicable for the purpose of determining the place of supply of 'services connected to immovable property' (Article 47 VAT Directive and Article 31a and 31b VAT Implementing Regulation). However, the wording of Article 13b VAT Implementing Regulation suggests a broader scope of the definition. It simply reads that:

> For the application of Directive 2006/112/EC, the following shall be regarded as 'immovable property':
>
> a) any specific part of the earth, on or below its surface, over which title and possession can be created;
> b) any building or construction fixed to or in the ground above or below sea level which cannot be easily dismantled or moved;
> c) any item that has been installed and makes up an integral part of a building or construction without which the building or construction is incomplete, such as doors, windows, roof, staircases and lifts;
> d) any item, equipment or machine permanently installed in a building or construction which cannot be moved without destroying or altering the building or construction.

The Explanatory notes on EU VAT place of supply rules on services connected with immovable property are inconclusive as to the exact scope of the definition.[8] Even though some doubt on the precise scope of the definition may exist, it certainly Article 13b echoes the CJEU case law on this concept, which we describe below.

In *Commission/France*, the CJEU indicated that the leasing of caravans, tents, mobile homes and light-framed leisure dwellings could not be considered as the (exempted) lease of immovable property.[9] The CJEU considered this type of property to be 'movable property', to which the exemption cannot be extended. In *Maierhofer*, the CJEU further explained that a characteristic of such property, classified as movable, is that it is either mobile, in the case of caravans or mobile homes, or could be easily moved, in the case of tents and light-framed leisure dwellings.[10] The leased property consisted of buildings with a concrete base erected on concrete foundations sunk into the ground. They could be dismantled on expiry of the lease for subsequent re-use, given recourse to eight persons over 10 days. According to the CJEU, such buildings made of structures fixed to or in the ground must be regarded as immovable property.

7. Article 31a and 31b VAT Implementing Regulation contain specific guidance on the interpretation of 'services connected to immovable property' as referred to in Article 47 VAT Directive. We discussed these provisions in Chapter 4, section 4.5.3.4.1.
8. *See*: Explanatory notes on EU VAT place of supply rules on services connected with immovable property that enter into force in 2017, points 30 and 31, available at: https://taxation-customs.ec.europa.eu/document/download/ecebc89d-3d5f-44e0-94a7-33043ed18b05_en?filename=explanatory_notes_new_en.pdf (accessed 17 August 2024).
9. CJEU 3 July 1997, Case C-60/96 *Commission of the European Communities v French Republic*, ECLI:EU:C:1997:340.
10. CJEU 16 January 2003, Case C-315/00 *Rudof Maierhofer v Fianzamt Augsburg-Land*, ECLI:C:2003:23, para. 31.

In that connection, it was significant that the structures could not be easily dismantled or easily moved, but there was no need for them to be inextricably fixed to or in the ground.

In *Fonden Marselisborg Lystbådehavn,* the CJEU answered the question of whether a piece of land which is permanently delimited, even if it is underwater (land- and water-based moorings for boats) must be regarded as immovable property.[11] The CJEU attached much value to the facts that the water-covered area was clearly delimited and could not be moved.[12] The CJEU answered the question in the affirmative: the concept of letting of immovable property includes the letting of both water-based mooring berths for boats, as well as land sites for their storage.

In *Heger,* the CJEU further defined the term 'immovable property'.[13] Heger acquired and sold fishing rights relating to certain geographical areas in rivers or lakes. The CJEU considered that one of the essential characteristics of such property is that it is attached to a specific part of the earth's surface. Fishing rights such as those acquired and sold on by Heger allow - according to the CJEU - the exercise of a right over certain, very specific, parts of the stretch of water. Those rights, which related not to the quantities of water which flowed in the river and were constantly replaced, but to certain geographical areas, where those rights might be exercised, were thus connected with a surface covered in water, which was permanently delimited. Consequently, the stretches of river to which the fishing permits related had to be regarded as immovable property.

In *Susanne Leichenich,* the CJEU added a new criterion to the concept of immovable property.[14] Not only the question of whether a certain item or structure can be easily dismantled or easily moved but also the intention to use the structure in a permanent or non-permanent way has to be taken into account. In 1999, Mrs Leichenich concluded an agreement with the German state for the occupation of a parcel of land and an area of water, namely a portion of the river adjacent to that land. By that agreement, the German state placed those parcels at the disposal of the users for the purposes of operating a houseboat with a landing stage as a restaurant. The houseboat in question had been moored in the same place for many years, had never been moved, and was immobilized by means of ropes, chains and anchors. It had no engine or system of propulsion. It was, moreover, connected to the water and electricity networks and had an address, a telephone line and a septic tank. According to the CJEU, the concept of the leasing or letting of immovable property includes the leasing of a houseboat, together with space and the landing stage contiguous therewith, which is fixed by attachments which are not easily removable to the bank and bed of

11. CJEU 3 March 2005, Case C-428/02 *Fonden Marselisborg Lystbådehavn v Skatteministeriet,* ECLI:EU:C:2005:126.
12. *Ibid.*, para. 34.
13. CJEU 7 September 2006, Case C-166/05 *Heger Rudi GmbH v Finanzambt Graz-Stadt,* ECLI:EU:C:2006:533, paras 21-22.
14. CJEU 15 November 2012, Case C-532/11 *Susanne Leichenich,* ECLI:EU:C:2012:720, paras 9 and 29.

a river, stays in a demarcated and identifiable location in the river water and *is exclusively used*, according to the terms of the leasing contract, *for the permanent operation of a restaurant-discotheque at that location.*

9.4.2 Extension of the Definition of Immovable Property by Legal Fiction

Article 15(2) VAT Directive contains a number of optional legal fictions, on the basis of which the Member States may treat certain assets as 'tangible property' (*see* section 3.2.2). In fact, these legal fictions all relate to immovable property.[15] Article 15(2) concerns:

(1) certain interests in immovable property (Article 15(2)(a) VAT Directive, *see* section 9.4.2.1);
(2) rights in rem giving the holder thereof a right of use over immovable property (Article 15(2)(b) VAT Directive, *see* section 9.4.2.2);
(3) shares or interests in immovable property or parts thereof (Article 15(2)(c) VAT Directive, *see* section 9.4.2.3).

Although Article 15(2) VAT Directive only allows the Member States to treat rights, shares and interest as 'tangible property', we believe that in a Member State which availed itself of one or more of the options, the supply of such 'tangible property' is to be regarded as the supply of 'immovable property' since all three options explicitly refer to immovable property as the object to which the rights, shares or interests pertain.

As we discussed in Chapter 3 ('Taxable Transactions'), not only the transfer but also the creation of a right relating to immovable property as specified in Article 15(2) VAT Directive can be regarded as a (supply of) tangible property by the Member States that implemented that provision.[16] Furthermore, we indicated that, following the CJEU's ruling in *Stichting Goed Wonen*, Member States may lay down certain conditions when implementing Article 15(2) VAT Directive.[17] The limitation is that the conditions laid down by the Member State in question must not alter the nature of choice afforded.

The reasons for (optionally) expanding on the concept of tangible property lie within the principle of neutrality. Since rights in rem, as well as shares and interest in immovable property, may give the holder thereof rights which are similar to the rights the (full) owner of an immovable property has, the Member States must be able to treat both situations equally.[18]

---

15. Article 15(2)(b) VAT Directive replaced Article 5(3) of the Sixth Directive.
16. CJEU 4 December 1990, Case C-186/89 *W.M. van Tiem v Staatssecretaris van Financiën*, ECLI:EU:C:1990:429.
17. CJEU 4 October 2001, Case C-326/99 *Stichting 'Goed Wonen' v Staatssecretaris van Financiën*, ECLI:EU:C:2001:506.
18. Explanatory Memorandum to the proposal for a Sixth Directive of 20 June 1973, COM (73)950.

9.4.2.1 *Certain Interests in Immovable Property*

Based on Article 15(2)(a) VAT Directive, Member States may regard 'certain interests in immovable property' as tangible property. It is not completely clear which interests in immovable property the authors of the VAT Directive(s) had in mind when drafting this provision. A provision allowing the Member States to expand on the concept of tangible property was not included in the Second VAT Directive. The proposal for the Sixth VAT Directive only contained (mandatory) provisions on treating rights in rem and shares or interest in immovable property as tangible property. It did not contain the category 'certain interests in immovable property'. However, in the text, as finally adopted, the category of 'certain interests' suddenly appeared, without any explanation being given.

It would seem that the rights to which Article 15(2)(a) refers are already covered by Article 15(2)(b) and (c). Therefore, we assume that the category of 'certain interests in immovable property' in Article 15(2)(a) VAT Directive must be seen as a kind of safety net provision. If an interest in immovable property does not fall within the scope of subparagraphs (b) or (c) of Article 15(2), it is to be categorized under Article 15(2)(a). This way, the provision gives the Member States the maximum guarantee that they may treat all rights in immovable property as tangible property.

In *Heger*, the CJEU determined whether Austria had treated fishing rights over certain very specific parts of the stretch of water as certain interests in immovable property, or as rights in rem.[19] It decided that even if fishing permits were, in principle, capable of being classed as interests in immovable property or rights in rem (which is open for debate), the Commission's observations indicated that Austria had not availed itself of that option. If the Member State has not – like Austria in this case – treated such rights as tangible property, the transfer of such a right is not a supply of good (Article 14 VAT Directive) but the performance of a service (Article 24 VAT Directive).

9.4.2.2 *Rights In Rem*

Article 15(2)(b) VAT Directive provides that the Member States may consider rights in rem, giving the holder thereof a right of use over immovable property, to be tangible property. That provision was prompted by the existence in the private law of several Member States of limited rights in rem, such as usufruct, *emphyteusis* and superficies, which give the holder certain rights of economic utilization over immovable property.[20] The legislator was apparently aware of the fundamental differences in civil law between, on the one hand, the grant of a right in rem, such as a usufructuary right and building rights, and on the other hand, leasing or letting. The latter concept must be read as relating only to personal rental contracts, which do not give rise to rights in rem (as meant in Article 15(2)(b)). A rental contract creates rights in personam, which is to be considered as leasing or letting. The grant of (for instance) a usufructuary right,

19. CJEU 7 September 2006, Case C-166/05 *Heger Rudi GmbH v Finanzambt Graz-Stadt*, ECLI: EU:C:2006:533, para. 19.
20. Explanatory Memorandum to the proposal for a Sixth Directive of 20 June 1973, COM (73)950.

however, will be a supply of a good if the Member State concerned treats the transfer of such rights as the supply of tangible goods.

The question may arise whether the difference between rights in personam and rights in rem is really useful while distinguishing the comparable rights under the various jurisdictions. According to Advocate General Jacobs:

> The fact that usufruct grants the holder a right in rem while rental contracts grant only rights in personam is irrelevant. Even in the civil law jurisdictions the practical differences between usufruct and rental contract are much narrower than suggested by the abstract and theoretical distinction between rights in personam and rights in rem. For example, in most civil law jurisdictions the tenant does not lose his rights arising from a rental contract – which are in theory in personam only – where the owner sells the property to a third person. Conversely a usufructuary right (a personal servitude) can rarely be transferred freely to third persons and cannot survive the death of the original usufructuary. Those are probably the main reasons why the classification both of the rights flowing from a rental contract as rights in personam and of usufruct as a right in rem were historically disputed. It must also be recalled that in the common law jurisdictions the lease serves the purposes of both rental contracts and usufruct and may grant the tenant rights which are stronger than limited rights in rem.[21]

It should be noted that Member States availing themselves of the option of Article 15(2)(b) VAT Directive are not required to treat all rights in rem as tangible property. As the CJEU confirmed in *Stichting Goed Wonen:*

> Furthermore ... member states are at liberty to exercise the choice afforded them by Article 5(3) of the Sixth Directive, by, *inter alia,* laying down certain conditions, in so far as these do not fundamentally alter the nature of the choice afforded, since no provision of the Sixth Directive in any way restricts the member states' discretion in this regard.[22]

From later case law, it can be learned that the freedom of choice granted by provisions such as Article 15(2)(b) VAT Directive find their limitation in the general principles underlying the VAT system (e.g., the principle of neutrality).[23]

In *Stichting Goed Wonen,* the CJEU decided that the adoption of a special anti-avoidance provision by the Netherlands to prevent artificial arrangements relating to immovable property[24] whereby classification as a supply of goods of the grant, transfer, modification, waiver or termination of rights in rem in immovable property is made subject to the condition that the total consideration, plus turnover tax, must

21. Opinion of Advocate General Jacobs of 22 February 2001, Case C-326/99 *Stichting 'Goed Wonen' v Staatssecretaris van Financiën,* ECLI:EU:C:2001:115, para. 88.
22. CJEU 4 October 2001, Case C-326/99 *Stichting Goed Wonen I v Staatssecretaris van Financiën,* ECLI:EU:C:2001:506, para. 34.
23. For example: CJEU 17 February 2005, Joined Cases C-453/02 and C-462/02 *Finanzamt Gladbeck v Edith Linneweber (C-453/02) and Finanzamt Herne-West v Savvas Akritidis (C-462/02),* ECLI:EU:C:2005:92, paras 24 and 25.
24. Such as Article 3(2) of the *Wet houdende vervanging van de bestaande omzetbelasting door een omzetbelasting volgens het stelsel van heffing over de toegevoegde waarde* ('Law replacing turnover tax by the system of taxing added value') of 28 June 1968, as amended by the *Wet ter bestrijding van constructies met betrekking tot onroerende zaken* ('Law to prevent artificial arrangements relating to immovable property') of 18 December 1995.

amount to at least the economic value of the immovable property to which those rights in rem relate was not precluded. Nor in this respect was precluded the adoption of a national provision[25] which, for the purposes of the application of the exemption from VAT, allows the grant, for an agreed period and for payment, of a right in rem entitling the holder to use immovable property, such as the usufructuary right in question in the present case, to be treated as the leasing or letting of immovable property.

A Member State which has exercised its discretion under Article 15(2) must accept that also the creation and transformation of rights in rem pertaining to immovable property are considered as a supply of the underlying immovable property. *See* Chapter 3, section 3.2.2.2.

9.4.2.3 Shares or Interests in Immovable Property or Parts Thereof

Article 15(2)(c) VAT Directive allows the Member States to regard as tangible property 'shares or interests equivalent to shares giving the holder thereof de jure or de facto rights of ownership or possession over immovable property or part thereof'. If a Member State opts for the implementation and application of this provision, the sale of shares (or documents with a similar function) in companies primarily holding immovable property will be treated in their jurisdiction as the supply of immovable goods (with all the associated VAT consequences). Not every Member State availed itself of the possibility provided by Article 15(2)(c). It should be noted that this is one of the rare situations in which the cross-border supply of an immovable property may occur.

In those Member States that did not make use of Article 15(2)(c), the question may arise whether the transfer of shares in a company primarily holding immovable property should be considered as a supply of goods (immovable property) or as a supply of services (shares) if the intention of the seller and the buyer is, in fact, to sell and buy the immovable property owned by that company. This is particularly relevant to the application of intermediary services in connection with such a supply because negotiation in share interests in companies is exempt, 'save rights or securities referred to in Article 15(2)'. In *DTZ Zadelhoff*, the CJEU provided an answer to the question as to the classification of a transfer of immovable property by transferring the shares in the company holding that immovable property.[26] It follows from that judgment that it is necessary, in accordance with the VAT system's objectives of ensuring legal certainty and facilitating the application of the tax, to have regard, save in exceptional cases, to the objective character of the transaction in question.[27] Therefore, if a Member State has not implemented Article 15(2)(c) VAT Directive, the transfer of shares in a company primarily holding immovable property must be considered as a supply of services, rather than as a supply of tangible (immovable) property (goods). Such a supply of services is to be categorized as an exempt transfer of shares under Article

25. *See* Article 11(1)(b), point 5, of the VAT Law of 28 June 1968, as amended by the Law of 18 December 1995.
26. CJEU 5 July 2012, Case C-259/11 *DTZ Zadelhoff vof v Staatssecretaris van Financiën*, ECLI: EU:C:2012:423.
27. *Ibid.*, para. 25.

135(1)(f) VAT Directive.[28] Therefore, the negotiation of such a transaction involving the transfer of company shares also is exempted under that provision.[29] *See* Chapter 8, 'Exemptions' and Chapter 11, 'Shares and Other Securities'.

9.5 SUPPLIES OF IMMOVABLE PROPERTY

In this section, we discuss the VAT consequences of supplies of immovable property. To that end, we will use the VAT determination scheme (*see* Chapter 1, 'Introduction') as a guideline. However, to avoid unnecessary repetition, we will only discuss those elements of the VAT determination scheme that require special attention with respect to supplies of immovable property.

9.5.1 Supplies of Immovable Property and Taxable Person Status

Persons who supply goods or services for consideration on a regular basis are normally regarded as taxable persons. In this respect, it is irrelevant whether a person supplies services, movable goods or immovable property. If a person only makes supplies on an occasional basis, in principle, that person cannot be considered as a taxable person.[30] However, Article 12(1) VAT Directive allows the Member States to regard as a taxable person anyone who carries out, *on an occasional basis*, a transaction relating to the activities referred to in the second subparagraph of Article 9(1) and in particular[31] one of the following transactions:

(a) the supply, before first occupation, of a building or parts of a building and of the land on which the building stands;
(b) the supply of building land.

Article 12(1) and (2) VAT Directive explicitly and implicitly[32] introduce various concepts. In this section, we will discuss the following concepts:

(1) 'building' and 'parts of a building';
(2) 'land on which the building stands';
(3) 'building land';
(4) 'first occupation', 'completion', 'first supply';
(5) 'creation of a new building'; and
(6) 'conversion'.

28. Previously Article 13B(d)(5) of the Sixth Directive.
29. *See also* A.J. van Doesum, *What Looks Like a Duck Is a Duck: Economic Purpose and Legal Reality in EU VAT Law* (2012) 2 World Journal of VAT, pp. 202-204 https://doi.org/10.5235/wjovl.1.2.202.
30. *See* sections 2.4.7. and 2.4.8.
31. This indicates that points a and b are merely examples and do not form an exhaustive list.
32. Even though Article 12 VAT Directive does not explicitly introduce the concept of 'creation of a new building', this concept spawns from the notions such as 'first occupation', 'completion' and 'first supply'.

The importance of these concepts is not limited to the occasional supplies of immovable property and the taxable status of the supplier. They also play a role in the (potential) application of the exemption to the supply of immovable property (*see* Article 135(1)(j), (k) and (l) in conjunction with Article 137(1)(b), (c) and (d) VAT Directive).

9.5.1.1 *Building and Parts of a Building*

The concepts of 'building' and 'parts of a building' are only relevant with respect to the *supply* of (certain) immovable property. As regards the *leasing and letting* of immovable property (as a service), the VAT Directive deems it irrelevant whether that immovable property is considered as a building, a part of a building or as building land.[33]

For the purposes of Article 12(1)(a) VAT Directive, Article 12(2), first paragraph defines quite broadly that 'building' shall mean 'any structure fixed to or in the ground'. Article 12(1)(a) as well as Article 135(1)(j) VAT Directive also cover 'parts of a building'. It may be assumed that the term 'building' is broad enough to cover, for example (but is not limited to), residential buildings, buildings for industrial, commercial or agricultural use, viaducts and squares. From *Lomoco*, it seems to follow that a 'building' only exists if a structure is capable of being 'first occupied' in the sense of Article 12(1)(a) VAT Directive. As such, the CJEU ruled that mere foundations of residential housing structures cannot be regarded as 'buildings'.[34]

In our view, the concept of 'building' also covers structures that are completely under the ground, such as tunnels. Sometimes, it may be more difficult to determine whether a structure that is fixed to or in the ground is to be considered as a 'building'. For example, sports pitches with an artificial surface generally require a foundation and certainly need to be fixed to or in the ground. Arguably, such sports pitches are also to be classified as 'buildings'. However, in *Gemeente Vlaardingen*, the CJEU seems to consider sports pitches with an artificial surface either as land, which has been built on or as building land.[35] It would not surprise us if, at some point, the CJEU were to be asked to further explain the classification of such sports pitches.

The concept of a 'building' as referred to in Article 12(1)(a) VAT Directive is relevant not only for determining whether a person making an occasional supply of a building is to be regarded as a taxable person but also for the application of the exemption of Article 135(1)(j) VAT Directive.[36] The latter provision stipulates that the

33. Article 135(1)(l) VAT Directive simply exempts the leasing or letting of 'immovable property'. It only excludes the leasing and letting of accommodation, sites for the parking of vehicles, installed equipment and machinery and safes from the exemption (*see* section 9.6.4.1).
34. CJEU 7 November 2024, Case 594/23 *Lomoco Development and Others*, ECLI:EU:C:2024:942.
35. CJEU 8 November 2012, Case C-299/11 *Staatssecretaris van Financiën v Gemeente Vlaardingen*, ECLI:EU:C:2012:698, para. 36.
36. Both the provisions providing for exemptions (Article 135(1)(j) and (k)) use the same expression, namely 'the supply of buildings or parts thereof and the land on which they stand'. Cf. CJEU 8 July 1986, Case 73/85 *Hans-Dieter and Ute Kerrutt v Finanzamt Mönchengladbach-Mitte*, ECLI:EU:C:1986:295, para. 12.

supply of a building or parts thereof (and of the land on which it stands) *other than the supply referred to in point (a) of Article 12(1)* is exempt. Since Article 12(1)(a) VAT Directive only refers to supplies of buildings etc. *before first occupation*, only supplies of buildings, etc., *after first occupation* fall within the scope of the exemption of Article 135(1)(j) VAT Directive. Supplies of buildings, etc., before first occupation, are, in principle, taxed.[37] The reason that supplies of buildings before first occupation are excluded from the exemption (are taxed) is the same that the Member States may consider persons making supplies of buildings, etc., before first occupation as a taxable person: buildings that have not yet been occupied are still at the very beginning of their economic cycle and/or had not yet left the production process to become subjects of consumption (*see* section 9.5.1.4).

9.5.1.2 Land on Which the Building Stands

The supply of land on which the as yet unoccupied building stands is also covered by Articles 12(1)(a) and 135(1)(j) VAT Directive. The concept of 'land on which the building stands' is a Union concept and must, therefore, be interpreted in a uniform manner in all Member States.[38]

The English language version of the VAT Directive does not explicitly indicate that not only the land that is actually occupied by the building is covered by the concept, but – as other language versions clearly indicate[39] – also the adjoining parts of the land that are connected to the plot of land on which the building stands. Yet, 'land on which the building stands' this refers to land which, viewed in isolation, does not qualify as a 'building', 'parts of a building' or as 'building land'. For example, the supply of a parking lot belonging to an office building will be assessed on its own merits: the parking lot is considered as a 'building' in its own right.

The CJEU has confirmed that for the purposes of VAT, buildings or parts of buildings and the land on which they stand cannot be dissociated from each other.[40] Consequently, for VAT purposes, the land on which a building stands is deemed to be part of the building, which, as an inseparable part, shares the tax treatment of the building to which it is attached. It would seem that even without this specific mentioning of the 'land on which a building stands', the supply of such land would follow the fiscal regime of the supply of the building because the land and the building are a single supply from an economic point of view and it would be artificial to split the

37. Under point 9 of Annex X, Part B VAT Directive, Member States are allowed to continue exempting supplies of buildings before first occupation and building land. It should also be noted that on the basis of Article 391 VAT Directive, Member States may grant taxable persons the right to opt for taxation for supplies which Member States have continued to exempt.
38. CJEU 8 June 2000, Case C-400/98 *Finanzamt Goslar v Brigitte Breitsohl*, ECLI:EU:C:2000:304, para. 48.
39. For example: the Dutch language version uses the words 'erbij behorend terrein', the German-language version 'dazugehörigen Grund und Boden' and the French language version 'du sol y attenant'.
40. CJEU 8 June 2000, Case C-400/98 *Finanzamt Goslar v Brigitte Breitsohl*, ECLI:EU:C:2000:304, para. 50.

supply of the building land from that of the building itself.[41] We refer to Chapter 3, section 3.5.

9.5.1.3 *Building Land*

As is the case with the concepts of 'building' and 'parts of a building', the notion of 'building land' only bears relevance to the *supply* of (certain) immovable property. As regards the *leasing and letting* of immovable property (as a service), the VAT Directive deems it irrelevant whether that immovable property is considered as building land (*see* section 9.4.1).

On the basis of Article 12(3) VAT Directive, 'building land', as referred to in Article 12(1)(b) VAT Directive, means 'any unimproved or improved land defined as such by the member states'. Article 135(1)(k) VAT Directive uses the same terminology and indeed refers back to Article 12(1)(b) VAT Directive. Therefore, the definition of the term 'building land' in Article 12(1)(b) VAT Directive is equally relevant for the purposes of Article 135(1)(k) VAT Directive.

From the wording of Article 12(3) VAT Directive, it follows that irrespective of whether or not a plot of land has been improved, it can be considered as building land. Thus, the provision takes no account of any transformations which the land in question might have undergone.[42]

Furthermore, Article 12(3) VAT Directive refers expressly to the Member States' definitions of building land: it is for the Member States to define what land is to be regarded as being building land. This implies that the concept of 'building land' is not a uniform concept of Union law.[43] However, as the CJEU indicated in *Gemeente Emmen* and in *Don Bosco* when defining the concept of 'building land', Member States must have regard to the objective pursued by Article 135(1)(k), which seeks to exempt from VAT only supplies of land which has not been built on and is not intended to support a building.[44] In *Gemeente Maasdriel*, the CJEU further explained that it is necessary that all land which has not been built on, and which is intended to support a building and,

---

41. Cf. CJEU 8 July 1986, Case 73/85 *Hans-Dieter and Ute Kerrutt v Finanzamt Mönchengladbach-Mitte*, ECLI:EU:C:1986:295, paras 12 and 13. We note that notwithstanding the inseparability of a building and the land on which it stands, the CJEU has confirmed in De Jong that for the purposes of asset labelling and the application of the deemed supplies in case of private use, a distinction can be made between the building and the land on which it stands. CJEU 6 May 1992, Case C-20/91 *Pieter de Jong v Staatssecretaris van Financiën*, ECLI:EU:C:1992:192. Furthermore, it is conceivable that from a civil law perspective, the owner(s) of the land are not the same person(s) as the owner(s) of the building. *See*, for example: Pending case C-405/19 *Vos Aannemingen BVBA v Belgische Staat.*
42. CJEU 28 March 1996, Case C-468/93 *Gemeente Emmen v Belastingdienst Grote Ondernemingen*, ECLI:EU:C:1996:139, para. 24.
43. *Ibid.*, para. 22.
44. *Ibid.*, paras 20 and 25 and CJEU 19 November 2009, Case C-461/08 *Don Bosco Onroerend Goed BV v Staatssecretaris van Financiën*, ECLI:EU:C:2009:722, para. 43. The vendor both supplied a plot of land and arranged for demolition work that was necessary in order to demolish the existing buildings which stood on the plot of land which the customer (Don Bosco) wanted to acquire. The CJEU decided that it was a single taxable transaction because the economic purpose of those actions was to supply land ready for construction.

therefore, intended to be built on, is to be covered by the national definition of 'building land'.[45] This leads us to believe that the Member States are free to define the concept of building land, as long as they consider building land each plot of land, which has not been built on but is intended to support a building. In our view, this implies that effectively, there is little room for the Member States to define the concept of building land after all. In practice, this will not always cause difficulties. For example, a meadow without any additional provisions and in respect of which no intention exists to support a building will certainly be seen as a plot of land not having the characteristics of building land. For other plots of land, however, it can be more difficult to establish whether it is building land or not.

9.5.1.4 New Versus Old Buildings: 'First Occupation', 'Completion', 'First Supply'

Article 12(1)(a) VAT Directive only allows the Member States to consider as a taxable person, anyone who occasionally carries out a supply of a building (or part thereof) and the land on which the building stands if the building has not previously been occupied. Thus, only supplies of buildings (or parts thereof) *before first occupation* fall within the scope of Article 12(1)(a) VAT Directive.

Article 12 VAT Directive introduces the concept of 'first occupation' in the context of determining the taxable status of a person incidentally making a supply of immovable property. However, whether an immovable property is supplied before first occupation is also (in particular) relevant for the application of the exemption for (regular) supplies of immovable property (by regular taxable persons). A supply of a building or parts thereof, and of the land on which it stands as well as supplies of land which has not been built on, is, in principle, exempt (Article 135(j) and (k)).[46] Indeed, Articles 12 and 135(j) VAT Directive must be considered in conjunction.[47] This is directly connected to the basic idea of VAT, which is to tax the added value of a supply.[48] Whereas the sale of an old building generally does not represent any significant added value, this is quite the opposite with respect to the sale of a new building. Therefore, the supply of newly erected buildings – before their first occupation – must be taxed. If a building is supplied before its first occupation, it is still within the economic cycle and has not yet left the production process to become a subject of consumption. Therefore, it was considered desirable to subject the construction and marketing of new buildings to the tax, in whatever capacity the vendor may be acting.

45. CJEU 17 January 2013, Case C-543/11 *Woningstichting Maasdriel v Staatssecretaris van Financiën*, ECLI:EU:C:2013:20, para. 31.
46. However, in case of a supply of such immovable property after first occupation, Member States may allow the supplier to opt for taxation. There is no option for taxation with respect to the supply of building land. The supply of building land does not fall into the scope of the exemption of Article 135(1)(j) or (k) VAT Directive.
47. CJEU 16 November 2017, Case C-308/16 *Kozuba Premium Selection sp. z o.o. z siedzibą w Warszawie v Dyrektor Izby Skarbowej w Warszawie*, ECLI:EU:C:2017:869, paras 29 and 30.
48. CJEU 4 September 2019, Case C-71/18 *Skatteministeriet v KPC Herning*, ECLI:EU:C:2019:660, para. 57.

The CJEU indirectly acknowledges this underlying reason, by connecting the *ratio legis* of taxing supplies of new buildings before their first occupation and exempting those of old buildings to the difference in the added value generated by the two types of supplies:

> the relative lack of added value generated by the sale of an old building. Indeed, the sale of a building following its first supply to a final consumer, which marks the end of the production process, does not generate any significant added value and must therefore, as a rule, be exempt (...).[49]

To mark the difference between a new and an old building, the notion of 'first occupation' has been introduced. It determines the moment at which the building leaves the production process and becomes a subject of consumption; that is to say, when the building begins to be used by its owner or a tenant.[50] The VAT Directive does not contain any definition of the concept of 'first occupation'. It does seem clear, however, that it is irrelevant who first occupies the building.[51]

Example

A, who is a taxable person, constructs a new building. Immediately after completion of the construction, A leases that building to B. Subsequently, B effectively occupies the building. Next, A supplies the building to C.

In these circumstances, for the purpose of Article 12(1)(a) VAT Directive, A supplies a building *after first occupation.*

On the basis of Article 12(2), last paragraph, Member States may apply criteria other than that of first occupation, such as the period elapsing between the date of completion of the building and the date of first supply, or the period elapsing between the date of first occupation and the date of subsequent supply, provided that those periods do not exceed five years and two years respectively.

A 'first occupation' (as well as a 'completion' and a 'first supply') presumes that a building has been newly created. Therefore, this concept is inextricably connected to that of 'creation of a new building'. We will elaborate on the notion of creation in the next subsection.

9.5.1.5 Creation of a New Building

The landmark case with regard to the creation of a good which previously did not exist is *Van Dijks' Boekhuis.*[52] The CJEU ruled that the making of a new good implies the creation of an article that did not previously exist. According to the CJEU, a new article is produced when the work of the contractor results in an article whose function, according to generally accepted views, is different from that of the materials provided.

49. *Ibid.*
50. Explanatory Memorandum to the proposal for a Sixth Directive of 20 June 1973, COM (73)950.
51. CJEU 16 November 2017, Case C-308/16 *Kozuba Premium Selection sp. z o.o. z siedzibą w Warszawie v Dyrektor Izby Skarbowej w Warszawie*, ECLI:EU:C:2017:869, para. 41.
52. CJEU 14 May 1985, Case 139/84 *Van Dijks' Boekhuis BV v Staatssecretaris van Financiën*, ECLI:EU:C:1985:195.

A mere repair of a good, however radical it may be, which simply restores the function of the article handed over, does not amount in the creation of a new article.

Even though this case deals with the creation of movable property, we believe its relevance extends to immovable property. It is, for example, relevant to determine whether a 'work of construction' in terms of Article 14(3) VAT Directive exists. Under this provision, Member States may regard the handing over of certain works of construction as a supply of goods. There can only be a work of construction if an immovable good is created, which previously did not exist. We refer to Chapter 3, section 3.2.5.1.

So, the overall criterion for the 'creation' of an immovable property is whether an immovable good is created that did not previously exist. If an immovable property is newly erected, it is usually not extremely difficult to establish that a new building is created. It is also clear that minor alterations to a building, such as internally changing the layout of the rooms by moving some walls, does not lead to the creation of a new building. However, in case of renovation works to immovable property, it is not always easy to establish whether such work leads to the creation of a new building that did previously not exist. Therefore, it is useful to further discuss the notion of 'conversion'.

9.5.1.6 Conversion

If an existent building is converted, for example, from an office building to an apartment building, the conversion may be so drastic, that the converted building no longer resembles the original building, i.e., the conversion has, in fact, led to the creation of a new building. A sale of a converted building represents the significant value added and is, therefore, to be taxed. In this regard, Article 12(2), second paragraph VAT Directive allows the Member States to lay down detailed rules to determine under what circumstances the conversion of a building leads to the creation of a new building. From this rule, it can be deduced that the VAT legislator considered that if the conversion of a building leads to the creation of a new building, the first occupation of the 'new building' after the conversion is a 'first occupation' in terms of Article 12(1)(a) VAT Directive.[53] Arguably, the reason that the VAT legislator allowed the Member States to lay down detailed rules is to enable them to counter abusive practices. This is connected to the exemption for supplies of buildings (and parts thereof) in Article 135(1)(l) VAT Directive. If the supply of buildings had to be consistently exempted after first occupation, Member States would have no effective legal instrument[54] to combat practices in which entrepreneurs use a building themselves for a short period of time, after which they supply the building without VAT to, for example, a private individual. The CJEU has limited the level of discretion Article

53. CJEU 9 March 2023, Case C-239/22 *État belge and Promo 54 v Promo 54 and État belge*, ECLI:EU:C:2023:181, para. 21.
54. Other than the adjustment rules laid down in Articles 184 and further VAT Directive if applicable.

21(1)(a) VAT Directive seems to give to Member States. The CJEU indicated that it does not authorize Member to alter the concept of 'first occupation' in their national laws.[55]

It follows from the above that the answer to the question of whether a new building is 'created', through the conversion of an existent building, is decisive for the application of VAT to the supply of such building. The concept of 'conversion' as used in Article 12(2) VAT Directive has not been defined anywhere in the VAT Directive. However, it is closely connected to the concept of creation of a new building and the concept of 'added value', as the CJEU confirmed in *Kozuba*:

> The interpretation of the concept of 'conversion' given in Article 52 of this judgment is, moreover, in line with the objective of the VAT Directive, in particular that of taxation of a transaction that seeks to increase the value of the property at issue. For new buildings, as the Advocate General observed in points 71 and 72 of his Opinion, that added value is the result of construction work that leads to a substantial modification of what physically exists as a result of the transition from immovable property without a building, or even undeveloped land, to a habitable building. For old buildings, that added value arises when a substantial transformation has taken place, such that the old building in question may be regarded as a new building.[56]

In *Promo 54*, the CJEU further clarified that:

> In so far as the supply of an old building that has undergone a conversion generates, like the supply of a new building before its first occupation, added value, it fulfils the criterion of 'first occupation' referred to in Article 12(1)(a) of the VAT Directive and gives rise to a transaction subject to taxation.[57]

It follows from *Kozuba* that for a conversion/creation to result in a newly created building, it is at the very least required that the building concerned has been subject to 'substantial modifications intended to modify the use or alter considerably the conditions of its occupation'.[58] According to the CJEU, the concept of 'conversion' covers, *inter alia*, a situation where completed or sufficiently advanced works have been carried out and on completion of those works, the building concerned is intended to be used for other purposes.[59] In *Kozuba*, the CJEU confirms that the costs incurred by the 'upgrade' of the building may form a relevant and – depending on the amount involved

55. CJEU 16 November 2017, Case C-308/16 *Kozuba Premium Selection sp. z o.o. z siedzibą w Warszawie v Dyrektor Izby Skarbowej w Warszawie*, ECLI:EU:C:2017:869, para. 54 and CJEU 9 March 2023, Case C-239/22 *État belge and Promo 54 v Promo 54 and État belge*, ECLI:EU:C:2023:181, para. 24.
56. CJEU 16 November 2017, Case C-308/16 *Kozuba Premium Selection sp. z o.o. z siedzibą w Warszawie v Dyrektor Izby Skarbowej w Warszawie*, ECLI:EU:C:2017:869, para. 55.
57. CJEU 9 March 2023, Case C-239/22 *État belge and Promo 54 v Promo 54 and État belge*, ECLI:EU:C:2023:181, para. 23.
58. CJEU 16 November 2017, Case C-308/16 *Kozuba Premium Selection sp. z o.o. z siedzibą w Warszawie v Dyrektor Izby Skarbowej w Warszawie*, ECLI:EU:C:2017:869, para. 52 and CJEU 9 March 2023, Case C-239/22 *État belge and Promo 54 v Promo 54 and État belge*, ECLI:EU:C:2023:181, para. 25.
59. CJEU 16 November 2017, Case C-308/16 *Kozuba Premium Selection sp. z o.o. z siedzibą w Warszawie v Dyrektor Izby Skarbowej w Warszawie*, ECLI:EU:C:2017:869, para. 54.

– even a strong indicator for a creation of a building.[60] Indeed, it would seem to us that an overall assessment of the circumstances under which the construction or conversion took place, supported by objective evidence, is required to establish whether a new building has been created. For example, other indications could in our view be changes to the external appearance and/or architectural identity of the building, to the internal outlay of the building and changes in the structural construction.[61] However, whatever relevant circumstances may apply, following *Kozuba* and *Promo 54*, a conversion requires in any case that there are substantial modifications intended to (1) modify the use or (2) alter considerably the conditions of its occupation have been made. In our view, a modified use entails, for example, a situation in which an office building is converted into private dwellings. Considerable alterations to the conditions of the occupation of a building are present if the building is still used for the same purposes (e.g., a hotel) after completion of the construction works, but the way in which it is used for that function has been drastically changed. This could in our view, for example, be the case if, for example, in the hotel, all rooms have been adapted, rooms or parts of the building have been added, the infrastructure has been renewed, the entire entrance area has been renovated, and the restaurant has been enlarged.

There are indications in CJEU case law that alterations to a building may lead to the creation of a new good, separate from the already existing building. In *VOF X*, a taxable person in the form of a partnership adapted part of the attic of its warehouse for temporary occupation by the two partners and their children pending completion of a commercial residence adjacent to the warehouse. With that in mind, two dormer windows, a vestibule, a bathroom and a toilet were installed. The CJEU ruled that the permanent installation of two dormer windows and a vestibule was to be regarded as the creation of a new, separate capital item.[62] The CJEU did not elaborate on the classification of that new capital item. Should that item be considered as a separate (newly created) part of a building, leading its own fiscal life? In our view, this would very much complicate the VAT treatment of immovable property. We refer to Chapter 10, section 10.6.5.1 and 10.7 for the implications of this case on the adjustment of the deduction of input VAT.

60. However, if it cannot be the exclusive criterion on which such a conclusion is to be based. Member States may only use a quantitative criterion as part of a set of qualitative criteria. CJEU 9 March 2023, Case C-239/22 *État belge and Promo 54 v Promo 54 and État belge*, ECLI: EU:C:2023:181, para. 26.
61. In the Netherlands, the Supreme Court has ruled that 'changes in the structural construction' form a necessary condition. *See:* Hoge Raad 4 November 2022, ECLI:NL:HR:2022:1577, V-N 2022/49.11 and Hoge Raad 11 November 2022, ECLI:NL:HR:2022:1609, V-N 2022/50.13. It is debated whether this is in line with the CJEU's rulings in *Kozuba* and *Promo 54*. *See*, for example: W.J.C.M. Gelderblom, commentary to *Promo 54* in NLF 2023/601, Redactie Vakstudie-Nieuws, commentary to *Promo 54* in V-N 2023 /13.14 and M.D.J. van der Wulp commentary to *Promo 54* in FED 2023/65.
62. CJEU 19 July 2012, Case C-334/10 *X v Staatssecretaris van Financiën*, ECLI:EU:C:2012:473, paras 16 and 18.

9.5.2 Various Types of Supplies of Immovable Property

In Chapter 3, 'Taxable Transactions', we indicated that the VAT Directive acknowledges various types of supplies. Clearly, the 'transfer of the right to dispose of tangible property as owner' as mentioned in Article 14(1) VAT Directive is the main rule on supplies of goods. However, with respect to immovable property, there are two other types of supplies particularly relevant: 'certain works of construction' and 'internal supplies'. Furthermore, as immovable property is often an important component of transfers of businesses, it is useful to discuss the supply of immovable property as a part of a transfer of a business here as well.

9.5.2.1 The Transfer of Ownership of Immovable Property

Pursuant to Article 14, the supply of goods shall mean the transfer of the right to dispose of tangible property as owner. This tangible property can be movable or immovable. Not only a legal title transfer of an immovable property falls within the scope of this concept of supply but also other forms of transfer, such as an economic title transfer, or certain forms of lease.

As we indicated in Chapter 3, section 3.2.3, the notion of 'transfer of ownership' is an independent concept of Union law. Therefore, its meaning does not depend on how and when a supply of immovable property is acknowledged under the national civil laws of the Member States. After all, if that were to be the case, VAT would be chargeable at different moments in the various Member States, depending on whether the immovable property was transferred by contract (e.g., France, Italy and Belgium) or by the formal act of delivery (e.g., the Netherlands).[63]

Therefore, a supply of goods can take place, even if there is no transfer of *formal legal* ownership of the property. What *is* decisive in our view, is whether the other purchaser obtains enough rights to use the goods as it sees fit *and* is actually in a position to use the goods as it sees fit. We refer to Chapter 3, section 3.2.3.

9.5.2.2 Construction Work

Under Article 14(3) VAT Directive, Member States may regard the handing over of certain works of construction as a supply of goods. In Chapter 3, section 3.2.5.1, we dealt extensively with the notion of works of construction. Therefore, we refer to that section.

9.5.2.3 Internal Supplies of Immovable Property

To prevent certain distortions of competition, Article 18(a) VAT Directive allows Member States to treat as supplies of goods the application by a taxable person for the

63. B. Terra & J. Kajus, *A Guide to the European VAT Directives, Introduction to European VAT*, Vol. 1 (IBFD 2012), p. 447.

purposes of his business of goods produced, constructed, extracted, processed, purchased or imported in the course of such business, where the VAT on such goods, had they been acquired from another taxable person, would not be wholly deductible. Even though the scope of this provision is not restricted to movable or immovable goods, in most Member States that availed themselves of this option, the provision is of particular importance for immovable goods. In Chapter 3, section 3.2.5.2, we discussed the internal supplies in detail. Therefore, we refer to that section.

9.5.2.4 Immovable Property and the Transfer of a Going Concern

In Chapter 3, section 3.6.3, we discussed the 'no-supply' rule of Article 19 VAT Directive. This provision allows the Member States to consider the transfer of a totality of assets or part thereof not to be a supply of goods, whether the transfer takes place for consideration or not, or as a contribution to a company.

In Chapter 2, section 2.4.7, we explained that the leasing or letting of immovable property usually amounts to the carrying on of an economic activity, conferring on the lessor taxable person status. If a taxable person leases parts of a building to various lessees, the question may arise whether a supply by the lessor of that building (without the lease contracts being terminated) to a third party (who takes over the position of lessee) can be considered as a totality of assets or part thereof as referred to in Article 19 VAT Directive. In our view, the mere transfer of an immovable property (without any lease contracts), in principle, does not fall within the scope of Article 19 VAT Directive. However, if the immovable property is transferred in combination with the lease contracts, we believe that Article 19 VAT Directive can be applied, provided that the other criteria for the application of the no-supply rule have been met (*see* Chapter 3, section 3.6.3).

9.5.3 The Place of a Supply of Immovable Property

For the determination of the place of supply of immovable property, Article 31 stipulates that for goods which are not dispatched or transported, the place of supply shall be deemed to be the place where the goods are located at the time when the supply takes place. As immovable property cannot be dispatched or transported (at least not other than being transported from a legal perspective), the supply will take place in the country where the immovable property is situated. Services connected with immovable property are also situated where the property is located (Article 47 VAT Directive, *see* section 9.7).

In section 9.5.2.2, we indicated that the Member States may regard the handing over of certain works of construction as a supply of goods. Because the rules for the determination of the place of a supply of immovable property and the rules for the determination of the place of a supply of a service connected with immovable property lead to the same result (the place where the immovable property is located), it is in this regard irrelevant whether a work of construction is treated as a supply of a good or as a supply of a service.

9.5.4 The Exemption for Supplies of Buildings and Parts Thereof

Immovable property has a special position in the framework of consumption taxes. Given the fact that immovable property, in principle, lasts for years if not decades, and generally cannot be completely consumed, it seems odd to levy a consumption tax each time a specific immovable property is supplied (*see* section 9.2). Moreover, immovable property is often also supplied by private persons. For these reasons, as a general rule, the Directive exempts the supply of buildings, including the land on which they stand (*see* Article 135(1)(j) VAT Directive). This rule has various exceptions. We will discuss the rules governing the supplies of buildings and parts thereof in the next subsections.

9.5.4.1 Exempt Supplies of Old Buildings and Parts Thereof

Article 135(1)(j) VAT Directive exempts the supply of a building or parts thereof, and of the land on which it stands, other than the supply referred to in Article 12(1)(a) VAT Directive. Excluded from the exemption for supplies of buildings or parts thereof are supplies of 'new' buildings (and parts thereof). To resolve difficulties in distinguishing between new buildings and old, the notion of first occupation has been used to determine the moment at which the 'production' process of a building finishes, and it becomes a subject of consumption, that is to say when the building begins to be used by its owner or a tenant.[64]

Effectively, that means that only the supply of 'old' buildings, i.e., buildings that have already been occupied (or that are 'old' on the basis of criteria set by the Member State in question in accordance with Article 12(2) last paragraph VAT Directive),[65] is exempt.

As regards residential buildings (and parts thereof), the underlying reason for that is that residential buildings are considered as having already been 'consumed' by virtue of the first occupation thereof. Since the supply of 'new' buildings, before their first occupation, is taxed (*see* section 9.5.1.1), the VAT Directive ensures that the consumption of buildings is taxed when they leave the productive sphere and enter that of consumption. In order to avoid double taxation, which could occur if the supply of old residential buildings were to be taxed, it was deemed necessary to apply an exemption to the supply of 'old' residential buildings.[66]

If only residential buildings were to be exempted from tax, a clear set of definitions would be required to distinguish residential from commercial buildings. Instead, the VAT legislator chose to exempt supplies of both old residential and old commercial buildings (and parts thereof). However, Member States may allow taxable persons making supplies of 'old' buildings (and parts thereof) to opt for taxation (Article 137(1)(b), *see* section 9.5.4.3).

64. Explanatory Memorandum to the proposal for a Sixth Directive of 20 June 1973, COM (73)950.
65. *See* section 9.5.1.1. In the remainder of this chapter, we will abstract from this nuance and focus on the 'first occupation' as a criterion to determine whether a building is old or new.
66. Explanatory Memorandum to the proposal for a Sixth Directive of 20 June 1973, COM (73)950.

9.5.4.2 Taxed Supplies of New Buildings and Parts Thereof

Although the legislator had reasons to exempt the supply of buildings (and parts thereof) and to formulate this as the starting point for the treatment of the supplies of buildings, there were also solid grounds to tax buildings at least once in their lifetime, ensuring that the consumption of a building is taxed like that of any other good. Therefore, the legislator stipulated that the supply of newly created buildings (and parts thereof) is always taxed (*see* section 9.5.1.5). This result was achieved by excluding supplies of buildings (and parts thereof) and of the land on which the building stands, referred to in Article 12(1)(a) VAT Directive, from the exemption.

What may look like a supply of an old building may for VAT purposes be classified differently. For example, in *Don Bosco*, a taxable person supplied an old building to a purchaser.[67] They also agreed that Don Bosco would demolish the building. The process of demolition had already started, and it was stipulated in the contract that Don Bosco would finalize the demolition after the sale. The CJEU considered that the supply and the demolition formed a single transaction, given that, taken as a whole, the aim of the transactions was not to supply the existing building and the land it stands on but the land that has not been built on, regardless of how far demolition of the old building had progressed at the moment the land was actually supplied. The supply had to be classified as a supply of land that has not been built on. Following the CJEU's decision in *Gemeente Maasdriel*, this land that has not been built on is more precisely to be considered as building land.

This is because, in *Gemeente Maasdriel*, the CJEU clarified that all land which has not been built on, and which is intended to support a building and, therefore, intended to be built on, is to be considered as 'building land'. To determine whether there is an intention to be built on, the declared intention of the parties must be taken into consideration. Aspects that are relevant are the extent to which the transformation work carried out by the vendor had advanced at the time of supply, the completion before the time of supply, by the vendor, of demolition work for the purposes of future construction, and the vendor's understanding to carry out such demolition work with a view to future construction.[68]

In *J.J. Komen en Zonen Beheer Heerhugowaard BV*, the supplier of an old shopping mall had already started the demolition work before the immovable property was supplied to J.J. Komen.[69] Following the acquisition of the building, J.J. Komen continued the renovation and transformation work, so that the totality of the work carried out, both for the account of vendor and for that of J.J. Komen, resulted in the construction of a new building. At no time, in the context of that process of transformation of the building, did the work create a vacant plot of land. The old building was, at least in part, used as such at the time of the supply because the

67. CJEU 19 November 2009, Case C-461/08 *Don Bosco Onroerend Goed BV v Staatssecretaris van Financiën*, ECLI:EU:C:2009:722.
68. CJEU 17 January 2013, Case C-543/11 *Woningstichting Maasdriel v Staatssecretaris van Financiën*, ECLI:EU:C:2013:20.
69. CJEU 12 July 2012, Case C-326/11 *J.J. Komen en Zonen Beheer Heerhugowaard BV v Staatssecretaris van Financiën*, ECLI:EU:C:2012:461.

shopping mall was still accessible to the public, and at least one shop was operational. So, at the time of the supply of the building, only partial demolition work had been carried out by the supplier, the building was still partially occupied, and the construction work to transform that building into a new building was entirely carried out by the purchaser after the supply. This led the CJEU to the conclusion that the supply of the partly demolished old shopping mall, still partly in use as such, was to be considered as a supply of an old building, even though the building was undergoing a transformation into a new building.

KPC Herning deals with a situation in which there are two consecutive supplies of immovable property.[70] The first supply was a supply by the port of Odense to KPC Herning of a plot of land on which an (old) warehouse was located. This contract was subject to a number of conditions, including the condition that KPC Herning was to conclude a contract with a low-rent housing body for the purpose of carrying out, on the land in question, a building project composed of social housing for young persons. The second supply was a supply by KPC Herning to Boligforeningen Kristiansdal of that same plot of land and (old) warehouse. They agreed that the seller, KPC Herning, was to undertake to build and provide, on a turnkey basis, social housing units for young persons on that land. However, parties also agreed that the (partial) demolition of the old warehouse was to be done by the buyer, Boligforeningen Kristiansdal. The latter carried out the partial demolition of the warehouse at its own expense and risk. At the date of the successive transfers of the land and the warehouse, the warehouse was fully operational. The dispute concerned the question of whether the supplies are to be considered as supplies of building land, given the fact that the intention of the parties involved was that the building should be wholly or partly demolished to make room for a new building. The CJEU considered that this situation was fundamentally different from *Don Bosco* in that the supplies to and by KPC Herning constituted two separate supplies for VAT. Furthermore, KPC Herning was not at all involved in the partial demolition of the warehouse. It was the (ultimate) buyer, Boligforeningen Kristiansdal, which instructed, at its own expense and risk, a third-party undertaking to carry out the necessary works. Consequently, the demolition of the warehouse was regarded as a transaction independent of its sale and did not form, with that transaction, a single economic service. Hence, the doctrine of composite supplies, which was applied in *Don Bosco*, could not be used in this situation. Now, looking at each of the two supplies separately, the CJEU made it clear that neither the first sale nor the second appeared to have increased the economic value of that property, with the result that those two transactions did not give rise to significant added value such as to make them subject to VAT. The mere fact that the parties intended to eventually erect a new building in combination with the fact that each of the supplies it to be treated separately for VAT purposes, brought the CJEU to the conclusion that the supplies could not be classified as a sale of building land.

70. CJEU 4 September 2019, Case C-71/18 *Skatteministeriet v KPC Herning*, ECLI:EU:C:2019:660.

9.5.4.3 *Option to Taxation: Taxed Supplies of Other Buildings Than New Buildings*

On the basis of Article 137(1)(b) VAT Directive, Member States may allow taxable persons a right of option for taxation. If such an option is introduced and used with respect to a supply of a building from one taxable person to another taxable person, the latter being entitled to a deduction of input VAT, tax cascading will be avoided. If the option were not to be available, the supply of the building would be VAT-exempt, and the supplier would incorporate the non-deductible VAT in the (sales) price of the building. Subsequently, the taxable person purchasing this building will most probably incorporate the hidden VAT embedded in the price of the building when he resells this building. These sales would incur VAT, which could result in tax cascading, as hidden VAT will be taxed with VAT. Several Member States have introduced an option to tax supplies of buildings and of the land on which they stand. The design of the option, however, differs per Member State. This is likely to be partially caused by the fact that several Member States levy a real estate transfer tax next to VAT on supplies of immovable property.

In order to tackle abuse, some Member States have introduced the rule that only customers with a full or almost full right to deduction (for instance, 90%) are entitled to cooperate in taxing the supply. Article 137(2) VAT Directive provides a legal basis for setting such conditions.[71]

9.5.5 The Exemption for Supplies of Land

In this section, we will discuss Article 135(1)(k), which exempts the supply of land which has not been built on, other than the supply of building land as referred to in point (b) of Article 12(1) VAT Directive.

9.5.5.1 *Exempt Supply of Land Other Than Building Land*

In the explanatory memorandum to the proposal for a Sixth VAT Directive, it was considered that land would seem to be a most unsuitable subject for VAT since it is neither produced nor consumed. Therefore, as a main rule, Article 135(1)(k) exempts the supply of land which has not been built on.

9.5.5.2 *Taxed Supply of Building Land*

Pursuant to Article 135(1)(k) VAT Directive, an exemption applies to the supply of land which has not been built on, other than the supply of *building land* as referred to in Article 12(1)(b) VAT Directive. Consequently, the supply of building land is taxed with VAT. The explanatory memorandum explains the reason for this as follows:

71. CJEU 30 June 2022, Case C-56/21 *UAB 'ARVI' ir ko v Valstybinė mokesčių inspekcija prie Lietuvos Respublikos finansų ministerijos*, ECLI:EU:C:2022:509, para. 19.

> But, if earth as such cannot be 'produced', it can however be the subject of certain productive economic activities which may add value to it: a building site cleared and prepared will be more valuable than such a site in its natural state, and the source of the difference in value is the economic activity. The selling price will not be broken down into the price for the land as such and the price of the work which has been carried out on it. If supplies of land are exempted from value added tax, then one thereby exempts also the work which may have contributed to its value, if the land is supplied to an individual; by the same token however, the work will be taxed twice over if the land is supplied to an undertaking. Moreover, a distinction between a site prepared for construction (foundation, roads, levelling, installation of drainage and water supply systems, installation of electricity supply, etc.) and a site with a completed building on it is a completely artificial distinction, since in both cases a certain quantity of work is incorporated indivisibly into the earth. Indeed, plots of land would appear to be a 'raw material' of economic activities. Even if one considers that they cannot be the subject of consumption in the strict sense of the word, they are nevertheless put to use, to satisfy either the needs of individuals (residential premises), in which case they have the nature of consumer goods, or the needs of business undertakings, in which case they constitute investments. .... .[72]

For these reasons, the VAT legislator deemed it necessary that supplies of plots of building land should be taxed. Consequently, the supply of building land, as referred to in point (b) of Article 12(1) VAT Directive, is excluded from the exemption. *See* section 9.5.1.4 for the definition of the concept of 'building land'.

9.5.5.3 *Option to Taxation: Taxed Supplies of Land Other Than Building Land*

On the basis of Article 137(1)(c) VAT Directive, Member States may allow taxable persons a right of option for taxation of a supply of land which has not been built on, other than the supply of building land. That there is no option right for the Member States to introduce an option to taxation with regard to building land speaks for itself, as the supply of this type of land is taxed by definition (*see* section 9.5.1.3).

Just as for 'old' buildings (*see* section 9.5.1.1), the reason for introducing the possibility to allow an option for taxation is that taxable persons who want to supply immovable property to other taxable persons having the right to reclaim VAT on input transactions should be enabled to avoid cascading of VAT. Under this regime, they will be able to reclaim or adjust their initial reclaim of VAT made on the purchase of the plot of land or other related costs by charging VAT on the supply which VAT can be deducted by the customer (in full or partly). In order to tackle abuse, some Member States have introduced a rule that only customers with a full or almost full right to deduction (for instance, 90%) are entitled to cooperate in taxing the supply. Article 137(2) VAT Directive provides a legal basis for setting such conditions.[73]

---

72. Explanatory Memorandum to the proposal for a Sixth Directive of 20 June 1973, COM (73)950.
73. There are also Member States that have made the option to tax conditional on the transfer of the immovable property to a taxable person who, at the time of conclusion of the transaction, is already registered for VAT purposes. The CJEU has approved of such national legislation. CJEU

A taxable person (B), who intended to supply a property with the option for taxation to a buyer (C), may face an adjustment of the VAT he deducted on the purchase (from A) of that property (*see* Chapter 10, section 10.6) if it is in retrospect established that at the time of the supply of the immovable property not all conditions for the option for taxation had been met. However, the (later) use made by the purchaser (C) of the immovable property after the supply was made cannot affect (adjustment of) the right to deduct the input VAT paid by the seller (B) upon the acquisition of that property.[74]

9.5.6 The Person Liable to Pay the VAT on Supplies of Immovable Property

If a supply of immovable property is taxed, the VAT on that supply will, in principle, be payable by the supplier of immovable property (Article 193 VAT Directive). However, Member States may decide to apply the reverse charge mechanism where the supply is carried out by a taxable person who is not established in the Member State in which the VAT is due (Article 194 VAT Directive). Article 199 VAT Directive allows Member States to apply the reverse charge mechanism in certain cases if the supplier of the immovable property is established in the Member State in which the VAT is due. As cases in which the reverse charge mechanism may be applied, Article 199 VAT Directive mentions:

(a) the supply of construction work, including repair, cleaning, maintenance, alteration and demolition services in relation to immovable property, as well as the handing over of construction works regarded as a supply of goods pursuant to Article 14(3);

...

(c) the supply of immovable property, as referred to in Article 135(1)(j) and (k), where the supplier has opted for taxation of the supply pursuant to Article 137;

...

(g) the supply of immovable property sold by a judgment debtor in a compulsory sale procedure.

The rationale for the application of the reverse charge mechanism seems to be the tackling of abusive practices. In Chapter 12, section 12.3.2.1, we extensively discuss the application of the reverse charge mechanism on the basis of Article 199 VAT Directive.

9.5.7 The Right of Deduction of Input VAT and Supplies of Immovable Property

If a supply of immovable property is exempt, this may have an effect on the right of deduction of any VAT that was charged on the purchase of that immovable property.

---

30 June 2022, Case C-56/*21 UAB 'ARVI' ir ko v Valstybine mokesčių inspekcija prie Lietuvos Respublikos finansų ministerijos*, ECLI:EU:C:2022:509.

74. *See:* CJEU 30 June 2022, Case C-56/*21 UAB 'ARVI' ir ko v Valstybine mokesčių inspekcija prie Lietuvos Respublikos finansų ministerijos*, ECLI:EU:C:2022:509.

This is because the deduction of VAT on the purchase of immovable property must be monitored during a period varying by Member State between five and 20 years. We refer to Chapter 10, section 10.6.

As regards the input VAT incurred by a taxable person on purchases of immovable property, it is particularly relevant to note that any subsequent lease by the purchaser to a third party may have an effect on the right of deduction (and/or the adjustment of that deduction). As we will explain further in section 9.6, the leasing or letting of immovable property is - as a main rule - exempt from VAT. Consequently, in principle, this does not give rise to a right of deduction of input VAT, or - if the exempt lease follows a taxed use of an immovable property - gives rise to repayments of VAT that was deducted, on the basis of the adjustment rules.

On the basis of Article 168a, sub 1 VAT Directive, VAT on expenditure related to immovable property forming part of the business assets of a taxable person and used both for the purposes of the taxable person's business and for his private use or that of his staff, or, more generally, for purposes other than those of his business, will be deductible only in proportion to the property's use for the purposes of the taxable person's business (*see* Chapter 10, section 10.5)

9.6 THE LEASING OR LETTING OF IMMOVABLE PROPERTY

According to Article 135(1)(l) VAT Directive, Member States must exempt the leasing or letting of immovable property. Article 135(2) VAT Directive excludes from the exemption the leasing or letting of specific items. In section 9.4, we discussed the concept of 'immovable property'. It is well-established case law that the terms used to specify the exemptions provided for by (mainly) Articles 132 and 135 constitute independent concepts of Union law, which must be given a Union law definition. In this and the subsequent (sub)paragraphs, we will first discuss the concepts of 'leasing' or 'letting' as referred to in Article 135(1)(l) and 135(2) VAT Directive. Then, we will elaborate on the leasing or letting of immovable property and the taxable person status, the place of supply of leasing or letting of immovable property, the exemptions (and the exceptions thereto) for the leasing and letting of immovable property, as well as on the person liable and the right of deduction in relation to the leasing of letting of immovable property.

9.6.1 The Concept of 'Leasing or Letting of Immovable Property'

The VAT Directive does not expressly define the concept of leasing or letting. Nor does it leave that definition to the legal orders of the Member States. Leasing and letting are independent concepts of Union law, which must be given a Union law definition. Such a definition of leasing or letting cannot be found by simply referring to legal concepts used by only some of the national laws.[75] From CJEU case law, it can be learned that

75. Opinion of Advocate General Jacobs of 22 February 2001, Case C-326/99 *Stichting 'Goed Wonen' v Staatssecretaris van Financiën*, ECLI:EU:C:2001:115, para. 72.

there does not seem to be a principal distinction between leasing and letting (of immovable property). For example, this can be inferred from the CJEU's ruling in *Stichting Goed Wonen*.[76] The question that had to be answered in the *Stichting Goed Wonen* case was whether the national legislature might treat the terms leasing or letting as covering not only leasing and/or letting in a sense applied to those terms by civil law but also any other form in which immovable property is made available for use otherwise than by way of the supply thereof.[77] More specifically, the question arose whether the granting of (some specific) usufructuary rights in the Dutch VAT Act (for which the sum paid plus turnover tax amounted to less than the economic value of those rights) could be regarded as leasing or letting. The CJEU answered this question in the affirmative, which confirms the broad scope of the notions 'leasing' and 'letting' in Article 135(1)(l) VAT Directive.

According to settled CJEU case law, the fundamental characteristic of the concept of 'leasing or letting of immovable property' lies in conferring on the other party to the contract, for an agreed period and for payment, the right to occupy property as if that person were the owner, and to exclude any other person from enjoyment of such a right.[78] This leads us to believe that the following elements are essential to the notion of the 'leasing or letting of immovable property':

(a) An immovable property must be made available to the lessee or tenant 'for an agreed period'.
(b) That immovable property must be made available to the lessee or tenant 'for payment'.
(c) The lessee or tenant obtains the right to occupy the property as if he were the owner and to exclude any other person from enjoyment of such a right.

In the next subsections, we will only discuss the first and third criteria because it is self-evident that the lease or letting of immovable property can only be exempt if it constitutes a taxable transaction, which requires that the service is supplied 'for consideration' (i.e., 'for payment').

9.6.1.1 For an Agreed Period (Duration of the Activity Involved)

A key element of leasing or letting is the duration of the contract. For instance, does the provision of access to roads on payment of a toll represents a '(leasing or) letting of immovable property'? Is the nature of the transaction in paying for car parking not very similar to the transaction involved in paying a toll, which is according to Article 135(2) a (taxed) form of leasing or letting? Given the similarities, and given that, according to

76. CJEU 4 October 2001, Case C-326/99 *Stichting 'Goed Wonen' v Staatssecretaris van Financiën*, ECLI:EU:C:2001:506.
77. Opinion of Advocate General Jacobs of 22 February 2001, Case C-326/99 *Stichting 'Goed Wonen' v Staatssecretaris van Financiën*, ECLI:EU:C:2001:115, para. 49.
78. For example: *ibid.*, para. 55 and CJEU 22 January 2015, Case C-55/14 *Régie communale autonome du stade Luc Varenne v Belgian State*, ECLI:EU:C:2015:29, para. 21.

the VAT Directive, the letting of immovable property expressly includes the service offered for parking fees, arguably it can be inferred that the same applies to the services offered in exchange for a toll. However, the CJEU ruled differently.

The term (leasing or) letting cannot be considered to cover contracts in which, as is the case when paying a toll for access to roads, the parties have not agreed on any duration for the right of enjoyment of the immovable property, which is an essential element of a contract to let. Where access to roads is provided, what interests the user is the possibility offered to him of making a particular journey rapidly and more safely. The duration of the use of the road is not a factor taken into account by the parties, in particular, not in determining the price.[79]

9.6.1.2 Right to Occupy the Property as an Owner/Exclusive Occupation

Another key condition for the leasing or letting of immovable property is the granting of the right to occupy the property combined with the right to exclude other persons from the immovable property. Illustrative for the relevance of the condition of 'exclusive occupation' is the *Temco Europe*[80] case. In this case, a number of contracts simultaneously granted associated companies a licence to occupy a single property. This was done in return for a payment set essentially on the basis of the area occupied and by which the contracts, as performed, had as their essential object the making available, in a passive manner, of premises or parts of buildings. This activity of making available was performed in return for a payment linked to the passage of time. As regards the tenant's right of exclusive occupation of the property, it must – according to the CJEU – be pointed out that this could be restricted in the contract concluded with the landlord and might only relate to the property as it was defined in that contract. Thus, the landlord may reserve the right regularly to visit the property let. Furthermore, a contract of letting may relate to certain parts of a property that must be used in common with other occupiers. The presence in the contract of such restrictions on the right to occupy the premises let did not prevent that occupation being exclusive as regards all other persons not permitted by law or by the contract to exercise a right over the property which is the subject of the contract of letting. Therefore, these activities compromised the 'letting of immovable property' and not the provision of a service capable of being categorized in a different way.

What did not amount to a letting of immovable property within the meaning of the exemption involved was the grant by the owner of premises to an owner of a cigarette vending machine of the right to install, operate and maintain the machine in its premises (the *Sinclair Collis* case).[81] The latter received this right for two years.[82] However, he did not receive rights of possession or control other than those expressly

79. For example: CJEU 12 September 2000, Case C-358/97 *Commission of the European Communities-Ireland*, ECLI:EU:C:2000:425, paras 47-54.
80. CJEU 18 November 2004, Case C-284/03 *Temco Europe SA v Belgian State*, ECLI:EU:C:2004:730, paras 24 and 25.
81. CJEU 12 June 2003, Case C-275/01 *Sinclair Collis ltd v Commissioners of Customs and Excise*, ECLI:EU:C:2003:341, paras 27-29.

set out in the agreement between the parties. The agreement did not confer on the owner of the machine the right to control or restrict access to the area where the machines were placed. Under the agreement, he retained an exclusive right of access to the machines to maintain them, keep them stocked with cigarettes and remove the cash inside. That right concerned only access to the machine itself, in particular its inner mechanism, and did not involve access to that part of the premises where the machine was situated. The right was restricted to the opening hours of the commercial establishment and could not be exercised without the site owner's consent. The agreement did not prescribe any precisely defined area or space for the installation of the vending machines at the premises. Contrary to the position in relation to the characteristics of a letting, the location of the machine was material only in so far as it enabled the maximum possible number of sales to be generated. Subject to that criterion, under the agreement, there was nothing to prevent the machines from being moved about, to a degree, as the site owner wished. As a consequence, the nature of this supply – the subject matter of the agreement – was the guarantee of the exercise of the exclusive right to sell cigarettes at the premises by installing and operating automatic vending machines in return for a percentage of the profits. It was not the provision of the *exclusive occupation* of a clearly defined area or space, and therefore, it did not fall within the scope of the exemption with respect to the letting of immovable property.

9.6.1.3 Services by the Lessee or Tenant to the Landlord

Usually, it is the landlord and not the lessee or tenant who performs services that fall within the scope of the notion leasing and letting. However, things may not always be immediately clear.

For example, in *Mirror Group*, it looked as if – besides the landlord – the tenant was also involved in leasing and letting with regard to the same immovable property. The question had to be answered whether a prospective tenant who did not initially have any interest in the immovable property and who entered into an agreement for the lease of that immovable property with a landlord and/or accepted the grant of a lease of the property in return for a sum of money paid by the landlord made a supply which would fall within the scope of the notion 'leasing and letting' in the provision regarding the exemption concerned. In this case, the CJEU's answer was negative. The amount paid could only be seen as a kind of discount on the supply made by the landlord, and not as a consideration for a supply by the tenant. This would only have been different if the tenant were a so-called *anchor* tenant, a very interesting and from a commercial viewpoint attractive prospective client whose presence might attract other tenants. Under those conditions, it would have been seen as a service, but certainly not the lease or letting of a building – where it is the landlord who makes a taxable supply of services

82. It was in return for a percentage of the gross profits on the sales of cigarettes and other tobacco goods in the premises. *See* CJEU 12 June 2003, Case C-275/01 *Sinclair Collis ltd v Commissioners of Customs and Excise*, ECLI:EU:C:2003:341.

and the tenant who, in return for the supply, pays consideration – but a supply of advertising services.[83]

In *Lubbock Fine*, the CJEU ruled that the leasing or letting of immovable property for the purposes of Article 13B(b) of the Sixth Directive covered the case where a tenant surrenders his lease and returns the immovable property to his immediate landlord. As such, it was accepted that that also the tenant was able to render a service that fell within the scope of the notion 'leasing or letting'. This required further explanation as it seemed to be in contrast to *Mirror Group*. The CJEU explained that that judgment was given in respect of a tenant who had returned the immovable property leased to the landlord and who, consequently, for the purposes of taxation, had assigned his right to occupy the property back to the landlord by surrendering it. That is why the Court ruled, in paragraphs 9 and 12 of the judgment, that the tenant's surrender of the supply of services made by the landlord[84] had to be exempt where the supply itself was exempt. Those conditions were not met in the *Mirror Group* case, as a prospective tenant was not surrendering to the landlord its right to occupy the property.

9.6.1.4 *Letting or Lease of Immovable Property in Combination with Other Supplies (Composite Supplies)*

Often, the activity of making the immovable property available is accompanied by other services supplied by the same landlord. In Chapter 3, section 3.5, we discussed the possible VAT consequences of composite supplies.

In light of the letting or leasing of immovable property, of particularly note is the *Tellmer Property* case[85] concerning the question of whether the costs of cleaning the common parts in an apartment block are, like letting, exempt from VAT. The CJEU considered that even if the cleaning services of the common parts of an apartment block accompany the use of the property let, they do not necessarily fall within the concept of letting for the purposes of Article 13(B)(b) of the Sixth Directive (currently Article 135(1)(l)VAT Directive). It is not disputed that the cleaning services of the common parts of an apartment block can be supplied in various ways, such as, for example, a third party invoicing the cost of the service direct to the tenants, or by the landlord employing his own staff for the purpose or using a cleaning company. In this case, RLRE Tellmer Property invoiced the cleaning services to the tenants separately from the rent. Such letting and such cleaning could not be regarded as constituting a single transaction within the meaning of the case law of the Court. As a result, the letting of immovable property and the cleaning service of the common parts of the latter must, in circumstances such as those in this case, be regarded as independent, mutually divisible operations, so that the said service does not fall within the scope of the exemption for leasing and letting of immovable property. This could also apply to

83. CJEU 9 October 2001, Case C-409/98 *Mirror Group Plc v Commissioners of Customs and Excise*, ECLI:EU:C:2001:524, para. 27.
84. Which involves a change in the contractual relationship.
85. CJEU 11 June 2009, Case C-572/07 *RLRE Tellmer Property sro v Finanční ředitelství v Ústí nad Labem*, ECLI:EU:C:2009:365, paras 21-25.

other services where they are supplied together with the leasing or letting of the immovable property by the landlord, like smaller and more encompassing forms of continuing maintenance.

After the *Tellmer* case, one criterion needed to be further explained. Was the fact that a cleaning service could (in theory) also be supplied by a third party in itself enough to establish that such a cleaning service forms a distinct service? The answer is no. In *Field Fisher Waterhouse,*[86] the Court considered that as to the relevance of the fact that a third party could, in principle, supply certain services, it must be observed that the existence of such a possibility is not decisive in itself. As may be seen from the Court's case law, the possibility that elements of a single supply may, in other circumstances, be supplied separately is inherent in the concept of a single composite transaction.[87]

The question may arise whether certain supplies which are additional to the letting of immovable property and must be seen as inseparable could still have such a substantial and decisive nature that they could change the character of the whole supply (in principle, the exempt leasing or letting of immovable property) into a supply with another nature (mostly taxed). This type of issue mostly arises with regard to sports accommodation. If the supply transcends the activity of making available immovable property, it could certainly change the supply into a taxed supply. Services linked to sport or physical education must, so far as is possible, be considered as a whole. The Court ruled in the *Lindöpark* case that the activity of running a golf course generally entails not only the passive activity of making the course available but also a large number of other commercial activities, such as supervision, management and continuing maintenance by the service provider, provision of other facilities and so forth. In the absence of quite exceptional circumstances, letting out a golf course cannot, therefore, constitute the main service supplied. In practice, it is not always easy to determine whether the activity of making an immovable property available can be seen as simply the leasing or letting of that immovable property (mostly exempt or taxed if the conditions to opt for taxation are fulfilled) or that it is a composite supply resulting in more than just leasing or letting (which would be taxed anyway).

In *Luc Varenne,*[88] the CJEU decided that the act of making available, for consideration, a football stadium under a contract reserving certain rights and prerogatives to the stadium owner and providing for the supply, by the owner, of various services, including services of maintenance, cleaning, repair and upgrading, representing 80% of the charge agreed in the contract to be payable, did not constitute, as a general rule, a 'letting of immovable property' within the meaning of that provision.

86. CJEU 27 September 2012, Case C-392/11 *Field Fisher Waterhouse LLP v Commissioners for Her Majesty's Revenue and Customs*, ECLI:EU:C:2012:597, para. 26.
87. *See also* CJEU 19 January 2012, Case C-117/11 *Purple Parking Ltd and Airparks Services Ltd v Commissioners for Her Majesty's Revenue and Customs*, ECLI:EU:C:2012:29, para. 31.
88. CJEU 22 January 2015, Case C-55/14 *Régie communale autonome du stade Luc Varenne v* État belge, ECLI:EU:C:2015:29, para. 39.

In *Wojskowa Agencja Mieszkaniowa w Warszawie*,[89] the CJEU ruled that in the context of the letting of immovable property, the provision of electricity, heating and water and refuse collection, provided by third-party suppliers for the tenant directly using those goods and services must be regarded as being supplied by the landlord where he has concluded agreements for the provision of those supplies and simply passes on the costs thereof to the tenant. The letting of immovable property and the provision of water, electricity and heating as well as refuse collection accompanying that letting must, in principle, be regarded as constituting several distinct and independent supplies which need to be assessed separately for VAT purposes unless the elements of the transaction, including those indicating the economic reason for concluding the contract, are so closely linked that they form, objectively, a single, indivisible economic supply which it would be artificial to split. According to the CJEU, it is important to ascertain in the context of each letting whether, with respect to utilities, the tenant is free to determine his own levels of consumption. In that regard, the existence of individual meters and billing according to the amount of the goods used is a factor of importance, which suggests that the provision of utilities should be regarded as constituting separate supplies from the letting. So far as concerns refuse collection if the tenant has a choice of supplier or may conclude a contract directly with the supplier, even if, for reasons of convenience, he does not exercise that choice or option, but obtains the service from the supplier designated by the landlord on the basis of a contract concluded between the landlord and the supplier, that circumstance points to the existence of a supply separate to the letting. If, in addition, the amount due for refuse collection and that due under the letting are itemized separately on the invoice, it must be considered that the landlord does not provide a single supply consisting of the letting and that supply. Another example of a situation in which the lease of immovable property, in combination with additional services, forms a single supply can be found in *Mailat*. In *Mailat*, a lease contract for an immovable property which was used for commercial purposes included the lease of all capital equipment and inventory items necessary for that commercial use. The CJEU ruled that this constituted a single supply in which the letting of the immovable property was the principal supply.[90]

9.6.2 Leasing or Letting of Immovable Property and Taxable Person Status

In Chapter 2, section 2.4.7, we indicated that according to the third paragraph of Article 9(1) VAT Directive, the exploitation of tangible or intangible property for the purposes of obtaining income therefrom on a continuing basis must, in particular, be regarded as an economic activity. A clear example of this kind of economic activity is the leasing or letting of immovable or movable property.

89. CJEU 16 April 2015, Case C-42/14 *Minister Finansów v Wojskowa Agencja Mieszkaniowa w Warszawie*, ECLI:EU:C:2015:229, paras 45-47.
90. CJEU 19 December 2018, Case C-17/18 *Criminal proceedings against Virgil Mailat and Others*, ECLI:EU:C:2018:1038.

9.6.3 The Place of a Supply of Leasing or Letting of Immovable Property

The leasing or letting of immovable property is considered as a supply of a service 'connected with immovable property'. Article 47 VAT Directive in this respect explicitly mentions 'the granting of rights to use immovable property'. Article 31(1)(h) of Regulation (EU) No 1042/2013 also explicitly indicates that the leasing or letting of immovable property is considered as a supply of a service 'connected with immovable property'. Therefore, the place of supply of the leasing or letting of immovable property is to be determined on the basis of Article 47 VAT Directive. The place of supply is where the immovable property is located.

9.6.4 The Exemption for the Leasing or Letting of Immovable Property

The leasing or letting of immovable property is an exempt supply under Article 135(1)(l) VAT Directive. As a consequence, no VAT needs to be charged on the rental fee, and no input VAT associated with the leasing of letting is deductible.

However, the application of the general rule (exemption) may have cascading effects if the lessee or tenant is a taxable person carrying out taxed transactions. For this reason, various exceptions to this main rule are included in the VAT Directive, some of which are mandatory, others optional. These exclusions concern the lease and letting of hotel and holiday accommodation, parking space, permanently installed equipment and machinery, safes, other taxed lease or letting and the leasing or letting with an option to taxation (but even if the Member State has exercised its right to introduce an option to taxation, it is in the end up to the contract parties to opt for taxation).

9.6.4.1 Exceptions to the Exempt Leasing or Letting of Immovable Property

In this subsection, we will discuss the exceptions to the main rule that the leasing or letting of immovable property is an exempt supply.

9.6.4.1.1 Hotel and Holiday Accommodation

According to Article 135(2)(a) VAT Directive, the provision of accommodation, as defined in the laws of the Member States, in the hotel sector or in sectors with a similar function, including the provision of accommodation in holiday camps or on sites developed for use as camping sites, is taxed. Under Article 98 jo Annex III (12) VAT Directive, Member States may apply a reduced rate on this type of rental service.

In *Blasi*, the CJEU was asked whether the short-term lease of a dwelling accommodation was also covered by the provision regarding the taxed lease of hotel accommodation and lease of accommodation in a sector with a similar function (the relevance of this question mostly concerns the fact that most Member States apply the lower rate to this type of short-term lease).[91] The CJEU ruled that this provision also covers short-term accommodation for guests as constituting the provision of accommodation in sectors with a function similar to that of the hotel sector. This may be applied to letting agreements concluded for a period of less than six months if the duration is deemed to reflect the parties' (true) intention. The provision of short-term accommodation, being defined as less than six months, appears to be a reasonable means by which to ensure that the transactions of taxable persons whose business is similar to the essential function performed by a hotel, namely the provision of temporary accommodation on a commercial basis, are subject to tax. It is, however, for the national court to determine whether, in a case before it, certain factors (such as the automatic renewal of the letting agreement) suggest that the duration stated in the letting agreement does not reflect the parties' true intention, in which case, the actual total duration of the accommodation, rather than that specified in the letting agreement, would have to be taken into consideration.

9.6.4.1.2 Parking Space

Pursuant to Article 135(2)(b) VAT Directive, the letting of premises and sites for the parking of vehicles is taxed. The first question occurring while reading this provision is what is meant by the term 'vehicles'. According to the CJEU in *Marselisborg*,[92] the provision concerned, which excludes the letting of premises and sites for parking vehicles from the exemption from VAT, must be interpreted as meaning that the term of 'vehicles' used in that provision includes all means of transport, including aircraft, trains, caravans and boats. The second question that may arise is what the author of the Directive had in mind when he used the phrase 'the letting of premises and sites for parking'. The question becomes even more relevant when the vehicle is a boat. According to the CJEU, the concept of letting of immovable property also includes the letting of both water-based mooring berths for boats and land sites for the storage of boats on land. A mooring berth in a port basin, for instance, fulfils the definition of immovable property within the meaning of the provision concerned since the letting does not concern a particular quantity of water, but a specific part of the port basin which is clearly delimited and cannot be moved. The third question that needs to be answered is what the term 'letting' means in this regard. As we have discussed before, the term 'leasing and letting' is an independent concept of European law. In this provision, only the word 'letting' is used. 'Letting' as used in this provision comes very close to or also has the characteristics of custody, which might in itself be the reason why the legislator, with a view to this slightly different and more specific nature of letting, decided to exclude this type of letting from the exemption.

---

91. CJEU 12 February 1998, Case C-346/95 *Elisabeth Blasi v Finanzamt München I*, ECLI: EU:C:1998:51.
92. CJEU 3 March 2005, Case C-428/02 *Fonden Marselisborg Lystbådehavn v Skatteministeriet*, ECLI:EU:C:2005:126.

The *Morten Henriksen* case[93] shows that the provision concerned, which introduces an exception to the exemption laid down in the provision regarding the leasing or letting of immovable property, and more particularly the phrase 'premises and sites for parking vehicles', covers the letting of all places designed to be used for parking vehicles, including closed garages. However, such lettings cannot be excluded from the exemption if they are closely linked to lettings of immovable property for another purpose, which is itself exempt from VAT. This may apply particularly where the owner lets both the dwelling and the attached closed garage to the same tenant. From later case law, it becomes even more apparent that in such a situation, only one transaction is deemed to be carried out, of which the most decisive element (the exempt letting of the dwelling) will dictate the VAT treatment of this composite supply. Member States may not be exempt from VAT lettings of premises and sites for parking, which are not covered by the exemption. In the various Member States, the letting of publicly owned parking space along city roads will mostly be treated as an activity falling within the scope of the special regime for public authorities (as a non-taxable activity), whereas the letting by the same municipality of parking space in a car park (indoor garage) is considered an economic activity to be taxed for VAT purposes.

9.6.4.1.3 *Permanently Installed Equipment and Machinery*

The lease of permanently installed equipment and machinery is taxed as it is excluded from the exemption under Article 135(2)(c) VAT Directive. The rationale behind this exclusion is most probably that exempting leasing and letting of immovable property with a strict business character would distort the neutrality, as the non-deductible input tax would result in cascading effects. It must have been for this reason that the authors of the Directive have chosen to define the exemptions, and therefore, also the exemption relating to the lease and letting of immovable property, as strictly as possible, in order to avoid these types of distortion. That exemptions could have a distorting impact can also be derived from settled case law in which the CJEU has repeatedly stated that exemptions must be interpreted strictly, as they are exclusions to the general rule that supplies are to be taxed, and as they might cause cascading effects. That the legislator chose to exclude the lease of permanently installed equipment and machinery from the exemption results in the uniform treatment of the purchase and the hiring of machinery. This also ensures equitable VAT treatment of machinery, regardless of whether it is categorized as movable tangible property or as equipment that must be affixed to the ground to function effectively. Both types of leases are subject to VAT in a uniform manner.

The leasing of immovable property falling within Article 135(1)(l) of the VAT Directive and the supplies of services linked to that leasing may constitute a single supply from the point of view of VAT[94] (*see* Chapter 3, section 3.5). Consequently, the

93. CJEU 13 July 1989, Case C-173/88 *Morten Henriksen, Avocat v Skatteministeriet*, ECLI: EU:C:1989:329.

94. CJEU 27 September 2012, Case C-392/11, *Field Fisher Waterhouse LLP v Commissioners for Her Majesty's Revenue and Customs*, ECLI:EU:C:2012:597, para. 28, CJEU 19 December 2018, Case

letting of permanently installed equipment and machinery is, after all, exempt where that letting constitutes a supply ancillary to a principal supply of leasing a building, carried out under a leasing agreement concluded between the same parties and exempt under Article 135(1)(l), and those supplies form a single economic supply.[95]

9.6.4.1.4 Safes

Lettings of safes, safety deposit boxes and the like are expressly excluded in the VAT Directive from the exemption for the leasing and letting of immovable property. The rationale behind this provision is presumably the same as for parking sites: this type of letting bears a strong resemblance to custody.

9.6.4.1.5 Other Taxed Lease or Letting

According to the last subparagraph of Article 135(2), Member States may apply further exclusions to the scope of the exemption referred to in point (l) of paragraph 1. This provision has turned out to be providing the Member States with a broad margin of discretion. From the CJEU's ruling in *Amengual Far,* it became apparent that (the former version of) this provision (Article 13B(b) of the Sixth Directive) allows (allowed) Member States to lay down a general rule making lettings of immovable property subject to VAT and exempting from that rule only lettings of immovable property to be used for dwelling purposes.[96]

9.6.4.1.6 Option to Taxation: Leasing or Letting of Immovable Property

As previously noted, exemptions within the production chain can exacerbate the tax burden due to the non-recoverability of related input VAT. Such exemptions have the potential to cause significant distortions, potentially disrupting competitive equilibriums. For instance, a taxable person purchasing a new immovable property will, unless engaged in exempt activities, deduct the related input VAT from the VAT payable on his output transactions, whereas a taxable person who hires the same immovable property would encounter a disadvantage caused by the fact that the owner was not entitled to reclaim the related input tax and would most presumably increase his rental fee accordingly. To address this inequity and foster a level playing field, the authors of the Directive have included an option for the Member States to provide taxable persons with an option to tax the lease of immovable property. Such an option serves to neutralize the aforementioned disparities, thereby ensuring a more equitable VAT environment for all parties involved in immovable property transactions.

C-17/18, *Criminal proceedings against Virgil Mailat and Others*, ECLI:EU:C:2018:1038, paras 39-41 and CJEU 4 May 2023, Case C-516/21 *Finanzamt X v Y.*, ECLI:EU:C:2023:372, para. 32.

95. CJEU 4 May 2023, Case C-516/21 *Finanzamt X v Y.*, ECLI:EU:C:2023:372.
96. CJEU 3 February 2000, Case C-12/98 *Miguel Amengual Far v Juan Amengual Far*, ECLI: EU:C:2000:62.

Under Article 137(1)(d), Member States may allow taxable persons a right of option for taxation in respect of the leasing or letting of immovable property. The second paragraph of Article 137 stipulates that the Member States shall lay down the detailed rules governing the exercise of the option under paragraph 1. Member States may even restrict the scope of that right of option:

> Article 137 of the VAT Directive allows the Member States not only to grant taxable persons the right to opt for taxation of transactions covered by that provision, but also allows them to restrict the scope of that right or withdraw it. Accordingly, the Member States have a wide discretion under that article, since it is for them to assess whether they should or should not introduce the right of option, depending on what they consider to be expedient in the situation existing in their country at a given time.[97]

Various Member States introduced measures[98] to ensure that this option to taxation would not result in abusive practices, restricting the right to opt for taxation to those tenants who are entitled to a full or, for instance, a 90% right of deduction. If a Member State allows the application of this right to opt for taxation even to tenants who are not entitled to a deduction, or to a deduction at a very low percentage, there is a risk that the landlord will lease or let the immovable property for a very low rental fee. This would grant him a full right of deduction on the VAT incurred in the purchase of the goods, while the tenant will only be confronted with a, relatively, very low amount of non-deductible VAT. For completeness sake, we note that the latter issue can be resolved by implementing Article 80 of the VAT Directive, which provision allows Member States to increase the low prices which related parties sometimes tend to charge each other.

9.6.5 The Person Liable to Pay the VAT on Leasing or Letting of Immovable Property

If the leasing or letting of immovable property is a taxed supply, the taxable person making the supply is, in principle, the person liable to pay the VAT. This may be different if that taxable person is not established in the Member State where the VAT is due, and the Member State in question availed itself of the option of Article 194 VAT Directive to apply the reverse charge mechanism in such cases. There are no specific rules on the determination of the person liable to pay the VAT in relation to the leasing or letting of immovable property.

---

97. CJEU 30 June 2022, Case C-56/21 *UAB 'ARVI' ir ko v Valstybine mokesčių inspekcija prie Lietuvos Respublikos finansų ministerijos*, ECLI:EU:C:2022:509, para. 19.
98. *See*, for example: CJEU 9 September 2004, Case C-269/03 *Administration de l'enregistrement et des domaines and État du grand-duché de Luxembourg v Vermietungsgesellschaft Objekt Kirchberg Sàrl*, ECLI:EU:C:2004:512. The CJEU approved the measure taken by Luxembourg making the option for taxation conditional upon non-retroactive, prior approval of the tax authorities.

9.6.6 The Right of Deduction of Input VAT and the Leasing or Letting of Immovable Property

In section 9.6.4.1.6, we indicated that any lease to a third party by the purchaser of a building may have an effect on the right of deduction (and/or the adjustment of that deduction). Since the leasing or letting of immovable property is - as a main rule - exempt from VAT, in principle, the letting or leasing does not give rise to a right of deduction of input VAT, or - if the exempt lease follows a taxed use of immovable property - gives rise to repayments of VAT that was deducted on the basis of the adjustment rules.

9.7 SERVICES CONNECTED TO IMMOVABLE PROPERTY

On the basis of Article 47 VAT Directive, services connected to immovable property shall be regarded as taking place where the immovable property is located. We elaborated on services connected to immovable property in Chapter 4, section 4.5.3.4.1.

CHAPTER 10

Deduction of Input VAT

10.1 INTRODUCTION

Perhaps the most notable characteristic of the VAT system is the right of deduction. This right ensures that a taxable person only pays VAT on balance between the VAT on his output transactions and VAT incurred on his purchases so that, in effect, VAT is only levied on the value added. The right of deduction has been referred to as the 'cornerstone' of the VAT system.[1]

It is settled CJEU case law that the deduction system is meant to relieve the trader entirely of the burden of the VAT payable or paid in the course of all his economic activities, provided these are subject to VAT.[2] According to the CJEU, the right of deduction is an integral part of the VAT scheme and, in principle, may not be limited and must be exercised immediately in respect of all taxes charged on transactions related to inputs.[3] Yet, it is entirely clear that the VAT Directive itself contains rules on the basis of which the right of deduction *is* limited. This creates various difficulties. Not only does it gnaw away at the roots of a neutral VAT system but also often makes it difficult to calculate the portion of the VAT that is deductible. In this chapter, we discuss the right of deduction, its function and place in the VAT system, the exceptions to the right of deduction, the methods for calculation of the proportion of deductible VAT and the complications restrictions of the right of deduction cause.

10.1.1 Function and *Ratio Legis* of the Right of Deduction

The basic principle underlying the right of deduction is the principle of neutrality of VAT. In this regard, the term 'neutrality' should not be interpreted as a reflection in the field of VAT of the general principle of equality. Rather, it should be regarded as the idea that taxable persons should not be affected by the levy of VAT, that the VAT should not be a cost to taxable persons, that the VAT should not affect their business decisions, that the VAT should not distort competition, that the VAT should not 'cascade', and that the VAT should be exactly proportional to the prices throughout the

1. Opinion of Advocate General Darmon of 24 June 1992, Case C-131/91 *'K' Line Air Service*, ECLI:EU:C:1992:271, para. 35; Opinion of Advocate General Cosmas of 12 February 1998, Case C-361/96 *Société générale des grandes sources d'eaux minérales françaises tegen Bundesamt für Finanzen*, ECLI:EU:C:1998:56, para. 21 and Opinion of Advocate General Léger of 19 September 2002, Case C-185/01 *Auto Lease Holland*, ECLI:EU:C:2002:515, para. 8.
2. CJEU 14 February 1985, Case 268/83 *D.A. Rompelman and E.A. Rompelman-Van Deelen v Minister van Financiën*, ECLI:EU:C:1985:74, para. 19; CJEU 22 February 2001, Case C-408/98 *Abbey National plc v Commissioners of Customs and Excise*, ECLI:EU:C:2001:110, para. 24 and CJEU 21 March 2000, Cases C-110/98 to C-147/98 *Gabalfrisa S.L. and Others – Adminstración Estatal de la Agencia Tributaria (AEAT)*, ECLI:EU:C:2000:145, para. 44.
3. *Inter alia:* CJEU 6 July 1995, Case C-62/93 *BP Soupergaz Anonimos Eteria Geniki Emporiki Viomichaniki kai Antiprosopeion – Greek State*, ECLI:EU:C:1995:223, para. 18; CJEU 21 March 2000 *Gabalfrisa S.L. and Others v Agencia Estatal de Administracion Tributaria (AEAT)*; Cases C-110/98-C-147/98, ECLI:EU:C:2000:145, para. 43; CJEU 6 October 2005, Case C-243/03 *Commission v France*, ECLI:EU:C:2005:58, para. 28 and CJEU 18 December 2008, Case C-488/07 *Royal Bank of Scotland*, ECLI:EU:C:2008:750, para. 14.

entire production and distribution chain (also *see*: Article 1(2) VAT Directive).[4] Indeed, the CJEU has consistently ruled that through the right of deduction, the common system of VAT ensures complete neutrality of taxation of all economic activities, whatever their purpose or results, provided that they are themselves subject, in principle, to VAT.[5]

The neutrality of VAT not only requires that taxable persons should have a right of deduction but also that the right of deduction is obtained immediately and for the full amount, even where it results in a refund of VAT. That is the only way to avoid the outcome of taxable persons having to pre-finance and (except for the administrative burden) carry the burden of VAT.

According to Article 167, the right of deduction arises at the time the deductible tax becomes chargeable. Article 168 VAT Directive further clarifies that a taxable person can deduct the input VAT from the output VAT which he is liable to pay. Thus, the purchaser can deduct input VAT in the actual period in which the supplier charged it to him (or, in the case of the application of the reverse charge mechanism, when it became due). In other words, the right of deduction is *immediate*. Note that Article 167a VAT Directive offers the possibility of an exception to this main rule.[6] It provides Member States with the option to postpone the right of deduction of a taxable person whose VAT solely becomes chargeable in accordance with Article 66(b) until the VAT on the goods or services supplied to him has been paid to his supplier.[7] On the basis of Article 168, the taxable person has both an immediate and a full right of deduction. This implies that even if in a certain tax period the total amount of recoverable input VAT is higher than the output VAT due, a taxable person has the right of an (immediate) refund of the excess of input VAT.

It is on the basis of this system of immediate and full deduction of input VAT that traders are, in principle, entirely relieved of the burden of VAT. The tax burden is passed on to the final person in the production and distribution chain: the final consumer.

4. Cf. A.J. van Doesum, *Contractuele samenwerkingsverbanden in de btw* (*dissertation*) (Kluwer 2009), pp. 31-34.
5. CJEU 18 December 2008, Case C-488/07 *Royal Bank of Scotland*, ECLI:EU:C:2008:750, para. 15.
6. *See* CJEU 10 February 2022, Case C-9/20 *Grundstücksgemeinschaft Kollaustraße 136*, ECLI: EU:C:2022:88.
7. The second paragraph of Article 167a VAT Directive determines that Member States which apply this option to postpone deduction, shall set a threshold for taxable persons using the scheme within their territory, based on the annual turnover of the taxable person calculated in accordance with Article 288. That threshold may not be higher than EUR 500,000 or the equivalent in national currency. However, Member States may increase the threshold up to EUR 2,000,000 or the equivalent in national currency after consulting the VAT Committee. Such consultation of the VAT Committee shall not be required for Member States which applied a threshold higher than EUR 500,000 or the equivalent in national currency on 31 December 2012.

10.1.2 Exemptions and the Right of Deduction: Cascading of VAT, and the Paradox of VAT

If the deduction of input VAT were always to be full and immediate, the EU VAT system would, in our view, be simpler, more efficient and more robust than it is now. In this respect, New Zealand's VAT system (there it is called a 'goods and services tax', 'GST') could be regarded as representing 'best practice': it is very broad-based and has few if any exceptions to the right of deduction.[8] By contrast, the VAT Directive contains various exceptions to the broad-based nature of VAT and as a result to the right of deduction. Notable are the exemptions for certain supplies of goods and services (Articles 132-135 VAT Directive; *see* Chapter 8). The exception to the right of deduction as regards exempt activities follows from an *a contrario* interpretation of Article 168 VAT Directive.

Article 168 stipulates, among other things, that the taxable person shall be entitled to deduct the VAT due or paid in respect of supplies to him of goods or services, carried out or to be carried out by another taxable person from the VAT which he is liable to pay, but only insofar as the goods and services are used for the purposes of the taxed transactions of a taxable person. Conversely, insofar as goods and services are used for the purposes of the *exempt* transactions of a taxable person, there shall be no right of deduction.

Following this line of reasoning, it is accepted that if a supplier makes an exempt supply, in principle, he cannot recover the input VAT attributable to that exempt supply. This concept is referred to as the 'paradox of the VAT system'. The paradox of the VAT system is that those that make exempt supplies, and therefore, think they are exempt from VAT, are, in fact, taxed (because the non-deductible input VAT is a cost to them), yet those that make taxed supplies, and therefore, think they are being taxed, are actually exempt from VAT (through the deduction of input VAT).

The danger of non-deductible VAT occurring in the production and distribution chain is that the VAT cascades. Taxable persons who cannot (fully) recover their input VAT can be assumed to incorporate that non-recoverable VAT (also known as hidden or sticky VAT) in the prices of their products, so passing on their input VAT as a cost component to their customers. If the customer is a taxable person making taxed supplies, that person, in turn, will charge VAT on the full price, including the hidden VAT. It follows that VAT is then being charged on VAT. This is commonly referred to as the 'cascading of VAT', having the effect that VAT is neither completely neutral to taxable persons nor exactly proportional to the price of goods or services.

The fact that taxable persons are not entitled to a deduction of input VAT if their costs are attributable to exempt supplies complicates the application of the VAT system. For example, it requires that detailed rules are put in place on how to make the correct attribution of costs, particularly if a taxable person makes both taxed and exempt supplies. Difficulties also arise from the fact that taxable persons may be

8. *See* D.I. White & E. Trombitas, 'The Future of Indirect Taxation', in T. Ecker, M. Lang & I. Lejeune (eds), *Recent Trends in VAT and GST Systems Around the World* (Wolters Kluwer Law & Business 2012), p. 389.

engaged in non-taxable transactions (i.e., transactions outside the scope of VAT, such as a transfer of a going concern (*see also* Chapter 3, section 3.6)) or the issue of shares. We refer to section 10.3.2 with respect to the right of deduction for non-taxable supplies.

10.2 FUNDAMENTALS OF THE RIGHT OF DEDUCTION

In this section, we discuss the fundamentals of the right of deduction. We address the way in which input VAT can be recovered ('input VAT recovery mechanisms', section 10.2.1), the conditions to the right of deduction (section 10.2.2), the moment when the right of deduction arises (section 10.2.3) and the scope of the right of deduction (section 10.2.4).

10.2.1 Input VAT Recovery Mechanisms

In principle, the EU VAT system is based on the general idea that VAT on purchases is subtracted from VAT on sales. This is why Chapter I to Title X of the VAT Directive refers to the right of *deduction*. The effect of exercising a right of deduction may be that the amount of VAT deductible (on the input transactions) exceeds the amount of VAT payable (on the output transactions). Then, there are basically two options: the VAT is refunded, or the (negative) amount of deductible VAT is carried forward to a subsequent tax period.

These two mechanisms are discussed in this section. We note that as regards foreign taxable persons who have no VAT payable in a Member State but who have incurred input VAT in that Member State, the VAT Directive explicitly allows for a refund of VAT (*see* section 10.2.4.3).

10.2.1.1 Subtracting Input VAT from Output VAT (Deduction and Refund)

On the basis of Article 179 VAT Directive, the taxable person shall make the deduction by subtracting from the total amount of VAT due for a given tax period the total amount of VAT in respect of which, during the same period, the right of deduction has arisen. This is exercised in accordance with Article 178 VAT Directive.[9]

10.2.1.2 Carry-Forward Mechanism

Although the full and immediate deduction described in the previous section is the standard approach, the VAT Directive provides the Member States with an option to postpone at least a part of the right of deduction until a later stage. If in a tax period, the amount of deductions exceeds the amount of VAT due, the Member States may, in

9. However, Member States may require that taxable persons who carry out occasional transactions, as defined in Article 12, exercise their right of deduction only at the time of supply.

accordance with conditions which they shall determine, either make a refund or carry the excess forward to the following period. However, Member States may refuse to refund or carry forward if the amount of the excess is insignificant (Article 183 VAT Directive).

10.2.2 Conditions to the Right of Deduction

In this section, we discuss the material and formal conditions to the right of deduction.

10.2.2.1 Taxable Person: Status and Capacity

Article 2 VAT Directive makes a distinction between the status of a taxable person and the capacity in which he may act. It provides that only supplies of goods or services 'by a taxable person' (status) 'acting as such' (capacity) are within the scope of VAT. This distinction between the status and capacity of a taxable person is also made in the VAT Implementing Regulation. The VAT Implementing Regulation uses these notions within the scope of the determination of the place of supply of services (*see* Chapter 4). Pursuant to Article 17 VAT Implementing Regulation, the place of services depends on the taxable *status* of the customer, which must be determined on the basis of Articles 9-13 and 43 VAT Directive. If, however, a person with taxable person status purchases cross-border services for his private use, it must be established that that person did not buy the services in his *capacity* as a taxable person (*see* Article 19 VAT Implementing Regulation).

We regard the distinction between the status and capacity of a taxable person as fundamental to the functioning of the VAT system. Nevertheless, Article 168 VAT Directive - which is the base provision on the right of deduction - makes no explicit reference to the difference between the status and the capacity of a taxable person. It does, however, seem to incorporate this distinction in the phrase 'In so far as the goods and services are used for the purposes of the taxed transactions of a taxable person'. In this regard, it clearly follows from CJEU case law that merely having a taxable person status is insufficient to deduct input VAT. A taxable person also needs to act in the *capacity* of a taxable person (*see*, for example, *Lennartz*).[10] Therefore, we believe that it is elemental to the right of deduction to take into account both the status and the capacity of a taxable person.

Article 9(1) VAT Directive defines 'Economic activities' as comprising 'all activities of producers, traders and persons supplying services ... and activities of the professions'. A person who is engaged in several activities of which only some can be regarded as economic activities as referred to in Article 9 VAT Directive, will have taxable person *status* (he will have, or should have, or should at least be able to obtain a VAT registration number), but might not always operate in his *capacity* of taxable

10. CJEU 11 July 1991, Case C-97/90 *Hansgeorg Lennartz v Fianzamt München III*, ECLI: EU:C:1991:315, para. 17: 'Article 20(2) of the sixth Directive ... applies where a person acquires capital goods *in his capacity as a taxable person* and allocates them to his economic activity within the meaning of Article 4 of the Sixth Directive'.

person – in other words, in the furtherance of his economic activities. Whether he is entitled to a deduction depends on whether he is also acting in the capacity of a taxable person. This can also be derived from *Wellcome Trust*.[11] Completely separate from its investment activities in marketable shares, i.e., the holding and the sale of shares, the Wellcome Trust carried out activities as a taxable person by leasing immovable property (taxed) and granting direct loans to third parties.[12] The Wellcome Trust wanted to deduct the VAT on costs it incurred with respect to its investment activities, in particular, the sale of shares to customers outside the EU.[13] This raised the question of whether the holding and the sale of shares also constituted economic activities. The CJEU decided that the Wellcome Trust – as regards the purchase and the sale of shares and other securities – did not carry out economic activities. Therefore, the VAT on services purchased from third parties relating to the sale of shares to customers outside the Community could not be deducted. Even though the Wellcome Trust had taxable person status (because of its leasing and lending activities), it did not act in that capacity with regard to the sales of shares. As a result, it was considered as not having purchased the services in its taxable person capacity and consequently had no right of deduction.

With regard to mixed-use goods (for both business and private purposes), it is settled case law that taxable persons have the right to assign (label) the item involved fully, partially or not at all to their business assets (this is referred to as 'asset-labelling', or the '*Lennartz* principle'). In other words, one could argue that these taxable persons are in a way free to choose whether they buy these items in their capacity as taxable persons or otherwise.

The right to label goods as business assets does not exist with regard to goods and services used for (i.e., costs incurred for) both economic activities and non-economic activities, not being private use (e.g., the promotion by an association of the general interests of its members and some forms of investment in securities).[14] From *Uudenkaupungin Kaupunki*, it follows that VAT made on costs relating to non-economic activities cannot be deducted. With respect to costs that simultaneously relate to both economic and non-economic activities, the CJEU held in several instances – most

11. CJEU 20 June 1996, Case C-155/94 *Wellcome Trust Ltd v Commissioners of Customs and Excise*, ECLI:EU:C:1996:243.
12. According to the facts given in point 13 of this case, the Wellcome Trust was already operating as a taxable person: 'Around the same time, investments of approximately £72 million had been made in a property portfolio including offices, shops and a distribution warehouse. In respect of some of the properties, the Trust elected to waive the exemption provided for by the 1983 Value Added Tax Act, an option permitted under Article 13C(a) of the Directive. The Trust also invests in venture capital projects, which are limited in time and liability. Finally, quite apart from any investment in marketable securities, the Trust earns interest from cash balances by making direct loans to institutions and banks.' It is remarkable that the CJEU did not refer to those facts when answering the preliminary questions.
13. *See* Article 169(c) VAT Directive.
14. On the basis of *Gmina Ryjewo*, adjustments to the scope of deduction are possible if a capital asset in question was purchased in the capacity of a taxable person, but was used initially for non-economic activities. *See* CJEU 25 July 2018, Case C-140/17 *Szef Krajowej Administracji Skarbowej v Gmina Ryjewo*, ECLI:EU:C:2018:595. *See also* section 10.6.2.

notably in *Vereniging Noordelijke Land- en Tuinbouw Organisaties (VNLTO),*[15] *Securenta,*[16] *Portugal Telecom,*[17] and *Zwiazek Gmin*[18] – that the input VAT relating to expenditure incurred by a taxable person cannot give rise to a right to deduct *insofar as* it relates to the non-economic activities. The CJEU ruled that where a taxable person simultaneously carries out economic activities, whether taxed or exempt, and non-economic activities outside the scope of the directive, deduction of the input VAT relating to expenditure is allowed only to the extent to which that expenditure may be attributed as an output to the economic activity of the taxable person.[19] Insofar as taxable persons purchase goods and services for non-economic activities, they do not buy these items in their *capacity as a taxable person,* and cannot reclaim the incurred input taxes. This is in line with Article 168 VAT Directive as it grants the right of deduction insofar as the goods and services are used for the purposes of the taxed transactions of a taxable person. We note that the mere fact that costs relate to a non-taxable transaction does not necessarily mean that such transaction is always a non-economic activity.[20] Before drawing the conclusion that costs have not been incurred 'as a taxable person', it must always be checked first whether such costs relate to the 'economic activity as a whole', in which case they must be regarded as having been made in the capacity of a taxable person (*see* section 10.3.2).

We point out that acting in the capacity of a taxable person is not only relevant for the question of whether or not a specific (legal) person is entitled to a deduction of input VAT. According to *Ferimet*, a material condition for the right of deduction is that the goods or services for which a deduction is sought are supplied by a taxable person acting as such.[21]

10.2.2.2 The Person to Whom the Supply Is Made (The 'Recipient of the Supply')

Article 168(1)(a) VAT Directive only allows for deduction of the VAT due or paid in respect of supplies 'to' the taxable person of goods or services. This implies that only the recipient of a supply can deduct the VAT on that supply, provided that all other requirements for deduction of input VAT are met.

15. CJEU 12 February 2009, Case C-515/07 *Vereniging Noordelijke Land- en Tuinbouw Organisatie v Staatssecretaris van Financiën*, ECLI:EU:C:1996:243, para. 37.
16. CJEU 13 March 2008, Case C-437/06 *Securenta Göttinger Immobilienanlagen und Vermögensmanagement AG v Finanzamt Göttingen*, ECLI:EU:C:2008:166, paras 30 and 31.
17. CJEU 6 September 2012, Case C-496/11 *Portugal Telecom SGPS SA v Fazenda Pública*, ECLI:EU:C:2012:557.
18. CJEU 28 May 2019, Case C-566/17 *Związek Gmin Zagłębia Miedziowego w Polkowicach v Szef Krajowej Administracji Skarbowej*, ECLI:EU:C:2019:390, para. 28.
19. CJEU 13 March 2008, Case C-437/06 *Securenta Göttinger Immobilienanlagen und Vermögensmanagement AG v Finanzamt Göttingen*, ECLI:EU:C:2008:166 and CJEU 12 February 2009, Case C515/07 *Vereniging Noordelijke Land- en Tuinbouw Organisatie v Staatssecretaris van Financiën*, ECLI:EU:C:1996:243.
20. *See Inter alia* CJEU 22 October 2015, Case C-126/14 *'Sveda' UAB v Valstybine mokesčių inspekcija prie Lietuvos Respublikos finansų ministerijos*, ECLI:EU:C:2015:712.
21. CJEU 11 November 2021, Case C-281/21 *Ferimet SL v Administracíon General del Estado*, ECLI:EU:C:2021:910, para. 27.

Usually, it is quite clear who the recipient of a supply is. If a customer pays a supplier for goods or services supplied under an agreement, that customer is usually the recipient of the supply. However, there may be circumstances in which a party other than the recipient of the supply may pay for that supply, or in which a party other than the contracting party benefits from the supply. In those circumstances, it is important to correctly identify the person to whom the supply is made.[22]

Generally speaking, the following criteria to determine the recipient of a supply can be derived from CJEU case law:

(1) contractual relation (legal relationship);
(2) use/benefit/consumption;
(3) payment;
(4) invoice;
(5) right to dispose of tangible property as owner.

As mentioned above, the contractual relationship seems to be the most common and decisive criterion to identify the recipient of a supply. Beforehand it must be stressed that there are differences between the identification of the recipient (or customer) of a supply of a good and the identification of the recipient of a service. Due to the more concrete and tangible nature of goods (and, by contrast, the intangible and volatile nature of services), it is generally easier to identify the recipient of a good than it is to determine the recipient of a service. As was discussed in Chapter 3, a supply of goods requires the transfer of the right to dispose of tangible property as owner. As a result, the fifth criterion of those listed above is only relevant for identifying the recipient of a good, and not for services. As all other criteria - albeit in different ways - can be relevant for the identification of the recipient of a good or a service alike, we will discuss the criteria combined for both categories.

10.2.2.2.1 Contractual Relation ('Legal Relationship')

Although relevant for the supply of both goods and services, the legal relationship - as a factor for the determination of the recipient of the supply - is most explicitly and cogently mentioned in CJEU case law with regard to services.

From *Tolsma*, it follows that a supply of services is effected 'for consideration' only if there is a legal relationship between the provider of the service and the recipient, pursuant to which there is reciprocal performance, the remuneration received by the provider of the service constituting the value actually given in return for the service supplied to the recipient.[23] This implies that the 'legal relationship' is key to the existence of a taxable supply. The fact that the legal relationship should exist between the provider of the service (or good, for that matter) and the recipient indicates, in our

22. *See also* J. Bijl, *VAT Deduction: The Relevance of Being 'The Recipient' of a Supply and the Use of the Supply*, (2020) 5 EC Tax Review, pp. 227-235 https://doi.org/10.54648/ecta2020049.
23. CJEU 3 March 1994, Case C-16/93 *R. J. Tolsma v Inspecteur der Omzetbelasting Leeuwarden*, ECLI:EU:C:1994:80, para. 14.

view, that the contractual position, i.e., the 'legal relationship' is not only an important factor in establishing the direct link between a supply and a consideration but also in determining the recipient of a supply. This matches perfectly with the idea that EU VAT takes the form of a transaction tax.

This is further substantiated in *Paul Newey*, in which the CJEU considered that:

> the contractual position normally reflects the economic and commercial reality of the transactions and in order to satisfy the requirements of legal certainty, the relevant contractual terms constitute a factor to be taken into consideration when the supplier and the recipient in a 'supply of services' transaction ... have to be identified.[24]

Indeed, in our view, the contractual terms are, in principle, decisive to determining the recipient of the supply. Even though the legal character of VAT may be that of a consumption tax, it takes the form of a transaction tax, which form in itself creates norms which should be adhered to.[25] In this case, it creates the norm that the legal relationship should be an important factor to determine the recipient of the supply.[26]

Also from the viewpoint of contractual freedom and the idea that VAT should be neutral, i.e., should not influence business decisions, the legal relationship between parties should be a strong indicator for the determination of the recipient of a supply. This becomes even more apparent if one accepts that freedom of contract is one of the basic principles of the internal market.[27] This leads us to the conclusion that, in principle, the legal relationship as laid down in the contract should be a leading consideration when determining the recipient of a supply.

24. CJEU 20 June 2013, Case C-653/11 *Her Majesty's Commissioners of Revenue and Customs v Paul Newey*, ECLI:EU:C:2013:409, para. 43.
25. A.H.R.M. Denie, *De overheid in de omzetbelasting* (*dissertation*) (Kluwer 1987), p. 50.
26. In CJEU 3 September 2015, Case C-526/13 *Fast Bunkering Klaipeda UAB v Valstybine mokesčiu inspekcija prie Lietuvos Respublikos finansų ministerijos*, ECLI:EU:C:2015:536 (FBK) however, the middleman (B) acting in his own name was 'skipped' and the supply was considered as having been made directly by the first (original) supplier, A (Fast Bunkering Klaipeda) to the last party in the chain of transactions (the customer, C, being the operator of the seagoing vessel). The main practical impact of this decision is that the (original) suppliers of tangible goods involved in chain transactions have to determine whether they make their supply to their contract party (the intermediary) or directly to the final consumer with whom they have no legal arrangements. Making taxable supplies (of goods) to the contracting party rather than to parties with whom the supplier did not enter into a contract remains the default situation, but caution is advised. In cases where the supplier brings the customer of his intermediary irrevocably into position to dispose of the goods as if he is the owner, before the supplier sells and invoices the goods to the intermediary, it completely changes the supply chain and the position of the intermediary. *See* sections 3.2.4.3 and 3.3.2.1.
27. *See* W. Snijders, 'Building a European Contract Law; Five Fallacies and Two Castles in Spain', in *Ius Commune Lectures on European Private Law*, Vol. 7.4 (Electronic Journal of Comparative Law 2003), p. 11, G.J. van Norden, *Het concern in de BTW* (*dissertation*) (Kluwer 2007), p. 338 and J. Basedow, *Freedom of Contract in the European Union* (2008) 16/6 European Review of Private Law, pp. 901-923 https://doi.org/10.54648/erpl2008069.

10.2.2.2.2 Use/Benefit/Consumption

As we indicated in section 10.2.2.2.1, with a transaction tax such as VAT, legal certainty demands that, in principle, the contractual terms are decisive when determining the recipient of a supply. Nonetheless, there is an argument in favour of also taking into account which party has the use, benefit or consumption of a transaction),[28] when determining the recipient of the supply. This argument is to be derived from *Landboden-Agrardienste,* in which the CJEU considered:

> Contrary to their submissions, that reasoning does not mean that a payment made by a public authority in the common interest cannot constitute consideration for a supply of services for the purposes of the Sixth Directive, or that the concept of a supply of services depends on the use made of a service by the person who pays for it. Only the nature of the undertaking given is to be taken into consideration: for such an undertaking to be covered by the common system of VAT it must imply consumption.[29]

We note that applying the criterion of use, benefit, or consumption causes difficulties in practice. How can one determine who actually consumed a supply if the concept of consumption itself is unclear? And even if it could be established what use, benefit or consumption entails, it would be virtually impossible, or excessively difficult, to determine the recipient of a supply on the basis of such criteria.[30] Applying such criteria is bound to go against legal certainty; reason enough for the CJEU to take the legal relationship as the base criterion.

In our view, the use, benefit or consumption criterion can play a role (especially with respect to services) if the contractual terms do not fully reflect economic reality.[31] If the contract does not reflect economic reality but constitutes a wholly artificial arrangement set up with the sole aim of obtaining a tax advantage, then the legal relationship following from the contract should not be decisive in the determination of the recipient of the supply. However, we note that even under those circumstances, the CJEU only seems to allow for the 'consumption' criterion to be applied, under the application of the doctrine of abuse of rights.[32]

As said before, the (wording of the) legal relationship is key also for the determination of the recipient of a supply of goods. If a person (really) purchases goods in his own name and for his own account he will generally and in accordance with the contractual terms be seen as the recipient of those goods. However, now and then it turns out that the contract party is not actually purchasing the goods in his own name and for its own account. Although in *Auto Lease Holland* the costs were incurred in the

28. CJEU 20 June 2013, Case C-653/11 *Her Majesty's Commissioners of Revenue and Customs v Paul Newey*, ECLI:EU:C:2013:409, para. 48.
29. CJEU 18 December 1997, Case C-384/95 *Landboden-Agrardienste GmbH & Co. KG v Finanzamt Calau*, ECLI:EU:C:1997:627, para. 20.
30. Cf. G.J. van Norden, *Het concern in de BTW (dissertation)* (Kluwer 2007), p. 340.
31. CJEU 20 June 2013, Case C-653/11 *Her Majesty's Commissioners of Revenue and Customs v Paul Newey*, ECLI:EU:C:2013:409, para. 49.
32. *Ibid.*, para. 52.

lessor's own name, the supplies were effected at Auto Lease's expense only ostensibly.[33] The actual consumption was the financial responsibility of the lessee who, consequently, wholly bore the costs of the supply of fuel. So, in fact, the costs were totally recharged to the lessee. Under those circumstances, in which the fuel was already irrevocably in the car's tank and because the lessee could use the goods (fuel) as if he were the owner, the use of the goods (in fact, the right to dispose of the goods as if he were the owner, *see also* section 10.2.2.2.5) seems to have taken precedence over the literal wording of the contract, in which the lessor was 'presented as' the purchaser of the fuel. Also, with respect to chain transactions, it may occur that someone other than the contracting party is considered to be the recipient of the supply (*see* sections 3.2.4.3 and 3.3.2.1).[34] *See also* the following section for the relevance of the fact that the payment has been made by another person than the purchaser mentioned in the (written) contract.

10.2.2.2.3 Payment

Usually, the person making a payment is the person who concluded the contract for the supply. In fact, the payment can be regarded as a (rebuttable) proof of the existence of a legal relationship.[35] However, it follows from what is set out above, that to be acknowledged as the recipient of a supply, it is not necessary that the addressee of the invoice must make the corresponding payment to the supplier. If a contract is concluded with – and the invoice is addressed to – a taxable person and paid by another person, the person making the payment is just a third party who, for whatever reason, pays the bill for the 'true' recipient of the supply (the payment flow is different from the flow of supplies). For example, it is common for multinational groups of businesses to reduce administrative costs by appointing a company within a group to be the 'paymaster' (cash clearing agent, billing agent, or other such terms), responsible for payments under the relevant agreement to pay for services received.[36]

In cases where an employee purchases goods and services, the fact that the person who makes the payment is not necessarily the recipient of the supply causes particular difficulties. Sometimes, an employee orders and pays for supplies which are meant for his employer (e.g., fuel bought by a truck driver), but it also occurs that an *employer* orders and pays for supplies actually made for – or at least partially for the benefit of – his employees (e.g., if the employer pays for outplacement activities, or for the removal expenses of his staff members). It may also happen that a lessee pays for something in the name and for the account of the lessor.

33. CJEU 6 February 2003, Case C-185/01 *Auto Lease Holland BV v Bundesamt für Finanzen*, ECLI:EU:C:2003:73. *See also* CJEU 15 May 2019, Case C-235/18 *Vega International Car Transport and Logistic – Trading GmbH v Dyrektor Izby Skarbowej w Warszawie*, ECLI:EU:C:2019:412.
34. CJEU 3 September 2015, Case C-526/13 *Fast Bunkering Klaipeda UAB v Valstybine mokesčių inspekcija prie Lietuvos Respublikos finansų ministerijos*, ECLI:EU:C:2015:536.
35. Cf. HR 1 March 2002, No 36 020, BNB 2002/141.
36. *See also* OECD (2017), *International VAT/GST Guidelines*, OECD Publishing, Paris, https://doi.org/10.1787/9789264271401-en, p. 51 (accessed 17 August 2024).

It will not always be easy to identify the recipient of the supply in situations like these. For example, who would be the recipient of the supply in the following situation?

Example

An employee purchases fuel in its own name, but for the account of his employer. The employee will use the fuel exclusively for the taxable transactions of his employer. The employer reimburses the employee for the costs of the fuel.

The main issue here is whether, despite this triangular structure between the supplier, the employee and the employer, there may nevertheless be considered to be a supply between taxable persons, namely the seller of the fuel and the employer.[37] It is apparent from *Leesportefeuille Intiem* that the physical delivery of goods to the employee does not in itself preclude the employer's right to deduct.[38] If the employee incurs costs in his own name and receives a flat-rate reimbursement from the employer (which by its nature will not guarantee that the actual costs will be borne by the employer), it is not possible for the employer to be regarded as the recipient of the supply, in which case he cannot deduct the VAT (*Commission v The Netherlands*).[39] However, if the employer pays the exact amount of the fuel cost, there may be a right of deduction. Under such circumstances, the employee can be regarded as an 'organ' of the employer's company: he represents the employer while purchasing the goods and/or services. To a certain extent, the situation is comparable with a situation in which an employee incurs accommodation, subsistence and/or travel costs on the occasion of a business trip, or a situation in which an employee of a construction firm working on an outside building site, purchases tools.[40] The purchase of fuel admittedly involves particular problems of delimitation, but that cannot, in principle, preclude the right to deduct.

According to the CJEU in *Commission v United Kingdom*, in many cases, purchases by employees are in reality supplies made to their employers, and hence to a taxable person entitled to deduct input tax. We conclude on the basis of the case law set out above that if goods or services are used in the context of a taxable transaction, it should not make any difference whether the contractual recipient of the goods or services is the employer himself or his employee or agent (the employer will eventually be seen as the recipient of the supply). In *Commission v United Kingdom*, the CJEU considered that if an employee acts on behalf of his employer and purchases goods to

37. *See also* CJEU 10 March 2005, Case C-33/03 *Commission v United Kingdom of Great Britain and Northern Ireland*, ECLI:EU:C:2005:144.
38. In CJEU 8 March 1988, Case 165/86 *Leesportefeuille 'Intiem' CV- staatssecretaris van Financiën*, ECLI:EU:C:1988:122 the Court evidently assumed that the supply of fuel took place in the course of the employer's business activity, or that the fuel was used for business purposes of the employer.
39. In CJEU 8 November 2001, Case C-338/98 *Commission of the European Communities v Kingdom of the Netherlands*, ECLI:EU:C:2001:596, para. 77, the Court stated that by providing 'in breach of Articles 17(2)(a) and 18(1)(a) of the Sixth Directive ..., in the version resulting from Directive 95/7 ... that an employer who is a taxable person for the purposes of VAT may deduct part of an allowance paid to an employee for business use of a private car, the Kingdom of the Netherlands has failed to fulfil its obligations under the EC Treaty'.
40. *See* Opinion of Advocate General Stix-Hackl of 14 December 2004, Case C-33/03 *Commission v United Kingdom*, ECLI:EU:C:2004:801, para. 36.

be used by the employer for the requirements of his business, the supply is, in fact, made to the employer.[41] However, in that particular case, there was no direct link between the supplier of the fuel and the employer. The contested British provision could not ensure that the right to deduct input tax related only to supplies of fuel used for the taxable transactions of the employer (but most probably also for the private use of the car by the employee). In *Commission v United Kingdom*, the CJEU stated that invoices in such cases would be better made out in the name of the employer. In this case, the Court held that the British regulation enabling the employer to reclaim the VAT incurred on direct deliveries of fuel to its personnel was not in line with the Directive, mainly because the regulation could not rule out that the input tax recovered was not used exclusively for taxed supplies, but seemingly also for the private use of the staff members. That explains why the outcome was different from that of *Leesportefeuille Intiem*.

In *ALH*, the lessee of a car used a credit card, which was put in the name of ALH (the lessor). This card enabled the lessee to fill up his petrol tank in ALH's name and on its behalf.[42] Although that appeared to be a fact, in essence, the main question was whether the lessee indeed purchased petrol on behalf of ALH. The reason for doubt lied in the fact that, on a monthly basis, the lessee had to pay a prepayment of 1/12 of the estimated annual fuel consumption. At the end of each year, he paid or received the difference between the prepayments and the actual total amount. ALH reclaimed the VAT charged on the deliveries of fuel in Germany, which were paid for by the lessee in ALH's name, but the German tax authorities declined the claim for the refund. The CJEU ruled that the fuel was not supplied to ALH (nor subsequently supplied onwards by ALH to the lessee) because the costs were only *seemingly* born by ALH; the fuel costs were actually and eventually born by the lessee, who finally had to pay the full amount for the fuel delivered. Under these conditions, the CJEU decided that there was no supply of fuel by the lessor to the lessee, where the lessee fills up at filling stations, even if the vehicle is filled up in the name and (seemingly) at the expense of that lessor. Accordingly, the CJEU considered the fuel management agreement not as a contract for the supply of fuel, but rather as a contract to finance its purchase. ALH did not purchase the fuel in order to subsequently resell it to the lessee; the lessee purchased the fuel, having a free choice as to its quality and quantity, as well as the time of purchase. At the moment the lessee was invoiced, the fuel was already irrevocably in the car's tank.[43] ALH acted, in fact, as a supplier of credit vis-à-vis the lessee. The lessee was designated as the recipient of the supply. Therefore, the lessor/employer could not deduct (reclaim) the VAT on the fuel supplies. In *Vega International* – with a fact

41. CJEU 10 March 2005, Case C-33/03 *Commission v United Kingdom*, ECLI:EU:C:2005:144, para. 15.
42. CJEU 6 February 2003, Case C-185/01 *Auto Lease Holland BV v Bundesamt für Finanzen*, ECLI:EU:C:2003:73.
43. *See also* CJEU 3 September 2015, Case C-526/13 *Fast Bunkering Klaipeda UAB v Valstybinė mokesčių inspekcija prie Lietuvos Respublikos finansų ministerijos*, ECLI:EU:C:2015:536.

pattern similar to that in *Auto Lease Holland* – the CJEU confirmed that a fuel management contract to pre-finance fuel constitutes an exempt financial service for VAT.[44]

In *Leesportefeuille Intiem,* the employer (and not the employee) paid the total and exact amount of fuel costs which were incurred by the employee in his name (and the fuel was also physically supplied to the employee). The employer was considered the recipient of the supply. Conversely, in *ALH* it was the lessee who made the costs in the name of the lessor, and who paid eventually the precise amount of fuel costs (and who received the fuel directly). The employee was considered as the recipient of the supply.

10.2.2.2.4 Invoice

We believe that the invoice for a supply can be seen as an indicator of the person to whom a supply is made. After all, an invoice is usually issued to the person receiving the supply. Indeed, in our view, the invoice provides strong, although rebuttable evidence with respect to the identification of the recipient of a supply. However, it cannot be a decisive factor in itself since an invoice is only intended to document the supply that originates from a contract.

10.2.2.2.5 Right to Dispose of Tangible Property as Owner

As mentioned in section 10.2.2.2, 'the right to dispose of tangible property as owner' is only a relevant criterion for the identification of the recipient (customer) of a supply of goods. In *Safe*, the CJEU indicated that a 'supply of goods' requires the transfer of the right to dispose of tangible property as owner. It covers any transfer of tangible property by one party which empowers the other party actually to dispose it of as if he were the owner of the property.[45] With respect to the determination of the recipient of a supply of goods, it may seem logical to deem the person who obtains physical possession of a good as the recipient of the supply. However, the person who has physical possession of goods is not always the person who has the right to dispose of it as if he were the owner. Moreover, in cases where it is questioned whether the person who obtains the right to dispose of it as if he were the owner is a different person than the one indicated in the contract as the buyer of the good, this criterion does not provide enough legal certainty to take precedence over the criterion of the legal relationship (*see* section 10.2.2.2.1).[46]

---

44. CJEU 15 May 2019, Case C-235/18 *Vega International Car Transport and Logistic – Trading GmbH v Dyrektor Izby Skarbowej w Warszawie,* ECLI:EU:C:2019:412.
45. CJEU 8 February 1990, Case C-320/88 *Staatssecretaris van Financiën v Shipping and Forwarding Enterprise Safe BV,* ECLI:EU:C:1990:61, paras 7 and 9.
46. We already mentioned that there are exceptions to this general rule, such as the situation in CJEU 6 February 2003, Case C-185/01 *Auto Lease Holland BV v Bundesamt für Finanzen,* ECLI:EU:C:2003:73 and in CJEU 3 September 2015, Case C-526/13 *Fast Bunkering Klaipeda UAB v Valstybine mokesčių inspekcija prie Lietuvos Respublikos finansų ministerijos,* ECLI: EU:C:2015:536.

10.2.2.2.6 *Not the Recipient of the Supply, Still a Right of Deduction*

It appears from CJEU case law that under special circumstances, another person than the person with whom the supplier entered into an agreement can have a right of deduction. A significant case in this respect is *Kopalnia Odkrywkowa Polski Trawertyn*.[47] Two future partners of a partnership bought a quarry. Apparently, the supply of the quarry was a taxed supply. At the time of the purchase, neither one of them had taxable person status, and neither of them presented themselves as future partners of a partnership. At a later stage, they decided to form a partnership and to contribute the quarry (in kind) to that partnership.

One would expect that – on the basis of the legal relationship with the supplier – the two purchasers, who were later to become partners of a partnership, should be considered as the recipients of the supply, each purchaser for its part in the quarry. Since they did not have taxable person status at the time of the purchase, they could not deduct the VAT on the supply. However, the CJEU ruled differently.

In essence, the CJEU followed Advocate General Cruz Villalón's opinion. He stated that:

> In fact, persons who acquire assets and procure services for the purpose of making a capital contribution to a partnership upon its formation are not, strictly speaking, part of the production chain, since they do not exploit the assets acquired and do not profit from the transaction at any stage. The role of the 'future partner' is simply as a vehicle or a person who, as it were, 'accidentally' becomes an economic operator simply by virtue of the fact that there is an interval of time when only that person can represent the future undertaking.[48]

The CJEU ruled that in so far as, under national legislation, the partners, even though they might be considered taxable persons for the purposes of VAT, were unable to rely on the taxable transactions effected by the partnership in order to deduct the

47. CJEU 1 March 2012, Case C-280/10 *Kopalnia Odkrywkowa Polski Trawertyn P. Granatowicz, M. Wąsiewicz, spółka jawna v Dyrektor Izby Skarbowej w Poznaniu*, ECLI:EU:C:2012:107. *See also* CJEU 13 March 2014, Case C-204/13 *Finanamt Saarlouis v Heinz Malburg*, ECLI:EU:C:2014:147, paras 28-44, in which the CJEU compares both cases. *Malburg* involves the question of whether a partner in a partnership who acquires from that partnership a portion of its client base may be entitled to deduct the input VAT paid on the acquisition of that client base. The client base was purchased for the sole purpose of making it available directly and free of charge to a newly founded partnership. The partner would become the principal partner in the newly founded partnership. The newly founded partnership could use that client base in its business, without that client base, however, becoming part of its capital assets. Among other reasons, the CJEU ruled that in *Malburg* (in contrast to *Polski Trawertyn*), the new partnership had already been created when Mr Malburg acquired the client base and, unlike the situation at issue in *Polski Trawertyn*, there was no contribution of capital goods, in this case, the client base, to the capital assets of that partnership. Finally, it is not the newly formed partnership which has requested the right to deduct input VAT paid by a partner in the course of acts preparatory to the partnership's activity.
48. Opinion of Advocate General Cruz Villalón of 15 September 2011, Case C-280/10 *Kopalnia Odkrywkowa Polski Trawertyn P. Granatowicz, M. Wąsiewicz, spółka jawna v Dyrektor Izby Skarbowej w Poznaniu*, ECLI:EU:C:2011:592, para. 40.

input VAT, it was the partnership which – alternatively – had a right of deduction so as to ensure the neutrality of taxation.[49]

Although we can agree with the outcome – the right of deduction with the partners or – alternatively – with the partnership, in our view, there is little to no basis for this decision to be found in the VAT Directive. Had it not been a partnership but a limited company instead, it is unlikely that the CJEU would have allowed the future shareholders a right of deduction.[50] If the principle of neutrality can alter the scope of the right of deduction in such a drastic manner, why then would Article 168 VAT Directive still require that the supply be made 'to' the taxable person, and why would anyone still bother with determining the identity of the recipient of the supply?

10.2.2.3 Use for Taxed Transactions

A right of deduction can only exist if the person concerned has taxable person status and acts in his capacity as taxable person.[51] If a right of deduction exists, its scope depends on the extent to which the goods and services which are purchased are used for taxed transactions. For, Article 168 VAT Directive only allows for deduction of input VAT insofar as the goods or services which are purchased, acquired or imported are used for 'taxed transactions'. As indicated in section 10.1.2, from an *a contrario* interpretation of Article 168 VAT Directive, it follows that no right of deduction exists if goods and services are used for supplies which are exempt under Articles 132 and 135 VAT Directive. Certain exceptions to that rule apply (*see* Article 169 VAT Directive).

If goods and services are used for both taxed and exempt supplies, the taxable person is only entitled to a proportional ('pro rata') deduction of input VAT. In section 10.4.1, we will further explain the rules on the calculation of the pro rata deduction.

If goods and services are used for activities that are not taxable supplies, such as the transfer of a going concern (*see also* Chapter 3, section 3.6), the purchase of shares, or supplies for no consideration, the question arises to what extent the same *a contrario* reading of Article 168 should apply. In this respect, it must be checked whether the costs can be attributed to the economic activity as a whole (*see* section 10.3.2). If that is possible, there may be proportional right of deduction of input VAT. In section 10.5, we elaborate on the right of deduction in cases where the costs relate to non-economic activities.

49. CJEU 1 March 2012, Case C-280/10 *Kopalnia Odkrywkowa Polski Trawertyn P. Granatowicz, M. Wąsiewicz, spółka jawna v Dyrektor Izby Skarbowej w Poznaniu*, ECLI:EU:C:2012:107, para. 35.
50. In our view, the analogy which the CJEU seeks with *Faxworld* is weak because Faxworld Gbr was not a future shareholder, but merely a predecessor to Faxworld AG. *See* CJEU 29 April 2004, Case C-137/02 *Finanzamt Offenbach am Main-Land v Faxworld Vorgründungsgesellschaft Peter Hünninghausen und Wolfgang Klein GbR*, ECLI:EU:C:2004:267.
51. The first investments with a view to a planned economic activity already grant taxable person status. *See*: CJEU 14 February 1985, Case 268/83 *D.A. Rompelman and E.A. Rompelman-Van Deelen v Minister van Financiën*, ECLI:EU:C:1985:74.

10.2.2.4 *Possession of a Correct Invoice*

Pursuant to Article 178(a) VAT Directive, the right of deduction can only be exercised if – in respect of the supply of goods or services – an invoice is held, drawn up in accordance with Articles 220-236 and Articles 238, 239 and 240 VAT Directive. From *Barlis,*[52] it follows that the invoice accounts for the economic transaction, allowing the competent tax authority to monitor payment and declaration of the amount of the tax due by the issuer of the invoice and the existence of the right to deduct VAT of the taxable person receiving the goods or services. As such, the invoice is an essential means of proof for the right to deduct input VAT.[53] In Chapter 15, we discuss the invoicing requirements.

The possession of an invoice is also required if the recipient of an ICS, i.e., a person making an ICA, is liable to pay the VAT on that intra-Community acquisition (ICA) and wants to deduct that input VAT under Article 168(1)(c) VAT Directive. Moreover, Article 178(c) VAT Directive requires that the acquirer sets out in the VAT return provided for in Article 250 VAT Directive all the information needed for the amount of VAT due on his ICAs of goods to be calculated.

In *John Reisdorf,* the CJEU somewhat eased the formal requirement for the possession of a correct invoice. According to the CJEU, this provision permits the Member States to regard as an invoice not only the original but also any other document serving as an invoice that fulfils the criteria determined by the Member States themselves. Moreover, the provision confers on the Member States the power to require production of the original invoice in order to establish the right to deduct input tax, as well as the power, where a taxable person no longer holds the original, to admit other evidence that the transaction in respect of which the deduction is claimed actually took place.[54] It is also settled case law that flaws in the formal invoicing requirements, do not stand in the way of deduction of input VAT, as long as a right to deduct input VAT substantively exists.[55] Furthermore, in situations where the substantive requirements for deduction are met, even if an invoice is issued by a non-existent trader, or if an invoice is issued to another (non-taxable) person, principally, the right to deduct should not be limited.[56]

Notwithstanding the above, sometimes the possession of a correct invoice is not a requirement at all, to be able to deduct the VAT on the purchase. For example, if a taxable person makes an internal supply under Article 18(a) or 27 VAT Directive,

---

52. CJEU 15 September 2016, Case C-516/14 *Barlis 06 – Investimentos Imobiliários e Turísticos,* ECLI:EU:C:2016:690.
53. Opinion Advocate General Wahl, Joined Cases C-374/16 and C-375/16 *Rochus Geissel v Finanzamt Neuss and Finanzamt Bergisch Gladbach v Igor Butin,* ECLI:EU:C:2017:515, para. 39.
54. CJEU 5 December 1996, Case C-85/95 *John Reisdorf v Fianzamt Köln-West,* ECLI:EU:C:1996:466.
55. *See* a.o. CJEU 15 September 2016, Case C-516/14 *Barlis 06 – Investimentos Imobiliários e Turísticos,* ECLI:EU:C:2016:690 and CJEU 15 September 2016, Case C-518/14 *Senatex GmbH v Finanzamt Hannover-Nord,* ECLI:EU:C:2016:691.
56. CJEU 1 March 2012, Case C-280/10 *Kopalnia Odkrywkowa Polski Trawertyn P. Granatowicz, M. Wąsiewicz spółka jawna v Dyrektor Izby Skarbowej w Poznaniu,* ECLI:EU:C:2012:107 and CJEU 22 October 2015, Case C-277/14 *PPUH Stehcemp sp. j Florian Stefanek, Janina Stefanek, Jaroslaw Stefanek v Dyrektor Izby Skarbowej w Łodzi,* ECLI:EU:C:2015:719.

effects a B2Me ICA (*see* Chapter 13), or imports goods from outside the EU (*see* Chapter 14),[57] Article 178(b), (d) and (e) respectively do not require an invoice to effectuate the right of deduction. Also, the VAT Directive does not require the possession of an invoice if the customer, rather than the supplier, is liable to pay the VAT on the supply to the tax authorities (reverse charge mechanism). For example, if a taxable person in Portugal purchases services from a taxable person in Latvia, under Article 44 VAT Directive, the place of supply is Portugal. However, the Latvian taxable person should not charge (Portuguese) VAT because Article 196 VAT Directive applies: the Portuguese company should report the Portuguese VAT on its VAT return. Insofar as the Portuguese company uses the services for its taxed activities and all other requirements for the right of deduction are fulfilled, he can immediately, i.e., in the same VAT return, deduct the self-assessed VAT as input VAT. To be eligible for that deduction, Article 178(f) VAT Directive only stipulates that the company must comply with the formalities as laid down by the Portuguese authorities. However, these formalities cannot entail that the Portuguese company must be in possession of an invoice, meeting the invoicing requirements. After all, in *Bockemühl*, the CJEU held that the taxable person was not obliged to be in possession of an invoice drawn up in accordance with the Directive in order to be able to exercise his right of deduction, as the recipient of services, for the VAT on the purchase of the services.[58]

In addition, Article 180 of the VAT Directive stipulates that the Member States may authorize a taxable person to make a deduction which he has not made in accordance with Articles 178 and 179. According to Article 181 VAT Directive, Member States may authorize a taxable person who does not hold an invoice drawn up in accordance with the VAT Directive to make the deduction referred to in Article 168(c) VAT Directive of his intra-Community acquisitions (ICAs) of goods. In practice, this means that in many Member States, the deduction will be effected in the same tax period as with respect to which the VAT becomes payable upon the acquisition (*see* section 10.2.3 at the moment when the right of deduction arises).

If VAT is charged incorrectly on an invoice, the supplier will be liable to pay the incorrectly charged VAT to the tax authorities (Article 203 VAT Directive), which the addressee of the invoice cannot deduct (*Genius Holding*).[59] However, subject to conditions, incorrectly charged VAT may be adjusted. We refer to Chapter 12, section 12.4.

10.2.2.5 Possession of Import Documents (Deduction of Import VAT)

For the purposes of deductions pursuant to Article 168(e) VAT Directive in respect of the importation of goods, the taxable person must hold an import document specifying him as consignee or importer, and stating the amount of VAT due, or enabling that

57. *See also* Article 52 VAT Implementing Regulation.
58. CJEU 1 April 2004, Case C-90/02 *Gerard Bockemühl v Finanzamt Gummersbach*, ECLI:EU:C:2004:206.
59. CJEU 13 December 1989, Case C-342/87 *Genius Holding BV v Staatssecretaris van Financiën*, ECLI:EU:C:1989:635.

amount to be calculated. Article 52 of Regulation 282/2011 (which covers electronic import documents) stipulates that where the Member State of importation has introduced an electronic system for completing customs formalities, the term 'import document' in Article 178(e) VAT Directive shall cover electronic versions of such documents, provided that they allow for the exercise of the right of deduction to be checked. We believe that this provision should be interpreted such that the required documents give rise to the rebuttable presumption that the goods will be used for taxed transactions of the taxable person concerned, as required in Article 168(e) VAT Directive.[60]

Neither the term 'consignee' nor 'importer' has been defined in VAT law. However, in customs law, the term consignee is usually used to indicate the person who physically receives the goods.[61]

Given the fact that importation of goods is both a taxable event for VAT and for customs law, it would seem logical to define this term in accordance with customs law. A complication in this regard is that customs law provides no definition of the term 'importer'. In our view, the 'importer' in Article 178(e) VAT Directive can be interpreted as the 'debtor', i.e., the person who is liable to pay the customs duties on importation as referred to in Article 5(19) Union Customs Code (UCC). Who the debtor is depends largely on who files the customs declaration. Usually, it is the same person in whose name the customs declaration is filed (the declarant). However, in the case of 'indirect representation', this may be different (*see* sections 4.4.3.3, 12.2.3, 13.3.2.2.3 and 14.13.1).

If the term 'importer' in Article 178(e) VAT Directive is to be interpreted as 'debtor', as referred to in Article 5(19) UCC, normally that person will be able to claim the VAT on importation, provided that he uses the goods for his taxed transactions. Technically, such an interpretation would mean that in the event of indirect representation, there would be two 'importers'. However, in such a case, the intermediary person will normally not use the goods for his taxed transactions, which implies that he cannot deduct the VAT on importation. This conclusion seems to be confirmed by *DSV Road A/S* and *Weindel Logistik*.[62] It follows from these cases that a right to deduct exists only in so far as the goods imported are used for the purposes of the taxed transactions of the taxable person. According to the CJEU, that condition is satisfied only where the cost of the input services is incorporated either in the cost of particular output transactions or in the cost of goods or services supplied by the taxable person as part of his economic activities.

60. Cf. D.B. Bijl, M.E. Van Hilten & D.G. van Vliet, *Europese BTW en Nederlandse omzetbelasting* (3rd edn, Kluwer 2001), p. 314.
61. 'Consignee' (as mentioned in box 8 of a customs declaration) is defined/described in the explanatory notes to the customs declarations as included in Annex 37 (Title II, sub C-8) of the CCC Implementation Regulation: 'the person(s) or company(ies) to whom the goods are to be delivered'.
62. CJEU 25 June 2015, Case C-187/14 *DSV Road A/S*, ECLI:EU:C:2015:421 and CJEU 8 October 2020, Case 621/19 *Weindel Logistik Service SR spol. s r.o*, ECLI:EU:C:2020:814.

10.2.3 The Moment at Which the Right of Deduction Arises

Under Article 167 VAT Directive, a right of deduction arises with the recipient of a supply at the moment the deductible tax becomes chargeable with the *supplier*.

As a main rule, the obligation to pay the VAT to the tax authorities lies with the supplier.[63] Consequently, the time that VAT becomes due for the supplier determines the moment at which the recipient may reclaim VAT charged to him. Since – following from this rule – the recipient is not allowed to reclaim the input tax when it is most convenient for him, he will not be permitted to postpone the moment when he actually recovers the VAT charged to him. Moreover, in *Staatssecretaris van Financiën v X*, it is pointed out that the possibility of exercising the right to deduct VAT without any temporal limit would be contrary to the principle of legal certainty, which requires the tax position of the taxable person, having regard to their rights and obligations vis-à-vis the tax authority, not to be open to challenge indefinitely.[64]

The question may arise as to what happens if the recipient does not receive the invoice in good time. Pursuant to Article 178(a) VAT Directive, the right of deduction can only be exercised if – in respect of the supply of goods or services – he holds an invoice drawn up in accordance with Articles 220-236 and Articles 238, 239 and 240 VAT Directive (*see* Chapter 15). From *Terra Baubedarf*, it is apparent that Articles 167 and 178(a) VAT Directive must be read in conjunction. That implies that VAT can only be deducted at the moment the goods have been delivered, or the service performed and that the recipient holds the invoice or the document which may be considered to serve as an invoice.[65] In *Terra Baubedarf*, the appellant was under the impression that the VAT charged to him could be deducted at the moment he received the service, even though the supplier issued the invoice in January of the year following that in which the supply took place. The CJEU did not accept this reasoning and decided that VAT can only be deducted in respect of the tax period in which both conditions required by these provisions are satisfied: the supply has been made *and* the invoice issued. From *Senatex*, it follows that that deduction is not precluded if an invoice is issued that lacks formally required details, such as the VAT number of the supplier, and such omission is corrected at a later date. In those circumstances, the recipient has a right to deduct at the moment of issue of the original, flawed, invoice.[66]

In section 10.2.2.4, we indicated that with respect to B2B services to which the reverse charge mechanism applies, i.e., the customer is liable to pay the VAT on the supply, the deduction of that reverse-charged VAT does not require the possession of an invoice. In these situations the VAT becomes due at the moment that the service is performed. The moment of deduction is still connected to the moment when the VAT becomes due. In practice, this frequently raises problems for taxable persons, as they must account for the VAT on the services supplied to them and – if they are entitled to

63. *See*, however, Chapter 12, Person Liable to Pay VAT.
64. CJEU 7 July 2022, Case C-194/21 *Staatssecretaris van Financiën v X*, ECLI:EU:C:2022:535.
65. CJEU 29 April 2004, Case C-152/02 *Terra Baubedarf-Handel GmnH-Finanzamt Osterholz-Scharmbeck*, ECLI:EU:C:2004:268.
66. CJEU 15 September 2016, Case C-518/14 *Senatex GmbH v Finanzamt Hannover-Nord*, ECLI:EU:C:2016:691.

a deduction – have to reclaim VAT at the moment they are not yet in possession of the invoice which would have otherwise revealed them the correct VAT amounts.

According to Article 167a, Member States may provide for an optional scheme that the right of deduction of a taxable person whose VAT solely becomes chargeable according to Article 66(b) (allowing Member States to decide that VAT becomes chargeable no later than the time the payment is received) be postponed until the VAT on the goods or services supplied to him has been paid to his supplier. Member States wishing to apply this option scheme must set a threshold for taxable persons using the scheme within their territories.

Articles 180-182 provide the Member States with some discretionary room to allow deductions outside the rules provided in Articles 178 and 179. From *Biosafe*, it follows that these provisions may be used by Member States to allow deduction to tax payers even if they did not exercise their right during the period in which the right arose, subject, however, to compliance with certain conditions and procedures determined by national legislation.[67]

10.2.4 The Scope of the Right of Deduction

Both Article 168 and 168a VAT Directive deal with the scope of the right of deduction. Article 168 provides the general rule. Only VAT on goods and services that are used for taxed transactions can be deducted. In section 10.2.4.1, we further discuss this provision.

Article 168a defines the scope of the right of deduction for a more specific case. It provides a restriction of this right insofar as immovable property assigned in full or partly to the business assets is used for private purposes. With respect to this latter provision, we refer to section 10.7.1.2.

In section 10.2.4.2, we discuss the extensions to the scope of the right of deduction contained in Article 169 VAT Directive. We consider the following types of transactions:

(1) transactions carried out outside the Member State (Article 169(a) VAT Directive, section 10.2.4.2.1);
(2) certain types of transactions to non-EU customers (Article 169(c) VAT Directive section 10.2.4.2.2);
(3) transactions with a 'credit' (Article 169(b) VAT Directive, section 10.2.4.2.3).

With respect to the extension contained in Article 169(a) VAT Directive (transactions carried out outside the Member State), it is inevitable to discuss the territorial

67. CJEU 12 April 2018, Case C-8/17 *Biosafe – Indústria de Reciclagens SA v Flexipiso – Pavimentos SA*, ECLI:EU:C:2018:249.

scope of the right of deduction in relation to transactions carried out by foreign establishments.

On the basis of Articles 170-172 VAT Directive, taxable persons who incur VAT in a Member State in which they are established or registered for VAT, may apply for a refund. In section 10.2.4.3, we elaborate on refunds of VAT to foreign taxable persons.

The VAT Directive also contains various provisions that restrict the scope of the right of deduction. We discuss these restrictions in section 10.2.4.4.

10.2.4.1 Used for Taxed Transactions

Article 168(1) VAT Directive states that insofar as goods and services are *used* for the purposes of a taxable person's *taxed transactions*, he shall be entitled, in the Member State in which he carries out these transactions, to deduct the following from the VAT which he is liable to pay:

(a) the VAT due or paid in that Member State in respect of supplies to him of goods or services carried out or to be carried out by another taxable person (section 10.2.4.1.1);
(b) the VAT due in respect of transactions treated as supplies of goods or services pursuant to Articles 18(a) and 27 VAT Directive (section 10.2.4.1.2);
(c) the VAT due in respect of intra-Community acquisitions (ICAs) of goods pursuant to Article 2(1)(b)(i) VAT Directive (section 10.2.4.1.3);
(d) the VAT due on transactions treated as intra-Community acquisitions (ICAs) in accordance with Articles 21 and 22 VAT Directive (section 10.2.4.1.2);
(e) the VAT due or paid in respect of the importation of goods into that Member State (section 10.2.4.1.4).

Below, we will discuss these elements of Article 168 VAT Directive.

10.2.4.1.1 Supplies of Goods and Services

The VAT paid, as referred to in Article 168(1)(a) VAT Directive, is any VAT which was *charged* to the taxable person by his supplier (based on Article 193 VAT Directive, the supplier is, in principle, liable to pay this VAT to the tax authorities) and which was also actually *paid* by the taxable person to his supplier. Schematically, this system can be depicted as in Figure 10.1.

Figure 10.1 Deduction of VAT Paid to the Supplier

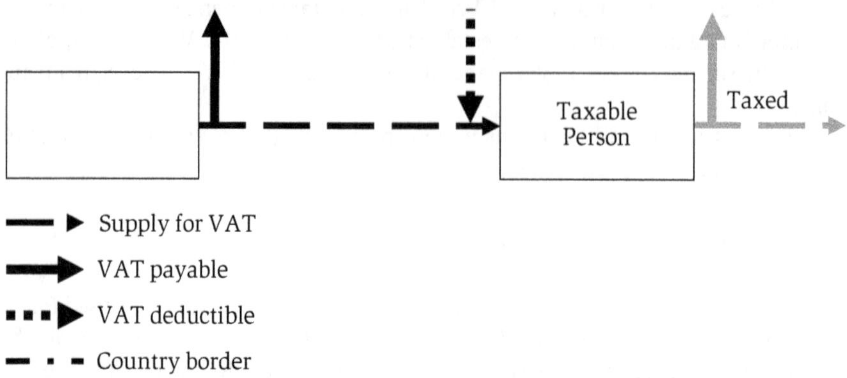

If the VAT was charged but had not been paid by the recipient at the moment that he reclaims the VAT on the input transaction, the VAT is due (and not yet paid). The VAT *due,* as referred to in Article 168(1)(a) VAT Directive refers to any VAT that is reverse charged to the recipient on the basis of Article 194 VAT Directive by the supplier. This VAT can also be deducted insofar as the goods and services are used for taxed transactions (*see* Figure 10.2). From *Zipvit Ltd*, it follows that VAT cannot be regarded as being *due* or *paid* and can therefore not be deducted by the taxable person, in the case where, first, that person and its supplier have mistakenly assumed, on the basis of an incorrect interpretation of EU law by the national authorities, that the supplies at issue were exempt from VAT in a situation where the contract between those two persons provided that, if that tax were due, the recipient of the supply should bear the cost of it.[68] As a result, if parties have incorrectly assumed that no VAT was due, and no correction is made in this respect, the recipient cannot claim that there is a right to deduct VAT, included in the purchase price.

68. CJEU 13 January 2022, Case C-156/20 *Zipvit Ltd v The Commissioners for Her Majesty's Revenue & Customs*, ECLI:EU:C:2022:2.

Figure 10.2 Deduction of Reverse-Charged VAT

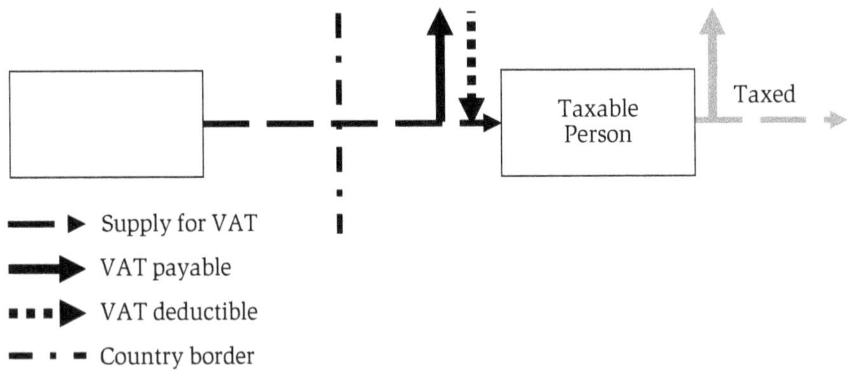

10.2.4.1.2 VAT on 'Internal Supplies' and 'Internal' Intra-Community Acquisitions

The VAT due in respect of transactions treated as supplies of goods or services pursuant to Articles 18(a) and 27 can be deductible (Article 168(1)(b) VAT Directive).

On the basis of Articles 18(a) and 27 Member States may introduce specific internal supplies (for instance, they may treat some transactions as a supply of goods for consideration). As an example, the application by a taxable person for the purposes of his business of goods produced, constructed, extracted, processed, purchased or imported in the course of such business, where the VAT on such goods, had they been acquired from another person, would not be wholly deductible, may be treated as a taxable transaction (internal supply). However, as far as the VAT on such goods would have been deductible had they had been purchased from another person, the VAT on the internal supply will be deductible accordingly (*see* Figure 10.3).

Also, deductible is the VAT that is due on transactions treated as intra-Community acquisitions (ICAs) in accordance with Articles 21 and 22 VAT Directive (*see* Chapter 13).

Figure 10.3 Example of the Scope of the Right of Deduction under Article 168(1)(b) VAT Directive (Internal Supply)

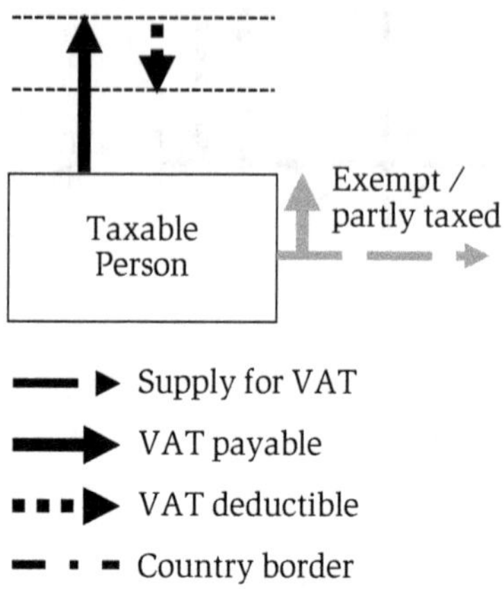

To be able to deduct VAT on the basis of Article 168(b) and (d) VAT Directive, the taxable person must comply with the formalities as laid down by each Member State (*see* section 10.2.2).

10.2.4.1.3 VAT Due in Respect of Intra-Community Acquisitions (ICAs)

Article 168(1)(c) VAT Directive allows for deduction of the VAT due in respect of intra-Community acquisitions (ICAs) of goods pursuant to Article 2(1)(b)(i) VAT Directive. VAT on straightforward B2B ICAs (Article 2(1)(b)(i) VAT Directive; *see* Chapter 12) is deductible insofar as those goods will be used for taxed supplies. This is depicted in Figure 10.4.

Figure 10.4 Deduction of VAT on a B2B Intra-Community Acquisition of Goods (ICA)

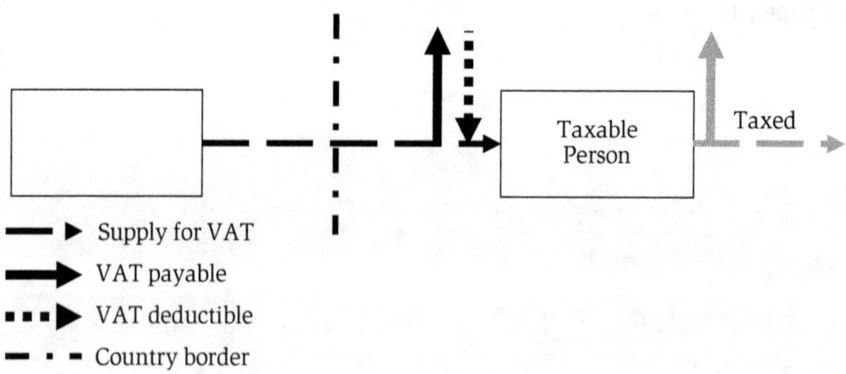

10.2.4.1.4 VAT on the Importations of Goods

The VAT due or paid in respect of the importation of goods into that Member State is deductible following Article 168(1)(e) VAT Directive. VAT payable upon importation of goods is deductible for the person that imports those goods. In principle, the VAT on importation is due upon entry of the goods in the EU (*see* Figure 10.5).

Figure 10.5 The Liability and Deduction of VAT on Importation

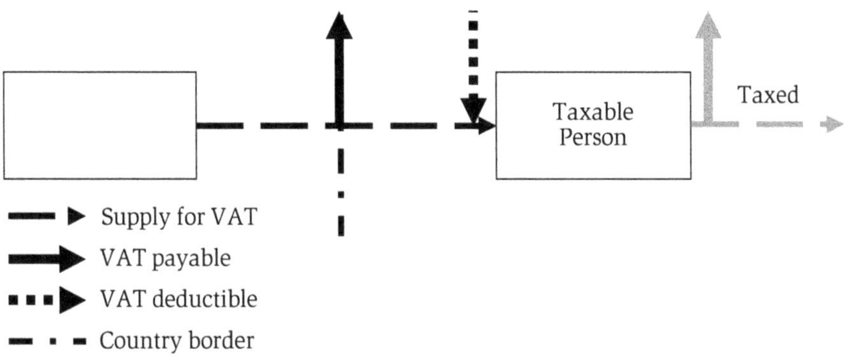

The liability to pay VAT on importation may be postponed, based on Article 211 VAT Directive (a deferral mechanism; *see* section 14.7). If such a deferral mechanism is applied, the VAT due and the deduction of that VAT take place at the same moment, resulting in a zero sum operation. Figure 10.6 serves to illustrate this.

Figure 10.6 The Liability and Deduction of VAT on Importation under an Import VAT Deferral Scheme

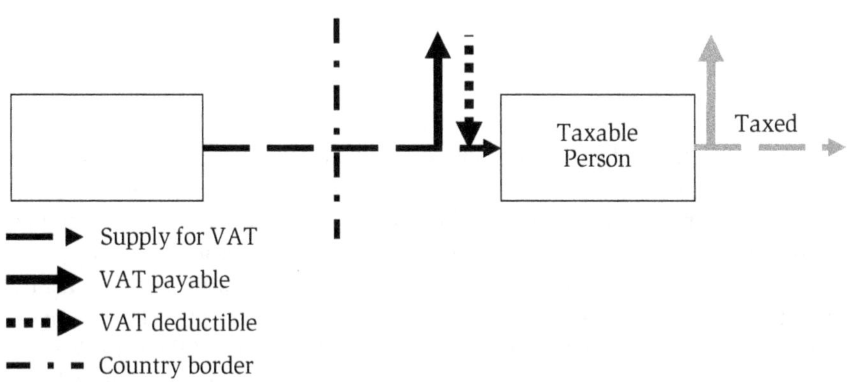

With respect to the formal requirements to the right of deduction of import VAT, we refer to section 10.2.2.5.

10.2.4.2 Extensions to the Scope of the Right of Deduction

In this section, we discuss those provisions in the VAT Directive that extend the scope of the right of deduction (or refund) of VAT.

10.2.4.2.1 Transactions Carried Out Outside the Member State

It may occur that a taxable person makes a supply of a good or a service that is considered to take place in another country (*see* Chapter 4 on the Place of Supply), but that he purchases goods and services on which the VAT of his Member State of establishment is charged. For example, if a taxable person in Bulgaria supplies a B2B advisory service to a customer in Slovenia, that service is taxable in Slovenia. If the Bulgarian supplier purchased legal services from a Bulgarian lawyer which he used to supply the advisory services to its Slovenian company, the question arises whether he can deduct the Bulgarian VAT on the legal services. Article 169(a) VAT Directive allows for deduction of input VAT on goods and services used for services which are taxed in another country, subject to the condition that the input VAT would be deductible if the services (advisory services in the example) had been carried out within that Member State. Figure 10.7 illustrates this mechanism.

Figure 10.7 Deduction of Input VAT for Transactions Carried Out Outside the Member State

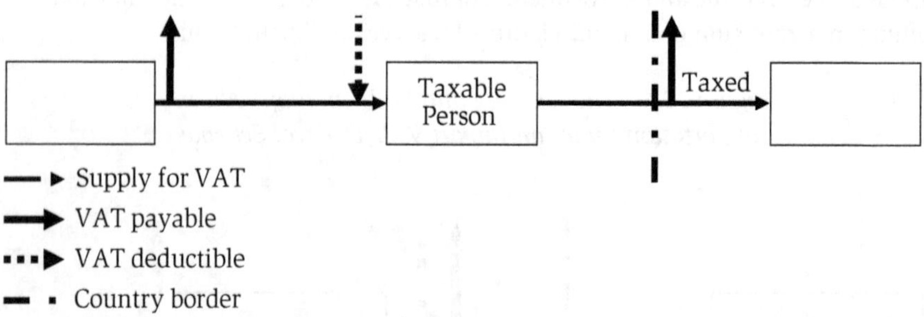

By allowing the deduction for supplies which are deemed to be made in another Member State, the legislator prevents a possible violation of the fiscal neutrality which would occur if transactions taking place in another Member State were burdened with non-deductible (foreign) VAT. It should be noted that if the transactions taking place in another Member State would have been exempt, had they been carried out in the Member State of the establishment of the supplier, they do not give rise to a right of deduction.[69] There are, however, some exceptions. Subject to conditions, the VAT paid on goods and services used for exempt banking, financial and insurance transactions to

69. *See* to that effect CJEU 15 November 2017, Case C-507/16 *Entertainment Bulgaria System EOOD*, ECLI:EU:C:2017:864.

non-EU customers (which are also deemed to take place in the customer's country; *see* Articles 44 and 59(1)(e) VAT Directive) is deductible under Article 169(c) VAT Directive (*see* section 10.2.4.2.3).

10.2.4.2.2 Transactions Carried Out by Foreign Establishments (Territorial Scope)

In *Morgan Stanley,* the CJEU decided on the question of whether a taxable person, when calculating the deductible proportion (*see* section 10.4) applicable to a fixed establishment in a Member State, is allowed to take into account the turnover of its head office in another Member State.[70] The CJEU ruled that insofar costs incurred by the fixed establishments are used solely, or in part for the economic activity of the head office in another Member State, the turnover obtained with those activities in the other Member State should be taken into account for the calculation of the deductible proportion. The CJEU ruled that in this respect, deduction is only possible if a double test is applied. VAT on costs incurred by the fixed establishment in one Member State can only be deducted if the activity of the head office in another Member State for which the costs are used would give rise to a right to deduct in that Member State and if such right would also exist in the Member States where the costs are incurred. In effect, this double test will lead to application of the deduction right of the Member State that allows the least amount of deduction out of the two. The decision in *Morgan Stanley* came unexpectedly. In its earlier decision in *Credit Lyonnais,* which regarded the question of whether a head office should include the turnover of its fixed establishments in calculating the deductible proportion, the CJEU explicitly ruled that the deduction system is based on the principle of territoriality of the applicable national provisions (especially the way in which the deductible proportion must be calculated). The manner in which that calculation must be carried out falls, along with the deduction system, within the scope of the national VAT legislation to which an activity or transaction must be linked for tax purposes. That means that a taxable person – on the basis of *Credit Lyonnais* – must determine a separate deductible amount in every Member State in which he has an (fixed) establishment. The CJEU reconciled the decisions in *Morgan Stanley* and *Credit Lyonnais* – albeit rather unconvincingly, in our view – by ruling that the *Credit Lyonnais* case only regarded the deduction of VAT on general costs of the head office, which costs were not (also) used by its fixed establishments.

The combination of *Morgan Stanley* and *Credit Lyonnais* raises a number of questions. From *Credit Lyonnais,* it clearly follows that if a head office incurs costs which are attributable to all of its output transactions, it may only take into account the turnover made by this principal place of business when calculating the deductible proportion in the head office's Member State. How to determine whether or not those costs are also used for the fixed establishments of such head office? It seems likely that

70. CJEU 24 January 2019, Case C-165/17 *Morgan Stanley & Co International plc v Ministre de l'Économie et des Finances,* ECLI:EU:C:2019:58 and CJEU 12 September 2013, Case C-388/11 *Le Crédit Lyonnais v Ministre du Budget, des Comptes publics et de la Réforme de l'État,* ECLI: EU:C:2013:541.

the costs incurred by an international head office, directly or indirectly are also used for the activity of its fixed establishments. In other words, when does the *Morgan Stanley* approach come into play? What happens if the head office does not generate any turnover itself? How to apply the double test from *Morgan Stanley* when an establishment is involved that is established outside of the EU? These kinds of issues will certainly result in more European and/or national case law.

See also section 10.4 in which the calculation methods of the deductible proportion that the Member States may apply are set out.

10.2.4.2.3 Transactions with a 'Credit'

VAT cannot be deducted if the output transaction for which the taxable person used the goods and services, is exempt. However, this is only true for exempt transactions 'without a credit' (i.e., without the right to deduct the related input VAT). Exempt supplies without a credit are mainly dealt with in Articles 132 and 135 VAT Directive. However, the VAT Directive also contains exempt supplies *with* a credit. For example, Article 169(b) VAT Directive contains such exempt supplies with a credit. On the basis of this provision, transactions which are exempt pursuant to Articles 138, 142 or 144, 146-149, 151-153 or 156, 157(1)(b), 158-161 or 164 VAT Directive give rise to a deduction.

The most common exempt supplies with a credit are intra-Community supplies (ICSs, Article 138 VAT Directive) and export supplies to third countries (Article 146 VAT Directive). Some Member States, however, refer to these exempt supplies as supplies to which a 'zero rate' applies. In fact, they do not need a special provision like Article 169(b) VAT Directive because they consider such supplies as 'taxed supplies' (to which a VAT rate of 0% applies). In our view, it would have made life easier for those who have to deal with the practical aspects of VAT on a daily basis if the VAT Directive and all Member States had introduced the expression 'zero rate supply' instead of 'exempt supplies with the right of deduction'.[71]

10.2.4.2.4 Certain Types of Transactions to Non-EU Customers

According to Article 169(c) VAT Directive, a right to deduction also exists if goods and services are used for transactions which are exempt pursuant to Article 135(1)(a)-(f) VAT Directive, provided that the customer is established outside the EU or where those transactions relate directly to goods to be exported out of the EU.

As regards the financial transactions mentioned in Article 169(c) VAT Directive, regardless of whether they are supplied to businesses or non-taxable persons, are in almost all cases considered to take place in the country of the customer (Articles 44 and 59 VAT Directive, but *see also* Article 59a VAT Directive regarding the effective use and enjoyment rules). For example, if a German bank grants a loan to a Swiss client, the German bank is entitled to a deduction of input VAT attributable to the (exempt) loan

71. Not least because of the invoicing requirements that apply.

to the Swiss client. The rationale of this provision is to safeguard the 'external neutrality' of EU VAT. It serves to avoid cross-border competition between EU financial institutions and, for instance, US financial institutions. In the United States, no VAT or GST is levied, which would place US banks in a more favourable position than EU banks (they generally do not incur non-deductible input VAT). Article 169(c) prevents this distortion of competition from occurring.

10.2.4.3 Refunds of VAT to Foreign Taxable Persons

It may occur that a taxable person incurs costs in a Member State in which he is neither established nor carries out any taxable activities. In particular, the reverse charge mechanism (*see* section 12.3) often has the effect that even though a supply is subject to VAT in another Member State, the supplier is not the person liable for the VAT on that supply. Then, there is no requirement for the supplier to register for VAT in the other Member State.

The fact that there is no VAT registration or reporting requirement implies that the taxable person can deduct any VAT he incurred in that Member State. For example, a foreign taxable person who incurs VAT on petrol, hotel accommodation and/or seminars cannot deduct the VAT charged to him because he simply is not registered for VAT and does not have the possibility to file a VAT return.

Yet, the neutrality principle requires that a foreign taxable person should be relieved of the burden of VAT incurred in the furtherance of their business. That is why the VAT Directive - subject to conditions - allows for a *refund* of VAT incurred by a taxable person in another Member State than the Member State where that taxable person is established. Articles 170, 171 and 171a VAT Directive contain the general rules on the refund of VAT to foreign taxable persons. Directive 2008/9/EC and Directive 86/560/EEC further detail these rules. Directive 2008/9/EC applies to refunds of VAT a taxable person established in another Member State, whereas Directive 86/560/EEC applies to refunds to taxable persons established outside the EU.

We note that foreign taxable persons who have a VAT registration requirement in the Member State of which they incur the (local) VAT, are not eligible for a refund of VAT. They have to file (local) VAT returns and reclaim the foreign VAT via that VAT return. In such situations, they are excluded from the special refund procedures as arranged by the above-mentioned directives. This scenario applies, for example, if the foreign taxable person has a fixed establishment in the Member State concerned,[72] if he imports goods in that Member State or if he makes local supplies of goods or services in that Member State to which the reverse charge mechanism does not apply.

Small amounts cannot be reclaimed via the refund procedures. Refund claims by EU entrepreneurs can be submitted electronically. They have to produce a certificate issued by the authorities of the Member State in which they are established, showing that they have taxable person status in the other Member State.

72. CJEU 16 July 2009, Case C-244/08 *Commission of the European Communities v Italian Republic*, ECLI:EU:C:2009:478.

In *Debouche* a Belgian taxable person supplied services as a lawyer that were VAT exempt in Belgium. However, if such services would have been carried out in the Netherlands, they would have been taxed.[73] Debouche incurred Dutch VAT on the lease of a car and wanted to get a refund of the Dutch VAT. Thus, there are some essential differences between the *Debouche* case and the situation which Article 169(a) VAT Directive contemplates as: (1) Debouche did not supply services which were subject to VAT in another country, and (2) Debouche did not incur the VAT in the Member State of establishment. The CJEU considered that if Debouche were to be granted a refund of VAT, he would be treated more favourably than Dutch lawyers. After all, Dutch lawyers were indeed entitled to deduct input tax, but they had to charge VAT on their output transactions, whereas Mr Debouche carried out exempted transactions.[74]

In *Monte dei Paschi di Siena*, the CJEU provided further guidance on the question of whether a refund must be granted if the national and foreign VAT rules are not identical. An Italian bank which was involved in both taxed and exempt activities submitted a refund claim in France. It did not make any supplies in France. Yet, if it had carried out the same activities in France, those activities would have given rise to a higher right of deduction than the Italian bank had on the basis of Italian VAT law. The CJEU ruled that the bank could reclaim French VAT on the basis of the same deductible proportion as it was allowed in Italy.[75]

Effectively, the case law described above implies that the VAT rules in the Member State of establishment form a first 'cap' on the right to a refund and that the rules of the Member State of refund contain a second 'cap' on the right to a refund.

On the basis of Article 171a VAT Directive, Member States may exclude foreign entrepreneurs from the above refund procedures if they are not engaged in taxable events in that Member State (domestic supplies, intra-Community supplies (ICSs), intra-Community acquisitions (ICAs) or importations), but are just liable for VAT based on the reverse charge mechanism. They may require them to submit regular VAT returns (where they will also end up in a refund position). The existing restrictions pursuant to Articles 2(2) and 4(2) of Directive 86/560/EEC (the Thirteenth Directive for non-EU businesses) may be retained.

10.2.4.4 Restrictions to the Scope of the Right of Deduction

The scope of deduction is based on Articles 41, second paragraph, 168a and 172 VAT Directive and is restricted to certain transactions.

73. CJEU 26 September 1996, Case C-302/93 *Etienne Debouche v Inspecteur der Invoerrechten en Accijnzen*, ECLI:EU:C:1996:348.
74. *Ibid.*
75. CJEU 13 July 2000, Case C-136/99 *Ministre du Budget and Ministre de l'Economie et des Finances v Société Monte Dei Paschi Di Siena*, ECLI:EU:C:2000:408.

10.2.4.4.1 Number Acquisition

Sometimes the purchaser (acquirer) of goods requests the supplier to send or transport the goods to another Member State than where the acquirer is established and registered for VAT. Following Article 41 VAT Directive, and without prejudice to Article 40 VAT Directive, the place of an ICA shall be deemed to be within the territory of the Member State which issued the VAT ID number under which the person acquiring the goods made the acquisition[76] unless the person acquiring the goods establishes that VAT has been applied to that acquisition in accordance with Article 40 VAT Directive. This means that if the purchaser does not establish that VAT is applied in the Member State of arrival of the goods, the intra-Community supply (ICS) not only takes place in the Member State of arrival of the goods but *also* in the Member State of registration of the purchaser. Since the intra-Community acquisition (ICA) must be reported in two VAT returns (one in the Member State of arrival of the goods and one in the Member State of registration of the purchaser), and even though it is conceptually incorrect, in practice, it is quite common to speak about an 'intra-Community number acquisition' (or simply: 'number acquisition') when referring to the fact that the ICA must (also) be reported in the Member State of the purchasers' VAT registration. In Chapter 13, we elaborate further on this system of 'double acquisitions'.

Following *Facet*, the VAT on the number acquisition cannot be immediately deducted, even if the purchaser uses the goods only for taxed supplies.[77] Based on Article 41, second paragraph, VAT Directive the acquirer must first file the definitive acquisition in the Member State of arrival of the goods before he is entitled to reclaim the VAT on the first acquisition. This interpretation of Article 41 VAT Directive (not written with a view to resolving deduction matters) is not a restriction of the scope of the right to deduction in the strict sense but a breach of the right to *immediate* deduction (in fact, a postponing mechanism for the deduction).

10.2.4.4.2 Immovable Property

Article 168a VAT Directive contains a particular provision excluding the right of deduction of VAT on the purchase of immovable property that the taxable person also uses for his private purposes. The right of deduction is excluded up to the proportion of the property's use for private purposes. In section 10.7.1.2, we further explain the functioning of Article 168a VAT Directive.

76. The phrase 'the VAT identification number under which the person acquiring the goods made the acquisition' in Article 41 VAT Directive suggests that it applies only if the purchaser makes the purchases under its VAT ID number in the Member State where it is registered for VAT. However, this would deprive the provision of its purpose: the provision has also to be applicable if the purchaser makes the purchase under another VAT ID number of a Member State other than the one of VAT registration and arrival of the goods.
77. CJEU 22 April 2010, Joined Cases C-536/08 and C-539/08 *Staatssecretaris van Financiën v X (C-536/08) and fiscale eenheid Facet BV/Facet Trading BV (C-539/08)*, ECLI:EU:C:2010:217.

10.2.4.4.3 Intra-Community C2C Supplies of New Means of Transport

On the basis of Article 9(2) VAT Directive, any person who, on an occasional basis, supplies a new means of transport to a destination outside the territory of (mostly their own) Member State but within the EU to another private consumer must be regarded as a taxable person. The intra-Community acquisition (ICA) of a new means of transport by the customer (being a taxable person or not) is taxed.

In order to avoid double taxation, the supplier is entitled to a deduction of the VAT charged to him. However, this poses the risk that he might charge a lower amount to his customer (without a right of deduction) than he paid for the new means of transport himself. To prevent abuse, Article 172 VAT Directive stipulates that the deductible amount of VAT for the supplier is limited. It states that any person who is regarded as a taxable person as regards the supply of a new means of transport to another Member State shall, in the Member State in which the supply takes place, be entitled to deduct the VAT included in the purchase price of this means of transport, (only) up to an amount corresponding to the amount of VAT for which he would be liable if the supply were not exempt. Also, the moment of the right of deduction is postponed. A right of deduction arises and may be exercised only at the time of supply of the new means of transport. In section 13.8, we further elaborate on intra-Community Consumer to Consumer (C2C) supplies of new means of transport.

10.3 DIRECT AND GENERAL COSTS[78]

Article 168 VAT Directive allows for deduction of input VAT if a taxable person uses the goods and services which he purchases 'for the purposes of the taxed transactions'. This implies that there must be a direct and immediate link between the (costs of)[79] the goods and/or services purchased and the (prices of) the output transactions. The 'use' to which Article 168 VAT Directive refers is what may constitute the link between the costs and the prices. The ultimate aim pursued by the taxable person is irrelevant in this respect.[80]

In principle, a direct and immediate link must be established between a *particular* input transaction and a *particular* output transaction or transactions giving rise to an entitlement to deduct.[81] After all, the right to deduct VAT charged on the acquisition of input goods or services presupposes that the expenditure incurred in acquiring them was a component of the cost of the output transactions that gave rise to the right to

78. *See also* A.J. van Doesum, *Ondanks een onlosmakelijke samenhang, Correcties op de onlosmakelijke samenhang als norm voor het recht op aftrek van voorbelasting* (Inaugural speech) (Kluwer 2012).
79. Cf. Article 2 First VAT Directive (now: Article 1(2) VAT Directive). *See also* CJEU 6 April 1995, Case C-4/94 *BLP Group plc v Commissioners of Customs & Excise*, ECLI:EU:C:1995:107, para. 21 and CJEU 8 June 2000, Case C-98/98 *Commissioners of Customs and Excise v Midland Bank plc*, ECLI:EU:C:2000:300, para. 21.
80. CJEU 6 April 1995, Case C-4/94 *BLP Group plc v Commissioners of Customs & Excise*, ECLI:EU:C:1995:107, para. 19.
81. CJEU 8 June 2000, Case C-98/98 *Commissioners of Customs and Excise v Midland Bank plc*, ECLI:EU:C:2000:300, para. 24.

deduct.[82] If a direct and immediate link can be established between a particular input transaction and a particular output transaction or particular output transactions of a comparable nature (i.e., either exclusively taxed supplies or exclusively exempt supplies), the costs are 'direct costs'. If the output transaction is a taxed transaction, all VAT on the purchase can be deducted. Conversely, if the output transaction is exempt or does not give rise to a right of deduction for other reasons, the VAT on the purchase cannot be deducted.[83]

If a direct and immediate link with a particular output transaction or particular output transactions of a comparable nature cannot be established, it is necessary to investigate whether it is possible to identify a direct and immediate link with a larger set of transactions which do not have the same nature (i.e., both taxed and exempt transactions).[84] Where such a direct and immediate link between the costs and the taxable person's 'economic activity as a whole'[85] can be found, the costs are 'general costs'.[86] General costs, in fact, form part of a taxable person's overhead and are, therefore, as such, component parts of the price of its products.[87] If the costs are to be considered as forming part of the general costs associated with the taxable person's overall economic activities, the corresponding VAT is proportionally deductible (pro rata deduction; *see* section 10.4).

10.3.1 Criteria to Establish a Direct and Immediate Link with Output Transactions[88]

In *Midland Bank*, the CJEU was asked to clarify the nature of the direct and immediate link.[89]

Midland Bank had supplied financial services to a customer outside the EU who was in the process of taking over another business. Under (what is now) Article 169(1)(c) VAT Directive, such financial services gave a right of deduction. During the

82. CJEU 26 May 2005, Case C-465/03 *Kretztechnik AG v Finanzamt Linz*, ECLI:EU:C:2005:320, para. 35.
83. CJEU 29 October 2009, Case C-29/08 *Skatteverket v AB SKF*, ECLI:EU:C:2009:665, para. 57. *See also* D. Ramsdahl Jensen & H. Stensgaard, 'Partial Deduction of Input VAT in the Common VAT System in Europe', in T. Ecker, M. Lang & I. Lejeune (eds), *The Future of Indirect Taxation* (Wolters Kluwer 2012), pp. 690-693.
84. CJEU 29 October 2009, Case C-29/08 *Skatteverket v AB SKF*, ECLI:EU:C:2009:665, para. 60.
85. CJEU 26 May 2005, Case C-465/03 *Kretztechnik AG v Finanzamt Linz*, ECLI:EU:C:2005:320, para. 36.
86. Cf. CJEU 29 October 2009, Case C-29/08 *Skatteverket v AB SKF*, ECLI:EU:C:2009:665, para. 65.
87. CJEU 6 April 1995, Case C-4/94 *BLP Group plc v Commissioners of Customs & Excise*, ECLI:EU:C:1995:107, para. 25; CJEU 8 June 2000, Case C-98/98 *Commissioners of Customs and Excise v Midland Bank plc*, ECLI:EU:C:2000:300, para. 31 and CJEU 18 October 2018, Case C-153/17 *Commissioners for Her Majesty's Revenue and Customs v Volkswagen Financial Services (UK) Ltd*, ECLI:EU:C:2018:845.
88. A.J. van Doesum & H.W.M. van Kesteren, *De onlosmakelijke samenhang tussen kosten en belastbare handelingen* (2012) 6960 Weekblad Fiscaal Recht, pp. 885-897 and A.J. van Doesum, *Ondanks een onlosmakelijke samenhang, Correcties op de onlosmakelijke samenhang als norm voor het recht op aftrek van voorbelasting* (Inaugural speech) (Kluwer 2012).
89. CJEU 8 June 2000, Case C-98/98 *Midland Bank plc v Commissioners of Customs and Excise*, ECLI:EU:C:2000:300, para. 25.

process of taking over of the business by Midland Bank's customer, something went wrong. The customer sued Midland Bank for damages. Midland Bank hired a lawyer to assist in the lawsuit. The lawyer charged VAT on his services to Midland Bank. The latter deducted the VAT, stating that the lawyer's services related to the financial services outside the EU which it had supplied to its customer. However, the tax authorities took the position that from a VAT perspective, the costs of the lawyer could not be attributed to the financial services because the costs could not be a component part of the cost of the financial services. After all, the costs were incurred at a later moment than the moment when the financial services had been supplied. Therefore, the tax authorities argued that the costs could only be a component part of Midland Bank's overall activities (i.e., they were part of Midland Bank's overheads). Indeed, the CJEU ruled that the costs could only be general costs because they could only relate to services in the future. Midland Bank could deduct the VAT on the lawyer's services on a pro rata basis.

Even though the CJEU indicated that it would not be realistic to attempt to be more specific in respect of the determination of a direct and immediate link,[90] from Midland Bank and other CJEU case law, criteria can be distilled on the basis of which the existence of a direct and immediate link can be checked. In our view, the CJEU uses the following criteria to determine whether a direct and immediate link exists:[91]

(1) The *cost inclusion* criterion.[92] Have the costs been included in the prices of the taxed output transactions?
(2) The *use or intention* criterion.[93] Have the costs been made with a view to carrying out taxed output transactions? Or, phrased differently, have the goods and services which the taxable person purchased been used to carry out taxed transactions?
(3) The *causal connection* criterion.[94] Had the costs also been made if the person were not engaged in that specific economic activity and would that specific economic activity also have been carried out if the taxable person had not made the costs?

In most cases, a combination of two, or preferably all, criteria should be used to establish whether and to what extent a direct and immediate link exists between the costs and the (taxed) output transactions. We believe that the intention or use criterion is in this respect the most determinative touchstone because the text of Article 168 VAT

90. *Ibid.*
91. A.J. van Doesum & H.W.M. van Kesteren, *De onlosmakelijke samenhang tussen kosten en belastbare handelingen* (2012) 6960 Weekblad Fiscaal Recht, pp. 885-897.
92. *See*, for instance, CJEU 29 October 2009, Case C-29/08 *AB SKF v Skatteverket*, ECLI: EU:C:2009:665.
93. CJEU 8 June 2000, Case C-98/98 *Midland Bank plc v Commissioners of Customs and Excise*, ECLI:EU:C:2000:300, para. 33.
94. CJEU 8 February 2007, Case C-435/05 *Investrand BV v Staatssecretaris van Financiën*, ECLI: EU:C:2007:87, para. 33.

Directive requires that the input transactions must be *used* for taxed output transactions. In this view, the other two criteria are subservient to the main criterion (rather as auxiliary criteria) and can be used to established eventually that the input transactions were actually used for the output transactions concerned.[95]

10.3.1.1 The Cost Inclusion Criterion

The cost inclusion criterion seems to be directly based on Article 1(2) VAT Directive, which states that VAT is chargeable on the price of goods or services 'after deduction of the amount of VAT borne directly by the various cost components'. Clearly, this suggests that the costs should be component parts of the prices of (taxed) output transactions. Hence, the cost inclusion criterion entails that the costs relating to the goods or services which he has utilized as a consequence of making a deductible transaction are part of the cost components of that transaction.[96]

In *Midland Bank*, the outcome of the cost inclusion criterion was that the costs could not be regarded as general costs because the costs (of the lawyer's services) were incurred *after* the financial services giving rise to deduction of input VAT had been supplied. Generally, cost components must have arisen before the taxable person carried out the taxable transactions to which they relate.[97] From *Volkswagen Financial Services UK*, it follows in this respect that the cost inclusion criterion cannot be used to make general costs into direct costs by including all those general costs in the price of a specific taxable output transaction, whereas the costs are actually used for multiple (both taxable and exempt) output transactions.[98]

10.3.1.2 The Use or Intention Criterion

The use or intention criterion is reflected by the text of Article 168 VAT Directive because that provision allows for deduction of input VAT in so far as the goods and services are *used* for the purposes of taxed transactions. In *Midland Bank*, the use or intention criterion did not indicate that a direct and immediate link existed between the costs and the output transactions (financial services). Admittedly, Midland Bank did not use the lawyer's services with a view to supplying the financial services, but rather with a view to managing the (adverse) consequences of these financial services. As regards the test against the use or intention criterion, the CJEU considered:

> a taxable person cannot deduct in its entirety the VAT charged on input services where they have been utilised not for the purpose of carrying out a deductible transaction but in the context of activities which are no more than the consequence

95. A.J. van Doesum & H.W.M. van Kesteren, *De onlosmakelijke samenhang tussen kosten en belastbare handelingen* (2012) 6960 Weekblad Fiscaal Recht, p. 97.
96. CJEU 8 June 2000, Case C-98/98 *Midland Bank plc v Commissioners of Customs and Excise*, ECLI:EU:C:2000:300, para. 32.
97. *Ibid.*, para. 30.
98. CJEU 18 October 2018, Case C-153/17 *Commissioners for Her Majesty's Revenue and Customs v Volkswagen Financial Services (UK) Ltd*, ECLI:EU:C:2018:845.

of making such a transaction, unless that person can show by means of objective evidence that the expenditure involved in the acquisition of such services is part of the various cost components of the output transaction.[99]

Even though it is less explicit, the use or intention criterion also seems to have played a decisive role in *INZO*, *Schloßstraße* and *Ghent Coal*.[100] In *INZO*, the planned economic activity was not realized, in *Schloßstraße* and *Ghent Coal*, the planned taxed transaction was not realized for reasons beyond the control of the taxable persons. Yet, in all three cases, the input VAT was deductible because the costs were made with a view to carrying out taxed transactions. The mere fact that in the end, the taxed transactions were not effectuated – also making it impossible to include the costs in the prices of those planned transactions – did not alter this conclusion.[101] Another example of the CJEU applying the use or intention criterion is the case *Kopalnia Odkrywkowa Polski Trawertyn*.[102] Here the CJEU ruled that national legislation which permits neither partners nor their partnership to exercise the right to deduct input VAT on investment costs incurred by those partners, before the creation and registration of the partnership, 'for the purposes of and with the view to its economic activity' is not in line with the VAT Directive.

The use or intention criterion cannot only be used in cases in which a taxable person purchases goods or services *prior* to carrying out (taxed) output transactions but also if a taxable person makes costs *after* he carried out the (taxed) output transactions. For example, a taxable person who incurred costs after he had finished his economic activity could still deduct the VAT on those costs on the basis of the use or intention criterion.[103]

Sometimes, the use or intention criterion takes the form of an 'investment criterion'. This criterion entails that it must be checked to what extent a taxable person carries out an activity (e.g., the issue of new shares) for the benefit of its economic activity in general.[104] We believe that on the basis of the CJEU case law as it stands, the investment criterion can only be used where the costs relate to non-taxable activities.[105]

99. *Ibid.*, para. 33.
100. CJEU 29 February 1996, Case C-110/94 *Intercommunale voor zeewaterontzilting (INZO) v Belgian State*, ECLI:EU:C:1996:67; CJEU 8 June 2000, Case C-396/98 *Grundstückgemeinschaft Schloßstraße GbR v Finanzamt Paderborn*, ECLI:EU:C:2000:303 and CJEU 15 January 1998, Case C-37/95 *Belgische Staat v Ghent Coal Terminal NV*, ECLI:EU:C:1998:1.
101. It should be noted that the principle of legal certainty also played an important role in these cases.
102. CJEU 1 March 2012, Case C-280/10 *Kopalnia Odkrywkowa Polski Trawertyn P. Granatowicz, M. Wąsiewicz spółka jawna v Dyrektor Izby Skarbowej w Poznaniu*, ECLI:EU:C:2012:107.
103. CJEU 3 March 2005, Case C-32/03 *I/S Fini H v Skatteministeriet*, ECLI:EU:C:2005:128.
104. CJEU 26 May 2005, Case C-465/03 *Kretztechnik AG v Finanzamt Linz*, ECLI:EU:C:2005:320, para. 36, *see also* CJEU 8 November 2018, Case C-502/17 *C&D Foods Acquisition ApS v Skatteministeriet*, ECLI:EU:C:2018:888.
105. Possibly, *AB SKF* is an exception in this regard, as it relates to a taxable (exempt) supply of shares. *See* CJEU 29 October 2009, Case C-29/08 *AB SKF v Skatteverket*, ECLI:EU:C:2009:665.

10.3.1.3 The Causal Connection Criterion

The causal connection (or 'legal cause') criterion appears to be based on generally accepted principles of (EU) law to establish the relation between an event (the cause) and another event (the effect).

As regards the determination of a direct and immediate link between costs and (the prices of) output transactions, it would seem that it is a relevant criterion if the taxable person incurs costs *after* he carried out the output transactions. Indeed, it would seem that if a taxable person incurs costs *before* he carries out the output transactions, the cost inclusion and the use or intention criteria will be sufficient to test whether the link can be established. In *Midland Bank*, the CJEU used the causal connection criterion to establish that the costs had been caused by the output transactions (the financial services). Even though the CJEU did not explicitly say so, it seems that the causal connection test was the decisive criterion, in that case, to consider the costs as general costs.

In *Iberdrola*, the CJEU ruled that Iberdrola could deduct input VAT on costs incurred for the construction or improvement of a pump station owned by a third party (a Bulgarian municipality), even when that third party enjoys the results of those services free of charge and – as such – the costs incurred are used both by the taxable person and by the third party in the context of their economic activity.[106] However, Iberdrola could only deduct in so far as the services purchased did not exceed that which was *necessary* to allow them to carry out the taxable output transactions. Although it will not always be clear wat is necessary for a specific economic activity, Iberdrola shows that there should be a sufficient causal connection between the costs incurred and the taxable output of the taxable person incurring those costs. This means that the causal connection criterion may prevent deduction in cases where a third party benefits from costs incurred by another taxable person. This may particularly be true in situations where the third party in itself is not a taxable person or in any case lacks a right to recover input VAT.[107]

This type of application of the causal connection criterion is also apparent in *Wolfram Becker*.[108] In *Wolfram Becker*, a German prosecuting authority brought criminal proceedings against two managing directors whom it suspected of benefiting, prior to the conclusion of a building contract, from confidential information concerning the tenders submitted by competing undertakings and of having, therefore, been able to submit the most advantageous tender. Mr Becker was the majority shareholder of the limited company that had won the tender. The company took upon itself the legal costs of defending the criminal proceedings against Mr Becker. One of the questions asked of the CJEU was whether a causal connection existed between the (costs of the)

106. CJEU 14 September 2017, Case C-132/16 *Iberdrola Inmobiliaria Real Estate Investments EOOD*, ECLI:EU:C:2017:683.
107. *See also* CJEU 16 September 2020, Case C-528/19 *Mitteldeutsche Hartstein-Industrie*, ECLI: EU:C:2020:712; CJEU 4 October 2024, Case C-475/23, *Voestalpine Giesserei Linz*, ECLI: EU:C:2024:866. These judgments contain outcomes similar to *Iberdrola*.
108. CJEU 21 February 2013, Case C-104/12 *Finanzamt Köln-Nord v Wolfram Becker*, ECLI: EU:C:2013:99.

services of the lawyers and the company's activities. According to the CJEU, such a connection did not exist because there was no legal link between the criminal proceedings and the company.[109] Therefore, the lawyer's services had to be considered to have been performed entirely outside the company's taxable activities.[110] Similarly, in *Finanzamt R*, no right to deduct input VAT existed for a holding company that incurred VAT on services obtained from third parties and supplied to subsidiaries in return for the grant of a share in the general profit, where the input services have direct and immediate links not with the holding company's own transactions but with the largely tax-exempt activities of the subsidiaries and are as such not a part of the general costs of the holding company itself.[111]

10.3.2 The Direct and Immediate Link Test in Case of Non-taxable Activities

According to the CJEU, from a VAT perspective, it is impossible to attribute costs to a non-taxable activity (a supply or activity that in itself does not constitute a taxable transaction or remains outside the scope of VAT)[112,113] because it is considered to be non-existent. However, it follows from the application of the use or intention criterion that if costs that are incurred for a non-taxable activity are incurred for the benefit of the economic activity as a whole, the VAT on those costs can be recovered as part of the general costs.[114] In these situations, the non-taxable activity is in the scope of the economic activity as a whole, on the basis of which fiscal neutrality requires that input VAT should be recoverable.

Sometimes, it is even possible to find a link not just with the economic activity as a whole, but more precisely with a clearly defined part of the taxable person's economic activities. Then, the (general) costs form part of the overheads of that part of the business. If all the transactions relating to that part are subject to VAT, the taxable person may deduct all the VAT charged on his costs of acquiring the goods and services.[115]

In situations where costs are incurred for a non-economic activity – an activity that does not lead to taxable output transactions, and is outside the scope of the

109. *See also* T. Ecker, 'VAT Deductions', in M. Lang, et al. (eds), *ECJ: Recent Developments in Value Added Tax, the Evolution of European VAT Jurisprudence and Its Role in the EU Common VAT System* (Linde 2014), p. 343.
110. *Ibid.*, para. 31.
111. CJEU 8 September 2022, Case C-98/21 *Finanzamt R (Déduction de TVA liée à une contribution d'associé)*, ECLI:EU:C:2022:645.
112. Examples of non-taxable activities carried out by a taxable person are the issue of shares and the transfer of a going concern under Articles 19 and 29 VAT Directive.
113. CJEU 30 March 2006, Case C-184/04 *Uudenkaupungin kaupunki*, ECLI:EU:C:2006:214.
114. CJEU 22 February 2001, Case C-408/98 *Abbey National plc v Commissioners of Customs & Excise*, ECLI:EU:C:2001:110; CJEU 27 September 2001, Case C-16/00 *Cibo Participations SA v Directeur régional des impôts du Nord-Pas-de-Calais* [2001] ECR I-6663; CJEU 26 May 2005, Case C-465/03 *Kretztechnik AG v Finanzamt Linz*, ECLI:EU:C:2005:320 and CJEU 17 October 2018, Case C-249/17 *Ryanair Ltd v The Revenue Commissioners*, ECLI:EU:C:2018:834.
115. CJEU 22 February 2001, Case C-408/98 *Abbey National plc v Commissioners of Customs & Excise*, ECLI:EU:C:2001:110, para. 40 and CJEU 17 October 2018, Case C-249/17 *Ryanair Ltd v The Revenue Commissioners*, ECLI:EU:C:2018:834, para. 31.

economic activity of the taxable person – deduction of input VAT, as a general rule, is not possible.[116] From a fiscal neutrality perspective, this makes sense, as non-economic activities should be seen as activities undertaken by a taxable person, outside of its capacity as a taxable person.

10.4 PROPORTIONAL DEDUCTION ('PRO RATA DEDUCTION')

In section 10.3, we explained that direct costs are the costs of purchases of goods or services which are exclusively used for either taxed or exempt activities. They hold a direct link with a specific output transaction. The VAT on direct costs is fully deductible if the output transaction is taxed. The VAT on direct costs is not deductible at all if the output transaction is exempt under Articles 132-135 VAT Directive.[117]

Costs of purchases of goods or services that cannot be linked to a specific output transaction can still give rise to a right to deduct if they have a direct and immediate link with the economic activity of the taxable person as a whole. Typically, these costs, which are attributable to both the taxed *and* the exempt activities of a taxable person, are referred to as 'general costs'. The VAT on general costs is, in principle, deductible on the basis of the ratio between the taxed and the exempt supplies of the taxable person. This is called the 'proportional deduction' or 'pro rata deduction'.

In this section, we discuss this mechanism of proportional deduction.

10.4.1 Pro Rata: Main Rule (Turnover)

The provisions concerning the pro rata are intended to enable a taxable person who acquires goods or services in order to carry on both taxed and exempt activities to fully deduct the amount of the VAT paid on the acquisition of those goods or services which is *deemed to correspond* to the proportion used for the purpose of the taxed activities.[118] The pro rata thus only offers a rough estimate of the use of mixed costs for taxed and exempt transactions.[119]

According to Article 173 VAT Directive, VAT shall be deductible in the case of goods or services used by a taxable person both for transactions in respect of which VAT is deductible pursuant to Articles 168-170 VAT Directive and for transactions in respect of which VAT is not deductible, for only such proportion of the VAT as is attributable to the former transactions. Article 174(1) VAT Directive further details this

116. CJEU 30 March 2006, Case C-184/04 *Uudenkaupungin kaupunki*, ECLI:EU:C:2006:214; CJEU 28 May 2019, Case C-566/17 *Związek Gmin Zagłębia Miedziowego w Polkowicach v Szef Krajowej Administracji Skarbowej*, ECLI:EU:C:2019:390, para. 28 and CJEU 3 July 2019, Case C-316/18 *Commissioners for Her Majesty's Revenue and Customs v The Chancellor, Masters and Scholars of the University of Cambridge*, ECLI:EU:C:2019:559.
117. There are some exceptions. For example, Article 169(1)(c) VAT Directive.
118. CJEU 6 March 2008, Case C-98/07 *Nordania Finans A/S BG Factoring A/S v Skatteministeriet*, ECLI:EU:C:2008:144, para. 20.
119. For example, if a taxable person purchases a service that he uses 50% for taxed transactions and 50% for VAT-exempt transactions, for which his (single) overall pro rata would be 80%, he still would be allowed to deduct 80% of the input VAT.

mechanism. The result of these two provisions is that, as a main rule, the pro rata shall be made up of a fraction comprising as numerator, the total amount (exclusive of VAT) of taxed turnover per year and as denominator, the total amount (exclusive of VAT) of total turnover per year. In our view, the result of these provisions should be that, in principle, each taxable person has a single turnover-based pro rata, regardless of the variety of the transactions carried out in the different parts of his business. Indeed, Article 173(1), second paragraph VAT Directive states that the deductible proportion shall be determined for *all* the transactions carried out by the taxable person. However, it seems to follow from *Morgan Stanley* that multiple pro rata percentages could be applicable at a single taxable person.[120] In any case, this is true if such taxable person has (fixed) establishments in different Member States and costs are incurred that are used (also) for the activities of an establishment in a different Member State. Similarly, in specific cases (*see* most notably *Abbey National I* and *Ryanair*), it seems possible to find a link not just with the economic activity as a whole but more precisely with a clearly defined part of the taxable person's economic activities. Then, the (general) costs form part of the overheads of that specific part of the business. If all the transactions relating to that part are subject to VAT, the taxable person may deduct all the VAT charged on his costs of acquiring the goods and services.[121] In this sense, the CJEU seems to tend to an interpretation of Article 173(1) second paragraph VAT Directive that leads to a more precise, fragmented application of the general pro rata. Although it could be argued that fiscal neutrality is served by that approach, it is, in our view, questionable how such an approach fits in the text of the provision.

In our view, the use of the word 'transactions' in the phrases 'for transactions in respect of which VAT is deductible' (Article 173(1) VAT Directive) and 'attributable to transactions in respect of which VAT is deductible' (Article 174 VAT Directive) indicates that the importation and the ICA (although being taxable *events*) are excluded from this calculation. Thus, the deductible proportion must be exclusively based on the turnover proportions of the taxed and the exempt supplies of goods and services.

10.4.1.1 Turnover to Be Taken into Account[122]

The method for calculating the deductible proportion is detailed in Article 174(1) VAT Directive. It specifies that the numerator consists of turnover attributable to taxed transactions and that the denominator consists of the same amount *plus* the turnover attributable to exempted transactions.

120. CJEU 24 January 2019, Case C-165/17 *Morgan Stanley & Co International plc v Ministre de l'Économie et des Finances*, ECLI:EU:C:2019:58, para. 44.
121. CJEU 22 February 2001, Case C-408/98 *Abbey National plc v Commissioners of Customs & Excise* ECLI:EU:C:2001:110, para. 40. *See also* CJEU 17 October 2018, Case C-249/17 *Ryanair Ltd v The Revenue Commissioners*, ECLI:EU:C:2018:834, para. 31.
122. *See* H.W.M. van Kesteren & M.M. Gabriel, *Calculation of the (Pre-) Pro Rata under EU VAT Law* (2011) 22/5 International VAT Monitor, pp. 332-337 https://doi.org/10.59403/237cm58.

Member States *may* include subsidies, other than subsidies directly linked to the price of the supply, in the denominator.[123] What may not be taken into account in the calculation is the amount of:

- turnover attributable to supplies of capital goods used by the taxable person for the purposes of his business;
- turnover attributable to incidental real estate and financial transactions; and
- turnover attributable to the transactions specified in Article 135(1)(b)-(g) VAT Directive insofar as those transactions are incidental.[124]

The objective of Article 174(2) VAT Directive (previously Article 19(2) Sixth VAT Directive) is apparent from the Explanatory Memorandum to the proposal for the Sixth VAT Directive,[125] according to which:

> [t]he factors mentioned in this paragraph must be excluded from the calculation of the proportion lest, being unrepresentative of the taxable person's business activity, they should deprive the amount of any real significance. Such is the case with sales of capital items and real estate and financial transactions which are only ancillary operations, that is to say, which are only of secondary importance in relation to the total turnover of the business. These factors are only excluded if they are not part of the usual business activity of the taxable person.

According to the Explanatory Memorandum, the Community (now: Union) legislature thus intended to exclude from the calculation of the proportion the turnover attributable to incidental transactions where that transaction is of an unusual nature in relation to the normal activities of the taxable person concerned and does not, therefore, require the use of goods or services for mixed use in a way that is proportionate to the turnover which it generates.

10.4.1.1.1 Exclusion: Supplies of Capital Goods

In principle, turnover generated through the supply of capital goods is excluded from the pro rata calculation. With a view to the purpose of this rule of law, which is to exclude from the pro rata those transactions which are of an unusual nature in relation to the normal activities, in *Nordania Finans*, the CJEU was asked to provide a further explanation.[126]

123. Subsidies directly linked to the price of the supply will probably be taken into account anyway since they form remuneration for consideration.
124. Article 174(2) VAT Directive.
125. Which was submitted by the Commission of the European Communities to the Council of the European Communities on 29 June 1973 (*see Bulletin of the European Communities*, supplement 11/73, p. 19).
126. CJEU 6 March 2008, Case C-98/07 *Nordania Finans A/S and BG Factoring A/S v Skatteministeriet*, ECLI:EU:C:2008:144.

The referring court asked whether the notion of 'capital goods used by the taxable person for the purposes of his business' included vehicles which a leasing undertaking purchased with a view to leasing them and subsequently selling them upon the termination of the respective leasing contracts. The CJEU answered that in those circumstances, the notion of 'capital goods used by the leasing company for the purposes of his business' cannot include capital goods (cars) the sale of which is, for the taxable person concerned, *in the nature of a normal business activity*. For the leasing company in question, the purchase and subsequent sale of such goods (cars) means that it has to use goods and services for mixed use on an everyday basis. Since that sale is part of the normal taxable activities of the taxable person, the turnover attributable to it must be taken into account in the calculation of the deductible proportion.

10.4.1.1.2 Exclusion: Incidental Financial Transactions

Income, such as interest, obtained from financial transactions which is of an incidental nature should, in principle, be excluded from the pro rata calculation. However, if the financial activity constitutes the direct, permanent and necessary extension of a taxable activity, it cannot be characterized as an 'incidental' (financial) transaction.[127] Then it should be included in the pro rata calculation.

Interest must also be excluded where the loan activities do not constitute economic activities.[128] This is, for example, the case if a holding company 'merely reinvests dividends received from its subsidiaries and outside the scope of VAT in loans to those subsidiaries'.[129]

10.4.1.1.3 Exclusion: Dividend and Other Income from Non-taxable Activities

Some forms of income of the business are not excluded on the basis of Article 174(2) VAT Directive, but for reasons other than being incidental in nature. Some forms of income cannot be characterized as a consideration for a supply, and consequently should not be taken into account when calculating the denominator of the pro rata key. The denominator of the turnover fraction should only include the totality of turnover resulting from economic activities. As far as dividends are concerned, the CJEU has considered that '[s]ince the receipt of dividends is not the consideration for any economic activity within the meaning of the Sixth Directive, it does not fall within the

127. CJEU 11 July 1996, Case C-306/94 *Régie Dauphinoise – Cabinet A. Forest SARL v Ministre du Budget*, ECLI:EU:C:1996:290, para. 22 and CJEU 29 October 2009, Case C-174/08 *NCC Construction Danmark A/S v Skatteministeriet*, ECLI:EU:C:2009:669, para. 35.
128. CJEU 14 November 2000, Case C-142/99 *Floridienne SA and Berginvest SA v Belgian State*, ECLI:EU:C:2000:623, para. 32.
129. *Ibid.*, para. 30.

scope of VAT'.[130] For that reason, the CJEU ruled that 'dividends must be excluded from the calculation of the deductible proportion'.[131]

10.4.2 Pro Rata: Special Rules (Optional Provisions)

The main rule on the calculation of the deductible proportion simply on the basis of the turnover ratios only provides for a rather rough estimate of the actual use of goods and services for the taxed and exempt transactions. The only explanation for this rough method lies in practical and tax efficiency reasons. Indeed, it is hardly imaginable that a taxable person would want to exactly attribute costs of each and every individual purchase to his taxed and exempt supplies if he uses the good or service for both types of transactions.

Yet, the application of the main rule on the calculation of the deductible proportion may be considered as being too rough. For that reason, Article 173(2) VAT Directive offers the Member States some special rules to calculate the deductible proportion with greater accuracy.[132] If in such a Member State, the calculation of the deductible proportion on the basis of the default turnover-based method is less accurate than one of the methods based on Article 173(2) VAT Directive, as implemented by that Member State, that method can take precedence over the default turnover-based method.[133] We note that these are optional provisions to the Member States. They may authorize or even require taxable persons to determine different proportions, such as proportions related to business sectors or on the basis of use (Article 173(2) VAT Directive).[134] It should be noted that an alternative method should be able to guarantee a more precise result than the turnover method in order to take

130. CJEU 22 June 1993, Case C-333/91 *Sofitam (Satam) S.A. v Ministre du budget*, ECLI:EU:C:1993:261, para. 13. *See also* CJEU 27 September 2001, Case C-16/00 *Cibo Participations SA v Directeur régional des impôts du Nord-Pas-de-Calais*, ECLI:EU:C:2001:495, paras 39 and 44; CJEU 14 November 2000, Case C-142/99 *Floridienne SA and Berginvest SA v Belgian State*, ECLI:EU:C:2000:623, para. 32 and CJEU 29 April 2004, Case C-77/01 *Empresa de Desenvolvimento Mineiro SGPS SA (EDM) v Fazenda Pública*, ECLI:EU:C:2004:243.
131. CJEU 22 June 1993, Case C-333/91 *Sofitam (Satam) S.A. v Ministre du budget*, ECLI:EU:C:1993:261, para. 14.
132. The purpose of Article 173(2) VAT Directive (previously Article 17(5), third subpara. Sixth Directive) is to allow Member States to take account of the specific characteristics of some activities of taxable persons in order to achieve greater accuracy in determining the extent of the right to deduct. *See*: CJEU 18 December 2008, Case C-488/07 *Royal Bank of Scotland plc v The Commissioners of Her Majesty's Revenue & Customs*, ECLI:EU:C:2008:750; CJEU 8 November 2012, Case C-511/10 *Finanzamt Hildesheim v BLC Baumarkt GmbH & Co. KG.*, ECLI-:EU:C:2012:689; CJEU 10 July 2014, Case C-183/13 *Fazenda Pública v Banco Mais SA*, ECLI:EU:C:2014:2056 and CJEU 9 June 2016, Case C-332/14 *Wolfgang und Dr. Wilfried Rey Grundstücksgemeinschaft GbR v Finanzamt Krefeld*, ECLI:EU:C:2016:417.
133. For example: CJEU 10 July 2014, Case C-183/13 *Fazenda Pública v Banco Mais SA*, ECLI:EU:C:2014:2056.
134. From the explanatory memorandum to the proposal for a Sixth Directive, it follows that this discretion is conferred on Member States as a means to avoid inequalities which 'may work to the detriment or to the advantage of the taxable person' (Proposal for a Sixth Council Directive on the harmonization of Member States concerning turnover taxes COM (73) 950, 20 June 1973, Article 14, para. 5).

precedence. This does not mean that the alternative method should also be the *most* precise method possible in the situation at hand.[135]

10.4.3 The Method of Calculation of the Deductible Proportion

In the year in which the goods and services are purchased, it will most commonly not be known to what extent they will be used for taxed transactions. In other words, the deductible proportion is usually unknown upfront. For that reason, Article 175 VAT Directive determines that the calculation must be based on the turnover of the *previous* year. The deductible proportion is to be rounded up to a figure not exceeding the next whole number.[136]

The provisional proportion for a year must be calculated on the basis of the preceding year's transactions. In the absence of any such transactions to refer to, or where they were insignificant in amount, the deductible proportion must be estimated provisionally, under the supervision of the tax authorities, by the taxable person on the basis of his own forecasts. This means that the taxable person has to show to and discuss with the authorities the way he calculates his deductible proportion based on his estimations.[137] Naturally, the Member States must ensure that at the end of the year – as soon as the final figures are present – the provisional calculations are adjusted on the basis of the definitive figures (Article 175(3) VAT Directive).

10.5 PROPORTIONAL DEDUCTION IN CASE OF NON-ECONOMIC TRANSACTIONS ('PRE-PRO RATA MECHANISM')

The VAT on costs which have been made with respect to non-economic activities is, in principle, not deductible.[138] *See* section 10.3.2.

This raises the question of what happens if a taxable person incurs costs which relate to both his taxable (taxed and/or exempt) activities and his non-economic (out of the scope of VAT and of the economic activity as a whole) activities. In such a situation, the pro rata mechanism of Article 173 and Article 174 VAT Directive cannot

135. CJEU 9 June 2016, Case C-332/14 *Wolfgang und Dr. Wilfried Rey Grundstücksgemeinschaft GbR v Finanzamt Krefeld*, ECLI:EU:C:2016:417, para. 33 and CJEU 18 October 2018, Case C-153/17 *Commissioners for Her Majesty's Revenue and Customs v Volkswagen Financial Services (UK) Ltd*, ECLI:EU:C:2018:845, para. 53.

136. Member States are not required to apply the rounding up rule where the proportion of input tax deductible is calculated in accordance with one of the special methods in (what is now) Article 173(2) VAT Directive. CJEU 18 December 2008, Case C-488/07 *Royal Bank of Scotland plc v The Commissioners of Her Majesty's Revenue & Customs*, ECLI:EU:C:2008:750.

137. Member States may retain the rules in force at 1 January 1979 or, in the case of Member States which acceded to the Community after that date, on the date of their accession.

138. CJEU 30 March 2006, Case C-184/04 *Uudenkaupungin kaupunki*, ECLI:EU:C:2006:214; CJEU 28 May 2019, Case C-566/17 *Związek Gmin Zagłębia Miedziowego w Polkowicach v Szef Krajowej Administracji Skarbowej*, ECLI:EU:C:2019:390, para. 28 and CJEU 3 July 2019, Case C-316/18 *Commissioners for Her Majesty's Revenue and Customs v The Chancellor, Masters and Scholars of the University of Cambridge*, ECLI:EU:C:2019:559.

be applied. After all, the pro rata mechanism only serves as a tool to apportion general costs attributable to taxed and exempt supplies.

In *Securenta*, the CJEU ruled that if a taxable person simultaneously carries out economic activities, taxed or exempt, and non-economic activities outside the scope of VAT, deduction of the VAT relating to expenditure connected with the non-economic activity is allowed only to the extent that that expenditure is attributable to the taxpayer's economic activity.[139] This implies that a 'special' deductible proportion must be applied to exclude non-taxable activities from the system of deduction of input VAT. For that reason, in practice, this is referred to as the application of the 'pre-pro rata'.[140]

Since the VAT Directive does not provide for any rules on the calculation of the pre-pro rata, it is in the discretion of the Member States to provide for a method of calculation which objectively reflects the part of the input expenditure actually to be attributed, respectively, to the taxable and non-taxable activities. However, when exercising this obligation, Member States must have regard to the aims and broad logic of the VAT Directive.[141] From *Gemeente Dinkelland*, it can be derived that EU law does not preclude a Member State from authorizing or requiring a taxable person to establish, by means of an allocation key drawn up under the responsibility of such taxable person, the detailed rules for calculating the pre-pro rata.[142]

10.6 ADJUSTMENT OF DEDUCTIONS

In this section we discuss the system of adjustment of deductions.

10.6.1 The Purpose of the System of Adjustment of Deductions

Articles 184-192 VAT Directive set out the rules on the system of adjustments of deductions. According to the CJEU, this is an essential element of the VAT system. Its purpose is to ensure the accuracy of deductions and hence, the neutrality of the tax burden.[143]

139. CJEU 13 March 2008, Case C-437/06 *Securenta Göttinger Immobilienanlagen und Vermögensmanagement AG v Finanzamt Göttingen*, ECLI:EU:C:2008:166, para. 34.
140. *See* with respect of the origin of this term: A.J. van Doesum, *Contractuele samenwerkingsverbanden in de btw (dissertation)* (Kluwer 2009), p. 252.
141. CJEU 13 March 2008, Case C-437/06 *Securenta Göttinger Immobilienanlagen und Vermögensmanagement AG v Finanzamt Göttingen*, ECLI:EU:C:2008:166, para. 34 and CJEU 28 May 2019, Case C-566/17 *Związek Gmin Zagłębia Miedziowego w Polkowicach v Szef Krajowej Administracji Skarbowej*, ECLI:EU:C:2019:390.
142. CJEU 22 February 2024, Case C-647/22 *Gemeente Dinkelland*, ECLI:EU:C:2024:147.
143. For example, CJEU 30 March 2006, Case C-184/04 *Uudenkaupungin kaupunki*, ECLI:EU:C:2006:214, para. 26.

10.6.2 The Scope of the System of Adjustment of Deductions

The system of adjustments cannot create a right of deduction.[144] The right to make a deduction is dealt with in other provisions of the VAT Directive (the main provision is Article 168 VAT Directive). The provisions on the system of adjustments do no more than establish the procedure for calculating the adjustments to the initial deduction. They cannot, therefore, give rise to any right to deduct or convert the tax paid by a taxable person in respect of his non-taxable transactions into a tax that is deductible.[145] They also cannot give rise to any right of deduction if a public body purchases goods in its capacity as a public body (not in its capacity of a taxable person) but decides to use the goods for its taxed activities as a taxable person at a later moment.[146]

It is important to realize that the system of adjustment of deductions, in principle, only applies when there are changes in the ratio of use for taxed and exempt transactions. Changes in the ratio of use for taxable (economic) and non-taxable (non-economic) activities, in principle, are not covered by the system of adjustment of deductions.[147] The determination of methods and criteria for apportioning input VAT between economic and non-economic activities is left to the discretion of the Member States who, when exercising that discretion, must have regard to the aims and broad logic of the VAT Directive and, on that basis, provide for a method of calculation which objectively reflects the part of the input expenditure actually to be attributed, respectively, to those two types of activity.[148] However, adjustments are possible if the capital asset in question was purchased in the capacity of a taxable person, but was used initially for non-economic activities.[149]

The adjustment system, in principle, cannot be applied to changes in the use of a business asset for business and for private purposes. The adjustment system is not an alternative to applying the deemed supplies to correct for private consumption (Articles 16 and 26 VAT Directive), and so the Member States do not have a choice between transposing either the adjustment mechanism or the mechanism for making applications for private use liable to tax since both are mandatory.[150] However, since 2011, Article 168a(1) VAT Directive has stipulated that changes in the ratio of business to private use of immovable property (and movable property if a Member State chooses to do so, *see* Article 168a(2) VAT Directive) shall be taken into account in accordance

144. CJEU 7 July 2022, Case C-194/21 *Staatssecretaris van Financiën v X*, ECLI:EU:C:2022:535.
145. CJEU 11 July 1991, Case C-97/90 *Hansgeorg Lennartz v Fianzamt München III*, ECLI:EU:C:1991:315, paras 11 and 12.
146. CJEU 2 June 2005, Case C-378/02 *Waterschap Zeeuws Vlaanderen v Staatssecretaris van Financiën*, ECLI:EU:C:2005:335 and CJEU 25 July 2018, Case C-140/17 *Szef Krajowej Administracji Skarbowej v Gmina Ryjewo*, ECLI:EU:C:2018:595.
147. *Ibid.*
148. CJEU 13 March 2008, Case C-437/06 *Securenta Göttinger Immobilienanlagen und Vermögensmanagement AG v Finanzamt Göttingen* [2008] ECR I-01597, para. 33.
149. CJEU 25 July 2018, Case C-140/17 *Szef Krajowej Administracji Skarbowej v Gmina Ryjewo*, ECLI:EU:C:2018:595.
150. CJEU 30 March 2006, Case C-184/04 *Uudenkaupungin kaupunki*, ECLI:EU:C:2006:214, para. 29.

with the principles of the system of adjustment of deductions (Article 168a(1) second paragraph VAT Directive).

10.6.3 The Functioning of the System of Adjustments

Article 184 VAT Directive determines that the initial deduction shall be adjusted where it is higher or lower than that to which the taxable person was entitled. This provision covers situations in which a taxable person initially deducts the VAT charged to him on the basis of his intended use for taxed transactions, but at a later stage it turns out that the actual use of the goods and/or services he purchased is different. For example, if a taxable person purchases a building in which he intends to carry out taxed transactions (e.g., legal advice) after two years also starts supplying exempt services (e.g., insurance services) from that building, the initial use (fully taxed) is different from the actual use in the second year (partially taxed). Then, Article 184 VAT Directive, in principle, calls for an adjustment of the VAT that was initially deducted.

Article 185 VAT Directive contains a clarification of Article 184 VAT Directive, which confirms that the purpose of the first provision is to take into account changes which occurred after the initial right of deduction was exercised. It states that adjustment shall be made, in particular, where, after the VAT return is made, there is some change in the factors used to determine the amount to be deducted, for example, where purchases are cancelled, or price reductions are obtained.

From *SEB Bankas*, it follows that Article 184 VAT Directive is applicable to cases where the initial deduction could not be made lawfully because the transaction giving rise to that deduction was exempt from VAT, and the input VAT was, therefore, unlawfully charged.[151] Article 184 VAT Directive does not cover situations in which the taxable person did not reclaim any input VAT, even though he has a right to do so.[152] As a result, it seems that Article 184 has quite a broad scope to cover corrections of different kinds.

From *Skellefteå Industrihus AB* and *Vittamed*, it follows that deducted input VAT should be adjusted if a taxable person acquires goods and services for (intended) taxable activities if those goods and services at some point have not been used - and will never be used - in the course of taxable economic activities, for example, because the shareholder of such business has decided to liquidate the company.[153] Although, prima facie, this line of reasoning may not seem unreasonable, we note that it seems to be in sharp contrast with *INZO* (*see* section 2.4.9.1). In that case, it was decided that a taxable person may deduct input VAT that it incurred with respect to goods and services for which it could objectively proof an intention to perform taxable activities and that such right to deduct could not be denied or corrected at a later stage if ultimately the intended taxable output transaction never came to be. In *Vittamed*, the

151. CJEU 11 April 2018, Case C-532/16 *Valstybine mokesčių inspekcija prie Lietuvos Respublikos finansų ministerijos v AB SEB bankas*, ECLI:EU:C:2018:228.
152. CJEU 7 July 2022, Case C-194/21 *Staatssecretaris van Financiën v X*, ECLI:EU:C:2022:535.
153. CJEU 6 October 2022, Case C-293/21 *UAB 'Vittamed technologijos', in liquidation v Valstybine mokesčių inspekcija*, ECLI:EU:C:2022:763.

Court confirms this reading of *INZO* but adds that although the right to deduct cannot be denied in these circumstances, in fact an adjustment through Articles 184 and 185 should be made if the goods and services will never be used for taxable activities. Obviously, a full right to deduct input VAT is worthless if in the end it needs to be adjusted in full.[154] As such, *Vittamed* raises some important questions. The main question is in which circumstances it should be concluded that goods and services 'will never be used for taxable activities'. In *Vittamed*, the proof for this was apparently found in the liquidation of the company, but it is unclear what other situations would justify the conclusion that goods or services 'will never be used'. In our view, from the perspective of the principle of neutrality, situations in which a taxable business incurs costs for an intended new activity but has to conclude that such activity is not economically viable after all should not be confronted with an adjustment of its deduction.

Article 186 VAT Directive simply states that the Member States shall lay down the detailed rules for applying Articles 184 and 185.

10.6.4 Transactions Remaining Totally or Partially Unpaid, Destruction, Loss or Theft, Gifts and Samples

No adjustments need be made in the case of transactions remaining totally or partially unpaid, or in the case of destruction, loss or theft of property duly proved or confirmed, or in the case of goods reserved for the purposes of making gifts of small value or of giving samples as referred to in Article 16 VAT Directive. However, in the case of transactions remaining totally or partially unpaid, or in the case of theft, Member States may require an adjustment to be made (Article 185(2) last subparagraph VAT Directive).

10.6.5 Capital Goods

With respect to capital goods, the VAT Directive contains special rules as to how to make adjustments to the initial right of deductions. In essence, this special regime for capital goods implies that during a period, which may vary from 5 to 20 years (depending on the nature of the good and choices made by the Member State in question), each year the actual right of deduction of input VAT attributable to that year must be compared to the initial right of deduction of input VAT attributable to that year (*see* for a further explanation, section 10.6.5.2).

154. *See also* M. Lamensch, *Order in Skellefteå Industrihus AB: A Reversal of the INZO, Ghent Coal Terminal and Breitsohl Jurisprudence?* (2022) 3 EC Tax Review, pp. 158-162 https://doi.org/10.54648/ecta2022016.

10.6.5.1 *The Concept of Capital Goods*

Member States may define the concept of capital goods (*see* Article 189(a) VAT Directive). However, in *VNO*, the CJEU ruled that the term 'capital good' in (what is now) Article 189(a) VAT Directive refers to goods which are used for the purposes of some business activity and are distinguishable by their durable nature and their value such that the acquisition costs are not normally treated as current expenditure but are written off over several years.[155] Consequently, the discretion of the Member States provided for in (what is now) Article 189(a) VAT Directive is indeed not unlimited:

> The Member States have a certain margin of discretion as regards the requirements which must be satisfied concerning the durability and value of the goods, together with the rules applicable for writing off, provided that they pay due regard to the existence of an essential difference between capital goods and the other goods used in the management and in the day to day running of undertakings.[156]

It appears from *VOF X* that it is conceivable that an immovable property consists of multiple capital goods. The installation of two dormer windows, a vestibule, a bathroom and a toilet in an already existing building is, in the words of the CJEU, a 'capital item'.[157]

Some services have the same characteristics as capital goods. They will be used for business purposes for longer than one year, and they are subject to depreciation for direct tax purposes. For instance, some investments in software or trademarks have similar characteristics to some durable goods. For this reason, in respect of the system of adjustments, Member States may regard as capital goods those services which have characteristics similar to those normal attributed to capital goods (Article 190 VAT Directive).

10.6.5.2 *Method of Applying the Adjustment Mechanism to Capital Goods*

As a general rule, Article 187(1) VAT Directive provides that in the case of capital goods, adjustment shall be spread over five years, including that in which the goods were acquired or manufactured. In our view, this means that during the five-year period (including the year of purchase, acquisition or manufacturing), the actual use for taxed transactions of the capital good must be compared to the initial or intended use (on which the initial deduction was based) of that capital good.

However, the word 'spread' in Article 187(1) VAT Directive already indicates that in each of those five years, only one-fifth of the VAT is adjusted. Article 187(2) VAT Directive confirms this by providing that the annual adjustment shall be made only in

155. CJEU 1 February 1977, Case 51/76 *Verbond van Nederlandse Ondernemingen v Inspecteur der Invoerrechten en Accijnzen*, ECLI:EU:C:1977:12.
156. *Ibid.*
157. CJEU 19 July 2012, Case C-334/10 *X v Staatssecretaris van Financiën*, ECLI:EU:C:2012:473, para. 25. In the English translation of the ruling, the word 'capital item' is used, suggesting that this is something else than a 'capital good'. However, in – for example – the Dutch translation, the word *investeringsgoed* (capital good) is used consistently.

respect of one-fifth of the VAT charged on the capital goods. The example below serves to clarify this.

Example

In 2022, a taxable person, acting in his capacity as a taxable person, purchased a new building. An amount of EUR 100,000 of VAT was charged in respect of that supply. The taxable person had the intention (which he could substantiate with objective evidence) of using the building for his taxed transactions. Indeed, in 2022, he used the building exclusively to supply taxed legal advisory services. In 2023, he also used the building to make exempt (insurance) services. These exempt services amounted to 25 % of his total turnover in 2023. The market for insurance services increased in 2024, and by the end of the year, 40 % of his total 2024 turnover consisted of exempt supplies.

Under these circumstances (and assuming that the adjustment period in this Member State is five years, *see* below), the adjustment system should function as follows. In 2022, the taxable person initially deducts all VAT (100 %) because he intends to exclusively use the building for his taxed transactions. Indeed, the right of deduction based on the actual use of the building in this year of purchase is identical to the right of deduction on the basis of the intended use of the building. Therefore, there is no need to make an adjustment of the deduction of input VAT in this first year. However, in 2023, the actual use of the building (25 % exempt, 75 % taxed) differs from the use of the building on which the initial deduction was based (100 % taxed). This means that an adjustment of 25% must be made. However, Article 187(2) VAT Directive states that the annual adjustment shall be made only in respect of one-fifth of the VAT charged on the capital good. Therefore, only one-fifth of EUR 100,000 VAT is to be adjusted. Since the difference between the right of deduction on the basis of the intended use in the year of purchase and the actual use in 2023 is 25 %, an adjustment of 25 % of one-fifth of EUR 100,000 = EUR 5,000. In 2024, the adjustment will be 40 % of one-fifth of EUR 100,000 = EUR 8,000. Depending on the actual use of the building in 2025 (year 4) and 2026 (year 5), again similar adjustments to the initial deduction must be made.

10.6.5.3 Alternate Adjustment Periods

In the example above, it was assumed that in the Member State in question, the adjustment period covered a period of five years, including the year of purchase, acquisition or manufacturing of the capital good. However, instead of applying this main rule, Member States may base the adjustment on a period of five full years *starting from the time at which the goods are first used*. The adjustment period applicable to immovable property (acquired as capital goods) may be extended up to 20 years (Article 187(1) second paragraph VAT Directive). From *Stichting Schoonzicht*, it follows that the Directive allows a national capital goods adjustment scheme, in which the adjustment is to be spread over several years, to provide that, in the year the goods in question are first used, where that year is also the first adjustment year, the *total* amount of the initial deduction for those capital goods is adjusted in a single step, if, when first used, it becomes apparent that that deduction deviates from the deduction which the taxable person was entitled to apply on the basis of the actual use of those goods.[158]

If a Member State chooses to apply an extended adjustment period (i.e., an adjustment period longer than five years), the annual adjustment will also have to be made in respect of the corresponding fraction of that period. For example, if a Member State applies an adjustment period of 10 years, each year an adjustment of one-tenth of the initial VAT must be made if the right of deduction on the basis of the actual use of the good in that year does not correspond to the right of deduction on the basis of the intended use in the year of purchase, or – if the Member State decided to apply a period of 10 years starting from the time at which the goods are first used – does not correspond to the actual use of the good in that first year.

10.6.5.4 *No Immediate Use of a Capital Good: Initial Deduction and Later Adjustments?*

In *Ghent Coal*, a Belgian taxable person bought immovable property to be used for its taxed transactions but did not use this property immediately.[159] According to the CJEU, the VAT on the purchase was deductible in full. However, any later use for exempt supplies would lead to an adjustment of the initially deducted VAT. Indeed, Ghent Coal sold the immovable property, exempt from VAT and therefore, had to adjust the initially deduct VAT on the basis of (what are now) Articles 187 and 188 VAT Directive. The fact that it had to sell the property for reasons beyond its own discretion (i.e., following a decision taken by the local government) could not alter the fact that an adjustment had to be made.

10.6.5.5 *Changes in the VAT Legislation: Adjustments?*

Changes to the VAT legislation of a Member State may entail that a transaction that used to be taxed becomes an exempt transaction. Such a change may be regarded as having an effect on the use of a capital good, and thus trigger adjustments in the years after the change in the legislation. For example, in 1995, the Netherlands made changes to the right of taxable persons to waive the exemption for the lease of immovable property. Many leases changed from being taxed to being exempt. The CJEU ruled that the Dutch tax authorities could require lessors of such buildings to make an adjustment of the initially deducted VAT in each of the years of the remainder of the adjustment period.[160]

---

158. CJEU 17 September 2020, Case C-791/18 *Stichting Schoonzicht v Staatssecretaris van Financiën*, ECLI:EU:C:2020:731.
159. CJEU 15 January 1998, Case C-37/95 *Ghent Coal Terminal NV v Belgian State*, ECLI: EU:C:1998:1.
160. CJEU 29 April 2004, Joined Cases C-487/01 and C-7/02 *Gemeente Leusden (C-487/01) and Holin Groep BV cs (C-7/02) v Staatssecretaris van Financiën*, ECLI:EU:C:2004:263.

If a Member State omits to require adjustments which are caused by a change in legislation, this may amount to that Member State providing (illegal) state aid. For example, in *Heiser*, the Austrian VAT legislation was changed so that the services of medical practitioners moved from taxable to exempt status. According to the EU, this change in VAT status entailed the reduction of input tax already deducted in relation to goods that continued to be used in the business. The CJEU ruled that not requiring an adjustment of the input VAT must be classified as state aid.[161]

In our view, adjustments to the right of deduction following changes in the VAT legislation of a Member State should be spread over the remaining years of the adjustment period, following Article 187(2) VAT Directive.[162]

10.6.5.6 A Supply of a Capital Good During the Adjustment Period

If a taxable person sells a capital good during the adjustment period applicable to that capital good, this has implications with respect to the remaining years of the adjustment period. Article 188 VAT Directive contains legal fictions with respect to the use of the capital good in the remaining part of the adjustment period after the sale. If the sale of the capital good is a taxed supply, the taxable person is deemed to use the good exclusively for its taxed transactions during the remainder of the adjustment period. In case the supply of the goods is exempt (which may particularly occur if it is a supply of an immovable property), the taxable person is deemed to use the good exclusively for its exempt transactions during the remainder of the adjustment period.[163] The taxable person must make the adjustment with respect to *all* remaining years of the adjustment period at once (Article 188(2) VAT Directive). The example below further illustrates this.

Example

In the previous example (*see* section 10.6.5.2), an amount of EUR 100,000 of VAT was charged to the taxable person in respect of the supply of an immovable property. The adjustment period in the Member State in question was five years. The first year of adjustment was 2022 (the year of purchase). In 2023 and 2024, the taxable person adjusted the deduction because the use of the building in those years differed from the use of the building on which the initial deduction was based. If this taxable person sells the immovable property in January 2025, there are two remaining years of adjustment (2025 and 2026). Whether he actually has to adjust the VAT on the building depends on whether the supply of the building in 2025 is a taxed or an exempt supply. If the supply is taxed, the taxable person is considered using the building exclusively for

---

161. CJEU 3 March 2005, Case C-172/03 *Wolfgang Heiser v Finanzamt Innsbruck*, ECLI:EU:C:2005:130.
162. Cf. CJEU 3 December 1998, Case C-381/97 *Belgocodex SA v Belgian State*, ECLI:EU:C:1998:589 and CJEU 8 June 2000, Case C-396/98 *Grundstückgemeinschaft Schloßstraße GbR v Finanzamt Paderborn*, ECLI:EU:C:2000:303.
163. However, if the supply of capital goods is exempt, Member States may waive the requirement for adjustment insofar as the purchaser is a taxable person using the capital goods in question solely for transactions in respect of which VAT is deductible (Article 188(2) VAT Directive).

taxed transactions in 2025 and 2026. Since that use corresponds with the use on which the initial deduction was based, no adjustment is necessary. However, if the supply is exempt, the taxable person is regarded as using the building exclusively for exempt supplies. Now, he needs to make a one-off adjustment of 2 (years) × 100% (difference intended use and actual use) × 1/5 (VAT attributable to each adjustment year) × EUR 100,000 (amount of input VAT) = EUR 40,000.

It appears that it is conceivable that the right to dispose of the same capital good is transferred twice. This may, for example, be the case if the economic title of a capital good is first sold to customer A and the residual right (the legal title) is sold to customer B. If both transactions take place during the adjustment period, the question may arise as to how the adjustment rules for capital goods must be applied. Exactly this question was put to the CJEU in *Centralan*.[164] A taxable person first granted a 999-year lease over capital goods (a British 'invention') to another person against the payment of a substantial premium. This was considered as the (first) exempt supply of that capital good. The taxable person transferred the freehold reversion in that property three days later to another person at a much lower price. This constituted a second, taxed supply of the same capital good. The CJEU ruled that the building should be regarded, until the expiry of the period of adjustment, as having been used in business activities which are presumed to be partly taxable and partly exempt in proportion to the respective values of the two transactions.

In our view, this solution is only viable if the two transactions of the same capital good are inextricably linked, and both supplies can be seen as supplies of goods. The solution provided by the CJEU can, in a way, be considered as a solution to tackle a specific kind of (aggressive) tax planning. The taxable person in question must have had the expectation that the 999-year lease was to be considered as a service and that only the taxed supply of the residual rights for a very low price would trigger an adjustment for the remainder of the adjustment period. We note that this case was ruled before the CJEU confirmed in *Halifax* that the abuse of right doctrine also applies in the field of VAT.[165] In *Centralan*, the CJEU effectively (although the calculation of the adjustment itself might create problems) solved the situation in which an unintended tax advantage occurred with the taxable person. Even though the text of Article 188 VAT Directive does not leave much room for splitting the adjustment over two supplies with regard to the same capital item, we believe that in this particular situation the result is satisfactory.

10.6.5.7 Specific Measures with Respect to Adjustments to Capital Goods

Apart from their right to define the concept of 'capital good' (Article 189(a) VAT Directive, *see* section 10.6.5.1), Member States may specify the amount of the VAT

164. CJEU 15 December 2005, Case C-63/04 *Centralan Property Ltd v Commissioners of Customs & Excise*, ECLI:EU:C:2005:773.
165. CJEU 21 February 2006, Case C-255/02 *Halifax plc, Leeds Permanent Development Services Ltd and County Wide Property Investments Ltd v Commissioners of Customs & Excise*, ECLI: EU:C:2006:121.

which is to be taken into consideration for adjustment (Article 189(b) VAT Directive), adopt any measures they deem necessary to ensure that adjustment does not give rise to any unjustified advantage (Article 189(c) VAT Directive) and allow for administrative simplification (Article 189(d) VAT Directive).

Moreover, Member States may, after consulting the VAT Committee, refrain from requiring an adjustment of the initially deducted VAT if the practical effect of such adjustments would be negligible anyway (Article 191 VAT Directive). However, when implementing such simplifications, Member States must have regard to the overall impact of VAT in their Member State and the need for administrative simplification. The simplification cannot be applied if it leads to distortion of competition.

10.7 ASSET LABELLING (LENNARTZ PRINCIPLE)

In section 10.2.2.1., we indicated that if a taxable person can either act in his capacity of taxable person or in the capacity as a private consumer, it is relevant to determine in which capacity he acts because it has an impact on his right of deduction when he purchases a capital good. We indicated that on the basis of the so-called asset labelling doctrine, or *Lennartz* principle, one-man businesses (self-employed persons) and – so it seems[166] – partnerships can, in fact, choose in which capacity they purchase capital goods. Asset labelling is restricted to one-man businesses and – possibly – partnerships that allow for private use of capital goods they purchased. Legal persons cannot apply the asset labelling doctrine. They cannot label goods (nor services) which they use for both economic and non-economic activities as their business assets.[167] One of the reasons for that is that the deemed services (Article 26 VAT Directive) cannot apply insofar as the goods are used for non-economic activities. That provision can only be applied if there is *private* use. Indeed, the CJEU considered that Article 6(2)(a) Sixth VAT Directive (now: Article 26(1)(a) VAT Directive) is not intended to establish a rule that transactions outside the scope of the system of VAT may be considered to be carried out for 'purposes other than' those of the business within the meaning of that provision because such an interpretation would have the effect of rendering Article

166. CJEU 19 July 2012, Case C-334/10 *X v Staatssecretaris van Financiën*, ECLI:EU:C:2012:473.
167. CJEU 12 February 2009, Case C-515/07 *Vereniging Noordelijke Land- en Tuinbouw Organisatie v Staatssecretaris van Financiën*, ECLI:EU:C:1996:243. The Dutch Supreme Court had already asked a similar question in CJEU 2 June 2005, Case C-378/02 *Waterschap Zeeuws Vlaanderen v Staatssecretaris van Financiën*, ECLI:EU:C:2005:335. It asked whether 'a body governed by public law has, as regards a capital item acquired by it which it supplies for consideration to a third party, in respect of which supply it must be regarded as a taxable person, a right to adjust the turnover tax paid in respect of that acquisition ... insofar as it has used that item for activities in which it engages as a public authority ...'? There was no need for the Court to answer this question as it decided that *Waterschap Zeeuw Vlaanderen* was not engaged in economic activities at the moment of the acquisition of the capital good. Thus, it had bought the goods as a non-taxable person. However, *see also* CJEU 25 July 2018, Case C-140/17 *Szef Krajowej Administracji Skarbowej v Gmina Ryjewo*, ECLI:EU:C:2018:595 from which it becomes clear that a public body can also purchase a capital good in its capacity as a taxable person.

2(1) of the directive meaningless.[168] Thus, a taxable person who carries out non-economic activities, other than private use of business assets, is regarded as acquiring such goods and/or services in full or in part *outside* the framework of the business, i.e., the taxable person cannot choose in which capacity it purchases such goods or services.

In section 2.4.12.5, we focused on the question to what extent and under which circumstances asset labelling is possible. In this chapter and section, we focus in particular on the consequences of asset labelling as regards the right of deduction.

10.7.1 The Effects of Asset Labelling on the Right of Deduction

In *Charles & Charles-Tijmens,* the CJEU outlined the features of the 'asset labelling' doctrine with respect to self-employed (taxable) persons.[169] These basic features are that if an item is used for both business and private purposes, the taxable person may choose to allocate this item in full, or in part, to either his business and/or his private assets. The CJEU considered:

> Should the taxable person choose to treat capital goods used for both business and private purposes as business goods, the input VAT due on the acquisition of those goods is, in principle, immediately deductible in full.[170]

Thus, if a one-man business purchases a capital good, which he uses for both his business and his private purposes ('mixed-use'), he has three options:

(1) He can fully label the capital good as a business asset.
(2) He can fully label the capital good as a private asset.
(3) He can partially label the capital good as a business and partially as a private asset.

Labelling an asset has various consequences. These depend not only on the choice the taxable person makes but also on the nature – movable or immovable – of the capital good in question. Below we will indicate the consequences of asset labelling for both immovable and movable goods.

168. CJEU 12 February 2009, Case C-515/07 *Vereniging Noordelijke Land- en Tuinbouw Organisatie v Staatssecretaris van Financiën,* ECLI:EU:C:1996:243, para. 38.
169. CJEU 14 July 2005, Case C-434/03 *P. Charles and T.S. Charles-Tijmens v Staatssecretaris van Financiën,* ECLI:EU:C:2005:463.
170. *Ibid.,* para. 24. *See also* CJEU 11 July 1991, Case C-97/90 *Hansgeorg Lennartz v Finanzamt München III,* ECLI:EU:C:1991:315, para. 26; CJEU 8 March 2001, Case C-415/98 *Laszlo Bakcsi v Finanzamt Fürstenfeldbruck,* ECLI:EU:C:2001:136, para. 25 and CJEU 8 May 2003, Case C-269/00 *Wolfgang Seeling v Finanzamt Starnberg,* ECLI:EU:C:2003:254, para. 41.

10.7.1.1 Consequences of Labelling a Movable Good

If a one-man business purchases a movable capital good which he uses for both business and private purposes, he may choose to what extent he treats that asset as a business asset. This choice has an impact on:

(1) the potential right of deduction;
(2) the occurrence of (deemed) self-supplies of goods or services (Articles 16 and 26 VAT Directive);
(3) the liability to tax of any supply of the good at a later stage.

We note that since 1 January 2011, Member States have been able to implement special rules with respect to the right of deduction of mixed-use movable capital goods. In effect, to treat movable assets as they specify, they may apply the same regime as is applied to immovable property (Article 168a(2) VAT Directive). In section 10.7.1.2, we discuss the consequences of labelling of immovable goods. In this section, we will discuss the VAT consequences of asset labelling of movable capital goods as if Article 168a(2) VAT Directive has not been implemented because Article 168a(2) VAT Directive is only an optional provision for the Member States.

10.7.1.1.1 Movable Goods and Asset Labelling: Potential Right of Deduction

The labelling of a mixed-use capital good determines the maximum amount of VAT deductible on that good. If a taxable person labels the capital good in question as his business asset, he can potentially deduct all VAT on the purchase of the good. How much of the VAT on the purchase he can actually deduct, depends not only on the labelling of the business asset but also on the business use (use for taxed or for exempt supplies). Hence, asset labelling only determines the *potential* right of deduction. If the taxable person labels the goods partially as his business assets, he, in fact, indicates that insofar as the good is labelled as a private asset, he did not purchase it in his capacity as a taxable person. Therefore, any right of deduction is limited to that part of the asset which is labelled as a business asset, and there is only a potential right of deduction insofar as the good is labelled as a business asset. Consequently, if the good is labelled as a fully private asset, any right of deduction is excluded. Figure 10.8 shows the consequences of asset labelling of a movable capital good as regards the potential right of deduction.

Figure 10.8 The Effect of Asset Labelling of a Movable Capital Good on the Potential Right of Deduction

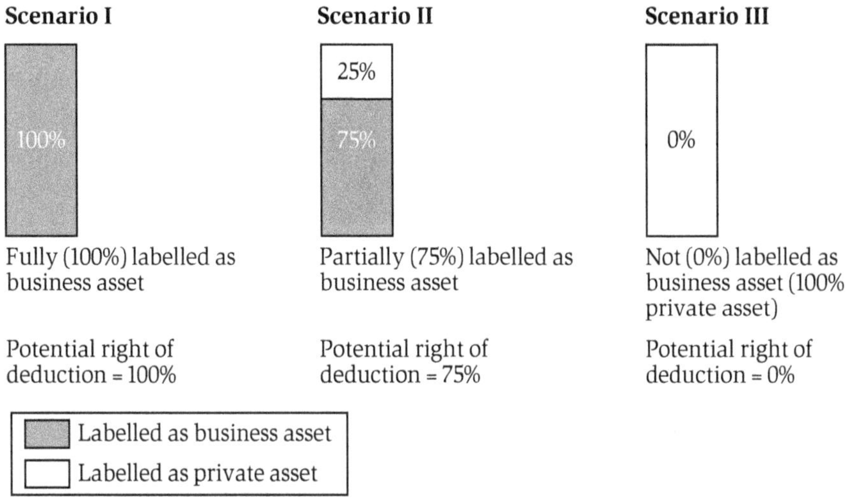

If a taxable person solely carries on taxed transactions, the potential right of deduction will coincide with the actual right of deduction of a taxable person. If he also carries out transactions for which no right of deduction exists, the potential right of deduction will be higher than his actual right of deduction. It is important to acknowledge that the labelling as a business asset is decisive to the actual right of deduction if the business use of the good does not exceed the percentage of which it forms part of the business assets. This is, for example, the case in Figure 10.9, in the scenario in which the asset is fully labelled as a business asset, yet the business use is only 90%. In that situation, the labelling of the asset determines the actual right of deduction. Conversely, if the use of a capital good for business purposes exceeds the percentage of which it was labelled as a business asset, the labelling as a business asset 'caps' the right of deduction. The potential right of deduction is smaller than it would be on the basis of the usage of the good alone. This is depicted in Figure 10.9 in the second and third scenarios.

Figure 10.9 The Effect of Asset Labelling and the Use of a Movable Capital Good on the Right of Deduction

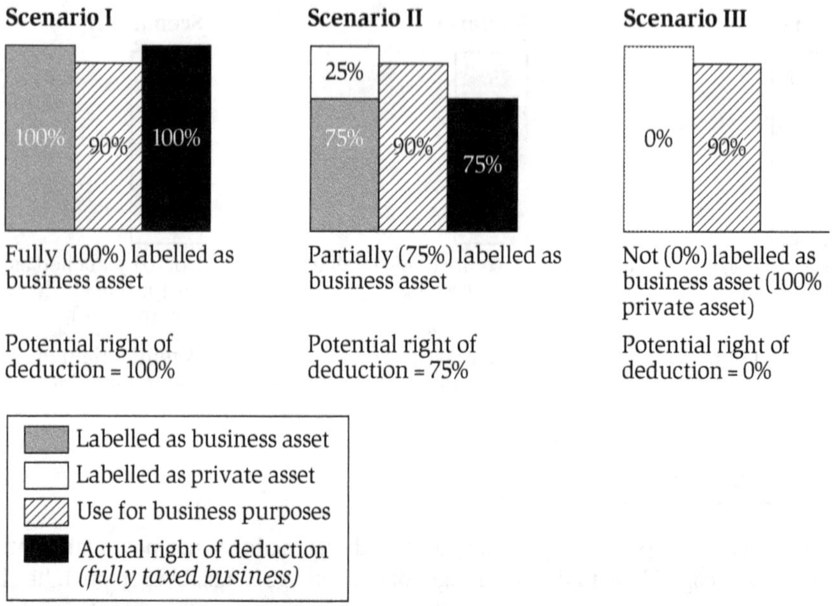

10.7.1.1.2 Movable Goods and Asset Labelling: (Deemed) Self-Supplies

A precondition to the labelling of movable capital good is that the taxable person is going to use it for both business and private purposes. If a movable capital good has wholly or partially been labelled as a business asset, the private *use* of that good will 'trigger' a self-supply under Article 26(1)(a) VAT Directive. The purpose of that self-supply is to tax the private consumption of business assets on which the taxable person deducted input VAT (*see* section 3.3.2.2). Thus, insofar as the labelling of an asset as a business asset exceeds the business use (and in fact, more VAT has been deducted than is justifiable, looking at the usage of the good alone), a self-supply will take place. In Figure 10.10, this is only the case in the first scenario.

Figure 10.10 The Effect of Asset Labelling of a Movable Capital Good on Deemed Supplies in Respect of Private Use

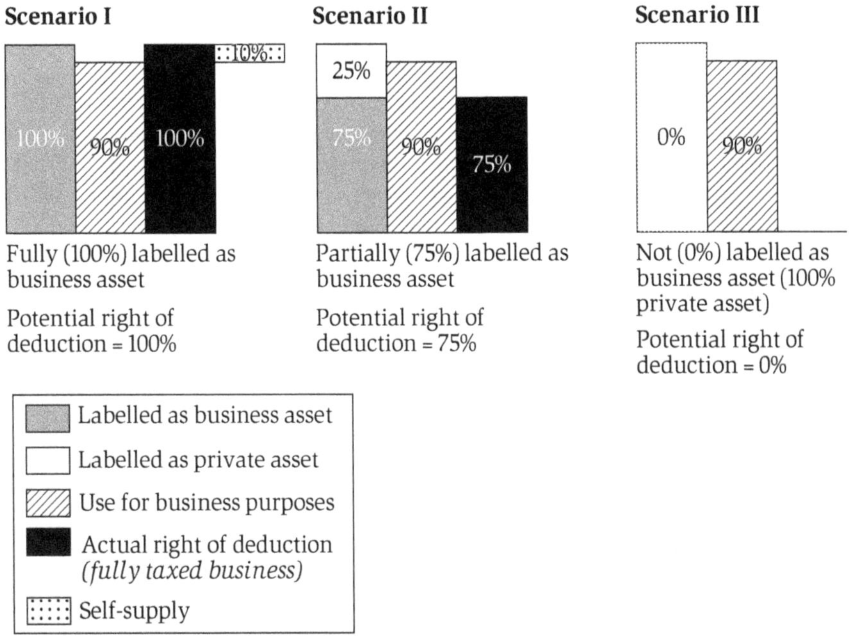

10.7.1.1.3 *Movable Goods and Asset Labelling: Supplies at a Later Stage*

As a principle, a supply of a mixed-use capital good is subject to VAT insofar as it has been labelled as a business asset. Referring to the figures in the previous sections, this implies that in the first scenario, a supply of the capital good at a later stage is fully (100%) subject to VAT, in the second scenario, only 75% of the supply is subject to VAT (25% of the supply takes place outside the scope of VAT), and in the third scenario, the supply is not subject to VAT at all because the supply is carried out by a taxable person that does *not* act as such with respect to the supply.

It should be noted however, that it follows from *Keziç* that it is possible that the supply of a good that was not labelled a business asset, is in fact undertaken as a taxable person acting as such, thus making such supply subject to VAT.[171] This can be the case if the supply cannot be regarded as the mere exercise of the right of ownership. In this respect, a relevant assessment criterion is whether the seller has taken active steps to market property by mobilizing resources similar to those deployed by producers, traders or persons supplying services within the scope of VAT, such as, for example, the carrying out of preparatory work to plots of land to make development

171. CJEU 9 July 2015, Case C-331/14 *Petar Kezić s.p. Trgovina Prizma*, ECLI:EU:C:2015:456.

possible, and the deployment of proven marketing measures.[172] In those circumstances, upon the moment of sale, an asset can be relabelled to become a business asset after all.

10.7.1.2 Consequences of Labelling an Immovable Good

Pursuant to Article 168a(1) VAT Directive, any VAT on expenditure related to immovable property forming part of the business assets of a taxable person and used both for the purposes of the taxable person's business and for his private use or that of his staff, or, more generally, for purposes other than those of his business, will be deductible only up to the proportion of the property's use for purposes of the taxable person's business. Consequently, the asset labelling doctrine no longer affects the right of deduction. However, as we will show below, asset labelling can still be relevant, even if it concerns immovable (capital) goods.

Due to Article 168a(1) VAT Directive, asset labelling of immovable property has an impact which is different from that of the asset labelling of movable property. Labelling immovable property has an impact on:

(1) the potential right of deduction;
(2) the adjustment of the right of deduction;
(3) the liability to tax of any supply of the good at a later stage.

10.7.1.2.1 Immovable Goods and Asset Labelling: Potential Right of Deduction

Article 168a(1) VAT Directive does not prevent the labelling of mixed-use immovable property as (wholly or partially) business assets. However, the effect of treating mixed-use immovable property as a business asset does not automatically mean that the VAT on the purchase of that immovable property can be fully deducted, as would be the case if it had been a movable capital good (and the business solely carries out transactions for which a right of deduction exists). This is clear in the first scenario depicted in Figure 10.11. In that scenario, an immovable good has been fully labelled as a business asset. However, its use for business purposes is only 90%, i.e., private use is 10%. Consequently, the (initial) right of deduction is only 90% (whereas it would have been 100% on the basis of the labelling as a business asset, had it been a movable capital good, *see* section 10.7.1.1.1).

172. CJEU 15 September 2011, Joined Cases C-180/10 and C-181/10 *Jarosław Słaby v Minister Finansów (C-180/10) and Emilian Kuć and Halina Jeziorska-Kuć v Dyrektor Izby Skarbowej w Warszawie (C-181/10)*, ECLI:EU:C:2011:589.

Figure 10.11 The Effect of Asset Labelling of an Immovable Capital Good on the Potential Right of Deduction

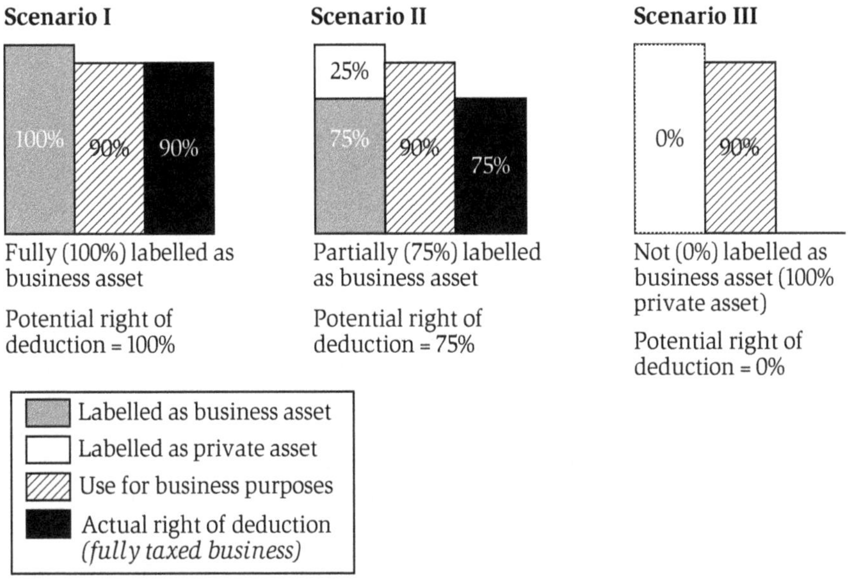

10.7.1.2.2 Immovable Goods and Asset Labelling: Adjustment of the Right of Deduction

Since the initial right of deduction of VAT on the purchase of an immovable property is not affected by the way in which it is labelled, the private use of such immovable property will not lead to a deemed supply under Article 26(1)(a) VAT Directive. However, it is conceivable that in the years following its purchase (and first use), the use for business and private purposes fluctuates. Such fluctuations shall be taken into account in accordance with the principles on which the system of adjustments of input VAT are based (*see* section 10.6).

10.7.1.2.3 Immovable Goods and Asset Labelling: Supplies at a Later Stage

A supply of a mixed-use capital good, whether it is a movable or an immovable good, is subject to VAT insofar as it has been labelled as a business asset. For the sake of brevity, we refer to section 10.7.1.1.3 (Movable goods and asset labelling: supplies at a later stage).

10.8 RESTRICTIONS ON THE RIGHT OF DEDUCTION

Both Articles 176 and 177 VAT Directive contain rules that reduce the scope of the right of deduction. Article 176 VAT Directive is a so-called standstill provision, and Article 177 VAT Directive is a provision on the exclusion of the right of deduction for cyclical economic reasons.

10.8.1 Standstill Provision of Article 176 VAT Directive

Pursuant to Article 176 VAT Directive the Council (acting unanimously on a proposal from the Commission) shall determine the expenditure in respect of which VAT shall not be deductible. VAT shall in no circumstances be deductible in respect of expenditure which is not strictly business expenditure, such as that on luxuries, amusements or entertainment. Clearly, the reason for such exclusion of the right of deduction lies within the legal character of VAT, which is that private consumption should be taxed.

This provision is a hollow phrase because it never entered into force. A final proposal to implement provisions that restrict the right of deduction with respect to expenditure which is not strictly business expenditure was never adopted, and it seems unlikely that such a provision will be implemented in the near future. Pending the entry into force of such restrictions as are referred to in Article 176, first paragraph VAT Directive, a special standstill provision was created in what is now Article 176, second paragraph VAT Directive. This standstill provision entails that the Member States may retain all the exclusions from the right of deduction provided for under their national laws at 1 January 1979 or, in the case of the Member States which acceded to the Community after that date, on the date of their accession.

The standstill provision applies, regardless of whether the particular exclusion in a Member State is indeed related to expenditure which is not strictly business expenditure, as Article 176, first paragraph suggests. Whatever the reasons that a particular Member State excluded certain categories of expenses from the right to deduction, and for whatever reasons it may have wished to retain that exclusion, Article 176, second paragraph respects the existence of the exclusions from the right of deduction. In *Royscot Leasing*, the CJEU ruled that Article 176 VAT Directive allows the Member States to retain the exclusion of the right of deduction on the purchase of a car, even where the car is an essential tool in the business of the taxable person concerned and is not used – not even partly – for private purposes.[173] This exclusion could also be maintained *after* the date on which the Council had to come up with a new, harmonized provision for the restrictions on the right of deduction (1 January 1979).

Although Article 176, second paragraph VAT Directive, is a standstill provision, Member States are permitted to *limit* the scope of their existing exclusions on the right of deduction, even if they decide to limit the scope of the exclusion after 1 January 1979

173. CJEU 5 October 1999, Case C-305/97 *Royscot Leasing Ltd & Royscot Industrial Leasing Ltd, Allied Domecq plc, T.C. Harrison Group Ltd v Commissioners of Customs and Excise*, ECLI: EU:C:1999:481.

or after the date of their accession.[174] The reason that limiting the exclusion is allowed, even after those reference dates, is that a restriction on a restriction brings the existing VAT rules closer to the harmonized system of VAT as it was intended to function. Conversely, alterations to the exclusions of the right of deduction are not allowed if they increase the scope of the exclusions.[175] In *X Holding & Oracle Netherlands*, the CJEU ruled that in order for an exclusion to be respected under the standstill provision of Article 176, second paragraph VAT Directive, the goods and services which a Member State wishes to exclude from the right of deduction must be sufficiently and clearly defined.[176] For example, categories of expenditure concerning, on the one hand, the provision of 'private transport', 'food', 'drink', 'accommodation' and 'opportunities for recreation' to the members of staff of a taxable person and, on the other hand, the provision of 'business gifts' or 'other gifts' are considered as being sufficiently and clearly defined.[177] Conversely, Member States are not allowed to retain exclusions from the right of deduction that are more general in nature and could be applied to each purchase of goods and services.[178]

10.8.2 Exclusions for Cyclical Economic Reasons

After consulting the VAT Committee, each Member State may, for reasons of cyclical economic circumstances, totally or partly exclude all or some capital goods or other goods from the system of deductions. The underlying objective of this provision must be to provide the Member States with a specific tool in extreme circumstances, such as wars or other social or natural disasters. By refusing the right of deduction for a certain defined period, a Member State may be able to force a shift in the timing of investments. When a general restriction on the right of deduction is announced, to enter into force on a set date, companies may react to that by forcing forward those investments, which may be useful at times of economic downturn. By contrast, in a period in which the economy is booming, Member States may be able to move companies to defer their investments to a date in the future, on which the restriction to the right of deduction is revoked.

In *Stradasfalti*, the Italian government tried to substantiate its claim on the right to retain a certain exclusion of the right of deduction, which was introduced *after* 1 January 1979[179] by referring to Article 177 VAT Directive.[180] The CJEU ruled that Article 177 VAT Directive can only be invoked by the Member States if:

174. CJEU 14 June 2001, Case C-345/99 *Commission of the European Communities v French Republic*, ECLI:EU:C:2001:334.
175. CJEU 14 June 2001, Case C-40/00 *Commission of the European Communities v French Republic*, ECLI:EU:C:2001:338 and CJEU 22 December 2008, Case C-414/07 *Magoora sp. Zoo v Dyrektor Izby Skarbowej w Krakowie*, ECLI:EU:C:2008:766.
176. CJEU 15 April 2010, Joined Cases C-538/08 and C-33/09 *X Holding BV v Staatsssecretaris van Financiën and Oracle Nederland BV v Inspecteur van de Belastingdienst Utrecht-Gooi*, ECLI: EU:C:2010:192.
177. *Ibid.*
178. CJEU 30 September 2010, Case C-395/09 *Oasis East sp. z o.o. v Minister Finansów*, ECLI: EU:C:2010:570.
179. For this reason, Article 176 VAT Directive could not be used as a basis for the exclusion.

(1) the VAT committee has been consulted;
(2) the application of the deviating rule is restricted in time; and
(3) the measure is not part of a wider package of structural measures to decrease budget deficits.

Italy did not meet these requirements (e.g., it had not consulted the VAT committee). The exclusion of the right of deduction could, therefore, not be based on Article 177 VAT Directive.

10.9 THE (ABSENCE OF A) RIGHT OF DEDUCTION IN CASE OF FRAUD ('KITTEL DOCTRINE')

The VAT Directive has no specific provisions on the restriction of right of deduction in cases of fraudulent evasion of VAT (e.g., carousel fraud). However, from CJEU case law, rules of law can be deduced restricting the right of deduction in case of fraudulent behaviour.[181]

In our view, a distinction must be made regarding the position of:

(1) the fraudster himself;
(2) persons who were aware or could have been aware of the fraud; and
(3) persons who are not aware or could not be aware that a fraud was or is to be committed.

10.9.1 The Fraudster

In *Kittel*, the Court ruled that the objective criteria which form the basis of the concepts of supply of goods carried out by a taxable person acting as such and 'economic activity' are not met where tax is evaded by the taxable person himself.[182]

This rule of law is, in our view, rather particular because it does not exclusively impact on the right of deduction of a taxable person but also implies the obligation to include the obligation to charge VAT on output supplies. It appears to imply a 'bonus' for fraudsters on not complying with the rules, in that they have no obligation to charge any VAT simply because they are fraudsters. We assume that the CJEU did not intend

180. CJEU 14 September 2006, Case C-228/05 *Stradasfalti Srl-Agenzia delle Entrate v Ufficio di Trento*, ECLI:EU:C:2006:578.
181. *See also* E. Kristoffersson, 'Unlawful and Abusive Transactions and the Right to Deduct Input VAT', in M. Lang, et al. (eds), *ECJ: Recent Developments in Value Added Tax, the Evolution of European VAT Jurisprudence and Its Role in the EU Common VAT System* (Linde 2014), pp. 330-335.
182. CJEU 6 July 2006, Case C-439/04 *Axel Kittel v État belge* and C-440/04 *État belge v Recolta Recycling SPRL*, ECLI:EU:C:2006:446, para. 53: 'By contrast, the objective criteria which form the basis of the concepts of "supply of goods effected by a taxable person acting as such" and "economic activity" are not met where tax is evaded by the taxable person himself'. *See also* CJEU 21 February 2006, Case C-255/02 *Halifax plc, Leeds Permanent Development Services Ltd and County Wide Property Investments Ltd v Commissioners of Customs & Excise*, ECLI: EU:C:2006:121, para. 59.

such a bonus. Presumably, the CJEU only intended to rule that fraudsters cannot derive any rights from EU law connected to taxable person status and/or to the making of taxable supplies (like the right of deduction). As such, the CJEU has repeatedly held that no right to deduct can exist in case of fraud.[183]

10.9.2 Persons Who Were Aware or Could Have Been Aware of the Fraud

If a (taxable) person, although not being a fraudster himself, knew or should have known that, by his purchase, he was participating in a transaction connected with fraudulent evasion of VAT, it is for the national court to refuse that taxable person entitlement to the right to deduct.[184] In its ruling in *Maks Pen*, the CJEU indicated that:

> 35 Therefore, although, as the referring court itself states at paragraph 72 of its request for a preliminary ruling, it is apparent from Article 160(2) of the Tax and Social Security Procedure Code that that court is required to determine whether there is tax evasion when it examines of its own motion whether the amended tax notice contesting the VAT deduction made by the taxable person is in conformity with national law, it must also raise of its own motion the requirement of European Union law referred to in the preceding paragraph of this judgment, in accordance with the objective of Directive 2006/112 of preventing any tax evasion, tax avoidance and abuse.
>
> 36 It must be recalled, in this connection, that it is for the national court to interpret the national law, so far as possible, in the light of the wording and the purpose of the directive concerned in order to achieve the result sought by the directive, which requires that it does whatever lies within its jurisdiction, taking the whole body of domestic law into consideration and applying the interpretative methods recognised by that law (see, to that effect, Case C212/04 *Adeneler and Others*, [2006] ECR I-6057, paragraph 111). It is, therefore, for the national court to ascertain whether the rules of national law on which it is relying and which, in its view, might be contrary to the requirements of European Union law, can be interpreted in accordance with the objective of preventing tax evasion on which those requirements are based.[185]

If a national court must or may raise of its own motion points of law based on binding rules of national law, it is required to do whatever lies within its jurisdiction, taking the whole body of domestic law into consideration and applying the interpretative methods recognized by that law to refuse the right of deduction if that right is relied on for fraudulent or abusive ends.[186] This implies that a national court must deny

183. CJEU 22 October 2015, Case C-277/14 PPUH *Stehcemp sp. j Florian Stefanek, Janina Stefanek, Jaroslaw Stefanek v Dyrektor Izby Skarbowej w Łodzi*, ECLI:EU:C:2015:719, para. 47, CJEU 13 February 2014, Case C-18/13 *Maks Pen EOOD v Direktor na Direktsia 'Obzhalvane i danachno-osiguritelna praktika' Sofia, formerly Direktor na Direktsia*, ECLI:EU:C:2014:69.
184. CJEU 6 July 2006, Case C-439/04 *Axel Kittel v État belge* and C-440/04 *État belge v Recolta Recycling SPRL*, ECLI:EU:C:2006:446.
185. CJEU 13 February 2014, Case C-18/13 *Maks Pen EOOD v Direktor na Direktsia 'Obzhalvane i danachno-osiguritelna praktika' Sofia, formerly Direktor na Direktsia 'Obzhalvane i upravlenie na izpalnenieto' Sofia*, ECLI:EU:C:2014:69, paras 35 and 36.
186. CJEU 13 February 2014, Case C-18/13 *Maks Pen EOOD v Direktor na Direktsia 'Obzhalvane i danachno-osiguritelna praktika' Sofia*, ECLI:EU:C:2014:69.

the right of deduction in cases of fraud or abuse even if there is no national provision on the basis of which that right of deduction can be denied.[187] We refer to section 13.11.

10.9.3 Persons Who Are Not Aware or Could Not Be Aware That a Fraud Was or Is to Be Committed

It can also be deduced from *Kittel* that where a recipient of a supply of goods is a taxable person who did not and could not know that the transaction concerned was connected with a fraud committed by the seller, he will not be deprived of his right of deduction. Thus, if the taxable person concerned is involved in the same chain of supply in which one of the supplies has a possibly fraudulent nature, prior or subsequent to his own transaction and he had no knowledge and no means of knowledge, he should retain his right of deduction.

187. CJEU 18 December 2014, Joined Cases C-131/13, C-163/13 and C-164/13 *Staatssecretaris van Financiën v Schoenimport 'Italmoda' Mariano Previti vof (C-131/13) and Turbu.com BV (C-163/13) and Turbu.com Mobile Phone's BV (C-164/13) v Staatssecretaris van Financiën*, ECLI:EU:C:2014:2455.

CHAPTER 11

Shares and Other Securities

11.1 INTRODUCTION

It follows from settled CJEU case law that the acquisition, holding and sale of shares are not considered economic activities in themselves.[1] Such dealings cannot confer on a person the status of a taxable person. According to the CJEU, the mere acquisition and holding of financial holdings in other undertakings does not amount to an economic activity from which a taxable person status can be derived because any dividend yielded by that holding is merely the result of ownership of the property.[2]

However, the issue, acquisition, holding and sale of shares may, in certain circumstances, be an economic activity after all. From CJEU case law, it can be deduced that this is the case in three situations:

(1) if the holding of shares is accompanied by direct or indirect involvement in the management of the company in which the holding has been acquired, insofar as the involvement of that kind entails carrying out transactions which are subject to VAT (holding of shares by a 'controlling, active parent company');[3]
(2) if these activities are effected within the course of commercial share dealings;[4]

1. CJEU 20 June 1996, Case C-155/94 *Wellcome Trust Ltd v Commissioners of Customs and Excise*, ECLI:EU:C:1996:243, para. 33; CJEU 29 October 2009, Case C-29/08 *AB SKF v Skatteverket*, ECLI:EU:C:2009:665, para. 28 and CJEU 30 May 2013, Case C-651/11 *Staatssecretaris van Financiën v X BV*, ECLI:EU:C:2013:346, para. 36.
2. For example: CJEU 29 April 2001, Case C-77/01 *Empresa de Desenvolvimento Mineiro SGPS SA (EDM) v Fazenda Pública*, ECLI:EU:C:2004:243, para. 57: 'In that regard, it must be noted at the outset that under consistent case-law the mere acquisition and holding of shares in a company is not to be regarded as an economic activity within the meaning of the Sixth Directive, conferring on the holder the status of a taxable person. The mere acquisition of financial holdings in other undertakings does not amount to the exploitation of property for the purpose of obtaining income therefrom on a continuing basis because any dividend yielded by those holdings is merely the result of ownership of the property and is not the consideration for any economic activity within the meaning of that directive (see *Harnas & Helm*, paragraph 15, and *Floridienne and Berginvest*, paragraph 21). If such activities do not therefore in themselves constitute an economic activity within the meaning of that directive, the same must be true of activities consisting in the sale of such holdings (see *Wellcome Trust*, cited above, paragraph 33, and Case C-442/01 *KapHag*, [2003] ECR I-6851, paragraphs 38 and 40).'
3. CJEU 14 November 2000, Case C-142/99 *Floridienne SA and Berginvest SA v Belgian State*, ECLI:EU:C:2000:623, para. 19. *See* A.J. van Doesum, H.W.M. van Kesteren & G.J. van Norden, *Share Disposals and the Right to Deduction of Input VAT* (2010) 2 EC Tax Review https://doi.org/10.54648/ecta2010008 and J. Eggers & B. Ahrens, *The VAT Treatment of Holding Companies: German and EU VAT Practice Perspective* (2015) 26/3 International VAT Monitor, p. 138 https://doi.org/10.59403/3vk6km3 and further. As we will explain in section 11.7, it can be argued that that a sale of shares is an economic activity in only two situations: if the sale is the effected within the course of commercial share dealings or if the direct and exclusive reason of the sale lies in the taxable economic activity of the company concerned.
4. CJEU 20 June 1996, Case C-155/94 *Wellcome Trust Ltd v Commissioners of Customs and Excise*, ECLI:EU:C:1996:243; CJEU 6 February 1997, Case C-80/95 *Harnas & Helm CV v Staatssecretaris van Financiën*, ECLI:EU:C:1997:56 and CJEU 29 April 2004, Case C-77/01 *Empresa de Desenvolvimento Mineiro SGPS SA (EDM) v Fazenda Pública*, ECLI:EU:C:2004:243.

(3) if these activities constitute the direct, permanent and necessary extension of a parent company's taxable activity.[5]

The relevance of having the taxable person status and acting as such with respect to dealings in shares is of little relevance for the output VAT due. If the output activities (issue and sale of shares) are outside the scope (not subject to VAT), no VAT becomes due. If the output activities are inside the scope of VAT, no VAT is due either because such activities are exempt from VAT under Article 135(1)(f) VAT Directive.[6]

The true relevance of a holding company having taxable person status and acting as such, therefore, lies in the right of deduction on costs relating to the issue, acquisition, holding and sale of the shares. The same applies to other securities, such as bonds,[7] which we will discuss in section 11.8. A holding company which is not and/or does not act as a taxable person cannot deduct VAT on any costs (e.g., 'transaction costs', *see* section 11.2) which it incurs with respect to the acquisition, the holding and the sale of the shares. Conversely, if a holding company is to be considered as a taxable person acting as such with respect to its dealings in shares, a right of deduction may exist. For example, in case shares are transferred to a purchaser who is located outside the EU,[8] or if the transaction costs can be attributed to a downstream taxed transaction.[9]

Even though the true relevance lies with the right of deduction, given the overall design of the EU VAT system, it is pivotal to address all relevant steps in the VAT determination scheme (*see* Chapter 1, section 1.13). Therefore, in this chapter, we will address the following elements of the EU VAT system in connection with dealings in shares:

(1) the taxable person status and capacity;
(2) the taxable transaction;[10]

---

5. CJEU 11 July 1996, Case C-306/94 *Régie Dauphinoise – Cabinet A. Forest SARL v Ministre du Budget*, ECLI:EU:C:1996:290; CJEU 6 February 1997, Case C-80/95 *Harnas & Helm CV v Staatssecretaris van Financiën*, ECLI:EU:C:1997:56; CJEU 14 November 2000, Case C-142/99 *Floridienne SA and Berginvest SA v Belgian State*, ECLI:EU:C:2000:623; CJEU 26 June 2003, Case C-305/01 *MKG-Kraftfahrzeuge-Factory GmbH*, ECLI:EU:C:2003:377, para. 46 and CJEU 29 October 2009, Case C-29/08 *Skatteverket v AB SKF*, ECLI:EU:C:2009:665.
6. *See*, however, Article 137(1)(a) VAT Directive: Member States may allow taxable persons to opt for taxation with respect to certain financial services, such as transactions in shares. CJEU 26 June 2003, Case C-442/01 *KapHag Renditefonds 35 Spreecenter Berlin-Hellersdorf 3. Tranche GbR v Finanzamt Charlottenburg*, ECLI:EU:C:2003:381, para. 40 and CJEU 20 June 1996, Case C-155/94 *Wellcome Trust Ltd v Commissioners of Customs and Excise*, ECLI:EU:C:1996:243, para. 33. *See also* A.J. van Doesum & F. Nellen, *VAT in a Day* (Fonds Indirect Tax, 2021). Available at: https://ssrn.com/abstract=3867201 (accessed 16 August 2024), p. 29.
7. CJEU 6 February 1997, Case C-80/95 *Harnas & Helm CV v Staatssecretaris van Financiën*, ECLI:EU:C:1997:56.
8. Article 169(c) VAT Directive.
9. CJEU 26 May 2005, Case C-465/03 *Kretztechnik AG v Finanzamt Linz*, ECLI:EU:C:2005:320, para. 36 and CJEU 3 July 2019, Case C-316/18 *Commissioners for Her Majesty's Revenue and Customs v The Chancellor, Masters and Scholars of the University of Cambridge*, ECLI:EU:C:2019:559, paras 31 and 32.
10. Clearly, this only relates to the sale of shares and other securities. The purchase and holding of shares or other securities do not constitute taxable events for the purchaser or holder of the

(3) the exemptions;
(4) the right of deduction.

The topic of the VAT treatment of the issue, acquisition, holding and sale of shares has become a rather complicated subject matter over the last 30 years. Apart from the option to treat as tangible property shares or interests equivalent to shares giving the holder thereof de jure or de facto rights of ownership or possession over immovable property (Article 15(2) VAT Directive) and apart from the exemption for transactions in shares (Article 135(1)(f) VAT Directive), the VAT Directive does not contain specific rules on dealings in shares. There is, however, a vast body of CJEU case law on the VAT consequences of the acquisition, holding and sale of shares (in chronological order):

1. Polysar *(C-60/90)*	15. DTZ Zadelhoff *(C-259/11)*
2. Sofitam *(C-333/91)*	16. Portugal Telecom *(C-496/11)*
3. BLP *(C-4/94)*	17. X BV *(C-651/11)*
4. Wellcome Trust *(C-155/94)*	18. Larentia + Minerva *(C-108/14 and C-109/14)*
5. Harnas & Helm *(C-80/95)*	19. MVM *(C-28/16)*
6. Floridienne & Berginvest *(C-142/99)*	20. Polfarmex *(C-421/17)*
7. EDM *(C-77/01)*	21. Marle *(C-320/17)*
8. Welthgrove *(C-102/00)*	22. Ryanair *(C-249/17)*
9. Cibo *(C-16/00)*	23. C&D Foods *(C-502/17)*
10. KapHag *(C-422/01)*	24. University of Cambridge *(C-316/18)*
11. BBL *(C-8/03)*	25. Sonaecom *(C-42/19)*
12. Kretztechnik *(C-465/03)*	26. W GmbH *(C-98/21)*
13. Investrand *(C-435/05)*	27. P. sp. z o.o. *(C-241/23)*
14. SKF *(C-29/08)*	

This case law contains crucial ambiguities in its very fundaments, causing serious legal uncertainty among businesses and side effects which may raise concerns.[11] It is our impression that it is currently impossible to come to one single comprehensive

shares because the purchase and holding of shares cannot be regarded a supply of goods or services, nor an intra-Community acquisition nor an import of goods.

11. In the same sense: R. de la Feria, *When Do Dealings in Shares Fall Within the Scope of VAT?* (2008) 1 EC Tax Review https://doi.org/10.54648/ecta2008051. In her opinion in Sonaecom, Advocate General Kokott points out that as a 'consequence of the CJEU's case-law according to which holding companies have a right to deduct only where they provide remunerated services to their affiliated companies, they set-up seemingly artificial constructions of taxable services in order to prevent a definitive VAT burden within the group of companies to which they belong'. She indicates that the CJEU could have prevented companies being compelled to conclude service contracts for consideration if it had accepted that 'controlling holding companies, which are economically active through the affiliated companies controlled by them, had been recognised in principle as having the right to deduct from their expenditure as a holding company'.

interpretation of the CJEU's case law without accepting that certain inconsistencies remain. Determining the VAT consequences of dealings in shares has become one of the most complex topics in the field of VAT, particularly when it comes to determining the right of deduction. In this chapter, we take an integrated look at the VAT aspects of dealings in shares and other securities, providing as much clarity as we can, while still recognizing the ambiguities in the case law of the CJEU.

11.2 TRANSACTION COSTS

In section 11.1, we introduced the term 'transaction costs'. Transaction costs may include costs, such as those of lawyers, advisers, consultants, accountants and – not surprisingly – tax advisers. Normally, certain financial services may also be classified as transaction costs. However, since financial services may be exempt from VAT (*see* Article 135(1)(b)-(g) VAT Directive), they are excluded from the definition of transaction costs for the purposes of this chapter. Furthermore, the term transaction costs typically refers to the costs of the acquisition and sale and even the issue of shares.[12] For the purpose of this chapter, we also include the costs of the holding of shares in that very same term. Lastly, the term 'transaction costs' suggests that a transaction has been carried out. Nonetheless, we also include costs relating to intended but never effected transactions.[13]

11.3 WHY IS THE MERE HOLDING OF SHARES NOT AN ECONOMIC ACTIVITY?

It has become an *acte clair* that the mere acquisition and holding of financial holdings in other undertakings do not amount to an economic activity from which a taxable person status can be derived because any dividend yielded by that holding is merely the result of ownership of the property.[14] This is, in our view, less self-explanatory than it may seem and therefore, requires further clarification.

The idea that the mere holding of shares is not an economic activity is related to the answers to two questions. The first question is: to what extent is a distinction to be made between a private and a professional investor? The second dilemma is: to what extent is it necessary to distinguish between share capital (equity) and debt capital (loans)? We will discuss both issues hereinafter.

Opinion of Advocate General of 14 May 2020, Case C-42/19 *Sonaecom SGPS SA v Autoridade Tributária e Aduaneira*, ECLI:EU:C:2020:378, paras 41-47.

12. We exclude so-called investment-costs, i.e., the costs of goods and services which a contributor (shareholder) contributes in the fulfilment of an obligation to pay up on shares. These are not expenditures which a contributor needs to incur to acquire shares, but expenditures which themselves constitute the very object of the shareholder's contribution to its subsidiaries. Cf. CJEU 8 September 2022, Case C-98/21 *Finanzamt R v W-GmbH*, ECLI:EU:C:2022:645, para. 53.
13. *See*, for example: CJEU 8 November 2018, Case C-502/17 *C&D Foods Acquisition ApS v Skatteministeriet*, ECLI:EU:C:2018:888.
14. CJEU Order of the Court of 12 July 2001, Case C-102/00 *Welthgrove BV v Staatssecretaris van Financiën*, ECLI:EU:C:2001:416.

According to the CJEU, a holding company confining itself to managing an investment portfolio in the same way as a private investor is not a taxable person.[15] From the viewpoint of VAT as a tax on consumption (and not on savings), a private investor should indeed not be regarded as a taxable person. If one considers that the activities of a mere holding company are not materially different from those of a private investor, it explains why the CJEU ruled that the mere holding of shares is not an economic activity. It also may explain why things are different if the holding of shares by a holding company is accompanied by a direct or indirect involvement in the management (*see* section 11.4.1). However, one may question whether a mere holding company is indeed comparable to a private investor.[16] After all, a (mere) holding company typically plays a central role and has a specific function in a group of roles that a private investor neither plays nor has.

The similarity between a private investor and a holding company as an investor is not the only reason for the CJEU to consider the holding of shares not automatically as an economic activity. Another reason for this is that even though investing in shares (and receiving dividend) and granting of loans or investing in bonds (and receiving interest) may be comparable from an economic perspective, they cannot be equated. Their economic resemblance can, in our view, not immediately explain why the acquisition and holding of shares is not an economic activity. Granted, simple placements of money with a bank do not constitute an economic activity because such placements are a mere exercise of the right of ownership (*see* Chapter 2, section 2.4.12.2). Similarly, if a holding company merely reinvests dividends it received from its subsidiaries as interest-bearing loans to those subsidiaries, such loans are also considered as the mere exercise of ownership and thus as activities outside the scope of VAT.[17] The economic similarities between investing in shares (receiving dividends) and investing in loans or bonds (receiving interest), may explain why they are both considered as non-economic activities in their own right if they entail nothing more than the mere exercise of a right of ownership. However, the granting of a loan may, in certain circumstances, be more than the simple exercise of a right of ownership. For example, if the lender of the funds actively determines the conditions and the interest rates of the bonds, this exceeds the mere exercise of the rights of ownership, resulting in the granting of the interest-bearing loans to be taxable (yet exempt) activities. In our view, this also applies to holding companies which take on an active role in granting loans to their subsidiaries.[18] If indeed the granting of loans and the provision of capital to a company are to be considered as similar activities from an economic perspective, one may question why an investor taking on an active role in providing capital to a company is not to be regarded as a taxable person on the basis of that activity. Perhaps

15. *See*, for example: CJEU 29 April 2004, Case C-77/01 *Empresa de Desenvolvimento Mineiro SGPS SA (EDM) v Fazenda Pública*, ECLI:EU:C:2004:243, para. 60.
16. *See also*: Opinion of Advocate General of 14 May 2020, Case C-42/19 *Sonaecom SGPS SA v Autoridade Tributária e Aduaneira*, ECLI:EU:C:2020:378, para. 46.
17. CJEU 14 November 2000, Case C-142/99 *Floridienne SA and Berginvest SA v Belgian State*, ECLI:EU:C:2000:623, para. 29.
18. *See*, for example: Hoge Raad, 23 September 2011, Case 10/00383, ECLI:NL:HR:2011:BP3871, V-N 2011/47.14.

this explains the case law on the basis of which a controlling active holding company is considered as a taxable person with regard to its shareholding activities (*see* section 11.4.1).

Notwithstanding the above, we believe that the CJEU correctly attaches value to the important differences that exist between the granting of interest-bearing loans (debt capital) and the provision of capital as a shareholder (share capital). As the CJEU confirmed in *Kretztechnik*, there is a conceptual difference between the payment of a consideration and an investment or an employment of capital.[19] If a lender loans money to a company, legally, the lender still owns the money, even though the company may make use of it. If a shareholder invests in a company, the company becomes the owner of the money, and the shareholder becomes the owner of the shares. It is in this regard important to understand that shareholders are not owners of the assets of the undertaking in which they hold their shares.[20] They are merely owners of the shares and, as such, are entitled to a dividend and to the communication of information and are involved in the adoption of important decisions for the management of the undertaking. In other words, the taking, purchasing and holding of shares by a shareholder is merely an act involving the disposal of his assets.[21] This sets an investment in a company apart from the lending of money to a company.

Moreover, the idea that the holding of shares is not an economic activity because dividends do not constitute a consideration seems to be based on the idea that there must be a direct link between a supply and a payment. The carrying out of supplies for consideration (requiring a direct link between a supply and the consideration) is a prerequisite to the existence of an economic activity. It appears that this is also a reason for the CJEU to consider the mere holding of shares as a non-economic activity.

In *Cibo*, the CJEU essentially considered that there is no direct link between the receipt of a dividend and any supplies of goods or services performed.[22] This was confirmed in *Floridienne*.[23] First, the amount of dividend to be received by a shareholder (in this context, a holding company) is not pre-established but depends on a number of external, unknown factors, such as the existence of distributable profits. This makes the payment of dividend dependent on the company's year-end results rather than on the performance of any activity by the shareholder. Furthermore, the

19. CJEU 26 May 2005, Case C-465/03 *Kretztechnik AG v Finanzamt Linz*, ECLI:EU:C:2005:320, para. 26.
20. CJEU 30 May 2013, Case C-651/11 *Staatssecretaris van Financiën v X BV*, ECLI:EU:C:2013:346, para. 39.
21. Cf. Opinion of Advocate General Colomer of 6 February 2003, Case C-442/01 *KapHag Renditefonds v Finanzamt Charlottenburg*, ECLI:EU:C:2003:75, paras 33 and 41 and Opinion of Advocate General Jacobs of 24 February 2005, Case C-465/03 *Kretztechnik AG v Finanzamt Linz*, ECLI:EU:C:2005:111, para. 60.
22. CJEU 27 September 2001, Case C-16/00 *Cibo Participations SA v Directeur régional des impôts du Nord-Pas-de-Calais*, ECLI:EU:C:2001:495, para. 42.
23. 'In view, specifically, of the fact that the amount of the dividend thus depends partly on unknown factors and that entitlement to dividends is merely a function of shareholding, the direct link between the dividend and a supply of services (even where the services are supplied by a shareholder who is paid dividends), which is necessary if the dividends are to constitute consideration for the services, does not exist'. CJEU 14 November 2000, Case C-142/99 *Floridienne SA and Berginvest SA v Belgian State*, ECLI:EU:C:2000:623, para. 23.

proportions in which the dividend is distributed are determined by reference to the type of shares held, in particular, by reference to classes of shares, and not by reference to the identity of the owner of a particular shareholding. Again, this indicates that the receipt of dividends is not connected to the performance of any activities by the shareholder. A last argument for the CJEU to consider dividends as unconnected to any performance of supplies by the shareholder is that dividends represent, by their very nature, the return on investment in a company and are merely the result of ownership of that property.[24]

11.4 DEALINGS IN SHARES AND THE TAXABLE PERSON STATUS

In section 11.1, we indicated that the acquisition, holding and sale of shares can be an economic activity granting taxable person status in three situations:

(1) if a controlling active parent company acquires, holds and sells the shares; or
(2) if a commercial share dealer acquires, holds and sells the shares; or
(3) if the acquisition, holding and selling of the shares constitute the direct, permanent and necessary extension of a taxable activity.

In this section, we will discuss each of these situations separately.

11.4.1 Controlling Active Parent Companies

Under Article 9, second paragraph VAT Directive, the exploitation of tangible or intangible property for the purposes of obtaining income therefrom on a continuing basis shall be regarded as an economic activity. In the landmark case *Van Tiem*, the CJEU clarified that the term 'exploitation' refers to all transactions, whatever may be their legal form, by which it is sought to obtain income from the goods in question on a continuing basis.[25] The holding of shares generates dividends on a continuing basis. Yet, from *Polysar*, it follows that the mere acquisition and holding of shares in a company are not to be regarded as an economic activity.[26] The CJEU considered:

24. Also *see*: CJEU 20 June 1991, Case C-60/90 *Polysar Investement Netherlands BV v Inspecteur der Invoerrechten en Accijnzen*, ECLI:EU:C:1991:268, para. 13 and CJEU 14 November 2000, Case C-142/99 *Floridienne SA and Berginvest SA v Belgian State*, ECLI:EU:C:2000:623, para. 22.
25. CJEU 4 December 1990, Case C-186/89 *Van Tiem v Staatssecretaris van Financiën*, ECLI: EU:C:1990:429, para. 18.
26. This has become settled CJEU case law. The CJEU confirmed that the mere acquisition and holding of shares is not an economic activity in virtually all cases regarding holding companies. *See*, for example: CJEU 20 June 1991, Case C-60/90 *Polysar Investement Netherlands BV v Inspecteur der Invoerrechten en Accijnzen*, ECLI:EU:C:1991:268, para. 13; CJEU 22 June 1993, Case C-333/91 *Sofitam SA (formerly Satam SA) v Ministre chargé du Budget*, ECLI: EU:C:1993:261, para. 12; CJEU 20 June 1996, Case C-155/94 *Wellcome Trust Ltd v Commissioners of Customs and Excise*, ECLI:EU:C:1996:243, para. 32; CJEU 6 February 1997, Case C-80/95 *Harnas & Helm CV v Staatssecretaris van Financiën*, ECLI:EU:C:1997:56, para. 15; CJEU 14 November 2000, Case C-142/99 *Floridienne SA and Berginvest SA v Belgian State*, ECLI:

> It does not follow from that judgment,[27] however, that the mere acquisition and holding of shares in a company is to be regarded as an economic activity, ... conferring on the holder the status of a taxable person. The mere acquisition of financial holdings in other undertakings does not amount to the exploitation of property for the purpose of obtaining income therefrom on a continuing basis because any dividend yielded by that holding is merely the result of ownership of the property.[28]

However, the Court added to that:

> It is otherwise where the holding is accompanied by direct or indirect involvement in the management of the companies in which the holding has been acquired, without prejudice to the rights held by the holding company as shareholder.[29]

In *Floridienne-Berginvest*, the CJEU further clarified that:

> It follows that involvement of that kind in the management of subsidiaries must be regarded as an economic activity ..., in so far as it entails carrying out transactions which are subject to VAT ..., such as the supply by Floridienne and Berginvest of administrative, accounting and information technology services to their subsidiaries.[30]

From this case law, it can be deduced that a holding company obtains taxable person status if it:

EU:C:2000:623, para. 17; CJEU Order of the Court of 12 July 2001, Case C-102/00 *Welthgrove BV v Staatssecretaris van Financiën*, ECLI:EU:C:2001:416, paras 13, 14 and 17; CJEU 27 September 2001, Case C-16/00 *Cibo Participations SA v Directeur régional des impôts du Nord-Pas-de-Calais*, ECLI:EU:C:2001:495, paras 18 and 19; CJEU 29 April 2004, Case C-77/01 *Empresa de Desenvolvimento Mineiro SGPS SA (EDM) v Fazenda Pública*, ECLI:EU:C:2004:243, para. 57; CJEU 21 October 2004, Case C-8/03 *Banque Bruxelles Lambert SA (BBL) v Belgian State*, ECLI:EU:C:2004:650, para. 38; CJEU 26 June 2003, Case C-442/01 *KapHag Renditefonds 35 Spreecenter Berlin-Hellersdorf 3. Tranche GbR v Finanzamt Charlottenburg*, ECLI:EU:C:2003:381, para. 38; CJEU 26 May 2005, Case C-465/03 *Kretztechnik AG v Finanzamt Linz*, ECLI:EU:C:2005:320, para. 19; CJEU 8 February 2007, Case C-435/05 *Investrand BV v Staatssecretaris van Financiën*, ECLI:EU:C:2007:87, para. 25; CJEU 6 September 2012, Case C-496/11 *Portugal Telecom SGPS SA v Fazenda Pública*, ECLI:EU:C:2012:557, paras 31 and 32; CJEU 16 July 2015, Joined Cases C-108/14 and C-109/14 *Beteiligungsgesellschaft Larentia + Minerva mbH & Co. KG v Finanzamt Nordenham and Finanzamt Hamburg-Mitte v Marenave Schiffahrts AG*, ECLI:EU:C:2015:496, paras 18 and 19; CJEU Order of the Court of 12 January 2017, Case C-28/16 *Magyar Villamos Művek Zrt. (MVM) v Nemzeti Adó- és Vámhivatal Fellebbviteli Igazgatóság*, ECLI:EU:C:2017:7, paras 30 and 31; CJEU 5 July 2018, Case C-320/17 *Marle Participations SARL v Ministre de l'Économie et des Finances*, ECLI:EU:C:2018:537, para. 28 and CJEU 8 November 2018, Case C-502/17 *C&D Foods Acquisition ApS v Skatteministeriet*, ECLI:EU:C:2018:888, para. 30. Remarkably, in some cases, the CJEU indicated that the sale of shares is also not an economic activity: CJEU 29 October 2009, Case C-29/08 *Skatteverket v AB SKF*, ECLI:EU:C:2009:665, para. 28 and CJEU 30 May 2013, Case C-651/11 *Staatssecretaris van Financiën v X BV*, ECLI:EU:C:2013:346, para. 36.

27. The CJEU refers to *Van Tiem*: CJEU 4 December 1990, Case C-186/89 *Van Tiem v Staatssecretaris van Financiën*, ECLI:EU:C:1990:429.
28. CJEU 20 June 1991, Case C-60/90 *Polysar Investement Netherlands BV v Inspecteur der Invoerrechten en Accijnzen*, ECLI:EU:C:1991:268, para. 13.
29. *Ibid.*, para. 14.
30. CJEU 14 November 2000, Case C-142/99 *Floridienne SA and Berginvest SA v Belgian State*, ECLI:EU:C:2000:623, para. 19.

(1) holds shares in one or more subsidiaries;
(2) that holding of shares is accompanied by a direct or indirect involvement in the management of those subsidiaries; and
(3) that involvement in the management entails carrying out transactions which are subject to VAT (taxable transactions).

Since the first condition of holding of shares is rather self-explanatory, we will elaborate only on the conditions of involvement in the management and the supply of taxable transactions.

Direct or Indirect Involvement in the Management

Although it is settled CJEU case law that a direct or indirect involvement in the management of its subsidiaries is a necessary precondition to the taxable person status of a holding company,[31] the CJEU has never explained what a direct or indirect involvement in the management entails.[32] Apparently, it is something which stands separately from the rights held by the holding company as a shareholder.[33] In our view, involvement means that the holding company fulfils a steering and policy-making function in relation to the operating companies within the group.[34]

In its more recent case law, the CJEU seems to equate the involvement in the management with the taxable supplies which form the third precondition to taxable status (*see* above). For example, in *Marle*, the CJEU considered that:

> The term 'involvement of a holding company in the management of its subsidiary' must, accordingly, be understood as covering all transactions constituting an economic activity, within the meaning of the VAT Directive, performed by the holding company for the benefit of its subsidiary.[35]

The qualifying services can be administrative, accounting, financial, commercial, information technology and technical services,[36] but can also be the lease of immovable property for the benefit of the subsidiary or any other economic activity.[37]

It is difficult to reconcile *Marle* with previous CJEU case law on this topic. It seems as if in *Marle*, the CJEU has approached the concept of involvement in the

31. Apart from commercial share dealing and the direct, permanent and necessary extension (*see* sections 11.4.2 and 11.4.3).
32. *See*, however: CJEU 5 July 2018, Case C-320/17 *Marle Participations SARL v Ministre de l'Économie et des Finances*, ECLI:EU:C:2018:537.
33. *See*: CJEU 20 June 1991, Case C-60/90 *Polysar Investement Netherlands BV v Inspecteur der Invoerrechten en Accijnzen*, ECLI:EU:C:1991:268, para. 14.
34. *See*, for example: Dutch ministerial Decree of 18 February 1991, No VB91/347, FED 1991/266, which applies until 1 July 2025.
35. CJEU 5 July 2018, Case C-320/17 *Marle Participations SARL v Ministre de l'Économie et des Finances*, ECLI:EU:C:2018:537, para. 32.
36. CJEU 14 November 2000, Case C-142/99 *Floridienne SA and Berginvest SA v Belgian State*, ECLI:EU:C:2000:623, para. 19; CJEU 27 September 2001, Case C-16/00 *Cibo Participations SA v Directeur régional des impôts du Nord-Pas-de-Calais*, ECLI:EU:C:2001:495, para. 22; CJEU 6 September 2012, Case C-496/11 *Portugal Telecom SGPS SA v Fazenda Pública*, ECLI:EU:C:2012:557, para. 34 and CJEU 5 July 2018, Case C-320/17 *Marle Participations SARL v Ministre de l'Économie et des Finances*, ECLI:EU:C:2018:537, para. 30.
37. CJEU 5 July 2018, Case C-320/17 *Marle Participations SARL v Ministre de l'Économie et des Finances*, ECLI:EU:C:2018:537.

management in a different way than it did in its earlier case law. In its previous case law, the CJEU gave the impression that it should first and separately be established whether there is an involvement in the management before establishing whether that involvement is accompanied by or entails the supply of services for consideration.[38] The issue with that two-step approach is not only that the concept of involvement is all but clear, but also that, in practice, it is generally rather difficult to determine whether board members or employees from the parent company indeed fulfil a 'steering and policy-making function in relation to the operating companies within the group'. In that regard, it is much easier to start with verifying whether the parent company supplies services for consideration to its subsidiaries and if that is the case, derive from that fact that there must also be an involvement in the management. This may explain the approach taken by the CJEU in *Marle* when it effectively equated the involvement in the management with the supply of taxable services.[39]

We note that even though this more recent approach may be easier to apply than having to separately establish the involvement in the management and the supply of services and/or goods, it largely disregards the original idea of how the position of a holding company can be distinguished from that of a private investor (*see* section 11.3). A holding company differs from a private investor who holds shares if the holding company (1) is involved in the management; and (2) supplies services (or goods) for consideration to the company in which the shares are held. Both elements are typically absent with a private investor. What even underlines the difference between a holding company and a private investor is (3) the requirement of a link or a material connection between the involvement and the supply of taxable transactions, meaning that the involvement in the management should *entail* the supply of taxable transactions. Nonetheless, with its ruling in *Marle*, the CJEU seems to have mitigated the importance of the involvement and the material connection between the involvement and the existence of any taxable transactions. One may wonder if the CJEU did not go one step too far in *Marle* and whether it would be wise to require a material link between the involvement in the management and the lease of immovable property after all. In other words: although it may complicate the practical application of EU VAT law, in *Marle* it would have been more in line with the ratio of the condition of involvement in the management to require an investigation as to whether that involvement entails the lease of immovable property.

In *W GmbH*, the CJEU has cast even more doubt on the relevance of a link between the holding of shares, an involvement in the management and the supply of services for consideration.[40] The CJEU considered with respect to a contribution in kind that it 'comes under holding of shares', which does not amount to an economic activity, even though the contributing party concerned already regularly supplied services for consideration to the subsidiary. This suggests that the holding of shares

38. *See*, for example: CJEU 14 November 2000, Case C-142/99 *Floridienne SA and Berginvest SA v Belgian State*, ECLI:EU:C:2000:623, para. 19.
39. Since in the field of VAT, there is no fundamental difference between the supply of services and goods, we believe that the involvement in the management can also be embedded in the supply of goods for consideration.
40. CJEU 8 September 2022, Case C-98/21 *Finanzamt R v W-GmbH*, ECLI:EU:C:2022:645.

and supplying services for consideration should be considered separately, and that the holding of shares should never be considered an economic activity, even if it is accompanied by services for consideration. However, such an interpretation would contradict the earlier established CJEU case law and would, more particularly, be diametrically opposed to the ruling in *Marle*.

In our view, it is more likely that the leading idea behind *W GmbH* is that in case of a contribution in kind, for this contribution to be an economic activity, one must not look for a link with any services that the investor (in addition to and separately from the contribution) supplies to the subsidiary. Instead, it may be so that the CJEU believes that a contribution in kind can only be an economic activity (for which a right of deduction may exist) if that contribution *itself* can be regarded as a supply for consideration under Article 2(1)(a) of the VAT Directive.[41] A contribution 'free of charge' may then arguably 'come under holding of shares',[42] which does not amount to an economic activity; the mere holding of shares does not constitute an economic activity. Admittedly, however, it remains unclear whether the CJEU indeed holds this thought as its guiding principle. Moreover, this interpretation creates ambiguities of its own right (*see* Chapter 3, section 3.4.8).

In view of the above considerations, we maintain our belief that *W GmbH* should not be interpreted as meaning that the holding of shares and supplying services for consideration should be considered separately and that the holding of shares is always a non-economic activity. Therefore, we will abstract from this ruling in the remainder of this section.

Taxable Transactions

In *Welthgrove*, the CJEU made it clear that the holding of shares in combination with an involvement in the management alone is not sufficient for a holding company to qualify as a taxable person.[43] The involvement must entail carrying out transactions which are subject to VAT (i.e., taxable transactions).

According to Advocate General Kokott, the condition of the supply of taxable transactions is based on the idea that the precondition to any economic activity is the supply of goods or services for consideration:

> As was stated above (point 18), the holding of a share alone does not(!)[44] mean that an economic activity is considered to exist. On the other hand, the Court states in its settled case law that the acquisition and holding of a share by a holding company does constitute an economic activity within the meaning of Article 9(1)

41. *See*, however: A.J. van Doesum, *Contractuele samenwerkingsverbanden in de btw* (*dissertation*) (Kluwer 2009), pp. 540-580 and A.J. van Doesum, *Contributions to Partnerships from a European VAT Law Perspective*, (2010) 6 EC Tax Review https://doi.org/10.54648/ecta2010033.
42. Cf. CJEU 8 September 2022, Case C-98/21 *Finanzamt R v W-GmbH*, ECLI:EU:C:2022:645, para. 53.
43. CJEU Order of the Court of 12 July 2001, Case C-102/00 *Welthgrove BV v Staatssecretaris van Financiën*, ECLI:EU:C:2001:416.
44. In the English text version of the Advocate-General's opinion in Ryanair, the word 'not' appears to be unintentionally omitted. The Dutch, German and French text version do not contain this omission. Opinion of Advocate General Kokott of 3 May 2018, Case C-249/17 *Ryanair Ltd v The Revenue Commissioners*, ECLI:EU:C:2018:301, para. 25.

> of the VAT Directive where the shareholding is accompanied by direct or indirect involvement in the management of the target company. Such involvement may, for example, consist in the supply of administrative, financial or commercial services to the target company. However, this criterion is merely based on the fact that for a pure holding company to be recognized as a taxable person, there must additionally be activities which are subject to VAT by virtue of Articles 2 and 9 of the directive.[45]

We agree with Advocate General Kokott that this seems to be the underlying reason for the CJEU to require that the involvement in the management entails taxable supplies. What makes it difficult to understand this, though, is that any company, whether it holds shares or not, obtains taxable person status if it makes supplies for considerations on a continuous basis. This again suggests that – differently from *Marle* – it is not sufficient for a holding company to merely supply services (or)goods for consideration to its subsidiary, but that there must also be a material link with an involvement in the management of that subsidiary.[46] We believe that unpaid intervention is indeed not sufficient (would that then be a service free of charge?), but if the services to the subsidiary cover the intervention, one may argue that the intervention takes place for consideration.[47] In our view, it is difficult if not impossible, to reconcile *Marle* with previous CJEU case law and with the rationale of distinguishing actively involved holding companies from other investors (*see* section 11.3). This creates an ambiguity in the CJEU's case law because it raises doubts on whether *Marle* indicates that the CJEU has entered a new path or whether *Marle* was merely 'a slip of the pen'.[48]

11.4.2 Commercial Share Dealings

In *Wellcome Trust,*[49] the CJEU ruled that the concept of economic activities is to be interpreted as not including an activity, consisting in the purchase and sale of shares and other securities by a trustee in the course of the management of the assets of a charitable trust. However, transactions in shares, interests in companies or associations, debentures and other securities may fall within the scope of VAT, in particular,

45. *Ibid.*, para. 25. Footnote references have been omitted in this citation.
46. Even though the Advocate General at first sight seems to equate the involvement in the management with the supply of taxable services to the target company, when looking closer she seems to be of the opinion that the services for consideration are to be supplied 'in addition' to an involvement: 'However, this criterion is merely based on the fact that for a pure holding company to be recognised as a taxable person, there must additionally be activities which are subject to VAT by virtue of Articles 2 and 9 of the directive'.
47. Footnote 15 of the Opinion of Advocate General Kokott of 3 May 2018, Case C-249/17 *Ryanair Ltd v The Revenue Commissioners*, ECLI:EU:C:2018:301, para. 25.
48. An indication that this was merely a faux pas can be found in CJEU 8 September 2022, Case C-98/21 *Finanzamt R v W-GmbH*, ECLI:EU:C:2022:645, para. 42. There, the CJEU refers to 'remunerated services subject to VAT coming under that involvement'.
49. CJEU 20 June 1996, Case C-155/94 *Wellcome Trust Ltd v Commissioners of Customs and Excise*, ECLI:EU:C:1996:243. Confirmed in CJEU 6 February 1997, Case C-80/95 *Harnas & Helm CV v Staatssecretaris van Financiën*, ECLI:EU:C:1997:56 and CJEU 29 April 2004, Case C-77/01 *Empresa de Desenvolvimento Mineiro SGPS SA (EDM) v Fazenda Pública*, ECLI:EU:C:2004:243.

where such transactions are effected as part of a commercial share-dealing activity. The CJEU confirmed this judgment in *Harnas & Helm*.[50]

It should be noted that a holding company operating commercially in shares is not a holding company in the strict sense of the word because it is not a parent company which holds shares in its subsidiaries. The purpose of such a holding company is the commercial trade of shares and not the mere holding of the shares. The company holds the shares as stock in the same manner as other taxable persons keep stock of goods.[51]

11.4.3 Direct, Permanent and Necessary Extension

In *Régie Dauphinoise*,[52] the CJEU introduced the concept of the direct, permanent and necessary extension. Régie Dauphinoise was involved principally in the management of property. That business consisted partly in managing let property as an agent of the owners and partly in acting as manager of condominiums. As such, it received advances from the co-owners and lessees for whom it managed the properties. With the agreement of its clients, it invested those sums for its own account with financial institutions. Régie became the owner of the sums advanced with effect from their payment into its account. It remained under an obligation to repay but was entitled to retain the interest on the placements. The main question was whether the interest realized with Régie's treasury placements should be taken into account when calculating the deductible proportion. According to the CJEU, the placements with financial institutions were to be regarded as services supplied to those institutions, consisting of the loan of money for a fixed period, duly remunerated by the payment of interest. Those placements would not have been subject to VAT, had they been supplied by a person not acting as a taxable person.[53] However, in this particular case, the receipt, by such a manager, of interest resulting from the placements of monies received from clients in the course of managing their properties constituted a 'direct, permanent and necessary extension of the taxable activity'. Consequently, the manager (Régie Dauphinoise) was considered to have been acting as a taxable person in making such an investment.[54]

From this case, it becomes clear that mere placements are not inside the scope of VAT. This might be different if the placements are the direct, permanent and necessary extension of other taxable activities. Régie Dauphinoise was a taxable person (management of property) and was also acting in the capacity of a taxable person with

50. CJEU 6 February 1997, Case C-80/95 *Harnas & Helm CV v Staatssecretaris van Financiën*, ECLI:EU:C:1997:56, para. 16. *See also* CJEU 29 April 2004, Case C-77/01 *Empresa de Desenvolvimento Mineiro SGPS SA (EDM) v Fazenda Pública*, ECLI:EU:C:2004:243.
51. G.J. van Norden, *Het concern in de btw (dissertation)* (Kluwer 2007), pp. 153-154.
52. CJEU 11 July 1996, Case C-306/94 *Régie Dauphinoise – Cabinet A. Forest SARL v Ministre du Budget*, ECLI:EU:C:1996:290.
53. *See*: S.B. Cornielje, *Fusies en overnames in de Europese btw (dissertation)* (2016), pp. 213-226.
54. For completeness' sake, we note that to the extent that Régie Dauphinoise's placements with financial institutions were to be regarded as services falling within the scope of VAT, those placements were exempt. Accordingly, the amount of interest received should be included in the denominator of the fraction used to calculate the deductible proportion.

respect to the placements. If the placements were not to be regarded as a direct, permanent and necessary extension of the economic activity, Regie Dauphinoise would have acted in two capacities.

In *Harnas & Helm,*[55] the CJEU confirmed the concept of the 'direct, permanent and necessary extension'. In this case, the CJEU ruled that the holding of shares and bonds may fall within the scope of VAT where they constitute the direct, permanent and necessary extension of the taxable activity.[56] Activities consisting in the mere acquisition of ownership in and the holding of bonds and the receipt of income therefrom, which are not subservient to any other economic activity, are not to be regarded as economic activities. Apparently, the concept of the direct, permanent and necessary extension applies not only to loans but also to activities regarding shares and bonds.

In *Floridienne-Berginvest,* the CJEU decided that granting loans by a holding company to its subsidiaries to which it supplies administrative, accounting, information technology and general management services cannot be subject to VAT on the ground that it is the direct, permanent and necessary extension of the supply of these taxable services. Such loans are neither necessarily nor directly linked to services thus supplied.[57] On the basis of this ruling, it has become clear that for a direct, permanent and necessary extension to exist, a non-economic activity must be directly linked to and necessary for the fulfilment of an economic activity.

In *SKF,*[58] the CJEU confirmed that transactions relating to shares or holdings in a company are subject to VAT where they constitute the direct, permanent and necessary extension of the taxable activity. By the disposal of all its shares in the subsidiary and in the controlled company, SKF ended its holdings in those companies. That disposal, carried out to enable the parent company to restructure a group of companies, could be regarded as a transaction that consisted of obtaining income on a continuing basis from activities which went beyond the compass of the simple sale of shares. That transaction had a direct link with the organization of the activity carried out by the group and constituted accordingly a direct, permanent and necessary extension of the taxable activity of SKF (involvement in the management of subsidiaries).[59] A similar line of reasoning can be found in *C&D Foods.*[60]

If one considers that the acquisition, holding and sale of shares by a controlling active holding company is an economic activity in itself (*see* section 11.4.1, above), it should be irrelevant whether the disposal of shares is the direct, permanent and necessary extension of the taxable activity of a controlling active parent company. Conversely, the idea that a sale of shares by a controlling active holding company is the

55. CJEU 6 February 1997, Case C-80/95 *Harnas & Helm CV v Staatssecretaris van Financiën,* ECLI:EU:C:1997:56.
56. *Ibid.,* para. 19. According to the CJEU, there is no reason to treat bondholding differently from shareholding.
57. CJEU 14 November 2000, Case C-142/99 *Floridienne SA and Berginvest SA v Belgian State,* ECLI:EU:C:2000:623, para. 29.
58. CJEU 29 October 2009, Case C-29/08 *Skatteverket v AB SKF,* ECLI:EU:C:2009:665.
59. *Ibid.,* para. 33.
60. CJEU 8 November 2018, Case C-502/17 *C&D Foods Acquisition ApS v Skatteministeriet,* ECLI:EU:C:2018:888.

direct, permanent and necessary extension of an economic activity, suggests that it is in itself *not* an economic activity.[61] Yet, the CJEU has repeatedly held that if the holding of shares does not constitute an economic activity (which was, for example, the case in SKF), the sale of those shares constitutes an economic activity neither.[62] Again, CJEU case law is inconsistent, which makes it difficult to determine the VAT treatment of dealings in shares with a sufficient degree of certainty. Moreover, if a sale of shares is considered as an extension of an economic activity, this has important implications with respect to the recovery of input VAT on transaction costs (*see* section 11.7.4.4). In our view, the CJEU has caused a troublesome inconsistency in the VAT treatment of dealings in shares.

11.5 THE ISSUE AND SALE OF SHARES AND THE TAXABLE TRANSACTION

In this section, we elaborate on the question of whether a transaction in shares may constitute a taxable transaction for VAT. We note that the acquisition and the holding of shares cannot form a taxable transaction for the acquirer, as they are rather 'input' rather than 'output' transactions. Therefore, we focus on the issue and sale of shares.

11.5.1 The Issue of Shares[63]

In *Kretztechnik*, the CJEU confirmed that a new share issue does not constitute a taxable transaction. A share issue is, therefore, a non-taxable ('out of scope') activity. Although we subscribe to this point of view, the CJEU's underlying reasoning is not watertight.

The CJEU refers to its ruling in *KapHag*.[64] In *KapHag*, the CJEU was asked whether a partnership makes a taxable supply to a new partner who enters into the partnership, making a contribution in cash to that partnership. The CJEU's starting point was to reiterate that the mere acquisition and holding of shares in a company is not to be regarded as an economic activity. From that, the CJEU concluded that the entry of a new partner into a partnership in consideration for a contribution in cash does not constitute an economic activity on the part of the partner. This is difficult to understand because the taking of shares is not the same thing as the contribution to the capital of a company (*see* Chapter 3, section 3.4.8), which is usually the obligation which follows from the taking of the shares. Furthermore, it follows that the CJEU

61. Which in itself could be found to be in line with CJEU 8 September 2022, Case C-98/21 *Finanzamt R v W-GmbH*, ECLI:EU:C:2022:645.
62. *See*, for example: CJEU 20 June 1996, Case C-155/94 *Wellcome Trust Ltd v Commissioners of Customs and Excise*, ECLI:EU:C:1996:243, para. 33 and CJEU 26 June 2003, Case C-442/01 *KapHag Renditefonds 35 Spreecenter Berlin-Hellersdorf 3. Tranche GbR v Finanzamt Charlottenburg*, ECLI:EU:C:2003:381, para. 40.
63. *See*, with regard to the VAT consequences of contributions (following the issue and subsequent taking of shares), Chapter 3, section 3.4.8.
64. CJEU 26 June 2003, Case C-442/01 *KapHag Renditefonds 35 Spreecenter Berlin-Hellersdorf 3. Tranche GbR v Finanzamt Charlottenburg*, ECLI:EU:C:2003:381.

equated the acquisition by a shareholder of shares in a share company with an interest of a partner in a partnership. From the viewpoint of neutrality of legal form, we believe that this is in itself a correct approach. It can also be deduced from *KapHag* that the CJEU equates the acquisition of shares by a holding company with the taking of new shares in a partnership by a partner. Since there does not seem to be a material difference between a partner/partnership and a shareholder/share company, this implies that the taking of newly issued shares by a holding company should also be outside the scope of VAT.

The next step in the CJEU's reasoning in *KapHag* is, in our view, rather incomprehensible. The CJEU considered:

> If the taking of shares does not in itself constitute an economic activity within the meaning of the Sixth Directive, the same must be true of activities consisting in the transfer of such shares (Case C-155/94 Wellcome Trust [1996] ECR I-3013, paragraph 33).
>
> The admission of a new partner into a partnership does not, therefore, constitute a supply of services to him.
>
> In that context, it is irrelevant whether the admission of the new partner must be regarded as the act of the partnership itself or as that of the other partners since the admission of a new partner does not in any event constitute a supply of services for consideration for the purposes of the directive.[65]

The problem with this argumentation is twofold. First, it suggests that the issuing of shares is the same thing as the transfer of shares. We believe this is incorrect. A transfer of shares is a disposal of shares which a shareholder/holding company holds in another person (subsidiary). An issue of shares is not a disposal of shares in another person but is the allowing of other persons to obtain shares in the issuing company. Neither is an issue of shares a transfer of the assets of the issuing company. As the CJEU confirmed in *X BV*, shareholders are not owners of the assets of the undertaking in which they hold their shares; they are owners of the shares and, as such, are entitled to a dividend and to the communication of information, and are involved in the adoption of important decisions for the management of the undertaking.[66] Second, the cited consideration seems to ignore the fact that the person taking the shares (the partner, or in case of a holding company, that holding company) is not the same person as the one issuing the shares (the partnership, or the subsidiary). Consequently, it does not make much sense, when the CJEU states that if the taking of shares is not an economic activity, the transfer of the shares is also not an economic activity.[67]

Whatever the criticism on the CJEU's reasoning in *KapHag* may be, it is clear that neither the partnership, nor the existing partners, nor the new partner makes a taxable supply when the new partner enters into a partnership, in consideration of payment of a contribution in cash. Building further on this, in *Kreztechnik*, the CJEU ruled that the same conclusion must be drawn regarding the issue of shares for the purpose of raising

65. *Ibid.*, paras 40-42.
66. CJEU 30 May 2013, Case C-651/11 *Staatssecretaris van Financiën v X BV*, ECLI:EU:C:2013:346, para. 39.
67. *See* further: A.J. van Doesum, *Contributions to Partnerships from a European VAT Law Perspective* (2010) 6 EC Tax Review, pp. 259-271 https://doi.org/10.54648/ecta2010033.

capital: that too is a non-taxable transaction (i.e., outside the scope of VAT). However, referring to the Advocate General's opinion in *Kretztechnik*, the CJEU further underpinned this conclusion by stating that a company that issues new shares is increasing its assets by acquiring additional capital, while granting the new shareholders a right of ownership of part of the capital thus increased. From the issuing company's point of view, the aim is to raise capital and not to provide services. As far as the shareholder is concerned, payment of the sums necessary for the increase of capital is not a payment of consideration but an investment or an employment of capital.[68] Apparently, the issuing (and taking) of shares is something which takes place in the capital relation and therefore, does not constitute a taxable transaction. We note that the CJEU seems to consider that the objective of a person's actions is relevant: since it is the aim of the issuing company to raise capital and not to provide services, the issue of shares is not regarded as the supply of services. If this is true for the issue of shares in relation to which a cash contribution is made, the same should apply to contributions in kind to the company's capital. Indeed, in *W GmbH*, the CJEU ruled that 'a contribution from a holding company in favour of its subsidiaries, whether in cash or in kind, comes under holding of shares which does not amount to an economic activity'.[69] This raises the question of why, if there is no material difference between companies with and companies without a capital divided into shares (neutrality of legal form), such contributions in kind to – for example – partnerships should also be outside the scope of VAT.[70] Moreover, in *P. sp. z o.o.*, the CJEU ruled that a contribution in kind in return for newly issued shares *did* constitute a supply for consideration.[71] This seems to contradict the ruling in *W GmbH*. A potential explanation may lie in the fact that in W GmbH the contributor did not receive newly issued shares (the value of the existing shares merely increased) while in P. sp. z o.o. new shares were issued. Yet, if from the contributor's point of view, the contribution in kind constitutes a supply for which the newly issued shares are the consideration, how can this then be reconciled with the notion from *Kretztechnik* that from the issuing company's point of view the issuing of new shares does not constitute a supply for consideration for the reason that its aim is to raise capital and not to provide services? We refer to Chapter 3, section 3.4.8.

11.5.2 The Sale of Shares

It is settled CJEU case law that the mere sale of shares does not constitute an economic activity. A sale of shares does not amount to exploitation of an asset intended to

68. CJEU 26 May 2005, Case C-465/03 *Kretztechnik AG v Finanzamt Linz*, ECLI:EU:C:2005:320, para. 26.
69. CJEU 8 September 2022, Case C-98/21 *Finanzamt R v W-GmbH*, ECLI:EU:C:2022:645, para. 53.
70. *See* further: A.J. van Doesum, *Contributions to Partnerships from a European VAT Law perspective* (2010) 6 EC Tax Review, pp. 259-271 https://doi.org/10.54648/ecta2010033.
71. CJEU 8 May 2024, Case C-241/23 *P. sp. z o.o. v Dyrektor Izby Administracji Skarbowej w Warszawie*, ECLI:EU:C:2024:392.

produce revenue on a continuing basis, as the only consideration for those transactions consists of a possible profit on the sale of those shares.[72]

Nonetheless, it follows from CJEU case law that there are situations in which a sale of shares against payment does constitute a taxable supply of a service.[73] A sale of shares may fall within the scope of VAT if it is effected as a part of a commercial share-dealing activity. A sale of shares by a controlling active parent company should, in principle, also come into the scope of VAT.[74] Moreover, there is CJEU case law suggesting that the sale of shares by a controlling active holding company is the direct, permanent and necessary extension of a taxable activity.[75] At this point, we must already note that in *W GmbH*, the CJEU has cast some doubt on how its earlier case law should be interpreted. The CJEU suggests that holding shares in a subsidiary should be considered separately from any services provided for consideration to that subsidiary and that holding shares, in any case, does not constitute an economic activity. However, we maintain the view that the CJEU did not intend this in a general sense. We will discuss the situations in which a sale of shares constitutes an economic activity in this section.

11.5.2.1 The Sale of Shares by a Commercial Share Dealer

The sale of shares by a commercial share dealer is generally considered to be an economic activity.[76] Such a supply of a service for consideration is exempt from VAT (*see* section 11.4.2).

11.5.2.2 The Sale of Shares by a Controlling Active Holding Company

It follows from cases such as *Wellcome Trust*,[77] *EDM*,[78] *Kretztechnik*[79] and *KapHag*[80] that if the acquisition and the holding of the shares do not constitute an economic activity, the sale of such shares is also not an economic activity.

72. CJEU 29 April 2004, Case C-77/01 *Empresa de Desenvolvimento Mineiro SGPS SA (EDM) v Fazenda Pública*, ECLI:EU:C:2004:243, para. 58; CJEU 29 October 2009, Case C-29/08 *Skatteverket v AB SKF*, ECLI:EU:C:2009:665, para. 28 and CJEU 30 May 2013, Case C-651/11 *Staatssecretaris van Financiën v X BV*, ECLI:EU:C:2013:346, para. 38.
73. CJEU 26 May 2005, Case C-465/03 *Kretztechnik AG v Finanzamt Linz*, ECLI:EU:C:2005:320, para. 22.
74. CJEU 6 February 1997, Case C-80/95 *Harnas & Helm CV v Staatssecretaris van Financiën*, ECLI:EU:C:1997:56, para. 16.
75. CJEU 29 October 2009, Case C-29/08 *Skatteverket v AB SKF*, ECLI:EU:C:2009:665.
76. CJEU 29 October 2009, Case C-29/08 *AB SKF v Skatteverket*, ECLI:EU:C:2009:665, para. 31.
77. CJEU 20 June 1996, Case C-155/94 *Wellcome Trust Ltd v Commissioners of Customs and Excise*, ECLI:EU:C:1996:243.
78. CJEU 29 April 2004, Case C-77/01 *Empresa de Desenvolvimento Mineiro SGPS SA (EDM) v Fazenda Pública*, ECLI:EU:C:2004:243, para. 57.
79. CJEU 26 May 2005, Case C-465/03 *Kretztechnik AG v Finanzamt Linz*, ECLI:EU:C:2005:320, para. 19.
80. CJEU 26 June 2003, Case C-442/01 *KapHag Renditefonds 35 Spreecenter Berlin-Hellersdorf 3. Tranche GbR v Finanzamt Charlottenburg*, ECLI:EU:C:2003:381, para. 40.

On the basis of the overall design and functioning of the VAT system, one may expect that if a holding company acquires and holds shares as a taxable person, any later sale of such shares is also effected in the taxable person capacity of that holding. In fact, this would be fully consistent with CJEU case law confirming that if the acquisition and holding is not an economic activity, the sale of such shares is also not an economic activity.

Indeed, in *SKF*, the CJEU indicated that if a holding company holds shares as a taxable person, the sale of those shares (referred to as 'transactions relating to shares or holdings in a company') also constitutes an economic activity (i.e., a 'taxable activity'). It considered:

> Moreover, it is clear from the Court's case-law that transactions relating to shares or holdings in a company are subject to VAT when they are carried out as part of a commercial share-dealing activity or in order to secure a direct or indirect involvement in the management of the companies in which the holding has been acquired, or where they constitute the direct, permanent and necessary extension of the taxable activity (*see, inter alia*, Case C-155/94 Wellcome Trust [1996] ECR I-3013, paragraph 35, and Harnas & Helm, paragraph 16 and the case-law there cited).[81]

Also in other cases, the CJEU has suggested that if the acquisition and the holding of shares by a holding company form an economic activity, the sale of such shares also constitutes an economic activity and therefore, forms a taxable service. For example, in *BLP*, a disposal of shares by a controlling active parent company was considered as a taxable supply, and more particularly as an exempt supply of services.[82] The CJEU denied BLP the right to deduct VAT on costs related to a disposal of shares in one of its subsidiaries because of the fact that the sale of shares to which the costs could be directly attributed constituted a VAT-exempt supply. The CJEU's ruling in *EDM*, however, appeared to accept that the sale of shares by a controlling active parent company was *not* to be regarded as an economic activity.[83] Without even mentioning its ruling in *BLP*, the CJEU held that an undertaking which pursues activities consisting in the *simple* sale of shares is to be regarded as confining itself to managing an investment portfolio in the same way as a private investor and thus performing a non-economic activity. Some drew the conclusion that despite the CJEU's ruling in *BLP*, a sale of shares by a controlling active parent company is not an economic activity.[84] However, from the facts of the case, it becomes clear that EDM was a mere holding company, which was not involved in the management of its subsidiaries. The only management it did was the management of its own portfolio of securities. The management of a portfolio should not be confused with the (involvement in the)

81. CJEU 29 October 2009, Case C-29/08 *AB SKF v Skatteverket*, ECLI:EU:C:2009:665, para. 31.
82. CJEU 6 April 1995, Case C-4/94 *BLP Group plc v Commissioners of Customs & Excise*, ECLI:EU:C:1995:107.
83. *See* for an extensive analysis, R. de la Feria, *When Do Dealings in Shares Fall Within the Scope of VAT?* (2008) 1 EC Tax Review, pp. 24-40 https://doi.org/10.54648/ecta2008051.
84. Dutch Supreme Court 14 March 2003, No 38 253, BNB 2003/197 and Dutch Supreme Court 9 July 2004, No 38 026, BNB 2004/363. *See also* A. van Dongen, *BTW-gevolgen van de verkoop van aandelen na EDM* (2004) 6583 *Weekblad Fiscaal Recht*, pp. 964-970.

management of subsidiaries. Therefore, we contend that it cannot be inferred from EDM that the sale of shares by a controlling active parent company is not to be considered an economic activity.

It follows that there are indications in CJEU case law that a sale of shares should fundamentally follow the same logic as any other sale of business assets. However, starting with the CJEU's ruling in *SKF*, the idea has emerged that a sale of shares should not strictly follow the same VAT regime as a sale of other assets of a business, such as machinery. The explanation for a different approach to sales of shares (as opposed to sales of assets like machinery) seems to be that shares are not directly used in the production process.[85] Moreover, machines are written off over time, as they are 'productively consumed' during their lifespan – which is not the case with shares. Furthermore, if a holding company holds shares in another entity that does not mean that the subsidiary's assets and/or economic activity (if any) can be attributed to the holding company, nor that the subsidiary's production can be attributed to the holding company.[86] As the CJEU summarizes in X BV:

> unlike the holding of the assets of an undertaking, the holding of shares in an undertaking is not sufficient to allow an independent economic activity to be carried on.[87]

In its more recent case law, the CJEU seems to depart from the idea that a sale of shares by a holding company is by default not an economic activity. For example, in *SKF*, the CJEU did not simply rule that since the holding of shares by the controlling active holding company constituted an economic activity, the sale of those shares also constituted an economic activity. Instead, it considered that the sale of shares by a controlling active holding company (SKF) was not an economic activity in its own right, but only by virtue of it being the direct, permanent and necessary extension of the taxable activity of SKF as a controlling active holding company. The CJEU considered that by disposing of all its shares in its subsidiaries, the controlling active parent company (SKF) brought to an end its holdings in those subsidiaries. Such a disposal which is carried out in order to enable the parent company to restructure a group of companies can be regarded as a transaction that consists of obtaining income on a continuing basis from activities which go beyond the compass of the *simple* sale of shares. Following the CJEU's reasoning, the disposal has a direct link with the organization of the activity carried out by the group and constitutes accordingly the direct, permanent and necessary extension of the taxable activity of SKF.[88] The CJEU reiterated this in *C&D Foods* (*see* below, section 11.5.2.3).[89]

85. By analogy: CJEU 9 July 2015, Case C-331/14 *Petar Kezic s.p. Trgovina Prizma v Republika Slovenija*, ECLI:EU:C:2015:456, para. 21.
86. *See*: A.J. van Doesum, *What Looks Like a Duck Is a Duck: Economic Purpose and Legal Reality in EU VAT Law* (2012) 2 World Journal of VAT, pp. 202-204 https://doi.org/10.5235/wjovl.1.2.202.
87. Cf. CJEU 30 May 2013, Case C-651/11 *Staatssecretaris van Financiën v X BV*, ECLI:EU:C:2013:346, para. 35.
88. *Ibid.*, para. 33.
89. CJEU 8 November 2018, Case C-502/17 *C&D Foods Acquisition ApS v Skatteministeriet*, ECLI:EU:C:2018:888, para. 33.

In summary, from *SKF* and *C&D Foods*, it can be inferred that the sale of shares by a controlling active holding company is not by default an economic activity (i.e., a taxable supply of a service). This is only the case if it forms the direct, permanent and necessary extension of the taxable activity of that holding company. A potential explanation lies in the different nature of 'normal' business assets and shares.

It seems appropriate to make some critical observations here. First, we believe that the CJEU's approach in *SKF* and *C&D Foods* is difficult to reconcile with previous case law from which the idea emerged that if the acquisition and the holding is an economic activity, the sale of those shares is also an economic activity. Second, even though we can see the conceptual differences between (normal) business assets and shares, we believe these differences cannot justify a different VAT treatment of sales of shares. Notwithstanding the different nature of a 'normal' business asset and that of shares, the disposal of shares which are held within the course of an economic activity is a *supply* of a service which is very similar to any other taxable *supply* of services (or goods) by a taxable person. If a company is a taxable person and acts as such when effecting a transaction for consideration, the transaction is either a supply of goods or a supply of services within the meaning of Article 2(1) VAT Directive. In either case, it is irrelevant whether the transaction is the direct, permanent and necessary extension of the taxable activity of the parent company. That criterion does not have a relevant function in this respect.[90] In our opinion, sales by a taxable person acting as such of goods, of assets or of shares in other companies, do not materially differ in such a manner that a sale of the shares is the extension of its economic activity whereas the sales of products or assets are regular components and results of that economic activity. Third, the use of the extension doctrine in relation to a sale of shares by a holding company poses difficulties with respect to the right of deduction (*see* section 11.7.4.4).

In the analysis above, we essentially discussed the situation in which a controlling active holding company purchased and held shares in its taxable person capacity and subsequently sold those shares. We indicated that the CJEU seems to hold that by 'default' a sale of shares is not an economic activity. Apparently, it is conceivable that shares are relabelled from 'business assets' to 'non-business assets'. Only if the sale of such shares constitutes a direct, necessary and permanent extension of the economic activity, no relabelling takes place, the shares remain 'business assets' of the controlling active holding company, and the sale is within the scope of VAT. This somewhat echoes the approach by the CJEU taken towards sales of other assets than shares, in particular, *Petar Kezic* (*see* Chapter 2, section 2.4.12.5.1).[91]

Mr Kezic had acquired plots of land, some of which had been assigned to his private assets and others to his business. He had built, in his capacity as a taxable person, upon all of those plots of land, a shopping centre. Moreover, he had taken

90. It may have a useful function in other situations. *See*, for example, CJEU 11 July 1996, Case C-306/94 *Régie Dauphinoise – Cabinet A. Forest SARL v Ministre du Budget*, ECLI:EU:C:1996:290 and CJEU 6 February 1997, Case C-80/95 *Harnas & Helm CV v Staatssecretaris van Financiën*, ECLI:EU:C:1997:56.

91. CJEU 9 July 2015, Case C-331/14 *Petar Kezic s.p. Trgovina Prizma v Republika Slovenija*, ECLI:EU:C:2015:456, paras 24-28.

active steps to market the property by mobilizing resources among which private property and the carrying out on that land of preparatory work to make development possible. Eventually, this centre was sold, together with the plots of land on which the building was erected. The CJEU ruled that the sale of the plots of land which were originally assigned to his *private* assets must be subject to VAT since that person, at the time of that transaction, acted as a taxable person. This ruling shows that under specific circumstances the label 'private asset' can be removed from the asset and changed into the label 'business asset'. We see no unsurmountable obstacles in applying the same mechanism to sales of shares. Thus, a sale of shares by a holding company which purchased the shares in a non-taxable person capacity may be an economic activity (i.e., a taxable transaction) after all if there are specific circumstances that justify a 'relabelling' of the shares. We doubt whether such a relabelling can be justified alone by – for example – the holding company at some point in time becoming involved in the management of the subsidiary and supplying services for consideration to it. However, if the involvement and supply of services are accompanied by allocating the proceeds of the sale directly to the taxable economic activity of the parent company or to the economic activity carried out by the group headed by the parent company,[92] the sale should, in our view, be considered an economic activity after all.[93] We note that the opposite may also be the case: a sale of shares by a controlling active parent company who purchased and held the shares as a taxable person, may in specific circumstances be a non-economic activity, for example, if the proceeds of the sale of shares are exclusively used for the benefit of its shareholders.[94] Again, the relevance lies in the right of deduction of VAT on transaction costs relating to the sale of shares. We refer to section 11.7.[95]

We have previously observed that the ruling in *W GmbH* has potentially undermined the above-mentioned intellectual framework of the CJEU concerning the holding and selling of shares (*see* section 11.4.1).[96] The ruling suggests that the holding of shares and the supply of services for consideration by an active controlling holding company should be considered in isolation from each other and that the holding of shares should never be considered an economic activity, even if it is accompanied by services for consideration. However, such an interpretation would contradict the earlier established CJEU case law. It would also raise the question of why the CJEU has

92. Cf. CJEU 8 November 2018, Case C-502/17 *C&D Foods Acquisition ApS v Skatteministeriet*, ECLI:EU:C:2018:888.
93. Arguably, a sale of shares by a passive holding company which uses the proceeds of the sale to purchase shares in another subsidiary in which it intends to be actively involved in the management and to supply services for consideration to must – by analogy to *C&D Foods* and *Ryanair* – also be regarded as an economic activity.
94. This was in fact, albeit on different grounds, the outcome of CJEU 8 November 2018, Case C-502/17 *C&D Foods Acquisition ApS v Skatteministeriet*, ECLI:EU:C:2018:888.
95. An unanswered question is whether with regard to the holding of shares a similar mechanism (applying C&D Foods by analogy) could be applicable. Should it be relevant what the dividends obtained from the subsidiary are used for? For example: if they are used to strengthen the company's own economic activity or that of its group, the holding of the shares constitutes an economic activity; if they are distributed to the shareholder(s), the holding of the shares does not constitute an economic activity.
96. CJEU 8 September 2022, Case C-98/21 *Finanzamt R v W-GmbH*, ECLI:EU:C:2022:645.

previously merely stated the obvious by saying that the (continuous) supply of services for consideration by a parent company constitutes an economic activity. Without a doubt, *W GmbH* will give rise to new questions for the CJEU on this matter, also because it is at odds with *P. sp. z o.o.*[97] Until those questions are posed and answered, we are inclined to adhere to the initial case law of the CJEU and consider *W GmbH* as a misstep (*see* section 11.4.1).

11.5.2.3 The Sale of Shares as a Direct, Permanent and Necessary Extension

As we indicated above, in its more recent case law, the CJEU seems to consider a sale of shares in principle as a non-economic activity. The initial signs of that were already visible in *SKF*. In *SKF*, a controlling active holding company ended its holding by disposing of all of its shares in a subsidiary. The CJEU considered:

> That disposal, carried out in order to enable the parent company to restructure a group of companies, can be regarded as a transaction that consists in obtaining income on a continuing basis from activities which go beyond the compass of the simple sale of shares. (…)
>
> That transaction has a direct link with the organisation of the activity carried out by the group and constitutes accordingly the direct, permanent and necessary extension of the taxable activity of the taxable person (…). Such a transaction consequently comes within the scope of VAT.[98]

Here, the CJEU apparently considers that a sale of shares is not an economic activity in itself, even if it is carried out by a controlling active holding company. However, the CJEU seems to use the notion of a direct, permanent and necessary extension of the taxable activity, to 'pull' the sale of shares into the economic activity after all.[99]

In *C&D Foods*, the CJEU confirms and further explains its ruling in *SKF*. It considers that:

> in order for a share disposal transaction to be able to come within the scope of VAT, the direct and exclusive reason for that transaction must, in principle, be the taxable economic activity of the parent company in question, or that transaction must constitute the direct, permanent and necessary extension of that activity. That is the case where that transaction is carried out with a view to allocating the proceeds of that sale directly to the taxable economic activity of the parent company in question or to the economic activity carried out by the group of which it is the parent company.[100]

In our view, *W GmbH* does not alter this. Even if it were to be inferred from *W GmbH* that holding shares, in isolation, by an active controlling holding company does

97. CJEU 8 May 2024, Case C-241/23 *P. sp. z o.o. v Dyrektor Izby Administracji Skarbowej w Warszawie*, ECLI:EU:C:2024:392.
98. CJEU 29 October 2009, Case C-29/08 *Skatteverket v AB SKF*, ECLI:EU:C:2009:665, para. 38.
99. Also *see*: CJEU 8 November 2018, Case C-502/17 *C&D Foods Acquisition ApS v Skatteministeriet*, ECLI:EU:C:2018:888, para. 35.
100. *Ibid.*, para. 38.

not constitute an economic activity, this still allows for the application of the direct, permanent and necessary extension principle as the CJEU applied in *SKF* and *C&D* Foods.

Following *C&D Foods*, two (alternative) situations in which a sale of shares by a holding company can come into the scope of VAT can be distinguished:

(1) if the direct and exclusive reason for the sale is the taxable economic activity of the holding company; or
(2) if the sale constitutes the direct, permanent and necessary extension of the economic activity of the holding company.

If we understand the CJEU's ruling correctly, either one of these two options[101] applies if the sale of shares is carried out with a view to allocating the proceeds of that sale:

(a) directly to the taxable economic activity of the parent company in question; or
(b) to the economic activity carried out by the group of which it is the parent company.

Two aspects stand out here. First of all, it seems to us that the CJEU attaches much weight to the intention with which the shares are disposed of. In our view, this poses practical problems because it is often difficult to determine one single, exclusive reason for a sale of shares. It that regard, it is useful that the CJEU offers a more objective test (the allocation of the proceeds) to make out what the direct and exclusive reason for the sale is. However, in practice, it is often difficult to establish the allocation of the proceeds of a sale of shares. Nonetheless, there may be situations in which it is rather clear that the proceeds of the sale are simply used to grant a dividend to the shareholders of the holding company selling the shares. If that is the case, the sale of shares should indeed not be an economic activity on which a right of deduction of VAT on the transaction costs is based.

The second aspect that stands out is that it appears that a sale of shares may come into the scope of VAT if it finds its cause in the economic activity of group companies, other than the holding company itself. If the line of reasoning in *C&D Foods* is to be followed, a sale of shares does not only come into the scope of VAT if it is the extension of a holding company's *own* economic activity (consisting of the holding of shares, the involvement in the management and the supply of services subject to VAT in connection thereto) but also if it forms the extension of the group's economic activity. We note that this implies that the economic activities of other persons (i.e., the group members) are determinative of the holding companies' economic activities. Although this matches well with the idea of a group of companies being a unit from an economic

101. *Ibid.*, it is not entirely clear whether both options refer to both scenarios or to the second scenario (direct, permanent and necessary extension) alone.

perspective, it goes against the idea set out in *Polysar* that each group member must be evaluated on its own merits, unless a VAT group exists.[102]

The ruling in *C&D Foods* also raises the question of the relevance of *BLP*. In our view, it is rather difficult to reconcile *C&D Foods* with *BLP*. In *BLP*, a holding company, being a taxable person, disposed of its shares, for the purpose of raising funds necessary for paying BLP's debts, which derived precisely from the taxable transactions it had effected.[103] BLP argued that the sale of the shares was directly or indirectly linked to its taxable transactions. The CJEU did not accept that reasoning:

> Moreover, if BLP's interpretation were accepted, the authorities, when confronted with supplies which, as in the present case, are not objectively linked to taxable transactions, would have to carry out inquiries to determine the intention of the taxable person. Such an obligation would be contrary to the VAT system' s objectives of ensuring legal certainty and facilitating application of the tax by having regard, save in exceptional cases, to the objective character of the transaction in question.[104]

We believe that *C&D Foods* and *BLP* are inconsistent in this regard.[105] Either the objective of a sale of shares is irrelevant (*BLP*), or it is the decisive criterion (*C&D Foods*) in determining whether a sale of shares falls inside the scope of VAT.

The last issue that exists with respect to the application of the extension doctrine to the sale of shares by a controlling active holding company is that it has a negative effect on the pro rata of that holding company. We refer to section 11.7.4.4.

To get a better understanding of the scenarios which are outlined in *C&D Foods*, we will address these scenarios in more detail below.

Scenario 1: The Taxable Economic Activity of the Holding Company is the Direct and Exclusive Reason for the Sale

A real-life example of this scenario is the situation in which an intermediate holding company (B) sells the shares in its subsidiary (C) to obtain funds to strengthen its own economic activity. In the words of the CJEU, this implies that the 'proceeds of the sale are directly allocated to the economic activity of the parent company' (B), the parent company being the intermediate holding company in this example. This situation may be depicted as in Figure 11.1.

102. CJEU 20 June 1991, Case C-60/90 *Polysar Investement Netherlands BV v Inspecteur der Invoerrechten en Accijnzen*, ECLI:EU:C:1991:268, paras 15 and 16.
103. CJEU 6 April 1995, Case C-4/94 *BLP Group plc v Commissioners of Customs & Excise*, ECLI:EU:C:1995:107, para. 12.
104. *Ibid.*, para. 24.
105. *SKF* is difficult to reconcile with *C&D* Foods. In the operative part of the ruling in *SKF*, there is no reference whatsoever to how the proceeds of the sale could be relevant for considering a sale of shares as the extension of an economic activity.

Figure 11.1 Proceeds from the Sale of Shares Are Allocated to the Economic Activity of the (Intermediate) Holding Company (B). The Sale of Shares Is Considered as an Economic Activity

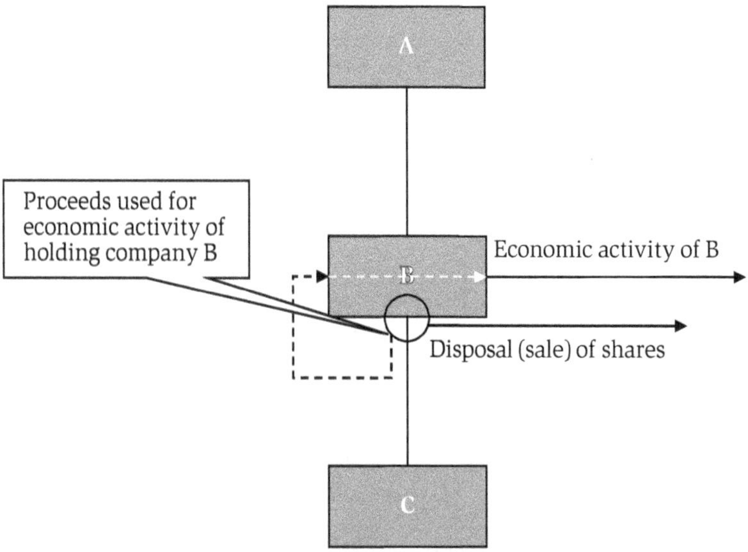

Since the proceeds of the sale of shares are used by the parent company selling the shares (B) for its own economic activity, the sale of shares is considered as an economic activity (i.e., a taxable yet exempt supply of services).

Scenario 2: The Sale Constitutes the Direct, Permanent and Necessary Extension of the Economic Activity of the Holding Company

In case an intermediate holding company (B) sells its shares in one of its subsidiaries in order to obtain funds that are used to strengthen the economic activities of the group, but not for the economic activity of the holding company itself, the sale of shares is considered as the direct, permanent and necessary extension of the economic activity of the holding company.[106] This situation may be depicted as in Figure 11.2.

106. In this case, the direct and exclusive reason for the sale of shares does not lie in the economic activity of the holding company (B) itself.

Figure 11.2 Proceeds from the Sale of Shares Are Allocated to the Economic Activity of the Group of Companies (E & D) of Which the (Intermediate) Holding Company (B) Is the Parent Company. The Sale of Shares Is Considered as the Direct, Permanent and Necessary Extension of the Economic Activity of the (Intermediate) Holding Company (B)

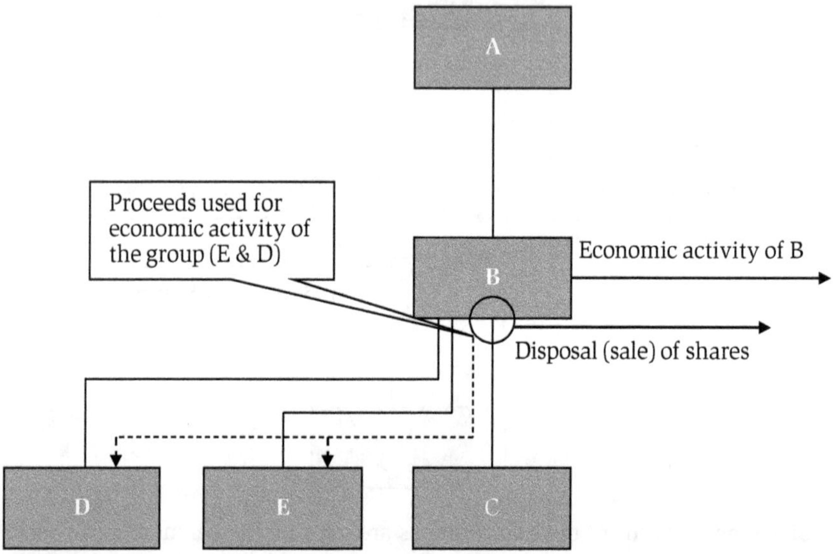

For this scenario to apply, we believe that it is necessary that the proceeds of the sale of shares can be allocated to the economic activity carried out by the group of which B is the parent company. Effectively, this means that the proceeds must be allocated to the economic activities of E and D. As we indicated above, this is prone to raise practical difficulties.

The ruling in *C&D Foods* makes it rather clear that only if the proceeds of the sale are allocated to the economic activity of the group *of which the selling holding company is the parent company*, such sale can be regarded as an economic activity. This means that if the proceeds are used for the economic activity of the group companies of which the ultimate holding company is the parent company, the sale is not considered as an economic activity. This may be depicted as in Figure 11.3.

Figure 11.3 Proceeds from the Sale of Shares Are Allocated to the Economic Activity of the Group of Companies (F & G) of Which the (Ultimate) Holding Company (A) Is the Parent Company. The Sale of Shares Is Not Considered as the Direct, Permanent and Necessary Extension of the Economic Activity of the (Intermediate) Holding Company (B)

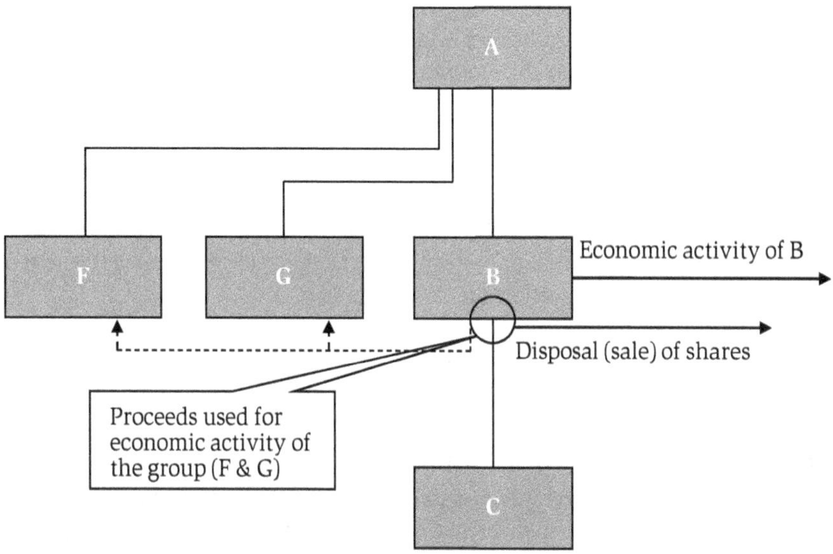

In our view, this outcome is somewhat unbalanced. Just like in the previous situation, the proceeds are used for an economic activity (and not for the purposes of granting dividends to the ultimate shareholders). Arguably, such a sale constitutes a transaction consisting in obtaining income on a continuing basis from activities which go beyond the compass of the simple sale of shares,[107] in the same manner when the proceeds of that sale are used for the economic activity of the group below (D & E). We note that in practice, the company holding and selling the shares is often located somewhere down the group structure, making the example depicted above all but theoretical. Moreover, combinations of the scenarios may occur. For example, the proceeds of the sale of shares by an intermediate holding company (B) may partially be allocated to its own economic activity, partially to the economic activity of the group below (D & E) and even partially to the rest of the group (e.g., F & G). Does that mean that the 'direct and exclusive reason' of the sale is no longer the economic activity of the holding company (B) and that the sale can only come into the scope if it constitutes the direct, permanent and necessary extension of the economic activity of B? Should the sale perhaps only be partially classified as the extension of an economic activity,

107. Cf. CJEU 8 November 2018, Case C-502/17 *C&D Foods Acquisition ApS v Skatteministeriet*, ECLI:EU:C:2018:888, para. 39.

that is only insofar as the proceeds can be allocated to the economic activity of the group below (D & E)?

11.6 THE SALE OF SHARES AND THE EXEMPTIONS

Article 135(1)(f) VAT Directive provides for an exemption for transactions, including negotiation but not management or safekeeping, in shares, interests in companies or associations, debentures and other securities (*see* Chapter 8, section 8.4.3.5).[108] If a sale of shares constitutes a taxable supply of services, then this sale of shares is, in principle, VAT-exempt, unless the Member State in question exercised its powers under Article 137(1) VAT Directive, to allow taxable persons a right of option for taxation. If the sale of shares is an exempt transaction, any input VAT on transaction costs directly attributable to that sale cannot be deducted, unless the purchaser of the shares is established outside the EU (Article 169(c) VAT Directive).[109] We will elaborate on the right of deduction with respect to the sale of shares and the effect thereon of the exemption in section 11.7.

11.7 THE ISSUE, ACQUISITION, HOLDING, AND DISPOSAL OF SHARES AND THE RIGHT OF DEDUCTION

In order to determine to what extent VAT on transactions costs (e.g., costs of lawyers, accountants, experts) is recoverable, it is necessary to establish if the holding company has taxable person status, acts in that capacity when carrying out the issue, acquisition, holding or sale of the shares and whether a direct and immediate link exists with taxed transactions that give rise to a right of deduction.[110]

11.7.1 The Issue of Shares

If a mere holding company issues new shares without having the intention to carry out any economic activities, it issues those shares in its capacity of a non-taxable person. Logically, the related input VAT will not be deductible. Conversely, if a holding company issues shares with a view to carry out economic activities, a right of deduction may exist.

As we discussed in section 11.5.1, the CJEU ruled in *Kretztechnik*[111] that since a share issue is a non-taxable supply, and that it was carried out by *Kretztechnik* in order

108. Documents establishing title to goods, and the rights or securities referred to in Article 15(2) VAT Directive are excluded from this exemption.
109. This also follows from CJEU 6 April 1995, Case C-4/94 *BLP Group plc v Commissioners of Customs & Excise*, ECLI:EU:C:1995:107.
110. Cf. CJEU 17 October 2018, Case C-249/17 *Ryanair Ltd v The Revenue Commissioners*, ECLI:EU:C:2018:834, para. 15.
111. CJEU 26 May 2005, Case C-465/03 *Kretztechnik AG v Finanzamt Linz*, ECLI:EU:C:2005:320, paras 36 and 37. *See also* CJEU 16 July 2015, Case C-109/14 *Finanzamt Hamburg-Mitte v Marenave Schiffahrts AG*, ECLI:EU:C:2015:496.

to increase its capital for the benefit of its economic activity in general, it must be considered that the related costs were general costs. Those costs have a direct and immediate link with the whole economic activity of the taxable person.[112] Since *Kretztechnik* only made taxed supplies, it followed that it was entitled to deduct all the VAT charged on the expenses incurred in the context of the share issue. A taxable person who issues new shares and who effects both transactions in respect of which VAT is deductible, and transactions in respect of which it is not, may deduct only that proportion of the VAT attributable to the former transactions.[113]

In *Polfarmex*, the question was raised whether a redemption of shares, which can, to a certain extent, be seen as the opposite of an issue of shares, was subject to VAT. Polfarmex was a limited company which manufactured pharmaceutical products. It planned to buy-back part of the shares held in its capital by a shareholder, through either 'automatic', 'mandatory' or 'voluntary' redemption of the shares. The compensation due by reason of that redemption would be the transfer, to the shareholder, of ownership of some land and the buildings thereon and their equipment. The CJEU considered that the transfer of immovable property to the shareholder took place in exchange for the shares held by the shareholder. Therefore, the sale of the immovable property constitutes a supply for consideration. That supply is made by a table person acting as such if the goods are goods allocated to that company's 'economic activity' in the broad sense.[114] As regards the redemption of the shares, the CJEU reiterated its case law that if the acquisition of financial holdings in other undertakings does not in itself constitute an economic activity, the same must be true of activities consisting in the sale of such holdings. It appears that the CJEU sees the redemption of shares by the company as a sale of shares by the shareholder.[115]

11.7.2 The Acquisition of Shares

Buying shares outside the scope of the business activity (i.e., without the intention to hold them within the scope of the business activity) will not give rise to a deduction of the input tax incurred on the costs associated with the acquisition.[116]

112. *See* CJEU 6 April 1995, Case C-4/94 *BLP Group plc v Commissioners of Customs & Excise*, ECLI:EU:C:1995:107, para. 25; CJEU 8 June 2000, Case C-98/98 *Midland Bank plc v Commissioners of Customs and Excise*, ECLI:EU:C:2000:300, para. 31; CJEU 22 February 2001, Case C-408/98 *Abbey National plc v Commissioners of Customs & Excise*, ECLI:EU:C:2001:110, paras 35 and 36 and CJEU 27 September 2001, Case C-16/00 *Cibo Participations SA v Directeur régional des impôts du Nord-Pas-de-Calais*, ECLI:EU:C:2001:495, para. 33.
113. *See* CJEU 22 February 2001, Case C-408/98 *Abbey National plc v Commissioners of Customs & Excise*, ECLI:EU:C:2001:110, para. 37 and CJEU 27 September 2001, Case C-16/00 *Cibo Participations SA v Directeur régional des impôts du Nord-Pas-de-Calais*, ECLI:EU:C:2001:495, para. 34.
114. CJEU 13 June 2018, Case C-421/17 *Szef Krajowej Administracji Skarbowej v Polfarmex Spółka Akcyjna w Kutnie*, ECLI:EU:C:2018:432, para. 42.
115. *See*: H. van Kesteren & H. van Erp, *De aandeelhoudersrelatie in en uit: het wassende water*, WFR 2018/230 and H. van Kesteren & H. van Erp, 'Taxable and Non-taxable Transactions', in M. Lang, et al. (eds), *CJEU, Recent Developments in Value Added Tax 2018* (Linde, Wien 2019).
116. CJEU 20 June 1996, Case C-155/94 *Wellcome Trust Ltd v Commissioners of Customs and Excise*, ECLI:EU:C:1996:243.

The question may arise as to whether a holding company that intends to be involved in the management of the subsidiary that it wants to acquire (its target) will be entitled to a deduction of VAT on the related expenses. An acquisition of shares as such is a non-taxable event for the acquirer of the shares (it is not even an output transaction). However, transaction costs incurred by a holding company in respect of the various services which it purchased in connection with the acquisition of a shareholding in a subsidiary form part of its *general costs* and therefore have, in principle, a direct and immediate link with the business *as a whole*.[117] Thus, if the holding company carries out both transactions in respect of which VAT is deductible, and transactions in respect of which it is not, it may deduct only that proportion of the VAT which is attributable to the former. The costs cannot be treated as direct costs, as the costs have no direct connection with a specific output transaction. As the transaction costs are still made in the taxable person capacity, the costs are assumed to be general costs.

Sometimes, a controlling active parent company is involved in the management of only some, but not all, of its subsidiaries. The question is whether such a company holds the shares in subsidiaries in which it involves itself in the management within the furtherance of its economic activity or that those shares belong to its non-economic activity. This question becomes relevant in cases where it acquires a new participation and where it incurs VAT on the costs attributable to that acquisition. From *Larentia + Minerva*,[118] it can be learned that the expenditure connected with the acquisition of shareholdings in subsidiaries incurred by a holding company which is (or will be) only involved in the management of *some* of those subsidiaries and which, with regard to the others, does not, by contrast, carry out an economic activity, must be regarded as only partially belonging to its general expenditure. The effect of this is that the VAT paid on that expenditure may be deducted only in proportion to that which is inherent to the economic activity, according to the criteria for apportioning defined by the Member States (the calculation of the pre-pro rata is discussed in section 10.5).

In *Ryanair*, the CJEU elaborated on the deduction of VAT on transaction costs of an intended acquisition of shares that was eventually never carried out.[119] According to the CJEU, in order for the VAT paid to be deducted, the exclusive reason[120] for the transaction costs must be found, in principle, in the intended economic activity,

117. CJEU 27 September 2001, Case C-16/00 *Cibo Participations SA v Directeur régional des impôts du Nord-Pas-de-Calais*, ECLI:EU:C:2001:495.

118. CJEU 16 July 2015, Case C-108/14 *Beteiligungsgesellschaft Larentia + Minerva mbH & Co. KG v Finanzamt Nordenham*, ECLI:EU:C:2015:496, para. 33.

119. *See also*: CJEU 12 November 2020, Case C-42/19 *Sonaecom SGPS SA v Autoridade Tributária e Aduaneira*, ECLI:EU:C:2020:913.

120. CJEU 17 October 2018, Case C-249/17 *Ryanair Ltd v The Revenue Commissioners*, ECLI: EU:C:2018:834, para. 30. We doubt whether the exclusive reason for Ryanair to envisage an acquisition of Air Lingus was indeed the provision of management services to the target company. We agree with Advocate General Kokott, who indicated that this was an intended strategic takeover by which Ryanair pursued the aim of extending or modifying its operating business. *See*: Opinion of Advocate General Kokott of 3 May 2018, Case C-249/17 *Ryanair Ltd v The Revenue Commissioners*, ECLI:EU:C:2018:301, para. 38.

namely the provision to the target company of management services subject to VAT.[121] Referring to *INZO*, *Midland Bank*, and *Ghent Coal Terminal*, the CJEU reiterated that the right to deduct, once it has arisen, is retained even if the intended economic activity was not carried out and, therefore, did not give rise to taxed transactions. That also applies in case of intended taxable supplies by a holding company: the right of deduction on the transaction costs was retained, even though the shares were never acquired and the holding company never supplied taxed services to the target companies. According to the CJEU, the transaction costs concerned are general costs. Typically, general costs give rise to a pro rata right of deduction.[122] Yet, the CJEU rules that a full right of deduction exists. Although the CJEU does not provide much clarification in this regard, it appears that the CJEU considers the costs as costs attributable to a well-defined part of the economic activity, being the (intended) supply of management services. This approach bears resemblance to the concept of a 'clearly defined part of the economic activities', which the CJEU introduced in *Abbey National I* (*see* Chapter 10, section 10.4.1).[123] However, for reasons unclear to us, the CJEU does not make any reference to the latter case.

Just like in *Ryanair*, in *Sonaecom*,[124] a mixed holding company (i.e., a holding company that holds shares passively and, in addition, carries out economic activities) planned to acquire shares in a target company and then to supply taxable services to it. With a view to the acquisition of the shares, Sonaecom received consultancy services and services relating to the issue of corporate bonds. However, the acquisition of the shares in the target did not materialize. Sonaecom thereupon made available the capital obtained through the issue of the bonds to the parent company of the group as a loan. Sonaecom was refused to deduct the VAT on the consultancy services and the services relating to the issue of corporate bonds. The CJEU effectively confirmed its ruling in *Ryanair*, deciding that a mixed holding company whose involvement in the management of its subsidiaries is recurrent is entitled to deduct the input VAT paid on the purchase of consultancy services relating to a market study carried out with a view to acquiring shares in another company, including where that acquisition did not ultimately take place.[125] As regards the deductibility of the VAT on the services relating to the issue of corporate bonds, the CJEU ruled in line with the Advocate General's opinion,[126] concluding that the direct link with the exempt loan actually provided takes

121. In *W GmbH*, the CJEU considered that the costs of a contribution in kind (i.e., 'investment costs' rather than 'transaction costs', *see* section 11.2) could not be attributed to the supply of services to the target company. With Ryanair in mind, it is not entirely clear to us why the transaction costs of acquiring shares are considered to have their exclusive reason in (eventually) providing services for consideration to the subsidiary (*Ryanair*), while the investment costs resulting from the acquisition (taking) of shares do not (*W GmbH*).
122. CJEU 8 June 2000, Case C-98/98 *Midland Bank plc v Commissioners of Customs and Excise*, ECLI:EU:C:2000:300.
123. CJEU 22 February 2001, Case C-408/98 *Abbey National plc v Commissioners of Customs & Excise*, ECLI:EU:C:2001:110.
124. CJEU 12 November 2020, Case C-42/19 *Sonaecom SGPS SA v Autoridade Tributária e Aduaneira*, ECLI:EU:C:2020:913.
125. *Ibid.*
126. Opinion of Advocate General of 14 May 2020, Case C-42/19 *Sonaecom SGPS SA v Autoridade Tributária e Aduaneira*, ECLI:EU:C:2020:378. *See* for a critical analysis: A.J. van Doesum,

precedence over the original intention to supply taxable services to a subsidiary to be acquired with that capital.[127]

11.7.3 The Holding of Shares

The acquisition and holding of shares by mere holding companies that do not envisage carrying out economic activities are considered as non-economic activities themselves. If other securities are held by such a mere holding company, no right to deduction for the related input VAT exists either (*see* section 11.8). Conversely, if a controlling active holding company incurs costs which are directly attributable to the holding of the shares in the subsidiaries in which it is involved in the management (by supplying taxable services to them), the costs are to be regarded as general costs. This is because the holding of shares is a non-taxable transaction (it is not even an output transaction) but is related to the economic activity of that holding company.

If a holding company only supplies services for consideration to some of the subsidiaries in which it is involved in the management (and not to the other subsidiaries it holds), the (mixed) holding company only has a partial right of deduction. Insofar as the costs relate to the holdings in subsidiaries in which the parent company is not involved in the management or does not supply taxable services to, no right of deduction exists.[128] In those circumstances, any costs relating to holdings in subsidiaries in which the parent company is involved in the management and supplies services to, are to be regarded as general costs. The calculation of the deductible proportion of the VAT incurred on costs which relate to both the economic and the non-economic activities of a mixed holding company must be calculated on the basis of a pre-pro rata key (*see* section 10.5).

11.7.4 The Disposal of Shares

In this section, we discuss the right of deduction of VAT on transaction costs relating to a disposal of shares by a commercial share dealer (section 11.7.4.1) and by holding companies (sections 11.7.4.2-11.7.4.4).

11.7.4.1 Commercial Share Dealer

If a commercial share dealer disposes of shares, such a disposal will be considered as an exempt supply of services.[129] An exempt sale of shares does not give rise to the deduction of input VAT on the transaction costs. However, to safeguard external

---

Broken Deals and EU VAT, Kluwer International Tax Blog, available from: https://kluwertaxblog.com/2020/07/06/broken-deals-and-eu-vat/ (accessed 17 August 2024).

127. CJEU 12 November 2020, Case C-42/19 *Sonaecom SGPS SA v Autoridade Tributária e Aduaneira*, ECLI:EU:C:2020:913, paras 65 and 66.

128. CJEU 16 July 2015, Case C-108/14 *Beteiligungsgesellschaft Larentia + Minerva mbH & Co. KG v Finanzamt Nordenham*, ECLI:EU:C:2015:496.

129. *See* however, Article 137(1) VAT Directive.

neutrality if the buyer is located outside the EU, Article 169(c) VAT Directive does allow for VAT deduction.

11.7.4.2 Holding Company

In case of a sale of shares by a holding company, it first needs to be determined whether the sale is a taxable transaction (economic activity). Subsequently, the question must be addressed whether the transaction costs can be related to an economic activity.

It is clear that a holding company which does not have taxable person *status*[130] when disposing of shares does not have a right of deduction of VAT on transaction costs. It is settled case law that if the acquisition and holding of shares is not an economic activity, the same applies to the disposal of those shares. However, in specific circumstances, where, for example, active steps on the market are being taken, it may that analogously to case law on the selling immovable property,[131] the shares need to be 'relabelled' so that the sale comes into the scope of VAT after all. We refer to section 11.5.2.2.

If a holding company does have taxable person status, the question arises whether it acts in its capacity as a taxable person and makes a taxable supply of services if it sells shares in one or more of its subsidiaries. The question as regards the capacity in which the holding company operates is often 'translated' into the question of whether the sale of shares constitutes an economic activity or whether it is the direct, permanent and necessary extension of an economic activity. In section 11.5.2.2, we indicated that there seems to be a (partial) shift in the CJEU's approach towards the VAT treatment of sales of shares by (controlling active) holding companies. Previously, it could be inferred from CJEU case law that the sale of shares by a controlling active holding company was either a non-taxable supply (non-economic activity), a taxable, yet exempt supply in its own right or the direct, permanent and necessary extension of such a holding's economic activity (*see* section 11.5.2). However, since *C&D Foods*, the question arises under which circumstances a sale of shares by a controlling active holding company can still be a taxable, yet exempt supply in its own right. In this section, we will focus on the approach taken by the CJEU up to and until *SKF* and on the approach taken in *C&D Foods*. We will disregard the CJEU's ruling in *W GmbH* in this regard, because we believe that it cannot be inferred from that ruling with certainty that the holding (and sale) of shares can never be an economic activity.[132]

It has been inferred from *EDM that* the sale of shares by a controlling active holding company cannot be an economic activity. The CJEU would have abandoned its

130. That is a mere holding company or a holding company that is involved in the management of its subsidiaries, but which does not supply services or goods for consideration to its subsidiaries (*see* section 11.4).
131. CJEU 9 July 2015, Case C-331/14 *Petar Kezic s.p. Trgovina Prizma v Republika Slovenija*, ECLI:EU:C:2015:456, paras 24-28.
132. Arguably, even if it is maintained that it follows from *W GmbH* that the holding of shares is never an economic activity (considered in isolation from the supply by the parent company of services for consideration), a sale of those shares can still constitute an economic activity on the basis of *SKF* and *C&D Foods* (direct, necessary and permanent extension doctrine).

approach taken in *BLP*. It is in this regard important to realize that EDM was not a controlling active holding company, but merely 'managed' its investment portfolio (*see* section 11.5.2). We will, therefore, elaborate on this scenario no further but instead, focus on the ideas that: (1) a disposal of shares is a taxable transaction in its own right (section 11.7.4.3), or (2) a disposal of shares by a controlling active holding company comes into the scope through the application of the extension doctrine (section 11.7.4.4).

11.7.4.3 Holding Company: The Disposal of Shares Is a Taxable Transaction in Its Own Right

In section 11.5.2.2, we explained that the way the CJEU in its more recent case law seems to address a sale of shares has become fundamentally different from how the CJEU addressed and still addresses a sale of assets. In case of a sale of assets, the CJEU starts from the idea that if the assets were part of the business assets of a taxable person, the sale of those assets is by default an economic activity. If a (taxable) person sells shares it holds in other companies, the default position is that the sale of those shares is not an economic activity.[133] However, it follows from CJEU case law that there are situations in which a sale of shares does fall within the scope of VAT.

In *SKF* the European Commission argued that the exemption of Article 135(1)(f) VAT Directive only covers transactions that are carried out as part of a commercial share-dealing business. According to the CJEU, the term 'transactions ... in shares' referred to in Article 135(1)(f) VAT Directive is broad enough not to be restricted to the business of trading in shares. If the interpretation advocated by the Commission were to be accepted, transactions that were substantively identical would be treated differently depending on whether they were part of the taxable person's normal and usual business. That would be contrary to the VAT system's objectives of ensuring legal certainty and facilitating the application of the tax by having regard to the objective character of the transaction. Therefore, the CJEU held that a disposal of shares changes the legal and financial position of the parties to the transaction[134] and is thus VAT-exempt.[135] This confirms that the disposal of shares by a controlling active holding company is a taxable transaction in its own right.

In *C&D Foods*, the CJEU offers two options for a sale of shares to constitute an economic activity. Such a sale is an economic activity if the direct and exclusive reason for that transaction is the taxable economic activity of the parent company, or (!) if that

133. This explains why it is settled case law that if the acquisition and holding is not an economic activity, the sale of those shares is also not an economic activity, and why CJEU case law does not contain a standard consideration stating that if the acquisition and holding *is* an economic activity, so is the sale of those shares.

134. CJEU 5 June 1997, Case C-2/95 *Sparekassernes Datacenter (SDC) v Skatteministeriet*, ECLI: EU:C:1997:278 and CJEU 13 December 2001, Case C-235/00 *Commissioners of Customs & Excise v CSC Financial Services Ltd.*, ECLI:EU:C:2001:696.

135. *See*: A.J. van Doesum, H.W.M. van Kesteren & G.J. van Norden, *Share Disposals and the Right of Deduction of Input VAT* (2010) 2 EC Tax Review, p. 64 https://doi.org/10.54648/ecta2010008.

transaction constitutes the direct, permanent and necessary extension of that activity. In our view, the first option (direct and exclusive reason is the economic activity of the holding company) allows for an interpretation in which – subject to the condition that the proceeds of the sale are allocated to the economic activity of the holding company – a disposal of shares by a controlling active holding company is still to be considered as an exempt taxable transaction in its own right.

The consequence of a disposal of shares being a VAT-exempt supply of services is that any input VAT directly attributable to that disposal is not deductible unless the purchaser of the shares is established outside the EU.[136] This could lead to a situation in which a controlling active parent company that normally only supplies taxable services (to its subsidiaries) cannot deduct input VAT when it disposes of shares in those subsidiaries. Then, the input VAT becomes a cost for that parent company. In our view, this is the mere consequence of the existence of exemptions without a right of deduction in the EU VAT system. The infringement to the principle of (system) neutrality which those exemptions cause, are inherent to their very existence.

In *SKF*, the CJEU observes a difference with respect to the right of deduction of VAT on transaction costs between a taxable, yet exempt transaction and a transaction which is outside the scope of VAT. In case of an exempt transaction, no right of deduction exists, whereas in case of a non-taxable transaction, a pro rata deduction may exist, depending on whether it can be established that there is a direct and immediate link between the costs and the economic activity as a whole. According to the CJEU, such a different treatment of those two situations would amount to treating objectively similar transactions differently for tax purposes and would be an infringement of the principle of fiscal neutrality (as a reflection of the principle of equal treatment). Likewise, if the right to deduct input VAT paid on consultancy costs relating to a disposal of shares which is exempted because of involvement in the management of the company whose shares are sold was not allowed, and if the right to deduct input VAT in respect of such costs relating to a disposal which is outside the scope of VAT was allowed on the ground that those costs constitute general costs of the taxable person, that would amount to treating objectively similar transactions differently for tax purposes and would be an infringement of the principle of fiscal neutrality.[137] It is difficult to understand the merits of this reasoning because it is unclear what the CJEU means when it uses the words 'disposal outside the scope of VAT' in paragraph 66 of its judgment.[138] It appears that the CJEU refers to the disposal of shares by a holding company that holds and sells these shares in its capacity as a non-taxable person where it can be proved that the costs are nonetheless general costs. Whatever situation the CJEU had in mind, these considerations may explain why the CJEU in *SKF* explored two routes to deduction of input VAT.[139] The first route is that of

136. Article 169(c) VAT Directive.
137. CJEU 29 October 2009, Case C-29/08 *AB SKF v Skatteverket*, ECLI:EU:C:2009:665, para. 66.
138. A.J. van Doesum, H.W.M. van Kesteren & G.J. van Norden, *Share Disposals and the Right of Deduction of Input VAT* (2010) 2 EC Tax Review, pp. 65 and 66 https://doi.org/10.54648/ecta2010008.
139. *Ibid.*, p. 70.

'general costs'. The second route is the 'transfer of a going concern'. In light of case law of the CJEU of later date, both routes turn out to be dead-end streets.

First Route: Costs Not Directly Related to Certain Output Transactions

Whether a pro rata mechanism is needed to establish the deductibility of costs related to the disposal depends on the possibility of attribution to the overall economic activities or on the disposal itself. Bearing *Kretztechnik* and *Investrand* in mind, it seems like deductibility can be optimized by making sure that the costs relate to overall business activities. The CJEU allowed for such an approach in *SKF*,[140] specifically in cases in which it can be proved that the costs were not incorporated in the price of the shares but presumably in the prices of all the transactions forming part of total economic activity.[141]

However, caution is certainly needed. Advocate General *Kokott*[142] writes not unjustly (with reference to *Wolfram Becker*):

> if an input transaction objectively serves the purpose of the performance of certain or all output transactions of a taxable person, there is a direct and immediate link between the two as understood in case-law. This is because in such a case the input transaction constitutes, from an economic perspective, a cost component in the provision of the respective output transaction. As the wording of Article 168 of the VAT Directive already indicates, that therefore depends on the objective purpose of the use of an input transaction.

In section 10.3.1.2, we referred to this 'objective purpose' as the 'use or intention criterion'. If we follow the Advocate General's approach, we have to draw the conclusion that the costs concerned can only be treated as general costs if the objective purpose of the use of advisory costs is for the business (economic activity) as a whole and not just for the disposal of the shares. In most cases, however, costs related to the disposal 'simply' relate to the disposal.

This becomes all the more true now the CJEU has followed the Advocate General's approach in *Sveda*. The CJEU ruled:

> It is apparent from the case-law of the Court that, in the context of the direct-link test that is to be applied by the tax authorities and national courts, they should consider all the circumstances surrounding the transactions concerned and take account only of the transactions which are objectively linked to the taxable person's taxable activity. The existence of such a link must thus be assessed in the light of the objective content of the transaction in question (see, to that effect, judgment in Becker, C104/12, EU:C:2013:99, paragraphs 22, 23 and 33 and the case-law cited).[143]

---

140. CJEU 29 October 2009, Case C-29/08 *AB SKF v Skatteverket*, ECLI:EU:C:2009:665, para. 68.
141. *See* however section 11.7.4.4 in which we explain that if the extension doctrine applies, the sale of the shares cannot be classified as 'incidental' for the purposes of Article 19(2) Sixth VAT Directive (currently Article 174(2)b VAT Directive).
142. *See* Opinion of Advocate General Kokott, of 22 April 2015, Case C-126/14 *UAB 'Sveda' v Valstybine mokesčių inspekcija prie Lietuvos Respublikos finansų ministerijos*, ECLI: EU:C:2015:254, para, 45. She substantiates her position by referring to CJEU 21 February 2013, Case C-104/12 *Finanzamt Köln-Nord v Wolfram Becker*, ECLI:EU:C:2013:99.
143. CJEU 22 October 2015, Case C-126/14 *'Sveda' UAB v Valstybine mokesčių inspekcija prie*

We believe that direct costs cannot be 'transformed' into general costs, by simply incorporating the costs in the prices of all transactions carried out by the taxable person. We agree with Advocate General Kokott's line of reasoning in *C&D Foods*. According to Advocate General Kokott,[144] the wording of the CJEU, according to which the expenditure incurred must be included in the price of the holding or the shares, does not mean that an actual increase in the price is necessary or, for example, that a specific sum would have to be imposed onto the selling price. The Advocate General rightly points out that if this were to be different, public companies could never meet the criterion of cost inclusion. After all, the share price of a public company is usually based on the current share price index and not through negotiation between seller and buyer. Therefore, according to the Advocate General, the CJEU's formulation should be construed as meaning that 'the expenditure must have an immediate negative impact on the profit from a specific transaction involving a holding or shares and not solely on the overall profit of the company. The input transactions must therefore be so closely linked to the sale of the shares that, in financial terms, they represent directly a component of the cost of the intended transaction'. In *Volkswagen Financial Services (UK) Ltd*, the CJEU confirmed that account must be taken of the actual and non-negligible allocation of a share of the general costs for the purposes of the transaction giving rise to a right to deduct.[145] Exclusively looking at cost inclusion is not enough to determine the right of deduction. In conclusion, in connection with the deduction of input VAT, this first route seems to lead nowhere.

Second Route: The Sale Is a Transfer of a Going Concern

If it were possible to apply the no-supply rule (i.e., the TOGC regime applies, which means that a totality of assets or part thereof is transferred), the costs incurred in relation to the disposal of the shares would be regarded as general costs and therefore the VAT on these costs should be eligible for pro rata deduction.[146] In *SKF*, the CJEU did not categorically rule out that this option could be applied, and did not specify when a transfer of shares can be considered as the transfer of a business as a whole. The mere fact that 100% of the shares were transferred did not seem to be enough in itself.[147] After all, the CJEU indicated that it did not have sufficient information to establish whether the transfer by SKF is a transfer of a totality of assets, even though it was clear that SKF transferred all shares in at least one of the subsidiaries.[148]

Lietuvos Respublikos finansų ministerijos, ECLI:EU:C:2015:712, para. 29.

144. Opinion of Advocate General Kokott of 5 September 2018, Case C-502/17 *C&D Foods Acquisition ApS v Skatteministeriet*, ECLI:EU:C:2018:676, points 45-47.
145. CJEU 18 October 2018, Case C-153/17 *Commissioners for Her Majesty's Revenue and Customs v Volkswagen Financial Services (UK) Ltd*, ECLI:EU:C:2018:845, paras 56-59.
146. CJEU 22 February 2001, Case C-408/98 *Abbey National plc v Commissioners of Customs & Excise*, ECLI:EU:C:2001:110. As a consequence of the no-supply rule, the turnover realized as a result of the transfer of the totality of assets, including the shares, should not be included in the pro rata calculation.
147. *See* A.J van Doesum, H.W.M. van Kesteren & G.J. van Norden, *Share Disposals and the Right of Deduction of Input VAT* (2010) 2 EC Tax Review pp. 62 et seq https://doi.org/10.54648/ecta2010008.
148. CJEU 29 October 2009, Case C-29/08 *AB SKF v Skatteverket*, ECLI:EU:C:2009:665, para. 21.

In *X BV* the CJEU decided on the question of whether a disposal of 30% of the shares in a company by a shareholder who, until the date of disposal, supplied services subject to VAT to that company forms a transfer of a totality of assets and/or of services (or part thereof).[149] In this case, the CJEU left no room for doubt as to whether a disposal of 100% (not to mention any lower percentage) could be seen as a transfer of a totality of assets. The answer was clearly in the negative. The CJEU ruled: 'In that regard it must be stated that, unlike the holding of the assets of an undertaking, the holding of shares in an undertaking is not sufficient to allow an independent economic activity to be carried on.' So the second route to the deduction of input VAT turns out to be a cul-de-sac.

11.7.4.4 Holding Company: The Disposal of Shares Is the Extension of an Economic Activity

In *SKF* and *C&D Foods*, the disposal of shares by the controlling active holding company did not constitute a taxable transaction in its own right. As we indicated in section 11.5.2.3, the CJEU considers a disposal of shares by a controlling active holding company as the direct, permanent and necessary extension of an economic activity if the disposal is carried out with a view to allocating the proceeds of that disposal directly to its own taxable economic activity or to the economic activity carried out by the group of which it is the parent company.

The issue in *C&D Foods* was that effectively, the costs incurred by the controlling active holding company concerned were costs that 'belonged' to its shareholders. The parent company's shareholder had debts with a bank. On account of the failure on the part of the shareholder to repay a loan which had been granted to it, the bank assumed ownership of the parent company and thus of the entire group of companies, for the sum of EUR 1. The idea was that the holding company was to sell the shares in a group company (a subsidiary or sub-subsidiary of the holding company – the facts of the case are not entirely clear) so that the proceeds of the sale could be used to settle the debts of the shareholders of the parent company with the bank. During the intended sale of the shares, the holding company incurred transaction costs. For completeness sake, we note that ultimately no buyer was found, and the intended sale of the shares never materialized.

In our view, the *CJEU* could have simply applied *BLP* in combination with *Iberdrola*. Then, the intended sale of shares would have been considered as an intended taxable yet exempt supply of a service in its own right. The right of deduction of the VAT on the transaction costs could have been denied, on the ground that they did not

149. CJEU 30 May 2013, Case C-651/11 *Staatssecretaris van Financiën v X BV*, ECLI:EU:C:2013:346, para. 35.

have a direct and immediate link with the economic activities of the holding company.[150] After all, the transaction costs, effectively, ultimately and solely made for the shareholder's benefit, clearly exceeded the needs of the holding company.[151]

The CJEU took a different direction by ruling that the share disposal envisaged but not carried out, for which the direct and exclusive reason did not lie in the taxable economic activity of the parent company concerned, or which did not constitute the direct, permanent and necessary extension of that economic activity, does not come within the scope of VAT.[152] It considered that a share disposal comes into the scope of VAT if the transaction is carried out with a view to allocating the proceeds of that sale directly to the taxable economic activity of the parent company in question or to the economic activity carried out by the group of which it is the parent company. We refer to section 11.5.2.3.

If a sale of shares by a controlling active holding company constitutes the direct, permanent and necessary extension of the economic activity, this has a bearing on the right of deduction of the VAT on the transaction costs. Under the extension doctrine, the sale of shares will become an exempt supply of services. It seems, however, rather difficult to argue that the (exempt) sale of shares can be excluded from the pro rata calculation if the sale is considered as a direct, permanent and necessary extension of the economic activities. This is because an economic activity cannot be classified as 'incidental' for the purposes Article 174(2)b VAT Directive if it constitutes the direct, permanent and necessary extension of the business.[153] An exempt disposal of shares by a controlling active holding company to a purchaser within the EU may, therefore, have an incidental effect on the overall right of deduction of the holding company. Clearly, this does not contribute to the neutrality of the EU VAT system.

11.8 OTHER SECURITIES

It is settled CJEU case law that the receipt of dividends is not a consideration for any economic activity, any dividend yielded being merely the result of ownership of shares.[154] Interest on loans is not simply the result of the ownership of capital, but rather the consideration for placing capital at the disposition of a third party.[155] Yet the mere holding of bonds cannot be considered an economic activity. According to the

150. CJEU 14 September 2017, Case C-132/16 *Direktor na Direktsia 'Obzhalvane i danachno-osiguritelna praktika' – Sofia v 'Iberdrola Inmobiliaria Real Estate Investments' EOOD*, ECLI:EU:C:2017:683, para. 38.
151. *Ibid.*, para. 39.
152. CJEU 8 November 2018, Case C-502/17 *C&D Foods Acquisition ApS v Skatteministeriet*, ECLI:EU:C:2018:888, para. 42.
153. CJEU 29 October 2009, Case C-174/08 *NCC Construction Danmark A/S v Skatteministeriet*, ECLI:EU:C:2009:669, paras 30 et seq. and CJEU 11 July 1996, Case C-306/94 *Régie Dauphinoise – Cabinet A. Forest SARL v Ministre du Budget*, ECLI:EU:C:1996:290, para. 22.
154. For example: CJEU 20 June 1991, Case C-60/90 *Polysar Investement Netherlands BV v Inspecteur der Invoerrechten en Accijnzen*, ECLI:EU:C:1991:268 and CJEU 22 June 1993, Case C-333/91 *Sofitam SA (formerly Satam SA) v Ministre chargé du Budget*, ECLI:EU:C:1993:261.
155. CJEU 11 July 1996, Case C-306/94 *Régie Dauphinoise – Cabinet A. Forest SARL v Ministre du Budget*, ECLI:EU:C:1996:290.

CJEU in *Harnas & Helm*, the income from bonds derives from the mere fact of holding them.[156] Apparently, the CJEU sees more similarities between shares and bonds than between bonds and (other) interest-bearing loans.

We do not see such a significant difference between loans and bonds to treat them differently. A loan granted by a holding company to its subsidiary may in itself be considered an economic activity, consisting in exploiting that capital with a view to obtaining income by way of interest therefrom on a continuing basis.[157] However, in *EDM*, the CJEU appeared to adopt a broader view on the treatment of loans to subsidiaries, bank deposits and securities (such as treasury notes and certificates of deposit).[158] According to the CJEU, the annual granting by a holding company of interest-bearing loans to companies in which a parent company has a shareholding, as well as placements by that parent company of money in bank deposits or securities, constitutes an economic activity. The CJEU seems to view even the holding of bank deposits and securities as an economic activity.

The scale on which EDM undertook these activities, together with its holding activities and the granting of loans to these subsidiaries, in our view, suggests that EDM acted as a taxable person in respect of the holding of bank deposits and securities. If – subject to conditions – the holding of bank deposits and securities can be considered as an economic activity, this should also be the case as regards the holding of bonds.

156. CJEU 6 February 1997, Case C-80/95 *Harnas & Helm CV v Staatssecretaris van Financiën*, ECLI:EU:C:1997:56.
157. CJEU 14 November 2000, Case C-142/99 *Floridienne SA and Berginvest SA v Belgian State* [2000] ECR I-9567.
158. CJEU 29 April 2001, Case C-77/01 *Empresa de Desenvolvimento Mineiro SGPS SA (EDM) v Fazenda Pública*, ECLI:EU:C:2004:243.

CHAPTER 12

Person Liable to Pay VAT

12.1 INTRODUCTION

Articles 192a-205 VAT Directive contain the rules that establish which person is required to report the VAT due in his VAT return and pay any net VAT due to the tax authorities. The payment obligation must, in principle, be met by the person liable for payment. As a main rule, Article 193 VAT Directive provides that VAT is payable by the taxable person carrying out a taxable supply of goods or services, whether or not that person is established within the country. In other words: he who supplies, pays. However, there are various exceptions to this main rule, often applicable: (a) in situations in which a non-established taxable person carries out the taxable transaction and (b) in supply chains that are susceptible to VAT fraud. In such instances, the liability of VAT is shifted ('reversed') to a person other than the one carrying out the supply. Moreover, Member States may provide that a person other than the person liable to pay the VAT may be held jointly and severally liable for payment of VAT.

When a taxable person is designated as the person liable to pay VAT to the tax authorities, he must register (if he is not already registered) for VAT purposes in the Member State where the taxable transaction is regarded to take place (Article 214 VAT Directive). Moreover, the taxable person must file a VAT return and possibly a recapitulative statement in that Member State (*see* Chapter 15, on administrative obligations), and must pay the VAT to the tax authorities (Article 206 VAT Directive). The liability of VAT is thus connected with various administrative obligations.

In this chapter, we will focus on the appointment of the person liable to pay the VAT in respect of supplies of goods and services and on any joint and several liability for these taxable events.

12.2 MAIN RULES ON THE APPOINTMENT OF THE PERSON LIABLE TO PAY THE VAT

12.2.1 Supplies of Goods and Services

Article 193 VAT Directive provides that VAT shall be payable by any taxable person carrying out a taxable supply of goods or services. Thus: the supplier pays. Nonetheless, the provision explicitly mentions that VAT is payable by another person if Articles 194-199b or Article 202 VAT Directive apply.

12.2.2 Intra-Community Acquisition of Goods

In the case of an intra-Community acquisition ('ICA'), the person making the ICA is the person liable to pay the VAT.[1] The VAT Directive allows for no exceptions to this rule. It appears that this rule not only applies to ICAs in the Member State of arrival of the goods (Article 40 VAT Directive) but also to acquisitions in the Member State of VAT registration (Article 41 VAT Directive, *see* section 13.3.3.2.3).

12.2.3 Importation of Goods

As regards the importation of goods, the main rule is that the VAT is payable by any person or persons designated or recognized as liable by the Member State of importation (Article 201 VAT Directive).[2] An exception to this rule is laid down in Article 202 VAT Directive. If goods cease to be covered by a customs arrangement, the person who caused that the goods ceased to be covered by the customs arrangements is the person who is liable for payment of VAT to the tax authorities.

Article 201 VAT Directive stipulates that VAT (on importation) shall be payable by any person or persons designated or recognized as liable by the Member State of importation. Many Member States decided to consider the person liable to customs duties on importation as the person who is (also) liable to pay the VAT on importation. The person who is liable to pay the customs duties on importation is referred to in Article 5(19) UCC as the 'debtor'.[3] Who the debtor is, largely depends on who files the customs declaration:

(1) If a person makes a customs declaration in its own name and on its own behalf: that person will be considered as the declarant (Article 5(15) UCC). On the basis of Article 77(3) UCC, that person will also be the debtor.

1. This is commonly the person who, as the result of an ICS, obtains the right to dispose of the tangible property as owner in the Member State where the transport of the goods ends. *See* Articles 20 and 40 VAT Directive.
2. From the CJEU judgment in *U.I.*, it becomes apparent that Member States are under the obligation to provide for national legislation that properly arranges (joint and several) liability for VAT on importation; if national provisions do not explicitly and unequivocally designate the person who is liable, they cannot be accepted. CJEU 2 May 2022, Case C-714/20 U.I., ECLI:EU:C:2022:374.
3. *See* sections 4.4.3.4, 10.2.4.1.4 and 14.11.

(2) If a person makes a customs declaration in the name and on behalf of another person ('direct representation', *see* Article 18(1) UCC): the person who is represented is considered as the declarant (Article 5(15) UCC). On the basis of Article 77(3) UCC, the represented person will be the debtor.

(3) If a person makes a customs declaration in its own name, but on behalf of another person ('indirect representation', *see* Article 18(1) UCC): the person making the customs declaration is the declarant (Article 5(15) UCC). He is considered as the debtor (Article 77(3) UCC). However, the person on behalf of whom the declaration is made is *also* considered as the debtor (Article 77(3) UCC).

12.3 REVERSE CHARGE MECHANISM

In some cases, the recipient of a supply, instead of the supplier, is appointed as the person liable for payment of VAT to the tax authorities. This is generally called the 'reverse charge mechanism'. If the reverse charge mechanism applies, the supplier issues an invoice that does not mention any VAT but instead includes a reference to the application of the reverse charge mechanism. The recipient of the supply is required to establish the VAT due on the supply and to report this VAT in his VAT return (self-assessment). If the recipient of the supply is entitled to a deduction of input VAT, he can deduct the self-assessed VAT as input VAT on the same VAT return.

The application of the reverse charge mechanism transfers the liability of VAT from the taxable person carrying out the supply to the recipient of that supply. The effect is that the declaration and payment obligations are to be met by the recipient of the supply instead of the supplier. Only if a Member State has implemented the option for joint and several liability can the payment obligations be imposed on a person other than the person liable for payment of VAT (*see* section 12.5).

The reverse charge mechanism has a function in local transactions of preventing tax avoidance, evasion or fraud (*see* section 12.3.2). It also plays a role removing the need for foreign suppliers to register for VAT in the Member State in which the VAT is due (*see* sections 12.3.3 and 12.3.4). Specific reverse charge rules are also in place in respect of fixed establishments (*see* section 12.3.5). Moreover, the reverse charge mechanism has a specific role in respect of supplies of investment gold, gas through a natural gas system, and supplies of electricity and of heat or cooling energy through heating and cooling networks (*see* section 12.3.6.1). Lastly, it is used to simplify intra-Community triangular supplies of goods (the so-called triangulation simplification; *see* section 12.3.7).

12.3.1 The Generalized Reverse Charge Mechanism (until 30 June 2022)

The reverse charge mechanism marks a departure from the system of fractioned payments (*see* Chapter 1). Clearly, the system of fractioned payments has advantages, such as a clear audit trail and the self-policing effect of invoice flows throughout supply chains. However, the system also has disadvantages, mainly in cross-border situations (e.g., the need for foreign VAT registrations, the need to appoint a fiscal representative – all this to be able to report and pay VAT in the Member States other than that in which the taxable person is established). The reverse charge mechanism takes away both the advantages *and* disadvantages of the system of fractioned payments. Further, the reverse charge mechanism itself has both advantages (e.g., less administrative burdens for entrepreneurs, the potential of preventing carrousel fraud or missing trader fraud) and disadvantages (e.g., more difficult supervision and enforcement by authorities, the need to reclaim foreign input VAT through a foreign VAT refund procedure).

In the context of B2B transactions (i.e., between taxable persons), the absolute and consistent application of the reverse charge mechanism (an 'absolute reverse charge mechanism') would effectively mean that the VAT system as such would be reduced to an administrative affair. The reason is that taxable persons would no longer charge VAT to each other; the VAT would be levied and collected wholly in the final B2C leg of the supply chain. Even though VAT fraud in B2B situations would become less evident, such a change would erode the fundamental characteristics of VAT. Because of this and other reasons, the European Commission and most Member States have rejected the absolute B2B reverse charge mechanism as a viable option.[4] However, in December 2018, the EU institutions adopted a Directive which allowed Member States to make use of a temporary 'generalised reverse charge mechanism' – implying that they could, until 30 June 2022, shift the liability of VAT to the customer in case of 'non-cross-border supplies' that are made above a threshold of EUR 17,500 per transaction.[5] If the mechanism was applied, fraudulent companies were no longer able to charge VAT to their customers with the intention of not paying it to the tax authorities.[6] Various conditions applied; for example, Member States had to have a 'VAT gap' of at least 5% above the Community median, and they had to demonstrate that other control measures aimed at combating VAT fraud were not effective. As such, the temporary generalized reverse charge mechanism constituted an *ultimum remedium* in the fight against tax evasion. It no longer applies today.

4. The main arguments are that applying a generalized reverse charge would mean that the tax would be collected from a far larger group of taxpayers, making control proportionally more difficult, and that it would entail new administrative compliance burdens for entrepreneurs. *See* Communication from the Commission to the Council in accordance with Article 27(3) of Directive 77/388/EEC, 19 July 2006, COM (2006) 404 final, p. 5.
5. *See* the former Article 199c VAT Directive, and Council Directive (EU) 2018/2057 of 20 December 2018 amending Directive 2006/112/EC on the common system of value added tax as regards the temporary application of a generalized reverse charge mechanism in relation to supplies of goods and services above a certain threshold, 27 December 2018, OJ L 329/3.
6. For further reading on the relation between VAT fraud and the generalized reverse charge mechanism, refer to R. de la Feria, *The New VAT General Reverse-Charge Mechanism* (2019) 28 EC Tax Review, pp. 172-175 https://doi.org/10.54648/ecta2019020.

12.3.2 Optional Reverse Charge Mechanism for Certain Transactions

12.3.2.1 Reverse Charge, Certain Supplies, Optional Application

Article 199 VAT Directive contains seven optional exceptions to the main rule that Member States may adopt on the condition that they inform the VAT Committee of such legislative measures (Article 199(4) VAT Directive). The rationale for these exceptions is to prevent and/or combat tax avoidance, tax evasion, or tax fraud. Moreover, if one is to believe the Explanatory Memorandum to the Proposal for Directive 2006/69 by which Article 199 was adopted, the provision also simplifies the functioning of the VAT system and makes it more efficient, with no impact in tax terms for the customer and with minimal additional compliance costs. The reverse charge mechanism for the situations mentioned in Article 199 VAT Directive is not limited to either local or cross-border supplies. As it is an optional provision, we believe that the Member States may restrict the scope of the reverse charge mechanism to certain types of transactions or types of suppliers/recipients. Article 199(2) VAT Directive explicitly confirms that viewpoint.

Undoubtedly, the reverse charge mechanism may help to prevent and/or combat tax evasion or tax evasion involving liquidations of businesses.[7] In some sectors of the economy, such as the construction sector, taxable persons (contractors) have been found issuing invoices mentioning VAT (e.g., 100 + 20 VAT), collecting full payment from their customers (120), but never paying the VAT (20) to the tax authorities. Generally, the unsuspecting customers/taxable persons would exercise their right of deduction on the basis of the (seemingly legitimate) invoices issued by the contractors. Ultimately, the tax authorities would discover the fraud, but by that time, the contractors had often already disappeared with the VAT proceeds. Such malign fiscal behaviour would leave the Member State concerned with (sometimes substantial) losses of VAT revenues.[8]

Making the recipient of a supply the person liable for payment of VAT to the tax authorities takes away the possibility for fraudulent contractors to collect VAT from their customers. The reason for this is that the recipients no longer accept invoices mentioning VAT. Thus, in the past, a number of Member States have obtained derogations to apply the reverse charge mechanism for certain transactions taking place in the context of fraud sensitive sectors of the economy.[9] Since 2006, however, Article 199(1)(a), (b), (c) and (d) VAT Directive allows the Member States to apply the

7. *See* sixth recital of the Preamble to Council Directive 2006/69/EC of 24 July 2006 amending Directive 77/388/EEC as regards certain measures to simplify the procedure for charging value added tax and to assist in countering tax evasion or avoidance, and repealing certain Decisions granting derogations [2006] OJ L 221/9. It should be noted that the sixth recital only mentions 'tax evasion and avoidance', and not tax fraud.
8. *See* Proposal for a Council Directive amending Directive 77/388/EEC as regards certain measures to simplify the procedure for charging value added tax and to assist in countering tax evasion and avoidance, and repealing certain Decisions granting derogations, COM (2005) 89 final, 16 March 2005, p. 7.
9. Those derogations are/were based on Article 27 Sixth VAT Directive (now Article 395 VAT Directive).

reverse charge mechanism to (a) the supply or handing over of construction work, including certain connected services (repairs, cleaning, maintenance and the like), (b) the supply of staff engaged in construction activities, (c) the supply of immovable property, where the supplier has opted for taxation of the supply (*see* Chapter 9), and (d) the supply of waste, scrap and recyclable material together with some products resulting from their treatment and some treatment services.[10]

Fraud is not the only cause of loss of tax revenues. The Treasury is also at risk when a business is in financial distress and unable to honour its debts, including his obligations to the tax authorities. If a supplier goes into bankruptcy proceedings shortly after he collected VAT from his customers in respect of supplies made to them, that VAT may become part of a (mortgage) claim filed by a creditor (e.g., a bank). This makes it impossible for the tax authorities to collect the VAT due. Worse still: the customer who holds a correct invoice legitimately exercises his right to deduct, leading to a budgetary loss for the tax authorities. Even if the supplier does not liquidate his business or does not file for bankruptcy, he may sell goods that serve as collateral or supply goods of which the ownership is retained by another party. The result is that either the VAT is counted as proceeds from the sale and is retained by the creditor to offset the taxable person's debt, or the taxable person disappears without remitting the VAT to the tax authorities.[11] Again, this leads to a budgetary loss for the tax authorities, assuming the customer legitimately exercises his right to deduct. Article 199(1), (e), (f) and (g) VAT Directive aim at preventing such losses of revenue. Member States can implement a reverse charge mechanism in respect of (e) the supply of goods provided as security by one taxable person to another in the execution of that security, (f) the supply of goods following the cession of a reservation of ownership to an assignee and the exercising of this right by the assignee, and (g) the supply of immovable property sold by a judgment debtor in a compulsory sale procedure.

Article 199(2) VAT Directive stipulates that the Member States may specify the supplies of goods and services covered, and the categories of suppliers or recipients to whom these measures may apply.

Article 199(3)(a) and (b) contain specific provisions relating to recipients of supplies that are not, or are only partially, to be considered as taxable persons. Article 199(3)(a) VAT Directive allows Member States to treat taxable persons that also carry

---

10. By its very nature, the reverse charge mechanism is a legal remedy against VAT evasion and fraud. Increasingly however, scholars discuss the possibilities offered by IT. For example, various publications address the question of whether blockchain technology or real-time reporting obligations should be employed to counter VAT evasion and fraud. *See* M. Merkx & N. Verbaan, *Technology: A Key to Solve VAT Fraud?* (2019) 28 EC Tax Review, pp. 300-306 https://doi.org/10.54648/ecta2019033; R. Ismer & M. Schwarz, *Combating VAT Fraud Through Digital Technologies: A Reform Proposal* (2019) 30 International VAT Monitor https://doi.org/10.59403/3ckxzm4; R. Müller, *Proposal for an Automated Real-Time VAT Collection Mechanism in B2C E-commerce Using Blockchain Technology* (2020) 31 International VAT Monitor https://doi.org/10.59403/3ecfzka; C. Armand, *VAT in the Digital Age Proposal: Can DRR Tackle VAT Fraud?* (2023) 30 International VAT Monitor https://doi.org/10.59403/1k1c4ph.
11. Proposal for a Council Directive amending Directive 77/388/EEC as regards certain measures to simplify the procedure for charging value added tax and to assist in countering tax evasion and avoidance, and repealing certain Decisions granting derogations, COM (2005) 89 final, 16 March 2005, p. 8.

out activities that are not subject to VAT (e.g., a controlling active parent company that also acts as a mere holding company vis-à-vis certain subsidiaries) completely as taxable persons when they receive a supply mentioned in Article 199(1) VAT Directive. As a consequence, such a taxable person is required to apply the reverse charge mechanism on the supplies made to him. On the basis of Article 199(3)(b) VAT Directive, Member States are allowed to provide that a non-taxable body governed by public law is regarded as a taxable person in respect of supplies received as referred to in points (e), (f) and (g) of Article 199(1) VAT Directive (*see* above). In our view, it would have been easier to expand the scope of Article 199(1) VAT Directive to 'person' in the first place, rather than limiting it to 'taxable persons'. That way, Article 199(3) VAT Directive becomes superfluous.

12.3.2.2 Reverse Charge, Certain Supplies, Optional and Temporary Application

VAT fraud is a rather prevalent problem in the context of EU VAT.[12] In recent years, the EU legislator has increasingly employed the VAT reverse charge mechanism as an instrument to combat fraud. As a testament to this, Article 199a allows the Member States to apply the reverse charge mechanism to supplies of certain categories of goods and services, which are often the object of fraud schemes.[13] The option to introduce a temporary reverse charge mechanism first involved the transfer of greenhouse gas emission allowances only, given that the prevalent fraud in that sector required immediate action.[14] Since then, fraud has surfaced in other sectors too, and as a consequence, new goods and services were added to the list of supplies eligible for the temporary reverse charge mechanism.

Member States have the discretion to lay down the conditions for the application of the mechanism, including the setting of thresholds, the categories of suppliers or recipients to whom this mechanism may apply, and the partial application of the mechanism within categories.

The reverse charge mechanism under Article 199a VAT Directive, unlike the measures mentioned under Article 199, is a *temporary* measure that allows Member

12. *See* R. Ismer & M. Schwarz, *Combating VAT Fraud Through Digital Technologies: A Reform Proposal* (2019) 30/6 International VAT Monitor https://doi.org/10.59403/1k1c4ph; Green Paper on the future of VAT, Towards a simpler, more robust and efficient VAT system, COM (2010) 695 Final, 1 December 2010, p. 5.
13. *See* Council Directive 2010/23/EU of 16 March 2010 amending Directive 2006/112/EC on the common system of value added tax, as regards an optional and temporary application of the reverse charge mechanism in relation to supplies of certain services susceptible to fraud [2010] OJ L 72/1. This provision has been amended several times, e.g., to extend the period in which the reverse charge can be applied (*see* Council Directive 2013/43/EU of 22 July 2013 [2013] OJ L 201/4; Council Directive (EU) 2018/1695 of 6 November 2018 [2018] OJ L 282/5).
14. For further reading *see* P. Efstratios, *Halting the Horses: EU Policy on the VAT Carousel Fraud in the EU Emissions Trading System* (2012) 21 EC Tax Review, pp. 39-51 https://doi.org/10.5464 8/ecta2012005.

States to apply it until 31 December 2026.[15] For the long term, it is the EU legislator's ambition to provide more structural solutions to the problem of VAT fraud.[16]

12.3.2.3 *Reverse Charge: QRM*

Article 395 VAT Directive allows the Council to authorize the Member States to introduce special measures to prevent certain forms of tax evasion and avoidance. In the context of VAT fraud, recent experience has demonstrated that the rather lengthy procedure provided for under Article 395 VAT Directive is unsuitable for a quick response to VAT fraud.[17] In the view of the EU legislator, rapid and exceptional responses to instances of sudden fraud are best guaranteed by a QRM. This mechanism consists of the option to apply, under strict conditions and for a short period of time, a reverse charge mechanism. Article 199b prescribes how the Member States making use of this mechanism must notify the European Commission appropriately, and within what timeframe.[18] This is also a temporary measure, allowing Member States to apply it until 31 December 2026.[19]

12.3.2.4 *Changes to the Reverse Charge Mechanism in B2B Situations as of 1 July 2028*

Currently, Member States have the option to apply a reverse charge to certain B2B supplies, such as local supplies of goods and services related to immovable property (*see* previous sections). However, as of 1 July 2028, Member States will be obliged to apply the reverse charge to B2B supplies if a non-established supplier is not VAT registered in the Member State where the VAT is due, and the customer is.[20] Additionally, Member States will have the option to require the customer to reverse

15. The period was extended on the basis of Council Directive (EU) 2022/890 of 3 June 2022, OJ L 155.
16. *See* section 13.11.2 and Proposal for a Council Directive amending Directive 2006/112/EC as regards the introduction of the detailed technical measures for the operation of the definitive VAT system for the taxation of trade between Member States, COM (2018) 329 final, 25 May 2018.
17. *See* Preamble to Council Directive 2013/42/EU of 22 July 2013 amending Directive 2006/112/EC on the common system of value added tax, as regards a QRM against VAT fraud, para. 3.
18. For further reading, *see* I. Lejeune, S. de Maeijer & L. Vermeire, *Quick Reaction Mechanism Against EU VAT Fraud* (2013) 24 International VAT Monitor https://doi.org/10.59403/x56jjy.
19. The period was extended on the basis of Council Directive (EU) 2022/890 of 3 June 2022, OJ L 155. Some question the effectiveness of the QRM, whereas others explore alternatives to combat EU VAT fraud (e.g., Gryziak, who studies split-payment models (B. Gryziak, *Split Payment across the European Union: Review and Analysis* (2020) 1 International VAT Monitor)) https://doi.org/10.59403/1947qg2.
20. The text of Article 194 VAT Directive will be amended to this effect. *See*: Draft Council Directive as regards VAT rules for the digital age – General approach. https://data.consilium.europa.eu/doc/document/ST-14961-2024-INIT/en/pdf (accessed 27 November 2024).

charge VAT, even if the customer in a B2B transaction is not VAT registered in the Member State where the VAT is due.[21]

12.3.3 Local Supplies of Goods and Services by Non-established Taxable Persons

12.3.3.1 Optional Reverse Charge Mechanism for Local Supplies by Non-established Taxable Persons

As seen in Chapter 4, the place of supply may well be in a different Member State than the one in which the taxable person who carries out the supply is established. Figure 12.1 illustrates this.[22]

Figure 12.1 Local Supply by a Foreign Supplier

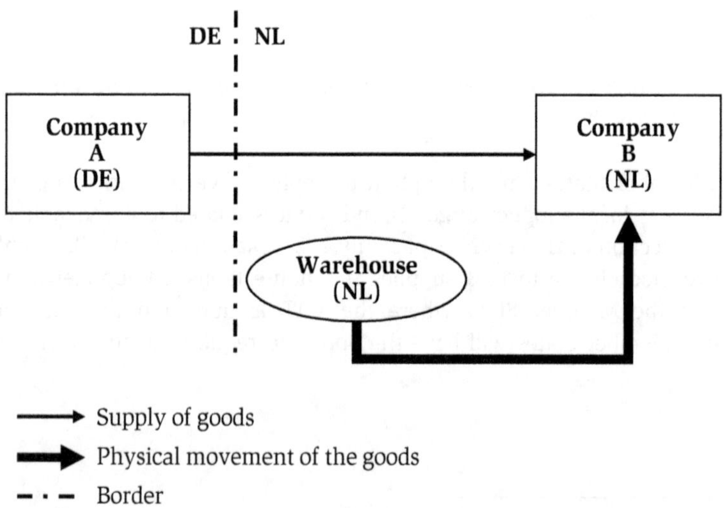

The example above shows a supplier, established in Germany, selling goods that are physically located in a warehouse in the Netherlands (not a fixed establishment) to a customer established in the Netherlands. The goods physically remain within the Netherlands. The place of supply is the Netherlands, on the basis of Article 31 or 32 VAT Directive. Consequently, Dutch VAT is due on the supply. In this example, the main rule of Article 193 VAT Directive requires that the German supplier (company A) charges Dutch VAT on his supply to the Dutch customer (company B) and pays the

21. These changes are part of the ViDA package which was adopted by the Economic and Financial Affairs Council (ECOFIN) of the EU on 5 November 2024. *See* section 1.8.1.
22. In this example, the foreign supplier is considered not to have a fixed establishment in the customer's country. In section 12.3.5, we will elaborate on the VAT liability in cases where a fixed establishment of a foreign supplier is present in the customer's country.

VAT to the Dutch VAT authorities, as he is the person liable for payment of VAT. Without any further arrangements, this implies that the German supplier must register for VAT in the Netherlands and file a Dutch VAT return. Article 194 VAT Directive allows Member States - such as the Netherlands in the mentioned example - to apply a reverse charge mechanism to local supplies by a taxable person not established in their territory to another taxable person. In the example, the application of this reverse charge mechanism would imply that the German supplier would be relieved from the obligation to register for VAT purposes in the Netherlands.[23]

As the provision is optional, some Member States have not implemented the reverse charge mechanism. Others only apply it in specific situations or under certain (differing) conditions. Needless to say, the fragmented and diffuse implementation by the Member States erode legal certainty and clarity for businesses that operate in a cross-border context. For that reason, it would have been better if Article 194 VAT Directive had been a mandatory provision - as proposed by the EU Commission.[24]

It should be noted that if the customer, established in the Member State in which the transaction is regarded as taking place, is the person liable for payment, a Member State may not require that a fiscal representative is appointed (Article 204 VAT Directive; *see* section 12.3.8).

12.3.4 Cross-Border Supplies of Services: B2B

If a taxable person supplies a service to another taxable person, Article 44 VAT Directive provides that the place of supply is where the recipient of that supply is established (i.e., the so-called B2B main rule, *see* section 4.5.3.3). For all services within the scope of the B2B main rule, the reverse charge mechanism applies mandatorily (Article 196 VAT Directive). That way, non-established service suppliers do not have to register for VAT in the Member States in which the recipients of their services are established.

The main rule for B2B services applies not only to services between taxable persons but as a result of Article 43(2) VAT Directive, it also applies to services rendered to non-taxable legal persons who are identified for VAT purposes (e.g., non-taxable legal persons merely holding shares that have a VAT ID number (holding companies)).[25] Article 44 VAT Directive also applies to services by a taxable person to

23. The Netherlands have indeed implemented Article 194 VAT Directive in such a manner that in the mentioned example, the Dutch taxable person (customer) is designated as the person liable for payment of VAT. *See* Article 12(3) of the Dutch VAT Act.
24. In the VAT in the Digital Age (ViDA) proposals, which are meant to partially reform the current EU VAT system, the EU Commission has included a redrafted Article 194 VAT Directive. If adopted, the provision would make the reverse charge mechanism discussed in this section mandatory for Member States to implement in their national legal order. *See* Proposal for a Council Directive amending Directive 2006/112/EC as regards VAT rules for the digital age, 8 December 2022, COM(2022) 701 final and Draft Council Directive as regards VAT rules for the digital age - General approach. https://data.consilium.europa.eu/doc/document/ST-14961-2024-INIT/en/pdf (accessed 27 November 2024). *See* section 12.3.2.4.
25. In our view, the scope of this provision should not be restricted to non-taxable *legal persons*, but should rather also be applied to entities without legal personality (e.g., partnerships, under the

a 'partially taxable person', i.e., a person who carries out activities or transactions which are in the scope of VAT *and* activities or transactions which are not. Such partially taxable persons are considered fully taxable persons for the purpose of applying the rules concerning the place of supply of services (Article 43(1) VAT Directive).[26] However, Article 196 VAT Directive does not designate a partially taxable person who receives a B2B main rule service as the person liable for payment of VAT. Further, Article 43 first sentence under (1) VAT Directive explicitly states that partially taxable persons are only considered fully taxable persons *for the purpose of applying the rules concerning the place of supply of services* – and thus not for the purpose of applying the rules concerning the liability of VAT. Following a literal interpretation of the VAT Directive, a taxable person who renders a B2B main rule service to a partially taxable person cannot apply the reverse charge mechanism of Article 196 VAT Directive, implying that the taxable person should register for VAT purposes in the Member State in which the service is deemed to take place on the basis of Article 44 VAT Directive. One might, however, argue that for the purpose of designating the person liable for payment of VAT, partially taxable persons are already covered by the term 'taxable person' in Article 196 VAT Directive. However, if that were to be true, why would the same argument not hold for the purpose of applying the rules on the place of supply of services? In other words, what is the function of Article 43(1) VAT Directive if the term 'taxable person' already covers partial taxable persons? Perhaps *TRR* offers a solution. The CJEU considers that:

> if the conditions for the application of Article 9(2)(e) of the Sixth Directive are met, the purchaser is liable for VAT on the supply of services which he receives, whether or not they have been supplied for the purposes of activities which fall outside the scope of those directives.[27]

The Sixth VAT Directive did not contain a specific rule on the liability of VAT in situations in which services to which the reverse charge normally applies, are supplied to a partially taxable person. Nonetheless, the CJEU seems to designate such a partially taxable person as the person liable for payment of VAT. In our view, this could also be the case under the current VAT Directive and the current place of supply/VAT liability rules.

12.3.5 Fixed Establishment

In section 4.5.2.3, we discussed the place of supply rules and explained the notion of 'fixed establishment'. A taxable person who has a fixed establishment in a Member State other than the one in which his primary establishment is located is essentially

---

laws of certain Member States). In our opinion, it does not fit well with the principle of fiscal neutrality to treat a non-taxable entity with a VAT ID number and legal personality differently from a non-taxable entity without legal personality.

26. *See also* CJEU 6 November 2008, Case C-291/07 *Kollektivavtalsstiftelsen TRR Trygghetsrådet v Skatteverket*, ECLI:EU:C:2008:609.
27. *Ibid.*, para. 34.

considered to be (secondarily) established in the first-mentioned Member State.[28] The taxable person's head office is considered the primary place of establishment.

Consequently, if a taxable person supplies services *from his head office*, the primary establishment is the supplier of the service. Conversely, if a taxable person supplies cross-border services from a fixed establishment, the secondary establishment (the fixed establishment) provides those services. If services are supplied *to* a fixed establishment, the fixed establishment is, in principle, considered as the recipient of the supply.

12.3.5.1 Person Liable for Payment: Supplies from a Head Office

In the previous section, we explained that if a taxable person supplies goods or services *from his head office*, the head office is the supplier of the service. If the head office supplies goods, the place of the supply depends solely on the physical location and/or flow of the goods (*see* Chapter 4). With respect to the supply of cross-border B2B services by a head office, the place of supply depends on the place where the customer is established. For example, if a taxable person's German head office supplies advisory services to a taxable person in France, the place of supply is France on the basis of Article 44 VAT Directive. As regards the supply of B2C services by a head office, the place of supply is where the head office is located.

Under normal circumstances, the person liable for payment of the VAT is the person making the supply (Article 193 VAT Directive), and in the case of a cross-border intra-EU B2B service, the customer under the reverse charge mechanism (Article 196 VAT Directive). This is even so if the supplier has a fixed establishment in the customer's Member State, as the supply is made *from the head office* and not *from the fixed establishment*. Figure 12.2 serves as an illustration.

28. The primary establishment concept in the VAT Directive relates to the establishment of the taxable person himself (the 'place where the business is established'). We note that, regarding VAT, a company that is primarily established in one Member State can only have a secondary establishment in another Member State through a fixed establishment. The establishment concept of Article 49 TFEU applies not just to the primary establishment of a parent company itself but also to (secondary) establishment(s) through a subsidiary or permanent establishment(s) of the parent company in another Member State. The difference between the concept of establishment in the VAT Directive and that of Article 49 TFEU, therefore, lies in the fact that for VAT purposes a company can only have a secondary establishment in another Member State by means of a fixed establishment. *See* A.J. van Doesum, H.W.M. van Kesteren & G.J. van Norden, *The Internal Market and VAT: Intra-Group Transactions of Branches, Subsidiaries and VAT Groups* (2007) 1 EC Tax Review, pp. 34-43 https://doi.org/10.54648/ecta2007005.

Figure 12.2 Supply from a Head Office Without a Fixed Establishment Intervening in the Supply

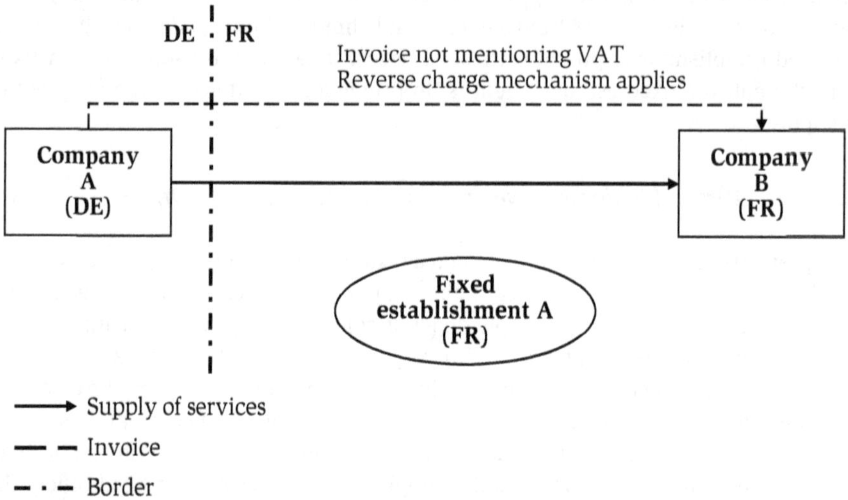

The example above shows that Company A in Germany has a fixed establishment in France. Company A supplies a service (B2B) from its head office in Germany to a customer in France. The fact that Company A has a fixed establishment in France is, in principle, irrelevant for the determination of the person liable to pay the VAT on the supply.

In practice, it can happen that a fixed establishment of the supplier in the customer's Member State *intervenes* in the supply. Conditional upon the supply of goods or services being regarded as taking place in the customer's Member State, the person liable for payment of VAT would, in that case, be the fixed establishment rather than the head office. This follows from Article 192a VAT Directive, which provides that the taxable person shall not be deemed to be established in the Member State where the VAT is due in case the fixed establishment does not intervene in the supply. Thus, *a contrario*, if the fixed establishment of the supplier in the customer's Member State intervenes in a supply of services, it is required to charge and report the local VAT on the supply. The ultimate consequence of this is that the reverse charge mechanism of Article 196 VAT Directive does not apply, as the fixed establishment 'absorbs' the liability from the customer. This can be illustrated in Figure 12.3.

Figure 12.3 Fixed Establishment Intervening in the Supply from a Head Office

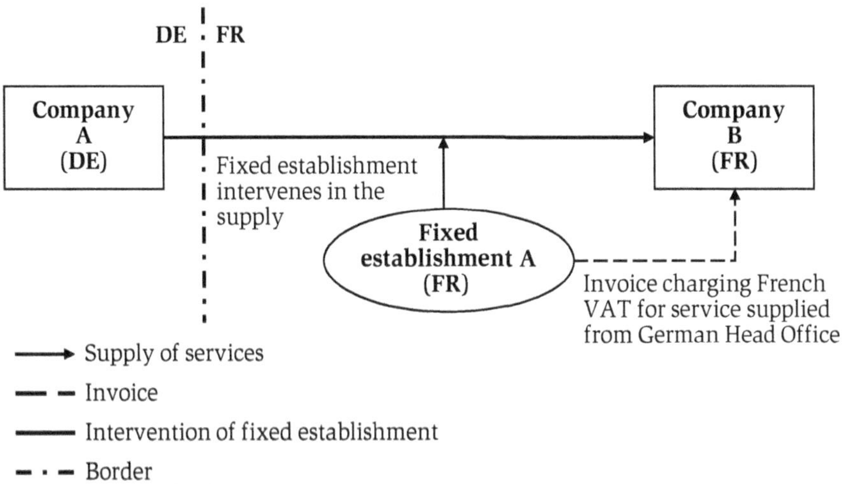

In the example above, Company A in Germany has a fixed establishment in France. Company A supplies a service (B2B) from its head office in Germany to a customer in France. The place of supply is still determined on the basis of Article 44 VAT Directive (B2B main rule), making France the place of supply. The fact that Company A has a fixed establishment in France does not alter the place of supply. However, if the fixed establishment intervenes in the supply of the service by the head office, the reverse charge mechanism of Article 196 will no longer apply. Further to Article 192a VAT Directive, the fixed establishment must charge French VAT to the French customer and report the French VAT in its French VAT return.

The liability for payment of VAT not only shifts from the recipient of the supply to the fixed establishment in the case of supplies of (B2B) services but may also shift in the case of a supply of goods made from the head office, while the place of supply is in the customer's country and the fixed establishment intervenes in the supply. It should be noted that this will only occur if the goods that are supplied are physically located in the customer's country because only in that situation can the place of supply of goods be located there. Figure 12.4 illustrates this.

Figure 12.4 Supply of Goods Made from the Head Office, While the Place of Supply Is in the Customer's Country and the Fixed Establishment Intervenes in the Supply

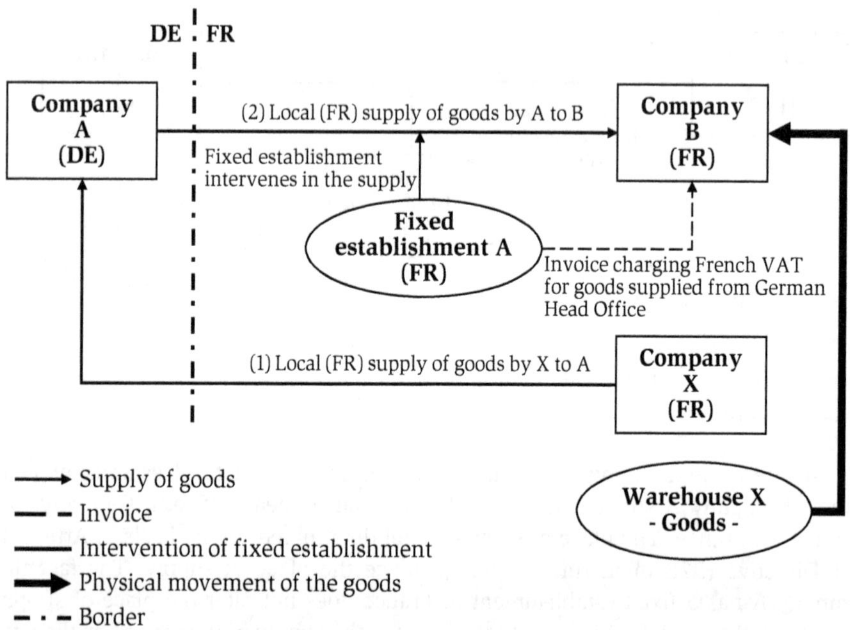

In this example, a supplier in France, X, supplies goods that are physically located in France to Company A (established in Germany). Company A, also having a fixed establishment in France, supplies the goods to a customer in France, B. Company A arranges the transaction from its primary establishment in Germany, but its French fixed establishment intervenes in the supply. The goods are moved directly from Company X's warehouse in France to Company B in France. Both supplies (by X to A and, subsequently, by A to B) are local supplies in France, subject to French VAT. Normally, Company A would have been required to register for VAT in France in order to report and pay the local French VAT on the supply A-B. However, since the fixed establishment intervenes in the supply, Company A is regarded as a taxable person established in France (Article 192a VAT Directive). As a consequence, the VAT on the supply A-B is to be reported on the fixed establishment's French VAT return.

The question may arise as to what type of fixed establishment Article 192a refers to since VAT legislation provides for different manifestations of the concept of a fixed establishment (i.e., a 'purchasing' fixed establishment in Article 44 VAT Directive, and 'supplying' fixed establishment in Article 45 VAT Directive). Article 53(1) VAT Implementing Regulation states that for the application of Article 192a, a fixed establishment of the taxable person can only be taken into consideration when it is characterized by a sufficient degree of permanence and a suitable structure in terms of human and technical resources to enable it to make the supply of goods or services in which it intervenes.

In cases where the taxable person has such a 'supplying' fixed establishment in the other Member State, this establishment will not automatically be seen as intervening in the supply, which is made by that taxable person (i.e., by the head office). The EU legislator starts from the assumption that where a taxable person has a fixed establishment within the territory of the Member State where the VAT is due, that establishment must be considered as not intervening in the supply of goods or services within the meaning of point (b) of Article 192a VAT Directive unless the technical and human resources of that fixed establishment are used by him for transactions inherent in the fulfilment of the taxable supply of those goods or services made within that Member State, before or during this fulfilment. Where, however, the resources of the fixed establishment are only used for administrative support tasks such as accounting, invoicing and collection of debt-claims, they cannot be regarded as being used for the fulfilment of the supply of goods and services (*see* Article 53(2) Implementing Regulation).

It must be stressed that if an invoice is issued under the VAT ID number attributed by the Member State of the fixed establishment, that fixed establishment must be regarded as having intervened in the supply of goods or services made in that Member State unless there is proof to the contrary.

We emphasize that the question of whether a fixed establishment intervenes in a supply is only relevant after it has been established that the supplier makes a supply from his head office, and the place of supply is the customer's country. If the supply is made from the fixed establishment directly, or if the supply is subject to VAT in a different country than the country where the customer is located (as is the case with many B2C services and with ICSs), it is irrelevant whether the fixed establishment intervenes in the supply. For more details on fixed establishments and the notion of 'intervention', we refer to section 4.5.2.3 on the place of supply rules.[29]

12.3.5.2 Person Liable for Payment: Supplies from a Fixed Establishment

As regards the place of supply, we note that if a fixed establishment supplies goods, the place of the supply solely depends on the physical location and/or flow of the goods (*see* section 4.4). If the supply of goods is considered to take place in the Member State where the supplier has his fixed establishment, the supplier, through his fixed establishment, is the person liable for payment on the basis of Article 193 VAT Directive.

29. Finally, the concept of 'intervention' is reserved for fixed establishments only. Following Article 54 Implementing Regulation, primary establishments cannot intervene in supplies by fixed establishments: 'Where a taxable person has established his place of business within the territory of the member state where the VAT is due, Article 192a VAT Directive shall not apply whether or not that place of business intervenes in the supply of goods or services he makes within that member state'.

With respect to the supply of cross-border B2B services by a fixed establishment, the place of supply depends on the place where the customer is located. In respect of cross-border intra-EU B2B services, the customer is the person liable for payment of VAT (Article 196 VAT Directive). If the fixed establishment supplies B2C services to a customer established in a different country than the Member State in which the supplier's fixed establishment is located, the supply is situated in the fixed establishment's Member State (Article 45 VAT Directive). The supplier, through his fixed establishment, is the person liable for payment on the basis of Article 193 VAT Directive.

12.3.5.3 *Person Liable for Payment: Supplies to a Fixed Establishment*

In case goods are supplied *to* a fixed establishment, the place of the supply depends solely on the physical location and/or flow of the goods. If goods (that are not already in free circulation) are shipped from a third country to the Member State where the fixed establishment is located, normally an importation of those goods will take place.[30] If the goods are transported from a different Member State to the Member State of the fixed establishment, the fixed establishment will be required to report an ICA of the respective goods.[31] Services supplied *to* a fixed establishment generally classify as B2B services since the notion of fixed establishment is inextricably connected to the notion of the taxable person. Further to this, Article 44 VAT Directive provides that if a taxable person supplies a cross-border B2B service *to* a fixed establishment of a customer (being a taxable person), the place of supply of those services is the place where that fixed establishment is located. In the case of a cross-border intra-EU B2B service *to* a fixed establishment, the reverse charge mechanism will apply (Article 196 VAT Directive).

12.3.6 Special Regimes

12.3.6.1 *Supplies of Gas Through a Natural Gas System, Electricity, Heat or Cooling Energy Through Heating or Cooling Networks*

Before 7 October 2003, the place of supply of electricity and gas was determined on the basis of the place of supply rules that apply to supplies of goods, supplies of electricity and gas being considered supplies of goods (*see* section 4.4.6). Normally, the place of supply of goods is the place where the goods are located at the time of the supply (Article 31 VAT Directive) or if the goods are transported, the place of departure of the goods (Article 32 VAT Directive, *see* section 4.4.1). However, electricity and gas being hard to track physically, it was burdensome to determine the place of supply of such transactions. Directive 2003/92/EC, amending the Sixth Directive, changed the place of supply of gas through a natural gas system situated within the territory of the

30. *See* Article 30 VAT Directive on the concept of importation.
31. *See* Article 20 VAT Directive on the concept of ICA.

Community, or any network connected to such a system, the supply of electricity, and the supply of heat or cooling energy through heating or cooling networks to a taxable dealer. The supply is now considered to take place where the taxable dealer (customer) is established, has a fixed establishment for which the goods are supplied or, where he has his permanent address or where he usually resides (Article 38 VAT Directive). Since EU VAT aims at taxing private consumption, the place of supply of gas through a natural gas system situated within the territory of the Community or any network connected to such a system, the supply of electricity or the supply of heat or cooling energy through heating or cooling networks, is in all other situations the place where the customer has the effective use and consumption of the goods (Article 39 VAT Directive). Where all or part of the gas, electricity or heat or cooling energy is not effectively consumed by the customer, those non-consumed goods are deemed to have been used and consumed at the place where the customer has established his business or has a fixed establishment for which the goods are supplied. To avoid foreign VAT registrations of suppliers of such (deemed) goods, the place of supply rules set out above are combined with the compulsory reverse charge mechanism laid down in Article 195 VAT Directive. If the customer is a person identified for VAT purposes, he is appointed as the person liable for payment of the VAT.

12.3.6.2 Supplies of Investment Gold, Gold Material and Semi-manufactured Products and Emitted Greenhouse Gases

In order to prevent and/or combat tax avoidance, tax evasion, or tax fraud, Article 198 VAT Directive contains a compulsory specific reverse charge mechanism for supplies of investment gold. For the same reasons, Member States may introduce a reverse charge mechanism with respect to supplies of certain gold material and semi-manufactured products and supplies (transfers) of emitted greenhouse gases and other units in the sense of Directive 2003/87/EC on emission allowance trading. The reverse charge mechanism for emitted greenhouse gases and other units is, in principle, of a temporary nature (*see also* section 12.3.2.2).

12.3.6.3 Derogations from the VAT Directive

Article 395 VAT Directive allows the European Council to authorize any Member State to introduce special measures derogating from the VAT Directive, in order to simplify the procedure for collecting VAT or preventing certain forms of tax evasion or avoidance. On the basis of this provision, certain Member States are – among other things – allowed to apply a reverse charge mechanism to particular supplies within their territory.[32]

32. For example, until 31 December 2024, Hungary is allowed to apply a reverse charge to supplies of capital goods and supplies of goods or services of an open market value exceeding HUF 100,000 by taxable persons under insolvency procedures. For a full overview, *see* the Derogations Schedule, made available online by the European Commission, https://taxation-customs.ec.europa.eu/taxation/vat/vat-directive/vat-derogations_en (accessed 17 August 2024).

12.3.7 Cross-Border Supplies of Goods: Simplified Triangulation

In section 13.7.2, we discuss the STS. In short, the simplified triangulation can be applied if there are three taxable persons and the first taxable person supplies goods to the second, following which the second taxable person supplies the same goods to the third. The goods are transported directly from the Member State of origin to the Member State of destination. Figure 12.5 depicts a typical triangulation situation.

Figure 12.5 Chain Transaction Involving Three Parties. Application of the Simplified Triangulation Scheme

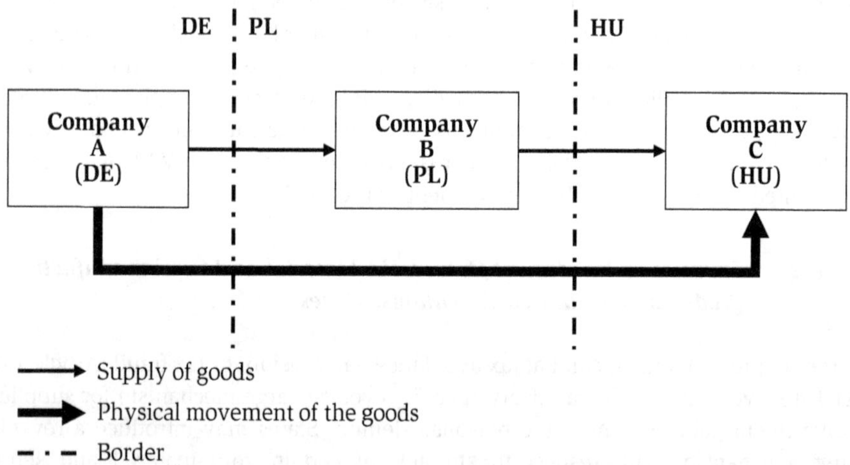

In this example, Company A makes an ICS in Germany. The supply will be exempt with a right to deduct related input VAT ('zero rated'). Company B effects an ICA in Hungary. Next, Company B makes a local supply of goods in Hungary to Company C. Under normal circumstances, Company B is the person liable for payment of VAT and would have to register for VAT purposes in Hungary to report the ICA and the subsequent local supply in Hungary. However, under the simplified triangulation rules, the ICA of B in Hungary is exempt on the basis of Article 141 VAT Directive; further, on the basis of Article 197 VAT Directive, the VAT liability for the subsequent local supply (i.e., by Company B to Company C) in Hungary is shifted to the Hungarian customer (Company C). The reverse charge mechanism only applies if the criteria for applying the simplified triangulation scheme laid down in Article 141 VAT Directive are met.[33] Moreover, C must be a taxable person or a non-taxable person registered for

33. From CJEU 8 December 2022, Case C-247/21 *Luxury Trust Automobil GmbH v Finanzamt Österreich*, ECLI:EU:C:2022:966, it follows that correct invoicing is of pivotal importance when applying the simplified triangulation rules. Here, the Court has ruled that the final customer (in our example: Company C) has not been validly designated as liable for payment of VAT where the invoice issued by the intermediary acquiring the goods (in our example: Company B) does not contain the words 'Reverse charge', as required by Article 226(11a) of the VAT Directive.

VAT in the Member State of arrival of the goods and if B's invoice to C meets the criteria of Articles 220-236 VAT Directive (*see* section 13.7).

12.3.8 VAT Representative (Tax Representative)

If the taxable person liable for payment of VAT is not established (neither by means of a primary establishment nor by means of a fixed establishment) in the Member State in which the VAT is due, Member States may *allow* that person to appoint a tax representative who is then liable for payment of the VAT (Article 204 VAT Directive).[34] That implies that if the reverse charge mechanism applies, typically, a VAT representative cannot be appointed as the person liable for payment of the VAT.

Member States may only *require* a non-resident taxable person to appoint a VAT representative who is then liable for payment if the taxable person is established in a country with which no legal instrument exists relating to mutual assistance for the collection of consumption taxes. Thus, Member States are not allowed to require taxable persons to appoint a VAT representative if these taxable persons are established in the other Member States.[35]

If a VAT representative can or must be appointed, it is at the Member States' discretion to lay down the conditions and procedures (Article 204(2) VAT Directive).

12.4 VAT INCORRECTLY ENTERED ON AN INVOICE[36]

Article 203 VAT Directive provides that VAT shall be payable by any person who enters the VAT on an invoice - so even if it is not due on the basis of the material provisions of EU VAT law.[37] The motives or intentions of the person mentioning the VAT on an invoice are irrelevant in this respect.[38] This is also true for the capacity or VAT status

34. An exception exists with respect to taxable persons who supply services taxable in the EU, who are not established within the Community, and who make use of the OSS special scheme of Articles 358a-369 VAT Directive.
35. CJEU 15 June 2006, Case C-249/05 *Commission of the European Communities v Republic of Finland*, ECLI:EU:C:2006:411.
36. This section is based on: A.J. van Doesum, *A Law of Counteracting Forces* (2013) 3 EC Tax Review, pp. 131-144 https://doi.org/10.54648/ecta2013015.
37. An example is when a taxable person issues an invoice mentioning the standard VAT rate (e.g., 21%), even though the supplied goods fall within the scope of a reduced VAT rate (e.g., 9%). In this case, 9% of VAT was duly charged, but the remainder (12%) not. Still, the full amount of VAT as mentioned on the invoice (21%) is due on the basis of Article 203 VAT Directive.
38. In its rulings of 31 January 2013, the CJEU confirmed (among other things) that Article 203 VAT Directive must be interpreted as meaning that the VAT entered by a person on an invoice is payable by him regardless of whether a taxable transaction actually exists. *See* CJEU 31 January 2013, Case C-642/11 *Stroy trans EOOD v Direktor na Direktsia 'Obzhalvane i upravlenie na izpalnenieto' - Varna pri Tsentralno upravlenie na Natsionalnata agentsia za prihodite*, ECLI:EU:C:2013:54 and CJEU 31 January 2013, Case C-643/11 *LVK - 56 EOOD v Direktor na Direktsia 'Obzhalvane i upravlenie na izpalnenieto' - Varna pri Tsentralno upravlenie na Natsionalnata agentsia za prihodite*, ECLI:EU:C:2013:55. In *Stadeco*, the CJEU ruled that the Member State to which the VAT mentioned on the invoice or other document serving as invoice relates, is allowed to collect the VAT on the basis of Article 203 VAT Directive, even if the

of that person; from the judgment in *P sp. z o.o.*, we learn that even an employee can be held liable for VAT that was incorrectly entered on an invoice.[39]

The *ratio legis* of Article 203 VAT Directive is to prevent a risk of any loss in tax revenues. This risk is particularly eminent if the customer has a full right of deduction; the person incorrectly mentioning the VAT on the invoice may not be inclined to pay that VAT to the tax authorities, while the customer is likely to fully deduct the VAT on that invoice. Clearly, such a situation can lead to a loss in tax revenues. As the CJEU explained in *Stadeco*, such danger even exists if the customer does not have a right of deduction (e.g., a hospital). However, in case the client base consists wholly of final consumers who do not have a right of deduction, Article 203 VAT Directive does not apply – the reason being that the CJEU deems no risk of loss of VAT revenue to be present at all.[40] The addressee of an invoice incorrectly mentioning VAT could de facto use the invoice to deduct the VAT mentioned thereon while the tax authorities cannot establish in a timely fashion that the deduction of the VAT is incorrect.[41] Hence, the purpose of Article 203 VAT Directive is to protect the interests of the Treasuries of the Member States by instituting an extra safeguard against the loss of tax revenues.[42]

That is also why, in *Genius Holding*, the CJEU provides that the right to deduct cannot be exercised 'in respect of tax which does not correspond to a given transaction, either because that tax is higher than that legally due or because the transaction in question is not subject to VAT'.[43] In simplified terms: VAT, which is due solely because

---

transaction in question was not taxable in that Member State. CJEU 18 June 2009, Case C-566/07 *Staatssecretaris van Financiën v Stadeco BV*, ECLI:EU:C:2009:380.

39. CJEU 30 January 2024, Case C-442/22 P sp. z o.o., ECLI:EU:C:2024:100. The case involved an employee of a taxable person who had issued a fake invoice showing VAT using the employer's identity as a taxable person, without the employer's knowledge or consent. The Court provides that the employee must be considered to be the person liable for VAT, unless the employer did not exercise the due diligence reasonably required to monitor the conduct of that employee.
40. CJEU 8 December 2022, Case C-378/21, *P GmbH v Finanzamt Österreich*, ECLI:EU:C:2022:968, para. 24.
41. CJEU 18 June 2009, Case C-566/07 *Staatssecretaris van Financiën v Stadeco BV*, ECLI: EU:C:2009:380, para. 29.
42. In this regard, we believe that the CJEU's ruling in *Maria Karageorgou* is not in line with the purpose of Article 203 VAT Directive. The CJEU ruled that an amount mentioned in error by way of VAT on the invoice may not be classified as VAT if that person erroneously believes that he is providing those services as a self-employed person while in reality there is an employer-employee relationship. According to the CJEU if a non-taxable person mentions an amount mentioned as 'VAT' on an invoice, that amount can in no event constitute VAT and can, therefore, not fall within the scope of Article 203 VAT Directive. However, even if the supplier of the service is not a taxable person, the recipient of the invoice may still have deducted the amount mentioned as VAT on the invoice. As the tax authorities may not be able to determine whether the deduction of the VAT is correct in sufficient time, there is a risk of loss of revenue. As set out above, the goal of Article 203 VAT Directive is, in fact, to prevent any risk of loss of revenue. In light of this, we find that the limitation of the scope of Article 203 VAT Directive in the CJEU's ruling in *Maria Karageorgou* is not in line with the purpose of Article 203 VAT Directive. CJEU 6 November 2003, Joined Cases C-78/02–C-80/02 *Elliniko Dimosio v Maria Karageorgou (C-78/02), Katina Petrova (C-79/02) and Loukas Vlachos (C-80/02)*, ECLI: EU:C:2003:604.
43. CJEU 13 December 1989, Case C-342/87 *Genius Holding BV v Staatssecretaris van Financiën*, ECLI:EU:C:1989:635, para. 15.

it is mentioned on the invoice, cannot be deducted by the taxable person to whom the invoice is issued.

The liability for VAT erroneously mentioned on an invoice (overcharged VAT) in combination with the non-deductibility of this VAT, would lead to the cascading of tax if no additional measures were taken.[44] The cascading of VAT can, however, be remedied if the issuer of the invoice can adjust the VAT on the invoice (i.e., request a refund from the tax authorities, and subsequently pay it back to the customer). According to the CJEU, the principle of the neutrality of VAT indeed requires that taxable persons must have the possibility of adjusting incorrectly charged VAT.[45] Following *EN.SA. Srl*, this possibility must even exist in case the taxable person carried out fictitious supplies and moreover was not acting in good faith, but only on the condition that he has 'in sufficient time, wholly eliminated the risk of any loss of tax revenue'.[46]

Because the VAT Directive contains no provisions on the adjustment of improperly invoiced (overcharged) VAT, it is up to the Member States to provide for the possibility of correcting any tax improperly invoiced in their internal legal systems.[47] They may, for example, make the adjustment subject to the condition that the supplier corrects the invoice.[48] However, Member States are not entirely free to set the conditions for adjustment. In *Genius Holding*, the CJEU requires that the person who issued the invoice must demonstrate that he acted in good faith.[49] In *Schmeink & Strobel*, the CJEU added that where the issuer of the invoice has in sufficient time wholly eliminated the risk of any loss in tax revenues, the VAT which has been improperly invoiced can be adjusted without such adjustment being made conditional by the Member States upon the issuer of the relevant invoice having acted in good faith.[50] Moreover, the CJEU has ruled that adjustment in respect of improperly invoiced

44. The VAT mentioned on the invoice is likely to become part of the prices of the supplies to the recipient of the invoice. If the recipient carries out taxed transactions, VAT will be calculated over an amount including (non-deductible) VAT.
45. CJEU 13 December 1989, Case C-342/87 *Genius Holding BV v Staatssecretaris van Financiën*, ECLI:EU:C:1989:635, para. 18 and CJEU 19 September 2000, Case C-454/98 *Schmeink & Cofreth AG & Co. KG v Finanzamt Borken and Manfred Strobel v Finanzamt Esslingen*, ECLI: EU:C:2000:469, para. 58.
46. CJEU 8 May 2019, Case C-712/17 *EN.SA. Srl*, ECLI:EU:C:2019:374, para. 36.
47. CJEU 13 December 1989, Case C-342/87 *Genius Holding BV v Staatssecretaris van Financiën*, ECLI:EU:C:1989:635, para. 18; CJEU 19 September 2000, Case C-454/98 *Schmeink & Cofreth AG & Co. KG v Finanzamt Borken and Manfred Strobel v Finanzamt Esslingen*, ECLI:EU:C:2000:469, paras 49 and 65 and CJEU 15 March 2007, Case C-35/05 *Reemtsma Cigarettenfabriken GmbH v Ministero delle Finanze*, ECLI:EU:C:2007:167, para. 37.
48. CJEU 18 June 2009, Case C-566/07 *Staatssecretaris van Financiën v Stadeco BV*, ECLI: EU:C:2009:380.
49. CJEU 13 December 1989, Case C-342/87 *Genius Holding BV v Staatssecretaris van Financiën*, ECLI:
EU:C:1989:635, para. 18.
50. CJEU 19 September 2000, Case C-454/98 *Schmeink & Cofreth AG & Co. KG v Finanzamt Borken and Manfred Strobel v Finanzamt Esslingen*, ECLI:EU:C:2000:469, para. 58. *See also* CJEU 6 November 2003, Joined Cases C-78/02–C-80/02 *Elliniko Dimosio v Maria Karageorgou (C-78/02), Katina Petrova (C-79/02) and Loukas Vlachos (C-80/02)*, ECLI:EU:C:2003:604, para. 50 and CJEU 18 June 2009, Case C-566/07 *Staatssecretaris van Financiën v Stadeco BV*, ECLI:EU:C:2009:380, para. 37.

VAT cannot be dependent upon the discretion of the tax authorities.[51] Also, the conditions under which a Member State allows for adjustment of the improperly invoiced VAT may not have the effect of undermining VAT neutrality.[52] They must adhere to the principles of equivalence and effectiveness.[53] That implies that they must not be less favourable than those relating to similar claims founded on provisions of domestic law (equivalence) or so framed as to render virtually impossible the exercise of rights conferred by the Community (Union) legal order (effectiveness).

12.5 JOINT AND SEVERAL LIABILITY

The person who is designated as the person liable for payment of VAT to the tax authorities bears the obligation to pay any (net) VAT due to the tax authorities. However, on the basis of Article 205 VAT Directive, Member States may hold another person jointly and severally liable for payment of VAT – e.g., to counter revenue losses caused by VAT fraud.[54]

The person liable for payment of VAT also bears the requirement to file a VAT return and meet certain other administrative obligations. It should be noted that on the basis of Article 205 VAT Directive, a person who is jointly and severally liable for payment of VAT cannot be held responsible for also (or alternatively) meeting such administrative obligations. His liability is restricted to payment of the tax due. Any other obligations must be met by the person liable for payment of the VAT alone.

51. CJEU 19 September 2000, Case C-454/98 *Schmeink & Cofreth AG & Co. KG v Finanzamt Borken and Manfred Strobel v Finanzamt Esslingen*, ECLI:EU:C:2000:469, para. 68 and CJEU 18 June 2009, Case C-566/07 *Staatssecretaris van Financiën v Stadeco BV*, ECLI:EU:C:2009:380, para. 38.
52. CJEU 18 June 2009, Case C-566/07 *Staatssecretaris van Financiën v Stadeco BV*, ECLI:EU:C:2009:380, para. 39.
53. For example: Case C-35/05 *Reemtsma Cigarettenfabriken GmbH v Ministero delle Finanze*, ECLI:EU:C:2007:167, paras 37 and 38.
54. *See* A.B. Prosper-Almagro, *Joint and Several Liability as a Measure to Tackle VAT Fraud: The Spanish Perspective* (2019) 3 Intertax https://doi.org/10.54648/taxi2019028.

CHAPTER 13

Intra-Community Transactions (Goods)

13.1 INTRODUCTION

On 1 January 1993, the 'single market' (or 'internal market', in terms of the TFEU) was established.[1] On that date, fiscal customs-based controls at internal EU frontiers were abolished, and a new VAT control system was put in place for intra-Community trade in goods. The concepts of export and import of goods were abolished for intra-Community trade.

In a 'true' internal market, all supplies of goods are treated equally as taxed 'local' supplies. In 1993, this was, however, not achieved – primarily since the single market still comprised of distinct national jurisdictions that not only had their own Treasuries but also employed varying VAT rates, exemptions, etc. Therefore, a transitional system

1. Article 26(2) TFEU.

for ICTs was put in place. This regime functioned as a transitional measure and was intended to be replaced by a definitive system as of 1 January 1997. However, as the Member States still could not agree on a final regime in 1997, the 'transitional' system became a more or less permanent system and later became part of the current VAT Directive (that came into force on 1 January 2007). Currently, the EU legislator is exploring alternatives to the current system – which, as always, proves to be a slow and politically complex process.[2]

In a way, the current transitional regime is a reflection of the regime of importation and exportation of goods, which (still) applies to cross-border supplies to and from third countries (*see* Chapter 14). Instead of 'supplies for export' and 'importations of goods', ICSs and ICA take place when an intra-Community B2B supply of goods is carried out.[3] The underlying rationale of this mechanism of ICSs and acquisitions is to levy VAT on goods according to the destination principle.[4] This principle entails that private consumption is taxed at the place (in the Member State) where the consumption actually takes place.[5] Additionally, it follows from CJEU case law that the transitional regime was intended to ensure a clear demarcation of the sovereignty of the Member States in matters of taxation, as it arranges the allocation of taxing competences as regards ICTs involving goods.[6]

To get a clear understanding of the current transitional regime, it is important to realize that it only applies to supplies of *goods* (cf. Article 14 VAT Directive) As regards supplies of *services* (cf. Article 24 VAT Directive), a different regime for the allocation of taxing competences applies (*see* Chapter 4 on the place of supply rules). Further, the transitional regime only applies to *intra-Community* trade in goods. Transactions involving goods that are transported to or from third countries (i.e., non-EU countries) are subject to a different set of rules (*see* Chapter 14).

2. In 2018, the Commission proposed an alternative system for intra-Community trade in goods. *See* Proposal for a Council Directive amending Directive 2006/112/EC as regards the introduction of the detailed technical measures for the operation of the definitive VAT system for the taxation of trade between Member States, COM (2018) 329 final, 25 May 2018.
3. Even though the 'European Community' is now the 'European Union', it is still common practice to refer to 'intra-Union' supplies as 'intra-Community' supplies. This terminology is also still used in the VAT Directive.
4. CJEU 6 April 2006, Case C-245/04 *EMAG Handel Eder OHG v Finanzlandesdirektion für Kärnten*, ECLI:EU:C:2006:232, para. 40 and CJEU 22 April 2010, Cases C-536/08 and C-539/08 *Staatssecretaris van Financiën v X and Staatssecretaris van Financiën v fiscale eenheid Facet BV/Facet Trading BV*, ECLI:EU:C:2010:217, para. 30.
5. For example: CJEU 6 March 2014, Joined Cases C-606/12 and C-607/12 *Dresser-Rand SA v Agenzia delle Entrate, Direzione Provinciale, Ufficio Controlli di Genova*, ECLI:EU:C:2014:125, para. 28.
6. *See* CJEU 18 November 2010, Case C-84/09 *X v Skatteverket*, ECLI:EU:C:2010:693, para. 23; CJEU 14 June 2017, Case C-26/16 *Santogal M-Comércio e Reparação de Automóveis Lda v Autoridade Tributária e Aduaneira*, ECLI:EU:C:2017:453, para. 38.

13.2 TYPOLOGY OF VARIOUS ICTs

The purpose of this section is to provide a high-level overview of the various types of ICTs. Therefore, we limit ourselves to highlighting the most important VAT consequences of the respective transactions, which are discussed in more detail in later sections of this chapter.

13.2.1 Starting Point: A Standard Supply Chain

As a starting point for the overview, we employ a basic, simplified supply chain adapted to the purposes of this chapter. It involves two businesses (taxable persons, cf. Article 9 VAT Directive) and one private consumer. All parties are established or residing in different Member States, and, in the course of the supplies, the goods are generally transported from one Member State to another Member State.

In a standard supply chain, various supplies take place. Figure 13.1 provides a graphical representation of the simplified supply chain.

Figure 13.1 Standard Supply Chain

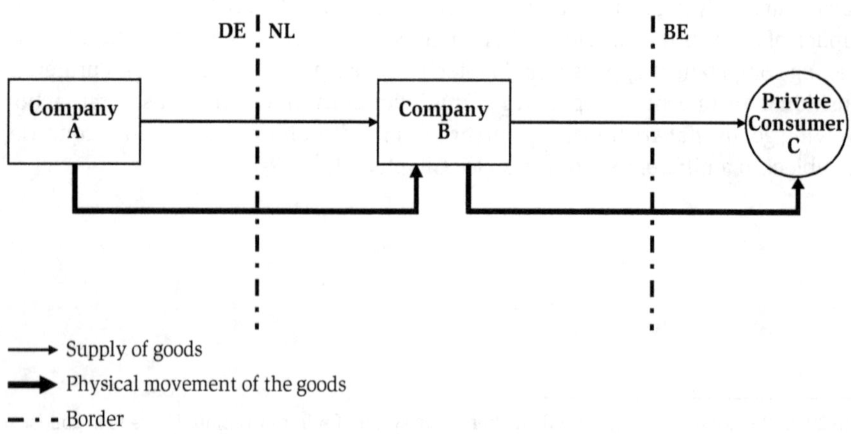

13.2.2 Intra-Community B2B Transactions

The first supply in this supply chain – the supply between company A and company B – is an 'ICT'. This basic manifestation of the ICT only occurs if the supply takes place between two taxable persons acting as such (i.e., B2B). Analogous to the place of supply rules, where a distinction is made between B2B and B2C supplies (*see* Chapter 4), we refer to such ICSs as 'B2B ICSs'.

A basic B2B ICT consists of an ICS (Intra-Community Supply) for consideration by a taxable person acting as such in the Member State of origin of the goods, and an ICA (Intra-Community Acquisition) of those goods by a taxable person acting as such in the Member State of arrival or destination. It is essential that the goods are physically transported or dispatched in the course of the supply from one Member State to the other. Figure 13.2 shows that the ICS by company A is 'exempt' from VAT (cf. Article 138(1) VAT Directive). With respect to an exempt ICS, the supplier (company A) can deduct related input VAT (cf. Article 169(b) VAT Directive). Figure 13.2 also shows that the ICA by company B is taxed in the Member State of arrival of the goods (the Netherlands in this example). Company B can deduct the VAT on the ICA, insofar it uses the goods for its taxed output supplies (Article 168(c) VAT Directive).

Figure 13.2 A Basic B2B ICT: ICS by Company A, Followed by ICA by Company B

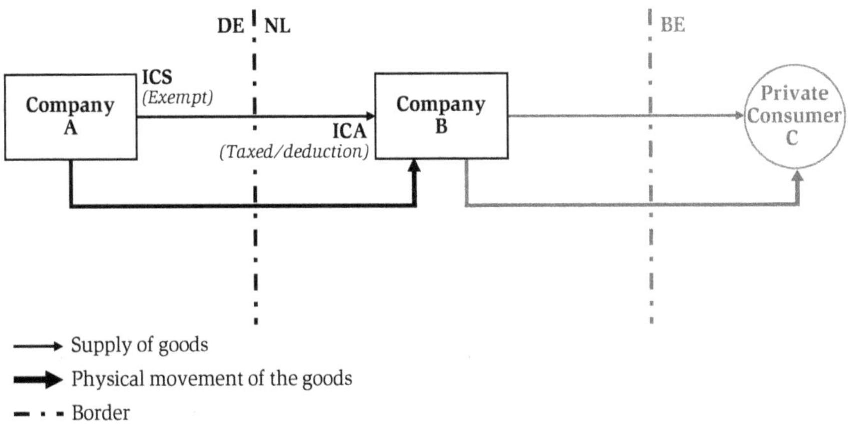

In practice, not all ICS chains involve only an ICS and acquisition. In the following subsections, we will discuss other types of cross-border supplies of goods within the EU.

13.2.3 Intra-Community B2C Transactions/Distance Sales

If a private consumer travels to the supplier's Member State, purchases goods in that Member State and subsequently takes the goods with him to his own Member State, the supply is considered as a local supply of goods in the supplier's Member State. In Figure 13.3, Company B would thus make a local supply of goods in the Netherlands.

If the *supplier* (company B in the example) transports (dispatches) the goods to the private consumer in the course of that supply, the supply is an Intra-Community B2C supply – which is also referred to as an Intra-Community Distance Sales of Goods (ICDS).[7] Such an Intra-Community B2C supply does not enjoy the exemption for B2B ICSs of goods (cf. Article 138(1) VAT Directive). In this regard, CJEU case law points out that an ICS requires that the acquirer of the goods is a taxable person (*see* section

7. *See* Article 14(4)(1) VAT Directive.

13.3.2.2.2).[8] Notwithstanding the difference between 'classic' intra-Community B2B supplies, we will refer to cross-border B2C supplies as 'intra-Community B2C supplies' since this term immediately makes clear what type of supply is referred to.

Let us have a look at an example of an Intra-Community B2C supply. Under Article 2(1)(b) VAT Directive, private consumers, in principle, cannot carry out an ICA, meaning that the rules on B2B ICS and ICA are not applicable. Therefore, Figure 13.3 shows that there is a taxed (intra-Community) B2C supply of goods by company B which is *not* followed by an ICA on the part of private customer C. Whether company B should charge the VAT of the Member State of departure of the goods (in this example the Netherlands) or the VAT of the Member State of arrival of the goods (in this example Belgium), depends on whether the supplier or the customer transports the goods and on whether a threshold is exceeded (Article 59c VAT Directive). If the threshold is exceeded, the intra-Community B2C supply is considered to take place in the Member State where the goods arrive (Article 33(a) VAT Directive). This mechanism is generally referred to as the 'distance sales scheme'. In section 13.4, we will further elaborate on B2C ICSs.

Figure 13.3 A Basic B2C ICS

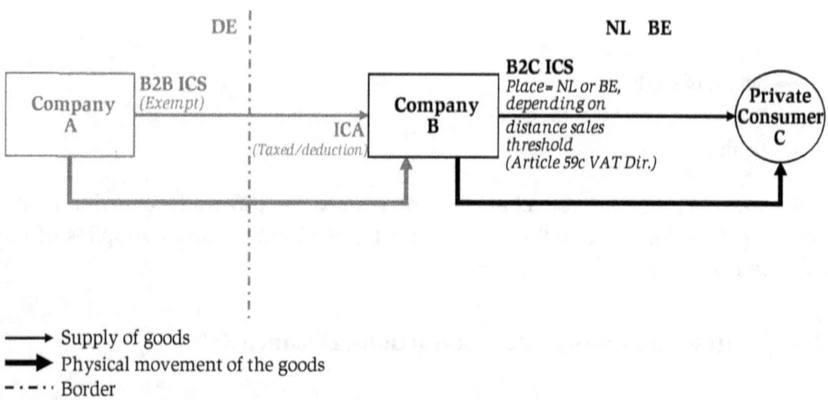

13.2.4 Intra-Community B2H(ybrid) Transactions

Article 2(1)(a) VAT Directive designates as a taxable transaction for VAT purposes the ICA of goods *by a taxable person or a non-taxable legal person*. This implies that in principle, also a non-taxable person (cf. Article 9 VAT Directive) can carry out ICAs

8. CJEU 27 September 2007, Case C-409/04 *The Queen, on the application of Teleos plc and Others v Commissioners of Customs & Excise*, ECLI:EU:C:2007:548, para. 42.

(assuming that person indeed legal persons, e.g., a SARL or Ltd.), as well as a taxable person that has no right of deduction (e.g., a hospital exclusively providing VAT-exempt hospital and medical care). However, notwithstanding Article 2(1)(a) VAT Directive, Article 3(1)(b) VAT Directive provides that the ICAs of the following categories of persons are *not* subject to VAT:

(1) a farmer applying the common flat-rate scheme for farmers;
(2) a taxable person who carries out only supplies of goods or services in respect of which VAT is not deductible; or
(3) a non-taxable legal person.

These three categories of persons have in common that they do not have a (full) right of deduction of input VAT. Their ICAs are not subject to VAT, and the supplies to them are subject to VAT in the Member State of departure of the goods in line with the taxation regime applicable to Intra-Community B2C supplies (distance sales; *see* section 13.4). Knowing this, the mentioned persons experience an incentive to buy goods locally in Member States with relatively low VAT rates. In order to counter such 'VAT rate shopping' - which is in conflict with the principle of neutrality and the ambition of realizing an internal market - Article 3(2) VAT Directive stipulates that when the intra-Community purchases of such customers exceed a certain threshold - the acquisition threshold - their ICAs *are* subject to VAT.[9] In that situation, the taxation regime for B2B ICSs and acquisitions applies to the purchases of the mentioned persons (*see* section 13.3).

When looking at the interplay between Articles 2(1)(b) and 3 VAT Directive, one may notice that the three types of customers mentioned in the former provision are either treated as private consumers (in case the acquisition threshold of Article 3(1)(b) *is not* exceeded) or as taxable persons (in case the acquisition threshold of Article 3(1)(b) *is* exceeded). Therefore, we refer to such customers as 'hybrids'. Figure 13.4 shows a supply by company B to a hybrid customer.

9. The threshold may not be less than EUR 10,000; the reference time is the current calendar year and the previous calendar year.

Figure 13.4 A B2H ICS

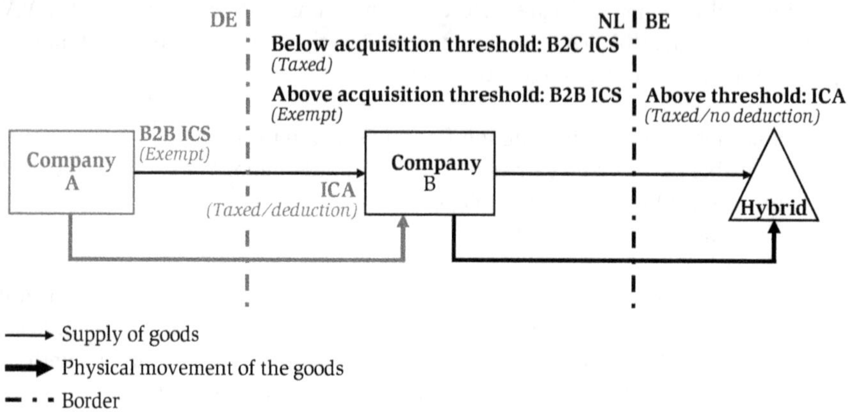

13.2.5 Intra-Community B2Me Transactions

Article 17(1) VAT Directive provides that the transfer by a taxable person of goods forming part of his business assets to another Member State shall be treated as a supply of goods for consideration. This is often referred to as a 'deemed ICS or a 'transfer of own goods'. A transfer of own goods does not qualify as a 'supply of goods' in its own right since there is no transfer of the right to dispose of the goods as owner to some other party (cf. Article 14 VAT Directive). However, through Article 17(1) VAT Directive, the transfer of goods is nonetheless qualified as a supply of goods by legal fiction ('shall be treated as a supply of goods'). A deemed ICS in the Member State of departure is followed by an ICA in the Member State of arrival of the goods. Since no 'true' supply of goods takes place, we refer to this kind of deemed ICSs as 'B2Me ICSs'.

One may wonder why the EU legislator has gone through the trouble of creating this legal fiction. First, the legal fiction has the important implication that transfers of own goods (stock movements) throughout the EU are, in fact, reported in the corporate administrations and VAT returns as 'deemed' ICSs in the Member State of departure and ICAs in the Member State of arrival. This allows the tax authorities of the respective Member States to monitor the movements of business assets and stocks within the EU. Further, the legal fiction serves the destination principle since the moved goods are ultimately subject to taxation (i.e., by means of taxed ICAs) in the Member State of arrival (which is, at least more likely than the Member State of departure, the Member State of consumption). Figure 13.5 shows the VAT treatment of an intra-Community B2Me supply.

Figure 13.5 A B2Me ICS

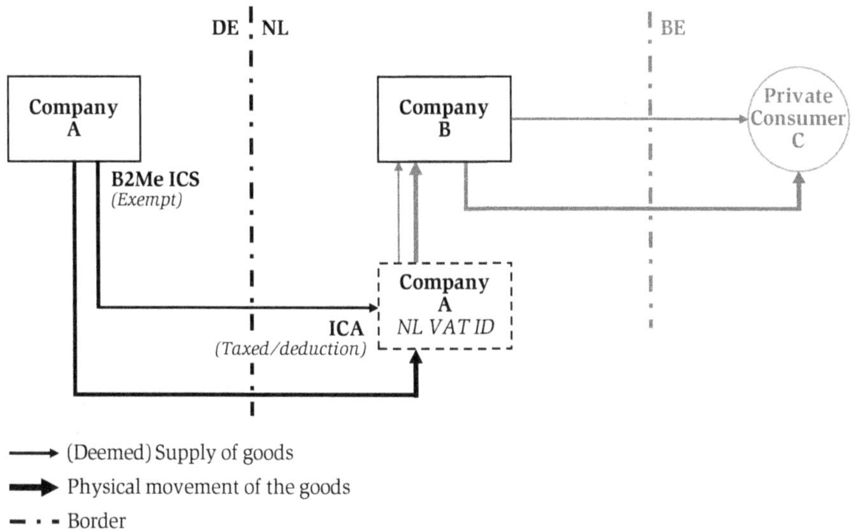

13.2.6 Intra-Community B2B Chain Transactions

In practice, supply chains are usually more extensive than the stylized supply chain described in sections 13.2.1 and 13.2.2. They may involve three, four, five or even more parties (total number: *n*) and almost as many supplies (total number: *n-1*). In principle, each supply in a supply chain is assessed on the basis of its own objective characteristics. For example, in the supply chain depicted in Figure 13.6, three taxable persons are involved. Each B2B supply is a separate B2B ICS, followed by an ICA. The last supply in the chain is a B2C ICS, which is taxed and is not followed by an ICA.

Figure 13.6 Multiple Transactions in a Supply Chain

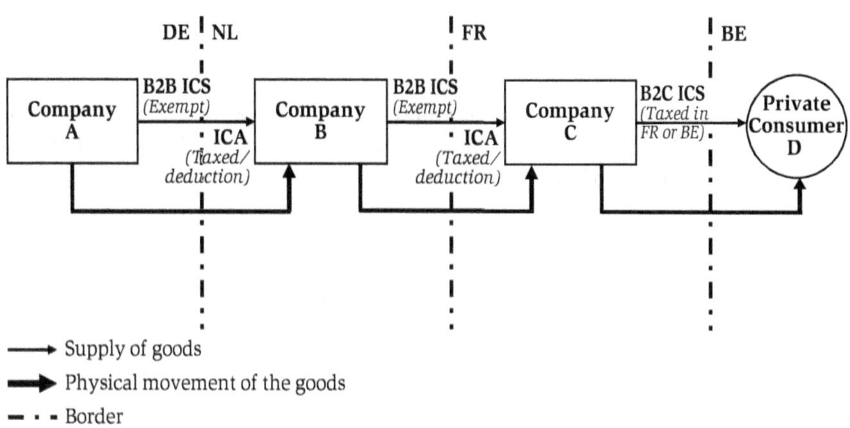

In this example, each time a supply is made, the goods are also physically transported in the course of that supply. Since that may not be economically efficient, parties may choose to directly transport the goods to the last taxable person in the supply chain if it is known in advance who that person is.[10] Then, a situation occurs in which there are multiple supplies, but only one transport movement. We refer to such chain transactions as 'intra-Community B2B chain supplies'. Clearly, such a chain of transactions may involve more than five parties. The mere fact that the goods are directly transported from A to C does not alter the fact that each transaction in the supply chain must be assessed on its own objective characteristics – even if the VAT treatment of the transactions is, to some extent, interdependent.

Figure 13.7 shows an intra-Community B2B chain supply involving three taxable persons. In this example, the transportation of the goods takes place in connection with the supply by A to B. Since there is only one physical movement of the goods, there can only be one B2B ICS, i.e., the supply by A to B (which, in the below example, takes place in Germany). Therefore, the supply by B to C must be a local supply (which, in the below example, takes place in France). In section 13.7, we will further elaborate on the VAT consequences of intra-Community B2B chain supplies.

Figure 13.7 Intra-Community B2B Chain Transaction

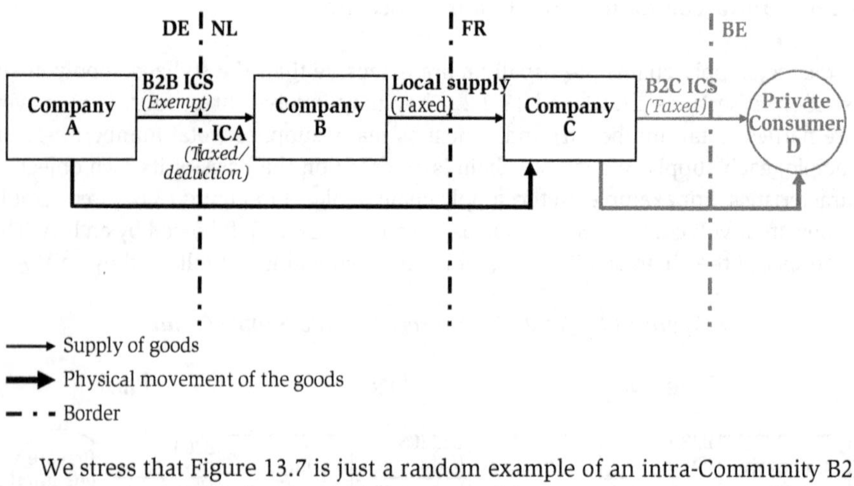

We stress that Figure 13.7 is just a random example of an intra-Community B2B chain transaction. All kinds of variations are possible. In section 13.7, we will discuss some different manifestations of chain transactions.

10. The goods may also be transported directly to the ultimate (private) customer in the supply chain. However, that is not very common since there may be so many customers the last taxable person in the supply chain supplies to. Therefore, we will not discuss this possibility further.

13.2.7 Intra-Community C2C Supplies of New Means of Transport

Normally, only taxable persons are able to carry out taxable transactions.[11] With the abolishment of internal fiscal frontiers on 1 January 1993, significant distortions of competition between the Member States were anticipated with respect to supplies of new means of transport (e.g., luxury cars). The EU legislator feared that private consumers would start purchasing new means of transport from non-taxable persons in the Member States with relatively low VAT rates. In order to prevent such distortion of competition, special provisions regarding the ICS of new means of transport were introduced. The effect of these provisions is twofold. In the first place, non-taxable persons are regarded as taxable persons for the ICS of new means of transport (*see* Article 9(2) VAT Directive). Second, non-taxable persons buying new means of transport in another Member State become liable with respect to the ICA of the new means of transport that they have procured (*see* Article 2(1)(b)(ii) VAT Directive). As a result, taxation takes place in accordance with the destination principle, and final consumers no longer have the possibility of 'VAT rate shopping'. Since the special provisions with respect to ICSs of transport apply to supplies by and to a non-taxable person, we refer to these types of supplies as intra-Community C2C supplies of new means of transport (*see* Figure 13.8).

Figure 13.8 Intra-Community C2C Supplies of New Means of Transport

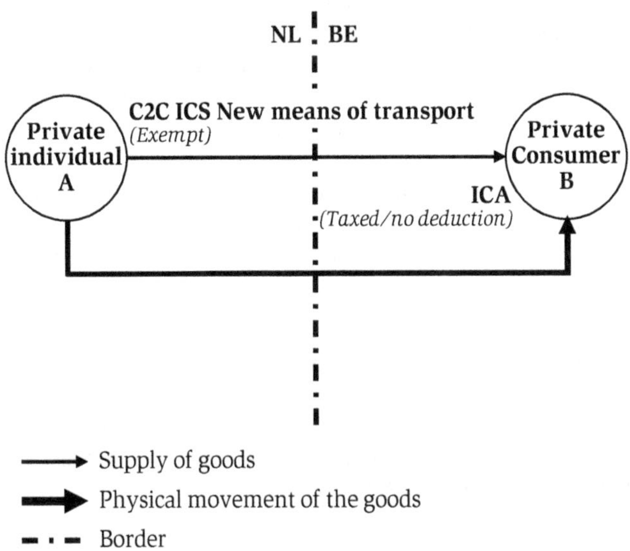

11. A notable exception to this is the taxable transaction 'importation' (*see* Article 2(1)(d) VAT Directive), which can be carried out even by final consumers. Refer to Chapter 14 for further reading.

13.2.8 Miscellaneous Cross-Border Supplies with Specific VAT Treatment

The VAT Directive contains some special provisions with respect to:

(1) ICAs of goods by non-legal persons following importation.
(2) ICAs of goods by NATO (North Atlantic Treaty Organization).
(3) The application of goods for business use.
(4) ICAs as pendants to deemed internal or self-supplies.

Moreover, there are specific provisions on certain ICSs of excise goods and on ICSs by small enterprises.

We will discuss these specific types of transactions in sections 13.9 and 13.10.

13.3 INTRA-COMMUNITY B2B TRANSACTIONS[12]

In this section, we discuss the VAT consequences of intra-Community B2B transactions in detail. Sections 13.3.2 and 13.3.3 provide further information on the concepts of 'ICSs' and 'ICAs' respectively.

13.3.1 Two Sides of the Same Coin

The regime for the taxation of an intra-Community B2B transaction relies on a duality, involving an ICS of goods in the Member State of departure and an ICA of goods in the Member State of arrival. Together, the ICS and ICA are inherent to only *one* commercial transaction that involves only *one* cross-border transport movement. However, both the ICS and the ICA are *two* separate taxable events for VAT purposes. The ICS creates rights and obligations for the supplier and the tax authorities in the Member State where the supply is considered to take place (Member State of departure; *see* section 13.3.2.2.3), whereas the ICA creates rights and obligations for the purchaser and the tax authorities in the Member State where the acquisition is considered to take place (Member State of arrival; *see* section 13.3.3.2.3).[13]

13.3.2 Intra-Community Supplies (ICSs)

In this section, we will first set out the definition of an intra-Community B2B supply (section 13.3.2.1). Subsequently, we will discuss the VAT aspects of such intra-Community B2B supplies (section 13.3.2.2).

12. This section is based on: A.J. van Doesum & F. Nellen, *VAT in a Day* (Fonds Indirect Tax, 2021). Available at: https://ssrn.com/abstract=3867201 (accessed 16 August 2024), pp. 37-39.
13. CJEU 27 September 2007, Case C-409/04 *The Queen, on the application of Teleos plc and Others v Commissioners of Customs & Excise*, ECLI:EU:C:2007:548, para. 23.

13.3.2.1 The Concept of ICSs

The VAT Directive does not contain a definition of the concept of an 'ICS' of goods. In fact, an ICS of goods is just an ordinary taxable supply of goods under Article 2(1)(a) and Article 14 VAT Directive. It is the transfer for consideration by a taxable person, acting as such, of the right to dispose of tangible property as owner. We refer to Chapter 3, section 3.2.3. What makes a supply of goods an 'intra-Community' supply of goods is that in the course of the supply, the goods are transported from one Member State to another.

In order to come to a definition of an 'ICS', it is useful to look at how its pendant, the ICA, is defined (Article 20 VAT Directive) and how the exemption for the ICS is phrased (Article 138(1) VAT Directive). From these provisions, one can deduce that an ICS of goods takes place if all the following conditions have been fulfilled:[14]

(1) both the supplier is a taxable person, and the customer is taxable persons or a non-taxable legal person;[15]
(2) the right to dispose of the goods as owner has been transferred to the purchaser;
(3) the goods have been dispatched or transported from one Member State to another Member State, and;
(4) the taxable person or non-taxable legal person for whom the supply is made is identified for VAT purposes in a Member State other than that in which the dispatch or transport of the goods begins and has indicated this VAT ID number to the supplier.[16]

These conditions reflect that there must be a supply of goods for consideration by a taxable person acting as such and detail that the goods must actually and physically move from one Member State (i.e., Member State of departure) to another (i.e., Member State of arrival). Moreover, the supplier must (a) be informed of the VAT ID number of the acquirer, and (b) have reported that number in the EC Sales Listing (*see* section 13.3.2.2).

14. *Ibid.*, para. 42.
15. In some cases, there is an ICS, even if the supplier and customer are non-taxable persons (*see* section 13.8 on the intra-Community C2C supplies of new means of transport). Also, in some cases there is an ICS if the customer is a non-taxable legal person. As indicated in section 13.2.4, we refer to ICSs to such customers as intra-Community B2H supplies because the VAT rules effectively entail that it must be established whether such a customer is treated as a taxable person (intra-Community B2B supply rules apply) or as a non-taxable person (intra-Community B2C supply rules apply). *See* section 13.5.
16. We also refer to Article 138(1a) VAT Directive, which provides that the exemption for ICSs of goods shall not apply where the supplier has not complied with the obligation to submit a recapitulative statement or the recapitulative statement submitted by him does not set out the correct information concerning this supply as required, unless the supplier can duly justify his shortcoming to the satisfaction of the competent authorities.

13.3.2.1.1 A Basic ICT

In essence, the system of ICSs and ICAs functions as follows. The supplier carries out an ICS of goods in the Member State of dispatch of the goods. This ICS is VAT-exempt, even though a right of deduction of related input VAT exists.[17] Consequently, the goods leave the Member State of dispatch VAT-free. The buyer of the goods (who must also be a taxable person or a non-taxable legal person) effects an ICA of the goods in the Member State of arrival of the goods. The ICA of goods is a taxable event in itself. The buyer must report the ICA in its VAT return and (in principle) pay the VAT that is due on the acquisition. If the buyer has a right to recover input VAT in full, he can deduct the VAT on the acquisition in the same VAT return. As a consequence, he will not be required to actually pay the VAT to the tax authorities. Figure 13.9 illustrates this example of a straightforward ICS.

Figure 13.9 A Basic Intra-Community B2B Supply

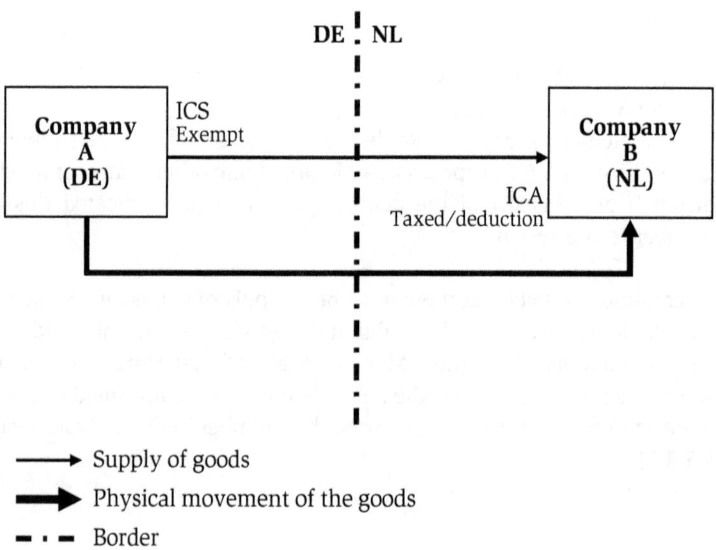

13.3.2.1.2 Transportation of Goods to Another Member State in the Course of the Supply

From the criteria for an ICS, it follows that it is essential that the goods are dispatched or transported to another Member State in the course of the supply, and that the goods physically leave the territory of the Member State of supply. Thus, there must be an actual physical movement of the goods from one Member State to another. Figure 13.10

17. In some Member States, the VAT exemption for ICSs is referred to as a so-called zero rate (0% VAT rate).

shows that there is no ICS if the goods physically remain in the same Member State, even if the goods are supplied to a buyer who is located in another Member State than the supplier. The supply in the example below is a local supply in Germany.

Figure 13.10 No ICS of Goods Because the Goods Physically Remain Within the Same Member State

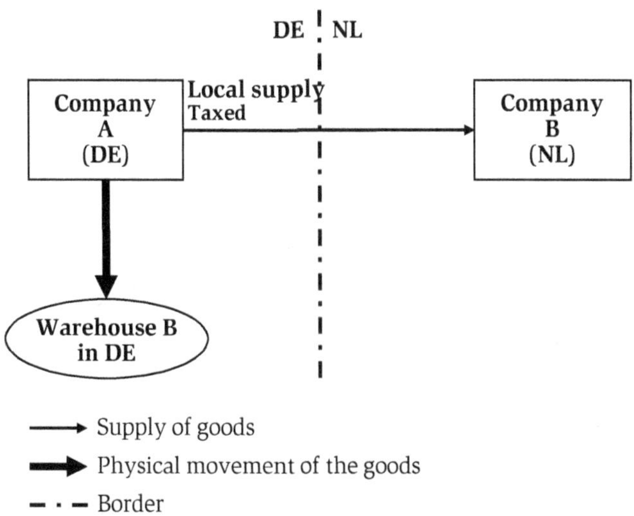

In order for a supply to be an ICS, it is not sufficient that the goods are at some point in time transported from one Member State to another. The dispatch or transportation must also take place *in the course* of the supply. Therefore, there is no ICS if the supplier first moves his goods to another Member State (*see* Moment 1 in Figure 13.11) and subsequently makes a supply of goods in that Member State (*see* local supply 2a and transport movement 2b at Moment 2). Figure 13.11 thus shows such a situation in which there is no transportation *in the course* of the supply and hence no ICS.[18] In order to establish whether transportation takes place in the course of the supply, the CJEU has provided that '... in order for such a classification [authors: classification as ICS] to be made (...), a temporal and material link must be established between the supply of the goods in question and the transport of those goods, as well as continuity in the course of the transaction.'[19] In our view, this implies that the transport should be continuous in the sense that it constitutes an integral logistic process that is not broken up by interruptions such as alteration of goods or long-term storage. Further, the transport must have a sufficient connection with the underlying supply of goods, where all circumstances have to be taken into account to establish whether that is the case (e.g., the contractual arrangements concerning the transport,

18. We note that the transfer of the goods from Germany by company A to its warehouse in the Netherlands is considered an intra-Community B2Me supply (*see* section 13.6).
19. CJEU 18 November 2010, Case C-84/09 *X*, ECLI:EU:C:2010:693, para. 33.

the causality of the transport, the time that has elapsed between the supply and the transport, etc.).

Figure 13.11 No ICS of Goods Because the Goods Are Not Dispatched or Transported to Another Member State in the Course of the Supply

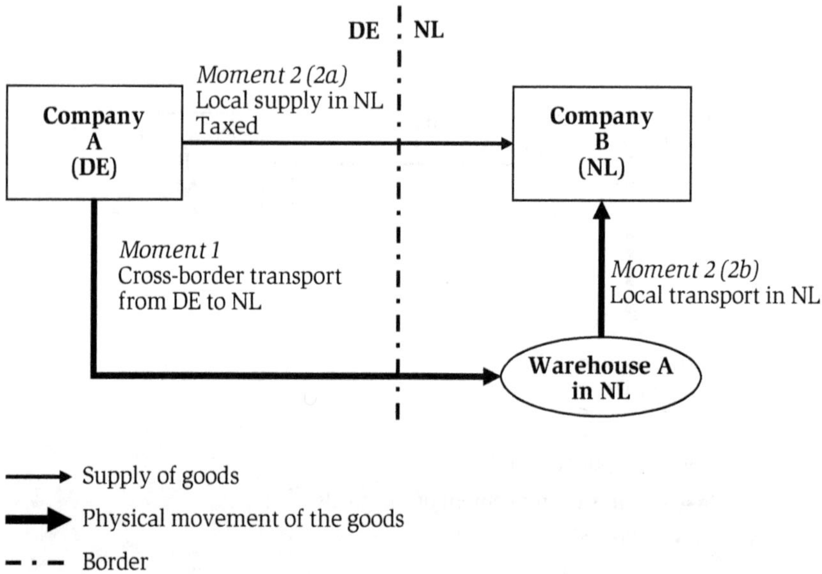

13.3.2.1.3 Customer Collects the Goods (Pickup B2B ICS)

The definition of 'ICS', as formulated by the CJEU, does not require that the supplier transports the goods or has the goods transported to another Member State.[20] If the customer picks up the goods himself, or if the customer arranges for the goods to be transported to another Member State, the supply can still qualify as an ICS if all conditions have been met. The provisions of the VAT Directive do not prevent such a 'pick up B2B ICSs' from being exempt under Article 138 VAT Directive. However, in

20. For example, CJEU 27 September 2007, Case C-409/04 *The Queen, on the application of Teleos plc and Others v Commissioners of Customs & Excise*, ECLI:EU:C:2007:548.

order for the supplier to apply the exemption, he must be able to provide sufficient proof to the tax authorities that the goods have indeed been transported to another Member State and that they left the Member State of the supplier.[21] If the customer takes care of the transportation, it will be difficult for the supplier to obtain the evidence he requires, as he will depend on the provision of items of proof by the customer.[22] Consequently, various Member States only allow for the application of the exemption under strict conditions, in the case of 'pick up B2B ICSs'. We refer to section 13.3.2.2.9.

13.3.2.2 The VAT Consequences of ICSs

13.3.2.2.1 Introduction

In this section, we will further analyse the VAT consequences of an ICS of goods. We will discuss the pendant to this supply, the ICA, in section 13.3.3.

Even though the ICS and the ICA are part of one commercial transaction, they are separate taxable transactions (*see* Article 2 VAT Directive) that both have their own VAT implications (*see* Figure 13.12). As is the case with all taxable transactions in VAT, it is useful to apply the so-called VAT determination scheme. Therefore, we will discuss each 'step' of this scheme separately with respect to ICSs (sections 13.3.2.2.2-13.3.2.2.9) and ICAs (sections 13.3.3.2.2-13.3.3.2.9).

21. As regards the burden of proof for the intra-Community transport of goods, the CJEU has ruled that 'it is for the supplier of the goods to furnish the proof that the conditions laid down for the application of [authors: article 138(1) VAT Directive] (...) are fulfilled.' CJEU 7 December 2010, Case C-285/09 *Criminal Proceedings against R.*, ECLI:EU:C:2010:742, para. 60.
22. For a detailed analysis of the (legal) implications of such interdependencies, refer to F.J.G. Nellen, *Information Asymmetries in EU VAT* (diss) (Datawyse 2017), section 16.2.3.

Figure 13.12 A Standard ICS of Goods: Steps in the 'VAT Determination Scheme'

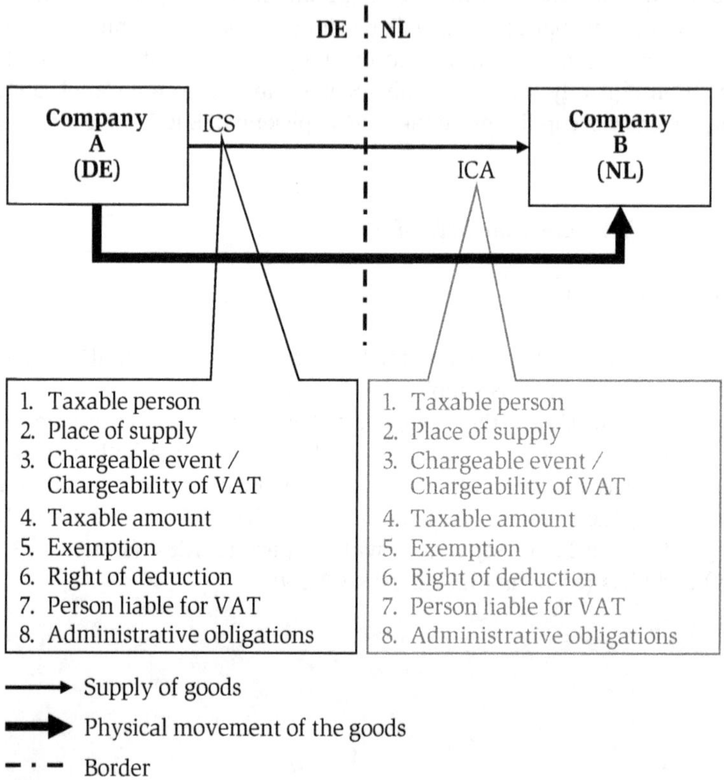

13.3.2.2.2 Taxable Person Status of the Supplier and the Customer

Further to Article 2(1)(a) VAT Directive, only a taxable person (Article 9 VAT Directive) can carry out a supply of goods (including an ICS of goods). If the supplier is not a taxable person, the supply will not be subject to VAT – with the exception of intra-Community C2C supplies of new means of transport (*see* section 13.8).

It follows from the definition of an ICS[23] (*see* section 13.3.2.1) that not only the supplier but also the customer must be a taxable person[24] in order for the supply to be

23. CJEU 27 September 2007, Case C-409/04 *The Queen, on the application of Teleos plc and Others v Commissioners of Customs & Excise*, ECLI:EU:C:2007:548, para. 42.
24. The condition set out in the VAT Directive, according to which the person acquiring the goods must be a 'taxable person … acting as such in, [another] Member State' does not, in itself, imply that the person acquiring the goods must trade under a VAT ID number in the course of the acquisition at issue. It is sufficient for the supplier that he can demonstrate that the acquirer is a taxable person acting as such in the transaction at issue. CJEU 27 September 2012, Case C-587/10 *Vogtländische Straßen-, Tief- und Rohrleitungsbau GmbH Rodewisch (VSTR) v Finanzamt Plauen*, ECLI:EU:C:2012:592.

an ICS. We will discuss the situation in which the customer is a 'hybrid' (i.e., a non-taxable legal person, flat-rate farmer or taxable person with no right of deduction) in section 13.5 on intra-Community B2H supplies.

13.3.2.2.3 The Place of ICSs

In section 4.4, we discussed the rules on the place of supply of goods. The place where a supply is deemed to take place for VAT purposes determines which country (Member State) is competent to tax (or to exempt) the supply. The place of supply of goods that are not dispatched or transported in the course of the supply is where the goods are located at the time when the supply takes place (Article 31 VAT Directive). An ICS presupposes that the goods are dispatched or transported in the course of the supply (*see* section 13.3.2.1.2). Where goods are dispatched or transported in the course of the supply, the supply is deemed to take place in the Member State where the goods are located at the time when the dispatch or transport of those goods begins (Article 32 VAT Directive). It is thus the Member State of dispatch or transport of the goods that must exempt the ICS on the basis of Article 138 VAT Directive.

In section 4.4.3.4 on supplies by the importer and subsequent supplies, we indicated that Article 32, second paragraph holds a special provision on the determination of the place of the supply. Under this provision, both the place of supply by the supplier and any subsequent supply is within the Member State of importation of the goods if:

(1) the dispatch or transport of the goods begins in a third territory or third country;
(2) the goods are imported by the supplier;[25] and
(3) the importer/supplier is designated or recognized under Article 201 as liable for payment of VAT on importation.[26]

For the background and rationale of this provision, we refer to sections 4.4.3.4, 10.2.2.5, 12.2.3 and 14.13.1. We note that Article 32, second paragraph VAT Directive also covers a situation in which goods are imported from outside the EU in a certain Member State prior to their onward shipment to another Member State. That means that if goods are supplied by a Chinese supplier, but imported in the Netherlands by a Dutch supplier, who subsequently supplies the goods to a German taxable person, who then makes an onward sale to a German final consumer, the following applies (assuming that there is a direct transportation to the German customer):

(a) The supply by the Chinese supplier to the Dutch customer takes place outside the EU, on the basis of Article 32, first paragraph VAT Directive.

25. *See also* sections 4.4.3.4, 10.2.2.5, 12.2.3 and 14.13.1.
26. *Ibid.*

(b) The subsequent supply by the Dutch supplier takes place in the Netherlands because he is the importer/supplier of the goods (Article 32, second paragraph VAT Directive applies). The supply is a B2B ICS, which is exempt under Article 138 VAT Directive. The German customer effects an ICA of goods in Germany (prior to its supply to the German consumer).

(c) Arguably, the supply by the German supplier to the German consumer is – on the basis of a literal interpretation of Article 32, second paragraph VAT Directive – in the Netherlands because it is a 'subsequent' supply. However, this would be in conflict with Article 40 VAT Directive. After all, the B2B ICS from the Netherlands to Germany should result in an ICA by the German customer in Germany. We believe that Article 40 VAT Directive is a *lex specialis* to Article 32 VAT Directive and, therefore, takes precedence.[27] This leads, in combination with the idea that if two successive supplies give rise only to a single movement of goods, they must be regarded as having followed each other in time,[28] to the conclusion that the place of supply by the German supplier to the German consumer is in Germany.

13.3.2.2.4 *Chargeable Event and Chargeability of VAT in Respect of ICSs*

With respect to a supply, be it intra-Community or not, the chargeable event takes place when the goods are supplied (Article 63 VAT Directive). Notwithstanding this, Article 67 VAT Directive contains a *specific* rule on the moment of VAT chargeability in the event of an (exempt) ICS.[29] The reason for having this special rule lies in the fact that the regime for the taxation of ICTs depends on the duality of two taxable transactions. Even though there is only *one* commercial transaction, there are *two* separate taxable transactions on each side of the intra-Community border: an ICS in the Member State of departure and an ICA in the Member State of arrival. Effective controls require that the supplier reports the ICS on its periodic VAT return and recapitulative statement (*see* section 13.3.2.2.9) in the same tax period as the customer reports the ICA in its VAT return. Only then can the tax authorities match the information on the supplier's VAT return and recapitulative statement with the information on the customer's VAT return. Therefore, Article 67 VAT Directive strongly coheres with Article 69 VAT Directive. These provisions stipulate that VAT shall become chargeable on issue of the invoice, or at the moment when the invoice should have been issued at the latest (*see* Article 222, first paragraph VAT Directive).

With a view to the required parallelism between ICSs and ICAs, it is, in our view, understandable that the last paragraph of Article 67 VAT Directive stipulates that the moment when the VAT becomes chargeable in case of an ICS remains the moment when the invoice is issued or should have been issued, even if the supply gives rise

27. Cf. B. Terra, J. Kajus & Z. Szatmári, *Commentary on European VAT* (IBFD 2023), Chapter 5.2.3.2.
28. *Ibid.*, para. 23.
29. For the moment of VAT chargeability for regular supplies of goods, refer to Articles 63-66 VAT Directive.

to successive statements of account or successive payments (Article 64(1) VAT Directive), the supply is a continuous supply (Article 64(2), third subparagraph VAT Directive) or in the case of prepayments (Article 65 VAT Directive).

13.3.2.2.5 Taxable Amount of and VAT Rate Applicable to ICSs

Article 138 VAT Directive exempts ICSs of goods. It may, therefore, seem unnecessary to determine the taxable amount for such supplies. However, the taxable amount is also relevant when calculating the pro rata of a business that carries out both activities for which a right of deduction exists and activities for which such a right does not exist.[30] Consequently, it may be relevant to determine the taxable amount for ICSs correctly.

Moreover, it is important to determine a correct taxable amount because ICSs must be periodically listed on so-called recapitulative statements (*see* section 13.3.2.2.9). The information on those statements is matched with the information on the customer's VAT return, in which the customer reported the corresponding ICA. Only if the same values are reported can the tax authorities see that there is a match between the ICS and the acquisition.

The taxable amount with respect to an ICA is established on the basis of the same factors as the ones used to determine the taxable amount for local supplies of the same goods within the Member State of acquisition (Article 83 VAT Directive). Thus, the taxable amount for ICAs is linked to the taxable amount for local supplies of (the same) goods. The VAT Directive does not contain a special rule on the taxable amount of B2B ICSs. The taxable amount for such supplies is determined on the basis of the same provisions as the ones that are applicable to local supplies. Thus, the method for establishing the taxable amount of an ICS matches with the method for establishing the taxable amount of an ICA. With respect to deemed ICSs (B2Me ICSs), Article 76 VAT Directive contains specific rules (*see* section 13.6.3.5).

13.3.2.2.6 Exemptions Applicable to ICSs

Article 138(1) VAT Directive contains an exemption for the ICS of goods. However, on the basis of Article 169(b) VAT Directive, the taxable person who carries out an exempt ICS of goods is allowed to deduct related input VAT. By exempting the supply *and* allowing for deduction of input VAT, the goods are fully relieved from the burden of VAT when they leave the Member State of dispatch. Some Member States have implemented this mechanism of exemption and deduction as a zero-rated (0% VAT rate) supply for which a right of deduction exists – which essentially entails the same end result. The supplier is required to fulfil various (administrative) requirements in connection with the application of the exemption, which are discussed in section 13.3.2.2.9.

30. CJEU 14 July 1998, Case C-172/96 *Commissioners of Customs & Excise v First National Bank of Chicago*, ECLI:EU:C:1998:354.

Article 138(2) VAT Directive extends the scope of the exemption for ICSs to certain supplies of new means of transport,[31] excise goods and certain transfers of own goods. Conversely, Article 139 VAT Directive excludes certain ICSs from the scope of the exemption. For example, ICSs by taxable persons that apply the special scheme for small enterprises are excluded from the exemption under Article 139(1) VAT Directive. In section 13.5, we will discuss Article 139(2) VAT Directive in more detail because it relates to intra-Community B2H(ybrid) supplies.

13.3.2.2.7 Right of Deduction in Respect of ICSs

Article 169(b) VAT Directive allows for deduction of input VAT with respect to ICSs, even though these are exempt under Article 138(1) VAT Directive. This means that any EU VAT on goods and services which the supplier uses for the purpose of making the ICSs is deductible. Since a right of deduction exists with respect to ICSs, such supplies may also have a positive effect on the pro rata of the supplier (*see* Chapter 10).

Fraud: No Right of Deduction

In *Kittel & Recolta*, the CJEU ruled that preventing tax evasion, avoidance, and abuse is an objective recognized and encouraged by the VAT Directive.[32] Consequently, if that right of deduction is being relied on for abusive or fraudulent ends, it is for the national courts and authorities to refuse the right of deduction.[33] The idea behind the refusal of rights in fraudulent situations is to create a disincentive for taxable persons to get involved in these.[34]

It is the responsibility of the tax authorities to deny rights (e.g., the right of deduction, the right to apply the exemption for ICSs) to the taxable person perpetrating the fraud. In addition, the authorities can also deny rights to other parties if it can be proven that these parties knew or should have known that, by their actions, they were taking part in a transaction connected with fraudulent evasion of VAT committed by the supplier or by another trader acting upstream or downstream in the chain of supply

31. *See* Article 2 VAT Implementing Regulation with respect to transfers of new means of transport by non-taxable persons and returns of new means of transport by non-taxable persons to the Member State from which the means of transport was initially supplied to those non-taxable persons. It is considered that such transfers and returns do not constitute ICAs, provided that the exemption in Article 138(2)(a) VAT Directive does not apply.
32. *See* CJEU 6 July 2006, Joined Cases C-439/04 and C-440/04 *Axel Kittel v Belgian State (C-439/04) and Belgian State v Recolta Recycling SPRL (C-440/04)*, ECLI:EU:C:2006:446, para. 54.
33. CJEU 6 July 2006, Joined Cases C-439/04 and C-440/04 *Axel Kittel v Belgian State (C-439/04) and Belgian State v Recolta Recycling SPRL (C-440/04)*, ECLI:EU:C:2006:446, para. 55. *See also* CJEU 6 December 2012, Case C-285/11 *Bonik EOOD v Direktor na Direktsia 'Obzhalvane I upravlenie na izpalnenieto' – Varna pri Tsentralno upravlenie na Natsionalnata agentsia za prihodite*, ECLI:EU:C:2012:774, paras 35-37 and CJEU 13 February 2014, Case C-18/13 *Maks Pen EOOD v Direktor na Direktsia 'Obzhalvane i danachno-osiguritelna praktika' Sofia*, ECLI: EU:C:2014:69, para. 26.
34. CJEU 6 July 2006, Joined Cases C-439/04 and C-440/04 *Axel Kittel v Belgian State (C-439/04) and Belgian State v Recolta Recycling SPRL (C-440/04)*, ECLI:EU:C:2006:446, para. 58.

of those goods or services.[35] In that situation, these 'collaborating' or informed parties must be regarded as participants in that fraud, irrespective of whether or not they profited by the resale of the goods. They become accomplices to the fraud.[36] Thus, even though a taxable person, who knew or should have known that he was taking part in a transaction connected with fraud, carries out an economic activity (taxable supplies), he cannot deduct the VAT charged to him.

Fraud: Diligent, Circumspect Traders Can Rely on Their Right of Deduction

Traders who take every precaution which could reasonably be required of them to ensure that their transactions are not connected with fraud, be it the fraudulent evasion of VAT or other fraud, can rely on the legality of those transactions without the risk of losing their right to deduct the input VAT.[37] If the recipient of a supply of goods is a taxable person who did not and could not know that the transaction concerned was connected with a fraud committed by the seller, his right of deduction will not be refused.[38]

Finally, we note that it is up to the tax authorities to prove (i.e., substantiate with proper evidence) that any taxable person knew, or should have known, that the transaction he engaged in was connected with fraud committed by the supplier or by another trader acting upstream or downstream in the chain of supply.[39] In our view, the authorities cannot, as a general rule, require from the trader that he proves that he took every precaution which could reasonably be required of them to ensure that his transactions were not connected with fraud.[40] Rights cannot be denied lightly; from the CJEU judgment in *Aquila*, it follows, among other things, that a considerable burden of proof rests on the tax authorities. It is for them, first, to provide an accurate description of the constituent elements of the fraud and to prove fraudulent conduct and, second, to establish that the taxable person actively participated in that fraud or that he or she

35. CJEU 18 December 2014, Joined Cases C-131/13, C-163/13 and C-164/13 *Schoenimport 'Italmoda' Mariano Previti vof (C-131/13) and Turbu.com BV (C-163/13) and Turbu.com Mobile Phone's BV (C-164/13)*, ECLI:EU:C:2014:2455, para. 50.
36. *Ibid.*, paras 56 and 57 and CJEU 13 February 2014, Case C-18/13 *Maks Pen EOOD v Direktor na Direktsia 'Obzhalvane i danachno-osiguritelna praktika' Sofia*, ECLI:EU:C:2014:69, para. 28.
37. For example: CJEU 11 May 2006, Case C-384/04 *Commissioners of Customs & Excise and Attorney General v Federation of Technological Industries and Others*, ECLI:EU:C:2006:309, para. 45 and CJEU 6 July 2006, Joined Cases C-439/04 and C-440/04 *Axel Kittel v Belgian State (C-439/04) and Belgian State v Recolta Recycling SPRL (C-440/04)*, ECLI:EU:C:2006:446, para. 51.
38. CJEU 6 July 2006, Joined Cases C-439/04 and C-440/04 *Axel Kittel v Belgian State (C-439/04) and Belgian State v Recolta Recycling SPRL (C-440/04)*, ECLI:EU:C:2006:446, para. 52.
39. For example: CJEU 21 June 2012, Joined Cases C-80/11 and C-142/11 *Mahagében Kft v Nemzeti Adó- és Vámhivatal Dél-dunántúli Regionális Adó Főigazgatósága (C-80/11) and Péter Dávid v Nemzeti Adó- és Vámhivatal Észak-alföldi Regionális Adó Főigazgatósága (C-142/11)*, ECLI-:EU:C:2012:373, para. 49 and CJEU 6 December 2012, Case C-285/11 *Bonik EOOD v Direktor na Direktsia 'Obzhalvane I upravlenie na izpalnenieto' – Varna pri Tsentralno upravlenie na Natsionalnata agentsia za prihodite*, ECLI:EU:C:2012:774, para. 43.
40. Depending on the circumstances and on national procedural law, there may exist exceptions to this (e.g., in case of a reversal of the burden of proof when there are significant indications that the taxable person violated statutory provisions).

knew, or ought to have known, that the transaction relied on as a basis for that right was connected with that fraud.[41]

13.3.2.2.8 Person Liable for VAT with Respect to ICSs

The VAT Directive does not contain any specific rules as regards the determination of the person liable for VAT with respect to ICSs. Therefore, the normal rules apply. This means that the VAT is payable by the supplier (Article 193 VAT Directive). One might argue that this provision cannot apply to ICSs because an exemption applies to such supplies. If there is no VAT on the supply, how can the supplier then be liable to pay the VAT on the supply? Nonetheless, it must be determined which party – the supplier or the purchaser – must apply the exemption. Therefore, determining the person liable for VAT is not completely without reason. Moreover, it is relevant to determine the person liable for VAT with respect to an intra-Community B2B supply if the application of the exemption is refused because of fraud on the part of the supplier. In such situations, the supplier will be liable to pay local VAT on the supply, even if ownership of the goods is transferred, the goods have been transported to another Member State in the course of the supply, and the goods actually left the Member State of departure.[42]

Notwithstanding the above observations, the CJEU seems to have created a VAT liability in cases of pickup B2B ICSs (*see* section 13.3.2.1.3), which is not based on any provision in the VAT Directive. If the customer collects the goods and the supplier fulfilled his obligations relating to evidence of an ICS (and thus can rely on the application of the exemption), but the purchaser does not dispatch or transport the goods out of the Member State of supply, the *purchaser* is liable for payment of local VAT in the Member State of supply (i.e., Member State of departure of the goods).[43] In our view, it is questionable whether the CJEU, in fact, enjoys the competence to create VAT liabilities that do not have a legal basis in the VAT Directive.[44]

13.3.2.2.9 Administrative Obligations with Respect to ICSs

Since the abolition of the fiscal border controls between (most of) the Member States, it has been difficult for the tax authorities to check whether or not goods have physically left the territory of a Member State. As a result, it is principally on the basis of the evidence provided by taxable persons and of their statements that the national tax authorities carry out the necessary checks.[45] For that reason, various administrative

41. CJEU 1 December 2022, Case C-512/21 *Aquila Part Prod Com SA*, ECLI:EU:C:2022:950, operational part.
42. CJEU 7 December 2010, Case C-285/09 *Criminal Proceedings against R.*, ECLI:EU:C:2010:742.
43. CJEU 27 September 2007, Case C-409/04 *The Queen, on the application of Teleos plc and Others v Commissioners of Customs & Excise*, ECLI:EU:C:2007:548, paras 66 and 67 and CJEU 16 December 2010, Case C-430/09 *Euro Tyre Holding BV v Staatssecretaris van Financiën*, ECLI: EU:C:2010:786, para. 38.
44. *See* F.J.G. Nellen, *Information Asymmetries in EU VAT* (diss) (Datawyse 2017), p. 228.
45. CJEU 7 December 2010, Case C-285/09 *Criminal Proceedings against R.*, ECLI:EU:C:2010:742, para. 42.

obligations exist.[46] Not fulfilling these administrative obligations often means that the supplier is not able or allowed to apply the exemption to his ICS. Therefore, fulfilling these obligations can be seen as gathering the required proof for applying the exemption, meaning that local VAT is due if these obligations are not fulfilled.[47] In this section, we will discuss the specific administrative obligations concerning ICSs.

Obtaining and Reporting the Customer's VAT ID Number

There are various provisions in EU law that relate to the identification of the customer by means of his VAT ID number.[48] Should the taxable person effecting the ICS of goods not be able to meet the requirements of those provisions, the exemption for ICSs may be denied to him.[49] In particular, we point out the following:

- Article 226, under point 4 VAT Directive, requires that the supplier mentions the customer's VAT ID number under which the customer received an exempt ICS of goods on the invoice.[50]
- For the application of the exemption, Article 138(1)(b) VAT Directive requires that the person for whom the ICS is made is identified for VAT purposes in a Member State other than that in which the dispatch or transport of the goods begins. Furthermore, that person must have indicated this VAT ID number to the supplier.
- For the application of the exemption, Article 138(1a) VAT Directive demands that the supplier has complied with the requirement to properly report the VAT ID number of the customer in his periodic EC Sales Listing (cf. Article 262 VAT Directive).[51]

The VAT ID numbers of taxable persons engaged in intra-Community trade have an administrative function that follows from the apparent need for proper supervision and enforcement by national tax authorities. Member States maintain electronic databases containing the VAT registration data of all taxable persons, which are aggregated in one centralized European administration (the 'VAT Information Exchange System': 'VIES'). In that database, the VAT ID number, the date of issue, the

46. *Ibid.*, para. 50.
47. *Ibid.*
48. According to the CJEU, the refusal of exemption in the case of non-compliance with an obligation provided for by national law, such as the obligation to identify the person acquiring the goods and receiving the ICS, has a deterrent effect which is intended to ensure compliance with that obligation and to prevent tax evasion or avoidance. CJEU 7 December 2010, Case C-285/09 *Criminal Proceedings against R.*, ECLI:EU:C:2010:742, para. 50.
49. Consequently, the taxable person may be confronted with additional VAT assessments. Also, depending on national law, fines and interest assessments may be imposed on him.
50. Articles 213-216 VAT Directive contain rules on the identification for VAT.
51. Years before the entry into effect of Articles 138(1)(b) and 138(1a) VAT Directive on 1 January 2020, the CJEU ruled that the exemption should not be refused on the sole ground that the supplier did not obtain the customer's VAT ID number if the supplier (a) acted in good faith and took all the measures which could reasonably be required of him, and (b) provided other information from which it became apparent that the customer is a taxable person acting as such. CJEU 27 September 2012, Case C-587/10 *Vogtländische Straßen-, Tief- und Rohrleitungsbau GmbH Rodewisch (VSTR) v Finanzamt Plauen*, ECLI:EU:C:2012:592.

trader's name, the trader's address and, where applicable, the date of cessation of validity of a VAT ID number can be verified. Suppliers carrying out an ICS can check with their local tax authorities whether a particular VAT ID number is valid and if so, whether it is correctly associated with a specified trader name and/or address. Additionally, the European Commission maintains a publicly accessible website that derives information from the Member States' VAT databases.[52] Using the European Commission's website, suppliers can check online whether a VAT ID number is valid.

The Member States use the VAT ID numbers and the information from the VAT returns and EC sales listings connected to the supplies made from and to these VAT ID numbers for the purpose of supervision and enforcement. Pursuant to the mutual assistance directive and the administrative cooperation regulation, a Member State can request information capable of establishing the intra-Community nature of a supply from the tax authorities in another Member State.[53] However, these legal instruments do not require a Member State to request information from the authorities. Consequently, a supplier cannot rely on the tax authorities to obtain proof that the goods actually arrived in another Member State.[54]

Proof of Transportation: Presumption (Article 45a VAT Implementing Regulation)

The VAT Directive does not stipulate which items of proof are required in order for the supplier to substantiate that the goods have been transported from one Member State to the other. Article 131 VAT Directive only indicates that Member States shall lay down conditions for the purposes of ensuring the correct and straightforward application of those exemptions and of preventing any possible evasion, avoidance or abuse. For these reasons, the CJEU ruled that it, therefore, falls within the competence of the Member States to determine what evidence is necessary.[55] This being said, as of 1 January 2020, the VAT Implementing Regulation (Article 45a) contains rules on the substantiation of intra-Community transport.[56] In short, the rules concern two presumptions for the cross-border transport of goods, allowing taxable persons to rely on a specific set of documents that is standardized throughout the EU in order to substantiate that the goods have indeed been transported from one Member State to the other. The presumptions depend on who arranges the transport (i.e., the 'vendor' or the acquirer):

---

52. https://ec.europa.eu/taxation_customs/vies/#/vat-validation (accessed 17 August 2024).
53. Council Directive 2010/24/EU of 16 March 2010 concerning mutual assistance for the recovery of claims relating to taxes, duties and other measures [2010] OJ L 84/1; Council Regulation (EU) No 904/2010 of 7 October 2010 on administrative cooperation and combating fraud in the field of value added tax [2010] OJ L 268/1.
54. CJEU 27 September 2007, Case C-184/05 *Twoh International BV v Staatssecretaris van Financiën*, ECLI:EU:C:2007:550.
55. CJEU 27 September 2007, Case C-146/05 *Albert Collée v Finanzamt Limburg an der Lahn*, ECLI:EU:C:2007:549, para. 24.
56. The legislative change was referred to as one of the 'Quick Fixes' of the current system of taxation for Intra-Community B2B trade. *See* Council Implementing regulation (EU) 2018/1912 of 4 December 2018 amending Implementing Regulation (EU) No 282/2011 as regards certain exemptions for ICTs [2018] OJ L 311/10.

(1) The vendor has the goods transported, either by himself or by a third party on his behalf: It shall be presumed that the goods have been transported from one Member State to the other if the vendor has at least two items of non-contradictory evidence which were issued by two different parties that are independent of each other, of the vendor and the acquirer.
(2) The acquirer has the goods transported, either by himself or by a third party on his behalf: It shall be presumed that the goods have been transported from one Member State to the other if the vendor has a written statement from the acquirer confirming the transport (and containing specific information), as well as at least two items of non-contradictory evidence which were issued by two different parties that are independent of each other, of the vendor and the acquirer.

In practice, the rules on the substantiation of the intra-Community transport are a safe harbour facility, allowing taxable persons to rely on a presumption for the application of the exemption for ICSs – assuming they meet the requirements. Some other specifics of the facility are the following:[57]

- The tax authorities are allowed to rebut the presumption, e.g., if they have proof that the goods have not been transported at all.
- The two items of non-contradictory evidence are, to a certain extent, prescribed (*see* Article 45a(3) VAT Implementing Regulation). The vendor should at least have one document relating to the dispatch or transport of the goods (e.g., a signed CMR document,[58] a bill of lading, an airfreight or carrier invoice), and can also choose to have one of the documents listed in Article 45a(3)(b) VAT Implementing Regulation (i.e., an insurance policy related to the transport, bank documents related to the transport, official documents issued by authorities confirming the arrival of the goods, or a warehouse keeper receipt confirming the storage of the goods in the Member State of destination).

A notable aspect is that the items of evidence should be issued by 'two different parties that are independent of each other, of the vendor and of the acquirer'. Unfortunately, it remains unclear what the requirement of 'independence' entails. Is a third-party freight forwarder or a warehouse keeper still independent if that party has a financial dependency on either the vendor or the acquirer because the latter person pays (or still needs to pay) the former for its services? Additionally, the vendor (supplier) may not be informed of whether the party who issues items of evidence is (also) independent of the acquirer of the goods. Further, the requirement of independence may even imply market distortions; it is not unthinkable that a vendor, in search

57. For a more detailed analysis of Article 45a VAT Implementing Regulation, refer to M. Horsthuis & F.J.G. Nellen, *A Critical Analysis of the Quick Fixes for the EU Intra-community B2B VAT System* (2019) 3 International VAT Monitor https://doi.org/10.59403/25gdm93.
58. CMR is the acronym for 'Convention relative au contrat de transport international de Marchandises par route'. It is a standardized document for cross-border transport of cargo by road.

of documents issued by independent parties, hires a(n) (independent) third-party freight forwarder rather than using its own or the acquirer's means of transport.[59]

Finally, we note that Article 45a VAT Implementing Regulation is an optional safe harbour facility. Should taxable persons not choose to rely on it, they need to adhere to the (national) rules for the substantiation of the cross-border transport. In practice, all kinds of combinations of evidence are used. Examples of items of evidence that can be used are: order confirmations, copies of invoices, payments by the customer made from another Member State, invoices from transportation companies, properly signed and filled out CMR documents, insurance policies for the transport of the goods, etc. The fact that the purchaser made a declaration concerning an ICA does not constitute conclusive proof for the purposes of the exemption. Nonetheless, it may be regarded as additional evidence.[60] A supplier who submits evidence of the intra-Community nature of the supply, which at a later stage is found to be false, will not be confronted with a refusal of the exemption if he acted in good faith, was not involved in tax evasion and took every reasonable measure in his power to ensure that the ICS he was effecting did not lead to his participation in such tax evasion.[61]

As indicated in section 13.3.2.1.3, particular difficulties exist if the customer picks up the goods at the supplier's premises. In those situations, the supplier may be unable to obtain sufficient evidence to prove that the goods were transported to another Member State and left the Member State of departure: the evidence that the supplier might submit to the tax authorities depends essentially on information that he receives for that purpose from the purchaser.[62] It follows from *Collée* that the evidence for an ICS may be provided *after* the supply took place. Even if the accounts of a company are adjusted after the supply took place, the intra-Community nature of a supply must be recognized, provided that all material conditions for the classification of the supply as an ICS are met.[63]

Even if the four material conditions for an ICS have been fulfilled (*see* section 13.3.2.1), the application of the exemption for ICSs can be denied in case the supplier was involved in VAT fraud or evasion.[64]

Periodical VAT Return

A taxable person making an ICS of goods must report the supply in its periodical VAT return. If a foreign company carries out an ICS in a (different) Member State, this may lead to the obligation for that company to register for VAT purposes in the Member State of the ICS.

---

59. This paragraph is derived from M. Horsthuis & F.J.G. Nellen, *A Critical Analysis of the Quick Fixes for the EU Intra-Community B2B VAT System* (2019) 3 International VAT Monitor https://doi.org/10.59403/25gdm93.
60. CJEU 27 September 2007, Case C-409/04 *The Queen, on the application of Teleos plc and Others v Commissioners of Customs & Excise*, ECLI:EU:C:2007:548.
61. *Ibid.*
62. CJEU 16 December 2010, Case C-430/09 *Euro Tyre Holding BV v Staatssecretaris van Financiën*, ECLI:EU:C:2010:786, para. 37.
63. CJEU 27 September 2007, Case C-146/05 *Albert Collée v Finanzamt Limburg an der Lahn*, ECLI:EU:C:2007:549.
64. CJEU 7 December 2010, Case C-285/09 *Criminal Proceedings against R.*, ECLI:EU:C:2010:742.

Recapitulative Statements (EC Sales Listing)[65]

Businesses making ICSs must not only record those supplies in their periodical VAT returns, they must also periodically submit separate declarations of their ICSs to the tax and customs administration (Article 262 VAT Directive). These declarations are commonly referred to as 'recapitulative statements' or 'EC Sales Listings'. The tax authorities of the Member States perform various checks on these declarations. In this respect, it is important to realize that the information on the EC Sales Listings is exchanged between the Member States via the so-called VIES.[66] This exchange of information enables the tax authorities of the Member State of arrival of the goods (i.e., the Member State where the ICA takes place) to compare the ICAs recorded by the purchaser in his local VAT return with the ICSs recorded by the supplier in the EC Sales List.

Register of Goods

In case of certain intra-Community B2Me supplies, the taxable person must keep a register of the goods dispatched or transported by him, or on his behalf, to another Member State (Article 243 VAT Directive). We refer to section 13.6.3.9 on intra-Community B2Me supplies.

Intrastat Reporting

For statistics purposes, suppliers who carry out ICSs must – in addition to the VAT return and the EC Sales Listing – periodically file intrastat reports if the value of the supplies exceeds certain thresholds. The rules on intrastat reporting are laid down in the 'intrastat regulation'.[67]

13.3.3 Intra-Community Acquisitions (ICAs)

In this section, we will explain the concept of the 'ICA' and the VAT consequences of such acquisitions of goods.

13.3.3.1 The Concept of ICAs of Goods

As we indicated in section 13.3.1, the ICS of goods and their ICA are, in fact, two sides of the same coin. This is apparent from the definition of an ICA of goods set out in Article 20 VAT Directive, which reads that it shall mean 'the acquisition of the right to dispose as owner of movable tangible property dispatched or transported to the person

65. The term 'EC Sales Listing' was already in use before the Lisbon Treaty. Even though it would be better to speak of 'EU Sales Listing' (in the same way as it would be better to speak of 'intra-European Union supplies and acquisitions'), it is common practice to use the old terminology.
66. *See* https://ec.europa.eu/taxation_customs/vies/#/vat-validation (accessed 17 August 2024).
67. Regulation (EU) 2019/2152 of the European Parliament and of the Council of 27 November 2019 on European business statistics, OJ L 327.

acquiring the goods, by or on behalf of the vendor or the person acquiring the goods, in a member state other than that in which dispatch or transport of the goods began.'

Since Article 2 VAT Directive as a main rule subjects ICAs by taxable persons to VAT,[68] this definition echoes the elements that constitute an ICS of goods (*see* section 13.3.2.1).

As this taxable transaction was introduced to replace the importation of goods within the EU after the abolition of the fiscal frontiers as of 1 January 1993, it is no surprise that the ICA of goods is limited to movable tangible property. Real estate cannot be the object of an ICA, simply because such assets are immovable and thus cannot cross any borders.

An ICA of goods is only a taxable transaction if the acquisition of goods takes place for consideration (Article 2(b) VAT Directive). Consequently, an acquisition for free results in an ICA of goods, but not in a *taxable* ICA of goods.

Articles 21, 22 and 23 VAT Directive contain provisions on deemed ICAs of goods. Article 21 VAT Directive is the pendant of the so-called intra-Community B2Me supplies (*see* section 13.6.3). Therefore, we will address Article 21 VAT Directive in section 13.6.4. We will discuss the deemed ICAs based on Articles 22 and 23 VAT Directive in section 13.9.

13.3.3.2 The VAT Consequences of ICAs

In this section, we discuss the VAT consequences of intra-Community B2B acquisitions.

13.3.3.2.1 Introduction

Article 23 VAT Implementing Regulation stipulates that where an ICA of goods has taken place, the Member State in which the dispatch or transport ends shall exercise its power of taxation irrespective of the VAT treatment applied to the transaction in the Member State in which the dispatch or transport began. Indeed, the ICA of goods is a taxable event ('taxable transaction') in its own right. The VAT Directive contains specific rules with respect to the place, the taxable amount, potential exemption, the chargeability of VAT and the moment when the VAT becomes due, etc. with respect to the ICA of goods (*see* Figure 13.13). Therefore, we will discuss each 'step' of the VAT determination scheme separately with respect to ICAs, just as we did with respect to ICSs of goods (*see* section 13.3.2.2).

68. In section 13.5, we discuss the exceptions to this principle. Some ICAs of goods by persons other than taxable persons are subject to VAT.

Figure 13.13 A Standard ICA of Goods: Steps to Be Taken in the 'VAT Determination Scheme'

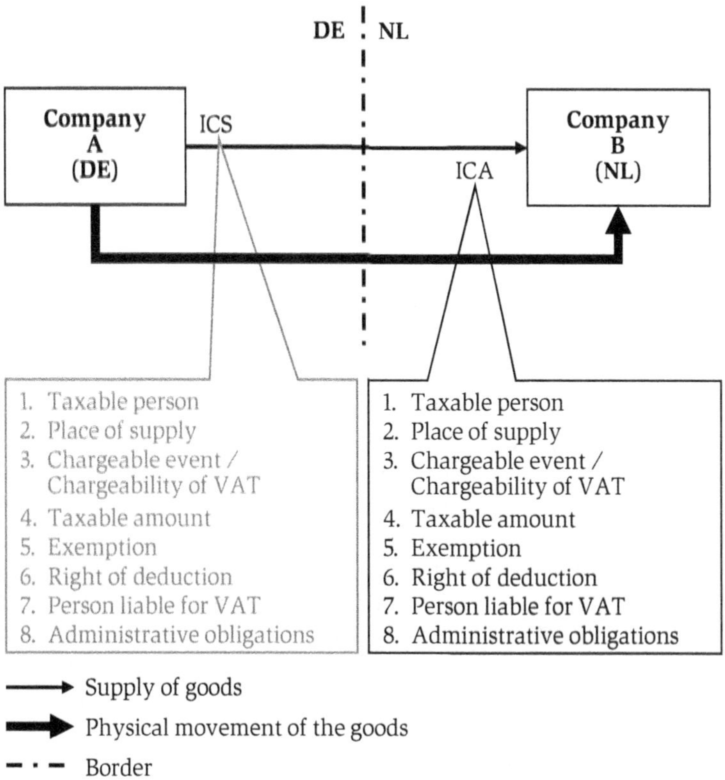

13.3.3.2.2 Taxable Person Status of the Acquirer

The main category of taxable ICAs of goods is formed by the acquisitions carried out by taxable persons acting as such (Article 2(1)(b)(i) VAT Directive). The other categories of taxable ICAs are listed in Article 2(1)(b)(ii) and (iii) VAT Directive. We note that ICAs can also be carried out by so-called hybrids, i.e., a non-taxable legal persons, flat-rate farmers and taxable persons with no right of deduction; this topic is however discussed in section 13.5 on intra-Community B2H supplies.

13.3.3.2.3 The Place of ICA of Goods and 'Number Acquisitions'

Main Rule: Place of Arrival of the Goods

The ICA of goods is a taxable transaction (Article 2(1)(b) VAT Directive). Therefore, it is necessary to determine the place where an ICA takes place. The VAT Directive contains a main rule and a safety net provision in this respect. Pursuant to the main rule of Article 40 VAT Directive, the place of an ICA of goods shall be deemed to be the place where dispatch or transport of the goods to the person acquiring them ends.[69]

The main rule determining the place of an ICA of goods is in line with the destination principle since it establishes that VAT is levied at the destination of the goods (i.e., where consumption of these goods is most likely to take place).

On the basis of Article 23 VAT Implementing Regulation, the Member State in which the dispatch or transport ends shall exercise its power of taxation irrespective of the VAT treatment applied to the transaction in the Member State in which the dispatch or transport began. If, for example, the Member State of dispatch treats the supply as a supply of services, the Member State of arrival may still treat the acquisition of the goods as an ICA of the goods.

Safety Net Provision: Place of the VAT ID Number of the Customer (Article 41 VAT Directive)

The VAT Directive also contains a safety net provision with respect to the place where an ICA takes place. The rule is laid down in Article 41 VAT Directive, which provides that without prejudice to Article 40 VAT Directive, the place of an ICA of goods shall be deemed to be within the territory of the Member State which issued the VAT ID number under which the person acquiring the goods made the acquisition (i.e., Member State of identification)[70] unless the person acquiring the goods establishes that VAT has been applied to that acquisition in accordance with Article 40 VAT Directive. This means that if the purchaser does not establish that VAT is applied in the Member State of arrival of the goods, the ICS not only takes place in the Member State of arrival of the goods but *also* in the Member State of identification of the purchaser. Thus, this provision creates a situation in which two Member States are simultaneously entitled to levy VAT with respect to the same taxable event, the ICA. The ICA in the Member State of identification is special in the sense that it is a taxable event at a location where the goods have *physically* never been. Commonly, it is referred to as an 'intra-Community number acquisition' (or simply 'number acquisition').

Following *Facet*, the VAT on the number acquisition cannot be immediately deducted, even if the purchaser uses the goods only for taxed supplies.[71] Consequently, Article 41 VAT Directive deliberately causes double taxation, which is only corrected when the purchaser demonstrates that VAT has been applied and reported on the 'true' ICA in the Member State of arrival of the goods. The reason for this rather complicated system is to prevent that no VAT is levied at all on ICAs and to create an incentive for

69. Note that this matches perfectly with the place of an ICS of goods: where the transport or dispatch begins.
70. The phrase 'the VAT identification number under which the person acquiring the goods made the acquisition' in Article 41 VAT Directive suggests that it only applies if the purchaser makes the purchases under its VAT ID number in the Member State where he is registered for VAT. However, this would deprive the provision of its purpose: the provision would not apply if the purchaser makes the purchase under another VAT ID number of another Member State than the one of VAT registration and arrival of the goods.
71. CJEU 22 April 2010, Joined Cases C-536/08 and C-539/08 *Staatssecretaris van Financiën v X (C-536/08) and fiscale eenheid Facet BV/Facet Trading BV (C-539/08)*, ECLI:EU:C:2010:217.

the purchaser to register for VAT in the Member State of arrival of the goods and report an ICA.[72]

The following example illustrates the purpose and the effect of Article 41 VAT Directive.

Example

Taxable person A, established in Estonia, sells goods to taxable person B, established in Italy. Company B is established in Italy but also has warehouses in other Member States. Company A arranges the transport of the goods to company B. This time company B wants the goods to be delivered to its newly established warehouse in Poland. Company B, however, is not (yet) registered for VAT purposes in Poland. Company A issues an invoice to company B, which states B's Italian VAT ID number. This and the VAT consequences of these activities are shown in Figure 13.14.

Figure 13.14 The Purpose and Effect of the Number Acquisition under Article 41 VAT Directive

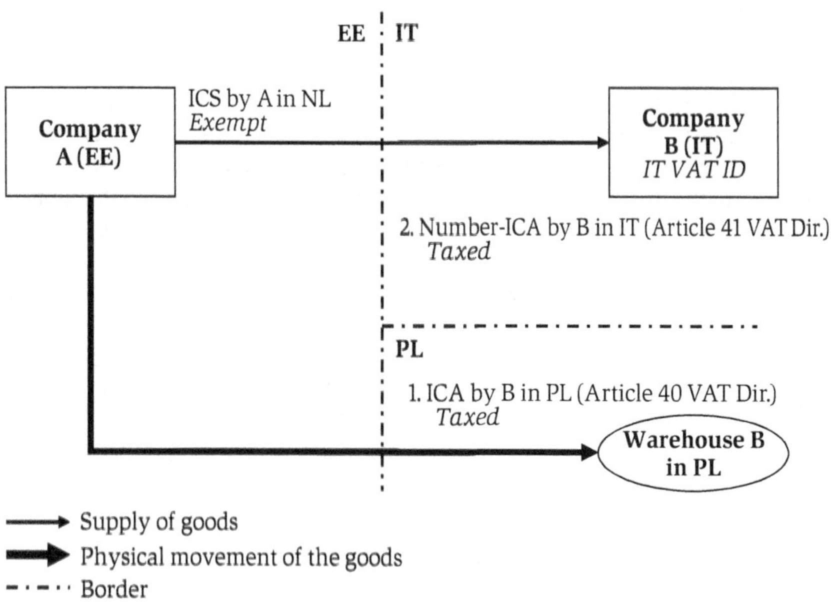

In any case, company A carries out an ICS of goods in Estonia. Under Article 40 VAT Directive, the place of the opposite ICA is where the goods arrive, i.e., Poland. However, if Article 41 VAT Directive were not to exist, there would be no incentive for company B to report an ICA in Poland (as B is not registered there), nor any incentive

72. *Ibid.*

for company B to report an ICA in Italy (as the goods are not transported there). There would be a risk of non-taxation.

Article 41 VAT Directive mitigates this risk. Because of Article 41 VAT Directive, company B must (also) report an ICA in Italy. This VAT cannot be immediately deducted.[73] As a result, VAT is at least levied somewhere in the EU, although this might not be in the Member State of arrival of the goods. The consequence of the application of Article 41 VAT Directive is that double taxation occurs. Since the purpose of Article 41 VAT Directive is merely to create an incentive for the purchaser to report an ICA of goods in the Member State of arrival of the goods, the VAT Directive contains a mechanism to remove the VAT on the number acquisition in case the purchaser shows that he reported an ICA in the Member State of arrival of the goods. We will explain this corrective mechanism below.

Correction for Double ICAs

Article 40 VAT Directive and the safety net provision of Article 41 VAT Directive apply simultaneously. Thus, it is conceivable that two ICAs are reported in relation to only one cross-border supply of goods. In view of the legal character of European VAT and the destination principle, the number acquisition can under certain conditions be reverted.

This is provided for in the second sentence of Article 41 VAT Directive. On the basis of that provision, the taxable amount of the number acquisition is reduced if the purchaser is able to demonstrate that he correctly reported an ICA in the Member State of arrival of the goods. The VAT Directive does not explicitly indicate what the practical consequence of the reduction of the taxable amount is. In our view, it should imply that the Member State of identification provides a refund of the VAT reported on the number acquisition.

On the basis of Article 42 VAT Directive, subject to conditions, there is no number acquisition in case of a chain transaction to which the so-called simplified triangulation rules apply (*see* section 13.7.2). The wording of this provision does not excel in terms of clarity, but particularly the reference to Article 197 VAT Directive makes clear that it only relates to cases in which the simplified triangulation rules apply. In section 13.7.2, we will further elaborate on the application of Articles 41 and 42 VAT Directive in the case of so-called chain transactions.

13.3.3.2.4 Chargeable Event and Chargeability of VAT in Respect of ICAs

Article 68 VAT Directive arranges the moment at which the chargeable event is deemed to occur in case of an ICA of goods. It occurs when the ICA of goods is made, i.e., when the supply of similar goods is regarded as being effected within the territory of the relevant Member State.

In section 13.3.2.2.9, we explained that effective controls require the supplier to report the ICS on its VAT return and on its recapitulative statement in the same tax

73. *Ibid.*

period in which the customer reports the ICA in its VAT return. For that reason, the moments at which the VAT becomes chargeable with respect to the ICS and the ICA must correspond. Therefore, Articles 67 and 69 VAT Directive are aligned.

On the basis of Article 69 VAT Directive, the VAT on the ICA shall become chargeable on issue of the invoice (for the supply), or at the moment when the invoice should have been issued at the latest (*see* Article 222, first paragraph VAT Directive).

13.3.3.2.5 Taxable Amount and VAT Rate Applicable to ICAs

Every taxable transaction, including the ICA of goods, requires rules governing the taxable amount and the tax rate. In view of the principle of neutrality and the destination principle, it is clear that the rules governing the taxable amount of the domestic supply of goods should also govern the ICA of these goods. As a main rule, the taxable amount of a supply of goods is the consideration obtained or to be obtained by the supplier (Article 73 VAT Directive). Following Article 83 VAT Directive, the taxable amount of ICAs of goods shall be established on the basis of the same factors as are used to determine the taxable amount for the supply of the same goods within the territory of the Member State concerned (*see* Chapter 6). Therefore, indeed the taxable amount of an ICA of goods is, in principle, the consideration obtained or to be obtained by the supplier.[74]

Sometimes, a taxable ICA occurs, even though the supplier receives no consideration, or the consideration received cannot be used as a taxable amount for other reasons. This is particularly the case with respect to the so-called deemed intra-Community B2Me acquisitions (*see* section 13.6.4). On the basis of the second paragraph of Article 83 VAT Directive, the taxable amount shall in those situations be the purchase price of the goods or of similar goods or, in the absence of a purchase price, the cost price, determined at the time of the supply.

Following Article 94(1) VAT Directive, the VAT rate applicable to the ICA of goods shall be equal to the VAT rate applied to the supply of like goods within the territory of the Member State (*see* Chapter 7). Again, the principle of neutrality and the destination principle require domestic supplies of goods and ICAs to be subject to the same VAT rate. Since the person acquiring the goods is the person liable for VAT, it is up to the acquirer to determine the applicable VAT rate in the Member State where he acquires the goods. We note that Article 94(2) VAT Directive does not deal with the VAT rate applicable to ICAs but rather to the VAT rate applicable to importations (*see* Chapter 14).

---

74. Article 84 VAT Directive specifically holds that Member States shall take the measures necessary to ensure that the excise duty due from or paid by the person making the ICA of a product subject to excise duty is included in the taxable amount. Adjustments in the amounts of excise duties payable also lead to an adjustment of the taxable amount for VAT on the ICA. In this way, excise goods purchased domestically are treated similarly to excise goods purchased from another Member State.

13.3.3.2.6 Exemptions Applicable to ICAs

Section 2 of Chapter 4 of the VAT Directive deals with exemptions for ICAs of goods. In essence, there are two types of exemptions for ICAs. The first type, contained in Article 140 VAT Directive, aims at achieving (external) neutrality of VAT. Goods purchased from other EU Member States should not be confronted with a heavier burden of VAT than goods purchased within a Member State. Moreover, goods purchased from other EU Member States should not be confronted with a heavier burden of VAT than goods purchased in non-EU countries. The second type, laid down in Article 141 VAT Directive, is part of the so-called simplified triangulation rules. Given the specific nature of this scheme, this latter type of exemption is discussed in a separate section (*see* section 13.7.2).

Article 140 VAT Directive comprises of three exemptions that the Member States should implement in their national legislation.

The ICA of Goods the Supply of Which Would in All Circumstances Be Exempt

Pursuant to Article 140(a) VAT Directive, Member States shall exempt the ICA of goods the supply of which by taxable persons would in all circumstances be exempt within their respective territory. This provision aims at safeguarding external neutrality of VAT. Goods that are procured in another Member State should not be taxed differently than goods bought within a Member State.

Local supplies of human organs, blood and milk, are imperatively exempt in all Member States under Article 132(1)(d) VAT Directive. Therefore, the ICA of these goods is also exempt. In our view, the neutrality principle requires that the words 'would in all circumstances be exempt' in Article 140(a) VAT Directive should be interpreted in such a manner that the ICA of goods is exempt, even if the exemption for the local supply of such goods is subject to conditions. For example, the supply of dental prostheses is exempt from VAT under Article 132(1)(e) VAT Directive, provided that the supply is made by dentists and dental technicians. One could argue that the condition that the supply must be made by a dentist or dental technician implies that the supply is not 'in all circumstances exempt'. However, such an interpretation would go against the *ratio legis* of the provision, i.e., to treat ICAs of dental prostheses by dentists and dental technicians identical to local supplies of dental prostheses by dentists and dental technicians. In the joined cases *VDP Dental Laboratory NV*, *X* and *Nobel Biocare Nederland BV*, the CJEU ruled that the exemption from VAT applies to the ICA and the final importation of dental prostheses supplied by dentists and dental technicians.[75] Whether or not a Member State of supply[76] or importation implemented transitional rules on the basis of Article 370 VAT Directive or whether the dental prostheses originate from a Member State which implemented such transitional arrangements is in this regard irrelevant according to the CJEU.

75. CJEU 26 February 2015, Joined Cases C-144/13, C-154/13 and C-160/13 *VDP Dental Laboratory NV v Staatssecretaris van Financiën (C-144/13) and Staatssecretaris van Financiën v X BV (C-154/13) and Nobel Biocare Nederland BV (C-160/13)*, ECLI:EU:C:2015:116, para. 58.
76. We believe that this should be 'ICA'.

The ICA of Goods the Importation of Which Would in All Circumstances Be Exempt

Not only should the ICA be treated in the same manner as the local supply of goods, it should also be taxed equally to the importation of goods. Therefore, Article 140(b) VAT Directive exempts the ICA of goods, the importation of which would, in all circumstances, be exempt. For that purpose, it refers to Article 143 VAT Directive, which contains the exemptions for the importations of goods. We note that the exemption for the importation of goods laid down in Article 143(1)(d) VAT Directive (importation followed by an intra-Community B2B or B2Me supply) is excluded in reference to Article 143 VAT Directive (*see* Chapter 14).

The ICA of Goods Where the Acquirer Would in all Circumstances Be Entitled to a Refund

If a taxable person acquires goods in another Member State, without him carrying out any (other) taxable transactions in that Member State, in principle, the taxable person is entitled to a refund of foreign VAT following Articles 170 and 171 VAT Directive, insofar he uses the goods for his taxed transactions. If, for example, a French company attends a fair in Italy and has 'give-aways' delivered from Germany to the fair in Italy, the French company, in principle, effects an ICA of goods in Italy and can recover the VAT on that acquisition via Articles 170 and 171 VAT Directive.[77] Another example is the ICA of office supplies in the Netherlands by a German company which only supplies B2B services to customers established outside the Netherlands. Article 140(c) VAT Directive exempts the ICA so that the French company does not need to go through a refund procedure. We note that if the acquirer does not have a full right of deduction (e.g., an insurance company), the exemption does not apply. After all, in such situations, there is no right of recovery of input VAT in the first place.

13.3.3.2.7 Right of Deduction of VAT on ICAs

The right to deduct input VAT should not only apply when a taxable person purchases goods domestically but also when a taxable person purchases goods from a supplier in another EU Member State. Therefore, Article 168(c) VAT Directive allows for the deduction of VAT that became due on ICAs of goods, insofar as the goods are used for the purposes of taxed transactions.

In addition, Article 168(d) VAT Directive arranges for a right of deduction of VAT due on 'transactions' which are treated as ICAs of goods under Articles 21 and 22 VAT Directive (*see* section 13.9). It speaks for itself that the VAT due on such ICAs can only be deducted insofar as the goods are used for the purposes of taxed transactions.

13.3.3.2.8 Person Liable for VAT with Respect to ICAs

Following Article 200 VAT Directive, VAT shall be payable by any person making a taxable ICA of goods. This also applies in cases of intra-Community B2H acquisitions

77. *See* B. Terra, J. Kajus & Z. Szatmári, *Commentary on European VAT* (IBFD 2023), Chapter 9.4.2.2.

and intra-Community C2C acquisitions of new means of transport (*see* sections 13.5 and 13.8).

Pursuant to Article 204 VAT Directive, Member States may allow a taxable person who is liable for payment of VAT in respect of an ICA of goods but is not established in the Member State in which the VAT is due, to appoint a tax representative. According to the text of Article 204 VAT Directive, this option is not available to non-taxable persons. Also, Member States may provide that a person other than the person liable for payment of VAT in respect of the ICA of goods is to be held jointly and severally liable for payment of VAT (Article 205 VAT Directive). We refer to Chapter 12 with respect to these provisions on the liability of VAT, as they are the same for regular supplies of goods and services for consideration and for ICAs of goods.

13.3.3.2.9 Administrative Obligations with Respect to ICTs

As a pendant to the ICS of goods, the ICA of goods is also coupled with administrative obligations, even if they are less extensive and fewer in number.

Periodical VAT Return

The taxable person acquiring goods must report the ICA in its periodical VAT return.[78] If a non-established company makes an ICA in a (different) Member State, this may lead to the obligation for that company to register for VAT in the Member State of acquisition.[79]

Recapitulative Statements (EC Sales Listing)

In principle, intra-Community B2B acquisitions of goods need not be reported on a recapitulative statement. However, if the simplified triangulation rules apply (*see* section 13.7.2), Articles 262 and 265 VAT Directive require that specific information on the ICA of the second taxable person in the supply chain (of three taxable persons) is reported in the recapitulative statement.

Intrastat Reporting

For statistical purposes, and if certain thresholds are exceeded, the intra-Community B2B acquisition of goods must be reported on the periodical intrastat return.

13.4 INTRA-COMMUNITY B2C SUPPLIES/DISTANCE SALES

As a general rule, private consumers cannot carry out 'ICAs of goods' as referred to in Article 2(1)(b) VAT Directive.[80] Rather, when private consumers procure goods from other Member States, they are, in principle, confronted with the VAT as applied by the Member State of departure of the goods (cf. Article 32 VAT Directive). Since the VAT

78. Article 251(c) VAT Directive.
79. Article 214(1)(b) VAT Directive.
80. If this were different, the tax authorities would potentially have to deal with an extremely large number of persons carrying out taxable events.

rates in the EU have not been harmonized, strict adherence to this manner of taxation would lead to VAT rate shopping by private consumers. To prevent such (and other) distortions, a special regime exists for intra-Community B2C supplies of goods. This regime is commonly referred to as the 'distance sales scheme' or the 'distance selling scheme' (*see* section 4.4.3.2 and 4.4.3.3).

13.4.1 Local (Without Transportation) Versus Intra-Community B2C Supplies (With Transportation)

The distance sales scheme does not generally apply to all purchases by private consumers in other Member States. If a private consumer travels to another Member State and purchases goods locally, the supply by the company in that other Member State will be a local supply of goods, regardless of whether the customer decides to take the goods to another Member State. Figure 13.15 serves to illustrate this.

Figure 13.15 Local Supply of Goods in Germany (No ICS) to a Dutch Private Consumer

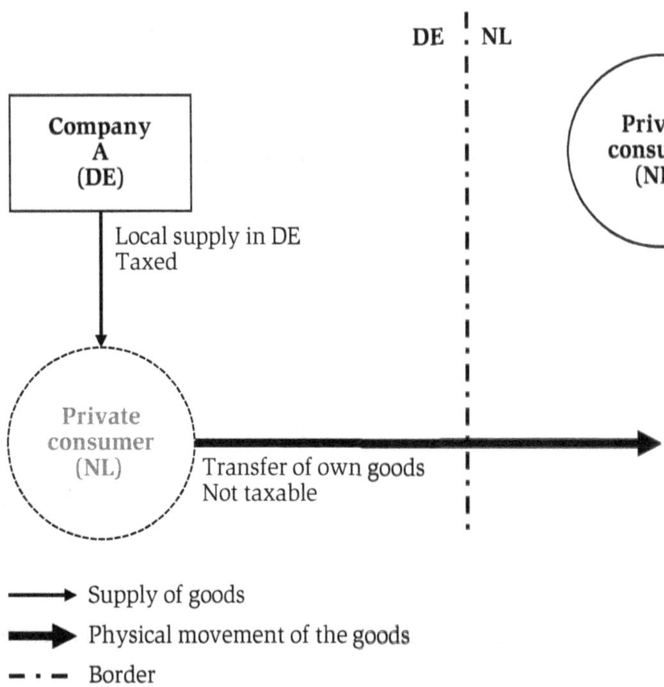

In this example, a Dutch private consumer travels to Germany and purchases a good from a German company. The Dutch private consumer himself takes the good back with him to the Netherlands. This means that the German company makes a local (taxed) supply of goods, without transportation. The place of that supply is in Germany

(Article 31 VAT Directive). The transfer of the goods to the Netherlands by the private consumer is not a taxable event for VAT (Article 17 VAT Directive only applies to intra-Community B2Me supplies and not to transfers of goods by private consumers).

If the goods are dispatched or transported by or on behalf of the supplier, the main rule on the place of supply (Article 32 VAT Directive) provides that the supply is subject to VAT where the goods are located at the time when dispatch or transport of the goods to the customer begins (i.e., the Member State of departure). Because Article 138 VAT Directive does not exempt ICSs to private consumers (i.e., the provision does not apply to intra-Community B2C supplies), local VAT will be due on the supply. In section 13.4.2, we will explain that this may cause various distortions and that the EU legislator, therefore, introduced the so-called distance sales scheme. Figure 13.16 explains the application of VAT in case the scheme does not apply.

Figure 13.16 Situation in Which Distance Sales Rules Do Not Apply

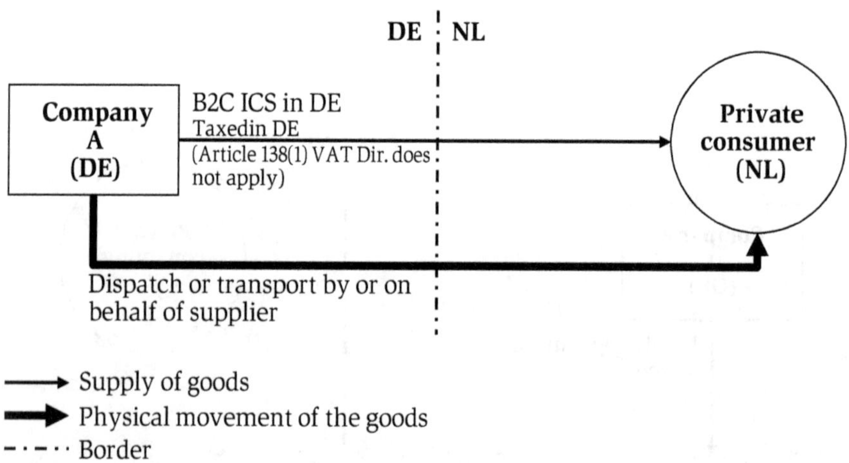

In this example, goods are dispatched or transported by or on behalf of the German supplier. If the distance sales rules do not apply (e.g., if the supplier threshold is not exceeded, *see* section 13.4.2.2), the place of supply under Article 32 VAT Directive is Germany. Even though the goods are transported to another Member State in the course of the supply, the supply is not exempt under Article 138 VAT Directive. German VAT applies.

13.4.2 Intra-Community B2C Supply (Transport by Supplier: Distance Sales)

As we indicated in section 13.4.1, without any special rules, companies that (a) supply goods by mail-order or via online marketing channels (web portals) and (b) that arrange the transportation of the goods to the customer, would have an incentive to make such supplies from a Member State with low VAT rates (compared to other Member States). Equally, private consumers would have an incentive to purchase goods in Member States with relatively low VAT rates and have the goods delivered at home by or on behalf of the supplier. Moreover, the products of suppliers making supplies from 'low VAT rate Member States' would possibly be cheaper than the identical products supplied by companies supplying goods from the same Member State in which the customer is residing. To prevent such distortions from occurring, the VAT Directive contains a specific regime (the distance sales scheme). We emphasize that these distance sales rules can only apply if the goods are dispatched or transported *by or on behalf of the supplier* from a Member State other than that in which dispatch or transport of the goods ends.

On 5 December 2017, the Council adopted Council Directive 2017/2455, the primary legislative instrument of the so-called VAT e-commerce package.[81] Accompanied by other legal instruments, the Directive was aimed at the modernization of EU VAT legislation as far as the e-commerce sector is concerned.[82] The intra-EU distance sales scheme was also affected by the legislative changes, which mostly entered into effect on 1 July 2021.[83] We will discuss both the scheme as it applied until 1 July 2021, and after. Further, the VAT e-commerce package also contains rules on distance sales of goods originating from non-EU countries; for further reading, refer to Chapter 14.

13.4.2.1 The EU Distance Sales Scheme until 1 July 2021

The essence of the former distance sales scheme was that, above a threshold of EUR 100,000 (or the equivalent in national currency), the place of a distance supply of goods

81. Council Directive (EU) 2017/2455 of 5 December 2017 amending Directive 2006/112/EC and Directive 2009/132/EC as regards certain value added tax obligations for supplies of services and distance sales of goods [2017] OJ L 348/7.
82. *See* Council Regulation (EU) 2017/2454 of 5 December 2017 amending Regulation (EU) No 904/2010 on administrative cooperation and combating fraud in the field of value added tax [2017] OJ L 348/1; Council Implementing Regulation (EU) 2017/2459 of 5 December 2017 amending Implementing Regulation (EU) No 282/2011 laying down implementing measures for Directive 2006/112/EC on the common system of value added tax [2017] OJ L 348/32; Council Implementing Regulation (EU) 2019/2026 of 21 November 2019 amending Implementing Regulation (EU) No 282/2011 as regards supplies of goods or services facilitated by electronic interfaces and the special schemes for taxable persons supplying services to non-taxable persons, making distance sales of goods and certain domestic supplies of goods [2019] OJ L 313/14; Council Directive (EU) 2019/1995 of 21 November 2019 amending Directive 2006/112/EC as regards provisions relating to distance sales of goods and certain domestic supplies of goods [2019] OJ L 310/1; Commission Implementing Regulation (EU) 2020/194 of 12 February 2020 laying down detailed rules for the application of Council Regulation (EU) No 904/2010 as regards the special schemes for taxable persons supplying services to non-taxable persons, making distance sales of goods and certain domestic supplies of goods [2020] OJ L 40/114.
83. Initially, the new rules would enter into effect on 1 January 2021. Due to the COVID-19 pandemic, this was postponed to 1 July 2021. Council Decision (EU) 2020/1109 of 20 July 2020 amending Directives (EU) 2017/2455 and (EU) 2019/1995 as regards the dates of transposition and application in response to the COVID-19 pandemic [2020] OJ L 244.

to a private consumer changed from the place where the transport begins, to the place where the transport ends.[84] Thus, the distance sales scheme applied if:

(1) a taxable person supplied goods to private consumers;
(2) the goods were dispatched or transported by or on behalf of the supplier from a Member State other than that in which dispatch or transport of the goods ends; and
(3) the total value, exclusive of VAT, of supplies of goods to that particular Member State in any one calendar year exceeded EUR 100,000, or the equivalent in national currency (Article 34(1)(b) VAT Directive); or
(4) the threshold of EUR 100,000 (or the equivalent in national currency) was exceeded in the previous calendar year (Article 34(1)(c) VAT Directive); or
(5) the supplier opted for the application of those rules (Article 34(4) VAT Directive).[85]

In the following section, we discuss the current EU distance sales scheme.

13.4.2.2 *The EU Distance Sales Scheme from 1 July 2021*

Most of the legislative changes in connection with the 'VAT e-commerce package' have entered into effect on 1 July 2021. The EU distance sales regime has changed on various points, even though the central notion of taxation in the Member State of arrival of the goods remains intact (*see* the current Article 33(a) VAT Directive). The current distance sales scheme applies, and taxation takes place in the Member State where the goods are located when transport to the customer ends if:

(1) a taxable person supplies goods to private consumers;
(2) the goods are dispatched or transported by or on behalf of the supplier, including where the supplier intervenes indirectly in the transport or dispatch of the goods, from a Member State other than that in which dispatch or transport of the goods ends; and
(3) the e-commerce threshold of EUR 10k (Article 59c VAT Directive) has been exceeded in the current or previous calendar year, *and* the taxable person has not opted for taxation under the distance sales scheme (Article 59c(3) VAT Directive).[86]

84. Former Article 33(1) VAT Directive.
85. The option shall in any event cover a period of two calendar years.
86. The option shall in any event cover a period of two calendar years.

Article 14(4)(1) VAT Directive provides a definition of EU distance sales, as it states that 'intra-Community distance sales of goods' means 'supplies of goods dispatched or transported by or on behalf of the supplier, including where the supplier intervenes indirectly in the transport or dispatch of the goods, from a Member State other than that in which dispatch or transport of the goods to the customer ends'. A central notion in this definition is the 'transport by or on behalf of the supplier, including where the supplier intervenes indirectly'. Article 5a VAT Implementing Regulation stipulates that such transport, including possible intervention, shall be deemed to have taken place in the following cases:[87]

(a) where the dispatch or transport of the goods is subcontracted by the supplier to a third party who delivers the goods to the customer;
(b) where the dispatch or transport of the goods is provided by a third party, but the supplier bears either the total or partial responsibility for the delivery of the goods to the customer;
(c) where the supplier invoices and collects the transport fees from the customer and further remits them to a third party who will arrange the dispatch or transport of the goods;
(d) where the supplier promotes by any means the delivery services of a third party to the customer, puts the customer and a third party in contact or otherwise provides to a third party the information needed for the delivery of the goods to the consumer.

This rule was adopted to combat situations such as the one in *KrakVet Marek Batko sp.k.*, where a taxable person tried to avoid the application of the distance sales scheme by having his customers directly engage with transportation companies via his website, so that the goods were not transported by or on behalf of him.[88]

Figure 13.17a illustrates an example in which the distance sales scheme applies.

87. However, goods shall not be considered to have been dispatched or transported by or on behalf of the supplier where the customer transports the goods himself or where the customer arranges the delivery of the goods with a third person and the supplier does not intervene directly or indirectly to provide or to help organize the dispatch or transport of those goods.
88. CJEU 18 June 2020, Case C-276/18 *KrakVet Marek Batko sp.k.*, ECLI:EU:C:2020:485. The Court ruled that 'transport by or on behalf of the supplier' occurs where the role of that supplier is predominant in terms of initiating and organizing the essential stages of the dispatch or transport of those goods, taking account of all the facts.

Figure 13.17a Distance Sale Rules Apply. The Place of Supply Is Where the Transport of the Goods Ends

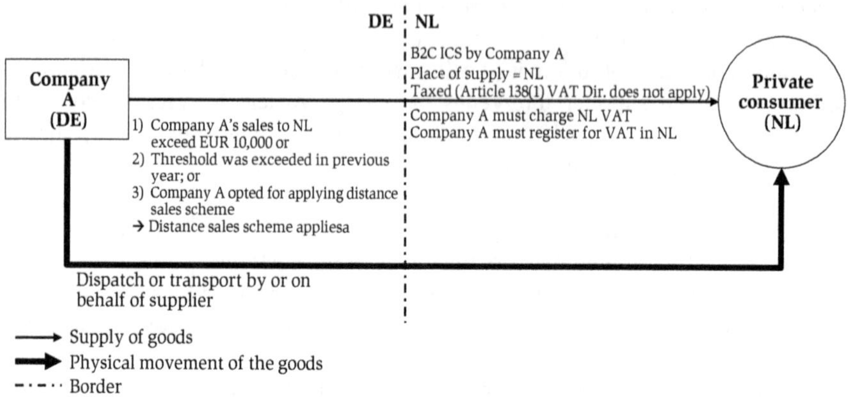

13.4.2.2.1 *Situations in Which the Distance Sales Scheme Does Not Apply*

In this section, we discuss the situations in which the distance sales rules do not apply, as there are various rules to that effect in the VAT Directive.

E-commerce Threshold Not Exceeded, Supplier Did Not Opt in, Supplier Established Only in One Member State

The use of a threshold implies that distortions of competition below this threshold are taken for granted. Apparently, the EU legislator did not deem it necessary to apply the distance sales scheme in all situations in which goods are dispatched or transported by or on behalf of the supplier to a private consumer in another Member State. Following Article 59c VAT Directive, the distance sales rules do *not* apply if: (a) the so-called e-commerce threshold of EUR 10,000[89] (or the equivalent in national currency) is not exceeded, (b) the e-commerce threshold was not exceeded in the previous calendar year, (c) the supplier did not opt for the application of the distance sales scheme, and (d) the supplier is established only in one Member State.[90] Under those circumstances, the main place of supply rule applies, which means that the supply takes place where the transport begins, and the supplier must charge the VAT of the Member State of

89. The former EU distance sales scheme (in effect until 1 July 2021) made use of a threshold that applied per destination country. The new scheme, that is currently in place, employs a lower threshold of EUR 10k. This threshold takes into account *all* EU distance sales, as well as B2C intra-EU TBE services (cf. Article 58 VAT Directive).

90. This threshold for small e-commerce entrepreneurs has already been in place, as of 1 January 2019, for cross-border intra-EU TBE services (*see* section 4.5.4.2.10).

departure of the goods on the supply. Figure 13.17b serves to illustrate a situation in which the distance sales rules do not apply.

Figure 13.17b Distance Sales Rules Do Not Apply. Place of Supply Is Germany

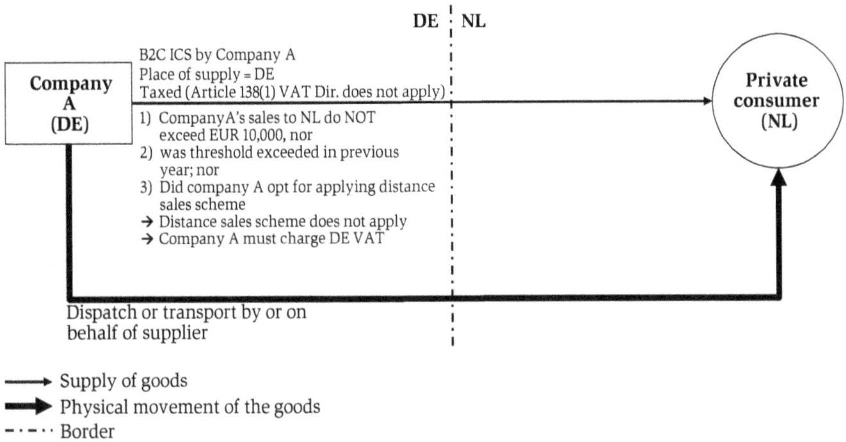

Supplies That Are Excluded from the Distance Sales Scheme

Supplies of new means of transport and supplies of goods supplied after assembly or installation, with or without a trial run, by or on behalf of the supplier, are excluded from the distance sales rules.[91] Similarly, the distance sale rules do not apply with respect to second-hand goods, works of art, collectors' items or antiques, supplies of second-hand means of transport (cf. Article 327(3) VAT Directive). All of these supplies have in common that they are covered by special rules, different from the distance sales rules.

13.4.2.2.2 Supplies to Other Customers Who Have No Full Right of Deduction

Article 33(1)(a) VAT Directive does not only apply if the customer is a private consumer ('any other non-taxable person') but also if the customer is a taxable person or non-taxable legal persons whose ICAs of goods are not subject to VAT pursuant to Article 3(1) VAT Directive. Whether or not the ICA by such customers is subject to VAT pursuant to Article 3(1) VAT Directive effectively depends on whether these customers

91. Article 14(4)(1)(b) VAT Directive.

must for VAT purposes be treated as 'normal' taxable persons or as 'private consumers'. Only in the latter situation, the distance sales rules apply. In section 13.5, on intra-Community B2H(ybrids) supplies, we will elaborate on the VAT treatment of supplies (with transportation) to customers that may either be effectively treated as taxable persons or as non-taxable persons.

13.4.2.2.3 Platform Taxation

Taxable persons who operate an electronic interface such as an (online) marketplace, platform or portal, and who facilitate, through the use of that medium, intra-Community distance sales of goods by non-EU-based suppliers to non-taxable persons shall in certain situations be deemed to have received and supplied those goods themselves (*see* Article 14a(2) VAT Directive).[92] This 'platform fiction' aims at promoting the collection of VAT on distance sales from the authorities' perspective, comparable to the already existing platform fiction of Article 9a VAT Implementing Regulation in connection with electronically supplied services. By 'inserting' the platform entrepreneur in the supply chain – so: he will be deemed to act as the *purchaser* of the goods from the non-EU-based supplier making intra-Community distance sales, and simultaneously as the *seller* of the same goods to the final consumer – the final VAT liability is generally imposed on that very platform entrepreneur. Thus, the tax authorities need only to check and supervise the platforms, rather than the (numerous) non-EU-based suppliers. Relevant aspects are that the supply of goods by the non-EU-based supplier to the platform is exempt for VAT purposes (Article 136a VAT Directive), so that there is no risk that that supplier does not remit the VAT to the tax authorities.[93] Additionally, the transport of the goods to the final customer is ascribed to the supply made by the platform; in this way, it is ensured that that supply in fact qualifies as the distance sale.[94] Figure 13.18 provides an overview of the (functioning of the) platform fiction.

92. *See* the new Article 14a VAT Directive, as adopted by means of Council Directive (EU) 2017/2455 of 5 December 2017. For distances sales of goods originating in non-EU countries, the consignments need to have an intrinsic value not exceeding EUR 150 for the platform fiction to apply.
93. *See* recital 2 of Council Directive (EU) 2019/1995 of 21 November 2019 amending Directive 2006/112/EC as regards provisions relating to distance sales of goods and certain domestic supplies of goods, OJ L 310.
94. *See* Article 36b VAT Directive.

Figure 13.18 EU Distance Sale, Carried Out by an Electronic Interface Operator (Platform Fiction)

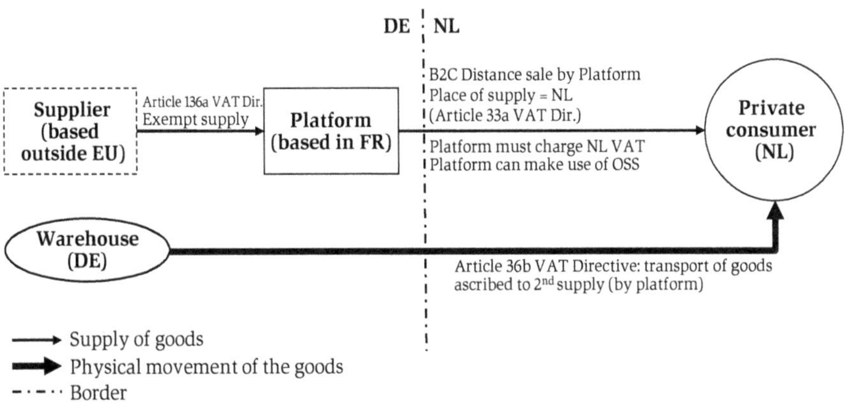

13.4.2.2.4 One-Stop Shop

Under the *OSS* scheme, Member States are required to permit taxable persons carrying out intra-Community distance sales of goods to use the OSS for the reporting and payment of VAT due on these transactions.[95] This implies that such taxable persons are allowed to settle their VAT affairs (the reporting and payment of VAT on intra-Community distance sales) in only one Member State (i.e., the Member State of identification), even if VAT is (also) due in other Member States (for further reading, refer to Chapter 15). For example, in Figure 13.18, the French platform operator can pay the German (and Italian, Spanish, Dutch etc.) VAT on its intra-Community distance sales via its French OSS-return.

13.5 INTRA-COMMUNITY B2H(YBRIDS) SUPPLIES

In section 13.4, we explained that the system of EU VAT has a special mechanism in place for ICTs involving certain categories of customers who are in a certain sense equitable with private consumers because they have no (full) right of deduction. The mechanisms primarily concern the following provisions:

- Article 2(1)(a) VAT Directive designates as a taxable transaction for VAT purposes the ICA of goods *by a taxable person or a non-taxable legal person*. This implies that in principle, also a non-taxable person (cf. Article 9 VAT

95. *See* Article 369b VAT Directive, as adopted by means of Council Directive (EU) 2017/2455 of 5 December 2017; for the legal definition of 'intra-Community distance sales of goods', refer to Article 14(4)(1) VAT Directive, as adopted by means of Council Directive (EU) 2017/2455 of 5 December 2017.

Directive) can carry out ICAs (assuming that that person is indeed a legal person, e.g., a SARL or Ltd.), as well as a taxable person that has no right of deduction (e.g., a hospital exclusively providing VAT-exempt hospital and medical care).

- Notwithstanding Article 2(1)(a) VAT Directive, Article 3(1)(b) VAT Directive provides that the ICAs of the following categories of persons are *not* subject to VAT: farmers applying the common flat-rate scheme for farmers; taxable persons who carry out only supplies of goods or services in respect of which VAT is not deductible; non-taxable legal persons. These three categories of persons have in common that they do not have a (full) right of deduction of input VAT. Their ICAs are not subject to VAT, and the supplies to them are subject to VAT in the Member State of departure of the goods in line with the taxation regime applicable to Intra-Community B2C supplies (distance sales; *see* section 13.4).
- Article 3(2) VAT Directive stipulates that when the intra-Community purchases of such customers exceed a certain threshold – the so-called acquisition threshold (which is different from the e-commerce threshold) – their ICAs are subject to VAT.[96] In that situation, the taxation regime for B2B ICSs and acquisitions applies to the purchases of the mentioned persons (*see* section 13.3). This provision is aimed at 'VAT rate shopping' by the mentioned three categories of persons, who otherwise would experience an incentive to buy goods locally in Member States with relatively low VAT rates.

The mechanism entails that certain types of customers, who are to a certain extent comparable to private consumers, can, subject to conditions, be treated as taxable persons that carry out ICAs. For that reason, we refer to these kinds of ICTs as 'intra-Community B2H(ybrid) transactions'. For each transaction, it must be determined whether the rules on intra-Community B2B supplies (*see* section 13.3.2) or the rules on intra-Community B2C supplies (*see* section 13.4) apply. Below, we will elaborate on this mechanism.

13.5.1 Intra-Community Purchases by Hybrids: B2C or B2B?

Article 3(1)(b) VAT Directive provides that ICAs made by any of the following categories of customers (referred to as: 'hybrids') are not subject to VAT:

(1) a farmer applying the common flat-rate scheme for farmers;
(2) a taxable person who carries out only supplies of goods or services in respect of which VAT is not deductible; or
(3) a non-taxable legal person.[97]

96. The acquisition threshold may not be less than EUR 10,000; the reference time is the current calendar year and the previous calendar year.
97. We note that Article 2(1)(b)(i) VAT Directive includes ICAs by non-taxable legal persons in the scope of VAT. Subsequently, Article 3(1)(b) VAT Directive excludes ICAs by non-taxable legal

However, if during the current calendar year, the total value of ICAs of goods by any of these types of customers exceeds the acquisition threshold of EUR 10,000,[98] the ICAs of such persons are subject to VAT (Article 3(2) VAT Directive). The same applies if the threshold was exceeded in the previous year. Pursuant to Article 3(3) VAT Directive, hybrids have the possibility to opt for treatment as a business (taxable persons). Even if the acquisition threshold is not exceeded in the current or previous calendar year, hybrids can perform ICSs of goods when they make use of the option. The option is often used in case goods are purchased from Member States with a higher VAT rate or in situations where it is clear that the threshold will be exceeded during the current year in order to achieve administrative simplification. The option shall, in any event, cover a period of two calendar years.[99]

Effectively, this means that if the intra-Community purchases by a hybrid exceed the acquisition threshold of EUR 10,000, or exceeded the threshold in the previous year, or if the customer opted to be treated as a taxable person (Article 3(3) VAT Directive), the customer (hybrid) is treated as a taxable person. The customer will then carry out taxed ICAs. However, he will not be able to recover the VAT on those ICAs. Conversely, the supplier(s) will be regarded as making intra-Community B2B supplies, which are exempt under Article 138(1) VAT Directive. Figure 13.19 serves to illustrate this.

Figure 13.19 B2H Supply: The Customer Is Treated as a Taxable Person

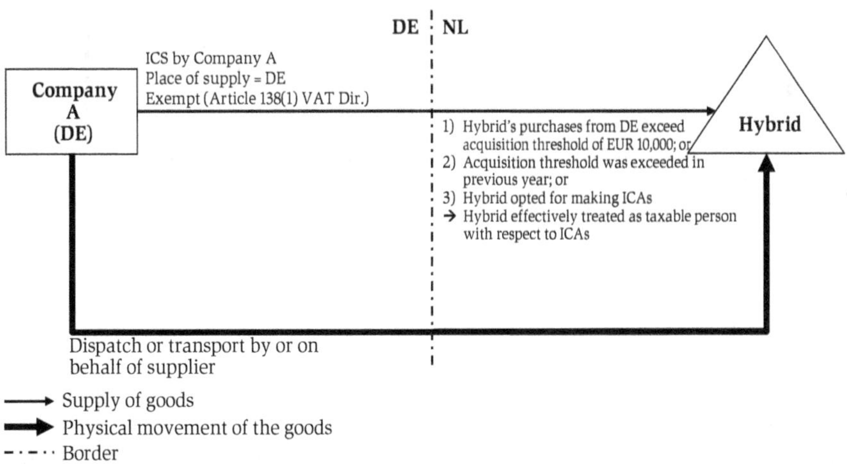

persons from the scope of VAT. Next, Article 3(2) VAT Directive again includes ICAs by non-taxable legal persons in the scope of VAT, depending on whether a threshold is exceeded.

98. Although many Member States indeed apply an acquisition threshold of EUR 10,000, Article 3(2) VAT Directive, in fact, stipulates that the ICA is subject to VAT if 'a threshold which the member states shall determine but which may not be less than EUR 10,000 or the equivalent in national currency' is exceeded.

99. Under Article 4 VAT Implementing Regulation, a hybrid which is not treated as a taxable person with respect to its ICAs, will still be treated in that manner, even if it obtained a VAT ID number because of the fact that he purchased services to which the reverse charge mechanism applied. However, if the hybrid communicates this VAT ID number to a supplier in respect of an ICA of goods, it shall be deemed to have exercised the option provided for in Article 3(3) VAT Directive (and will be treated as a taxable person with respect to its ICAs).

13.5.2 Intra-Community B2H Supplies and the Application of the Distance Sales Scheme

If the acquisition threshold is not exceeded (i.e., in the current and preceding year), hybrids are treated as private consumers. It now depends on the application of the EU distance sales rules, whether the supplier should charge the VAT of the Member State of departure of the goods or the VAT of the Member State of arrival of the goods. If the EU distance sales scheme does not apply, and the place of the supply is, therefore, in the Member State of departure of the goods, the (intra-Community) supply to the hybrid is excluded from the exemption for ICSs (Article 139(2) VAT Directive). Figure 13.20 illustrates this situation.

Figure 13.20 B2H Supply: The Customer Is Treated as a Non-taxable Person – Distance Sales Scheme Does Not Apply

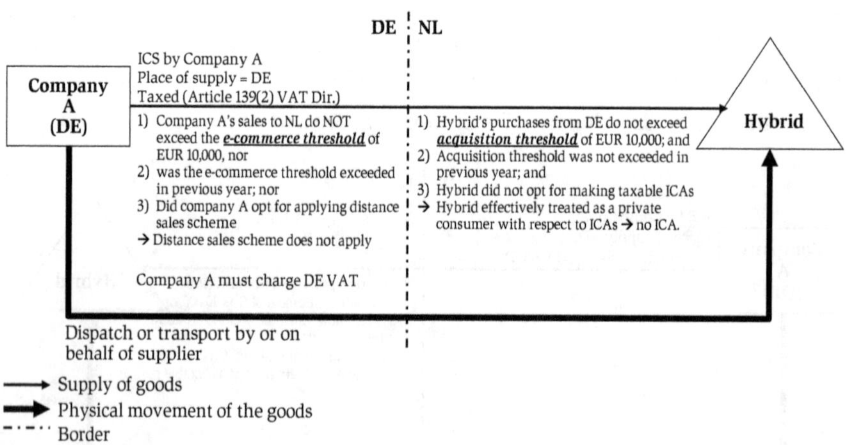

In the event that the threshold for B2H ICAs (acquisition threshold) is or was not exceeded, and the hybrid did not opt to be treated as a taxable person (hybrid treated as a private consumer, no ICAs), yet the supplier exceeded the distance sales threshold (e-commerce threshold) in the current or previous year or opted to apply the distance sales scheme, the supplier does not make an ICS in the Member State of departure of the goods, but rather a supply in the Member State where the goods arrive. That supply is, therefore, taxed in the Member State where the goods arrive. This can be illustrated as shown in Figure 13.21.[100]

100. *Ibid.*

Figure 13.21 B2H Supply: The Customer Is Treated as a Non-taxable Person – Distance Sales Scheme Applies

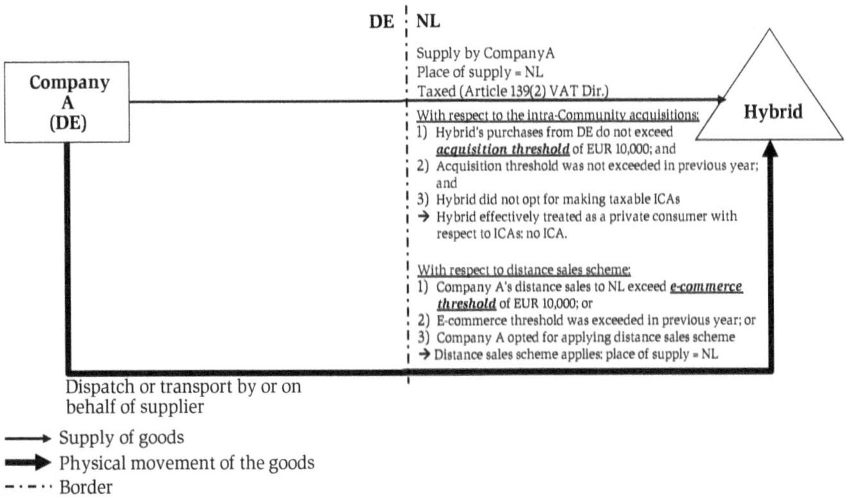

13.5.3 Towards a Simplified Regime for Intra-Community B2H Supplies?

Effecting intra-Community B2H transactions requires additional care from suppliers in respect of a correct VAT treatment. Similarly, purchasing goods in other Member States calls for extra attention from hybrids in order to ensure that VAT is accounted for in a correct manner. The mechanisms that are currently in place put a heavy burden on taxable persons doing business in the EU. In our view, the current system should be replaced by a simpler system. We favour a system in which farmers and taxable persons without a full right of deduction are, in all cases, treated as taxable persons with respect to ICAs of goods. This simplifies the regime for suppliers and hybrids. Moreover, this would be in line with the destination principle. A simplification with respect to ICSs to non-taxable legal persons could be to treat them as taxable persons with respect to ICAs of goods if they make use of a VAT ID number. If they do not provide a VAT ID number, they could be treated as non-taxable persons. This alternative would align with the place of supply of services regime which came into force as of 1 January 2010. Under this regime, non-taxable legal persons are treated as taxable persons for the place of supply of services, should they provide a VAT ID number (*see* section 4.5.3.1).

13.6 INTRA-COMMUNITY B2ME SUPPLIES (TRANSFERS OF OWN GOODS)

Since the abolishing of the internal EU fiscal frontiers in 1993, goods can move freely within the EU. When goods are transported to another Member State, they will not be subject to export and/or import formalities. Without a doubt, this contributes to the smooth functioning of the internal market. In the context of 'regular' supplies of goods between two taxable persons, the duality of ICSs and acquisitions ensures that the authorities of both the Member State of departure and the Member State of arrival are properly informed on the cross-border movement of the goods (i.e., via the VAT returns and EC Sales Listings of the taxable persons). However, in case *one* taxable person transports goods forming part of the assets of his business (i.e., 'own goods') to other Member States, the authorities would not be informed without any further rules. It is for that reason that the VAT Directive contains additional rules on cross-border transfers of own goods within the EU.[101]

The central provision of the rules on cross-border (intra-Community) transfers of own goods is Article 17(1) VAT Directive. On the basis of this provision, the transfer of own goods to another Member State is considered as an ICS of goods.[102] In practice, this type of supply is commonly referred to as 'deemed' or 'fictitious' ICS. The reason is that no 'true' supply of goods takes place (as there is no transfer of the right to dispose of the goods to another person, cf. Article 14 VAT Directive). For consistency purposes, we refer to such supplies as 'intra-Community B2Me supplies'.

Article 17(2) VAT Directive contains various exceptions to the intra-Community B2Me supplies. In this section, we will first address the key aspects of this type of ICSs. Subsequently, we will discuss the main exceptions to the intra-Community B2Me supplies. Lastly, we will discuss the VAT consequences of the pendant to the intra-Community B2Me supplies: the intra-Community B2Me acquisitions.

In the course of transportation, goods may move through various Member States before they arrive in the (ultimate) Member State of destination. A short stop in a Member State other than that of destination does not automatically trigger an intra-Community B2Me – assuming the logistical process is not compromised by significant interruptions (e.g., work on goods). For example, if company A in Poland supplies goods to company B in Germany, and company A transports the goods to Germany, but the truck driver stops for half a day just after crossing the Polish-German border, that does not automatically mean that there is a B2Me supply (by A, from Poland to Germany) followed by a local supply by A to B in Germany. As long as there is a sufficient temporal and material link between the supply of the goods in question and the dispatch of those goods, as well as continuity in the course of the transaction, the transportation of the goods, will be regarded as a single movement of the goods.[103] Then, the supply by A to B in the example above will still be considered as a normal ICS by A in Poland, followed by an ICA by B in Germany.

---

101. In a general sense, the rules are aimed at: (a) promoting supervision and enforcement, (b) countering VAT fraud and evasion, and (c) promoting taxation on the basis of the destination principle (i.e., taxation where consumption is most likely to take place).
102. In simple terms, the taxable person is regarded as making an ICS of goods to himself (a 'self-supply').
103. *See* CJEU 18 November 2010, Case C-84/09 *X v Skatteverket*, ECLI:EU:C:2010:693 and CJEU 2 October 2014, Case C-446/13 *Fonderie 2A v Ministre de l'Économie et des Finances*, ECLI: EU:C:2014:2252.

Sometimes, however, a stopover in a Member State triggers an intra-Community B2Me supply. This becomes apparent from the CJEU judgment in *Fonderie*, in which the logistical process was interrupted by work on the goods in the Member State of final destination (France). The case concerned a supplier (A) who sold goods originating in Italy to another taxable person (B). Before the goods were delivered at the premises of B in France, however, A had ordered a service provider in France to work on the goods (i.e., paint the goods). According to the CJEU, the place of supply of the goods on which the vendor, to make them fit to be supplied, has had finishing work carried out by a service provider established in the Member State of destination (France), before having them dispatched by the service provider to the person to whom they are being supplied, must be deemed to be in the Member State where the latter is established (France). Consequently, the transfer of the goods from the first Member State (Italy) to the last Member State (France) constitutes a B2Me supply followed by a local supply in the Member State (France) where the goods were made fit to be supplied.[104]

13.6.1 No Transfer of Ownership

An intra-Community B2Me supply only occurs if the right to dispose of the goods as owner is not transferred (cf. Article 14 VAT Directive) but remains with the same taxable person, yet the goods are 'transferred to another Member State'. The expression 'transfer to another Member State' means that movable tangible property is dispatched or transported by or on behalf of the taxable person, for the purposes of his business, to a destination outside the territory of the Member State in which the property is located, but within the EU (Article 17(1), last paragraph VAT Directive). Thus, without there being a supply to another person, the goods are moved from one Member State to another Member State by or on behalf of the taxable person who is and remains the owner of the goods.

13.6.2 Two Sides of the Same Coin

The pendant of a deemed ICS of goods under Article 17(1) VAT Directive must be an ICA of those goods. However, a literal interpretation of Article 20 VAT Directive indicates that the provision cannot apply because there is no 'acquisition of the right to dispose as owner of movable tangible property'. After all, there is only a transfer of own goods, and no acquisition of ownership whatsoever.

If one accepts that Article 20 VAT Directive cannot be regarded as the basis for an intra-Community B2Me acquisition, the deemed ICA can only be based on either Article 21 or Article 23 VAT Directive. The text of both provisions is broad enough to cover a deemed ICS following a deemed ICS. Unfortunately, the true rationale underlying the texts of both provisions remains unclear. There is no legislative history to draw conclusions from. The CJEU has not (yet?) construed a clear purpose for these

104. CJEU 2 October 2014, Case C-446/13 *Fonderie 2A v Ministre de l'Économie et des Finances*, ECLI:EU:C:2014:2252.

provisions. In our view, these provisions do not adhere to the common guidelines for the quality of drafting of Community legislation.[105]

The wording of Article 21 VAT Directive mirrors the text of Article 18(a) VAT Directive. The latter provision entails the 'internal supply' which – if implemented – may occur when a taxable person applies goods for the purposes of his business while the VAT on the goods, had they been acquired from another taxable person, would not be wholly deductible. We note that Article 18(a) VAT Directive applies if goods have been produced, constructed, extracted, processed, purchased or imported in the course of the business of a taxable person, but does *not* make any mention of goods having been acquired from another Member State.[106] These observations suggest that Article 21 VAT Directive is complementary to Article 18(a) VAT Directive.

Article 168(d) VAT Directive explicitly allows for deduction of the VAT due on ICAs covered by Article 21 VAT Directive. It makes no mention of Article 23 VAT Directive. Nevertheless, it is clear that a business carrying out fully taxed activities should have a full right of deduction with respect to a deemed ICA of goods. Since Article 21 VAT Directive, in conjunction with Article 168(d) VAT Directive, guarantees such a full right of deduction, we are inclined to consider Article 21 VAT Directive as covering deemed ICAs following a deemed ICSs under Article 17 VAT Directive. Should Article 23 VAT Directive cover the deemed intra-Community B2Me acquisition, one must note that Article 168(d) VAT Directive is incomplete in the sense that it does not refer to Article 23 VAT Directive.

Whether the deemed ICA is covered by Article 21 or Article 23 VAT Directive, it is safe to conclude that the deemed ICS and deemed ICA are, in fact, two sides of the same coin, just like 'normal' intra-Community B2B supplies and acquisitions. We refer to section 13.3.1.

13.6.3 The VAT Consequences of Deemed Intra-Community B2Me Supplies

In this section, we discuss the VAT consequences of deemed intra-Community B2Me supplies.

13.6.3.1 Introduction

In this section, we will further analyse the VAT consequences of an intra-Community B2Me supply of goods (*see* Figure 13.22). We will discuss the pendant to this supply, the intra-Community B2Me acquisition, in section 13.6.4. Even though the ICS and the ICA are two sides of the same coin, they both have their own VAT consequences. In this respect, there is little difference in comparison to 'normal' intra-Community B2B

105. Interinstitutional Agreement of 22 December 1998 on common guidelines for the quality of drafting of Community legislation [1999] OJ C073/0001–0004.

106. We note that the English text of Article 18(a) VAT Directive uses the word 'acquired'. However, looking at other language versions of the VAT Directive, it appears that this word should be interpreted as 'purchased' or 'obtained'.

transactions. Therefore, we will only highlight the elements that contain differences in comparison to normal intra-Community B2Me supplies in this section.

Figure 13.22 A Standard Intra-Community B2Me Supply of Goods: Steps to Be Taken in the 'VAT Determination Scheme'

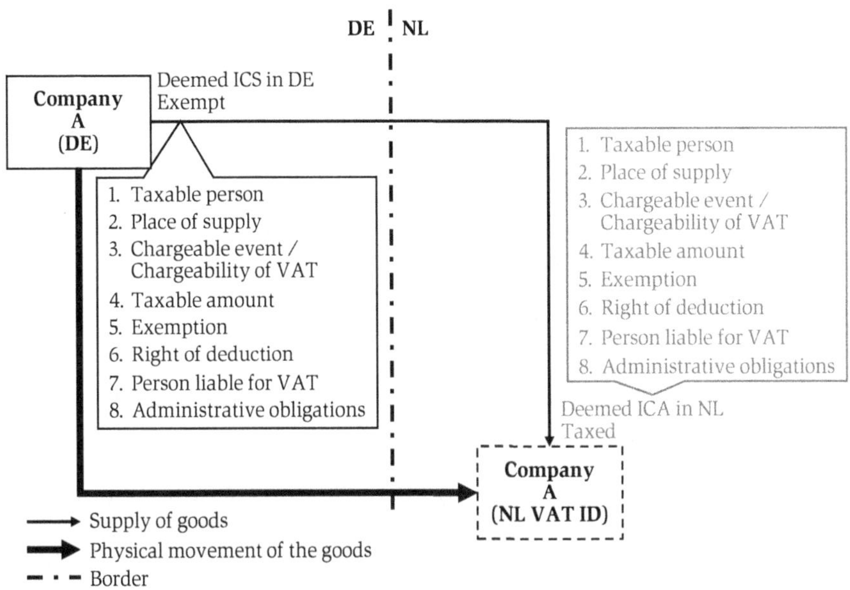

13.6.3.2 Taxable Person Status of the Supplier

The transfer of own goods to another Member State is only subject to VAT if the person transferring its own goods has the status of a taxable person. In this respect, Article 17(1) VAT Directive explicitly states that it only applies to transfers 'by a taxable person'.

13.6.3.3 The Place of Intra-Community B2Me Supplies

The place of intra-Community B2Me supplies follows the normal place of (intra-Community) supply rules. The place of supply will be in the Member State where the transport begins. *See* section 13.3.2.2.3.

13.6.3.4 Chargeable Event and Chargeability of VAT in Respect of Intra-Community B2Me Supplies

As a main rule, the moment when the taxable event takes place is determined on the basis of Article 63 VAT Directive: when the goods are supplied, i.e., when the goods are transferred to another Member State. Article 67 VAT Directive stipulates that: '... where goods are transferred VAT exempt to another Member State by a taxable person for the purposes of his business, VAT shall become chargeable on issue of the invoice, or on expiry of the time limit referred to in the first paragraph of Article 222 if no invoice has been issued by that time'. A deemed ICS is exempted under Article 138 VAT Directive (*see* section 13.6.3.6), and indeed a deemed ICS presupposes that goods are transferred VAT-exempt to another Member State by a taxable person for the purposes of his business. Strictly speaking, Article 67 VAT Directive should apply. However, in our view, the VAT Directive does not contain an obligation to issue an invoice for an intra-Community B2Me supply, nor does Article 222 set a time limit for the issue of an invoice to be issued in respect of a deemed ICS. Consequently, it would seem that Article 67 VAT Directive does not correctly provide for a moment on which the VAT becomes chargeable in respect of an intra-Community transfer of own goods. Therefore, it seems that the moment at which the VAT becomes chargeable in respect of a deemed ICS must be established on the basis of Article 63 VAT Directive, after all. The moment at which the VAT becomes chargeable is the moment when the goods are transferred to another Member State.

13.6.3.5 Taxable Amount of and VAT Rate Applicable to Intra-Community B2Me Supplies

Intra-Community B2Me supplies generally involve transfers of own goods, implying that there is, generally, no consideration that was agreed in the context of a supply and that can serve as a taxable amount. For that reason, Article 76 VAT Directive stipulates that the taxable amount shall be the purchase price of the goods or of similar goods or, in the absence of a purchase price, the cost price, determined at the time the transfer takes place. As far as the VAT rate is concerned, we note that an exemption applies (*see* next section).

13.6.3.6 Exemption Applicable to Intra-Community B2Me Supplies

Pursuant to Article 138(2)(c) VAT Directive, a deemed ICS of goods, consisting of a transfer to another Member State, is also exempt with a right of deduction if the supply had been exempt when made to another taxable person. The relevant criterion is whether the ICS would have been exempt if it had been made for another taxable person.

13.6.3.7 Right of Deduction in Respect of Intra-Community B2Me Supplies

With respect to transactions that are exempt pursuant to Article 138, Article 169(b) VAT Directive provides that a right of deduction exists. We refer to section 13.3.2.2.7.

13.6.3.8 *Person Liable for VAT with Respect to Intra-Community B2Me Supplies*

There are no specific rules with respect to the determination of the person liable for VAT in respect of intra-Community B2Me supplies. Under Article 193 VAT Directive, the taxable person transferring its goods to another Member State is the person liable for VAT on the deemed ICS.

13.6.3.9 *Administrative Obligations with Respect to Intra-Community B2Me Supplies*

Invoicing Requirements with Respect to Intra-Community B2Me Supplies

Article 220(1)(3) VAT Directive indicates that a taxable person who makes a supply in accordance with the conditions specified in Article 138 VAT Directive must ensure that an invoice is issued, either by himself or by his customer or, in his name and on his behalf, by a third party. An intra-Community B2Me supply is exempt under Article 138 VAT Directive (*see* section 13.6.3.6). However, the supply is only a *deemed* supply since no ownership is transferred. There does not seem to be any need to produce a merely internal document to record the deemed supply. Nevertheless, there is no provision in the VAT Directive that contains a specific rule to exclude intra-Community B2Me supplies from the scope of Article 220 VAT Directive. Article 221(3) VAT Directive does not even allow Member States to release taxable persons from the obligation to issue an invoice in respect of an intra-Community B2Me supply. Notwithstanding these facts, we believe that there should be no requirement for taxable persons to issue an invoice in respect of an intra-Community B2Me supply because it only relates to the transfer of own goods. In our view, there are no compelling reasons to impose such an administrative burden on businesses. Some Member States do not require an invoice to be issued in relation to intra-Community B2Me supplies, whereas others do. Businesses often find it practical to use so-called pro forma invoices to record the intra-Community B2Me supply anyway. Therefore, in practice, it is not uncommon that an (pro forma) invoice is issued in respect of intra-Community B2Me supplies.

Proof of Transportation

The intra-Community B2Me supply is exempt under Article 138(2)(c) VAT Directive. Normally, the supplier must be able to prove that he applied the exemption correctly. In that respect, he should be able to prove that the goods were transported to another EU Member State, and indeed left the Member State of dispatch. There is no indication in the VAT Directive that this is any different in case of an intra-Community B2Me supply.

Periodical VAT Return

It is self-evident that an intra-Community B2Me supply must be recorded in the periodical VAT return. Article 251(a) VAT Directive mentions 'supplies of goods referred to in Article 138' in this regard. It is by means of this action that the Member State of departure is informed of the movement of the goods (in addition to the EC Sales Listing). The Member State of destination or arrival is informed of the movement following the reporting of the ICA (Article 251(c) VAT Directive).

Recapitulative Statements (EC Sales Listing)

Article 262(a) VAT Directive stipulates that the taxable person who makes an intra-Community B2Me supply must file an EC sales list. Article 264(1)(c) VAT Directive provides that a taxable person must state in its EC sales list his VAT ID number in the Member State of dispatch of the goods, as well as his VAT ID number in the Member State in which the dispatch or transport ended.[107]

Register of Goods

In case of certain intra-Community B2Me supplies (*see* section 13.6.5), the taxable person must keep a register of the goods dispatched or transported by him, or on his behalf, to another Member State (Article 243 VAT Directive). Because the VAT Directive does not provide any formal conditions with respect to this register, we believe that taxable persons are free to choose a format, as long as all necessary data is contained therein.

Intrastat Reporting

The intra-Community B2Me supply must also be recorded for intrastat purposes. We refer to section 13.3.2.2.9.

13.6.4 The VAT Consequences of Intra-Community B2Me Acquisitions

In this section, we reflect on the pendant to the deemed intra-Community B2Me supply: the intra-Community B2Me acquisition of goods. Where possible, we will refer to other sections in this chapter to avoid repetitions.

13.6.4.1 Introduction

When a taxable person transfers own goods to another Member State, he will not only carry out a deemed ICS in the Member State of dispatch but also a corresponding ICA in the Member State of arrival of the goods (either Article 21 or Article 23 VAT Directive; it is unclear which provision applies, *see* section 13.6.2).

107. *See* section 13.3.2.2.9 for further reading on the relevance of the EC Sales Listing.

Figure 13.23 A Standard Intra-Community B2Me Acquisition of Goods: Steps to Be Taken in the 'VAT Determination Scheme'

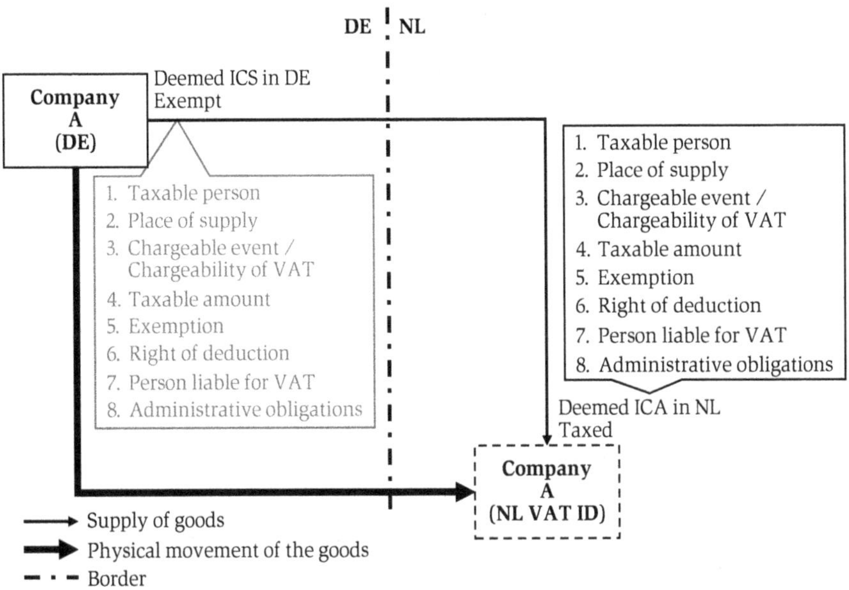

If the taxable person at issue is entitled to a deduction of input VAT, he is not only allowed to deduct all input VAT related to the deemed ICS in full, but should also be allowed to do so with respect to the VAT due as a result of the corresponding ICA. If Article 21 VAT Directive is the legal basis for the ICA, the right of deduction can be based on Article 168(d) VAT Directive. Figure 13.23 shows a standard transfer of own goods from one Member State to another Member State and the steps from the 'VAT determination scheme' that need to be taken in order to determine the VAT consequences of the acquisition.

13.6.4.2 Taxable Person Status of the Acquirer

The transfer of own goods to another Member State is only subject to VAT if the person transferring its own goods has the status of a taxable person. In this respect, Article 17(1) VAT Directive explicitly states that it only applies to transfers 'by a taxable person'. Since the intra-Community B2Me supply implies a transfer of *own* goods, the acquirer is the same person as the supplier and hence a taxable person.

13.6.4.3 The Place of Intra-Community B2Me Acquisitions

The place of an intra-Community B2Me acquisition is the place of arrival of the goods. We refer to section 13.3.3.2.3 on 'normal' ICAs.

13.6.4.4 *Chargeable Event and Chargeability of VAT in Respect of Intra-Community B2Me Acquisitions*

In section 13.3.3.2.4, we indicated that on the basis of Article 69 VAT Directive, the VAT on the ICA shall become chargeable on issue of the invoice (for the supply), or at the moment when the invoice should have been issued at the latest (*see* Article 222, first paragraph, VAT Directive). In section 13.6.3.9, we noted that in our view, there should not be a requirement to issue an invoice for such a deemed supply. The VAT Directive neither explicitly requires an invoice to be issued in case of an intra-Community B2Me supply, nor does it explicitly release a taxable person from the requirement to issue an invoice with respect to an intra-Community B2Me supply. Arguably, a literal interpretation of Article 69 VAT Directive can resolve this. After all, it states that 'VAT shall become chargeable on issue of the invoice, or on expiry of the time limit referred to in the first paragraph of Article 222 if no invoice has been issued by that time'. If there is no obligation to issue an invoice, the 'expiry of the time limit referred to in the first paragraph of Article 222' is the moment when the VAT becomes chargeable because, in the absence of a requirement to do so, the condition that 'no invoice has been issued by that time' will be necessarily fulfilled.

13.6.4.5 *Taxable Amount of and VAT Rate Applicable to Intra-Community B2Me Acquisitions*

Intra-Community B2Me acquisitions generally involve transfers of own goods, implying that there is, generally, no consideration that was agreed in the context of a supply and that can serve as a taxable amount. For that reason, the second paragraph of Article 83 VAT Directive stipulates that the taxable amount shall in those situations be the purchase price of the goods or of similar goods or, in the absence of a purchase price, the cost price, determined at the time of the (deemed) supply. For the VAT rate, we refer to section 13.3.3.2.5 on 'normal' ICAs.

13.6.4.6 *Exemption Applicable to Intra-Community B2Me Acquisitions*

Since there are also no specific provisions relating to exemptions applicable to intra-Community B2Me acquisitions, we refer to section 13.3.3.2.6 on 'normal' ICAs.

13.6.4.7 *Right of Deduction in Respect of Intra-Community B2Me Acquisitions*

In section 13.6.2, we indicated that if the intra-Community B2Me acquisition is to be based on Article 21 VAT Directive, the right of deduction of the VAT on the acquisition follows from Article 168(d) VAT Directive. If Article 23 VAT Directive is the proper basis for the intra-Community B2Me acquisition, the VAT Directive does not contain a specific provision on which the right of deduction can be based.

13.6.4.8 Person Liable for VAT with Respect to Intra-Community B2Me Acquisitions

For briefness sake, we refer to section 13.3.3.2.8.

13.6.4.9 Administrative Obligations with Respect to Intra-Community B2Me Acquisitions

For briefness sake, we refer to section 13.3.3.2.9.

13.6.5 Exceptions to the Intra-Community B2Me Supplies

The phenomenon of deemed intra-Community B2Me supplies involves considerable administrative burdens and related costs, simply for moving your own goods across an EU border. It creates the requirement for taxable persons to register for VAT in other Member States, and it implies various reporting requirements (*see* section 13.3.2.2.9). For that reason, Article 17(2) VAT Directive contains a list of specific exceptions to the general rule that transfers of own goods to other Member States are to be regarded as ICSs of goods against consideration. The exceptions are the following:

(a) the supply of goods by a taxable person within the territory of the Member State in which the dispatch or transport ends, in accordance with the conditions laid down in Article 33 (distance sales regime);
(b) the supply of goods, for installation or assembly by or on behalf of the supplier, by the taxable person within the territory of the Member State in which dispatch or transport of the goods ends, in accordance with the conditions laid down in Article 36;
(c) the supply of goods by a taxable person on board a ship, an aircraft or a train in the course of a passenger transport operation, in accordance with the conditions laid down in Article 37;
(d) the supply of gas through the natural gas distribution system, or of electricity, in accordance with the conditions laid down in Articles 38 and 39;
(e) the supply of the goods by a taxable person within the territory of the Member State, in accordance with the conditions laid down in Articles 138, 146, 147, 148, 151 or 152;
(f) the supply of a service performed for a taxable person and consisting of work on the goods in question physically carried out within the territory of the Member State in which dispatch or transport of the goods ends provided that the goods, after being worked upon, are returned to that taxable person in the Member State from which they were initially dispatched or transported;
(g) the temporary use of goods within the territory of the Member State in which dispatch or transport of the goods ends, for the purposes of the supply of services by the taxable person established within the Member State in which dispatch or transport of the goods began;

(h) the temporary use of goods, for a period not exceeding 24 months, within the territory of another Member State, in which the importation of the same goods from a third country with a view to their temporary use would be covered by the arrangements for temporary importation with full exemption from import duties.

In all the above-mentioned situations, no deemed intra-Community B2Me supplies take place. Also, no ICA of goods has to be reported in the Member State of arrival of the goods. If the exceptions mentioned under f, g and h apply, however, the taxable person transferring his own goods to another Member State on the basis of Article 243(1) VAT Directive is required to keep a register of those transfers.

13.6.6 Call-Off Stock Arrangement

In international trade, so-called call-off stocks or consignment stocks are common phenomena.[108] In simple terms, such stocks consist of goods that are transported to another country for storage, only to be supplied at a later moment in time. In practice, taxable persons having consignment stock or call-off stock in other Member States struggle with the regime for deemed ICTs (*see* sections 13.6.3 and 13.6.4). To overcome practical difficulties, some Member States had simplification arrangements in place. Since 1 January 2020, the VAT Directive contains a harmonized simplification arrangement for the call-off stock – which is discussed here.[109]

The call-off stock arrangement is laid down in Article 17a VAT Directive. Its central notion is that the ultimate supply of the goods (which often occurs by virtue of the fact that the customer takes the goods out of storage, e.g., for production purposes) is *at that very moment* treated as a regular ICS by the supplier in the Member State of departure, followed by a taxable ICA by the customer in the Member State of arrival. The preceding cross-border transport of the goods is not treated as a transfer of own goods in the sense of Article 17 of the VAT Directive (cf. Article 17a(1) VAT Directive). Thus, the arrangement eliminates the need for the stock owner (supplier) to register in

108. In the context of EU VAT, there are no legal definitions of 'call-off stock' and 'consignment stock'. The difference between the two concepts is ambiguous, yet seems to come down to the notion that consignment stock relates to goods which are held in a (foreign) warehouse operated by the supplier himself with the intention of selling these to customers whose identity is unknown at the moment that the goods are transported to the warehouse. Call-off stock concerns goods which are transported to the business premises of a known customer, so that that party can take the goods out of the stock when they are needed (e.g., for production processes). From this point onwards, we refer to 'call-off stock' only. For further reading, refer to M. Horsthuis & F.J.G. Nellen, *A Critical Analysis of the Quick Fixes for the EU Intra-Community B2B VAT System* (2019) 3 International VAT Monitor https://doi.org/10.59403/25gdm93.

109. Council Directive (EU) 2018/1910 of 4 December 2018 amending Directive 2006/112/EC as regards the harmonization and simplification of certain rules in the value added tax system for the taxation of trade between Member States [2018] OJ L 311/3. This section is copied from M. Horsthuis & F.J.G. Nellen, *A Critical Analysis of the Quick Fixes for the EU Intra-Community B2B VAT System* (2019) 3 International VAT Monitor https://doi.org/10.59403/25gdm93.

the Member State of arrival for reporting an intra-Community B2Me acquisition of the goods followed by a local supply.[110]

There are various strict conditions for making use of the arrangement. The most important conditions are the following:

(1) The goods are dispatched or transported by a taxable person (i.e., supplier), or by a third party on his behalf, to another Member State with a view to those goods being supplied there, at a later stage and after arrival, to another taxable person who is entitled to take ownership of those goods (i.e., customer) in accordance with an existing agreement between both taxable persons.[111]
(2) The supplier dispatching or transporting the goods has not established his business nor has a fixed establishment in the Member State to which the goods are dispatched or transported.
(3) The customer to whom the goods are intended to be supplied is identified for VAT purposes in the Member State to which the goods are dispatched or transported, and both his identity and the VAT ID number assigned to him by that Member State are known to the supplier at the time when the dispatch or transport begins.
(4) The supplier maintains a record of the goods in accordance with certain formal standards.

We reiterate that the call-off stock arrangement is characterized by rather strict conditions. In practice, the arrangement may prove to be rather impractical. Article 17a(4) VAT Directive, for example, stipulates that an intra-Community B2Me transaction will take place irrespective of the arrangement if, within 12 months after the arrival of the goods in the Member State to which they were dispatched or transported, the goods have not been supplied to the taxable person for whom they were intended. Further, the call-off stock arrangement is not or no longer applicable in case the goods are lost, stolen or destroyed, and in case the goods are transported or dispatched to a country other than the Member State from which they have been initially moved. Such restrictions are undoubtedly intended to ensure that the goods in call-off stocks remain administratively traceable, yet for taxable persons, they may seem rigid and impractical.[112]

---

110. The call-off stock arrangement will be replaced by a OSS, which taxable persons can use to report all of their intra-Community B2Me transactions. *See* Proposal for a Council Directive amending Directive 2006/112/EC as regards VAT rules for the digital age, COM/2022/701 final. *See*: section 1.8.1.
111. This excerpt of the provision suggests that consignment stocks are not covered by the arrangement. Even though we have not verified this, the possibility exists that Member States introduce or maintain national simplification arrangements for consignment stock in addition to the call-off stock simplification embedded in the VAT Directive.
112. *See* M. Horsthuis & F.J.G. Nellen, *A Critical Analysis of the Quick Fixes for the EU Intra-Community B2B VAT System* (2019) 3 International VAT Monitor https://doi.org/10.59403/25gdm93.

13.6.7 Returned Goods

Sometimes, customers return goods to their suppliers. There can be various reasons for such returns. For example, the customer might refuse to accept the goods. The purchase agreement is annulled if the goods are returned for repair under a warranty agreement.

If goods were initially supplied to the customer from another Member State (i.e., an ICS took place), the reversal of such a supply may involve various administrative complications. For example, if the customer refuses to accept the goods, there is no 'normal' ICS, but rather an intra-Community B2Me supply. That implies that the supplier needs to register for VAT in the Member State to which the goods were transported, report an intra-Community B2Me acquisition and a subsequent intra-Community B2Me supply in that Member State back to the Member State from which the goods were transported in the first place.

At the 41st VAT Committee meeting, held on 28 February and 1 March 1994, the VAT Committee discussed the VAT consequences of a number of cases in which goods are returned to the supplier or are onwards supplied to a different customer shortly after they were sold to a customer in another Member State. The outcome of this meeting was published as part of the VAT Committee 'guidelines' which are not legally binding and only give guidance.[113] We refer the reader who is interested in the solutions devised by the VAT Committee to these guidelines.

13.7 INTRA-COMMUNITY B2B CHAIN SUPPLIES

In a supply chain consisting of multiple subsequent transactions, the same goods are supplied multiple times before they reach the private consumer. For VAT purposes, each supply in the supply chain is, in principle, assessed on its merits.[114] We refer to Figure 13.24; in this section, we will not elaborate on the last leg of the supply chain, the supply to the end-customer. In the example, the goods are transported twice: first in the course of the supply by A to B, and second in the course of the supply by B to C. Thus, here we have two ICSs of goods and ICAs since in the context of both supplies the goods are transported to another Member State.

113. https://ec.europa.eu/taxation_customs/business/vat/vat-committee_en (accessed 17 August 2024).

114. *See* however, CJEU 3 September 2015, Case C-526/13 *Fast Bunkering Klaipeda UAB v Valstybine mokesčių inspekcija prie Lietuvos Respublikos finansų ministerijos*, ECLI: EU:C:2015:536. We discussed the particularities of this case in section 3.2.4.3.

Figure 13.24 Intra-Community Chain Transaction: In the Context of Each Distinct Supply, the Goods Are Transported to Another Member State

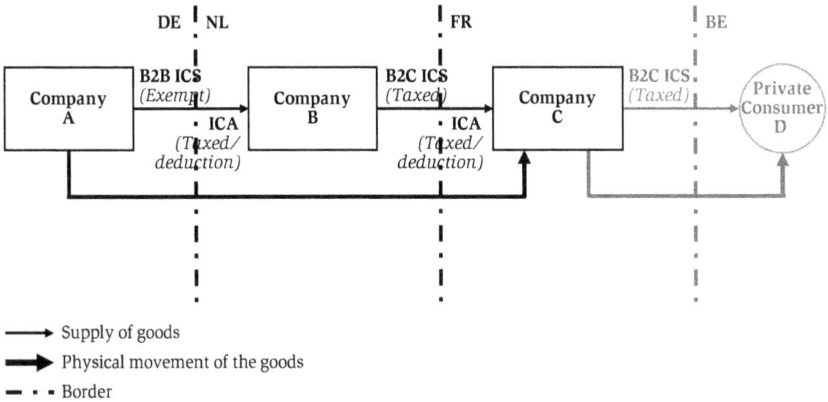

Having separate transport movements for each supply within a supply chain is not always practical and efficient. Additional transportation costs can often be avoided by transporting the goods directly from the first supplier to the ultimate buyer of the goods. In section 13.2.6, we depicted an example of a so-called chain transaction involving multiple supplies, yet only one transport movement. Figure 13.25 shows an example of an intra-Community B2B chain transaction.

Figure 13.25 Intra-Community B2B Chain Transaction: Goods Are Transported Directly from Company A to Company C. Assuming the Goods Are Transported by B or on His Behalf, the First Supply (Supply by A to B) Concerns the (Exempt) ICS (Article 36a(1) VAT Directive)

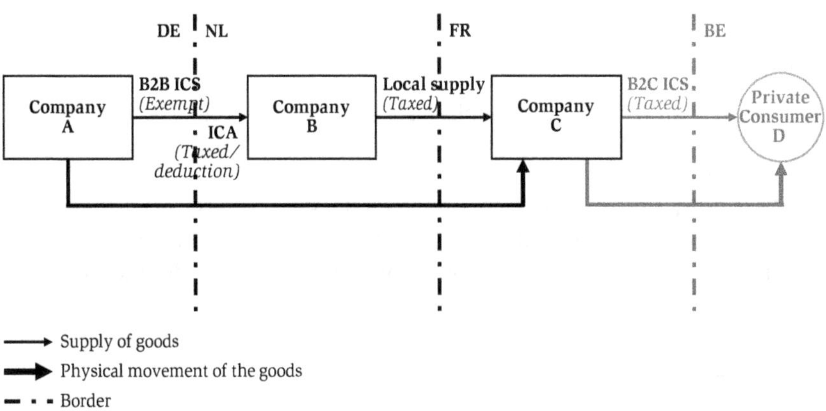

In this situation, there are two B2B supplies, yet the goods are only transported once. This has important VAT consequences, which we will explain below.

13.7.1 The VAT Consequences of Intra-Community B2B Chain Transactions

Even though each supply in the supply chain is, in principle, assessed on its merits, within chain transactions, the VAT treatment of all the supplies is interdependent. Following this, it is often difficult to establish the VAT consequences of intra-Community B2B chain transactions. In general, however, the following approach can be employed:

(1) Establish the number of supplies (transfers of the right to dispose of the goods as owner from one taxable person to the other) *and* establish the number of (integral) intra-Community transport movements.
(2) Ascribe each intra-Community transport movement to a separate supply. Each supply to which an intra-Community transport has been ascribed is treated as an ICS. All other supplies (i.e., to which no intra-Community transport has been ascribed) are treated as local supplies of goods.

We will elaborate on this approach below.

Establish the Number of Supplies and the Number of Transport Movements

In *EMAG*, the CJEU ruled that the dispatch or transport that takes place as part of the ICS can be ascribed to only one supply.[115] Thus, if there is only one physical movement of the goods from one Member State to the other, there can only be one ICS and acquisition. By definition, the other supply or supplies within the chain must be local supplies of goods.[116] This is fundamentally different from the situation in which the goods are transported more than once, for example, in the situation depicted in Figure 13.24,. In that situation, there are two transport movements, allowing both B2B supplies to qualify as ICSs. Conversely, in the situation depicted in Figure 13.25 (the intra-Community B2B chain transaction), either the supply by A to B *or* the supply by B to C can be an ICS. Now, the remaining task is to ascribe the transport to one of the supplies in order to establish which one is the ICS.

Ascribing the Intra-Community Transport Movement

In order to establish which of the supplies is the (exempted) ICS, one must determine to which of those supplies the transportation can be ascribed (assuming there is only one transport movement). Since 1 January 2020, the VAT Directive contains rules on the ascribing of transport in situations in which the same goods are supplied successively and transported from one Member State to another directly from the first supplier to the last customer in the chain. Article 36a VAT Directive provides the following:

115. CJEU 6 April 2006, Case C-245/04 *EMAG Handel Eder OHG v Finanzlandesdirektion für Kärnten*, ECLI:EU:C:2006:232.
116. The math is quite basic: if there are five supplies and two intra-Community transport movements, only two of the five supplies can qualify as ICSs/acquisitions. By definition, the other three supplies must be local supplies of goods.

(1) As a main rule, Article 36a(1) VAT Directive stipulates that the transport shall be ascribed only to the supply made *to* the 'intermediary operator' (so: to the supply by A to B, *see* Figure 13.25). The intermediary operator is defined as a supplier within the chain other than the first supplier who dispatches or transports the goods either himself or through a third party acting on his behalf (i.e., B, assuming he arranges transport).

(2) As an exception, Article 36a(2) VAT Directive provides that the transport shall be ascribed only to the supply of goods *by* the intermediary operator (so: to the supply by B to C) where the intermediary operator has communicated to his supplier (so: A) the VAT ID number issued to him (so: B) by the Member State from which the goods are dispatched or transported.

In our view, and in line with the explanatory notes of the VAT Expert Group, Article 36a VAT Directive is formulated in such a way that it cannot only be relied on in a three-party supply chain (i.e., A-B-C) but also in situations involving more than two successive supplies (e.g., A-B-C-D, A-B-C-D-E, etc.) as long as the conditions are fulfilled.[117]

In sum, Article 36a VAT Directive allows taxable persons to rely on a harmonized rule implemented for ascribing transport throughout the EU, thus promoting legal certainty and simplicity. However, the provision is tailored to situations in which the intermediary operator dispatches or transports the goods either himself or through a third party on his behalf. This means that there is no provision for ascribing transport in situations in which either party A or party C transports the goods. In this context, the European Commission has stated that '[n]o rule [...] is needed where the transport is made on behalf of the first supplier in the chain (in which case the transport can only be ascribed to the fist supply) or on behalf of the last taxable person in the chain (in which case the transport can only be ascribed to the supply made for that taxable person)'.[118] Irrespective of whether this notion is correct with regard to the current state of EU VAT law – in particular, the case law of the CJEU – we are of the opinion that the EU legislator should have also given clarification by adopting rules which govern situations in which the transport is executed by or on behalf of either party A or party C.

117. *See* M. Horsthuis & F.J.G. Nellen, *A Critical Analysis of the Quick Fixes for the EU Intra-Community B2B VAT System* (2019) 3 International VAT Monitor https://doi.org/10.59403/25gdm93; Explanatory Notes on the '2020 Quick Fixes', VAT Expert Group, 15 November 2019, VEG Nr. 084 REV1.

118. *See* Proposal for a Council Directive amending Directive 2006/112/EC as regards harmonizing and simplifying certain rules in the value added tax system and introducing the definitive system for the taxation of trade between Member States, COM (2017) 569 final, 4 October 2017, p. 13.

Before the adoption of Article 36a VAT Directive, transport allocation was based on an elaborate doctrine of the CJEU. Especially in *Euro Tyre*, the Court provided guidance on ascribing the transport in situations involving chain transactions. It noted that parties should carry out 'an overall assessment of all the specific circumstances from which it is possible to determine which supply fulfils all the conditions relating to an intra-Community supply'. Further, it followed from paragraph 33 of the judgment that in case the right to dispose of the goods concerning the second supply (i.e., the supply by party B to party C in a three-party chain transaction) took place in the Member State in which the transport had started, the transport could no longer be ascribed to the first supply (thus making the second supply the ICS). The question is whether the transport allocation doctrine developed by the CJEU has, for all situations, been outdated by the adoption of Article 36a VAT Directive.[119]

13.7.2 The STS (Simplified Scheme for A-B-C Transactions)

Shortly after the introduction of the 'transitional' regime for ICTs on 1 January 1993, Member States realized that the VAT treatment of chain transactions might lead to undesirable administrative burdens for businesses. For instance, in the example depicted in Figure 13.25, company B had to register for VAT in France and to report an ICA in its French VAT return. With respect to a particular type of transaction, the so-called triangular ICTs, the VAT Directive contains a special regime: the 'simplified triangulation scheme'. This triangulation scheme is scattered over three provisions in the VAT Directive: Articles 42, 141 and 197 VAT Directive. In this subsection, we elaborate on this scheme.

13.7.2.1 'Triangulation'

In practice, the regime contained in Articles 42, 141 and 197 VAT Directive is referred to as the simplified 'triangulation' scheme. The word 'triangulation' seems to stem from a certain way of depicting chain transactions involving three parties (*see* Figure 13.26).

119. CJEU 16 December 2010, Case C-430/09 *Euro Tyre Holding BV v Staatssecretaris van Financiën*, ECLI:EU:C:2010:786. *See also* CJEU 26 July 2017, Case C-386/16 *Toridas UAB*, ECLI: EU:C:2017:599.

Figure 13.26 Traditional Way to Depict a Chain Transaction Involving Three Parties. The Hypotenuse Symbolizes the Physical Movement of the Goods, Whereas the Other Two Edges Symbolize the Supplies of the Goods

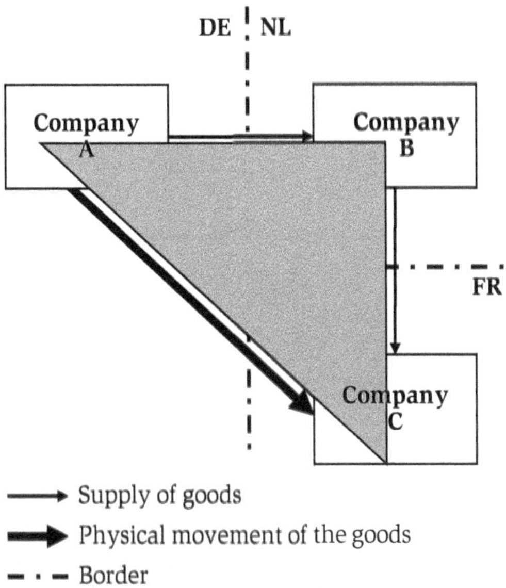

In our view, there are no compelling reasons for depicting chain transactions involving three parties like this. Therefore, we will not use this method of depicting 'triangular' supplies in this chapter, even though we will use the terms 'triangular' and 'triangulation'.

In this book, we use a linear method of depicting supply chains (Figure 13.27).

Figure 13.27 Linear Method to Depict a Chain Transaction Involving Three Parties. This Is the Method Used in This Book

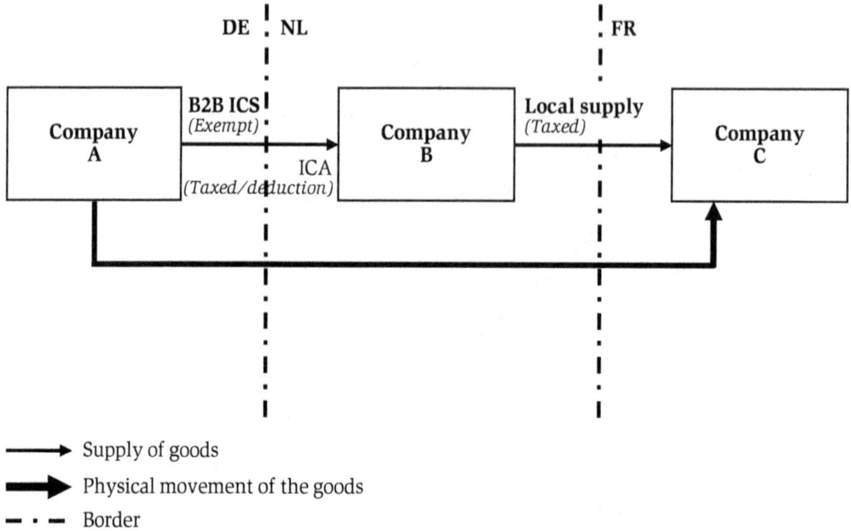

In this example, company A, established in Member State A (Germany), makes a supply of goods to company B, established in Member State B (the Netherlands). Subsequently, company B supplies those goods to company C, established in Member State C (France). The goods are directly transported by company A from Member State A (Germany) to Member State C (France).

13.7.2.2 Purpose and Functioning of the STS

The main purpose of the STS is to prevent company B (the middleman) from having to register for VAT and fulfil administrative obligations in the Member State of arrival of the goods (France, *see* Figure 13.28). To this end, the VAT Directive sets out the following measures:

(1) No VAT is charged on the ICA by company B in the Member State of arrival (France, in Figure 13.28).
(2) The reverse charge mechanism applies to the local supply by company B to C in the Member State of arrival (France, in Figure 13.28).
(3) Company B does not make a number acquisition in his own Member State (the Netherlands, in Figure 13.28).

Figure 13.28 Simplified Triangulation Scheme (STS)

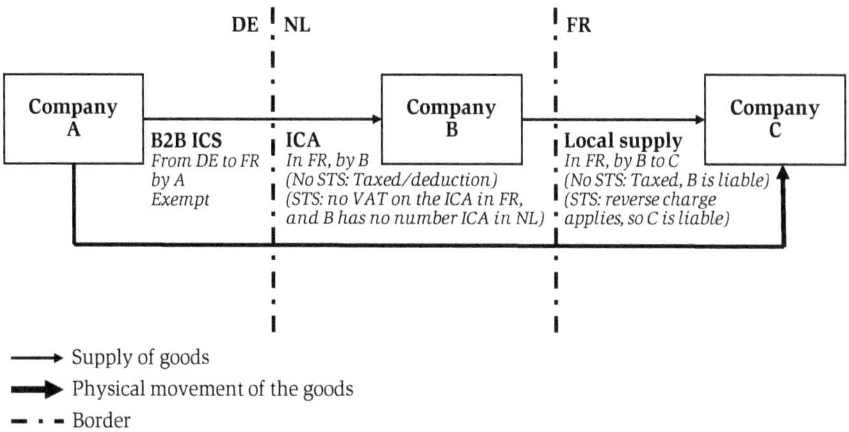

In the following sections, we will elaborate on these measures in the context of the STS.

13.7.2.2.1 No VAT Is Charged on the ICA by Company B

Article 141 VAT Directive provides that 'no VAT is charged' on the ICA by B in the Member State of arrival of the goods (France in the example depicted in Figure 13.28). The wording of this provision suggests that the ICA is outside the scope of VAT (non-taxable), but leaves room for the conclusion that the ICA is, in fact, exempt. After all, Article 141 VAT Directive is placed under the heading 'Exemptions for intra-Community acquisitions of goods'. Moreover, the reference in Article 262 VAT Directive to Article 42 VAT Directive indicates that company B makes a taxable acquisition. Therefore, we believe that Article 141 VAT Directive contains an exemption (with a right of deduction).[120] In any case, company B in the supply chain does not need to report an ICA in the Member State of arrival of the goods.

Article 141 VAT Directive implies that the STS can only apply if the transportation of the goods is to be attributed to the first supply (by company A to company B) in the supply chain.[121] If the transportation is to be attributed to the second supply in the supply chain (supply by company B to company C), company B is regarded as making a local purchase of goods in Member State A (Germany, in the example depicted in Figure 13.28), followed by an ICS in Member State A to company C. Subsequently, the latter effects an ICA of the goods in the Member State of arrival (or Member State C, i.e.,

120. Strangely enough, the VAT Directive (*see* Article 168(c) and Article 169(b) VAT Directive) does not explicitly provide for a right of deduction in respect of ICAs exempted under Article 141 VAT Directive.
121. *See also* Article 36a VAT Directive, which contains a presumption to this effect in situations in which the transport is arranged by B (intermediary operator) or on his behalf.

France). Thus, under those circumstances, B has an obligation to register for VAT and to report an ICS in Member State A (Germany). Article 141 VAT Directive only removes the obligation to report an ICA of the goods in the Member State of arrival of the goods. It does not remove any obligation to report an ICS in the Member State of departure of the goods. Therefore, we hold that the STS can only be applied if the first transaction (supply by company A to company B) is an ICS of goods (i.e., the transportation of the goods to the Member State of C is carried out in the course of the supply by A to B).

13.7.2.2.2 *The Reverse Charge Mechanism Applies to the Local Supply by Company B*

Under the simplified triangulation rules, the second supply by company B to company C is a local supply in the Member State of arrival of the goods (France) because it is considered that the supply by B to C followed in time on the supply by A to B.[122] Since the ICA of the goods took place in C's Member State (France), the subsequent supply by B to C was also considered to take place in that Member State. To prevent B from having to register for VAT in that Member State (France), and to charge local French VAT on his invoice to company C, the reverse charge mechanism applies (Article 197 VAT Directive). The customer, company C, must self-assess for the VAT on the supply and can deduct the VAT in his VAT return insofar as he uses the goods for this taxed activity. Further, the CJEU judgment in *Luxury Trust Automobil GmbH* has made it clear that, in order to correctly apply the triangulation simplification, the intermediary party (i.e., B) must issue an invoice containing the proper reference 'Reverse charge' (cf. Article 226(11a) VAT Directive), so that the final customer (party C) is made properly aware of his tax obligations.[123]

13.7.2.2.3 *Company B Does Not Make a Number Acquisition*

If the STS is applied, B does not effect a 'number acquisition' in Member State B (*see* Article 42 VAT Directive), which also contributes to the simplification of the administrative obligations B needs to fulfil.

13.7.2.3 *Conditions to the STS*

Article 141 VAT Directive contains the following conditions for the application of the STS:

122. CJEU 16 December 2010, Case C-430/09 *Euro Tyre Holding BV v Staatssecretaris van Financiën*, ECLI:EU:C:2010:786, para. 23.
123. CJEU 8 December 2022, Case C-247/21 *Luxury Trust Automobil GmbH v Finanzamt Österreich*, ECLI:EU:C:2022:966.

(a) the acquisition of goods is made by a taxable person (party B) who is not established in the Member State concerned but is identified for VAT purposes in another Member State;

(b) the acquisition of goods is made for the purposes of the subsequent supply of those goods, in the Member State concerned, by the taxable person referred to in point (a) (so: party B);

(c) the goods thus acquired by the taxable person referred to in point (a) (so: party B) are directly dispatched or transported, from a Member State other than that in which he is identified for VAT purposes, to the person for whom he is to carry out the subsequent supply (so: party C);[124]

(d) the person to whom the subsequent supply is to be made (party C) is another taxable person, or a non-taxable legal person, who is identified for VAT purposes in the Member State concerned;

(e) the person referred to in point (d) (so: party C) has been designated in accordance with Article 197 as liable for payment of the VAT due on the supply carried out by the taxable person who is not established in the Member State in which the tax is due (part B).

In addition to Article 141 VAT Directive, and with the purpose of preventing a number acquisition by company B, Article 42 VAT Directive sets out the following conditions:

(a) the person acquiring the goods (party B) establishes that he has made the ICA for the purposes of a subsequent supply, within the territory of the Member State identified in accordance with Article 40, for which the person to whom the supply is made (party C) has been designated in accordance with Article 197 as liable for payment of VAT;

(b) the person acquiring the goods (party B) has satisfied the obligations laid down in Article 265 relating to the submission of the recapitulative statement.[125]

Moreover, Article 265 VAT Directive contains obligations with respect to the EC sales listing that B needs to file in Member State B (the Netherlands, in the example).

Below, we will elaborate on each set of conditions.

---

124. We note that the CJEU has held that this criterion has been met where party B: (a) is resident and identified for VAT purposes in the Member State from which the goods are transported, yet (b) uses the VAT ID number of another Member State for that specific ICA. In other words: the VAT identification refers to the specific VAT ID number used by party B in the context of the transaction subject to the triangulation simplification. *See* CJEU 19 April 2018, Case C-580/16 *Firma Hans Bühler KG*, ECLI:EU:C:2018:261, para. 43.

125. In CJEU 19 April 2018, Case C-580/16 *Firma Hans Bühler KG*, ECLI:EU:C:2018:261, the Court has provided that obligations concerning recapitulative statements must be regarded as being formal. Moreover, the tax authorities of a Member State cannot, in principle, tax an ICA solely on the ground that the acquirer has not submitted in good time a duly completed recapitulative statement relating to the transaction.

13.7.2.3.1 Conditions with Respect to the Exemption of the ICA

Following Article 141 VAT Directive, company B's ICA in Member State C (France, in the example depicted in Figure 13.28) can only be exempt if:

(a) company B is not established in Member State C (France) but is registered for VAT in another Member State (e.g., Member State B, the Netherlands in the example);
(b) company B's ICA in Member State C (France) is followed by a local supply of those goods in Member State C;
(c) the goods are directly moved from a Member State (e.g., Member State A, Germany in the example), other than the Member State in which B is registered (e.g., Member State B, the Netherlands in the example)[126] to company C;
(d) company C is a taxable person, or a non-taxable legal person, who is identified for VAT purposes in Member State C (France);
(e) company C must self-assess for the VAT on the local supply by company B to company C in Member State C (France) under Article 197 VAT Directive.

The conditions listed above imply that the simplified triangulation regime can only be applied if there are three companies involved in three different Member States. The 'intermediary operator' must not be established in Member State C, and the goods must physically move directly from Member State A to Member State C. We note that the simplified triangulation rules do in principle[127] not apply if two, four or more parties are involved in the chain transaction.

Lastly, we note that Article 141 VAT Directive does not stipulate that the simplified triangulation rules cannot be applied if B does not use his VAT ID number of the Member State where he is established but uses a foreign VAT registration instead. Article 141 VAT Directive only prohibits company B from being *established* in Member State C. For that reason, some Member States allow the application of the simplified triangulation rules if company B has a VAT ID in Member State C (but is not established in that Member State).

126. We note that the CJEU has held that the triangulation simplification can still be applied if party B has a VAT registration the Member State from which the goods are transported; he should only not use it in the context of the transaction at hand. *See* CJEU 19 April 2018, Case C-580/16 *Firma Hans Bühler KG*, ECLI:EU:C:2018:261, para. 43.
127. Subject to conditions, there are situations in which the simplified triangulation rules can be applied, even if there are more than three parties in the supply chain (so-called quadrangulation). *See:* Explanatory Notes on the EU VAT changes in respect of call-off stock arrangements, chain transactions and the exemption for intra-Community supplies of goods ('2020 Quick Fixes'), para. 3.6.17, available from: https://taxation-customs.ec.europa.eu/document/download/d7d6f1be-1247-4e65-b303-a06512bcbe6c_en?filename=explanatory_notes_2020_quick_fixes_en.pdf (accessed 17 August 2024).

13.7.2.3.2 Conditions with Respect to the Exception to the Number Acquisition

The purpose of Article 42 VAT Directive is to prevent B from having a number acquisition in Member State B. Indeed, it would be troublesome for B to show under Article 41, second paragraph VAT Directive that VAT is applied to the acquisition in Member State C, in order for him to get a reduction of the taxable amount of the number acquisition. After all, under the simplified triangulation rules, the acquisition in Member State C is VAT-exempt! Therefore, it makes sense that Article 42 VAT Directive stipulates that there is no number acquisition if the simplified triangulation regime is applied.

However, Article 42 VAT Directive in combination with CJEU jurisprudence requires that:

(a) company B makes in ICA in Member State C, and the VAT on the subsequent local supply in that Member State is reverse charged to company C under Article 197 VAT Directive;
(b) company B reports an ICS(!) on its EC sales list in Member State B (i.e., the Netherlands in the example depicted in Figure 13.28). We refer to section 13.7.2.3.3 below;
(c) company B must issue an invoice containing the proper reference 'Reverse charge' (cf. Article 226(11a) VAT Directive), so that the final customer (party C) is made properly aware of his tax obligations.[128]

13.7.2.3.3 Conditions with Respect to the EC Sales List of Company B

The VAT Directive contains various formal requirements with respect to the EC sales list (EC Sales Listing or recapitulative statement) that B needs to file in Member State B.

At first sight, it may seem to be incorrect that B needs to file an EC sales list. After all, the application of the simplified triangulation regime implies that company A carries out an ICS in the Member State of departure (i.e., Germany in the example depicted in Figure 13.28). B has made no ICS whatsoever, and the ICA by B in the Member State of arrival of the goods does not need to be reported. Nonetheless, Article 262(b) VAT Directive stipulates that a taxable person must file a recapitulative statement reporting 'the persons identified for VAT purposes to whom he has supplied goods which were supplied to him by way of intra-Community acquisitions referred to in Article 42'. With the words 'intra-Community acquisitions referred to in Article 42 VAT Directive', Article 262(b) VAT Directive clearly relates to the ICA by company B in the Member State of arrival of the goods (i.e., France in the example depicted in Figure 13.28). It does not refer to a number acquisition by B in Member State B (the

128. *See* CJEU 8 December 2022, Case C-247/21 *Luxury Trust Automobil GmbH v Finanzamt Österreich*, ECLI:EU:C:2022:966.

Netherlands) because Article 42 VAT Directive explicitly states that there is no number acquisition in the event that the STS applies.

Article 265 VAT Directive stipulates the items of information that B needs to disclose by means of his recapitulative statement:

(1) His VAT ID number issued by the Member State of identification (i.e., the Netherlands in the example depicted in Figure 13.28) and under which he made the acquisition and subsequent supply of goods.
(2) The VAT ID number, in the Member State in which dispatch or transport of the goods ended (i.e., France), of the person to whom the subsequent supply was made (party C) by the taxable person (party B).
(3) For each person to whom the subsequent supply was made (so: party C1, party C2, etc.), the total value, exclusive of VAT, of the supplies made by the taxable person (party B) in the Member State in which dispatch or transport of the goods ended (i.e., France).

Even though from a business administrative point of view, these administrative obligations for company B may seem (over)complicated, it is not difficult to explain the rationale of these requirements. The reasons are the following. On the basis of Article 262(a) VAT Directive, company A must submit an EC sales list in Member State A (Germany) in which it reports the ICS to company B. To this end, company A reports in its EC sales list, company B's VAT ID number (in Member State B, the Netherlands in the example) and the total value of the supplies of goods to company B. In order to match this transaction in the EU VIES system,[129] company B would need to report an ICA of goods in Member State C. However, on the basis of the triangulation simplification, the ICA in Member State C is exempt, and company B makes no number acquisition in Member State B at all. This is bound to lead to mismatches when Member States exchange information on these transactions. Therefore, the legislator has adopted Article 265 VAT Directive. Following the formal requirements contained therein, the supply by company A, reported in A's VAT return and EC sales list in Member State A, can be matched with company B's 'special' reportings on company B's EC sales list in Member State B, thus resolving the mismatch.[130]

13.8 INTRA-COMMUNITY C2C SUPPLIES OF NEW MEANS OF TRANSPORT

The EU legislator feared that in the case of new means of transport, private individuals would adversely exploit VAT rate differences between Member States. The EU institutions believed that such individuals would purchase cars in Member States with

129. Member States maintain electronic databases containing the VAT registration data of all taxable persons, which are aggregated in one centralized European administration (the 'VIES').
130. It should be noted that some Member States would require, or formerly would have required, company B to report an ICA and a subsequent ICS in its VAT return in Member State B. However, this does not seem to be in line with the provisions in the VAT Directive.

relatively low VAT rates, only to sell these onwards to other consumers in Member States with relatively high VAT rates. In order to counter this (perceived) 'VAT rate shopping', a special regime for intra-Community C2C supplies of new means of transport was adopted.[131]

The special regime only applies to new means of transport. Article 2(2)(a) VAT Directive defines the term 'means of transport'. It encompasses motorized land vehicles, vessels and aircraft, which meet the specific requirements laid down in the mentioned provision. Moreover, these vehicles, vessels and aircraft should be intended for the transport of persons or goods.

Article 2(2)(b) VAT Directive builds further on the concept of 'means of transport' by indicating when a 'means of transport' must be regarded as 'new'. For each type of means of transport, two alternative criteria are in place to establish whether a means of transport is new. The first criterion relates to the period of use, whereas the second one relates to the extent of the use.

Under the special regime, the private consumer or any other non-taxable person (*see* section 13.5 on B2H supplies) who, on an occasional basis, supplies a new means of transport, which is dispatched or transported to the customer by the vendor or the customer, or on behalf of the vendor or the customer, to a destination outside the territory of a Member State but within the territory of the Community, is regarded as a taxable person (Article 9(2) VAT Directive). Thus, it does not matter whether the means of transport are dispatched or transported to the customer by the vendor or the customer, or on behalf of the vendor or the customer. The supply to the customer in another Member State is exempt under Article 138(2)(a) VAT Directive.[132] In *Santogal M-Comércio*, the CJEU has ruled that authorities cannot make the application of the exemption dependent on the condition that the purchaser of the new means of transport is established or domiciled in the Member State of destination. Also, the exemption cannot be denied on the sole ground that that means of transport has been registered only temporarily in the Member State of destination.[133]

Because the non-taxable person/supplier who performs an ICS of a new means of transport is regarded as a taxable person, this person is also be entitled to deduct input VAT incurred in respect of that supply. Article 172(1) VAT Directive specifically provides for a right of deduction in this respect. According to this provision, a person supplying a new means of transport is entitled to deduct the VAT included in the purchase price or paid in respect of the importation or the ICA of this means of

131. In CJEU 14 June 2017, Case C-26/16 *Santogal M-Comércio e Reparação de Automóveis Lda v Autoridade Tributária e Aduaneira*, ECLI:EU:C:2017:453, the Court has explained that in addition to covering the allocation of authority to tax, the rules on the taxation of acquisitions of new means of transport aim to prevent distortions of competition between the Member States liable to result from the application of differing rates of tax (para. 39).
132. *See* Article 2 VAT Implementing Regulation with respect to transfers of new means of transport by non-taxable persons and returns of new means of transport by non-taxable persons to the Member State from which the means of transport was initially supplied to those non-taxable persons. It is considered that such transfers and returns do not constitute ICAs, provided that the exemption in Article 138(2)(a) VAT Directive does not apply.
133. CJEU 14 June 2017, Case C-26/16 *Santogal M-Comércio e Reparação de Automóveis Lda v Autoridade Tributária e Aduaneira*, ECLI:EU:C:2017:453.

transport. However, the deduction of the input VAT is capped. It may only be deducted up to an amount not exceeding the amount of VAT for which this person would be liable if the supply were not to be exempted. Although this limitation does not seem to be in line with the VAT deduction mechanism concept, which allows a trader to be fully relieved of input VAT, the limitation should be understood in the context of the prevention of distortion of competition. Without a capped right to deduct input VAT, distortion of competition can still arise as, for example, a car can be purchased in a low VAT rate Member State and then sold at a relatively low price to a customer in a higher VAT rate Member State. In case of a non-capped deduction of input VAT, all VAT on the purchase of the car would be deductible, whereas VAT would only be due with respect to the very low price. Capping the amount of input VAT deduction to the amount of VAT, which would be due in case of a regular, not zero-rated, supply, prevents this type of VAT saving scheme. A right of deduction shall arise and may be exercised only at the time of supply of the new means of transport. Further to Article 172(2) VAT Directive, Member States must lay down detailed rules for the implementation of the aforementioned input VAT deduction regime.

In the Member State of arrival of the new means of transport, the customer is regarded as making a taxable ICA on the basis of Article 2(1)(b)(ii) VAT Directive. By means of this provision, taxation in the Member State of destination is realized –against the VAT rate applicable there. For an ICA of a new means of transport to take place, it is not necessary that the person acquiring the means of transport qualifies as a taxable person for VAT purposes. However, in connection with an ICS of a new means of transport, non-taxable persons are regarded as taxable persons pursuant to Article 9(2) VAT Directive. Non-taxable persons acquiring new means of transport should report VAT due in respect of the ICA in the Member State of arrival of these goods and are not entitled to deduct this VAT. The overall VAT position is thus similar to a local purchase of a new means of transport, which is in line with the destination principle and prevents distortion of competition. Following Article 210 VAT Directive, Member States shall adopt arrangements for payment of VAT on ICAs of new means of transport.

13.9 DEEMED ICAs

Articles 20, second paragraph, 21, 22 and 23 VAT Directive extend the scope of the concept of 'ICAs'. Under these provisions, the following activities or events are also regarded as ICAs:

(1) ICAs of goods by non-legal persons following importation.
(2) ICAs of goods by NATO.
(3) the application of goods for business use.
(4) ICAs as pendant to deemed internal or self-supplies.

In this section, we will highlight the most prominent features of these specific types of ICAs.

13.9.1 ICAs of Goods by Non-taxable Legal Persons Following Importation

If a non-taxable person purchases goods outside the EU, the goods will need to be imported once they enter the EU (*see* Chapter 14). It may happen that the goods enter the EU in a Member State different from that in which the non-taxable person is established. That does not prevent the physical movement of the goods being considered as a single shipment of the goods. For example, the mere fact that goods are transferred from a boat to a truck does not mean that a new leg of the transport starts when the goods are loaded on the truck. After all, under such circumstances, there is continuity in the course of the transaction, and there is a temporal and material link between the supply of the goods and the transport of those goods.[134]

Disregarding the specific measures taken in Article 20, second paragraph VAT Directive, the VAT consequences are that the supply by the non-EU supplier is considered as taking place outside the EU (Article 32, first paragraph VAT Directive), but that the non-taxable person makes a taxed importation of goods in the Member State of importation. The VAT on that importation is not deductible because the importer is not a taxable person. The transfer of the goods to another Member State (the Member State where the non-taxable person is established) is not a deemed ICS under Article 17 VAT Directive. First of all, there is only one transportation of the goods (taking place in the course of the supply by the non-EU supplier), and second, Article 17 VAT Directive only applies to taxable persons. Therefore, when the goods arrive in the Member State of the non-taxable person, there will be no taxable ICA. Then, the destination principle is not adhered to. Additionally, without any reporting of an ICS and ICA of the goods, it is difficult for the tax authorities to monitor the physical movement of the goods across the EU borders. Moreover, if no additional measures apply, non-taxable persons could save VAT by importing goods in Member States with relatively low VAT rates. This would not be in line with the principle of neutrality.[135]

For these reasons, Article 20, second paragraph VAT Directive provides that where goods acquired by a non-taxable legal person are dispatched or transported from a third territory or a third country and imported by that non-taxable legal person into a Member State other than the Member State in which dispatch or transport of the goods ends, the goods shall be regarded as having been dispatched or transported from the Member State of importation. Thus, Article 20, second paragraph VAT Directive 'creates' a (separate) transportation of the goods from one Member State to the other. As a consequence, the first paragraph of Article 20 VAT Directive applies. On the basis of Article 20, first paragraph VAT Directive, there is an ICA of goods because the non-taxable person (1) acquires the right to dispose as owner of (2) movable tangible property dispatched or transported to the person acquiring the goods (3) by or on

134. Cf. CJEU 18 November 2010, Case C-84/09 *X v Skatteverket*, ECLI:EU:C:2010:693, para. 33 and CJEU 2 October 2014, Case C-446/13 *Fonderie 2A v Ministre de l'Économie et des Finances*, ECLI:EU:C:2014:2252.

135. We note that the importation of goods, such as new means of transport, by private consumers, not being legal persons, in another (low VAT rate) Member State is not covered by these rules. Private consumers can still choose the Member State with the most advantageous VAT rate to import goods that are ultimately sent to another Member State.

behalf of the vendor or the person acquiring the goods (4) in a Member State other than that in which dispatch or transport of the goods began. However, in general, a non-taxable legal person cannot make a taxable ICA (*see* sections 13.4 and 13.5). Nonetheless, as we explained in section 13.5, there are situations in which non-taxable legal persons *can* make an ICA. This is the case if the threshold for intra-Community purchases by non-taxable legal persons is exceeded, or if the non-taxable legal person opted to be treated as a taxable person (*see* Article 3(2) and 3(3) VAT Directive, explained in section 13.5 on B2H supplies). Consequently, the combination of Article 20, second paragraph VAT Directive and the rules on intra-Community B2H supplies have the effect that the non-taxable legal person will have to report a (taxed) ICA in the Member State of arrival of the goods if the threshold is exceeded or in case he opted to be treated as a taxable person. The VAT on this ICA will not be deductible because the acquirer is not a taxable person.

Absent any further regulations, this mechanism would amount to double taxation since the importation is also a taxable event, and the VAT on importation is non-deductible. To prevent such double taxation, Article 20, second paragraph VAT Directive stipulates that Member State must grant the importer a refund of the import VAT, provided that the importer establishes that VAT has been applied to the acquisition in the Member State in which dispatch or transport of the goods ends.

13.9.2 ICAs of Goods by NATO

Article 22 VAT Directive contains a special rule on acquisitions of goods by the armed forces of a NATO party. This provision follows from the fact that, subject to conditions, the importation, ICA and/or local supply of goods in a Member State (e.g., France) by the NATO forces of another Member State (e.g., Germany) are exempt. If such goods have not been 'subject to the general rules governing taxation on the domestic market of a Member State' and are at some point transferred to another Member State (e.g., Germany), Article 22 VAT Directive prevents the goods from remaining VAT-free. Upon application in the Member State of arrival of the goods (e.g., Germany), an ICA is deemed to take place. Insofar as the goods are used for taxed transactions, Article 168(d) VAT Directive allows for the deduction of the VAT on the acquisition.

13.9.3 ICAs of Goods: Application for Business Use

In our view, Article 21 VAT Directive is the pendant to the so-called intra-Community B2Me supplies (*see* section 13.6.3). We have already discussed the intra-Community B2Me supplies and their pendant, the intra-Community B2Me acquisitions, under Article 21 VAT Directive in section 13.6.4. Therefore, we refer to section 13.6.

13.9.4 ICAs of Goods: Pendants of Deemed Internal/Self-Supplies

As mentioned above in sections 13.3.3.2.6, 13.6.2 and 13.6.4.1, the purpose of Article 23 VAT Directive is not clear. It could be that it covers the ICAs that follow on a transfer of own goods by a taxable person to another Member State (intra-Community B2Me supply under Article 17(1) VAT Directive, *see* section 13.6.3). However, Article 21 VAT Directive seems better suitable to cover such ICAs.

Possibly, Article 23 VAT Directive aims at preventing situations of non-taxation, which are caused by different national interpretations or different implementations of provisions in the VAT Directive. For example, a transaction that is considered to be a supply of services in Member State A (e.g., Spain) may be considered to be a supply of goods in Member State B (e.g., Italy). Another example is that an ICT may fall within the scope of the no-supply rule of Articles 19 and 29 VAT Directive in one Member State (e.g., Spain) but not in the other Member State (e.g., Italy). The goal of Article 23 VAT Directive could then be to treat goods purchased locally (e.g., in Italy) equally to goods purchased in another Member State (e.g., Spain). However, this potential purpose of Article 23 VAT Directive makes Article 16 VAT Implementing Regulation redundant. Article 16, first paragraph VAT Implementing Regulation provides that where an ICA of goods within the meaning of Article 20 VAT Directive has taken place, the Member State in which the dispatch or transport ends shall exercise its power of taxation irrespective of the VAT treatment applied to the transaction in the Member State in which the dispatch or transport began.

In section 3.2.4.4, we discussed the purpose and scope of the so-called self-supplies. The goal of self-supplies is to tax the application for private use of goods for which VAT was deducted. It could be that Article 23 VAT Directive aims at taxing goods forming part of his business that a taxable person applies *in another Member State* for his private use or for that of his staff, or their disposal free of charge or, more generally, their application for purposes other than those of his business (cf. Article 16 VAT Directive).

To sum it up, we cannot but conclude that it is unclear in what situations Article 23 VAT Directive applies. Since, in practice, this hardly seems to be an issue, we are inclined to the view that Article 23 VAT Directive is a redundant provision.

13.10 MISCELLANEOUS ICSS SUBJECT TO SPECIFIC VAT TREATMENT

13.10.1 Excise Goods

In principle, the VAT regime for ICTs applies to all types of goods. However, for excise goods, a special regime is in place. Which goods should be regarded as excise goods are determined in Article 2(3) VAT Directive. 'Products subject to excise duty' are energy products, alcohol and alcoholic beverages and manufactured tobacco, as defined in Article 1(1) of the Excise Directive 2008/118/EC.[136] Article 2(3) VAT Directive excludes from the scope of the term gas supplied through the natural gas distribution system, and electricity.

On the basis of Article 2(b)(iii) VAT Directive, the ICA of excise goods, where the excise duty on the ICA is chargeable pursuant to Directive 92/12/EEC (which has been

136. Council Directive 2008/118/EC of 16 December 2008 concerning the general arrangements for excise duty and repealing Directive 92/12/EEC [2009] OJ L 9/13.

replaced by Directive 2020/262), by a taxable person or a non-taxable legal person, whose other acquisitions are not subject to VAT pursuant to Article 3(1) VAT Directive, is subject to VAT.

The ICA of excise goods by farmers, fully exempt taxable persons and non-taxable legal persons is always taxable, even if the acquisitions do not exceed the threshold of EUR 10,000 for (*see* section 13.4.2.2.2). Following Article 210 VAT Directive, Member States shall adopt arrangements for payment of VAT on ICAs of excise goods.

The ICS of excise goods to the aforementioned categories of customers is VAT-exempt with a right of deduction, provided that the excise goods have been dispatched or transported under a regime for postponed payment of excise duties.

The VAT Directive does not consider the ICA of excise goods by private individuals as a taxable transaction subject to VAT. As excise goods are also explicitly excluded from the threshold under the distance sales scheme (*see* section 13.4.2.2.2), this regime *automatically* applies to supplies of excise goods to private individuals in other Member States. Pursuant to Article 34(1)(a) VAT Directive, the place of supply of excise goods lies in the Member State of arrival of these goods in case of a supply to a private individual established in that Member State. As a result, taxation takes place in accordance with the destination principle.

13.10.2 Small Enterprises

Article 281 VAT Directive allows Member States to introduce a special scheme for small enterprises (*see* section 15.2).

13.10.2.1 ICSs by Small Enterprises

The ICS of goods by a taxable person applying a small enterprise scheme is treated differently from the ICS of goods by a regular taxable person. Pursuant to Article 139(1) VAT Directive, the VAT exemption with right of deduction for ICSs of goods does not apply to the supply of goods carried out by taxable persons who are covered by the exemption for small enterprises.[137] Arguably, the subsequent ICA in the Member State of arrival of the goods is exempt on the basis of Article 140(a) VAT Directive.

137. From 1 January 2025, a revised SME scheme will apply. In the context of the legislative changes, also the provisions discussed in this section are amended. The legal effect remains largely the same, however. *See* Council Directive (EU) 2020/285 of 18 February 2020 amending Directive 2006/112/EC on the common system of value added tax as regards the special scheme for small enterprises and Regulation (EU) No 904/2010 as regards the administrative cooperation and exchange of information for the purpose of monitoring the correct application of the special scheme for small enterprises [2020] OJ L 62/13.

13.10.2.2 ICAs by Small Enterprises

As regards the ICA of goods, however, a taxable person applying a small enterprise scheme is treated equal to a regular taxable person. Subsequent to the ICS to a small enterprise, the ICA of goods by the small enterprise is subject to VAT in the Member State of arrival of the goods.

13.11 CAROUSEL FRAUD; A NEW SYSTEM FOR INTRA-COMMUNITY B2B TRADE IN GOODS?

The EU VAT system is susceptible to fraud and tax evasion. A very simple way for a business to commit VAT fraud is to charge VAT on an invoice, collect the VAT from the customer, and not remit that VAT to the tax authorities. The customer will deduct the VAT on the invoice, as a result of which the Member State not only misses out on the VAT revenue but also incurs a cost because of the VAT it refunds to the customer. Generally, the tax authorities will detect such a scheme and quickly end it. However, in practice, fraudsters tend to set up more advanced schemes to conceal their fraud and tax evasion. Often, such schemes involve multiple entities and various Member States.

13.11.1 Carousel Fraud Explained

In its basic form, a more advanced VAT fraud scheme – generally referred to as carousel fraud or Missing Trader Intra-Community (MTIC) fraud – is depicted in Figure 13.29.

Figure 13.29 A Basic Example of Carousel Fraud

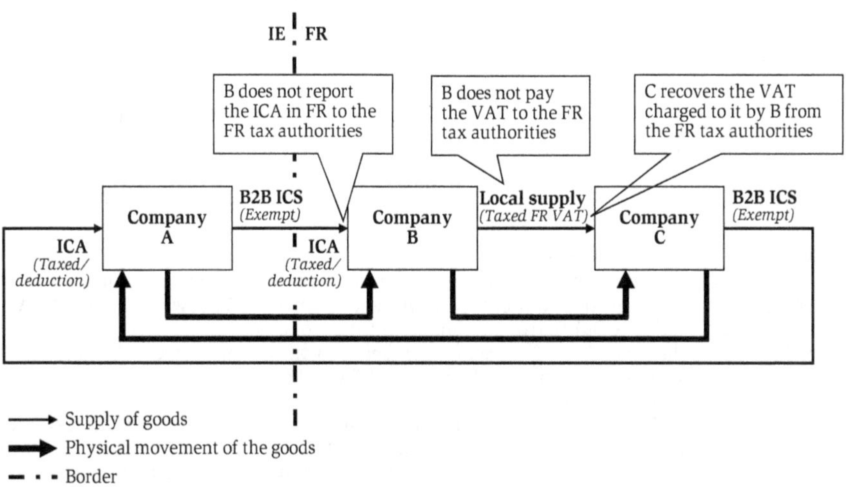

In this VAT fraud scheme, company A, established in Ireland, supplies goods to company B in France. The goods are transported from Ireland to France in the course of the supply. The supply by company A is treated as an exempt ICS in Ireland. Company B should report an ICA in France but does not do so, in order to stay out of sight of the tax authorities. Subsequently, company B supplies the goods to company C, which is also located in France. The supply is a local supply of goods, and B charges local French VAT on its invoice to company C. C pays the purchase price and the VAT mentioned on the invoice to B. However, B does not remit the VAT collected from C to the French tax authorities. Company C deducts the VAT mentioned on B's invoice because the purchase is directly attributable to the subsequent ICS in France, which company C makes to company A in Ireland. Company A then supplies the same goods again to company B in France, and the scheme is up for another 'round'. For this reason, this type of fraud is often referred to as 'carousel fraud'. By the time the tax authorities find out that company B is a fraudster, that company will 'disappear', making it impossible for the tax authorities to collect VAT. Often, company B is referred to as the 'missing trader', and for that reason, this type of fraud is not only referred to as 'carrousel fraud' but also as 'missing trader fraud' or 'MTIC fraud'. It may be that companies A and C are actively involved in the VAT fraud, but that is not necessarily the case. Companies A and C may be bona fide taxable persons that are unaware of the fraud.

This fraud is a major threat to the EU VAT system. Studies conducted for the European Commission have pointed out that cross-border intra-Community fraud leads to a yearly budgetary loss for the Member States of EUR 50 billion.[138] This is why the Member States and the EU institutions are keen to combat such fraud. Various legislative measures have been taken, varying from strengthening administrative cooperation between the Member States[139] to the introduction of a 'quick reaction mechanism' which allows for the rapid introduction of a reverse charge mechanism in case of sudden and massive fraud.[140]

The CJEU has also taken up a role as 'crime fighter'. For example, in *Kittel & Recolta,* the Court provided that the objective criteria which form the basis of the concepts of 'supply of goods effected by a taxable person acting as such' and 'economic activity' are not met where tax is evaded by the taxable person himself.[141] Moreover, it ruled that a taxable person who knew or should have known that, by his purchase, he was participating in a transaction connected with VAT fraud, cannot *deduct* the VAT on his inputs.[142] If a national court must or may raise of its own motion points of law based

138. *See* Communication from the Commission to the European Parliament, the Council and the European Economic and Social Committee on an action plan on VAT, Towards a single EU VAT area – Time to decide, COM (2016) 148 final, 7 April 2016, p. 3.
139. Cf. Council Regulation (EC) 1798/2003 of 7 October 2003 on administrative cooperation in the field of value added tax and repealing Regulation (EEC) 218/92.
140. *See* Article 199b VAT Directive.
141. CJEU 6 July 2006, Joined Cases C-439/04 and C-440/04 *Axel Kittel v Belgian State (C-439/04) and Belgian State v Recolta Recycling SPRL (C-440/04)*, ECLI:EU:C:2006:446, para. 53. *See* for an overview of the CJEU case law regarding the application of the VAT exemption to ICTs: S. Nathoeni and W. de Wit, *VAT Exemption of Intra-Community Supplies of Goods: State of Play after VSTR* (2013) 2 EC Tax Review, pp. 100-106 https://doi.org/10.54648/ecta2013011.
142. CJEU 6 July 2006, Joined Cases C-439/04 and C-440/04 *Axel Kittel v Belgian State (C-439/04) and Belgian State v Recolta Recycling SPRL (C-440/04)*, ECLI:EU:C:2006:446.

on binding rules of national law, it is required to do whatever lies within its jurisdiction, taking the whole body of domestic law into consideration and applying the interpretative methods recognized by that law to refuse the right of deduction if that right is relied on for fraudulent or abusive ends.[143] In our view, this implies that a national court must deny the right of deduction in cases of fraud or abuse even if there is no national provision on the basis of which that right of deduction can be denied.[144] On the basis of the *Italmoda* judgment, one can even take the position that the authorities are allowed to simultaneously deny multiple rights (e.g., the right of deduction *and* the right to apply the exemption for ICSs) to a single taxable person who knew or should have known that he was participating in VAT fraud.[145] This being said, the CJEU has made clear that the tax authorities are subject to a considerable burden of proof; they cannot deny rights merely because VAT fraud has taken place. Instead, the authorities should provide an accurate description of the constituent elements of the fraud and prove the fraudulent conduct. Additionally, they must establish that the taxable person actively participated in that fraud or that he or she knew, or ought to have known, that the transaction relied on as a basis for that right was connected with that fraud.[146]

From Case C-285/09, it follows that a fraudster cannot rely on the application of the exemption for ICSs.[147] In our view, the same principles, as expressed by the CJEU in *Maks Pen EOOD,* should apply in this regard.[148] Conversely, in the event that the purchaser has committed tax fraud, it is justifiable to make the supplier's right to the exemption conditional upon its good faith.[149] The supplier can rely on the application of the exemption if he acted in good faith and took every step, which could reasonably be asked of the supplier to satisfy itself that the transaction which it had carried out had not resulted in its participation in tax fraud.[150]

13.11.2 A New System for Intra-Community B2B Trade in Goods?

Both the susceptibility to VAT fraud and the administrative complexity of the current VAT system have led the EU institutions to take legislative steps to realize a revised taxation system for B2B intra-Community trade in goods – an initiative that has become

143. CJEU 13 February 2014, Case C-18/13 *Maks Pen EOOD v Direktor na Direktsia 'Obzhalvane i danachno-osiguritelna praktika' Sofia*, ECLI:EU:C:2014:69.
144. CJEU 18 December 2014, Joined Cases C-131/13, C-163/13 and C-164/13 *Staatssecretaris van Financiën v Schoenimport 'Italmoda' Mariano Previti vof (C-131/13) and Turbu.com BV (C-163/13) and Turbu.com Mobile Phone's BV (C-164/13) v Staatssecretaris van Financiën*, ECLI:EU:C:2014:2455.
145. *Ibid.*
146. CJEU 1 December 2022, Case C-512/21 *Aquila Part Prod Com SA v Nemzeti Adó- és Vámhivatal Fellebbviteli Igazgatósága*, ECLI:EU:C:2022:950, para. 37.
147. CJEU 7 December 2010, Case C-285/09 *Criminal Proceedings against R.*, ECLI:EU:C:2010:742.
148. CJEU 13 February 2014, Case C-18/13 *Maks Pen EOOD v Direktor na Direktsia 'Obzhalvane i danachno-osiguritelna praktika' Sofia*, ECLI:EU:C:2014:69.
149. For example: CJEU 6 September 2012, Case C-273/11 *Mecsek-Gabona Kft v Nemzeti Adó- és Vámhivatal Dél-dunántúli Regionális Adó Főigazgatósága*, ECLI:EU:C:2014:69, para. 50.
150. For example: *ibid.*, para. 53.

part of the so-called Action Plan on VAT.[151] The system was proposed by the Commission in 2018 and was intended to be in place as of 1 July 2022, yet the proposal is, at the time of writing of this book, still pending.[152] The Council has put the legislative procedure on hold, likely because of political disagreement on the acceptability of the revised system.

The revised system radically changes the manner in which intra-Community B2B supplies of goods are treated for VAT purposes.[153] Instead of relying on the duality of an exempt ICS in the Member State of departure of the goods and a taxed ICA in the Member State of arrival, the new system creates a new category of taxable transaction: the 'intra-Union supply of goods'. On the basis of the proposed Article 14(4) VAT Directive, an intra-Union supply of goods means a supply of goods where (a) the supply of goods is carried out by a taxable person for a taxable person or for a non-taxable legal person, and (b) the goods are dispatched or transported, by or on behalf of the supplier or the person acquiring the goods within the Union, from one Member State to another. Then, the proposed Article 35a VAT Directive stipulates that the place of supply of an intra-Union supply of goods shall be deemed to be the place where the goods are located at the time when the dispatch or transport of those goods to the customer ends. Further, the VAT due on the intra-Union supply of goods becomes chargeable on issue of the invoice to the customer (*see* Article 67 VAT Directive (proposed)), and the supplier can make use of the OSS for the reporting and payment of the VAT due.[154] In sum, this paradigm for the taxation of ICSs of goods compels the supplier to charge VAT in the Member State of destination and subsequently remit that VAT to the authorities (*see* Figure 13.30). The Commission expects that it will reduce cross-border VAT fraud by up to EUR 41 billion per year.[155] This would be caused by the circumstance that fraudulent companies are unable to purchase goods free of VAT from other Member States (which is now possible because of the exemption for ICSs, cf. Article 138(1) VAT Directive); since they would have to ask for a refund of the input VAT on intra-Union supplies (i.e., deduct it), it would become much more difficult to profit from a carousel fraud scheme.

151. Communication from the Commission to the European Parliament, the Council and the European Economic and Social Committee on an action plan on VAT, Towards a single EU VAT area – Time to decide, COM (2016) 148 final, 7 April 2016; M. Horsthuis & F.J.G. Nellen, *A Critical Analysis of the Quick Fixes for the EU Intra-Community B2B VAT System* (2019) 3 International VAT Monitor https://doi.org/10.59403/25gdm93.
152. Proposal for a Council Directive amending Directive 2006/112/EC as regards the introduction of the detailed technical measures for the operation of the definitive VAT system for the taxation of trade between Member States, COM (2018) 329 final, 25 May 2018.
153. For further reading, refer to M. Merkx & J. Gruson, *Definitive VAT Regime: Ready for the Next Step?* (2019) 28 EC Tax Review https://doi.org/10.54648/ecta2019017 and F. Matesanz, *The Certified Taxable Person Status* (2018) 6 International VAT Monitor https://doi.org/10.59403/vfs5dt.
154. For a detailed explanation of the OSS, refer to Chapter 16.
155. *Ibid.*, p. 4.

Figure 13.30 The Proposed Revised Taxation System for Intra-Community B2B Supplies of Goods

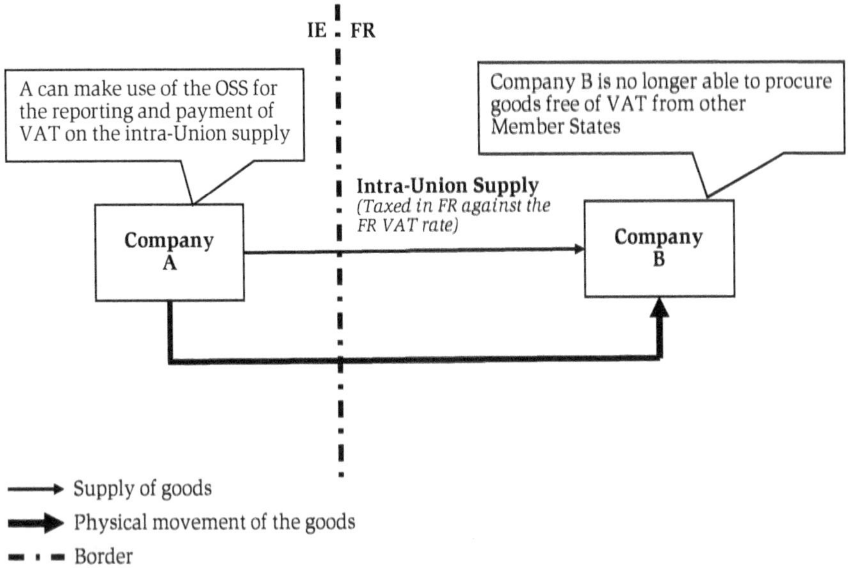

The revised system seems simple enough, yet there are also various nuances to it. The most important one concerns the concept of 'Certified Taxable Person' (CTP), laid down in Article 13a VAT Directive (proposed). In the context of intra-Community trade in goods, taxable persons can apply for this special VAT status if they have a place of business or a fixed establishment in the Union and if they meet certain criteria of trustworthiness.[156] If a customer to an intra-Union supply has the CTP status, the intra-Union supply falls under the reverse charge mechanism (Article 194a VAT Directive (proposed)), so that he has to self-assess the VAT instead of paying it to the supplier. Refer to Figure 13.31 for a graphical representation.

156. *See* Article 13a(2) VAT Directive (proposed), which relates to, among others, the absence of any serious infringement, levels of operational and logistic control and financial solvency.

Figure 13.31 The Proposed Revised Taxation System for Intra-Community B2B Supplies of Goods (Reverse Charge, Assuming Company B Is a CTP)

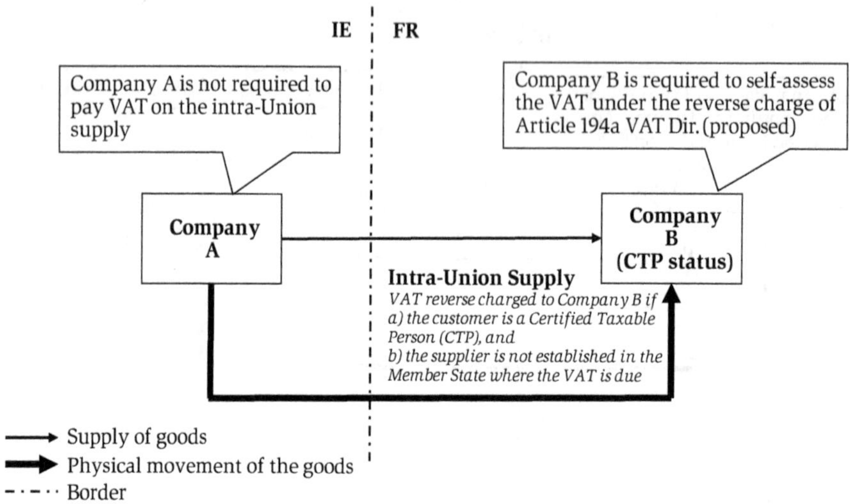

The question is whether or not the Council will agree on the system as proposed by the Commission. Many are of the opinion that no agreement will be reached on the *current* proposal, as it has one drawback that primarily manifests itself when one takes into account the political sensitivities on the EU level. With the OSS for the reporting and payment of VAT, the proposed system requires a clearing system for the distribution of VAT revenues among the Member States. Depending on international trade flow volumes, some Member States – like the Netherlands – will initially receive more VAT than is ultimately due to them.[157] Other Member States will be in a refundable position and thus depend on the payment of VAT due by other Member States. Unfortunately, the leaderships of most EU countries are unwilling to accept such budgetary dependencies on other countries – and thus, it remains to be seen whether the Council will adopt the system as proposed by the Commission.

157. The Netherlands is a major logistics hub, importing great quantities of goods from non-EU countries, only to transport these to other Member States after customs clearance. The volume of intra-Union supplies is expected to greatly outweigh the volume of intra-Union purchases, thus leading to a VAT payable position for the Netherlands vis-à-vis other Member States.

CHAPTER 14

Importation and Exportation of Goods

14.1 INTRODUCTION

The taxation of private consumption in the EU is primarily achieved by means of the 'main' taxable transactions: supplies of goods and supplies of services. If goods imported from non-EU countries were not taxed, not all consumption of goods in the EU would be burdened with VAT – which is at odds with the destination principle. Imposing a burden of VAT on goods imported from non-EU countries also prevents that taxable persons supplying goods to customers within the EU suffer from a competitive disadvantage in comparison with their non-EU competitors. To put it differently, the 'external neutrality' of VAT would be jeopardized if goods imported from non-EU countries are not burdened with EU VAT. Therefore, Article 2(1)(d) of the VAT Directive provides that also the importation of goods (in simple terms: the entry of goods into the Community)[1] is a taxable transaction for VAT purposes.

Conversely, goods that leave the EU must be relieved from the burden of (EU) VAT. This is achieved by exempting supplies of goods that are exported to a non-EU country ('supplies for export', or 'export supplies'), while at the same time allowing a right of deduction of input VAT in relation to those supplies. We note that the 'exportation of goods' is not defined as a standalone taxable transaction in Article 2 VAT Directive. Therefore, if a (taxable) person transfers its own goods from an EU

1. *See* Article 30 VAT Directive for a comprehensive definition of the concept of importation.

country to a non-EU country, no taxable transaction for EU VAT will occur.[2] If a (taxable) person supplies goods to a customer in a non-EU country, the supply will be exempt with a right of deduction (the so-called zero-rating), yet still, the exportation itself – i.e., the physical movement of the goods to a non-EU destination – will not in itself qualify as a taxable transaction.

In sections 14.2-14.14, we elaborate on the importation of goods. In section 14.15, we provide an overview of the VAT rules on the importation of goods in connection with non-EU distance sales of goods. Finally, in section 14.16, we discuss the exportation of goods.

14.2 BASIC FEATURES OF IMPORTATION OF GOODS

Article 30 VAT Directive further details the taxable transaction relating to the importation of goods. This provision defines 'importation of goods' as the entry into the Community of goods, which are not in free circulation within the meaning of Article 24 EC Treaty.[3] The entry into the Community of goods which are in free circulation, coming from a third territory forming part of the customs territory of the Community, is also considered as 'importation of goods' (Article 30, second paragraph, VAT Directive). From this definition, a number of characteristics relating to the importation of goods can be derived.

14.2.1 Status and Identity of Importer of Record Is Irrelevant

It is important to realize that the importation of goods is also a taxable transaction if it is effected by a non-taxable person (e.g., a private individual). Unlike the other taxable transactions, an importation of goods does not need to be carried out by a taxable person acting as such, which is only logical from the viewpoint of the aforementioned rationale underlying the destination principle. Such a broad definition also means that travellers from outside the EU, bringing their luggage into the EU, in principle, effect the taxable transaction importation. However, there are rather generous exemptions for travellers' luggage (*see* section 14.9.2).

14.2.2 No Link with a Supply of Goods Necessary

The broad definition of importation of goods also means that the importation is not necessarily connected to a supply of those goods (i.e., the transfer of the right to dispose of tangible property as owner, *see* Article 14 VAT Directive). So, a business moving goods from its inventory in Switzerland (non-EU) to its warehouse in Germany

2. Depending on the consumption tax system in the non-EU country of arrival of the goods, VAT/GST may be levied upon importation.
3. We note that the word 'Community' should have been replaced by 'Union', and the reference to Article 24 EC Treaty should have been replaced by a reference to Article 29 TFEU.

(EU) effects an importation of goods even though no transfer of ownership (title) takes place.

14.2.3 Services Cannot Be Imported

The taxable transaction 'importation of goods' is by its very wording restricted to goods. Thus, services cannot be imported. Although the notion of 'goods' is not explicitly defined in Article 2 or 14(1) VAT Directive, it follows from that provision that it refers to tangible property. In our view, the term 'goods' in Article 30 VAT Directive does not have a different meaning than in Article 14(1) VAT Directive. It also appears that electricity, gas, heat or cooling energy and the like, as referred to in Article 15 VAT Directive, are to be considered as goods in respect of Article 30 VAT Directive. The exemption in Article 143(l) VAT Directive for the importation of gas through pipelines would be meaningless if gas were not to be considered a good in terms of Article 30 VAT Directive. It is, however, questionable whether assets like interests in immovable property (*see* Article 15(2) VAT Directive) must also be regarded as goods within the meaning of Article 30 VAT Directive in those Member States that used any of the options that Article 15(2) VAT Directive makes available to them.

14.2.4 No Importation from Other EU Member States

Before 1993, the entry of goods into the territory of a Member State coming from another Member States was considered as an 'importation of goods'. However, since 1993, when the internal fiscal frontiers in the EU were abolished, 'importation' is no longer a concept applying to trade within the Community, but only to trade with third countries.[4] Exportation is also a term that is no longer used for cross-border ICTs between the Member States. Instead, cross-border ICTs are governed by the regime for intra-Community supplies and intra-Community acquisitions (*see* Chapter 13).

14.3 CONNECTION WITH CUSTOMS DUTIES

Upon importation of goods into the EU, not only VAT but also custom duties may be due.[5] The levy of VAT on importation is closely connected to the levy of customs duties. Before we go into further detail with respect to the importation of goods, it is useful to outline the rules governing the levy of customs duties and their relation to the levy of VAT upon importation of goods.

4. However, customs territory does fully match completely the VAT territory. *See* section 14.5.2.
5. In fact, there is a plethora of taxes, levies and contributions that may be due upon importation, including excises, anti-dumping duties, countervailing duties and CBAM certificate purchase obligations (as from 2026).

14.3.1 The CCC and the UCC

Until May 2016, the CCC[6] was the main legal basis for the levying of customs duties. This piece of legislation was replaced by the UCC,[7] which was adopted on 9 October 2013 and whose substantive provisions apply as from 1 May 2016. On 24 November 2015, the UCC's 'IA' was adopted by the Commission. The IA ensures the existence of uniform conditions for the implementation of the UCC and a harmonized application of procedures by all Member States.[8] On 17 December 2015, the European Commission also adopted a 'Delegated Act' (DA) to establish transitional rules for operators and customs authorities, pending the introduction of new IT systems to create a fully electronic customs environment.[9]

The UCC is part of the modernization of customs and will serve as the new framework regulation on the rules and procedures for customs throughout the EU. With a view to clarity and conciseness, we limit ourselves to the provisions of the UCC (and not the (replaced) CCC).[10]

14.3.2 Customs Duties and VAT

On the basis of the UCC customs duties are levied if – simply put – goods from outside the EU are released for free circulation in the EU. Thus, the levy of VAT on importation and customs duties may coincide.[11] Unlike VAT on importation, customs duties can, in principle, not be recovered by the person who has paid them. The VAT rules concerning the importation of goods make many references to the rules governing customs duties. For example, the formalities laid down in the UCC with respect to the levy of customs duties upon importation of goods into the customs territory of the Community are the same as those applying to the levy of VAT upon importation of goods in free circulation which enters the Community from a third territory forming part of the customs territory of the Community (Article 275 VAT Directive). Consequently, the customs rules governing the process of goods entering the EU are also relevant for VAT.

6. Council Regulation 2913/92 of 12 October 1992 establishing the Community Customs Code [1992] OJ L302/1.
7. Regulation (EU) No 952/2013 of 10 October 2013 of the Parliament and of the Council of 9 October 2013 laying down the Union Customs Code [2013] OJ L269.
8. Commission Implementing Regulation (EU) 2015/2447 of 24 November 2015 laying down detailed rules for implementing certain provisions of Regulation (EU) No 952/2013 of the European Parliament and of the Council laying down the Union Customs Code [2015] OJ L 343.
9. Commission Delegated Regulation (EU) 2015/2446 of 28 July 2015 supplementing Regulation (EU) No 952/2013 of the European Parliament and of the Council as regards detailed rules concerning certain provisions of the Union Customs Code [2015] OJ L 343.
10. For further reading on EU customs law, refer to T. Lyons, *EU Customs Law* (Oxford EU Law Library 2018).
11. For a detailed analysis of the interplay between customs duties and VAT on importation, refer to F. Nellen, *Over het parallellisme van douanerechten en btw in de internationale handel* (2023), Weekblad Fiscaal Recht 2023/133.

14.3.3 The Customs Rules Governing the Process of Goods Entering the EU

Before goods are brought into the customs territory of the Community, the person who brings the goods into the customs territory of the Community, or who assumes responsibility for the carriage of the goods, must file an entry summary declaration (Article 127 UCC).[12]

When goods enter the customs territory of the EU, they are put under immediately 'customs supervision' (Article 134 UCC). The person bringing the goods into the EU must without delay convey them by the route specified by the customs authorities to a customs office or another location specified by the authorities (Article 135 UCC).[13] Goods are commonly brought to approved temporary storage facilities operated either by the importer or by a storage-keeper, or to a warehouse operated by the customs authorities. The goods may not be removed from this place until they are released by the customs authorities.

Next, the goods must be presented to customs, i.e., the customs authorities must be notified of the arrival of the goods at the customs office or at any other place designated or approved by the customs authorities (Articles 139 and 5(33) UCC). Goods that have been presented to customs are put in so-called temporary storage (Article 144 UCC). When in temporary storage, the goods remain under the supervision of the customs authorities (Articles 134, 144, 147 and 148 UCC) until they are released.

Within a set period of time (90 days), the goods must be re-exported or placed under a customs procedure (Articles 149 and 150 UCC).[14] This is also referred to as 'customs designation' or 'customs arrangement'. Under the UCC, the following customs procedures are available (Article 5(16) UCC):

(a) release for free circulation;
(b) special procedures;
(c) export.

It is beyond the scope of this book to discuss the customs procedures in detail.[15] All goods intended to be placed under a customs procedure must be covered by a declaration for that customs procedure (Article 158 UCC). This is referred to as the 'customs declaration'. Subject to conditions, a summary (i.e., a simplified) customs declaration may be filed (Article 166 UCC).

Where the goods are released for free circulation, or where they are under the temporary importation procedure with partial relief from import duties, a customs debt on importation shall be incurred (Article 77 UCC). If the goods are placed under any

12. Except for goods brought into the customs territory of the Community by sea or air which remain on board the same means of transport for carriage, without transshipment. *See* Article 127(2) UCC. *See also* Article 104 Delegated regulation UCC (No 2015/2446).
13. Article 243 UCC allows Member States to designate parts of the customs territory of the EU as free zones. It is beyond the scope of this book to address the free zones in more detail.
14. The UCC only allows for placement under a 'customs procedure' or re-export (Articles 149 and 150 UCC). *See* Article 5(16) UCC for a definition of 'customs procedures'.
15. For more information, refer to Titles V-VIII of the UCC.

other customs procedure, the incurrence of a customs debt is postponed. The same is true for the VAT due on importation (Article 71 VAT Directive).

In order to place the goods under a customs procedure, a relevant declaration for that procedure must be filed (Article 158 UCC). In certain situations, the declaration can be made orally or by any other act (e.g., walking through a 'green lane' at the airport - *see* Articles 135-144 DA).[16] The customs authorities must accept the declaration immediately if it complies with all requirements (Articles 162 and 172 UCC). However, they have the power to examine the documents covering the declaration and the documents and examine the goods and take samples for analysis or for detailed examination (Article 188 UCC). The customs authorities shall release the goods as soon as the particulars in the declaration have been verified or accepted without verification (Article 194 UCC). That does not prevent the customs authorities from amending the declaration after the release of the goods if they find that the particulars contained in the declaration are incorrect (Article 198(1)(d) UCC).

14.4 NO TAXABLE IMPORTATION (YET): CUSTOMS ARRANGEMENT

The taxable transaction 'importation of goods' occurs when the goods are imported, i.e., when they physically enter the EU. At that same moment, VAT becomes chargeable, i.e., the tax authorities become legally entitled to claim the tax (Article 70 VAT Directive; also *see* Chapter 5). However, on the basis of Article 71 VAT Directive, as long as the goods are placed under a customs arrangement or situation mentioned in Articles 156, 276 or 277 VAT Directive, the chargeable event will not (yet) occur, and the VAT will not (yet) become chargeable. For example, if goods are placed in temporary storage or - following their placing in temporary storage - in a customs warehouse (which is a customs procedure), no chargeable event for VAT occurs and no VAT becomes chargeable. We refer to Chapter 12 on liability of VAT and to section 14.7 below.

When the goods 'cease to be covered' by the respective arrangement or situation, or when customs duties and similar imposts become chargeable, the chargeable event for VAT also occurs, and the VAT becomes chargeable (Article 71(1) VAT Directive).

14.5 IMPORTATION OF GOODS

Article 30 VAT Directive contains two definitions of situations in which importation of goods for VAT purposes occurs (*see* sections 14.5.1 and 14.5.2). In addition, it follows from the CJEU case law that importation also occurs if goods are removed from customs arrangements (section 14.5.3).

16. Commission Delegated Regulation (EU) 2015/2446 of 28 July 2015.

14.5.1 Goods That Are Not in Free Circulation Coming from Third Territory

Article 30, first paragraph, VAT Directive states that importation refers to the entry in the Community of goods that are not in free circulation. Thus, for importation to take place, the goods: (a) must not be in free circulation; and (b) must enter the EU. For completeness' sake, we note that the chargeable event and the chargeability of VAT may be postponed if – for example – the goods are placed in a customs warehouse (*see* sections 14.4 and 14.7).

According to Article 29 TFEU, goods are in free circulation if – simply put – the import formalities have been complied with, and any customs duties or other charges due upon importation have been paid.[17] Basically, that implies that if goods physically move from a location outside the EU to a location within the EU, importation occurs when the goods enter the EU.[18]

The territory of the Member States altogether forms the 'territory of the Community' (i.e., the territory of the EU).[19] The territories of the Member States are defined in Article 52 TEU and Article 355 TFEU. Article 6(1) VAT Directive excludes certain EU territories from the territorial scope of VAT. Conversely, Article 7 VAT Directive includes certain third territories in the territorial scope of VAT.

Example

A factory in the United States produces staplers. It is evident that such goods are not in 'free circulation' for EU customs and VAT purposes. The US factory supplies these goods for consideration to a business in France. The goods are shipped from the United States to France. Upon entry of the goods in the Community, the taxable transaction 'importation' occurs (even though the chargeable event and the chargeability of VAT may only occur at a later moment) (*see* Figure 14.1).

17. Article 29 TFEU provides: 'Products coming from a third country shall be considered to be in free circulation in a Member State if the import formalities have been complied with and any customs duties or charges having equivalent effect which are payable have been levied in that Member State, and if they have not benefited from a total or partial drawback of such duties or charges.'
18. There is a special exemption on importation for goods that re-enter the EU (*see* Article 143(c) VAT Directive and Articles 185-187 CCC).
19. Article 5(1) VAT Directive.

Figure 14.1 Importation of Goods Which Are Not Yet in Free Circulation

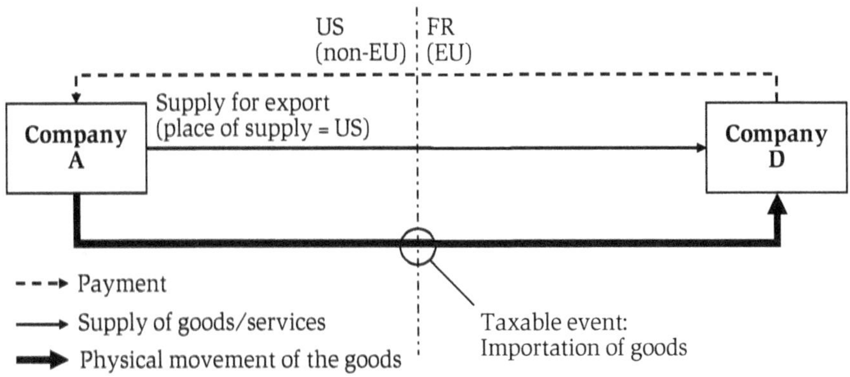

14.5.2 Importation of Goods That Are in Free Circulation Coming from a Third Territory Forming Part of Union Customs Territory

The territorial scope of VAT, as described in Articles 5-8 VAT Directive, does not correspond exactly to the territorial scope for customs purposes (the 'customs territory' of the EU). For example, there are territories that are part of the customs territory, but not part of the VAT area.[20] Goods that are within the customs territory are normally in 'free circulation'. If no specific measures were taken, Article 30 VAT Directive (first paragraph) would contain insufficient ground to levy VAT on importation when such goods were to be moved to a territory that is part of the VAT area. Ultimately, that would lead to consumption within the EU remaining untaxed, which goes against the legal character of EU VAT. Therefore, importation for VAT purposes also takes place in case goods that are in free circulation enter the VAT area from a third territory forming part of the customs territory (but not of the VAT area).[21]

Example

Goods are shipped from the Canary Islands to Madrid (Spain).

The Canary Islands are part of the customs territory of the EU. Goods that are on the Canary Islands are in free circulation (leaving aside goods that are still under customs control). However, Article 6(1) VAT Directive excludes the Canary Islands from EU VAT territory. Nonetheless, Article 30, second paragraph VAT Directive

20. Article 6(2) VAT Directive sets out specific exclusions from the scope of VAT regarding territories that are not part of the customs territory of the EU.
21. Article 30, second paragraph VAT Directive. *See also* CJEU 28 January 1999, Case C-181/97 *A.J. van der Kooy v Staatssecretaris van Financiën*, ECLI:EU:C:1999:32.

considers as importation the entry of goods that are in free circulation coming from a third territory that is part of the customs territory. Consequently, upon arrival of the goods in Madrid, there will not be importation of goods for the purpose of the customs rules, but there will be an importation from a VAT perspective (*see* Figure 14.2).

Figure 14.2 Importation of Goods Which Are Already in Free Circulation

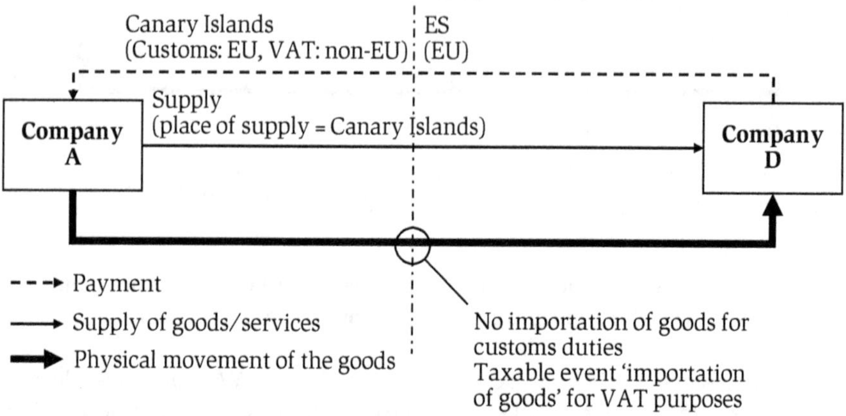

14.5.3 Importation When Goods Cease to Be Covered by a Customs Arrangement

In section 14.4, we explained that with respect to goods that entered the EU but that are subsequently placed under any of the customs arrangements, or in any of the situations mentioned in Articles 156, 276 and 277 VAT Directive, no chargeable event takes place, and VAT does not (yet) become chargeable.

Example

Goods (that are not in free circulation) are shipped from outside the EU to a location within the EU. Upon entry of goods into the EU, the taxable transaction 'importation of goods' takes place. The goods are presented to the customs authorities and are placed under customs supervision immediately. They are in 'temporary storage' until the importer gives the goods a customs designation. In this example, the importer decides to place the goods under a customs warehousing arrangement. Consequently, no chargeable event occurs, and no VAT on importation becomes chargeable. When the importer decides to remove the goods from the warehousing arrangement and release them for free circulation, the chargeable event occurs, and the VAT on importation becomes chargeable (*see* Figure 14.3).

Figure 14.3 Goods Which Cease to Be Covered by a Customs Arrangement

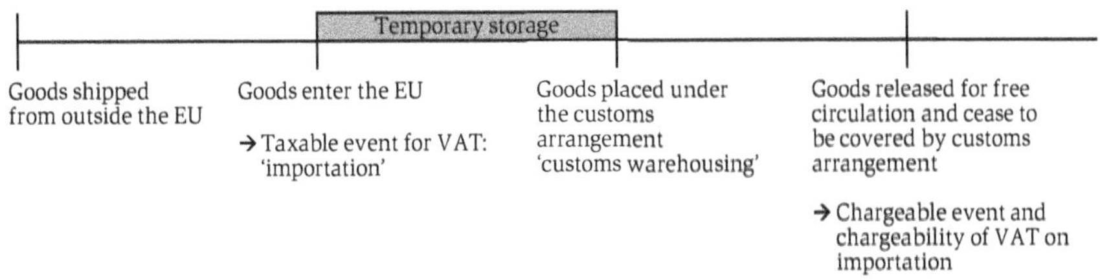

In *Wandel*, the CJEU declared that any withdrawal - even an unlawful withdrawal - from authorized storage of goods subject to customs supervision without the authorization of the customs authority constitutes removal for the purposes of Article 203(1) of the CCC (now incorporated in Article 79 of the UCC), and thus gives rise under that provision to a customs debt on importation.[22] From *Liberexim*, it follows that such withdrawal also causes VAT on importation to become chargeable.[23] More specifically, the CJEU ruled that the place where the chargeable event takes place is where the first operation which can be regarded as a removal of the goods (i.e., the first irregularity) from customs supervision was carried out (also *see* Article 61 VAT Directive, first paragraph and section 14.6 below). Thus, goods cease to be covered by an arrangement or are not covered by one of the situations mentioned in Articles 156, 276 and 277 VAT Directive if, when and where the first irregularity takes place which prevents the competent customs authority from gaining access to goods under customs supervision and from monitoring them.[24] Notwithstanding these judgments, CJEU case law also provides that the cessation of customs arrangements (e.g., the removal of goods from customs supervision in a free zone) does not give rise to a chargeable event for VAT purposes if those goods did not enter 'the economic network of the European Union'.[25] In other words: for import VAT to become chargeable, the goods must have been exposed to the risk of being consumed, which occurs when they have entered the economic network of the EU. This is not the case if the goods after removal are still under a free zone regime.

22. CJEU 1 February 2001, Case C-66/99 *D. Wandel GmbH v Hauptzollamt Bremen*, ECLI: EU:C:2001:69. On the basis of the *Wallenborn* judgment, where a customs debt arises by virtue of Article 203 of the Customs Code and no VAT debt is consequently incurred, on account of the circumstances of the dispute in the main proceedings, Article 204 of that code may not be applied for the sole purpose of providing a basis for charging VAT (*see* CJEU 1 June 2017, Case C-571/15 *Wallenborn Transports SA v Hauptzollamt Gießen*, ECLI:EU:C:2017:417).
23. CJEU 11 July 2002, Case C-371/99 *Liberexim BV v Staatssecretaris van Financiën*, ECLI: EU:C:2002:433.
24. In that respect it must be understood that removal of goods from customs supervision does not require intent, but, instead, only that certain objective conditions be met.
25. CJEU 1 June 2017, Case C-571/15 *Wallenborn Transports SA v Hauptzollamt Gießen*, ECLI: EU:C:2017:417.

14.6 PLACE OF IMPORTATION

The place of importation is the Member State within whose territory the goods are located when they enter the EU (Article 60 VAT Directive).

Example

Goods (not in free circulation) from outside the EU enter the EU in the Netherlands. They are released for free circulation in Rotterdam (*see* Figure 14.4).

Figure 14.4 Place of Importation: Goods Released for Free Circulation

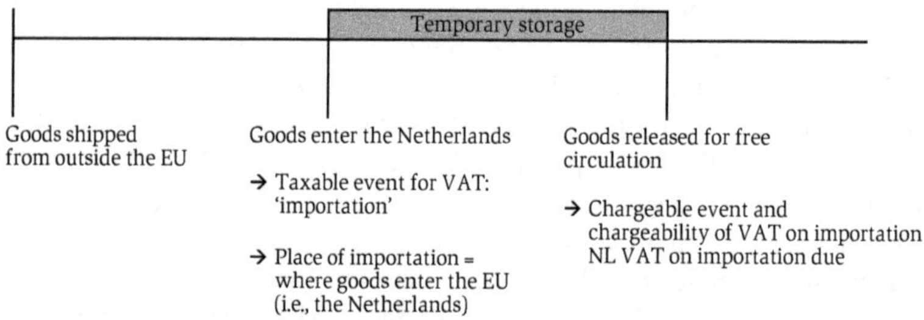

If goods are immediately placed under a customs arrangement or situation referred to in Article 156 VAT Directive (or under a temporary importation arrangement with a total exemption for import duty/an external transit arrangement), the place of importation is not where the goods physically entered the EU, but rather where the goods cease to be covered by those arrangements or situations (Article 61, first paragraph VAT Directive).[26]

Example

Goods (not in free circulation) from outside the EU enter the EU in the Netherlands. Subsequently, they are immediately transported by truck to Berlin under a transit customs procedure. In Germany, the goods are released for free circulation (*see* Figure 14.5).

26. Specific rules exist for situations in which goods in free circulation are places under arrangements or situations referred to in Articles 276 and 277 VAT Directive.

Figure 14.5 Place of Importation: Goods under a Customs Arrangement Prior to Release for Free Circulation

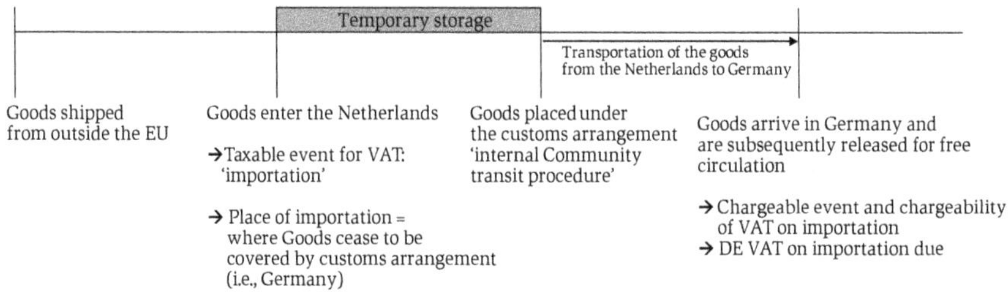

The CJEU doctrine on entry of goods 'into the economic network' – *see* section 14.5 – is also relevant when it comes to the place of importation. This becomes apparent when looking at the CJEU judgment in *FEDEX*.[27] In that case, the Court has provided that if goods are withdrawn from customs supervision in a certain Member State, one may presume that: (a) the goods have entered the economic network there, and (b) the goods have ceased to be covered by the customs arrangements there.[28] However, if it has been established that the goods have entered the economic network in another Member State (i.e., the Member State of the final destination), import VAT becomes chargeable there, even if customs supervision has ended somewhere else.[29] In *Hauptzollamt Münster*[30] and *Hauptzollamt Hamburg*,[31] the CJEU has reaffirmed the notion that the place of importation in some cases[32] depends on the place where the goods have entered the economic network of the EU.[33] In our view, the central question is what 'entry into the economic network' precisely means and where it should be deemed to take place. As regards an imported car, the Court has ruled that 'actual and permanent use' of the vehicle is relevant; the place of importation is situated in the Member State in which the user resides and uses the vehicle.[34] Perhaps the CJEU judgment in the pending case *Hauptzollamt Braunschweig* will provide more answers to the mentioned questions.[35]

27. CJEU 10 July 2019, Case C-26/18, *Federal Express Corporation Deutsche Niederlassung v Hauptzollamt Frankfurt am Main*, ECLI:EU:C:2019:579.
28. *Ibid.*, para. 47.
29. For a critical analysis of this CJEU judgment, and others, *see* F. Nellen, *Over het parallellisme van douanerechten en btw in de internationale handel* (2023), Weekblad Fiscaal Recht 2023/133.
30. CJEU 3 March 2021, Case C-7/20, *Hauptzollamt Münster*, ECLI:EU:C:2021:161.
31. CJEU 8 September 2022, Case C-368/21 *Hauptzollamt Hamburg*, ECLI:EU:C:2022:647.
32. It should be noted that the mentioned cases only relate to situations in which a customs debt arose because of non-compliance with customs legislation (*see* Article 79 UCC).
33. For further reading, *see* S. Ojak, *Case C-368/21: A New Definition of Importation in the Sense of VAT Law?* (2022) 5 EC Tax Review.
34. CJEU 8 September 2022, Case C-368/21 *Hauptzollamt Hamburg*, ECLI:EU:C:2022:647, dictum.
35. Case C-791/22 *Hauptzollamt Braunschweig*, still pending at the time of writing.

14.7 THE CHARGEABLE EVENT AND CHARGEABILITY WITH RESPECT TO THE IMPORTATION OF GOODS

This section deals with the chargeable event and the chargeability of VAT concerning goods that are imported. Two situations need to be discerned: standard situations and situations in which import VAT deferral schemes are used.

14.7.1 Standard Situations

Article 70 VAT Directive simply states that the chargeable event shall occur, and the VAT shall become chargeable when the goods are imported. Under normal circumstances, it is relatively easy to determine when the goods are imported, so that the moment of the chargeable event and the chargeability of VAT can be determined.

If the goods are placed immediately under a customs arrangement or situation referred to in Article 156 VAT Directive (or under a temporary importation arrangement with a total exemption for import duty/an external transit arrangement), the chargeable event and the chargeability of VAT are postponed (*see* section 14.4). In those situations, the chargeable event occurs, and the VAT becomes chargeable when the goods cease to be covered by the customs arrangement/situation.[36]

It is left to the Member States to lay down detailed rules for payment in respect of the importation of goods (Article 211 VAT Directive). If the goods are released for free circulation after their entry into the EU, normally, the VAT will be payable at the moment they are released for free circulation. This VAT can be deducted as input VAT on the periodical VAT return of the taxable person, to the extent that this taxable person uses the goods for taxed transactions (*see* section 14.10).

Example

Goods (not in free circulation) from outside the EU enter the EU in Antwerp (Belgium). They are released for free circulation. Belgian VAT is payable when the goods are released for free circulation (*see* Figure 14.6).

36. Article 71 VAT Directive. Where imported goods are subject to customs duties, to agricultural levies or to charges having equivalent effect established under a common policy, the chargeable event shall occur and VAT shall become chargeable when the chargeable event in respect of those duties occurs and those duties become chargeable. *See also* section 14.5.3.

Figure 14.6 Importation: Taxable Transaction, Chargeable Event and Chargeability of VAT

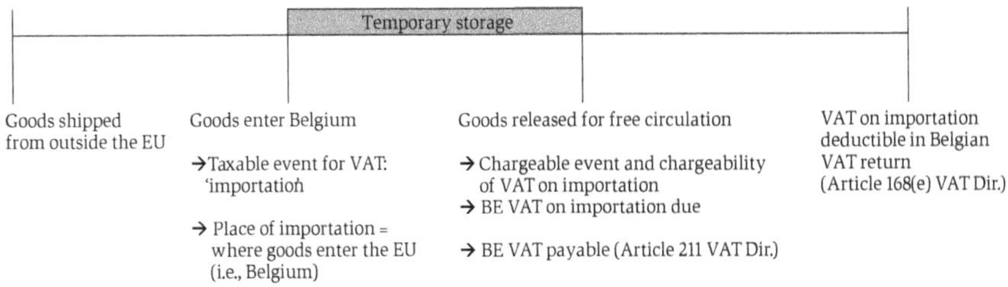

14.7.2 Import VAT Deferral Schemes

Assuming the taxable person enjoys a full right of deduction, the method of levy in the context of importation of goods has the disadvantage that the taxable person has to pay VAT to the authorities at the customs border, which is deductible at a later moment in the periodical VAT return. To alleviate that 'cash flow' disadvantage, Member States may provide that VAT on importation need not be paid at the moment of importation, on the condition that the import VAT is reported via the (regular) VAT return of the person effecting the importation (Article 211, second paragraph). A taxable person who has a full right of deduction can deduct the reported VAT on importation in the same VAT return. Consequently, he does not need to pre-finance the VAT on importation. This is commonly referred to as an 'import VAT deferral scheme'. The precise elements and requirements of import VAT deferral schemes depend on national law. For this section, we use the Dutch import VAT deferral scheme as an example.

Example

Goods (not in free circulation) from outside the EU enter the EU in Rotterdam (the Netherlands). They are released for free circulation. Dutch VAT is, in principle, chargeable and payable when the goods are released for free circulation. However, on the basis of Article 211 VAT Directive, and subject to conditions, the Netherlands allows regular importers to make use of an import VAT deferral scheme. Under the scheme, and on the basis of provisions of national law, not the declarant for customs purposes (e.g., customs agent) is liable for import VAT, but rather the person for whom the goods are destined (destinee), assuming that that person is authorized to use the scheme and meets the criteria.[37] The VAT becomes chargeable when the goods are imported, yet the destinee can settle this VAT via his periodical VAT return.[38] Subsequently, the destinee can claim the import VAT as deductible VAT on the same

37. Article 23(1) Dutch VAT Act.
38. Article 23(2) and (3) Dutch VAT Act.

VAT return – assuming he enjoys a right of deduction. Per sum, the importer pays no (import) VAT (*see* Figure 14.7).

Figure 14.7 Import VAT Deferral Scheme on Importation

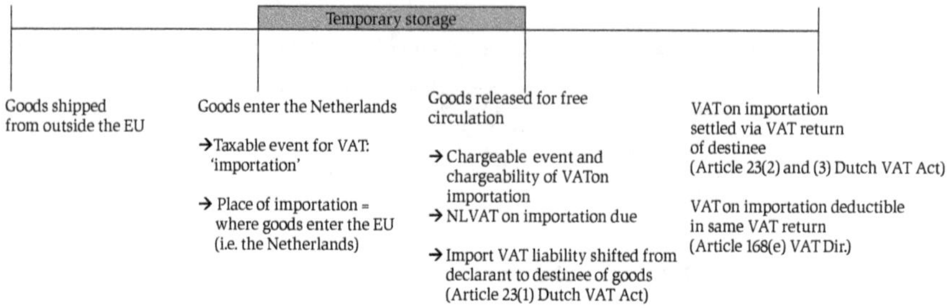

It should be noted that the VAT Directive allows Member States to require the appointment of a tax representative if the importer wants to apply a national import VAT deferral scheme while being established in a country with which there is no legal instrument relating to mutual assistance (Article 204(1) VAT Directive). Some Member States also require that taxable persons established in other Member States appoint a tax representative in case they want to make use of a national import VAT deferral scheme. We refer to Chapter 12 for further reading.

The VAT that is due on importation must, in principle, be paid by the person or persons designated or recognized as liable by the Member State of importation. Usually, the importer of record is the person liable to pay the VAT (Article 201 VAT Directive). However, if goods are removed from a customs arrangement (*see* section 14.5.3), the person who caused the goods to cease to be covered by such arrangement is liable to pay the VAT on importation (Article 202 VAT Directive, *see also* section 14.5.3).

14.8 TAXABLE AMOUNT AND VAT RATE

As regards the taxable amount[39] in respect of importation of goods, the VAT rules refer to the value for customs purposes, i.e., the 'customs value'. Thus, the taxable amount for VAT on importation is based on the provisions in the UCC. However, the VAT

39. Title VII, Chapter 4 VAT Directive reads 'Taxable Amount' and 'Importation of goods'. This appears to be an error as it is Chapter 1 of Title VII and contains a definition of the 'open market value'. Chapter 4 contains the rules governing the taxable amount in respect of the importation of goods.

Directive, on the one hand, includes (Article 86) and, on the other hand, excludes (Article 87) certain factors in the taxable amount in respect of importation of goods. Specific rules (which are not discussed here) apply in case of certain goods that are temporarily exported from the Community and with respect to the importation of works of art, collectors' items and antiques in certain Member States (*see* Articles 88 and 89 VAT Directive).

Title II, Chapter 3 UCC deals with the 'value of goods for customs purposes'. In principle, the customs value is the 'transaction value'. The transaction value is the price actually paid or payable for the goods when sold for export to the customs territory of the EU (Article 70 UCC). Certain costs must be added to the transaction value (Article 71 UCC), and others must be excluded (Article 72 UCC).

The transaction value cannot, in all cases, be used to determine the customs value of goods. For example, if the seller and the buyer are related persons who share financial or other substantive ties (e.g., a parent company and its subsidiary), the transaction value may not reflect the market value of the goods (*see* Article 70(3)(d) UCC). If the transaction method cannot be used, other methods of valuation of the goods for customs purposes are to be used. In this case, the UCC requires that the following methods of valuation, in descending order of precedence, must be applied (Article 74 UCC):

(1) the transaction value of identical goods;
(2) the transaction value of similar goods;
(3) deductive value;
(4) computed value;
(5) the residual method/fall back method.

On importation, the customs value is the basis for the taxable amount for VAT purposes. Article 86 VAT Directive adds taxes, duties, levies and other charges due outside the Member State of importation *and* those due by reason of importation. Consequently, the customs duties levied at importation are part of the taxable amount for the VAT on importation. VAT itself is excluded from the taxable amount. Incidental expenses, such as commission, packing, transport and insurance costs incurred up to the first place of destination within the territory of the Member State of importation as well as those resulting from transport to another place of destination within the Community if that other place is known when the chargeable event occurs, must also be included in the taxable amount insofar as they are not already included in the taxable amount. Article 86(2) VAT Directive defines the term 'first place of destination' as 'the place mentioned on the consignment note or on any other document under which the goods are imported into the Member State of importation'. If no such mention is made, Article 86(2) VAT Directive provides that the first place of destination is the place of the first transfer of cargo in the Member State of importation.

Whereas Article 86 VAT Directive requires certain costs to be added to the taxable amount in respect of the importation of goods, Article 87 VAT Directive excludes certain amounts. Price reductions by way of discounts for early payment (Article 87(a) VAT Directive) and price discounts and rebates granted to the customer and obtained by him at the time of importation (Article 87(b) VAT Directive) are excluded.

The VAT rate applicable to the importation of goods will be the same VAT rate as applicable to the other taxable transactions mentioned in Article 2 VAT Directive. If a Member State applies a reduced VAT rate for certain goods, that reduced VAT rate will also apply to the importation of such goods. When a Member State changes its VAT rate(s), the rate that is applicable at the moment that the VAT becomes chargeable will apply (Article 93(c) VAT Directive). For more reading on the VAT rates, refer to Chapter 7.

14.9 EXEMPTIONS

Just like other taxable transactions referred to in Article 2 VAT Directive, the importation of goods may qualify for exemptions. Unlike exempt supplies of goods and services, which are output transactions, exempt importations of goods do not affect the right of deduction of a business.

Article 143 VAT Directive contains thirteen exemptions on importation. Here, we will only discuss the four exemptions that are most commonly applied on importation:

(1) the final importation of goods of which the supply by a taxable person would in all circumstances be exempt within their respective territory (Article 143(1)(a));
(2) the final importation of goods governed by Council Directives 69/169/EEC,[40] 83/181/EEC[41] and 2006/79/EC (Article 143(1)(b));
(3) the final importation of goods, in free circulation from a territory forming part of the EU customs territory, which would be entitled to exemption on importation if they had been imported from a third country not forming part of the EU customs territory (Article 143(1)(c));
(4) the importation of goods that are supplied to another Member State directly after their importation (Article 143(1)(d)).

14.9.1 Local Supply Would in All Circumstances Be Exempt

In Chapter 8, we discussed the exemptions for supplies of goods and services. We indicated that the majority of the exemptions are for supplies of services (cf. Article 2(1)(c) VAT Directive). Nonetheless, certain supplies of goods are also exempt from

40. Replaced by Directive 2007/74/EC.
41. Replaced by Directive 2009/132/EC.

VAT. For example, the supply of human organs, blood and milk (Article 132(1)(d) VAT Directive), and the supply of dental prostheses by dentists and dental technicians (Article 132(1)(e) VAT Directive) are exempt from VAT. We refer to Chapter 8 for further reading.

The exemption of Article 143(1)(a) VAT Directive finds its *raison d'être* in the exemptions for supplies of goods mentioned in Article 132 VAT Directive. Without the exemption of Article 143(1)(a) VAT Directive, goods supplied from a third country would be treated differently from identical goods that are supplied locally.

Example

A dental technician in the Netherlands supplies dental prostheses to another dental technician in the Netherlands. That supply is exempt under Article 132(1)(e) VAT Directive. If this supply is compared to the supply of dental prostheses by a dental technician in a third country (e.g., the United States) to another dental technician in the Netherlands, it becomes immediately clear that both situations are not treated equally if the importation is not exempt. The schedule below serves to illustrate this (the sales price is set at EUR 300, and the Dutch VAT rate of 21% is used in the example) (*see* Figures 14.8 and 14.9).

Figure 14.8 Local Exempt Supply. No VAT on Sale and No VAT on Purchase

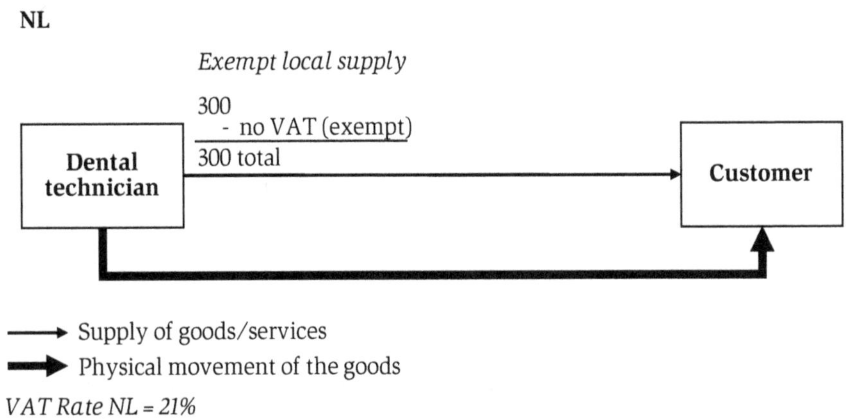

Figure 14.9 Supply for Export. No VAT on Supply, but VAT on Importation if the Exemption of Article 143(1)(a) VAT Directive Were Not to Apply

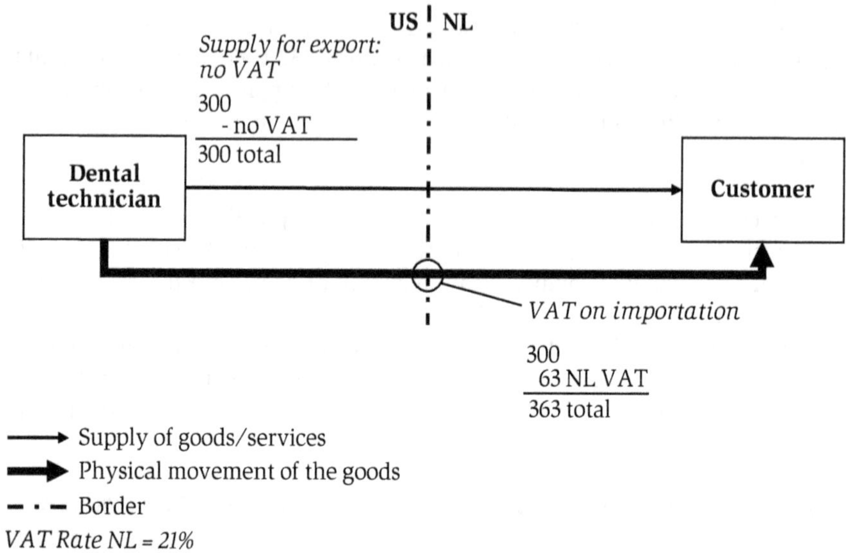

The fact that without applying Article 143(1)(a) VAT Directive the VAT burden on prostheses shipped from outside the EU would be higher than that on locally acquired prostheses is of no relevance if the customer (or acquirer) can deduct the VAT on importation under Article 168(e) VAT Directive. However, if the customer has no right of deduction (e.g., if the customer is a dentist or a private consumer), not applying the exemption of Article 143(1)(a) VAT Directive leads to an unequal treatment of goods purchased in third countries and goods purchased locally.[42]

It should be noted that Article 143(1)(a) VAT Directive uses the phrase 'in all circumstances'. It is unclear what is exactly meant by that phrase. In our view, when looking at the *ratio legis* of the provision, it means (or should mean) that an importation of dental prostheses is exempt if the equivalent domestic supply of identical goods is exempt. Advocate General Kokott, however, has taken another position. According to her, the terminology 'in all circumstances' leaves no doubt that the domestic supply of dental prostheses must be exempt without any additional condition. If the local supply of dental prostheses is only exempt if it is supplied by a

42. In the explanatory memorandum to the proposal for the Sixth VAT Directive, it was mentioned that what is now Article 143(1)(a) needed 'no special explanation'. It appears that the Commission believed that it was commonly known that the concept of neutrality requires such an exemption. *See* Proposal for a Sixth Council Directive on the harmonization of Member States concerning turnover taxes, COM (73)950. *See also* Z. Szatmári, *Chapter 9: Exemptions in Commentary on European VAT* (IBFD 2024), Global Topics IBFD. Available online at: https://research-ibfd-org.mu.idm.oclc.org/#/doc?url=/document/evdcom_recast_chap09 (accessed 21 August 2024 – please note that this a password-restricted website).

dentist or a dental technician (*see* Article 132(1)(e) VAT Directive), the conclusion must be drawn that the exemption on the local supply is not unconditional. She is, therefore, of the opinion that the importation of dental prostheses cannot be exempted.[43]

14.9.2 The Final Importation of Goods Is Exempt from Customs Duties

Customs law contains various exemptions to the importation of goods. Title VI, Chapter 2 of the UCC and Council Regulation No 1186/2009 of 16 November 2009 contain the main framework of the exemptions on importation for customs duties. The Directives mentioned in Article 143(1)(b) VAT Directive aim at achieving exemptions on importation for VAT purposes similar to the exemptions on importation for customs duties. Typically, the exemptions on importation are subject to conditions. Examples (the list below is not exhaustive) of such exemptions are:

(1) Goods contained in travellers' personal luggage.
(2) School outfits, educational materials and related household effects.
(3) Educational, scientific and cultural materials, scientific instruments and apparatus.
(4) Goods for charitable or philanthropic organizations.
(5) Goods to be used by monarchs or Heads of State.
(6) Products obtained by Community farmers on properties located in a third country.
(7) Capital goods and other equipment imported on the transfer of activities from a third country into the Community.

14.9.3 Goods from Third Territories Forming Part of Union Customs Territory

In section 14.5.2, we explained that there are territories that are part of the customs territory, but that are not part of the VAT territory. VAT on importation is also due if goods that are in free circulation come from a third territory forming part of the customs territory (but not of the VAT territory). To achieve an equal treatment of goods imported from territories that are not part of customs territory and goods imported from territories that are part of the customs territory, the exemptions on importation of goods apply equally to both (Article 143(1)(c) VAT Directive).

43. Opinion of Advocate General of 4 September, Joined Cases C-144/13, C-154/13 and C-160/13 *VDP Dental Laboratory NV v Staatssecretaris van Financiën, Staaatssecretaris van Financiën v X BV* and *Staatssecretaris van Financiën v Nobel Biocare Nederland BV*, ECLI:EU:C:2015:116, paras 44-61.

14.9.4 Goods That Are Supplied to Another Member State Directly after Their Importation

If goods are imported into a Member State, but directly thereafter are transported to another Member State, the transfer of the goods from the Member State of importation to the Member State of destination is either carried out in the framework of an intra-Community supply (to a third party) or in the framework of a transfer of own goods forming part of the business assets of the transferor. The latter transfer is also considered as an ICS (Article 17 VAT Directive; *see* Chapter 13). In the Member State of arrival of the goods, a taxable intra-Community acquisition takes place.

The destination principle demands that goods are taxed in the Member State of destination. Taxing the importation of goods in the Member State of importation does not necessarily mean that this goal is not achieved, as long as the importer enjoys a right of deduction of the VAT paid on importation. In that case, Article 143(1)(d) VAT Directive only prevents the importer from having to pre-finance the VAT on importation.[44] In line with this, the CJEU has provided that the primary objective of the exemption is to provide a simplification that facilitates cross-trade.[45] It ensures that no VAT is applied in the Member State of importation (which is, in that case, not the Member State of destination of the goods). Since the intra-Community acquisition of the goods will be taxed in the Member State of arrival of the goods, the resulting taxation is in line with the destination principle.

14.10 DEDUCTION OF VAT PAID ON IMPORTATION

Article 168(e) VAT Directive allows for the deduction of input VAT due or paid in respect of the importation of goods in a Member State, in so far as the goods are used for the purposes of the taxed transactions of a taxable person. We refer to Chapter 10 on the deduction of VAT.

14.11 PERSON LIABLE TO PAY THE VAT ON IMPORTATION

On the basis of Article 201 VAT Directive, it is up to the Member States to designate or recognize a person as being liable to pay the VAT on importation. If goods cease to be covered by a customs arrangement, the person who caused that the goods ceased to be covered by the customs arrangements is the person who is liable for payment of VAT to the tax authorities (Article 202 VAT Directive). From the CJEU judgment in *U.I.*, it

44. If a Member State made use of the option provided for in Article 211 VAT Directive, the importer might not need to pre-finance the VAT on importation.
45. *See* CJEU 14 February 2019, Case C-531/17 *Vetsch Int. Transporte GmbH*, ECLI:EU:C:2019:114, para. 40. In this case, the CJEU has also provided that the exemption may not be refused to an importer in a situation in which, first, the recipient of the intra-Community transfer of goods effected after the import commits tax evasion in connection with a transaction which is subsequent to that transfer and is not linked to that transfer and, second, there is no evidence to support the conclusion that the importer knew or ought to have known that that subsequent transaction entailed tax evasion on the part of the recipient.

becomes apparent that Member States are under the obligation to provide for national legislation that properly arranges (joint and several) liability for VAT on importation; if national provisions do not explicitly and unequivocally designate the person who is liable, they cannot be accepted.[46] We refer to Chapter 12, Person Liable to Pay VAT.

14.12 OBLIGATIONS RELATING TO CERTAIN IMPORTATIONS

With respect to the importation of goods in free circulation which enter the EU from a third territory forming part of the customs territory of the Community, Articles 275, 276 and 277 VAT Directive contain a number of specific obligations.

Article 275 provides that the formalities relating to the importation of goods from a territory that is part of the customs territory, but not part of the VAT territory, are identical to those relating to the importation of goods from a territory that is neither part of the customs territory, nor part of the VAT territory (*see* section 14.5.2). Article 276 allows for such goods to be placed under the internal Community transit procedure laid down by the Community customs provisions in force.

14.13 IMPORTATION AND THE PLACE OF SUPPLY OF GOODS

In Chapter 4, the main rules on the place of supply of goods are discussed. With respect to international supplies of goods – goods that are dispatched or transported from one country to the other – the main rule is that the place of supply is the place where the goods are located at the time when dispatch or transport of the goods to the customer begins (Article 32, first paragraph, VAT Directive).

However, with respect to supplies of goods that are brought into the EU, two particularities exist, which will be addressed in this section.

14.13.1 Supplies by the Importer and Subsequent Supplies

Article 32, second paragraph, VAT Directive provides that if dispatch or transport of the goods begins outside the VAT territory of the EU, both the place of supply *by* the importer and the place of any subsequent supply will be within the Member State of importation of the goods. Clearly, this provision relates mainly to chain transactions (*see* section 3.2.3.2). Its purpose is to prevent that parties without a right of deduction can obtain goods from non-EU countries free of VAT by purchasing them from a 'middle man' or intermediary taxable person who acts as importer of record.[47] Below, we provide some examples to demonstrate the application of Article 32, second paragraph, VAT Directive.

46. CJEU 2 May 2022, Case C-714/20 *U.I.*, ECLI:EU:C:2022:374.
47. Without Article 32, second paragraph, VAT Directive, Article 32, first paragraph, VAT Directive would have the effect that both supply by the non-EU supplier (party A) to the intermediary (party B) and the supply by the intermediary (party B) to the person without a right of deduction (party C) have a place of supply outside the EU (i.e., where transport begins).

Example

Supplier A in Brazil supplies goods to company B in Germany. The goods are transported from Brazil to Germany. B acts as the importer of record and will be liable to pay the VAT on importation of the goods in Germany (Article 201 VAT Directive). Importer B in Germany subsequently supplies the goods to his customer C in Germany. On the basis of Article 32, first paragraph VAT Directive, the place of the supply by the Brazilian supplier will be in Brazil (making it not subject to EU VAT). This is not altered by Article 32, second paragraph VAT Directive since that paragraph only pertains to supplies by the importer. However, the place of the supply by importer B to customer C will be considered to be in Germany on the basis of Article 32, second paragraph VAT Directive because B imports the goods and subsequently supplies those goods to C (*see* Figure 14.10).

Figure 14.10 Article 32, Second Paragraph VAT Directive: Importation by B

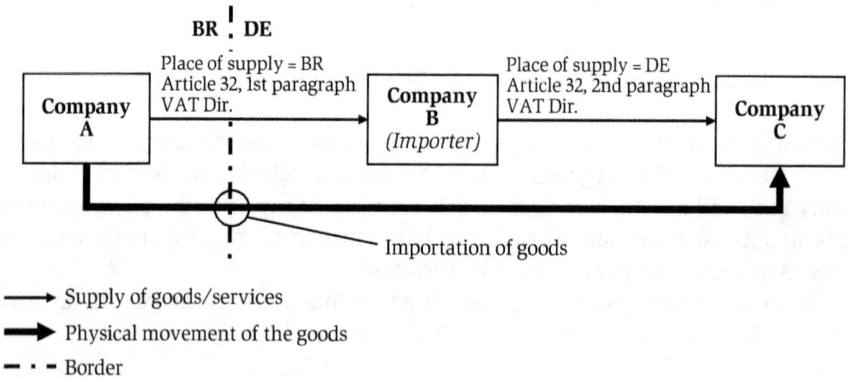

The scope of Article 32, second paragraph VAT Directive is not restricted to chain transactions. If the non-EU supplier A is the importer of record regarding the importation of the goods onto one of the EU Member States, his supply will take place within the EU, instead of in the country of departure, although the transport of the goods started outside the EU. The same rule applies to chain transactions in which A is the importer of record (already the first supply between him and his customer is deemed to take place in the Member State of importation).

Example

Supplier A in Brazil supplies goods to customer B in Germany. The goods are transported from Brazil to Germany. However, this time A himself acts as the importer of record and will be liable to pay the VAT on importation of the goods in Germany (Article 201 VAT Directive). A's customer B supplies the goods to C in Germany. On the basis of Article 32, second paragraph VAT Directive, the place of the supply by A will be in Germany, as A imported the goods in Germany. The subsequent supply by B to

C will also be located in Germany on the basis of Article 32, second paragraph VAT Directive (*see* Figure 14.11).

Figure 14.11 Article 32, Second Paragraph VAT Directive: Importation by A

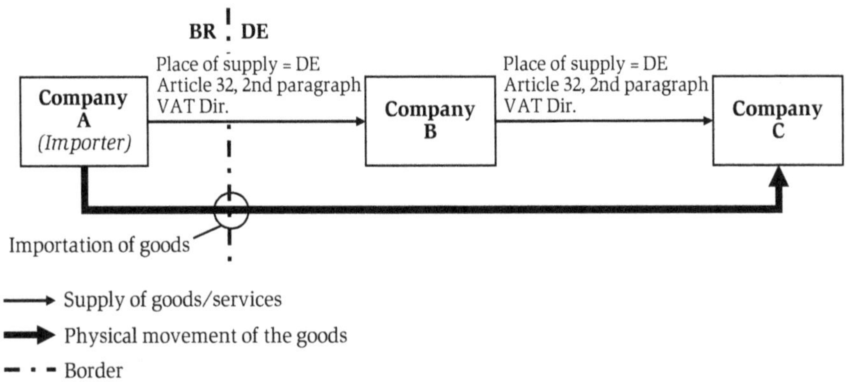

Example

Supplier A in Brazil supplies goods to customer B in Germany. The goods are transported from Brazil to Germany. Subsequently, B supplies the goods to C in Germany. On arrival of the goods from Brazil in Germany, C acts as the importer of record and will be liable to pay the VAT on importation of the goods in Germany (Article 201 VAT Directive). In this situation, Article 32, second paragraph VAT Directive, will not apply to the supply by A to B, nor will it apply to the supply by B to C since C imports the goods. On the basis of Article 32, first paragraph VAT Directive, both supplies will be considered to take place in Brazil (not subject to EU VAT) (*see* Figure 14.12).

Figure 14.12 Article 32, First Paragraph VAT Directive: Importation by C

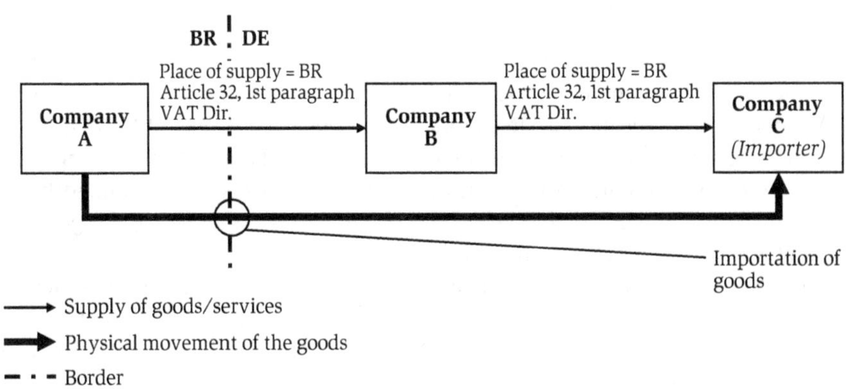

14.13.2 Supplies of Goods That Have Been Placed under a Customs Procedure

Article 30, first paragraph, VAT Directive defines 'importation of goods' as the 'entry into the Community of goods which are not in free circulation within the meaning of Article 24 of the Treaty' (*see* section 14.2). That means that even if goods are placed under a customs procedure, upon their entry into the Community, the goods have been imported.

In all the examples above, we have pinpointed the taxable transaction of importation at the moment of first entry into the Community – in other words, at the moment of the actual importation (the moment of the entry of the goods into the Community).

In situations in which goods have been placed under a customs procedure, one can, however, argue that the taxable transaction 'importation' takes a longer period and is only deemed to be fully completed at the moment that the goods cease to be covered by the already mentioned customs arrangements. In this view, the *taxable transaction* 'importation' starts at the moment of importation into the Member State of first arrival of the goods and elapses at the moment that the goods are brought into free circulation.

However, we do not share this view. In Chapter 5, we stated that the *chargeable event* in a temporal sense takes place at the moment that the taxable transaction has been completed. This is certainly true for regular supplies, like transactions involving goods and services, but the taxable transaction 'importation' has its own characteristics.

According to Article 30 VAT Directive, the importation of goods (the taxable transaction or event) is *'the entry into the Community'* of goods which are not in free circulation. With this in mind, we are of the opinion that the *taxable transaction* importation has already been completed upon (directly after) the first entry into the Community.

Further to Article 71 VAT Directive, the *chargeable event,* however, occurs no earlier than the moment at which *all* conditions are fulfilled for VAT to become due. That is the moment at which the goods cease to be covered by customs arrangements and at which they are thus brought into free circulation. Only at that moment are all the conditions fulfilled on the basis of which VAT upon importation becomes *materially* due (which is by definition the chargeable event). At the time of the chargeable event, the VAT becomes chargeable also in a more *formal* sense (*see* Article 71 VAT Directive: 'the chargeable event shall occur and VAT shall become chargeable') – meaning that the tax authorities are entitled to claim the VAT which needs to be remitted by the importer of record. The latter moment is also referred to as the *moment of chargeability*. *See* Chapter 5 for further clarification of these different moments of liability.

One has to keep in mind that the *place of importation* is not always the Member State in which the first entry into the Community takes place (cf. Article 60 VAT Directive). By way of fiction, and in deviation from Article 60 VAT Directive, Article 61 VAT Directive links the place of importation to the chargeable event. Further to this provision, the place of importation is the Member State within whose territory the goods cease to be covered by the already mentioned customs arrangements.

If non-EU goods that have entered the EU are *supplied* while they are under a suspensive customs regime (e.g., placed in a customs warehouse), in our view, that does not have any implications for the place where that supply of goods must be regarded to take place. It follows from *Profitube* that the place of supply rules for goods must be applied.[48] The place of supply is, in principle, to be determined on the basis of Article 31 VAT Directive if the goods are not transported in the course of the supply. The customs code, with regard to its scope, does not establish a special status for customs warehouses for VAT purposes. A customs warehouse is considered as being within the territory of the country where it is situated.[49]

Example

Supplier A in Brazil supplies goods to customer B in Germany. Immediately after their entry into the EU, the goods are placed in a customs warehouse in Germany. After a few days, B supplies the goods to customer C in Germany, while the goods remain in the warehouse. C (lawfully) removes the goods from the warehouse and brings the goods into free circulation. The supply by A to B must be considered as taking place outside the EU, on the basis of Article 32, first paragraph. Neither A nor B acts as the importer of the goods. The supply by B to C takes place in Germany (Article 31 VAT Directive) (*see* Figure 14.13).

Figure 14.13 Supply of Goods That Have Been Placed under a Customs Procedure

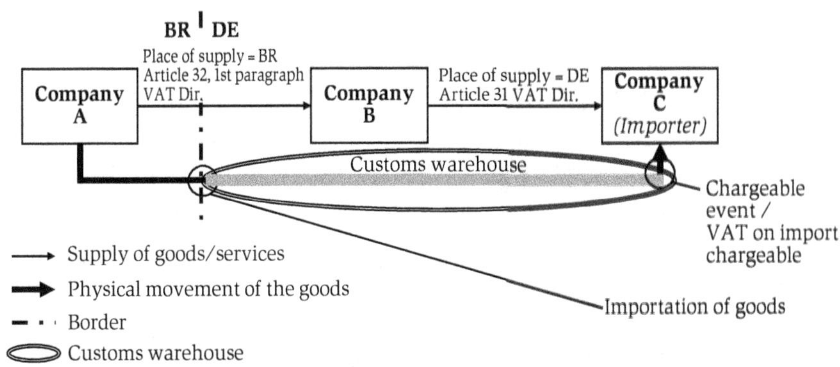

48. CJEU 8 November 2012, Case C-165/11 *Daňové riaditeľstvo Slovenskej republiky v Profitube spol. s r.o.*, ECLI:EU:C:2012:692.
49. *Ibid.*, para. 59.

14.14 TAXABLE TRANSACTIONS RELATING TO GOODS THAT ARE IMPORTED

In order to avoid double taxation, Article 144 VAT Directive exempts the supply of services relating to the importation of goods where the value of such services is included in the taxable amount of the importation. Since on the basis of Article 86(1) VAT Directive, various costs, such as costs of commission, packing, transport and insurance costs, must be included in the taxable amount of the importation of goods, Article 144 VAT Directive exempts those activities. Article 146(1)(e) VAT Directive provides for an exemption of services directly connected to goods that are placed under a customs procedure. Article 169(b) VAT Directive allows for input VAT deduction relating to these supplies.

14.15 THE IMPORTATION OF GOODS IN CONNECTION WITH NON-EU DISTANCE SALES OF GOODS (FROM 1 JULY 2021)

On 5 December 2017, the Council adopted Council Directive 2017/2455, the primary legislative instrument of the so-called VAT e-commerce package.[50] Accompanied by other legal instruments, the Directive is aimed at the modernization of EU VAT legislation as far as the e-commerce sector is concerned.[51] A considerable part of the VAT e-commerce package relates to so-called distance sales of goods imported from third territories or third countries (hereinafter 'non-EU distance sales').[52] In connection with these transactions, the following subparagraphs explain how the levy of VAT has been arranged from 1 July 2021 onwards.[53] In this regard, we note that as of 1 July

50. Council Directive (EU) 2017/2455 of 5 December 2017 amending Directive 2006/112/EC and Directive 2009/132/EC as regards certain value added tax obligations for supplies of services and distance sales of goods [2017] OJ L 348/7. For further reading on the VAT e-commerce packager, *see* M. Lamensch, *European Commission's New Package of Proposals on E-commerce: A Critical Assessment* (2017) 28 International VAT Monitor https://doi.org/10.59403/svhth4.
51. *See* Council Implementing Regulation (EU) 2019/2026 of 21 November 2019 amending Implementing Regulation (EU) No 282/2011 as regards supplies of goods or services facilitated by electronic interfaces and the special schemes for taxable persons supplying services to non-taxable persons, making distance sales of goods and certain domestic supplies of goods [2019] OJ L 313/14; Council Directive (EU) 2019/1995 of 21 November 2019 amending Directive 2006/112/EC as regards provisions relating to distance sales of goods and certain domestic supplies of goods [2019] OJ L 310/1; Commission Implementing Regulation (EU) 2020/194 of 12 February 2020 laying down detailed rules for the application of Council Regulation (EU) No 904/2010 as regards the special schemes for taxable persons supplying services to non-taxable persons, making distance sales of goods and certain domestic supplies of goods [2020] OJ L 40/114.
52. In short, this means supplies of goods dispatched or transported by or on behalf of the supplier, including where the supplier intervenes indirectly in the transport or dispatch of the goods, from a third territory or third country, to a customer in a Member State. *See* the new Article 14(4)(2) VAT Directive, as adopted by Council Directive (EU) 2017/2455 of 5 December 2017.
53. Note that these rules only apply under the following conditions: the supply of the goods (distance sale) is carried out for a taxable person, or a non-taxable legal person, whose intra-Community acquisitions of goods are not subject to VAT pursuant to Article 3(1) or for any other non-taxable person; the goods supplied are neither new means of transport nor goods supplied after assembly or installation, with or without a trial run, by or on behalf of the

2021, the import exemption for small consignments has been abolished, too.[54] For further reading, refer to section 16.7.

14.15.1 Two-Country Scenario: The Goods Are Imported from Third Territories or Third Countries into the Member in Which Dispatch or Transport of the Goods to the Customer Ends

In this scenario, typically, two countries are involved: the country of origin of the goods - a non-EU country - and the Member State in which the goods are imported and subsequently transported to the customer. The VAT consequences of distance sales are as follows from 1 July 2021:

(1) *The IOSS is used:* As the name suggests, the IOSS allows suppliers to arrange the reporting and payment of VAT on their non-EU distance sales with only one Member State, even if such sales are made to customers in the multiple Member States. For the IOSS to be used, various conditions apply (*see* section 16.7 for further reading). Among others, the intrinsic value of the goods must not exceed EUR 150.[55] If the IOSS is used, the place of supply of the distance sale shall be deemed to be in the mentioned Member State in which the goods are imported and subsequently transported to the customer.[56] Further, an exemption for the importation of the goods applies to the condition that the supplier or his intermediary provides his individual IOSS number to the customs authorities. By means of the IOSS, the distance seller (supplier) is required to report and pay VAT on the supply of the goods (distance sale), but not on the importation (*see* Figure 14.14).[57]

---

supplier. *See* the new Article 14(4)(2) VAT Directive, as adopted by Council Directive (EU) 2017/2455 of 5 December 2017. Initially, the new rules would enter into effect on 1 January 2021. Due to the COVID-19 pandemic, this has been postponed to 1 July 2021. Council Decision (EU) 2020/1109 of 20 July 2020 amending Directives (EU) 2017/2455 and (EU) 2019/1995 as regards the dates of transposition and application in response to the COVID-19 pandemic [2020] OJ L 244.

54. *See* Article 23 of Council Directive 2009/132/EC of 19 October 2009.
55. *See* the new Article 369l-369x VAT Directive, as adopted by means of Council Directive (EU) 2017/2455 of 5 December 2017.
56. *See* the new Article 33(c) VAT Directive, as adopted by Council Directive (EU) 2017/2455 of 5 December 2017.
57. In case another taxable person facilitates the distance sale through the use of an electronic interface (e.g., online marketplace), that person shall be deemed to have received and supplied those goods himself (*see* the new Article 33(c) VAT Directive, as adopted by Council Directive (EU) 2017/2455 of 5 December 2017).

Figure 14.14 The IOSS in a Two-Country Scenario

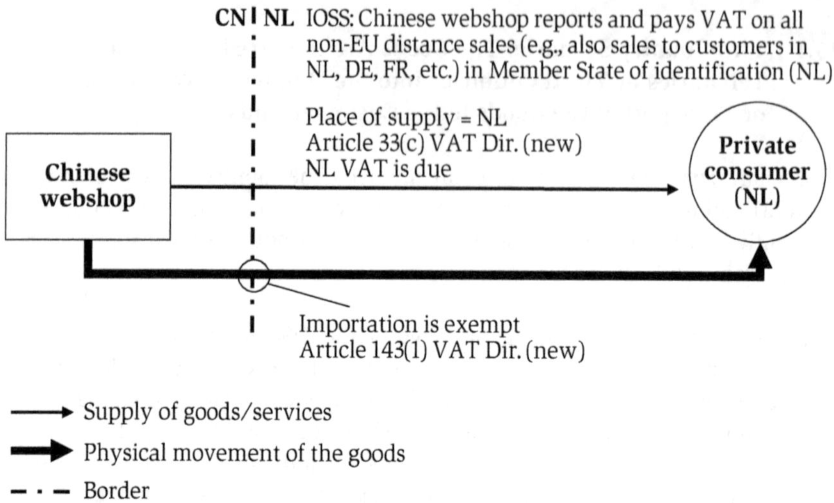

VAT Rate NL = 21%

(2) *The Carrier Import Scheme is used:* Notwithstanding the IOSS, it is also possible that the parties involved in the distance sale use the 'Carrier Import Scheme', which they can do on the conditions, among others, that the intrinsic value of the goods does not exceed EUR 150 and that the IOSS is not used.[58] For further reading, we refer to section 16.7. In case the Carrier Import Scheme is used, the place of supply of the goods is where the goods are located at the time when dispatch or transport of the goods to the customer begins (i.e., in the non-EU country).[59] Additionally, the person for whom the goods are destined (often the customer) shall be liable for the payment of the import VAT, yet the carrier is to collect this VAT from that person, to subsequently pay it to the authorities.[60] Thus, the VAT on the importation is settled by the carrier, who enjoys the possibility of reporting it electronically in a monthly declaration (*see* Figure 14.15).[61]

58. *See* the new Chapter 7 of Title XII of the VAT Directive, as adopted by means of Council Directive (EU) 2017/2455 of 5 December 2017.
59. Article 32 VAT Directive (assuming that the distance seller does not act as importer).
60. *See* the new Article 369z VAT Directive, as adopted by means of Council Directive (EU) 2017/2455 of 5 December 2017.
61. *See* the new Article 369zb(1) VAT Directive, as adopted by means of Council Directive (EU) 2017/2455 of 5 December 2017.

Figure 14.15 The Carrier Import Scheme in a Two-Country Scenario

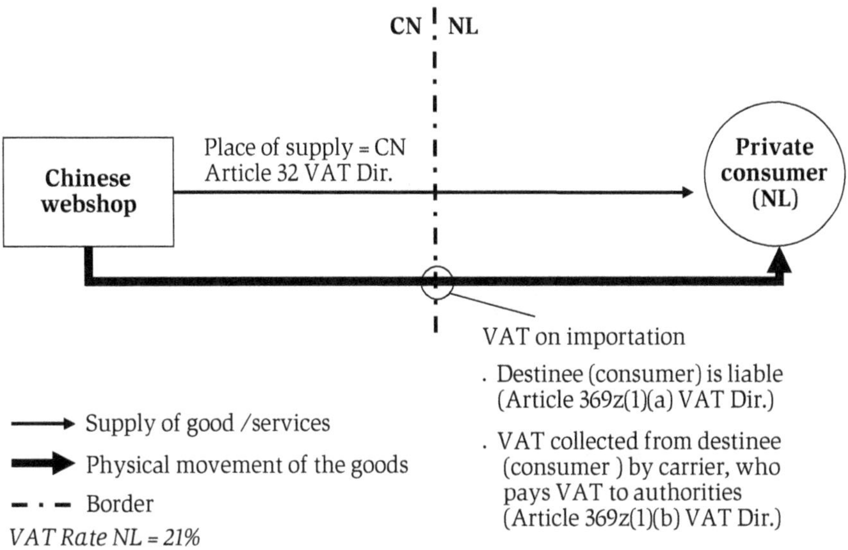

(3) *The IOSS nor the Carrier Import Scheme is used:* Both the IOSS and the Carrier Import Scheme have various conditions and, therefore, do not have general applicability. In particular, when the intrinsic value of the goods exceeds EUR 150, both schemes cannot be applied. In such situations, the standard rules on the levy of VAT on importation apply. Assuming that the distance seller presents the goods to the customs authorities (and thus acts as the importer of record), the supply of goods is deemed to be effected in the Member State of importation.[62] Consequently, the distance seller has to register for VAT purposes in that Member State and report and pay the VAT to the authorities.[63] Importation of goods takes place when the goods enter the Community; if he meets the requirements, the distance seller can deduct the VAT paid on importation.[64] In this manner, double taxation is avoided (*see* Figure 14.16).[65]

62. *See* Article 32 second paragraph VAT Directive. In case the customer acts as the importer of record, the supply of goods is deemed to be effected in the non-EU country where the goods are located at the time when dispatch or transport of the goods to the customer begins (Article 32 first paragraph VAT Directive). In that case, import VAT is due on importation; generally, the carrier will pre-finance that VAT and only release the goods after the customer has settled the payable VAT.
63. *See* Article 213 VAT Directive.
64. *See* Article 168(e) VAT Directive.
65. In case the customer acts as the importer of record, the supply is deemed to take place in the non-EU country where the transport starts (Article 32 first paragraph VAT Directive). The customer, being a final consumer, is not able to deduct the import VAT. In this way, taxation is realized in the Member State of destination.

Figure 14.16 The IOSS and Carrier Import Scheme Are Not Used in a Two-Country Scenario, Distance Seller Acts as Importer of Record

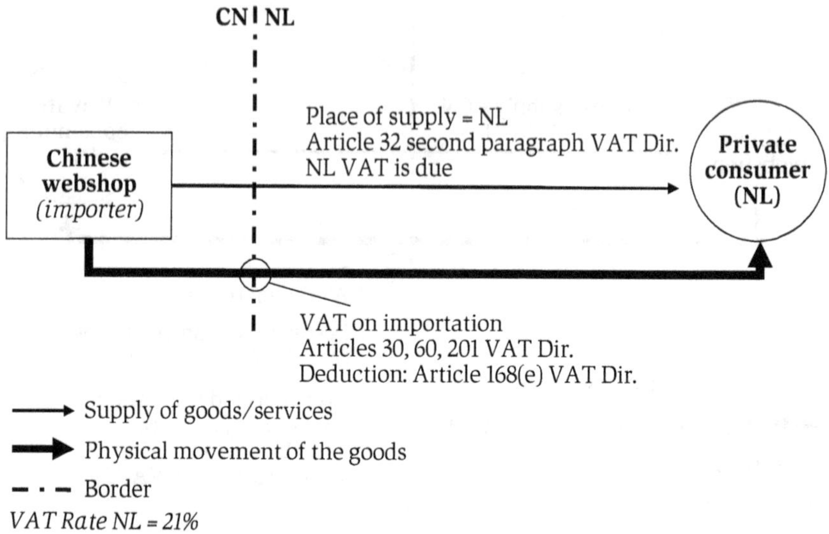

14.15.2 Three-Country Scenario: The Goods Are Imported from Third Territories or Third Countries into a Member State Other Than That in Which Dispatch or Transport of the Goods to the Customer Ends

In this scenario, typically three countries are involved: the country of origin of the goods – a non-EU country – the Member State in which the goods are imported, and the Member State where the transport of the goods to the customer ends. From 1 July 2021, the VAT consequences of distance sales are as follows:

(1) *The IOSS is used:* If the IOSS is used, the place of supply of the distance sale shall be deemed to be in the Member State where the goods are located at the time when the transport to the customer ends.[66] As with the IOSS in the two-country scenario, an exemption for the importation of the goods applies to the condition that the supplier or his intermediary provides his individual IOSS number to the customs authorities. By means of the IOSS, the distance seller (supplier) is required to report and pay VAT on the supply of the goods (distance sale), but not on the importation (*see* Figure 14.17).[67]

66. *See* the new Article 33(b) VAT Directive, as adopted by Council Directive (EU) 2017/2455 of 5 December 2017.
67. In case another taxable person facilitates the distance sale through the use of an electronic interface (e.g., online marketplace), that person shall be deemed to have received and supplied

Figure 14.17 The IOSS in a Three-Country Scenario, Distance Seller Acts as Importer of Record

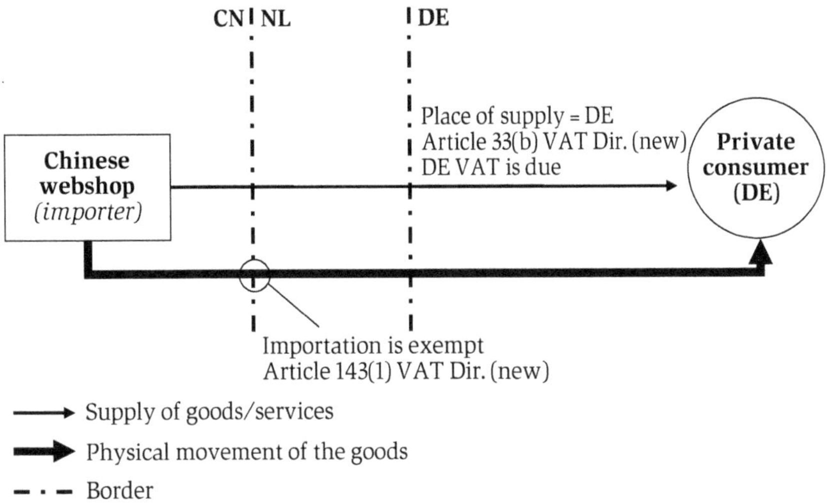

VAT Rate DE = 19%

(2) *The IOSS is not used:* In case the IOSS is not used, a distinction must be made between the situation in which the distance seller acts as the importer of record and the situation in which the customer (private consumer) acts as the importer of record. In the first situation, the place of supply of the distance sale is equally in the Member State where the goods are located at the time when the transport to the customer ends.[68] Consequently, in order to report and pay the VAT, the distance seller (who acts as the importer of record) needs to register for VAT purposes in that Member State.[69] He can reclaim the import VAT in the Member State of importation. In case the customer acts as the importer of record, the VAT consequences are different. In that situation, the private consumer would be confronted with import VAT in the Member State of importation, which he would not be able to reclaim.[70] At the same time, the distance seller would effect a taxed supply of the goods in the Member State where the transport to the customer ends.[71] Since the private consumer would also not be able to reclaim this VAT, double taxation is the

those goods himself (*see* the new Article 33(c) VAT Directive, as adopted by Council Directive (EU) 2017/2455 of 5 December 2017).

68. *See* the new Article 33(b) VAT Directive, as adopted by Council Directive (EU) 2017/2455 of 5 December 2017.
69. *See* Article 213 VAT Directive.
70. For import VAT to be reclaimed (deducted), Article 168(e) VAT Directive provides that one must use the goods for the purposes of taxed transactions. Further, one must have the quality and capacity of a taxable person.
71. *See* the new Article 33(b) VAT Directive, as adopted by Council Directive (EU) 2017/2455 of 5 December 2017.

result. In order to avoid this undesirable outcome, EU law provides that the customs office that is competent for the release for free circulation of the goods is the office situated in the Member State where transport ends.[72] In other words: in this particular situation, the goods must be customs cleared in the Member State of destination. The direct result is that the three-country scenario thus becomes, by virtue of EU law, a two-country scenario. Consequently, the supply by the distance seller is deemed to take place in the non-EU country where the transport starts (Article 32, first paragraph, VAT Directive). The customer, being a private consumer, is not able to deduct the import VAT. In this way, taxation is realized in the Member State of destination without double taxation occurring. *See* Figures 14.18a and 14.18b.

Figure 14.18a The IOSS Is Not Used in a Three-Country Scenario, Supplier Acts as Importer of Record

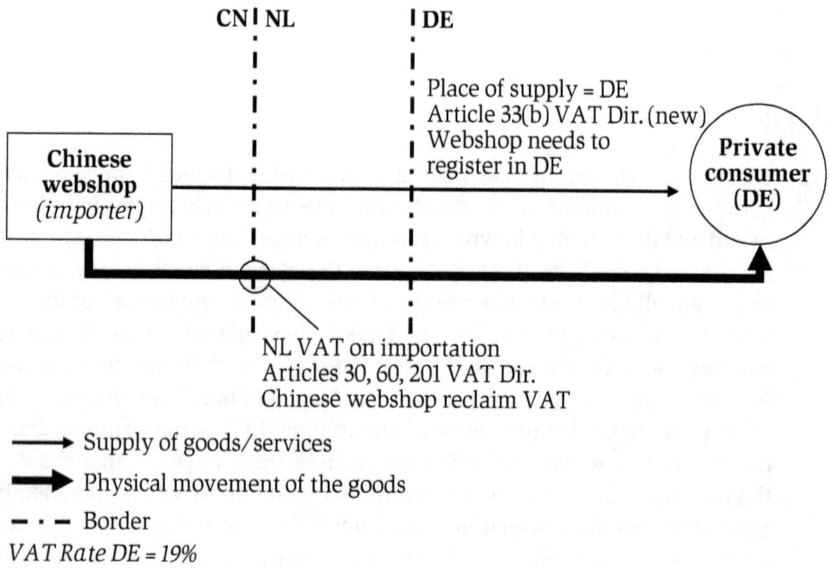

72. Article 221(4) Commission Implementing Regulation (EU) 2015/2447 of 24 November 2015, OJ L 343.

Figure 14.18b The IOSS Is Not Used in a Three-Country Scenario, Customer Acts as Importer of Record

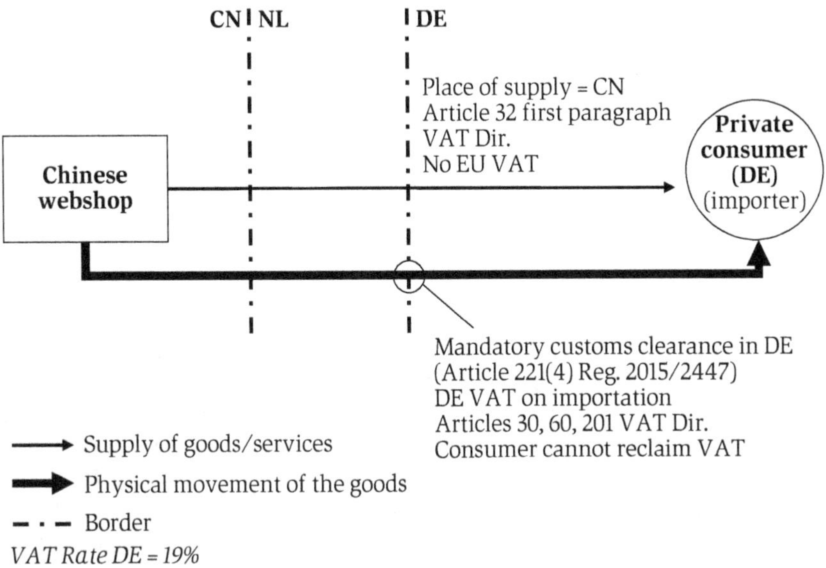

14.16 EXPORTATION OF GOODS

In section 14.1, we indicated that the exportation of goods itself is not a taxable transaction for VAT. Unlike importation of goods, exportation of goods is not mentioned in Article 2 VAT Directive. Consequently, if one transports EU goods to a non-EU location, that act in its own right does not result in a taxable transaction for EU VAT. This does not necessarily mean that there is (still) a burden of VAT on those goods. After all, taxable persons can, in principle, deduct the VAT on their purchases, even if the purchased goods are subsequently exported to a location outside the EU.

Notwithstanding the observations above, the transportation of goods to a non-EU location often takes place in the context of a supply of goods. As explained in Chapter 4, the supply of goods *is* a taxable transaction for VAT purposes (*see* Article 2(1)(a) VAT Directive). The place of supply of goods that are transported is where the goods are located at the time when dispatch or transport of the goods begins (Article 32, first paragraph VAT Directive).[73] Therefore, a supply of goods that are dispatched or transported to a destination outside the EU is considered to take place in the Member State of departure.

If such supply were to be burdened with EU VAT, EU suppliers would find themselves at a competitive disadvantage vis-à-vis their non-EU counterparties. In other words, the external neutrality of VAT would not be adhered to (*see* section 14.1)

73. Article 32, second paragraph VAT Directive is not relevant in this respect since it deals with goods that are dispatched or transported *from* a third country *to* a Member State.

in case goods originating from the EU would carry a (final) burden of EU VAT. Moreover, it is contrary to the destination principle to impose an EU VAT burden on products that are consumed outside the EU. Therefore, Article 146(1)(a) VAT Directive contains an exemption for supplies of goods that are dispatched or transported to a destination outside the Community by or on behalf of the vendor. On the basis of Article 169(b) VAT Directive, input VAT relating to exempt supplies for export is eligible for deduction.[74]

If the customer dispatches or transports the goods outside the EU, an exemption (with a right of deduction) will also apply to the supply, provided that the customer is established outside the EU (*see* Article 146(1)(b) VAT Directive). The condition that the customer must be established outside the EU may incite EU residents that purchase goods that are dispatched or transported outside the EU to arrange for the supplier to dispatch or transport the goods. For, in that situation, the supplier can apply the exemption of Article 146(1)(a) VAT Directive, whereas if the EU resident customer dispatches or transports the goods, no exemption is available. Goods transported by the customer himself for the equipping, fuelling and provisioning of pleasure boats and private aircraft or any other means of transport for private use are excluded from the exemption of Article 146(1)(b) VAT Directive anyway. The reason for that exception is that the private use of such goods must be taxed with VAT because VAT's legal character is that of a general tax on consumption. Article 146(1)(c) VAT Directive contains a specific exemption for export supplies to approved bodies that export them out of the Community as part of their humanitarian, charitable or teaching activities outside the Community. It is not uncommon that this exemption is implemented by means of a refund of VAT (Article 146(2) VAT Directive).

Articles 146(1)(d) and (e) VAT Directive do not relate to the export supply of goods itself, but rather to services on goods that are imported but will be exported again after having being worked upon. Article 146(1)(d) VAT Directive pertains to what is referred to as 'inward processing'.[75] In certain circumstances, it is possible, under those arrangements, to carry out various operations (working, processing, repair or use) within the Community customs territory on non-Community goods intended for re-export outside the Community customs territory in the form of compensating products without those products being subject to customs duties or agricultural levies.[76] Supplies of services relating to goods which are placed under this customs procedure – which is also relevant for VAT (*see also* section 8.7) – are exempted from VAT. That way, the external neutrality of VAT is safeguarded. Article 146(1)(e) VAT Directive further exempts services relating to goods that are exported (or imported).

74. Some Member States implemented the exemption for export supplies as a zero rate.
75. *See* Article 256 UCC.
76. *See* CJEU 8 February 1996, Case C-166/94 *Pezzullo Molini Pastifici Mangimifici SpA v Ministero delle Finanze*, ECLI:EU:C:1996:38, para. 11.

Article 147 VAT Directive contains an exemption relating to the personal luggage of travellers. If the traveller is not established within the Community and the goods are transported out of the Community before the end of the third month following that in which the supply takes place, the supply is exempt, provided that the total value of the supply, including VAT, is more than EUR 175. Member States may exempt a supply with a total value of less than EUR 175.

CHAPTER 15
Administrative Obligations

15.1 INTRODUCTION

In Chapters 5 (Chargeable event and Chargeability of VAT) and 12 (Person Liable to pay VAT), we explained at what point in time VAT obligations arise and by whom they should be fulfilled. Title XI of the VAT Directive contains a number of administrative obligations of taxable persons and certain non-taxable persons who are liable to account for VAT. The most noteworthy administrative obligations are to administratively register for VAT purposes with the competent public authorities, to issue VAT invoices in conformity with the legal requirements, to periodically submit VAT returns, to pay the net amount of the VAT due, to periodically file so-called recapitulative statements, and to keep adequate financial accounts. In this chapter, we discuss these administrative obligations in more detail. Moreover, we briefly discuss the administrative aspects of the ViDA-proposals (VAT rules in the Digital Age), the most recent legislative reform package of the European Commission.

We note that Member States enjoy the competence to adopt (administrative) measures of national law. Article 273 VAT Directive provides that they may impose other obligations which they deem necessary to ensure the correct collection of VAT and to prevent evasion, subject to the requirement of equal treatment and provided that such obligations do not, in trade between Member States, give rise to formalities connected with the crossing of frontiers. Such measures must comply with general principles of EU law; for example, following the principle of proportionality, they must not go beyond what is necessary to achieve the objectives pursued.[1]

15.2 NOTIFICATION, IDENTIFICATION AND (DE)REGISTRATION

Title XI, Chapter 2 of the VAT Directive is titled: 'Identification'. In fact, it deals with:

(1) Notification of activities (of commencing, changing or ceasing an activity as a taxable person).
(2) Identification of the subject of taxation by means of an individual number ('VAT registration').

In this section, we will discuss both the notification under Article 213 VAT Directive and the identification under Article 214 VAT Directive.

1. CJEU 11 November 2021, Case C-281/20 *Ferimet SL v Administracíon General del Estado*, ECLI:EU:C:2021:910, para. 32.

15.2.1 Notification of Commencing, Changing or Ceasing an Activity as a Taxable Person

Based on Article 213 VAT Directive, every taxable person must declare to the tax authorities when his activity as a taxable person commences, changes or ceases. As we have discussed in Chapter 2 (Taxable Person), the first investment expenditure incurred for the purpose of commencing a business must be regarded as an economic activity, granting the person making the investment the status of a taxable person for VAT purposes.[2] Thus, the tax authorities should be notified when the first investments are made with a view to future economic activities. The VAT Directive does not contain any provisions as to how such a notification is to be made. In our view, it is up to the Member States to adopt rules or arrangements for notifying the tax authorities of the start-up of a business.

In practice, the notification of the start-up of a business is also referred to as 'registering for VAT purposes'. However, strictly speaking, the notification of the start-up of a business and the VAT registration (identification by means of a VAT ID number) are two separate administrative affairs. For example, on the basis of the text of Article 213(1) VAT Directive, taxable persons who (will) exclusively carry out transactions in respect of which VAT is deductible are required to notify the tax authorities when starting up their businesses, yet taxable persons who only carry out transactions under the reverse charge mechanism do not necessarily need to register for VAT purposes (*see* Article 214(1)(a) VAT Directive and Chapter 12, Person Liable to Pay VAT). In practice, there is a wide variety of ways in which Member States deal with issuing of VAT ID numbers to taxable persons who solely carry out transactions that do not give rise to any VAT due. Furthermore, under the special scheme for small enterprises (Articles 281-294 VAT Directive), Member States may introduce and maintain VAT registration thresholds.[3]

A taxable person not only has an obligation to notify the tax authorities when his economic activity commences but also when his activity as a taxable person changes or ceases (Article 213(1) VAT Directive). It would seem that, in practice, the requirement to notify the tax authorities of changes in the activities of a taxable person is not applied very strictly.

When a taxable person ceases his activity, he will usually request that the tax authorities deregister him for VAT purposes. After deregistration, the former taxable person can, in principle, no longer file VAT returns. This may be problematic if a taxable person incurs costs relating to his former business after he has been registered. Further to the principle of fiscal neutrality, the VAT on such costs should be recoverable.[4] In some Member States, upon deregistration, the tax authorities perform a final VAT audit in order to ensure that all VAT due has been duly reported and collected. It

2. *See* CJEU 14 February 1985, Case 268/83 *D.A. Rompelman and E.A. Rompelman-Van Deelen v Minister van Financiën*, ECLI:EU:C:1985:74 and CJEU 29 February 1996, Case C-110/94 *Intercommunale voor zeewaterontzilting (INZO) v Belgian State*, ECLI:EU:C:1996:67.
3. *See* Editorial, *VAT Registration Thresholds in Europe* (2014) 6 International VAT Monitor.
4. *See* CJEU 3 March 2005, Case C-32/03 *I/S Fini H v Skatteministeriet*, ECLI:EU:C:2005:128.

follows from Article 3 VAT Directive, the last paragraph that taxable persons and non-taxable legal persons who have opted for taxation of their intra-Community acquisitions cannot deregister until at least two years from the time when they *opted for taxation* of their intra-Community acquisitions and, therefore, have been VAT registered. It seems, however, that taxable persons and non-taxable legal persons who were obliged to register for VAT purposes when *exceeding the threshold for taxation* of their intra-Community acquisitions may be deregistered for VAT purposes after one year following the calendar year in which the threshold was exceeded and their intra-Community acquisitions became subject to VAT.[5] We refer to section 13.5.

15.2.2 VAT Registration

Article 214 VAT Directive contains the obligation for Member States to take the measures necessary to ensure that the persons listed in that provision are 'identified by means of an individual number' (i.e., 'registered for VAT'). In this subsection, we will discuss this requirement in more detail.

15.2.2.1 **Ratio Legis** ***of the Requirement of VAT Registration***

Registering for VAT (i.e., obtaining a VAT ID number, *see* Articles 214(1) and 215 VAT Directive) is extremely important to start-ups because, in principle, only VAT-registered businesses can recover the VAT that they incurred on their expenses (investments). For the same reason, registering for VAT purposes is also important to non-established businesses commencing taxable transactions in another Member State for which they are liable to pay the VAT. However, in *Nidera*, the CJEU ruled that a taxable person who meets the substantive conditions for the right of deduction and who identifies himself as a taxable person for VAT purposes within a reasonable period following the completion of transactions giving rise to that right of deduction, cannot be denied recovery of the VAT on his inputs for the sole reason that he was not identified as a taxable person before using those goods in his taxable activity.[6] In *Polski Traweryn Kopalnia*, the CJEU reaffirmed this.[7] The fact that a supplier has not been identified for VAT purposes does not necessarily mean that the recipient cannot deduct the VAT charged to him.[8]

Naturally, the process of registering for VAT purposes is also relevant for tax administrations. The primary reason is that by means of VAT registrations, they

5. Article 3(2)(b) VAT Directive.
6. CJEU 21 October 2010, Case C-385/09 *Nidera Handelscompagnie BV v Valstybine mokesčių inspekcija prie Lietuvos Respublikos finansų ministerijos*, ECLI:EU:C:2010:627.
7. CJEU 1 March 2012, Case C-280/10 *Kopalnia Odkrywkowa Polski Trawertyn P. Granatowicz, M. Wąsiewicz spółka jawna v Dyrektor Izby Skarbowej w Poznaniu*, ECLI:EU:C:2012:107, para. 47.
8. Where the relevant invoices contain all the information, in particular, the information needed to identify the person who drew up those invoices and to ascertain the nature of the services provided, a taxable person can deduct the VAT on the services supplied by another taxable person who is not registered for that tax. CJEU 22 December 2010, Case C-438/09 *Bogusław Juliusz Dankowski v Dyrektor Izby Skarbowej w Łodzi*, ECLI:EU:C:2010:818.

become aware of taxable persons who carry out economic activity. This administrative link between the authorities and the taxable persons constitutes the obvious connection point for supervision and enforcement. Generally, a VAT registration also triggers the obligation to file periodic VAT returns because the process of filing VAT returns and paying VAT due is, in principle, directly connected to VAT registration. Moreover, the VAT ID number that is issued to a taxable person who registers for VAT purposes also has an important function in the context of taxation itself. For example, the application of the exemption for intra-Community supplies of goods is dependent on the indication by the customer of his VAT ID number to the supplier, and on the reporting of this number in the recapitulative statement of the supplier (*see* Article 138(1)(b) and (1a) VAT Directive).[9] Also, in connection with the place of supply of services, a non-taxable legal person who is identified for VAT purposes by means of an individual number shall be regarded as a taxable person. Even though the VAT registration process and the VAT ID number may appear to be administrative affairs, they have a real and material impact on the application of VAT.[10]

15.2.2.2 Who Should Register for VAT?

Based on Article 214(1)(a) VAT Directive, Member States are obliged to provide a VAT registration number ('VAT identification number') to every taxable person who carries out supplies of goods or services that give rise to a right to deduct VAT.

Under certain circumstances, not only taxable persons but also non-taxable persons are required to register for VAT. In particular, a VAT liability and an obligation to register for VAT purposes arise in case certain persons exceed the threshold for taxation of their intra-Community acquisitions (se*e* Article 3(1)(b) and (2) VAT Directive):

(1) flat-rate scheme farmers;
(2) taxable persons who are not entitled to deduction;
(3) non-taxable legal persons.

Furthermore, the intra-Community acquisition by a non-taxable legal person who has opted for taxation of his acquisitions, triggers an obligation to register for VAT purposes. These intra-Community acquisitions are subject to VAT on the basis of Article 3 VAT Directive, and therefore, notification and VAT registration are obligatory pursuant to Articles 213(2) and 214(1)(b) VAT Directive (*see* Chapter 13 on Intra-Community Transactions).

Based on Article 196 VAT Directive, taxable persons and VAT-registered non-taxable legal persons are liable to pay VAT under the so-called reverse charge mechanism if they receive services referred to in Article 44 VAT Directive from taxable

9. *See* Chapter 12 for further reading.
10. *See*, for example, Article 43(2) VAT Directive, which provides that a non-taxable legal person who is identified for VAT purposes shall be regarded as a taxable person for the purpose of applying the place of supply rules. *See* Chapter 4.

persons established outside their Member State (so-called B2B main rule services; *see* Chapters 4 'Place of Supply' and 12 'Person Liable to Pay VAT'). VAT identification of both the supplier and the recipient of such B2B services enables Member States to carry out supervisory checks on the reporting of such services since the supplier must periodically file a recapitulative statement listing the services supplied per customer's VAT ID number (Article 262(c) VAT Directive). Therefore, Member States are obliged to provide VAT registration numbers to:

(1) taxable persons supplying services to a customer in another Member State for which the customer is liable to pay the VAT pursuant to Article 196 VAT Directive (*see* Article 214(1)(e) VAT Directive); and
(2) taxable persons receiving such services for which they are liable to pay VAT pursuant to Article 196 VAT Directive (*see* Article 214(1)(d) VAT Directive).

It should be noted that non-taxable legal persons can also be liable to pay VAT on their purchases of services from a supplier in another Member State, pursuant to Article 196 VAT Directive. This is the case if they are already registered for VAT for other reasons. Yet, Article 214(1)(d) VAT Directive makes no mention of this category of customers. The reason for that is that in order for such non-taxable legal persons to fall within the scope of Article 196 VAT Directive in the first place, they must already be identified for VAT purposes on the basis of Article 214(1)(b) VAT Directive.

The tax authorities cannot simply refuse to register a person meeting the criteria of Article 214 VAT Directive. However, it appears that the VAT registration of a company can be refused if there is sound evidence leading to the suspicion that the VAT ID number assigned will be used fraudulently.[11]

15.2.2.3 VAT Grouping and VAT Registration

In Chapter 2 ('Taxable Persons'), we discussed the concept of VAT grouping. If implemented by the Member State (the national provision implementing), Article 11 VAT Directive allows persons who are bound to one another by financial, economic and organizational links no longer to be treated as separate taxable persons for the purposes of VAT. Instead, these persons are treated as a single taxable person. It follows from *Ampliscientifica* that the treatment as a single taxable person precludes persons who are thus closely linked from continuing to be identified, within and outside their group, as individual taxable persons.[12] According to the CJEU, if various persons together are considered as a single taxable person under Article 11 VAT Directive, this single taxable person, the VAT group, must be identified as such.

11. CJEU 14 March 2013, Case C-527/11 *Valsts ieņēmumu dienests v Ablessio SIA*, ECLI:EU:C:2013:168.
12. CJEU 22 May 2008, Case C-162/07 *Ampliscientifica Srl, Amplifin SpA v Ministero dell'Economia e delle Finanze, Agenzia delle Entrate*, ECLI:EU:C:2008:301, para. 19.

15.2.2.4 OSS Identification

As of 1 July 2021, Title XII (Special Schemes), Chapter 6 of the VAT Directive contains 'Special schemes for taxable persons supplying services to non-taxable persons or making distance sales of goods or certain domestic supplies of goods' and 'special arrangements for declaration and payment of import VAT'. In practice, the special schemes referred to in this section of the VAT Directive are commonly referred to as the OSS.[13] In section 16.7, we will elaborate on the OSS schemes in further detail.

Simply put, the OSS scheme allows taxable persons to obtain a special 'OSS' identification and report the VAT on the qualifying transactions in all Member States of consumption via one single web portal of the tax authorities in the Member State in which they choose to register for the OSS scheme. Effectively, the scheme takes away the need to register for VAT in each and every one of the Member States of consumption. The taxable person pays the VAT due in each Member State of consumption to the tax authorities of the Member State in which he registered for the OSS scheme (i.e., Member State of OSS identification). Subsequently, the tax authorities of the Member State of OSS identification transmit the information and the corresponding VAT paid to each Member State of consumption.

15.2.2.5 VAT ID Numbers

Article 215 VAT Directive stipulates that each individual VAT ID number shall have a prefix in accordance with ISO code 3166 – alpha 2 – by which the Member State of issue may be identified. Nevertheless, Greece may use the prefix 'EL'. On the basis of Article 216 VAT Directive, Member States must take the measures necessary to ensure that their identification systems enable the taxable persons referred to in Article 214 to be identified and to ensure the correct application of the transitional arrangements for the taxation of ICTs (*see* Chapter 13, 'Intra-Community Transactions').

In this regard, it is worth mentioning that Member States maintain electronic databases containing the VAT registration data of all taxable persons the VIES. The European Commission maintains a website, which is connected to the Member States' VAT databases.[14]

15.3 INVOICES

In this section, we will discuss the invoicing requirements laid down in Title XI, Chapter 3 VAT Directive (Article 217 and further).[15] Within the domain of EU VAT, the

13. Until 1 July 2021, the scheme only applied to telecommunication, broadcasting and electronic service. With regard to its limited scope, it was often referred to as (M)OSS. We note that the 'special arrangements for declaration and payment of import VAT' also include the Carrier Import Scheme (*see* section 16.7).
14. https://ec.europa.eu/taxation_customs/vies/#/vat-validation (accessed 21 August 2024).
15. The most recent major overhaul of the invoicing rules took place on the basis of the European Council Directive 2010/45/EU (the so-called Invoicing Directive), which was adopted on 13 July 2010. The Invoicing Directive entered into force on 1 January 2013.

invoice serves as an administrative reflection of a taxable transaction; at the same time, it is used by the taxable person to charge VAT to the recipient of the supply of goods or services.[16]

15.3.1 The Role of the Invoice in the EU VAT System

The invoice plays an essential role in EU VAT. It has the following three functions:

(1) it contains information on the application of VAT (e.g., VAT rates, exemptions, reverse charge mechanism);[17]
(2) it enables the tax authorities to carry out controls throughout the full chain of production and distribution;[18] and
(3) it allows a taxable person (in his capacity as supplier) to charge VAT to others, and to deduct the VAT that was charged to him (in his capacity as recipient of a supply).

Given the essential role of the invoice in EU VAT, it is not surprising that the invoicing rules have been largely harmonized. The VAT Directive provides a set of rules with regard to invoicing in Articles 220-240 VAT Directive. These provisions deal with the concept of invoices, the obligation to issue invoices, the content of invoices, electronic invoices and provide certain simplification measures.

15.3.2 The Invoice as a Requirement for the Deduction of Input VAT

According to Advocate General Sir Gordon Slynn, an invoice that complies with the rules is the 'ticket of admission' to the right of deduction of input VAT.[19] Indeed, based on Article 178(a) VAT Directive, a taxable person who is entitled to VAT deduction pursuant to Article 168(a) VAT Directive must hold an invoice drawn up in accordance with the invoice rules laid down in Articles 220-240 VAT Directive in order to be able to exercise his right to deduct VAT. In *Terra Baubedarf*, the CJEU confirmed that the right to deduct VAT must be exercised in respect of the tax period in which both conditions laid down in Article 178(a) VAT Directive are equally satisfied, namely that the goods have been delivered or the services performed and that the taxable person

16. If adopted, the 2022 ViDA-proposals of the Commission will drastically change the invoicing rules of the VAT Directive. *See* section 15.8 for further reading.
17. In some cases, chargeability of VAT is linked to the issuance of an invoice. For example: Article 203 VAT Directive. *See* Chapter 5.
18. Cf. CJEU 1 March 2012, Case C-280/10 *Kopalnia Odkrywkowa Polski Trawertyn P. Granatowicz, M. Wąsiewicz spółka jawna v Dyrektor Izby Skarbowej w Poznaniu*, ECLI:EU:C:2012:107, para. 48.
19. *See* Opinion of Advocate General Gordon Slynn of 31 May 1988, Joined Cases 123/87 and 330/87 *Léa Jorion, née Jeunehomme, and Société anonyme d'étude et de gestion immobilière 'EGI' v Belgian State*, ECLI:EU:C:1988:408.

holds a valid invoice or a document which may be considered to serve as a valid invoice.[20]

However, it is also clear that sometimes a right of deduction must be allowed, even if an invoice cannot be presented to the authorities. In *Bockemühl*, the CJEU answered the question of whether a recipient of cross-border services[21] who is liable to pay the VAT with respect to those services under the reverse charge mechanism may only exercise his right to deduct input VAT under Article 178(a) VAT Directive if he is in possession of an invoice issued in accordance with Article 226 VAT Directive. The CJEU decided that where the reverse charge mechanism applies, a taxable person who is liable, as the recipient of services for the VAT relating thereto, in accordance with (what is now) Article 196 VAT Directive does not have to be in possession of an invoice drawn up in accordance with Article 226 VAT Directive in order to be able to exercise his VAT deduction right.[22] Thus, where the reverse charge mechanism is applicable, there seems to be no link between the invoice obligations and the right to deduct the input VAT. Furthermore, an invoice is not required in order to exercise the right to deduct VAT due upon importation of goods into the EU. Instead, the taxable person entitled to a deduction of the import VAT must hold a valid import document (whether in paper form or electronic) specifying him as consignee of the goods or as an importer of record, and stating the VAT amount due or enabling that amount to be calculated.[23] With respect to the ICA, Article 181 VAT Directive holds that Member States may authorize a taxable person who is not in possession of a valid VAT invoice to make the deduction referred to in Article 168(c) VAT Directive in respect of his ICA. As a result, the VAT deduction will generally be effected in the same tax period as the one in which the VAT becomes payable with respect to the intra-Community acquisition.

We refer to sections 10.2.2.4 and 10.2.2.5 for further reading.

15.3.3 The Concept of an Invoice

Article 218 VAT Directive instructs the Member States to accept documents or messages on paper or in electronic form as invoices if they meet the conditions laid down in the specific provisions on invoicing. It follows from *John Reisdorf* that the Members States are permitted to regard as an invoice not only the original invoice but also any other document serving as an invoice that fulfils the criteria determined by the Member States themselves (e.g., a copy of the original invoice).[24]

Furthermore, any document or message that amends and refers specifically and unambiguously to the initial invoice (i.e., a credit note) must also be treated as an invoice by the Member States (Article 219 VAT Directive).

20. CJEU 29 April 2004, Case C-152/02 *Terra Baubedarf-Handel GmbH v Finanzamt Osterholz-Scharmbeck*, ECLI:EU:C:2004:268.
21. Subject to the main place of supply rule for B2B services of Article 44 VAT Directive.
22. CJEU 1 April 2004, Case C-90/02 *Gerard Bockemühl v Finanzamt Gummersbach*, ECLI:EU:C:2004:206.
23. Article 178(e) VAT Directive.
24. CJEU 5 December 1996, Case C-85/95 *John Reisdorf v Finanzamt Köln-West*, ECLI:EU:C:1996:466.

15.3.4 The Obligation to Issue an Invoice

Article 220 VAT Directive deals with the obligation to issue invoices. According to this provision, every taxable person must ensure that an invoice is issued in respect of supplies of goods and services, which he has made to another taxable person or to a non-taxable legal person. Furthermore, every taxable person must issue an invoice for supplies of goods that are subject to the distance selling rules of Article 33 VAT Directive[25] and for exempt intra-Community supplies referred to in Article 138 VAT Directive (*see* Chapter 13, Intra-Community Transactions). A taxable person is also obliged to issue an invoice if a payment on account (also referred to as prepayment) is made to him before the supply of goods was carried out, or the provision of the services was completed. However, an invoice is not required if a payment on account is made with respect to exempt intra-Community supplies of goods.

The VAT Directive does not require the invoice to be issued by the taxable person supplying the goods or services himself. The invoice may also be issued by his customer (a process generally referred to as *self-billing*), or by a third party in the name and on behalf of the taxable person.

It should be noted that the invoicing rules leave certain options for the Member States as regards the obligation to issue invoices with respect to supplies that are VAT-exempt (Articles 220(2) and 221(2) VAT Directive) and with respect to supplies to non-taxable persons (Article 221(1) VAT Directive). These options could raise issues where, for example, VAT-exempt services that fall under the main place of supply rule for services of Article 44 VAT Directive are supplied cross-border, and one of the Member States has used the option to require the issuing of a VAT invoice.

15.3.5 Applicable Invoicing Rules

Before 1 January 2013, the VAT Directive did not expressly state which Member State's invoicing rules applied in the case of cross-border supplies of goods and services. To provide legal certainty for businesses regarding their invoicing obligations, a set of harmonized rules was created on the basis of which one can determine which Member State's invoicing rules apply (Article 219a VAT Directive).

15.3.5.1 Main Rule: Invoicing Rules of the Place of Supply

Article 219a VAT Directive determines which Member State's set of rules on invoicing are applicable.[26] As a main rule, Article 219a(1) VAT Directive states that the invoicing rules of the Member State in which the supply of goods or services is deemed to be made in accordance with the provisions governing the place of supply of goods and services (Articles 31-61 VAT Directive) apply. For example, if a Bulgarian company

25. An exception applies when the taxable person makes use of the OSS (*see* section 16.7.2).
26. According to the Explanatory Notes on the VAT invoicing rules, the provisions of Article 219a VAT Directive do not relate to the storage of invoices, https://taxation-customs.ec.europa.eu/system/files/2016-09/explanatory_notes_en.pdf (accessed 21 August 2024). The Explanatory

sells and transfers newly built real estate located in Hungary to a Hungarian company, the Hungarian invoicing rules apply. This is because the place of supply, according to Article 31 VAT Directive is where the real estate is located, which in this case, is Hungary.

15.3.5.2 Exception for EU Suppliers: Invoicing Rules of the Supplier's Member State

Notwithstanding the above, invoices with respect to cross-border reverse charge supplies are subject to the rules applying in the Member State in which the supplier has established his business, has his permanent address, usually resides, or has a fixed establishment from which the supply is made. The same applies to invoices for supplies for which the place of supply is located outside the EU. If the aforementioned Bulgarian company, for example, were to provide advisory services to the Hungarian company, the Bulgarian invoicing rules would apply. The place of supply would be Hungary under the B2B main rule of Article 44 VAT Directive. However, the liability of the Hungarian VAT is shifted to the customer on the basis of Article 196 VAT Directive. Because the reverse charge mechanism applies, the *Bulgarian* invoicing rules apply, following Article 219a(2)(a) VAT Directive. This particular invoicing rule increases efficiency and reduces the invoice burden for service suppliers. After all, if the invoicing rules of the customer's Member States were to be applicable, this would require the supplier to inform himself of the customer's Member State invoicing requirements. Even though the invoicing requirements have been harmonized to a large extent, still, the differences between the Member States would mean that service suppliers that have (business) customers in multiple Member States were to experience a substantial administrative burden.

The exception of Article 219a(2)(a) VAT Directive does not apply in case of so-called self-billing. That means that the main rule of Article 219a(1) VAT Directive also applies in case of self-billed invoices where the customer issuing the invoice is also liable to pay the VAT due under the reverse charge mechanism. In that case, the invoicing rules of the Member State where the supply takes place shall apply. We deem this to be a reasonable approach, as the self-billing customer will generally be better informed on the invoicing rules of his own Member State than on those of the Member State of the supplier.

From the wording of Article 219a(2) VAT Directive, it follows that the exception to the main rule does not apply in case the supplier is established outside the EU. As a result, the main rule applies. This means that suppliers established outside the EU that make supplies of goods and services within the EU are required to issue invoices that meet the invoicing requirements of each respective Member State in which the supplies

Notes are not legally binding and although the notes are published by the European Commission, they do not represent the views of the European Commission. The Explanatory Notes are considered to be the result of discussions of the European Commission with both Member States and businesses across the EU.

are made.[27] Suppliers established outside the EU, therefore, have to comply with 27 sets of invoicing rules within the EU – a rather extensive administrative burden.

15.3.5.3 Exception in Case the OSS Is Applied

In case a taxable person makes use of the OSS for the reporting and payment of VAT, he is entitled to apply the invoicing rules applicable in the Member State where he has been identified for the OSS (*see* Article 219a(2)(b) VAT Directive). We refer to Chapter 16 for further reading on the OSS.

15.3.6 The Content of Invoices

The VAT Directive distinguishes between two types of invoices: standard invoices and simplified invoices. In principle, a standard invoice must be issued where the person to whom the supply is made is a taxable person or a non-taxable legal person. However, an exception to this rule applies when credit notes or correction invoices are issued (Article 219 VAT Directive) or when the taxable amount of the respective supply is less than EUR 100. In those cases, a simplified invoice may be issued (Article 220a VAT Directive).

15.3.6.1 Standard Invoices

Article 226 VAT Directive requires the following information to be included on the invoice:

(1) the date of issue;
(2) a sequential number, based on one or more series, which uniquely identifies the invoice;
(3) the VAT ID number under which the taxable person supplied the goods or services;
(4) the customer's VAT ID number in case the VAT liability is shifted to the customer under the reverse charge mechanism or in case of an exempt ICS;[28]
(5) the full name and address of the taxable person and of the customer;
(6) the quantity and nature of the goods supplied or the extent and nature of the services rendered;

27. The Explanatory Notes explicitly state that for suppliers not established in the EU making taxable supplies of goods or services in the EU, the exceptions indeed do not apply and the basic invoicing rule always applies, that being the Member State where the supply takes place. Explanatory Notes on VAT invoicing rules, https://taxation-customs.ec.europa.eu/system/files/2016-09/explanatory_notes_en.pdf (accessed 21 August 2024), p. 26.
28. Member States may require that the VAT ID number of the customer is mentioned in other cases than those mentioned here (Article 227 VAT Directive).

(7) the date on which the supply of goods or services was made or completed or the date on which the payment on account was made, in so far as that date can be determined and differs from the date of issue of the invoice;
(8) where the VAT becomes chargeable at the time when the payment is received in accordance with Article 66(b) VAT Directive and the right of deduction arises at the time the deductible tax becomes chargeable, the phrase 'Cash accounting';
(9) the taxable amount per rate or exemption, the unit price exclusive of VAT and any discounts or rebates if they are not included in the unit price;
(10) the VAT rate applied;
(11) the VAT amount payable, except where a special arrangement is applied under which such detail is excluded;
(12) where the customer receiving a supply issues the invoice instead of the supplier, the phrase 'Self-billing';
(13) in the case of an exemption, reference to the applicable provision of the VAT Directive, or to the corresponding national provision, or any other reference indicating that the supply of goods or services is exempt;
(14) where the customer is liable for the payment of the VAT, the phrase 'Reverse charge';
(15) in the case of the intra-Community supply of a new means of transport, the details that show that the means of transport supplied is 'new';
(16) where the margin scheme for travel agents is applied, the phrase 'Margin scheme - Travel agents';
(17) where one of the special arrangements applicable to second-hand goods, works of art, collectors' items and antiques are applied, the phrase 'Margin scheme - Second-hand goods', 'Margin scheme - Works of art' or 'Margin scheme - Collector's items and antiques', respectively;
(18) where the person liable for payment of VAT is a tax representative for the purposes of Article 204 VAT Directive, the VAT ID number, referred to in Article 214 VAT Directive, of that tax representative, together with his full name and address.

If the invoice is issued by a taxable person, who is not established in the Member State where the VAT is due, or whose establishment in that Member State does not intervene in the supply (*see* Article 192a VAT Directive), and who is making a supply of goods or services subject to the reverse charge mechanism, the details referred to in points (9), (10) and (11) above may be omitted on the basis of Article 226a VAT Directive. Instead, the invoice must indicate, by reference to the quantity or extent of the goods or services supplied and their nature, the taxable amount of those goods or services.

For purposes of supervision and enforcement, Member States may require translation into their official languages of invoices in respect of supplies of goods or services supplied in their territory and invoices received by taxable persons established in their territory. Member States may, however, not impose a general requirement that invoices be translated.[29]

15.3.6.2 Simplified Invoices

In the event of the issuance of a credit invoice or of a (debit) invoice for an amount less than EUR 100, Member States must allow taxable persons to issue simplified invoices (Article 226b VAT Directive). However, for intra-Community supplies of goods that are exempt (Article 138 VAT Directive) and for distance sales (Article 33 VAT Directive), it is not allowed to issue a simplified invoice. Furthermore, it is not allowed to issue simplified invoices for cross-border services subject to the reverse charge mechanism. However, for these supplies, the simplifications of Article 226a VAT Directive apply (*see* section 15.3.6.1).

According to Article 226b VAT Directive, simplified invoices should include at least the following details:

(1) the date of issue;
(2) identification of the taxable person supplying the goods or services;
(3) identification of the type of goods or services supplied;
(4) the VAT amount payable or the information needed to calculate it;
(5) where the invoice issued is a credit note, a specific and unambiguous reference should be made to the initial invoice and the specific details which are being amended.

Member States are not allowed to require further statements for VAT purposes (Article 226b VAT Directive).

15.3.7 Sending Invoices by Electronic Means

Invoices may be issued in paper form or can be sent or made available by electronic means. For an invoice to be considered an electronic invoice, it needs to be *issued* and *received* in an electronic format.[30]

Based on Article 232 VAT Directive, the use of an electronic invoice is subject to acceptance by the recipient. In our view, this does not mean that the customer must explicitly confirm the acceptance of each and every electronic invoice upon receipt. Since the VAT Directive requires that paper invoices and electronic invoices are treated equally, the acceptance of an electronic invoice by the customer should be determined in a similar manner as the acceptance of a paper invoice, e.g., by written acceptance of the invoicing procedure, or by the processing or payment of the electronic invoice.

29. Article 248a VAT Directive.
30. Explanatory Notes VAT invoicing rules, https://taxation-customs.ec.europa.eu/system/files/2016-09/explanatory_notes_en.pdf (accessed 21 August 2024), p. 9.

A key item for any type of electronic invoicing is that the authenticity of the origin, the integrity of the content and the legibility of an electronic invoice should be safeguarded (Article 233 VAT Directive). Given the crucial role that invoices have in respect of both VAT liability and VAT recovery, there should be no doubt as to the validity of an electronic invoice. Finally, we note that the Commission wants to shift from paper invoicing to electronic invoicing as the default invoicing method as of 1 January 2028 (for further reading, *see* section 15.8 on the ViDA-proposals of the Commission).

15.3.8 Time Limit to Issue Invoices

Article 222 VAT Directive states that invoices with respect to exempt intra-Community supplies of goods and cross-border services subject to the reverse charge mechanism must be issued no later than on the 15th calendar day of the month following that in which the supply took place.[31] Member States are still allowed to impose different time limits for other (domestic) supplies of goods and services. The Netherlands, for example, has not used this option provided for in Article 222 VAT Directive, second paragraph VAT Directive. Thus, in principle, all invoices to which the Dutch invoicing rules apply (*see* section 15.3.5) need to be issued no later than on the 15th calendar day of the month following that in which the supply takes place.

If on the basis of a contract, cross-border supplies are made on a *continuous* basis over a period of time (e.g., long-term lease of means of transport), the following applies pursuant to Articles 64 and 222 VAT Directive.

Cross-border services subject to the reverse charge mechanism that is provided on a continuous basis are deemed to be completed at least once per calendar year. As a result, an invoice must be issued no later than on the 15th calendar day of the month following the month in which the service was deemed to be completed.

As *continuous* intra-Community supplies of goods that are exempt are deemed to be completed on expiry of each calendar month, the invoice for these supplies must be issued at the latest on the 15th calendar day of the month following that in which the supplies are deemed to be made.

31. Prior to 1 January 2013, Member States were allowed to establish the time limit for issuing an invoice, which led to disharmonized rules across the EU. With a view to improving the functioning of the internal market, it was necessary to impose a harmonized time limit for the issue of an invoice with respect to certain cross-border supplies. *See* para. 6 to European Council Directive 2010/45/EU of 13 July 2013 amending Directive 2006/112/EC on the common system of value added tax as regards the rules on invoicing [2010] OJ L189/1. The ViDA-proposals of the Commission contain rules that greatly shorten the time limit for issuing invoices. Article 222 VAT Directive (proposed) stipulates that in case of intra-Community B2B supplies of goods and services, or in case of supplies under the reverse charge mechanism (Article 194 VAT Directive), invoices must be issued no later than two working days following the supply.

15.4 VAT RETURNS

Pursuant to Article 250 VAT Directive, taxable persons are required to file a periodical VAT return, setting out all the information needed to calculate the VAT that has become chargeable. Member States shall allow VAT return to be filed electronically and can set a deadline for filing, which may not be more than two months after the tax period. Since the tax period can be defined by the Member States, even if it cannot exceed one year, the VAT filing periods differ per Member State.[32]

15.5 PAYMENT OF THE NET VAT AMOUNT

Assuming that VAT is payable by the taxable person, the net amount of VAT must be paid to the tax authorities at the moment the VAT return is submitted (Article 206 VAT Directive). However, Member States may decide to set a different date for payment of the VAT and may even require interim payments to be made (Article 206 VAT Directive). As a result, the moment when the tax must be paid to the tax authorities can differ per Member State.

15.6 RECAPITULATIVE STATEMENTS

Since the introduction of the special regime for intra-Community trade in goods in 1993, every VAT taxable person must submit a so-called recapitulative statement (EC Sales List) of the persons to whom he has supplied *goods* in accordance with Article 138 VAT Directive (exempt intra-Community supplies of goods).[33] The recapitulative statement must include the total value of the supplies made by the taxable person to each taxable person or non-taxable person making intra-Community acquisitions subject to VAT. Furthermore, the recapitulative statement must mention the VAT ID number of each person acquiring the goods as these persons should, in principle, report an intra-Community acquisition of the goods in the Member State of arrival and pay the VAT due. It seems fair to say that in the VAT system for intra-Community trade, VAT ID numbers are essential, not only for businesses trading across the EU but also for the tax authorities as they are to ensure the proper collection of VAT.

Since 1 January 2010, the recapitulative statement must also be filed with respect to cross-border *services* (other than VAT-exempt services) within the EU for which the recipient is liable to account for VAT pursuant to Article 196 VAT Directive (*see* Article 262(c) VAT Directive). The recapitulative statement must include the VAT ID number of the recipient of the services and must mention the value of the services provided to each recipient. Based on Article 55 of the VAT Implementing Regulation, taxable persons and non-taxable legal persons that are liable to account for VAT on the basis

32. Some time ago, the Commission published a proposal for a standard(ized) VAT return, which it ultimately retracted again (*see* Proposal for a Council Directive amending Directive 2006/112/EC on the common system of value added tax as regards a standard VAT return, COM (2013) 0721 final).
33. Article 262 VAT Directive. *See also* section 13.3.2.2.9.

of Article 196 VAT Directive with respect to services received, are obliged to communicate their VAT ID number to their service provider. Finally, we note that since 1 January 2020, the exemption for intra-Community supplies of goods (*see* Chapter 13) does not apply where the supplier has not complied with the obligation to file a recapitulative statement containing the correct information (*see* Article 138(1a) VAT Directive and section 13.3.2.2.9) unless he can duly justify his shortcoming to the satisfaction of the competent authorities.

15.7 FINANCIAL ACCOUNTS

Pursuant to Article 242 VAT Directive, every taxable person is held to keep accounts in sufficient detail for VAT to be applied and its application checked by the tax authorities. This is a general administrative obligation. Its purpose is to ensure that the bookkeeping of taxable persons is of sufficient quality to support the VAT treatment they applied. Also, it should safeguard that tax authorities can check and audit the VAT treatment applied by taxable persons. The VAT Directive does not provide for further detail (e.g., the period required to retain financial accounts) besides this general obligation. This is left to the discretion of the individual Member States.

15.8 ADMINISTRATIVE ASPECTS OF 'VAT IN THE DIGITAL AGE'

On 8 December 2022, the European Commission proposed a legislative package to combat VAT fraud on the one hand and to modernize the VAT system on the other.[34] The package, referred to as the ViDA, employs mainly digitalization as a means to achieving the mentioned goals.[35] At the time of writing of this book, the proposal remained in the negotiation and consultation phase at the level of the ECOFIN and had not been adopted yet.[36]

Some of the proposed rules are substantive by nature, i.e., not formal or administrative. The most important substantive rules are as follows:

- ***Mandatory reverse charge:*** In line with the ambition to make it possible for companies to have only a 'single VAT registration' while doing business throughout the EU, the Commission has proposed to adopt a mandatory reverse charge for supplies of goods or services by a taxable person who is not established in the Member State in which the VAT is due, in case the supply is

34. *See* the Proposal for a Council Directive amending Directive 2006/112/EC as regards VAT rules for the digital age, 8 December 2022, COM/2022/701 final.
35. For further reading, *see* B. van der Doef, N. Verbaan, J. Gruson & M. Merkx, *VAT in the Digital Age Package: Viva la ViDA or Livin' la ViDA Loca?* (2023) 3 EC Tax Review https://doi.org/10.54648/ecta2023018; P. Wille, *EU VAT in the Digital Age* (2023) 1 International VAT Monitor https://doi.org/10.59403/3v3bwy6; C. Amand, *VAT in the Digital Age Proposal: Can DRR Tackle VAT Fraud?* (2023) 5 International VAT Monitor https://doi.org/10.59403/1k1c4ph.
36. https://eur-lex.europa.eu/legal-content/EN/HIS/?uri=celex:52022PC0701, accessed on 15 August 2024.

effected for a person who is already identified for VAT purposes in that state.[37] By shifting the liability of VAT to the recipient, the supplier no longer needs to register to report and pay output VAT.

- ***Deemed supplier regime***: In order to effectively collect VAT on short-term accommodation rentals and passenger transport services offered by the (digital) platform economy, the Commission has proposed a deemed supplier regime.[38] Under this regime, the platform (e.g., AirBNB) will charge and account for the VAT on the underlying service provided by the person who offers the respective services.

Many other rules are predominantly administrative or formal by nature. The most important ones are the following:

- ***Expansion of the OSS scheme:*** The current OSS scheme allows (certain) taxable persons to report certain types of transactions (e.g., non-EU and EU distance sales of goods, services rendered to non-taxable persons in the EU) in one Member State of identification, irrespective of where in the EU the transactions are taxable. If the proposals are adopted, the OSS will also cover local B2C supplies of goods by taxable persons not identified for VAT purposes in the respective Member State, as well as intra-Community transfers of own goods by taxable persons.[39] This change follows from the ambition of the Commission to move towards a 'single VAT registration' for companies doing business on the EU's internal market.
- ***Electronic invoicing (e-invoicing)***: Currently, the VAT Directive leaves from the notion that paper invoicing is the default instrument for the administration of transactions and the charging of VAT.[40] Following the ViDA-proposals, the Commission wants to change to electronic invoicing as the default method as of 1 January 2028.[41] In case of intra-Community B2B supplies of goods and services, or in case of supplies under the reverse charge mechanism (Article 194 VAT Directive), invoices must be issued no later than two working days following the supply.[42]
- ***Digital reporting requirements:*** The ViDA-proposals contain various rules aimed at improving, in a temporal sense, the vertical flow of information to the tax authorities.[43] For each individual ICTs, taxable persons will, as of 1 January 2028, be required to submit detailed data (e.g., taxable amount, date of issue of invoice) to the authorities. The data must be submitted no later than two working days after the issuing of the invoice, or after the invoice should

37. Proposed Article 194(1) VAT Directive.
38. Proposed Article 28a VAT Directive.
39. *See* the proposed Articles 369a(e) VAT Directive and 369xa-369xk VAT Directive.
40. *See* section 15.3.
41. Proposed Article 218 VAT Directive.
42. Proposed Article 222 VAT Directive.
43. Proposed Articles 262 and further VAT Directive.

have been issued.[44] With this 'near real-time' reporting obligation, the Commission hopes to contribute to the fight against (intra-Community) VAT fraud.

At the time of writing of this book, the ViDA-proposals were not yet adopted; it remains to be seen in what form, if at all, the proposed rules will ultimately be adopted by the EU legislature.

44. Proposed Article 263 VAT Directive.

CHAPTER 16
Special Schemes

16.1 INTRODUCTION

The VAT Directive contains six special schemes in connection with the levy of VAT in particular sectors of the economy. These special schemes are laid down in Title XII of the VAT Directive and concern: (i) SMEs, (ii) farmers, (iii) travel agents, (iv) second-hand goods, works of art, collector's items and antiques, (v) investment gold, (vi) the (import) 'OSS' and the carrier import scheme. The first three schemes are designed to streamline the levying of VAT for various particular categories of taxable persons. The fourth and fifth schemes are introduced to remove foreseen difficulties in connection with specific supplies of goods. The last scheme is introduced to provide for administrative simplification and to promote VAT compliant behaviour of, in particular, taxable persons established outside the EU.

Not all special schemes are mandatory. Member States have the option to introduce SME or flat-rate schemes for farmers, yet do need to implement such schemes into their national legal order. As the special schemes deviate from and are an exception to the regular VAT system, they should be interpreted and applied strictly.[1]

16.2 SMALL- AND MEDIUM-SIZED ENTERPRISES

On 18 February 2020, the EU legislator adopted a revised VAT scheme for the SME scheme, which applies from 1 January 2025. In this paragraph, we discuss both the former SME scheme (applying until 1 January 2025) and the current, revised one (applying from 1 January 2025).

16.2.1 The Former SME Scheme (Applicable until 1 January 2025)

The former special scheme for SMEs was laid down in Articles 281-294 VAT Directive. Its primary aim was to reduce the administrative burden for SMEs. Pursuant to Article 281 VAT Directive, Member States could introduce simplified procedures for charging and collecting VAT, which may not, however, lead to a reduction of the amount of VAT.

The SME scheme consisted of two central tenets. First, Member States were allowed to exempt taxable persons whose annual turnover was no higher than EUR 5,000 (hereinafter 'the exemption').[2] If these taxable persons indeed enjoyed the exemption, they were not entitled to deduct any input VAT charged to them and, moreover, were not allowed to mention VAT on the invoices that they issued.[3] Second, Member States were allowed to grant a graduated tax relief to taxable persons whose annual turnover exceeded the threshold of the exemption.[4]

The SME scheme had an optional character. Taxable persons who were entitled to the exemption from VAT could opt either to apply the normal VAT regime (i.e., charging, invoicing and deducting VAT) or the SME exemption scheme. In practice, taxable persons would only opt for the SME scheme when that was favourable from a financial point of view.

The VAT Directive allowed Member States to provide SMEs with a VAT exemption where their turnover did not exceed a certain amount per year. No exemption applied, however, if the turnover was generated by non-established taxable persons.[5] In *Ingrid Schmelz*, the question was raised as to whether this territorial limitation was

1. CJEU 8 March 2012, Case C-524/10 *European Commission v Portuguese Republic*, ECLI: EU:C:2012:129.
2. *See* Article 285 VAT Directive and European Commission, *Green Paper on the Future of VAT, Towards a Simpler, More Robust and Efficient VAT System*, Brussels, 1 December 2010, COM (2010) 695 final, p. 17. Note that Member States are allowed to continue using special schemes that they had in place previously (Article 284 VAT Directive).
3. *See* Article 289 VAT Directive.
4. *See* Article 285 VAT Directive.
5. Article 283(1)(c) VAT Directive.

compatible with the fundamental freedoms and with the general principle of non-discrimination.[6] The CJEU assessed that the restriction of the SME scheme to established taxable persons was a restriction to the freedom of establishment (Article 49 TFEU). However, according to the CJEU, the objective of maintaining effective fiscal supervision and combating fraud, evasion and abuse justified this territorial limitation. Notwithstanding the CJEU judgment in *Ingrid Schmelz*, the EU legislator has recognized the apparent drawbacks of the territorial scope of the current SME scheme. In fact, it was one of the primary drivers for the adoption of the revised SME scheme – which will be discussed in the following subparagraph.[7]

16.2.2 The Revised SME Scheme (Applying from 1 January 2025)

In 2018, the Commission proposed a revised SME scheme.[8] The proposal, which has been adopted by the Council on 18 February 2020 and has entered into force per 1 January 2025, is aimed at reducing administrative burdens for SMEs and at providing them with an environment that stimulates growth and cross-border trade.[9] The revised SME scheme, that is laid down in Articles 280a-292d VAT Directive, relies on three thresholds, each of which is connected with certain simplifications or facilitations:

(1) *Administrative threshold*: The EU legislator has introduced a yearly turnover threshold of EUR 2 million, enshrined in the legal definition of the concept of 'SME',[10] allowing SMEs remaining below this threshold to enjoy certain administrative simplifications (i.e., concerning VAT registration, invoicing, keeping of accounts and VAT returns). The threshold relates to 'Union turnover', i.e., the total annual value of supplies of goods and services, exclusive of VAT, made by a taxable person within the territory of the Community.

(2) *National threshold:* The EU legislator has introduced an optional yearly 'national' turnover threshold, which shall be no higher than EUR 85,000.[11] It allows Member States to exempt the supplies of goods and services made within their territory, assuming the enterprise does not exceed the threshold.

6. CJEU 26 October 2010, Case C-97/09 *Ingrid Schmelz v Finanzamt Waldviertel*, ECLI: EU:C:2010:632.
7. *See* the recitals of the Proposal for a Council Directive amending Directive 2006/112/EC on the common system of value added tax as regards the special scheme for small enterprises, COM (2018) 21 final. The EU legislator considers that '(...) despite the fact that Member States may exempt SMEs from VAT – an option that is widely used – SMEs continue to suffer from disproportionate VAT compliance costs due to how the SME exemption is designed. In particular, SMEs involved in cross-border trade cannot benefit from the SME exemption in Member States other than the one in which they are established.'
8. *See* Proposal for a Council Directive amending Directive 2006/112/EC on the common system of value added tax as regards the special scheme for small enterprises, COM (2018) 21 final.
9. *See* Communication from the Commission to the European Parliament, the Council and the European Economic and Social Committee on an action plan on VAT, Towards a single EU VAT area – Time to decide, COM (2016) 148 final, 7 April 2016, p. 6.
10. *See* Article 280a(1) VAT Directive.
11. *See* Article 284(1) VAT Directive.

Member States that implement this threshold into their national legislation are required to also exempt the supplies of enterprises established in other Member States (non-established EU enterprises), assuming their turnover does not exceed the national threshold.

(3) *Union threshold:* Finally, the EU legislator has provided for a yearly 'Union' turnover threshold of EUR 100,000.[12] It is by means of this aggregate threshold that the revised scheme indeed remains restricted to small enterprises. It entails that Member States shall only exempt the supplies of a non-established EU enterprise if the total turnover made by that enterprise within the territory of the Community remains below EUR 100,000 (Union threshold). Effectively, this means that for a non-established EU enterprise to be eligible for the exemption in any given Member State that has implemented a national threshold (max EUR 85,000), its turnover in the respective Member State should not exceed that national threshold, and its total turnover in the Community should not exceed the Union threshold (EUR 100,000).

It is by means of the revised SME Scheme that the EU legislator has mitigated the territorial limitation following from the *Ingrid Schmelz* judgment, in which the CJEU provided that Member States are allowed to limit the applicability of the VAT exemption for small undertakings to entrepreneurs established in their own territory, and to the annual turnover realized there.[13] Under the new rules, the combination of the national threshold and the Union threshold implies that entrepreneurs can make use of SME Schemes in other Member States than the one in which they are established themselves, assuming that they do not exceed, with their total EU turnover, the Union threshold. Non-EU businesses cannot make use of the scheme.

16.3 FLAT-RATE FARMER SCHEME

The so-called common flat-rate scheme for farmers (hereinafter 'flat-rate farmer scheme') is laid down in Articles 295-305 VAT Directive. This special scheme applies to the agricultural sector. A special scheme was considered necessary because the EU institutions were of the opinion that the burden of keeping detailed records for VAT compliance should be removed for farmers. Given the scale, professionalism and technical standards of modern farms, one may question whether a special scheme is still appropriate.[14]

The flat-rate farmer scheme is optional both for (farming) businesses and Member States. On the basis of Article 295(1)(1) VAT Directive, the scheme can be used by 'farmers', who are defined as taxable persons whose activity is carried out in an agricultural, forestry or fisheries undertakings. In contrast to SMEs (which commonly make use of the SME scheme), farmers often find themselves in the first leg(s)

12. *See* Article 284(2)(a) VAT Directive.
13. CJEU 26 October 2010, Case C-97/09, *Ingrid Schmelz v Finanzamt Waldviertel*, ECLI: EU:C:2010:632, para. 71.
14. The Netherlands have abolished the Dutch flat-rate farmer scheme as of 1 January 2018.

of the supply chain - and thus do not typically supply products to final consumers. Thus, if the farmer scheme would entail an exemption similar to that of the SME scheme, cascading of VAT would take place within the supply chain.[15] For that reason, the flat-rate farmer scheme relies instead on an exemption for the supplies made by the farmer in combination with a flat-rate compensation to offset the (non-deductible) VAT charged to the farmer. The compensation, which is either paid to the farmer or deducted by the customer, is calculated as a percentage fixed by the Member State and applied to the farmer's turnover.[16]

According to Article 297 VAT Directive, Member States themselves calculate the flat-rate compensation percentages. Following Article 298 VAT Directive, these percentages are calculated on the basis of macroeconomic statistics for flat-rate farmers alone for the preceding three years.

The percentages may be rounded up or down to the nearest half-point. Member States may also reduce such percentages to a nil rate.[17] The flat-rate compensation percentages are only to be applied to specific agricultural products and services.[18]

Pursuant to Article 302 VAT Directive, flat-rate farmers entitled to flat-rate compensation are not allowed to deduct input VAT. On the basis of Article 303 VAT Directive, taxable persons paying flat-rate compensation to farmers that apply the flat-rate farmer scheme are entitled to deduct the compensation amount from their VAT due.

16.4 TRAVEL AGENTS SCHEME

The special scheme for travel agents - referred to as the TOMS in connection with the plans to overhaul the scheme[19] - is laid down in Articles 306-310 VAT Directive. Member States are required to implement this scheme in their national legislation. According to the CJEU, the objective of the TOMS is to prevent the complications that the application of the normal VAT rules would cause where travel packages, including services provided outside the Member State, are concerned.[20] When a travel agent purchases services, such as hotel accommodations and transport services from third parties in other countries to subsequently include these in a travel package that he sells

15. The customers of the farmers (e.g., food processing plants) would incur non-deductible VAT which farmers have included n the price of their products.
16. Article 301(1) VAT Directive.
17. From CJEU 8 March 2012, Case C-524/10 *European Commission v Portuguese Republic*, ECLI:EU:C:2012:129, it is clear that Member States are not allowed to apply a nil rate under all circumstances. This is only allowed where calculations are actually made and show that the overall burden of input VAT borne by flat-rate farmers can be regarded as insignificant.
18. *See* Article 300 VAT Directive.
19. *See* https://ec.europa.eu/info/law/better-regulation/have-your-say/initiatives/11883-VAT-scheme-for-travel-agents-evaluation-_en (accessed 21 August 2024).
20. For example: CJEU 12 November 1992, Case C-163/91 *Van Ginkel Waddinxveen BV, Reis- en Passagiersbureau Van Ginkel BV and others v Inspecteur der Omzetbelasting Utrecht*, ECLI:EU:C:1992:435; CJEU 22 October 1998, Cases C-308/96 and C-94/97 *Commissioners of Customs and Excise v T.P. Madgett, R.M. Baldwin trading as The Howden Court Hotel*, ECLI:EU:C:1998:496 and CJEU 26 September 2013, Case C-189/11 *European Commission v Kingdom of Spain*, ECLI:EU:C:2013:587.

in his own name and on his own behalf to a traveller, he would, under the normal VAT rules, have to pay VAT on every supply of services and register in each Member State from which he purchased services. Further to this, the CJEU has underlined that the main aim of the TOMS is to avoid the practical difficulties to which economic operators in the travel sector would be exposed if the regular VAT rules would apply to them.[21] In other words: the standard provisions on the place of supply, the taxable amount and the deduction of VAT are unsuitable for the travel sector, which relies on composite transactions that often materialize in complex international settings.

Following Article 307 VAT Directive, all transactions performed by a travel agent in respect of a single travel package are treated as a single supply of services for VAT purposes. This single service is taxable in the Member State where the travel agent is established or has a fixed establishment from which the travel agent has carried out the supply of services. So, a travel agent established in France has to charge French VAT. Pursuant to Article 308 VAT Directive, VAT is only due in respect of the travel agent's margin, i.e., the difference between the total amount, exclusive of VAT, to be paid by the traveller and the actual external cost to the travel agent.[22] In conclusion, the travel agent has no right to deduct VAT on supplies made to him, but on the other hand, only pays VAT on the profit margin he realizes on the supply of his travel package.

No definition of 'travel agent' is provided for by the VAT Directive, although Article 306(2) states that tour operators must be regarded as travel agents, nor is the VAT Directive clear as to which services of travel agents are subject to this special regime. CJEU case law, however, provides some guidance in this respect. It can be derived from this case law that services by travel agents that fall within the scope of this regime encompass a variety of services within or outside the Member State where the travel agent is established and which, in particular, are aimed at transportation and accommodation. In *Van Ginkel*, however, the CJEU decided that the TOMS also applies in case a travel agent (who can also be a tour operator) merely provides the traveller with holiday accommodation but does not arrange transport to the holiday destination. In *First Choice Holidays*,[23] *Ist*[24] and especially *Minerva Kulturreisen*,[25] the CJEU clarified that only services that can be seen as a package of services can fall within the scope of

21. *See* CJEU 19 December 2018, Case C-422/17 *Szef Krajowej Administracji Skarbowej v Skarpa Travel sp. z o.o.*, ECLI:EU:C:2018:1029, para. 28.
22. These costs should have been incurred for the direct benefit of the traveller. *See also* CJEU 16 January 2014, Case C-300/12 *Finanzamt Düsseldorf-Mitte v Ibero Tours GmbH*, ECLI:EU:C:2014:8, in which the CJEU decided that a cash-back provided for by the travel agent could not reduce the taxable amount. The CJEU ruled that the principles established by the CJEU in *Elida Gibbs* concerning the determination of the taxable amount for VAT purposes do not apply when a travel agent, acting as an intermediary, grants to the final consumer, on the travel agent's own initiative and at his own expense, a price reduction on the principal service provided by the tour operator. *See* CJEU 24 October 1996, Case C-317/94 *Elida Gibbs Ltd v Commissioners of Customs and Excise*, ECLI:EU:C:1996:400.
23. CJEU 9 June 2003, Case C-149/01 *Commissioners of Customs & Excise v First Choice Holidays plc*, ECLI:EU:C:2003:358.
24. CJEU 13 October 2005, Case C-200/04 *Finanzamt Heidelberg v ISt internationale Sprach- und Studienreisen GmbH*, ECLI:EU:C:2005:608.
25. CJEU 9 December 2010, Case C-31/10 *Minerva Kulturreisen GmbH v Finanzamt Freital*, ECLI:EU:C:2010:762.

this special regime for travel agents and that a single supply, like the sale of tickets for an opera, without additional services, does not meet the criteria of this special scheme. Notwithstanding these judgments, the CJEU has ruled in *Alpenchalets Resorts* that the mere supply of holiday accommodation by the travel agent is sufficient for the TOMS to apply.[26] This case seems to suggest that single supplies can also fall within the scope of the scheme.

A definition of a 'traveller' is also missing. It follows from *Commission v Spain*[27] that not only final (private) consumers can be seen as travellers but also businesses. The scheme for travel agents can also be applied for travel arrangements that travel agents provide in their own names for other travel agents while making use of goods and services supplied by other businesses.

The TOMS has the advantage that VAT revenues accrue to the Member State in which the final consumption of each (service) component of the single travel package takes place.[28] The VAT on the hotel accommodation, for example, accrues to the Member State where the holiday takes place, while the services of the travel agent are taxed in the Member State where the travel agent is established.

The special scheme only applies to packages for travel and lodging in the EU. Pursuant to Article 309 VAT Directive, travel agents providing travel packages to places outside the EU are exempt from VAT.

Finally, we note that the European Commission has held consultations on the functioning of the TOMS. The reason is that the growing plurality of business models and operating practices in the travel sector calls for a re-evaluation of the current TOMS.[29] Commission proposals are expected in the future.

16.5 SECOND-HAND GOODS, WORKS OF ART, COLLECTORS' ITEMS AND ANTIQUES

Special arrangements are in place for second-hand goods, works of art, collectors' items and antiques. These are covered by Articles 311-343 VAT Directive. The EU legislator deemed it appropriate to adopt a uniform taxation system to be applied to second-hand goods, works of art, antiques and collectors' items, with a view to preventing double taxation and the distortion of competition as between taxable persons.[30] The ownership of such goods typically transfers between taxable persons and final consumers, and vice versa. As a result, when conducting business, a taxable person may potentially purchase a good from a final consumer against a purchase

26. *See* CJEU 19 December 2018, Case C-552/17 *Alpenchalets Resorts GmbH v Finanzamt München Abteilung Körperschaften*, ECLI:EU:C:2018:1032. In para. 33, the Court has added that the importance of other supplies of goods or services, which may be combined with the supply of accommodation, cannot have a bearing on the legal classification of the situation at issue, that is to say, that that situation is covered by the special scheme for travel agents.
27. Cf. CJEU 26 September 2013, Case C-189/11 *European Commission v Kingdom of Spain*. ECLI:EU:C:2013:587.
28. *Ibid.*
29. *See* https://ec.europa.eu/info/law/better-regulation/have-your-say/initiatives/11883-VAT-scheme-for-travel-agents-evaluation-_en (accessed 21 August 2024).
30. *See* recital 51 to the VAT Directive.

price, which includes a certain amount of hidden VAT (i.e., non-deductible VAT that was paid by the final consumer at the time he/she purchased the good). In case the taxable person resells such a good to another final consumer, cascading of VAT would take place in case the supply would be fully taxed once more. In order to prevent this adversity, the EU legislator has devised the special 'margin scheme' for second-hand goods, works of art, antiques and collectors' items.

The margin scheme applies to supplies of second-hand goods, works of art, collectors' items and antiques by so-called taxable dealers. Article 311(1) VAT Directive defines what second-hand goods, works of art, collectors' items and antiques exactly are. The same provision provides for a definition of a taxable dealer. In short, a taxable dealer is any taxable person who, in the course of his economic activity and with a view to resale, purchases the aforementioned goods, whether he is acting for himself or on behalf of another person pursuant to a contract under which commission is payable on purchase or sale.

Under the margin scheme, VAT is only applied to the profit margin of the taxable dealer. Pursuant to Article 314 VAT Directive the margin scheme applies to the supply by a taxable dealer of second-hand goods, works of art, collectors' items or antiques where those goods have been supplied to him within the EU by one of the following persons:

(a) a non-taxable person;
(b) another taxable person, in so far as the supply of goods by that other taxable person is exempt pursuant to Article 136 VAT Directive (*see* Chapter 8);
(c) another taxable person, in so far as the supply of goods by that other taxable person is covered by the SME scheme and involves capital goods (*see* section 16.2);
(d) another taxable dealer, in so far as VAT has been applied to the supply of goods by that other taxable dealer in accordance with the margin scheme.

Following Article 315 VAT Directive, the taxable amount in respect of a supply of goods under the margin scheme is the profit margin made by the taxable dealer, less the amount of VAT relating to the profit margin. This profit margin is equal to the difference between the selling price charged by the taxable dealer for the goods and the purchase price. Pursuant to Article 322 VAT Directive, taxable dealers are not entitled to deduct the following input VAT in respect of their supplies under the margin scheme:

(a) the VAT due or paid in respect of works of art, collectors' items or antiques which he has imported himself;
(b) the VAT due or paid in respect of works of art which have been, or are to be, supplied to him by their creator or by the creator's successors in title;
(c) the VAT due or paid in respect of works of art which have been, or are to be, supplied to him by a taxable person other than a taxable dealer.

The margin scheme does not lead to a perfectly neutral system, as a taxable dealer is only relieved from the burden of input VAT at the moment he makes a supply under the margin scheme. Only then does the taxable dealer apply VAT to his margin, which in essence means that he is de facto setting off the input VAT against the VAT normally due in respect of his supply. This imperfection is partially covered by the simplified procedure for collecting VAT, which Member States may introduce on the basis of Article 318 VAT Directive. Member States may provide that, for certain transactions or for certain categories of taxable dealers, the taxable amount in respect of supplies of goods subject to the margin scheme is to be determined for each tax period during which the taxable dealer must submit his VAT return. Rather than on a transaction-by-transaction basis, this simplification scheme allows taxable dealers to apply the margin scheme on a VAT return basis, e.g., monthly or quarterly.

Article 325 VAT Directive establishes that the taxable dealer may not enter separately on the invoices which he issues, the VAT relating to supplies of goods to which he applies the margin scheme. This means that taxable persons, which are entitled to deduct input VAT, who purchase goods under the margin scheme from a taxable dealer, cannot deduct the VAT charged to them in respect of their purchases. This disadvantage can be avoided because Article 319 VAT Directive allows taxable dealers to apply the normal VAT arrangements to any supply covered by the margin scheme. If a taxable dealer applies the normal VAT regime on supplies to taxable persons entitled to full input VAT deduction, this dealer charges VAT in respect of his full sales price. This results in a higher VAT amount compared to the application of the margin scheme, as in the latter situation, VAT is only applied to the margin. Since the customers at issue have the possibility to deduct input VAT in full, application of the normal regime is nevertheless beneficial for them.

Articles 333-341 VAT Directive deal with special arrangements for sales by public auction. On the basis of these arrangements, VAT becomes due by an organizer of a sale by public auction in respect of the margin between purchase and sale of second-hand goods, works of art, collectors' items and antiques. The special arrangements for taxable dealers and public auctions, at least during the so-called transitional period referred to in Article 402 VAT Directive, do not apply to intra-Community supplies of used, but nevertheless qualified as 'new', means of transport. These supplies are subject to the normal VAT regime.

16.6 INVESTMENT GOLD

Since 1 January 2000, Member States have been required to have a special scheme for investment gold in their national VAT legislation. In the context of a consumption tax, gold can be seen as an anomaly, as it can be used for multiple purposes. Gold is used as a raw material for productive purposes, ultimately enabling natural persons to consume certain products that contain that very gold (e.g., jewellery, mobile phones). However, equally relevant is the function of gold as an investment vehicle. The application of the normal VAT rules to the supply of gold constitutes a major obstacle to its use for investment purposes, and it is for this reason that the EU legislator has adopted a special scheme with a view to enhancing the international competitiveness of the EU gold market. The supply of gold for investment purposes is inherently similar to other financial investments that are exempt from VAT. Consequently, to exempt the supply of investment, gold appears to be the most appropriate VAT treatment.[31]

Under the special scheme for investment gold, the supply, intra-Community acquisition and importation of investment gold are exempt, while the person carrying out these transactions enjoys a partial right to deduct the input VAT related to these transactions. The special scheme is laid down in Articles 344-356 VAT Directive.

Article 344(1) VAT Directive defines 'investment gold' as:

(1) gold, in the form of a bar or a wafer of weights accepted by the bullion markets, of a purity equal to or greater than 995-thousandths, whether or not represented by securities; Member States may exclude from this special scheme small bars or wafers of a weight of 1 g or less;
(2) gold coins of a purity equal to or greater than 900-thousandths and minted after 1,800, which are or have been legal tender in the country of origin, and are normally sold at a price which does not exceed the open market value of the gold contained in the coins by more than 80%.

The above-mentioned coins are not to be regarded as sold for numismatic interest. As a result, the margin scheme (*see* section 16.5) does not apply.

Following Article 346 VAT Directive, Member States exempt from VAT the supply, the intra-Community acquisition and the importation of investment gold. Thus, the exemption applies regardless of whether the investment gold originates in the same Member State, another Member State or a non-EU country. The exemption also applies to investment gold represented by certificates for allocated or unallocated gold or traded on gold accounts. Moreover, the exemption is applicable to gold loans and swaps, involving a right of ownership or claim in respect of investment gold, as well as to transactions concerning investment gold involving futures and forward contracts leading to a transfer of right of ownership or claim in respect of investment gold. Pursuant to Article 347 VAT Directive, Member States also exempt the services of agents who act in the name and on behalf of another person when they take part in the supply of investment gold for their principal.

On the basis of Article 348 VAT Directive, Member States should allow taxable persons who produce investment gold or transform gold into investment gold the right to opt for taxation of supplies of investment gold to another taxable person who would otherwise be exempt. Member States are required to introduce this option to tax in their legislation. Article 349 VAT Directive offers Member States an option to introduce an additional option to tax. Member States may allow taxable persons who, in the course of their economic activity, normally supply gold for industrial purposes, the right to opt for taxation of supplies of gold bars or wafers. Pursuant to Article 350 VAT Directive, the right to opt for taxation is also available to agents whose services are exempt on the basis of Article 347 VAT Directive where the relevant suppliers of the investment gold have opted for taxation.

31. *See* recitals 52 and 53 of the VAT Directive.

The special scheme for investment gold includes a special mechanism for the deduction of input VAT related to transactions involving (the supply of) investment gold. Following Article 354 VAT Directive, a taxable person making an exempt supply of investment gold can only deduct: (a) the VAT incurred in respect of investment gold supplied to him by a person who has made use of the option to tax; (b) the VAT incurred in respect of a supply, an intra-Community acquisition or importation of gold other than investment gold which is subsequently transformed by him or on his behalf into investment gold; and (c) the VAT incurred in respect of services supplied to him consisting in a change of form, weight or purity of gold, including investment gold.

Article 355 VAT Directive provides that taxable persons who produce investment gold or transform gold into investment gold are entitled to deduct the VAT incurred in respect of the supply, intra-Community acquisition or importation of goods or services linked to the production or transformation of that gold as if their subsequent exempt supply of gold were taxed.

16.7 THE OSS SCHEME AND CARRIER IMPORT SCHEME

16.7.1 The (Former) OSS (Applying until 1 July 2021)

Since 1 January 2015, telecommunication, radio, and television broadcasting services supplied to non-taxable persons residing in the EU have been subject to VAT in the Member State of consumption. By proxy, this is the customer's country of residence (Article 58 VAT Directive).[32] Since a reverse charge mechanism is not available for such services supplied to non-taxable persons, service suppliers are required to charge the VAT of the Member State where the customer is residing or established. If it were not for the special scheme contained in Title XII, Chapter 6 of the VAT Directive, this would require B2C suppliers of telecommunication, radio and television broadcasting services to register for VAT purposes in each Member State where they have customers, implying a substantial administrative burden. It is for this reason that the EU legislator devised the so-called OSS scheme. The former Articles 358-369 VAT Directive contained the rules on the OSS scheme with respect to telecommunications, broadcasting or electronic services supplied by taxable persons not established within the Community. Article 369a–369k VAT Directive contained the rules for the OSS scheme with respect to telecommunications, broadcasting or electronic services supplied by taxable persons established within the Community but not in the Member State of consumption. Until 1 July 2021, the OSS scheme allowed taxable persons supplying telecommunication services, television and radio broadcasting services and electronically supplied services to non-taxable persons in Member States in which they do not have an establishment to account for the VAT due on those supplies via a web portal in the Member State in which they are identified. For instance, if a Luxembourg electronic

32. *See* M. Merkx, *New Implementing Measures for EU Place-of-Supply Change 2015* (2013) 4 International VAT Monitor https://doi.org/10.59403/1cr6zv4 and S. Claessens & I. Lejeune, *Taxation of B2C TBE Services under EU VAT from 2015* (2014) 1 International VAT Monitor https://doi.org/10.59403/3mpejxt.

service provider was liable to pay the VAT due in various Member States where his customers (non-taxable persons) were residing, the OSS scheme allowed him to file an aggregated single VAT return in Luxembourg and make a single payment of the VAT due in all these Member States. The Luxembourg tax authorities made sure the correct amount of VAT due was paid to the tax authorities of the relevant Member States. This saved the electronic service provider from having to register for VAT, file VAT returns and pay VAT in all the Member States where his customers (non-taxable persons) were residing.[33]

16.7.2 The (Current) OSS (Applying from 1 July 2021)

On 5 December 2017, the Council adopted Council Directive 2017/2455, the primary legislative instrument of the so-called VAT e-commerce package.[34] Accompanied by other legal instruments, the Directive was aimed at the modernization of EU VAT legislation as far as the e-commerce sector is concerned.[35] As the EU legislator affirmed in the recitals, globalization and technological change had led to an 'explosive growth of electronic commerce and, hence, of distance sales of goods', and the ever-expanding digital economy sector required legislative action in order to protect Member States' tax revenues and to ensure that international trade can take place in a neutral fashion. The

33. The place of supply rules for B2C electronic, telecommunication and broadcasting services and the (M)OSS scheme have been accompanied by detailed rules and guidelines. We refer to Council Implementing Regulation (EU) No 1042/2013 of 7 October 2013 amending Implementing Regulation (EU) No 282/2011 as regards the place of supply of services [2013] OJ L284/1, and the *Guide to the VAT (M)OSS* of the European Commission. Some argue that these rules have led to an increased compliance burden for businesses and may even cause legal uncertainty. *See* M. Lamensch, *The 2015 Rules for Electronically Supplied Services: Compliance Issues* (2015) 1 International VAT Monitor https://doi.org/10.59403/1hcksc0.
34. Council Directive (EU) 2017/2455 of 5 December 2017 amending Directive 2006/112/EC and Directive 2009/132/EC as regards certain value added tax obligations for supplies of services and distance sales of goods [2017] OJ L 348/7. Initially, the new rules would enter into effect on 1 January 2021. Due to the COVID-19 pandemic, this has been postponed to 1 July 2021. Council Decision (EU) 2020/1109 of 20 July 2020 amending Directives (EU) 2017/2455 and (EU) 2019/1995 as regards the dates of transposition and application in response to the COVID-19 pandemic [2020] OJ L 244.
35. *See* Council Regulation (EU) 2017/2454 of 5 December 2017 amending Regulation (EU) No 904/2010 on administrative cooperation and combating fraud in the field of value added tax [2017] OJ L 348/1; Council Implementing Regulation (EU) 2017/2459 of 5 December 2017 amending Implementing Regulation (EU) No 282/2011 laying down implementing measures for Directive 2006/112/EC on the common system of value added tax [2017] OJ L 348/32; Council Implementing Regulation (EU) 2019/2026 of 21 November 2019 amending Implementing Regulation (EU) No 282/2011 as regards supplies of goods or services facilitated by electronic interfaces and the special schemes for taxable persons supplying services to non-taxable persons, making distance sales of goods and certain domestic supplies of goods [2019] OJ L 313/14; Council Directive (EU) 2019/1995 of 21 November 2019 amending Directive 2006/112/EC as regards provisions relating to distance sales of goods and certain domestic supplies of goods [2019] OJ L 310/1; Commission Implementing Regulation (EU) 2020/194 of 12 February 2020 laying down detailed rules for the application of Council Regulation (EU) No 904/2010 as regards the special schemes for taxable persons supplying services to non-taxable persons, making distance sales of goods and certain domestic supplies of goods [2020] OJ L 40/114.

primary amendments to the legal framework of EU VAT in connection with the taxation of e-commerce transactions concerned the following:

(1) As of 1 January 2019, an annual turnover threshold of EUR 10,000 was adopted for cross-border telecommunications, broadcasting and electronic (TBE) services within the EU.[36] If a taxable person remains below this threshold, Article 58(1) VAT Directive (special place of supply rule for TBE services) will not apply; instead, the services are taxed in the Member State of the establishment of the service provider (Article 45 VAT Directive). This rule has been adopted to facilitate the VAT position of 'microbusinesses' providing B2C cross-border intra-EU services in the e-commerce sector, as they do not have to register for VAT purposes abroad if their turnover remains below the threshold and they meet the other requirements.
(2) As of 1 July 2021, the current threshold for intra-EU distance sales of goods (Article 34 VAT Directive) was abolished, to be replaced by the annual turnover threshold of EUR 10,000 which had already been in place, from 1 January 2019, for cross-border intra-EU TBE services (*see* point 1 above).[37]
(3) As of 1 July 2021, the import exemption for small consignments was abolished.[38] The EU legislator was of the opinion that this import exemption frustrates competitive relations, as it allowed non-EU distance sellers to offer goods free of VAT to final consumers in the EU, to the obvious detriment of EU-based businesses. The removal of the import exemption implied that VAT is now also due on the importation of small consignments (cf. Article 2(1)(d) VAT Directive).
(4) As of 1 July 2021, taxable persons who operate an electronic interface, such as an (online) marketplace, platform or portal, and who facilitate, through the use of that medium, distance sales of goods are in certain situations be deemed to have received and supplied those goods themselves.[39] This 'platform fiction' was aimed at promoting the collection of VAT on distance sales from the authorities' perspective, comparable to the already existing platform fiction of Article 9a VAT Implementing Regulation in connection with electronically supplied services. By 'inserting' the platform entrepreneur in the supply chain – so: he will be deemed to act as the *purchaser* of the goods from the (non-EU or EU based) distance seller, and simultaneously as the *seller* of the same goods to the final consumer – the final VAT liability in many cases is imposed on that very platform entrepreneur. Thus, the tax authorities need only to supervise (relatively small numbers of) platform entrepreneurs

36. *See* Article 1 of Council Directive (EU) 2017/2455 of 5 December 2017.
37. *See* the new Article 59c VAT Directive, as adopted by means of Council Directive (EU) 2017/2455 of 5 December 2017.
38. *See* Article 23 of Council Directive 2009/132/EC of 19 October 2009.
39. *See* the new Article 14a VAT Directive, as adopted by means of Council Directive (EU) 2017/2455 of 5 December 2017. For distances, sales of goods originating in non-EU countries, the consignments need to have an intrinsic value not exceeding EUR 150 for the platform fiction to apply.

and need not collect any VAT from distance sellers who are often established outside the EU.

The e-commerce amendments to the VAT Directive have implications for the liability of VAT, in particular. In some situations, new VAT liabilities arise (e.g., due to the abolition of the import exemption for small consignments), and in others, the VAT liabilities are purposefully shifted to a certain designated person (e.g., in the case of supplies facilitated by platforms). In order to streamline and simplify the reporting and payment of VAT due on e-commerce transactions, the EU legislator has extended the scope of the current OSS, so as to also cover the certain categories of e-commerce transactions and supplies of services. The schemes put in place to that purpose allow taxable persons to settle their VAT affairs (the reporting and payment of VAT on qualifying transactions) in only one Member State (i.e., the Member State of identification), even if VAT is (also) due in other Member States. In this context, three schemes have been adopted, which, at the moment they entered into effect (1 July 2021), were considered as a significant expansion of the former OSS:[40]

(1) *Special scheme for services supplied by taxable persons not established in the Community:* Under this scheme, taxable persons not established in the EU can use the OSS for the reporting and payment of VAT on services rendered to non-taxable persons established or residing in a Member State.[41] The scheme will apply to *all* those services, and the taxable person making use of the OSS are required to submit VAT returns in the Member State of identification, showing, among others, for each Member State of consumption (i.e., Member State in which the supply of services is deemed to take place according to the place of supply rules) the total value of supplies of services.[42]
(2) *Special scheme for intra-Community distance sales of goods, for supplies of goods within a Member State made by electronic interfaces facilitating those supplies, and for services supplied by taxable persons established in the Community*: Under this scheme, Member States are required to permit taxable persons carrying out intra-Community distance sales of goods to use the OSS for the reporting and payment of VAT due on these transactions.[43] In addition,

40. Additional rules as regards the special schemes have been adopted by means of Commission Implementing Regulation (EU) 2020/194 of 12 February 2020 laying down detailed rules for the application of Council Regulation (EU) No 904/2010 as regards the special schemes for taxable persons supplying services to non-taxable persons, making distance sales of goods and certain domestic supplies of goods [2020] OJ L 40/114. For guidelines, *see* Guide to the VAT One Stop Shop (European Commission, 2021), accessible via https://vat-one-stop-shop.ec.europa.eu/system/files/2021-07/OSS_guidelines_en.pdf (accessed 21 August 2024).
41. *See* the new Article 359 VAT Directive, as adopted by means of Council Directive (EU) 2017/2455 of 5 December 2017.
42. *See* the new Article 365 VAT Directive, as adopted by means of Council Directive (EU) 2017/2455 of 5 December 2017.
43. *See* the new Article 369b VAT Directive, as adopted by means of Council Directive (EU) 2017/2455 of 5 December 2017; for the legal definition of 'intra-Community distance sales of goods', refer to the new Article 14(4)(1) VAT Directive, as adopted by means of Council Directive (EU) 2017/2455 of 5 December 2017.

taxable persons who are established in the EU but not in the Member State of consumption (i.e., the Member State in which the supply of services is deemed to take place) are allowed to use the OSS for the reporting and payment of VAT due on services rendered to non-taxable persons. Finally, as arranged for by Council Directive 2019/1995, also electronic interfaces that facilitate distance sales of goods in one Member State can apply the special scheme – as they would otherwise be required to register for VAT purposes in that Member State.[44]

(3) *The IOSS*: In addition, the EU legislator has adopted a special scheme for distance sales of goods originating in non-EU countries. In this context, one can think of goods ordered by consumers from online platforms, such as *Alibaba*, when the respective goods are shipped from production or warehousing facilities outside the EU. The scheme only applies to distance sales of goods transported by or on behalf of the supplier, including where the supplier indirectly intervenes in the transport, from a third country to a qualifying customer in a Member State.[45] One particular requirement for the application of the scheme is that the consignments should have an intrinsic value not exceeding EUR 150.[46] To make use of the scheme, the respective taxable person (distance seller) must be established in the Community or in a third country with which the EU has concluded a mutual assistance agreement, or, alternatively, he must be represented by a fiscal intermediary (irrespective of where the taxable person is established).[47] Clearly, this provision is meant to safeguard the financial interests of the Member State of identification, as it provides the authorities with means of ensuring the collection of VAT.[48] Another notable aspect of the IOSS is that the chargeable event shall occur, and VAT shall become chargeable at the moment that the payment has been accepted by the distance seller.[49] The 'tax point' is, therefore, closely related to the cash flow impact of distance sales. This approach not only has the advantage that the authorities can claim the payment of VAT at a financially suitable moment (i.e., when the distance

44. *See* the third recital to Council Directive (EU) 2019/1995 of 21 November 2019 amending Directive 2006/112/EC as regards provisions relating to distance sales of goods and certain domestic supplies of goods [2019] OJ L 310/1. For the special scheme to apply, among others, the following conditions apply (in simplified terms): A non-EU supplier must carry out a distance sale; the electronic interface must facilitate that distance sale (cf. the new Article 14a(2) VAT Dir.; in the context of the distance sale, the transport starts and ends in the same Member State).
45. *See* the new Article 14(4)(2) VAT Directive, as adopted by means of Council Directive (EU) 2017/2455 of 5 December 2017 (the provision contains further conditions for the application of the special scheme).
46. *See* the new Article 369l VAT Directive, as adopted by means of Council Directive (EU) 2017/2455 of 5 December 2017.
47. *See* the new Article 369m VAT Directive, as adopted by means of Council Directive (EU) 2017/2455 of 5 December 2017.
48. *See* the thirteenth recital to Council Directive (EU) 2017/2455 of 5 December 2017.
49. *See* the new Article 369n VAT Directive, as adopted by means of Council Directive (EU) 2017/2455 of 5 December 2017.

seller has received the payment from his customer) but also that for determining the moment of the chargeable event and the chargeability of VAT, it is not necessary to establish when exactly the right to dispose of the good has been transferred to the customer.[50]

Globally, the EU OSS scheme may be regarded as an example for other consumption tax systems dealing with the challenges that electronic services pose. For example, the OECD advocates simplified registration mechanisms, which are sufficiently clear and accessible so that non-resident vendors, including SMEs, may easily fulfil their VAT obligations while also ensuring taxation where the consumption of electronic services takes place.[51] Partly because of its apparent advantages, the EU legislature has been expanding the OSS over the years. This development fits within the ambitions of the Commission, as it has expressed its desire to use the scheme for a growing number of categories of transactions, even for B2B supplies of goods within the Community and the effectuation of the right of deduction.[52] Notwithstanding these ambitions, the extension of the OSS, in our view, remains a politically sensitive topic, as its fundamental functioning implies the collection of VAT by a Member State other than the one which is entitled to the revenues – thus leading to financial interdependencies between the various national Treasuries in the Community.[53] It remains to be seen to what extent the Council is willing to accept such financial interdependencies to a greater extent than currently applicable.

16.7.3 The Carrier Import Scheme (Applying from 1 July 2021)

In addition to the special schemes discussed in the previous section, the EU legislator has, by means of the e-commerce VAT package, also adopted a fourth one – which has entered into effect on 1 July 2021.[54] This special scheme, hereinafter referred to as the 'Carrier Import Scheme', can be used by persons (i.e., carriers, commonly freight, postal or shipping companies) presenting goods to the customs authorities on behalf of the person for whom the goods are destined within the EU (hereinafter 'destinee') – all

50. *See* Article 63 VAT Directive.
51. OECD/G20 'Base Erosion and Profit Shifting Project, Addressing the Tax Challenges of the Digital Economy', Action 1: 2015 Final Report, https://www.oecd.org/en/publications/addressing-the-tax-challenges-of-the-digital-economy-action-1-2015-final-report_9789264241046-en.html (accessed 15 August 2024), p. 32.
52. *See* Proposal for a Council Directive amending Directive 2006/112/EC as regards the introduction of the detailed technical measures for the operation of the definitive VAT system for the taxation of trade between Member States, COM (2018) 329 final, pp. 9-11. Also, the Commission wants to extend the OSS to, among other categories of transactions, intra-EU transfers of own goods by taxable persons. *See* section 15.8 on the VAT rules in the Digital Age (ViDA) proposals (Proposal for a Council Directive amending Directive 2006/112/EC as regards VAT rules for the digital age, 8 December 2022, COM/2022/701 final).
53. For a critical assessment of the (M)OSS, refer to M. Lamensch, *European Commission's New Package of Proposals on E-commerce: A Critical Assessment* (2017) 2 International VAT Monitor https://doi.org/10.59403/svhth4.
54. *See* the new Chapter 7 of Title XII of the VAT Directive, as adopted by means of Council Directive (EU) 2017/2455 of 5 December 2017.

of this in the context of distance sales originating in non-EU countries. The primary requirements for the application of the Carrier Import Scheme are as follows:

(1) The goods must be the subject of importation of goods in a certain Member State.
(2) The goods must be consignments of an intrinsic value not exceeding EUR 150.
(3) The Member State of importation must also be the Member State in which the dispatch or transport of the goods ends.
(4) The IOSS for distance sales of goods originating in non-EU countries[55] must not be used.

Under the Carrier Import Scheme, the person for whom the goods are destined shall be liable for the payment of the import VAT, yet the carrier is to collect this VAT from that person, to subsequently pay it to the authorities.[56] In the latter regard, Member States must allow the VAT to be paid to be reported in an electronic monthly declaration.

Effectively, the Carrier Import Scheme requires the party arranging the transport of the goods (i.e., carrier) to act as an unpaid tax collector on behalf of the tax authorities. Generally, the carrier oversees the logistical flow of the goods and arranges their customs clearance. These aspects enable him to properly assess the VAT consequences of the importation of the goods. Moreover, the carrier can use the physical possession of the goods as leverage to obtain (collect) any VAT due from the destinee, i.e., by simply not handing over the good if the latter proves unwilling to carry the burden of VAT.

The IOSS and the Carrier Import Scheme are intended to promote an efficient and administratively smooth settlement of VAT due on importation, while safeguarding the financial interests of the Member States. However, the schemes are *optional*, which implies that parties engaged in cross-border distance sales of goods need not necessarily apply one of them. In addition, both schemes have various requirements (e.g., the goods concerned must have an intrinsic value not exceeding EUR 150). If the schemes are not applied, the person involved can rely on the 'standard import procedure' in order to avail himself of the common collection and reporting method of VAT on importation.[57] Often, this leads to a requirement to settle the payment of import VAT during the customs clearance of the goods at the non-EU - EU customs border.

55. *See* the new Article 369l-369x VAT Directive, as adopted by means of Council Directive (EU) 2017/2455 of 5 December 2017.
56. *See* the new Article 369z VAT Directive, as adopted by means of Council Directive (EU) 2017/2455 of 5 December 2017.
57. *See* the fifteenth recital to Council Directive (EU) 2017/2455 of 5 December 2017.

CJEU Case Law

A

O

P

R

Index

B

C

D

E

T

U

V

www.ingramcontent.com/pod-product-compliance
Lightning Source LLC
LaVergne TN
LVHW020649300926
849161LV00004B/872